Short Story Criticism

Guide to Thomson Gale Literary Criticism Series

For criticism on	Consult these Thomson Gale series
Authors now living or who died after December 31, 1999	*CONTEMPORARY LITERARY CRITICISM (CLC)*
Authors who died between 1900 and 1999	*TWENTIETH-CENTURY LITERARY CRITICISM (TCLC)*
Authors who died between 1800 and 1899	*NINETEENTH-CENTURY LITERATURE CRITICISM (NCLC)*
Authors who died between 1400 and 1799	*LITERATURE CRITICISM FROM 1400 TO 1800 (LC)* *SHAKESPEAREAN CRITICISM (SC)*
Authors who died before 1400	*CLASSICAL AND MEDIEVAL LITERATURE CRITICISM (CMLC)*
Authors of books for children and young adults	*CHILDREN'S LITERATURE REVIEW (CLR)*
Dramatists	*DRAMA CRITICISM (DC)*
Poets	*POETRY CRITICISM (PC)*
Short story writers	*SHORT STORY CRITICISM (SSC)*
Literary topics and movements	*HARLEM RENAISSANCE: A GALE CRITICAL COMPANION (HR)* *THE BEAT GENERATION: A GALE CRITICAL COMPANION (BG)* *FEMINISM IN LITERATURE: A GALE CRITICAL COMPANION (FL)* *GOTHIC LITERATURE: A GALE CRITICAL COMPANION (GL)*
Asian American writers of the last two hundred years	*ASIAN AMERICAN LITERATURE (AAL)*
Black writers of the past two hundred years	*BLACK LITERATURE CRITICISM (BLC)* *BLACK LITERATURE CRITICISM SUPPLEMENT (BLCS)*
Hispanic writers of the late nineteenth and twentieth centuries	*HISPANIC LITERATURE CRITICISM (HLC)* *HISPANIC LITERATURE CRITICISM SUPPLEMENT (HLCS)*
Native North American writers and orators of the eighteenth, nineteenth, and twentieth centuries	*NATIVE NORTH AMERICAN LITERATURE (NNAL)*
Major authors from the Renaissance to the present	*WORLD LITERATURE CRITICISM, 1500 TO THE PRESENT (WLC)* *WORLD LITERATURE CRITICISM SUPPLEMENT (WLCS)*

ISSN 0895-9439

83457 Volume 90

Short Story Criticism

Criticism of the
Works of Short Fiction Writers

Jessica Bomarito
Jelena Krstović
Project Editors

THOMSON

GALE

Detroit • New York • San Francisco • San Diego • New Haven, Conn. • Waterville, Maine • London • Munich

Short Story Criticism, Vol. 90

Project Editors
Jessica Bomarito and Jelena Krstović,

Editorial
Kathy D. Darrow, Jeffrey W. Hunter, Michelle Lee, Thomas J. Schoenberg, Noah Schusterbauer, Lawrence J. Trudeau, Russel Whitaker

Data Capture
Frances Monroe, Gwen Tucker

Indexing Services
Factiva®, a Dow Jones and Reuters Company

Rights and Acquisitions
Margaret Abendroth, Margaret Chamberlain-Gaston, Edna Hedblad

Imaging and Multimedia
Dean Dauphinais, Leitha Etheridge-Sims, Lezlie Light, Mike Logusz, Dan Newell, Christine O'Bryan, Kelly A. Quin, Denay Wilding, Robyn Young

Composition and Electronic Capture
Amy Darga

Manufacturing
Rhonda Dover

Associate Product Manager
Marc Cormier

LIBRARY OF CONGRESS CATALOG CARD NUMBER 88-641014

ISBN 0-7876-8887-8
ISSN 0895-9439

Printed in the United States of America
10 9 8 7 6 5 4 3 2 1

Contents

Preface

Short Story Criticism (SSC) presents significant criticism of the world's greatest short-story writers and provides supplementary biographical and bibliographical materials to guide the interested reader to a greater understanding of the authors of short fiction. This series was developed in response to suggestions from librarians serving high school, college, and public library patrons, who had noted a considerable number of requests for critical material on short-story writers. Although major short-story writers are covered in such Thomson Gale series as *Contemporary Literary Criticism (CLC)*, *Twentieth-Century Literary Criticism (TCLC)*, *Nineteenth-Century Literature Criticism (NCLC)*, and *Literature Criticism from 1400 to 1800 (LC)*, librarians perceived the need for a series devoted solely to writers of the short-story genre.

Scope of the Series

SSC is designed to serve as an introduction to major short-story writers of all eras and nationalities. Since these authors have inspired a great deal of relevant critical material, *SSC* is necessarily selective, and the editors have chosen the most important published criticism to aid readers and students in their research.

Approximately three to six authors are included in each volume, and each entry presents a historical survey of the critical response to that author's work. The length of an entry is intended to reflect the amount of critical attention the author has received from critics writing in English and from foreign critics in translation. Every attempt has been made to identify and include the most significant essays on each author's work. In order to provide these important critical pieces, the editors sometimes reprint essays that have appeared elsewhere in Thomson Gale's Literary Criticism Series. Such duplication, however, never exceeds twenty percent of an *SSC* volume.

Organization of the Book

An *SSC* entry consists of the following elements:

- The **Author Heading** cites the name under which the author most commonly wrote, followed by birth and death dates. Also located here are any name variations under which an author wrote, including transliterated forms for authors whose native languages use nonroman alphabets. If the author wrote consistently under a pseudonym, the pseudonym will be listed in the author heading and the author's actual name given in parentheses on the first line of the biographical and critical introduction. Uncertain birth or death dates are indicated by question marks. Single-work entries are preceded by the title of the work and its date of publication.

- The **Introduction** contains background information that introduces the reader to the author and the critical debates surrounding his or her work.

- A **Portrait of the Author** is included when available.

- The list of **Principal Works** is ordered chronologically by date of first publication and lists the most important works by the author. The first section comprises short-story collections, novellas, and novella collections. The second section gives information on other major works by the author. For foreign authors, the editors have provided original foreign-language publication information and have selected what are considered the best and most complete English-language editions of their works.

- Reprinted **Criticism** is arranged chronologically in each entry to provide a useful perspective on changes in critical evaluation over time. All short-story, novella, and collection titles by the author featured in the entry are printed in boldface type. The critic's name and the date of composition or publication of the critical work are given at the beginning of each piece of criticism. Unsigned criticism is preceded by the title of the source in which it appeared. Footnotes are reprinted at the end of each essay or excerpt. In the case of excerpted criticism, only those footnotes that pertain to the excerpted texts are included.

- Critical essays are prefaced by brief **Annotations** explicating each piece.

- A complete **Bibliographical Citation** of the original essay or book precedes each piece of criticism. Source citations in the Literary Criticism Series follow University of Chicago Press style, as outlined in *The Chicago Manual of Style,* 14th ed. (Chicago: The University of Chicago Press, 1993).

- An annotated bibliography of **Further Reading** appears at the end of each entry and suggests resources for additional study. In some cases, significant essays for which the editors could not obtain reprint rights are included here. Boxed material following the further reading list provides references to other biographical and critical sources on the author in series published by Thomson Gale.

Indexes

A **Cumulative Author Index** lists all of the authors that appear in a wide variety of reference sources published by Thomson Gale, including *SSC*. A complete list of these sources is found facing the first page of the Author Index. The index also includes birth and death dates and cross references between pseudonyms and actual names.

A **Cumulative Nationality Index** lists all authors featured in *SSC* by nationality, followed by the number of the *SSC* volume in which their entry appears.

An alphabetical **Title Index** lists all short-story, novella, and collection titles contained in the *SSC* series. Titles of short-story collections, separately published novellas, and novella collections are printed in italics, while titles of individual short stories are printed in roman type with quotation marks. Each title is followed by the author's last name and corresponding volume and page numbers where commentary on the work is located. English-language translations of original foreign-language titles are cross-referenced to the foreign titles so that all references to discussion of a work are combined in one listing.

In response to numerous suggestions from librarians, Thomson Gale also produces an annual paperbound edition of the SSC cumulative title index. This annual cumulation, which alphabetically lists all titles reviewed in the series, is available to all customers. Additional copies of this index are available upon request. Librarians and patrons will welcome this separate index; it saves shelf space, is easy to use, and is recyclable upon receipt of the next edition.

Citing *Short Story Criticism*

When citing criticism reprinted in the Literary Criticism Series, students should provide complete bibliographic information so that the cited essay can be located in the original print or electronic source. Students who quote directly from reprinted criticism may use any accepted bibliographic format, such as University of Chicago Press style or Modern Language Association (MLA) style. Both the MLA and the University of Chicago formats are acceptable and recognized as being the current standards for citations. It is important, however, to choose one format for all citations; do not mix the two formats within a list of citations.

The examples below follow recommendations for preparing a bibliography set forth in *The Chicago Manual of Style,* 14th ed. (Chicago: The University of Chicago Press, 1993); the first example pertains to material drawn from periodicals, the second to material reprinted from books:

Morrison, Jago. "Narration and Unease in Ian McEwan's Later Fiction." *Critique* 42, no. 3 (spring 2001): 253-68. Reprinted in *Short Story Criticism.* Vol. 57, edited by Janet Witalec, 212-20. Detroit: Gale, 2003.

Brossard, Nicole. "Poetic Politics." In *The Politics of Poetic Form: Poetry and Public Policy,* edited by Charles Bernstein, 73-82. New York: Roof Books, 1990. Reprinted in *Short Story Criticism.* Vol. 57, edited by Janet Witalec, 3-8. Detroit: Gale, 2003.

The examples below follow recommendations for preparing a works cited list set forth in the *MLA Handbook for Writers of Research Papers,* 5th ed. (New York: The Modern Language Association of America, 1999); the first example pertains to material drawn from periodicals, the second to material reprinted from books:

Morrison, Jago. "Narration and Unease in Ian McEwan's Later Fiction." *Critique* 42.3 (spring 2001): 253-68. Reprinted in *Short Story Criticism.* Ed. Janet Witalec. Vol. 57. Detroit: Gale, 2003. 212-20.

Brossard, Nicole. "Poetic Politics." *The Politics of Poetic Form: Poetry and Public Policy.* Ed. Charles Bernstein. New York: Roof Books, 1990. 73-82. Reprinted in *Short Story Criticism.* Ed. Janet Witalec. Vol. 57. Detroit: Gale, 2003. 3-8.

Suggestions are Welcome

Readers who wish to suggest new features, topics, or authors to appear in future volumes, or who have other suggestions or comments are cordially invited to call, write, or fax the Associate Product Manager:

Associate Product Manager, Literary Criticism Series
Thomson Gale
27500 Drake Road
Farmington Hills, MI 48331-3535
1-800-347-4253 (GALE)
Fax: 248-699-8054

Acknowledgments

The editors wish to thank the copyright holders of the excerpted criticism included in this volume and the permissions managers of many book and magazine publishing companies for assisting us in securing reproduction rights. Following is a list of the copyright holders who have granted us permission to reproduce material in this volume of *SSC*. Every effort has been made to trace copyright, but if omissions have been made, please let us know.

COPYRIGHTED MATERIAL IN *SSC*, VOLUME 90, WAS REPRODUCED FROM THE FOLLOWING PERIODICALS:

African American Review, v. 38, fall, 2004 for "'Like a Violin for the Wind to Play': Lyrical Approaches to Lynching by Hughes, DuBois, and Toomer" by Kimberly Banks. Reproduced by permission of the author.—*ATQ,* v. 8, June, 1994. Copyright © 1994 by The University of Rhode Island. Reproduced by permission.—*Canadian Review of Comparative Literature,* v. 23, December, 1996 for "Navigation as Exploration: The Fantastic Education of Sindbad the Sailor of the *Arabian Nights* and Twain's *Huckleberry Finn*" by Yusur Al-Madani. Copyright © Canadian Comparative Literature Association. Reproduced by permission.—*The Carrell,* v. 10, 1969 for "Constance Fenimore Woolson: First Novelist of Florida" by Evelyn Thomas Helmick. Reproduced by permission of the author.—*Comparative Literature,* v. 50, spring, 1998 for "'Peut-on ...': Intertextual Relations in *The Arabian Nights* and Genesis" by Daniel Beaumont. Copyright © 1998 by University of Oregon. Reproduced by permission of the author.—*Fabula,* v. 45, 2004. Copyright © 2004 by Walter de Gruyter & Co., D-10785 Berlin. All rights reserved. Reproduced by permission.—*The Georgia Review,* v. 34, spring, 1980. Copyright © 1980 by The University of Georgia. Reproduced by permission.—*The Griot,* v. 14, fall, 1995. Copyright 1999 by SCAASI/*The Griot.* Reproduced by permission.—*Journal of American Folklore,* v. 113, spring, 2000 for "Otherness and Otherworldliness: Edward W. Lane's Ethnographic Treatment of *The Arabian Nights*" by Jennifer Schacker-Mill. Copyright © 2000 American Folklore Society. Republished with permission of *Journal of American Folklore,* conveyed through Copyright Clearance Center, Inc.—*Journal of Arabic Literature,* v. 16, 1985. Copyright © 1985 by E. J. Brill, Leiden, The Netherlands. Courtesy of Brill Academic Publishers.—*Journal of the Short Story in English,* spring, 2002. Copyright © by Presses de l'Université d'Angers, 2002 - Tous droits réservés. Reproduced by permission.—*Legacy,* v. 4, spring, 1987. Copyright © 1987 by *Legacy.* All rights reserved. Reproduced by permission of the University of Nebraska Press.—*Marvels & Tales,* v. 18, 2004. Copyright © 2004 Wayne State University Press. Reproduced with permission of the Wayne State University Press.—*Modern Fiction Studies,* v. 48, winter, 2002. Copyright © 2002 for the Purdue Research Foundation by the Johns Hopkins University Press. Reproduced by permission.—*Raritan: A Quarterly Review,* v. 21, spring, 2002. Copyright © 2002 by *Raritan: A Quarterly Review.* Reproduced by permission.—*Revue de Littérature Comparée,* v. 54, April-June, 1980. Copyright © Didier-Erudition, Paris, 1979. Reproduced by permission.—*Southern Literary Journal,* v. 32, spring, 2000. Copyright © 2000 by the University of North Carolina Press. Used by permission.—*Studies in Short Fiction,* v. 33, spring, 1996; v. 35, summer, 1998. Copyright 1996, 1998 by *Studies in Short Fiction.* Both reproduced by permission.—*Studies on Voltaire and the Eighteenth Century,* v. 278, 1990 for "Destiny in Voltaire's *Zadig* and *The Arabian Nights*" by William H. Trapnell. Copyright © 1990 University of Oxford. Reproduced by permission of the publisher and the author.—*The Langston Hughes Review,* v. 12, spring, 1993; v. 16, fall-spring, 1999-2001. Copyright, 1993, 1999-2001 by The Langston Hughes Society. Both reproduced by permission.—*The Virginia Quarterly Review,* v. 79, winter, 2003. Copyright 2003, by *The Virginia Quarterly Review,* The University of Virginia. Reproduced by permission of the publisher.—*The Wordsworth Circle,* v. 29, spring, 1998. Copyright © 1998 Marilyn Gaull. Reproduced by permission of the editor.—*World Literature Today,* v. 76, winter, 2002. Copyright © 2002 by *World Literature Today.* Reproduced by permission of the publisher.

COPYRIGHTED MATERIAL IN *SSC*, VOLUME 90, WAS REPRODUCED FROM THE FOLLOWING BOOKS:

Boyd, Anne E. From *Writing for Immortality: Women and the Emergence of High Literary Culture in America.* The Johns Hopkins University Press, 2004. Copyright © 2004 The Johns Hopkins University Press. Reprinted with permission of The Johns Hopkins University Press.—Crumbley, Paul. From "Haunting the House of Print: The Circulation of Disembodied Texts in 'Collected by a Valetudinarian' and 'Miss Grief,'" in *American Culture, Canons, and the Case of Elizabeth Stoddard.* Edited by Robert McClure Smith and Ellen Weinauer. The University of Alabama Press, 2003. Copyright © 2003 The University of Alabama Press. All rights reserved. Reproduced by permission.—Dean, Sharon L. From *Constance*

Thomson Gale Literature Product Advisory Board

The members of the Thomson Gale Literature Product Advisory Board—reference librarians from public and academic library systems—represent a cross-section of our customer base and offer a variety of informed perspectives on both the presentation and content of our literature products. Advisory board members assess and define such quality issues as the relevance, currency, and usefulness of the author coverage, critical content, and literary topics included in our series; evaluate the layout, presentation, and general quality of our printed volumes; provide feedback on the criteria used for selecting authors and topics covered in our series; provide suggestions for potential enhancements to our series; identify any gaps in our coverage of authors or literary topics, recommending authors or topics for inclusion; analyze the appropriateness of our content and presentation for various user audiences, such as high school students, undergraduates, graduate students, librarians, and educators; and offer feedback on any proposed changes/enhancements to our series. We wish to thank the following advisors for their advice throughout the year.

The Arabian Nights

The following entry presents criticism of the short story collection *Alf layla wa-layla* (c. 9-10th century; *The Arabian Nights*; also translated as *The Thousand and One Nights, One Thousand and One Nights, The Book of the Thousand Nights and a Night,* and *The Arabian Nights' Entertainments*).

INTRODUCTION

The Arabian Nights is esteemed as a treasure of world literature and one of the most influential literary works of all time. Recognized for their fantastic, exotic nature and intricate narrative structure, the stories that comprise *The Arabian Nights* have inspired major figures in every realm of artistic expression, including composer Nikolai Rimski-Korsakov, poet Alfred Lord Tennyson, and artist Gustave Doré. Although traditionally associated with medieval Arabic culture, *The Arabian Nights* is the product of several oral traditions and contains stories and motifs from a variety of geographic areas and historical periods, including ancient Mesopotamia, India during the height of classical Sanskrit literature, early medieval Persia and Iraq, and Turkish-dominated Egypt of the late Middle Ages. While their exact sources are difficult to ascertain, it is believed that the tales were circulated orally throughout the Arabic world for centuries before being recorded. One of the earliest incarnations of *The Arabian Nights,* a Persian text entitled *Hazar afsana,* or "Thousand Stories," was purportedly translated into Arabic in the eighth century as *Alf layla,* or "Thousand Nights." The earliest extant record of *The Arabian Nights* is a ninth-century fragment of *Alf layla.* Classical Arabic authors explicitly mention the collection during the tenth century and later references in Arabic literature indicate that *The Arabian Nights* underwent continuous augmentations and other modifications throughout the Middle Ages.

In 1704 French Orientalist Antoine Galland introduced *The Arabian Nights* to European readers, publishing the first installment of his twelve-volume *Les Mille et une nuits* (1704-17), a French translation of the tales largely based on a Syrian manuscript and supplemented by oral sources. English translations by Edward W. Lane in 1831-41 and John Payne in 1882-84 led to Richard F. Burton's *The Book of the Thousand Nights and a Night* (1885), the most famous and widely read English-language version. More recently, Muhsin Mahdi published a meticulously researched edition entitled *Kitāb*

Alf laylah wa-laylah (1984) taken from a highly regarded fourteenth-century Syrian manuscript. Although scholars continue to debate the merits of various versions and translations, the tales of *The Arabian Nights* have become ingrained in the popular imagination of both Eastern and Western culture.

PLOT AND MAJOR CHARACTERS

The most extensive editions of *The Arabian Nights* contain approximately three hundred tales, many of which are interwoven or contain recurring characters. The tales are linked together within a frame-story about a young woman named Scheherazade, whose father is the principal officer of state for the murderous King Shahryar. After executing his adulterous wife, the king has become determined to exact his revenge upon women in general. He decides to marry a different virgin every night so that he may have her killed the following morning. In an attempt to save the women of the kingdom, Scheherazade offers herself to the king with the intention of ending this deadly cycle. As their first night together draws to a close, she begins to tell the king a story. The tale is soon interrupted by daybreak, but King Shahryar has become so enthralled that he postpones Scheherazade's execution so that she may conclude her story. The next night, however, Scheherazade deftly shifts the king's attention to a new tale as morning arrives, and her death is again delayed. This pattern repeats itself for the duration of the narrative, until Shahryar makes Scheherazade his queen.

Some of the most popular characters within the frame-story include Harun al-Rashid, Sindbad the Sailor, Ali Baba, and Aladdin. Harun al-Rashid was an actual caliph, or king, who ruled Baghdad from the year 775 to 785. He is a legend in Muslim history for his bravery and cultivation of the arts. His character in *The Arabian Nights,* an insomniac caliph who wanders the streets of Baghdad in disguise, is highly fictionalized and bears only a passing resemblance to the historical figure. Though he reappears throughout the collection, Harun al-Rashid is featured most prominently in "The Porter and the Three Ladies of Baghdad." The plot of this story, which comprises four interconnected tales, concerns three wealthy sisters who invite a group of guests—including the caliph posing as a merchant— into their home for food and shelter. When the guests inquire about their hostesses' personal lives, the sisters become offended and bind them to their chairs. By way of a narrative device common to many of the tales, the guests must tell entertaining stories to avoid being murdered.

Though they rank among the most celebrated stories of *The Arabian Nights* in Western culture, the tales "Aladdin and the Magic Lamp," "Ali Baba and the Forty Thieves," and "Sindbad the Sailor" do not originate from the earliest known manuscripts of the text, but were compiled by Galland for his French adaptation. Due to their immense popularity among European readers, Burton included the tales of Aladdin, Ali Baba, and Sindbad in his English translation, and these stories have since inspired innumerable imitations, pastiches, and adaptations by Western artists. Another character made famous by *The Arabian Nights* is that of the *jinni,* or genie. Although the concept of mystical spirits known as the *jinn* has existed in the Arabic world since pre-Islamic times, the Westernized notion of the "genie in the bottle" as the granter of wishes comes directly from *The Arabian Nights.*

MAJOR THEMES

One of the distinguishing elements of *The Arabian Nights* is its emphasis on class and social custom. This delineation of social hierarchies not only anchors the traditionalism of the stories but also reflects the medieval Arabic society in which most of the tales originate. The work also contains a didactic component which promotes a strong bond between individual and community, the resolution of domestic issues, the pious observance of God's will, and a resignation to fate. Other recurring moral messages in the collection include the folly of pompous behavior and the inevitability of violence to end in regret. The latter lesson figures prominently in several tales, including the frame-story of Scheherazade, as characters facing imminent violence choose an alternate course of action—namely the act of storytelling—in defense. Furthermore, *The Arabian Nights* recommends the proper application of magnanimous justice, which is illustrated in the first story cycle, "The Merchant and the Jinn." Rather than facing death or torture, the wicked characters in this tale are penalized by being transformed into animals. This considerate solution contrasts sharply with King Shahryar's execution of innocent women as punishment for the wrongdoing of his unfaithful wife. Finally, the narrative structure of the work suggests the magical and timeless nature of storytelling. Scheherazade's tales not only disrupt and delay the murderous rage of King Shahryar, but also serve as a metaphor for the ability of stories to operate on a level unaffected by time. Indeed, the universal concerns of love, death, happiness, fate, and immortality which permeate the work have transcended linguistic and cultural boundaries for over ten centuries.

CRITICAL RECEPTION

Critical analyses of *The Arabian Nights* have focused on the complex history of its sources and translations. In many cases, the translated texts have been deemed inferior to ancient Egyptian and Syrian manuscripts, particularly due to the inclusion of stories that do not appear in the earliest source material. As scholar and translator Husain Haddawy has asserted: "These translators did not, as one might expect, compare the various editions to establish an accurate text for their translations . . . instead they deleted and added at random, or at will, from the various sources to piece together a text that suited their individual purposes: in the case of Lane, a detailed but expurgated version; in the case of Payne and Burton, versions that are as full and complete as possible." Others have praised the English translation of Lane, specifically, for capturing the anthropological value of the text. Critic Jennifer Schacker-Mill, for example, has highlighted Lane's intent to "make readers more familiar with the manners, customs, and beliefs of the Arabs," characterizing his translation as one which is "guided by cultural expertise, as well as running ethnographic commentary." The variations in the collection across different cultures and time periods have been viewed as an indication of shifts in societal norms. In her discussion of Galland's French version, critic Rida Hawari has demonstrated the significance of cultural climate to the translator's text, stating: "Galland allows himself to invent details and even episodes which, in my view, are of a kind that his readers, accustomed to the sophistication of French literary taste in narrative, expect in a story. He allows himself to increase the piety, splendour and glamorous nature of the original, adding, as part of his narrative, a running commentary to explain obscurer points for the benefit of Western understanding."

In addition to the wealth of discourse concerning the merits and shortcomings of various translations, scholars have centered on the immense influence of *The Arabian Nights,* linking it to such disparate works as Voltaire's *Zadig,* the films of German expressionist Fritz Lang, the stories of Edgar Allan Poe, and Mark Twain's *Adventures of Huckleberry Finn.* Also, commentators have analyzed the stories according to Sigmund Freud's psychological theories and examined the role of Scheherazade as an early form of feminist characterization. Moreover, critics have addressed the universal appeal of *The Arabian Nights,* encapsulated by Haddawy as follows: "The essential quality of these tales lies in their success in interweaving the unusual, the extraordinary, the marvelous, and the supernatural into the fabric of everyday life. . . . Yet both the usual incidents and the extraordinary coincidences are nothing but the web and weft of Divine Providence, in a world in which people often suffer but come out all right at the end. They are enriched by the pleasure of a marvelous adventure and a sense of wonder, which makes life possible."

PRINCIPAL WORKS

Alf layla wa-layla [*A Thousand and One Nights*] c. 9-10th century

Principal Editions

Les Mille et une nuits, contes arabes traduits en français. 12 vols. (translated by Antoine Galland) 1704-17

The Thousand and One Nights, Commonly Called, in England, The Arabian Nights' Entertainments: A New Translation from the Arabic, with Copious Notes. 3 vols. (translated by Edward William Lane) 1831-41

The Book of the Thousand Nights and One Night (translated by John Payne) 1882-84

The Book of the Thousand Nights and a Night: A Plain and Literal Translation of the Arabian Nights' Entertainments (translated by Richard F. Burton) 1885

The Arabian Nights' Entertainments (selected and edited by Andrew Lang) 1898

Kitāb Alf laylah wa-laylah (edited by Muhsin Mahdi) 1984

The Arabian Nights: Based on the Text of the Fourteenth-Century Syrian Manuscript (translated by Husain Haddawy and edited by Mahdi) 1990

The Thousand and One Nights (edited by Mahdi) 1995

CRITICISM

Judith Grossman (essay date spring 1980)

SOURCE: Grossman, Judith. "Infidelity and Fiction: The Discovery of Women's Subjectivity in *Arabian Nights*." *The Georgia Review* 34, no. 1 (spring 1980): 113-26.

[*In the following essay, Grossman focuses on the frame-story of* The Arabian Nights, *demonstrating the thematic significance of Scheherazade's narration when interpreted "as a social act undertaken in a specified context of events."*]

The story of Scheherazade has become one of the universal cultural possessions. Although the work in which she figures has not usually been granted serious status in Islamic high culture, in the West (no doubt as a side benefit of the Orientalism so rigorously analyzed by Edward Said) it has frequently been seen as a unique locus for insights into the nature and functions of narrative. In our time, Frank Kermode and John Barth have both used Scheherazade as an emblem of the anxious ego prolonging its existence by means of the ever-renewed process of narration: a deep and accurate perception of the labor of the subjective self. To some extent the interpretation of the story which I offer here concurs with theirs; but my focus is not on a solipsistic narrator—it is on narration as a social act undertaken in a specified context of events. Read in this way, the framing story of *The Thousand and One Nights* again releases a new set of meanings to extend our understanding of fiction and its relation to the history of consciousness.

The story begins with the Persian King Shahryar and his brother, formerly happy and fortunate men, discovering the secret adulteries of each of their wives with the black slaves of the palace. As a result of these betrayals the royal brothers institute a policy of marrying young virgins every evening and executing them the morning after; until at last the supply of virgins runs short, and Shahrazad (the preferred form of her name in most translations) comes forward, and succeeds in changing the King's mind with her stories. Clearly the precipitating factor in the tale is the discovery of women's deceit and sexual depravity—a familiar theme indeed, and the preoccupation with it haunts this and many other texts, Islamic and Christian alike, from the medieval period and after.[1] It is a preoccupation which both attracts, by its concern with "the truth" about human nature, and repels us by its fierce animus. We may respond by categorizing the associated themes as "primitive" (though they persist with vigor to this day), and thus dismiss them. Or we may recall Heinrich Zimmer's warning against such distancing of the perennially retold tale:

> The fairy tale, the childlike legend (i.e., the message bearer) is methodically regarded as too lowly to merit our submission, both the tale itself and those zones of our nature that respond to it being comparatively unadult. Yet it would have been through the interaction of that outer and this inner innocence that the fertilizing power of the symbol might have been activated and the hidden content disclosed.[2]

Such a warning applies properly to the *Nights* [*The Thousand and One Nights*] as a work which draws heavily on folklore materials; and indeed the symbols continue to have power and a content for us. The story of King Shahryar and Shahrazad, I would argue, presents in an early form the problem which the recognition of female subjectivity has set for male-dominated cultures. The struggle with this problem can be traced in a range of literary texts from the late classical period onward, and the problem itself is at its root linked to the philosophical problem of "other minds." We can state it this way, from the male perspective: "Are women selves, in the same way that I am a self? And if they are, how should I act towards them?"

In taking up the manifestation of the issue in a chosen text we must, however, supply an historical context for the relatively modern assumption of conscious individual selfhood. And such a context can be located precisely in the early stages of prose fiction itself, the genre to which the *Nights* belong.

It has been widely recognized that prose fiction as a genre is historically associated with the development and fortunes of the differentiated (or detribalized) individual consciousness.[3] Typically, fiction has first arisen in urban environments where individual mobility and social freedom were expanded, and where interchange between different cultures enabled a new perspective on traditional cultural imperatives. In the Western world, early novels such as those of Petronius and Apuleius are cases in point: they took shape in culturally mixed, urban environments under the Roman empire—as later the *Nights* originated in the context of an Islamic supranationalist empire with many urban centers. These early fictional works are often marked by a distinct comic bias, in part resulting from the application of newly discovered double vision and meaning, *irony,* to the social scene, and in part reflecting the euphoric sense of fresh understanding and deliverance from an old tribal darkness. Images of light and enlightenment accompany the development and freeing of the individual consciousness (cf. the term "Enlightenment" as referring to a period after the breakdown of religious orthodoxy in Europe, in which the independent critical mind dominates). But invariably there also sets in a recognition of the miseries as well as the gains of differentiation.

Hence Apuleius' hero in *The Golden Ass* suffers a homeless instability (of physical form as well as ethical state) until he is saved by the universal religion of Isis: the detribalized individual must bear the loss of the old certainties, of fixed behavioral structures, of attachment to family and tribe—in general, the ills of alienation. Moreover, at any time the push for individual autonomy (inseparable from consciousness itself) may come to be stigmatized by social authorities old or new as morally wicked; and it is worth noting that this is particularly the case wherever the emergence of such drives in women is acknowledged.

Petronius illustrates this issue in his *Satyricon,* particularly in the tale of the Widow of Ephesus, a predecessor of King Shahryar's unfaithful wife. Here—in the story of a woman who exchanges the fixed traditional role of a chaste wife devoted unto death (with its prescribed gestures of hair- and cheek-tearing) for a self who feels her own hungers and satisfies them—we can discern a marvelous parable of the second birth into consciousness. From a tribal unit, she becomes a person in our sense of the word—guilty and authentic at once. After the Widow breaks her fast and consummates her new love for the soldier, in her dead husband's tomb, danger threatens the couple: one of the crucified bodies which the soldier should have been guarding has been removed, and his life is forfeit should his superiors find out. In this crisis the Widow saves her lover by proposing the crucifixion of her husband's corpse to replace the missing criminal's body. For Petronius' narrator this action adds outrageous impiety to sexual immorality. Yet the story is far more than the misogynistic *exemplum* it claims to be, and the humane quality of Petronius' tolerance opens it to the deeper interpretation: that the woman's behavior is, in contrast to her previous suicidal rigor, life-seeking, and an effective, even creative initiative in the given situation. The lovers' being saved by a crucifixion also calls to mind that the Gospel teaching during this same period was shifting emphasis from religious law to individual salvation: *the letter killeth, but the spirit giveth life.*

The Widow of Ephesus comes alive as a conscious self, but in doing so betrays her (admittedly deceased) husband. The link thus forged between the achievement of autonomous selfhood and sexual disloyalty becomes a regular feature of later storytelling about women, and it concerns us vitally here. For the obsessive questioning of women's fidelity/honesty, and the outright denials of its existence are wholly bound up with the acknowledgment of their possession of a subjective self. (It may be speculated that to question whether women "have souls," which was occasionally debated in the medieval period, is the same as to question whether women "are selves.")

The activating force in *The Thousand and One Nights* is the shattering revelation of their wives' adultery experienced by King Shahryar and his brother. What they saw can be redefined as women demonstrating their capacity for autonomous life by making passionate love with their black slaves. But why are the women doing this, at the grave risk of their lives? That is a question posed by one of the injured husbands and never answered directly since the wives are not permitted to speak. But after the first crisis of rage and grief, King Shahryar makes a proposal which begins obliquely to address it:

> Let us up as we are and depart forthright hence, for we have no concern with Kingship, and let us overwander Allah's earth, worshipping the Almighty till we find some one to whom the like calamity hath happened; and if we find none then will death be more welcome to us than life.[4]

If, he says, these betrayals are unique offenses against themselves as individuals, they will be unbearably shameful (reflecting discredit on the victims as insufficient in their roles as husbands?). But Shahryar raises another possibility: that the actual nature of the world and of human behavior may be different from what he has up to now supposed. Certainly wives *used to be* faithful—hence his former attitude of trust; but perhaps some or all women now have autonomous desires and the capacity to deceive their husbands in order to satisfy them. He proposes to settle the question by an empirical investigation—in itself an individualist strategy—and they go out into the world to find out what lies behind these disruptive events.

Here we should briefly note the narrowed emphasis in the *Nights* on disloyalty and deceit, separate from the issue of sexual fidelity as a guarantee of the paternity of heirs. Such a separation may perhaps be related to the Islamic practice of polygamy that almost guaranteed a choice of suitable heirs to the patriarch (whereas Western monogamous men staked everything on one contract); suspected bastards might be destroyed along with the guilty wife, without putting the succession in jeopardy. And this is a clarifying factor in the situation with which we are dealing; King Shahryar can ignore the matter of paternity entirely and focus on women's capacity for guile and for unsanctioned sexual choice.

Deceit itself as an element in human behavior also requires a moment's consideration. I want first to invoke the etiology assigned to deceit in modern psychological theory, and specifically the way in which its appearance is taken to mark a certain developmental stage in all young children:

> Freud once explained that the child's first lie, that is to say, his first secret, is one of the first signs of his beginning capacity for separation and individuation. . . . All lying, all secreting, derives . . . from the capacity to put apart, to separate me from thee, mine from thine, self from object.[5]

Lying thus appears as a normative phenomenon of nascent individuality, of the formation of a private autonomous space—in the context, it must be remembered, of a coercive parental environment, for the child's will is not yet the sovereign factor in its life. Later, as the child matures into adulthood, deceit should become unnecessary as ethical/social rules are internalized, and as the parents gradually relinquish their power. This is, of course, an optimal picture of human development; in fact, societies and families alike act to thwart what I would call the "empowering" of the self or granting of independence. Where such empowering of selves is also selective (granted to one social group and denied to another), precisely there we find deceitfulness attributed to the hindered group. The history of such attribution is well known: servants have traditionally been

called dishonest; blacks have been called untrustworthy; and in the medieval period deceitfulness was regularly ascribed to women as a quality, as is shown in the Wife of Bath's proverbial tag—

> Deceite, wepyng, spynnyng God hath yive
> To wommen kyndely, whil that they may lyve.[6]

It may be assumed that in subordinate groups dishonesty arises and is noted in proportion to the sense of a valid autonomy violated—and that it will be condemned by the dominant group precisely as implying the threat of independent thought and will.

We are most familiar with negative valuations of deceitfulness, for obvious reasons, but the exceptional positive valuation is as revealing about its place in human history. The Greek Odysseus, famous for cunning and for the manipulation of appearances, represents such a favorable valuation. Odysseus has been shown to be a figure marking a distinct shift in human consciousness as we find it represented in literature. Unlike the heroes of an older sort—Achilles, Agamemnon—he inhabits a world of monstrous disorder where the traditional rules have broken down after the fall of Troy. In a setting of cultural confusion Odysseus is, as George Dimock puts it, "a master of the delayed response, of the long way round, of the resisted impulse. That is the reason he is able to keep his identity intact."[7] The automatic, coded response has become disastrous, and Odysseus' control, his self-manipulative cunning, is an adaptive strategy for survival.

More recently Julian Jaynes has argued the case for Odysseus as a hero with a new achievement, that of subjective identity *per se*; and he further illuminates the relation of deceit to the possession of such an identity: "Long-term deceit requires the invention of an analog self that can 'do' or 'be' something quite different from what the person actually does or is, as seen by his associates."[8] In Jaynes's view, the capacity for deceit figures both as an adaptive response to historical pressures (involving, as we would now expect, the experience of alien cultures, *difference,* as well as the experience of weakness, nondominance), and also as a developmental phase in human evolution. But whether it is considered as a product of individual human development or of whole cultures at large, we can affirm that the capacity to lie characterizes the subjective self in conflict with forces too strong to be challenged openly with any hope of success.[9]

Now we bring these observations to bear on King Shahryar and his brother, wandering through the world. As they rest one day under a tree near the ocean, they happen to see a huge demon or Jinni emerging from the waves—a coal-black monster of terrifying aspect. The brothers climb into the tree to hide; the Jinni approaches, and as they watch sets down a large box close by in the shade. This he opens; within it is a locked chest out of which he takes a beautiful young woman. The Jinni addresses her as his beloved, and within a short time lies down to sleep with his head in her lap. Soon however the young woman looks up and sees the men in the tree, and after quietly removing the Jinni's head from her lap she goes over and commands them to descend and have intercourse with her. Reluctantly they comply, in fear of her threats to awaken the Jinni, after which she demands their seal-rings for her collection— numbering five hundred and seventy—and then tells her brief story:

> Of a truth this Ifrit bore me off on my bride-night, and put me into a casket and set the casket in a coffer and to the coffer he affixed seven strong padlocks of steel and deposited me on the deep bottom of the sea that raves, dashing and clashing with waves; and guarded me so that I might remain chaste and honest, quotha! that none save himself might have connexion with me. But I have lain under as many of my kind as I please, and this wretched Jinni wotteth not that Destiny may not be averted nor hindered by aught, and that whatso woman willeth the same she fulfilleth however man nilleth.

(I, 12-13)

The Destiny cited in this passage which cannot be hindered or averted is surely the familiar and inexorable cycle of coercion and revenge. The Jinni began the cycle by treating this woman as an object, kept in a box except when needed, and ignoring her status as a *self*. She is therefore unimpressed with the Jinni's attractions, even though he is black, "foul" and "filthy" like the blackamoor slaves whom the wives of the kings had loved—thereby pointing up the fact that what each of these women wanted was the self-made, the alternatively defined choice. This woman's freedom has been compressed into the short measure of the Jinni's sleep, and she has used it economically enough to assert whatever she can of herself, in reaction against her sexual bondage. By threatening other men with the Jinni's terrible power, she can practice sexual coercion on them in her turn, while getting revenge on her oppressor. The actions of oppressor and oppressed become fully reciprocal. Deceit meanwhile is the very mode of her continued existence as a person.

From this scene King Shahryar and his brother return home convinced simply that "they all do it." Shahryar resolves never to marry again, but finding that he cannot live without a woman he implements a new solution to the problem of unfaithful wives—marriage and consummation followed by execution. What has happened here? Shahryar has misread the experience he was offered, and failed to understand his own part in it—for he himself has cuckolded the Jinni just as the slave had cuckolded him, and all are contributors to the dynamic of coercion and revenge.

Shahrazad now enters the story as the heroic figure who must break this destructive bind. Her name was glossed by Burton as either "city-freer" or "lion-born," and connotes courage and achievement either way. She is the daughter of the King's minister, or Wazir, and has been spared from the slaughter so far because of her father's position; now she steps forward of her own accord with a plan to marry the King and save the situation. Shahrazad is deeply learned in history: "[she] had perused the books, annals and legends of preceding Kings, and the stories, examples and instances of by-gone men and things; indeed it was said that she had collected a thousand books of histories relating to antique races and departed rulers" (I, 15). She has also studied poetry, philosophy, the sciences, and the arts, but it is primarily as an historian that she triumphs, combating the King's narrow reading of experience with the immense resources of reported lives: the line between history and storytelling must be blurred here, as it was in the medieval period itself, to stress a common focus on *life-histories*.

It is of the first importance that Shahrazad herself decides to marry the King, even against her father's wish: "I will not listen to thy words and, if thou deny me, I will marry myself to him despite the nose of thee" (I, 23). Since her decision is followed by the King's ratification of it and his summons to her to appear that night, it is made clear that there is an equal commitment on both sides to the match. Each partner was free to have avoided it. By contrast the sexual relationships presented in the story up to now have all evidenced an imbalance of power and by implication an imbalance of intention: the kings ruled over their wives; the wives in turn could command their slaves; the Jinni's magic kept his wife in bondage. In fact, Shahryar has observed in his own life, as in the Jinni's case, a breakdown in the efficacy of what is substantially an ownership system: a body may be physically confined, but a self cannot be owned. The Jinni's wife asserts that the autonomous will cannot be defeated, and she proves it. Hence the deadlock, in which Shahryar has condemned himself to need the human being but to destroy the interior self (such a self is contingent upon a history, the unfolding of behavior over time, and this extension in time is what the King denies to his brides). Shahrazad's task will be to show the King that although the old certainty about behavioral roles has gone, and cannot be restored by force, a reasonable security in personal relationships can be gained by basing them on agreement between selves of equal status.

But for the moment, Shahrazad is threatened with execution the next morning, and she needs a strategy to avoid it. Her plan, as we know, is to tell part of a story to the King in the hours before dawn, so that when morning comes he must, if he wishes to hear the end of it, postpone her execution until the next day (fortunately the King keeps strict working hours). The plan will function by distracting the King, and there is an element of trickery in it too: Shahrazad will signal to her sister Dunyazad, present in the marriage chamber by previous arrangement, and Dunyazad will respond by asking for a story "to while away the waking hours" (I, 24) of their cultivated insomnia. This trick is essentially Odyssean, involving the control of instinctive responses to the threatening situation; it constitutes heroic deception as a survival strategy undertaken in the face of overwhelming odds.

A second motive of the plan emerges in the tales themselves when the immediate threat to life has receded: as cited in the conclusion of the *Nights,* it has to do with "warning for the man of wits and admonishment for the wise" (X, 55). For the framing story is not merely an excuse for assembling a random collection of entertaining tales; it exemplifies and comments on the function of stories, true or imagined, in helping us to lead non-disastrous lives. In a world of differentiated individuals—each with a singular nature and set of motivations, capable of honesty and dishonesty alike—the only way to develop good judgment is by gaining wide experience. But since our personal experience must be limited, fiction and history alike must expand and complete it. We can see this process at work in the first group of tales which Shahrazad tells: their thematic relevance to the framing story is brought out by contiguity.

Shahrazad begins with the tale of the merchant who while eating his lunch under a tree innocently throws away some date-stones, which by accident strike and kill the son of a powerful Jinni. The Jinni appears, and condemns the merchant to death; and when the merchant asks pardon on the grounds that he had no murderous intentions, the Jinni persists in invoking the old law of an eye for an eye. One sees a similarity already between this situation and the King's own encounter with a Jinni—had *that* Jinni awakened at the inopportune moment, the King too would have been condemned for an offence unwillingly committed. So right away fiction begins to work on the King's experience, and to connect with his social function as the administrator of justice in his kingdom. The link extends to Shahrazad's situation also, condemned to death for being a woman and the King's bride, not for any crime committed by her. Both she and the King may therefore be said to have a stake in the merchant's survival.

Shahrazad's merchant wins a stay of his execution for the purpose of arranging his family affairs. When he returns at the appointed time for death, it happens that three old men come by, one leading a gazelle, the second leading greyhounds, the third driving a mule. The merchant tells them of his predicament and they are moved by his fidelity to his word, pledged to the Jinni; so when the Jinni himself descends from the air bran-

dishing his sword, the first old man comes forward to intervene. He proposes (like Shahrazad herself) to tell his story to the Jinni, and he demands a reward of one-third of the merchant's blood (i.e., his life) if the story is approved. The proposal is accepted, and so begins the next tale-within-a-tale, which concerns the old man and his evil wife who by magic turned her stepson into a calf for the slaughter. Dawn breaks and Shahrazad stops her narrative with the old man remembering how he took the knife in his hand to butcher his own unrecognized son: it is a moment of dreadful warning, the message of which is—do not kill unless you can know fully whom you are killing, and why.

King Shahryar responds appropriately to this message. He delays the order for Shahrazad's death, and is rewarded the next night with further instruction. The old man's son, it turns out, was saved from death by the power of a good woman, whose white magic offset the spells of the evil wife. As for the wife, she was turned into the harmless gazelle which the old man now leads with him everywhere. Her fate demonstrates a refined justice: she had suffered much because of her inability to bear a child of her own, and although she must be punished, the punishment imposed is less than death; moreover, the form she is assigned is at least that of a graceful gazelle, and reflects her former beauty. Thus Shahrazad's first story shows the King that in a world of variable circumstances, in which evil and good women are both to be found, the hard task is to make discriminating choices and decisions, and further, that since evil springs from sorrow, justice should be tempered with compassion.

The first old man's story wins one-third of the merchant's life; those of the second and third old men complete his redemption. The tale of the third comes closest of all in one way to the King's own story, for it concerns a wife's adultery; yet here again the evil done by one woman is counteracted by the good actions of another. In all three of the stories, evildoers are brought to judgment, and although they deserve death according to the strict code of law, they are punished by transformation into an animal form in each case—the gazelle, the greyhounds, and the mule. Surely a point is made here about avoidance of the kind of extreme solution which Shahryar has attempted to the problem of wrongdoing: although these criminals were rightly convicted and condemned (all of them were attempted murderers), they were and are people much loved by those who must judge them, and this love enables the mitigation of punishment and the continuance of caring. By contrast, King Shahryar's execution of his wife and all subsequent brides has brought him only the hatred of his subjects for his ruinous depopulation of the city.

The ending of the merchant's story is accomplished when the Jinni gives up his claim of vengeance. And now Shahryar can begin to see the true nature of the world in the vastness of scope and possibility which is reflected in the stories of the *Thousand and One Nights.* By the time the resolution of the framing story is reached, Shahrazad has given birth to three children in the course of almost three years of storytelling. She cites these infants as the grounds for her claim to be freed, at last, from the King's death sentence on her, for who will be able to bring them up and educate them as she could? To which the King replies that he had pardoned her in his mind even before she had borne her children. Just as the marriage between them had occurred as the result of a dual initiative, so their full reconciliation is the result of a coincidence of appeal and concession.

Shahrazad refers with pride to her great achievement as a storyteller and teacher of wisdom, and she brings her long discourse to an end triumphantly, after which follows this passage:

> Then she ceased to speak, and when King Shahriyar heard her speech and profited by that which she said, he summoned up his reasoning powers and cleansed his heart and caused his understanding revert and turned to Allah Almighty and said to himself, "Since there befel the Kings of the Chosroës more than that which hath befallen me, never, whilst I live, shall I cease to blame myself for the past. As for this Shahrazad, her like is not found in the lands; so praise be to Him who appointed her a means for delivering His creatures from oppression and slaughter!"[10]

Here we may say that the tale is a little wiser than the teller. For Shahryar knows more now than just the fact that women's adultery is one among the many and various misfortunes of the world, and that women along with men are creatures of Allah and subject to His law and mercy. Before his conversion, the King had proceeded on the assumption that the world (and women as representative of the world outside of self) could be objectified and controlled. Faced with the appearance of interiority in his wife, he responded by abolishing it—and by continuing to abolish it everywhere in his vicinity. His mentality here was similar to that of the Jinni who insisted on a life for a life regardless of individual circumstances: actions were recognized by both of them as real, but no recognition was allowed the selves or subjects who were the origins of those actions. Men were for the Jinni what women were for Shahryar: an undifferentiated class of beings, externally perceived as the objects of intention.

By means of her stories Shahrazad has offered the King massive amounts of evidence for the existence of a variety of subjective motivations in men and women alike; and she has established through multiple examples the observation that female subjectivity in particular is not intrinsically evil. This observation has been clinched by her own example; for by prolonging her life she has

given the King a chance to experience *her* behavior as a choosing self, thus breaking down his absolutist views on female reality. And we may speculate that the work she performed in these respects could only have been done during those long nighttime hours—the time when the King must rest from his occupational exercise of the royal will: from the tyranny of intention.

The book ends with a formal wedding to celebrate the permanent union of Shahryar and Shahrazad. The King summons his royal brother Shah Zaman to the feast, and—won over by Shahrazad's triumph—he marries her sister Dunyazad and renounces his vendetta against women also. Here a new theme appears, extending the harmony of reformed human relations. The two sisters make it a condition of the double wedding that they not be separated—that henceforth the two couples must live in the same place, not in separate cities. The condition is accepted, and all proceed to live happily together until death. The theme here is that of the coexistence of similar and therefore potentially competing selves. It can be assumed that the recognition of subjective selfhood mutually between man and man would precede such recognition between man and woman, and this is surely the point reached at the start of the *Thousand and One Nights.* King Shahryar and his younger brother seem there to be on roughly equal terms with each other, and they engage in mutual acknowledgment. Yet though they love each other dearly, King Shahryar at the start of his reign sends his brother far away to rule Samarkand, and the implication is obvious that harmony depends on a sufficient distance between the two sovereignties. It may then be part of Shahrazad's achievement to demonstrate that sovereign selves can live together through negotiation and mutual agreement. The household of the two Kings and their wives thus become a model of mutual recognition and accommodation between same-sex as well as different-sex pairs.

The story of Shahrazad and its relationship to the mythology of female evil may be seen more clearly with the help of this observation by Frank Kermode:

> We have to distinguish between myths and fictions. Fictions can degenerate into myths whenever they are not consciously held to be fictive. In this sense anti-Semitism is a degenerate fiction, a myth; and *Lear* is a fiction. Myth operates within the diagrams of ritual, which presupposes total and adequate explanations of things as they are and were; it is a sequence of radically unchangeable gestures. Fictions are for finding things out, and they change as the needs of sense-making change. Myths are the agents of stability, fictions the agents of change.[11]

Operating under such a myth, King Shahryar, wounded and enraged by betrayal, fixed his world in the image of that event, and over and over again enacted the ritual of killing the "evil wife." When Shahrazad came to intervene and disrupt the deathly ritual, she did so not as a revived figure from a "good" traditional past but as a fully empowered self armed with new resources for coming to terms with a world crowded with autonomous yet interdependent selves. Shahrazad demonstrates the power of fiction in this situation to hold off the apocalyptic passion for deaths and endings; she inter poses the imagination of reality to maintain life and time in existence until the King's madness passes and he is able to accept things as they are.

Notes

1. As a concern, it is already alive in later classical literature—in Propertius and in Petronius (q.v.), for instance. But it is in the medieval period that it comes to dominate cultural attitudes towards women at large.

2. Heinrich Zimmer, *The King and the Corpse: Tales of the Soul's Conquest of Evil,* ed. Joseph Campbell (Bollingen Series XI, Princeton: Princeton Univ. Press, 2nd ed. 1957, repr. 1973), pp. 2-3.

3. See Ben Edwin Perry, *The Ancient Romances* (Berkeley: Univ. of California Press, 1967); see also Ian Watt's account of the background to English fiction in *The Rise of the Novel* (Berkeley: Univ. of California Press, 1960).

4. *The Book of the Thousand Nights and a Night,* tr. Richard F. Burton (Medina Edition: Burton Club rpt. of set originally published by the Kamashastra Society in 1885-86; neither place nor date of the reprinted volumes is known; they are pirated facsimile reprints—thought to have been printed in America, possibly Boston), I, 10. All citations are to this most widely available edition.

5. Rudolph Ekstein and Elaine Caruth, "Keeping Secrets," in *Tactics and Techniques in Psychoanalytic Therapy,* ed. P. Giovacchini (New York: Science House, 1972), pp. 200-201.

6. F. N. Robinson, ed., *The Works of Geoffrey Chaucer,* 2nd ed. (Boston: Houghton Mifflin, 1961), p. 80.

7. George E. Dimock, Jr., "The Name of Odysseus," in *Homer: A Collection of Critical Essays,* ed. George Steiner and Robert Fagles (Englewood Cliffs, N.J.: Prentice-Hall, 1962), p. 118.

8. Julian Jaynes, *The Origin of Consciousness in the Breakdown of the Bicameral Mind* (Boston: Houghton Mifflin, 1977), p. 219.

9. Cf. Georges Dumézil's discussion in *The Destiny of The Warrior* (Chicago: Univ. of Chicago Press, 1970) of Indo-European traditions of heroic victories gained by deceitful means (pp. 46-49).

10. *Nights,* X, 55. (Burton specifies in Volume I of this edition that Shahryar's name should be spelled without the *i;* but the name appears only as *Shahri-*

yar throughout Volume X.) In connection with this passage, it has been pointed out to me by Professor Herbert Mason of Boston University that a political interpretation is relevant: Shahrazad, besides being a Wisdom figure to enlighten Man in the prison of his carnality, can be seen as the messenger of God sent to correct a tyrannical monarch—Islam triumphant over the ever-heretical Persian monarchy!

11. *The Sense of an Ending* (New York: Oxford Univ. Press, 1967), p. 39.

Rida Hawari (essay date April-June 1980)

SOURCE: Hawari, Rida. "Antoine Galland's Translation of the *Arabian Nights.*" *Revue de Littérature Comparée* 54, no. 2 (April-June 1980): 150-64.

[*In the following essay, Hawari underscores the enormous popularity of Antoine Galland's translation of* The Arabian Nights *in eighteenth-century England, highlighting Galland's efforts to censor the risqué aspects of his source documents.*]

According to Chauvin's most complete bibliography of **Les Mille et Une Nuits,** all twelve volumes of Galland's French translation of the work had made their appearance between 1704 and 1717.[1] The first six volumes, which had appeared in 1704, suddenly made their appearance (in English) under the title of **Arabian Nights Entertainments,**[2] a title which has since stuck to the English version of the **Nights** [**The Arabian Nights**] and has even been translated into Arabic for the Calcutta edition of 1839-1842. It would seem that the first issue of this **Arabian Nights Entertainments** had been well know between 1708 and 1709. For in 1709, *The Golden Spy,* a book ascribed to Charles Gildon, had made its appearance, and in the dedication, its author, who was addressing Jonathan Swift, makes the remark: "The Arabian and Turkish Tales were owing to your Tale of a Tub".[3] Now, *The Golden Spy,* is a collection of stories of the type of *The adventures of a guinea.* It is also

> A Political Journal of the British Nights Entertainments of War and Peace, and Love and Politics: wherein are laid open, The Secret Miraculous Power and Progress of Gold, in the Courts of Europe. Intermixed with Delightful Intrigues, Memoirs, Tales, and Adventures, Serious and Comical.[4]

Evidently, the author of the *Golden Spy* could place some reliance on the recognition by his public of his allusion to it in the title "British Nights Entertainments". The **Arabian Nights Entertainments** must have suggested to him this basically imitative title in the same way it has since done to many a writer. But apart from the title, the *Nights* must have suggested to Gildon the manner in which he has told his own "Entertainments" as well as the framework in which he has fitted them. In short, apart from his book serving as external evidence in determining the date of the first English *Nights,* it is also the first book ever to borrow the essentially Oriental story-structure of the *Arabian Nights* for the purpose of telling tales essentially Occidental in nature and content.

The popularity of the *Arabian Nights* since the appearance of this English editio princeps is not difficult to gauge when we remember that the number of English editions derived from the version of Galland amounted to no less than twenty different editions before the turn of the 18th century[5] and more than forty during the 19th.[6] Parallel to this is, of course, the very large number of editions (many of which are also derived from Galland's French copy) in almost every language. It is interesting to note that Chauvin's bibliography of *Les Mille et Une Nuits,* in all languages, occupies ninety-five full pages of his work.[7] And yet, the enthusiastic reception accorded to the *Nights* after its first publication in Europe is, in my view, due more to Galland as a translator and to the special nature and qualities of his copy than to any other translator after him or, for that matter, to the original Arabic version that he had used and translated. His work possesses—par excellence—those special qualities and characteristics which were instrumental in giving impetus to European imagination and which are reflected in the works of most European writers.

First, then, Galland's original source and his special way of handling it. In his Epistle Dedicatory to the Lady Marchioness d'O, Galland sheds much light on the original sources he used. At a certain point in his epistle, he begs of her « la même protection que vous avez bien voulu accorder à la traduction Françoise de sept Contes Arabes que j'eus l'honneur de vous présenter ».[8] Then he goes on to say:

> Vous vous étonnerez que depuis ce tems-là je n'aye pas eu l'honneur de vous les offrir imprimés.
>
> Le retardement, Madame, vient de ce qu'avant de commencer l'impression, j'appris que ces Contes étoient tirés d'un recueil prodigieux de Contes semblables, en plusieurs volumes, intitulé *Les Mille et Une Nuits.* Cette découverte m'obligea de suspendre cette impression & d'employer mes soins à recouvrer le recueil. Il a fallu le faire venir de Syrie, & mettre en François le premier volume que voici, de quatre seulement qui m'ont été envoyés.[9]

The seven tales mentioned above are the seven stories of Sindbad the Sailor. The original MS from which Galland had translated them is now unknown.[10] But the MS collection which was sent him from Syria had consisted of four volumes, of which the Bibliotheque Na-

tionale at Paris had only three (Biblio. Nat. Ancien fonds Arabe 1506, 1507, 1508[11]; now MSS Arabe 3609, 3610 and 3611[12]). The fourth volume is at present missing.[13] In addition to these two manuscript sources, which Galland had used in the production of his *Nights,* in his *Diary,* published by Herman Zotenberg, we are told of a third source—a man from Syria who had actually recounted certain stories to him:

> Dans les premiers mois de l'année 1709 [we learn] un chrétien maronite d'Alep, nommé Hanna, qui avait accompagné à Paris de célèbre voyageur Paul Lucas, communiqua à Galland, de vive voix, plusieurs contes, entre autre l'histoire de la Lampe Merveilleuse.[14]

Evidently, our study of Galland's translation and his achievement can only be conclusive if we take as basis for it the three manuscripts whose Arabic text is known with certainty to have been used by our translator; namely, MSS Arabe 3609, 3610 and 3611, the Sindbad MS being unknown and Hanna's contributions being either suspect transcripts or de vive voix. Here, therefore, is a passage from **"The Story of Noureddin and the Fair Persian,"** which was very popular with the Victorians in 19th century England and which features prominently in many of their works. Noureddin and his Fair Persian have just arrived in Baghdad, two fugitives fleeing from the persecution and "hot pursuit" of the governor of "Balsora" (Basra), their hometown:

> « Quand le Bâtiment eut mouillé un peu au dessous de la Ville, » says Galland, « les passagers se débarquèrent, & se rendirent chacun où ils devoient loger. Noureddin donna cinq pièces d'or pour son passage, & se débarqua aussi avec la belle Persienne. Mais il n'étoit jamais venu à Bagdad, & il ne sçavoit où aller prendre logement. Ils marchèrent long tems, le long des Jardins, qui bordoient le Tigre, & ils en côtoyèrent un, qui étoit fermé d'une belle & longue muraille. En arrivant au bout, ils détournérent par une longue ruë bien pavée, où ils apperçûrent la porte du jardin, avec une belle fontaine auprès.
>
> La porte, qui étoit très-magnifique, étoit fermée, avec un vestibule ouvert, où il y avoit un Sofa de chaque côté. Voici un endroit fort commode, dit Noureddin à la belle Persienne, la nuit approche, & nous avons mangé avant de nous débarquer: Je suis d'avis que nous y passions la nuit, & demain matin nous aurons le tems de chercher à nous loger, qu'en dites-vous? Vous sçavez, Seigneur, répondit la belle Persienne, que je ne veux que ce que vous voulez: ne passons pas plus outre si vous le souhaitez ainsi. Ils bûrent chacun un coup à la fontaine, & montèrent sur un des deux Sofas, où ils s'entretinrent quelque tems. Le sommeil les prit enfin, & ils s'endormirent au murmure agréable de l'eau.
>
> Le Jardin appartenoit au Calife, & il y avoit au milieu un grand Pavillon qu'on appelloit le Pavillon des Peintures, à cause que son principal ornement étoit des Peintures à la Persienne, de la main de plusieurs Peintres de Perse, que le Calife avoit fait venir exprès. Le grand & superbe Salon, que ce Pavillon formoit, étoit

éclairé par quatrevingt fenêtres, avec un lustre à cha-
cune, & les quatrevingt lustres ne s'allumoient que lors
que le Calife y venoit passer la soirée, que le tems étoit
si tranquille, qu'il n'y avoit pas un souffle de vent. Ils
faisoient alors une trèsbelle illumination, qu'on apper-
cevoit bien loin à la Campagne de ce côté-là, & d'une
grande partie de la Ville. »[15]

A comparison of this French passage with the original
Arabic[16] will not fail to reveal that, to begin with, Galland was not in fact attempting so much a translation as
a loose paraphrase. Yet it is true to say that he took care
to render, simultaneously, all sentences and phrases that
he readily understood or that suited his purpose. This
practice has, inevitably, left distinct discrepancies between his version and the Arabic text. These discrepancies are discernible in additions he makes to the original, in no small number of errors consequent upon his
misinterpretation of the significations of some words
and, above all, in his individualistic, characteristic
method of telling the original episodes mainly à la Galland.

I should, however, point out that the Arabic text which
Galland had translated is written in a notorious hand
and in a hopelessly unidiomatic Arabic that is quite un-
intelligible in some places and unevenly colloquial in
countless many others. And yet the difficult, unfinished,
sometimes undecipherable, far-from-exact, and sometimes almost illiterate quality of the Arabic did not de-
ter Galland, writing, as he was, for a reading public of
aristocratic tastes and education. But where he was not
satisfied with the information supplied by his model he
provided his own with extreme felicity. His phrase, for
instance, « Par une longue ruë bien pavée[17] », which is
not to be found in his original, is perhaps put in to give
his readers the feeling that Baghdad was as civilized as
Versailles and had the same kind of streets. In the same
sort of way he has invented a fountain and elaborated
the gardens along the banks of the Tigris. His Arabic
original does not mention Noureddin's condition of being a complete stranger in Baghdad. All the same, Galland invents and emphasises this fact and dwells on it,
adding that, being perfect strangers in Baghdad, Noureddin and the Fair Persian were "at a loss for lodging".
So they

> rambled a considerable time along by the gardens that
> bordered on the Tigris, and keeping close to one of
> them that was inclosed with a very fine long wall at the
> end of it, they turned into a street well paved, where
> they perceived a garden-door, and a charming fountain
> near it. The door, which was very magnificent, hap-
> pended to be shut, but the porch was open, in which
> there was a sofa on each side.[18]

Except for the fact that the garden-door is also shut in
the Arabic original, the magnificence of the garden, its
charming fountain, its long wall and open porch are entirely Galland's invention. These details supplied by

him are of interest to the student of literature. For, besides being figments of Galland's imagination, some of
his additions: the river Tigris, the long wall of the garden as well as the porch with "a sofa on each side", all
of these objects found their way from this English passage into Tennyson's "Recollections of the Arabian
Nights". In fact, in « un sofa de chaque côté », we have
an interesting example of Galland's misinterpretation of
some key words in the text he translated. For the Arabic
text which he misinterpreted does not signify sofas, but
simply benches of bare stone or brick, A sofa is a kind
of divan furnished with mats and cushions, and it is interesting to note that Galland employs the word in other
tales in association with cushions of fine silk curiously
embroidered with all sorts of flowers. But he is so fond
of sofas that he consistently brings them in whenever
he describes the interior or, as in the case of the example above, the exterior of any *Arabian Nights* home,
mansion, or courtyard.

Be that however as it may, Tennyson's early misconception of Oriental sofas, as shown in the lines

> By garden porches on the brim,
> The costly doors flung open wide,
> Gold glittering thro' lamplight dim,
> And broider'd sofas on each side . . .[19]

is due to the fact that he was dependent on this particular passage in the English version of the tale of
"Noureddin and the Fair Persian" when he was writing his poem of the "Recollections" ["Recollections of
the *Arabian Nights*"]. This is borne out by the fact
that in one of his notes to the lines above, Tennyson says,
apologetically: "I had only the translation—from the
French of Galland—of the Arabian Nights when this
was written, so I talked of sofas etc. Lane was yet unborn".[20] Of course, Lane's translation of the passage under discussion has no porch with a sofa on each side.

The purpose of Galland's additions is, in my opinion,
twofold. They help him tell the original episodes as
though they were his own creation and enable him to
elaborate the total atmosphere of the *Nights.* Indeed, in
his invariable efforts to emulate the *Nights* and surpass
its romantic and (to him) exotic character by using its
glamorous atmosphere for his own purposes, he has
certainly "outbid his Omar". He has, in my view, rendered the generally primitive and unsophisticated Arabic original into a polished, smoothly flowing and
highly stylized narrative, which is not at all what his
original source is. In fact, the original sounds, more often than not, almost like a faint echo when compared
with what it becomes in Galland's immeasurably artistic and highly cultivated narrative. And it is this constant practice of expanding the original that really
adorns his *Les Mille et Une Nuits* with that extra touch
of glamour and exaggeration and reinforces its charac-

teristic elements of what is (to a European) "marvellous", "fantastic" and "strange". The Pavilion of Pictures[21] is so called, Galland says, (adding his irrepressible extras by way of embellishment): « à cause que son principal ornement étoit des Peintures à la Persienne, de la main de plusieurs Peintres de Perse, que le Calife avoit fait venir exprès ». But of this touch of exaggeration and the persistent effort to heap more glamour on what is glamorous already, I have more to say in connection with the following passage taken from the **"Story of the Envious Man, and of Him That Was Envied,"** an episode related in the house of "Zobeide" by the Second Calender:

A "genie" is about to transform the Calender, a king's son, into a beast or bird for finding him in the forbidden subterranean abode of the Princess of the isle of Ebene,[22] where he (the Jinni) had transported and imprisoned her since her wedding night. Imploring pardon, the prince promises, if he is spared, to tell the Jinii **"The Story of the Envious Man and of Him That Was Envied"**[23]—an offer not inconsistent with the overall theme of the *Nights,* considering that Shahrazâd herself has so far similarly staved off the execution of Shahrayar's vow. The Jinni accepts and the prince proceeds. But for the purposes of our comparative study, the important part of his tale is that which Galland translates as follows:

> Dans une Ville assez considérable deux hommes demeuroient porte à porte. L'un conçut contre l'autre une envie si violente que celui qui en étoit l'objet résolut de changer de demeure, & de s'éloigner, persuadé que le voisinage seul lui avoit attiré l'animosité de son voisin: Car quoi qu'il lui eût rendu de bons offices, il s'étoit aperçû qu'il n'en étoit pas moins haï. C'est pourquoi il vendit sa maison avec le peu de bien qu'il avoit, & se retirant à la Capitale du Païs qui n'étoit pas éloignée, il acheta une petite terre environ à une demi-lieuë de la ville. Il y avoit une maison assez commode, un beau jardin, & une cour raisonnablement grande, dans laquelle étoit une citerne profonde, dont on ne se servoit plus.
>
> Le bon homme ayant fait cette acquisition, prit l'habit de Derviche pour mener une vie plus retirée & fit faire plusieurs cellules dans la maison, où il établit un peu de tems une Communauté nombreuse de Derviches. Sa vertu le fit bientôt connoître, & ne manqua pas de lui attirer une infinité de monde, tant du Peuple que des Principaux de la Ville. Enfin, chacun l'honoroit & le chérissoit extrêmement. On venoit aussi de bien loin se recommander à ses prières, & tous ceux qui se retiroient d'auprès de lui, publioient les bénédictions qu'ils croyoient avoir reçûës du Ciel par son moyen.[24]

Again, a comparison of this passage with its Arabic original,[25] will yield a few more facts about Galland's method and work. As in the passage we have studied earlier, here, too, we have the usual additions, the occasional misinterpretations and the typical habit of glamorizing still further the original episodes that in themselves are already highly romantic in character. One example of an addition, of which the original Arabic does not have the merest suggestion, is Galland's invention of the reason why the Envied Man had to quit the neighbourhood of his envious neighbour, telling many things in the process and wandering off from the original story. The Envied Man, he explains,

> persuadé que le voisinage seul lui avoit attiré l'animosité de son voisin: Car quoi qu'il lui eut rendu de bons offices, il s'étoit aperçû qu'il n'en étoit pas moins haï. C'est pourquoi il vendit sa maison avec le peu de bien qu'il avoit, & se retirant à la Capitale du Païs qui n'étoit pas éloignée.[26]

According to the Arabic MS,[27] and contrary to Galland, the Envied Man knows no reason for his neighbour's envy. Nor does he remove to the capital city that was near, but rather journey's to a land far from his previous dwelling-place resolved to leave this world for the Envious Man's sake. Galland was telling the story freely and, in the course of its relation, he was cramming it with irrelevances. This, of course, transforms the Arabian tale into one that carries not so much the stamp of the Arabian narrator as that of a European well-versed in the art of fiction-writing, one who is well able to supply his own motifs and embellish the story he is presenting to his reading public. This method of paraphrase makes Galland's tale a different one, at times retaining but the mere skeleton of its original. It is as if his creative imagination and wilful enthusiasm frequently take charge and lead him away from his text to other regions of thought suggested by his understanding or, indeed, his misunderstanding of some important key words or phrases in his Arabic text. And the keyword in the Arabic text under study, which made him wander off onto the world of dervishes and their habits and cells, is the word (zâwiya),[28] which should be rendered in its context as an isolated home or cottage that the Envied Man built for himself. Galland, obviously, took it for an hermitage. Hence the inevitable extras,

> Le bon homme . . . prit l'habit de Derviche pour mener une vie plus retirée, & fit faire plusieurs cellules dans la maison, où il établit en peu de tems une Communauté nombreuse de Derviches.[29]

All this cannot be found in the Arabic MS. Indeed, nowhere in the original text do I find the Envied Man described as a "Derviche". Nor does Lane's *Thousand and One Nights* (which translates a later Cairo edition[30]) describe him so. The dervish, the dervish's habit, his society of dervishes and their cells are all Galland's invention. His purpose is, of course, self-evident, to build up more of the "strange" and "fantastic" atmosphere of which he is conscious through his wider reading in other tales. The atmosphere of the dervish's cell is all his work. And it was this very atmosphere that had appealed to Christina Rossetti, Galland's "dervise" being the very dervise she, in turn, called "Hassan" and who had fascinated her in her infancy. Her brother, William, relates the following anecdote of his sister's childhood, which confirms that Christina had had her imagination fired at an early age (« she may have been between seven and eight »[31]) by her reading of only a few books "such as the *Arabian Nights* and the lyric dramas of Metastasio".[32] He says:

> Possibly the earliest thing which Christina wrote (or rather . . . got some one to write from her dictation) was the beginning of a tale called perhaps *The Dervise* on the model (more or less, i.e. very little) of the *Arabian Nights*. The dervise, I think, went down into a cavern, where he was to meet with some adventures not much less surprising than those of Aladdin. In the thick of the plot it occurred to Christina that she had not yet given her dervise a name, so she interjected a sentence, "The Dervise's name was Hassan", and continued his perilous performances.[33]

Thus, Galland's romanticization of the Arabian tale had worked on the imagination of Christina Rossetti even before she could write. But she is no isolated case. George Meredith, too, was so fascinated by the tale of Galland's dervish that he borrowed from it the motif of the potent magic hair,[34] the root-idea of his Identical, which is the great image of the whole of *Shagpat* and the most important thing in the entire story.

So much of the glamour of the *Nights* is, therefore, the work of Galland, and it follows that, as a translation, his work is crammed with material that is, strictly speaking, alien to the Arabic original in that it comes from another world—that of Galland's learning. But some of this material was also due to his inability to grasp the meaning of portions of his Arabic, and that caused him to deviate from the original text and digress onto remote realms unheard of by the Arabian story-teller. A third passage, taken from Galland's account of the **"Petrified City,"** will lend support to this argument. Galland's "Zobeide"—her name is also taken from elsewhere—has just heard the voice of a human reading the *Quran* in an oratory of the desolate palace in the petrified city. This is how she tells her adventures in Galland's French:

> Il étoit environ minuit, lorsque j'entendis la voix comme d'un homme qui lisoit l'Alcoran de la même manière & du ton que nous avons coûtume de le lire dans nos temples. Cela me donna beaucoup de joie, Je me levai aussi-tôt, & prenant un flambeau pour me conduire, j'allai de chambre en chambre du côté où j'entendois la voix. Je m'arretai à la porte d'un cabinet d'où je ne pouvois douter qu'elle ne partît. Je posai le flambeau à terre, & regardant par un fente, il me parut que c'étoit un Oratoire. En effet il y avoit comme dans nos Temples une niche qui marquoit où il falloit se tourner pour faire la prière, des lampes suspendues & allumées, & deux chandeliers avec de gros cierges de cire blanche, allumés de même.

> Je vis aussi un petit tapis étendu de la forme de ceux qu'on étend chez nous pour se poser dessus, & faire la prière. Un jeune homme de bonne mine assis sur ce tapis, récitoit avec grande attention l'Alcoran qui étoit posé devant lui sur un petit pulpitre. A cette vûe ravie d'admiration, je cherchois en mon esprit comment il se pouvoit faire qu'il fût le seul vivant dans une Ville où tout le monde étoit pétrifié, & je ne doutois pas qu'il n'y eût en cela quelque chose de très merveilleux.

> Comme la porte n'étoit que poussée, je l'ouvris; j'entrai, & me tenant debout devant la niche, je fis cette prière à haute voix: Louange à Dieu qui nous a favorisé d'une heureuse navigation. Qu'il nous fasse la grace de nous protéger de même jusqu'à notre arrivée en notre pays. Ecoutez-moi, Seigneur, & exaucez ma prière.[35]

> Madame, me dit le jeune homme, [on being asked to explain by what miracle he alone was left alive when so many others had been turned to stone] vous m'avez fait assez voir que vous avez la connoissance du vrai Dieu, par la prière que vous venez de lui adresser. Vous allez entendre un effet très-remarquable de sa grandeur & de sa puissance, Je vous dirai que cette Ville étoit la capitale d'un puissant Royaume, dont le Roi mon père portoit le nom. Ce Prince, toute sa Cour, les habitans de la Ville, & tous ses autres sujets étoient Mages, Adorateurs du feu, & de Nardoun, ancien Roi des Géans rebelles à Dieu.[36]

Now, the Arabic original[37] of this text is, in fact, almost half as long as Galland's corresponding translation. This is due to the fact that, though a translator, Galland invariably told the Arabian episodes very profusely, adding to them all the glamour he was capable of mustering. His Zobeide's passing from one "chamber to another", and standing "still", then setting her "torch upon the ground", and "looking through a window" instead of looking through "the door" of the Arabic original, all these circumstances, added to "the Alcoran" being "upon a desk", the "great devotion" of the man and the joy and admiration with which Zobeide was transported, are only some of the cases in point. They are the work of Galland's usually splendid flair for storytelling and are not to be found in the corresponding paragraphs of his original. They are the result of his persistent practice of expansion and addition.

Galland's additions were, however, dictated by the fact that he was writing with the European reading public in the forefront of his mind. He had to annotate, as it were, and explain to them any Islamic habits or practices that came his way. Examples to support this observation are numerous. One passage from the **"Petrified City"** contains a few which again shed more light on Galland's method and elucidate even more clearly and conclusively his typical way of narration. If, for example, his Arabic text has an oratory, then he seizes this opportunity to explain its significance among the Muslims. But he incorporates these notes into his translation. It is, therefore, to his credit that the annotations and elucidations never border on parody or burlesque and that it is the pleasant interest and the pure element of entertainment that we seek without wishing for, or missing in the least, that element of entertainment through ridicule or satire, which later Orientalizers from Beckford to Thackeray and Meredith were unable to resist. Galland, though the book bears clear marks throughout of his personal genius, was never tempted to tread on such ground. "The oratory", his Zobeide would add freely and in her most natural sympathy, "had, as we have in our mosques, a niche that shows where we must turn to say our prayers". If the text has "a little carpet" spread on the floor, then she adds, by way of explanation, that it was "laid down like those we have to kneel upon when we say our prayers". If, on the other hand, she enters an oratory, then Galland might as well set his MS aside and compose a certain prayer for her to say aloud and so give his European readers a sample of Muslim piety. And, in fact, that is precisely what happens when he makes her stand before the niche. He puts in her mouth the following prayer:

> Praise be to God that has favoured us with a happy voyage, and may be graciously pleased to protect us in the same manner, until we arrive again in our own country. Hear me, O God, and grant my request.[38]

This prayer is not to be found in the original Arabic source. It is a composition of Galland's and its only source is his imagination. Yet it is also probable that he misunderstood his Arabic text, and thus, perhaps unknowingly, altered it. The original Arabic episode does, in fact, contain an entreaty, but it is to the handsome youth whom she has just found seated on the prayer-carpet and chanting the *Quran*. Her entreaty in the original source runs as follows: "I entreat you by the truth of that which you are reciting that you answer my question".[39] Her request, according to Galland, is that the Lord may be graciously pleased to protect them in the same manner as he has favoured them with a happy voyage, until they have arrived again in their own country. According to the Arabic *Nights,* the lady praises God for finding such a Muslim youth and requests the man to acquaint her with the story of the inhabitants of the desolate and "petrified" city and the reason why he alone was safe, a request which he readily grants her after he "shuts the Quran and seats her by his side".[40] No two versions could be more dissimilar.

Regarding the religion of the petrified inhabitants, Galland provides yet another interesting example of a complete departure from his source resulting, as it does, from a misreading on his part. According to him, the lonely survivor of the "petrified" race informs Zobeide that the king, his father, and all the inhabitants of the town were Magians, "Adorateurs du feu, & de Nardoun, ancien Roi des Géans rebelles à Dieu".[41] Yet in the original Arabic text, I find no such god as "Nar-

doun" whom the Magians of the city worship as their ancient King of the giants and who rebels against God. And it is this proper noun, "Nardoun", that is a conspicuous example of Galland's frequently imperfect understanding of his Arabic text. The phrase which he failed to understand, or rather failed to read correctly, describes all the inhabitants of the city as "Magians who worship fire in place of the Almighty King".[42] Obviously, Galland thought the two Arabic words "al-nar doun" (which simply mean "fire in place of") were one word, a proper noun. Thus leaving out "al", the Arabic definite article, he unwittingly coined the compound Nardoun, which he calls a god and uses more than once, in spite of the fact that the original Arabic story does not repeat the words "al-nar doun".

Misinterpretations and additions are not, however, the only defects of Galland's work as a translation. There are also some very significant omissions. Galland does sometimes omit phrases and sentences for reasons sometimes obvious and sometimes inexplicable. In addition to these, he is consistent throughout his translation in omitting a very important feature of the *Nights* stories, that is, the frequent passages of verse. The Arabic MSS of the *Nights* he used are interspersed with verses quoted, or invented, by its Arabian author to illustrate a point, laud or vilify a person or, indeed, any object. The shift in those MSS from prose to verse—a device widely used by some imitative English writers like Thackeray and Meredith, who actually followed Torren's and Lane's more faithful translations—is sometimes so sudden and unwarranted, so arbitrary, abrupt and uncalled for by the occasion that it hinders the flow of the narrative. There is no doubt that, if Galland had attempted a faithful rendering of the verse passages, he would not have inserted them without sacrificing the swiftness of his narrative style. However, his translation incorporates abbreviated readings of certain selected passages, as far as he can comprehend them. The verses are usually very difficult to follow. In fact, they are of very unequal quality, "ranging from poetry worthy of the name to the merest doggerel", so that Galland can hardly be blamed for being selective. To illustrate his method, I want to refer to the two sets of verse[43] which suddenly protrude at the first appearance (in the "petrified city") of the lone survivor. The lady of the Arabic *Nights* has just seen this handsome man and fallen in love with him at first sight. At this moment of Erhebung, as it were, and in keeping with his practice, throughout the whole book, the Arabian narrator makes the lady shift to song in praise of the man's face and features that beggar description. Her praise is contained in two verse passages, fourteen lines in all, which can hardly be echoed in the few words which Galland puts in the mouth of his Zobeide: "Je pris ce tems-là pour le considérer attentivement, & je lui trouvai tant de grace & de beauté, que je sentis des mouvemens que je n'avois jamais sentis jusqu'alors."[44]

In conclusion, Galland allows himself to invent details and even episodes which, in my view, are of a kind that his readers, accustomed to the sophistication of French literary taste in narrative, expect in a story. He allows himself to increase the piety, splendour and glamorous nature of the original, adding, as part of his narrative, a running commentary to explain obscurer points for the benefit of Western understanding. He omits all that he cannot handle, including the verses, which, naturally, remained unknown to Western readers until Torrens published his one-volume edition in 1838. He gives, in addition, a somewhat aristocratic and, here and there, moralistic, not to say prudish, tone to the style. Lastly, he sometimes makes blunders in translation but turns these to romantic account (as in the case of Nardoun) because that is how his mind seems to have worked. And it is these romantic embellishments which seem to me to have benefitted the *Nights* and welded the diffuse and uncultivated narration of the original into a closely-knit and cohesive work passing with all authors, especially in England, as the most imaginative of all literary creations, the fascinating tales generated by the wildest flights of extravagant fancy which, as R. L. Stevenson says,

> Charm us in age as they they charmed in childhood.[45]

The very tale of Zobeide, which we have been discussing, is a striking example of how these romantic and imaginative creations had influenced the Victorians. For it was soon to inspire Christina Rossetti, George Meredith and James Thomson ("B. V.") in their Juvenilia poems, "The Dead City" (1847), "The Sleeping City" (1851) and "Doom of a City" (1857), respectively, though each reacted to the story in a very individual manner, reading in it his or her own particular vision. James Thomson's word on the subject is perhaps typical of how the Victorian boyhood imagination reacted to the charms of individual tales in the *Nights.* In an explanatory note appended to a manuscript copy of his "Doom of a City", which he had presented to a friend, Mr. John Grant, he says:

> The City of the Statues [Part II of his "City of Doom"] is from the tale of Zobeide in the History of the Three Ladies of Bagdad and the Three Calenders. This episode and the account of the Kingdoms of the Sea in **"Prince Beder and—,"** impressed my boyhood more powerfully than anything else in the *Arabian Nights.*[46]

Each writer, then, had his favourite tale or tales. William Thackeray "had by heart the Barmecide's feast"[47] and, on the whole, felt sorry for those who did not care for the *Arabian Nights.*[48]

Judging by results of popularity and European reaction to *Les Mille et Une Nuits,* Galland seems to have been the right person to introduce the *Nights* to the European reader. He turned his very weaknesses as a translator

into strength and "loaded his rifts with ore", so that the book, owing to his additions, amendments and explanations, became one of the great sources of inspiration for European literature during the 18th and 19th centuries. One is bound to ask how much of the popularity of the *Nights* was due to Galland's additions and inventions, which with the consummate merits of his art of narration were instrumental in bringing about that huge mass of "exotic" literature since 1704. One thing is indisputable. The *Nights* would never have achieved such immense and universal popularity in England had it not been for Galland's copy—at least before Torrens and Lane appeared on the scene. It is interesting to note that the "Avertissement" prefacing his work has the following remark about his own translation:

> On a pris soin de conserver leurs caractères, de ne pas s'éloigner de leurs expressions & de leurs sentimens: & l'on ne s'est écarté du texte, que quand la bienséance n'a pas permis de s'y attacher. Le Traducteur se flatte que les personnes qui entendent l'Arabe, & qui voudront prendre la peine de confronter l'original avec la copie, conviendront qu'il a fait voir les Arabes aux François, avec toute la circonspection que demandoit la délicatesse de notre langue & de notre tems.[49]

Despite this claim, Galland seldom took special care to preserve the characters of the original Arabic version. On the contrary, he invented some. But by consistently delineating them on his own, at times at the expense of the original, he has certainly revealed himself keen on transmitting his wide knowledge of the Arabians and "showing them"—sometimes over-zealously—to the French. For of Islamic literature in general and Arabic literature in particular, Galland possessed a vast treasure of knowledge. He is the translator of that other book of tales, *Kalila Wa Dimna* or *Bidapai's Fables*—a book better known to the student of Arabic literature than the *Thousand and One Nights.* He is also the translator of *The Remarkable Sayings, Apothegms and Maxims of the Eastern Nations,* which he abstracted partly from printed books, and partly from MSS, Arabic, Persian and Turkish.[50] Through his work, Galland familiarized the European for the first time with all this Oriental heritage. He poured forth on the pages of his translation, to inform and delight, his special knowledge of the Eastern nations, Arabians, Persians, Tartars, and Indians, their religions, habits and practices. In a word, Galland was determined that his *Les Mille Et Une Nuits* should enable the reader, without the fatigue of going to see those peoples in their respective countries, to have the pleasure of seeing them act and them recount[51] not only many of their tales of engaging wonder but also much of what he happened to know of their manners and customs from other sources.

I say many of their tales and not all, because then, as Galland had excused himself, the times decreed otherwise. He was obliged to make omissions in deference to European tastes in the matter of propriety. All the objectionable portions of the *Nights*—and these are many—were never translated or even hinted at by Galland (apart from what he refers to as "la bienséance" in his Avertissement). And so, when his tale of Zobeide appeared, to take just one instance, it was a piously decent version and without the frank descriptions of the adventures of Zobeide and her sisters with the porter.[52] Later, however, it was adventures like these that gave a shock to 19th century feeling of moral decorum when Payne and Burton published their unexpurgated translations. Curiosity gave way to reprobation, as may be seen from the reviews and the reactions of the periodicals of the time.[53] Suddenly the whole truth about the *Nights,* as Burton had rendered it, was morally unpalatable. Besides, Galland had asserted that he had shown "the Arabians to the French, with all the Circumspection that the Niceness of the French Tongue and of the Times requires".[54] To him, those who have "any Inclination to profit by the Examples of Virtue and Vice, which they will . . . find exhibited" in the *Nights,* "may reap an Advantage by it, that is not to be reap'd in other Stories, which are more proper to corrupt than to reform our Manners".[55] Evidently, Burton was as yet unborn, and Galland's were the times when the "exotic" tale had to undergo strict expurgation and excision. It had to conform to the decrees of propriety and be made serviceable to the moral designs of those translators and successive Orientalisers and believers in the cult of the Oriental, who felt its forceful impact on their thinking.

Notes

1. V. C. Chauvin, *Bibliographie des Ouvrages Arabes,* 1900, IV, note (21a), pp. 25-6.

2. Id., p. 70

3. C. Gildon, *The Golden Spy,* 1709, Dedication.

4. Id., Title-page.

5. For some of these, see V. C. Chauvin, op.cit., n° 2, pp. 70-74.

6. Id., pp. 70-80.

7. Id., pp. 25 ff.

8. Galland, *Les Milles et Une Nuits,* 1745, I, Epître.

9. Ibid.

10. D. B. Macdonald, "First Appearance of the *Arabian Nights,*" *The Library Quarterly,* 1932, II, n° 4, 390.

11. Id., pp. 390-391.

12. M. le Baron de Slane, *Catalogue des Manuscrits Arabes de la Bibliothèque Nationale,* 1883, p. 619.

13. D. B. Macdonald, op. cit., p. 391.

14. *Notices et Extraits de MSS de la Bibliothèque Nationale . . .* Paris, 1887, XXVIII, Pt. I, 199.

15. Galland, *Les Mille et Une Nuits,* 1719, VII, 82-5.

16. Biblio. Nat. MS Arabe 3611, f. 39.

17. See ante, p. 20.

18. *A.N.E.,* 1978, III, 29-30. See the French text p. 20.

19. Tennyson, *Works,* 1907, I, 41-42.

20. Tennyson, *Works,* op. cit., p. 340. Lane's scholarly translation was to appear later between 1839 and 1841.

21. See ante, p. 20. The Arabic MS (Biblio. Nat. MS Arabe 3611, f. 39) has a Palace of Statues.

22. Galland, *A.N.E.,* 1789, I, 125.

23. Id., p. 135.

24. Galland. *Les Mille et Une Nuits,* (La Haye), 1714, II, 112-114.

25. Biblio. Nat. MS Arabe 3609, f. 51.

26. See ante, p. 23

27. Biblio. Nat. MS Arabe 3609, f. 51.

28. Ibid.

29. See ante, p. 23.

30. Lane, *The Thousand and One Nights,* 1839, I, XV-XVi.

31. Christina Rossetti, *Poetical Works,* 1904, p. XLiX.

32. Ibid.

33. Id., pp. XLiX-L.

34. Galland, *A.N.E.,* 1789, I, 134.

35. Galland, *Les Mille et Une Nuits,* 1745, I, 321-322.

36. Id., p. 324.

37. Biblio. Nat. MS Arabe, 3609, F. 68 & f. 69.

38. Galland, *A.N.E.,* 1789, I, 185. See ante, p. 17.

39. Biblio. Nat. MS Arabe, 3609, f. 68.

40. Ibid., f. 68 & f. 69.

41. See ante, p. 25.

42. Biblio. Nat. MS Arab, 3609, f. 69.

43. Biblio. Nat. MS Arabe, 3609, f. 69.

44. Galland, *Les Mille et Une Nuits,* 1745, I, 322-323.

45. R. L. Stevenson, *Collected Poems,* (ed. Janet A. Smith), 1950, p. 288.

46. J. Thomson, *Poetical Works,* 1895, II, 443.

47. Thackeray, *Works,* VIII, 194.

48. Id., XVII, 431.

49. Galland, *Les Mille et Une Nuits,* 1745, I, Avertissement.

50. Galland, *The Remarkable Sayings, Apothegms and Maxims of the Eastern Nations,* 1695, p. vi. The work was originally contained in d'Herbelot's *Bibliothèque Orientale* to serve as a continuation of, and supplement to, that work. See *Bibliothèque Orientale* (par C. Visdelon et A. Galland), 1779, pp. 407-520.

51. Galland, *A.N.E.,* 1763, I, Preface.

52. Biblio. Nat. MS Arabe, 3609, ff. 38-39.

53. See, for instance, "Burton's *Arabian Nights*", *Saturday Review,* III (Jan. 2, 1886), 26-7 & "Burton's *Arabian Nights* Re-Edited," LXXIX (March 9, 1895), 322-323.

54. Galland, *A.N.E.,* 1763, I, Preface.

55. Ibid.

Heinz Grotzfeld (essay date 1985)

SOURCE: Grotzfeld, Heinz. "Neglected Conclusions of the *Arabian Nights*: Gleanings in Forgotten and Overlooked Recensions." *Journal of Arabic Literature* 16 (1985): 73-87.

[*In the following essay, Grotzfeld focuses on the differences between the traditionally accepted translations of* The Arabian Nights *and preceding versions, asserting that the widely read translations obscure some key features of the earlier texts.*]

Certainly no other work of Arabic literature has become so universally known in the West as the *Stories of Thousand and One Nights,* more commonly called *The Arabian Nights' Entertainments* or simply *The Arabian Nights.* Since their first appearance in Europe (Galland's French translation 1704 sqq.; English and German translations of Galland only a few years later), the *Nights* [*The Arabian Nights*] met with lively interest from a large public. In the latter part of the 18th century, this interest generated something like a run on manuscripts of the *Nights,* especially in the English world, as is documented by the relatively large number of Arabic MSS of the *Nights* that were purchased by British residents or travellers in the East and are now to be found in British libraries. Even the I Calcutta edition of the Nights of 1814 and 1818 as well as the II Calcutta edition of 1839-1842 are due to British activities,

since they are both based on MSS brought from Syria or Egypt to India by Englishmen.[1] On the continent, too, one library or another contains MSS of the *Nights,* most of them, however, purchased after 1800 and representing the same recension as the Bulaq edition; a considerable number of older MSS of the *Nights* are to be found only in the Bibliothèque Nationale de Paris.

The interest in MSS of the *Nights,* which is to be observed in the 18th century, diminished at the beginning of the 19th century. Arabists, anyway, did not make the most of the MSS treasured in European libraries. They were satisfied with picking out stories which had not been translated at that time and, in their own translations or expansions of Galland, simply added them to the repertoire of *Nights* stories already existing. There are two exceptions. One is Joseph von Hammer, whose French translation, made in Constantinople from 1804 to 1806 on the basis of a complete Egyptian MS and sent to Silvestre de Sacy for publication, came out only in 1823, not in its original form, but in a stylistically rather unsatisfactory German version for which his publisher Cotta was responsible. The important information given by Hammer in his introduction about the *Nights,* the complete list of the stories, their order and segmentation into nights, as well as his view of the history of the work, had been published earlier in the *Fundgruben* and the *Journal Asiatique.* The other exception is Maximilian Habicht, "who, through close intercourse with Orientals during his long residence in Paris, had come to embrace entirely the irresponsible Oriental attitude towards MSS and editing" (Macdonald 1909, p. 687) and made out of fragments of the *Nights* and other material a compilation of his own, which he published in the years 1825-1839 (vols. I-VIII of the Breslau edition; the remaining four vols. were published after Habicht's death by H. L. Fleischer, 1842-1843).

The Bulaq edition of 1835, which was widely circulated both in the Arab world and in Europe, and the II Calcutta edition, which is of the same recension, superseded almost completely all other texts and formed the general notion of the *Arabian Nights.* For more than half a century it was neither questioned nor contested that the text of the Bulaq and II Calcutta editions was the true and authentic text. This opinion did not change even when in 1887 H. Zotenberg in his *Notice sur quelques manuscrits des Mille et Une Nuits et la traduction de Galland* showed that the text of the Bulaq and II Calcutta editions represented only one recension of the work[2] and that other recensions of the *Nights* were attested by manuscript evidence much older than any evidence for ZER [Zotenberg's Egyptian Recension].[3] It is not that the results of Zotenberg's research were disregarded. But a process not uncommon in the history of texts made it possible to preserve the generally accepted notion of the *Nights* more or less unaffected by them: ZER was given, by tacit convention, the status of a *canonical* text, whereas other recensions were degraded to the rank of *apocrypha*. Still another group of texts was classified as *pseudepigrapha*, e.g. the Breslau edition, which was revealed by Macdonald to be a compilation made by its editor Habicht.[4] Even texts which since Galland had been considered to be integral parts of the *Nights*, e.g. Aladdin or Ali Baba, became classified as spurious.[5] Disregarding "apocryphal" or "pseudepigraphical" material may frequently be of little or no consequence. But focusing the view on ZER rather blocked philological research concerning the text. It is one of the purposes of this paper to show that a careful study of "apocryphal" materials can throw new light on the history of the *Nights.*

The original conclusion of the *Nights* seems to be lost. Galland never had a text for the conclusion he gave to his *Mille et Une Nuits,* and he was considered—wrongly, see below, n. 21—to have invented this end himself. Thus it was not before the early 19th century, when copies of ZER came into the hands of Europeans, that an Arabic text of the end of the *Nights* became known in Europe. Hammer boasted of being the first European to have discovered the unexpected conclusion of the *Nights* (for his *unexpected* conclusion, see below). The conclusion of the *Nights* as it stands in the Bulaq and II Calcutta editions is no doubt a very simple piece of literature.[6] Nevertheless, it reflects the conclusion outlined in the latter half of the 10th century in the following famous passage of the *Fihrist*:

> . . . until she had passed a thousand nights, while he at the same time was having intercourse with her as his wife, until she was given a child by him, which she showed to him, informing him of the stratagem she had used with him. Then he admired her undertaking and inclined to her and preserved her alive. And the king had a quahramāna who was called Dīnārzād, and she assisted her in that.[7]

The central idea of the conclusion in ZER, thus, is obviously the same as that of a *Nights*-recension which circulated in Bagdad 800 years earlier, though more obscured than at that time.

We do not know what the conclusion was in the Indian archetype nor in *Hazār Afsānah,* the Persian recension. Reflexes of the frame story in the popular literatures of India and its neighbouring countries compel us to assume that in the original form of the frame story, Shahrazād continues to tell her stories, in the well-known manner, thus postponing her execution from one day to the other, until she has given birth to a child[8] and therefore feels safe enough to reveal her stratagem to the king, whereupon the king preserves her alive and definitely makes her his queen. The new title the work was given in the Arabic world, *alf layla,*[9] in which the number was taken literally, suggests that Shahrazād has to survive a fixed number of nights by the telling of sto-

ries, not the period until she has reached the status of mother, which then safeguards her against execution. The connection between Shahrazād's reaching this status and her ending the story-telling became obscured. That seems to be the case already in the conclusion summarized in the *Fihrist*. The wording of the *Fihrist,* however, does not exclude, even if it does not suggest, that Shahrazād needed exactly 1000 nights to become a mother. Compared with that conclusion, ZER presents a slight but not unimportant change: during the 1001 nights, Shahrazād has borne the king three children. It is difficult to decide whether Shahrazād now has three children because naive tradition could not imagine the king and Shahrazād enjoying the delight of communion 1001 nights successively without the number of children Shahrazād is plausibly to have in that time, and therefore amended the number, or whether she has them because three children were thought to touch the king's heart more effectively than only one child. The latter does not seem to be wholly incompatible with ZER, since here changed numbers occur in two other places in the frame-story as well. In the well-known orgy observed by Shāhzamān, the queen enters the garden together with twenty slave girls and twenty male slaves; in G (see n. 30) and other earlier texts, the queen is escorted only by twenty slave girls, ten of whom, however, are disguised male slaves, which becomes clear to Shāhzamān only some time later, when they strip off their clothes. In ZER, the trophies of the young woman held captive in the chest are five hundred and seventy seal-rings; in G and most of the other texts, the number is ninety-eight. The change in both instances is no doubt due to a defective or somewhat illegible text.[10] Nevertheless, it shows the predilection of the redactor of ZER, or more likely of one of his predecessors, for strengthening essential elements of the narration by quantitative arguments.

By linking the end of Shahrazād's story-telling with the thousand and first night, the internal logic of the conclusion is lost: when Shahrazād on the 1001th night requests the king to grant her a wish, namely to exempt her from slaughter for the sake of her three children whom she presents to him, her step has not been prepared in the narrative. Nor has any reason been given—except through the title—that she should do so this very night, since the period of story-telling has nowhere previously been limited, unlike the period of seven days in the *Book of the Seven Sages,* where the span to be bridged by telling stories is set in advance by the horoscope of the hero. One or other among the copyists or compilers of *Nights*-recensions also realized this lack. Hammer owned (and translated) a ZER-MS containing a revised ZER-version. Its conclusion says that on the 1001th night, after the story of Ma'rūf the Cobbler, king Shahriyār was bored by Shahrazād's story-telling and ordered her to be executed the following morning, whereupon Shahrazād sent for her three children and asked for mercy, which was granted her, in the same way as in the other ZER-versions. This surprising turn, which could have been borrowed from a parody of the frame-story, fully explains why Shahrazād must proceed to act as well as why she finishes telling stories to the king.[11]

Even the author of the poor conclusion which ends the recension contained in the so-called Ṣabbāgh-MS[12] conceived such a double motivation, though one which perfectly fits the poorness of the compositions: Shahrazād has related to the king all she knew (*hāḏā mā 'indī min tawārīḫ as-sālifīn wan-nās al-awwalīn*), "and when king Shahriyār had heard all the tales of Shahrazād, and since God had blessed him by her (sc. with children) during the time he had been occupied by listening to her tales, he said to himself: 'By God, this wife is intelligent, erudite, reasonable, experienced, so I must not slay her, specially since God has blessed me by her with two children.' And he continued that night admiring her wisdom, and his love for her increased in his heart. In the following morning, he rose and went to the cabinet, bestowed a robe of honour and all kinds of favour upon her father the wazīr, and lived together with her in happiness and delight until the angel of Death came to them and made them dwell in the grave" (MS arabe 4679, fol. 401b). In these artless, simple or poor conclusions[13] we meet the same deterioration that is often to be observed in stories transmitted by long oral tradition: the elements as such of the stories are still preserved, but the original connection between them has become distorted or totally lost. So it is reasonable to assume that the conclusions of ZER and the Ṣabbāgh-MS reproduce what was known about the end of the *Nights* from oral tradition in a more or less skilful arrangement by the respective compiler.

There exists, however, an elaborate skilful conclusion, entirely different from that of ZER. It is attested by some manuscript sources considerably older than ZER, and one printed one, namely Habicht's edition. But since this edition, following Macdonald's article in *JRAS* 1909, was discredited in its entirety, though parts of it reproduce "authentic" *Nights*-material, particularly fragments of *Nights*-recensions prior to ZER, its conclusion was no longer paid any attention.

So far, I know of four sources for this conclusion:

H: Habicht's edition or compilation of the *Nights*; the end of his compilation, nights 885-end, is based upon the transcript made by Ibn an-Najjār (Habicht's Tunisian friend) of a fragment of a *Nights*-recension transcribed in 1123/1711 (see Macdonald 1909, p. 696).

K: MS Edebiyât 38 in Kayseri, Raṣid Efendi kütüphane; this MS is described by H. Ritter in *Oriens* 2, 1949, pp. 287-289; on the basis of its script Ritter gives the 16th

or the 17th century as the date of its transcription ("frühestens 10.jh.H."). The text is divided into nights, but the nights are not numbered, the space for the numbers, which probably were to have been rubricated, not having been filled.

B: MS We.662 in Berlin, Stiftung Preussischer Kulturbesitz-Staatsbibliothek (formerly Royal Library), Nr. 9104 in Ahlwardt's catalogue; the transcription of the part concerning us is from 1173/1759. The night-formulae and the numbering have been crossed out (see below p. 87).

P: MS arabe 3619 in Paris, Bibliothèque Nationale; the MS. was formerly marked "Supplément arabe 1721 II" (so in Zotenberg 1887, p. 214); "d'origine égyptienne écrit au XVIIᵉ siècle ou au commencement du XVIIIᵉ siècle".

The conclusion of these sources differs from the conclusion attested by the *Fihrist* and narrated in ZER, in that Shahrazād does not implore the king's mercy by referring to her status as mother of his child or children, but "converts" the king by telling stories which make him reflect on his own situation so that he begins to doubt whether it was right to execute his wives after the bridal night. No sooner is Shahrazād sure that her stories have taken effect than she begins to tell the prologue/frame-story of the *Nights* themselves, somewhat condensed and slightly alienated in that the characters have no names, but are labelled "the king", "the wazīr", "the wazīr's daughter" and "her sister", and the scene is simply "a town":[14]

> It has reached me, o auspicious King, that someone said: People pretend that a man once declared to his mates: I will set forth to you a means of security against annoy. A friend of mine once related to me and said: We attained to security against annoy, and the origin of it was other than this; that is, it was the following: I over-travelled whilome lands and climes and towns and visited the cities of high renown . . . Towards the last of my life, I entered a city,[15] wherein was a king of the Chosroës and the Tobbas and the Caesars. Now that city had been peopled with its inhabitants by means of justice and equity; but its then king was a tyrant dire who despoiled lives and souls at his desire; in fine, there was no warming oneself at his fire, for that indeed he oppressed the believing band and wasted the land. Now he had a younger brother, who was king in Samarcand of the Persians, and the two kings sojourned a while of time, each in his own city and stead, till they yearned unto each other and the elder king despatched his Wazir to fetch his younger brother . . .

(Burton XII, pp. 192-193; I shall skip the rest of the story, which ends as follows)

> . . . on the fifth night she told him anecdotes of Kings and Wazirs and Notables. Brief, she ceased not to entertain him many days and nights, while the king still

said to himself, 'Whenas I shall have heard the end of the tale, I will do her die,' and the people redoubled their marvel and admiration. Also the folk of the circuits and cities heard of this thing, to wit, that the king had turned from his custom and from that which he had imposed upon himself and had renounced his heresy, wherefor they rejoiced and the lieges returned to the capital and took up their abode therein, after they had departed thence; and they were in constant prayer to Allah Almighty that He would stablish the king in his present stead. "And this" said Shahrazad "is the end of that which my friend[16] related to me." Quoth Shahriyar, "O Shahrazad, finish for us the tale thy friend told thee, inasmuch as it resembleth the story of a King whom I knew; but fain would I hear that which betided the people of this city and what they said of the affair of the king, so I may return from the case wherein I was."[17] Shahrazad replies that, "when the folk heard how the king had put away from him his malpractice and returned from his unrighteous wont, they rejoiced in this with joy exceeding and offered up prayers for him. Then they talked one with other of the cause of the slaughter of the maidens and they told this story and it became obvious for them, that only women had caused all that[18] and the wise said, 'Women are not all alike, nor are the fingers of the hand alike.'"

(Burton XII, p. 197)

The king comes to himself and awakens from his drunkenness; he acknowledges that the story was his own and that he has deserved God's wrath and punishment, and he thanks God for having sent him Shahrazād to guide him back on the right way. Shahrazād, then, lectures on the interrelation between ruler and army, between ruler and subjects, on the indispensability of a good wazīr (which is all somewhat inappropriate in this context), argues by reference to sūra 33:35 that there are also chaste women,[19] and by relating the Story of the Concubine and the Caliph (Burton XII, pp. 199-201; Chauvin's Nr. 178) and the Story of the Concubine of al-Maamun[20] (Burton XII, pp. 202-206; Chauvin's Nr. 179) she demonstrates for Shahriyār that his case is not as unique as he thought, because "that which hath befallen thee, verily, it hath befallen many kings before thee . . . all they were more majestical of puissance than thou, mightier of kingship and had troops more manifold" (Burton XII, p. 199). The king is now fully convinced that he was wrong and that Shahrazād has no equal. He arranges his marriage with her, and marries Dīnāzād to his brother Shāhzamān, who in Samarcand behaved the same way as he had done until Shahrazād entered the scene. Dīnāzād, however, stipulates that the two kings and the two sisters should live together for ever. So the wazīr is sent to Samarcand as their governor. The king orders the stories told by Shahrazād to be recorded by the annalists; they fill thirty volumes. There is no mention in these texts of a child, much less three children, as an argument for granting mercy to Shahrazād.[21]

The texts of the four sources mentioned above are essentially identical, the variants in number and nature being within the usual confines. But though derived from one and the same version, they constitute the end of two different recensions of the Nights. In H, this conclusion follows the **"Tale of the King and his Son and his Wife and the Seven Wazirs"** (i.e. the Arabic version of the *Book of Sindibād* or *Book of the Seven Sages*); the transition from this tale to the conclusion is seamless and logical:

> King Shahriban (i.e. Shahriyār's name in the Breslau edition) marvelled at this history and said, 'By Allah, verily, injustice slayeth its folk!'[22] And he was edified[23] by that, wherewith Shahrazad bespoke him, and sought help of Allah the Most High. Then he said to her, 'Tell me another of thy tales, O Shahrazad; supply me with a pleasant story and this shall be the completion of the story-telling.' Shahrazad replied, 'With love and gladness! It has reached me, O auspicious King, that a man once declared. . . .'

(Burton XII, p. 192; see above p. 79)

In the three other texts, this conclusion is interwoven with the **"Tale of Baibars and the Sixteen Captains of Police"**[24] as follows: the 16th Captain tells to King Baibars the prologue-story as if related to himself by a friend. The stories told in the Breslau edition by the 14th, 15th, 16th Captain (*n, o, p* in Burton's translation) in this recension of the Baibars-cycle are told by the 13th, 14th and 15th respectively (this shift is already prepared in the first half of the cycle: the 5th Captain relates two stories, his "own" and that of the 6th Captain). The stories of the Clever Thief and of the Old Sharper (Burton's *na* and *nb*) remain in their place in the order of tales between *n* and *o*. The 15th Captain thus tells, in the first person singular, the story of the traveller who was threatened by a robber sitting on his breast with a knife drawn in his hand, but is delivered by a crocodile which came

> 'forth of the river and snatching him up from off my breast plunged into the water, with him still hending knife in hand, even within the jaws of the beast which was in the river. And I praised God for having escaped from the one who wanted to slay me.' The king[25] marvelled and said: 'Injustice harms[26] its folk.' Then he was alarmed[27] in his heart and said: 'By God, I was in foolishness before these exhortations, and the coming of this maiden is nothing but (a sign of God's) mercy.' Then he said: 'I conjure thee, O Shahrazad, supply me with another one of these pleasant tales and exhortations, and this shall be the completion of the Story of King aẓ-Ẓāhir and the sixteen Captains.' And she said: 'Well, then came forward another Captain,' and he was the sixteenth of the Captains, and said: 'I will set forth to you a means of security against annoy. One of my friends once related to me. . . .'

(B, fol. 113a; I have borrowed from Burton XII, p. 44 and 192 the translations of the corresponding parts in the Breslau edition = H)

The text of the story told by the 16th Captain (see p. 81) is somewhat fuller in B than in H, which is, for its part, close to the text of K. B and K coincide, however, in minor details both internal (e.g. even the first wives of the two brother-kings are sisters) and external (e.g. the 16th Captain's story has night-divisions at the same places), so there is no doubt that B and K derive from the same version, the fuller text of B being due to a more recent polishing. In P, a considerable portion of the text is missing here: the **"Tale of the Two Kings"** which is told by the Captain, breaks off after the words characterizing the elder kind ('. . . and wasted the land'); then follows immediately the **"Tale of the Concubine of the Caliph"** (fol. 163b, lines 5-6). The lacuna is superficially dissimulated by the interpolation of *fa-ta'aǧǧab al-malik aẓ-Ẓāhir min hāḏihi l-umūr, fa-lā ta'aǧǧab ayyuhā l-malik Šahriyār* at the end of the second Concubine-tale (fol. 170a). Even the division into nights continues; the numbering, however, runs thus: fol. 163a: 908; fol. 165b: 909; fol. 168a: 1000 (!). Shahrazād finishes telling her stories in that night.

Incorporating the prologue-story into the Baibars-cycle involved a threefold oblique narration, which necessitated some adjustments in the text to be transcribed. The redactor mastered this task well, but eventually, certainly because of failing attention, made a mistake, which then was copied by over-scrupulous scribes. In K, as in B (P: lacuna), the Baibars-cycle ends as follows (somewhat less abruptly than in the Breslau edition, vol. 11, p. 399)

> '. . . and this is the end of what my friend related to me, O King aẓ-Ẓāhir.' Those who were attending and King aẓ-Ẓāhir marvelled, then they dispersed. And this is (said Shahrazad) what reached me from their invitation. Then King Shahriyar said: 'This is indeed marvellous, but O Shahrazad, this story which the Captain related *to me* (*aḥkā lī*), resembles the story of a king whom I know. . . .'

He then asks what the reaction of the subjects was, "so I may return from the case wherein I was." (K, fol. 122b). Shahrazād replies by using nearly the same words as in H (see above p. 79), though on the basis of the premises of this composition she cannot have any further information. In the text of B, the inappropriate *to me* has been eliminated. The story then continues and ends in the same way as in H.

The literary ambition and the skill of this composition—at least of parts of it—are clearly discernible in spite of the somewhat degenerated versions in which it is accessible to us. Redactional mistakes as the aforementioned one indicate that this conclusion was not originally composed for these versions, but is a "recycled" fragment.[28] Since the recensions into which this conclusion has been inserted were in all probability compiled as early as the 16th century,[29] the recensions

to which this conclusion originally belonged must be considerably older.

Such an early date of origin is suggested by some characteristic details in which the Story of the Two Kings and the Wazīr's Daughter, i.e. the prologue-story, agrees with the prologue in Galland's MS, the earliest extant MS of the *Nights*.[30] As in G, the story immediately begins with two kings who are brothers (ZER begins with a king who divides his kingdom and assigns it to either of his two sons); the younger brother returns to his castle, as in G, to take leave of his wife (in ZER he returns because he forgot *ḥāǧa* 'something' or *ḥaraza* 'a pearl') and, as in G, he perceives in the garden the wife of his brother together with ten white slave girls and ten male negro slaves (in ZER the number is twenty for each group). The lover of the younger brother's wife is "a man" (*raǧul,* K and B) or "a strange man" (*raǧul aǧnabī,* H), which fits in better with the "man from the kitchen-boys" (*raǧl min ṣubyān al-maṭbaḥ*) in G than with the "negro slave" in ZER. Last not least, the epithets *ǧabbār—lā yuṣṭalā lahū bin-nār* ("a tyrant dire—there was no warming oneself at his fire", see above p. 79) which characterize the elder brother occur even in G among the epithets of Shahriyār (they are not found in ZER nor in any other MS which is independent of the G-group).[31] This congruence does not necessarily imply that this conclusion ever constituted the end of that recension of which G is an initial fragment, since the prologue in G, too, is most probably a literary spolium;[32] it implies, however, that a prologue like that of G and a conclusion like that of H and K, B, P once formed the beginning and the end of a recension of the *Nights* considerably earlier than G.

Though the conclusion incontestably bears an Islamic stamp and at first sight hardly has anything in common with the conclusion summarized by Ibn an-Nadīm, we have to ask ourselves, considering the great age of the composition, whether it is a totally new creation achieved without any knowledge of other conclusions of the *Nights*—or at least without any regard to them—, or whether the author of this composition has perhaps also inserted, besides comparatively young elements such as the two concubine tales,[33] fragments of older recensions. I think we have good reasons to assume that this composition includes an element which was part not only of a very old recension of the *Nights,* but also, most probably, of the Indian archetype. Ibn an-Nadīm's words concerning the end of the *Nights,* "until she was given a child by him, which she showed to him, informing him of the stratagem she had used with him", imply, no doubt, the device by which in this composition the king is informed of the matter. For, how did Shahrazād instruct the king? It is hardly conceivable that the structural element par excellence of the (older parts of the) *Nights,* namely telling a story for the most varied purposes (to obtain ransom, to gain time, to entertain, to instruct), should not be employed here: for Shahrazād nothing is better suited to reveal her stratagem to the king than to relate to him the story in its alienated form in which Shahriyār recognizes himself and his own fate as in a mirror. I have no doubt that in the recension of the *Nights* which the author of the *Fihrist* had before his eyes the conclusion was introduced by this revelation story, but I consider it also very likely that this was the case already in the Indian archetype of the *Nights*.

Since the king is converted from his hatred for women to an indulgent attitude towards them, and does not simply show mercy, as he does in the *Fihrist*/ZER-conclusion, there is no need for Shahrazād to produce a child, or three children respectively, as an argument to obtain pardon. Children would even mar the picture of the sumptuous wedding by which this composition is closed. Therefore I assume that the author of this conclusion dropped the children-motif on purpose.

A third version of the end is found in the recension represented by the so-called MS Reinhardt.[34] After the tale of Hārūn ar-Rashīd and Abū Ḥasan, The Merchant of Oman, which is the last tale of this recension (nights 946-952 in ZER), Shahrazād immediately begins the **"Tale of the Two Kings and the Wazīr's Daughters,"** without any preparatory transition except for the usual *wa-ḥukiya,* "one relates". The first part of this tale repeats almost verbatim, without any abridgement, the prologue of this recension,[35] the two kings and their father, for instance, being given their names. Only the latter part of the tale is more condensed (the two daughters of the wazīr remain nameless here):

> (Shahrazād is still talking:) '. . . and she occupied him with tales and stories until she got pregnant and gave birth to a boy, got pregnant once again with a girl, and for a third time got pregnant with a boy. They bought white and black slave girls and populated the palace anew, as it had been before, the king not being aware of any of this.' The king turned his face to her (i.e. he pricked his ears) and asked: 'Where are *my* children?'— She replied: 'They are here.' Then he said: 'So that is the way to let me know! By God, if you had not acted in this manner and caught me with your stories, you would not have remained alive until now. Well done!' Shahrazād replied: 'A woman is worth only as much as her intelligence and her faith. Women are very different form one another.' And she ordered (*amarat*) her sister Dunyazad to bring the children. . . .
>
> (4281, fol. 477 b-478a)

The king rejoices at his children and tells Shahrazād that he loves her still more. Complying with her request, he brings back servants and domestics to the palace;[36] he writes a letter to his brother relating to him this happy ending; the brother sends his congratulations and gifts for all of them, "and King Shah Baz and the wazir's daughter abode in all solace of life and its de-

light until there came the Destroyer of delights and the Sunderer of societies" (the translation of this frequent end-clausula is borrowed from Burton).

I have evidence that the Reinhardt MS is the original copy of this recension or compilation;[37] so the date of transcription, 1247/1832, is at the same time that of the compilation. In view of this recent date one is not inclined to assume that the end of this recension is a proof of another ancient conclusion of the *Nights*. Nevertheless, it cannot be contested that this conclusion comes closest to that summarized by Ibn an-Nadīm: There are children involved;[38] Shahrazād reveals her stratagem to the king; the king admires her intelligence, he inclines towards her and preserves her alive. Shahrazād's sister has, in this conclusion, the same function as Shahrazād's accomplice in the *Fihrist*-version: she is only a nurse (thus, there is no need to marry her to the king's brother); there is no trace of a "conversion" or "listening to reason". These congruences are not accidental; there must be a connection between the end of the recension known to Ibn an-Nadīm and the conclusion of the Reinhardt MS. It is not likely that the compiler of this recension knew a version of the conclusions discussed above. It is true that he did not hesitate to recast stories radically, as is shown by the prologue, but if he had rewritten the end, there should be some traces left from the former text. As to Shahrazād's device of informing the king of her stratagem, namely relating his own story to him, there is no model for it in the finale of ZER (which was certainly known to the compiler), nor does it follow immediately from what the *Fihrist* (which the compiler can hardly have known) says about the end. On the other hand, it is obvious that the stories are gathered from very shifting traditions; even such tales as occur under the same title in ZER are not all taken from ZER-fragments; the tale of Tawaddud, for instance, is from a tradition which can be traced back to the 16th century,[39] quite independently of ZER. Thus, we cannot but deduce that the compiler of the Reinhardt MS knew a model stemming from a separate tradition, and we must for the present accept the curious fact that the latest recension of the *Nights* obviously presents the very conclusion which is closest to its original form.[40]

Since ZER was regarded as canonical not only in Europe but also in the Arabic World, other recensions were less appreciated even there. The *Nights*-fragment B, then, less than a hundred years after its transcription was considered to be trash and was rehashed; by means of a rather superficial revision it was turned into a "new" work: *Kitāb samarīyāt wa-qiṣaṣ 'ibarīyāt.* The redactor's work, however, consisted chiefly in crossing out the Night-formulae and numbers and in adding a few excerpts from other books as well as a new title page (cf. Ahlwardt Nr. 9103 and 9104). We should not let ourselves be deluded by this procedure, any more than that unknown Arabic reader of the "new" work who wrote the following beneath its new title: *hāḏa kitāb min sīrat alf layla ilā intihā' as-sīra* ("this is a part of the **Story of the Thousand Nights** right to the end of the story").

Notes

1. Cf. Macdonald, D. B., "A preliminary classification of some MSS of the *Arabian Nights*." In: *A Volume of Oriental Studies, presented to E. G. Browne*; ed. by T. W. Arnold and R. A. Nicholson, Cambridge 1922, pp. 313 and 305. The "Egyptian MS brought to India by the late Major Turner Macan", from which II Calcutta was printed, is lost. I rather doubt if this MS was a *complete* ZER-copy. Bulaq and II Calcutta differ chiefly in the first quarter, Calcutta presenting in its prose passages an unrevised "middle Arabic" like any other MS of ZER. In the three remaining quarters, the text of Bulaq and II Calcutta is almost identical, Calcutta presenting here the same "polished" Arabic as Bulaq, which is somewhat strange. But this can easily be explained by the—heretical—assumption that these parts of II Calcutta were printed directly or indirectly from the *printed* Bulaq text.

2. Zotenberg called this recension "la rédaction moderne d'Égypte", Macdonald introduced the abbreviation ZER = Zotenberg's Egyptian Recension.

3. All known manuscript evidences for ZER were transcribed shortly before or after 1800; in all probability, the compilation of ZER itself had been carried out only a few years earlier. Mardrus's affirmation that he owned the very MS "de la fin du XVIIᵉ siècle" from which the Bulaq edition was printed (cf. Chauvin IV, p. 109) is a lie.

4. Macdonald, D. B., *Maximilian Habicht and his recension of the* Thousand and One Nights, JRAS 1909, p. 685-704.

5. It was out of reverence for their first translator that Mia Gerhardt, *The Art of Story-Telling*, Leiden, 1963, p. 15, did not call them so, but euphemistically spoke of "Galland's orphan stories".

6. Burton expanded it with passages taken from the Breslau edition. Lane translated the end as he had found it in his Bulaq copy.

7. Ibn an-Nadīm, *Kitāb al-Fihrist, maqāla* 8, *fann* 1; I quote the translation of Macdonald, D. B., *The earlier history of the* Arabian Nights, JRAS 1924, pp. 353-397; p. 365.

8. Or until she was pregnant, as in the frame-story of the *Hundred and One Nights*, which corresponds much better to our feeling of plausibility. It is quite unreasonable of ZER to demand the audience or the reader to believe that Shahrazād managed to hide her three pregnancies from the king.

9. The oldest documentary evidence for the actual title *alf layla wa-layla* is from the 12th century and comes from the Cairo Geniza; see S. D. Goitein in JAOS 78, 1958, pp. 301-302.

10. The number 570 is obviously a *taṣḥīf* of 98, the *rasm* of a carelessly written *ṯamāniya wa-tis'īn* being very close to that of *ḵamsimi'a wa-sab'īn*; it is to be found already in the Paris MS 3612, which is prior to the compilation of ZER. The twenty male slaves have been added in order to make plausible a text in which the passage relating the disguise had been dropped, obviously by a copyist who was unable to guess how the story could have run.

11. Burton missed the point of this modification or interpolation. Though he knew that this reading was to be found in some MSS, he accused Trébutien, the French translator of Hammer-Zinserling, that he "cannot deny himself the pleasure of a French touch" (X, p. 54, n. 2).

12. Paris, Bibliothèque Nationale, MS arabe 4678-4679, formerly marked "Supplément arabe 2522-2523", transcribed at the beginning of the 19th century in Paris by Michel Ṣabbāġ from an unknown MS which had been transcribed in 1115/1703 in Bagdad, according to its colophon copied literally by Ṣabbāġ; cf. Zotenberg p. 202.

13. Burton says that the Wortley Montague MS in the Bodleian Library "has no especial conclusion relating the marriage of the two brother kings with the two sisters" (XV, p. 351). Does this mean that the MS has a poor conclusion, like that in ZER, or no conclusion at all?

14. This is certainly what was originally intended. The beginning of H and B is still in accord with this intention. In the sequel, names have slipped into the narration: the younger brother lives in Samarcand, the elder in Ṣīn. In K, the alleged friend who relates the story came to "a town in Ṣīn".

15. Burton has added here "of the cities of China" and explained in note 6 that this "is taken from the sequence of the prologue where the elder brother's kingdom is placed in China". He missed the point that in this tale, which he qualifies as "a rechauffé of the Introduction" (note 4), persons and places must remain nameless. *Fī āḫir al-'umr* (H = the text translated by Burton, B) is no doubt a corruption of *fī āḫir al-'umrān* (K); the best reading is to be found in P: *daḫaltu madīna fī āḫir al-'umrān* 'I came to a town at the end of the civilized world' (fol. 163b).

16. This short-cut *isnād* is in contradiction with the longer *isnād* in the introductory passage, but it is no doubt that of the older version.

17. The words *hādihi l-ḥikāya tušbih li-ḥikāyat malik anā a'rif-hu* are certainly an integral part of this revelation scene; so is the king's request to hear about the reaction of the subjects *urīd an asma' mā ǧarā li-ahl hādihi l-madīna wa-mā qālū min amr al-malik.* But the subsequent final clause *li-arǧi' 'am-mā kuntu fīhi* is not quite logical. An emendation *lammā raǧa' 'am-mā kān fīhi* 'when he returned from the case wherein he was', which, regarding the *rasm,* seems to suggest itself, would make the text reasonable.

18. This passage has been dropped from H, but the following statement of the wise presupposes at least *sabab hādā an-nisā*; the addition is from B, fol. 114b; nearly the same text is to be found in K, fol. 124b.

19. Women qualified as *muslimāt, mu'mināt, qānitāt, ṣādiqāt . . . ḥāfiẓāt* (sc. *furūǧahunna*) must exist in reality, as they are mentioned in this *āya.*

20. The name of the Caliph in this story is al-Ma'mūn al-Ḥakim bi-amrillāh. The *ism* of the historical caliph al-Ḥakim (who reigned from 996 to 1021) was al-Manṣūr. The scene of the story is Cairo.

21. The spread of this conclusion in the 17th century is attested indirectly by Galland. He had tried in vain to get a complete copy of the *Nights,* nor had he ever had at his disposal an Arabic text of an end-fragment. The ending of his translation therefore has been suspected, until quite recently, to be of Galland's own invention. But from oral information he knew at least the basic concept of this conclusion: as early as August 1702, two years before he published the first volume of his translation, he outlined in a letter "le dessein de ce grand ouvrage: (. . .) De nuit en nuit la nouvelle sultane le mesne [Schahriar] jusques à mille et une et l'oblige, en la laissant vivre, de se défaire de *la prévention où il étoit généralement contre toutes les femmes*". The words in italics are to be found in the conclusion of Galland's translation, in which Shahrazād does not present children, but is granted mercy because the king's "esprit étoit adouci" and the king is convinced of Shahrazād's chastity. (The quotation from Galland's letter in M. Abdel-Halim, *Galland, sa vie et son œuvre,* Paris 1964, pp. 286-287).

22. Text: *al-baġyu yaqtulu ahlahū.* This looks like a proverb, a variant of the one recorded by al-Maydānī, *Maǧma' al-amtāl,* Cairo 1953, nr. 555 = Freytag, Proverbia Maidanii, cap. II, nr. 129: *al-baġyu āḫiru muddati l-qawmi, ya'nī anna ẓ-ẓulma idā mtadda madāhu, ādana bi-nqirāḍi muddati-him.*

23. Text: *itta'aza*; but see the parallel texts, note 27.

24. Translated by Burton from the Breslau edition, XII, pp. 2-44.

25. In K, the king is nameless; P: *al-malik aẓ-Ẓāhir*; in B, his name is Šahribāz.

26. B: *yaḍurru*; P: *yuhliku*; K: *yusri'u* (=?).

27. B: *irtā'a fī nafsihī*; K: *irtada'a,* obviously a *taṣḥīf* instead of *irtā'a.* This passage is not in P, nor is the following dialogue between the king and Shahrazād.

28. In most cases fragments of older recensions were inserted into the new compilation without extensive revision. So quite often it is not difficult to detect such *spolia* by inconsistent distribution of the roles (speaker, hearer etc.), stylistic peculiarities and the like. The ZER-text however, specially the printed one, has undergone a careful revision.

29. The corruptions found in the text of K, the oldest of the four MSS and carefully calligraphed, show that already that text had been transmitted within a long written tradition.

30. Paris, Bibliothèque Nationale, arabe 3609-3611 (formerly marked "ancien fonds 1508, 1507, 1506"). This MS, commonly designated as G, was transcribed after 1425, the year in which the *ašrafī*-dinar (mentioned in 3610, fol. 43b) was introduced, and before 943/1535, the earliest date of a reader's expression of thanks at the end of 3610.

31. *lā yuṣtalā lahū bin-nār* is among the epithets of 'Umar ibn an-Nu'mān at the beginning of the 'Umar-Romance.

32. It does not come up to the same stylistic and narrative level as the tales inserted into the frame, which are, by the way, far better in the version of G than in ZER. Shahrazād's first tale however, that of the Merchant and the Jinnī, is as poor as in the printed texts, which proves that even it was part of the initial fragment left from preceding recensions.

33. The tale of the Concubine of al-Ḥakim can have taken its actual shape only after the eccentric person of the historical al-Ḥakim had been transfigured by time, so that he could become a nucleus of popular story or romance. The Zuwayla-Gate mentioned in all the texts was built in 1092; as a *terminus ante quem non,* such an early date is rather insignificant.—Also six of the seven poems describing the bride's seven dresses in the Tale of Nūr al-Dīn and his Son (Burton I, pp. 217-219) are used (again?) here for the same purpose.

34. Strasbourg, Bibliothèque Nationale et Universitaire, MS 4278-4281. Date of transcription 1247/

1831-2. As for the date of the compilation, see note 37. Table of contents in Chauvin, *Bibliographie* IV, pp. 210-212.

35. The prologue has been considerably remodelled in its details: the seats of the two kings have been exchanged; the younger brother is deceived by his chief concubine, the elder by his wife; the number of slave girls and male slaves who accompany the queen into the garden has been raised to eighty; Shahrazād is the younger of the two daughters of the wazīr.

36. The untrue slaves had all been executed, so the palace, at least the *ḥaramlik,* had been totally depopulated.

37. The text has been divided into nights by relatively long formulae with separate spaces left for the numbers of the nights. The night-formulae always fill half a page; the nights themselves measure two and a half pages, the formulae not included. The scribe has evidently inserted the night-formula rather automatically, on every third or fourth page, into the text he was copying. But he has made a mistake, for there is one too many: after the formula used for the 1001st night, there is yet another, which was crossed out later. If the MS was a transcription from a compilation already lying before the copyist's eyes, the lines that were crossed out and the free space for the night-number would not have been copied.

38. The composition does not say how many children Shahrazād herself is supposed to have. The number of the heroine's children in Shahrazād's revelation-story is no doubt borrowed from ZER.

39. The version of Tawaddud is very different from that in ZER, but close to freely circulating versions of the story, e.g. that of MS We.702 in Berlin (Ahlwardt Nr. 9179), transcribed in 1055/1645.

40. "A quite modern MS may carry a more complete tradition than one centuries older" (Macdonald 1922, p. 321).

William H. Trapnell (essay date 1990)

SOURCE: Trapnell, William H. "Destiny in Voltaire's *Zadig* and *The Arabian Nights.*'" *Studies on Voltaire and the Eighteenth Century* 278 (1990): 147-71.

[*In the following essay, Trapnell explores the function of miraculous events, narrative condensation, and hedonistic characters in Voltaire's* Zadig *and* The Arabian Nights.]

To the title *Zadig ou la destinée* (1748), Voltaire added the subtitle *histoire orientale.* This subtitle has received less critical attention than the second part of the title, *la*

destinée, which announces the greatest preoccupation of his later career. His protest against the injustice of human destiny in works like *Candide* (1759) has obscured the oriental reference in *Zadig,* which nonetheless reveals its narrative point of departure. He probably intended the conflicting anachronisms in the 'Epître dédicatoire' of *Zadig*[2] to distract critics from his comparison of this tale with the '*Mille et une Nuits,* [les] *Mille et un Jours,* etc.' on the same page. Although he dates the epistle 837 H. (1459 A.D.), he claims that his tale had been translated from ancient Chaldean (Babylonian) to Arabic, 'que ni vous ni moi n'entendons'.[3] The translator, he says, sought to amuse Sultan Ouloug-beb[4] who, unlike his wives, preferred it to *The Arabian Nights.* 'Comment pouvezvous préférer, leur disait le sage Ouloug, des contes qui sont sans raison, et qui ne signifient rien?—C'est précisément pour cela que nous les aimons, répondaient les sultanes' (p. 30). Behind Voltaire's ostensible agreement with Ouloug, lurks a hint of sympathy with his wives,[5] whose deference to the sultan screens a secret irony. For them, the irrational and insignificant allure of the tales obscures the subtle wisdom of the lessons they teach. This indeed they have in common with *Zadig,* 'ouvrage qui dit plus qu'il ne semble dire' (p. 29). Voltaire's playful condescendence towards the *Nights* [*The Arabian Nights*] does not imply contempt for the work as such, but rather an aversion for some of its aspects.[6]

The edition of the work in his library appeared in 1747.[7] He must have written *Memnon,* a preliminary version of *Zadig,* that year, because he published it in June of 1747. His edition of the *Nights* is an adaptation of the work by the Oriental scholar Antoine Galland[8] originally published in twelve volumes between 1704 and 1717. Galland translated most of his text from an Arabic manuscript in four volumes[9] which he had procured, with much difficulty, from Aleppo. He added material from other manuscripts and, in particular, the *Histoire de Sindbad le marin* which he had translated before he learned of the *Nights.* Impatient for more material, the publisher of volume viii (veuve Ricœur), inserted two Arab tales adapted by Galland's fellow scholar Pétis de La Croix, including '**Codadad et ses frères**' which contains '**La Princesse de Deryabar.**' This betrayal upset Galland, but all the other major collections contain the inserted tales too. Published after his death (1715), the last two volumes of his adaptation contain several tales for which he had no written source.[10] He learned them from the Maronite Hanna whom his friend Paul Lucas had brought back with him when he returned from Aleppo in 1709. Thus the final transmission of these tales before their publication continued the ancient oral accumulation that had produced the corpus.[11] Galland's *Nuits* [*Les Mille et une nuits*] were a great monument[12] and Hanna's, a great tradition with roots in a largely undocumented past.[13] Elements of some tales arose in ancient India before these and other stories formed the original collection in Sassanid Persia. The Arabs translated, transformed and developed the corpus in two stages, one in Abbassid Bagdad and the other in Fatimid Cairo. Galland's manuscript, the oldest substantial one extant, probably came from Cairo.

As a storyteller, he had three virtues in common with Voltaire, who should have paid him more attention.[14] His classical elegance, his narrative skill and even his detachment—for these tales seemed less important to him than his scholarly work[15]—assured the extraordinary success of his adaptation,[16] which continues today. Critics generally agree on the literary superiority of his text in comparison with his and the other Arabic sources,[17] intended as they were for recitation or reading aloud.[18] The edition owned by Voltaire was already the fifth at least[19] and translations, especially in English, proliferated. Galland's **Mille et une nuits** and, to a lesser extent, the similar *Cent et un jours* (1710-1712) translated by Pétis de La Croix generated a great vogue[20] of imitations and pseudo-translations claiming oriental sources.[21] Few deserve comparison with Montesquieu's *Lettres persanes* (1720), which evidently stimulated Voltaire's desire to publish an oriental story of his own. Printed in Amsterdam, *Memnon* does not seem to have reached the reading public in France. At the Queen's gambling party in Versailles, Voltaire dared to warn his friend Mme Du Châtelet, in English, that her opponent was cheating. This incident might have landed him in the Bastille for the third time, if he had not fled to Sceaux, where the duchesse Du Maine kept him out of sight. She loved to hear stories as much as he loved to tell them. When he came down for dinner at two o'clock in the morning, he read from his works,[22] including an intermediate version of *Zadig* recorded by his secretary Longchamp, the source of this information, on a manuscript now in Leningrad.[23] His oral talent probably enabled him to exploit unusual literary opportunities in the tradition inherited from Galland.

He assigns the text he says he has translated to the period when 'les Arabes et les Persans commencèrent à écrire les *Mille et une Nuits*' (p. 29). Hardly does he bother to state, however, precisely when and where he thinks they did so, hence the (deliberately) confused historical and geographical background of *Zadig*.[24] Yet his hero lives in much the same world as those of the *Nuits* who belong to the Bagdad period in the evolution of this work, despite his persistent allusions to more ancient ones.

In his tale, Babylon on the Euphrates surely refers to Bagdad on the Tigris, a traditional confusion noted by d'Herbelot in his *Bibliothèque orientale* (1697),[25] a copy of which the author owned and consulted.[26] The travellers in his narrative take the overland routes followed by many of those in the *Nuits*:[27] Bagdad-Damascus-Cairo,[28] Cairo-Medina-Mecca, Mecca-Basra[29] and Medina-Damascus-Bagdad,[30] although he names none of these cities except Basra. Trade and the merchant class enjoy the same prestige in *Zadig* as in the *Nuits*,[31] which must have appealed to him for this very reason. The activity of bandits, the humane treatment of slaves[32] and the prejudice against the integrity of the Jews also appear in both works. Voltaire persistently refers to pre-Islamic religions, but his hero advocates a de facto deism largely compatible with Islam, which discreetly pervades the *Nuits.* When he assigns the text he says he has translated to the time when the Arabs and the Persians *wrote,* as he typically assumes, the *Nuits*,[33] he probably means the reign of the caliph Harun al-Rashid in Bagdad (170-193 H./792-815 A.D.) romanticised by the authors of this tradition.[34] Scarcely does he realise, however, that there were many authors and that they were storytellers of the spoken word who transformed and transmitted narrative material inherited from their predecessors. While he associates his tale with both Persian and Arab culture, the latter predominates to the extent that *Zadig* contrasts with the *Lettres persanes* in this respect, a contrast that confirms Voltaire's originality.

The thematic unity of *Zadig* also distinguishes it from the *Lettres,* whose value consists in the variety of the correspondents' observations and interests. Voltaire concentrates on the problem of human destiny, which all of the protagonists in the *Nuits* face as well, but their reactions to destiny differ from Zadig's. The following study first examines the illustration of this theme by one kind of passage and two kinds of incidents common to both works. Then it proceeds to a comparative analysis of the attitude towards destiny in each. The use of recapitulations to review the destiny of the hero provides us with convenient initial examples.

Among the recapitulations in the *Nuits,* the two in '**Aladdin ou la lampe merveilleuse**' offer the best possibilities of comparison with those in *Zadig*. The magician masquerading as Aladdin's uncle sends him into a secret cavern with instructions to bring him the lamp. When Aladdin returns with the lamp and some precious stones which he has gathered, he asks for a helping hand. But the magician insists on surrender of the lamp first so that the boy may exit more easily. Fearful of dropping the stones, however, Aladdin insists on the helping hand. Thus unexpected obstinacy upstairs and down results in a disagreement. Enraged, the magician closes the entrance by the same incantation he used to open it and abandons his dream of supernatural power. After his escape, which I shall discuss later (see below, p. 167), Aladdin tells his mother how the magician imprisoned him in the cavern. 'Mais il n'en put dire davantage sans verser des larmes' (ii.258). The distress caused by the mere remembrance of his plight demonstrates the trauma of the experience more dramatically than any comment Galland could have made while relating the original event. It impresses us all the more because it occurs in the middle of a leisurely recapitulation that seems almost deliberately to violate modern rules of narrative economy.

Aladdin uses the genie subservient to the lamp's owner to marry Princess Badroulboudour and build a castle for the couple to live in. Unaware of the lamp's properties, Badroulboudour exchanges it for a new one offered by the magician while her husband is away on a hunt. The magician orders the genie of the lamp to take the castle with the princess inside to his homeland in North Africa, where he tries to marry her. But the genie of the ring enables Aladdin to find the castle and he encourages Badroulboudour to lure the magician into drinking poisoned wine. As soon as the magician dies, Aladdin evacuates the great hall and orders the genie of the lamp to return the castle to China. Badroulboudour's father, the sultan, has vowed to have Aladdin beheaded unless he produces the princess again. Badroulboudour reassures him by a detailed account of what has happened to her, leaving the rest of the story to her husband. He explains that he evacuated the great hall in order to spare her and her women further contemplation of 'le traître étendu mort sur le sofa' (ii.342). Since this spectacle hardly seems to have bothered them at the time, however, we infer that he wants to keep the secret of the lamp. Except for this implication, the recapitulation serves no more evident purpose than the pleasure of recalling the marvellous events of a dangerous adventure with a happy ending.

Reducing the volume of information allows an increase in the pace of the narrative. Galland entertains his readers with a thorough review of the preceding adventure, a tactic inherited from the oral tradition. Writing for a less leisurely public, Voltaire refreshes their memory by a concise summary of all previous adventures. The recapitulations in *Zadig* are shorter than those in the *Nuits* and the second one is shorter than the first. The first one occurs when Zadig and his valet become slaves: 'Je vois, lui disait-il, que les malheurs de ma destinée se répandent sur la tienne' (p. 54). A list of causes and effects follows: he was fined for noticing a female dog; he was nearly impaled[35] for talking about griffons; he was nearly executed for writing some verses in praise of the king; he was nearly strangled for some yellow ribbons worn by the queen 'et me voici esclave avec toi parce qu'un brutal a battu sa maîtresse' (p. 54). The disproportion between causes and effects in such lists has received much critical commentary, which usually concludes with an appreciation of Voltaire's talent for irony. This I would hardly dispute, but his irony clearly flows from the conviction that destiny is capricious and that our fellow men are untrustworthy. In his conclusion, Zadig resigns himself to this evidence. Arab merchants will have their slaves and he, a man like other men, might as well be one of them.

Yet Sétoc proves more generous than other men, for he rewards Zadig for his services by freeing him. The free man sets out for Syria and, on the way, says the second recapitulation to himself, in other words to God in whom he believes. A series of exclamations, it recapitulates the first recapitulation, a progression lacking in the *Nuits,* and adds a subsequent misadventure: 'Quoi! disait-il . . .' (p. 63). And we learn that the fine amounted to 400 ounces of gold, that the king threatened to have Zadig beheaded for four lines of verse, that the colour of the queen's ribbons was the same as that of Zadig's bonnet,[36] that Zadig had come to the rescue of the woman beaten by her lover. Thus Voltaire not only manages to recapitulate more concisely, but also more explicitly. The new injustice follows the old ones: Zadig was 'sur le point d'être brûlé pour avoir sauvé la vie à toutes les jeunes veuves arabes!' (p. 63). No longer resigned to his fate, he begins to protest, but only when he benefits from an exception to the rule of fate, an encounter with a generous man capable of gratitude. However irrational this change may seem, it conforms with human psychology. Protest begins only when the grip of oppression relaxes, thus releasing the force of accumulated resentment. One vindication whets an appetite for others and, in Zadig's case, the vindication of his love for Queen Astarté.

The complaints of an unfortunate fisherman move him to recapitulate his own misfortunes again, but this time Voltaire limits the exposition to the first and last event: 'Il répétait la liste de ses infortunes [. . .] depuis la chienne de la reine jusqu'à son arrivée chez le brigand Arbogad' (p. 68). We know them well enough by now and the pathetic register did not particularly appeal to the storyteller at this point in his career.[37] These lists nonetheless omit the rare incidences of good fortune in Zadig's life, such as his appointment as minister of Babylon and his liberation by Sétoc. Perhaps fate has taught him the wisdom of pessimism. Only too eager to relate happy outcomes of dangerous adventures, Aladdin and Badroulboudour live in a different world. This world reflects the optimism of Galland's sources, which cultivate Arab nostalgia for the legendary justice of Abbassid Islam. The resolution of the conflicts between the sympathetic young people and the evil old magician take place in the supernatural sphere where Allah evidently reigns supreme. Voltaire avoids this sphere because he suspects the Christian priesthood of claiming access to it in justification of the authority they usurp over their fellow men. His playful condescension towards the *Nuits* stems from the magic rings and lamps, the genies conjured up and the supernatural acts accomplished. The extent to which destiny depends on them hardly suits his taste. In *Zadig,* he restricts supernatural intervention to the famous chapter on the angel Jesrad masquerading as a hermit, who bears some resemblance to the magicians in the *Nuits.* The destiny demonstrated by his tale reveals a jealous manipulation by the God whose role he assumes in telling it. Zadig's pessimistic recapitulations evoke the destiny imposed by this God whom Voltaire fears[38] more than he loves. The optimistic recapitulations in the *Nuits* attest an Islamic providence assuring the eventual triumph of the righteous and defeat of the wicked.

Nothing illustrates the existence of a providential God more effectively than poor fishermen casting their nets in vain until he provides them with a valuable catch for a reason stated or implied by the context. In **'Les trois pommes'** the disguised Harun al-Rashid encounters an unsuccessful fisherman who has already given up. Harun offers him a hundred sequins for his catch if he has the courage to try one more time. The supernatural power invested in the caliph enables the fisherman to net a casket containing the dismembered corpse of a young woman. In **'Noureddin et la belle Persane'** the same power traps 'cinq ou six beaux poissons' (i.612) in another poor fisherman's net. It seems less impressive this time, however, since the fisherman casts his net from the bank of a royal garden where fish are abundant precisely because fishing is forbidden. Anxious to disguise himself as a fisherman, the caliph takes the two biggest fish and exchanges his clothes with the poacher, who gladly accepts his reward under circumstances that would ordinarily result in punishment. In the **'Histoire du pêcheur'** Allah responds to a prayer by a 'bon musulman' (i.41) who has caught nothing in three attempts. After asking Allah to intervene in his fourth and final attempt, he nets a sealed flask containing a genie who eventually shows him a lake full of magic fish. Desperate for a piece of lead to weight his net, the fisherman in **'Cogia Hassan Alhabbal'** finally obtains one from the ropemaker named in the title. Saad has given Cogia the lead in order to show Saadi that wealth does not necessarily accrue from money as his friend believes. When the fisherman's wife brings him the piece of lead, he willingly accepts the promise she has made to reward Cogia with the contents of his net after the first cast. This cast nets the biggest fish of an abundant catch and the fisherman brings it to Cogia: 'Dieu ne m'a envoyé pour vous que celui-ci, je vous prie de l'agréer' (ii.397). When Cogia's wife cuts the fish open, she finds an enormous diamond in its belly, which she mistakes for a piece of glass. Saad nonetheless wins his argument with Saadi, for the diamond eventually enables Cogia to become wealthy. This extraordinary catch resembles the one in the **'Histoire du pêcheur'** since Allah intervenes directly, while his vicar the caliph intervenes in the two preceding examples. In all four cases, he rewards the faith of a poor fisherman whose family depends on him for survival.

Despite the ascension of Jesrad, Voltaire did not believe in miracles, to say the least. He never witnessed one himself or trusted anyone who said he had and he suspected the Christian clergy of inventing and promoting

them to further their interests. Thus he does not even give his poor fisherman a chance to make a miraculous catch. 'Déplorant sa destinée', Zadig comes to a river and sees 'un pêcheur couché sur la rive, tenant à peine d'une main languissante son filet, qu'il semblait abandonner, et levant les yeux vers le ciel' (p. 66). Like Zadig, he considers himself the most unfortunate of men. He used to sell the most delicious cream tarts in Bagdad and he had the prettiest wife a tradesman could hope for. Ruined, and betrayed by his wife, he received increasingly lower offers for the sale of his house until it was looted and burned to the ground. Taking refuge in a shack, he lived on the fish he caught, but now he cannot catch any. 'O mon filet! je ne te jetterai plus dans l'eau, c'est à moi de m'y jeter' (p. 66). Astonished to discover a man unhappier than himself, Zadig intervenes, dissuades him, consoles him and questions him. Here Voltaire amplifies the sympathy two such unhappy men will have for each other. The pastrymaker reveals that the minister Zadig and Queen Astarté were regular customers of his. Zadig, who refrains from identifying himself, also learns that a Hyrcanian[39] prince has conquered Babylon: 'Quoi! vous ne savez rien de la destinée de la reine?' (p. 67). The fisherman cannot satisfy Zadig's curiosity, but the question prepares us for the reunion of the lovers in the next chapter.

Neither does this fisherman have any inclination to try again, nor does anyone encourage him to do so. His heavenward gaze implies a complaint rather than a plea. Although Jesrad will claim that Orosmade (God)[40] sent Zadig to save him, the hero seems more like a sympathising fellow sufferer than an agent of the divinity. Instead of urging him to cast his net again, he gives him half of his money. The thought of using charity to convince the recipient that he owes it to God never crosses his mind. He neither claims to wield supernatural power nor credits divine intervention in human affairs. 'Je n'aime pas le surnaturel,' he remarks in the posthumous chapter 'Danse'; 'les gens et les livres à prodiges m'ont toujours déplu' (p. 87). He speaks for Voltaire, who substitutes human intervention for the supernatural and divine interventions in the *Nuits*. Rather than demonstrate providential compensation for pious suffering, he stresses the injustice of suffering itself, thus implying the injustice of the God who allows it. The fisherman's story confirms his conviction that virtue suffers and evil prospers all too often in this world. The commercial nature of the pastrymaker-fisherman's virtue may seem to detract from its value, but the apologist of an economy founded on the luxury market[41] would certainly disagree. A healthy society consists, in Voltaire's opinion, of wealthy consumers and modest producers satisfying each other's needs. The pastrymaker's misfortunes deprived Babylon of a valuable resource. The fisherman has the virtue of making the living he can until, no longer able to cope, he prefers suicide to begging, an economic sin. While the fishermen in the *Nuits* share his economic virtue, they have pious virtue as well. Instead of deploring their fate, they rely on the Creator for relief and trust in him to improve their lot. Convinced that their life belongs to him, they never contemplate suicide like Voltaire's fisherman. Hardly does this consideration occur to him, for he regards his life as a personal asset which he may keep or forfeit as he sees fit. When he cast his net into the waters of destiny, therefore, he did not have exactly the same intention as they do. He was inviting God to do him justice, while they are imploring his sympathy.

Certainly Allah deserves the trust of the beautiful princesses in the *Nuits* who fall into the hands of unworthy suitors. An arrow from the king of Deryabar's bow slays a black giant as he prepares to decapitate the Saracen princess he lifts by the hair. She has driven him to this extremity by her scorn for his advances. 'Il ne tient qu'à vous d'être heureuse,' he has just reassured her. She need only love him and be faithful! 'O affreux satyr,' she retorts, 'tu seras toujours un monstre à mes yeux!' (ii.139). Furious, he grabs her and draws his scimitar. Saved by the king, she explains that the giant was one of her husband's officers. Having fallen in love with her, he abducted her and her little child. He took them to a forest far from their homeland and kept them there for several days before losing his patience. Nor can we doubt the danger she faced, for the king saw the giant drink an excessive amount of wine and eat with bestial appetite an ox roasted over his fire. Evidently the monster could have violated her whenever he chose. 'Quelque déplorable [. . .] que soit ma destinée,' comments his victim, 'je ne laisse point de sentir une secrète consolation, quand je pense que ce géant, tout brutal et tout amoureux qu'il ait été, n'a point employé la violence pour obtenir ce que j'ai toujours refusé à ses prières.' Yet he threatened many times to take her by force, if she did not yield to him of her own accord. When he finally did resort to force, 'j'ai moins craint pour ma vie que pour mon honneur' (ii.140).

This of course we scarcely dare to question. What tickles our curiosity, nonetheless, is a slight suspicion of feminine vanity provoked by the tone of voice in which we imagine her giving this testimony. Does the secret consolation, which she so eagerly confides in her hero, not suggest more satisfaction with the awe inspired by her charm than that inspired by her virtue? She will accept his hospitality and continue to accept it, despite her husband whom she eventually forgets. Because of her affection for the king, 'elle [aurait] su plus mauvais gré à la fortune de la rapprocher de ses parents que de l'en avoir éloignée' (ii.141). Another problem raised by this passage admits a more decisive solution. The destiny deplored by the Saracen princess condemns her to every disgrace except the ultimate one she fears. The coincidence between the giant's final recourse to violence and the king's last-second intervention, which re-

veals the vigilance and skill of an extraordinary huntsman, seems gratuitous at first sight. The giant's flight from Morocco or Andalusia must have taken him many days more than the several he has spent in the forest. The king's ardent pursuit of a wild ass happens to bring him to the forest where he sees the giant's campfire shortly before the crisis. Obviously, the coordination of the giant's rage with the king's arrival on the scene results from the desire to engineer an exciting narrative event. Yet belief in Providence by an anonymous succession of Muslim storytellers justifies the coincidence. For them, destiny consists in the progressive accomplishment of Allah's will and Galland, a more scholarly translator than his successors admit,[42] respects this conviction.

This tale parallels another one which encloses it, the story of the king's daughter, the princess of Deryabar. Another black giant has imprisoned her in his black-marble castle in the desert, where he threatens to abuse her if she does not yield to him by tomorrow. This giant, who eats human flesh and wields a huge scimitar, preys on passing caravans. He may well be a diabolical prototype of the bandit Arbogad in *Zadig*. Before slaying him, Prince Codadad 's'adressa au ciel pour le prier de lui être favorable' (ii.134). The princess does not vituperate against him for killing her 'lover' like Missouf, the beautiful Egyptian, who turns on Zadig after imploring his protection. On the contrary, she marries him. The problem and the solution must have seemed simplistic to Voltaire, but the naive conception of Providence inherited from the Islamic storytellers explains them both. Allah guarantees the dignity of princesses, the feminine elite of his society, from the lust of his enemies. Yet he does not rely on miraculous intervention to rescue them from a fate worse than death. The heroes of both the encapsulating and the encapsulated stories are superior huntsmen and warriors equal to the challenge of the giants they face.

The divine control of events by natural means remains the rule when the magician, who has abducted Aladdin's princess, tries to force her to marry him. Though skilled in the use of arms like Codadad and the king of Deryabar, he faces a supernatural power more dangerous than muscle and steel. Thus Aladdin does not rely on weapons but rather on cunning inspired by his love for Badroulboudour. Her beauty, which excites the magician's lust, lures him into drinking the poisoned wine. Allah's enemy therefore succumbs to the very temptation of abusing one of his noblest creatures. The princess justifies the privilege of divine protection by her resistance to the magician. Separation from her father and husband tormented her more, she asserts, than 'l'insolence de mon ravisseur, qui m'a tenu des discours qui ne me plaisaient pas. Je les ai arrêtés par l'ascendant que j'ai su prendre sur lui' (ii.341). Her superiority not only attracts him, but also inspires his respect. Yet his magic power would have been even more effective in overcoming her resistance, if he had used it for that purpose, than the brute force of the giants who prey on the Saracen princess and the princess of Deryabar.

The author of *Zadig* views such awe of feminine virtue by masculine vice with more than the usual scepticism. A satirical derivative of these passages appears in the account Queen Astarté gives Zadig of what has happened to her since her separation from him. Her husband King Moabdar's infatuation with the capricious Missouf resulted in a chaos that exposed Babylon to invasion by the prince of Hyrcania. Preferring her to Missouf, the conqueror told her that he would send for her as soon as he had completed a forthcoming expedition. She therefore found herself in an even more desperate situation than before, although her husband's death made her love for Zadig legitimate. She answered the prince with all the pride of rank and honour: 'J'avais toujours entendu dire que le ciel attachait aux personnes de ma sorte un caractère de grandeur qui, d'un mot et d'un coup d'œil, faisait rentrer dans l'abaissement du plus profond respect les téméraires qui osaient s'en écarter' (p. 72). Surely she had 'heard' Badroulboudour tell how she had overawed the magician, for Voltaire is probably mocking the passage quoted above. Astarté spoke like a queen and was treated like a chambermaid. Without even bothering to reply, the prince called her impertinent but pretty, and ordered his black eunuch to take care of her. A fresher complexion would increase his satisfaction when he had a chance to enjoy her. Although she threatened to kill herself, he only laughed and said he had heard that one before. He disposed of her as if putting a parakeet back in its cage. She escaped only because Missouf, whom she encouraged to replace her as the prince's favourite, helped her. Voltaire does not say how she managed to elude the prince's eunuchs.

Why then does he neglect the opportunity to give us the exciting details of an extraordinary episode? Apparently he does not want us to pay much attention to the manner in which the beautiful princess manages to preserve her dignity. He has no intention of pretending that this dignity overawes her crude, princely captor and he scorns any solution that might resemble a miracle. Although, at this point, he accepts the narrative ideal of the *Nuits,* which requires an unviolated heroine, he refuses to let God play a providential role in the affair. Astarté must appear fortunate rather than blessed. God does not care about her dignity, nor does he trouble to keep it intact for the hero. The author of *Zadig* scorns convenient villains who, lusting after beautiful captives, neglect the brute or magic power they wield for fear of degrading God's superior creatures. Their unnatural and foolish respect clashes with his conception of the life we must lead. The narrative, in his opinion, has to re-

flect this life in order to attract intelligent readers. He covets the interest of Ouloug-beb more than the fancy of his women. He even encourages the former to smile at the fantasies of the latter, although he does not disdain the latter's applause. No one masters the delicate art of teasing lady readers like Voltaire. Astarté's royal contempt for the Hyrcanian prince provokes none of the black giant's rage against the Saracen princess in the *Nuits*; on the contrary, it merely amuses him and whets his appetite. Zadig has no opportunity like Codadad to punish the villain for imprisoning his mistress and lusting after her. He participates in her adventure no more than vicariously by listening to her account of it. Voltaire reduces the hero's protection of the heroine in her hour of greatest need to the mere remembrance of an unfulfilled lover who may be dead. In comparison with the passages in the *Nuits,* however, the contrasts scarcely eclipse the similarities. The episode in *Zadig* manifestly presents Voltaire's reaction to them.[43]

In our comparison of these two works, we have so far concentrated on the illustration of a theme, the theme of destiny. From now on, we shall examine the idea behind the theme. Our analysis will treat the hedonistic motivation of characters, the apparent perversity of destiny, the extent of complaint by its victims and, finally, the nature of Providence.

Zadig's comments on his initial misadventures, which precede the summaries considered above, show that Voltaire intended to tell a story of virtue seeking the happiness it deserves. 'Qu'il est difficile d'être heureux dans cette vie!' (p. 37) exclaims the victim of two unsuccessful marriages and two miscarriages of justice. He changes his mind, however, when King Moabdar rescinds his execution for writing an alleged satire against him and grants him his favour in recognition of his talent for verse: 'il n'est pas difficile d'être heureux' (p. 40). Then Moabdar judges him the winner of a virtue contest. 'Zadig disait, "Je suis enfin heureux!" Mais il se trompait' (p. 42). Enumerated in the summaries, the misadventures that follow confirm this prediction. No further comment on Zadig's hedonistic quest occurs until the happy ending, in which virtue triumphs after so many defeats that this victory seems arbitrary. 'Zadig fut roi, et fut heureux' (p. 85). The past definite tense terminates the narrative without any guarantee of permanence. If Voltaire had seen fit to extend it, the logic of the plot would have tended to another disaster caused by royal jealousy. Other allusions to the hedonistic theme reinforce the significance of Zadig's quest. 'L'homme de Cambalu' (Bekin), who clearly speaks for Voltaire, makes the first attempt[44] to reconcile the representatives of diverse religions in the dispute at the Basra fair. 'Il suffit d'être heureux', he admonishes them (p. 59). 'L'heureux homme!' (p. 81), exclaims the hermit as he watches the fire he has set destroy the house of the man who has sheltered and fed him and Zadig. The man will discover a treasure under the ruins. This additional evidence confirms Voltaire's intention of assimilating human endeavour to a hedonistic quest.

The heroes in the *Nuits* are as hedonistic as Zadig, but neither they nor the narrators ever explicitly acknowledge it. When Aladdin tells his mother how he has obtained the magic lamp, he concludes: 'Puisque le hasard nous en a fait découvrir la vertu, faisons-en un usage qui nous soit profitable' (ii.262). The hitherto lazy and trifling boy therefore accepts the responsibility conferred on him by his good fortune. He will use the lamp to improve the life he and his widowed mother lead. Hardly does he consider leaving her and taking the profligate fling we might have expected. Other young men in the *Nuits* who inherit a great fortune yield to this temptation.[45] Adversity seems to have taught Aladdin that happiness consists as much in the opportunity to make others happy as in the satisfaction of personal desires. Yet he does not forget himself. On the contrary, he fully exploits the genie of the lamp in his campaign to marry Princess Badroulboudour with whom he has fallen in love. A mere glimpse of her unveiled face has inspired the ambition to qualify as her husband by the magic acquisition of wealth and nobility, which never tempted him before. He becomes a prince in order to marry the princess, his ultimate hedonistic goal. Provided by the genie of the lamp, his sumptuous attire, mount and escort assure a lavish welcome by her father the sultan. 'S'il y a quelque endroit', he responds, 'par où je puisse avoir mérité un accueil si favorable, j'avoue que je ne le dois qu'à la hardiesse qu'un pur hasard m'a fait naître, d'élever mes yeux, mes pensées et mes désirs jusqu'à la divine princesse qui fait l'objet de mes souhaits' (ii.303). His passion for her has made this eloquence desirable, but the genie of the lamp has made it possible. The urchin who entered the cavern could never have managed such a speech.

We find a similar blend of hedonistic ambition and generosity in Zadig. Even before falling in love with Queen Astarté, he distinguishes himself by his humanity as the king's minister. He also resembles the lovers in the *Nuits* who, separated from the woman or man they love, travel great distances in search of her or him.[46] The heroes and heroines in this work seek ultimate happiness in the fulfilment of love, the enjoyment of wealth and the humane exercise of power. Although wealth plays a lesser role in *Zadig,* whose hero is born wealthy, economic ambition, enterprise and success assure the same kind of social prestige. Whether economic or sentimental, the hedonistic goal in both works motivates a quest that encounters the successive encouragements and discouragements imposed by destiny. While both maintain the tradition of the happy ending, Voltaire's pessimism contrasts with the detachment of the Arab storytellers. Their respect for the mystery of providential motivation imposes a balanced dosage of good and bad fortune. In

fact this attitude frees their imagination of prejudices like the grudge against the God of destiny in *Zadig*. Since anything can happen, as they see it, everything they imagine does, but they organise their events according to a deliberate narrative aesthetic. They justify the apparent chaos of their plots, which makes the *Nuits* so exciting to read, by frequent allusions to destiny and Providence. The frequency of the word *destinée* and synonyms like *destin, sort* and *fortune* in Galland's adaptation could scarcely have escaped Voltaire. He certainly seems to have borrowed it for his subtitle as well as a few strategic references in his text. Yet his semantics clearly alter the significance of the term.

The most wicked and attractive character in his tale of destiny is the bandit Arbogad. Early in his life, Arbogad realised that 'la destinée ne m'[avait] pas réservé ma portion' (p. 64). A wise old Arab, whom he consulted, told him of a grain of sand that complained of being lost in the desert. Several years later, however, it had become a diamond in the sultan of India's crown. Seeing himself as a grain of sand, Arbogad decided to become a diamond. Like any Bedouin outlaw, he began by stealing horses, then joined with others in raiding small caravans. Reducing the disparity between himself and the wealthy, he captured the castle in which he receives Zadig and became a robber baron. He also obtained the right to collect the tribute due to the king of kings[47] from Arabia. Irritated no doubt, Moabdar sent a satrap with orders to have him strangled but, once Arbogad had had the satrap's men strangled, the officer joined him. When Arbogad mentions Moabdar's fall, Zadig asks for news of Astarté. Insensitive to his guest's concern, however, the bandit says he sells the beautiful women he captures without inquiring into their identity. '[Il] buvait toujours, faisait des contes, répétait sans cesse qu'il était le plus heureux de tous les hommes, exortant Zadig à se rendre aussi heureux que lui' (p. 65). Thus the least virtuous hedonist in *Zadig* is the most successful, so successful in fact that he tries to corrupt the most virtuous and least successful. The contrast between Arbogad and Zadig can only imply that destiny rewards evil and punishes virtue. While the happy ending finally rewards Zadig's virtue, it also precludes the possibility of relating a further disillusionment.

Less predictable than equitable in the *Nuits,* destiny causes more anxiety than despair. 'Que la fortune est inconstante!' cries the king of the Black Islands. 'Elle se plaît à abaisser les hommes qu'elle a élevés. Où sont ceux qui jouissent tranquillement d'un bonheur qu'ils tiennent d'elle?' (i.63). Having married his cousin, with whom he had fallen in love, he discovered that she was betraying him every night in the palace garden. Unrecognised in the dark, he struck her lover with his scimitar and left him for dead. She nonetheless managed to keep him alive without being able to heal him. Exasperated, the king curses them both and she converts the bottom half of his body into marble. The sultan, who discovers this living statue, tricks the sorceress, by an impersonation of her lover, into restoring the lower half of the king's body, then kills her. However desperate the living statue may seem, his lament does not imply that happiness is impossible, but rather precarious. Destiny torments us by depriving us of the good fortune it temporarily allows us.

But it also rescues us from misfortune. The king of Zanguebar offers his protection to the Princess of Deryabar, the sole survivor of a shipwreck after the overthrow and assassination of her father. 'La fortune, qui vous persécute, est inconstante,' he reassures her. 'Votre sort peut changer' (ii.143). It does improve for a while, since the king falls in love with her and marries her. During this very celebration, however, the son of the Saracen princess, who overthrew her father, conquers Zanguebar. Although the royal couple escape in a fishing boat, pirates capture them. The only survivor of a dispute among these pirates over who will keep her throws her husband into the sea. He is taking her to a friend in Cairo when the black giant attacks his caravan, kills him and locks her up in his castle. Further vicissitudes await her before her final reunion with her second husband Codadad in a happy ending. Only then does her destiny take the permanent turn for the better foreseen by the king of Zanguebar. While her persistent misfortune recalls Zadig's, it serves as an exception illustrating the rule. Destiny inflicts such disproportionate adversity on few of the characters in the *Nuits*.

Adversity moves the fisherman in the **'Histoire du pêcheur,'** the Saracen princess and Zadig all three to complain that destiny rewards evil and punishes virtue. The fisherman suffers because he cannot catch any fish, but he accuses fortune of moral perversity: 'Tu prends plaisir à maltraiter les honnêtes gens et à laisser les grands hommes dans l'obscurité, tandis que tu favorises les méchants, et que tu élèves ceux qui n'ont aucune vertu' (i.40). Assuming that he considers himself virtuous, we may wonder whether he finds that evil men catch too many fish or that they do not have to resort to this precarious livelihood. Since the context neglects this point, perhaps an Arab storyteller inserted the complaint in order to cultivate political resentment among his listeners. It would have seemed more appropriate if Voltaire had assigned it to the fisherman in *Zadig*. Selfish and evil men, including Zadig's enemy Orcan, have ruined the pastrymaker so that he must fish for a living. Deprived of influence over his own destiny, he wholly depends on it for survival, a desperate situation in Voltaire's story. It is not the fisherman who complains, however, but rather Zadig himself: 'Ah! dit-il au pêcheur, Orcan mérite d'être puni. Mais d'ordinaire ce sont ces gens-là qui sont les favoris de la destinée' (p. 68). In an allusion to the envious Arimaze, another en-

emy of Zadig, Voltaire notes that 'l'occasion de faire du mal se trouve cent fois par jour, et celle de faire du bien, une fois dans l'année, comme dit Zoroastre' (p. 38-39). The Saracen princess makes a similar remark as she tells her story to the king of Deryabar, who has just rescued her from the black giant: 'La fortune favorise plus souvent les entreprises injustes que les bonnes résolutions' (ii.139). The similarity between this quotation and the preceding one suggests that Voltaire borrowed the idea from the *Nuits* rather than Zoroaster. The Saracen princess and the fisherman in the **'Histoire'** [**'Histoire du pêcheur'**] nonetheless face an unexpected prosperity, while Zadig's misadventures have by no means come to an end. The comparison of these passages therefore confirms the contrast between Islamic optimism and deistic pessimism observed above.

Zadig endures his misadventures without questioning Providence[48] until late in the tale, when Itobad substitutes his green armour for the white armour that Astarté has sent her lover. Defeated by all of his opponents in the tournament, Itobad thus usurps the victory of the sleeping hero, who has defeated all of his opponents. Consequently, Zadig loses his advantage in the competition for the right to marry the Queen and rule over Bagdad. 'Il lui échappa enfin de murmurer contre la Providence.' Perhaps 'tout était gouverné par une destinée cruelle qui opprimait les bons et faisait prospérer les chevaliers verts' (p. 78). This suspicion tempts him again when the hermit sets their host's house on fire and calls him a happy man. Though torn between the urge to laugh and the urge to insult the old man, between the urge to beat him and the urge to flee, he meekly continues to follow him. He finally protests when the hermit drowns their hostess's nephew: 'O monstre! ô le plus scélérat de tous les hommes!' (p. 81). For he has no reason so far to suspect that his companion is more than a fellow man. The hermit excuses his arson on the grounds that Providence will reward the victim by the discovery of a buried treasure under the ruins of his house. His murder pre-empted the victim's murder of his aunt and Zadig.[49] 'Qui te l'a dit, barbare?' (p. 82) protests Zadig. Even if the old man has read these events in the book of destinies, which he has shown Zadig, he has no right to kill an innocent child. Apparently disconcerted, the hermit reverts to his true identity as Jesrad, the Islamic angel of death.[50] Zadig protests more respectfully, but no less persistently, making three more objections, each of which begins with the word 'Mais . . .' (p. 82, 83). The first time, he objects to the divine injustice of punishing good men and rewarding evil men. Jesrad denies the assertion. The second time, he questions the toleration of evil by the Creator and Jesrad explains that divine perfection excludes any other perfection. Jesrad has just revealed that God sent Zadig to change the fisherman's destiny, when the hero says his third *mais*. This time, however, the angel spreads his four wings[51] and ascends towards an Islamic heaven which Voltaire has rounded off at ten spheres.[52] This sudden ascension puts a convenient end to an embarrassing discussion in which an inferior creature dares to ask questions and raise doubts. If Zadig had had the time to finish his sentence, he might well have objected that God entrapped the fisherman in his undeserved poverty to begin with. The objections he does succeed in making seem more convincing than the hermit-angel's dogmatic, complacent and condescending replies. Jesrad behaves like a celestial bureaucrat with a routine response to every complaint. Despite his apology of God's justice, the only supernatural figure in *Zadig* leaves us with the impression that his divine master sacrifices the noblest creatures in his creation to the arbitrary harmony of the whole, just as Leibniz speculates.[53] Voltaire does not seem to attack the German philosopher, but rather to deplore the truth of his philosophy. Leibnizian optimism, which he assimilates with Islamic providentialism,[54] inspires nothing but pessimism in him.[55]

Although misfortune drives some of the characters in the *Nuits* to complain to the divinity, Allah responds by deeds rather than words. 'O fortune!' cries the poor fisherman in the **'Histoire,'** 'cesse d'être en colère contre moi, ne persécute point un malheureux qui te prie de l'épargner!' (i.40). He promptly nets the flask with the genie sealed inside. The half-marble king of the Black Islands adds a more specific request to his more specific complaint: 'O fortune, qui n'a pu me laisser jouir pour longtemps d'un heureux sort, et qui m'a rendu le plus infortuné de tous les hommes, cesse de me persécuter, et viens par une prompte mort mettre fin à mes douleurs!' (i.63). Zadig and his fisherman also consider themselves the most unfortunate of men. While God sends him to save the fisherman, Allah sends a sultan to deliver the king of the Black Islands. Rather than grant the victim's request for death, this agent of divine justice inflicts it on his tormentor. The unhappy Princess of Deryabar regrets her reaction to the discovery that, after her father's overthrow and death, she alone has survived the shipwreck. 'Souvent,' she comments, 'les malheurs nous rendent injustes: au lieu de remercier Dieu de la grâce particulière que j'en recevais, je ne levai les yeux au ciel que pour lui faire des reproches de m'avoir sauvée.' Preoccupied with this grace, she forgets the injustice done to her and the other victims. Even at the time, she ignored this injustice: 'Loin de pleurer le vizir et ma gouvernante, j'enviais leur destinée' (ii.142). Like the fishermen in the **'Histoire'** and *Zadig,* she would have thrown herself into the sea if God had not sent someone to dissuade her, the king of Zanguebar in her case. Her pious gratitude seems to have reinforced her feelings of guilt over the momentary lapse in her faith. The impossibility of divine injustice convinces her that only she could have been wrong.

Scarcely does Zadig share this conviction. While she questions Providence itself, she never questions more than a single act of God and one that happens to affect her. Her second husband Codadad's disappearance after his brothers try to kill him leads her to believe that he is dead. 'C'est à moi seule que je dois imputer ta mort,' she tells him. 'Tu as voulu joindre ta destinée à la mienne; et toute l'infortune que je traîne après moi [. . .] s'est répandue sur toi.' Thus she assumes responsibility for her destiny and its effect on others without denying Providence. Allah causes all events and yet those who suffer incur the blame! This very contradiction reveals the depth of her faith, even though she yields to the temptation of questioning divine wisdom: 'O ciel [. . .] si vous ne vouliez pas que j'aie d'époux, pourquoi souffrez-vous que j'en trouve!' (ii.147). This question conforms to the same logic as the earlier one: why kill the people I love and spare me? Far from doubting Allah's right to take lives, she simply regrets his choice. Her survival seems like needless cruelty.

Her testimony confirms that the ultimate issue in the *Nuits* is not destiny, but Providence. The vizir had intended to accompany her to the courts of neighbouring kings whom he might have persuaded to intervene on her behalf: 'mais le ciel n'approuva pas une résolution qui nous paraissait si raisonnable' (ii.142), hence the shipwreck. Since human reason cannot penetrate the mystery of Providence, we must take Allah's wisdom for granted. We must thank him for his favours and never complain, no matter how badly he treats us. The frequency of such recommendations in the *Nuits* might suggest a pious routine, if the stories did not constantly justify them. Time and again, they prove the futility of rebellion against fate or the irrelevance of failure to deserve good fortune. Even the caliph's generosity does not save his favourite Schemselnihar and the Persian prince, who love each other so desperately that they cannot face a life of separation from each other. 'Les plaintes que je fais au ciel de la rigueur de ma destinée' (i.426), which she evokes in a letter to him, avail them nothing. The mysterious illnesses of which they die resemble broken hearts. On the other hand, Noureddin seduces the beautiful Persian slave whom his father, the vizir, has purchased for the king of Basra. He dissipates the wealth he inherits from his father. And he even offers the slave, who has become his beloved and loving wife, to a fisherman. Fortunately for him, this fisherman is a disguised caliph in a generous mood. 'Où allez-vous?' the astonished Harun asks him after this offer. 'Où Dieu me conduira', he replies (i.616). Allah and the caliph reward his foolish generosity by making him and his wife the king and queen of Basra. This prodigal deserves more than the occasional anxiety he suffers and less than the prosperity he consistently enjoys. Allah has decided otherwise for mysterious reasons justifying the surprises that hold our attention in this story.[56]

More frequently, however, the *Nuits* veil Providence in partial mystery alone. After three days in the cavern, Aladdin loses all hope of survival and raises his joined hands in prayer. 'Avec une résignation entière à la volonté de Dieu, il s'écria: "Il n'y a de force et de puissance qu'en Dieu"' (ii.255). In accomplishing this very prayer, however, he unintentionally rubs the ring on his finger which the magician has given him. Immediately the genie of the ring appears, providing him with the power to reopen the entrance to the cavern. He continues to wear this ring, but he apparently forgets it until it saves his life a second time. After the disappearance of his castle with the princess inside, the sultan vows to have him executed unless he produces her again. Desperate, Aladdin decides, like Voltaire's fisherman, to throw himself into the river, 'mais il crut, en bon musulman fidèle à sa religion, qu'il ne devait pas le faire sans avoir auparavant fait sa prière' (ii.328-29). In an attempt to wash himself as Islam requires, he slips on the bank and rubs the ring on a stone. Appearing again, the genie enables him to overcome the magician as we have seen. Evidently, in both cases, Aladdin's piety saves his life and assures his prosperity. A foolish boy until the first incident, he has been a wise young man ever since. Unlike Noureddin, therefore, he deserves his prosperity and the crises he overcomes enable him to prove it. Allah intervenes twice in order to save the life of a faithful Muslim. In neither case does the context offer any argument in favour of a mere coincidence between sincere piety and supernatural rescue. In conclusion, Scheherazade invites her husband the sultan to admire the justice done both to Aladdin and the magician. Each deserves his destiny because of the use he makes of the treasure available to him.

The appropriate use of the creation founds much of the morality in the *Nuits*. 'Tu fais un bon usage des richesses que Dieu t'a données,' Harun al-Rashid tells Cogia Hassan Alhabbal. 'Les voies par lesquelles il a plu à la Providence de te gratifier de ses dons doivent être extraordinaires' (ii.382). Cogia willingly complies with the caliph's request to hear his story. We already know about the wager between Saadi and Saad. Cogia hides most of Saadi's first gift in his turban, but a kite steals the turban. Assuming that Allah wants to try him, he does not complain, but rather praises him just as he did when he received the gift: 'Je me soumets à sa volonté!' (ii.388). Unknowingly, his wife trades the vase in which he has hidden Saadi's second gift for some infusorial earth. A merchant who needs the bran stored in the vase just happens to come their way when she needs the infusorial earth. They must say nothing, Cogia tells her, and submit to Allah's will. Indeed they should praise him for letting them keep 10 of the 200 gold pieces which he did not put in the vase. After explaining what has happened, he tells Saadi: 'Il n'a pas plu à Dieu que votre libéralité servît à m'enrichir, par un de ses secrets impénétrables que nous ne devons pas approfondir'

(ii.394). Despite this respect for divine mystery, the story hints at some of the reasons behind Allah's treatment of Cogia. The piece of lead, which has no pecuniary value, succeeds where the two gifts of money fail. The natural and yet extraordinary discovery of the diamond in the fish's belly compares with the loss of the turban and the vase. All three events suggest divine intervention, but the first two frustrate Saadi's attempts to make Cogia rich and the last one rewards Saad's with success. Why then does Allah prefer lead to money? Wealth acquired by financial investment tempts us to believe that he had nothing to do with it. The piece of lead has the advantage of demonstrating, as we learn elsewhere, that 'tout ce qui arrive, c'est Dieu qui le fait arriver' (ii.120). Evidently Cogia passes the tests to which Allah submits him. His docility and faith qualify him as a good Muslim like Aladdin who will use his wealth wisely once he has acquired it. Allah can entrust a greater portion of the creation to such a believer.

Zadig's God seems to prefer less docile believers like the princess of Deryabar. Subject to persistent adversity, both she and Zadig reinforce their faith by the very efforts they make to overcome their doubt. The mysterious ways of Providence incite temporary dissatisfaction before they inspire lasting respect. An intellectual like Voltaire, Zadig wonders what book engrosses the hermit when he first sees him. 'C'est le livre des destinées,' the old man replies, offering to let him read it. Despite Zadig's knowledge of several languages, he cannot decipher a single character in the book. Since this obstacle merely increases his curiosity, however, the hermit discusses destiny with him. 'Zadig se sentit entraîné vers lui par un charme invincible' (p. 78), the supernatural charm of the archangel, of course, but the context implies that the hermit's eloquence captivates him too. He even illustrates the arbitrary mysteries of Providence as Zadig looks on helplessly. He steals from the generous but disdainful host, rewards the stingy host, burns the house of the generous and modest host down, drowns the kindly widow's nephew. The ways of Providence escape us, he comments. 'Les hommes [ont] tort de juger d'un tout dont ils n'[aperçoivent] que la plus petite partie.' This principle summarises Voltaire's conception of Leibnizian optimism. 'Tout est dangereux ici-bas, et tout est nécessaire' (p. 80). The second clause simplifies Leibnizian determinism and the first expresses Voltaire's reaction to it.[57] Unable to read the book of destinies, Zadig at first rejects the hermit's claim that Providence has authorised all four of his acts. Did Providence punish the disdainful host by a theft, embarrass the stingy host by a gift, reward the modest host with a treasure, save the kindly widow and the virtuous hero from murder? Despite Zadig's protests, these incidents demonstrate, as Jesrad insists, '[qu']il n'y a point de mal dont il ne naisse un bien' (p. 82). Confronted with this principle, Zadig submits to Jesrad's supernatural authority: 'à genoux, [il] adora la Providence' (p.

83). When Zadig and Astarté finally ascend the throne of Bagdad, they establish a reign of justice and love. '[Ils] adorèrent la Providence [. . .] Ce fut le plus beau siècle de la terre' (p. 85).

This extremely happy ending includes no apparent hint of the irony we expect from Voltaire on such occasions. Perhaps he thought the fate that preys on Zadig during most of the preceding fifty-six pages enough to indicate how seriously we should take the last one. Do dreams of eventual bliss not enable us to endure the harsh reality of our everyday lot? Although Voltaire's conception of Providence has much in common with the one in the *Nuits,* his pessimism clashes with the optimism of the Muslim storytellers. He also carries his analysis of destiny further than they do and even to the point of metaphysical inquiry, which scarcely interests them. A vague Islamic Providentialism satisfies them because it satisfied their pious audiences. It does not satisfy him because he has seen too much abuse of the Christian equivalent. Rather than substitute the Islamic for the Christian Providence in his oriental tale, therefore, he tries, unsuccessfully, to situate the plot in a vague pre-Islamic past. Successfully, nonetheless, in that his amateur references to this past result in a heteroclite anachronism that enhances the flavour of his story. Providence does not answer fervent prayers by pious sufferers in *Zadig,* where divine intervention commands little credence. The only miracle in the tale serves merely to justify human despair. Significantly, it is a departure and not an arrival.

Otherwise, his Providence resembles the one in the *Nuits.* God or Allah determines all events according to a mysterious justice that may seem to persecute the good and favour the wicked, an illusion caused by the distorted perspective of suffering creatures. In neither case, however, does the mystery remain absolutely impenetrable, since this justice privileges humans over the other natural creatures and assures a minimal order among them by a system of checks and balances whose complication partly surpasses their comprehension. Providence assigns the noblest role to heroes and a few heroines whose intelligence, courage, honesty and piety earn more prestige than felicity.[58] It subjects them to endless trials in order to reinforce their faith precisely because they can withstand greater adversity than their fellows.

Though certainly no source in the conventional sense, the *Mille et une nuits* provided the author of *Zadig* with useful narrative material organised along lines that interested him. They revealed the opportunity of assigning a narrative role to Providence and illustrated the possibilities of a dialectic between narrative and destiny. Providence determines the destiny that unfolds in the narrative, which itself records the fulfilment of this destiny and the reactions of the characters subject to it.

But these reactions also form a commentary on destiny and hence Providence itself. The Arab storytellers taught Voltaire this secret, but he exploited it more aggressively than they did. The cultural background of the *Nuits* also furnished the elements of an exotic alternative to Christendom, a less dangerous target than the real thing. Behind the angel Jesrad lurks a clergyman whose condescension reflects more lust for power than subordination to God. Voltaire never relaxes his vigilance against the Church, while the storytellers persistently cultivate faith in Allah. Yet he borrowed considerably more from the *Nuits* than a vehicle for antichristian polemic. Without admitting it, he appreciated and perhaps even admired the essential notion of medieval Islamic civilisation that Galland had transmitted. Though even less authentic than the legendary vision of Abbassid Bagdad in Galland's sources, the way of life in *Zadig* has its own peculiar charm, which we owe to the author's ability to appropriate and transform whatever struck his fancy.[59] Is that not in fact what originality really means? Yes. Could he have written *Zadig* without a knowledge and appreciation of the *Nuits*? No.

Notes

1. This article originally appeared in the *International Journal of Islamic and Arabic studies* (Bloomington, Indiana). Permission to reprint it has graciously been given by the editor. An Open Grant from the Lilly Foundation of Indianapolis provided the material support for this study. A seminar on *Les Mille et une nuits,* organised by J. E. Bencheikh in the winter and spring of 1987 for the Institut d'études arabes et islamiques provided the intellectual stimulation.

2. For example: 'Son *Epître dédicatoire* [. . .] a été rédigée, nous dit-il, par le poète Sadi l'an 837 de l'hégire [. . .] Or cette date est impossible. Sadi [. . .] a vécu 200 ans plus tôt.' Pol Gaillard, 'A propos de *Zadig ou la destinée, histoire orientale*', *Raison présente* 67 (1983), p. 47.

3. Voltaire, *Romans et contes* (Paris 1966), p. 29. Henceforth, page numbers from this edition will appear in parentheses after quotations.

4. '*Ouloug-Beb*: Mirza Mohammed, grandson of Tamburlaine, who reigned from 1416 to 1449.' H. T. Mason (ed.), *Zadig and Other Stories* (Oxford 1971), p. 239.

5. 'Le public auquel avait conscience de s'adresser Galland était, lui, en grande partie féminin.' Georges May, *Les Mille et une nuits d'Antoine Galland ou le chef-d'œuvre invisible* (Paris 1986), p. 44. Yes. But May also assumes that Ouloug speaks exclusively for the author: 'Un esprit [. . .] aussi exceptionnel que Voltaire pouvait se mé-

prendre sur la valeur des contes [. . .] "qui ne signifient rien," tout simplement parce qu'il avait le tort de les mesurer à son aune et non à la leur' (p. 203). To interpret any Voltarian text *tout simplement* is to risk missing the point.

6. 'Il ne manque pas de faire appel à l'expression péjorative de "contes des Mille et Une Nuits" lorsqu'il veut dénoncer quelque monstrueuse absurdité.' Jacques van den Heuvel, *Voltaire dans ses contes: de 'Micromégas' à 'L'Ingénu'* (Paris 1968), p. 183.

7. *Les Mille et une nuits, contes arabes, traduits en français par Mr. Galland. Nouvelle édition corrigée,* 6 vols (Paris 1747).

8. '[Galland substituait] à la logique propre du texte de référence et à la conception du récit qui le soustend une autre logique et une autre conception, celle du public destinataire.' Claude Hagège, 'Traitement du sens et fidélité dans l'adaptation classique: sur le texte arabe des *Mille et une nuits* et la traduction de Galland', *Arabica* 27 (1980), p. 127.

9. Three are in the Bibliothèque nationale: MSS Arabe 3609, 3610, 3611. The fourth has disappeared.

10. 'Ali Cogia, marchand de Bagdad', 'Le Cheval enchanté', 'Le Prince Ahmed et la fée Pari-Banou', 'Les Deux sœurs jalouses de leur cadette'.

11. 'Tous [les] manuscrits, de quelque époque qu'ils soient, s'écartent fortement les uns des autres [. . .] Les contes se transforment journellement dans la bouche des narrateurs comme sous la plume des scribes.' Nikita Elisséeff, *Thèmes et motifs des* Mille et une nuits (Beyrouth 1949), p. 64.

12. 'C'est entre ses mains que, pour la première fois, une collection disparate et encore informe de contes d'origine diverses devient un ensemble homogène marqué de cette unité conceptuelle et stylistiqu'e faute de laquelle il n'y a pas de véritable chef-d'œuvre' (May, p. 99).

13. 'Here is a book [. . .] whose author's name is legion.' Mia Gerhardt, *The Art of Storytelling* (Leiden 1963), p. 39.

14. The 'Catalogue de la plupart des écrivains français', which he appended to *Le Siècle de Louis XIV* (1752), contains a brief entry on Galland including the following comments on the *Nuits*: 'il y mit beaucoup du sien: c'est un des livres les plus connus en Europe, il est amusant pour toutes les nations.' *Œuvres complètes de Voltaire* (Paris 1877-1885), xiv.75.

15. See May, p. 78-81, for a thorough discussion of his attitude.

16. 'Tous les savants orientalistes qui se penchèrent par la suite sur [sa] traduction des *Nuits* reconnaissent, non sans un certain dépit, que le génie de leur prédécesseur fut l'élément décisif de la fortune des contes orientaux.' Mohamed Abdel-Halim, *Antoine Galland, sa vie et son œuvre* (Paris 1964), p. 292.

17. 'He [. . .] has rendered the generally primitive and unsophisticated Arabic original into a polished, smoothly flowing and highly stylized narrative [. . .] The original sounds, more often than not, almost like a faint echo when compared with what it becomes in Galland's immeasurably artistic and highly cultivated narrative.' Rida Hawari, 'Antoine Galland's translation of the *Arabian nights*', *Revue de littérature comparée* 54 (1980), p. 155.

18. The third kind of storyteller observed by Edward Lane distinguished himself from the others by reading from a written text, attracting educated listeners and exploiting *The Arabian Nights. An Account of the Manners and Customs of the Modern Egyptians Written in Egypt during the Years 1833-1835* (London 1836). See ii.149-50.

19. According to Victor Chauvin, *Bibliographie des ouvrages arabes ou relatifs aux Arabes publiés dans l'Europe chrétienne de 1810 à 1885* (Liège 1900-1902), iv.25-27.

20. Facilitated by 'le nouvel état d'esprit qu'avaient créé, après une longue période d'ignorance de l'Orient musulman, les entreprises commerciales de Louis XIV favorisées par Colbert et doublées d'un important effort culturel' (Hagège, p. 115).

21. Marie-Louise Dufrenoy lists 15 such works between the beginning of 1745 and the publication of *Memnon* in 1747 in her *L'Orient romanesque en France, 1704-1789* (Montréal 1946-1947), p. 360-62.

22. Longchamp mentions 'les contes et romans qui l'avaient tant amusé lorsqu'il venait tous les soirs prendre son repas dans la ruelle de son lit'. Longchamp and Wagnière, *Mémoires sur Voltaire et sur ses ouvrages* (Paris 1826), ii.152.

23. 'The manuscript, though copied by Longchamp, has been corrected in Voltaire's own hand. It represents beyond any doubt an intermediary between the publication of *Memnon* and the composition of *Zadig*.' Ira Wade, *The Search for a New Voltaire: Studies on Voltaire and upon Material Deposited in the American Philosophical Society,* Transactions of the American Philosophical Society, new series 48 (1958), p. iv.

24. 'Chronologie brouillée: Sadi n'est pas du temps d'Ouloug-beg. Géographie fantaisiste: Memphis est trop près de Babylone, on va trop vite de Perse

en Egypte, et d'Oreb à Balzora.' V. L. Saulnier (ed.), *Zadig ou la destinée, histoire orientale* (Paris 1946), p. xxv.

25. 'Les historiens persiens prétendent que cette ville, aussi bien que celle de Babel ou Babylone, a été bâtie par les rois de Perse de la première dynastie, qui ne sont en effet que les rois des Assyriens.' Barthélemy d'Herbelot, 'Bagdad', *Bibliothèque orientale, ou dictionnaire universel, contenant généralement tout ce qui regarde la connaissance des peuples d'Orient* (Paris 1777-1779). Voltaire's copy and original edition: 1697. 'Pour le commun des Français au XVIIe et au XVIIIe siècle, une confusion s'était opérée entre cette antique Babylone et la capitale des califes musulmans: Bagdad.' Georges Ascoli (ed.), *Zadig* (Paris 1929), ii.11.

26. M. P. Alekseev and T. N. Koreeva find 'traces de lectures' in Voltaire's copies of both d'Herbelot's *Bibliothèque* (no. 1626) and Galland's *Nuits* (no. 2457): *La Bibliothèque de Voltaire* (Moscou 1961).

27. 'Quanto alle carovane nelle *Mille e une Notte*, esse percorrono sempre gli stessi tragetti. Da Mosul in Iraq, attraverso la Mesopotamia, si segue il corso dell'Eufrate e si giunge ad Aleppo, a Damasco, al Cairo [. . .] Tra le città prestigiose, prima da tutte, Bagdàd, sede della reggia del grande Harún. I luoghi volteriani son spesso i medesimi.' Doa Rigo Bienaimé, 'Alcuni aspetti della "feerie" orientale nei racconti di Voltaire', *Rivista di letterature moderne e comparate* 31-32 (1978-1979), p. 12.

28. Doctor Hermès, who examines Zadig's wounded eye in the first chapter, comes from Memphis, which Voltaire seems to have cited because it was a more ancient capital of Egypt than Cairo. Later Zadig travels to Egypt and, although Voltaire does not give us more precise geographical details, his hero would ordinarily have been sold in the slave market at Cairo.

29. Zadig does not travel between Basra and Bagdad.

30. Zadig's master Sétoc enters the Sinai ('Horeb' to Voltaire) peninsula with his caravan. Later, when Zadig leaves Sétoc, he crosses the border between Syria and Arabia Petraea. Although Voltaire says nothing of travel southward towards Medina and Mecca, Zadig's trip to Basra and his eventual return to Bagdad would ordinarily follow the routes from these cities to Basra and Bagdad in the north.

31. André Miquel describes 'le grand marchand' in the time of Harun al-Rashid as 'socialement nanti, religieusement justifié et littérairement exalté' in his *Islam et sa civilisation* (Paris 1968), p. 148.

32. '[Les esclaves] parvenaient souvent à des situations enviables; ils n'étaient pas, comme en d'autres régions, maltraités, ni fatalement voués aux besognes inférieures, aux métiers malsains ou pénibles.' Aly Mazahéri, *La Vie quotidienne des musulmans au Moyen-Age du Xe au XIIIe siècles* (Paris 1951), p. 300.

33. Galland himself, who should have known better, speaks of 'l'auteur arabe, qui n'est pas connu' in his 'Epître' to the marquise d'O. *Les Mille et une nuits, contes arabes, traduits par Galland,* 2 vols (Paris 1960), i.xxx. Henceforth, references to this work will appear in parentheses after quotations in the text.

34. 'Le nom de Haroun al-Raschid est devenu de bonne heure le symbole commun du bon vieux temps, surtout de ce qui est merveilleux et fabuleux.' J. Oestrup, *Alf Layla wa Layla, Encyclopédie de l'Islam* (Leyde 1913), i.256.

35. A Turkish method of execution. This is another example of the cultural confusion in *Zadig*.

36. What Voltaire continues to leave unsaid, however, generates further irony: 'C'est le roi rendu jaloux par les courtisans qui avait fait le rapprochement entre la couleur des babouches de la reine et du bonnet porté par Zadig.' Pierre Haffter, 'L'usage satirique des causales dans les contes de Voltaire', *Studies on Voltaire* 53 (1967), p. 17.

37. It had nonetheless appealed to the author of the tragedy *Zaïre* (1732) and it would appeal to the author of the novel *L'Ingénu* (1767).

38. 'Le Dieu cruel, honni du jeune Voltaire, vit encore [en 1748] sourdement dans le contraste voltairien du Dieu immense et de l'homme infime.' René Pomeau, *La Religion de Voltaire* (Paris 1969), p. 248.

39. The ancient name of the region south of the Caspian Sea.

40. 'Ormazd is the Parsi form of the highest god of Mazdaeism, the principle of good opposed to Ahriman [. . .] the lord of the bad creation.' 'Ormazd', *Encyclopedia of Religion and Ethics* (Edinburgh 1917).

41. See Voltaire's *Essai politique sur le commerce* (1734) and *Le Mondain* (1736).

42. 'Exemple curieux de la déformation que peut subir un texte en traversant le cerveau d'un lettré au siècle de Louis XIV, l'adaptation de Galland, faite pour la cour, a été systématiquement émasculée de toute hardiesse et filtrée de tout le sel premier.' [J. C. Mardrus,] 'Présentation', *Le Livre des Mille et une nuits* (Paris 1986), i.vi. As a translator, Mardrus systematically repairs this 'emasculation' by an erotic distortion of his sources.

43. Did Voltaire know that the 'Princesse de Deryabar' was taken from the *Cent et un jours* and inserted

in Galland's text without his consent? (see above, p. 158). Did he care?

44. Zadig makes the second and decisive one.

45. The ones in the 'Histoire racontée par le Marchand chrétien' and 'Histoire de Noureddin et de la belle Persane'.

46. See especially 'Histoire [. . .] de Camaralzaman [. . .] et de Badoure'.

47. The title of the king of Persia, but the context refers to Moabdar, the king of Babylon.

48. 'On devrait intituler [*Zadig*] plutôt *la Providence* que *la Destinée*.' Voltaire to cardinal de Bernis, 14 October 1748, *Correspondence and Related Documents,* ed. Th. Besterman, *The Complete Works of Voltaire* 85-135 (Genève, Banbury, Oxford 1968-1977), Best.D3784.

49. In his edition of *Zadig* (ii.136-52), Georges Ascoli demonstrates that Voltaire borrowed most of this episode from derivatives of 'The Cave', Koran xviii.66-83, including 'The Hermit', a poem by the Englishman Parnell.

50. In a letter to d'Argenson in July of 1747, Voltaire identifies 'Iesrad' with 'l'ange exterminateur' (Best.D3550). Voltaire is apparently confusing two Islamic archangels, Djabra'il or Djbril, the archangel of revelation, and Izra'il or Azra'il, the archangel of death. Like Jesrad, Izra'il has four wings, while Djabra'il has 1600. See Frithjof Schuon, *L'Œil du cœur* (Paris 1974), p. 37, 38.

51. In addition to Izra'il, Voltaire may have been thinking of L'Eclair, 'un grand génie à quatre ailes' (ii.63) in the 'Histoire de Beder'.

52. '[Allah] a créé les sept cieux superposés.' *Le Coran,* trans. Régis Blachère (Paris 1980), lxvii.3.

53. 'La scène de l'Hermite est une allégorie romancée de *La Théodicée* de Leibniz, écrite pour répondre aux commentaires de Bayle sur le manichéisme, c'est-à-dire sur la théorie la plus élémentaire pour expliquer l'origine du mal. Certes Zadig renonce à lutter contre l'ange, mais seulement à cause de son caractère surnaturel et devant la logique de ses arguments. Si l'on élimine le principe d'autorité, il ne subsiste plus que le "mais" final de Zadig, qui représente l'insatisfaction inexprimée du héros.' Jean Sareil, 'De *Zadig* à *Candide,* ou permanence de la pensée de Voltaire', *Romanic Review* 52 (1961), p. 273.

54. '"Le grand reproche qu'on avait d'abord fait à Leibniz et à Pope," nous dit Voltaire, c'était "d'enseigner le fatalisme."' [*Œuvres complètes de Voltaire,* ed. Moland, ix.468] 'Où donc situer un roman qui mettra en évidence leur doctrine, sinon dans cet Orient, où le fatalisme est communément accepté pour loi suprême?' (Ascoli, i.XLVII).

55. 'Man's only course is to take Jesrad's assertions on trust, but in times of adversity they place a burden on his faith which may well prove intolerable [. . .] Voltaire offers the solution of faith, but he does so in such a way as to reveal his doubts about its practical value in the circumstances in which it is most needed.' W. H. Barber, *Leibniz in France from Arnauld to Voltaire* (Oxford 1955), p. 220.

56. 'Voltaire se rappelle que le principal ressort des contes arabes était dans des catastrophes imprévues et de subits revirements de fortune' (Dufrenoy, p. 219).

57. The author of *Zadig* believes that 'man is primarily a passive victim of destiny, helpless for all his sense of freedom, in the grip of forces he cannot control, whose purposes he can never fully understand' (Barber, p. 205).

58. 'Nei racconti delle *Mille e une Nuits,* tutti gli elementi sembrano concorrere alla creazione di un modello de perfezione umana, ma sopratutto al raggiungimento di una straordinaria abilità da parte dell'oroe orientale di fronte ale aversità del destino.' Gisella Maiello, *Voltaire, narratore fantastico* (Napoli 1985), p. 70.

59. 'Son attitude en face d'une tradition romanesque [comme celle des *Nuits*] est toujours la même. Il en a pénétré profondément les mécanismes, et il exploite habilement les procédés et les thèmes, mais à des fins proprement philosophiques et sans cesser chemin faisant de railler leur invraisemblance' (Van den Heuvel, p. 184).

Husain Haddawy (essay date 1990)

SOURCE: Haddawy, Husain. Introduction to *The Arabian Nights,* translated by Husain Haddawy, edited by Muhsin Mahdi, pp. ix-xxix. New York: W. W. Norton & Company, 1990.

[*In the following essay, Haddawy provides a brief history of the origins and publication of* The Arabian Nights *and illustrates the shortcomings of some of its popular translations.*]

Bless thee, Bottom! Bless thee! Thou art translated.

—*A Midsummer Night's Dream*

THE WORLD OF *THE ARABIAN NIGHTS*

It has been some years now since as a little boy in Baghdad I used to listen to tales from *The Thousand and One Nights.* It sometimes seems like yesterday, sometimes like ages ago, for the Baghdad I knew then seems now closer to the time of the *Nights* [*The Thousand and One Nights*] than to our own times. It was on long winter nights, when my grandmother was visited by one lady or another, Um Fatma or Um Ali, always dressed in black, still mourning for a husband or a son, long lost. We would huddle around the brazier, as the embers glowed in the dim light of the oil lamp, which cast a soft shadow over her sad, wrinkled face, as if to smooth out the sorrows of the years. I waited patiently, while she and my grandmother exchanged news, indulged in gossip, and whispered one or two asides. Then there would be a pause, and the lady would smile at me, and I would seize the proffered opportunity and ask for a story—a long story. I used to like romances and fairy tales best, because they took me to a land of magic and because they were long.

The lady would begin the story, and I would listen, first apprehensively, knowing from experience that she would improvise, depending on how early or late the hour. If it was early enough, she would spin the yarn leisurely, amplifying here and interpolating there episodes I recognized from other stories. And even though this sometimes troubled my childish notions of honesty and my sense of security in reliving familiar events, I never objected, because it prolonged the action and the pleasure. If the hour was late, she would, in spite of my entreaties, tell either a brief story or one of normal length, summarizing here and omitting there. If I knew the story, I would protest, reminding her of what she had left out, and she, smilingly, would promise to tell me the story in its entirety the next time. I would then entreat her to narrate at least such and such an episode. Sometimes my grandmother, out of love for me and her own delight in the story, would add her voice to mine, and the lady, pleased to be appreciated and happy to oblige, would consent to go on, narrating in a gentle, steady voice, except when she impersonated a man or woman in a moment of passion or a demon in a fit of anger, at times getting up to act out the part. Her pauses were just as delicious as her words, as we waited, anticipating a pleasure certain to come. At last, with the voice still steady but the pauses shorter and less frequent, she would reunite the lovers or reconcile the hero to fate, bringing the story, alas, to an end and leaving me with a feeling of nostalgia, a sense at once of fulfillment and of loss. Then I would go to sleep, still living with magic birds and with demons who pursued innocent lovers and haunted my dreams, and often dreaming, as I grew older, of a face in Samarkand that glowed with love and blessed my waking hours.

So has the drab fabric of life been transformed into the gossamer of romance, as these stories have been spun for centuries in family gatherings, public assemblies, and coffeehouses, in Baghdad, Damascus, or Cairo. (Indeed, on a recent trip to Marrakech, I came across

storytellers in a public square, mesmerizing their audiences.) Everybody has loved them, for they enchanted the young and the old, alike, with their magic.

In the *Nights* themselves, tales divert, cure, redeem, and save lives. Shahrazad cures Shahrayar of his hatred of women, teaches him to love, and by doing so saves her own life and wins a good man; the Caliph Harun al-Rashid finds more fulfillment in satisfying his sense of wonder by listening to a story than in his sense of justice or his thirst for vengeance; and the king of China spares four lives when he finally hears a story that is stranger than a strange episode from his own life. Even angry demons are humanized and pacified by a good story. And everyone is always ready to oblige, for everyone has a strange story to tell.

The work consists of four categories of folk tales—fables, fairy tales, romances, and comic as well as historical anecdotes, the last two often merging into one category. They are divided into nights, in sections of various lengths, a division that, although it follows no particular plan, serves a dual purpose: it keeps Shahrayar and us in suspense and brings the action to a more familiar level of reality. The essential quality of these tales lies in their success in interweaving the unusual, the extraordinary, the marvelous, and the supernatural into the fabric of everyday life. Animals discourse and give lessons in moral philosophy; normal men and women consort or struggle with demons and, like them, change themselves or anyone else into any form they please; and humble people lead a life full of accidents and surprises, drinking with an exalted caliph here or sleeping with a gorgeous girl there. Yet both the usual incidents and the extraordinary coincidences are nothing but the web and weft of Divine Providence, in a world in which people often suffer but come out all right at the end. They are enriched by the pleasure of a marvelous adventure and a sense of wonder, which makes life possible. As for the readers, their pleasure is vicarious and aesthetic, derived from the escape into an exotic world of wish fulfillment and from the underlying act of transformation and the consequent pleasure, which may be best defined in Freudian terms as the sudden overcoming of an obstacle.

Such an effect, which is contingent on merging the supernatural and the natural and securing a willing suspension of disbelief, the storyteller of the *Nights* produces by the precise and concrete detail that he uses in a matter-of-fact way in description, narration, and conversation, bridging the gap between the natural and supernatural situations. It is this quality, by the way, that explains the appeal of these tales to the romantic imagination. For instance, the demon is a serpent as thick as the trunk of a palm tree, while the she-demon is a snake as thin as a spear and as long as two; the transparent curtain hiding the gorgeous girl in the bed is red-speckled; and the seductive girl from Baghdad buys ten pounds of mutton, while the pious gardener buys two flagons of wine for the mysterious lovers. Thus the phantasmagoric is based on the concrete, the supernatural grounded in the natural.

DISSEMINATION AND MANUSCRIPTS

The stories of the *Nights* are of various ethnic origins, Indian, Persian, and Arabic. In the process of telling and retelling, they were modified to conform to the general life and customs of the Arab society that adapted them and to the particular conditions of that society at a particular time. They were also modified, as in my own experience, to suit the role of the storyteller or the demand of the occasion. But different as their ethnic origins may be, these stories reveal a basic homogeneity resulting from the process of dissemination and assimilation under Islamic hegemony, a homogeneity or distinctive synthesis that marks the cultural and artistic history of Islam.

No one knows exactly when a given story originated, but it is evident that some stories circulated orally for centuries before they began to be collected and written down. Arab historians of the tenth century, like al-Mas'udi and ibn al-Nadim speak of the existence of such collections in their time. One was an Arabic work called *The Thousand Tales* or *The Thousand Nights,* a translation from a Persian work entitled *Hazar Afsana* (A thousand legends). Both works are now lost, but although it is not certain whether any of these stories or which of them were retained in subsequent collections, it is certain that the *Hazar Afsana* supplied the popular title as well as the general scheme—the frame story of Shahrazad and Shahrayar and the division into nights—to at least one such collection, namely *The Thousand and One Nights.*

The stories of the *Nights* circulated in different manuscript copies until they were finally written down in a definite form, or what may be referred to as the original version, in the second half of the thirteenth century, within the Mamluk domain, either in Syria or in Egypt. That version, now lost, was copied a generation or two later in what became the archetype for subsequent copies. It too is now lost, but its existence is clearly attested to by the remarkable similarities in substance, form, and style among the various early copies, a fact that points to a common origin. Specifically, all the copies share the same nucleus of stories, which must have formed the original and which appear in the present translation. The only exception is the **"Story of Qamar al-Zaman,"** of which only the first few pages are extant in any Syrian manuscript, and for this reason I have not included it in the present translation.

From the archetype there evolved two separate branches of manuscripts, the Syrian and the Egyptian. Of the Syrian branch four manuscripts are known to exist. The

first is the copy in the *Bibliothèque Nationale* in Paris, in three volumes (nos. 3609-3611). It is of all existing manuscripts the oldest and the closest to the original, having been written sometime during the fourteenth century. The other three Syrian manuscripts were copied much later, in the sixteenth, eighteenth, and nineteenth centuries, respectively. They are, however, very close to the fourteenth-century manuscript and similarly contain only the nucleus and the very first part of **"Qamar al-Zaman"** ["Story of Qamar al-Zaman"].

If the Syrian branch shows a fortunately stunted growth that helped preserve the original, the Egyptian branch, on the contrary, shows a proliferation that produced an abundance of poisonous fruits that proved almost fatal to the original. First, there exists a plethora of Egyptian copies all of which, except for one written in the seventeenth century, are late, dating between the second part of the eighteenth and the first part of the nineteenth century. Second, these copies delete or modify passages that exist in the Syrian manuscripts, add others, and indiscriminately borrow from each other. Third, the copyists, driven to complete one thousand and one nights, kept adding folk tales, fables, and anecdotes from Indian, Persian, and Turkish, as well as indigenous sources, both from the oral and from the written traditions. One such example is the story of Sindbad, which, though early in date, is a later addition. What emerged, of course, was a large, heterogeneous, indiscriminate collection of stories by different hands and from different sources, representing different layers of culture, literary conventions and styles tinged with the Ottoman cast of the time, a work very different from the fundamentally homogeneous original, which was the clear expression of the life, culture, and literary style of a single historical moment, namely, the Mamluk period. This is the more significant because the Ottoman period is marked by a sharp decline in Arabic culture in general and literature in particular.

The mania for collecting more stories and "completing" the work led some copyists to resort even to forgery. Such is the case of none other than **"The Story of Aladdin and the Magic Lamp."** This story is not among the eleven basic stories of the original work, nor does it appear in any known Arabic manuscript or edition, save in two, both written in Paris, long after it had appeared in Galland's translation. Galland himself, as his diaries indicate, first heard the story in 1709 from Hanna Diab, a Maromite Christian of Aleppo, who may have subsequently written it down and given it to Galland for his translation. The first time the story appeared in Arabic was in 1787, in a manuscript written by a Syrian Christian priest living in Paris, named Dionysius Shawish, alias Dom Denis Chavis, a manuscript designed to complete the missing portions of the fourteenth-century Syrian manuscript. The story appeared again in a manuscript written between 1805 and 1808, in Paris, by

Mikhail Sabbagh, a Syrian collaborator of Silvestre de Sacy. Sabbagh claimed to have copied it in turn from a Baghdad manuscript written in 1703. Such good fortune, in retrieving not one but two versions of a lost wonderful tale, might be cause for rejoicing, as it indeed was among the scholars. However, a careful examination of the two versions, both in the light of the general style of the *Nights* and in the light of Galland's translation, leads to a less joyful conclusion. Chavis fabricated the text by translating Galland back into Arabic, as is manifest from his French syntax and turns of phrase, and Sabbagh perpetuated the hoax by improving Chavis's translation and claiming it to be a Baghdad version. And this forgery was the source used by Payne and Burton for their own translations of the story.

THE PRINTED EDITIONS

If the history of the manuscripts is a confusing tale, that of the printed editions of *The Thousand and One Nights* is a sad comedy of errors. The first edition was published by Fort William College in Calcutta, in two volumes comprising the first two hundred nights (vol. 1 in 1814; vol. 2 in 1818). The editor was one Shaikh Ahmad ibn-Mahmud Shirawani, an instructor of Arabic at the college. He pieced this edition together from a late Syrian manuscript and a work containing classical anecdotes, choosing the texts at random. He deleted, added, and modified numerous passages and tried to change, whenever he could, the colloquial to literary expressions. He edited as he pleased. Then came the Breslau edition, the first eight volumes of which were published by Maximilian Habicht, between 1824 and 1838, and the last four by Heinrich Fleischer, between 1842 and 1843. For reasons known only to himself, Professor Habicht claimed to have based his edition not on a Syrian or an Egyptian but on a Tunisian manuscript, thus confusing the scholars until they finally disproved the claim by discovering that he had patched the text together from copies of the fourteenth-century Syrian manuscript and late Egyptian ones.

It was on such a late Egyptian manuscript that the first Bulaq edition of 1835 was exclusively based. It is a manuscript whose copyist, by culling, collecting, and interpolating numerous tales of recent vintage and written in a late style, swelled the old text, and by subdividing the material, obtained one thousand and one nights, thus producing a "complete" version of the *Nights*, a version very different from the Mamluk original in substance, form, and style. The Bulaq editor, Abd al-Rahman al-Safti Al-Sharqawi, not content to edit and print an accurate text of the manuscript, took it upon himself to correct, emend, and improve the language, producing a work that was in his judgment superior in literary quality to the original. Then came the second Calcutta edition, published in four volumes by William Macnaghten, between 1839 and 1842. Edited by several

hands, it was based on a late Egyptian manuscript copied in 1829, with interpolations and with "corrections" in the substance and the style, according to the first Calcutta and the Breslau editions. Thus "thoroughly edited" and "completed," as its editors claimed, it has ever since vied with the Bulaq edition in the estimation of scholars and general readers, not to mention all the major translators. Thus authentic came to mean complete and, ironically, spurious. (For a full history of the manuscripts and printed editions, see Muhsin Mahdi's Arabic introduction to his edition of the text of the *Nights, Alf Layla wa Layla,* Leiden, 1984, and his English introduction in the forthcoming third volume.)

THE MAHDI EDITION

It is one of the curiosities of literary history that a work that has been circulating since the ninth century, that has been heard and read for centuries by young and old everywhere, and that has become a world classic should wait until very recently for a proper edition. This is curious yet understandable as one of the anomalies of comparative cultural studies. While the history of textual scholarship in the West has been, since the Renaissance, increasingly one of keen accuracy and authenticity, its counterpart in the East, especially in the case of the *Nights,* has been one of error and corruption, at the hands of Eastern and Western scholars alike, the result of ignorance and contempt. It is all the more gratifying, therefore, that the most recent edition of the Arabic text of the *Nights* should be by far the best. After years of sifting, analyzing, and collating virtually all available texts, Muhsin Mahdi has published the definitive edition of the fourteenth-century Syrian manuscript in the *Bibléothèque Nationale* (*Alf Layla wa Layla,* Leiden, 1984). Mahdi fills lacunae, emends corruptions, and elucidates obscurities; however, he refrains from providing punctuation and diacritical marks or corrected spellings. What emerges is a coherent and precise work of art that, unlike other versions, is like a restored icon or musical score, without the added layers of paint or distortions, hence, as close to the original as possible. Thus a long-standing grievance has been finally redressed, and redressed with a sense of poetic justice, not only because this edition redeems all others from a general curse, but also because it is the work of a man who is at once the product of East and West. And it is particularly gratifying to me personally, because it has provided me with the text for my translation.

PAST TRANSLATIONS

Not so fortunate were the major translators of the work into English, Edward Lane (1839-41), John Payne (1882-84), and Richard Burton (1885-86). Lane based his translation on the Bulaq, the first Calcutta and the Breslau; Payne on the second Calcutta and the Breslau; and Burton on the Bulaq, the second Calcutta, and the

Breslau editions. These translators did not, as one might expect, compare the various editions to establish an accurate text for their translations (assuming that, given what they had, such a task was possible); instead they deleted and added at random, or at will, from the various sources to piece together a text that suited their individual purposes: in the case of Lane, a detailed but expurgated version; in the case of Payne and Burton, versions that are as full and complete as possible. In effect, they followed the same Arabic editorial tradition, except that whereas the editors of Bulaq and Calcutta produced a corrupt text in Arabic, the translators of London produced an even more corrupt text in English. Even the two less significant twentieth-century translations followed this pattern. Edward Poweys Mather based his English version (Routledge, 1937) on a French translation by J. C. Mardrus, which was based on the Bulaq and second Calcutta editions. Since he knew no Arabic, he altered the French text, ignorant of what he was doing to the Arabic or how far he had strayed from it. And N. J. Dawood, who translated a selection of tales (Penguin, 1956), which includes less than three of the eleven basic stories of the *Nights,* followed the second Calcutta, "editing" and "correcting" here and there in the light of the Bulaq edition.

Interestingly, the only exception to this pattern is Galland himself, the very first to translate the work in Europe (1704-17). His French translation of the basic stories was based on none other than the fourteenth-century Syrian text, as well as other sources. But instead of following the text faithfully, Galland deleted, added, and altered drastically to produce not a translation, but a French adaptation, or rather a work of his own creation. He did succeed, however, in establishing the work as a classic, for no sooner had his translation begun to appear than a Grub Street English version followed (1706-8), went into many editions, and was itself followed by other translations, pseudotranslations, and imitations, so numerous that by 1800 there were more than eighty such collections. It was such hack versions that inflamed the imagination of Europe, of general readers and poets alike, from Pope to Wordsworth. The *Nights* could shine in the dark.

These translators did not deviate from the letter of the original because they did not know sufficient Arabic. On the contrary, a careful comparison between any given Arabic passage and their own respective translation of it reveals an admirable command of Arabic diction, grammar, and syntax, except where the text itself poses severe problems, as it often does. Although the tales are generally written in the conversational style of the storyteller, they modulate between the colloquial and the literary, and even ornate, within a given passage, from passage to passage, and from story to story, and both types pose problems in regards to diction, grammar, and syntax. A great many words are thirteenth-

century Syrian and Egyptian colloquial idioms, which have long since disappeared from usage or whose meanings have been altered; and many others are of Persian origin, either used without alteration or Arabized. The sentences are often ungrammatical, hence capable of several different and often contradictory readings. The typical structure is that of an interminable running sentence, consisting of brief coordinated clauses, often without apparent regard for place, time, or causality. The translator is therefore forced to interpret and reorder the clauses in a subordinated and logical sequence, in order to suit the European habits of reading and thinking, if his reader is to understand the passage at all. To make matters worse, the text, including Mahdi's, normally bears neither diacritical nor punctuation marks. In Arabic, the diacritical marks distinguish one letter from another, thus differentiating between words that share the same letters but have different roots and therefore different meanings. Thus a word may offer two very different readings in a given sentence. This is not a problem when one of the meanings is unlikely in the context, but when both are possible, the translator must choose a single interpretation. The diacritical marks also indicate the forms of conjugation and declension. Their absence, therefore, coupled with the faulty grammar of some sentences, makes every sentence an encounter, assuming, that is, that one always knows where a sentence or a unit of expression begins or ends, for the Arabic text uses no punctuation, not even question marks.

What makes a coherent reading or translation of such a text possible is an eye familiar with Arabic prose and an ear attuned to the rhythm of the spoken language, ideally the eye and ear of someone who reads, writes, and speaks Arabic like a native. It is a wonder, therefore, that foreign translators, like Lane, Payne, and Burton, made so few mistakes, yet no wonder that they made them. In diction, for instance, when they met words they could not understand, they often dropped them from their text. In grammar, a misreading, for instance, of the conjugation of the verb "to overtake," which also means "to realize," leads Burton to translate the refrain "But morning overtook Shahrazad, and she lapsed into silence," as "And Shahrazad perceived the dawn of day and ceased saying her permitted say." This example would seem innocuous enough were it not that it is repeated one thousand times and were it not that it spoils the dramatic poignancy of the situation, when the morning, the hour of her execution, finally catches up with Shahrazad. In syntax, reordering the clauses for a coherent reading often requires knowledge of Arab life and culture. For example, the following passage, translated literally, reads:

> After a while, our mother also died, and left us three thousand dinars, which we divided equally among ourselves. I was the youngest. My two sisters prepared their dowries and got married.

Burton translates it as follows:

> After a while my mother also deceased, leaving me and my sisters-german three thousand dinars; so each daughter received her portion of a thousand dinars and I the same, albe the youngest. In due course of time, my sisters married with the usual festivities.

But it should read:

> After a while, our mother also died, leaving us three thousand dinars, which we divided equally among ourselves. Since I was the youngest of the three, my two sisters prepared their dowries and got married before me.

For what is at issue here is not the Islamic law of inheritance but marriage customs in Arab society.

Moreover, the problem for the translators was compounded in that, as often as not, a given passage had already been altered by the editor of a manuscript or a printed edition or by both. For the tales, for all their popularity among the people, were regarded with condescension and contempt by the Arab literati of the eighteenth and nineteenth centuries. These included the editors themselves, self-appointed men of taste and judgment, who, trained during the period of the decline of Arabic literature, had little judgment and no taste. They regarded these folk tales as entertaining in substance but vulgar in style, and they undertook to improve them according to their own light.

Their method was to condense, amplify, or alter. They took a given passage, summarized it, and recast it in correct, polite, or literary Arabic, often sacrificing vivid details vital to the art of the storyteller for empty academic phrases or poetic diction. For instance, **"The Story of the Hunchback"** opens with this passage:

> It is related, O King, that there lived once in China a tailor who had a pretty, compatible, and loyal wife. It happened one day that they went out for a stroll to enjoy the sights at a place of entertainment, where they spent the whole day in diversions and fun, and when they returned home at the end of the day, they met on the way a jolly hunchback. He was smartly dressed in a folded inner robe and an open outer robe, with gathered sleeves and an embroidered collarband, in the Egyptian style, and sporting a scarf and a tall green hat, with knots of yellow silk stuffed with ambergris. The hunchback was short, like him of whom the poet 'Antar said:
>
> > Lovely the hunchback who can hide his hump,
> > Like a pearl hidden in an oyster shell,
> > A man who looks like a castor oil branch,
> > From which dangles a rotten citric lump.
>
> He was busy playing on the tambourine, singing, and improvising all kinds of funny gestures. When they drew near and looked at him, they saw that he was drunk, reeking of wine. Then he placed the tambourine under his arm and began to beat time by clapping his hands, as he sang the following verses:
>
> > Go early to the darling in yon jug;
> > Bring her to me,
> > And fete her as you fete a pretty girl,
> > With joy and glee,
> > And make her as pure as a virgin bride,
> > Unveiled to please,
> > That I may honor my friend with a cup
> > Of wine from Greece.
> > If you, my friend, care for the best in life,
> > Life can repay,
> > Then at this moment fill my empty cup,
> > Without delay.
> > Don't you, my tantalizer, on the plain
> > The gardens see?
>
> . . . [W]hen the tailor and his wife saw the hunchback in this condition, drunk and reeking of wine, now singing, now beating the tambourine, they were delighted with him and invited him home to sup and drink with them that night. He accepted gladly and walked with them to their home.

I have deliberately chosen this lengthy passage in order to show how drastically the Egyptian editor reduces and excises (in this case two entire poems) and to show the extent of the substance and flavor the reader misses as a result. Payne's translation is accurate, but he uses the edited version, and so he reads:

> There lived once in the city of Bassora a tailor, who was openhanded and loved pleasure and merrymaking: and he was wont, he and his wife, to go out by times, a-pleasuring, to the public places of recreation. One day they went out as usual and were returning home in the evening, when they fell in with a hunchback, the sight of whom would make the disappointed laugh and dispel chagrin from the sorrowful. So they went up to look at him and invited him to go home and make merry with them that night. He consented and accompanied them to their house.

Or else the editors altered some details and thereby showed insensitivity to psychological subtlety or dramatic nuance. In **"The Story of the Slave-Girl Anis al-Jalis and Nur al-Din ibn-Khaqan,"** the passage in which the caliph throws off his disguise reads:

> I heard, O happy King, that the old man went into a storeroom to fetch a stick with which to beat the fisherman, who was the caliph, while the caliph cried out from the window, "Help, help!" and was at once joined by Ja'far and the officers, who dressed him in his royal suit, seated him on a chair, and stood in attendance. When the old man came out of the storeroom with the stick, rushing toward the fisherman, he was stunned to see instead the caliph seated on a chair and Ja'far standing in attendance. He began to bite his nails in bewilderment and to exclaim, "Am I asleep or awake?" The caliph turned to him and said, "O Shaikh Ibrahim, what state do I see you in?" The old man became sober at once and, rolling on the ground, recited the following verses.

The Egyptian editor alters the passage to read, again in Payne's translation:

> When the Khalif heard this, he cried out at him and made a sign to Mesrour, who discovered himself and rushed upon him. Now Jaafer had sent one of the gardeners to the doorkeeper of the palace for a suit of the royal raiment for the Commander of the Faithful; so he went and returning with the suit, kissed the earth before the Khalif and gave it to him. Then he threw off the clothes he had on and dressed himself in those which the gardener had brought, to the great amazement of Gaffer Ibrahim, who bit his nails in bewilderment and exclaimed, 'Am I asleep or awake?' 'O Gaffer Ibrahim,' said the Khalif, 'what state is this in which I see thee?' With this, he recovered from his drunkenness and throwing himself on the ground, repeated the following verses:

Or they inserted some details, often exaggerating action, description, or emotion and thereby weakening the literary effect. Again in a passage in **"Anis al-Jalis,"** [**"The Story of the Slave-Girl Anis al-Jalis and Nur al-Din ibn-Khaqan"**] for instance, the added details change the delicate humor of high comedy to the coarse humor of low comedy. After the caliph exchanges his clothes with the fisherman, he takes the salmon and returns to the garden in disguise to surprise Ja'far, who has been waiting for him there. But the Egyptian editor inserts the following passage, which reads, this time in Burton's translation:

> Hardly had the fisherman ended his verse, when the lice began to crawl over the Caliph's skin, and he fell to catching them on his neck with his right and left throwing them from him, while he cried, 'O fisherman, woe to thee! What be this abundance of lice on thy gaberdine'? 'O my lord,' replied he, 'They may annoy thee just at first, but before a week is past thou wilt not feel them nor think of them'. The Caliph laughed and said to him, 'Out on thee! Shall I leave this gaberdine of thine so long on my body?' Quoth the fisherman, 'I would say a word to thee but I am ashamed in presence of the Caliph!' and quoth he. 'Say what thou hast to say'. 'It passed through my thought, O Commander of the Faithful', said the fisherman, 'that since thou wishest to learn fishing so thou mayest have in hand an honest trade whereby to gain thy livelihood, this my gaberdine besitteth thee right well.' The Commander of the Faithful laughed at this speech, and the fisherman went his way.

Thus the translators, by adhering to such sources, deviate not only from the letter but also from the spirit of the original, particularly since the letter and the spirit are often inextricable. But such adherence is not the only cause of their violation of the spirit; another and more fundamental cause lay in their respective views of the work itself, their objectives in translating it, and their strategies and styles, all of which may be explained by the fact that they simply failed to see that fidelity to the precise detail was crucial to achieve the essential quality of the *Nights,* by bridging the gap between the natural and the supernatural.

From Galland to Burton, translators, scholars, and readers shared the belief that the *Nights* depicted a true picture of Arab life and culture at the time of the tales and, for some strange reason, at their own time. Time and again, Galland, Lane, or Burton claimed that these tales were much more accurate than any travel account and took pains to translate them as such. For this purpose, each of them adopts a specific strategy, depending on his other intentions. Lane translates the work as a travel guide to Cairo, Damascus, and Baghdad. In order to substantiate this claim, he adds compendious notes intended to explain a given passage and to introduce the reader to various aspects of Arab culture, such as social customs, mythology, religion, and ethics, without asking himself whether such substantiation would be necessary if the claims were true. Consequently, he proceeds to depict this life in an accessibly plain style, much more faithful to the conversational style of the original than, say, the style of Burton. But instead of being faithful to the life depicted in the tales, Lane omits sometimes a few details, sometimes whole passages, curiously because he finds them inconsistent with his own observations of life in Cairo. For instance, he omits the details of the drinking scene in **"The Story of the Porter and the Three Ladies,"** because he has never seen Cairene ladies drink, but, to make sure that the reader is properly informed, he appends a twenty-page footnote dealing with drinking habits among the Arabs. Then he goes on to explain that such passages, like the one he has omitted, "seem as if they were introduced for the gratification of the lowest class of auditors of a public reciter of a coffee-shop. These passages exhibit to us persons of high rank, both men and women, as characterized by a grossness which is certainly not uncommon among Arabs of the inferior classes" (ch. 10, n. 87). He also omits the verse passages, except for a token line here and there, because he finds them to be for the most part either worthless or obscure, and because in truth they do not suit his sociological purpose. He is an orientalist or a sociologist, rather than a storyteller.

If Lane attempts to guide the prudish Victorian reader through Cairo by introducing him to a higher class of Egyptian society, Burton attempts to bring Cairo, in all its color, to England. But unlike Lane, who is interested in what he considers to be typical manifestations of Arab culture, Burton is interested in the exotic, the quaint, and the colorful. He too appends copious notes, but these are meant to appeal to Victorian prurience or to shock prudish sensibility. Typical is the note on the passage in the **"Prologue,"** in which Shahrayar's wife lies on her back and invites the black slave Mas'ud to make love to her while ten other black slaves are busy making love to ten of her female attendants; Burton explains the white woman's predilection for black men by expatiating on the efficacy of the enormous male organs in Zanzibar, promising the reader to regale him on the retention of the semen, in due course.

Burton declares in the introduction that his purpose is to produce a "full, complete, unvarnished, uncastrated copy of the great original." That original, as I have mentioned earlier, uses a style that modulates between the colloquial and the literary. The literary is marked by metaphors and similes, formulaic epithets, parallelisms, and rhymed prose, and Burton literally preserves all this, including the jingling rhymes, merrily telling the reader that he has "carefully Englished the picturesque turns and novel expressions of the original in all their outlandishness." And outlandish, indeed grotesque, they appear, both to English and to Arabic eyes. Having gone so far, Burton is unable to retrench in his rendering of the colloquial passages; therefore, he renders them in a pseudo-archaic style dear to the heart of many a Victorian translator, a style that is totally alien both to the style of the Arabic original and to any recognizable style in English literature. One may suppose that Burton follows a general Victorian tendency to archaize and make more colorful the "rude" works of primitive times and places; and subsequently one may trace the same tendency in the style of Payne's translation of the *Nights,* in which Burton detects and admires a "sub-flavor of the Mabinogianic archaism." But even a cursory comparison easily shows that the style of Payne's translation, which was unfortunately published in a limited edition of five hundred copies and was therefore unavailable to the general reader, is by far more successful than Burton's in reproducing both the letter and the spirit of the original. But what is more to the point here is that a careful and thorough comparison between Burton and Payne explains another reason for Burton's choice of style. He himself admits in the introduction that Payne "uses the exact vernacular equivalent of the foreign word so happily and so picturesquely that all future translations must perforce use the same expression." Burton consistently follows Payne's translation, copying it almost verbatim but adding his own sauce and spices.

Thus Burton's translation is akin to that of Galland, at least in one respect, for it is not so much a true translation of the *Nights* as it is a colorful and entertaining concoction. For instance, a passage that reads:

> The curtain was unfastened, and a dazzling girl emerged, with genial charm, wise mien, and features as radiant as the moon. She had an elegant figure, the scent of ambergris, sugared lips, Babylonian eyes, with eyebrows as arched as a pair of bent bows, and a face whose radiance put the shining sun to shame, for she was like a great star soaring in the heavens, or a dome of gold, or an unveiled bride, or a splendid fish swimming in a fountain, or a morsel of luscious fat in a bowl of milk soup,

becomes in Burton's hands:

> Thereupon sat a lady bright of blee, with brow beaming brilliancy, the dream of philosophy, whose eyes were fraught with Babel's gramarye and her eyebrows were arched as for archery; her breath breathed ambergris and perfumery and her lips were sugar to taste and carnelian to see. Her stature was straight as the letter I and her face shamed the noon-sun's radiancy; and she was even as a galaxy, or a dome with golden marquetry or a bride displayed in choicest finery or a noble maid of Araby.

Another passage, which reads:

> When I saw that he was dead and realized that it was I who had killed him, I let out a loud scream, beat my face, tore my clothes, and cried, "O people, O God's creatures, there remained for this young man only one day out of the forty, yet he still met his death at my hand. O God, I ask for your forgiveness, wishing that I had died before him. These my afflictions I suffer, draught by bitter draught, 'so that God's will may be fulfilled.'"

becomes almost a parody or rather a self-parody:

> When I saw that he was slain and knew that I had slain him, maugre myself, I cried out with an exceeding loud and bitter cry and beat my face and rent my raiment and said, 'Verily we be Allah's and unto Him we be returning, O Moslems! O folk fain of Allah! there remained for this youth but one day of the forty dangerous days which the astrologers and the learned had foretold for him; and the predestined death of this beautiful one was to be at my hand. Would Heaven I had not tried to cut the water melon. What dire misfortune is this I must bear lief or loath? What a disaster! What an affliction! O Allah mine, I implore thy pardon and declare to Thee my innocence of his death. But what God willeth let that come to pass.'

Burton, having raised his style to such a pitch, is forced, when he comes to the more ornate verse passages, to raise it yet to a higher pitch, adopting an even more artificial and more tortured expression that is forced to slide downward. For instance, a humorous poem that reads:

> Wail for the crane well-stewed in tangy sauce;
> Mourn for the meat, either well baked or fried;
> Cry for the hens and daughters of the grouse
> And the fried birds, even as I have cried.
> Two different kinds of fish are my desire,
> Served on two loaves of bread, zestful though plain,
> While in the pan that sizzles o'er the fire
> The eggs like rolling eyes fry in their pain.
> The meat when grilled, O what a lovely dish,
> Served with some pickled greens; that is my wish.
> 'Tis in my porridge I indulge at night,
> When hunger gnaws, under the bracelets' light.
> O soul, be patient, for our fickle fate
> Oppresses one day, only to elate.

becomes:

> Wail for the little partridges on porringer and plate;
> Cry for the ruin of the fries and stews well marinate:
> Keen as I keen for loved, lost daughters of the Kata-
>   grouse,
> And omelette round the fair enbrowned fowls agglom-
>   erate:
> O fire in heart of me for fish, those deux poissons I
>   saw,
> Bedded on new-made scones and cakes in piles to
>   laniate.
> For thee, O vermicelli! aches my very maw! I hold
> Without thee every taste and joy are clean annihilate.
> Those eggs have rolled their yellow eyes in torturing
>   pains of fire
> Ere served with hash and fritters hot, that delicatest
>   cate.
> Praised be Allah for His baked and roast and ah! how
>   good
> This pulse, these pot-herbs steeped in oil with eysill
>   combinate!
> When hunger sated was, I elbow-propt fell back upon
> Meat-pudding wherein gleamed the bangles that my
>   wits amate.
> Then woke I sleeping appetite to eat as though in
>   sport
> Sweets from brocaded trays and kickshaws most
>   elaborate.
> Be patient, soul of me! Time is haughty, jealous wight;
> Today he seems dark-lowering and tomorrow fair to
>   sight.

Burton hoped, by adapting such a procedure and such a style for his translation, by writing "as the Arab would have written in English," to create a work that would be added to the treasures of English literature, for "the translator's glory is to add something to his native tongue." What Burton bequeathed to the nation, how-ever, was no more than a literary Brighton Pavilion.

THE PRESENT TRANSLATION

THE GUIDING PRINCIPLES

Three centuries have gone by since Antoine Galland first introduced the *Nights* to Europe, and a full century since Richard Burton translated the work, in the last se-rious attempt to introduce it to the English reader. Much has happened in the world since then, a world in which, though technology seems hostile to romance, the ven-tures of science have become as fantastic as the adven-tures of fiction, and illusion and reality have become al-most one. Nonetheless, it is science that has been largely responsible for the demand for authenticity, or truth, in facing our world, which is becoming threateningly small, recognizing the value of other cultures, and ex-ploring their treasures. Now the flamboyant Victorian distortions of Burton seem closer to the disarming neo-classical liberties of Galland than to our modern func-tionalism, which needs a style more suited to our mod-ern sensibility than the styles of Burton or Galland, the

one still circulating as a Victorian relic, the other, though lively in its own day, now lying buried in the ar-chives of literary history.

The failure of past translations lies in assuming the work to be other than what it was intended to be, a col-lection of tales told to produce aesthetic pleasure in the Arabic reader. In translating the work as they did, they violated its integrity—Lane by emasculating it; Burton by reproducing its Arabic peculiarities and adding other idiosyncrasies of his own; and Galland by altering it to suit French taste, although this method comes the clos-est to producing the intended effect. Translation is the transfer of a text from one cultural context to another by converting its language into the language of the host culture. This requires command of the languages in-volved and of the literary idioms and conventions of both cultures. In converting the meaning of the text, the translators, who must act both as editors and as inter-preters, offer a reading of it, designed for a given reader in a given language, and in the context of a given cul-ture. They try to achieve equivalency, but since, due to the untranslatable difference in cultural connotations, associations, and other nuances, full equivalency is im-possible, the translators try to achieve approximation by securing a willing suspension of disbelief that allows the reader to believe that the translated text is the origi-nal text. This is possible, especially since in literature, the translators must convey not only the meaning of the text but also its aesthetic effect on readers. They re-spond to the text as natives would, by identifying the means by which this effect is produced, and by finding the comparable linguistic and literary means available in the host culture to produce a comparable effect in the intended reader. Therefore, they should not, as transla-tors from Dryden to Burton have advocated, try to write as the original author would have written in the host language, for such a creature can never be; instead, they should try to produce an equivalent text that will pro-duce an effect on the intended reader comparable to the effect the original text produces on the native reader. For the aesthetic effect, which is grounded in human nature and which can be achieved by our knowledge of and skill in using the tools of the respective literary conventions, is the common denominator between the native and the host culture and the principal means of success in transferring the literary work from one con-text to another.

THE PROSE

In translating the *Nights,* whose principal function is not to express the subtle nuances of experience and of our perceptions of it but to produce a certain kind of aesthetic pleasure, mainly by grounding the supernatu-ral in the natural, adherence to the aesthetic effect be-comes paramount. Such adherence has been the under-lying principle of my translation. This does not mean, however, that I have taken liberties with the text; on the contrary, I have been as faithful as possible, except for very few interpolations (placed in brackets) without which the gaps would have rendered the narrative illogical, and except when literal fidelity would have meant deviating from the limits of idiomatic English and consequently violating the spirit or the intended effect of the original. Thus, for instance, "O my liver," becomes, "O my heart" or "O my life"; "Allah" becomes "God"; and "God the Most High," the most familiar epithet for God in Arabic, becomes "The Almighty God." I have, unlike the other translators, who use the same style regardless of level, adopted a plain narrative as well as a conversational style that modulates with the original between the colloquial and the literary, according to speaker or situation, yet I have used colloquialisms and slang terms sparingly because the English equivalents are certain to disappear sooner or later, thus rendering the translation obsolete before its time. Likewise, I have used literary ornament judiciously because what appealed to Arabic thirteenth- or fourteenth-century literary taste does not always appeal to the taste of the modern English reader. For instance, I have avoided the rhymed prose of the original because it is too artificial and too jarring to the English ear.

Furthermore, I have varied the level of the style to suit the level of a given story, a lower level for some of the comic tales of **"The Story of the Hunchback,"** and a higher level for **"The Story of Nur al-Din ibn-Bakkar and the Slave-Girl Shams al-Nahar,"** a story written in thirteenth-century Baghdad, with literary echoes from the highly euphuistic and popular *Maqamat* of Hariri. Finally, I have avoided the temptation to add a distinctive color or stamp a personal manner or mannerism on the original in order to appeal to the reader. Burton's case is sobering enough; besides, the intention of the style of the *Nights* is to provide the storyteller or the reader with the opportunity to tell or read the story in his own voice and to dramatize the action and dialogue in his own way, very much as the actors do when they bring their written parts to life. Neutrality is crucial here.

THE VERSE

One of the distinctive features of the *Nights* is that the prose narrative is interspersed with verse passages, some of which were interpolated by the original editor, some by subsequent copyists. They are inserted to suit the occasion, and whether adding color to the description of a place or a person, expressing joy or grief, complimenting a lady, or underscoring a moral, they are intended to heighten the action, raise the literary level, and intensify the emotional effect. Yet a great number of these passages fail to achieve such effects because they are too mediocre, for less than one-half are anthologized from the classical poets of the period down to the four-

teenth century, while the rest are composed by lesser versifiers, including hacks and even the copyists themselves.

In general, the verse is characterized by poetic diction, comparisons, metaphors, conceits, and all kinds of parallelisms, especially balanced antitheses. For this reason, I have adopted a style similar to that of neoclassic poetry, particularly because, like its Arabic counterpart, it was ultimately derived from the same source, namely the Greco-Roman tradition; besides, a traditional Arabic poem consists of lines, each of which comprises two equal halves and follows the same rhyme throughout, thus producing an effect akin to that of the heroic couplet. I have, however, used an abab rhyme scheme for greater freedom and flexibility in reproducing both the sense and the stylistic ornaments of the original. In the case of the love lyrics, I have drawn on the tradition of courtly compliment, imitating one type or another depending on the freedom or emotional intensity of the Arabic lyric in question.

My main problem was how to render the turgid or vapid verse passages of the lesser versifiers, which are marked by artificial word order, forced rhymes, inexact parallelisms, and hackneyed metaphors. The choice was either to purify them through the filter of translation and avoid the charge of inept English renderings, or to be consistent with my aim of adhering both to the letter and to the spirit of the original. I have decided in favor of the latter and have rendered each passage as it is, making it appear neither better nor worse. Thus the original discrepancy between the good and the bad is maintained. For instance, a classic passage reads:

> If you suffer injustice, save yourself,
> And leave the house behind to mourn its builder.
> Your country you'll replace by another,
> But for yourself you'll find no other self.
> Nor with a mission trust another man,
> For none is as loyal as you yourself.
> And did the lion not struggle by himself,
> He would not prowl with such a mighty mane.

while that of a hack versifier reads:

> If I bemoan your absence, what will you say?
> If I pine with longing, what is the way?
> If I dispatch someone to tell my tale,
> The lover's complaint no one can convey.
> If I with patience try to bear my pain,
> After the loss of love, I can't endure the blow.
> Nothing remains but longing and regret
> And tears that over the cheeks profusely flow.
> You, who have long been absent from my eyes,
> Will in my loving heart forever stay.
> Was it you who have taught me how to love,
> And from the pledge of love never to stray?

And thus the English reader, like his discerning Arab counterpart, can see for himself both the faults and the felicities of the work.

CONCLUSION

For all a given translator's knowledge and skill, a translation is essentially a matter of sensitivity and taste, applied in one thousand and one instances. As such, for the translator, who stands astride two cultures, possesses two different sensibilities, and assumes a double identity, a translation is a journey of self-discovery. And the road to truth is, like the road to fairyland, fraught with perils and requires an innocent suspension of disbelief in the self and what it creates. By translating the work, one translates oneself; the little Arab boy who listened to the **Thousand and One Nights** has become the English storyteller. He may have produced a strange creature, a man with an ass's head, or may even, like Bottom, sport an ass's head of his own. What does it matter, so long as he has dreamed, in one Baghdad or another, a dream in the lap of a fairy queen.

David Pinault (essay date 1992)

SOURCE: Pinault, David. "An Introduction to the *Arabian Nights.*" In *Story-Telling Techniques in the* Arabian Nights, pp. 1-30. Leiden, The Netherlands: E. J. Brill, 1992.

[*In the following essay, Pinault outlines the culturally disparate origins of* The Arabian Nights, *and places the text within the tradition of medieval Arabic literary compilations.*]

A. A NOTE ON THE HISTORY OF THE *NIGHTS*
[*THE ARABIAN NIGHTS*]

"The first people to collect stories," claims the tenth-century Arab encyclopedist Ibn Isḥāq al-Nadīm in his work *al-Fihrist*, "devoting books to them and safeguarding them in libraries, some of them being written as though animals were speaking, were the early Persians." Al-Nadīm makes this statement while discussing the genre of "evening stories and fables"; and he notes that the Sassanid kings of Iran (reigned third-seventh centuries AD) took an interest in such tales. Al-Nadīm goes on to state of this material that "the Arabs translated it into the Arabic language and then, when masters of literary style and eloquence became interested, they refined and elaborated it."[1]

It seems that Arab interest in Persian popular narrative began at a very early period and can be discerned even in seventh-century Mecca during the life of the Prophet. In the Qur'an (31: 6-7) we find the statement:

There is one person who purchases frivolous stories so as to lead people away from the path of God; ignorant, he makes mock of God's path. For persons such as this there will be a humiliating punishment.

In his Qur'an commentary Maḥmūd ibn 'Umar al-Zamakhsharī (d. AD 1143) explained the context of the above revelation:

"Frivolous stories": such as evening conversations dealing with legends, tales lacking any basis of truth, the telling of fairytales and jokes, excessive talk in general, unseemly popular poems; also singing and acquaintance with musicians, and so forth. It is said that this passage was revealed concerning al-Naḍr ibn al-Ḥarith, who had the custom of traveling as a merchant to Persia. He would purchase books of the Persians and then would recite tales therefrom to members of the Quraysh tribe. He would say: "If Muḥammad has been reciting for you tales of 'Ād and Thamūd, well then *I'm* going to recite for you tales of Rustam and Behrām, and of the Persian shahs and the monarchs of Ḥīrah!" They found his tales very amusing and began to give up listening to the recitation of the Qur'an.[2]

The moral question implicit in this Qur'anic verse and in Zamakhsharī's commentary—whether "frivolous stories" are likely to distract one from the path of God—was to surface again in later Islamic history. This concern is reflected in an anecdote from Baghdad recorded in AD 932 by al-Ṣūlī, the tutor of Muḥammad, son of the 'Abbasid caliph al-Muqtadir. One day while al-Ṣūlī was instructing the young prince in Arabic literature, they were interrupted by a group of servants dispatched by Muḥammad's grandmother. The servants snatched up all the books in the classroom and then retreated. Instructor and student alike were startled, but al-Ṣūlī explained to Muḥammad that this was probably the caliphal family's way of inspecting Muḥammad's reading material to make sure that it was properly edifying. When the servants returned with the books a few hours later, the prince exclaimed:

Tell them who sent you, 'You have seen these books and found them to be books of tradition, jurisprudence, poetry, language, history and the works of the learned—books through the study of which God causes one to benefit and to be complete. They are not like the books which you read excessively, such as *The Wonders of the Sea, The Tale of Sindbad,* and *The Cat and the Mouse.*'[3]

Nabia Abbott in her analysis of this passage points out that the titles quoted above by Prince Muḥammad refer to tales from the **Nights** [*The Arabian Nights*] and similar stories from the genre of *khurāfāt* ("fairy tales") and *asmār* ("evening narrative-recitations").[4]

In the twentieth century the **Arabian Nights** has come in for its share of criticism on moral grounds. Iflah 'Umar al-Adalbī, in a 1974 survey published in Damascus entitled *Naẓrah fī adabinā al-sha'bī* ("A Look at Our Folk Literature"), criticized the **Nights** severely because it "exceeds all bounds in some of its stories in portraying immorality, debauchery and perversion."[5] More recently, in May 1985, an Egyptian court ordered the confiscation of copies of a recent "unexpurgated" edition of the *Nights.* According to one newspaper account, "Brig. Adly al-Kosheiry, head of the morals department of the Interior Ministry, which prosecuted the case, told reporters before the ruling today that the new edition of the book, which was printed in Beirut, posed a threat to the morals of Egypt's youth."[6] For several months the moral controversy surrounding the *Nights* claimed newspaper headlines in Cairo and formed the subject of editorial cartoons. Ṣabrī al-ʿAskarī, a lawyer who represented the Egyptian Writers' Union in its attempts to defend the book, warned that confiscating an edition of the *Nights* might inhibit the future publication of numerous other works from the Arab literary tradition.[7] Salwā al-ʿInānī published a long essay in the Egyptian newspaper *al-Ahrām* in which she asserted the worth of the *Arabian Nights* in general as one of the great works of world literature. "Let us take a united, educated and cultured stance," she says by way of conclusion, "in the face of those who would set fire to our heritage."[8] The columnist Aḥmad Bahjat replied to al-ʿInānī's essay with a series of articles in which he harshly attacked her view. According to Bahjat critics such as al-ʿInānī implicitly believe that cultural tradition in general—along with the *Nights* as part of this tradition—is sacred and hence inviolate; whereas in fact only the Qurʾan deserves this status. Each age, Bahjat argues, must prune the tradition of what may be harmful to the new generation.[9] Earlier editors, he asserts, including Rushdī Ṣāliḥ, "the dean of folk literature," voluntarily censored their editions of the *Nights.* Bahjat goes on to point out that:

> There is a difference between sex as it occurs in life and the artistic representation of sex. The artistic representation is not direct nor could it ever be direct. What appears in this edition of *The Thousand and One Nights* is not an artistic representation of sex; rather it consists of representations which are harmful to morals. Previous generations suppressed such things in earlier editions.[10]

In reality I believe that religious devotion and ascetic piety are far more typical than obscene entertainment as narrative concerns in tales from the *Nights*; **"The City of Brass"** forms a good example thereof. But for now let us return to the tenth-century *Fihrist* and al-Nadīm's description of early Iranian stories. He mentions a work with the Persian title *Hazār afsāneh,* which he translates as "a thousand stories." Al-Nadīm explains the origin of this title by sketching the narrative which serves as the outer frame for the entire collection: a king has the bloodthirsty habit of marrying a succession of women, killing each after spending one night with her. But then, according to al-Nadīm's summary, "he married a concubine of royal blood who had intelligence and wit." The *Fihrist* names her Shahrāzād (Scheherazade, to English readers) and explains that every evening for a thousand nights she recited a story to

her husband, taking care always to leave a tale unfinished at dawn so that the king would postpone her execution.[11]

The tenth-century chronicler al-Masʿūdī also mentions the *Hazār afsāneh.* He notes that although the Persian title literally means "one thousand tales," the collection was popularly known in Arabic translation as *Alf laylah* or "one thousand nights."[12] Abbott points out the logic of this popular title, given the prominence of nighttime as the locus of action in the story-collection and given also the tradition of *asmār* or "evening-tales" as a genre of narrative entertainment among the Arabs. She notes that the earliest extant Arabic text of the *Nights,* a ninth-century manuscript-fragment, probably Syrian in origin, carries the title *Kitāb fīhi ḥadīth alf laylah* ("A book containing tales of a thousand nights"). At some unknown date this title was extended to *Alf laylah wa-laylah* (*One Thousand and One Nights*). A story-collection with the title *Alf laylah wa-laylah* is known to have circulated in twelfth-century Fatimid Egypt.[13]

But if medieval Arab authors acknowledged Persian story-collections as the immediate source of the *Nights,* it must also be noted that many other cultures contributed to the formation of the various Arabic texts known by the name *Alf laylah wa-laylah.* Enno Littmann in his research on the sources of the narratives comprising this collection listed various "layers" or historical strata evident in the *Nights*: Indian, Persian, Baghdādī, and Cairene. Each stratum corresponds to a deposit of stories which reflect the influence on the *Nights* of a given society and geographical locale during a particular historical period. Thus the Indian stratum is represented by certain animal-stories, which reflect influence from ancient Sanskrit fables; the Persian stratum is represented in part by the frame-story of Scheherazade and king Shāhrayār (which itself reflects an older Indian model); the Baghdādī, by tales of ʿAbbasid caliphs; the Cairene, by **"Maʿrūf the Cobbler."** But this list does not exhaust the sources of the *Alf laylah* [*Alf laylah wa-laylah*]'s various stories. Tales such as **"Iram of the Columns"** are derived from pre-Islamic legends of the Arabian peninsula, **"Bulūqiyā"** shows some continuity with motifs from the Mesopotamian epic of Gilgamesh; and **"Sindbad the Sailor"** shares points in common with adventures described in Homer's *Odyssey* (though one should keep in mind the possibility that Greek and Arabic narratives alike were influenced by a more ancient common source).[14]

The reference above to cumulative strata and narrative deposits should also remind us that throughout the medieval and early modern eras the *Alf laylah* was never a static or fixed collection, that it continued to grow until the late eighteenth and early nineteenth centuries. One of the pioneers in tracing the history of the *Nights* was H. Zotenberg, who in his *Histoire d' ʿAlā al-Dīn* developed a theory to account for the development of the disparate story-collections comprising the *Alf laylah.* He began by noting that numerous *Alf laylah* manuscripts of the seventeenth and eighteenth centuries consisted of a "fonds primitif" or "original core" of *Alf laylah* stories, always comprising fewer than three hundred nights, to which individual redactors added tales borrowed from other, independent, story-collections. In adding to the "original core" of stories, Zotenberg suggested, these late redactors were apparently motivated by a desire to make the actual number of nights in the collection match the literal number specified by the title ***Thousand and One Nights***.[15] Littmann elaborated on Zotenberg's theory by noting that in the 'Abbasid period (i.e., the eighth through thirteenth centuries AD) the number 1,001 was simply understood as meaning "many," and that early redactors consequently felt under no obligation to take literally the number designated by the collection's title; whereas by the seventeenth and eighteenth centuries, as Littmann notes, "the number was taken in its literal meaning, and it became necessary to add a great many stories in order to complete the number 1,001."[16]

Whatever the actual motivation of these later redactors, the fact remains that numerous seventeenth- and eighteenth-century manuscripts demonstrate a consistent relation with a certain fourteenth-century text of the *Alf laylah* known as Bibliothèque Nationale 3609-3611 (henceforth G). This text once belonged to the French scholar Antoine Galland, who used it as the basis for the first European translation of the *Nights, Les mille et une nuits* (published in 1704). Galland's Arabic manuscript formed the basis for Muhsin Mahdi's 1984 Leiden edition of the *Alf laylah.* G is of Syrian provenience and is by far the oldest sizable *Nights* manuscript extant (the ninth-century fragment examined by Abbott consists of only a title-page and some sixteen lines of text). G does not, however, contain 1,001 nights; it proceeds as far as Night 282 and no further.[17]

It was Zotenberg's conviction that the fourteenth-century G text was a representative of the "original core" of *Alf laylah* stories on which later writers relied in compiling more extended collections of the *Nights.* Zotenberg cites as an example BN 1491A, an *Alf laylah* manuscript containing 870 nights, written in the second half of the seventeenth century and brought to France from Egypt at the beginning of the eighteenth century by the French consul-general Benoît de Maillet. Zotenberg lists the contents of 1491A and gives its story-titles, together with the nights covered by each tale. Now a comparison of this table of contents with Galland's Arabic manuscript shows that the first part of 1491A includes virtually all the story-titles in G, and in the same order. After reproducing this series of stories which bear the same titles as those in G, the redactor of 1491A then added a miscellany of tales, including

lengthy borrowings from other, independent, story-cycles: the adventures grouped together in "'Umar al-Nu'mān," which recounts military expeditions against the Frankish Crusaders, and the *Kalīlah wa-Dimnah* of Ibn al-Muqaffa', an eighth-century collection of animal-fables inspired by Pahlavi Sassanid sources. Zotenberg then lists the contents of a seventeenth-century Turkish text of the *Alf laylah,* BN 356, which likewise begins by reproducing the titles contained in G. BN 356 follows these G-titles with another miscellany of tales, again drawn, as in 1491A, from independent story-cycles. Some of these stories in the second part of BN 356 are the same as in 1491A (e.g., "'Umar al-Nu'mān"), but others represent borrowings from completely different independent sources, such as **"The Tale of Sindbad the Sailor."** Zotenberg deduced from such evidence that, by the seventeenth century, there existed a tendency among redactors to add to the "original core" of *Alf laylah* stories by borrowing tales from other, independent, cycles; but that in the seventeenth century these supplementary tales varied from collection to collection. Hence nothing on the order of a fixed definitive text of the *Alf laylah* existed as yet.[18]

Duncan Black MacDonald, who, like Zotenberg, focused his scholarship on the evolution of the *Alf laylah*'s component stories, supplemented Zotenberg's speculations by demonstrating that the G manuscript represents the culmination of the *Alf laylah*'s evolution from the Sassanid to the Mamluk periods: the early Persian *Hazār afsāneh* led to an early, possibly eighth-century Arabic translation; this translation, modified and expanded during the 'Abbasid era, was supplemented by additional stories of autochthonous Arab origin; and the G manuscript constitutes a fourteenth-century descendant of this Persian-Arabic amalgam. In turn, the cluster of stories contained in G formed the starting point for later collections, such as BN 1491A and BN 356, as described above. Thus the G manuscript represents the "fonds primitif" of stories postulated by Zotenberg as the common stock of tales in diverse enlarged manuscripts of the seventeenth and eighteenth centuries.[19]

I remarked above that copyists of this later period tried to fill out the *Alf laylah* to cover 1,001 nights and drew from diverse sources to achieve this goal. These expanded texts differed (except for their "core" drawn from the family of manuscripts represented by G) from manuscript to manuscript and did not coalesce into anything resembling a fixed arrangement of tales until the late eighteenth century. At this time a group of Arab scholars in Cairo, under the direction of a shaykh whose name is lost to us, produced a new version of the *Alf laylah.* As did BN 1491A and BN 356, this manuscript followed G for its initial cycles of stories; but it included sufficient additional stories, unlike its predecessors, to make a full complement of 1,001 nights. Zotenberg named this late eighteenth-century Cairene collection "la rédaction moderne d'Égypte;" and since his own day this text is referred to as the "Zotenberg Egyptian Recension" or ZER. Zotenberg counted a dozen manuscripts in European libraries which were derived directly from this late eighteenth-century recension, and he observed that this same recension also served as the basis for the best-known Arabic editions of the *Nights* of the nineteenth century, Būlāq (henceforth B) and MacNaghten (henceforth MN, also referred to as Calcutta II). B was first published in Cairo in 1835; MN, in Calcutta over the years 1839-1842. Because they were based on the ZER rather than on G alone, the B and MN editions contain numerous stories not found in Mahdi's Leiden edition or in the fourteenth-century manuscript from which it is derived. Since B and MN between them inspired the majority of the nineteenth- and twentieth-century European translations of the *Alf laylah* and since B is the text most commonly reprinted in contemporary Arabic editions, the version of the *Nights* represented by the ZER is the one most familiar to modern audiences.[20]

Mahdi's research has resulted in an even more nuanced understanding of the history of the *Nights.* He demonstrates the existence of two major branches or families of *Alf laylah* manuscripts, a Syrian and an Egyptian. The fourteenth-century G belongs to the Syrian branch; whereas the eighteenth-century ZER (and the B and MN editions derived therefrom) is a very late descendant of the Egyptian manuscript tradition (hence both MN and B are sometimes referred to as Egyptian editions, even though MN was published in India). Both the Syrian and Egyptian branches ultimately derive from a common early medieval manuscript source; this common derivation explains whatever similarities the two traditions share.[21]

I have discussed Zotenberg's findings in order to emphasize his distinction between the earlier "core" of the *Alf laylah*'s stories and its later additions. This distinction will help us in approaching the question: to what extent are the later supplementary stories thematically linked to the overarching Scheherezade-frame which informs the entire *Alf laylah*?

We can begin to address this issue first by surveying the 282 nights comprising the G manuscript. King Shāhrayār's behavior in the outermost frame is triggered by his first wife's deceit and infidelity. This leads the king to kill one wife after another; and Scheherazade tries to ward off this violence by offering stories as ransom for her life. Bearing this in mind it is instructive to glance over the other tales in G. The majority of the story-cycles contained therein—including **"The Merchant and the Genie," "The Fisherman and the Genie," "The Porter," "The Three Apples,"** and **"The Hunchback"**—all feature very prominently the threat of vio-

lence and the use of stories to postpone or avert this violence. Moreover some of the tales enframed by the above-mentioned cycles enunciate themes which may be understood as a further commentary on the action of the outermost Scheherazade-frame. Such is the case I believe with **"The Husband and the Parrot"** (contained within the **"Fisherman"** [**"The Fisherman and the Genie"**] cycle): the husband gives way to an impulse to kill a loyal pet and experiences keen regret thereafter. That the *Alf laylah* composers intended these tales to function as commentaries on the outermost frame is suggested by a story such as **"The Enchanted Prince,"** a tale featuring marital violence and graphically depicted tortures in which King Shāhrayār—who sits listening to the recital by Scheherazade—is described as feeling anguish for the sorrows undergone by the protagonist.[22]

Despite the close thematic links uniting many of the G tales with the Scheherazade-frame, it is not necessary to posit that these stories were created ex nihilo especially for the *Alf laylah.* It seems more likely (and more consistent with the historical testimony concerning the earlier *Hazār afsāneh*) that many if not most of these tales pre-dated the Arabic *Alf laylah* and were modified and re-told for inclusion in the *Nights.* In fact a separate Arabic manuscript-tradition completely independent of the *Nights* exists for many of the stories now found in the *Alf laylah.* Such is the case for example with **"The Fisherman and the Genie"** and **"The Enchanted Prince"** (found in the G and ZER *Alf laylah* collections) as well as **"The False Caliph"** and **"The City of Brass"** (present in the ZER but not G). Moreover these stories continued to be transmitted in manuscript-collections unaffiliated with the *Alf laylah* long after the tales had been incorporated into the *Nights.*[23] Such manuscript-collections can be described as "*Alf laylah* analogues": they are usually untitled, lacking the Scheherazade-frame and any division into nights, but containing one or more narratives also present in *Alf laylah* texts of the Syrian and Egyptian traditions. The significance of these analogues is that, in those instances where such independent manuscript-collections survive, it becomes possible for us to compare two distinct versions of the same story—one assimilated to the *Nights,* one independent thereof. Till now little use has been made of these analogues in literary studies of the *Nights.* Part of the reason for this neglect is that most such collections have never been published or edited. For the chapters which follow in the present study I have sought out analogues (whenever I could locate such) for comparison with versions of the same tale as found in the *Alf laylah* proper. Frequently substantial differences (both in wording and in narrative structure) will be found between the independent- and *Alf laylah*-version of certain stories. In these cases we may obtain some insight into the process whereby composers of the *Nights* modified a tale for inclusion in the collection.

The discussion above of violence and narrative-ransom motifs in the oldest stories of the G core is crucial when we turn to the question of thematic unity in the later ZER text. In brief I would assert that the degree to which a given ZER tale is linked to the overarching Scheherazade-frame depends primarily on whether the story is also found in the "fonds primitif" or *Alf laylah*-core represented by G. Later additions to the collection are for the most part linked only in a formal sense to the Scheherazade narrative: these later tales are divided into enumerated nights; each night begins and concludes with conventional patterned sentences (e.g., "Then dawn overtook Scheherazade . . ."). But rarely do the themes of the supplementary tales relate directly to those of the outermost frame. This is not to say, however, that the later story-cycles incorporated into the *Nights* lack any thematic unity of their own. For example the structure of the tale of **"The City of Brass"** (which does not seem to have been added to the *Alf laylah* prior to the eighteenth-century ZER) is itself defined by a set of thematic concerns informing each of the tale's enframed subordinate narratives (the Black Castle, the Imprisoned *'Ifrīt,* Queen Tadmur's story, etc.). These minor enframed narratives restate and add further emphasis to the themes of ascetic piety and the need for humble acceptance of God's will which are articulated in the major narrative-frame of **"The City of Brass."** In adding such tales to the *Alf laylah* the later redactors of the seventeenth and eighteenth centuries seem mostly to have preserved the thematic integrity of their sources. In general it will I think be more fruitful to look for the themes which define each supplementary story-cycle individually rather than insist on anything more than a perfunctory and largely formal link with the G-core and its narrative-motifs.[24]

B. ORAL PERFORMANCE AND LITERARY LANGUAGE IN THE *ARABIAN NIGHTS*

"Abū 'Abd Allāh Muḥammad ibn 'Abdūs al-Jahshiyārī," we are informed in al-Nadīm's *Fihrist,* "author of *The Book of Viziers,* began the compiling of a book in which he was to select a thousand tales from the stories of the Arabs, Persians, Greeks, and others. Each section . . . was separate, not connected with any other. He summoned to his presence the storytellers, from whom he obtained the best things about which they knew and which they did well. He also selected whatever pleased him from the books composed of stories and fables . . . There were collected for him four hundred and eighty nights, each night being a complete story . . . Death overtook him before he fulfilled his plan for completing a thousand stories."[25]

This reference to al-Jahshiyārī (an 'Abbasid government official and secretary of the tenth century AD) offers us a glimpse of how medieval Arabic story-anthologies were created. This particular composer drew on both written sources and the oral performances of professional storytellers. The two influences—literary and oral—should be borne in mind when evaluating a collection such as the *Alf laylah.*

Richard Hole, an English scholar who in 1797 published a series of lectures entitled *Remarks on the* Arabian Nights' Entertainments, recorded travelers' comments on the *Alf laylah:*

> Colonel Capper, in his observations on the passage to India through Egypt and across the great Desert, says, that "before any person decides on the merit of these books, he should be eye-witness of the effect they produce on those who best understand them. I have more than once seen the Arabians on the Desert sitting round a fire, listening to these stories with such attention and pleasure as totally to forget the fatigue and hardship with which an instant before they were entirely overcome."[26]

This observation reminds us that the tales comprising the *Alf laylah* were originally oral evening-entertainments and were meant to be recited and listened to. The performance-dimension of the *Nights* is reflected in the very manuscripts used to record various versions of the tales. For storytellers who could afford them, texts incorporating some or all of the *Alf laylah* adventures served as reference material and sources of narrative inspiration. In his study on "The Earlier History of the *Arabian Nights*" MacDonald makes reference to the story-manuscripts comprising the library of a professional reciter in Damascus.[27] Lane remarks on public recitations from the *Nights* in Cairo during the early nineteenth century; but he also notes that the cost of a complete *Alf laylah* manuscript was too high for most reciters. According to Lane the 'Anātirah (or storytellers who recited the adventures of the Arab hero 'Antar) frequently read aloud from written texts of the tale as part of their public performance.[28]

Peter Molan has drawn attention to phrases such as *qālā al-rāwī* ("the storyteller said") and *qāla ṣāḥib al-ḥadīth* ("the master of the tale said") which recur throughout many manuscript texts of the *Nights.* Such phrases are in Molan's description "anomalous" or extrinsic to the dialogue and narrative context within which they occur. He argues that instances of anomalous *qāla* are linked to the oral provenience of stories recorded in *Alf laylah* manuscripts.[29] . . . By way of summary I note the following. Phrases such as *qāla ṣāḥib al-ḥadīth* tend to appear at transition points in the given text: anomalous *qāla* often occurs between the conclusion of a poem and the resumption of the prose narrative; or it may come at the end of a minor story told by a character within a larger narrative, thus indicating a return to the major narrative frame. The copyists who inserted *qāla al-rāwī* or *qāla ṣāḥib al-ḥadīth* in their texts sometimes penned such phrases in disproportionately large letters or in an ink which varied from that of the surrounding text. Thus we can hypothesize that anomalous *qāla* served as a visual guide and marker alerting any reciter who glanced at the page of an imminent change in narrative voice.[30]

The *Alf laylah* text occasionally discloses other allusions to its oral performance background, as in this passage from the tale of **"Maryam the Christian"**:

> As for that young maiden's departure from her father's city, there is a curious story and wondrous matter behind that, which we will utter in proper order, so that the hearer might delight therein and grow cheerful therefrom.
>
> (wa-qad kāna li-khurūj tilka al-jāriyah min madīnat abīhā ḥadīth gharīb wa-amr 'ajīb nasūquhu 'alā al-tartīb ḥattā yaṭraba al-sāmi' wa-yaṭīb)[31]

The phrasing of this sentence (". . . which we will utter . . . so that the hearer might delight therein . . .") implies the presence of a reciter and an audience of listeners rather than a relationship of writer and reader. Those familiar with medieval Arabic literature will recognize in the text above the use of *saj'*, the prose-rhyme often favored for public recitation. Taken together the phrasing and rhyme-form recall the oral performance environment within which the *Nights* evolved.

Yet the published Arabic editions of the *Alf laylah* are far from being straightforward unaltered transcriptions of oral vernacular performances. The B and MN texts are the products of learned editors of the eighteenth and nineteenth centuries who rewrote much of the material in their source-manuscripts in accordance with the principles of *fuṣḥā* or classical literary Arabic. They normalized the spelling of individual words, substituted elevated diction for colloquial expressions, formalized dialogue so as to remove traces of influence from the vernacular, and altered the grammatical structure of sentences to align them with the rules of *fuṣḥā*. Even the fourteenth-century G manuscript, which is much more colloquial than B or MN in its language, is influenced by classical literary models. Extravagant and sometimes incorrect use is made of literary grammatical constructions as ornaments with which to embellish the text. In this the G manuscript only follows the practice of the Ayyubid and Mamluk periods, eras characterized by literary works in which the author strained for rhetorical effects by the elaborate use of classical *fuṣḥā* constructions. As Mahdi remarks, the wording of G comprises a "third language," neither purely colloquial nor exclusively literary, in which both *fuṣḥā* and colloquial are employed in the presentation of each tale. Thus the *Alf laylah,* as revealed through the very diverse texts in which it is recorded, cannot be described only as a collection of transcribed oral folktales: for it survives as the crafted composition of authors who used various forms of written literary Arabic to capture an oral narrative tradition. In evaluating the stories of the *Nights* it will be wise to acknowledge the interaction implicit therein of the text's oral performance background and the transforming process of written composition.[32]

Throughout the present study I use the term 'redactor' in discussing the authorship of individual *Alf laylah* tales. As Andras Hamori remarks:

> 'Redactor' is a term of convenience. The composition of the book [i.e., the *Alf-laylah*] . . . suggests arrangement for effect. How many hands' work this is, we cannot know.[33]

Each redactor will doubtless have benefitted from the creativity of oral reciters who transmitted and embellished the given tale before it was committed to writing. He also will have been influenced by the textual revisions introduced by preceding generations of scribes. The term redactor indicates that person who stands at the end of this chain of oral and textual transmission, that person responsible for the shape in which the story reaches us in its final written form in a given manuscript or printed text.

C. A Description of Selected Storytelling Techniques from the *Nights*

In this section I describe narrative devices used by redactors in numerous stories found in the *Alf laylah*. . . .

i. Repetitive Designation

Under this heading I group repeated references to some character or object which appears insignificant when first mentioned but which reappears later to intrude suddenly on the narrative. At the moment of the initial designation the given object seems unimportant and the reference casual and incidental. Later in the story, however, the object is brought forward once more and proves to play a significant role.

A good example of this technique can be found in one of the early episodes in the frame-story of King Shāhrayār and Scheherazade as presented in the Leiden edition of the G manuscript.[34] Shāhrayār's brother Shāhzamān arrives for a visit, and the G redactor offers a detailed description of the guest-quarters where Shāhzamān is housed: a palace overlooking an enclosed garden and facing a second house containing the women's quarters. Furthermore, it is carefully explained that his chambers have windows overlooking the garden. Finally, we are told that the nobleman repeatedly sighs and laments, "No one has ever had happen to him what happened to me!," a reference to the adulterous betrayal by his wife which opened the story. These references seem incidental enough at first, but in fact the redactor has made mention of all these details—the women's quarters, the garden, the guest-chamber windows which happen to overlook the garden, Shāhzamān's lament—by way of foreshadowing and preparation for the next development in the plot. One day King Shāhrayār departs to go hunting, and Shāhzaman, the redactor tells us, chances to look out his window at the garden which is visible below. Suddenly he sees his brother's wife, followed by an entourage of men and women, emerge from the harem opposite and enter the garden. From his window-perch he sees them all join lustily in sexual congress. Shāhzamān then realizes that his repeated lament is untrue, for his brother too has had happen to him what happened to Shāzamān.

Another instance of repetitive designation emerges in the Leiden version of **"The Merchant and the Genie."**[35] The tale opens with a description of the protagonist putting loaves of bread and dates in his saddlebag as provisions for a journey he is about to undertake. Trivial enough data this seems at first, a description of the food a man takes on a business trip. But to the contrary: in the next scene the merchant pauses in his journey for lunch and eats his dates, flinging away the date-stones at random. Shortly thereafter a wrathful genie appears, which informs the man that his life is now forfeit: the date-stones he flung away so thoughtlessly at lunch struck and killed the genie's invisible son; in turn the genie must now kill him. The hapless merchant pleads for mercy, a plea which will ultimately trigger the stories-told-for-ransom which comprise the bulk of this narrative-cycle.

Thus in the two examples cited above the initial reference establishes an object (e.g., a garden-window or a saddlebag full of dates) in the background of a scene and readies it for its appearance at the proper moment. Repetitive designation creates thereby an effect of apparently casual foreshadowing and allows the audience the pleasure of recognition at that later moment when the object reappears and proves significant.

II. Leitwortstil

In his work *The Art of Biblical Literature* Robert Alter explains that the term *Leitwortstil* ("leading-word style") was coined by Martin Buber and Franz Rosenzweig and applied to the field of Biblical textual studies. Alter states that the term designates the "purposeful repetition of words" in a given literary piece. The individual *Leitwort* or "leading word" usually expresses a motif or theme important to the given story; the repetition of this *Leitwort* ensures that the theme will gradually force itself on the reader's attention.[36]

In the preface to his German Bible translation Buber discusses the triliteral root system in Hebrew and the opportunities it offers for verbal repetition. He labels this technique of repetition as a *Leitwortstil* and defines the term as follows:

> A *Leitwort* is a word or a word-root that recurs significantly in a text, in a continuum of texts, or in a configuration of texts: by following these repetitions, one is able to decipher or grasp a meaning of the text . . . The repetition, as we have said, need not be merely of the word itself but also of the word-root; in fact, the very difference of words can often intensify the dynamic action of the repetition. I call it "dynamic" because between combinations of sounds related to one another in this manner a kind of movement takes place: if one imagines the entire text deployed before him one can sense waves moving back and forth between the words.[37]

What is true for Hebrew triliteral roots and the Bible holds good, I believe, for Arabic and the *Arabic Nights*. *Leitwortstil* can be discerned at work in the MN version of **"The Magian City,"** a minor narrative enframed within **"The Tale of the First Lady"** (which in turn belongs to the story-cycle known as **"The Porter and the Three Ladies of Baghdad"**).[38]

Three sisters leave Baghdad to undertake a business trip by sea. Their ship goes off course, and for several days the vessel drifts without direction. Neither captain nor crew has any idea where they are; but after a number of days an unknown shore is sighted. The lookout cries, "Good news! . . . I see what looks like a city"; and the ship is brought to harbor. The captain goes ashore to investigate:

> He was gone for some time; then he came to us and said, "Come, go up to the city and marvel at what God has done to His creatures, and seek refuge from His wrath!" (*wa-ista'īdhū min sukhṭihi*). And so we went up to the city.

> Then when I came to the gate I saw people with staves in their hands at the gate of the city. So I drew near to them, and behold!: they had been metamorphosed and had become stone (*wa-idhā hum maskhūṭīn wa-qad ṣārū ahjāran*). Then we entered the city and found everyone in it metamorphosed into black stone (*maskhūṭan ahjāran sūdan*). And in it [i.e., in the city] there were neither houses with inhabitants nor people to tend the hearths. We marveled at that and then traversed the markets.[39]

A note by Edward Lane from his translation of the *Nights* suggests the significance of the verbal root *s-kh-ṭ* which occurs three times in the above passage:

> The term "maskhooṭ," employed to signify "a human being converted by the wrath of God into stone," is commonly applied in Egypt to an ancient statue. Hence the Arabs have become familiar with the idea of cities whose inhabitants are petrified, such as that described in **"The Story of the First of the Three Ladies of Baghdad."**[40]

In his *Arabic-English Lexicon* Lane also notes that the primary sense of the passive participle *maskhūṭ* is "transformed, or metamorphosed . . . in consequence of having incurred the wrath of God." In addition, Lane records the gerund *sukhṭ,* which he defines as "dislike, displeasure, disapprobation, or discontent."[41]

The term *maskhūṭ* may of course be understood in a very general sense simply to mean "transformed" or "metamorphosed." Burton's commentary on this tale notes that *maskhūṭ* is "mostly applied to change of shape as man enchanted to monkey, and in vulgar parlance applied to a statue (of stone, etc.)"; elsewhere in his edition of the *Nights* he offers the gloss "transformed (mostly in something hideous), a statue."[42] But the connotations enumerated by Lane are brought forward in the MN edition by the captain's exclamation at the beginning of the Magian City episode: *ta'ajjabū min ṣan' Allāh fi khalqihi wa-ista'īdhū min sukhṭihi* ("Marvel at what God has done to His creatures, and seek refuge from His wrath!"). The redactor uses this sentence to achieve a resonance of meanings between *sukhṭ* ("divine wrath") and *maskhūṭ* ("metamorphosed"), words derived from the same verbal root, *s-kh-ṭ.* The presence of the noun *sukhṭ* gives *maskhūṭ* a religious connotation; and the implication that arises from this juxtaposition of words is that the city's inhabitants were transformed specifically as a punishment for having aroused God's anger.

Of interest to our discussion is a remark by 'Abd al-Qāhir al-Jurjānī (d. AD 1078) on the subject of context and meaning in his work *Dalā'il al-i'jāz* ("Demonstrations of Qur'anic Inimitability"):

> It becomes clear then, with a clarity that leaves no place for doubt, that verbal expressions are not remarkable for their excellence insofar as they are mere abstracted utterances, nor insofar as they are isolated words. Rather the worth or lack of worth of a given expression depends on the harmony established between the meaning of a given expression and the meaning [of the word or phrase] which follows that expression.[43]

As G. J. H. van Gelder notes in his analysis of al-Jurjānī's work: "The qualities do not depend on the single words but on the 'wonderful harmony' (*ittisāq 'ajīb*) in the passage."[44] Al-Jurjānī's insight can be applied to the 'harmony of meanings' found in a story such as **"The Magian City."** By placing the phrase *ista'īdhū min sukhṭihi* immediately before the sentences describing the lost city and its metamorphosed populace, the MN redactor reminds the reader of the root-meaning of *maskhūṭ,* with its original denotation of God's wrath against the impious. The words *sukhṭ* and *maskhūṭ* will recur throughout this narrative-frame as related *Leitwörter* highlighting the tale's moralistic concerns.

The story continues with a description of how passengers and crew disembark and then wander the lifeless city. The protagonist ventures on her own into a palace where she discovers the preserved corpses of a king and queen, each of which has been transformed into black stone (and each described with the term *maskhūṭ*). Finally she encounters a young man who alone has survived the fate of all the other inhabitants. He tells her the story of this city, explaining that all its people were Magians and devoted to the worship of fire. He himself, however, was secretly Muslim. Year after year divine warnings visited the city to the effect that the infidel inhabitants must abandon their fire-worship and turn to the true God; to no avail. And so, the young man explains:

> They never ceased with their adherence to the way they were, until there descended upon them hatred and divine wrath (*al-maqt wa-al sukhṭ*) from heaven, one morning at dawn. And so they were transformed into black stone (*fa-sukhiṭū ahjāran sūdan*), and their riding beasts and cattle as well.[45]

The Magian City frame ends when the protagonist rejoins her companions and conveys to them the story she has just heard:

> I reported to them what I had seen, and I told them the tale of the young man and the reason for the metamorphosis of this city (*wa-sabab sukhṭ hādhihi al-madīnah*) and what had happened to them; and they marveled at that.[46]

Thus in this story the condition of the city's inhabitants (*maskhūṭ, sukhiṭū*) is explained as a consequence of divine wrath (*al-sukhṭ*), with the two states described in terms of the single root *s-kh-ṭ.* Not only does this motif-word accent relationships among events within **"The Magian City"**; it also demarcates this enframed minor narrative at both beginning and end and distinguishes the tale from the surrounding major narrative.

In other *Alf laylah* stories one notes the operation of what may be termed (as an extension of Buber's model) *Leitsätze* ("leading-sentences"): entire clauses or sentences which are repeated at salient points throughout a narrative and encapsulate its theme. . . . The sentence "This is a warning to whoso would be warned" is a familiar moralistic utterance encountered frequently throughout the *Nights*; in **"The City of Brass,"** however, the redactor repeatedly introduces variants of this conventional admonition (all built around the *Leitwörter 'ibrah*—"warning"—and *i'tabara*—"to take warning") so as to draw attention to the thematic concerns which unite the various episodes in the tale.

III. THEMATIC PATTERNING AND FORMAL PATTERNING

In those stories from the *Alf laylah* (as with works of fiction in general) which are especially well crafted, the structure is disposed so as to draw the audience's attention to certain narrative elements over others. Recurrent vocabulary, repeated gestures, accumulations of descriptive phrases around selected objects: such patterns guide the audience in picking out particular actions as important in the flow of narrative. And once the audience has had its attention drawn to the patterns which give shape to a story, it experiences the pleasure of recognition: so *this* is the revelation toward which the storyteller is guiding us; *this* must be the object which constitutes the story's focus. The reader attempting to discern such patterns in a story, however, should beware of examining too narrowly any one given incident from the tale, for an individual dialogue or isolated event, taken alone, may not have enough context to let the observer establish its significance for the story at hand. The observer's emphasis, rather, should be on the particular event as it exists in relation to the rest of the narrative and the way in which the events and other narrative elements in a story join to form a structural pattern.

In my study of individual tales I have noted two kinds of structural patterning, thematic and formal. By thematic patterning I mean the distribution of recurrent concepts and moralistic motifs among the various incidents and frames of a story. In a skillfully crafted tale, thematic patterning may be arranged so as to emphasize the unifying argument or salient idea which disparate events and disparate narrative frames have in common.

Thematic patterning binds the tales contained within **"The Fisherman and the Genie."** The argument of this narrative-cycle may be baldly stated as: violence against one's benefactors or intimate companions, whether triggered by mistrust, envy, or jealous rage, leads inevitably to regret and repentance. This concept is illustrated both in the major narrative of the **"Fisherman"** and in its enframed minor narratives such as **"Yunan and Duban"** and **"The Jealous Husband and the Parrot."** Of course all these stories are also linked thematically to the outermost narrative frame, where Scheherazade is quite literally trying to talk her way out of violent death at the hands of a husband who himself is dominated by mistrust and jealous rage.

Another example of thematic patterning can be found in **"The City of Brass,"** a story which at first glance may appear to have little structural unity. The primary action, in which a party of travellers crosses the North African desert in search of ancient brass bottles, is continually interrupted by subsidiary narratives: the tale recorded on inscriptions in the lost palace of Kūsh ibn Shaddād; the imprisoned 'ifrīt's account of Solomon's war with the jinn; and the encounter with Queen Tadmur and the automata which guard her corpse. But each of these minor narratives introduces a character who confesses that he once proudly enjoyed worldly prosperity: subsequently, we learn, the given character has been brought low by God and forced to acknowledge

Him as greater than all worldly pomp. These minor tales ultimately reinforce the theme of the major narrative: riches and pomp tempt one away from God; asceticism is the way to salvation. Thus a clearly discernible thematic pattern of pride—punishment from God—submission to the Divine Will unifies the otherwise divergent stories which are gathered into this tale.

By formal patterning I mean the organization of the events, actions and gestures which constitute a narrative and give shape to a story; when done well, formal patterning allows the audience the pleasure of discerning and anticipating the structure of the plot as it unfolds. An example can be found in **"The Tale of the Three Shaykhs,"** where three old men come upon a merchant in the desert about to be slain by a demon which has a claim of blood-vengeance against him (we have encountered the earlier part of this tale already, in my analysis of incidents from **"The Merchant and the Genie"**). First the redactor takes care to note that each shaykh has with him some object of interest: the first, a chained gazelle; the second, a pair of black hunting dogs; the third, a mule. Then the first shaykh approaches the genie and pleads with it for the merchant's life: if you grant me one-third of the blood-claim due you from this man, he states, I will recite for you a wondrous tale concerning this chained gazelle. The demon accepts, and the audience can already recognize the symmetries of the formal patterning at work in this story-cycle: each of the three shaykhs in turn will advance to tell a wondrous tale concerning his animal and claim one-third of the blood-punishment. And such in fact is what happens: the merchant is saved by the recitation of the three tales.[47]

A more elaborate instance of formal patterning is at work in a story-cycle entitled **"The Tale of the Hunchback."**[48] Four characters, a Christian broker, a steward, a Jewish doctor, and a tailor, are summoned before a sultan and each must tell a satisfyingly amazing anecdote in order to have his life spared. This story-as-ransom motif obviously connects the entire cycle with the Scheherazade frame, where the heroine also recites tales to avert death. But there is more. Each of the four characters in **"The Hunchback"** [**"The Tale of the Hunchback"**] tells a story in which he describes an encounter with a young man who has been mysteriously maimed or crippled. In each encounter the narrator asks the young man how he suffered his hurt, and the latter's explanation constitutes the tale offered to the sultan as ransom. The last of the four reciters, the tailor, tells how at a marriage-feast he met a young man who had been lamed. The youth recounts the misfortunes whereby he came to be crippled; and it turns out that the person responsible for this injury, an insufferably garrulous barber, is seated at the same table as the tailor. No sooner does the youth conclude his tale than the barber insists on offering the tailor and his friends a succession of stories, first one about himself, then a good half-dozen anecdotes about his six unfortunate brothers. The tales narrated by the barber are not demanded as any kind of ransom by the tailor, in contrast to the four tales required by the sultan in the overarching **"Hunchback"** cycle. Nor do the barber's stories seem controlled by a common thematic concern or moral argument. All six brothers suffer harm, but some deserve punishment for their foolishness or lust, while others (especially the third and fourth brothers) are clearly innocent victims of malicious sharpsters. But common to the vignettes in this series is that each tells how one of the brothers was blinded, castrated or somehow deprived of lips and ears.[49] This structural pattern of mutilation links the six tales formally to one another and in turn unites the **"Barber"** [**"The Barber's Six Brothers"**] cycle as a whole with **"The Hunchback,"** where each of the four enframed tales also displays a formal patterning of mutilation/crippling. Thus the stories contained in **"The Barber's Six Brothers"** constitute an example of a narrative cycle where the unity lacking at the thematic level is compensated for by a consistent formal patterning.

IV. DRAMATIC VISUALIZATION

I define dramatic visualization as the representing of an object or character with an abundance of descriptive detail, or the mimetic rendering of gestures and dialogue in such a way as to make the given scene 'visual' or imaginatively present to an audience. I contrast 'dramatic visualization' with 'summary presentation,' where an author informs his audience of an object or event in abbreviated fashion without dramatizing the scene or encouraging the audience to form a visual picture of it. In *The Rhetoric of Fiction* Wayne Booth analyzes the modern novel by making analogous distinctions between what he calls "showing" and "telling": when an author "shows" his audience something he renders it dramatically so as to give the "intensity of realistic illusion"; when he "tells" his audience about a thing he is using his authorial powers to summarize an event or render judgment on a character's behavior, without, however, using descriptive detail to make the given event or character imaginatively present.[50]

To understand how these techniques function let us compare the wording of analogous scenes in two different *Alf laylah* stories. Both portray exemplary punishment in the form of amputation which is to be inflicted on the protagonist. The first scene is from **"The Lover Who Pretended to be a Thief."** Khālid, governor of Basrah, is confronted with the men of a family who have caught a handsome young man breaking into their home. They accuse the boy of theft, and the prisoner confesses freely. To Khālid the youth seems too well-spoken and of too noble a bearing to be a thief; yet given the boy's insistence on his own guilt, the gover-

nor has no choice but to order the legally mandated punishment. Suspecting nevertheless that the prisoner is for some reason concealing the truth, Khālid counsels him privately to "state that which may ward off from you the punishment of amputation" the next morning when he is to be interrogated one last time by the judge before the sentence is executed (not till the end of the story do we learn that the youth is a lover who had entered the home for a tryst with the daughter of the house, and that he has allowed himself to be labeled a thief so as to protect her honor). The punishment-scene reads as follows:

> When morning dawned the people assembled to see the youth's hand cut off; and there was not a single person in Basrah, neither man nor woman, who failed to be present so as to see the punishment of this young man. Khālid came riding up, and with him were prominent dignitaries and others from among the people of Basrah. Then he summoned the judges and called for the young man to be brought. And so he approached, stumbling in his chains; and not one of the people saw him without weeping for him. And the voices of the women rose up in lamentation.
>
> The judge thereupon ordered the women to be silenced; and then he said to him, "These persons contend that you entered their home and stole their possessions. Perhaps you stole less than the amount which makes this a crime legally necessitating such punishment?"
>
> "On the contrary," he replied. "I stole precisely an amount which necessitates such punishment."
>
> He said, "Perhaps you were co-owner with these persons in some of those possessions."
>
> "On the contrary," he replied. "Those things belong entirely to them. I have no legal claim to those things."
>
> At this point Khālid grew angry. He himself stood up, went over to him and struck him in the face with his whip, quoting aloud this verse:
>
> > Man wishes to be given his desire
> > But God refuses all save what *He* desires.
>
> Thereupon he called for the butcher so that the latter might cut off his hand. And so he came, and he took out the knife. Then he stretched out the boy's hand and placed upon it the knife.
>
> But suddenly there rushed forward a young woman from the midst of the women, clad in soiled and tattered clothes. She screamed and threw herself upon him. She drew back her veil, to reveal a face like the moon for beauty. And there rose up from the people a great outcry.[51]

The beloved has appeared: she will sacrifice her reputation and their love-secret so as to save the boy from punishment.

We will return to the lovers in a moment, but let us look first at our second amputation-scene, this one from **"The Reward of Charity."** A capricious king has ordered that henceforth no one in his realm is to offer alms or bestow charity under any circumstances; all those caught violating this command will have their hands chopped off. In what follows a starving beggar approaches a woman who proves to be the protagonist:

> The beggar said to the woman, "Give me something in the way of charity!"
>
> She replied, "How can I give you alms when the king is cutting off the hand of everyone who gives alms?"
>
> He said, "I beg you in God's name, give me something in the way of alms!"
>
> So when he asked her in God's name she felt pity for him and gave him two loaves of bread as an act of charity.
>
> Thereafter report of this reached the king and he ordered that she be brought to him. Then when she appeared he cut off her hands and she returned to her home.[52]

Brief, brutal, and to the point.

But the two passages, juxtaposed as they are here, trigger a question: why is dramatic visualization employed in the amputation-scene from **"The Lover"** [**"The Lover Who Pretended to be a Thief"**], while the redactor contents himself with the technique of summary presentation in an analogous episode from "The Reward of Charity"? The answer I believe is related to the fact that the punishment-scene in **"The Lover"** is the climax of the entire story. Throughout the *Alf laylah* dramatic visualization is reserved especially for scenes which form the heart of a given narrative. Such is the case here. What *follows* the girl's appearance in the public square is narrated succinctly: the boy's punishment is averted, the couple's love is made known, and Khālid prevails on the girl's father to allow them to marry. But the redactor lingers over the spectacle of punishment: the wailing crowds, the pathetic glimpse of the youth stumbling in his chains, the extended dialogue between judge and prisoner, and the sketch of the frustrated Khālid giving up all attempt to save the boy and lashing out with his whip. The effect of all this visualized detail is to slow the pace of narration; and we are not permitted any resolution till the last possible moment, when the heroine is introduced just as the butcher is about to apply his knife. Thus the technique of dramatic visualization enables the storyteller to heighten the tension in a scene and increase his audience's experience of pleasurable suspense.

By way of contrast the amputation in **"The Reward of Charity"** is not the narrative focus of the story at all. The punishment is presented in summary fashion because it is only a prelude to the true climax: the scene where the woman's generous impulse is vindicated. Mutilated as she is and subsequently expelled to the desert with her infant son clinging to her, she wanders until she comes upon a stream:

> She knelt down to drink, because of the extreme thirst which had overtaken her from her walking and her fatigue and her sorrow. But when she bent over, the boy fell into the water. She sat weeping greatly for her child.
>
> And while she was crying, behold!: two men passed by; and they said to her, "What is making you weep?"
>
> She answered them, "I had a boy who was holding me about the neck, and he fell into the water."
>
> They said to her, "Would you like us to bring him forth for you?"
>
> She replied, "Yes," and so they called on God most high. Thereupon the child came forth to her unharmed; nothing ill had befallen him.
>
> Then they said to her, "Would you like God to restore your hands to you as they had been?"
>
> She replied, "Yes," and so they called on God—all praise and glory to Him!—and her hands were restored to her, more beautiful than they ever had been before.
>
> Then they said to her, "Do you know who we are?"
>
> She replied, "Only God knows!"
>
> They said, "We are your two loaves of bread, which you bestowed in charity on the beggar."[53]

The redactor has reserved dramatic visualization for the scene which most merits it, that episode illustrating the moralistic theme which drives the whole narrative.

Notes

1. Bayard Dodge, ed. and translator, *The Fihrist of al-Nadīm: a Tenth-Century Survey of Muslim Culture* (New York: Columbia University Press, 1970), vol. 2, pp. 712-713.

2. Maḥmūd ibn ʿUmar al-Zamakhsharī, *al-Kashshāf ʿan ḥaqāʾiq al-tanzīl* (Beirut: Dār al-maʿrifah, n.d.), vol. 3, p. 210.

   Al-Naḍr ibn al-Harith is described by Philip Hitti, *History of the Arabs,* 6th ed. (London: Macmillan & Co., 1956), p. 273, as a "poet-minstrel whose pagan recitals competed with the revelations of Muḥammad in winning the favour of the people." The Quraysh (to whose tribe the Prophet himself belonged) were among the inhabitants of Mecca in Muḥammad's lifetime; many of them were initially hostile to the Qurʾanic revelation. According to Arab legend, ʿĀd and Thamūd were great civilizations of the ancient Arabian peninsula; chapter 7 of the Qurʾan tells the story of how these peoples were punished for refusing to accept the messengers sent them by God. Rustam and Behrām were heroes of ancient Iranian epic. Ḥīrah was the capital of a kingdom in northeast Arabia allied with the Sassanid Persian shahs.

3. Cited by Nabia Abbott, "A Ninth-Century Fragment of the 'Thousand Nights,'" *Journal of Near Eastern Studies* 8 (1949), p. 155.

4. Ibid., p. 155.

5. Iflah 'Umar al-Adalbī, *Naẓrah fī adabinā al-shaʿbī* (Damascus: Ittiḥād al-kuttāb al-ʿarab, 1974), p. 45.

6. Judith Miller, "Egypt Bans Copies of '1,001 Nights,'" *The New York Times,* Monday, May 20, 1985, p. A6.

7. Ṣabrī al-ʿAskarī, *"Natāʾij thaqāfīyah li-muṣādarat* Alf laylah wa-laylah (Cultural Consequences of the Confiscation of the *Thousand and One Nights*)," *al-Ahrām* (Cairo), Sunday, June 16, 1985, p. 14. For editorial cartoons concerning the *Alf laylah* controversy see *al-Ahrām,* Saturday, March 23, 1985, p. 13; Friday, March 29, 1985, p. 17; and Tuesday, April 9, 1985, p. 9.

8. Salwā al-ʿInānī, *"Qaḍīyat* Alf laylah wa-laylah (The Affair of the *Thousand and One Nights*)", *al-Ahrām,* Friday, April 19, 1985, p. 14.

9. Aḥmad Bahjat published a total of five essays, each entitled *"Alf laylah wa-laylah,"* in his daily column on p. 2 of *al-Ahrām* beginning Saturday, April 20, 1985. His criticism of Salwā al-ʿInānī and references to the Qurʾan appeared in the fifth of these essays, on Wednesday, April 24, 1985.

10. Bahjat, *al-Ahrām,* Monday, April 22, 1985, p. 2. For other articles from *al-Ahrām* concerning this controversy, see Munā Rajab, *"Baʿda qaḍīyat kitāb* Alf laylah wa-laylah*: hal hiya muqaddimah lil-ʿabath bi-kutub ukhrā?* (After the Affair of the *Thousand and One Nights*: Is This the Prelude to Tampering with Other Books?)", Sunday, April 7, 1985, p. 13; Bāhir al-Jawharī, "Alf laylah wa-laylah *wa-adab al-būrnūjarāfiyā* (The *Thousand and One Nights* and Pornographic Literature)", Friday, April 19, 1985, p. 14; and an untitled essay by Ahmad Bahāʾ al-Dīn in his column, *"Yawmīyāt* (Daily News)", Saturday, May 25, 1985, p. 20.

11. al-Nadīm, op. cit., vol. 2, pp. 713-714.

12. Abū al-Ḥasan al-Masʿūdī, *Murūj al-dhahab (Les prairies d'or)*, ed. C. Barbier de Meynard (Paris: l'Imprimerie impériale, 1861-1877), vol. 4, pp. 90-91; cited and translated by Abbott, op. cit., p. 150.

13. Abbott, op. cit., pp. 132, 151-152; Enno Littmann, s.v. *"Alf Layla wa-Layla,"* The Encyclopaedia of Islam, 2nd ed. (Leiden: E. J. Brill, 1960), vol. 1, p. 361.

14. Littmann, op. cit., pp. 361-363; also see Littmann's essay "Anhang: zur Entstehung und Geschichte von Tausendundeiner Nacht," in his *Erzählungen aus den Tausendundein Nächten* (Wiesbaden: Insel-Verlag, 1953), vol. 6, p. 717. For affinities between Greek and Arabic popular literature, see Gustave von Grunebaum, *Medieval Islam: a Study in Cultural Orientation,* 2nd ed. (Chicago: University of Chicago Press, 1953), chapter 9, "Creative Borrowing: Greece in the *Arabian Nights,*" pp. 294-319.

15. H. Zotenberg, *Histoire d' ʿAlā al-Dīn ou la lampe merveilleuse. Texte arabe publié avec une notice sur quelques manuscrits des Mille et une Nuits* (Paris: Imprimerie Nationale, 1888), pp. 16-23, 47.

16. Littmann, "Alf Layla," p. 362.

17. For the Galland text and the history of *Alf laylah* MSS see Muhsin Mahdi, ed., *The Thousand and One Nights (Alf layla wa-layla) from the Earliest Known Sources* (Leiden: E. J. Brill, 1984), vol. 1, pp. v-ix, 25-36. See also Abbott, op. cit., pp. 132-133.

18. Zotenberg, op. cit., pp. 16-23, 47.

19. Duncan Black MacDonald, "The Earlier History of the *Arabian Nights,*" *Journal of the Royal Asiatic Society* (1924), pp. 353-397. See also Littmann, "Alf Layla," p. 361, for a discussion of MacDonald's research.

20. Littmann, "Alf Layla," p. 360; Zotenberg, op. cit., pp. 45-46. For a recent reprint of the Būlāq edition see Muhammad Qiṭṭah al-ʿAdwī, ed., *Alf laylah wa-laylah* (Baghdad: Maktabat al-muthannā, n.d.); 2 vols. For the MacNaghten edition see W. H. MacNaghten, ed., *The Alif Laila or Book of the Thousand Nights and One Night* (Calcutta: W. Thacker & Co., 1839-1842), 4 vols.

21. Mahdi, op. cit., vol. 1, pp. 25-36.

22. For "The Jealous Husband and the Parrot" see the Leiden edition, vol. 1 (Night 14), pp. 98-99; for "The Enchanted Prince" see Leiden, vol. 1 (Night 25), p. 122. Both stories are discussed in chapter 2 of the present study.

23. Thus e.g. "The Fisherman and the Genie" and "The Enchanted Prince" (which formed part of the fourteenth-century G text of the *Alf laylah*) can be found in untitled independent story-collections of the eighteenth century such as Paris BN 3651 and 3655. "The Ebony Horse" and "Khalīfah the Fisherman and Hārūn al-Rashīd" (both part of the eighteenth-century ZER text) can be found in Rabat 6152 (from the Moroccan Royal Library), a story-collection dated AH 1281 (= AD 1864) which is independent of the *Alf laylah.*

24. An exception to this generalization might be the stories involving Hārūn al-Rashīd (who appears in many of the ZER's supplementary narratives), a

figure who could be construed as a commentary on King Shāhrayār, particularly in his restless desire for entertainment and repeated threats of violence. In my discussion of "The False Caliph" in chapter 3 I discuss this point and note the B edition's use of formulae to draw attention to the presence of Shāhrayār as audience for this tale.

25. al-Nadīm, op. cit., vol. 2, p. 714.

26. Richard Hole, *Remarks on the* Arabian Nights' Entertainments (London: Cadell & Davies, 1797; reprint: New York: Garland Publishing, 1970), p. 7.

27. MacDonald, op. cit., p. 370.

28. Edward William Lane, *Manners and Customs of the Modern Egyptians* (London: J. M. Dent & Sons, Everyman's Library edition, 1954), pp. 419-420.

29. Peter D. Molan, "The *Arabian Nights*: the Oral Connection," *Edebiyāt* n.s. vol. II, nos. 1 & 2 (1988), p. 195.

30. For examples of MSS in which *qālā al-rāwī* and other instances of anomalous *qāla* are penned in disproportionately large lettering see Paris 3651, fol. 40b et seq. ("The City of Brass") and Paris 3663, fol. 85a et seq. ("The False Caliph"). See also the Leiden edition of the *Alf laylah*, vol. 2, plates 55-56 (Christ Church Arabic MS 207) and plates 71-72 (Paris 3612). In Paris 3668, fol. 53b et seq. ("The City of Brass"), red ink is used for phrases such as *qāla al-rāwī* and for other words which indicate changes of speaker in dialogue portions of the text, in contrast to the black ink used for the bulk of the narrative.

31. B vol. 2 (Night 878), p. 431. See also the beginning of the *Nights* in the Leiden edition (vol. 1, p. 56): *wa-yataḍammanuhu* [sic] *ayḍan siyar jalīlah yata'allamu sāmi'uhā al-firāsah* ("It also contains many splendid accounts; the person who hears them may learn discernment"). The latter phrase is retained in the incipit of many texts of the Syrian family. Note also Scheherazade's statement as she begins the recitation of "Nūr al-Dīn and the Lady Shams al-Nahār" (Leiden, vol. 1, p. 379): *wa-huwa ḥadīt[h] Abū* [sic] *al-Ḥasan . . . wa-mā jarā lahu ma'a jāriyat al-khalīfah Shams al-Nahār yaṭraba al-sāmi' wa-huwa bahjat ḥusn al-ṭawāli'* ("This is the tale of Abū al-Ḥasan . . . and what happened to him with the caliph's servant-girl Shams al-Nahār. The person who hears it will delight therein, if he is lucky enough [to hear it]").

32. Mahdi, op. cit., vol. 1, pp. 37-51. See also Johann Fück, *'Arabīya: Recherches sur l'histoire de la langue et du style arabe* (Paris: Librairie Marcel Didier, 1955), pp. 177-191.

33. Andras Hamori, "A Comic Romance from the *Thousand and One Nights*: the Tale of Two Viziers," *Arabica* 30:1 (1983), p. 38, n. 1.

34. Leiden, vol. 1, pp. 57-59.

35. Leiden, vol. 1, pp. 72-73.

36. Robert Alter, *The Art of Biblical Narrative* (New York: Basic Books, 1981), p. 92.

37. Quoted and translated by Alter, op. cit., p. 93.

38. The MN version of "The Magian City" is found in vol. 1, pp. 123-128. B (vol. 1, pp. 44-46) and Leiden (vol. 1, pp. 203-207) lack MN's pattern of *Leitwörter*. The three versions are compared in D. Pinault, "Stylistic Features in Selected Tales from *The Thousand and One Nights*" (Ph.D. diss., University of Pennsylvania, 1986), pp. 172-194.

39. MN vol. 1, p. 123.

40. Edward William Lane, *The Arabian Nights' Entertainments* (New York: Tudor Publishing Co., 1927), p. 1209, n. 1.

41. Edward William Lane, *An Arabic-English Lexicon* (Beirut: Librairie du Liban, 1968), vol. 4, p. 1325.

42. Richard Burton, *Book of the Thousand Nights and a Night* (London: Burton Club for Private Subscribers, "Bagdad Edition," n.d.), vol. 1, p. 165, n. 1, and vol. 10, p. 362.

43. 'Abd al-Qāhir al-Jurjānī, *Dalā'il al-i'jāz,* ed. Muḥammad 'Abd al-Mun'im Khafājī (Cairo: Maktabat al-Qāhirah, 1969), p. 90.

44. G. J. H. van Gelder, *Beyond the Line: Classical Arabic Literary Critics on the Coherence and Unity of the Poem* (Leiden: E. J. Brill, 1982), p. 131.

45. MN vol. 1, p. 127.

46. MN vol. 1, p. 128.

47. Such at least is the structure of this story-cycle as found in B (vol. 1, pp. 7-10) and MN (vol. 1, pp. 12-20); but it is of interest to note that, from the point of view of formal patterning, G (as found in the Leiden ed., vol. 1, pp. 78-86) is markedly deficient. As in the two Egyptian texts, in G the first of three shaykhs advances to claim one-third of the blood-punishment, and the audience is prepared for a pattern of three stories. The first two shaykhs bring forward their beasts and recite wondrous tales concerning them, as in B and MN. But when it comes the third shaykh's turn, he is not described in G's version as having with him any animal; hence he quite literally has no tale worth speaking of. And G in fact at this juncture (Leiden, p. 86) contains no more than the bald statement:

The third shaykh told the genie a tale more wondrous and stranger than the other two tales. Then the genie marvelled greatly and shook with pleasure and said, "I grant you one-third of the blood-claim."

Thus in G we are told only that the shaykh recited his story, but we are not permitted to hear the story itself, in contrast to the pattern followed with the full recitals given by the first two shaykhs. The audience is denied hearing the third tale which it had been led to expect by the narrative's structure. The passage quoted above shows that G acknowledges the structure dictated by the formal patterning of the three shaykhs and the blood-punishment divided into thirds; but G disposes of this structure at the end in very perfunctory fashion.

48. The story is found in Leiden, vol. 1, pp. 280-379; B vol. 1, pp. 73-106; and MN vol. 1, pp. 199-278.

49. Some of these mutilations are central to the given story, others incidental. One significant variant among the three editions occurs in the account of "The Barber's Fifth Brother." The Egyptian texts (MN, vol. 1, p. 271 and B, vol. 1, p. 103) conclude this story by having thieves fall upon the barber's fifth brother and cut off his ears, an incident not found in the Leiden version. This act is not essential to the story proper of the fifth brother, but it does link the tale to its larger frame by bringing forward the motif of maiming/mutilation which characterizes all the stories of the "Hunchback" cycle. As such the Egyptian versions of "The Barber's Fifth Brother" offer a more consistent example than does the Syrian text of the use of formal patterning as a means of achieving structural unity for a series of otherwise unrelated tales.

50. Wayne Booth, *The Rhetoric of Fiction* (Chicago: University of Chicago Press, 1961), pp. 3-9, 40.

51. B vol. 1 (Night 298), p. 471.

52. B vol. 1 (Night 348), p. 527.

53. Ibid., p. 527.

Bibliography of Works Cited

MANUSCRIPTS

Rabat, al-Khizānah al-Ḥasanīyah

No. 6152 (*Kitāb al-ḥikāyāt al-ʿajībah*)

Tunis, Dār al-kutub

No. 04576 (*Miʾat laylah wa-laylah*)

No. 18047 ("The Man who Claimed to be a Prophet")

Lucknow, Sulṭān al-madāris Library

No. 238 (*al-Dhakhīrah al-iskandarīyah*)

Paris, Bibliothèque Nationale

No. 3118 ("The City of Brass")

No. 3651 ("The City of Brass," "The Fisherman and the Genie/The Enchanted Prince")

No. 3655 ("The Fisherman and the Genie/The Enchanted Prince")

No. 3663 ("The False Caliph")

No. 3668 ("The City of Brass")

No. 4678 (*Kitāb alf laylah wa-laylah*)

No. 5725 ("The City of Brass")

PUBLISHED EDITIONS OF THE *ALF LAYLAH WA-LAYLAH* AND THE *MIʾAT LAYLAH WA-LAYLAH*

Habicht, Maximilian, and Fleischer, M. H. L., eds. *Tausend und Eine Nacht, Arabisch. Nach einer Handschrift aus Tunis herausgegeben.* 12 vols. Breslau: Josef Max & Co., 1825-1843.

MacNaghten, W. H. ed. *The Alif Laila or Book of the Thousand Nights and One Night . . .* 4 vols. Calcutta: W. Thacker & Co., 1839-1842.

Mahdi, Muhsin, ed. *The Thousand and One Nights (Alf layla wa-layla) from the Earliest Known Sources.* 2 vols. to date. Leiden: E. J. Brill, 1984.

Ṣāliḥ, Rushdī, ed. *Alf laylah wa-laylah.* Cairo: Dār al-shaʿb, 1969.

al-Shaṛqawī, ʿAbd al-Rahmān al-Ṣafatī, ed. *Alf laylah wa-laylah.* 2 vols. Cairo: Būlāq edition, 1835. Reprint (2 vols.): Muḥammad Qiṭṭah al-ʿAdwī, ed., Baghdad: Maktabat al-muthannā, n.d.

Ṭarshūnah, Maḥmūd, ed. *Miʾat laylah wa-laylah.* Tunis: al-Dār al-ʿarab⁻yah lilkitāb, 1979.

OTHER SOURCES

Abbott, Nabia. "A Ninth-Century Fragment of the 'Thousand Nights': New Light on the Early History of the *Arabian Nights.*" *Journal of Near Eastern Studies* 8 (1949): 129-164.

al-Adalbī, Iflah ʿUmar. *Naẓrah fī adabinā al-shaʿbī.* Damascus: Ittiḥād al-kuttāb al-ʿarab, 1974.

Alter, Robert. *The Art of Biblical Narrative.* New York: Basic Books, 1981.

al-ʿAskarī, Ṣabrī. "Natāʾij thaqāfīyah li-muṣādarat *Alf laylah wa-laylah.*" *al-Ahrām* (Cairo), Sunday, June 16, 1985, p. 14.

Bahāʾ al-Dīn, Aḥmad. "Yawmīyāt." *al-Ahrām* (Cairo), Saturday, May 25, 1985, p. 20.

Bahjat, Aḥmad. "*Alf laylah wa-laylah.*" *al-Ahrām* (Cairo), Saturday, April 20, through Wednesday, April 24, 1985. His essays appeared on p. 2 of each issue.

Booth, Wayne C. *The Rhetoric of Fiction.* Chicago: University of Chicago Press, 1961.

Burton, Richard. *The Book of a Thousand Nights and a Night.* 10 vols. [London]: Burton Club for Private Subscribers, "Bagdad Edition," n.d.

Fück, Johann. *'Arabiya: Recherches sur l'histoire de la langue et du style arabe.* French translation by Claude Denizeau. Paris: Librairie Marcel Didier, 1955.

Hamori, Andras. "A Comic Romance from the *Thousand and One Nights*: The Tale of Two Viziers." *Arabica* 30: 1 (1983): 38-56.

Hitti, Philip K. *History of the Arabs.* 6th ed. London: MacMillan & Co., 1956.

Hole, Richard. *Remarks on the* Arabian Nights' *Entertainments.* London: Cadell & Davies, 1797. reprint: New York: Garland Publishing, 1970.

al-'Inānī, Salwā. "Qaḍīyat *Alf laylah wa-laylah.*" *al-Ahrām* (Cairo), Friday, April 19, 1985, p. 14.

al-Jawharī, Bāhir, "*Alf laylah wa-laylah* wa-adab al-būrnūjarāfīyā." *al-Ahrām* (Cairo), Friday, April 19, 1985, p. 14.

al-Jurjānī, 'Abd al-Qāhir. *Dalā'il al-i'jāz.* Edited by Muḥammad 'Abd al-Mun'im Khafājī. Cairo: Maktabat al-Qāhirah, 1969.

Kipling, Rudyard. *Life's Handicap.* New York: Doubleday, Page & Co., 1923.

Lane, Edward William. *The Arabian Nights' Entertainments.* New York: Tudor Publishing Co., 1927.

Lane, Edward William. *An Arabic-English Lexicon.* 8 vols. Beirut: Librairie du Liban, 1968.

Lane, Edward William. *Manners and Customs of the Modern Egyptians.* London: J. M. Dent & Sons, Everyman's Library edition, 1954.

Littmann, Enno. s.v. "Alf laylah wa-Layla," in the *Encyclopaedia of Islam,* 2nd ed., vol. 1, pp. 358-364. Leiden: E. J. Brill, 1960.

MacDonald, Duncan Black. "The Earlier History of the *Arabian Nights.*" *Journal of the Royal Asiatic Society,* 1924, pp. 353-397.

Mahdi, Muhsin. "Maẓāhir al-riwāyah wa-al-mushāfahah fī uṣūl *Alf laylah wa-laylah.*" *Majallat Ma'had al-Makhṭūṭāt al-'arabīyah* 20 (1974): 125-144.

al-Mas'ūdī, Abū al-Ḥasan. *Murūj al-dhahab* (*Les prairies d'or*). Edited by C. Barbier de Meynard and Pavet de Courteille. 9 vols. Paris: L'Imprimerie Imperiale, 1861-1877.

Miller, Judith. "Egypt Bans Copies of '1,001 Nights.'" *The New York Times,* Monday, May 20, 1985, p. A6.

Molan, Peter. "The *Arabian Nights*: The Oral Connection." *Edebiyāt* n.s. vol. 2, nos. 1 & 2 (1988): 191-204.

al-Nadīm, Abū al-Faraj Muḥammad ibn Isḥāq. *The Fihrist of al-Nadīm: a Tenth-Century Survey of Muslim Culture.* Edited and translated by Bayard Dodge. 2 vols. New York: Columbia University Press, 1970.

Pinault, David. "Stylistic Features in Selected Tales from *The Thousand and One Nights.*" Ph.D. dissertation, University of Pennsylvania, 1986.

Rajab, Munā. "Ba'da qaḍīyat kitāb *Alf laylah wa-laylah*: hal hiya muqaddimah lil-'abath bi-kutub ukhrā?" *al-Ahrām* (Cairo), Sunday, April 7, 1985, p. 13.

van Gelder, G. J. H. *Beyond the Line: Classical Arabic Literary Critics on the Coherence and Unity of the Poem.* Leiden: E. J. Brill, 1982.

von Grunebaum, Gustave. *Medieval Islam: a Study in Cultural Orientation.* 2nd ed. Chicago: University of Chicago Press, 1953.

al-Zamakhsharī, Maḥmūd ibn 'Umar. *al-Kashshāf 'an ḥaqā'iq al-tanzīl.* 4 vols. Beirut: Dār al-ma'rifah, n.d.

Zotenberg, H. *Histoire d''alā al-Dīn ou la lampe merveilleuse. Texte arabe publié avec une notice sur quelques manuscrits des Mille et Une Nuits.* Paris: Imprimerie Nationale, 1888.

Yusur Al-Madani (essay date December 1996)

SOURCE: Al-Madani, Yusur. "Navigation as Exploration: The Fantastic Education of Sindbad the Sailor of the *Arabian Nights* and Twain's *Huckleberry Finn.*" *Canadian Review of Comparative Literature* 23, no. 4 (December 1996): 901-12.

[*In the following essay, Al-Madani analyzes the moral implications of "Sindbad the Sailor" and Mark Twain's* Adventures of Huckleberry Finn, *and portrays the protagonists' journeys as indicative of their respective cultures.*]

Journeying as a quest for knowledge and education is a common theme in world literature. No wonder then that two works about journeys from two vastly different literatures produce intellectual and moral parallels and opposites. Both **"Sindbad the Sailor"** of the *One Thousand Nights and One Night,* better known as the *Arabian Nights,* and Twain's the *Adventures of Huckleberry Finn* employ the journey, as a process of initiating their heroes into the realities of the world. Both Sindbad and Huck express, at least partially, the ancient migratory restlessness of man, whether motivated by a drive to confront the world (Sindbad's case) or one to escape its brutalities (Huck's case). Commenting on the universality of **"Sindbad the Sailor,"** Hussein Fowzi declares that not only is the story of Sindbad "the great maritime story of Arabic literature" but also "one of the most important tales in world literature" (256, my translation). So is Huck Finn's journey. Although critical views on Huckleberry Finn present a variety of responses ranging from classifying the book as "one of the central documents of American culture" (Trilling 318) in which "Huck's voice combined with Twain's satiric genius changed fiction in America" (Fishkin 3), to condemning it as a "grotesque example of racist trash" (Wallas 16), Twain's masterpiece, precisely because of its local colour, remains America's epic of self-exploration. The fact that Sindbad goes on to an ocean, while Huck Finn explores a great river, only indicates the marginal, though significant, difference that Sindbad belongs to an imperial culture while Huckleberry Finn belongs to one still in the making.

The purpose of this paper is to examine the growth to maturity and knowledge of two journeying young people, Sindbad the Sailor and Huck Finn, who, as fictional creations, have come to represent their respective cultures. Through measured comparison, the nature, stages and significance of their journeys, which comprise the essence of their education, are explored as intellectual and moral processes of adventure ultimately leading each figure to embrace a veritable system of values. Though comparative in approach, this paper confines itself to eliciting plain similarities and dissimilarities in the two journeyers' experiences. It neither delves into extended intertextual comparisons that needlessly go beyond its central purpose, nor does it draw ideological parallels and opposites from the two main figures' education. Moreover, the cultural background informing each text, the Arab Islamic in the first, the American in the second, is introduced, for the same reason, only in its most general outlines.

The journeys Sindbad and Huck undertake are motivated by their dissatisfaction with their prevalent human conditions, different as they are. Inexperienced, Sindbad squanders on land the good fortune his father has left him, a blunder which forces him to sell what little property he is left with, buy himself some goods and embark on a trading sea-trip in the hope of making profit. After each journey, Sindbad returns home a richer man, yet the itch to travel and the desire to improve himself always drive him back to the sea for more fantastic adventures.

Likewise, Huck Finn is discontented with his life with the widow Douglas, whose sole objective is to "civilize" him. Describing his insipid and boring "civilized" life with the widow and her sister, Miss Watson, Huck complains: "I felt so lonesome I most wished I was dead" (9). In order to rejuvenate himself and break away from a confining social order, Huck makes forays into nature from time to time. His ultimate break away from social conditioning takes place when he sets up his mock-murder to escape the torture of his drunkard father and, accidentally, meets later with the runaway slave, Jim. He realizes that nature, with its romantic reverberations, is no place for him to know himself. The rest of the book relates the adventures of Huck and Jim as they turn their backs on the mainland and float down the river on their raft in search for a meaningful life.

The overall pattern of Sindbad's journeys is circular, while that of Huck's is circular yet linear. Both protagonists depart from society, travel along a road of exile and danger, and come back to everyday life as more experienced. Sindbad's journeys start and end in Baghdad, where he finally settles down to enjoy what Campbell pointedly calls the "boons" (30) of these wanderings. Huck's journey, however, and in an apparently circular manner, brings him back to society only as an alien and only to start a new voyage, "to light out for the Territory ahead of the rest" (229). In this sense, Huck's ultimate orientation is never-ending and, consequently, linear. The apparent contradiction is explained away by the fact that Huck's life is similarly contradictory: it forces him back to the shore in a circular manner but very soon, he disengages himself from the mainland and moves ahead, always ahead, always looking beyond the circle. Contrary to Sindbad who finds his final prize in establishing himself in society, Huck remains a social outcast as well as a rejectionist on a perpetual never-ending journey of self-exploration and self-definition.

The preliminaries of the two narratives are absolutely realistic as long as both protagonists are on land. Once the journey takes a maritime line, a fantasy-world starts evolving in **"Sindbad the Sailor"** and a sometime dream-like, sometime grotesque, world in Huckleberry Finn. Although the fantasy element is exceptionally powerful in **"Sindbad the Sailor"** and only implied or elementary in *Huckleberry Finn*, Huck's dream-world on board the raft becomes the vehicle for Huck's moral conflict between his societal self, which forbids him to help a slave in his flight to freedom, and his natural self, which prizes love and brotherhood as the norms for human existence. Such a conflict, however, is totally absent in Sindbad, whose journeys remain primarily fantastic (*ajeeb* in Arabic, or astonishing) in nature culminating in his passage from innocence to maturity, knowledge, and social prominence.

The encounter with the *ajeeb* and the fantastic is a recurrent pattern in Sindbad's seven journeys. Each journey begins with Sindbad's buying himself a passage on a trading ship. With minimum details, the reader is thrust into the middle of action. A catastrophe soon takes place, the ship is wrecked, and Sindbad is inevitably the only survivor. Laboriously struggling with the elements of nature, Sindbad invariably finds himself on an island to start his astonishing and marvelous adventures. He withdraws from everyday reality into "a region of supernatural wonder," a region of "fabulous forces" (Campbell 30), from which he emerges victorious. The marvelous, therefore, functions as a test to the protagonist's intelligence and endurance. Sindbad's comeback to society is always victorious and successful. His second voyage impeccably illustrates this pattern.

Hungry for "commercial profit" and "exploration of the wonders of God's world" (**"Sindbad"** [**"Sindbad the Sailor"**] 147-48),[1] Sindbad embarks on his second voyage. After a long and arduous journey, his ship lands on a paradisiacal island where the crew rejoice amid a magnificent and bounteous nature. While Sindbad is enjoying his invigorating sleep, the ship sails away leaving him alone. He laments his misfortune but will not fall victim to despair. He climbs a tree to explore the place and notices "a gigantic white dome" towards which he walks. Unable to find any entrance into this dome, Sindbad concludes that this must be the egg of a colossal roc hovering in the sky.

Alone and bewitched, Sindbad finds a way to deliver himself from impending danger. It is a frequent pattern in all Sindbad's journeys that his intelligence and knowledge of the lore of fantastic journey tales rescue him from definite perdition. He ties himself to the leg of a peacefully resting roc hoping that the roc will take him to the land of men and civilization. Unfortunately, the roc lands him in a treacherous and deserted valley which, though abounding with precious diamonds, is the home of Cyclopean snakes. He has read fantastic stories about these dangerous mountains and valleys, and he knows perfectly well that a man venturing into such regions is most certainly venturing his own life. The resourceful Sindbad, nevertheless, uses his intelligence and knowledge again to rescue himself, collecting, at the same time, as many of the priceless diamonds as his pockets and *a'mama* (head cloth) can take. The roc flies him to the top of the mountain where tradesmen usually linger waiting for their hunt. Despite dire dangers, he ultimately succeeds in preserving his life and, inevitably his fortune. This dynamic, energetic, instinctively acquisitive, centrifugally-oriented child of his age is constantly graced with survival everytime he finds himself doomed to a certain death. It is part of his education to find the concept of survival thus confirmed in a culture that celebrates journeying and venturing as outstanding means to obtain learning, pleasure, and fortune.

Not all Sindbad's journeys, however, strictly reproduce this pattern. In three of his journeys, the fourth, the fifth, and the seventh, the pattern is broken and restored. Here action regresses into mere adventure in which Sindbad is thrust among ordinary human beings, "[t]he most benevolent and generous" (170) he has ever met. In the fourth voyage, for example, Sindbad reaches an unknown Kingdom where he manages, utilizing his diligence and craftsmanship, to make a good fortune, earn a high social position and, inevitably, win a beautiful young wife. Because of this kingdom's strange social custom, Sindbad, a short while later, has to be buried alive with his deceased wife. The restoration of the pattern occurs when he manages to escape from death. It is a recurrent feature in all Sindbad's adventures, which is also a feature of a cultural vision of life, that his survival is always accompanied by a fantastically positive turn of event and a handsome fortune.

Whenever there is a break in the pattern, the fantastic element noticeably disappears from the narrative. It is only at the end of the seventh and last voyage that we have a strong resurgence of one of the most popular fantastic themes: metamorphosis. This episode furnishes a superb example of ordinary human beings whose "organisms" metamorphose each month so that "wings, by which they fly across the sky, shoot out from their bodies" (200). Sindbad manages to accompany these human bird-like creatures on one of their adventures only to discover that they are nothing but embodiments of demons. He participates, therefore, in one of his most astonishing adventures that makes him, upon returning, determined to go back to Baghdad.

Referring to the fantastic in the *Arabian Nights,* Todorov claims that the book employs the "conventional imagery" (83) of the fantastic. He specifically assigns **"Sindbad the Sailor"** not to the "pure marvelous" that intends "to awaken doubts" (83) but rather to the "hyperbolic" or the "exotic" marvelous "in which the supernatural is somewhat justified" (54). In the first type, "phenomena are supernatural only by virtue of their dimension" (54), and the supernatural, in this case "does not do excessive violence to reason" (55). In the second type, "supernatural events are reported without being presented as such" (55). The reader, Todorov continues to say, is "ignorant of the regions where the events take place, and consequently he has no reason for calling them into question" (55).

These differentiations, however, produce an impression of intellectual hairsplitting. According to Todorov, we are in the realm of the fantastic as long as the "fantastic confronts us with a dilemma: to believe or not to believe" (83). One can ask here: does not the marvelous in **"Sindbad the Sailor"** after all leave us in the realm of doubt? The answer to this question should not be affected by Sindbad's natural credulity. A reader may well find incredible all that Sindbad accepts as credible. The focal point is culture: Sindbad's Islamic culture, which transcends mere religious practices toward a comprehensive vision of the cosmos, absorbs such *ajayib* (fantasies) through cultural channels as being credible. A modern reader, however, will most probably attribute these fantasies to the "pure marvelous," which is established, moreover, as a recurrent pattern in Sindbad's circuitous journeys. It is through these *ajayib* that Sindbad acquires his education.

Unlike the complementary relation between sea and land in Sindbad's journeys, Huck's is determined by an antithetical river-land relation. As T. S. Eliot states:

> A river, a very big and powerful river, is the only natural force that can wholly determine the course of human peregrination. At sea, the wanderer may sail or be carried by winds and currents in one direction or another; a change of wind or tide may determine fortune. In the prairie, the direction of the movement is more or less at the choice of the caravan; among mountains there will often be an alternative, a guess at the most likely pass. But the river with its strong, swift current is the dictator to the raft or to the steamboat.
>
> (107-08)

Huck's "river" is indeed as powerful a natural force as his determination to forge his own moral code, while Sindbad's "sea" is a multitude of forces symbolizing the multi-directional texture of his culture. Indeed Sindbad is a "Wanderer" but, unlike Huck Finn, never feels exiled or alienated despite his encounters with the extraordinary and the incredible.

The river, as Eliot emphasizes, is a formidable force capable of destructive floods. Nevertheless, it is confined for the most part between two lands, that is, between two even more formidable expanses of the mainland. The river is a pathway which Huck takes up towards knowledge. It is the space in which Huck is genuinely himself, probably the only place which is not subordinate to the authority of the mainland Huck rejects morally and relationally. The raft, his popular vehicle for endurance and learning can amazingly survive the torrents of the river, which is in this respect symbolic of creative tensions of American life, whereas a much more formidable vehicle, the big ship named "Walter Scott," again symbolic of the aristocratic and conservative elements of American culture, is wrecked by the same torrents.

Huck's journey starts as an act of separation from everyday reality and a renunciation of society, progresses toward a more human mode of living in nature symbolized by Huck's and Jim's "community of Saints" (Trilling 86) on board the raft, prior to the arrival of the King and the Duke, and finally goes back to society where Huck decides once more to start a new journey. Once Huck and Jim start their journey, life on the raft acquires a paradisiacal, dream-like quality. The journey down the Mississippi river is portrayed as a dream-world of liberation from traditional restrictions and social atrocities. Describing the scene at the beginning of their journey, Huck says: "It was kind of solemn, drifting down the big still river, laying on our backs looking up at the stars, and we didn't ever feel like talking loud, and it warn't often that we laughed only a little kind of low chuckle" (55). On board the raft, Huck and Jim are represented as "children of nature" (Jones 157) pervaded by the imbibing tranquility of the beautiful quiet night. They are both enchanted by the blissful peacefulness of the raft. Huck experiences this state of transcendent peace every time he returns to the raft from his grotesque adventures on the shore. Following the near-death ventures on board the wrecked "Walter Scott," Huck feels relieved and "mighty glad" to "get aboard the raft again" (61). This "island" of safety and peace stands in contrast with Sindbad's islands which are treacherously peaceful. For Huck and Jim, "there wasn't no home like a raft after all." To them, all "other places do seem cramped up and smotherly, but a raft don't." On the raft, they "feel mighty free and comfortable" (96). All sorrows and dangers troubling their mind vanish once they are on board the raft. The raft, therefore, functions as "a privileged space, an Eden to which Huck can return after each separation from Jim and become reunited, revitalized into a better understanding of the bond which can convert 'half chile' into an integrated whole" (Knoepflmacher 54). On the raft, Huck introspectively gains gradual but profound understanding of what is essential and sacred in life: his sanctified relation with Jim based on equality and freedom. His journey down the Mississippi river, therefore, is not an escape from life, but rather a rejection of a certain type of life and a quest for a democratic mode of living.

Once Huck and Jim start their glide down the river, their journey comprises a significant pattern: a temporary departure from nature symbolized by the raft and the river, phantasmagorical adventures in towns and villages along the river shore, and a return to nature. Huck's journey in this sense stands in sharp contrast to Sindbad's. Huck's escape is always from a perilous and corrupt society to his blissful island-raft while Sindbad's is always from a perilous island to his serene and placid shelter in Baghdad. Huck seldom thrives within the orderliness of society, and the raft always serves as a free and sure haven from the inhumanity of the shore. Sindbad, however, too often succeeds in reintegrating himself in society, whether at home or abroad. Organized society in **"Sindbad the Sailor"** functions as a moral term of reference as well as a refuge from the menace of the external world of Sindbad's ventures. Huck's ventures on the shore, therefore, correspond to Sindbad's on exotic islands. With all the corruption, the brutality, and the insanity Huck experiences on land, one can say that Huck's fantastic sallies into society compare in a profound sense with Sindbad's fantastic thrusts into unknown islands.

Huck's is, therefore, a formative journey of discovery; while Sindbad's is an affirmative one of recovery. Sindbad's fantastic experiences reconfirm prevalent values which his dissatisfaction on the mainland makes dubious. The sea in his journeys, therefore, reveals, restores, and reasserts the values of the mainland. In contrast, Huck's journeying brings him to an irreversible separation from the mainland. From a symbolic viewpoint, Huck's journeying is linear in that it totally lacks concord and interrelatedness with the values of the shore.

The two courses of journeys are full of encounters and confrontations. Sindbad's encounters predominantly take place on islands. The sea, as symbol of vastness and richness encompassing all places, directs Sindbad towards fantastic risks and adventures, but it is absolutely certain that the text does not surprise its reader with dire conclusions. With Huck, however, it is always a confrontation with violence and crime on the mainland. In this sense, the raft becomes a refuge. It is not too farfetched to say that the river, which penetrates the American continent, is a symbolic affirmation of the ability of the new continent to rediscover and shape a new moral and epistemological order.

In these episodes, the realistic element appears directly in the foreground, whereas the fantastic only flickers in the background. What seems factual and realistic in them appears to be most hilarious and fanciful. The Grangerfords and the Shepherdsons, whose bearing and conduct are strictly concordant with the genteel standards of the Southern aristocracy, proceed mindlessly in killing one another for a gratuitous reason which is itself deeply rooted in the traditions of the South. Such violence and horror are uniquely a special caliber of fantastic action. Colonel Sherburn, described by Huck as "a proud looking man" and "the best-dressed up man in town" (115), shoots the drunkard Boggs in cold blood in front of Boggs's daughter. Even the loafers of the town are diverted for a while by a re-enactment of the killing.

The most nonsensical characters in the novel are probably the King and the Duke. The range of things these two say or do are utterly outrageous and incredibly absurd. They repudiate the world of fact and prefer rather to live in a fantasy world of their own making. Tom Sawyer, who reappears at the end of the novel, is the most insensitive and insensible of all the characters in the novel in his pursuit of an insane plan to free an already free slave by subjecting him to humiliation and lethal danger only to satisfy his romance-coated supercilious imagination. In Twain's novel, Huck's and Jim's dream-like world, supposed to be unreal, materializes finally as fact, and the factual world on the shore represents to Huck a real nightmare. Huck's journey, in this sense, contrasts sharply with Sindbad's in that the fantasy element is man-made whereas in **"Sindbad the Sailor"** it is supernatural. Encountering it, Sindbad is mentally always swept off by sheer wonder and credulity; Huck, on the other hand, is always nauseated and estranged by the insanities and the grotesqueries on the shore. Such grotesque representations may have their roots in historical reality, but their textual significance transcends these roots and establish an ahistorical characteristic of a text which is to be correlated, significance-wise, to that of Sindbad's. we are here in company of universal values which though initially a product of history, appeal for timelessness.

These narrative differences, however, do account for a significant variance in the education of the two protagonists which in both means knowledge and growth acquired through experience. Criticism on this subject is diverse. Most critics who have written on **"Sindbad the Sailor"** have failed either to see any moral significance in Sindbad's stories apart from entertainment, or to consider Sindbad as a character that morally matures at the end of his travels. In *A Journey into* One Thousand Nights and One Night, Al-Mallah finds the *Arabian Nights*' stories "lacking in presenting any moral or education" (226, my translation). Eissa Mal-Allah, however, asserts that **"Sindbad the Sailor"** is an "artistic presentation of a portrait of a man who is industrious, rigorous, and hungry for knowledge" and "on top of that," the narrative "is to be classified as a great artistic presentation of fantastic literature at its best" (381, my translation). On the other hand, Cooley wonders whether Huck's "knowledge of the world grows in any consistent way." He goes on to say that "Huck's narrative might properly be viewed as a sequence of assaults upon his innocence rather than a sure progress toward a healthy maturity" (ix). Contrary to this view, Hill and Blair assert that although Huck Finn "does not grow up physically in the book," he "does mature morally, and does reach the point of revolting against the mores of ante-bellum slave-holding society" (16). The same view is expressed by Mark Altschuler. Basing his argument on theoretical matters of psychological moral development, he states that although Huck is a "motherless" and "isolated child" with "neither well-developed cognitive skills nor solid perceptions of social reality," he "does in fact develop morally" (32).

In the final analysis, both Sindbad and Huck repeatedly participate in epistemological tests to correct their tentative ideas and ideals by facing illuminating facts about man, life, and society, and both do grow from innocence to knowledge through their teaching experiences, which essentially include moral, social, and individual strata. While Sindbad's education is experiential and expedient, Huck's is experimental and moral. Sindbad grows up into empirical knowledge about success, social eminence and social norms; Huck into moral knowledge of himself and the world around him.

During his journeys, Sindbad imbibes many vital truths about life in general and human nature in particular. He realizes that benevolence and generosity are the ultimate bases of human conduct, a truth which absolutely contrasts with what Huck learns about human nature. Sindbad discovers, moreover, that honest money is never lost, and that the more precious the thing is, the more unattainable it becomes. What makes detecting the process of Sindbad's education difficult is that what he learns from his experiences is not directly stated in the text but rather implied in action. The only time we have a direct reference to his education is, strangely enough, at the very beginning of the narrative, where the poor mainland Sindbad, a mere laborer who has never known the sea, utters a few verses in which he laments his exceedingly destitute and miserable state, to which Sindbad the Sailor answers back also in verses:

> Acquiring sublimities is commensurate with great toil
>   And he who would seek eminence should stay
>   awake all night
> He who would seek pearls should dive into the sea
>   And by that obtain supremacy and favors
> And he who would seek eminence without toil
>   Would waste a life-time seeking the impossible.
>
> (139)[2]

Sindbad the Sailor expostulates to his desperate mainland counterpart that it is futile for one to laze about doing nothing and then ask Providence to shower one with the treasures of the world. Only by good work and persistent toil can man change his state from utter deprivation to one of absolute success and eminence. This truth is what Sindbad's seven travels confirm, and is what he wants his mainland guest to perceive. The need to reveal it finally prompts Sindbad to narrate his fantastic life story to his impoverished friend. In the closing episode, Sindbad's counterpart not only acknowledges Sindbad's right to prosperity after going through so many hardships and demonstrating shrewdness and tact, but also endorses Sindbad's views, which Sindbad has learned from his experiences, that social inequality is inevitable in a universe where only perseverance and prudence lead to affluence.

On the other hand, the process of Huck's moral growth is most emphatically indicated by his decision, made on two separate occasions, to free Jim from slavery. The first moral decision occurs early in the novel when he and Jim are heading down the river towards Cairo. The closer they come to Cairo, the more troubled and anxious he becomes. The more Huck thinks of himself as an abolitionist, the more base and corrupt he feels. Twain vividly chronicles Huck's conflict:

> Jim said it made him all over trembly and feverish to be so close to freedom. Well I can tell you it made me all over trembly and feverish, too, to hear him, because I began to get it through my head that he *was* most

free—and who was to blame for it? Why, *me* . . . It got to troubling me so I couldn't rest . . . I tried to make out of myself that I warn't to blame, because I didn't run Jim off from his rightful owner; but it warn't no use, conscience up and says, every time, "But you knowed he was running for his freedom, and you could a paddled ashore and told somebody." That was so—I couldn't get around that, noway. That was where it pinched.

> (73)

This moral torment shows the extent to which Huck's mind is pervaded by the mores of his slave-holding society. When Jim speaks of his plans to steal his children from their owner, Huck is horrified by his talk. To him, this is the consequence of violating the laws of society. At this stage, he is unable to see that Jim, as a human being, has rights to his children. Paddling off to see if they have indeed reached Cairo, Huck has an opportunity to turn in Jim. Instead, he moves firmly to protect him by inventing a story that the man on the raft is his father, who is critically inflicted with smallpox, a story he knows will keep the two gun-men from capturing Jim. When Huck returns to the raft, he is still "feeling bad and low, because I knowed very well I done wrong . . ." (74). To free his conscience, he has to free himself from the lamentable moral deformity of his society. He has to learn how to accept and respect Jim as a human being. In other words, Huck has to learn how to define his identity and confirm his individuality.

Huck's moral anxiety contrasts with the moral acquiescence of Sindbad, whose individuality is determined by his society's religious and ethical codes. Unlike Huck, Sindbad does not suffer from moral conflicts. In the fourth voyage, for example, when the pragmatically perceptive Sindbad is buried alive with his dead wife, he feels remorse neither towards killing his buried-alive comrades nor towards stealing their bread and jewelry. Sacrificing the life of a human being does not impinge upon his conscience. It is an action justified by the law of survival which is an accepted norm in his culture. The psychologically perceptive Huck, on the other hand, goes through a long process of self-education and self-definition which proceeds slowly though a series of illuminating adventures effected by his movement between the shore and the raft, and which culminates in his second and final moral decision to steal Jim from captivity.

Huck's adventures with the phantasmagorial world on the shore reveal to him examples of the depravity and degradation of man to the point that he is nauseated with and "ashamed of the human race" (131). These outlandish shore adventures, however, are instrumental for the growth of his moral consciousness. The more Huck encounters cruelty and corruption on the shore, the more he recognizes Jim's profound humanity and the purifying reality of the raft. Jim's self-sacrifice and compassion, his love and care for Huck are always put in contrast with the cruel and mean-spirited behaviour of the white masters on the shore. This opposition, unmasks to Huck the hypocrisy, violence, and pretense which pervade Southern society. It also stresses that white skin does not justify claims of superior virtue and affirms, as well, the worthiness of the individual regardless of colour, possession, or education.

On the raft, Huck finally embraces the fact that Jim is a sensitive, loyal and loving human being. On Jim's grieving for his family, he amazedly comments: "I do believe he cared just as much for his people as white folks does for their'n. It don't seem natural, but I reckon it's so. . . . He was a mighty good nigger, Jim was" (125). Their shared experience in nature enables Huck to discover aspects of Jim's nature which otherwise would have remained undiscovered by him. Huck's comment here displays growth, but his moral metamorphosis is not yet complete. Slowly but steadily, Huck will learn to acknowledge Jim's right to freedom and individuality.

This climactic moment constitutes Huck's second and final moral decision in favor of Jim. He arrives at this decision through strained wrestling with his conscience whether to help Jim escape or to write to Miss Watson and let her know of Jim's whereabouts. Rehearsing his odyssey with Jim, he irreversibly decides "to go to hell" (169) rather than keep Jim a slave for the rest of his life. Huck's decision is obviously a moral regeneration. By siding with the humanity of Jim, he transcends the moral limitations of his white society and embraces a code of living in keeping with the American tradition that stresses the worthiness of the individual.

Huck's personal ethics determines his ultimate and final decisions, whereas Sindbad's is determined by his culture. One can say, therefore, that the impact of sociocultural norms on both characters does not include historical factuality, for these norms are predominantly addressed above and over, rather than within, historicity. History, if at all, remains part of the socio-educational canvases of the two texts, for both are in a profound sense ahistorical, and the two central characters, in no sense portrayed as representatives of a given history, are essentially and referentially cultural figures. If Huck is to be viewed as a person in conflict with the prevailing values of his society, Sindbad is an ideal embodiment of his culture. Nevertheless, Huck's nonconformity, his self-reliance, is indeed an outstanding trait of American culture. The Arabian Sindbad's culture undergoes no contradictions with itself, and no longer appears to have unanswered questions morally and ontologically. Its firm moral and ideological stability emanates from an unshakable belief in an unequivocal world order in which even fantasy and fantastic action are taken for granted. Sindbad's moral world,

therefore, is an affirmation, Huck's, on the other hand, is an exploration. It is a world which is tentative, individual and still in the making. Accordingly, the Arabian Sindbad succeeds in reintegrating himself in society; his American counterpart fails to find an appropriate "land" for moral settlement. He realizes society is irredeemable. What is left for him, therefore, is to re-embark on a quest of self-education and self-restoration. Sindbad's objectives are Huck's rejections, though both consider self-exploration as the only mode of existence and meaningful life. Huck therefore, has "to light out for the territory ahead of the rest" (229). He must be an eternal traveler on a perpetual never-ending journey. In contrast, Sindbad, like a rehabilitated Ishmael, seems to stretch on his divan ready to narrate his life story.

Notes

1. All references to "Sindbad the Sailor" are my translation of the Arabic text of *Alf Layla Wa Layla* [*One Thousand Nights and One Night*]. By Arabic classical standards of criticism, the *Arabian Nights* is not a "literary" text, and as such it produces subtleties unfamiliar to a non-native speaker. Marked by a total absence of any punctuation system, the whole composition is in slang, and comprehensible only to readers in the then Arab Islamic empire. As Robert Irwin points out, "all translation from Arabic poses a range of problems not encountered in translations from European languages and translating the *Nights* [*The Arabian Nights*] poses quite specific difficulties" (9). Investigating this textual aspect of the *Nights* is, consequently, virtually impossible in the present paper.

2. A traditional Arabic poem follows a rigorous, formal and rhyming pattern based on a two-hemistitch line as the smallest unit of meaning and imagery which contains no punctuation of any kind.

Works Cited

Altschuler, Mark. "Motherless Child: Huck Finn and a Theory of Moral Development." *American Literary Realism* 22.1 (1989): 31-42.

Al-Mallah, Abd Alghani. *Journey into One Thousand Nights and One Night.* n.p.: Arabic Association Press, n.d.

Campbell, Joseph. *The Hero with a Thousand Faces.* Princeton: Princeton UP, 1968.

Clemens, Samuel Langhorne. *Adventures of the Huckleberry Finn.* Eds. Sculley Bradley et al. New York: W. W. Norton & Company, Inc., 1977.

Cooley, Thomas. "Preface to the Second Edition." Bradley Sculley *et al.,* ix-xi.

Eliot, T. S. "Mark Twain's Masterpiece." Inge 103-11.

Fishkin, Shelly Fisher. *Was Huck Black?: Mark Twain and African-American Voices.* Oxford: Oxford UP, 1993.

Fowzi, Hussein. *Sindbad in a Car.* Cairo: Dar Al-Hilal, 1972.

Hill, Hamlin and Walter Blair. "The Composition of Huckleberry Finn." Inge 15-21.

Inge, Thomas M., ed. *Huck Finn among the Critics: A Centennial Selection 1884-1984.* Washington D.C.: Forum Series, 1984.

Irwin, Robert. *The Arabian Nights: A Companion.* London: The Penguin Press, 1994.

Jones, Bently. "Huck and Jim: A Reconsideration." Leonard *et al.* 154-72.

Knoepflmacher, U. C. "Roads Half-taken: Travel, Fantasy, and Growing up." *Proceedings of the Thirteenth Annual Conference of Children's Literature* (1986). 48-59.

Leonard, James, *et al.,* eds. *Satire or Evasion: Black Perspectives on Huckleberry Finn.* Durham: Duke UP, 1992.

Mallah, Eisa M. A. *Literature of the Arabs in the East: Its Origins and Developments within the End of the 8th-Century Hijri.* Baghdad: Al-Ershad Press, 1978.

Sculley, Bradley et al. *Huckleberry Finn.* ix-xi.

"Sindbad the Sailor." *Alf Layla Wa-Layla* [*One Thousand Nights and One Night*]. Vol. 3. Beirut: Al-Maktabah Al-Thaqafiyah, 1981.

Todorov, Tzvetan. *The Fantastic: A Structural Approach to a Literary Genre.* Trans. Richard Howard. Ithaca: Cornell UP, 1975.

Trilling, Lionel. "The Greatness of Huckleberry Finn." Sculley *et al.* 318-28.

Wallas, John. "Case Against Huck Finn." Leonard *et al.* 16-24.

Daniel Beaumont (essay date spring 1998)

SOURCE: Beaumont, Daniel. "'Peut-on . . .': Intertextual Relations in *The Arabian Nights* and Genesis." *Comparative Literature* 50, no. 2 (spring 1998): 120-35.

[*In the following essay, Beaumont applies Sigmund Freud's concepts of displacement and humor to underscore common thematic concerns in "The Story of the First Sheikh," "The Merchant and the Jinn," and the biblical book of Genesis.*]

PSYCHOANALYSIS AND THE INTERTEXT

After showing in *The Interpretation of Dreams* how the processes of condensation and displacement operate in the "dream text," Freud moved further afield and in *The*

Psychopathology of Everyday Life and *Jokes and Their Relation to the Unconscious* ambitiously used the same principles to explain other seemingly "normal" mental processes, among them forgetting and jokes. Since every scheme Freud put forth to explain the mind was fundamentally dualistic, psychoanalysis as a form of reading and interpretation has always been concerned with "intertextual" relations no matter how one designates the two psychic "texts"—whether one calls them "primary" and "secondary," "latent" and "manifest," or "unconscious" and "conscious." This fact alone would make psychoanalysis a "science of tropes" in Harold Bloom's words, something noticed by readers of Freud as diverse as Trilling and Lacan. Moreover, the recognition of a certain correspondence between Freud's concepts of condensation and displacement and Jakobson's definitions of metaphor and metonymy has led to theories of narrative that equate these processes with the categories of similarity and difference that for a formalist like Todorov always operate in narrative.[1] The theory that Peter Brooks lays out in "Freud's Masterplot" is probably the best known example in this regard, though others with a more Lacanian bent have also been put forth.

My intention here is to show how the concepts of condensation and displacement can be used to explain the intertextual relations of different narratives. To do so, I will use two different methods to read stories from *The Thousand and One Nights* and Genesis against each other. I use the first method, which might be called "philological," to understand how **"The Story of the First Sheikh,"** a medieval Arabic narrative, takes up and revises the story of Abraham in Genesis 11-25. The two stories are clearly related by plot, though the question remains as to how much of the revision can be attributed to conscious artistic changes to the biblical plot by the medieval Arab storyteller, and how much to the prior activities of Muslim traditionists and theologians engaged in the reinterpretation of Jewish materials in the early Islamic era. In any case, the relation between the two stories has not, to my knowledge, been recognized by anyone recently—by which I mean since the Middle Ages. The second method could be called "postmodern" in that it creatively brings together two texts that most likely have had no prior connection, **"The Merchant and the Jinn"** in *The Thousand and One Nights* and the story of Tamar, Er, Onan and Judah in Genesis 38.

Insofar as the first way of reading presupposes that one or more "storytellers," "traditionists"—or whatever you might wish to call someone who unravels an old yarn to spin a new one—knew the kinship of the two stories, we can think of it as a kind of "canny" reading; that is, it brings together two narratives that belong together because of a literary, cultural and historical connection. The second method of reading, on the other hand, brings together two narratives on the basis of a similarity that is purely coincidental, and this might be called "uncanny" in that certain coincidences stir an uncanny feeling. For as Freud says, "we attach no importance to the event when we hand in an overcoat and get a cloakroom ticket with the number, let us say, 62; or when we find that our cabin on a ship bears that number. But the impression is altered if two such events, each in itself indifferent, happen close together—if we come across the number 62 several times in a single day . . . We do feel this to be uncanny" (17:237-38). Similarly, the coincidental and "uncanny" intertextual relations between these narratives encourages us to seek out thematic connections between them, comparing one to the other in order to understand each story more completely. More importantly, this endeavor juxtaposes the two works in the form of a joke as the processes of condensation and displacement work together to create a new text. Thus, while the general model of condensation and displacement Freud describes in *The Interpretation of Dreams* provides an apt analogy for intertextual relations in a philological reading, the structure of the joke provides the best analogy for a creative postmodern reading.

"THE STORY OF THE FIRST SHEIKH"

"The Story of the First Sheikh" is told in the course of **"The Merchant and the Jinn."** In **"The Merchant and the Jinn"** a merchant inadvertently kills the son of a jinn, and three sheikhs, each leading an animal or two on a rope, ransom his life by telling stories to the jinn. The first sheikh, who leads a gazelle on a rope, tells the jinn, "This is my wife." His story goes like this:

When his wife after thirty years of marriage has still not given him a son, the sheikh takes a mistress. Soon enough the mistress gives birth to a son. While the sheikh is away, the wife casts spells on the mistress and the son, turning the mistress into a cow and the son into a calf. When the sheikh returns, his wife tells him that the mistress has died and the son has run away. She then persuades him to have his herdsman slaughter the cow/mistress for a feast day, despite the husband's misgivings about the cow's somewhat unusual behavior. This turns out to be a bad decision, for despite her healthy appearance the cow mysteriously yields nothing but skin and bones. Thus, when his wife tries to convince him to kill the calf/son the sheikh resists. Instead he tells his herdsman to take the calf home. Now the herdsman's daughter is also skilled in magic and sorcery, and when she sees the calf she hides her face, laughs, then cries. She tells her father that the calf is his master's son whom the wife has bewitched. That was why she laughed. She cried because the wife had contrived to get the mistress slaughtered. The herdsman takes his daughter to the sheikh, and the girl proposes to remove the spell if she can take the son for her husband and be allowed to cast a spell on the wife. The

sheikh agrees. The herdsman's daughter marries his son and turns his wife into a gazelle. Some years pass, the sheikh's daughter-in-law dies, and his son wanders off to a foreign land. The sheikh leaves home to search for him, and it is on this journey that he comes upon the merchant awaiting his death at the hands of the jinn. The jinn says that this is a most amazing story, and he agrees to give the sheikh the right to a third of the merchant's blood.

Here I will assert a biblical "hypotext" whose intertextual presence has been unrecognized, at least in our era. **"The Story of the First Sheikh"** recalls the story of Abraham in several important respects, especially when medieval Islamic versions of that story are taken into account. The wife does not give birth to a son, à la Sarah, and so the sheikh, like Abraham, takes a mistress who does bear a son for him, à la Hagar. The sheikh's son is almost sacrificed on what the text calls *'îd Allâh al-akbar*.[2] This is *al-'îd al-kabîr*, the tenth day of the month of *Dhû 'l-hijja*. This feast, which marks the end of the pilgrimage season, commemorates the sacrifice of Abraham—and the near sacrifice of his son. Here, however, we must note a divergence from the story as it is familiar to the reader of Genesis. Among early Muslim authorities there was a dispute as to which son, Ishâq/Isaac or Ismâ'îl/Ishmael, Abraham intended to sacrifice, some authorities maintaining that there was a Jewish cover-up, that it was really Isma'il, ancestor of the Arabs. By the later Middle Ages, when *The Thousand and One Nights* had assumed the form close to what we now know, the consensus among medieval Muslims was that it was not Isaac/Ishaq, but Ishmael/Isma'il that Abraham was called upon to sacrifice. And indeed there is no confusion in our story; it is the son of the concubine, and so, we may say, it is Hagar's son Isma'il who is almost sacrificed. At the same time, Isaac/Ishaq is wholly absent, a striking effect about which more will be said later.

These similarities make it clear that we are reading a revision or, better, a "rescription" of a biblical story, for as a rescription is a reply by a Pope or emperor to a letter sent him, so too the medieval Arabic version, precisely because of its revisions, can be seen as a reply to the biblical version. The principle intertextual relations between the two stories can be described as a series of condensations and displacements. The first sheikh and his wife are condensations of Abraham and Sarah; the mistress and her son are condensations of Hagar and Ishmael. Perhaps more interesting are the displacements that have occurred. First and foremost, the sacrifice is not demanded by God, but by the jealous wife—in whom also loom all the evil step-mothers of countless stories. The curious ending of the story shows another important displacement. As a comic tale, the story should predictably end with the marriage of the herdsman's daughter to the son of the mistress and the transformation of the wife into a gazelle. Yet the story does not end here, but goes on to narrate the death of the daughter-in-law and the subsequent departure of the son who wanders off into a foreign land, *bilâd al-Hind* or "the land of India" as the text has it. While this event is used to explain why the sheikh encounters the merchant and the jinn, it is hardly necessary for that purpose; he could very well have been on a business trip such as the one he took earlier when his wife bewitched the mistress and the son. But **"The Story of the First Sheikh"** tells us that the sheikh *searches* for his son, and a glance at the biblical story of Abraham suggests why.

In the biblical tale when Sarah sees Isaac and Ishmael playing together one day, she says to Abraham, "Cast out this slave woman with her son; for the son of this slave woman shall not be heir with my son Isaac" (Genesis 21:10). Abraham hesitates, but God insists that he get rid of them. He leaves them in the desert, where they almost die of thirst, but God shows them a spring of water. Then they wander off into the wilderness of Paran, where Ishmael becomes father of the Arabs (in a kind of biblical footnote), while Isaac becomes the father of the Jews. We hear nothing more about Ishmael until the appearance of Islam—the return of the repressed, so to speak.

Readers unfamiliar with Islamic tradition may not realize the importance of Abraham to a polemic with Judaism in which Muslims claim Abraham as "the first Muslim." Medieval Muslim apologists exploited the fact that Abraham (Ibrâhîm in the Arabic) was not a Jew—there were no "Jews" yet—but only a Semitic monotheist, and therefore, to their way of thinking, the first Muslim. Crucial revisions to the biblical account follow from this. In Muslim tradition, Abraham does not simply send Hagar and Ishmael packing; he follows them into Arabia, where he founds the sanctuary at Mecca. After this bold stroke, the claim that the son that Abraham was called upon to sacrifice was not Isaac (Ishâq) but Ishmael (Ismâ'îl) follows as an obvious corollary, asserted simply on the basis of the "corruption" of the Torah—corruptions Muhammad was sent to correct. At length, after completing his work in Arabia, Abraham does return to resume his biblical tasks, but the crucial point has been made. As Michael Cook puts it, these revisions of the biblical story "endow Arabia and the Arabs with an honoured place in monotheist history, and one geneologically independent of the Jews and Christians" (38). In other words, through the paternity of Abraham, the younger offspring, Islam, makes a claim to *displace* the older one, Judaism—a nice ironic reversal of Isaac's displacement of Ishmael, but one consistent with numerous other examples in Genesis, as Robert Alter insists.

In any event, we can see now that the curious departure of the sheikh's son not only provides motivation for the

sheikh's trip, but also allows an important revision of the earlier biblical narrative. While in the Hebrew Bible Abraham reluctantly writes off Ishmael, in the Arabic tale Ibrâhîm now goes in search of Isma'il, "correcting" the record, so to speak. As already noted, biblical Isaac is absent from the Arabic tale; he is, from the Muslim standpoint, wittily ejected from the tale—or *foreclosed*, to borrow Lacan's term. That is, he is not repressed, but ejected from memory. His expulsion from the narrative can be seen as a rejoinder to the expulsion of Ishmael in the biblical story and also as a displacement of that event. The "expulsion of the brother," is, in effect, split and "overdetermined" insofar as it occurs on two different levels of the text: once in the form of the son's wandering off to *bilâd al-Hind,* and a second time in the absence of Isaac. And yet, if we are aware of the intertextual relation to the biblical story, the absence of his presence is palpable, to borrow a notable phrase from the late Howard Cosell.

At least one key question remains, however: how much of this revision can be attributed to a medieval Arab storyteller in **The Thousand and One Nights** tradition and how much to the prior activities of traditionists and theologians engaged in working over Jewish materials in the early Islamic era. Since it seems unlikely that an ordinary storyteller would have had firsthand knowledge of the biblical story of Abraham, we can assume that in **"The Story of the First Sheikh"** he is working on narrative material that has already undergone many of the crucial revisions examined above. Indeed, this sort of narrative can be found in any of the medieval Arabic works of the *qisas al-anbiyâ'*, or "stories of the prophets" variety. The storyteller himself presumably excised the proper names, reset the story in its present setting, and gave the principles various occupations. He also added magic to the narrative, which here entails the transformation of people into and from animal forms. The storyteller's contribution might thus be compared to Freud's process of "secondary revision" in which the dream content undergoes further changes under the scrutiny of a "censoring agent"—though I would not want to push this analogy too far. For it is likely that the gradual transformation of biblical Abraham into the first sheikh was the work of many hands, more agents in any event than are usually at work in Freud's account of dream production.

A final word on Abraham may serve as transition here to the story of **"The Merchant and the Jinn."** He too may be overdetermined, since his presence can also be detected in the figure of the merchant in **"The Merchant and the Jinn,"** the frame story for **"The Story of the First Sheikh."** In that story the merchant obtains his reprieve by insisting that he must return home to pay his debts. Qur'ân 53:36 likewise emphasizes an "*Ibrâhîm alladhî waffâ*" (an "Abraham who upheld his obligations")—a parallel that suggests that Abraham looms behind both the first sheikh and the merchant, the story of whom we now take up.

"THE MERCHANT AND THE JINN"

"The Merchant and the Jinn" is the first story Shahr-azad tells King Shahriyar in order to win a day's reprieve, and while the story pleases King Shahriyar, scholars—perhaps we should not be surprised—have been more critical than this deranged despot. D. B. Macdonald writes in "The Earlier History of the *Arabian Nights*," "It has often been remarked that Shahr-azad certainly did not put her best foot foremost in her storytelling and that this first experiment of hers is in a different class entirely from the story of the fisherman and the jinni, which immediately follows" (376). Mia Gerhardt would seem to agree, for she says, "Shahrazad is given a surprisingly insignificant piece for a beginning" (402-3).

Given their low opinions of the story, both Macdonald and Gerhardt are at pains to explain its prominent position in the book. Macdonald declares the story to be "of a pronounced desert and Arabic type," and Gerhardt concludes that this explains its "place of honor." However, as Gerhardt notes, Macdonald's conclusion about the provenance of the story rests on a *hadîth,* or tradition about the prophet Muhammad, found in ash-Sharîshsî's thirteenth-century commentary on the *Maqâmât of al-Harîrî.*[3] Ash-Sharîshsî cites the *hadîth* (which Macdonald translates) to explain the word *khurâfa,* which by the thirteenth century probably meant something like a fictional narrative, perhaps with some fantastic elements.

In the *hadîth,* Muhammad's favorite wife 'A'isha asks him to tell her "the *hadîth* of *Khurafa,*" and Muhammad tells her a story about a man named Khurafa who is captured by three jinn and subsequently ransomed by three passers-by who tell three stories. The plot is that of **"The Merchant and the Jinn"**—with some differences. To begin with, the three stories told to ransom the man differ, despite a few common motifs, from those in **"The Merchant and the Jinn,"** though, as Macdonald tells us, two of these stories are found elsewhere in the *One Thousand and One Nights.* The story of the well that changes the sex of the person who drinks from it is found in **"The Seven Viziers,"**[4] and the story of the *sawîq* or parched meal that casts a spell on the person who eats it is found in **"Badr Bâsim."** The story of the bull—the weakest, I think—does not appear in the *Nights* [*The Thousand and One Nights*]. The number of jinn also differs from the number in **"The Merchant and the Jinn,"** but the most significant difference for our reading is that the jinns' capture of Khurafa in the *hadîth* is unmotivated, whereas the merchant incurs the wrath of the jinn in the version in the *Nights* by unwittingly killing the jinn's son.

Given the late medieval date of ash-Sharîshsî's commentary, there is no certainty that the *hadith,* an obvi-

ous fiction itself, served as the prototype for the story in **The Thousand and One Nights**; in fact, it cannot be ruled out that the latter served as the prototype for the *hadith,* or, a third possibility, that they had a common ancestor—or even a slew of them. But it doesn't really matter, since the notion of textuality operating here makes identifications such as "pronounced Arabic type" something of a fiction also. However, the *intertextual* question still occupies us as an example of the coincidental and "uncanny" connections characteristic of the second ("Postmodern") way of reading I outlined at the beginning of this essay. Let us examine the beginning of the story in more detail.

A merchant, in the course of a business trip, sits down to rest for a moment beneath a tree. He takes a crust of bread and a date from his bag and eats them.

> When he finished eating the date, he threw the pit away, and then, all of a sudden, there appeared a towering jinn brandishing a sword. He drew close to the merchant and said, "Stand up so that I can kill you as you have killed my son!"
>
> (10)

Many of the virtues of narrative style in **The One Thousand and One Nights** as a whole are apparent in this brief scene. The swift transitions between sexual acts and death found in the frame story are matched here by another such transition, in this instance from eating to death. This particular moment joins other disparate elements in the story as well: the visible and the invisible, the small and the great, the mundane (bread crusts and date pits) and the fantastic (a towering jinn), and, of course, life and death. The words of the jinn create for the reader a sense of wonder (though perhaps not fear) similar to that of the merchant: how on earth did the poor merchant kill the jinn's son? This, of course, is just what the merchant asks, and the jinn's reply is superb:

> When you ate the date and threw the pit, it entered my son's chest. Just like that—one moment he was walking, and then he died instantly!
>
> (10)

The jinn's reply is superb not because it is such a fine answer, for it only answers the merchant's question in a gross sense; it explains—sort of—how the jinn's son died. It is superb because as it explains it creates a new question that carries the narrative to a new level, creating a new tension in the narrative that will not be resolved. It cannot be resolved, since this "explanation" brings into relation two events and two realms that are incommensurable, which is a large part of the uncanny effect here. By the seemingly innocent act of casting aside a date pit, the mundane world is invaded by death—the death of the jinn's son, and for the merchant the prospect of his own imminent death. I should mention that the famous nineteenth-century Orientalist Edward Lane says the merchant *is* culpable, an opinion that rests on the custom of nineteenth-century Egyptian peasants saying, *"Destour!"*—which in familiar Egyptian usage means "permission" before they toss date pits away. The merchant's omission of this word makes him guilty in Lane's view. But the story predates this custom by at least half a millennium, and traditions that tell us of Muhammad throwing date pits make no mention of him uttering any precautionary formulas. Those unacquainted with Islamic law might be surprised that even the throwing of a date pit, trivial as it may seem, is a matter of law, but every action of Muhammad is potentially a matter of law and a model for all Muslims to imitate. Thus, in Ibn Hanbal's collection of traditions, the *Musnad,* we find a tradition in which we are told that the Prophet, "used to, when he ate [a date], throw the pit . . . He would put the pit on his index and middle finger and then throw it" (4: 189). This suggests that it is permitted to throw date pits without uttering *destour,* since tradition does not record any preemptive utterance by Muhammad in connection with this act.

Rather than seeking a way to convict the merchant of negligence, it is more profitable to read the story as being about the merchant's loss of innocence. For the power of the story, I think, derives from the way it reenacts that moment in the life of every human when he realizes that, despite his "innocence," simply by being alive his life is already forfeit. And, insofar as death is the necessary correlate of being an animal that reproduces itself, that "debt" is expressed in the story by the act of casting a seed on the ground. Thus, a seemingly trivial act, whose dire consequences are unforeseeable, may represent for us the intrusion of the "Real," as Lacan calls it, the Real being that order of experience that eludes the symbol or the image. An aspect of this can be seen in the way that the death in the story is present only when it is *told* by the jinn after the fact. The death of the son is not narrated as an event as such, on the level with the throwing of the date pit; the merchant only knows of it through language, through the words of the jinn. Yet the event is also comic—at least to the reader whose loan is not yet due.

Perhaps on this point a digression in response to Macdonald and Gerhardt may be allowed. Whether the provenance of this story could, in some limited sense, be called Arab and pre-Islamic (pace Macdonald) or non-Arab and non-Islamic, it must be admitted that the suddenness with which the world of the merchant is turned topsy-turvy is consonant with a management style favored by Allah in the Qur'an. Here I refer to the celebrated inscrutability of His will, which at times borders on mere capriciousness, a trait that might be considered in relation to the trickster-like aspects of Yahweh sometimes apparent in Genesis—although, as the Bible says, "Far be it from God, that he should do wickedness." That the jinn in his visible form should be

so huge, towering over the merchant as he does, and yet, when invisible, that he and his son should be so small that a date pit could kill one of them; that one and the same creature is now invisible, now visible, now tiny, now enormous and, of course, now alive, now dead—and, as with life and death, that there should be no intermediate stage: and that all these transformations are caused by nothing more than the casting of a date pit—all of these things are not inconsistent with a view of God's relation to the world found in the Qur'ân, especially in the more apocalyptic passages. Nor, for that matter, is it inconsistent with the divine narrative style in that book. Note for example the suddenness with which the "vanished people" are dispatched: "A shout claimed the evil doers and in the morning they were prostrate in their houses, as though they had never prospered there. Thamud denied their Lord. Gone are the people of Thamud" (Qur'ân 11:67-68).

Well, how does the merchant react to this event? He utters the expression used by Muslims on any occasion where the subject of death is broached: "I belong to God, and to Him I shall return. There is no strength or power save in God, the Great and Elevated." But the merchant's resignation that it is all a matter of God's will is no explanation—or, at least, it is no longer an explanation *for us,* for whom it amounts to saying nothing more than "just because." We are still left to wonder what is going on here. The episode is coherent as it stands, but it is rather like a dream which, as Freud says, "even if it is quite coherent . . . confronts our mental life as something alien, for whose origin one cannot in anyway account" (*Jokes* [*Jokes and Their Relation to the Unconscious*] 198). Or as a prominent nineteenth-century scholar of Arabic literature, Victor Chauvin, put it in his *Bibliographie des ouvrages arabes,* "Peut-on tuer avec des noyaux de dattes?" (7:23, n. 1) ("Can one kill with date pits?"). I will try to answer that question by means of a joke.

THE JOKE

If we compare **"The Merchant and the Jinn"** to the biblical story of Tamar, a resemblance in plot structure between the Arabic story and the episode of Onan and Tamar can be seen. This resemblance is no doubt the result of mere chance, and yet, due to the resemblance, the two narratives can be profitably read together. Their relation can be given the structure of a joke whose condensations and displacements cast light on the meanings of both stories. The similarity of the plot structure is readily apparent if we consider the first ten verses of Genesis 38, the story of Judah, his sons Er and Onan, and Tamar:

> It happened at that time that Judah went down from his brothers, and turned in to a certain Adullamite, whose name was Hirah. There Judah saw the daughter of a certain Canaanite whose name was Shua; he married her and went into her. And she conceived and bore a

son, and he called his name Er. Again she conceived and bore a son, and she called his name Onan. Yet again she bore a son, and she called his name Shelah. She was in Chezib when she bore him. And Judah took a wife for Er his first-born, and her name was Tamar. But Er, Judah's first-born, was wicked in the sight of the Lord and the Lord slew him. Then Judah said to Onan, "Go and perform the duty of the brother-in-law to her, and raise up offspring for your brother." But Onan knew that the offspring would not be his; so when he went in to his brother's wife he spilled the semen on the ground, lest he should give offspring to his brother. And what he did was displeasing in the sight of the Lord, and he slew him also.

(38:1-10)

This short biblical narrative is prologue to the story of Judah and Tamar. As Gerhard Von Rad writes in his commentary, the verses give "the reader the most necessary facts in a rather dry enumeration and without particular vividness . . . the narrator dispenses with all causes and motivations in this section and limits himself to giving the bare facts" (357). Robert Alter ties the incident to the recurrent theme in Genesis that the first-born are "losers" (6). The verses do not tell us what Er did, but in the midrash we are told that God killed him because "he ploughed on roofs" (792)—that is, he practiced anal intercourse. Onan's sin, however, is explicit in the biblical text; he refuses his duty under the institution of levirate marriage wherein the brother-in-law must marry the widow. The purpose, as Von Rad explains, is that, "The son begotten by the brother is then considered the son and heir of the deceased man, 'that his name may not be blotted out of Israel' (Deut. 25:6). But the practice has also been explained in the interest of preserving property" (358). As we all know, poor Onan's punishment is two-fold. First, he suffers the death penalty, and second—and what is worse, for he would have died anyway—he suffers the ignominy of his name becoming synonymous with an abomination he does not even commit.

Tamar, the name of Er's wife, is of course the Hebrew cognate of the Arabic word *tamra,* and has the same meaning in Hebrew, "date-palm" or simply "date." So let us say then that, like Onan, the merchant has taken the seed out of Tamar and thrown it on the ground, and, as Onan thus "slays Er's son," so too the merchant slays the jinn's son. Is **"The Merchant and the Jinn"** therefore a conscious revision of this biblical story as **"The Story of the First Sheikh"** is a conscious revision of the Abraham story? It seems not. For unlike the story of Abraham, which was central in medieval Islamic culture, the story of Judah, his sons and Tamar does not seem to be known—and yet the uncanny correspondence remains.

This resemblance has two bases. Essentially both episodes are variants of the same plot; both the merchant and Onan "kill" another's son and are sentenced to die

for this by a supernatural being. But the uncanny resemblance between the two episodes is a result of more than simply the plot; in considerable measure it derives from the role of the cognate *tamra* in both narratives. It is a kind of "involuntary repetition"; it seems mere chance, and yet the fortuitous link established by the word suggests that the story of the merchant could have been written, and can be read, as a comic revision of the Onan-Tamar story—as a joke, that is. In *Jokes and Their Relation to the Unconscious* Freud shows how the processes of condensation and displacement operate in the formation of jokes even as they do in dreams, and the reading here will attempt to explain the similarities between these two episodes in terms of a joke constructed upon various condensations and displacements. A whimsical task perhaps, yet this kind of reading will reveal other thematic links between the two stories and indeed show a similarity between Tamar and the date that surpasses the coincidence of the Arabic and Hebrew cognates.

While the two episodes share a common plot, the comic transformation of our hypothesized travesty depends on a piece of word-play; *tamra,* a word that comes to be a feminine name because of its auspicious meaning as a staple fruit in the Near East, is the linchpin that holds it all together. Its role here matches numerous examples cited by Freud in his chapter on joke techniques under the rubric of words with a "double-meaning." The transformation of Tamar the biblical girl to *tamra* the snack in the Arabic story is not, I should add, without precedent in medieval Arabic literature. For example, a medieval story by al-Hamadhânî uses the same plot as another story found in **The Thousand and One Nights,** the story of **"The Lame Young Man and the Barber,"** which is told in **"The Hunchback."** In that case the lovely daughter of a judge in the latter story is replaced by a bowl of stew in the story by al-Hamadhani, though no word play is involved in the transformation. In any event, this free hand with narrative material is found elsewhere.[5]

Once the transformation of Tamar to *tamra* is recognized, those of the other biblical figures can then be established in our comic version. As the date *condenses* Tamar the biblical heroine, so the merchant condenses the figure of Onan. The jinn is more problematic. On the one hand, it could be argued that he condenses Er. But taking the biblical narrative and the midrash together, we can see that Er either resists fathering a son by Tamar, or, at best, is an indifferent pervert. In either case, his ghost should have no bone to pick with Onan, who simply uses a different method to achieve the same result.[6]

Hence, I think our joke will gain interest if we consider the jinn as also, and perhaps more significantly, representing Judah and God, for a closer look at the biblical version reveals another similarity between the two tales.

As Von Rad notes, it seems clear that after the death of his first born, Er, and his second born, Onan, Judah's reluctance to marry his last son, Shelah, to Tamar results from a suspicion that Tamar bears some sort of curse; for marriage to Tamar has proved fatal for two of his sons. This likely is meant to exemplify the dangers of marrying outside one's tribe, for all three of Judah's sons are the product of his marriage to a Canaanite woman. In this case, insofar as he suspects Tamar of contributing to the deaths of Er and Onan, Judah is akin to the figure of the jinn insofar as the *tamra* has killed the latter's son. My insistence here on "stuffing" so many males into the figure of the jinn follows from the fact that part of what is at stake in both stories is male lineage; that is what concerns Judah—and God. Judah wants to see his line propagated through his sons, but to do so his sons must live. This is what he seems to hold against Tamar.

At this point, an interesting displacement resulting from the transformations of the simple plot in the Arabic story deserves closer scrutiny. In the larger biblical narrative of Judah, his sons and Tamar, there is thematic emphasis on the failure of first his sons and then Judah with respect to Tamar. But the Arabic tale is all about men seeking satisfaction under *lex talionis*. Thus, insofar as he invokes the law, the figure of the jinn really represents the law—the *nom du pere*. In this travesty, the claims of Tamar are lost; we no longer have a story about a woman and the brothers and father who fail her, we have a story now solely about men. "He done her wrong" becomes "he done him wrong." Thus, the *condensations* of various males in the jinn entail a *displacement* of the biblical theme. We will take up the question of Tamar and *tamra* in a moment. Here let us examine what we have created; the joke structure between the two texts might be diagrammed so:

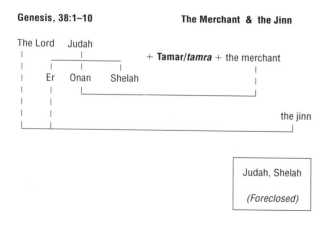

Genesis, 38:1–10

The Merchant & the Jinn

Judah, Shelah

(Foreclosed)

The value of the joke may now be seen. By transforming the girl Tamar into an object, *tamra* in the Arabic story, an important aspect of the biblical story becomes clear: Tamar is already an *object* in the biblical story, no less than the date, for they are both possessed by

men. As Von Rad says, the point of levirate marriage is that "the wife [of the deceased] is also a capital asset . . ." (358). So the joke highlights the problematic position of the woman in the Bible, in *The Thousand and One Nights,* and indeed in marriage in general. The problem is that in marriage the woman is exchanged like an object. But she is a special sort of object, one that also happens to be a subject, that is, a creature that speaks, and all the subsequent difficulties for Judah follow from this fact. She can invoke the law to Judah, who owes something for her, who owes a son-in-law to Tamar's father. Judah would like to forget the whole thing, but his "date" speaks. As Lacan writes: "The fact that the woman is thus bound up in an order of exchange in which she is object is really what accounts for the fundamentally conflictual character, I wouldn't say without remedy, of her position—the symbolic order literally subdues her, transcends her" (*Seminar, Book II* 262). Tamar is thus an object of exchange no less than the *tamra* can be one, and our joke's transformation of her simply strips her of her subjectivity. Yet we should note that, although the *tamra* in the Arabic story does not speak, it still has its effect. The *symbolic* effect of Tamar, the claim of the law in the biblical story, becomes in our travesty a *real* effect, the crushing effect of the date pit—which seems a strangely appropriate metaphor for the weight of the law.

Two other elements in the story also entail condensations and displacements of biblical motifs, although the motifs are not found in the Er-Onan-Tamar story, but elsewhere in Genesis. They are two words used to designate the place where the merchant meets the jinn, the *tree* and the *garden*. The story of **"The Merchant and the Jinn"** begins when the merchant sits down beneath a tree and eats some bread and dates. And then, when he returns on the first day of the new year to the same place, we are told, "he traveled until he arrived at that garden"—*al-bustân* (I:11). These two terms obviously link **"The Merchant and the Jinn"** not only with Genesis 2-3, but also with the frame story of *The Thousand and One Nights,* where the orgy of Shahriyar's wife and her twenty slaves and slave girls takes place in a garden, and the black slave with whom Shahriyar's wife couples climbs out of a tree. Subsequently Shahriyar and his brother Shahzaman hide from the jinn in a tree in a meadow (*marja*) with a spring, and beneath the tree the two have sex with the girl whom the jinn has kidnapped on her wedding night. Both the garden and the tree are obviously things "known of old and long familiar"—as Freud puts it in his essay "The Uncanny." In the frame story, as in Genesis 2:7-9, the tree marks a primal scene, a place where an originary violation occurs. This association seems to be played upon as well in **"The Merchant and the Jinn."** Insofar as the garden and the tree condense other gardens and trees, they signal that some sort of primal violation is to happen—though "violation" is perhaps not the best word to describe what happens in **"The Merchant and the Jinn,"** for it is really a matter here of things simply going awry.

CONCLUSION

The preceding discussion shows the viability of condensation and displacement for delineating intertextual relations in two different kinds of readings. As analytic instruments they can reveal heretofore unseen relations between narratives; in the case of **"The Story of the First Sheikh"** and the biblical story of Abraham, these intertextual relations may even suggest why the first of these stories is given "pride of place" in *The Thousand and One Nights.* If one considers that the frame story is based on products of Persia and India (as Cosquin showed a century ago), then the immediate introduction of an Arabic story that is a comic revision of Hebrew materials asserts the identity of the book in a most striking way, reenacting the manner in which Islamic culture borrows from all of these cultures to create cultural synthesis. The irony is that *The Thousand and One Nights*—rather like Ishmael, after all—became and has remained an outcast from the Arab-Muslim tradition that gave birth to it.

In the case of the second reading, these concepts reveal similarities in plot and theme between stories that are likely without any historical connection. Their efficacy in this regard stems from the power of abstraction that they bring to bear as concepts. As in the case of Tamar-tamra, they reveal how the word in its materiality, as Lacan calls it, functions in narrative.

Notes

1. Although it is true that Jakobson correlates them with synecdoche and metonymy in *Fundamentals of Language,* p. 95.

2. The Arabic text I am using is Macnaghten's 2nd Calcutta edition. The translations that follow are my own.

3. The *Maqâmât* are brief, rhetorically elaborate narratives that recount the repeated encounters of a gullible narrator with an eloquent trickster.

4. And Chauvin, *Bibliographie des ouvrages arabes,* p. 43, lists many other versions.

5. This and other such transformations are discussed in my article "A Mighty and Never Ending Affair" in *Journal of Arabic Literature.*

6. Incidentally, *coitus interruptus* is upheld by some Muslim jurists as permitted, *mubâh.*

Works Cited

Alf Layla wa Layla. Ed. William Macnaghten. Calcutta: Thacker, 1839.

Alter, Robert. *The Art of Biblical Narrative.* New York: Harper Collins, 1981.

Beaumont, Daniel. "A Mighty and Never Ending Affair." *Journal of Arabic Literature* 24.2 (July 1993): 139-59.

The Bible. Standard Revised Edition.

Bloom, Harold. *Agon.* New York and Oxford: Oxford University Press, 1982.

Chauvin, Victor. *Bibliographie des ouvrages arabes.* Vol. 7. Paris: H. Vaillant-Carmanne, 1902. 12 vols. 1892-1922.

Cook, Michael. *Muhammad.* London: Oxford University Press, 1983.

Cosquin, Emmanuel. "Le Prologue-cadre des mille et une nuits." *Études folkloriques.* Paris. 1922. 265-347.

Freud, Sigmund. *The Standard Edition of the Complete Psychological Works of Sigmund Freud.* Trans. James Strachey et al. 24 vols. London: Hogarth Press, 1953-74.

———. *The Interpretation of Dreams.* Standard Edition. Vols. 4 and 5. 1953.

———. *Jokes and Their Relation to the Unconscious.* Standard Edition. Vol. 8. 1960.

———. *The Psychopathology of Everyday Life.* Standard Edition. Vol. 6. 1960.

———. *An Infantile Neurosis and Other Works.* Standard Edition. Vol. 17. 1955.

Gerhardt, Mia. *The Art of Storytelling.* Leiden: E. J. Brill, 1963.

Ibn Hanbal. *al-Musnad.* Cairo (no date): Bulaq edition.

Jakobson, Roman and Morris Halles. *Fundamentals of Language.* The Hague and Paris: Mounton, 1971.

Lacan, Jacques. *Écrits.* Trans. Alan Sheridan. New York: W. W. Norton, 1977.

———. *The Seminar of Jacques Lacan, Book I: Freud's Papers on Technique 1953-1954.* Ed. Jacques-Alain Miller. Trans. John Forrester. New York and London: W. W. Norton, 1988.

———. *The Seminar of Jacques Lacan, Book II: The Ego in Freud's Theory and in the Technique of Psychoanalysis 1954-1955.* Ed. Jacques-Alain Miller. Trans. Sylvia Tomaselli. New York and London: W. W. Norton, 1988.

Lane, E. W. *The Arabian Nights.* 4 vols. London: Charles Knight & Co., 1838-41.

Macdonald, D. B. "The Earlier History of the *Arabian Nights.*" *Journal of the Royal Asiatic Society* 3 (July 1924): 353-97.

Midrash Rabbah. Ed. H. Freedman and M. Simon. Vol. 2. London: Soncino Press, 1951. 10 vols.

Qur'ân. Text in *Alfâz al-Qur'ân.* Ed. M. 'Abd al-Bâqî. Cairo: Dâr al-hadîth, 1987.

Von Rad, Gerhard. *Genesis: A Commentary.* Philadelphia: The Old Testament Library, 1972.

Judith Plotz (essay date spring 1998)

SOURCE: Plotz, Judith. "In the Footsteps of Aladdin: De Quincey's *Arabian Nights.*" *The Wordsworth Circle* 29, no. 2 (spring 1998): 120-26.

[*In the following essay, Plotz argues that Thomas De Quincey's version of the tale of Aladdin reflects both his disdain for Victorian-era children's literature and his complex personal relationship with William Wordsworth.*]

Thomas De Quincey is the most Scheherazadean of English writers. Borges glosses **The Thousand One Nights,** that "infinite book," through the comparable infinities of De Quincey (56); and Grevel Lindop's tributary poem to the one who knows "that there is a story opening / inside every other story, / and that of these it is given us to know / an infinite number, but still less than all" is dedicated not, as one might expect, to De Quincey but "To Scheherazade" (Caracciolo xxix). De Quincey himself reads and cites **The Arabian Nights** with avidity, even projecting an Arabian drama featuring his "Moor's last agonies," [Clej 137]. Above all, De Quincey shares the structural tactics of Scheherazade: both proliferate recursions, maddening editors and thwarting authoritative texts; both practice a "nocturnal poetics" privileging a pariah population of "Dionysiac . . . riffraff" (Ghazoul 151); both structure "arabesque" narratives (Sandra Naddaff's term) of "digressive but patterned movement"—figured by the caduceus, the involute, the labyrinth (Naddoff 112).

However close De Quincey may be to the infinite and labyrinthine spirit of the *Arabian Nights,* he deviates significantly from the letter in his most systematic consideration of an *Arabian Nights* tale, his strange dislocation of **"Aladdin"** in an 1851-52 essay on "Infant Literature" (*Collected Writings* 1.127-31). As best I have been able to determine, De Quincey's version of Aladdin resembles *no* version current in his lifetime.[1] "[The] most renowned story invented by man" (Dawood 132), **"Aladdin"** first came to Europe in Galland's translation of 1704-17,[2] and to England in the anonymous "Grub Street" translation of 1721-22 which was reprinted in numerous editions for more than a century. Of all the tales, **"Sinbad"** and **"Aladdin"** were most popular and most frequently issued separately. Though

De Quincey almost certainly read the Grub Street translation as a child,[3] it is possible that he later encountered either the Torrens (1838) or the Lane (1839-42) translations. He might also have attended one or more Aladdin pantomimes based on Aladdin that were performed for Christmas time at theaters throughout the U.K. The first such Aladdin pantomime was presented at Covent Garden in 1788, beginning a popular tradition that has lasted two centuries.

All 18th- and 19th-century Aladdins, *except De Quincey's,* follow the same pattern. (The summary that follows is based on multiple versions of **"Aladdin"** though all quotations are drawn from the Grub Street translation.) Aladdin, the "careless and idle" son of a poor Chinese tailor, Mustapha, has "many vicious habits . . . wicked, obstinate, and disobedient." Refusing to settle down to work at his father's trade, Aladdin hangs out with "blackguard boys and such little vagabonds as himself." "Mustapha chastised him, but Aladdin was incorrigible; and his father, to his great grief was obliged to abandon him to his libertinism." Mustapha dies of a broken heart but Aladdin, fifteen years old and bone-idle, lives off his widowed mother. One day an African magician, a talent spotter of young rogues, sees Aladdin and realizes his excellent potential for mischief. Passing himself off as an uncle, the Magician promises to make Aladdin's fortune, takes him to an isolated rural spot where he knows a lamp of power is hidden in a subterranean cavern. Aladdin, now wearing a special ring of power, is sent into the cavern whence he retrieves the lamp and lots of treasure. The rest is familiar—though protracted in the Galland version. Aladdin refuses to hand over the lamp unless he's helped out first. The magician gets testy, shuts Aladdin in the cavern, returns to Africa. Aladdin eventually gets out through the genie of the ring, eventually becomes rich through the genie of the lamp, eventually marries the king's daughter (this through a series of grossly cheerful tricks which involve locking a rival bridegroom all night in a freezing cold privy until his sexual member shrivels so he can't consummate the marriage). The magician, learning of Aladdin's triumph and treasure, returns to trick the princess through the "New Lamps for Old" gambit and carries the princess, lamp, and palace off to Africa. But Aladdin's ring enables him to recover palace, princess, lamp, and to foil both the magician (poison) and his brother, another magician (stabbing), and to live triumphantly as king for many happy years.

All 18th- and 19th-century Aladdins, in storybooks or on stage, share certain features: First, Aladdin is *Chinese* and the story is set in China. Most illustrated texts show Chinese characters and costumes and from 1813 the pantomimes heavily emphasize Chinese-ness. One frequently presented version calls Aladdin's mother the Widow CHING MUSTAPHA and the putative uncle

QUAM MUSTAPHA (1826). In the most famous of all Aladdin pantomimes. H. J. Byron's Opium-War-era 1861 version, the supernumeraries are Mandarins, the chief courtier Pekoe, and the widowed mother Widow Twankey (a brand of Green Tea—also slang for gin.)[4]

Second, Aladdin is a *layabout,* a feckless juvenile delinquent, not young, not good. Some epithets: "wicked, obstinate, disobedient" (1789 943); "shiftless, idle, incorrigible" (1793); "many vicious habits" (Newbury Moralist 1800-211); "graceless, illiterate" [1826], or "wilful" (1855), or "perverse and graceless from his earliest childhood," a "good-for-nothing" (Payne 1889). A breezy 1931 version describes Aladdin as "a young rip with a taste for the beau monde" (Clinton-Baddeley). Wealth eventually makes the adult Aladdin respectable—but too late to save Mustapha, dead of paternal heartbreak.

Third, Aladdin is *lucky*: his is a story about easy money. It is Aladdin's *effortless* wealth and power that explain the popularity of the Aladdin name as shorthand for ease and plenty. Thus the Aladdin title of a number of turn-of-the-20th-century get-rich-quick adventure novels: Max Pembleton's *Aladdin of London* (Polish mines); Herbert Quick's *Aladdin: A Romance of Yankee magic* (1904; a gilded era land grab scheme); *Aladdin in London* (1892; a ring of power and the Brahmin slaves of the ring give access to untold Indian wealth from a despoiled temple). Thus Aladdin's name betokens effortless prefabricated housing construction (as in *Instructions for the Erection of your Aladdin Home* from the Aladdin Company of Bay City, Michigan) and even miraculous economic schemes for universal prosperity such as Gorham Munson's *Aladdin's Lamp: The Wealth of the American People* (1945; Social Credit) and Ernest Greenwood's *Aladdin, USA* (1928; Unbridled de-regulation).

Finally, the story of Aladdin is cheerfully *comic,* both funny and triumphant. In its incarnations as a Christmas pantomime (and as a Disney film), **"Aladdin"** has generated multiple comic parts: melodramatically evil Abanazar the magician; his deaf-mute assistant Kasrac, played by the celebrated clown Joe Grimaldi; the lugubriously hysterical Widow Twankey. The story contains openings for broad humor as when Byron's Abanazor transports the palace to Africa and Widow Twankey contemplates the empty pit center stage:

Widow Twankey:

> Something's moved this house.

Aladdin:

> Indeed! Ha! Ha!
> Our jokes have often moved this house, mamma

(50)

This comic exuberance and the triumphant shape of the plot explain why an "Aladdin in Flanders" was produced by soldiers on the Western Front in 1915, and why Kipling's Indian army officers in *Stalky & Co.* can whip the fractious Pathans of the Northwest frontier while singing songs from their schoolboy production.

Though *all* 18th and 19th-century Aladdins are bad but lucky boys whose stories are comically triumphant, such triumphant comedy is antithetical to De Quincey's doleful redaction of the story he claims to have "despised" when he was six. Despite the foolish praise of Mrs. Barbauld, "queen of all the blue stockings":

> my sister and myself pronounced Sinbad to be very bad, and Aladdin to be pretty nearly the worst . . . in Aladdin, after the possession of the lamp has been once secured by pure accident, the story ceases to move. All the rest is a mere record of upholstery; how this saloon was finished today, and that window on the next day. . . .

(1.128)

In recapitulating the story he claims to had read at six, De Quincey omits as boring *all* the elements of Aladdin's triumph—escape, genies, treasure, marriage, rescuing the princess, killing the magicians, living in prosperity and power—and focuses instead on the "wicked" and "murderous" magician and the "innocent" and "solitary" Aladdin. De Quincey's Aladdin lives not in China (always wicked) but virtuously on the banks of the Tigris. Not a sociable Chinese adolescent hanging out "with other blackguards like himself", De Quincey's Aladdin is both "an innocent child" and "a solitary infant," the tender unique target of the magician's unique auditory surveillance. Unlike all other magicians who are masters both of "fumigation" and "geomacy" (divination by fire and smoke, divination by sand-casting) or—in the pantomimes—of a special "Book of Fate," De Quincey's sorcerer is a supreme auditor:

> Where shall such a child be found? . . . The magician knows: he applies his ear to the earth; he listens to the innumerable sounds of footsteps that at the moment of his experiment are tormenting the surface of the globe; and amongst them all, at a distance of six thousand miles, playing in the streets of Baghdad, he distinguished the peculiar steps of the child Aladdin. Through this mighty labyrinth of sounds, which Archimedes, aided by the *arenarius,* could not sum or disentangle, one solitary infant's feet are distinctly recognized on the banks of the Tigris, distant by four hundred and forty days march of an army or caravan. These feet, these steps, the sorcerer knows, and challenges in his heart, as the steps of that innocent boy, through whose hands only he could have a chance of reaching the lamp.

(1. 128-29)

De Quincey emphasizes that magician's interpretative terrorism can fasten a fixed and fixative "murderous attention" upon "one insulated tread" and "disarm Babel

. . . of its confusion," by deciphering the "secret hiero-glyphics uttered by the flying footsteps." Without moving his summary version beyond the poised balance of attentive hunter and fixed hunted, De Quincey leaves the Aladdin story as a vignette of a solitary child arrested in a static condition of terrified anticipation.

De Quincey's peculiar and terrifying Aladdin of solitary innocence pursued seems less peculiar within the context of the Wordsworth Circle reconstruction of childhood. Both in the corrective seizure of the narrative from Mrs. Barbauld and in the de-narrativized isolation of Aladdin, De Quincey is contributing to that continuing project.

As Mitzi Myers has suggested, developing the Romantic Child involved a forced repatriation of childhood, a kind of patriarchal kidnapping that wrested childhood away from the female sphere, i.e. children's writers such as Barbauld, Wollstonecraft, and Edgeworth, and sequestered it in a restorative realm of permanent difference. Using exactly the same manoeuver as Wordsworth, Coleridge, and Lamb in their discussions of *The Arabian Nights* for children, De Quincey opens his remarks on "infant literature" with a contemptuous conjuration of the most important children's writer of the era, Anna Letitia Barbauld (described as "A lady nearly forgotten") as well as a gratuitous smack at "Miss Edgeworth . . . now very nearly forgotten too" (1.127). (De Quincey makes the crowing claim that to identify Barbauld by a comparison to Edgeworth—both well-known purveyors of children's literature—is "to explain *ignotum per ignotius* or at least one *ignotum* by another *ignotum*" [1.127]) He further diminishes Barbauld by coolly attributing a title, the slightly adapted "Generous Revenge," from one of her well-told stories in *Evenings at Home* (1792-96) to a thematically-similar but crudely told "A Generous Return for an Injury," in Thomas Percival's *Parental Instructions* (1788), a work whose title De Quincey's tellingly recollects as *The Father's Assistant.*

The Wordsworth Circle complaint against Barbauld and Edgeworth as writers for children is familiar: these bare-and-bald lady writers whose lack of imagination is a sexual disability (women, De Quincey argues, like savages and orientals lack imagination)[5] privilege realism, moralism, and a forced maturity in damaging little tomes "which only told how Master Billy and Miss Ann spoke and acted . . . not only ridiculous but extremely hurtful" (Coleridge *Shakespearean Criticism* 2:293). Ignoring the distinction between childhood and adulthood, Barbauld and Edgeworth use their fictions—hardly fictions, little screeds of moral will and banal verisimilitude run wild—to bridge a gap which should not be bridged. Seeing childhood as *continuous* with rather than *distinct* from adulthood, Barbauld and Edgeworth are largely uninterested in the Child, in childhood

as a decontextualized *state* of being, and focus instead on social and ethical becoming. Their stories stage interactions among members of a family or other small communities in which children learn the life lessons that help them to function as self-regulated adults. Piaget has argued that what is often praised by Romantics as a childlike sense of wonder has more to do with an authoritarian family structure than the insights of the child's nature and that the habit of "cooperat[ion] with . . . equals" can make one who is a child chronologically an adult psychologically (80). In such an egalitarian spirit, Barbauld, Edgeworth, and Wollstonecraft model such self-legislating behavior for children and thus assimilate adulthood and childhood. But the Wordsworth Circle habitually deepens what Marie Corelli called "the enormous gulf of difference" (*Boy* 16) between child and adult worlds by characterizing childhood as an isolated "continent" (Scudder) or "island" (H. Coleridge) or "peninsula" (De Quincey).

De Quincey's Aladdin exemplifies the Romantic construction of "The new continent of childhood," childhood as a region of difference, a desired stable space of containment, recuperation, cure for adulthood (Scudder, *Childhood in Literature* 162-63). Aladdin, the unique designated innocent, like the habitual Wordsworth Circle Child, is a de-contextualized singleton, inhabiting a realm of difference, distance, and arrest. As the predestined object of the magician's irresistible ear, Aladdin is marked out and contained in what Hartley Coleridge described as "mute simplicity of passive being" by an adult desire. This arrest accords with the powerful Wordsworthian pattern evident in packs of solitary children, each one "single in the field" in one way or another. They can be "embalmed" in childhood like the Theater Child of *The Prelude*. They can be sequestered in their limitations like Wordsworth's Idiot Boy or the Blind Highland Boy or Hartley Coleridge's "Deaf and Dumb Little Girl" ("Herself her all, she lives in privacy . . . All her little being / Concentred in her solitary seeing"). Or they can be introjected within the inner space of an adult body as in Lamb's "superfoetations."

In De Quincey's version, Aladdin loses all his pert insolent individuality and becomes another faceless Romantic innocent with his back to us ("the hands of an innocent child" "the step of that innocent boy"), both archetypal and fungible like the innocent infants described by Hartley Coleridge at the last day: "All in one shape, one feature, and one size . . . alike all blessed, and alike all fair, / And only God remember who they were" ("To Little Katy Hill" *CP* [Hartley Coleridge *The Complete Poetical Works*] 191).[6] This erasure of personality is further enforced by De Quincey's refusal of narrative movement in an **"Aladdin"** that is more a predicament than a story. De Quincey's Aladdin never takes to his heels into a lived adventure but is held, contemplatively, a solitary textual readable being whose "secret hieroglyphics uttered by the flying footsteps" stand in need of reinterpretation. This repetitious contemplative arrest is essential to the production of the iconic Romantic Child, and is evident, for example, in Hartley Coleridge's repetitive lifelong performance of childhood, a performance including such key resistances to development as not finishing stories: "I care nothing about conclusions. A book must end somehow—with marriage or death or a nunnery. But the characters we love, the scenes we dwell in, end not, change not, die not. Robinson Crusoe is on the Island still, sometimes with poor Friday and sometimes all alone . . . and little Goody is still trudging about with her basket of letters, her lame Billy, and her raven Ralph" ("Untitled essay on books," HCP [The Hastley Coleridge Papers]).

De Quincey's Aladdin narrative is similarly truncated in an arrested character in a fixed scene, forever available as yet another solitary and helpless Romantic innocent, at once the prey, bait, and lost self of the reconnoitering adult reader.

But De Quincey's Aladdin is no mere recapitulation of the Wordsworthian Child. On the contrary, the redaction is an anti-Wordsworthian episode in De Quincey's life-saving autobiographical project. The Aladdin story bears all the marks of De Quincey's usual autobiographical pattern, notably the presence of the symbiotic mutually-tormenting autobiographical couple (the child as subject self, the adult as autobiographer; the child as textual cipher imprinting "hieroglyphics uttered by . . . flying footsteps," the adult as cryptographer deciphering them; the child as victim, the adult as criminal). The child subject here is the familiar child pariah, both hero and reader of a genre of literature, "Infant Literature," which De Quincey thematizes as pariah literature. The pariah pattern emerges not merely in the Aladdin story itself but in the two flanking examples of children's literature—a Latin tag about Aesop ("*Aesopo statuam ingentem posuere Attici; / Servumque collocarant eterna in basi.*" "*A colossal statue did the Athenians raise to Aesop; and a poor pariah slave they planted upon an everlasting pedestal*"),[7] and Thomas Percival's worm-turning sado-masochistic little story of "noble revenge" in which a soldier humiliated by an unprovoked blow from his officer is so gallantly selfless in battle that he humiliates the abusive officer by his magnanimity.

Within this pariah pattern, the Aladdin tale functions, I would argue, to carry out another such a "noble revenge" by De Quincey-Aladdin against Wordsworth-Magician, finally, in 1851, safely dead. Though complexities of the Wordsworth-De Quincey relationship have been frequently explored this veiled and violent account complicates matters further. Opening with a quotation from Wordsworth: "*The child*," says Wordsworth, "*is father of the man,*" De Quincey establishes Wordsworth as the great talent-spotter of childhood,

"the first person to notice" childhood as a privileged state on its "distinct peninsula"; the first to notice that childhood "is endowed with a special power of listening for the tones of truth" (1.122). A master "of all the mighty world / Of eye, and ear" ("Tintern Abbey" 105-6), himself endowed with this "special power of listening," Wordsworth prefigures the Magician's auditory fear. Just as De Quincey's African sorcerer (unique among all magicians and dervishes of the Aladdin tradition) sunk in the depths of Africa "applies his ear to the earth to distinguish the peculiar steps of Aladdin" walking the streets of Baghdad, so on one memorable night on Dunmail Rise during the Peninsular War, Fall 1808, did De Quincey watch Wordsworth "applying his ear to the ground, so as to catch the sound of wheels that might be groaning along at a distance" with the news from the rim of Europe (*Recollections of the Lakes . . .* 160). This explicit connection of Wordsworth and the Magician is also implicit in the two couples: as Aladdin is to the Magician, so De Quincey is to Wordsworth.

Key to every Aladdin story is the symbiosis of Magician and Aladdin: both seek the same treasure; neither can obtain the treasure without the help of the other. Wordsworth was the magician whose divinations revealed to De Quincey the treasure he wished and for which he felt a prefigured, destined affinity, "a peculiar destiny written in his constitution." From the time of De Quincey's earliest reading of Wordsworth, he was drawn as by a "deep, deep magnet" (3:283) to the poet who both "*delivered*" (Jordan 37) him and (he insisted) deeply resembled him. It is impossible to overstate the insistent affinity De Quincey felt between himself and Wordsworth as pariahs,[8] as elegists of sisterly affliction, as contemplative rural solitaries dedicated to "some great intellectual project, to which all intellectual pursuits may be made tributary" (Page 108).[9]

Wordsworth seemed to possess in the highest degree the life-treasures De Quincey most desired: "he has possessed, in combination, all the conditions for their most perfect culture—the leisure, the ease, the solitude, the society, the domestic peace, the local scenery—Paradise for his eye . . . Paradise for his heart. . . . (*Recollections* 195). But, as his early list of the twelve heavily Wordsworthian constituents of happiness suggests, De Quincey temperamentally, by "a peculiar destiny written in his constitution," was predisposed to desire the treasures Wordsworth already enjoyed. The sense of symbiosis was so powerful that De Quincey could not distinguish what was innately "written on his constitution" and what had been written there by Wordsworth: had he invented Wordsworth, or had Wordsworth invented De Quincey? In fantasy, De Quincey assumed that Wordsworth felt as murderously entitled to De Quincey's property as De Quincey had felt towards Wordsworth's intellectual property:

so true it is, that still, as Wordsworth needed a place or a fortune, the holder of that place or fortune was immediately served with a summons to surrender it—so certainly was this impressed upon my belief, as one of the blind necessities, making up the prosperity and fixed destiny of Wordsworth, that for myself—had I happened to know of any peculiar adaptation in an estate or office or mine. to an existing need of Wordsworth's—forthwith, and with the speed of a man running for his life, I would have laid it down at his feet. 'Take it,' I would have said—'Take it—or in three weeks I shall be a dead man.'

(*Recollections* 297)

This pursuing Wordsworth regards as his own the "fortune" which sustains De Quincey's own productive life—including perhaps the pilfered *Prelude* (the unauthorized copies I am convinced De Quincey made in 1810-11 of the manuscript); perhaps the loan of a "new lamp for old," little Katherine in place of lost Elizabeth, that "lamp lighted in paradise [that] was kindled for me which shone so steadily in thee" (*CEOE* [*Confessions of an English Opium-Eater and Other Writings*], *Suspiria* 101). Whatever power came to De Quincey through the Wordsworth connection, he was able to use that power only after the break, after the flight from the enchanter. As De Quincey's representation of his uniquely impotent Aladdin suggests, this exercise of power felt less like an achievement than a *theft*. In his **"Aladdin,"** De Quincey suggests that his own autobiographical project, the descent into the Aladdin cave of his own consciousness, has been enabled and compelled by Wordsworth, both his genius and his nemesis, worthy both of abject gratitude and noble revenge.

Notes

1. Although this 1851-52 account of his early reading, describes works De Quincey was reading in 1791-92, i.e. at 6 and 7, I have not confined my survey to versions of "Aladdin" that were circulating in the 1790s. Instead I have looked at versions extant any time during DQ [De Quincey]'s lifetime. There are hundreds of such versions but many are simply reprints of the Galland edition. I have carefully examined seventy-five versions—full texts, shorter children's versions, pantomime texts—and have leafed through more than a hundred more (enough to determine that they were mere reprints of the Galland edition).

2. The tale did not appear in earlier Arabic manuscripts and Galland is thought to have collected it from a "native informant," a Maronite from Aleppo. Clej 312 n27.

3. Although an abridged children's version, *The Oriental Moralist* appeared in 1791, Brian Alderson maintains that "The dominance of Galland's version for so long makes it almost certain that this is the edition that children [included DQ] would have read" (Caracciolo 83).

4. Byron's version leans heavily on tea jokes. Scene V, the engagement of Aladdin to the Princess of China, invokes riotous tea-drinking revelry:

> EMPEROR:
>> Now then, let all be revelry and joy;
>> Let tea from every fountain flow till late.
>> And Mandarins put on their robes of state.
>> Let all the rich confectionery shops,
>> Dispense for nothing their best lollipops;
>> Let all the public sights be opened free;
>> Pekin be wrapped in universal spree.
>> Death to the publican who makes tea weak;
>> Let the tea kettle to the trumpet speak,
>> The trumpet to the cannonier without:—
>> Now the king drinks to young Aladdin!
>
> WIDOW TWANKEY:
>> Shout!

(The assembled company breaks into cheers. MANDARINS appears bearing cups of tea which are served to one and all. ALADDIN is toasted and then bursts into song).

[41]

Byron's is the version performed by Kipling's "Slaves of the Lamp" in *Stalky & Co.*

5. Among his "False Distinctions," De Quincey includes:

> 1. *That women have more imagination than men.* . . . What work of imagination owing its birth to a woman can he lay his hand on?. . . . Who is the female Aeschylus, or Euripides, or Aristophanes? . . . where is Mrs. Shakespeare?—No, no! good women: it is sufficient honor that you produce *us*—the men of the planet—who produce the books (the good ones I mean). . . .
>
> 2. *That the savage has more imagination than the civilized man:.* . . .
>
> 3. *That Oriental nations have more imagination . . . than those of Europe* . . . if savages betray the *negation* of all imaginative power (/=0), the Oriental nations betray the *negative* of that power (/= -).

6. Hartley Coleridge is particularly insistent that childhood always trumps individuality: "Let mutability, then, work its will / The child shall be the same sweet creature still" ("To KHI, the Infant Grandchild of a Blind Grandfather" *CP* 181-82).

7. De Quincey invokes the figure of Aesop through a slightly misremembered Latin tribute from Phaedrus. De Quincey erroneously quotes the first three words as *Aesopo statuam ingentem* / = a huge statue to Aesop instead of *Aesopi ingenio statuam* / = a statue to the genius of Aesop. The misquotation suggests a will to transform the tiny and puny into the colossal (he was a *very short* man) and to emphasize the difference between the hugeness of the statue and the lowliness of Aesop's position as "pariah slave."

8. De Quincey delighted to depict Wordsworth and Coleridge as scorned and rejected pariah artists—or rather as despised and rejected by *all* readers with the sole exception of De Quincey, "alone in all Europe":

> no man, beyond one or two in each ten thousand, had so much as heard of either Coleridge or Wordsworth, and that one, or those two, knew them only to scorn them, trample on them, spit upon them. Men so abject in public estimation, I maintain, as that Coleridge and that Wordsworth, had not existed before, nor existed since, will not exist again. We have heard in old times of donkeys insulting effete or dying lions by kicking them; but in the case of Coleridge and Wordsworth it was effete donkeys kicking living lions. They, Coleridge and Wordsworth, were the Pariahs of literature in those days: as much scorned wherever they were known; but escaping that scorn only because they were as little known as Pariahs, and even more obscure.
>
> (*CW* 3:42)

9. Shortly before meeting Wordsworth and not long after beginning to correspond with him, DQ drew up a list of the twelve constituents of happiness. With the exception of two rather personal items (#11 "The Education of a child" and #12 ". . . personal appearance tolerably respectable") all the items are intensely Wordsworthian. Eaton has argued that this list, composed in August, 1805, to be DQ's response to WW [William Wordsworth]'s letter of March, 1804, describing the lifetime project of *The Prelude*. The list includes "A capacity for thinking," "A cultivation of an interest in all that concerns human life and human nature," "a fixed residence in some spot of eminent beauty," "interchange of solitude and interesting society," "*Books,*" "Some great intellectual project," "consciousness of a supreme mastery over unworthy passions," "A vast predominance of contemplation" over actions, and "a more than ordinary emancipation from all worldly cares."

Works Cited

Aladdin and the Enchanted Lamp. Tr. John Payne (1889); *Aladdin; or, the Wonderful Lamp. A Delightful Story selected from the Arabian Nights Entertainments and on which the Pantomime of that Name is founded which is now performing, with universal applause, at the Theater Royal, Convent Garden* (1789); *Aladdin; or, the Wonderful Lamp: A Grand Romantic Spectacle, in Two Acts* (1826); *Aladdin and the Wonderful Lamp* (1855); *Aladdin, or the Wonderful Lamp* (1889); *Aladdin, or the Wonderful Lamp* (1905); *The Arabian Nights.* Tr. Edward Forster. 5 vols. (1803); *The Arabian Nights' Entertainment,* The "Grub Street" Translation, Vols. 3 & 4 (1793); *The Arabian Nights' Entertainment.* Tr. Jonathan Scott. 6 vols. (1811); *The Arabian Nights' Entertainment.* Tr. Edward William Lane (1853); *The Arabian Nights' Entertainment.* Tr. Richard Burton. 2 vols. (1955); *Babrius and Phaedrus.* Ed. and Tr. Ben Edwin Perry (1975);

Barbauld, Anna Letitia and Dr. Aikin. *Evenings at Home; or, the Juvenile Budget Opened* (1879); Barrell, John. *The Infection of Thomas De Quincey: A Psychopathology of Imperialism* (1991); Beer, John. "De Quincey and the Dark Sublime: The Wordsworth-Coleridge Ethos." *Thomas De Quincey Bicentenary Studies.* Ed. Robert Lance Snyder (1985); Booth, Michael. *Prefaces to English Nineteenth-Century Theater* (1980); *Victorian Spectacular Theater 1850-1910* (1981); Borges, Jorge Luis. *The Thousand and One Nights. Seven Nights.* Tr. Weinberger (1984) 42-57; Byron, H. J. *Aladdin.* Ed. Gyles Brandreth (1861; 1971); Caracciolo, Peter L. The Arabian Nights *in English Literature* (1988); Clej, Alina. *A Geology of the Modern Self: Thomas De Quincey and the Intoxication of Writing* (1995); Clinton-Baddeley, V. C. *Aladdin* (1931); Coe, Richard. *When the Grass Was Taller: Autobiography and the Experience of Childhood* (1984); Coleridge, Hartley. *The Complete Poetical Works.* Ed. Ramsay Colles (1908); The Hartley Coleridge Papers. U. of Texas, Humanities Research Center; Coleridge, Samuel Taylor. *Shakespearean Criticism;* Dawood, N. J., Tr. *Tales from the Thousand and One Nights.* (1985); De Quincey, Thomas. "Infant Literature." *The Collected Writings of Thomas De Quincey.* Ed. David Masson (1889-90); *Confessions of an English Opium-Eater and Other Writings.* Ed. Grevel Lindop (1996); *Recollections of the Lakes and the Lake Poets.* Ed. David Wright (1970); Ghazoul, Ferial. *Nocturnal Poetics:* The Arabian Nights *in Comparative Context* (1996); Greenwood, Ernest. *Aladdin U.S.A.* (1928); Hume, Fergus. *Aladdin in London* (1892); *Instructions for the Erection of Your Aladdin Home.* Aladdin Company of Bay City, Michigan (1921); Isham, Frederick. *Aladdin from Broadway* (1913); Morton, J. M. *Aladdin and His Wonderful Lamp* (1856); Jordan, John E. *De Quincey to Wordsworth: A Biography of a Relationship* (1961); Kipling, Rudyard. *Stalky & Co.* Ed. Isabel Quigley (1987); Lindop, Grevel. *The Opium-Eater: A Life of Thomas De Quincey.* (1981); Munson, Gorham, *Aladdin's Lamp: The Wealth of the American People* (1945); Myers, Mitzi. "Little Girls Lost: Rewriting Romantic Childhood, Right Gender and Genre." *Teaching Children's Literature: Issues, Pedagogy, Resources.* Ed. Glenn Edward Sadler (1992): 131-142. Naddaff, Sandra. *Arabesque: Narrative Structure and the Aesthetics of Repetition in 1001 Nights* (1991); *The Oriental Moralist, or the Beauties of the* Arabian Nights' Entertainment. Tr. Rev. Mr. Cooper (1800); Page, H. A. [Pseudonym for A. H. Japp]. *Thomas De Quincey: His Life and Writings.* 2 vols. n.d.; Pembleton, Max. *Aladdin or London;*

or Lodestar (1907); Percival, Thomas. *Parental Instructions: or, Guide to Wisdom and Virtue designed for Young Persons of Either Sex* (1788; 1846); Piaget, Jean. *The Moral Judgment of the Child.* Tr. Marjorie Gabain (1932; 1977); Quick, Herbert. *Aladdin: A Romance of Yankee Magic* (1904); *The Thousand and One Nights, commonly called in English The Arabian Nights' Entertainments.* Tr. Edward William Lane. 3 vols. (1839-40); Scudder, Horace. *Childhood in Literature and Art* (1894); Spector, Stephen J. "Thomas De Quincey: Self-Effacing Autobiographer." *VS* 18 (1979): 501-20; Wearing, J. P. "Edwardian London West End Christmas Entertainments, 1900-1914." *When They Weren't Doing Shakespeare: Essays on Nineteenth-Century British and American Theater.* Ed. Judith Fisher and Stephen Watt. (1989): 230-40.

The author is indebted to the Harry Ransom Humanities Research Center, University of Texas, Austin.

Eva K. Sallis (essay date 1999)

SOURCE: Sallis, Eva K. "Readings of Selected Stories and Anecdotes: 'Hārūn al-Rashid and the Arab Girl,' 'The Pious Black Slave,' "Azīz and 'Azīza,' "Abdallah the Fisherman and 'Abdallah the Merman,' 'Ma'rūf the Cobbler.'" In *Sheherazade through the Looking Glass: The Metamorphosis of the* Thousand and One Nights, pp. 108-42. Richmond, England: Curzon, 1999.

[*In the following essay, Sallis discusses the plots and themes of five tales from* The Arabian Nights, *suggesting that close readings of individual stories illuminate the diversity of the work as a whole.*]

Defining the content of the *Nights* [*The Thousand and One Nights*] in any kind of literary classification as a preliminary to interpretation is more difficult than it seems. Quite clearly very different types of story are represented in the collection, and differentiation between them is useful, as in many cases they differ so markedly that a variety of models governs their structure and meanings, such as is immediately apparent in the case of the beast fables or the short historical anecdotes. Payne divided the tales into five general categories: histories, by which he meant long histories of which **"Umar al-Nu'mān'** is really the only example; anecdotes and short stories of historical figures and everyday incidents; romances and romantic fictions; fables and apologues (the beast fable sections); and finally, tales of heterogeneous learning, such as **'Tawaddud'** (9. 367-73). His third category, that of romances and romantic fictions, was extremely broad, covering all the leftovers of the other more specific groups. It included anything which used supernatural machinery and lacked historical people or anything apparently fictional, rang-

ing from **"Azīz and 'Azīza'** to the **'Hunchback'** cycle or to **'Ma'rūf the Cobbler.'** In other words, most of the tales of the collection remained under this amorphous heading.

Later scholars offer slightly more useful definitions. Robert Irwin discusses them in mutable groups according to the kind of entertainment they offer. Many stories belong to several of his broad headings. His chapters are 'Street Entertainments', 'Low Life', 'Sexual Fictions' and the 'Universe of Marvels', and the advantage of these headings is that applicable stories spring to mind. This loose categorisation is based firmly on certain elements of the content, rather than the form of the tales, and given that Irwin's main interest is the social world represented through the *Nights* (*Companion* [*The Arabian Nights: A Companion*] 5), this is an accommodating and flexible differentiation.

Mia Gerhardt attempts a more literary and comprehensive study and offers a far more extensive classification of types. She divides them into Love-stories, Crime-stories, Travel-stories, Fairy-tales and lastly, Learning, Wisdom and Piety. Each of these has several subdivisions, in which she attempts to take account of chronological alterations in these genres. She omits **"Umar al-Nu'mān'** and **"Ajīb and Gharīb'** from classification and discussion, arguing that they were never meant to form part of the collection, and are 'alien to its spirit' (*Story-telling* [*The Art of Story-telling: A Literary Study of* The Thousand and One Nights] 117). However, even though this is a useful tool in accessing the overwhelming mass of tales, it has its limitations, and can be seen as a provisional model only. A part as large as the crusading epic of **"Umar al-Nu'mān'** cannot be ignored because it differs from the rest; the fundamentally patchwork nature of the whole resists such a judgement. Furthermore, **"Umar al-Nu'mān'** has been part of versions of the *Nights* since at least 1550/957[1] and Gerhardt is willing to accept additions made much later by Galland and others. Another problem is that one suspects that a love story in which Jinn appear is at times not so generically different from one without them, so a distinction between tales with supernatural elements and those without becomes almost arbitrary. Any separation or affinity asserted between two tales, or two types of tale, is subject to criticism and is ultimately an argument which brings us no closer to understanding a given tale. Stating that the wonders of the sea motif appears in the voyages of **'Sindbād'** and in **"Abdallah of the Sea,'** and derives from a craze of the Baghdadian era actually tells us little or nothing about these tales in themselves. Gerhardt is the first to admit that even the primary transparent differentiation between stories and anecdotes shows a 'blurred line of demarcation between them' (*Story-telling* 43). The following section will apply the simplest categorisation of the tales, a categorisation which imposes no interpretation upon them: there are long tales and short tales.

As stated earlier in this study, no clear principle governs the relationship between the frame and the enframed. The frame as part of reading a story appears intermittently, fragmented and refracted throughout the collection. Following from the themes and styles of the frame tale the reader can, in some stories, identify a crucial relationship between art and violence or a development of character based on collage and repetition of reflections. In many instances stories include a repetition of images of violence, infidelity, power and death, with men and women the very different and very variable subjects, forming between them the dialectic tension of action, development and resolution. This recurrence and reflection of frame theme and image is random, and in most cases the demands of the specific tale take precedence over the meanings generated for Sheherazade's story. The second calender's tale (in the **'Porter and the Three Ladies of Baghdad'**) contains within it the metaphor of Sheherazade's transforming the king Shahriyār gone wrong: this variant has the virtuous princess destroy herself to effect the metamorphosis of the beastly man, the man as ape. However, at no time do we feel that this reference to the frame is the point of the event. Tales retain their autonomy and integrity: where they refer to the frame, it is predominantly through the inferences we draw. They are put into a relationship with the frame sometimes only by simple adjacency and the meanings generated by this collocation, while undeniably important and pleasurable, are a shadow of a given tale's internal momentum and laws.

The collection is so large that moving from the particular to the general seems to risk drowning in detail.[2] However, as the recent individual readings of tales offered by Hamori, Miquel and many others have shown, reading one tale as if unique can tell us much more about its genre than the meticulous identification of its generic features, particularly as careful individual readings have not been a feature of *Nights* criticism until recently. This chapter will look at a small selection of different tales primarily as unique literary events, as an indication of the potential of reading the *Nights* for its literary diversity. Some comment on related tales and types will be made but not with a view to formulating any generic classification.

It is problematic to select one version or even the versions in just one language and affirm them to the exclusion of others. The reasons for this have been discussed at length. This unresolved textual identity leaves practical problems. While Payne is the base text for the following readings, Payne's is not in itself a satisfactory text. The text analysed in these pages proves to be in part an ideal formulation: Payne, supplemented by others for his deficiencies, the reiterations at dawn and dusk reinserted and the variants of a given story informing the representative under scrutiny. Payne's story titles and proper names are also too archaic and cumbersome to be retained. These are replaced with transliterations from the Arabic. Dissatisfaction with any single text forces the critic either to affirm uneasily one unsatisfying representative or to react to a potential, rather than a real text.

'HARŪN AL-RASHĪD AND THE ARAB GIRL'

This tale appears in the Egyptian MSS and is represented in the Bulaq, Breslau and Calcutta II texts, and, following them, in Burton and Payne, Night 685-86 (Chauvin 6. 143). This is one of the stories in the *Nights* which also appears in an unrelated literary collection, in this case in the *I'ām al-Nās* (Chauvin 9. 60).

> Hārūn al-Rashīd was out walking when he saw some girls drawing water. He overheard one of them recite some verses on love and sleepless yearning. He was struck by her beauty and eloquence, and asked her if the verses were her own. She answered that they were and he challenged her to keep the meaning but change the rhyme to prove it. This she did three times in response to his demands. He asked her obliquely who she was and she answered equally obliquely that she was the daughter of the chief of her tribe. She asked him a similar riddle and he answered in kind, without fooling her. Impressed, the Caliph made the arrangements to marry her and she became one of his dearest women. One day, upon hearing of her father's death, he went to see her, troubled for her sake. As soon as she saw him, she took off all her rich clothes, put on mourning clothes and began to lament her father. His face alone had communicated the news to her. The Caliph wept with her and not long after she died from grief.

This is a short, simple and satisfying tale presented in an anecdotal form. Although it does not name any chain of transmitters, its form aligns it with the multifarious collections of anecdotal literature of the 10th/4th century. Anecdotes (*akhbār* and *nawādir*) began as an oral literature, popular in the 7th/1st century in Medina. They later became a written resource, having a distinct role amongst other *adab* literatures. Anecdotes were used to break the intensity and give relief from concentration on an *adab* treatise, and the correct use of them was an art. They were one of the entertaining components of instruction essential to the *adab* genre (*EI* (2) [*The Encyclopaedia of Islam* (second edition)] VII. 857-8). Significant collections of anecdotal and story literature of the 10th/4th century are extant. That of al-Tanūkhī (*al-Faraj ba'd al-shidda*) has generic links with the *Nights* (Irwin, *Companion* 83). This tale offers a similar, if perhaps more independently literary, version of the same style of smörgåsbord entertainment.

There are several components to the anecdote. Most prominently, the poems and the word play which the girl improvises, demonstrating her wit and poetic skill, form the substantial pleasure offered by the anecdote as a whole. Payne's translation of the first can give only a clumsy idea of the original:

> Bid thou thy spright from my couch, I pray, At the season of
> slumber turn away,
> So I may rest me and eke the fire In my bones that rages may
> have allay
> For me, the love-lorn, whom passion's hands Turn on the carpet
> of sickness aye,
> Thou knowest well how it is with me: Doth thy favour last for a
> single day?
>
> (6. 199)[3]

The four variations of the poem are on the theme of sleeplessness as a result of unrequited passion and are intense, direct and sensual in tone: they suggest a woman ill, even feverish, with longing for an absent, or departed lover. The mode of address is to a woman, which should not be taken too literally. It is both an inversion of a standard poetic convention and a sample of poetic 'cross-addressing' (Wilmsen). As an inversion of convention it stands out, reinforcing the Arab girl's claim to authorship.[4] Cross-addressing is a feature of Arabic love language in which the loved one is linguistically designated as being of the same gender as the lover.[5] By this transformation one of *them* is brought closer to the self and becomes one of *us*. David Wilmsen observes that in the present day

> reverse gender reference . . . is used in establishing, maintaining and expressing intimacy; in protecting or concealing the identity of the referee or the referent, [and] in banter with same-sex cohorts. . . .
>
> (*Arabic-L*)

Here, however, perhaps banter is most prominent and the intimacy suggested by cross-addressing is mere embellishment as the poems are offered as wordplay; there is no suggestion that the girl is expressing anything other than her own virtuosity. However, the poems communicate indirectly to the future lover on a different level from the witty interchange between the Caliph and the girl, a communication which, while unintended as flirtation (the girl recites the first version to her friends), participates in the cursorily described marriage of the two. The conjunction of the poems as cause, the marriage as effect, and the understated: 'she became of the dearest of his women to him' (6. 201) create a picture to be put together by the reader. The passion of the poems obliquely informs us about the relationship.

Two legendary groups are represented in the anecdote through the figures of the Caliph and the girl. The Caliph Hārūn al-Rashīd is quintessentially urban and in stories and popular imagination was the most famous and brilliant figure of the Golden Age of Baghdad, the first great metropolis. The girl is one of the few desert Arabs to be portrayed positively in the *Nights.* As poet, she represents the legendary virtues of the desert people, invoking the great pre-Islamic poets for the reader or listener with her identity. Her passion, poetry, independence from wealth and her extraordinary grief give her mythical status and align her with the archetypal pre-Islamic Arab. The pairing of the two carries with it a satisfying union of images of excellence from the two principal worlds of Arab folklore.

The communication in riddles tests each participant's ability to understand the other and comprehension alone establishes a relationship. The Caliph guesses naturally enough that she is the chief's daughter from her encoded description of herself: 'Of its midmost in dwelling and highest in tent-pole' (6. 200). She, however, asks him to answer in kind by encoding her question: 'of what [art thou among] the guardians of the horses?' His response: 'Of the highest in tree and of the ripest in fruit' (6. 200) is understood immediately by her: she greets him by his proper title. Comprehension signifies the deeper perception of the self behind the code, and not surprisingly results in a relationship. The girl is marked by her perspicacity. She reads the news of her father's death in the expression on Hārūn al-Rashīd's face; her ability to comprehend communication is highly developed and causes him some wonder. Encoded communication and especially the semiological powers of women from which men are excluded by incomprehension is a feature of some tales, notably **"Azīz and 'Azīza'** which will be discussed in some detail later.

This is a short 'historical' anecdote, very different in form from the complexities of the frame story and from the marvellous machinery of many of the tales. However, the character of the girl and the nature of the relationship are given to the reader by cumulative reflections rather than direct comment, in much the same way as that of Shahriyār. . . . Furthermore, despite being less than three pages long, and more than half its length devoted to the poetry, the tale manages to give a relatively rich image of the girl, the Caliph and the relationship. In the case of the girl, this image is of a character, not a body or a visual object. In fact, rich clothes are mentioned only when she is discarding them forever. Several things are not mentioned; she enters the richest palace in the story-telling repertoire without one description being given to place her physically in that context. The image is created through the use and transcendence of stereotypes. She becomes the wife of the Caliph, a fairly stereotypical reward in tales. It is worthwhile noting, however, that marriage to the Caliph is rarely the acme of the reward scale. More often the Caliph is the agent through which an ideal marriage takes place. The ideal is usually suggested as equal; fulfilment for both the male and the female are essential to it. The sheer number of the Caliph's real and possible sexual partners places him outside any normative ideal, since the desires, physical or emotional, of any woman paired with him, are unlikely to be satisfied for long, certainly not until the 'Destroyer of Delights' parts them. In this particular tale, the ideal is partly invoked, since in the case of the Caliph, it must be contained in the suggestion that the heroine beats the competition in gaining his deeper affections. The ideal is partly fulfilled also, as she retains his regard and intimacy is sustained between them until she dies. The dynamics of the Caliph's household and private life generate a whole genre of stories which play with the conflict between ideal love and the power signified by unlimited abundance of women. Thus the Caliph's passion for Qūt al-Qulūb in the tale of Ghānim the son of Ayyūb puts the girl in grave danger from the jealousy of Zubayda, powerful queen, cousin and wife.

The relationship between the Caliph and the Arab girl who became of the dearest of his women in this tale is given through just two scenes of their life together (without even a description of the marriage). The first scene captures his concern over having to tell her that her father is dead and her instantaneous comprehension of it without words; the second shows him grieving with her. Her ability to comprehend and her feeling for him evokes in him something like empathy: his eyes fill with tears and he grieves with and for her when he hears her explain that she read the news in his face. This minimalist picture sketched in a few deft strokes establishes an intimate relationship between a man and a woman, where all the normal gorgeous and unreal portrayals of the Caliph and his world have become irrelevant. The tale manages to establish its own verity and authority by using a pseudo-historical form of address, and by using stereotypes and stock figures in a way which breaks with expected descriptions; the tale suggests that this is the real Hārūn al-Rashīd, a Caliph and a man, not the story book hero.

The encounter between two characters who represent polarised social groups is often the frame upon which an anecdote is stretched and is invariably both interesting and subtly edifying. The form of the genre is too brief to engage with abstract opposites such as good and evil; rather, the form lends itself to depicting the experiential middle ground of life and concerns itself with social polarities: class, wealth, gender, education and behaviour. This is not to say that the anecdotes in the ***Nights*** necessarily record historical, realistic or even believable scenes. Many of them play with the validating convention of a named chain of transmitters to communicate quite preposterous encounters. They are often a record of the weird, the wonderful, the strange or the curious in a fictional experiential world which claims enough reality with its form and its recognisable

social types to ask for a suspension of disbelief. The confrontation with the devil or with the angel of death form a small genre of their own; these can also be seen to deal with an encounter with an Other, in which the experiential world of the subject is the focal point. The authoritative form is usually most apparent in the opening, and is the point of departure for some of the best of these anecdotes.

'THE PIOUS BLACK SLAVE'

This tale appears in the Egyptian MSS and in two independent anecdote or story collections: *al-Nawādir* of al-Qalyūbi (died 1658/1068) (Marzolph 171), and *al-Mustaṭraf fī kull fann mustaẓraf* of al-Ibshīhī (15th/9th century). It has been translated into English only by Burton and Payne, covering nights 467-68 (Chauvin 6. 186).

> Mālik ibn Dīnār and nine other theologians and jurists prayed for rain during a drought in Basra, to no avail. At about nightfall, he and Thābit al-Bananī, one of the theologians, witnessed a poor, although attractive, black slave pray, beseeching God to grant rain in the name of His love for him. The sky clouded over and rain poured down. The two scholars were amazed and Mālik ibn Dīnār approached the slave, asking him if he were not ashamed to presume God's love for him. The slave answered passionately that the scholar was not in touch with his own soul, that God's love was proved by the guidance to knowledge which He had granted and that God's love was measured by the slave's love for God. The scholar asked the slave to stay with him awhile but the slave answered that as a slave he had his duties to fulfil to his lesser master.
>
> The scholars followed the slave and found that he lived with a slave dealer. Accordingly they went to the dealer the next day and purchased him. Mālik ibn Dīnār asserted that he wished to serve, not be served by him. They went to the mosque and the slave prayed fervently that since the secret between him and God had been betrayed, that God might take his soul forthwith. He prostrated himself and the scholar found that he was dead. He laid the body out and found that the face was illuminated and smiling. A stranger came in with two rich robes as shrouds and asked God to bless the scholars for Maimūn, the name of the slave. The tomb became a place of prayer for rain.

This is a religious wonder tale with a clear purpose. It mimics the authoritative anecdote in order to strengthen its claims, as instructive or exemplary tales rely upon being 'real'.[6] It is anchored from the outset to the names of ten famous theologians and jurists. Payne tells us also that Mālik ibn Dīnār was a 'renowned theologian and ascetic' of 8th/2nd century Basra (5. 16). This pool of authority quickly metamorphoses into a literary construct: the greatness of this horde of scholars and their failure as rain bringers is played off against the malnourished, impoverished and in every way disadvantaged figure of the black slave who is successful.

The contrast is very effective. The devout young man is described vividly: he is 'a black of comely visage, slender-shanked, big-bellied . . . clad in a pair of woollen drawers; if all he wore had been priced, it would not have fetched a couple of dirhems' (5. 16). This character, not named until the end of the tale, proves to have a stronger spiritual connection to God than the great religious thinkers of the times; making a point which derives its effect from his apparent lowliness, strengthened by the fact that he is black, enslaved and poor. The tale has its religious message endorsed by the fact that it is related by the theologian, who realises that the slave is his spiritual master.

It is very obviously a pro-Sufi tale. There are several indications that the slave who has outstripped these traditional scholars is a Sufi initiate. The word for his woollen drawers puts the idea first into the reader's mind, but the prayer makes it apparent. The oneness with God and the seeming arrogance of the self thus being the fulfilment of God are familiar Sufi stances (al-Ḥallāj's apparent blasphemy, the ecstatic 'I am God' is the most famous example.)[7] Several words used by the slave, as Payne notes, also recall stages in the mystic's journey to oneness with God (5. 17). The tale affirms the Sufic way directly by having the two prayers answered and indirectly by impressing the scholar Mālik ibn Dīnār.

One phrase which stands out, particularly for the contemporary reader, is the following: in death, 'whiteness had gotten the better of blackness in his face, and it was radiant with light' (5. 18). The language is too subtle and imprecise to suggest that his face turned from black to white, a simplistic medieval miracle. Rather, it is clear that his face is still at least to a degree black and that the observer is describing a subjective impression of the illuminated quality of the face, and suggesting at the same time a transcendence of blackness which can be read several ways. One can argue that prejudice in society was such that the storyteller had to whiten his saint in order to justify the elevated role he is given in the tale.[8] Whitening a face, and blackening a face were blessings or imprecations which could be called down upon anybody. Predicated from the prejudices of the times, the phrase is nonetheless an attempt to communicate the slave's blessedness in death, and a radiant happiness, without violating the believable. The phrase, despite its uncomforting racial overtones for us, simply communicates for the storyteller and the crowd a transcendence of the conditions of his life: enslaved, marginalised, deprived of full citizenship and rights, despised[9] and, in the case of this slave, poor and ill-fed.

The story closes with a poem which is perhaps told by Mālik ibn Dīnār, or perhaps by the tale-teller as a final comment upon the intimate connection with God to which the anecdote has borne witness.[10] The poem describes Paradise first as a garden in which the just drink old wine and then moves to make explicit that this is a metaphor for 'close communion with the Lord'. The final line: 'The secret of their hearts is safe from other than God's sight; For that their sprights and his are blent in one supreme accord' recalls the final prayer of the black slave: 'How then shall life be sweet to me, now that others than thou have happened upon that which is between Thee and me?' This poem functions as a coda in which the theme of closeness to God, proved and witnessed in prose, is transformed into oneness with God expressed in poetry as a more general observation on the completion of the slave's journey, and the possibilities of spiritual transcendence for others.

"'Azīz and 'Azīza'

This tale appears in the Egyptian MSS, in the Bulaq and Macnaghten texts, and in Lane, Payne, Burton and Mardrus (Chauvin 5. 144) (Nights 112-129 in Payne). It is unclear whether this story is originally Baghdadian or Egyptian. It is embedded within the tale of Tāj al-Mulūk, which in turn is embedded within the long **"Umar al-Nu'mān'** epic. It is worthwhile reading this particular story with the frame tale in mind, as it is one of the tales which works well with Sheherazade's shadow presence implied.

> Having been importuned by the prince Tāj al-Mulūk to tell his story and in particular the story of her who had given him the piece of linen embroidered with two gazelles, the unhappy young merchant 'Azīz told his tale.
>
> 'Azīz and 'Azīza his cousin had been betrothed since early childhood and had lived together as brother and sister. When they reached adulthood, 'Azīz's parents organised the marriage festivities. On the day of the wedding, as 'Azīz was making his way home from the bath, fully prepared and perfumed for the event, he happened to sit down on a stone bench to rest from the heat. A white handkerchief fell upon him from above and, looking up, he saw a beautiful woman, who made a series of indecipherable signs to him. 'Azīz was instantly passionately in love with the unknown woman and after waiting until sundown for her to reappear went home with the handkerchief. When he got home he found his cousin weeping. She told him that the guests and dignitaries had departed and that his father was very angry. 'Azīz told her what had happened to him and begged her to help him. 'Azīza selflessly agreed, and interpreted the signs of the woman for him. The unknown woman was, according to her signals, also in love with him and wished him to return in two days. Neither eating nor drinking, he waited the two days, comforted all the while by 'Azīza. At the appointed time the lady again appeared at her window and made a complex pantomime of signs which 'Azīz could not comprehend. He waited again for her to reappear and returned home only near midnight. He found his cousin weeping bitterly and reciting poetry of unre-

quited love. However, she again translated the signs for him and told him that he was to wait in the dyer's shop in five days time for a further communication from his beloved. 'Azīz sickened from longing and was consoled by 'Azīza with stories of lovers to pass the time. This time, however, the woman did not appear and he returned home in deep distress. 'Azīza was weeping but she greeted him hopefully. 'Azīz kicked her down and her head was cut open in the fall. She treated him gently, saying nothing against him, and helped him again: the translation was that the woman wished to test him and 'Azīza counselled him to go to the stone bench the next day. 'Azīza brought him food but he kicked it away. They passed a sleepless night. The next day at the stone bench, the woman appeared at her window, laughing. She made another series of inexplicable gestures and signs and then closed the window. 'Azīz returned to find 'Azīza weeping and bandaged and reciting forlorn verses. She helped him again: he was to go after sunset to the garden of the house and wait there for his mistress and for the fulfilment of his wishes. She sent him to his assignation, charging him, when he had made love to his mistress and was about to leave, to repeat to her a certain verse. Three times in a row, however, 'Azīz ate from the array of wonderful foods laid out in the garden and fell asleep, and each time his mistress left objects as messages on his sleeping body. The messages as 'Azīza translated them were increasingly angry and, finally, threatening. However, with careful foreplanning and his cousin's assistance, on the fourth occasion he managed to stay awake, pass the test and spent a night of lovemaking with his mistress. In the morning, his mistress gave him the embroidered linen, telling him to keep it carefully, as it was her sister's work. 'Azīz returned home, forgetting to tell his lover the verse from his cousin. He gave 'Azīza the embroidered linen and she kept it. The following night he spent with his mistress and in the morning remembered to repeat 'Azīza's message, a verse asking what the unrequited lover should do. His mistress Bint Dalīla's eyes filled with tears and she answered, through 'Azīz, with a verse counselling secrecy and acceptance. 'Azīz returned home and found 'Azīza ill. Through verses, 'Azīza communicated her situation to 'Azīz's lover who, weeping for her unknown rival, sent verses back. On the third occasion, Bint Dalīla knew from the verse that 'Azīza was dead and demanded to know who she was. When she found out that 'Azīza was her lover's cousin and that it was with her help that he had succeeded she was very angry, and cursed him. 'Azīz left, troubled, and returned home. 'Azīza was indeed dead and his mother also cursed him. 'Azīza had left a message for him; he was to say to his mistress the phrase: 'Faith is fair and perfidy foul' upon leaving. This he remembered to do and his mistress said that she had intended to do him mischief but that with these words 'Azīza had protected him from her. She then charged him to stay away from all women, as he no longer had his cousin to protect him. His mistress then visited 'Azīza's tomb and grieved for her, giving alms, and engraving verses on the tomb with a mallet and chisel.

They lived together a year. 'Azīz became fat and forgot 'Azīza. However, every night his mistress would ask him to repeat 'Azīza's final message. One day, scented from the bath and slightly tipsy, 'Azīz entered a by-street and encountered an old woman who by subterfuge led him to the door of a handsome house. As he stood there a young woman ran up, dazzling 'Azīz with her beauty. The old woman and the young woman pushed 'Azīz into the house and locked the door. The young woman beat him up and then offered him a choice of life or death. He chose life which, as she explained, meant living married to her, having sex with her and remaining locked in the sumptuous house. She was his mistress' enemy and portrayed Bint Dalīla to him as a deadly figure, who commonly slew her lovers. She could not understand why 'Azīz had not suffered at her hand. He told her his story and she wept for 'Azīza. She said that the phrase 'Faith is fair and perfidy foul' had in fact saved him. He was then swiftly married to the young woman and lived a year in the lifestyle she had described and had a son with her. After a year she let him out for a day, after he had sworn upon the Qur'ān, by sword and the oath of divorce that he would return. He went straight to his mistress' house and found her forlorn, changed and weak from pining. However, once he had told his tale, and that he was only available for one night, she became very angry. Her women threw him to the ground and beat him while she sharpened a knife to kill him. At the last second, however, he cried out 'Azīza's phrase and she castrated him instead. He returned to his wife's house and passed out, awaking to find himself cast out, being of no further use to her. He returned to his mother's and in his convalescence finally mourned for 'Azīza. His mother gave him back the piece of linen, as 'Azīza had told her to do. He found a verse of his cousin's longing and grief embroidered on it, and also a letter acquitting him of responsibility in her death and telling him that the gazelles were wrought by Dunyā, the daughter of the King of the Camphor Islands and not his mistress's sister. She also told him to keep away from all women and not to try to gain the love of the lady of the gazelles. After a year of grief, he yearned for Dunyā and even visited her but his condition made everything hopeless.

Tāj al-Mulūk fell in love with Dunyā from 'Azīz's description and, taking the young merchant with him, set out to find and win her.

A *Nights* hero or heroine can do a terrible thing and still retain our liking and even respect. Examples spring to mind: Sindbād; 'Alī Nūr al-Dīn who gives away his love, Anīs al-Jalīs; the husband who kills his wife in the **'Three Apples'**; Budūr and Ḥayāt al-Nufūs' love for each other's sons. These are frequently acts of breaking trust or faith with a beloved and inhabit a grey area between storybook good and evil. None of these, however, is quite the anti-hero we find in 'Azīz, a character made enjoyable, although not really likeable, precisely because he violates the rules and expectations and fails utterly according to the standard of story heroes.

The world described in this tale is the stuff of Shahriyār's nightmares—with a difference. It is a world populated by women, which is nonetheless real; it is not a fantastic realm in which the women are queens and the men subjects, or where willing women wait in lots of forty for the arrival of the hero. Rather, it is a world in which 'Azīza cannot go out of her house without compromise, in which the customs surrounding 'Azīz's family are normal and believable. However, despite this world being the real world, every major event in the tale is controlled or engineered by a woman. There are several major female figures in the tale and only one male, 'Azīz (his father being mentioned only to normalise his betrothal and to underscore the hero's losses with his death). Women are all-powerful in this series of social interactions by virtue of their comprehension of each others' language, while men are rendered relatively powerless by their inability to comprehend: they are excluded and controlled by their ignorance. The reader, the listener (Shahriyār), the listener Dhū l-Makān, the listener Tāj al-Mulūk, and, until an explanation is given to him by a woman, 'Azīz, are all excluded from the meaning of words and signs used to communicate. The codes are literally impenetrable until 'Azīza decodes them or Bint Dalīla's enemy reveals them. We are made to appreciate that 'Azīza's intelligence, described by 'Azīz as far greater then his own, is also way beyond ours. This perspicacity between women is not limited to 'Azīza alone. The point is emphasised by the fact that 'Azīz's lover can read 'Azīza's communications with equal skill. A deeper meaning, a comprehension which links up cause and consequence, is perceived by the women and, as suggested above, this explicitly empowers them. This is one tale which assumes a male reader, since the male recipients (Shahriyār and Tāj al-Mulūk) have their emotions played upon.[11]

All explanations in this world come from women. It is populated and manipulated by women who are able to understand each other sight unseen and across the boundaries of polarised social positions: 'Azīza is the virtuous, protected, house-bound good girl, while Dalīla's daughter is a worldly woman of independent wealth who chooses and kills lovers as she pleases. The only man in presented in any detail is 'Azīz, who is the helpless pawn and ultimate victim of these women. He cannot understand them, or their world, and therefore cannot prevail. He ends up a broken and castrated man, telling a tale to horrify anyone remotely threatened by the feminine.

However, the story resists a simple response to this scenario. The women may be numerous, intelligent and deadly in comparison with the men but they differ substantially from each other as characters and the two opposites, 'Azīza and the daughter of Dalīla, both capture our respect and sympathy, even our admiration. The hero 'Azīz fails at all times to measure up to their calibre as individuals and the story explores his weaknesses in considerable detail. Despite their power, and often ruthlessness, these women are faithful, whereas Azīz

falls for temptation where it is offered, whether in the form of food or sex. He is an inversion of the heroic, for while he is very beautiful and is loved by 'Azīza, desired and ultimately loved by Dalīla's daughter, and desired by her enemy whom he marries, he portrays himself (since he is the teller) without hiding his cruelty and physical abuse of 'Azīza, without covering up his betrayal of his lover or his wife and indeed displays no positive attribute whatsoever except honesty about what took place. 'Azīz is depicted at several key points in the moment of bodily excretions: sweating profusely and sitting on his handkerchief to keep his clothes clean, at a loss as to how to wipe his face just before he sees Dalīla's daughter for the first time, hastily washing the food off his hands and mouth as his lover enters, pissing on a wall just before the old woman entraps him into his marriage with the enemy. These images of his body, including the castration scene, and his getting fat and slow in the year of good living with his lover, all undermine his physical beauty and seriously damage any heroic status he might have had by being the protagonist of the tale. He is weak, immoral, faithless, vicious and unjust, and his castration comes as a welcome punishment for his repetitious infidelity and his failure to learn. He is scarcely the stuff of a king's role model and the patent impossibility of identifying Shahriyār with 'Azīz forces reappraisal of the women in the tale, for, despite their dangerous nature and unassimilable powers, they show the qualities and conform with the ideals which underscore 'Azīz's failures. The most prominent of these ideals is the ideal of love and the actions of a lover, exemplified in the purest form by the selfless 'Azīza's death for love but evident also in Bint Dalīla's year of grief when 'Azīz deserts her.[12]

The thoroughly rotten hero, as distinct from the rather nobly thoughtless, such as 'Alī Nūr al-Dīn (**"Alī Nūr al-Dīn and Anīs al-Jalīs"**), appears to have been a recurrent character in certain types of stories. 'Azīz is probably an early form, as his pathetic weakness is fittingly punished: an exemplary, warning element remains in the tale. However, later heroes form a cavalcade of scoundrels, wastrels and social failures, who, through no virtues of their own, do very well in the course of their stories. In fact the tale shows a form of delight in their shortcomings. This generic anti-hero provides a special impetus for the story, not so much to rectify his weaknesses but to make way for his partner to upstage him. The inversion of roles which are otherwise relatively defined in society is one of the major pleasures of popular story-telling and in each case of the rotten hero, the heroine proves resourceful, astute, intelligent and often warlike. Zumurrud is breadwinner, decision maker and ruler, while 'Alī Shār feebly bemoans his fate.

This hero has a role which is considerably diluted in the purely literary text. Gerhardt notes with wonder that these heroes are offered with no express disapproval (*Story-telling* 141). However, to understand fully the impact of such a hero, we need to return to the creative interaction of the *rāwī* and the crowd. The hero is predicated from the disapproval in the crowd, and the entertaining element is maximised if the performance context is judgemental. A great many elements in the *Nights* appear devoid of disapproval simply because they presume it in their listeners and then play deliciously with it. Nūr al-Dīn, the lover of Maryam the Christian, is first drunk, then beats his father, is asked to leave the family home by his mother and steals a bag of gold in parting. This is how his tale begins. Having broken the gamut of honourable social codes and behaviours, he is set up as the inversion of the heroic. One can imagine the scandalised delight the crowd would show as the list accumulates. Inversions require an accepted code of roles or rules to be fun. It is noticeable that the hero is so bad in this tale that the space is created for not just a super heroine but a Christian one at that.

Infidelity in its multitude of manifestations in the tales cannot but recall the frame in the mind of the reader and cannot avoid being synthesised into a reading or commentary on the action of the frame. While the reiterations at dawn formally structure the collection with the frame, the repetitions of images of infidelity form the strongest and most recurrent thematic collusion between the two. For both men and women, faithlessness emerges as a redeemable mid-point between good and evil. It is on the arena of fidelity and infidelity that many *Nights* characters emerge as human, flawed and subject to inner change and suffering. Infidelity and resolution of betrayal and psychological and emotional damage are the pattern of many stories. However, in the tale of **"Azīz and 'Azīza,'** the man is the image of dishonour, shame and infidelity; unfaithful in his promises not just to 'Azīza, whom he did not love or marry, but significantly unfaithful also both to the woman he loved and to the woman he married (Bencheikh, *Mille et un contes* 309). The repetition-in-inversion of the themes of the frame is most effective.

'Azīz is entrapped by force, offered a choice between death or marriage with his captor and, after his marriage, locked up by his wife in order to ensure his fidelity. His role is to do as the cock does; to live the life of luxurious incarceration provided by his wife and to give sex on demand. When his wife discards him, she keeps his son, something 'Azīz does not even complain about. In this particular relationship we are offered an inversion, even a parody of gender roles (Hamori, 'Two Love Stories' 69); 'Azīz resembles nothing more than the stock female concubine of the tales, with some added bite to the image.[13] The crudity with which his position is described and his complete powerlessness and idleness are offered with no veneer of idealism. However, this parody is not set in a fantasy world made interest-

ing by its inversions; it is presented as a distinctly possible world. Neither Dalīla's daughter nor her enemy belong to the groups in society which most represent the stereotypes or stock figures. Neither are named, but the invocation of the name of Dalīla is sufficient to give the tale a pseudo-historical context. Dalīla was a Cairene confidence trickster and manipulator famous in the real Baghdad of the 10th/4th century (Irwin, *Companion* 145-6). Several legends of the story Baghdad explore her wiles and trickery. The schemers and masters of this tale have the authority of being her descendants; nominally her real daughter and certainly her narrative daughters. The use of the name of Dalīla simply prohibits this world from being read or heard as unreal or symbolic in the same way as the undersea society of 'Abdullah of the Sea is.

'Azīz is paired by a twin who is also his opposite, however, much in the same way as the two 'Abdullahs are. Assonant names are usually stridently meaningful in the *Nights*; here 'Azīza is his other half, having everything he lacks. They are complementary opposites in an ideal world but in the real world it is the contrast between them which generates the ultimate tragic separation. 'Azīz's permanent incompleteness without his pair and partner is crudely sketched in his castration.

One confusing element of the tale is the piece of linen with its embroidered gazelles. This component is welded into the tale with some care, yet, other than being a motif to lead into and out of the tale, it seems obscure. None of the questions which we might ask about this motif is directly answered, despite the significance attached to it by 'Azīza, her mother, Bint Dalīla and ultimately 'Azīz. 'Azīza translates for us all the other obscure symbols traded between the women but this one is left to the reader. It is a repetition by reappearance which pressures the reader to search for its meaning. The first indication that it has great significance is when Tāj al-Mulūk meets 'Azīz for the first time. 'Azīz appears to lose his mind when the piece of embroidered linen falls inadvertently from his wares. Tāj al-Mulūk then forces the reluctant 'Azīz to tell the tale of the piece of linen, which is described fully in this framing encounter. It has

> . . . the figures of two gazelles, facing one another, one wrought in silk and gold and the other in silver with a ring of red gold and three bugles of chrysolite about its neck.

> (2. 221)

They are beautiful enough to provoke wonder and admiration in Tāj al-Mulūk, who asks for the story of 'her who gave ['Azīz] these gazelles' (2. 222), in other words the story of Bint Dalīla, 'Azīza and his mother, since all three are effectively the givers. The piece of linen then reappears when he relates how Bint Dalīla gave it to him. She tells him to keep it carefully, for it is her sister's work. 'Azīz admires the work but disregards her instructions. He throws it down before 'Azīza, who asks to keep it. In the end the gazelles are given back to 'Azīz by his mother, who is acting as 'Azīza's agent, instructed to return them to him once he mourns for the loss of his cousin. 'Azīza's letter informs him that Dunyā is the maker of the linen, which is sent abroad each year as a mystical advertisement for that princess. Finally 'Azīz is instructed to preserve the gazelles in memory of his cousin and not to marry Dunyā.

All of this is very mysterious. However, several elements are clear: the gazelles represent love in some form[14] but not with just anybody. Significantly, the model of abusive sexuality, 'Azīz's wife, does not either receive or give the piece of linen. She is not a participant in the meanings they offer. Bint Dalīla, however, has an ambiguous role. She loves 'Azīz and is loved by him but 'Azīza tells him that Bint Dalīla's claim to the gazelles is a lie. The gazelles depict a love 'Azīz never attains: the love of two creatures of the same kind, equivalent in the ways cousins are presumed to be.[15] All his relationships are imbalanced: he is lacking in feeling and at the mercy of his dominating lovers. In the end the gazelles represent his irretrievable loss: severed from his other half, incomplete in a physical, emotional and spiritual sense. Significantly, all the women take the piece of linen very seriously: they understand it. Even Tāj al-Mulūk, who still has his three bugles of chrysolite, responds to it with a search for love and completion.[16]

The presence of this motif on linen in the tale is so oddly achieved that one could argue that its main function in the narrative is mechanical and that it is unsatisfying in its other gestures. We can speculate that some clarifying component which explores its power has been lost. However, given its resonance of the principal theme of the tale, it is hard to agree with Gerhardt that it is a vestige of an unrelated tale linking Tāj al-Mulūk to Dunyā upon which the tale of **"Azīz and 'Azīza'** has been pasted (*Story-telling* 135).

"Abdallah the Fisherman and 'Abdallah the Merman'

This tale appears in the Egyptian MSS, the Bulaq, Macnaghten and Breslau texts, and following them, in Lane, Payne and Burton (Chauvin 5. 6-7) (Nights 940-46 in Payne).

> 'Abdallah, a poor fisherman who owned only his net and relied on God's providence for each day's food, went down to the seashore to fish in the name of his newborn son, his tenth child. He cast his net repeatedly until the end of the day but caught nothing. He headed home, dejected and worried. However, a friendly baker, despite the general food shortage, singled 'Abdallah

out and insisted on giving him bread and money, refusing to allow the fisherman to pawn his net for it. 'Abdallah was to pay in fish, when times improved. For forty days there were no fish and each day the fisherman got deeper into debt to the baker (also named 'Abdallah), who had all this time provided the essential sustenance for the large family. At the end of the forty days 'Abdallah was ready to die from dejection and shame and was shaken in his faith in God. On the forty first day he cast his net praying for even one fish, to give to the baker. He hauled in a stinking corpse of a dead donkey. On the second cast, however, he hauled in a living merman, who told 'Abdallah that he too was a muslim and asked to be released. They agreed to exchange fruits of the land for jewels of the sea each day and, after reciting the Fātiḥa, the fisherman released the merman, who was also named 'Abdallah. The fisherman briefly regretted releasing the merman, thinking he could have paraded him as a curiosity and made some money but the merman quickly returned carrying all kinds of jewels. 'Abdallah went straight to the baker and gave him half of the jewels.

The next day the fisherman took all kinds of fruit in a basket to the seaside, called the merman and gave it to him. The merman exchanged it, filling the basket with jewels. After sharing with the baker, the fisherman went to the bazaar to sell them but was arrested on suspicion of theft of the queen's jewels. He was brought before the king, who was also named 'Abdallah. The queen, however, vindicated him and the good king believed his story. The king married 'Abdallah the fisherman to his daughter, his only child, saying that wealth needs status. The fisherman's ten boys and his wife came to live in the palace and were treated with love and honour.

Next day and every day after the fisherman went to the sea with fruit to keep his tryst with his friend the merman. All was well, and the king, hearing of the baker, made him wazir, saying that the four of them were brothers.

One day, as 'Abdallah the fisherman was chatting with 'Abdallah the merman, the conversation turned to to the tomb of the Prophet. The merman was shocked that the fisherman had not yet made the pilgrimage, although the latter protested that circumstances had in the past prevented him and that in fact he longed to go. They agreed that he would fulfil his wish and go that year, taking a pledge on the merman's behalf. The merman invited him to his house under the sea, as a guest, and to collect the pledge. He brought the fisherman a yellow ointment and, following instructions, the fisherman rubbed it all over his body. Then they went under the sea together, the fisherman protected from drowning by the ointment. 'Abdallah the merman showed his friend the wonders of the sea; the immense variety of fish life, many cities, and places, and described for him the different cultural and social practices. The fisherman marvelled at what he saw and heard but became tired after seeing fourscore cities in the same number of days and sick of eating only raw fish. The merman took him to a small city, his own, and to his own house. The fisherman was laughed at by the family: he was a 'lacktail', and they were beautiful, but naked and with fishtails, and he was fed fish yet again. However, the king of the land had heard of the lacktail and wished to see him. He was taken to the court and laughed at again but the merman came forward and explained the situation, after which the king entertained the fisherman and gave him jewels. Then the merman took him home and gave him a purse as pledge for the Prophet's tomb. As they were making their way back to the land, they passed a feast, with singing, eating and merrymaking. 'Abdallah the fisherman asked if this was a wedding and was told that it was in fact a funeral. He asked about the custom in surprise and told 'Abdallah the merman that on the land the people mourn and weep. The merman was deeply shocked and asked for the pledge back. He ended the friendship forthwith, horrified that the people of the land would grieve upon giving up to God His pledge, that is, their souls.

The fisherman returned to the king and his family and told the king of the marvels of the sea and what had happened between him and his friend. The king told him that he had been wrong to say what he did. The fisherman returned to the seashore for some time but the merman never again answered or appeared. At last he gave up hope and lived happily with the king and their families until they died.

This tale is divided into two movements which blend smoothly into one another, as motifs in each are reflected and explored in the other. The first is a complete tale in itself, exploring 'Abdallah's poverty and piety very effectively. The two brothers or counterparts, 'Abdallah of the sea and 'Abdallah of the land, discover an identity in difference in this first half, an identity primarily effected by shared faith. However, the great differences between them, noted but dormant in the first half, are the subject of the second. This movement explores the response to the exotic Other in vividly human terms. The two friends separate forever in the end because of irreconcilable differences of point of view. If the first movement establishes the ideal Muslim world, the second demolishes it again with the very human limitations of its members. It is on the one hand the most gloriously idealistic tale and in the end the most resignedly realistic and, apart from that, it is entertaining; its exotic and scientific details are a delight in themselves, both for the *rāwī*'s crowd and for the twentieth-century reader. Quite often, these elements are seen as so dominant that the tale is categorised simply as a marvels of the sea tale, with no further comment.

'Abdallah the fisherman is one of the very finely drawn characters of the collection, not because his motives, personal development or inner significance are explored, for they are not. 'Abdallah is tangibly real because he is reflected in his experiences and his surroundings. His contact with his experiential world is given in moments of immediacy, and this is sufficient to give him a kind of photographic reality. We are observers, eavesdroppers on living moments in the life of an ordinary man, 'snuffing the smell of . . . hot bread' (8. 331), or tugging a net until his palms bleed. Even his suicidal feel-

ings of shame are put into words overheard: he says to his wife 'I have a mind to tear up the net and be quit of this life' (8. 333). 'Abdallah is established through these ordinary experiences as someone just like you or me and from there his extraordinary experiences seem to belong in the world of possible fiction, rather than fairytale. His world entraps us in the fantasy of the tale, for in his world a dead donkey not only stinks, he has to move and fish elsewhere in order to get away from the stench.

The rigours of a famine are resolved in unimaginable bounty and goodwill, personified by the four good servants of God. 'Abdallah the fisherman, 'Abdallah the merman, 'Abdallah the baker and 'Abdallah the king, united by their names, are brothers indeed and help each other without consideration of self or class. In the first encounter, the baker provides for 'Abdallah the fisherman and his enormous family with bread and money for forty days during a famine, with no realistic expectation of material return. He does not give charity; he repeats again and again that the fisherman may redeem the debt when fish are plentiful, thus preserving equality between them and attempting to allay the fisherman's discomfort. In the second encounter, the fisherman returns the merman to the sea, an act of trust in their bargain which might be against his interests as, realistically, he notes to himself. Their subsequent trade of fruit for jewels and the establishment of the friendship is marked by its equivalences. Fruit may be easily come by on land but jewels are worthless under the waves. Despite their extreme differences, the two 'Abdallahs are Muslim and recite in unison the Fātiḥa of the Qur'ān to seal their compact, initiating their friendship as equals. Each of these two encounters suggests its implicit inequalities as well. 'Abdallah the fisherman is burdened to the point of being suicidal by his debt to the baker, as regaining equality can be achieved only by real rather than hypothetical repayment. As will be discussed below, this debt is presented as a prolonged test of the fisherman's faith. The second encounter, that with the merman, encapsulates a transition from extreme inequality to equality and friendship. The merman is at first the fisherman's prisoner, subject to goodwill, cruelty or caprice. After releasing him 'Abdallah the fisherman's brief regret at not having kept him as a sideshow, an exotic curiosity for which he could have charged admission, hints at a relationship in absolute contrast with the one they do establish. In the midst of this reflection, he describes the merman as his 'prey' (8. 336). The third encounter of this Muslim brotherhood is with the king of the land. The fisherman is as much at the mercy of the king as the merman was at his, and is indeed a prisoner as in the encounter preceding. The transition to equality is unexpectedly and quickly made. The king treats 'Abdallah the fisherman most honourably and accepts without question that such good fortune may be the lot of any individual. His assistance is as practical and as pragmatic as it is essentially altruistic. At the least it is sensible and unselfish. At first glance it seems as though the king is obtaining access to such riches by befriending and advancing their source.[17] However this criticism, applicable to kings in general in the *Nights,* dissolves upon scrutiny. The king argues that 'wealth hath need of station' (8. 340), more to protect the possessor than anything: he says he could extend his protection to the fisherman but it might not last beyond his reign. The king's plan is presented as something he thinks up to look after the fisherman: he marries him to his only daughter, makes him, and later also the baker, his wazir, and brings the fisherman's family to the court. Most importantly, he establishes 'Abdallah as his successor. It is the king who says, after finding out that the fisherman, the baker and the merman are each named 'Abdallah: 'And my name too is 'Abdallah . . . and the servants of God are all brethren' (8. 342). This general picture of equality and harmony is exceptional and, of course, utopian, yet in its directness and vigour and in the pleasure generated by its underlying patterning, it sidesteps our disbelief.

The sea features prominently in this tale, present from the beginning of the first movement to the final parting in the last. It is more than a backdrop, however; it is, further, the image of the unknown, even of God. Like God's providence, it gives or withholds life and death without reason or warning. It is bounteous beyond the limits of imagination, peopled and exotic, and ultimately outside the possibility of assimilation. In its aspects of emptiness and plenitude, it is the many-in-one, beyond the experiential capacity of 'Abdallah the fisherman, infinite and beyond the finite human. The movement from attraction to repulsion is prefigured from the beginning, for it is not the magical, richly giving sea which occupies the first pages. The tale begins with the sea's repeated failure to provide the basic subsistence 'Abdallah requires for his starving family; it is a vast, harsh, ungiving emptiness which, in failing to provide for life, offers up death implicitly for the large family and explicitly in the stinking, bloated corpse of the dead donkey. In forty one days of trying, not one single fish is forthcoming. This image changes, for in catching the merman, followed by the visually and imaginatively stimulating exchange of fruits and jewels superimposed suddenly upon the bleak scene, the sea becomes the source of exotic wealth and the unknown home of the exotic friend who rectifies with his bounty the suffering of 'Abdallah, his wife and their ten young sons. The ten times blessed 'Abdallah the fisherman then rectifies the dearth suffered by 'Abdallah the king, who has only one daughter, who is seen cuddling the children he has invited to live with him. Entering the sea and exploring its richness and diversity might have resulted in an assimilation of its mysterious plenty but it does not. We are far from the *who dares wins* concept which governs Sindbād's voyages.[18] The ocean's very plentifulness,

contrasted with its emptiness of the opening scenes, becomes the source of 'Abdallah the fisherman's ennui and revulsion, and inability to assimilate its otherness. Its plenty, appropriately, is captured in the abundance of fish and it is particularly fish as food which finally puts 'Abdallah off. Ultimately even its diversity is lost in his perception of a surfeit of fish. His needs are relative: the need for fish was relative to his starving condition, while his need for variety is relative to his satiety. The sea, empty or over-abundant, is always too much. Near the end 'Abdallah the merman reinforces 'Abdallah the fisherman's growing ennui and sense of the uniformity of life under the sea: 'After this wise do all the people of the sea; they traffic not with one another nor serve each other save by means of fish; and their food is fish and they themselves are a kind of fish' (8. 351). In the final scenes under the sea many wonders of the realm are offered for the reader's enjoyment. However, the pulse of 'Abdallah the fisherman's revulsion with all he sees is picked up in reiterations of the word 'fish'. 'Abdallah the merman's boy is munching a young fish 'as a man would munch a cucumber' (8. 352), 'Abdallah's wife serves 'two great fishes, each the bigness of a lamb' (8. 351), and finally he must eat fish of 'various kinds and colours' as the guest of the king. His inability to try to participate and understand begins with his rejection of the common food and his reminders of land food (lambs and cucumbers) are funny and effective reminders of the state of his stomach.

'Abdallah the fisherman's journey is through the looking glass and to the impossible other side. He travels to the realm of his not-self, outside of his possible life. One of the beauties of this tale is the patterning of reflection and equivalence when he passes under the reflective threshold between the worlds; the sea civilisations are exotic but recall in mirror image and in alter image the land story of the first movement. Just as the friendship with the king 'Abdallah is the acme of the fisherman's good fortune, so the alienating encounter with the king of the sea is the nadir of his underworld journey. The civilisation might be different but it is also disturbingly similar: structured and hierarchical.

The fisherman is not alienated and repelled simply because of his own limitations. His inability to go beyond the boundaries of his self is reflected in his friend and double, who is ultimately equally unable to accept or assimilate difference. The people of the sea are like the people of the land in that they make fun of, use or reject difference. The fact that a lacktail is sported as a side show and amusement had its direct equivalence in the first movement. Remember that the fisherman thought of precisely the same sport with the merman. The limitations of undersea society alienate the fisherman to the point of insult: he is an object, potentially of scorn and laughter. The reader is aware of the exact equivalences of the two societies despite the exotic world described. The character, however, cannot respond to the equivalence, as his relationship to the society is the moot point. As the outsider, the exotic, he has no place as subject, since he is unable to redeem his otherness. The friendship, which through faith, equality and respect of the other had bridged or clouded this gulf, is ultimately the casualty of this discovery. 'Abdallah the merman, in sensing the fisherman's profound rejection, in turn rejects his friend's world on religious grounds.

The first movement of the tale is presented as a test of the faith of a pious man, a test which he passes and for which he is rewarded. The second movement is also a test; a test of the boundaries and limitations of the self and identity of the good man, a social test which he necessarily fails.

At the beginning of the tale the fisherman and his wife are given as the stock figure of the pious couple: 'Abdallah trusts to God's providence to the extent that he will not use times of plenty to provide for a rainy day; in his words, 'To-morrow's provision will come tomorrow' (8. 330), and in his wife's, 'Put thy trust in God' (8. 330). This stereotype is very effective, as the picture of this impractical faith is contrasted with the real pressures on the couple: the story opens with the birth of their tenth child and the repeated failure of the sea to come up with provision in the name of the new baby. At the end of the first day in which 'Abdallah has fished with prayer for his new son and worried for his wife in the straw, he questions this faith for the first time: 'Hath God then created this new-born child, without an [appointed] provision?' He immediately answers himself: 'This may never be . . . He is the Bountiful, the Provider' (8. 331). He is 'broken-spirited and heavy at heart' but his faith is at this point whole. However, this is the first in a series of doubts he has as things go from bad to worse and he has to endure the debt and dependency upon the baker to feed his family. His wife, soothing the children crying from hunger, has faith in him and in God. She becomes a source of the answers to 'Abdallah's questions, for to her it is clear that the baker's kindness is also God's bounty. At the point when 'Abdallah has lost faith in the sea providing for him, it is her reiteration of God's bounty which gnaws at him. In the end, disgusted with the dead donkey, his wife's words in his mind, he says 'Is this dead ass the good of which she speaks?' (8. 334) 'Abdallah's faith is faltering, his pride, independence and identity too embattled by the circumstances. However, providentially, he catches the merman at this point and the release and friendship are enacted on the basis of shared faith and trust. The chain reaction generated by the ideal scene of the meeting of the two worlds and the recitation of the Fātiḥa providentially rewards all involved. The baker's

altruistic faith is rewarded, 'Abdallah's wife is rewarded, the merman is rewarded and ultimately the king and the fisherman become brothers.

As suggested earlier, this tale is often seen as a tale of marvels which are offered for their own sake. However, in many instances the wondrous in the *Nights* is not the absolutely imaginary, separate and distinct from the real world or offered purely for pleasure. It exists liminally between the real and the unreal, the possible and the impossible, or the pleasurable and the serious (Sarkīs 183). Here the marvels are stimulating and wonderful but ultimately directed towards a comment upon faith, human limitations and the Absolute which encompasses all worlds. After the irremediable rift between the two friends, after all the wonders and marvels and the exploration of the Other, and after all have lived happily and died, we are strongly reminded by the closing phrase of the breadth and all encompassing nature of God:

> And glory be to the [Ever-] Living One, who dieth not, whose is the Empire of the Seen and the Unseen, who can all things and is gracious to His servants and knoweth all that pertaineth to them!
>
> (8. 355)[19]

MAʿRŪF THE COBBLER AND HIS WIFE FAṬIMA

This is a late Egyptian tale which appears only in the Egyptian MSS. It is represented in the Bulaq and the Macnaghten texts. Following the Bulaq and the Macnaghten, it appears in English in the translations of Lane, Burton, and Payne (Chauvin 81). It is the last tale of the enframed narratives, stretching from Night 989 to Night 1001.

> Maʿrūf, a good, generous, poor cobbler of Cairo, was married to a vicious, cruel woman named Fāṭima, who from malice mistreated him. He found it necessary to flee Cairo after she had falsely denounced him several times to the courts for wife beating. As he sheltered in a ruined place from the winter rain, a jinnī took pity on him, and flew him to a place where Fāṭima would not find him. The cobbler ended up in a beautiful city, a year's journey away from Cairo. He was rescued from the pressures of the crowd by a rich merchant who proved to be his long lost boyhood neighbour and friend, ʿAlī. Delighted to be reunited, ʿAlī set Maʿrūf up with the scheme that had made his own fortune. He gave Maʿrūf a thousand dinars with which Maʿrūf impressed the other merchants with his liberality, giving money without concern, saying all the while that his baggage was on its way. Maʿrūf convinced everybody that he was a great merchant with uncountable quantities of every valuable thing. However, he also borrowed so much money on the strength of it and gave so liberally to the poor, that ʿAlī became deeply concerned. When he confronted Maʿrūf with his worries, Maʿrūf merely answered that when his baggage arrived, all would be repaid. ʿAlī gave up on him, and adopted a low profile. Eventually the merchants be-

came concerned and complained to the king. The king, however, was a greedy man, and was so impressed by Ma'rūf's munificence that he was inclined to believe him. Against the judgement of his wazir, he married Ma'rūf to the princess, hoping to obtain the fabled wealth. Ma'rūf was at first reluctant, as his baggage had not yet arrived and he could not bestow fitting gifts upon his bride. The king, however, put the treasury at his disposal and Ma'rūf exhausted it with largesse and celebrations for the whole city lasting several weeks. Incited to suspicion by the wazir, the king decided to get the truth out of Ma'rūf by the agency of his daughter. She managed to get the whole story out of the cobbler but, since she loved him, she decided to help him. She packed him off in disguise in the middle of the night, with 50,000 dinars of her own money and a fast horse, promising to send him money and letters, and to bring him back to the city if her father died. She then told her father and the wazir that he had had news of his baggage and had gone to meet it.

Meanwhile Ma'rūf wandered in the open country, distressed at the parting with his wife. At lunchtime he came upon a peasant, ploughing in a field. The peasant went to get him and his horse some food. While he was waiting Ma'rūf, out of pity for the man, continued with the ploughing. The ploughshare struck and got caught in a buried ring of gold, handle to an alabaster flagstone. Ma'rūf pulled it away, and discovered a stairway to a fantastic storehouse of treasure, including a talismanic ring, which he soon discovered commanded a Sultan of the Jinn. With the help of this Sultan, he provided the peasant with a banquet upon his return, and after that compiled his fantasy baggage and headed back to his wife the princess. The king was overjoyed, the princess delighted and confused, the wazir disgraced, and 'Alī the merchant deeply impressed upon Ma'rūf's return. However, after a little while the king, egged on by the wazir, began to feel afraid of his strikingly wealthy and overgenerous son-in-law. They carried out a plan to get Ma'rūf drunk in the garden and extracted both the secret of the ring from him, and the ring itself. The wazir ordered the slave of the ring to cast both Ma'rūf and the king into the wilderness. The wazir then revealed himself to be a true tyrant and tried also to marry the princess. By trickery and violence, she managed to get the ring from him also, and to have her father and husband brought back, and everything set to rights. She insisted, however, that the ring remain with her, since neither of them was sensible enough to look after it. The wazir was executed. They all lived happily for five years, during which time Ma'rūf and the princess Dunyā had a beautiful son. However, after five years had passed, Dunyā died, charging Ma'rūf to take care of the ring for his own and the boy's sake.

Suddenly Fāṭima, his first wife, reappeared. Her life had become difficult and she had regretted her past actions. She told Ma'rūf her tale of woe, which culminated with the sympathetic jinnī telling her of Ma'rūf's whereabouts and transporting her there. Ma'rūf treated her with honour and provided her with all she could want, and foolishly also told her about the ring. After a little while, her true character resurfaced. She was jealous of Ma'rūf's young son and of his many young and lovely concubines, and she coveted the ring. One night

Ma'rūf's son saw her sneaking into Ma'rūf's chamber. He watched her search for the ring, which she knew Ma'rūf removed from his hand at night. When she had found it and was about to rub it, the young boy cut her head off with his small sword. Her perfidy was proven by the ring in her hand.

Ma'rūf lived happily after this. He sent for the peasant and made him his wazir, marrying also the peasant's very beautiful daughter, and they all lived happily to the end of their days.

Ma'rūf and Fāṭima are set in opposition from the outset. The story-teller informs us that Fāṭima is 'a worthless, ill-conditioned wretch, little of shame and a sore mischief-maker', while Ma'rūf is a 'man of sense and careful of his repute' who 'fear[s] her malice and dread[s] her mischief' (9. 180). This inequality between them is illustrated and emphasised by the contrast in their modes of speech. Every sentence Ma'rūf utters in the introductory paragraph contains a reference to God, whereas Fāṭima's speech borders on crudity and faithlessness. When she mentions God, it is with some disrespect: 'Whether He provide or not, look thou come not to me save with the vermicelli and bees' honey thereon' (9. 181). This demonstration of faith and contrasting impiety is a very simple way of aligning the reader's sympathies; Ma'rūf's words show him to be a good man, Fāṭima's show her to be a bad woman. The tension set up between these two poles, particularly as the story opens with the bad maltreating and prevailing over the good, creates the expectation of a resolution of this inequality, and a redress for the injustices Ma'rūf suffers at the hand of his wife. This resolution is long deferred by the adventures to follow but, because it is ultimately forthcoming, it is possible to say that the story of Ma'rūf and Fāṭima frames the long sequence of adventures in which the cobbler becomes a rich merchant, a prince and a king through a combination of fraud and inner purity. This framing tale, however, is linked to its enframed narratives in a more organic way than usual in the collection as a whole. It is not specified in any way as distinct and it shares the protagonist Ma'rūf. The frame effect is created by the use of deferral of a resolution of inequilibrium and by the insertion of adventures essentially distinct from the story of the mismatched couple. The hero and the story going full circle are the main structuring devices of a rather rambling episodic tale featuring food, benign confidence trickery, noble peasants, avaricious nobles, street humour and coincidence, but underscored by a serious theme of resignation to destiny and fate, and a providence which ultimately rewards the good and punishes the evil.

The explicitly untruthful nature of stories is an essential and liberating feature of Arab tales past and present (Muhawi 331-32). A lie is not the responsibility of the teller and, being untrue, below serious criticism. For this reason, stories could explore real issues and injustices without being threatening (Muhawi 331). In **'Ma'rūf the Cobbler,'** [**'Ma'rūf the Cobbler and his wife Fāṭima'**], lies acquire quite literary features. It is a story in which the lie is virtually the prime motivator, as is perhaps appropriate for a story full of inversions. There are clearly good and bad forms of lying. Fāṭima denounces Ma'rūf as a cruel husband to several judges in a row, maliciously subverting his good character and causing him a great deal of physical and monetary misery. The direct outcome of this series of lies is Ma'rūf's flight from his oppressive wife and his flight from the frame to the enframed. Ma'rūf is the author of the next major series of lies, the lies of plenty which establish his reputation as an eccentric billionaire merchant and lead ultimately to his marriage to the princess. Ultimately all the lies are fulfilled and, interestingly enough, when Ma'rūf tells the truth, he is either not believed (as when he tells of the jinnī bringing him from Cairo in one night) or the fulfilment of his lies puts his truths into doubt (his confession to the princess is overridden by the physical manifestation of the lie) or he gets into serious trouble (his confession to the king and the wazir). Fāṭima's return at the end involves her attempt to deceive Ma'rūf the benevolent king more evilly than ever, resulting in her death and destruction. However, overall, lies are not a bad thing. They are a safer thing than truths and for the devout and pure at heart they tend to work out well. They are the stuff of life, or at least, of narrative life. The celebration of Ma'rūf's delightful lies has both a taste of the carnivalesque unreality of the noble peasant king and an element of palpable social realism. Ma'rūf and his friend 'Alī were street kids of Cairo. 'Alī ran away at age seven having been upset by a beating inflicted by his father for stealing bibles from the Christians and selling them, a scam which both boys had run successfully for some time. 'Alī, in a foreign city, hustles his way into respectability and helpfully teaches Ma'rūf his technique. In getting the hustle hopelessly wrong, Ma'rūf nonetheless manages to pull off the scam of all time, facilitated step by step by his innate generosity and admirable character. It is a story to delight an urban audience relatively lenient on a distinction between lies and truth but also manages to use lies enough to defuse the image of a cobbler king, a peasant queen and a peasant wazir with which the tale closes. It stops just short of suggesting anything revolutionary. It is a tale informed by a deeply cynical view of the ruling class and an idealisation of the common man.

In this world, the lies of a good man virtually become prophecies, while the truths of a bad man are proved wrong and come to nothing. The wazir almost invariably tells the truth, indeed, in a worldly sense, he offers sound advice to the king. However, in lacking the graces of lies, he also lacks the social and religious ethics to restrain his passions. He is such a bad man that he is proved to be an infidel by his violation of religious law and his proposed violation of the Princess Dunyā, who, unsurprisingly, prevails over him by deceit.

The most prominent lie, which is also one of the most memorable in the *Nights,* is Ma'rūf's cumulative lie of plenty. One of the delightful aspects of this lie is that it sublimates the *Nights* collection as a whole. Ma'rūf's lie resembles many of the story-teller's lies already encountered in that it invokes the imaginary realm of unlimited yet thoroughly tactile wealth and the forsaking of all daily care. Ma'rūf dupes the merchants and the king with the same story as has been told the reader many times before, but with this added element of comic suspense: he is believed. When finally the cobbler finds a real treasure as immense as anything he imagined, the reader is very ready to be duped again, as the windfall gets our hero out of a very sticky position. This play with the lie of wealth is a clever revival of a stock feature of earlier tales. Many elements of 'Ma'rūf' reflect a more self-reflexive, mature and playful use of the story-telling genre. Inversion of predictable stock figures is the most obvious of these. Gone is the King or Caliph remote in his glory, wealth and power. The nameless king in this tale is weak and avaricious, distinctly lacking in personal grandeur. He is, furthermore, the owner of a real treasury which is a poor and limited thing in comparison with Ma'rūf's imaginary one. Wealth here has a spiritual correlative. The real king, with his real wealth, does not measure up to the abilities and capacities of the hustler, the 'Sheikh of Imposters' (9. 217). Ma'rūf's ability to imagine unlimited wealth and his ability to give it away, reflect an equally unlimited generosity and openness of spirit. The king's rapidly exhaustible treasury of mere real valuables reflects his petty, little-minded and unimaginative personality. It is comically delightful that the working class hero nobly separates the king from all of his wealth by the agency of the king's own avarice.

The princess is a good character, although the story-teller keeps us in suspense, when we are briefly unsure whether she will cross over to the realm of good lies or tell the truth and destroy Ma'rūf. She quickly reveals herself to be up there with the best of liars, telling her father and the wazir that Ma'rūf's messenger has reported that the arrival of the baggage is imminent, delayed by the attacks of Bedouins. She embroiders this story so imaginatively that they believe her. Dunyā's language aligns her with the good, and we have an idea that all will be well when she asks Ma'rūf to tell her the truth by invoking the name of God. In this case, truth does Ma'rūf no harm.

Ma'rūf manages to fill and parody the roles of several stock heroes in sequence, without for a moment losing his own personality. Street kid, hustler, story-teller, tradesman, merchant, prince and bridegroom, separated from Dunyā he becomes the lovestruck hero and of course, when distraught lover, he is the poet.

Ma'rūf manages to become carnival king for life (or for a tale), ending a very satisfactory peasant tale with a dream of good government and egalitarian recognition of human worth (in the ploughing scene). In the end cobbler king takes peasant wife with peasant first minister, righting the wrongs of the previous irreligious, dishonourable and ungenerous government. This is an interesting parallel to the stories where women rule, for it is a similar inversion. A powerless and exploited class is ideally posited as both in power and better at it, a fantasy born of oppression but modelled on archetypes of what is enjoyable in a story: unlikely hero makes good against odds. It is also the carnival pleasure in story, where the good man is the simple, sweet, generous scoundrel, the peasant hero.

Notes

1. See the discussion of this MS in chapter two, page 33-34.

2. A danger noted also by Peter Heath ('Romance as Genre' 1. 4).

3. *Qūlī li-ṭaīfiki yanthanī 'an madja'ī waqt al-manām Kaī astarīḥa wa tanṭafī nārun tu'ajjiju fī-l-'iẓām*

   danifun tuqallibuhu-l-akuffu 'alā bisāṭin min suhām amma anā fa-kamā 'alimti fahal li-waṣliki min dawām (Beirut 1981, 3. 332-3).

   Tell your apparition to turn from my bed at the time of sleep. So that I can rest and a fire burning in the bones be extinguished

   Seriously ill from emaciation, turned by the hand on a carpet. As for me, I am as you knew: is there any permanence to union with you? (trans. mine).

4. I am indebted to Dr Samer Akkach for this observation. James Montgomery suggested that the woman here appropriates the convention which dictated that the love-lorn be a man, and simply composes as a man (private correspondence).

5. The male addressee of classical Arabic poetry is a formal stylistic feature, too well known to require comment. What is interesting is the inversion here, and the idea that cross-addressing, which is common in spoken Arabic between intimate friends, parents and children, and between lovers, is deliberately utilised. I am indebted to the *Arabic-L* Internet discussion list for a valuable pool of information on cross-addressing generated on the 25th and 26th March 1996/1416, and in particular David Wilmsen's posting 25th March 1996/1416.

6. The use of an invented attribution to justify a fiction is discussed in detail by Beaumont ('Comic Narratives' 232-4). It is a 'strategy for bringing [the fictive text] into the domain of literature' (233). Here of course we are not given a conventional *isnād,* or chain of direct transmission, merely a gesture at the possibility that one could have been constructed. The author or narrator can thus bend rather than violate the rules.

7. 'I am [God] the Truth' (*'Anā-l-ḥaqq*) (*EI* (2) III. 100).

8. James Montgomery suggests that 'in death he is no longer a black slave but is transformed into an Arab' (private correspondence).

9. Slaves were not necessarily despised: this would be far too great a generalisation on a complex sociological issue spanning the changes and upheavals of more than ten centuries. In the *Nights,* however, black slaves get a very bad press, and this figure is practically the only positive portrayal. However, in the Arabic version of 'Ali Bābā Marjāna (Morgiane) is a black Abbyssinian slave, whose beauty and cleverness are described in superlatives (Macdonald, 'Ali Baba and the Forty Thieves' 348).

10. As Daniel Beaumont suggests: 'verse is often used at the end of a prose text to give a sense of closure to it' ('Comic Narratives' 21).

11. The entertainment value, indeed attraction of the fictional powerful woman, can be seen to express the yearning for equality in society or at least a recognition of inequality. The peculiar status accorded to the slave-girl singer, in history and in the literature, reflects this phenomenon, for these women often had more freedom, opportunity and education than wives could have (*EI* (2). VI. 468; IV. 822). In celebrating the slave-girl's body, intellect and talent, the tales fulfil submerged social wishes in relation to all men and women (Sarkīs 129). As Wiebke Walther notes: 'So mag man sich bei den Liebesmärchen und -novellen aus 'Tausendundeiner Nacht' fragen, ob sie Wunschvorstellungen, Idealbilder oder vielleicht gar eine Art Antiliteratur darstellen' ('Das bild der Frau' 78). See also Bencheikh, *Mille et un contes de la nuit* 265-66.

12. Hamori explores this tale in relation to codes of ideal love in the Arab tradition, noting in particular 'Azīz's failure to meet the standard exemplified by 'Azīza ('Notes on Two Love Stories' 69-75).

13. Bencheikh discusses this element in some detail, suggesting that 'Azīz plays the role of a muslima: cloistered sex-object after marriage (*Mille et un contes de la nuit* 304-5). However, to read a simplistic social parallel into the tale is to lose its satiric play with social stereotypes.

14. For a discussion of the trope of the gazelle as lover in a variety of forms in Arabic poetry, see J. C. Bürgel's 'The Lady Gazelle and her Murderous Glances.'

15. I am indebted to Teresita White both for this idea, and for pushing me to explore the gazelles' meanings more deeply.

16. James Montgomery's idea that in the context of the literary tradition the two gazelles have to represent two beloveds rather than the lover and his beloved would result in a very different reading here.

17. Gerhardt also notes the essentially selfless nature of the king's actions, despite appearances (*Storytelling* 265).

18. The gulf between Sindbād and 'Abdallah is also noted by Miquel (*Sept Contes* 128).

19. André Miquel suggests: 'on dira que . . . le monde des hommes est trop petit pour embrasser ce miracle absolu de la grâce que Dieu nous fit, qu'il y faut autre chose que nos pauvres limites, et que la foi, la vraie, est insondable comme la mer' (*Sept contes* 130).

Bibliography

PRIMARY TEXTS

Alf layla wa-layla. Beirut: al-Maktaba al-thaqāfiyya, 1981.

Burton, Isabel, ed. *Arabian Nights Translated Literally from the Arabic.* 6 Vols. London: Waterlow & Sons, 1886.

Lane, Edward William, trans. *The Thousand and One Nights Commonly Called the Arabian Nights Entertainments.* 32 Pamphlets [3 Vols]. London: Charles Knight, 1839.

Payne, John, trans. *The Book of the Thousand Nights and One Night.* 9 Vols. Villon Society, [1884].

————. *Tales of the Arabic of the Breslau and Calcutta Editions.* 3 Vols. London: Villon Society, 1884.

MANUSCRIPTS

John Rylands 654 (709) c. 1778. Ḥikāya 'Ajib wa Gharīb.

John Rylands 657 (204) c. 1650. [*Alf layla wa-layla*].

John Rylands 648 (485) c. 1740. Qiṣṣa Tawaddud.

John Rylands 646 (706) c. 1550. [*Alf layla wa-layla*].

SECONDARY TEXTS: *THE THOUSAND AND ONE NIGHTS*

Beaumont, Daniel Edward. 'Love and Hope and Sex and Dreams: Comic Narratives in Classical Arabic Literature.' Diss. Princeton University, 1991.

Bencheikh, Jamel Eddine, Claude Brémond and André Miquel. *Mille et un contes de la nuit.* Paris: Éditions Gallimard, 1991.

Chauvin, Victor. *Bibliographie des ouvrages arabes ou relatifs aux arabes publiés dans l'Europe chrétienne de 1810 à 1885.* Vols 4-6, & 9. Liege: H. Vaillant-Carmanne, 1902.

————. *La récension Égyptien des Mille et une nuits.* Brussels: Société Belge de Librairie, 1899.

The Encyclopaedia of Islam. 2nd Edition. Leiden: E. J. Brill, 1960-.

Gerhardt, Mia I. *The Art of Story-telling: A Literary Study of* The Thousand and One Nights. Leiden: E. J. Brill, 1963.

Hamori, Andras. 'An Allegory from the *Arabian Nights*: the City of Brass.' *Bulletin of the School of Oriental and African Studies.* 34 (1971): 9-19.

————. 'Notes on Two Love Stories from the *Thousand and One Nights*.' *Studia Islamica.* 43 (1976): 65-80.

Heath, Peter. 'Romance as Genre in the *Thousand and One Nights*.' *JAL.* Part I, 18 (1987): 1-21; Part II, 19 (1988): 1-26.

Irwin, Robert. *The Arabian Nights: A Companion.* London: Allen Lane (The Penguin) Press, 1994.

Macdonald, D. B. 'Ali Baba and the Forty Thieves in Arabic from a Bodleian MS.' *JRAS.* (1910): 327-86.

Marzolph, Ulrich. 'Das Aladdin-Syndrom: zur Phänomenologie des narrativen Orientalismus.' *Hören Sagen Lesen Lernen: Bausteine zu einer Geschichte der kommunikativen Kultur.* Festschrift Rudolf Schenda. Ursula Brunold-Bigler and Hermann Bausinger, eds. Bern: Peter Lang, 1995.

Miquel, André. *Sept contes des Mille et une nuits, ou il n'y a pas de contes innocents.* Paris: Sindbad, 1981.

Payne, John. '*The Book of the Thousand Nights and One Night*: Its History and Character.' *The Book of the Thousand Nights and One Night.* Vol. 9. London: Villon Society, 1884.

Sarkīs, Iḥsān. *Al-thanā'iyya fī Alf layla wa layla.* Beirut: Dār al-ṭalī'a li-l-ṭabā'a wa-l-nashr, 1979.

Walther, Wiebke. 'Das Bild der Frau in Tausendundeiner Nacht.' *Hallesche Beiträge zur Orientwissenschaft.* 3 (1981): 69-91.

SECONDARY TEXTS: GENERAL

Arabic-L internet discussion forum: arabic-l@byu.edu.

Bürgel, J. C. 'The Lady Gazelle and her Murderous Glances.' *JAL.* 20 (1989): 1-11.

Muhawi, Ibrahim. 'Lies and Lying in the Palestinian Folktale.' *IBLA*. 168 (1991-2): 329-34.

Wilmsen, David. 'Reverse Gender.' Discussion network: *Arabic-L*: (arabic-l@byu.edu) 25. 3. 96; 26. 3. 96.

List of Abbreviations

EI (2): *The Encyclopaedia of Islam* (second edition)

JA: *Journal Asiatique*

JAL: *Journal of Arabic Literature*

JNES: *Journal of Near Eastern Studies*

JAOS: *Journal of the American Oriental Society*

JRAS: *Journal of the Royal Asiatic Society*

JSS: *Journal of Semitic Studies*

IJMES: *International Journal of Middle Eastern Studies*

ZDMG: *Zeitschrift der Deutschen Morgenlandischen Gesellschaft*

ZER: Zotenberg's Egyptian Recension

Jennifer Schacker-Mill (essay date spring 2000)

SOURCE: Schacker-Mill, Jennifer. "*Otherness and Otherworldliness*: Edward W. Lane's Ethnographic Treatment of *The Arabian Nights*." *Journal of American Folklore* 113, no. 448 (spring 2000): 164-84.

[*In the following essay, Schacker-Mill describes Edward W. Lane's translation of* The Arabian Nights *as a universally accessible combination of the magical and the mundane as well as an early example of anthropological study.*]

> The doubtful and obscure become truth and elucidation in his hands: we are improved, in spite of ourselves, and even by the very means we seek to avoid it; and customs, and manners, and habits of thought, become familiarized to us, even as amongst the chosen playthings of indolent recreation.
>
> —*Foreign Quarterly Review* 1838:255

When Edward William Lane's annotated and illustrated edition of the **Arabian Nights** was published in 1838, it was greeted with enthusiasm by many readers and critics. As late as 1909, Lane's translation of *Alf Layla wa- Layla* (known in English as **The Thousand and One Nights** or **Arabian Nights**) continued to be considered "the standard English version for general reading" (Lane 1909:4). The later influence and popularity of translations by John Payne (1882-84) and Richard Burton (1885-86) notwithstanding, Lane's annotated edition of

the **Nights** [**The Arabian Nights**] at the very least served as a point of comparison for subsequent efforts to render the tales in English.[1]

Lane's treatment of the **Nights** is distinguished from those of his well-known successors in several significant ways. First, unlike the editions of Payne and Burton, each of which was initially available only through private subscription, Lane's annotated translation of the **Arabian Nights** was aimed at a mass readership. Moreover, it was the format of Lane's edition—with detailed annotations at the close of each of the created chapters—as much as the retranslation of familiar tales that inspired commentaries such as that quoted above and later provided a model for Burton's infamous musings about Middle Eastern practices and beliefs. Lane sought to do more than present a better translation than those previously available: he valued **Alf Layla wa- Layla** as a source of "admirable pictures of the manners and customs of the Arabs" (1963:xxiv) and sought to explicate such matters for British readers, offering an experience both "improving" and diverting. It is this seemingly incongruous combination of ethnographic detail and translated fantasy narratives, or, as my title suggests, of "otherness" and "otherworldliness," that is of interest to me here.

In more recent scholarship, Lane's work has not fared very well: the **Nights** itself has been cast as "a frivolous text" manipulated by Europeans to support preconceived notions of Arab character (Kabbani 1986:43), and Lane's project of retranslation has been dismissed as "a pretext for a long sociological discourse on the East" (Kabbani 1986:37) and "the imposition of a scholarly will on an untidy reality" (Said 1979:164).[2] While it is not my intention to assess the place of Lane's edition in Orientalist discourse or to adduce the "true" value of the **Nights** as a source of ethnographic insight, I question the assertion that these imaginative tales serve as no more than a pretext for the discussion of manners and customs. Edward Lane clearly regarded his translation of the tales and his annotations to be mutually illuminating, intrinsically bound; and in doing so he inherited a critical tradition of particular relevance to the historiography of folklore.

Commissioned by the Society for the Diffusion of Useful Knowledge and published by Charles Knight, first in 32 periodic installments (1838-40) and subsequently in three extensively annotated and illustrated volumes (1839-41), the appearance of this edition of the **Arabian Nights** is contemporaneous with that period in English scholarship that Richard Dorson has characterized as "a complex and intricate chapter of intellectual history" (1968:1): the decades immediately preceding the emergence of "Folk-Lore" as an autonomous field of scholarly inquiry. Although Dorson's account of "the British folklore movement" seeks to delineate the "stirring debates . . . that had once kept all Victorian England in thrall" (1968:440), that work does not, in fact, take *all* of England into account: Dorson's interest did not extend to the more popular forms of folkloristic publication. Lane's edition of the *Nights,* aimed at a mass readership and offering detailed ethnographic information in an appealing manner, would thus appear to fall beyond the scope of Dorson's historiography.

Dorson does take account of Lane's work in a later essay (1980). However, here it is the earlier *Manners and Customs of the Modern Egyptians* that captures Dorson's imagination, with the remainder of Lane's corpus dismissed as "anticlimactic,"his edition of the *Nights* described as "emasculated" and unworthy of further consideration (1980:xiii). Those scholars who have granted this edition of the *Nights* sustained attention have done so within an English literary context, narrowly conceived: see, for instance, Muhsin Jassim Ali's focus on "the prevailing literary concerns of the time" (1981:7) or Nancy Victoria Workman's study of "the ways . . . Victorians made use of this text in their own writing" (1988:2). References to "folklore sources," as Ali explains, are utilized only "sparingly . . . simply because they fall outside the scope of purely literary trends" (1981:7). In fact, this text can offer much of interest to contemporary folklorists—if not in the way of reliable ethnographic data about 19th-century Egypt, than as a valuable source of information regarding certain conventions of textual presentation and the development of folkloristic discourse in popular publications. Likewise, I believe the folklorist can offer a valuable perspective on this text: folklorists have long sought to understand discursive traditions as socially situated, socially constructed phenomena. When applying this perspective to the written text, Lane's edition emerges as a "performance" of sorts, negotiated by a number of players, shaped by emergent generic conventions and the anticipated responses of an intended audience.

To begin with, then, this study seeks a scholarly tradition in which to place Lane's treatment of the *Nights.* There are undoubtedly many parallels to be drawn; and, in fact, it is precisely such a convergence of scholarly energies on such matters as history, culture, tradition, literature, and nationhood in the emergent textual practices of this period that has appealed to historiographers of many disciplines (see historians Culler [1985] and Jann [1985], anthropologist Stocking [1987], and cross-disciplinary work by literary theorist Herbert [1991], to name but a few) and has been of increasing interest to folklorists in recent years (see Abrahams 1993; Bauman 1993; Briggs 1993). Yet, despite the intersection of many lines of inquiry, there is one of particular relevance to Lane's treatment of the *Arabian Nights* and also to the history of folklore: namely, the strain of biblical scholarship established in the 18th century by Bishop Robert Lowth.

Leila Ahmed has pointed out that, as the land of the Bible, Egypt was often construed by Europeans as both foreign and "imaginatively familiar" and that European treatments of the *Nights* reflect this tension (1978:11). However, the significance of Lowth's work to that of Lane extends beyond the resonance of their respective subjects: Lowth was revolutionary in his treatment of the Old Testament as a form of poetry, and his insistence that one must understand the material culture, customs, and even the mentality of a culture in order to appreciate its discursive traditions was an opinion articulated with equal vehemence by Lane.

The relevance of Bishop Lowth's ideas to the historiography of folklore has not often been explored.[3] There is a direct lineage from Lowth to the collecting efforts of 19th- and early-20th-century folklorists, and it was to Lowth's *Lectures on the Sacred Poetry of the Hebrews* (1753) that Johann Gottfried Herder repeatedly responded when formulating his notions of *das Volk* and *volksgeist.*[4] Herder's writings in turn inspired the Brothers Grimm to collect German folk narratives. The rest, of course, is familiar disciplinary history: the Grimms' project was received enthusiastically by European scholars and general readers alike and provided a model for other national collections of folktales (Dégh 1972:54-55; Dorson 1968:91; Thompson 1977:407). Published just 15 years after the first English translation of the Grimms' *Kinder- und Hausmärchen* (Edgar Taylor's *German Popular Stories*), Lane's edition of the *Arabian Nights* may be regarded as yet another response to the ideas regarding culture and creativity established by Lowth. I will therefore begin with a consideration of Lane's statements of purpose compared briefly with Lowthian biblical interpretation.

It is important to note Hasan El-Shamy's observation that *Alf Layla wa- Layla* has coexisted with oral tradition but as a distinct form of discourse: it "is generally viewed as a 'folk book,' [and] normally not narrated" (1980:xlviii-xlix).[5] Despite this, Lane sought to illuminate the *Nights* as an oral discursive phenomenon. Lane's annotations frequently gravitate to the subject of oral storytelling and the place of fantastic narratives in Egyptian belief systems and social life, as the second half of this article explores. While the result may be misleading and even culturally inaccurate, the intent is folkloristically modern: not only does Lane offer details of general manners and customs, he also situates these translated narratives in the context of a broad oral discursive culture. As exploration of the form and content of Lane's annotational writings reveals, the result is a metalevel commentary for the translated tales in which storytelling and fantasy emerge as signs of Egyptian otherness.

THE CHARACTER OF THE TEXT

When Edward Lane began work on the *Arabian Nights,* English readers were familiar with the tales primarily through English translations and adaptations of Antoine

Galland's *Les Milles et Une Nuits: Contes Arabes,* published in French in the early 18th century.[6] The first seven volumes of *Contes Arabes* [*Les Mille et une nuits*] were based on a 14th-century Syrian manuscript, but Galland's version is anything but a literal translation of a single text. Because Galland had "exhausted his material" before exhausting his readers' interest (McDonald 1932:393), his publisher "borrowed" from the work of another translator in the same publishing house, falsely linking these tales to the *Contes Arabes* in order to "furnish more 'copy'" (McDonald 1932:394; see Gerhardt 1963:67, 71-74; Hanford 1964:48-49). The remainder of the tales in the collection were based on the repertoire of a Maronite scholar, Youhenna ("Hanna") Diab, who met Galland while visiting Paris in or around 1709 (Haddawy 1990:xiii; Irwin 1994:16-18; McDonald 1932:394-395; Zipes 1991:xx-xxi). It is from this man, and not from manuscript translation, that many of the now most famous tales—such as those of Aladdin and Ali Baba—were drawn.[7]

The demand for translations of Galland's *Contes Arabes* precipitated the appearance of versions in English, the first of which was available in 1706, if not earlier, with many others in the decades to come (for details, see Haddawy 1990; Hanford 1964; McDonald 1932).[8] By the turn of the 19th century, English editions of *The Arabian Nights' Entertainments,* as the work was then commonly known, numbered more than 18, and by mid-century the publication rate of new and reprinted editions had doubled (Carriciolo 1988:6).

Not all English readers were satisfied with Galland's *Contes Arabes* as a model for European editions of *Alf Layla wa- Layla.* For example, the accuracy of the *Contes Arabes* became an issue of open debate in the correspondence section of *Gentleman's Magazine* for several years in the 1790s. In September 1794, one reader of the magazine wrote in bemoaning the fact that available translations were incomplete: he suggests that in "the Bodleian, there are many more of these fables in the original Arabick, which have not yet been introduced to the English reader, and which would probably form a valuable acquisition to the stock of innocent amusement in our language" (1794:783). Four years later, "W. W." likewise calls for a more complete edition of the *Nights,* although what this reader craved was not more innocent amusement but the inclusion of poetic and morally reflective passages: "The French translation, from which our English one is made, is generally supposed to be very defective. Would not a new translation, therefore, be gladly received by the publick; especially if it represented those fine poetical passages and moral reflexions with which, we are told, the original abounds, but of which scarce a vestige remains in the present translation" (1798:757). Complaint had clearly begun to take the form of a cry for an edition that was textually and culturally more accurate, truer to the manuscripts in content, form, and worldview.

The premise that the *Nights* was a potentially valuable source of information regarding Arab lifeways was well established by the early years of the 19th century. As Leila Ahmed has detailed, such a notion was "proclaimed on the work's title-page almost since the *Arabian Nights*' first appearance in England": as early as 1713, the text had been presented as *Arabian Nights . . . containing a better account of the Customs, Manners, and Religion of the Eastern Nations, viz. Tartars, Persians, and Indians, than is to be met with any author hitherto published* (1978:155, 128). When Henry Weber surveyed the mixed response with which 18th-century England had greeted the *Nights,* he proposed that the "true and striking picture of manners and customs" offered therein was the one aspect of the tales' value that had never been called into question (1812:ii). This perceived dimension of the text was repeatedly emphasized in other prefaces and introductory essays of the early 19th century, while the growing interest in textual accuracy inspired close analysis of Galland's translation and the various Arabic manuscripts (Ahmed 1978:154-156). It is in such a context that Lane was heralded by many as "absolutely the fittest of writers for the task" of translating the *Nights* anew (*Foreign Quarterly Review* 1838:255).

By the late 1830s, Lane was known to the English reading public as something of an expert on Egypt, having published his writings on Egyptian culture, *Manners and Customs of the Modern Egyptians,* in 1836. The appeal of such material is evinced by the fact that *Modern Egyptians* was reissued in a "Cheaper Edition" within a year (Lane-Poole 1877:85) and remains in print to the present day. Under the rubric of "manners and customs," Lane covers topics ranging from Muslim Egyptian costume and physical characteristics to festivals and funerary customs.[9] As Lane writes in the preface, his early interest in Arabic as a language had been overtaken by determination to document aspects of Egyptian culture such as would be of general interest to the English reading public and of value in literary studies:

> During a former visit to this country, undertaken chiefly for the purpose of studying the Arabic language in its most famous school, I devoted much of my attention to the manners and customs of the Arab inhabitants; and in an intercourse of two years and a half with this people, soon found that all the information which I had previously been able to obtain respecting them was insufficient to be of much use to the student of Arabic literature, or to satisfy the curiosity of the general reader.
>
> [1963:xxiii]

Lane's interests in language, custom, and literature were to find expression throughout his career, as he turned his attention from *Modern Egyptians,* to the *Arabian Nights,* to a translation and annotation called *Selections from the Kur-an* in 1843, and finally to the compilation of *An Arabic-English Lexicon* in 1863 (for details regarding the latter two works, see Ahmed 1978:178-197). Lane's perception that such matters could speak to both students of literature and a wider readership was to have a shaping influence on his treatment and presentation of the *Nights.*

In fact, one need not look any further than the preface to *Modern Egyptians* to find explicit foreshadowing of the approach to the *Nights* Lane was soon to take. Surveying the available literature on Egypt, Lane declares that, despite the apparent dearth of adequate information regarding "the Arabs," there existed an as-yet-unappreciated source of data:

> There is one work . . . which presents most admirable pictures of the manners and customs of the Arabs, and particularly of those of the Egyptians; it is *The Thousand and One Nights*; or, *Arabian Nights Entertainments*: if the English reader had possessed a close translation of it with sufficient illustrative notes, I might almost have spared myself the labour of the present undertaking.
>
> [1963:xxiv-xxv]

Lane echoes earlier claims about the *Nights'* ethnographic value and also, as Ahmed (1978:128) has pointed out, overturns the earlier assumption that the available editions were capable of revealing such dimensions of the text. But Lane's still tacit assumptions here regarding the nature of "close" translation and "sufficient" annotation deserve attention. As one turns to the essays with which Lane frames his translation of the *Nights,* his criteria for assessing quality of translation and commentary become more explicit.

Understanding that the very existence of his edition implied "an unfavourable opinion" of the existing versions, Lane sought to differentiate his approach from that of his French predecessor. Proposing that the "chief faults" of the available English editions were "to be attributed" to Galland, Lane writes,

> I am somewhat reluctant to make this remark, because several persons, and among them some of high and deserved reputation as Arabic scholars, have pronounced an opinion that his version is an *improvement* upon the original. That *The Thousand and One Nights* may be greatly improved I most readily admit; but as confidently do I assert, that Galland has excessively *perverted* the work. His acquaintance with Arab manners and customs was insufficient to preserve him always from errors of the grossest description, and by the *style* of his version he has given to the whole a false character.
>
> [1839-41, 1:viii]

It is interesting to note that Lane does not object in principle to Galland's manipulation of the text; it is what Lane perceives to be the sacrifice of the overall "character" of the "original," the abandonment of pre-

cise depiction of "Arabian manners," that he finds so lamentable. In so defining the falseness of Galland's edition, Lane implies that the "true" translation of the work is to be guided by knowledge of the manners and customs of the source culture.

Lane was commended not only for what was found to be an accurate depiction of the Arabs but also for his selective editing of the text: he was praised for his creation of an edition in which the "grossness . . . of Eastern manners is entirely avoided" (*Foreign Quarterly Review* 1838:255). Yet Lane is careful to assure his readers that despite his omission of passages that were found to be "comparatively uninteresting or on any account objectionable," he had drawn on his personal expertise to retain the text's original, overall character (1839-41, 1:xvii).[10] Similarly, when Lane addresses the possibility of faulty translation, he writes,

> No translator can always be certain that, from twenty or more significations which are borne by one Arabic word, he has selected that which his author intended to convey; but, circumstanced as I am, I have the satisfaction of feeling confident that I have never given, to a word or phrase in this work, a meaning which is inconsistent with its presenting faithful pictures of Arab life and manners.
>
> [1839-41, 1:xvii]

Of course, Lane did not intend his readers to comprehend the Arab character through the translation alone; Lane considered his edition to be distinctive not only because it offers a more "faithful" rendering of the text than was previously available but also because of the notes and illustrations that accompany it. The notes, Lane writes, are intended to "give such illustrations as may satisfy the general reader, without obliging him to consult other works," to make readers more familiar with the manners, customs, and beliefs of the Arabs (1839-41, 1:xviii, xix). The engraved illustrations by William Harvey serve the same purpose, Lane suggests, and may therefore "considerably assist to explain both the text and the notes" (1839-41, 1:xxi). Again, readers are assured that Lane has taken the utmost care to attend to accuracy of representation (1839-41, 1:xxi-xxii). Lane, thus, offered his English audience an illustrated translation guided by cultural expertise, as well as running ethnographic commentary.[11]

A similar model for translation of "Oriental" works had been proposed in the 1760s by Johann Gottfried Herder. Herder suggested that ideally such a translation would serve to "set apart the frontiers of foreign people from our own, no matter how convolutedly they may run; it makes us more familiar with the beauty and the genius of a nation that we had quite viewed askance and yet ought to have known face to face" (1992:187). To achieve such a goal, Herder argued that more than a shift in language was required:

The finest translator must be the finest explicator; should this sentence also be true in the reverse order, and should both be joined, we would soon be able to hope to for a book entitled: "Poetic translation of the poems of the Morn in which they are explicated on the basis of the land, the history, the attitudes, the religious life, the condition, the customs, and the language of their nation, and transplanted into the genius of our day, our mentality, and our language."

[1992:187]

Herder's emphasis on both the translation of words and the explication of the "genius" behind them would certainly appear to add a dimension to the philologist's responsibilities and seems to foreshadow an approach such as Lane's; but Herder was neither the sole nor the first advocate of such a project.

In a series of lectures given in the 1740s at Oxford, published in 1753 and translated from Latin to English in 1787, Bishop Robert Lowth had proposed that textual criticism and interpretation of the Old Testament would best be served by a thorough appreciation of the time and place of its entextualization. For Lowth this entailed more than the mastery of facts: an adequate reading of Scripture required of the reader a total empathy of sentiment and mentality with the Old Testament-era Hebrews. He states that it is

not enough to be acquainted with the language of this people, their manners, discipline, rites and ceremonies; we must even investigate their innermost sentiments, the manner and connexion of their thoughts; in one word, we must see all things with their eyes, estimate all things by their opinions: we must endeavour as much as possible to read Hebrew as the Hebrews would have read it.

[1969:113]

Lowth proposes that, in expressing divine sentiment, the Hebrew authors drew on the mundane, using "most freely that kind of imagery which was most familiar, and the application of which was most generally understood" (1969:144-145). Images that at first seem "obscure" to the 18th-century English reader, he suggests, do so because "[we] differ so materially from the Hebrews in our manners and customs": To overcome this barrier one must familiarize oneself with the details of their daily life and venture an imaginative leap, placing oneself in the intellectual and physical world of the Hebrews (1969:155-156). Lowth exemplifies this approach as he turns his attention to scriptural references to "the infernal regions and the state of the dead" (1969:156). He begins with an architectural description of the "sepulchres of the Hebrews," moving from external appearances, to a description of the barricaded entranceway, to a call for readers to imagine themselves within "a vast, dreary, dark, sepulchral cavern" (1969:165). The process of reading takes the form of an imaginative journey, providing increasingly revealing views of otherwise inaccessible realms.

Lowth's proposition that "obsolete custom, or some forgotten circumstance opportunely adverted to, will sometimes restore its true perspicuity and credit to a very intricate passage" in the Old Testament (1969:155-156) was fully embraced by the Reverend Samuel Burder of Cambridge. This statement of Lowth's thus adorns the title page of and provides the ideological foundation for Burder's 1802 work *Oriental Customs: or, an Illustration of the Sacred Scriptures, by an Explanatory Application of the Customs and Manners of the Eastern Nations, and Especially the Jews, Therein Alluded to, Collected from the most Celebrated Travellers and the Most Eminent Critics*. As his lengthy title suggests, Burder draws freely from ancient and contemporary sources, first- and secondhand accounts, scholars and amateurs, to complete his picture of "Oriental customs and manners." He defends the lack of temporal and geographic specificity this would seem to imply by stating "that in the East the usages and habits of the people are invariable" (1822:xvi) and by quoting Sir J. Chardin's assertion that "in the East they are constant in all things: the habits are at this day in the same manner as in the precedent ages; so that one may reasonably believe, that in that part of the world the exterior forms of things, (as their manners and customs) are the same now as they were two thousand years since" (1822:xviii).

One may recognize in Lane a comparable conflation of Eastern past and present, but he is distinguished by his adamance regarding geographical and cultural specificity. The type of traveler's account so freely drawn on in Burder's annotation of Scripture was considered by Lane to be criminally "vague" in its account of manners and customs (1839-41, 1:viii). The "East" of the *Arabian Nights*, Lane argues, is not an uncertain locale; nor is it all-inclusive. Rather, he proposes that "it is in Arabian countries, and especially in Egypt, that we see the people, the dresses, and the buildings, which [the *Nights*] describes in almost every case, even when the scene is laid in Persia, in India, or in China" (1839-41, 1:viii). This is reiterated in the "review" essay that concludes volume 3, in which Lane states that "all the complete copies (printed and manuscript) of which I have any knowledge describe Cairo more minutely and accurately than any other place; and the language, manners, customs, & c, which they exhibit agree most closely with those of Egypt" (1839-41, 3:740-741).[12]

In Lane, as in Burder, there is an inheritance of Lowth's general proposition that detailed understanding of a place and its inhabitants may serve as a key to its literature. However, for Lane this understanding was to be gained not by means of an imaginative leap across cultural boundaries, as Lowth had suggested, but by a real one: Lane proposes that he is capable of the close translation and sufficiently explanatory annotation previously unavailable not because of his expertise in literary translation or familiarity with Arab history but because he claims to have experienced Egypt as an Egyptian: "I consider myself possessed of the chief qualifications for the proper accomplishment of my present undertaking," he writes, "from my having lived several years in Cairo, associating almost exclusively with Arabs, speaking their language, conforming to their general habits with the most scrupulous exactitude, and [having been] received into their society on terms of perfect equality" (1839-41, 1:ix). Lane thus situates himself between two cultures, fluent in not only the languages but also the customs of both. It is this position, he proposes, that enables him to achieve his goal of "presenting pictures of Arab life and manners" rendered "intelligible and agreeable to English readers" of the *Arabian Nights* (1839-41, 1:xvii, xviii).

The line of inquiry established by Bishop Lowth provides resonant statements regarding the nature of literary interpretation, the process of reading, and the comprehension of times and cultures other than our own. Of particular relevance is Lowth's proposition that one must seek to understand poetic works as did their authors and original audiences. Whether such an objective is attainable remains a debatable point. Nonetheless, a closely comparable belief underlies Edward Lane's criticism of Galland's translation of the *Arabian Nights* and the motivation for his own.

ARAB POPULAR TALES AS ENGLISH POPULAR LITERATURE

My concern thus far has been with the ideology underlying Edward W. Lane's annotated and illustrated translation of the *Arabian Nights,* especially as articulated in the essays that frame the three-volume edition of that work. At this point it should prove worthwhile to turn from these essays to Lane's actual treatment of the text. The volumes that constitute this edition of the *Nights* contain more than 1,000 pages of translation, annotation, and illustration, so it is necessarily by means of selected example rather than exhaustive detailing that I must proceed. Such a study does, however, include some consideration of textual emendation, for it is to this realm of fine print that many of the "lesser" tales were banished in the effort to render the *Nights* more "intelligible"; this is also the realm in which Lane defends his omission of certain segments of the text.

One of the most striking dimensions of Lane's annotational writings is his recurrent interest in the narration and interpretation of stories in the Arab world. As many critics have explored, the telling of stories provides the *Nights* with its master trope, shaping not only the frame story, in which Shaharazad narrates nightly in order to postpone her own execution, but many of the tales she "tells," as the characters in these stories-within-a-story are called on to become narrators themselves. The role

of storytelling in the *Nights* as a whole, and within particular cycles, has received abundant critical attention (to name but a few, see Gerhardt 1963; Malti-Douglas 1991; Naddaff 1991; Pinault 1992), but Lane's interest in such matters has been overlooked.[13]

In fact, there are few recent works that consider the mode of textual presentation employed in this edition of the *Nights* at all. Those that do vary in tone, from the more appreciative (Ali 1981; Ahmed 1978) to the decidedly hostile (Kabbani 1986), but are unanimous in one regard: credit or blame, as the case may be, is placed squarely on Lane. There is a contextual frame that has a bearing on the form this edition actually took, but it has been of only marginal concern to critics (when it has been considered at all): the text's publishing history. Unlike Sir Richard Burton, whose edition of the *Nights* was to become available in 1885-86 to a group of private subscribers calling themselves "The Wanderers' Club,"[14] Edward Lane did not have the means to publish any of his works privately (Lane-Poole 1877:36). It is essential to understand something of the conditions under which Lane's text was created in order to better appreciate the form in which we find it.

Lane's attempt to find a publisher for his first work—a collection of engravings and writings based on his travels in Egypt and entitled *Description of Egypt*—was unsuccessful, and this collection remains unpublished to the present day. It was only when the material on ancient Egypt was dropped altogether, and the writings on contemporary Egyptian manners and customs were revised and expanded, that the work was issued as *Account of the Manners and Customs of the Modern Egyptians* in 1836. Years had passed since Lane's search for a publisher had begun, and the author's health and finances had suffered greatly in the meantime (see Ahmed 1978:34-37; Lane-Poole 1877:34-38; Sattin 1988:70).

The offer to publish a work on modern Egyptian culture had ultimately come from the Society for the Diffusion of Useful Knowledge, an organization founded by Lord Brougham in 1826 and made up of "statesmen, lawyers, and philanthropists" with interests in mass publication and popular education (Curwen 1873:258). In association with the publisher Charles Knight, the society sought to make available in inexpensive editions works they deemed of value to a wide readership, serving "a blow aimed at the monopoly of literature—the opening of the flood-gates of knowledge" (quoted in Curwen 1873:258-259). Indeed, the joint efforts of Knight and the society are generally given a place of prominence in the early-19th-century movement in which "the most expensive treasures of literature, the choicest garnerings of . . . knowledge, were placed at the disposal of the meagrest purse" (Curwen 1873:235). As was to be the case with the initial printing of Lane's *Nights,* affordable publication was often enabled by the division of larger works into "small weekly or monthly parts, at an infinitesimal cost" (Curwen 1873:235).[15]

Exactly how wide the "popular" readership was envisioned to be is clarified by Knight, citing an 1828 report for the society. He writes,

> We *all* want Popular Literature—we all want to get at real and substantial knowledge by the most compendious processes. . . . But we are all tasked, some by our worthless ambitions and engrossing pleasures—most by our necessary duties. . . . We are ashamed of our ignorance—we cannot remain in it; but we have not the time to attain any sound knowledge upon the ancient principle of reading doggedly through a miscellaneous library, even if we had the opportunity.
>
> [1971:68-69]

Knight suggests that, excepting those few people for "whom learning is the business of life," the entire reading public remained "all too ignorant" of certain subjects: "the wonders of Nature . . . of the discoveries of Science and Philosophy . . . of the real History of past ages—of the manners and political condition of the other members of the great human family" (1971:69). As this quotation suggests, the popular manners and customs of foreign cultures were conceived to be appropriate subject matter for English popular literature; clearly it was to this latter category of knowledge that Lane's *Modern Egyptians* and his treatment of the *Arabian Nights* were seen to contribute.

As Leila Ahmed's research has revealed, Lane began his work on the *Nights* promptly following the publication of *Modern Egyptians,* despite his poor health. Left little time to complete each installment, Lane found himself under constant pressure, as passages from existing correspondence reveal. Ahmed details, "In order that the numbers might appear promptly every month, Lane worked, he wrote, 'till my sight has become confused,' and towards the end of the month 'the printers suffer me to have no rest nor leisure'" (1978:38). Evidently, the circumstances under which Lane was writing were far from ideal, and the pressures of constant deadlines and economic dependence on his publishers could not but have had a shaping influence on Lane's work. In addition, those aspects of the project of greatest importance to Lane and those valued by his publisher were not in perfect harmony.[16]

Stanley Lane-Poole has quoted Lord Brougham as saying of Edward Lane, "I wonder if that man knows what his *forte* is?—Description" (1877:34); and from all indications, Lane did value this dimension of his work most highly. According to Lane-Poole, when Lane took on this project he was committed to providing the type of detailed description found in *Modern Egyptians* and "resolved to make his translation of *The Thousand and One Nights* an encyclopaedia of Arab manners and cus-

toms" (1877:93). According to Lane himself, what is "most valuable in the original work [is] its minute accuracy with respect to those peculiarities which distinguish the Arabs" (1839-41, 1:viii), and it was this minute accuracy that he sought to make accessible to English readers in his notes. Although, as I will demonstrate shortly, Lane's notes always take specific words or events in the narrative as points of departure, many are written with such a thoroughness of description that they may be read and understood without reference to the ongoing narrative.[17]

As a survey of reviews in contemporaneous periodicals reveals, many critics applauded Lane's detailed annotations as the most distinctive and valuable feature of the edition. More recently, Ahmed has suggested that the notes offered contemporary readers clarification of "the forms, images, manners and beliefs referred to in the *Arabian Nights* . . . binding it irrevocably with the Arabian world, and with reality" (1978:141). Yet can one truly be certain that, as Ahmed proposes, the inclusion of these notes *did* "profoundly . . . alter the experience of reading the *Arabian Nights* for the English reader" (1978:141)? Who is the generic English reader conceived to be? The actual reading practices of Lane's audience are largely left to speculation, but if one looks to the individual with the most significantly vested interest in this matter—Lane's publisher, Charles Knight—the role of the annotations in the popularity of the text is called into question.

According to Knight's memoirs, Lane's general concern with faithful rendering of the text was occasionally in conflict with popular demand. Lane strove to differentiate his treatment of the tales from Galland's, and readers also were sensitive to intertextual comparison: Knight suggests that Lane's introduction of transliterated Arabic words "proved a stumbling block" for many readers, and "loud, too, was the complaint that '**Aladdin and his Lamp and the Forty Thieves**' [the most popular of Galland's additions] were no where to be found in these volumes." Particularly revealing is Knight's offhand reference to the annotations, which appear to have been of interest to only a fraction of the reading public. He writes, "However repellent to desultory readers might have been Mr. Lane's version, it was soon discovered that no other *Arabian Nights* would meet the wants of those who really desired to understand Oriental customs and forms of speech, and was worthy of the admiration of educated persons" (1971:258).

This sentiment is echoed by Lane-Poole, who claims that by the late 1870s Lane's edition was "on all hands acknowledged to be the only translation that students of the East can refer to without fear of being misled. Every oriental scholar knows that the Notes are an essential part of his library" (1877:96). Convinced of the truth of this statement, Lane-Poole edited and recombined Lane's notes on "the main characteristics of Mohammadan life" (1883:vii), divorced them from the text they were originally intended to illuminate, and published them as *Arabian Society in the Middle Ages: Studies from the* Thousand and One Nights (1883). And yet, as had been indicated by Knight himself, such learned readers (Lane-Poole's "students of the East" and "oriental scholars") did not make up a significant portion of the publisher's desired market.

It is interesting to note that, immediately prior to the publication of this edition, Knight and the Society for the Diffusion of Useful Knowledge had been engaged in the production of a project that similarly involved the illustration and annotation of a translated text for a popular audience: *The Pictorial Bible* of 1836-38. Inspired in part by an edition of the Bible being published in inexpensive installments by a German firm, Knight's vision here was of a "publication in which Art should be employed to delight the young, and learning should not be wanting" (1971:252). Prefiguring somewhat the approach to be taken with the *Nights*, this edition of the Bible includes "ample commentary on such passages as are connected with the History, Geography, Natural History, and Antiquities of the Sacred Scriptures," and the illustrations were intended to highlight "landscape scenes . . . costume . . . zoology and botany [and] the remains of ancient architecture" (Knight 1971:252-253). The comparability of such an approach to the Bible with Edward Lane's annotated and illustrated treatment of the *Arabian Nights* was not lost on the publisher: in his memoirs, Knight recalls Lane's "bold and simple rendering of Eastern modes of expression" which was found to be reminiscent of "our translation of the Bible" (1971:258). The success of this earlier publication, in which the dividing line between "delight" and "learning" was purposefully blurred, may very well have shaped the form Lane's work was to take—or, rather, the form in which Knight was to publish it.

In fact, Knight accounts for the widespread interest in the edition with reference not to Lane's annotations but, rather, to the collaborative efforts of Lane and the engraver, William Harvey. Knight writes of the edition,

> Its instant popularity, as well as its permanent utility, was commanded by the designs of William Harvey— the most faithful as well as the most beautiful interpreters of the scenery and costume of the stories. The artist worked with the assistance of the author's mind, and the result was to produce an illustrated book which is almost without a rival.
>
> [1971:258-259]

Ironically, the dimension of the text most valued by Knight, and apparently of the widest appeal, is dubbed by Lane's grandnephew "the least excellent part of the book" (Lane-Poole 1877:95), was apparently considered superfluous by Lane (Lane-Poole 1877:96), and is always granted secondary importance in critical writings about the edition.[18] One must account for the possibility that while Lane's annotations may have, for many readers, provided the edition with an appealing, "scholarly" tone—what Rana Kabbani has dubbed "the paraphernalia of academic discourse" (1986:43)—they were infrequently consulted.[19]

The very organization of this edition would seem to facilitate not only its publication in short installments but also the reading of tales without reference to the notes. Lane's notes are placed at the close of each of the 30 created chapters, set apart both typographically and spatially from the narratives they are intended to illuminate. As the work progresses, a reader would have to be especially dedicated to follow the notes: in volumes 2 and 3 Lane's notes grow fewer and more concise, very often referring readers back to notes from the first volume. The lengthy annotations to which critics generally refer are actually typical only of the first volume. For example, when a male child is born in **"The Story of Noor Ed-Deen and His Son"** of volume 1, Lane provides a six-page essay that details such topics as the relationship of Islamic teachings to child-rearing practices; feasts, ritual sacrifice of animals, and other celebrations of birth; the naming of children; protection of children from the Evil Eye and other supernatural dangers; the hierarchy of power within the family; attitudes toward fertility; conceptions of appropriate behavior for children; circumcision; and the methods and content of Arab education. Few of these topics have any direct bearing on the tale to which this note is appended; rather, they are covered so that Lane may, as he writes, later "avoid an unnecessary multiplication of notes on the same or nearly the same subject, by availing myself of this occasion to insert . . . illustrations of numerous passages, in the preceding and subsequent tales" (1839-41, 1:309). Of the approximately 550 pages that constitute volume 1, almost 130 are notes of this kind; of the 488 pages in volume 2, 147 are of the small print variety, but the majority of these are "abstracts" of tales cut from the main body of the translation; and of the 714 pages in volume 3, 138 fall after the close of the chapters proper, and most of these are story abstracts. The form of this edition seems to constitute a subordination of the annotations to a place of secondary importance.[20]

It is striking to note the breadth of subject matter Lane attempted to cover in his annotations. Although the scope of the present project does not allow for thorough study of them all, we may focus on certain "clusters" of subject matter that do emerge as one peruses the three volumes. For my present purpose, the subjects covered by Lane may be roughly divided into those "philological" in nature (dealing with matters such as transliteration, translation, the variant manuscripts, the publishing history of the *Nights* and related works, etc.) and those that may be generally characterized as "ethnographic."

In editing Lane's annotations for *Arabian Society in the Middle Ages,* Stanley Lane-Poole created 11 chapters and over 150 subheadings to encompass the scope of this latter category of notes (see 1883), and these could certainly be simplified further. For example, entries on such matters as slavery, law, childhood, and woman-hood may be taken as indicative of Lane's interest in social organization; those concerning play, festival, mu-sic, cooking, and bathing, his interest in Egyptian cus-toms; and so on. What I find to be most remarkable, however, and what distinguishes the scope of Lane's writings from those of such a work as *The Pictorial Bible,* is the predominance of entries centered around "belief": religion, astrology, magic, and dream interpre-tation are only a few examples. This is a subject area that Knight's annotated Bible had not aimed to cover in any depth but which figures powerfully in Lane's notes.

Lane regarded a chief purpose of the annotations to be the explication of differences between Arab and English mentalities, particularly in regard to conceptions of "fact" and "fantasy." Of his annotations, Lane writes,

> My general object in them has been to give such illus-trations as may satisfy the general reader, without oblig-ing him to consult other works. In many of them I en-deavour to shew [sic], by extracts from esteemed Arabic histories and scientific and other writings . . . as well as by assertions and anecdotes that I have heard, and conduct that I have witnessed, during my intercourse with Arabs, that the most extravagant relations in this work are not in general regarded, even by the educated classes of that people, as of an incredible nature. This is a point which I deem of much importance to set the work in its proper light before my countrymen.
>
> [1839-41, 1:xiii-xix]

Lane's interest in Arab notions of credibility is made manifest in the lengthy annotations on such subjects as religious practice, the occult, festival, and funerary ritual; but perhaps most salient are those that serve, ei-ther explicitly or implicitly, to comment on the role of fantasy literature in Arab society. Lane's annotations may, thus, be seen to provide a countertext to the *Nights* not only in terms of form (being highly narrativized and coherently structured) but also in content, providing a running metacommentary on the place of storytelling and fantasy in the culture that produced the *Arabian Nights.*

One of the clearest instances of this is the lengthy note "On Magic" (1839-41, 1:65-70), which is appended to **"The Story of the First Sheykh and the Gazelle"** in chapter 1. In Lane's translation, a sheikh is in the midst of telling an 'Efreet (a powerful malevolent form of

genie) of previous misfortunes (a common occurrence in these tales). The sheikh describes how his son, con-cubine, and wife came to be magically transformed: "My cousin [and wife], this gazelle, had studied en-chantment and divination from her early years; and dur-ing my absence, she transformed the youth above men-tioned into a calf; and his mother, into a cow" (1839-41, 1:48). At this point, readers are referred to Lane's entry, which describes the place of the occult in Egyp-tian education, some of the practical uses of magic in everyday life, the various classifications of magical power and practice as defined by Egyptians, methods and uses of astrology, types of divination, conceptions and indications of good and bad luck, the careers of "celebrated magicians," and so forth (1839-41, 1:69). Again, most of these topics are irrelevant to the passage cited above; yet their inclusion at this point in the text is not at all arbitrary. Rather, Lane intends the descrip-tion of such matters to contribute to readers' under-standing of a more far-reaching notion and, thus, pref-aces this lengthy entry by stating that "the Arabs and other Mohammadans enjoy a remarkable advantage over *us* in the composition of works of fiction: in the inven-tion of incidents which *we* should regard as absurd in the extreme, *they* cannot be accused by their country-men of exceeding the bounds of probability" (1839-41, 1:65). To support this claim, Lane recounts a fantastical story he himself had heard "related as . . . a fact, in Cairo," which is similar to that found in the *Nights* (1839-41, 1:65).

Only one page later in **"The Story of the First Sheykh and the Gazelle,"** as morning comes and Shaharazad's storytelling is necessarily interrupted, Lane finds the opportunity to comment further on the art of fiction in Arab society and its relationship to notions of "prob-ability." In the note "On the Influence of Eloquence and Tales upon the Arabs" (1839-41, 1:72-76), Lane again links the Arab conception of "the probable" to the prac-tice of storytelling in the culture as a whole and to the *Arabian Nights,* itself. Here he writes,

> The main incident upon which this work is founded, the triumph of the fascination of the tongue over a cruel and unjust determination which nothing else could annul, might be regarded, by persons unacquainted with the character and literature of the Arabs, as a con-trivance too improbable in nature; but such is not the case. Perhaps there is no other people in the world who are such enthusiastic admirers of literature, and so ex-cited by romantic tales, as those above named.
>
> [1839-41, 1:72]

As this entry continues, Lane elaborates on the uses of verbal artistry for entertainment, its relationship to reli-gious belief and customs, and the role literature has played in Arab culture over time (drawing in this last instance on studies of "the history and literature of early Arabs" [1839-41, 1:72-75]). The note's essay culminates with the argument that even in "the present declining age of Arabian learning . . . literary recreations still exert a magic influence upon the Arabs," and Lane seeks to demonstrate the extent to which this is true by describing public storytelling performances and the popularity of printed materials:

> Compositions of a similar nature to the tales of a *Thousand and One Nights* (though regarded by the learned as idle stories unworthy of being classed with their literature) enable numbers of professional story-tellers to attract crowds of delighted listeners to the coffee-shops of the East; and now that the original of the present work is printed, and to be purchased at a moderate price, it will probably soon, in great measure, supersede the romances of Aboo Zeyd, Ez-Zahir, and 'Antar.
>
> [1839-41, 1:75]

It is also at this point in the text that Lane must defend a significant omission from the original: the recurrent passages that open and close each "night." Whether the decision to eliminate this most distinctive feature of the *Arabian Nights* was, in fact, up to Lane remains unclear; from what is known of Knight's intended market, it seems highly likely that the publisher would have favored the restructuring of the text into a form more familiar to English readers. Whatever the case may be, Lane felt compelled to explain the significance of these recurring passages and the reason for their omission both in his annotation and within the text itself. In the midst of **"The Story of the First Sheykh,"** [**"The Story of the First Sheykh and the Gazelle"**] set apart by brackets, Lane explains,

> On the second and each succeeding night, Shaharazad continued so to interest King Shahriyar by her stories as to induce him to defer putting her to death, in expectation that her fund of amusing tales would soon be exhausted; and as this is expressed in the original work in nearly the same words at the close of every night, such repetitions will in the present translation be omitted.
>
> [1839-41, 1:49]

True to Knight's express concern with the time constraints of the general reader, Lane seeks brevity and simplicity in the midst of 1,001 nights of tale-telling.

Yet, in the course of the three volumes, redundancy emerges as only one of many reasons given for emendation of the original text. Particularly in the second and third volumes, literary value emerges as another criterion by which certain tales earn inclusion in the text, others appear in summary form at the close of chapters, and some are omitted completely. For example, following chapter 33, Lane provides abstracts of certain tales that had been cut from the text proper; while presumably of insufficient quality to be included in the chapter, Lane believes them "not entirely unworthy of being presented to the English reader" (1839-41, 3:158) and, therefore, includes them in this altered form.

Frequently, passages or entire tales disappear on the grounds of "indecency," as is the case with **"The Story of the Two Princes."** When "two ladies in the King's palace . . . became enamoured of the two princes," readers are alerted to the fact that Lane has had to omit "an explanation which is of a nature to disgust every person of good taste" (1839-41, 2:150, 237). Lane does not stop here, however; instead, he places the *Nights* in the context of oral narrative performance and details the place of obscenity in the tale-telling of Egyptians:

> He who is unacquainted with the original [of the *Arabian Nights*] should be informed that it contains many passages which seem as if they were introduced for the gratification of the lowest class of the auditors of a public reciter at a coffee-shop. . . . It is highly probable that Haroon Er-Rasheed often exercised the wit of Aboo Nuwas by relating to him exaggerated or even fictitious accounts of occurrences in his own hareem; and, still more so, that the latter person, in his reciting his anecdotes to his friends, disregarded truth in a much greater degree.
>
> [1839-41, 2:237]

Lane thus attempts to place the "obscenity" of the *Nights* in a wider narrative tradition that includes public performance, conversational storytelling, and gossip.

In fact, what seems to me most remarkable about these entries is the ease with which Lane alternates between discussion of the *Nights* and the multifarious uses of discourse in Arab culture. In these annotations, the *Arabian Nights* is portrayed as the product of a specific discursive tradition, deeply embedded in the belief system and narrative habits of a people. As Lane turns his attention from the practice of everyday life, to the material conditions of everyday life, to discourse about everyday life, the "character and the literature of the Arabs" (1839-41, 1:72) emerge as inherently related, mutually illuminating phenomena.

How is one to reconcile Lane's apparent sensitivity to the narrative tradition of which he believes the *Arabian Nights* to be a part with the various, and often significant, forms of textual emendation characteristic of this edition? One cannot fully appreciate the form this edition took, discuss the ideological and literary assumptions that underlie it, much less attempt to attribute such matters to Lane, without considering the institutional, intertextual, and metadiscursive factors that shaped it. Edward Lane's financial dependence on his publisher and the nature of that publisher's intended market must be regarded as two of many factors that had a shaping influence on this text. At the very least, any appraisal of Lane's annotational writings as a reflection of or influence on early Victorian conceptions of the Arab world should take these contextual factors into account. Lane's annotated translation of the *Arabian Nights* should, therefore, be regarded not only as a treatment of Arab literature, manners, and customs but within the context of 19th-century English popular publishing as well.

CONCLUSION

Underlying the translation, annotation, and illustration of this edition of the *Arabian Nights* is a unified philosophy of textual presentation that shaped Edward Lane's approach to the project as well as his criticism of earlier efforts to render the tales for an English audience. Lane's voice joined those of many of his contemporaries who believed that the *Nights* offered English readers "admirable pictures of the manners and customs of the Arabs" (1963:xxiv). Lane hoped that by means of annotation and illustration this dimension of the text could be brought to the attention and appreciation of the mass reading public.

In his attempt to make the manners, customs, and mentality of the Egyptians "intelligible and agreeable to English readers" (1839-41, 1:xviii), Lane recalls Bishop Lowth's proposition that cultural and textual appreciation go hand in hand. Lowth had envisioned the gathering of such knowledge within the confines of the imagination, but Lane offered his readers the authority of firsthand observation and experience and, thus, a privileged perspective otherwise unavailable. Cast as central to Egyptian national character is an affinity for the picturesque and for fantasy; for the English reader, the very act of reading the *Nights* was thus transformed into one of cross-cultural discovery. What may appear to be mutually exclusive fields of interest—the fantastic tales of the *Nights* and the very real details of Egyptian daily life—are here conjoined, as Lane places storytelling in a broader cultural and metadiscursive context. The effect is an exoticization of the mundane and a naturalization of the fantastic: each custom, practice, belief, and object affirms the otherness of the subject matter, and the supernatural character of the tales is itself cast as an index of Arab cultural difference.

Lane clearly hoped to offer both a general readership and committed Orientalists the kind of translation of the *Arabian Nights* that was previously unavailable. In this, he, like so many of his contemporaries in the nascent disciplines of folklore and anthropology, seems to have found himself searching for precedents, experimenting with appropriate modes of textual presentation. I have suggested that there are significant parallels to be drawn between Lane's approach to the *Arabian Nights* and that of Bishop Lowth to the Old Testament, and that the relevance of each to the development of folkloristic discourse in the 19th century should be reassessed.

Edward Lane himself remains difficult to situate: he seems to hover between categories, qualifying as neither gentleman scholar nor hack writer, as neither a clear predecessor of the social scientist nor one of the literary critic. It would certainly be a mistake to treat this text as the unmediated product of Lane's intellectual objectives; economic factors figure prominently, in terms of both Lane's financial dependence on the Society for the Diffusion of Useful Knowledge and publisher Charles Knight's interest in capturing a mass audience. Also to be considered are the philanthropic motivations of Lane's benefactors and the place of this text in the broader context of the society's publishing efforts. The result of these numerous, and sometimes conflicting, interests is an edition of the *Arabian Nights* that offered English readers escape from life as they knew it, in the form of imaginative and cultural journeys.

Notes

I would like to thank Richard Bauman, Hasan El-Shamy, Henry Glassie, Fedwa Malti-Douglas, Andrew Miller, and my anonymous reviewers for their comments, insights, and encouragement.

1. The publication dates of Payne's and Burton's editions for their respective subscribers are taken from the extensive bibliography provided by Muhsin Jassim Ali (1981:147-188).

2. In contrast to the generally dismissive and frequently disdainful tone of critics like Kabbani and Said, Robert Irwin's appraisal of Lane's work takes into account the intended audience and interpretive framing of the edition (see 1994:23-25).

3. Giuseppe Cocchiara's *The History of Folklore in Europe* (1980) is a noteworthy exception.

4. Herder's references to Lowth are numerous, ranging from the incidental (such as 1992:76) to the sustained (such as 1833).

5. *Alf Layla wa- Layla,* or *The Thousand and One Nights,* has had a long and complicated history as a manuscript, a printed text, and a translation, with correspondences in oral narrative tradition. Far from being a static text, the *Nights* may be more accurately regarded as a complex narrative phenomenon, and the scholarship surrounding it, as Fedwa Malti-Douglas has noted, is hardly less daunting (1991:11). For a recent overview of the known textual history of the *Nights* and its introduction to European readers, see Haddawy 1990.

6. Although Mia Gerhardt (1963) dates the publication of Galland's volumes to the period 1703-13, Husain Haddawy (1990), Muhsin Jassim Ali (1981), and Duncan McDonald (1932) cite 1704-17.

7. As Haddawy has detailed, the European popularity of such stories as these resulted in their subsequent appearance in Arabic manuscript form. Af-

ter the publication of Galland's edition, the "mania for collecting more stories and 'completing' the work led some . . . to resort even to forgery" (1990:xiii).

8. Among these were several versions and excerpts published in installments, as Lane's version was later to be issued: the *Churchman's Last Shift* published "The Voyage of Sindbad the Sailor" and other tales from the *Nights* in weekly installments in 1720; the *London News* published a version with episodes appearing three times a week, beginning in 1723 and continuing for three years; and late in the 18th century, selections from the *Nights* appeared in the *General Magazine* (see Ali 1981:11-12).

9. The 1917 edition of the *Dictionary of National Biography* attests to the durability of Lane's reputation: "The value of the 'Modern Egyptians' lies . . . chiefly in its microscopic accuracy of detail, which is so complete and final that no important additions have been made to its picture of the life and customs of the Muslims of modern Egypt, in spite of the researches of numerous travellers and scholars" (1917, 11:513-514).

10. Haddawy has suggested that Lane shaped the text to fit his area of expertise by omitting "sometimes a few details, sometimes whole passages" because Lane found them to be "inconsistent with his life in Cairo" (1990:xxi). While this appears to have often been the case, I maintain that an assessment of Lane's editing ought to take into account his express objective of providing an edition of the tales suitable for a mass audience.

11. That Lane's annotations have a narrative cohesiveness of their own has been explored in detail by Rana Kabbani (1986), Muhsin Jassim Ali (1981), and others and is perhaps epitomized by their separate publication (*sans nuits*!) as *Arabian Society in the Middle Ages* (Lane-Poole 1883). In his introduction to this work, Lane's grandnephew and future editor, Stanley Lane-Poole, suggests that the notes are a reflection of Lane's scholarly ambition and that they have an authoritativeness that extends beyond the general reader:

> [Lane] was not content with producing a mere rendering of the Arabic text: he saw that the manners and ideas there described required a commentary if they were to become intelligible to the learned reader. . . . These notes have long been recognized by Orientalists as the most complete picture in existence of Arabian society.
>
> [1883:vii-viii]

12. Lane argues that the world described in the tales most resembles Cairo and that Cairo, in turn, is exemplary among the modern Arab cities: "Cairo

is the city in which Arabian manners now exist in the most refined state; and such I believe to have been the case when the present work was composed" (1839-41, 1:ix). The matter of Cairo's representativeness as an Arab city is never fully addressed, and although Lane offers a very brief historical perspective, he appears to rely more on personal experience and observation than on anything else.

13. Critics have frequently characterized Lane's notes as "sociological" (Ali 1981:96; Kabbani 1986:37), but the closer one looks, the more inadequate this designation seems to be.

14. This was sometimes called the "Kamashastra Society" (Ali 1981:151).

15. To Lane's translation and annotations were matched designs by William Harvey, and their joint work was first published in monthly installments costing two shillings and six pence a piece and then in three volumes priced at four pounds and four shillings (Ahmed 1978:150).

16. Information regarding the making of Lane's *Arabian Nights* is, by necessity, from sources other than Lane himself. To the frustration of his biographers, Edward Lane left little behind in the way of diaries or letters: as Stanley Lane-Poole describes, "Mr. Lane had a deeply-rooted objection to the publication of letters meant only for private friends, and he unfortunately took care to have all his own letters from Egypt destroyed; whilst after his return to England he hardly ever wrote one except on questions of scholarship which he was asked to decide" (1877:v-vi).

17. For Lane-Poole these notes represented "monographs on the various details of Arabian life" (1877:93) which were inconveniently appended to a narrative text (1883:vii-viii).

18. Ultimately, one can only speculate about the effect this apparent conflict of interests may have had on Lane's treatment of the text; it is interesting, however, that the demands of the publisher and reading public had an enormous influence on the early-18th-century French translation by Antoine Galland. As mentioned earlier, it was the very popularity of the tales that drove Galland's publisher to forgery (presenting as "translation" original work by another author) and Galland to deviation from the Arabic manuscripts (Hanford 1964:48-49; McDonald 1932:394).

19. Similarly, there were those readers of Sir Richard Burton's edition who objected to editorial commentary. Upon the publication of Burton's translation, an anonymous writer in *The Saturday Review* commented that "unfortunately [Burton] must

needs bespatter the whole with comments and notes which would have been better omitted. There are many matters concerning public morals the discussion of which is out of place, to say the least of it, in the translation of a great literary work" (1887:633). Here, protest against ethnographic commentary is on both moral and aesthetic grounds: it is the status of the *Nights* as "literature," and not simply readers' inconvenience, that makes such annotation undesirable.

20. Not surprisingly, one single-volume reprint of Lane's translation that includes his notes does so by placing them at the back of the book, as an "appendix" to the tales (see Lane 1927). Collections of selected tales from the *Nights,* such as that in the Harvard Classics Series, make use of Lane's translations but exclude the notes altogether (see Lane 1909).

References Cited

Abrahams, Roger D. 1993. "Phantoms of Romantic Nationalism in Folkloristics." *Journal of American Folklore* 106(419):3-37.

Ahmed, Leila. 1978. *Edward W. Lane.* London: Longman.

Ali, Muhsin Jassim. 1981. *Shaharazad in England: A Study of Nineteenth-Century English Criticism of the* Arabian Nights. Washington, D.C.: Three Continents Press.

Bauman, Richard. 1993. "The Nationalization and Internationalization of Folklore: The Case of Schoolcraft's 'Gitshee Gauzinee.'" *Western Folklore* 52:247-269.

Briggs, Charles. 1993. "Metadiscursive Practices and Scholarly Authority in Folkloristics." *Journal of American Folklore* 106(422):387-434.

Burder, Samuel. 1822[1802]. *Oriental Customs: or, an Illustration of the Sacred Scriptures, by an Explanatory Application of the Customs and Manners of the Eastern Nations, and Especially the Jews, Therein Alluded to, Collected from the most Celebrated Travellers and the Most Eminent Critics,* vol. 1. 6th edition. London: Longman, Hurst, Rees, Orme, and Brown.

Burton, Sir Richard F. 1885-86. *The Book of the Thousand Nights and a Night. A Plain and Literal Translation of the Arabian Nights Entertainments.* 10 vols. London: Kamashastra Society.

Carriciolo, Peter. 1988. *The* Arabian Nights *in English Literature: Studies in the Reception of* The Thousand and One Nights *into British Culture.* New York: Mac-Millan.

Cocchiara, Giuseppe. 1980. *The History of Folklore in Europe.* Trans. John N. MacDaniel. Philadelphia: Institute for the Study of Human Issues.

Culler, A. Dwight. 1985. *The Victorian Mirror of History.* New Haven, Conn.: Yale University Press.

Curwen, Henry. 1873. *A History of Booksellers, the Old and the New.* London: Chatto and Windus.

Dégh, Linda. 1972. "Folk Narrative." In *Folklore and Folklife: An Introduction,* ed. Richard M. Dorson, pp. 53-83. Chicago: University of Chicago Press.

Dictionary of National Biography. 1917. Ed. Sir Leslie Stephen and Sir Sidney Lee. London: Oxford University Press.

Dorson, Richard M. 1968. *The British Folklorists: A History.* Chicago: University of Chicago Press.

————. 1980. "Foreword." In *Folktales of Egypt,* ed. Hasan El-Shamy, pp. ix-xxxix. Chicago: University of Chicago Press.

El-Shamy, Hasan. 1980. *Folktales of Egypt.* Chicago: University of Chicago Press.

Foreign Quarterly Review. 1838. *Foreign Quarterly Review,* July: 255.

Gentleman's Magazine. 1794. *Gentleman's Magazine* 64:783-784.

Gerhardt, Mia I. 1963. *The Art of Story-Telling: A Literary Study of the* Thousand and One Nights. Leiden, the Netherlands: E. J. Brill.

Haddawy, Husain, trans. 1990. *The Arabian Nights.* New York: W. W. Norton.

Hanford, James Holly. 1964. "Open Sesame: Notes on the *Arabian Nights* in English." *Princeton University Library Chronicle* 26(1):48-56.

Herbert, Christopher. 1991. *Culture and Anomie: Ethnographic Imagination in the Nineteenth Century.* Chicago: University of Chicago Press.

Herder, Johann Gottfried. 1833[1782-83]. *The Spirit of Hebrew Poetry.* 2 vols. Trans. James Marsh. Burlington, Vt.: Edward Smith.

————. 1992[1766]. "On the German-Oriental Poets." In *Johann Gottfried Herder: Selected Early Works, 1764-1767,* ed. Ernest A. Menze and Karl Menges, trans. Ernest A. Menze with Michael Palma. University Park: Pennsylvania State University Press.

Irwin, Robert. 1994. *The Arabian Nights: A Companion.* London: Penguin.

Jann, Rosemary. 1985. *The Art and Science of Victorian History.* Columbus: Ohio State University Press.

Kabbani, Rana. 1986. *Europe's Myths of the Orient.* Bloomington: Indiana University Press.

Knight, Charles. 1971[1864-65]. *Passages of a Working Life, during Half a Century with a Prelude of Early Reminiscences,* vol. 2. Shannon: Irish University Press.

Lane, Edward William, trans. and ed. 1839-41. *The Thousand and One Nights, commonly called in England The Arabian Nights' Entertainments. A new translation from the Arabic with copious notes.* 3 vols. London: Charles Knight.

————, trans. 1909. *Stories from the* Thousand and One Nights *(The Arabian Nights' Entertainments).* Rev. Stanley Lane-Poole. Harvard Classics, 16. New York: P. F. Collier.

————, trans. 1927. *The Arabian Nights' Entertainments, or The Thousand and One Nights.* New York: Tudor.

————. 1963[1836]. *Manners and Customs of the Modern Egyptians.* London: J. M. Dent.

Lane-Poole, Stanley. 1877. *Life of Edward William Lane.* London: Williams and Norgate.

————, ed. 1883. *Arabian Society in the Middle Ages: Studies from the* Thousand and One Nights. London: Chatto and Windus.

Lowth, Robert. 1969[1787]. *Lectures on the Sacred Poetry of the Hebrews,* vol. 1. Hildesheim, Germany: Georg Olms.

Malti-Douglas, Fedwa. 1991. *Woman's Body, Woman's Word: Gender and Discourse in Arabo-Islamic Writing.* Princeton: Princeton University Press.

McDonald, Duncan B. 1932. "A Bibliographical and Literary Study of the First Appearance of the *Arabian Nights* in Europe." *Library Quarterly* 2(4):387-420.

Naddaff, Sandra. 1991. *Arabesque: Narrative Structure and the Aesthetics of Repetition in* 1001 Nights. Evanston, Ill.: Northwestern University Press.

Payne, John, trans. 1882-84. *The Book of the Thousand Nights and One Night.* 9 vols. London: Villon Society.

Pinault, David. 1992. *Story-Telling Techniques in the Arabian Nights.* Leiden, the Netherlands: E. J. Brill.

Said, Edward W. 1979[1978]. *Orientalism.* New York: Vintage Books.

Sattin, Anthony. 1988. *Lifting the Veil: British Society in Egypt, 1768-1956.* London: J. M. Dent and Sons.

Saturday Review, The. 1887. *The Saturday Review*: 632-633.

Stocking, George W., Jr. 1987. *Victorian Anthropology.* New York: Free Press.

Thompson, Stith. 1977[1946]. *The Folktale.* Berkeley: University of California Press.

"W. W." 1798. *Gentleman's Magazine* 68:757.

Weber, Henry. 1812[1802]. *Tales of the East,* vol. 1. Edinburgh: James Ballantyne and Co.

Workman, Nancy Victoria. 1988. *A Victorian* Arabian Nights *Adventure: A Study in Intertextuality.* Ph.D. dissertation, Loyola University of Chicago.

Zipes, Jack, ed. 1991. *Spells of Enchantment: The Wondrous Fairy Tales of Western Culture.* New York: Penguin.

Susanne Enderwitz (essay date 2004)

SOURCE: Enderwitz, Susanne. "Shahrazâd Is One of Us: Practical Narrative, Theoretical Discussion, and Feminist Discourse." *Marvels & Tales* 18, no. 2 (2004): 187-200.

[*In the following essay, Enderwitz explores Scheherazade's dual role as both narrator and character in* The Arabian Nights *and interprets her portrayal in the works of Edgar Allan Poe and feminist author Ethel Johnston Phelps.*]

Setting out to investigate the frame-story of the *Nights* [*The Thousand and One Nights*] and its impact on Eastern and Western literature, I was unaware of the wealth of studies that have been published. They range from strictly philological research to postmodern literary studies. The former often include considerable reservations about the latter and their seemingly inflated interpretations of details. For this reason, I have largely restricted myself to reconsidering previous theses and theories and will regroup different approaches as to content, form, or both while focusing on Shahrazâd's different roles as "heroine," "narrator," and "woman."

INTRODUCTION

"Your name's really Sherazade?" "Yes." "Really? It's . . . it's so . . . How can I put it? You know who Sheherazade was?" "Yes." "And that doesn't mean anything to you?" "No." "You think you can be called Sherazade, just like that? . . ." "No idea." He looked at her, standing the other side of the high, round counter at the fast-food, unable to believe his eyes. "And why not Aziyade?" "Who's that?" "A beautiful Turkish woman from Istanbul who Pierre Loti was in love with, a hundred years ago." "Pierre Loti I've heard of. Not Aziyade." ". . . Aziyade belonged to the harem of an old Turk. She was a young Circassian slave, converted to Islam." "Why you telling me about this woman? She's got nothing to do with me." "She had green eyes, like you." "That's no reason." Sherazade was drinking her Coke out of the can. She wasn't listening any more. Julien Desrosiers went back to reading the small ads in *Libération.*

(Sebbar 1-2)

Shahrazâd seems to be common property for Arabs and Europeans, natives and migrants, the educated and the uneducated alike. Beyond the diffusion of Shahrazâd's own story and the repertoire of her stories into many cultures, there is also evidence for their origins in many cultures. The collection known as **Thousand and One Nights** is the result of a "cultural and ethnic melting-process" (Walther 12), in which Indian and Persian elements blend (not to mention Greek, Egyptian, and Turkish). Against this multinational backdrop, the principle of intertwined stories corresponds to Arab concepts of *adab* by underlining the power of the word and of brilliant speech. Shahrazâd herself is a cultural amalgamate, for she speaks the Arabic language, bears a Persian name (meaning "of noble appearance and/or origin"), and employs an Indian narrative mode, the frame-story device. Moreover, it has repeatedly been pointed out that, long before Galland's French translation of the *Nights* started its triumphant march through the Western world, its forerunners had already stimulated European and Judeo-Christian culture. The **"Sindbâd"**-cycle has been compared to Homer's *Odyssey,* and Shahrazâd has been considered—and refuted—to be a sister of the biblical Esther (De Goeje; Cosquin), while the opening story of the two kings Shariyâr and Shâhzamân has been believed a variation of paradise lost and regained (Ghazoul 18).

Whatever common grounds the *Nights* and the foundation myths of Judeo-Christian culture may have, there is no doubt that before they were even translated into French, English, and German, the *Nights* made their mark on European literature, in particular on the literature of Renaissance Italy (Walther 17; Littmann 359). In Europe and America as well as in the Near East, writers in the twentieth century (in fact more so than ever) still used the characters of Shahrazâd's tales and her narrative mode as models for their own writings. With this in mind, Fedwa Malti-Douglas states: "Were the Arabic Shahrazad to awaken, like some fairy tale princess, centuries after she first wove the stories in **The Thousand and One Nights,** she would undoubtedly be surprised by her numerous literary transformations" ("Shahrazad Feminist" 40). Robert Irwin states that it is probably easier to specify the few Western or non-Arab authors who were not affected by the *Nights* (Irwin 358; Pinault 65-66) than to present a comprehensive list of those who were—this list ranging from Johann Wolfgang von Goethe, Sir Walter Scott, and William Thackeray through Gustave Flaubert, Stendhal, and Gérard de Nerval to H. P. Lovecraft, John Barth, and A. S. Byatt, Jorge Luis Borges, and Salman Rushdie. Similarly, many an Arab writer, if only in the second part of the twentieth century, has adapted the tradition of the *Nights* for his or her own literary work. To mention but a few: Tâhâ Husain, Tawfîq al-Hakîm and Naguib Mahfouz, Emil Habibi and Jabra Ibrahim Jabra, Idwâr al-Kharrât and Jamâl al-Ghitânî, Ilyas Khouri or Nawâl al-Sa‘dâwî, as well as francophone North-African writers like Tahar Ben Jelloun or Leila Sebbar. All of them have contributed to "making the medieval **Alf layla wa-layla** a vital and influential part of the Arab literary heritage today" (Pinault 76).

THE HEROINE

What is true for the whole corpus of the *Nights* is certainly true for the frame-story, which, due to Shahrazâd's preeminent role, will be the main point of reference for my essay. "The frame story of the **Thousand and One Nights**—that is, the work's prologue and epilogue, as they are usually termed—is without doubt one of the most powerful narratives in world literature" (Malti-Douglas, *Woman's Body* 11), and it stands out by its special status. In the frame-story, contrary to the *Nights* themselves, the voice of the narrator is not Shahrazâd's voice; instead, Shahrazâd is the heroine of the text, or of parts of it. At the same time the frame-story is what Eva Sallis has called the "signature story" for all the stories of the *Nights*: "It is Sheherazade's life and narrative power which are remembered long after we become hazy about the myriad details of the contents" (*Looking Glass* 87).

But Shahrazâd in her role as a woman, a wife, a narrator and, in the epilogue, a mother, is not only the first person one remembers when talking about the *Nights,* she is also the first character to appear in the earliest preserved information about the *Nights.* This information is given in various Arabic sources of the ninth and tenth centuries. The earliest is a ninth-century paper fragment of a text called "A Book containing Tales of a Thousand Nights" (**kitâb fîhi hadîth alf layla**), representing the title page and an opening page to a story-telling session between Dînâzâd (Dunyâzâd) and, we assume, Shîrâzâd (Shahrazâd) (Abbott 152-53). Dating from the tenth century, an important reference is listed in the historical work *Murûj al-dhahab* (*Meadows of Gold*) by al-Mas‘ûdî (d. 956), and a more detailed notice in the *Fihrist* (Catalogue) of Ibn al-Nadîm (written 987). There are only a few other records or references to the *Nights* that can be dated to before the first extant manuscripts of the thirteenth and fourteenth centuries (Sallis, *Looking Glass* 19). The full version of the prologue that became the basis for most of the printed versions—in spite of its comparatively recent date—still bears a logical resemblance to the early version mentioned above (Grotzfeld, *Erzählungen* 11-49; Walther 11-20).

The first part of the frame-story, the prologue, runs as follows: Shahriyâr, the Sasanid king of the islands of India and China, longs to see his brother, Shahzamân, the king of Samarkand of the Persians whom he has not seen for many years. The latter, about to fulfill his brother's wish, surprises his wife enjoying herself with a black slave. Overwhelmed by pain, he kills both of them and proceeds to visit his brother. Once there, he discovers that his brother's wife also betrays her husband with a black slave. He eventually reveals this fact to his older brother, and the two set out on a journey, looking for someone even more unfortunate than themselves. On the voyage, both brothers are blackmailed into sexual intercourse by a young woman who has been locked up by a demon (*'ifrît*) who kidnapped her on her wedding night. From this interlude they deduce that no woman can be trusted. Shahriyâr returns to his kingdom, has his wife and her black lover killed, and begins his one-night stands with virgins whom he executes after the evening's entertainment. At this point, the highly educated Shahrazâd enters the scene as a vizier's daughter determined to offer herself as a new bride to the king. While her father tries in vain to discourage her, Shahrazâd replies that "either she would ransom the daughters of the people, or she would live" (Richard Burton, in his translation, observes that Shahrazâd is proposing to "Judith" the king). She joins the king, and when the night falls, she sends for her sister, Dunyazâd. With her sister's help, she recounts stories that conveniently stretch over the break of the day, and hence, keeps the king in suspense and herself alive (Malti-Douglas, "Shahrazad Feminist" 41-42; Sallis, "Sheherazade" 153-54).

The second part of the frame-story, the epilogue or "closure" (Malti-Douglas, *Woman's Body* 25), is shorter and various versions exist. The version which made its way into the most widely spread editions contains the following: at the end of the storytelling cycle, the readers and/or listeners—together with the king—discover that Shahrazâd has given birth to three sons. The king spares her life, not only because she has given birth to his children who would otherwise lose their mother, but because he has fallen in love with her for her purity, virtue, and piety. The city is lavishly decorated, marriage takes place, and they live happily together until they die. This version is basically identical with the account by Ibn al-Nadîm, but differs from it with regard to an important detail. In Ibn al-Nadîm's summary, Shahrazâd tells her stories until she has given birth to one child only, and is spared because of her motherhood. For Heinz and Sophia Grotzfeld, this conclusion, which offers a strong argument in favor of granting her pardon, seems to be closer to the unknown original text than other versions. In fact, the argument runs along the lines of motherhood itself, irrespective of the additional number of children. Therefore, the Grotzfelds maintain that once the title *A Thousand and One Nights* was accepted, the links between the telling of stories and giving birth (as two parallel acts of procreation) were lost. Instead the *Nights* were just equated with the span of time it takes to give birth to three children successively, or vice versa. This is a rather more prosaic view of the issue, according to which the numbers 1,000 and 3 ruled out the inherent logic of the original story. At least one of the later compilers appears to have sensed a lack of motivation behind the number of nights and the number of children presented. In his version, perhaps with a

parodistic undertone, the king is so bored at the end of the *Nights* by the sheer number of stories that he intends to have Shahrazâd executed, whereupon she presents her three sons and is saved. In another version, Shahrazâd's stories themselves, without the interference of motherhood, serve to heal the king from his hatred of women by confronting him with his own deeds. This helps him to gain the new insight that not all women are alike, as he had deduced from his experiences. After all, it depends on the version whether Shahrazâd's skillfulness as a storyteller or her biological faculties are highlighted or disregarded (Grotzfeld, *Erzählungen* 60-61; Grotzfeld, "Neglected Conclusions" 59-68).

Following the tremendous success of the *Nights* in Europe, the first author to rewrite the frame-story with regard to its epilogue was Edgar Allan Poe in "The Thousand and Second Night" (1845). Malti-Douglas comments on the fact that in Poe's sardonic version Shahrazâd is killed at the end of the *Nights* by interpreting this as an act of male vengeance on female talent in storytelling: Shahrazâd's "power over words and her perceived ability to control discourse have provoked the envy of male writers from Edgar Allan Poe to John Barth" (*Woman's Body* 11). Leaving aside Malti-Douglas's polemical retaliation against misogynist adaptations, Poe's extension of the thousand and one nights by an additional night, which he pretends to have read in a forgotten manuscript of the ancient book "Isitsöornot," is a highly complex reflection of the role of women in literature and history. In this little piece Poe labeled a "grotesque," Shahrazâd the heroine loses within a single night all the favors Shahrazâd the narrator had gained from the king in a thousand and one nights, and she does so by virtue of her wit and self-assurance, not by her lack of them. Her wit and self-assurance place her ahead of all other women, in particular of the women of later, or more "advanced" ages. At the same time these qualities make the king suspicious of Shahrazâd's "female" qualities, i.e., her power to divert his mind from his daily duties.

In her thousand and second night, Shahrazâd displays an enlightened attitude vis-à-vis the royal despot. This eventually leads to her execution since she transgresses the limits set for any woman. Referring to an old saying that reality in its miraculousness even surpasses invention, Shahrazâd as an enthusiast of modern technology narrates a whole range of miracles in her additional night that Poe's contemporary readers would easily identify as engines, telegraphs, or photomechanical devices. This not being enough, Shahrazâd, with her feminist awareness, turns upon her fellow women and satirically spreads out the follies of contemporary fashion, which she finds neither healthy nor aesthetically convincing. In the very last of her stories, a misguided spirit—as often before—turns up, this time, however, in the shape of:

"A crotchet," said Scheherezade. "One of the evil genii who are perpetually upon the watch to inflict ill, has put it into the heads of these accomplished ladies that the thing which we describe as personal beauty, consists altogether in the protuberance of the region which lies not very far below the small of the back. Perfection of loveliness, they say, is in the direct ratio of the extent of this hump. Having been long possessed of this idea, and bolsters being cheap in that country, the days have long gone by since it was possible to distinguish a woman from a dromedary. . . ."

This very moment, when Shahrazâd steps out of her role as a fancy narrator and proves to be a rational being showing insight into the human nature and ridiculing female vanity, seals her fate as the heroine of the *Nights*. Shahriyâr is challenged in both his roles as a king and a man by Shahrazâd's performance, for it mirrors him as an unenlightened despot on the one hand and a thoughtless consumer on the other. Therefore the king, in order to save his face, finds himself immediately inclined to sacrifice Shahrazâd's life:

"Stop!" said the king, "I can't stand that, and I won't. You have already given me a dreadful headache with your lies. The day, too, I perceive, is beginning to break. How long have we been married?—my conscience is getting to be troublesome again. And then that dromedary touch—do you take me for a fool? Upon the whole you might as well get up and be throttled."

(98-101)

THE NARRATOR

Poe equips Shahrazâd with a vision of the achievements of nineteenth-century technology and science, while the king remains medieval in his predilection for miracles. John Barth, for his part, endows Shahrazâd—whom he names "Sherry"—with a twentieth-century American touch, transforming her into "an undergraduate arts-and-sciences major at Banu Sasan University. Besides being Homecoming Queen, valedictorian-elect, and a four-letter varsity athlete, she had a private library of a thousand volumes and the highest average in the history of the campus" (13). In contrast to Poe, Barth simply reconstructs the story, fitting it into the circumstances of his own cultural setting, and therefore Shahrazâd ends up in her well-known destiny as a mother of three children and wife of Shahriyâr. Analogies with other writers are not found in the plot but elsewhere, especially in the structure of Barth's narrative. His multidimensional and polyphonous rewriting of the story comes close to more recent adaptations in Arabic, themselves more influenced by the form of Shahrazâd's narrative than by its content or her personality.

Searching for an indigenous Arabic narrative or for specific characteristics defining Arabic literature, a number of contemporary Arab authors are returning to their own cultural heritage in general and to the *Nights* in particular (Pflitsch 59). Whereas in 1934, 1936, and

1943 Tawfîq al-Hakîm and Tâhâ Husayn depicted Shahrazâd as a symbol for earth-bound baseness, unbound creative fantasy, and a prudent advocate of humaneness (Walther 162-63), respectively, writers of the younger generations rather identify with Shahrazâd's narrative mode. Here, they find parallels to literary modernity and set out to revitalize it in a "postmodern" or "postmahfouzian" manner. Under the label of "radical constructivism" their compositions are characterized by an awareness not only of the constructedness of literature but of reality itself or, in short, of the double constructedness of reality (Pflitsch 62).

Even so, the connection between Shahrazâd the heroine and Shahrazâd the narrator, between the frame and the enframed stories, remains a controversial issue. While the predominance of the frame-story over the ensuing narrative is often taken more or less for granted, this evaluation does not apply to the dependency of the stories on the frame. At the same time, even the frame-story's unity is under discussion, as it seems to be made up "from bits and pieces" (Gerhardt 398). Based on Emmanuel Cosquin's research, the Grotzfelds distinguish three different parts of even the prologue: (a) the story of a husband who, being desperate about the infidelity of his wife, finds solace in the fact that a high ranking person suffers the same fate; (b) the story of a superhuman being, whose wife or captive successively manages to seduce other men, even though he has imprisoned her; and (c) the story of a young woman who escapes from great danger threatening herself, her father, or both, by virtue of gaining time through only storytelling. To this tripartite introduction the epilogue as the fourth part of the frame may be added (Grotzfeld, *Erzählungen* 50-51). Other researchers detect four basically independent stories in the prologue (Ghazoul 18-19) or six in the whole frame (Malti-Douglas, *Woman's Body* 14).

As has been shown, the prologue displays two interrelated but at the same time independent focusses, Shahrazâd and Shahriyâr, turning it into an arabesque, "a play with symmetry emerging from the tension," so typical a form of the *Nights* in general (Karahasan 60). Therefore, not only the unity of the frame-story but also its main protagonist is called into question. Peter Heath, for instance, vigorously claims that the readers' fascination with Shahrazâd should not blind them to the fact that by the standards of the romantic genre it is not she but King Shahriyâr who is the tale's main protagonist. In contrast to the traditional interpretation of the story, he maintains that the king is the one tested by Fate and who subsequently fails the test, degrades love, is unfaithful himself, acts inhumanely, courts death—"and this being romance, where unfaithful lovers meet fitting ends, he is in terrible danger" (18-19). In Heath's view, the issue at stake is indeed Shahrazâd's life, but also that of Shahriyâr. Besides, the central idea is now the restoration of the king's sound perception both of himself and of women. Implicitly, the most commonly accepted ending is also the *Nights*' main objective: a prosperous people, a happy couple, and a healthy progeny.

With all these nuances in mind, most scholars ultimately agree about the cohesiveness of the frame-story and Shahrazâd's central position in it. The Shahrazâd-story "is all that a framing should be" (Gerhardt 398), as it functions as an "ever flexible border" (Naddaf 5) and has "endured from a time when the enframed stories are pure speculation" (Sallis, "Sheherazade" 154). It is a story capable of integrating other stories whatever their plot may be. At this point, however, a second fundamental objection against the unity of the *Nights* is raised. Some scholars discern a certain arbitrariness of the frame with regard to what follows. First, despite the basic structure of the *Nights* according to the old institution of *samar* (nightly entertainment), the manuscripts vary as to whether the compilers separate episodes into nights through to the end and whether the flow of stories is interrupted by the characters of the frame from time to time (Gerhardt 398-99). Secondly, the (psycho)logical unity of the frame and the stories is important. Mia Gerhardt denies this unity by arguing that the compilers did not strive to interrelate the two or to keep alive the reader's interest in the framing story itself. As she maintains, the readers, like the compilers, gradually forget Shahrazâd and her plight, and concentrate all their attention upon the stories she tells. Moreover, Gerhardt dismisses any possible interrelation, claiming that even the very first story (**"The Merchant and the Jinni"**) introduces the theme of wicked wives, which renders it an unsuitable or, in the case of a wife having intercourse with a black slave, even tactless choice by a woman in such a dangerous situation as Shahrazâd's (399-400). This criticism, however, is contested by Muhsin Mahdi (131-34), Dzevad Karahasan (65-66), and Ferial Ghazoul, all of whom meticulously argue in favor of the aptness of exactly this story for the first night Shahrazâd and Shahriyâr spend together. Taking this story as a starting-point, but without confining themselves to it, they detect a whole range of subtle messages beyond just the repetition of the king's experiences, which are not wasted upon him. As a matter of fact, Shahrazâd's successful survival night after night strongly supports this thesis as well as Malti-Douglas's remark that Shahrazâd is quite present as a narrator, appearing at least at the beginning and end of every night (*Woman's Body* 14).

THE WOMAN

From a feminist point of view, Shahrazâd's inclination to include all kinds of stories should not be discarded at all as the indifferent attitude of the compilers; on the contrary, it should be appreciated as the integrative ability of a woman. "Shahrazad is characterized by nothing

if not her fertility—both narrative and otherwise—and it is a tribute to her legacy of potentially infinite narrative generation that the text possesses an ability, indeed a willingness, to accommodate ultimately any tale between its ever-flexible borders, in the interest of maintaining narrative variety" (Naddaf 5). Other writers share this equation of biological and mental procreation, albeit with modifications. For Ghazoul, a master-slave dialectic seems at work, when Shahrazâd, embodying the very principle of female vulnerability, succeeds *vis-à-vis* her virile oriental despot in turning women from objects of sex into objects of fantasy (23-24). For Paul Auster, in a rather sophisticated argument, Shahrazâd's procreative abilities appear to be justified mainly through the proof of her talent in telling stories of life and death. Shahrazâd "has borne the king three sons. Again, the lesson is made clear. A voice that speaks, a woman's voice that speaks, a voice that speaks stories of life and death, has the power to give life" (153). Still another author, Dzevad Karahasan, links being a female to fundamental creative powers, when he states: "It is my firm belief that this book has been told by a woman, maybe not a single one, but several, whose stories, over the years, have harmoniously blended." This is not due, in his view, to the meandering mode of Shahrazâd's narration or other techniques of a so-called feminine speech, like decentrism, avoidance of clear-cut definitions, paraphrases of the subject, etc., but to easily overlooked details of observation like the one "more visible than a banner and more beautiful than a red camel." Comparisons like these happen to enter literature, according to Karahasan, only by way of "accident"; they are spontaneous creations, having escaped "male" (self-)censorship that corresponds with the ruling canon (53).

We may wonder whether Karahasan is familiar with theories of oral transmission, but something else seems to be of greater importance here. Most scholars, indeed, attribute not only Shahrazâd's way of storytelling but also her outlook in general to intentions traditionally linked to female rather than male characters in literature. These intentions or, better perhaps, the *raison d'être* of Shahrazâd's storytelling, have been identified as belonging to the scheme of time-gaining, a therapeutical or didactical quest, and a complex web of "desire."[1] Shahrazâd's struggle to gain time and to instruct the king do not exclude each other. In consequence, Heath laconically writes: "[O]ne should remember that [Shahrazâd's] main purpose with this strategy [of daily storytelling] is not procrastination. This could not be so; even she would eventually run out of stories. On the contrary, Shahrazad is narrating tales primarily to instruct the king" (18; cf. Bettelheim 87). So we have a clear case of instruction by storytelling. It is again Karahasan who reminds us of the peculiar qualities of storytelling as opposed to other kinds of instruction: "A speech in a way of a theologian or philosopher would have been useless [for Shahriyâr]. . . . He was in need of a knowledge that is supplied only by experience and literature, a knowledge comprising human totality, body, soul, sentiment. . . . Therefore, Shahrazad instructs by way of narration. . . ." (64).

Malti-Douglas, on the other hand, dismisses both ways of understanding Shahrazâd's situation, as both the procrastination- and the healing-scheme identify Shahrazâd with speech. She argues that "[a]ll these views of Shahrazad and the frame have one overriding characteristic in common: they are prefeminist and pregender conscious, in the intellectual, not the chronological sense" (*Woman's Word* 13). Like others mentioned above, Malti-Douglas postulates a relation between femininity and discourse, stating that Shahrazâd shifts the problem of desire, the realm of Shahriyâr's trauma, to the seemingly more distant and more malleable world of the text. However, in picking up the catchword "desire," Malti-Douglas envisages not childbearing but sexuality.

> [Shahrazad's] storytelling teaches a new type of desire, a desire that continues from night to night, a desire whose interest does not fall and which can, therefore, leap the intervening days. In sexual terms, this is a replacement of an immature male pattern of excitement, satisfaction, and termination with what can be called a more classically female pattern of extended and continuous desire and pleasure. Of course, it is this extension of desire through time that permits the forging of relationships, and with it the nonexploitive approach to sexuality.
>
> (*Woman's Body* 22)

While a reconciliation of the sexes is achieved, it runs along traditional lines. From the epilogue we learn that the king has fallen in love with Shahrazâd during the period of three years that has meanwhile elapsed; nevertheless, it is to her and our relief that she is able to reassure herself with her three sons, just in case the king still bears traces of his former character. In one of the epilogue's versions the king, as a proof of his utmost appreciation of Shahrazâd's tales, gives order to have them written down. Desire may be one of the catchwords for psychoanalytically based studies, "literature" is the one for postmodern oriented theorists. Shahrazâd has, indeed, narrated the stories, but Shahriyâr is the one to preserve them, as he has the male command over the authority and the permanence of the written word. "In the process, body has been transmuted into word and back into body. Corporeality is the final word, as Shahrazad relinquishes her role of narrator for that of perfect woman: mother and lover" (Malti-Douglas, *Woman's Body* 28).

Here, in the epilogue, we have the starting-point for a rewriting of Shahrazâd's story, Arab and other. In the early 1980s, Ethel Johnston Phelps published a new

version of the story, her protagonists being a cruel old king and a versatile young Shahrazâd. Discontent with the traditional ending, she suggested another one. In her version, at the eventual death of the king (sultan), Shahrazâd was free to do "what any clever storyteller would do: Using her earlier education provided by the best tutors, she of course wrote down for posterity a more polished version of her one thousand and one tales" (173). But the American feminist Phelps was not alone in pointing out the fact that Shahrazâd stands for oral transmission, which is fugitive by definition, as the narrative is caught in space and time, depends on spontaneous performance, and lacks the authority of the written word. Led by the same discontent with the epilogue, Assia Djebar put forward a question, which has been picked up by many literary critics: "After all, had Shéhérezade not been narrating every night until dawn, but written, would she have killed the sultan?"

Djebar's modern Shahrazâd in *Ombre sultane* distinguishes herself more than any other from the original, including the protagonist of Leila Sebbar's *Sherazade,* a novel which confronts the reader with the identity-search of a young woman from the "beurs"-milieu in Paris. Somewhat autobiographically, Djebar's heroine, Isma, comes from a privileged family and receives her education in France. There, she marries a fellow Algerian with whom she has a daughter. Seeking divorce, she comes into contact with her husband's second wife, Hajila, as she makes use of the traditional prerogative of the queen, i.e., to choose her successor. Hajila, in contrast to Isma, comes from a traditional background, in which female education is not regarded as a major issue. The (nameless) husband loses his impotence, which he has suffered from during the last years with Isma, and enjoys his conjugal rights in a way that may almost be regarded as rape. When Hajila sees Isma going around unveiled, she starts to secretly leave the house, but her husband beats her up and puts her under guard. Hajila, desperate because she is the victim of his violence, tries to kill herself but only loses her unborn child. The same day Isma leaves the city to go live with her daughter in the place she has come from. For Djebar, a reconciliation between the sexes is impossible to achieve, either with or without children. On the contrary, she pleads for solidarity among women in order to overcome male predominance. Isma "shadows" Hajila as she watches over her—but does not Hajila, too, "shadow" Isma by helping her to free herself from the "sultan"?

One cannot, however, speak about Djebar's novel without mentioning the second person who plays a key role in Shahrazâd's own story, in addition to the king's: Dunyâzâd, Shahrazâd's little sister. In the original plot, when alone with the king, Shahrazâd sends for Dunyâzâd in order to bid her farewell. From that moment on, Dunyâzâd serves as Shahrazâd's companion during the (roughly) three years of the *Nights,* but her real importance lies in her instigation of the storytelling. She is the one who raises the king's interest and keeps it alive by urging Shahrazâd to tell a story, by commenting upon it, and by interrupting it at the end of the night. The manuscripts of the *Nights* reflect her role in one of two ways, either by omitting her completely in the epilogue or by granting her an almost equal footing with Shahrazâd: in a long version of the epilogue she is married to Shahzamân, Shahriyâr's younger brother. Modern writers have felt that the character of Dunyâzâd contains a wealth of meanings and have made her a heroine in her own right. In Barth's *Dunyazadiad* (which turns her story into a "classical" one by the ending -iad, but at the same time Americanizes her name into "Doony," an equivalent to his "Sherry") she is the real narrator who tells her own and her sister's story to Shahzamân on their wedding night, whereas Shahrazâd has received all her stories from a jinni (who is none other than the author himself). In May Telmissany's *Dunyazad,* the heroine is a stillborn child of that name, whose only resemblance to her namesake is the fact that her death causes other people to tell their stories. But Djebar's novel is distinct. Shahrazâd is not a plagiarist, and Dunyâzâd does not serve merely as a catalyst. On the contrary, we learn that the privileged and emancipated Shahrazâd, who has been educated according to Western cultural standards, cannot free herself as long as the poor, uneducated, and veiled Dunyâzâd in her traditional setting remains in subjugation or, from a slightly different perspective, that the freedom of the former is at the expense of the latter. In aesthetical as well as in gender and political terms, Djebar's modern version of the two sisters' story is the most advanced and consequent: decentrist, feminist, and antieurocentrist.

Note

1. Desire as the main motive behind the actions taken by the characters in the *Nights* has been singled out, first of all, by writers like André Miquel, Edgar Weber, and Jemal Eddine Bencheikh, all of whom belong to the "French"—Lacan-inspired—school.

Works Cited

Abbott, Nabia. "A Ninth-Century Fragment of the 'Thousand Nights': New Light on the Early History of the *Arabian Nights*." *Journal of Near Eastern Studies* 8 (1949): 129-64.

Auster, Paul. *The Invention of Solitude.* London: Penguin, 1992.

Barth, John. "Dunyazadiad." *Chimera.* 1972. Boston and New York: Houghton Mifflin Co., 2001.

Bencheikh, Jemal Eddine. *Les Mille et une Nuits ou la parole prisonnière.* Paris: Gallimard, 1988.

Bettelheim, Bruno. *The Uses of Enchantment: The Meaning and Importance of Fairy Tales.* New York: Vintage Books, 1977.

Cosquin, Emmanuel. "Le Prologue-cadre des Mille et une Nuits." *Revue Biblique* 6 (1909):7-49. Also in *Études folkloriques.* Paris: Édouard Champion, 1922. 265-347.

De Goeje, Michael J. "De arabische nachtvertellingen." *De Gids* 50 (1886): 385-413.

Djebar, Assia. *Ombre sultane.* Paris: J. C. Lattès, 1987.

Gerhardt, Mia. *The Art of Story-Telling: A Literary Study of the* Thousand and One Nights. Leiden: Brill, 1963.

Ghazoul, Ferial. *Nocturnal Poetics:* The Arabian Nights *in Comparative Context.* Cairo: American UP, 1996.

Grotzfeld, Heinz. "Neglected Conclusions of the *Arabian Nights*: Gleanings in Forgotten and Overlooked Recensions." *Journal of Arabic Literature* 16 (1985):73-87.

Grotzfeld, Heinz and Sophia. *Die Erzählungen aux "Tausendundeiner Nacht."* Darmstadt: Wissenschaftliche Buchgesellschaft, 1984.

Heath, Peter. "Romance as Genre in *The Thousand and One Nights*." *Journal of Arabic Literature* 18 (1987): 1-21; 19 (1988): 1-26.

Irwin, Robert. *Die Welt von Tausendundeiner Nacht.* Frankfurt and Leipzig: Insel, 1997.

Littmann, Enno. *Alf layla wa-layla. The Encyclopaedia of Islam.* Vol. 1. Leiden: Brill, 1960. 358-64.

Karahasan, Dzevad. *Das Buch der Gärten: Grenzgänge zwischen Islam und Christentum.* Frankfurt and Leipzig: Insel, 2002.

Mahdi, Muhsin. *The Thousand and One Nights.* Vol. 3. Leiden: Brill, 1994.

Malti-Douglas, Fedwa. *Woman's Body, Woman's Word: Gender and Discourse in Arabo-Islamic Writing.* Princeton: Princeton UP, 1992.

———. "Shahrazad Feminist." The Thousand and One Nights *in Arabic Literature and Society.* Ed. Richard G. Hovannisian and Georges Sabagh. Cambridge: Cambridge UP, 1997. 40-55.

Miquel. André. *Sept contes des Mille et une Nuits; ou Il n'y a pas de contes innocents.* Paris: Sindbad, 1981.

Naddaf, Sandra. *Arabesque: Narrative Structures and the Aesthetics of Repetition in* 1001 Nights. Evanston, IL: Northwestern UP, 1991.

Pflitsch, Andreas. "Konstruierte Wirklichkeiten: Die zeitgenössische arabische Literatur, der radikale Konstruktivismus und die Erzählungen aus 1001 Nacht."

Understanding Near Eastern Literatures: A Spectrum of Interdisciplinary Approaches. Ed. Verena Klemm and Beatrice Gruendler. Wiesbaden: Reichert, 2000. 59-71.

Phelps, Ethel Johnston. *The Maid of the North: Feminist Folk Tales from Around the World.* New York: Henry Holt, 1982.

Pinault, David. *Alf layla wa-layla. Encyclopedia of Arabic Literature.* Ed. Julie S. Meisami and Paul Starkey. Vol. 1. London and New York: Routledge, 1998. 69-77.

Poe, Edgar Allan. *Prose Tales.* Vol. 5. New York: Thomas Y. Crowell, 1902. 80-101.

Sallis, Eva. "Sheherazade/Shahrazad: Rereading the Frame Tale of the *1001 Nights.*" *Arabic and Middle Eastern Literatures* 1 (1998): 153-67.

———. *Sheherazade Through the Looking Glass: The Metamorphosis of the* Thousand and One Nights. Richmond: Curzon Press, 1999.

Sebbar, Leila. *Sherazade.* London: Quartet Books, 2000.

Telmissany, May. *Dunyazad.* London: Saqi Books, 2000.

Walther, Wiebke. *Tausendundeine Nacht.* München and Zürich: Artemis, 1987.

Weber, Edgard, ed. *Le Secret des Mille et une Nuits: L'inter-dit de Sheherazade.* Toulouse: Eché, 1987.

Robert Irwin (essay date 2004)

SOURCE: Irwin, Robert. "Political Thought in *The Thousand and One Nights.*" *Marvels & Tales* 18, no. 2 (2004): 246-57.

[*In the following essay, Irwin concentrates on the political and moral didacticism of* The Arabian Nights, *alleging that its simplistic emphasis on servitude and obedience reflects early Islamic culture.*]

It is a preposterous title, of course. Should we also look for political thought in *Snow White and the Seven Dwarfs?* Or in the slapstick films of Laurel and Hardy? Or in *Superman* comics? Surely, whereas politics is "the art of the possible," *The Thousand and One Nights* (henceforth: *Nights* [*The Thousand and One Nights*]) is, in large part at least, the art of the impossible. Yet a moment's reflection allows one to realize that the title is not so very preposterous after all. To start with, the exordium to the *Nights,* with its references to doomed and vanished dynasties (**"Thamûd, 'Âd and Pharaoh of the Vast Domain"**) and its promise to provide lessons based on "what happened to kings from the beginning of time," strongly suggests that political concerns were not wholly alien to those who contributed to the

Nights (Mahdi 1: 56; Haddawy 2). In listening to Sheherezade, Shahriyâr is supposed to be learning from past examples (even if the political philosopher, Michael Oakeshott, once described the study of history as something the historian loves "as a mistress of whom he never tires and whom he never expects to talk sense" [182]). In the light of the opening exordium, the whole of the *Nights* can be considered to be an overblown and out-of-control example of the literary genre of mirror-for-princes (German *Fürstenspiegel*). In the mirror-for-princes section of *Nasîhat al-mulûk,* a work spuriously attributed to the eleventh-century theologian and Sufi, al-Ghazâlî (d. 1111), the reading of stories about past kings is advocated as a royal duty: "He must also read the books of good counsel . . . just as Anûshîrvân . . . used to read the books of former kings, ask for stories about them and follow their ways" (Crone, "Did al-Ghazali Write a Mirror for Princes?" 184).

To look at the politics of the *Nights* from another angle, when Elie Kedourie, in a study of modern Middle Eastern politics, came to discuss the medieval and Islamic legacy to the politics of the modern Middle East, he touched on the despotic powers of the caliphs and specifically of Abbasid Caliph Hârûn al-Rashîd, and he had this to say: "The emblem of his terrible power is the black executioner who, in the *Nights,* is shown to be in constant attendance on Hârûn al-Rashîd. Nearness to supreme power is perilous. The constant care of the ordinary subject is to avoid the attention of authority. A story in the *Nights* concerns a householder who, coming back from work in the evening, finds a corpse near his door. He is terrified to report his discovery to the police, lest they accuse him of murder. . . ." Having given (a slightly garbled) version of **"The Tale of the Hunchback"** with its migratory corpse, Kedourie made the point that for most people under a premodern Islamic regime, happiness was dependent on having as little as possible to do with the rulers, and he went on to quote Hârûn al-Rashîd's son and successor, the Caliph al-Ma'mûn, who declared that "the best life has he who has an ample house, a beautiful wife, and sufficient means, who does not know us and whom we do not know" (15). Historically it was probably quite easy for middle- or lower-class Baghdadis to avoid the real Hârûn. But in the fictions of the *Nights,* humble folk were not so lucky, and for many of them, their story and their peril begin when they come up against the nocturnally prowling caliph and suddenly find themselves talking for their lives.

Modern political textbooks tend to be drab productions. This was not always the case in medieval times, when storytelling was an accepted way of transmitting religious, political, and moral ideas. Political treatises are not the only possible expressions of political thought (even if the academic prejudice inclines that way). Mobs and mob violence, carnivals and kings-for-a-day, shadow theatre and storytelling can all furnish examples of the politics of the street. For all its apparent wildness, the politics of the street has tended to be conservative. Mobs in eighteenth-century England were more likely to riot against freethinkers and Roman Catholics than they were to demonstrate against the government (White 104-20; cf. Davis 152-87). In Mamluk times, the commonest targets of mob violence in Cairo and Damascus were Christians and Jews. Though there were occasional protests against individual sultans, viziers or *muhtasibs,* people did not protest against the institutions as such. Moreover, protestors generally preferred to blame the sultan's evil counsellors rather than the sultan himself (Shoshan, *Popular Culture* 62-66; "The Moral Economy;" Grehan; Irwin, *Middle East* 54, 94-95). As we shall see, the latent tendency of the politics of the stories of the *Nights* was to support the status quo.

Throughout the Islamic world, there was a strong tradition of transmitting wisdom and information through teaching stories. Consider the political agenda of Ibn al-Muqaffa'(d. ca. 760) in his Arabic version of the Indo-Persian collection of animal tales and fables, *Kalîla wa-Dimna,* where storytelling animals instruct a hypothetical ruler and his ministers in the duties and perils of governing (Ibn al-Muqaffa'). The Isma'îlîs and the Muslim Neoplatonist group of Ikhwân al-Safâ ("Brethren of Purity") frequently used stories and fables to make political or moral points (Netton 89-94). Later yet, from the late twelfth century onwards, Sufi masters began to make use of the teaching tale. Moreover, the philosophers Ibn Tufayl (d. 1185), Ibn Sînâ (Avicenna; d. 1037), and Ibn al-Nafîs (d. 1288) all produced fantasies that dealt in part with political and social issues. The fifteenth-century historian and belletrist, Ibn 'Arabshah, produced the *Fâkihat al-Khulafâ',* a story-collection with a strong political content (Irwin, "What the Partridge Told the Eagle"). To take one example, he includes the story of a king who wickedly thinks of violating a shepherdess. As soon as he does so, the milk of the animals runs dry. When he abandons his wicked thought, it flows again (El-Shamy 275-76; cf. 262-63). The message of the story is that the prosperity of the land is dependent on the moral health of the king. If the king strays, his land becomes a wasteland (a wasteland that may make us think of the Arthurian wasteland presided over by the wounded Fisher King).

Some of the stories in the *Nights* shed a rather odd sort of light on Islamic political thinking. Others, however, come very close to expounding the banal and somewhat servile ideas that can be found in mainstream political theory of the time as produced by scholars such as Ibn Jamâ'a (d. 1333) or the author of *Nasîhat al-Mulûk.* For example in the **"Tale of King Omar bin al-Nu'uman and his Sons,"** the young woman Nuzhat al-Zamân, who has been enslaved and sold to King Sharrkân, is asked to demonstrate her prowess to the *qâdîs,* so as to prove her worthiness to become the king's bride. "O King, to hear is to obey." She then gives a lecture on government that parrots most of the conventional Islamic thinking on the rights and duties of rulers and subjects (Burton, *Nights* 2: 156-71). Kingship and religion are inseparable (and here she is almost certainly quoting the Persian treatise *The Testament of Ardashir,* which was translated into Arabic by Ibn al-Muqaffa'in the early eighth century) (Lambton 45, 51). The king must govern justly, taking care of the weak and preventing robbery and dissension, so that all of his subjects may receive the just rewards of their labors. The king's pillars of government are his emirs and the religious scholars ('ulamâ'). There are three classes of king: kings of faith; kings who govern according to justice and protect the faith; and kings who govern according to their passions and selfish whims. Nuzhat al-Zamân's class one king is really a caliph. The class two king is a sultan who theoretically exercises authority as the executive agent of the caliph and the class three king is a tyrant and perhaps an infidel as well. Nuzhat al-Zamân then alludes to virtuous examples of the pre-Islamic Persian kings, Ardashir and Chosroes. The general trend of her political wisdom is Persianate, as she presents justice as deriving from the will of the ruler, rather than from religious law (*sharî'a*). She advises her king to be neither too generous nor too stingy in paying his army, and to take advice from his chamberlains (the *hâjibs*). Beware of ostentation, beware of excess, beware of the advice of women, deal equitably with everyone. Nuzhat al-Zamân's speech, though it is no more than a hotchpotch of moralising clichés and improving examples, draws great acclaim from Sharrkhân's courtiers. Nuzhat al-Zamân is just as tedious in her way as her rival in the world of tedious slave-girls, Tawaddud.

Sheherezade herself attempts something of the same kind in Habicht's Breslau edition of the *Nights,* in which Sheherezade, running out of stories perhaps, tells Shahriyâr his own story. (It appears in Burton under the title **"Tale of Two Kings and the Vizier's Daughter."**) Shahriyâr, in listening, recognizes his own cruel and unjust behavior and repents of it. Sheherezade is then emboldened to lecture him on the duties of a just king. She points out (as if this may not have occurred to him before) that a strong king needs a strong army. He must deal justly with his subjects. The king is like a gardener. He must employ a virtuous vizier to deal justly with his people. The vizier is like a doctor. The king's subjects will serve him well if he serves them well, and, if he does not, then they will not. It is hardly surprising that Shahriyâr falls asleep at the end of all this (Burton, *Supplemental Nights* [*Supplemental Nights to the Book of the Thousand Nights and a Night*] 2: 263-72). Similar banalities are uttered by the seven viziers who advise the king in **"King Jali'ad of Hind and his**

Vizier Shimas." They give the monarch tedious lessons on virtue and moderation. Kings are necessary to dispense justice and protect their subjects from foreign enemies. A king who is merciful and wise is a good king. People should be content with their lot. There is good deal more of such spiritless stuff, though leavened with fable and anecdote (Burton, *Nights* 9: 32-134). Incidentally, the Persian "national epic," the *Shâhnâmah* by Firdawsî, whose compilation was concluded towards the beginning of the eleventh century, is similarly infested with *andarz*; *andarz,* a Persian word, designates moral, political or religious precepts that are usually attributed to famous people (Shaked). The monarchical lore of old Persia also features in **"The Righteousness of King Anurshirwan"** (Burton, *Nights* 5: 254-55).

It is one of the curious features of the *Nights* that villains, like the treacherous amazons in the **"Tale of Omar bin Nu'uman and His Sons"** or the evil stepmother in the Syntipas cycle are just as likely to deliver lectures on right rule and moral living as their more virtuous opponents. It seems that the wickedness of the messenger was not held to disqualify the virtue of the message. In this respect, the wicked but moralising lecturers of the *Nights* can be compared to the evil but sententious jackal Dimna in Ibn al-Muqaffa's *Kalîla wa-Dimna* and to the sermonising rogue, Abû Zayd, in Ibn al-Muqaffa's *Maqamat* (Irwin, "Beast Fable" 45-46). It may be superfluous to remark that the readiness of the kings of the *Nights* to be lectured on politics by women is unlikely to be something that reflected historical reality.

Some of the moralizing about contentment with one's lot, avoidance of bad advice, and so forth in the *Nights* comes in the form of animal fables. One such group of fables follows **"The Tale of the Birds and Beasts and the Carpenter"** (Burton, *Nights* 3: 125-62). The general burden of these tales is minding one's own business, resorting to prayer, quietism and resignation to one's fate. **"The Tale of the Birds and Beasts and the Carpenter"** is an abridged and adapted tale that derives ultimately from the tenth- or eleventh-century encyclopedia, the *Rasâ'il* of the Ikhwân al-Safâ, and one of the tales that follows, that of **"The Cat and the Crow,"** concludes with an explicit message: "This story, O king showeth that the friendship of the Brethren of Purity delivereth and saveth from difficulties and from falling into mortal dangers" (Burton, *Nights* 3:150). I shall return to the storytelling proclivities of the Brethren of Purity in what follows. The second batch of animal fables, framed within the story of **"King Jali'ad of Hind and his Wazir Shimas,"** are not explicitly linked with the doctrines of the Brethren of Purity, but they contain similar public service messages—trust in God, trust in those of one's fellow men who are worthy to be

trusted, and so forth. Although these fables are notionally addressed to a king, it seems plain that their real target audience is much humbler folk.

To someone who has read Hobbes, Rousseau, Bakunin, or Oakeshott, the discourses of the viziers and storytelling slave girls and the moralising verbiage of the birds and the beasts will seem not so much examples of political thought as substitutes for it. Nevertheless, the naïve and servile sententiousness of the narrators cited above accurately reflects a great deal of mainstream political theory in the Islamic, which was turgid, craven, and sometimes unrealistic. Formal writing on politics was the shared monopoly of the 'ulamâ' and the pet essayists and scribes of the court, and it is their kind of writing that Nuzhat al-Zamân and other political lecturers in the *Nights* ultimately drew upon.

Apart from overt political lectures and *andarz* precepts that have been awkwardly inserted in the stories, the plotting and outcome of the story itself often have a latent political meaning. Jack Zipes, introducing a study of Grimms' *Märchen,* or fairy tales, remarked that "if we reread some of the tales with history in mind, and if we reflect for a moment on some of the issues at stake, it becomes apparent that these enchanting lovable tales are filled with all sorts of power struggles over kingdoms, rightful rule, money, women, children and land, and that their real 'enchantment' emanates from these dramatic conflicts whose resolutions allow us to glean the possibility of making the world, that is, shaping the world in accord with our needs and desires" (Zipes 20). This is largely true of the stories of the *Nights* too. Only the last phrase, suggesting the possibility "of shaping the world in accord with our needs and desires," seems to me to have too overoptimistic and revolutionary a flavour to apply to many of the stories that circulated in the medieval Islamic world.

Submission to God, submission to Fate, and submission to the ruler dominate rather a large number of the stories. The political direction is determined at the outset, when Sheherezade, rather than thinking of how to overthrow the tyrant Shahriyâr, instead proceeds to entertain him with stories. Incidentally, to be entertained by stories is one of the prerogatives of kingship. In the eleventh-century *Siyâsat-nâmah,* the famous Persian mirror-for-princes treatise, its author, Nizâm al-Mulk, states that the king cannot do without suitable cup-companions. And the cup-companion "must possess an ample fund of stories and strange tales both amusing and serious, and be able to tell them well" (89). And of course the need to entertain Hârûn al-Rashîd or some other ruler or prince by telling him the story of one's adventures is a recurring motif in the *Nights.* The political theorists of the medieval Islamic world were realists. Rather than waste their time thinking of alternatives to despotism, they preferred to concentrate on how to get the best despot. In political theory and in storytelling in the *Nights,* a despot could be improved by good servants who provided him not only with good advice, but also with stories that were conducive to political virtue.

In the ideal kingdoms of the *Nights,* the wise prince will beware of ghouls, wicked stepmothers, and apparently pointless interdictions (of the whatever-you-do-don't-go-through-that-door kind). On the other hand, the ideal ruler will listen to sagacious advice. He will be brave and generous. He will also be younger. Although the Arab tellers of tales unquestioningly accepted hereditary right, they did not accept primogeniture, as they shared the very general fairy-story teller's prejudice in favor of younger brothers. In addition to being younger, he will also be good looking. Good looks are certainly part of politics. The virtuous kings and heroes of the stories of the *Nights,* all of them good-looking, are following (however unconsciously) the precept of Nizâm al-Mulk's *Siyâsat-nâmah,* in which he ruled that the sovereign must have physical beauty (10). Al-'Aynî (d. 1451) similarly, in the presentation chronicle he composed for the fifteenth-century Mamluk Sultan al-Mu'ayyad Shaykh, seems also to have regarded good looks as one of the desirable qualities of a ruler (234-37). Although many of the tales in the *Nights* either originated in the Mamluk period or were rewritten in that period, they fail to reflect the political realities of that age in two important respects. First the stories stress hereditary right, something that was rather at a discount in the Mamluk period. Secondly, they commonly stress the power of the vizier and his great influence over the ruler, but the real authority of the vizier rapidly declined under the Mamluks, and David Ayalon has noted that by the fifteenth century the "principal and almost the only duty of the *wazir* was to supply meat to the army" (61).

It is easy to exaggerate the popular nature of the *Nights* and, because it is easy, I did so myself in my own book on the *Nights* (Irwin, *Companion* [*The Arabian Nights: A Companion*]). Looking again at the inflated and editorially unpoliced corpus of the *Nights,* as it has come down to us in the Bûlâq (1835) and Calcutta (1839-42) editions, I now think that I greatly underestimated the contribution of the literature of the boon-companions (*nudamâ'*) and belletrists of the court to that corpus. Material from al-Mas'ûdî (d. 956), al-Tanûkhî (d. 994), Abu 'l Faraj al-Isfahânî (d. 967), and other respectable folk were recycled by scribes who produced manuscripts of the *Nights* from the fifteenth century onwards. The conservative and monarchical tendency that pervades so much of the *Nights* reflects the fact that a great deal of popular literature derives ultimately from elite culture. In somewhat the same way, the chapbooks that were sold by colporteurs to French peasants in the seventeenth and eighteenth century celebrated old-fashioned

virtues, magic, mystery, kingship, and knight errantry. Moreover, some of the authors of those chapbooks were quite substantial and highly educated people (Mandrou; Tenèze).

However, it is now time to turn to the alternative, adversarial, and anti-establishment themes in the *Nights,* for such themes are indeed occasionally present. Systematic oppositional texts and sketches of utopias or alternative societies only rarely feature in Islamic literature. A rare example of an oppositional fable occupies a large part of one of the volumes of the encyclopedic *Rasâ'il* of the Brethren of Purity. The Brethren were a secretive group of philosophers in tenth- and eleventh-century Basra. They had Platonist interests and, perhaps, Isma'îlî sympathies. Their encyclopedia drew on Buddhist stories, as well as other stories about kings and animals in order to make their points. Their main political fable has been mentioned already as the source of the *Nights* story **"The Birds and Beasts and the Carpenter,"** and it has been translated under the title *The Case of the Animals versus Man before the King of the Jinn: A Tenth-Century Ecological Fable of the Pure Brethren of Basra* (Goodman). In this remarkable and quite lengthy story, which dominates the volume of the encyclopedia devoted to the subject "On How the Animals and their Kinds are Formed," the animals, birds and fishes combine to bring a court case against humanity at the court of the King of the Jinn, seeking to have humanity condemned for its cruelty, waste of resources and environmental heedlessness. But, while it is accurate to describe it as an ecological fable, this is only part of the story. A careful reading of this story suggests that the Brethren of Purity were using their animal mouthpieces in this story to denounce not just human cruelty to animals, but also human cruelty to humans. The fable amounts to an attack on society as it was constituted in the tenth century, as it denounces war, enslavement as a consequence of war, gross inequalities in wealth, lack of charity, overclever shyster bureaucrats, politically ambitious *'ulamâ',* corrupt judges, and the tyrannical caliphs who commit all conceivable crimes—murder, debauchery, and robbery—driven by excessive greed. The animals, victims of mankind, also symbolize the blindly obedient masses (Enayat; cf. Nasr 95). Thus *The Case of the Animals* more closely resembles Orwell's *Animal Farm* than might appear at first sight. Incidentally, the Brethren made use of other fables to make less contentious points about the virtues of cunning and cooperation and so forth.

Fairy tales and tales from the *Nights,* most of them anyway, are one-man utopias—that is to say not really utopias at all. Aladdin, for example, gets the woman, the palace, the jewels, and the glory, but others do not, and the society from which he emerged remains unchanged. As Robert Darnton has observed in the context of a discussion of French folktales in the early modern period, "[t]o dream of confounding a king by marrying a princess was hardly to change the moral basis of the Old Regime" (59). However, outside the fantasy world of the *Nights,* the Brethren of Purity did put forward some inconsistent and incoherent ideas for a spiritual utopia, which they referred to as the *madîna fâdila ruhâniyya*—a term which clearly derives from the political philosophy of the tenth-century philosopher, al-Fârâbî. Utopias featured so rarely in medieval Arab conjectures that Pierre Versins, the splendid compiler of an encyclopedia of utopias, knew of only one such—al-Fârâbî's Ârâ' ahl al-Madîna al-fâdila, or "Ideas of the Inhabitants of the Virtuous City" (Farabi; Versins 57). This was a lightly Islamicized version of Plato's ideal republic, that was to be governed by a philosopher-king. En passant, it is noteworthy that al-Fârâbî and the Brethren of Purity after him both conceived of utopia as a city. Cities were places where power and wealth were to be found, and happiness too. Muslim philosophers and storytellers were agreed on that point, and consequently they wasted no time on bucolic reveries. The woods and fields of the European fairy tale are almost wholly absent from the *Nights,* as they are from Islamic political philosophy.

Although most tales of the *Nights* deal only with the fulfilment of individual wishes, there is one tale that essays a brief but striking sketch of an alternative society. This is **"The Tale of Abdullah the Fisherman and Abdullah the Merman"** (Burton, *Nights* 9: 165-88; cf. Miquel 111-42). In this story the fisherman is introduced by the merman to the marvels of the deep, including merfolk's society. The merfolk, who dwell in numerous underwater cities, do not buy or sell; they have no use for precious stones, they practice free love. They are in effect communists. I hardly need to add that the communism of the merfolk was presented as something to be marvelled at, one of many marvels of deep, rather than something to be emulated. But any kind of reference to communism in premodern Islamic discourse is extremely rare, even if some writers in the Islamic period, most notably Ibn al-Muqaffa', were fascinated by Mazdak, a sixth-century (and therefore pre-Islamic) Persian communist insurgent who was alleged to have fought for communal access to women and property (Crone, "Kavad's Heresy"). Though there were Muslim anarchists in ninth-century Basra (Crone, "Ninth-Century Muslim Anarchists"), I have found no echoes of this in the *Nights.* It is also disappointing that the other underwater society to feature in the *Nights,* that of **"Julnar the Sea-Born,"** seems to have been a conventional monarchy (Burton, *Nights* 7: 264-308).

"The Tale of Abdullah the Fisherman" [**"The Tale of Abdullah the Fisherman and Abdullah the Merman"**] also mentions a "City of the Women of the Sea." Amazon communities also appear in the **"Tale of Omar bin Nu'uman,"** [**"Tale of Omar bin Nu'uman and**

His Sons"] **"The Man Who Never Laughed during the Rest of his Days," "Hasan of Basra,"** and **"The Lovers of Syria."** But such tales are rather a reflection of erotic fantasy than of political concerns (feminist or otherwise). Women who rule get a bad press in the stories and are sometimes presented as sorceresses or man-eating ghouls, though there are a number of important exceptions.

The story of **"Abu Kir the Dyer and Abu Sir the Barber"** celebrates the superiority of medieval or early modern Egyptian commerce and technology over those of far-flung heathen parts (Burton, *Nights* 9: 134-65). But Sindbad is, of course, the most famous explorer of exotic parts. The sea that Sindbad of the Sea sets out on is a highway to the mysteries of alien societies, and Sindbad of the Sea instructs Sindbad of the Land about such exotic matters as the Indian caste system, suttee, cannibal tribes, the city of apes, and the city of flying men. Sindbad's sea is thus, to some extent, a political sea. And here I cannot resist quoting from Oakeshott again: "In political activity then, men sail a boundless and bottomless sea; there is neither harbour for shelter nor floor for anchorage, neither starting place nor appointed destination. The enterprise is to keep afloat on an even keel; the sea is both friend and enemy; and seamanship consists in using the resources of a traditional manner of behaviour in order to make a friend of every hostile occasion" (127). But the unfortunate Sindbad is no good at all staying afloat and he makes friends of hostile occasions (such as the Old Man of the Sea) only belatedly and with great difficulty. In the end, the narrated dangers of the exotic function as a kind of affirmation of all that is familiar and traditional in Islamic society.

The king wandering the streets in disguise in order to learn the secrets of his subjects is one of the most familiar themes in storytelling and historical folklore. Apart from Hârûn al-Rashîd, rulers such as al-Hâkim bi-Amrillâh, Qâytbây, Pedro the Cruel, James V of Scotland, and many others are reputed to have done so. In many of the stories of the *Nights,* the king perambulating the city in disguise serves as no more than a perfunctory prelude or framing device to someone else's adventure. In two stories, however, real or pretended failure to penetrate the ruler's disguise licenses sociopolitical criticism. In **"The Night Adventures of Sultan Mohammed of Cairo"** (Burton, *Supplemental Nights,* 5: 90-94), the sultan and his vizier in disguise are looking for a certain house within which the sultan has previously glimpsed a beautiful damsel. To that end, the vizier has advised the sultan to decree that no candles should be lit in the city after the evening prayer. Then they identify a house that is not observing the blackout and, sure enough, the damsel is inside. They present themselves as dervishes seeking shelter for the night, but the sharp-witted damsel who has penetrated their disguise and knows perfectly well who they are takes advantage of their supposed dervishood to deliver an unusually acerbic political lecture: "O Darwaysh, verily the Sultan's order should not be obeyed save in commandments which be reasonable; but this proclamation forbidding lights is sinful to accept; and indeed the right direction wherein man should walk is according to Holy Law which saith, 'No obedience to the creature in a matter of sin against the Creator.' The Sultan (Allah make him prevail!) herein acteth against the Law and imitateth the doings of Satan." The damsel then goes on to explain that the ordinance against candles was making it difficult for spinners, like the women of her family, to continue to earn their living. When the vizier points out that obedience is due to the sultan from all his subjects, she replies that he may be sultan, but how does he know whether his subjects are starving or not? And she re-emphasizes the point that obedience is not due to a sovereign who is in breach of the *sharî'a*. The sultan in disguise takes her admonishment in good part and returns the following night to give the family money and hear their story . . .

"The History of al-Bundukani" (Burton, ***Supplemental Nights*** 7: 42-85) is another example of a story in which the disguise of the ruler licenses his subject to speak bluntly. The circumstances are different in that, though the Caliph Hârûn al-Rashîd is in disguise, the old woman whom he encounters has not penetrated that disguise. Instead, she mistakes for him a robber and a captain of thieves. At a certain level however, this is no mistake as the Caliph with his corrupt officers and oppressive taxes is indeed a kind of robber-king. In the naïve old lady's eyes, only his status as a terrible robber can explain the terror and obedience the man inspires in all around him, "for that Moslems one and all dread him and his mischief." Only successful thieving can explain his lavish fortune. Later on in this comedy of errors, the same woman talking to Hârûn whom she still believes to be a robber chief, denounces the Caliph for having ruined her household and unjustly imprisoned her son. However, it would be a mistake to make very much of all this, as in the end the Caliph uses his wealth and power to make everything right for the widow and free her son from his unjust imprisonment. In this and many other tales the values of the establishment are implicitly affirmed.

To hear is to obey! The fantastic stories of the ***Nights*** that were read or listened to by people living under Mamluk or Ottoman despotism offered them no escape from the despotic solution. Fiction merely offered different despots, Shahriyâr, Hârûn al-Rashîd, Sultân Muhammad . . . Some were better and some worse than the ones the audience actually lived under.

Works Cited

Ayalon, David. "Studies in the Structure of the Mamluk Army." *Bulletin of the School of Oriental and African Studies* 15 (1953): 203-28 (pt. 1); 448-76 (pt. 2); 16 (1954): 57-90 (pt. 3).

Al-'Aynî, Badr al-Dîn. *Al-Sayf al-muhannad fî sîrat al-Malik al-Mu'ayyad Shaykh al-Mahmûd.* Ed. Fahim Muhammad Shaltût. Cairo: Dâr al-Kâtib al-'arabî, 1967.

Burton, Richard. *A Plain and Literal Translation of the Arabian Nights Entertainments, Now Entitled the Book of the Thousand Nights and a Night.* 10 vols. Benares (Stoke Newington, London), 1885.

———. *Supplemental Nights to the Book of the Thousand Nights and a Night.* 6 vols. Benares (=Stoke Newington, London), 1886-88.

Crone, Patricia. "Did al-Ghazali Write A Mirror for Princes? On the Authorship of *Nasîhat al-mulûk.*" *Jerusalem Studies in Arabic and Islam* 10 (1987): 167-91.

———. "Kavad's Heresy and Mazdak's Revolt." *Iran* 29 (1991): 21-42.

———. "Ninth-Century Muslim Anarchists." *Past and Present* 167 (2000): 3-28.

Darnton, Robert. *The Great Cat Massacre and Other Episodes in French Cultural History.* London: Allen Lane, 1984.

Davis, Natalie Zemon: *Society and Culture in Early Modern France.* Stanford: Stanford UP, 1965.

El-Shamy, Hasan, ed. and trans. *Folktales of Egypt.* Chicago: U of Chicago P, 1980.

Enayat, Hamid. "An Outline of the Political Philosophy of the *Rasâ'il* of the Ikhwân al-Safâ." *Isma'ili Contributions to Islamic Culture.* Ed. Hossein Nasr. Tehran: Imperial Iranian Academy of Philosophy, 1977. 23-49.

Al-Farabi on the Perfect State (Ârâ' ahl al-Madîna al-fâdila). Ed. and trans. R. Walzer. Oxford: Oxford UP, 1985.

Goodman, Len, trans. *The Case of the Animals versus Man before the King of the Jinn: A Tenth-Century Ecological Fable of the Pure Brethren of Basra.* 4th ed. Los Angeles: Gee Tee Bee, 1978.

Grehan, James. "Street Violence and Social Interaction in Late Mamluk and Ottoman Damascus (c. 1500-1800)." *International Journal of Middle Eastern Studies* 35 (2003): 215-36.

Haddawy, Husain (trans.). *The Arabian Nights.* London and New York: Norton, 1990.

Ibn al-Muqaffa', Abû Muhammad 'Abd Allâh. *Kalîla wa-Dimna.* Ed. Louis Cheikho. Beirut: Imprimerie Catholique, 1905.

Irwin, Robert. *The Arabian Nights: A Companion.* London: Allen Lane, 1994.

———. "The Arabic Beast Fable." *Journal of the Warburg and Courtauld Institutes* 55 (1992): 36-50.

———. *The Middle East in the Middle Ages: The Early Mamluk Sultanate 1250-1382.* Beckenham, Kent: Croom Helm, 1986.

———. "What the Partridge Told the Eagle: A Neglected Source on Chinggis Khan and the Early History of the Mongols." *The Mongol Empire and Its Legacy.* Ed. Reuven Amitai-Preiss and David O. Morgan. Leiden: Brill, 1999. 5-11.

Kedourie, Elie. *Politics in the Middle East.* Oxford: Oxford UP, 1992.

Lambton, Ann K. S. *State and Government in Medieval Islam: An Introduction to the Study of Islamic Political Theory: The Jurists.* Oxford: Oxford UP, 1981.

Mahdi, Muhsin, ed. *Alf layla wa-layla.* 2 vols. Leiden: Brill, 1984.

Mandrou, Robert. *De la culture populaire aux 17e et 18e siècles: La bibliothèque bleue de Troyes.* Paris, Stock: 1964.

Miquel, André. *Sept contes des Mille et Une Nuits ou: Il n'y a pas de contes innocents.* Paris: Sindbad, 1981.

Nasr, Hossein. *An Introduction to Islamic Cosmological Doctrines: Conceptions of Nature and Methods Used for Its Study by the Ikhwân al-Safâ', al-Bîrûnî and Ibn Sînâ.* Cambridge, MA: Belknap P, 1964.

Netton, Ian Richard. *Muslim Neoplatonists: An Introduction to the Thought of the Brethren of Purity.* London: George Allen & Unwin, 1982.

Nizam al-Mulk. *The Book of Government or Rules for Kings: The Siyar al-Mulûk or Siyâsatnâma.* Trans. Hubert Darke. London: Routledge and Kegan Paul, 1960.

Oakeshott, Michael. *Rationalism in Politics and Other Essays.* 2nd ed. Indianapolis: Liberty Fund, 1991.

Shaked, Shaul. "Andarz. I: Andarz and andarz literature in pre-Islamic Iran." *Encyclopedia Iranica.* Vol. 2. London and New York: Routledge and Kegan Paul, 1987. 11-16.

Shoshan, Boaz. "Grain Riots and the 'Moral Economy': Cairo 1350-1517." *Journal of Interdisciplinary History* 10 (1979-80): 459-78.

———. *Popular Culture in Medieval Cairo.* Cambridge: Cambridge UP, 1993.

Tenèze, Marie-Louise. "Bibliothèque bleue." *Enzyklopädie des Märchens.* Vol. 2. Berlin and New York: Walter de Gruyter, 1979. 283-87.

Versins, Pierre. *Encyclopédie de l'utopie et de la science fiction.* 2nd ed. Lausanne: L'Age de d'Homme, 1972.

White, T. H. *The Age of Scandal: An Excursion through a Minor Period.* London: Jonathan Cape, 1950.

Zipes, Jack. *Breaking the Magic Spell: Radical Theories of Folk and Fairy Tales.* London: Heinemann, 1979.

Donald Haase (essay date 2004)

SOURCE: Haase, Donald. "The *Arabian Nights,* Visual Culture, and Early German Cinema." *Fabula* 45, nos. 3/4 (2004): 261-74.

[*In the following essay, Haase details the enthusiastic reception of* The Arabian Nights *in Germany during the early years of cinema and observes its influence upon such acclaimed directors as Ernst Lubitsch, Fritz Lang, and Paul Leni.*]

Robert Irwin has written that "If one asks what was the influence of the *Nights* [*The Arabian Nights*] on Western literature, then one is asking not for a single answer, but rather for a series of answers to a group of questions which relate to one another in complex ways" (Irwin 1994: 237). When I set out to write on the German reception of the *Arabian Nights*—a very broad topic with myriad possibilities—I kept this thought in mind. Accordingly, this paper focuses on a specific moment in German cultural history. That "moment" spans several decades in the late nineteenth and early twentieth centuries, from approximately 1880 to 1935. Within that period I will be considering two significant cultural developments and how they intersect. One is the robust reception of the *Arabian Nights* in print. The other is the emergence of visual culture in the form of motion pictures.

German interest in the exotic tales of the *Arabian Nights* had been strong ever since the eighteenth century, of course; but the late nineteenth and early twentieth centuries witnessed especially lively publishing activity around the *Nights.* Between 1895 and 1928, three major translations appeared in Germany: Max Henning's popular translation published by Reclam (1895-99), Felix Paul Greve's German rendering (1907-08) based on Sir Richard Burton's English version, and Enno Littmann's important scholarly translation from the Arabic (1921-28). In addition, a steady stream of selections and adaptations for a juvenile audience appeared during this period (see Fähndrich 2000: 103). The collection of the Internationale Jugendbibliothek in Munich alone attests to over forty children's editions issued by German publishers between 1880 and 1920. Most of these are illustrated editions. Some are lavishly produced and offer impressive cover illustrations that catch the reader's eye and generate interest even before the book is opened.

Many of the illustrated volumes from this period utilize innovative technologies in the reproduction of images and colors. For example, an 1889 reprint of a popular edition of *Arabian Nights* tales adapted for children by Albert Ludwig Grimm boasts the inclusion of eight original water colors reproduced by chromolithography (Grimm 1889). This new technology, which reached its zenith in Europe during the 1880s and 1890s, enabled illustrators to have their exotic Oriental scenes reproduced in brightly and intensely colored book illustrations (Ries 1992: 289 f.; Caracciolo 1988: 39 f.). In 1880 a selection of six stories from the *Arabian Nights* adapted and illustrated by Theodor von Pichler announces that it offers six *Transparent-Verwandlungs-Bilder* (Pichler 1880). These illustrations—produced on a plate bearing a double impression—are transparent pictures which, when held to the light, reveal additional images that change the scene and thus make the story's action visible (see Ries 1992: 54, not. 3). For instance, viewed before a light source, the transparent image illustrating the story of **"Aladdin and the Magic Lamp"** shows Aladdin moving up a set of stairs towards the magic lamp (Pichler 1880: facing p. 12). By visually advancing the action and creating the illusion of movement, the image is a picture of motion, if not precisely a motion picture. Innovations like these in the visual presentation of the stories suggest the degree to which books in general and these editions of the *Arabian Nights* in particular contributed to the genesis of visual culture. These editions of the *Arabian Nights* were not simply to be read, but to be viewed as spectacles in their own right.

The transformation of readers into spectators takes place concurrently with the birth of cinema. The first motion pictures were taken by Étienne-Jules Marey in 1882, and over the next three decades technological advances in the form of the Kinetograph, the Kinetoscope, and the improved equipment made by Europeans such as the Lumière brothers facilitated the development of cinema both artistically and commercially. Germans began participating in the new visual culture as spectators in 1895, when the first public screening of films occurred in a commercial setting in Berlin. Although Germany did not have its own "native film production until about 1910" (Hansen 1983: 159), once German filmmakers became involved in production—especially during the Weimar Republic—they turned out pioneering works of visual art. Among these are several important films from the early 1920s that draw on the stories, settings, and narrative techniques of the *Arabian Nights.* I am referring specifically to Ernst Lubitsch's *Sumurun* (*One Arabian Night*) of 1920, Fritz Lang's *Der müde Tod* (*Destiny*) of 1921, and Paul Leni's *Das Wachsfigurenkabinett* (*Waxworks*) of 1924.

It is remarkable that a book revolving around the act of storytelling is adapted by important filmmakers at this turning point in Western culture. Just as writers and editors adapted folktales in the early-nineteenth century to negotiate the shift from orality to literacy, so do the pioneers of visual culture seem to adapt the *Arabian Nights* in order to work through the transition from print to film. This intersection of the *Arabian Nights* with the visual turn in Western culture leads to the fundamental question I want to explore: How do the *Arabian Nights* come to be a focal point in the development of visual culture and in early German cinema? To understand why filmmakers such as Lubitsch, Lang, and Leni turned to the *Arabian Nights,* we first need to examine how literary editors and commentators during this era came to understand and portray the *Nights* as a visual experience.

READING THE *ARABIAN NIGHTS* AS SPECTACLE

In a 1935 book review of Enno Littmann's *Arabische Märchen,* Hermann Hesse laments the "decline and fall of the art of narration" ("Niedergang und Zerfall der Erzählungskunst"). Praising the *Arabian Nights* as a classical collection exhibiting "the Oriental style of narration at its pinnacle" ("den orientalischen Erzählungsstil auf seiner Höhe"), Hesse finds that these more recent tales told by a woman storyteller in Jerusalem at the turn of the twentieth century pale in contrast. Although they do not possess the classical style of the *Arabian Nights*—which display "the naive passion for narration in tandem with an extremely sophisticated literary and religious-intellectual background" ("die naive Erzählerlust im Bund mit einer überaus hohen literarischen und religiös-denkerischen Bildung")—Hesse maintains that the folktales collected by Littmann have nonetheless been able to preserve "the genuine tradition of Oriental storytelling" ("die echte Tradition des morgenländischen Erzählens"). As is typical of the discourse that mourns the decline of orality and storytelling, Hesse's critique implicates the destructive effects of modern media and modern cultural practices:

> That Orient of the fairy tale, of the pleasure taken in images, of contemplation has been destroyed more thoroughly by the books, newspapers, business practices, and work ethic of the West than by its armies and machine guns.

> Jenes Morgenland des Märchens, der Bilderfreude, der Kontemplation ist durch die Bücher, Zeitungen, Geschäftspraktiken und Arbeitsmoral des Abendlandes noch gründlicher zerstört worden als durch seine Armeen und Maschinengewehre.

> (Hesse 1970: vol. 12, 56)

It is only thanks to small communities of orality, Hesse concludes, that "[j]enes Morgenland des Märchens"—"[t]hat Orient of the fairy tale"—survives:

> And it lives on not simply in libraries but also here and there in a family, in a circle of friends of the Orient, wherever the old magical art, even though it is nearly displaced by cinema and newspaper, comes to life again in the mouth of a storyteller.

Und doch lebt es nicht bloß in den Bibliotheken weiter, sondern da und dort auch noch in einer Familie, einem Freundeskreis des Orients, wo immer noch, obwohl von Kino und Zeitung fast verdrängt, je und je im Mund eines Erzählers die alte Zauberkunst wieder lebendig wird.

(Hesse 1970: vol. 12, 56 f.)

Hesse's critique of modernity and its impact on storytelling seems at first predictable. After all, the demise of the folktale and the oral tradition had long been linked to the printing press and the rise of literacy. Since the eighteenth century cultural critics had been constructing a mythology that placed the spoken and the written word in opposition, a mythology in which the printed book became the nemesis of folk narrative. Hesse's critique, however, modifies the conventional myth of the folktale's decline on two points. One is his explicit acknowledgment that literary sophistication brought storytelling to its pinnacle in the *Arabian Nights.* The other is his reference to cinema—*Kino*—as a contemporary force threatening the existence of the narrative culture that he identifies with the "Orient of the fairy tale." Cinema assumes a special interest in this context because its inclusion by Hesse updates the romantic concern over storytelling's decline. By adding cinema to the list of threatening cultural products, Hesse—writing in 1935, just two years before the premiere of Walt Disney's *Snow White and the Seven Dwarfs*—expands the terms of the debate. No longer is it simply a question of literature's destructive effect on oral tradition, but of the threat posed to literary and oral narration by the visual (cf. Hesse 1970: vol. 11, 247 f.).

Yet despite his apparent mistrust of film, Hesse portrays the narrative art of the East and the *Arabian Nights* as predominantly visual experiences. In 1929 he described the *Arabian Nights* as "the richest picture book in the world" ("das reichste Bilderbuch der Welt" [Hesse 1970: vol. 11, 346]). And in the very review where he mentions the threat posed by motion pictures, Hesse also stresses the visual dimension of Eastern narrative art when he invokes "[j]enes Morgenland der Märchen, der Bilderfreude, der Kontemplation"—"that Orient of the fairy tale, of the pleasure taken in images, of contemplation." We find joy in images when we view them, of course. And *Kontemplation*/contemplation—deriving from the Latin verb *contemplari*—is first and foremost the act of gazing upon an object (Duden 1994: 764; *Oxford English Dictionary* 1971: def. 1). So for Hesse the *Arabian Nights* and the world of Eastern narrative are characterized by the visual. The words Hesse chooses to characterize classical Eastern narrative—*Bilderfreude*/ pleasure taken in images and *Kontemplation*—do not really describe the narrative itself but the experience and activity of the auditor or reader. In fact, his descriptions imply that we do not hear or read the *Arabian Nights*—the world's "richest picture book"—but that we gaze with pleasure upon it.

Since Hesse was also a painter, it is perhaps understandable that he would use visual metaphors to describe creations of the oral and literary tradition. However, this perception is not unique to Hesse, for late-nineteenth- and early-twentieth-century German commentators frequently conceived of the *Arabian Nights* in visual terms. In 1907 another German poet, Hugo von Hofmannsthal, published an introduction to Felix Paul Greve's German edition of the *Arabian Nights,* and in it he repeatedly uses visual references to describe the work and the interactions of readers with it. According to Hofmannsthal the *Arabian Nights* appeals to both the intellect and the senses—especially the senses:

> The boldest intellectuality and the most complete sensuousness are woven here into one. There is no sense in us that is not aroused, from the most superficial to the most profound; everything in us is brought to life and called to pleasure.

> [H]ier ist die kühnste Geistigkeit und die vollkommenste Sinnlichkeit in eins verwoben. Es ist kein Sinn in uns, der sich nicht regen müßte, vom obersten bis zum tiefsten; alles, was in uns ist, wird hier belebt und zum Genießen aufgerufen.

(Hofmannsthal 1924: 102)

But of all the senses stimulated by this sensuous collections of stories, Hofmannsthal privileges sight. He not only refers repeatedly to the text's appearance before the reader's "eyes" (101, 104), he also compares the book itself to "a magic plate embedded with gems that, like glowing eyes, form wondrous and uncanny figures" ("einer magischen Tafel, worauf eingelegte Edelsteine, wie Augen glühend, wunderliche und unheimliche Figuren bilden" [101]). He claims that "the most tremendous sensuousness" ("[d]ie ungeheuerste Sinnlichkeit") pervades the *Arabian Nights,* and he elaborates this claim with a telling comparison to painting: "In this poetic work [the sensuous] is what light is in the paintings of Rembrandt and color on the panels of Titian" ("[Die Sinnlichkeit] ist in diesem Gedicht, was das Licht in den Bildern von Rembrandt, was die Farbe auf den Tafeln Tizians ist" [103]). The scholar Wolfgang Köhler is correct when he glosses this climactic passage with the observation that Hofmannsthal considered the essential characteristic of the *Arabian Nights* to be "the visually ascertainable" (1972: 66).

The spectacular nature of the *Arabian Nights* derives for Hofmannsthal from its color (102), its rich materials and weave (103 f.), and the unfailing and unbounded concreteness of its description (103). These are the same visual characteristics ascribed to the work by Enno Littmann in a lecture of 1923, where he compares reading the *Arabian Nights* to the experience of viewing a remarkable weave of colors, whether artificial or natural:

> This jumbled tangle of fairy tales and legends, novels and novellas, sagas and fables, humorous tales and anecdotes creates an impression on the reader as on the

viewer of a colorful Oriental rug or like an artfully decorated title page of an Arabic or Persian manuscript, or like an Oriental meadow covered with many types of flowers. One is often astonished at how many different colors are united there in a single image, which nonetheless remains unified precisely because, like the meadow, it has grown that way naturally, or, like the rug and the artful title page, is modeled on nature.

Dies durcheinander gewürfelte Gewirr von Märchen und Legenden, Romanen und Novellen, Sagen und Fabeln, Schwänken und Anekdoten macht auf den Leser etwa den Eindruck wie auf den Beschauer ein bunter orientalischer Teppich oder wie ein kunstvoll verziertes Titelblatt einer arabischen oder persischen Handschrift, oder auch wie eine mit vielerlei Blumen übersäte Wiese im Morgenlande. Man staunt oft, wie viele verschiedene Farben dort zu einem Gesamtbilde vereinigt sind, das aber dennoch einheitlich bleibt, eben weil es, wie die Wiese, von Natur so gewachsen ist, oder, wie der Teppich und das kunstvolle Titelblatt, der Natur nachgebildet ist.

(Littmann 1923: 5)

Commentators in late-nineteenth- and early-twentieth-century Germany could not find enough metaphors to describe the visual experience induced by reading the *Arabian Nights.* At the end of the popular Reclam edition, translator Max Henning—in an afterword dated 1897—portrays the collection of tales that has been paraded before the reader as a theatrical spectacle:

We are at the end. The curtain has fallen over the scene that brought before our eyes a changing panorama of countless images that were magnificently colored, sometimes fantastic and grotesque, sometimes true-to-life, gentle and charming or crudely humorous.

Wir sind am Ende. Der Vorhang ist über die Scene gefallen, die uns ein Wandelpanorama von zahllosen farbenprächtigen, bald phantastisch-grotesken, bald wieder lebenswahren, zartempfundenen und entzückenden oder derb-humoristischen Bildern vor die Augen führte.

(Henning 1895-99: vol. 8, 206)

Like Hofmannsthal and Littmann, Henning too locates the visual dimension of the *Arabian Nights* in their seemingly endless variety of subject matter and in their color, a visual concept that stands for the rich materials of narration and their equally rich description. Henning differs from Hofmannsthal and Littmann, however, in his description of the *Arabian Nights* as a theatrical event and a changing panorama, and in depicting the reader as a spectator in an audience. Whereas Hofmannsthal and Littmann compare the text to visual objects that are static—such as paintings, carpets, and illustrated title pages—Henning sees the *Arabian Nights* as a moving succession of countless images that pass before the spectators' eyes. He is talking about theater, of course, but he makes the comparison in 1897—the era of primitive film and the first commercial performances in the public sphere—so one might also think he is describing the *Arabian Nights* as a motion picture.

That is exactly the case in the introduction to another early-twentieth-century edition of the *Arabian Nights*: Carl Theodor Ritter von Riba's translation entitled *Die Liebesgeschichten des Orients aus den tausend Nächten und der einen Nacht* (Oriental Love Stories from the Thousand Nights and The One Night). In an introduction dated 1913 and entitled "Einblick und Umblick"—which I translate as "Insight and Panorama"— von Riba explicitly compares the reader's experience of the *Arabian Nights* to the spectator's experience of cinematography. He aims primarily to draw attention to the historical, social, and cultural content of the *Arabian Nights,* but he begins by acknowledging that the collected tales from Arabic-Islamic tradition are considered simply fairy tales by those adults "who remember the books of our childhood and see fairies and nightmares surface before our mind's eye" ("die wir uns der Bücher unserer Kindheit erinnern und vor unserm Geist Feen and Schreckgespenster auftauchen sehen" [Riba 1913: 5]). Following a predictable litany of the strange and fabulous motifs that readers see paraded before them when reading the *Arabian Nights,* von Riba invokes cinematography to explain the psychological significance of this experience:

If this were all, it would be hardly worth warming up childhood memories again, unless the adult yearns to escape the colorless cold of everyday life and return to the uncritical, carefree dream-time of youth, which takes pleasure precisely in the inexplicable, the unexpected, and surrenders completely to the magic of this magical world. That this psychological moment is a factor that should not be underestimated has been evident now for years in the success of the cinematograph, which to a certain extent reawakens the memories of our youth, the magical land of our childhood dreams: perhaps it is not the worst of us who, there in the darkened room, follow the improbable images and find more pleasure in them than in the sensational, nerve-racking "Kinodramas" or even in the instructive and edifying images of landscapes. Yes, these are in themselves still somewhat wondrous—distant lands come alive before us, the dead return to life, even speak to us (Kinetophon!), and we sit silently and need hardly stir in order to view all these surprises. Isn't it in part the poet-types who rejoice in the natural-unnatural? It would be truly worthwhile to write a psychology of the cinematograph.

Wäre das alles, so verlohnte es sich nicht übermäßig, die Erinnerungen der Kindheit wieder aufzuwärmen, es sei denn, daß der Erwachsne sich aus der farblosen Kälte des Alltagslebens wieder zurücksehnt in die unkritische, sorgenlose Traumzeit der Jugend, die sich gerade am Unerklärlichen, Überraschenden erfreut und sich rückhaltlos dem Zauber dieses Zauberdämmers hingibt. Daß dieser psychologische Moment ein nicht zu unterschätzender Faktor ist, beweist ja seit Jahren der Erfolg des Kinematographen, der bis zu einem gewissen Grad die Erinnerungen unserer Jugend, das Zauberland unserer Kinderträume wiedererweckt: es sind vielleicht nicht die schlechtesten unter uns, die dort im finstern Raume den unwahrscheinlichen Bildern folgen und daran mehr Freude finden als an sensationellen, nervenzerreißenden 'Kinodramen' oder selbst an belehrsamen und erbaulichen Landschaftsbildern. Ja, diese selbst sind doch ein Stück Wunder—ferne Länder leben vor uns auf, Tote erwachen zum Leben, sprechen gar zu uns (Kinetophon!), und wir sitzen still und brauchten uns kaum zu rühren, um all diese Überraschungen zu schauen. Sind es nicht ein wenig Dichternaturen, die sich dort am Natürlich-Unnatürlichen erfreuen? Wahrlich, es lohne sich, eine Psychologie des Kinematographen zu schreiben.

(Riba 1913: 6)

Although wishing that adults would attend more soberly to the sociocultural content of the *Arabian Nights,* von Riba posits that grown readers are affected by the tales in the same way that spectators are seduced by the images projected before them in the darkened cinema. There, in the darkness, adults longing to escape the stress and monotony of modern life—"the colorless cold of everyday life"—allow themselves to be transported psychologically back to childhood by viewing the seemingly magic succession of marvelous images, which evokes the magical consciousness of childhood and its pleasure in the succession of fairy-tale images appearing before the mind's eye. That it is the sequence of moving pictures in the cinema and the serial, episodic nature of the images and stories in the *Arabian Nights* that stimulate this psychological reaction becomes evident when von Riba compares the *Kinematograph* to the *Kinodrama* and landscape film, which are certainly capable of evoking wonder in their own right, but which lack a cinematically shaped narrative and its stream of diverse and "improbable images."

Von Riba's juxtaposition of the *Arabian Nights* with the early-twentieth-century experience of cinema offers another remarkable example of how writers, translators, and editors conceived of this fairy-tale collection in visual terms at the turn of the century. It also focuses our attention directly on the intersection of the *Arabian Nights* and early German film.

THE *ARABIAN NIGHTS* AND EARLY GERMAN FILM

The visual aspects highlighted in the late-nineteenth and early-twentieth-century literary reception of the *Arabian Nights* are reflected in the productions of Weimar-era filmmakers who drew on the *Arabian Nights.* Perceived in visual terms and described as a visual experience comparable to that of viewing a motion picture, the *Arabian Nights* apparently presented itself as a source and narrative model for filmmakers involved in the creation of the new visual culture. Fritz Lang, Ernst Lubitsch, and Paul Leni did, in fact, create films that are informed in diverse ways by the *Arabian Nights* and inspired by the idea of its visual features and spectacular nature.

The visual dimension of the *Arabian Nights* that most obviously appealed to filmmakers was its color, which each of the literary commentators surveyed above had foregrounded in their descriptions of the collection. "Color," of course, is used metaphorically to describe the subject matter and rich descriptions in the literary text. Color refers above all to exotic sights and settings, to the fantastic objects, characters, and events, to the abundant variety of these, and to the generic diversity of the tales throughout the *Nights.* Since the primitive period in filmmaking, films had exploited the sensational—the out of the ordinary and the exotic (see Hansen 1983: 162)—and the colorful *Arabian Nights* certainly offered filmmakers a rich treasury of fantastic and foreign settings, characters, scenes, and props. Georges Méliès's film of 1905, *Le Palais des Mille et une Nuits,* which Robert Irwin has identified and described as "an opulent . . . vision of the gorgeous East" (Irwin 1994: 291), exemplifies the fit between the *Arabian Nights* and the new medium's proclivity for exotic spectacles. Lotte Reiniger's later silhouette film *Die Abenteuer des Prinzen Achmed* (1926; The Adventures of Prince Achmed) also illustrates the close ties between the spectacular and the exotic. The visual spectacle Reiniger creates from paper, scissors, and light relies almost entirely on the "colorful" lines and shapes that signal the exotic landscapes, architecture, and costumes associated with the Orient.

Costume films produced in Germany during the early years of the Weimar era continued to showcase the unusual and the exotic and in notable cases to do this by adapting the *Arabian Nights.* Ernst Lubitsch's *Sumurun* (1920; released in America in 1921 as *One Arabian Night*) and Fritz Lang's *Der müde Tod* (1921; known in English as *Destiny*) are both important films that incorporate exotic settings inspired by the *Nights.* Lubitsch, in fact, chose to film *Sumurun* shortly after deciding to abandon shorts and make only feature films. "The challenge of evoking the *Arabian Nights* on the screen," Herman G. Weinberg has noted, "was irresistible" (Weinberg 1977: 35). In her classic study of early German cinema, Lotte Eisner has observed that the many German costume films appearing between 1919 and 1924 expressed "the escapism of a poverty-stricken, disappointed nation which, moreover, had always been fond of the glitter of parades" (Eisner 1969: 75). In this context it is useful to recall von Riba's emphasis on those adults who use the *Arabian Nights* and the cinema "to escape the colorless cold of everyday life." According to this early view, the exotic *Nights* and nights at the cinema provide the "color"—the "glitter," as Eisner (1969) would later call it—that compensates for a "colorless" contemporary existence.

Von Riba's brief analysis of 1913 and Eisner's argument of 1953 may or may not accurately describe the actual experience of spectators between 1919 and 1924;

but these parallel views do suggest that Weimar-era filmmakers would have considered the *Arabian Nights* a useful vehicle for thematizing questions about the filmmaker's role, the public's response, and the social function of film. This would have occurred logically from considering the *Arabian Nights* in visual terms. By characterizing the *Nights* as a visual experience and equating its serial narrative with the successive flow of images in cinema, commentators at the turn of the century essentially erase the distinction between storyteller and filmmaker. The narrative art of the *Arabian Nights,* in other words, becomes identical to filmmaking, turning the filmmaker into a storyteller. And once the reader of the *Arabian Nights* is transformed into a spectator—who either derives pleasure from contemplating the colorful images (as Hesse and Hofmannsthal posited) or compensates for an impoverished, colorless reality by surrendering to the flow of colorful images (as von Riba and Eisner argue)—the *Nights* are positioned to thematize contemporary debates about the effects of film on the audience and the new medium's social function.

Early German filmmakers clearly drew on the fundamental narrative strategy of the *Arabian Nights*—the frame story and succession of stories told within it, which Thomas Elsaesser has called "the most distinctive feature of narration in Weimar films" (Elsaesser 2000: 82). Certainly there are many films utilizing a frame that do not replicate the exotic settings and subject matter of the *Arabian Nights.* And certainly the *Nights* are not the only literary model for framing and nesting narratives (83). However, films like *Destiny* and *Waxworks,* which embed a series of exotic and unusual tales within a frame story, clearly involve the *Arabian Nights* as a significant intertext. And by invoking the narrative strategy of the *Nights,* these films thematize the filmmaker's role as storyteller.

In Fritz Lang's film *Destiny,* the central figure and ultimate storyteller is Death—*Der müde Tod*—who takes the life of young man. When the young man's fiancée pleads with Death to return her lover to the world of the living, Death offers her the chance to rekindle his extinguished light by saving another human life. Death presents the young woman—and the audience—with three tales set in distant lands, including Persia, Renaissance Italy, and China. He seems not to tell the stories verbally, but to set them in motion visually by lighting a candle at the beginning of each tale. All three stories end tragically, with no life capable of being saved; and each tale ends when the candle that set it in motion is extinguished. That Death's exotic stories ensue visually from the illumination of candles that he himself lights suggests that this master of light and shadow is the filmmaker himself. As Thomas Elsaesser has quipped, "in the sombre and eery fairy tale *Der müde Tod,* . . . death plays magic lanternist to the hapless bride" (2000:

149). While the film's self-reflexivity may be obvious, the intertextual connection to the *Arabian Nights* operates more subtly. Like Shahrazād, who tells her tales night after night to defer her own execution, the figure of Death projects a series of tales in the attempt to reverse—and thus delay—the young man's inevitable death. The difference is that Shahrazād's serial storytelling enables her to deny death and define her destiny, whereas Death's sequence of visions—and by implication the filmmaker's own moving pictures—seem powerless to derail destiny.

In Paul Leni's *Waxworks,* the filmmaker's identification with a storytelling character is even more apparent. Responding to a classified ad placed by a showman, a writer arrives at a fair and is hired to compose imaginative stories about the wax figures in the showman's *Panopticum*. The menacing wax figures include Jack the Ripper, Ivan the Terrible, and Haroun-al-Raschid, the Caliph of Baghdad. The writer, inspired in part by his attraction to the showman's daughter, pens a series of tales revolving around each figure, tales that begin with his written narration and then quickly continue in visual form. Quite literally the imaginative words of the writer become images seen by the film's audience, creating a metacommentary on the narrative art of filmmaking. But if *Destiny* explores the filmmaker as a failed Shahrazād, unable to defer death through the art of narration, *Waxworks* offers a different commentary on the function of film.

The tales of tyrants embedded in *Waxworks* succeed one another chronologically, moving from Haroun al-Raschild in historically distant Baghdad to Ivan the Terrible and finally to present-day Jack the Ripper. We view this last tale as the writer's dream, which takes place at the fair and in the *Panopticum* itself. Confusing the reality of the amusement fair with the writer's nightmare, the tale ends and the writer awakens when, unable to protect the showman's daughter, he dreams that he is stabbed by Jack the Ripper. While this final tale projected by the mind of the dreaming writer threatens to erase the line between illusion and reality, in the end the tyrants paraded before our eyes seem to be simply harmless amusements confined to the sensational world of the *Panopticum,* a mere entertainment in the escapist world of the fair. The series of tales visualized for spectators by the writer and showman in the *Panopticum*—whatever threat of tyranny they may imply—are not told to defer death, as in the literary *Arabian Nights* and in *Destiny,* but to amuse a paying public in search of escape from modern reality.

To suggest that Leni's vision of the *Panopticum* offers a self-reflection of the filmmaker is not to imply that he uncritically embraces film as escapist fare for the masses. Ernst Lubitsch's costume drama *Sumurun* has been called "escapist" (Weinberg 1977: 37), but Lubitsch very clearly uses this "One Arabian Night" to reflect critically on the filmmaker and his audience (Kracauer 1974: 50). *Sumurun* does not use a frame story, but like *Waxworks* it thematizes the vision of the film's director and the gaze of the audience for whom the director makes his films. Lubitsch himself plays a hunchback/clown who is part of a traveling troupe of entertainers. Unlike *Sumurun*'s voyeuristic crowds, who are captivated by the spectacle of the troupe's public performance, Lubitsch's hunchback is depicted in a series of scenes as a secret observer of less visible realities. He observes what is obscured from public view, what transpires behind walls among the powerful. His deeper vision (in the film's final scene he appears as the lone artist with his eyes closed) enables him ultimately to avenge the tyranny of evil. The exotic settings of *Sumurun* may appeal to the masses in search of entertaining spectacles, but it is evident that Lubitsch critiques their short-sighted expectations. As his film tells us—warns us, in fact—in its opening titles: "With such a tale as this did Sheherazade beguile her angry lord . . ." (Lubitsch 1920).

Shahrazād's beguiling storytelling—which resists tyranny by entertaining it—is a model for each of these directors. By amusing King Shahriyār, Shahrazād protects her own life and enables the survival of many others. As she herself says, "I will begin to tell a story, and it will cause the king to stop his practice, save myself, and deliver the people" (Haddawy 1995: 16). Shahrazād's storytelling is an entertainment for its listeners, but the thousand and one nights of entertainment are also a courageous survival strategy and a pragmatic political response to social trauma and tyranny.

Much of the scholarship about Weimar cinema has grappled with its relation to contemporary society, modernity, the trauma of World War I, and Germany's sociopolitical trajectory from Romanticism to the tyranny of National Socialism (see, e.g., Kracauer 1974; Eisner 1969; Elsaesser 2000: 18-60). This brief paper cannot do justice to that debate or adequately explore the complex nuances in the films I have cited. However, I do think further contemplation of the role of the *Arabian Nights* in the visual culture and films of this period can help illuminate these matters. Those late-nineteenth- and early-twentieth-century writers, translators, and editors who conceived of the *Arabian Nights* as spectacle implicated it in contemporary discourse about visual culture, and their commentaries help us understand the *Nights*' appeal to filmmakers. Beyond its exotic subject matter and its technique of nesting a series of stories in a narrative frame, however, filmmakers responded to something even more fundamental in Shahrazād's model of storytelling. Shahrazād's secret struggle with tyranny and trauma, her ironic balance of entertainment with sociopolitical purpose, and her conscious manipulation of an audience seduced by amusement, made the

Arabian Nights a perfect intertext for filmmakers who were exploring the artistic and social potential of a new medium that offered itself as entertainment for a postwar audience who faced the political challenges and consumer culture of modernity.

CONCLUSION

In this paper I have shown how the *Arabian Nights* entered the discourse about visual culture at the turn of the twentieth century, and how the perception of the *Nights* as a visual experience was manifested in a select set of German films from the Weimar period. There are, of course, still other connections that need to be explored and questions that need to be asked about the reception of the *Arabian Nights* in visual culture and film. For example, the "colorful" qualities that preoccupied so many commentators in their descriptions of the *Nights* need to be further considered in the context of Orientalism and its manifestation in visual culture (cf. Fähndrich 2000). Similarly, the pleasure of contemplating the *Arabian Nights*—as evident in Hesse's *Bilderfreude* and in Hofmannsthal's emphasis on the intense sensual stimulation provoked when the reader's eyes encounter the "glowing eyes" of the text—needs to be further scrutinized in light of theoretical work on the "gaze" and scopophilia (see Mulvey 1989). The eroticism inherent in the visual pleasure ascribed to the *Nights*, and the fact that the commentators and filmmakers I have examined are all men, raises questions about the role that gender plays in the visual reception of the *Arabian Nights*. Just as male editors invoked archetypal female storytellers while appropriating traditional folktales for their own collections during the transition from oral to print culture, so did male filmmakers appropriate the literary tales and narrative techniques of Shahrazād and cast themselves as the serial storyteller during the developing years of visual culture. We might well probe not only the implications of this phenomenon but also the reception of the *Arabian Nights* by women filmmakers, in particular Lotte Reiniger's remarkable silhouette film of 1926, *Die Abenteuer des Prinzen Achmed*. The numerous film and television adaptations of the *Arabian Nights* subsequent to the Weimar era also deserve closer inspection. To what degree do these visual texts inspired by Shahrazād's stories still rely on the ideas about the *Nights* articulated during the formative yeas of modern visual culture?

Certainly the perception of the *Arabian Nights* as a visual experience has been strong and persistent. Consider, in conclusion, the 1996 paperback edition of *Die schönsten Märchen aus 1001 Nacht,* a collection of radio plays by Günter Eich. In his introduction to this edition, Karl Karst takes pains to emphasize the value of Eich's radio plays—these *Hörspiele*—by underlining the primacy of aural reception in storytelling. He invokes not only the archetypal circle of children listing to stories from the **Arabian Nights** but also the early-twentieth-century introduction of radio as an antidote to the decline of creative memory brought on by the culture of print (Karst 1996: 9f.). Yet it is remarkable that Karst's defense of aurality depends on visual metaphors and visual descriptions of the **Arabian Nights.** His very first sentence portrays the **Nights** as a visual stimulus: "There they sat and listened: the mother read while the children's eyes were kept busy visualizing Shahrazad's sparkling gems . . ." ("Da saßen sie also und hörten zu: Die Mutter las, während die Kinder alle Augen voll zu tun hatten, sich die funkelnden Edelsteine Shehrezáds . . . auszumalen . . ."). When he quotes Hesse's description of the **Nights** as "the richest picture book in the world," he quickly qualifies the analogy by asserting, "A picture book for the imagination, not for eye sight" ("Ein Bilderbuch der Imagination, keines der Augen-Sicht" [Karst 1996: 9]). Karst's struggle to tame these metaphors reveals just how deeply ingrained the image of the **Arabian Nights** as a visual experience has become. We need only look at the seductive photograph decorating the front cover of this book of German radio plays, where a colorful and richly bejeweled young woman of the Orient, her hands modestly covering nearly all her face, meets our own gaze by staring out at us with a single open eye.

Works Cited

Caracciolo, Peter L.: "Introduction: Such a Store House of Ingenious Fiction and of Splendid Imagery." In: The Arabian Nights *in English Literature: Studies in the Reception of* The Thousand and One Nights *into British Culture.* ed. P. L. Caracciolo. London: Macmillan, 1988: 1-80.

Duden: *Das große Fremdwörterbuch. Herkunft und Bedeutung der Fremdwörter.* Mannheim: Dudenverlag, 1994.

Eisner, Lotte H.: *The Haunted Screen: Expressionism in the German Cinema and the Influence of Max Reinhardt.* Translated by Roger Greaves. Berkeley: University of California Press, 1969.

Elsaesser, Thomas: *Weimar Cinema and After: Germany's Historical Imaginary.* London: Routledge, 2000.

Fähndrich, Hartmut: "Viewing The Orient and Translating its Literature in the Shadow of *The Arabian Nights.*" In: *Yearbook of Comparative and General Literature* 48 (2000) 95-106.

Greve, Felix P. (ed.): *Die Erzählungen aus den tausendundein Nächten. Vollständige deutsche Ausgabe in zwölf Bänden auf Grund der Burton'schen Ausgabe.* 12 vols. Leipzig: Insel, 1907-08.

Grimm, Albert Ludwig: *Märchen der Tausend und einen Nacht für die Jugend bearbeitet. Neunte durchgesehene Auflage mit acht in Chromo-Lichtdruck ausgeführten Bildern nach Original-Aquarellen von F. Simm.* Leipzig: Gebhardt [1889].

Haddawy, Husain (Translator): *The Arabian Nights.* New York: Norton, 1995.

Hansen, Miriam: "Early Silent Cinema: Whose Public Sphere?" In: *New German Critique* 29 (1983) 147-184.

Henning, Max: *Tausend und eine Nacht.* 8 vols. Leipzig: Reclam, 1895 99.

Hesse, Hermann: *Gesammelte Werke.* ed. Volker Michels. 12 vols. Frankfurt am Main: Suhrkamp, 1970.

Hofmannsthal, Hugo von: "Tausend und eine Nacht." In: *Gesammelte Werke.* vol. 3. Berlin: S. Fischer, 1924: 101-106.

Irwin, Robert: *The Arabian Nights: A Companion.* London: Penguin, 1994.

Karst, Karl (ed.): *Die schönsten Märchen aus 1001 Nacht von Günter Eich.* Frankfurt am Main: Insel, 1996.

Köhler, Wolfgang: *Hugo von Hofmannsthal und Tausendundeine Nacht: Untersuchungen zur Rezeption des Orients im epischen und essayistischen Werk mit einem einleitenden Überblick über den Einfluß von Tausenduneine Nacht auf die deutsche Literatur.* Bern: Lang, 1972.

Kracauer, Siegfried: *From Caligari to Hitler: A Psychological History of the German Film.* Princeton: Princeton University Press, 1974.

Lang, Fritz: *Destiny* (Der müde Tod). Screenplay by Thea von Harbou. Director Fritz Lang, Performers Lil Dagover/Walter Janssen/Bernhard Goetzke. 1921. DVD. Image Entertainment, 2000.

Leni, Paul: *Waxworks* (Das Wachsfigurenkabinett). Screenplay by Henrik Galeen. Director Paul Leni, Performers Emil Jannings et al. 1924. DVD. Kino International, 2002.

Littmann, Enno (ed.): *Die Erzählungen aus den Tausendundein Nächten. Vollständige deutsche Ausgabe in sechs Bänden zum ersten Mal nach dem arabischen Urtext der Calcuttaer Ausgabe vom Jahre 1839 übertragen.* 6 vols. Leipzig: Insel, 1921-28.

id.: *Tausendundeine Nacht in der arabischen Literatur.* Tübingen: J. C. B. Mohr, 1923.

Lubitsch, Ernst: *One Arabian Night* (Sumurun). Screenplay by Hans Kraly. Director Ernst Lubitsch, Performer Polas Negri et al. 1920. VHS. Video Yesteryear, 1985.

Mulvey, Laura: "Visual Pleasure and Narrative Cinema." In: *Visual and Other Pleasures.* London: Macmillan, 1989: 14-26.

Oxford English Dictionary, The Compact Edition. Oxford: Oxford University Press, 1971.

Pichler, Theodor von: *Sechs Märchen aus Tausend und eine Nacht für die Jugend bearbeitet mit 6 Transparent-Verwandlungsbildern.* Stuttgart: Weise, 1880.

Reiniger, Lotte: *The Adventures of Prince Achmed* (Die Abenteuer des Prinzen Achmed). Director Lotte Reiniger, 1926. VHS. Milestone, 2001.

Riba, Carl Theodor von (Translator): *Die Liebesgeschichten des Orients aus den tausend Nächten und der einen Nacht.* Illustrationen von F. von Bayros. Leipzig: Borngräber, [1913].

Ries, Hans: *Illustration und Illustratoren des Kinder- und Jugendbuchs im deutschsprachigen Raum 1871-1914.* Osnabrück: Wenner, 1992.

Weinberg, Herman G.: *The Lubitsch Touch: A Critical Study.* New York: Dover, 1977.

Ulrich Marzolph (essay date 2004)

SOURCE: Marzolph, Ulrich. "The Persian *Nights*." *Fabula* 45, nos. 3/4 (2004): 275-93.

[*In the following essay, Marzolph investigates the purported Persian origins of* The Arabian Nights, *the history of Persian translations, and the status of the work in contemporary Iran.*]

LINKS BETWEEN THE *ARABIAN NIGHTS* AND
IRANIAN CULTURE

The *Thousand and One Nights*—or, as I prefer to call them in the following for purely practical reasons: the *Arabian Nights*—as we perceive them three hundred years after Antoine Galland's epochal French adaptation bear a distinct Arabic imprint. Meanwhile, the commonly accepted model for their textual history acknowledges various stages in the conceptualization and effective formation of both the collection's characteristic frame story and the embedded repertoire. The vast majority of tales in the preserved manuscripts of the *Nights* [*The Arabian Nights*] has been integrated into the collection during two periods of Arabic influence, the so-called Baghdad and Cairo periods (Gerhardt 1963: 115-374). These "Arabic" stages are preceded by an Iranian version, probably dating to pre-Islamic times, which in its turn profits from both structural devices and narrative contents originating from Indian tradition. Considering the eminent position that Iran and Iranian culture hold in the early stages of the textual history of the *Arabian Nights,* surprisingly few details are known concerning the collection's relation to and its actual position within the Iranian cultural context. In the following, I will discuss links between the *Arabian Nights* and Iranian culture on several levels. In surveying these links, I will treat five major areas: (1) The Iranian prototype of the *Nights*; (2) Tales of alleged Persian origin; (3) Persian characters within the tales; (4) Persian translations of the *Arabian Nights*; and (5) The position of the *Arabian Nights* in modern Iran.

THE IRANIAN PROTOTYPE *HAZAR AFSAN*

The title of the commonly acknowledged Iranian prototype of the *Arabian Nights* is given in the tenth century by both the Arab historian al-Mas'ūdī and the Baghdad bookseller Ibn al-Nadīm in a more or less identical spelling as *Hazār afsān[e]* (Abbot 1949: 150f.). While this title is usually understood to mean "A Thousand Stories," the Persian term *afsān[e]* is semantically close to terms like *afsun* and *fosun,* both denoting a magic spell or incantation, and, hence, an activity linked in some way or other to magic. Hence, Persian *afsān[e]* may be understood as not simply a narrative or story, but more specifically a "tale of magic." The Persian title was translated into Arabic as *Alf khurāfa,* the Arabic term *khurāfa* denoting a genre of fantastic and unbelievable narratives. The eponym of the literary term is Khurāfa, said to have been a man of the Arabian tribe of Banū 'Udra who was carried off by demons and who later described his experience. His tale is recorded on the authority of the Prophet Muhammad who himself vouched for the existence of the character and the authenticity of his statements (Drory 1994). *Alf khurāfa* was not, however, necessarily the title of the Arabic translations of *Hazār afsān[e],* since al-Mas'ūdī further specified that those were usually known as *Alf laylah* (A Thousand Nights). Ibn al-Nadīm mentions that the Arabic version of the book continues through a thousand nights and contains less than 200 stories. At the same time, the content of the collection in any of its early versions, whether Persian or Arabic, is unknown. The oldest preserved Arabic manuscript dates from the fifteenth century and is the first document to inform about the content of the medieval *Alf laylah wa-laylah* (Grotzfeld 1996-97).

Ibn al-Nadīm's summary of the opening passages of the frame story is short. While he mentions the king's ritual behavior of marrying and killing a woman night after night, he neither states a reason nor elaborates on the previous events, such as the two kings witnessing the faithlessness of their wives, or their being violated by the tricky woman kept in a box by a demon (Horálek 1987). Either Ibn al-Nadīm had not bothered to actually read the introductory passages—given his judgemental verdict on the *Nights* as a "worthless book of silly tales" (Abbott 1949: 151) this appears to be quite probable—or whatever he had seen did not correspond to the refined and structured frame story known today. Moreover, Ibn al-Nadīm claims to have seen the book "in its entirety several times," thus indicating that complete copies containing the conclusion of the frame story were available in his day, even though they might have been rare. At the same time less than a dozen manuscripts that can reliably be related to the period predating Antoine Galland's French translation (1704-17) have been preserved. These manuscripts appear to indicate that the collection in its historical development was regarded as an open-ended concept with the potential to integrate an undefined number of tales, not necessarily comprising either a thousand nights or a thousand tales, and maybe not even aiming or requiring to close the frame opened at the beginning (Marzolph 1998).

As for the authorship of the Persian *Hazār afsān,* Ibn al-Nadīm reports the opinion that the book was composed for (or by?) Homā'i, the daughter of King Bahman; al-Mas'ūdī, according to whom a certain Ḥumāya was the daughter of Bahman, the son of Isfandiyār and Shahrazād, regards Ḥumāya as the sister of the Achaemenid emperor Darius who reigned before him; this information is corroborated by various other Arabic historians (Pellat 1985). While the earliest preserved document of the *Arabian Nights,* an Arabic fragment dated 266/879 (Abbott 1949), testifies to the popularity of the collection in the Arab world in the first half of the ninth century, most conjectures as to its early history remain speculative. Both al-Mas'ūdī and Ibn al-Nadīm were inclined to attribute a Persian or Indian origin to fictional narrative in general, and modern scholarship agrees on an Indian origin for the frame story or at least certain elements in it (Cosquin 1909). The Persian names of the main characters in the frame story of the Arabic version—Shahrazād, Shahriyār, Dināzād, or similar forms—are taken to indicate an early familiarity with the Persian prototype, most probably dating back to pre-Islamic times. The Persian text might then have been translated into Arabic as early as the eighth century. A number of intriguing similarities between the frame story of the *Arabian Nights* and the historical events narrated in the biblical book of Esther even led Dutch scholar Michael J. de Goeje (1886) to presume a Jewish (or Judaeo-Persian) author as the compiler of the original version of the *Nights.* De Goeje's thesis has been refuted in great detail by Emmanuel Cosquin (1909).

Various reasons have been suggested for the change of the original number of a thousand (tales) into a thousand and one (nights) (see Barth 1984). Most prominently, German scholar Enno Littmann (1953: 664) has supported the hypothesis that the latter number gained its superior position because of the prominence of the Turkish alliteration *bin bir,* meaning "a thousand and one." Scholars of Persian literature tend to refute this opinion, quoting as their argument a number of instances from as early as the twelfth century, in which the number 1001 appears in Persian prose and poetry (as *hezār-o yek*) to denote an undefined and indefinite amount. The mystical poet Farīd al-Dīn 'Aṭṭār (died 1201) in his biographical work on famous mystics quotes Hakīm Tirmidhī (died ca. 910) as saying that he saw God in his dreams a thousand and one times (Meier [no date]; Ritter 2003: 461). In his poetry, 'Aṭṭār himself used the phrase "a thousand and one persons must be set in order ere thou canst properly put a morsel of

food into thy mouth" (Boyle 1976: 46). The poet Neẓāmi (died 1209) even chose his pen-name deliberately so as to allude to the thousand and one secrets hidden in his tales (Barry 2000: 87f.), as the numerical value of its letters add to the amount of 1001 (n=50, ẓ=900, ā=1, m=40, i=10). Though these instances indicate a strong position of the number 1001 in medieval Persian culture, it remains to be studied whether or not the Persian usage might have influenced the collection's general denomination in Arabic.

While it is possible to reconstruct the date of the first Arabic translation of the Persian *Hazār afsān[e],* it is not altogether clear until what time the Persian book survived. Munjīk of Tirmidh, a highly literate poet of the tenth century, is quoted as having "read heroic tales and listened to their narration from written sources: 'Many versions of the tales of the Seven Trials, and the Brass Fortress did I read myself, and heard recited [to me] from the book [called] *Hazār afsān*'" (Omidsalar 1999: 329). Similar evidence is said to abound in the verse of the poet Farrokhi who lived in the early eleventh century (ibid.). And still Neẓāmi in a passage of his romance *Khosrou and Shirin* alluded to the collection under its ancient Persian name of *Hazār afsān* (Barry 2000: 87). The tales of the Seven Trials (Persian *haft khvān*) and of the Brass Fortress mentioned by Munjīk belong to the genre of mythical history and are also contained in the Persian national epic, the *Shāhnāme* or "Book of the Kings" compiled by Munjīk's contemporary Ferdousi (died 1010). In consequence, the *Hazār afsān* alluded to by Munjīk appears to denote a collection of mythical or historical narratives rather than a precursor of the *Arabian Nights.* Driving this argument somewhat further, one might speculate that the term *Hazār afsān* in medieval Persian poetry did not even mean a specific book or compilation. Probably the *Hazār afsān* was similar to the concept of *arzhang* (or *artang*), a denomination linked to the notion of a mysterious colorful masterpiece of art produced by the legendary Persian artist Māni. While the exact characteristics of this masterpiece are not clear, some sources mention his house and others refer to a lavishly illustrated manuscript (Sims et al. 2002: 20). By analogy, *Hazār afsān* might have implied a fictitious concept of a truly wonderful and unsurpassedly inspiring collection of narratives.

TALES OF ALLEGED IRANIAN ORIGIN

Jiří Cejpek in the chapter on "The Iranian Element in the *Book of a Thousand and One Nights* and Similar Collections" in Jan Rypka's *History of Iranian Literature* is quite apodictic as to the extent of the Iranian material in the *Arabian Nights.* In an extensive passage devoted to this problem, he regards the "core of the *Book of a Thousand and One Nights*" as "undoubtedly Iranian" and speaks of its being "modeled on the Middle Persian prose folk-book *Hazār afsānak* which was Iranian throughout in character" (Cejpek 1968: 663). Accordingly, he also claims that the frame story, including its embedded stories, is of Iranian origin. Next Cejpek supplies a list of stories "all of which form part of the Iranian core in the *Book of a Thousand and One Nights,* i. e. the original *Hazār afsānak*"; the stories listed by him include "the stories of the '**Merchant, the Ghost and the Three Old Men**' [. . .], '**The Fisherman and the Ghost**,' '**The Three Apples**' [. . .], '**The Porter**,' '**The Three Ladies and the Three Qalandars**' [. . .], '**The Magic Horse**,' '**Hasan from Basra**,' '**Prince Badr and Princess Jauhar from Samandal**,' '**Ardashīr and Hayāt an-nufūs**,' '**Qamar az-zamān and Queen Budūr**'". In addition, Cejpek mentions what he calls the "[d]efinitely Iranian" tales about "Ahmad and the Fairy Parībānū, and the Story of the Jealous sisters," conceding, however, that it is "doubtful and in fact unlikely" that these stories were part of the original Persian collection (664).

While Cejpek relies on previous research (such as Oestrup 1925: 42-71; see also Elisséeff 1949: 43-47), in terms of evidence to support his evaluation, it is interesting to note his arguments. Cejpek says: "Proper names are a great help and rarely let one down when determining the origin of a story. If they are Persian it means that they are original and prove the subject in question to be of Persian origin too. On the other hand, if one finds Arabic names in Iranian stories (which happens particularly in the magic fairy-tales), they have been invented and substituted for the Iranian ones later on." (Cejpek 1968: 664) As detailed arguments are missing, this statement ought to be considered a fairly general one. In fact, in view of the other evaluations in Cejpek's writing, it appears to be highly biased in favor of Iran. On a general level, comparative folk-narrative research has shown that the names that are not constitutive for a given folktale are as susceptible to change as numerous other ingredients or requisites (Nicolaisen 1999). Moreover, it remains unclear why Cejpek denies Arabic names the very quality he previously claims for Persian ones.

Enno Littmann, who has also dealt in some detail with the various national or ethnic components in the *Arabian Nights* argues in terms of content. In his evaluation, relying on Johannes Østrup, those tales in which benevolent ghosts and fairies interact independently with human characters are of Persian origin (Littmann 1923: 18; id. 1953: 677-695). The most prominent tales he regards as Persian according to this evaluation are the tales of "**Qamar al-zamān and Budūr**," "**Ahmad and the Fairy Peri Bānū**," "**The Ebony-horse**," "**Jullanār the Mermaid**," and "**The Two Envious Sisters**."

To name but a third source surveying the Iranian element in the *Arabian Nights,* Jean-Louis Laveille in his recent study of the theme of voyage in the *Arabian Nights* (Laveille 1998: 189-193) also concedes a Persian character to about ten stories, including the already named ones of "**Qamar al-zamān and Budūr**," "**The Ebony-horse**" and "**Ahmad and the Fairy Peri Bānū**."

Interestingly, at least two of the tales mentioned by the above quoted authors—those of "**Ahmad and the Fairy Peri Bānū**" and of "**The Two Envious Sisters**"—belong to the stock of what Mia Gerhardt has termed the "orphan tales" (Gerhardt 1963: 12-14). Those tales are not included in the fifteenth-century Arabic manuscript used by Galland. Their outlines were supplied to him by the Syrian Maronite narrator Hannā Diyāb, and the tales Galland constructed on the basis of Hannā's narration only became part of the traditional stock of the *Arabian Nights* after Galland had introduced them into his publication when his original manuscript material had been exhausted. This fact leads one to ponder about the feasibility of using the geographical or ethnical approach to identify the Persian element in the *Arabian Nights,* in fact about the very justification of any attempt to identify ingredients supposed to be constituted against or derived from a specific ethnical or national backdrop. Persian narrative literature at any given state, and certainly at the stage in which it might have contributed discernibly to the narrative repertoire of the *Arabian Nights,* was of a hybrid character, incorporating numerous elements originating from other national or ethnic cultures; besides the Indian narrative tradition, the Greek (Davis 2002) is most notable. Cejpek aims to compensate this hybridity by pointing out the fact that "the Indian material [in the *Arabian Nights*] was so completely iranized that there can be no question of the *Thousand and One Nights* being a direct descendant of an Indian model." (1968: 665)

On the other hand, readers such as Laveille correctly point out that Iran in a number of tales in the *Arabian Nights* serves as nothing more than an imaginative matrix, a "never-never land of collective memory constituted by the legends" ("un pays de cocagne dans la mémoire collective constituée par les légendes;" Laveille 1998: 189; see also Djebli 1994: 205f.; Henninger 1949: 224). While this evaluation certainly holds true for the two "orphan-tales" mentioned above, its impact for the earlier history of the Iranian contribution to the *Arabian Nights* should also not be underestimated. Already in the early Islamic period, Iran had gained renown as a place of legends, similar to the manner in which Babylon—according to a Koranic allusion (2,102) and subsequent Islamic legend about the angels Hārūt and Mārūt—was invariably linked to the concept of magic. Altogether, the present knowledge about this level of a Persian link to the narrative stock of the *Arabian Nights* includes little direct Persian influence and relies on general evaluations that have not been subjected to detailed scrutiny.

PERSIAN CHARACTERS IN THE *NIGHTS*

Besides the standard Persian kings and princes, serving—somewhat like the kings of European fairy-tales—to illustrate the acme of royal (and, by analogy, both legitimate and permanent) rule, Persian characters in the *Arabian Nights* are quintessentially named Bahrām and figure in two distinct categories: the merchant and the Magian (Arabic *majūsī*).

Appearing frequently, the Persian merchant is essentially a neutral role supporting two major aspects. First, it indicates the cultural impact of medieval trade between Iran and the Arabic lands. This impact is already documented in storytelling by the famous anecdote of Nadhr ibn al-Ḥārith, the Arab merchant who challenged the Prophet Mohammad by promising to narrate Persian legends (Omidsalar 1999: 328f.). Second, it stresses the general character of the *Arabian Nights* as being what Aboubakr Chraibi has labeled a "mirror for merchants" (2004: 6; see also Coussonnet 1989). Since the merchant is an unobtrusive and unsuspicious character, villains would at times dress up in disguise as a Persian merchant, a motif figuring most prominently in the tale of Ḥasan of Basra.

The Magian denotes a lay member of the Zoroastrian community rather than a Zoroastrian priest. In contrast to the neutral merchant, the Magian is one of the standard villain characters of the *Arabian Nights.* In medieval Arabic narrative literature, the Magians are imagined as infidels practicing a number of strange customs, including the worship of fire, human sacrifice and incestuous relations, specifically between grown sons and their mothers (Marzolph 1992: vol. 2, nos. 28, 706, 738; Marzolph 1999: no. 1). Practicing a different belief and rituals that were in stark contrast to the basic Islamic tenets, the Magians were vulnerable to being portrayed and stereotyped as a highly dubious ethnic Other. Besides customs conflicting with public morals, such as a certain Magian's homosexual preferences in the tale of **"'Alā' al-di Abū al-shāmāt,"** Magians in the *Arabian Nights* invariably practice magic and kill the true believers. Magians figure most prominently in the Tale of **"As'ad and Amjad"** (Sironval 1984) which in turn is embedded in the tale of **"Qamar al-zamān,"** when As'ad is kidnapped and held prisoner to be presented as a human sacrifice on the Mountain of Fire. Magians are furthermore encountered by Sindbād the sailor on his fourth voyage, when his comrades are killed by a tribe of cannibal Magians ruled by a ghūl. Magian adversaries are mentioned in the story of **"Gharīb and his Brother 'Ajīb."** And, finally, Badr Bāsim, the son of Jullanār the mermaid and her human husband, is shipwrecked during his adventures on an island inhabited by Magians whose queen is the vicious sorceress Lāb. In all cases in which an ethically good (and hence, by extension, Muslim) protagonist falls victim to the Magi-

ans, the only means to save him is through the help of a Muslim (and hence, by extension, ethically good) man who often spends his life in the city or country of the Magians without professing his true belief. The practice of hiding or even denying one's true belief in time of imminent personal danger constitutes a legally accepted practice in Islam known as *taqiyya.* This practice is particularly linked to the Persian context by the fact that the adherents of the creed of Shiism, which only became the dominant creed in Iran from the Safavid period onwards, were often subjected to severe persecutions and practiced *taqiyya* in order to both survive and remain true to their belief (Meyer 1980).

It would be interesting to study the reception (and hypothetical change) of the image of Iranian characters in Persian translations of the *Arabian Nights.* After all, Persian authors and readers might justly be supposed to be more sympathetical towards their fellow countrymen than the ethnically different Arabs, regardless of the formers' religious creed. Historical circumstances make it, however, obvious, that the image of Iranians in Persian translations of the *Arabian Nights* is unlikely to be different from that of the Arabic version. The outlook and world-view of the *Arabian Nights* is not defined by the language of the tales, be it Arabic, Persian, or any other language, but rather by the cultural background. This cultural background is dominated by (Islamic) religion which in turn is the same for Muslim Arabs and Muslim Iranians. And it is Muslims that constituted the overwhelming majority of the country's population soon after the Islamic conquest and certainly the main category of readers at the time when the Persian translations of the *Arabian Nights* were prepared.

The implications of the image of the Magians in Persian versions of the *Arabian Nights* may in some way be compared to the development the image of Alexander the Conqueror underwent in Persian and general Islamic tradition. In historical Persian sources originating against a Zoroastrian backdrop, Alexander is an evil destroyer, a conqueror annihilating traditional values—such as he had, in fact, been experienced in history (Yamanaka 1993). In contrast, later Islamic sources transformed him not only into a triumphant conqueror, but also into a just ruler, and eventually into a sage and a prophet (Waugh 1996). Regardless of the language in which later sources were compiled, the common religious perspective determined the evaluation of Alexander in the Islamic sources. Since Iran's Arabic conquerors were in a similarly alien and hostile position towards Iran as had been Alexander, it was tempting for them to propagate his image in a similarly sympathetic way as Greek and Hellenistic sources did. By analogy, a Persian translation of the stereotypical image of the pre-Islamic fire-worshippers pictured in the Arabic sources would not result in any major changes, as the religious perspective of Islam was and still is shared by both Muslim Persians and Arabs, and Magians despite their national or ethnic proximity to their fellow Iranians would be—and in fact often are—alienated because of their religious creed.

At any rate, the negative image of the Magian is characteristic of Arab sources, and no truly Persian version of a given tale would—for various reasons—employ the character of the Magian as a villain. Whereas narratives rooted in ancient Iranian belief would resort to fictitious characters such as evil demons or sorcerers, the standard ethnical villain characters in modern Persian folktales are the Jew, the black man, and the gypsy (Marzolph 1984: 29).

PERSIAN TRANSLATIONS OF THE *NIGHTS*

When and where the **Arabian Nights** were first translated into the Persian language is not known exactly. While Turkish translations from the Arabic, some probably enlarged, already existed before Galland's French adaptation (Chauvin 1900: 23, 201), Persian translations apparently were not prepared before the beginning of the nineteenth century. As is well known, the British colonial enterprise exercised a decisive influence on the textual history of the **Arabian Nights,** particularly as two of its early printed editions were published in Calcutta (1814-18, 1839-42). In a similar vein, the attention generated by the publication of the printed editions might have given rise to suggesting a version of the **Arabian Nights** in Persian, a language that continued to hold its position as the local *lingua franca* of all of India. The catalogues of Persian manuscript collections worldwide list at least four early nineteenth century versions of the **Arabian Nights** in Persian, variously known as **Alf leile va-leile, Hezār-o yek shab,** or—in a curious distortion of its Arabic name—as **Alf al-leil.** None of these manuscript versions has so far been studied in detail. While Aḥmad Monzavi's *Union Catalogue of Persian Manuscripts* (1349/1970: 3659) lists two manuscripts presently not available for inspection in Madina and Tehran, the *Catalogue of the Arabic and Persian Mss. in the Oriental Public Library at Bankipore,* India, mentions a manuscript "collection of one hundred tales from the **Alf laylah,**" compiled in satisfaction of his friends' request by a certain Auḥad ibn Aḥmad Bilgrāmī and completed on Dhū'l-qa'da 15, 1251, corresponding to March 3, 1836 (Muqtadir 1925: 195, no. 767). The content of this manuscript, comprising some 102 folios, is not known.

The Berlin Staatsbibliothek possesses yet another Persian translation, the only manuscript whose text is available to me at present (Pertsch 1888: 967f., no. 998). The text of this manuscript comprises 118 folios covering 81 nights, and containing the opening of the frame story up to a part of the tale of **"Nūr al-Dīn 'Alī and His Son Badr al-Dīn Ḥasan."** The sequence of tales

reminds one of the Breslau edition prepared by Maximilian Habicht (and, after his death, continued by Heinrich Leberecht Fleischer; 1824-43). The manuscript is written by different hands, suggesting its production as the copy of an already existing manuscript through the collective effort of different scribes. The manuscript's language both in terms of syntax and vocabulary indicates its origin from Northeastern Iran. This evaluation is also corroborated by the name of the translator/compiler that is given as Mirzā Zein al-'Ābedin Khān Neishāburi (fol. 29b/-1-30a/1: *motarjem-e in ketāb*), i. e. a person originating from or living in the town of Neishābur. As the manuscript is not complete, it does not contain a colophon mentioning the date of compilation; the circumstances would, however, suggest a production in the first half of the nineteenth century. The text of this Persian manuscript version is particularly curious inasmuch as both its wording and division into nights differs considerably from both contemporary printed editions of the Arabic text, Bulaq I (1835) and Calcutta II (1839-42). Further research is needed in order to determine the Arabic text used as the basis of translation, most probably a manuscript, and its relation to other versions of the **Arabian Nights.**

The only existing complete version of the **Arabian Nights** in Persian was prepared by Mollā 'Abd al-Laṭif Ṭasuji together with the poet Mirzā Sorush of Esfahan and was completed in 1259/1843. Soon after, the translation was published in a two volume lithographed edition, the calligraphical work of which was accomplished in 1259/1843 and 1261/1845 respectively.[1] After his accession to the throne in 1264/1847, young Nāṣer al-din Shāh, who was an avid reader of the Persian translation (Amanat 1997: 49f., 66)[2] and is said to have yearned for a finely illustrated copy of the book ever since he first listened to the stories, ordered the calligrapher Moḥammad Ḥosein Tehrāni to copy the text. When this job was achieved on a total of some 570 text folios in 1269/1852, a team of more than forty leading artists under the supervision of the famous Abu 'l-Ḥasan Khān Ghaffāri Ṣani' al-molk supplied an equal number of folios containing illustrations, besides preparing the bookbinding that is lavishly embellished by lacquer work. The working conditions in the chambers of the polytechnical school (the Majma'-e Dār al-ṣanāye') appear to have been "cramped" (Zokā' 1382/2003: 33), as numerous people had to work together in modest quarters. The resulting work, now preserved in the library of the Golestān Palace in Tehran, was finished only seven years later in 1276/1859. It comprises a total of 2279 pages in large folio format that are bound in six exuberantly decorated volumes (see Ātābāy 2535/1976: 1375-1392; Zokā' 1382/2003: 33-38, 83-105, plates 12-34). This manuscript represents the last outstanding specimen of the traditional art of the book in Qajar Iran. According to a recently published document (Bakhtiyār 1381/2002), the cost of preparing its illustrations and illumination totalled the sum of 6,850 *tumān*. This amount was equivalent to a sixth of the total amount spent to construct and decorate the contemporary multistoried palace in Tehran known as Shams ol-'emāre, itself the most sumptuously decorated royal building of the Qajar period. A painting by Abu 'l-Hasan Khān Ghaffāri depicts Dust-'Ali Khān Mo'ayyer al-mamālek, head of the polytechnical school, presenting a volume of the manuscript to the ruler (Zokā' 1382/2003: 134, no. 69; Bakhtiyār 1381/2002: 130).

Except for two places in the manuscript, the text folios alternate with those containing illustrations. The space on the illustrated folios has been divided into at least three and up to as many as six images per page, the individual images being framed and separated from each other by a band of illumination that also includes a caption indicating the content. The illustrations number a total of 3,600 different scenes. In the course of restoration in recent years, making a photographic documentation and reproduction of this manuscript has repeatedly been discussed, as doing so would serve both conservatory functions and make this monument of Qajar art available to national and international scholarship. In view of the uninhibited and outspokenly playful illustration of the sexual scenes particularly at the manuscript's beginning, such a reproduction contradicts the presently propagated values in Iran and is unlikely to happen soon. Even so, the manuscript's published images contain a wealth of information about popular customs and material culture of the Qajar period.

One of the most fascinating images illustrates a scene from the story of Ghānim ibn Ayyūb in which, as the caption says, the Caliph Hārūn al-Rashīd, who in the *Nights* embodies the quintessence of just rule (Marzolph 1990), speaks to his vizier Ja'far al-Barmakī (Zokā' 1382/2003: 85, no. 12). The fact that the Abbasid caliph and his vizier are rendered in the likeness of the young Qajar ruler Nāṣer al-din Shāh and his prime minister Amir Kabīr add a tragic touch to this image. Amir Kabīr, who was an extremely able and powerful prime-minister as well as the Shāh's favorite, had suddenly been dismissed by the Shāh in late 1851, and he was subsequently executed on Rabī' I 17, 1268, corresponding to January 9, 1852. In this manner, he had suffered a similar tragic fall from the ruler's favor and untimely death as had been experienced by Hārūn al-Rashīd's vizier Ja'far and the Barmakid clan. If it holds true that the manuscript's illustration was not begun before the year 1269, the image rather than unknowingly foreshadowing the tragic event probably represents a late tribute by the artist (and the ruler, who undoubtedly approved of the illustrations in person) to the once powerful and highly esteemed politician.

When the first lithographed edition of the *Arabian Nights* was prepared in 1259-61/1843-45, lithographic illustration had not yet become a regular phenomenon.

Soon after the preparations for illustrating the luxurious royal manuscript had begun, a second lithographed edition was ordered, this time containing illustrations. As the effort of preparing the lithographed book was considerably easier, the task was achieved much faster than the manuscript, and the result was published in 1272/1855. This first illustrated lithographed edition of the *Arabian Nights* in Persian, in fact the first ever Oriental edition of the *Nights* containing a regular set of illustrations, includes 70 illustrations executed by Mirzā 'Ali-Qoli Khu'i, an eminent artist of the day (Marzolph 1997), and two of his apprentices, Mirzā Reżā Tabrizi and Mirzā Ḥasan (see id. 2002: 232). This edition in turn appears to have created an increased popular demand, since only three years later Mirzā Ḥasan, the son of the well-known court painter Āqā Seyyed Mirzā, illustrated another edition on his own, albeit with a slightly reduced iconographical program (ibid.). A total of at least seven additional lithographed editions of the *Arabian Nights* in Persian were published between 1289/1872 and 1357/1938, all but two of which—the editions of 1292-93/1875-76 and of 1357/1938—contain illustrations that are usually modeled on either of the two early illustrated editions.[3]

The translation prepared by Ṭasuji and Sorush is regarded as an exceptional piece of literature (Bahār 2535/1977: 369) in the formative period of the modern Persian language. Its textual basis has never been discussed in previous scholarship, and a close comparison between the translation and the Arabic original constitutes a promising field for future study. In theory, both the editions of Bulaq and Calcutta II would have been available, even though the publication of the latter one was probably just finished when the Persian translation was already under way. Fortunately, both editions differ considerably in wording, and a particularly peculiar lacuna proves the Bulaq edition beyond reasonable doubt to constitute the basis for the Persian translation. The Bulaq edition offers a highly reduced version of the **"Third Qalandar's Tale"** that is narrated within **"The Story of the Porter and the Three Ladies of Baghdad."** In its full version, this tale consists of three episodes: The destruction of the talisman on the Magnetic Mountain, the fateful slaying of the youth in the underground palace, and the protagonist's adventures with the forty maidens. While the Calcutta edition contains the tale's full text, the Arabic manuscript serving as the basis for this particular passage of the Bulaq edition must have suffered from a lacuna of several folios occurring shortly after the beginning of the second episode and affecting the text of the third episode up to the point at which the protagonist is about to break the tabu of opening the forbidden door. In order to mend the break, the compiler of the printed edition has merged the originally distinct second and third episodes: As in the second episode, the hero watches a group of people preparing an underground mansion. As soon as they have left, he uncovers the mansion's lid, enters, and then, as towards the end of the third episode, wanders through 39 beautiful gardens. When opening a door, he finds the magic horse that brings him to the ten mournful youths and hits out one of his eyes. This version by way of its Qajar period Persian translation was also popular as a separate chapbook under the title of *Se gedā-ye yek-chashm* (The Three One-Eyed Beggars) in mid-twentieth century Iran (Marzolph 1994: no. XLIV) and lingers on as far as the modern study of the *Arabian Nights* in Iran, when the tale's summary simply reads: "By accident, [the hero] in an underground city mounts a horse whose tail makes him blind . . ." (Samini 1379/2001: 392)

Two further Persian language adaptations of the *Arabian Nights* need to be mentioned. One is an illustrated chapbook version of the frame story, published in pocket-book format in 1280/1863 (Chauvin 1900: 23, no. 20 zz; Edwards 1922: 129); the other one is a complete versified version prepared by the Persian poet Seif al-sho'arā'Mirzā Abo 'l-Fath Dehqān (died 1326/1908), published under the title *Hezār dāstān* (One Thousand Stories), in a folio-sized lithographed edition in 1317-18/1899-1900. The latter edition contains a set of 59 illustrations prepared by the contemporary popular artists 'Ali-Khān and Javād (Marzolph 2002: 243).

THE *ARABIAN NIGHTS* IN MODERN IRAN

As a final point, the position of the *Arabian Nights* in modern Iran deserves to be mentioned. Reliable and extensive information about international *Arabian Nights* scholarship is available to Persian readers through two studies published by Jalāl Sattāri (1368/1989, 1382/2003). A first edition printed in movable type had been prepared by Mohammad Ramażāni, head of the famous publishing house Kolāle-ye khāvar as early as 1315-16/1936-37. This edition also contained a learned introduction by the scholar 'Ali Asghar Hekmat. While Ramażāni's edition appears to reproduce major parts of Tasuji's nineteenth century translation faithfully, even a superficial comparison reveals various editorial changes that were obviously deemed necessary to adjust the content and wording to contemporary taste. Several printed editions in Persian circulate since the 1990s, all of them presenting adapted, if not censored versions following Ramażāni's edition. One of the editions available to me is a typical "Bazaar edition." It is presented in the traditional style of Persian chapbooks (Marzolph 1994) as *Hekāyat-e shirin-e Alf leile va-leile shāmel-e barkhi as hekāyāt-e Hezār va yek shab* (The Sweet Story of the [Arabic] *Thousand and One Nights,* containing some of the stories of the [Persian] *Thousand and One Nights.*) The fact that this booklet, dating from the 1980s, is printed as "grey literature" without the obligatory mention of publication details might indicate that the publisher was not sure whether the book's content might cause him trouble. Mitrā Mehrābādi's one volume edition of "Tasuji's translation" follows Ramażāni's edition quite closely inasmuch as she includes the preface by 'Ali Asghar Hekmat and even reproduces most of the illustrations from the former edition. At the same time, her short introductory notice makes it perfectly clear that some of the disputable passages could not be reproduced in a "society paying respect to moral values" (*yek jāme'e-ye akhlāq-garā*; Tasuji 1380/2001: 4). In contrast to most other recent editions, Mehrābādi's adapted reprint footnotes difficult passages and at the end of each of the five volumes of the original edition has a glossary of terms unfamiliar to modern Persian readers.

Particularly the sexually pronounced passages of the frame story and the introductory set of tales of the *Nights* are bound to conflict with the moral standards propagated in today's Iran (Marzolph 1995) and have been adjusted accordingly. As a case in point, I have compared in detail two passages in various available editions. The first one is the introductory passages in which Shāhzamān surprises both his own and his brother Shahriyār's wife committing adultery and in which later on both are violated by the beautiful woman kept in a box by a demon; the second one is the joyful discussion of the various denominations of the female and male sexual parts celebrated by the porter and the three ladies in the story of the same name.

Both Tasuji's (1275/1858: fol. 1b-2b) and—reproducing Tasuji's wording verbatim—Ramażāni's (1315-16/1936-37: vol. 1, 3-8) texts present the sexually pronounced elements of the frame story in a manner closely following the wording of the Arabic text. Ramażāni even includes an uninhibited (European) illustration of the scene in which Shāhzamān spies on Shahriyār's wife and her servants as they embrace their male lovers in the garden just after Shahriyār has left to go hunting (ibid.: vol. 1, 5). While the same text is also reproduced in the Bazaar edition and one of the modern editions (Tasuji 1379/2000: vol. 1, 1-6), Mehrābādi in her edition of "Tasuji's translation" has opted to replace the three instances of extramarital sexual relations with an all-embracing summary in a wording reminiscent of Tasuji's style: "Yet, there came a time when those two brothers due to the filthy and disagreeable character of their wives killed them . . ." (*lik zamāni farā resid ke ān do barādar besabab-e khu-ye zesht va nā-pasandi ke as hamsarān-e-shān bedidand, ānhā-rā koshtand . . .*). The sentence is then continued with Tasuji's words: ". . . and from then on, Shāhzamān chose to live in celibacy . . ." (*. . . va az ān pas, Shāhzamān, tajarrod gozide . . .*; Tasuji 1380/2001: 22).

The version published under the title *Dāstānhā-ye Hezār va yek shab* (The Stories of the *Thousand and One Nights*; 1377/1998) contains a modern retelling that follows Ṭasuji's text to some extent while justifying the rendering of the reprehensible action by additional comments aiming to illustrate the psychological conflict experienced by Shāhzamān. Whereas Shāhzamān in the older versions, including the Bulaq edition and Ṭasuji's translation, have Shāhzamān return to his wife simply because he has forgotten something,[4] this version (vol. 1, 11) states that Shāhzamān loved his wife dearly (*nesbat be-hamsar-e khod delbastegi-ye be-syār dāsht*) and for that reason wanted to see her one more time before he left. As he approached her bedroom, he was hoping that his unexpected appearance would make the queen even happier. In consequence, the loving husband Shāhzamān was shocked even deeper than in the previous versions to discover his wife's adultery. As a further digression motivating his following action, instead of straightaway slaying the sinful lovers, he could not believe his eyes and went into an inner dialogue how this situation was possible at all before he finally killed them. Probably this version is not so much indicative of the restraints experienced by publishers in modern Iran than by the requirements of motivating the action so that juvenile readers—at whom this edition is apparently directed—were given a better chance to understand.

The joyful sexual discussion between the porter and the three ladies has been translated by Ṭasuji in minute detail (ed. 1275: fol. 11f.). When their party reaches its climax, the text first says: "In short, they spent their time drinking wine, reciting poetry and dancing until they got drunk . . ." (*al-gharaż be-mei keshidan va ghazal khvāndan va raqṣ kardan hami-gozarāndand tā inke mast shodand . . .*). Then follows the scene in which they undress one after the other, take a bath in the pool and tease the other sex with proposing to guess the name of their private parts. Soon after Shahrazād has resumed her narrative in the eleventh night, it is time for the characters in her story to have dinner, and the young ladies ask the porter to leave (. . . *tā hangām-e shām shod dokhtaregān goftand aknun vaqt-e ān-ast ke az khāne birun ravi*). In Ramaẕāni's text (1315-16/1936-37: vol. 1, 54-56) and, following him, in one the modern editions (Ṭasuji 1379/2000: vol. 1, 35), the beginning of this scene is just the same, and the three ladies one after the other take a bath, sit close to the porter and "have fun with each other" (*be-shukhi va-lahv mashghul shodand*). While the playful slapping in the original version is justified by the fact that the porter does not guess the "correct" denomination for the women's sexual parts, in this version it is motivated by sheer joy, if anything, before—with the wording of Ṭasuji's text—the women ask the porter to leave.

It is interesting to note that the unrestricted sexual joy of this particular passage has also been regarded as revoltingly obscene in some of the European translations. While Richard Burton, renowned for his particular de-

lectation of obsessive sexuality, renders the passage in detail (1885: vol. 1, 89-93), Edward William Lane (1859: vol. 1, 124f.) in his puritan manner has the following wording:

> The wine continued to circulate among them, and the porter, taking his part in the revels, dancing and singing with them, and enjoying the fragrant odours, began to hug and kiss them, while one slapped him, and another pulled him, and the third beat him with sweet-scented flowers, till, at length, the wine made sport with their reason; and they threw off all restraint, indulging their merriment with as much freedom as if no man had been present.

At the end of this passage, and before the ladies ask the porter to leave, Lane has inserted a footnote entitled "On Wine, Fruits, Flowers, and Music, in Illustration of Arab Carousals." He begins by mentioning that in his translation he has passed over

> an extremely objectionable scene, which, it is to be hoped, would convey a very erroneous idea of the manners of Arab *ladies*; though I have witnessed, at private festivities in Cairo, abominable scenes, of which ladies, screened behind lattices, were spectators. Can the same be said with respect to the previous carousal? This is a question which cannot be answered in a few words.

He then delves into an extended and most learned discussion of the mentioned subjects occupying more than twice the space a translation of the actual passage would have required (ibid., 193-204).

Mehrābādi has again opted for an even more condensed and less objectionable wording than the one given by Ramaẕāni. In her version, there is neither wine, nor dance, nor even poetry, and—needless to mention—even less bathing or nudity. Instead, the porter is accepted by the ladies as an educated boon-companion with whom they spend some time in pleasant conversation (*ham-māl-rā be-nadimi bar-gozide be-ṣohbat neshastand*) before sending him away at dinner-time (Ṭasuji 1380/2001: 38f.). Again, the related illustration in Ramaẕāni's edition has not been reproduced. Similarly, in the modern retelling the original drink of wine (Persian *mei* or *sharāb*)—whose consumption is strictly forbidden under the present interpretation of Islamic laws in Iran—has been replaced by an act beyond reproach, namely passing around a cup of *sharbat,* or sweet juice (***Dāstānhā* [*Dāstānhā-ye Hezār va yek shab*]** 1377/1998: vol. 1, 137), and the company spends their time reciting love-poetry, a past-time "all of them sincerely enjoyed" (*hame-ye ānhā az in bazm ṣami-māne lezzat mi-bordand*) before, once more, the porter is asked to leave.

Since Iran has constituted decisively to the genesis and character of the ***Arabian Nights,*** it appears natural that his body of world literature is appreciated in today's

Iran as part of the country's literary heritage. However, a sound appreciation of the collection's original character appears more jeopardized than ever before, as the treatment of the text passages just discussed demonstrates. The consumption of alcoholic beverages and the indulging in extramarital sexual relations, both of which are frequently encountered in the *Nights,* contradict the moral values presently propagated in Iran, and publishers opt for different strategies to adjust the text so as to eliminate reprehensible components. As both Ramażāni's Persian edition and Lane's English rendering prove, similar strategies have been at work in different periods as well as different cultural contexts, albeit with varying success. Whereas the Western world has grown accustomed to regarding the *Nights* as a monumental and uninhibited affirmation of the joy of life in all its manifestations, Iranian readers are restricted to textual versions that have been adapted to their present political circumstances.

On the other hand, the *Arabian Nights* throughout their history have proven to be highly capable of adjusting to a diversity of cultural contexts. Two announcements in the current issue of the Iranian journal *Farhang-e mardom* (Folklore) indicate some of the directions into which the future reception of the *Arabian Nights* in Iran develops (Vakiliyan 2003: 164f.). The Iranian writer Moḥammad Bahārlu is preparing a new Persian edition. The text of his edition, comprising a total of 1,400,000 words, will be completely adapted to the grammar and style of the modern Persian language while remaining faithful to Ṭasuji's translation. Moreover, the edition is to contain an annotated index of the Koranic verses and Prophetic utterances as well as of other Arabic and Persian expressions that might need to be explained to the modern readers. Another publication, by the folklorist Moḥammad Ja'far Qanavāti, is to present versions of tales from the *Nights* collected from living oral tradition. Besides documenting a renewed interest in the *Nights,* both publications will indicate the degree to which official guidelines determine how this part of the country's literary heritage is to be dealt with. At any rate, this is an unfinished chapter in the collection's history that the future is still writing.

Notes

1. Early Persian lithographed books do not contain a regular date of publication. As they constitute the direct successors of previous manuscript production, their dating is to be inferred from the book's colophon in which the calligrapher would often state his own name and the name of the person who ordered or paid for the preparation of the book together with the year (and sometimes the day and month) of completion of the written text that served as the basis of lithographic reproduction.

There is some confusion in Iranian studies concerning the completion of the manuscript and the publication of the first lithographed text. Moḥammad Ja'far Maḥjub in his influential study still holds the work of translation to have begun in 1259; in consequence, he considers the data concerning printed editions of 1259, 1261, and 1263 as faulty (1339/1960: 48). He quotes the Islamic date 1263 with reference to Chauvin (1900: 23) who lists a lithographed edition Tehran 1847; this edition cannot be verified. For copies of the Persian *editio princeps,* said to be "the best printing ever made of this work" (Zoka' 1382/2003: 33), and later editions see Marzolph 2002: 231f.

2. The Iranian National Library contains a total of six copies of the *editio princeps.* As the National Library also incorporates the holdings of the former library of the royal palace, this comparatively large amount is also indicative of the ruler's interest.

3. Two editions printed in Lahore are listed by Naushahi 1986: vol. 1, 552f.

4. While the Bulaq text (1252: vol. 1, 2) has a simple "something" (Arabic: *ḥājja*), Ṭasuji argues that Shāhzamān had forgotten to take along a precious jewel (*gouhari gerānmāye*) intended as a present for his brother.

Works Cited

Abbott, Nabia: "A Ninth-Century Fragment of the 'Thousand Nights': New Lights on the Early History of the *Arabian Nights.*" In: *Journal of Near Eastern Studies* 8 (1949) 129-164.

'Abd al-Laṭif Ṭasuji: *Hezār va yek shab* (*The Thousand and One Nights*). Lithographed edition Tehran, 1275/1858.

id.: *Hezār va yek shab* (*The Thousand and One Nights*). 6 vols. Tehran: Jāmi, 1379/2000.

id.: *Hezār va yek shab. Tarjome-ye Ṭasuji-ye Tabrizi* (*The Thousand and One Nights. The Translation of Ṭasuji Tabrizi*). ed. by Mitrā Mehrābādi. Tehran: Afsun, 1380/2001.

Alf laylah wa-laylah. al-ṭab'a al-ūlā. muqābala [wa-]taṣḥīḥ al-Shaykh Muḥammad Qiṭṭa al-'Adawī/Alif Laila wa-Laila. *The Book of a Thousand and One Nights.* Reprint of the Original Copy of the Būlāq edition of 1252 A. H. 2 vols. Baghdad: Maktabat al-Muthannā, ca. 1965.

Amanat, Abbas: "Pivot of the Universe." *Nasir al-Din Shah Qajar and the Iranian Monarchy, 1831-1896.* Berkeley/Los Angeles: University of California Press, 1997.

Ātābāy, Badri: *Fehrest-e divānhā-ye khaṭṭi-ye Ketābkhāne-ye salṭanati va ketāb-e Hezār va yek shab* (Catalogue of the Manuscript Collections of Poems in the Royal Library and the Book of *The Thousand and One Nights*). Tehran 2535/1976.

Bahār, Moḥammad Taqi Malek al-shoʻarā': *Sabkshenāsi* ([Persian] Stylistics). 3 vols. Tehran: Amir Kabir, [4]2535/1977.

Bakhtiyār, Moẓaffar: *Ketāb-ārā'i-ye "Hezār va yek shab"* (noskhe-ye ketābkhāne-ye Golestān) (The Illumination of the *Thousand and One Nights* [the manuscript preserved in the Golestān palace museum]). In: Nâmeh-ye Bahârestân 5 (1381/2002) 123-130.

Barry, Michael: "le conte de la princesse du maghreb sous le pavillon turquoise par nezâmî de gandjeh" (1141-1209). In: *Horizons maghrébins* 42 (2000) 83-89, 97-99.

Barth, John: *Don't Count on It: A Note on the Number of* The 1001 Nights. Northridge, Calif.: Lord John Press, 1984.

Boyle, John Andrew (Translator): *The Ilāhī-Nāma or Book of God of Farīd al-Dīn ʻAṭṭār.* Manchester: Manchester University Press, 1976.

Burton, Richard F.: *Arabian Nights with Introduction & Explanatory Notes.* Reprinted from the Original Edition Issued by the Khamashastra Society for Private Subscibers only. Benares, India (i. e. London) 1885. 16 vols. Beirut: Khayat 1966.

Cejpek, Jiří: "The Iranian Element in the *Book of a Thousand and One Nights* and Similar Collections." In: Rypka, Jan: *History of Iranian Literature.* ed. by Karl Jahn. Dordrecht: Reidel, 1968. 607-709.

Chauvin, Victor: *Bibliographie des ouvrages arabes ou relatifs aux arabes publiés dans l'Europe chrétienne de 1810 à 1885.* 4 vols. Liège: Vaillant-Carmanne/Leipzig: Harrassowitz, 1900.

Chraibi, Aboubakr: "Situation, Motivation, and Action in the *Arabian Nights.*" In: *Marzolph, Ulrich, and Richard van Leeuwen: The* Arabian Nights *Encyclopedia.* Santa Barbara, Calif./Denver/Oxford, 2004. 5-9.

Cosquin, Emmanuel: "Le Prologue-cadre des Mille et une Nuits." In: *Revue Biblique* 6 (1909) 7-49; also in id.: *Études folkloriques.* Paris: Édouard Champion, 1922. 265-347.

Coussonnet, Patrice: *Pensée mythique, idéologie et aspirations sociales dans un conte des* Mille et une nuits. Cairo: Institut français d'archéologie orientale du Caire, 1989.

Dāstānhā-ye Hezār va yek shab (The Stories of the *Thousand and One Nights*). 2 vols. Tehran: Eqbāl, 1377/1998 ([3]1382/2003).

Davis, Dick: *Panthea's Children: Hellenistic Novels and Medieval Persian Romances.* New York: Bibliotheca Persica Press, 2002.

Djebli, Moktar: "Cités d'Orient dans *les Mille et une Nuits.*" In: *Les Mille et une Nuits: Contes sans frontière.* ed. by Edgard Weber. Toulouse: Amam, 1994. 195-211.

Drory, Rina: "Three Attempts to Legitimize Fiction in Classical Arabic Literature." In: *Jerusalem Studies in Arabic and Islam* 18 (1994) 146-164.

Edwards, Edward: *A Catalogue of the Persian Printed Books in the British Museum.* London: British Museum, 1922.

Elisséeff, Nikita: *Thèmes et motifs des* Mille et une Nuits*: Essai de classification.* Beyrouth 1949.

EM = *Enzyklopädie des Märchens.* 10 vols. Berlin/New York: Walter de Gruyter, 1977-2002.

Gerhardt, Mia I.: *The Art of Story-telling: A Literary Study of the* Thousand and One Nights. Leiden: Brill, 1963.

Goeje, Michael J. de: "De Arabische nachtvertellingen." In: *De Gids* 50 (1886) 385-413.

Grotzfeld, Heinz. "The Age of the Galland Manuscript of the *Nights*: Numismatic Evidence for Dating a Manuscript?" In: *Journal of Arabic and Islamic Studies* 1 (1996-97) 50-64.

Ḥekmat, "ʻAli Aṣghar: Alf leile va-leile." In: *Ramaẓāni* 1315-16: vol. 1, alef-lz.

Henninger, Josef: "Der geographische Horizont der Erzähler von *1001 Nacht.*" In: *Geographica Helvetica* 4 (1949) 214-229.

Horálek, Karel: "Frau im Schrein." In: *EM* 5 (1987) 186-192.

Lane, Edward William (Translator): *The Thousand and One Nights, commonly called, in England, The Arabian Nights' Entertainments.* Reprint of the Edition 1859. 3 vols. London: East-West Publications/Cairo: Livres de France, 1979.

Laveille, Jean-Louis: *Le Thème de voyage dans* Les Mille et une Nuits*: Du Maghreb à la Chine.* Paris: L'Harmattan, 1998.

Littmann, Enno: *Tausendundeine Nacht in der arabischen Literatur.* Tübingen: Mohr, 1923.

id.: Anhang: "Zur Entstehung und Geschichte von Tausendundeiner Nacht." In: id.: *Die Erzählungen aus den Tausendundein Nächten. Vollständige deutsche Ausgabe in sechs Bänden.* Wiesbaden: Insel, 1953. vol. 6, 648-738.

Maḥjub, Moḥammad Jaʻfar: "Dāstānhā-ye ʻāmmiyāne-ye fārsi. 11: Tarjome-ye fārsi-ye Alf leile va leile" (Popular Persian Tales. 11: The Persian Translation of the *Thousand and One Nights*). In: *Sokhan* 11 (1339/1960) 34-53 (also in id.: *Adabiyāt-e 'āmmiyāne-ye Irān. Majmu'e-y maqālāt dar bāre-ye afsānehā va ādāb va rosum-e mardom-e Irān.* ed. by Ḥasan Zo'l-faqāri. 2 vols. Tehran: Cheshme, 1382/2003. vol. 1, 391-422).

Marzolph, Ulrich: *Typologie des persischen Volksmärchens.* Beirut: Deutsche Morgenländische Gesellschaft/ Wiesbaden: Franz Steiner, 1984.

id.: "Hārūn ar-Rašīd." In: *EM* 6 (1990) 534-537.

id.: *Arabia ridens: Die humoristische Kurzprosa der frühen adab-Literatur im internationalen Traditionsgeflecht.* 2 vols. Frankfurt am Main: Klostermann, 1992.

id.: *Dāstānhā-ye širin: Fünfzig persische Volksbüchlein aus der zweiten Hälfte des zwanzigsten Jahrhunderts.* Stuttgart: Franz Steiner, 1994.

id.: "Zur Lage der Erzählforschung im nachrevolutionären Iran." In: *Spektrum Iran* 8,3 (1995) 39-51; English version: "Folk-Narrative and Narrative Research in Post-Revolutionary Iran." In: *Folklore in the Changing World.* ed. Jawaharlal Handoo/Reimund Kvideland. Mysore: Zooni, 1999. 299-305.

id.: Mirzâ 'Ali-Qoli Xu'i: "Master of Lithograph Illustration." In: *Annali* (Istituto Orientale di Napoli) 57,1-2 (1997) 183-202, plates I-XV.

id.: "Re-locating the *Arabian Nights*." In: *Orientalia Lovanensia Analecta* 87 (1998) 155-163.

id. (ed.): *Das Buch der wundersamen Geschichten: Erzählungen aus der Welt von* 1001 Nacht. München: C. H. Beck, 1999.

id.: "Alf leile va leile" (Hezâr-o yek shab). In: *The Beginning of Printing in the Near and Middle East: Jews, Christians and Muslims.* ed. by Lehrstuhl für Türkische Sprache, Geschichte und Kultur, Universität Bamberg, Staatsbibliothek Bamberg. Wiesbaden: Harrassowitz, 2001. 88.

Meier, Fritz: *Unpublished Notes about the Persian Contribution to the* Arabian Nights. Ms. University Library Basel NL 0323:D5.16 (no date).

Meyer, Egbert: "Anlaß und Anwendungsbereich der taqiyya." In: *Der Islam* 27 (1980) 246-280.

Monzavi, Aḥmad: *Fehrest-e noskhehā-ye khaṭṭi-ye fārsi* (Catalogue of Persian Manuscripts). vol. 5. Tehran: Mo'assasse-ye farhangi-ye manṭeqe'i, 1349/1970.

Muqtadir, Maulavi Abdul: Catalogue of the Arabic and Persian Manuscripts in the Oriental Public Library at Bankipore, vol. 8: Persian Manuscripts. Biography, Romances, Tales and Anecdotes. Patna: Oriental Public Library, 1925.

Nicolaisen, Wilhelm F. H.: "Name." In: *EM* 9 (1999) 1158-1164.

Naushahi, S. Arif: Catalogue of Litho-Print and Rare Persian Books in Ganj Bakhash Library, Islamabad. 2 vols. Iran/Islamabad: Pakistan Institute of Persian Studies, 1986.

Oestrup, Johannes: *Studien über* 1001 Nacht. *Aus dem Dänischen (nebst einigen Zusätzen) übersetzt von O[s-kar] Rescher.* Stuttgart: W. Heppeler, 1925.

Omidsalar, Mahmoud and Teresa: "Narrating Epics in Iran." In: *Traditional Storytelling Today: An International Sourcebook.* ed. by Margaret Read MacDonald. Chicago/London: Fitzroy Dearborn, 1999. 326-340.

Pellat, Charles: "Alf Layla wa layla." In: *Encyclopaedia Iranica.* ed. by Ihsan Yarshater. vol. 1. London/ Boston/Henley: Routledge & Kegan Paul, 1985. 831-835.

Pertsch, Wilhelm: *Verzeichniss der persischen Handschriften der Königlichen Bibliothek zu Berlin.* Berlin 1888.

Ramażāni, Moḥammad (ed.): *Hezār va yek shab. Tarjome az Alf leile va-leile* (The [Persian] *Thousand and One Nights*. A Translation of the [Arabic] *Thousand and One Nights*). 6 vols. Tehran: Kolāle-ye khāvar 1315-16/1936-37.

Ritter, Hellmut: *The Ocean of the Soul: Man, the World and God in the Stories of Farīd al-Dīn 'Aṭṭār.* Translated by John O'Kane with Editorial Assistance of Berndt Radtke. Leiden/Boston: Brill, 2003.

Ṣamini, Naghme: *Ketāb-e 'eshq va sha'bade: Pazhuheshi dar Hezār va yek shab* (A Book of Love and Trickery: A Study of the *Thousand and One Nights*). Tehran: Nashr-e Markaz 1379/2000.

Sattāri, Jalāl: *Afsun-e Shahrazād: Pazhuheshi dar Hezār Afsān* (The Magic of Shahrazād: A Study of the "Thousand Stories"). Tehran: Tus, 1368/1989.

id.: *Goft-o-gu-ye Shahrazād va Shahriyār* (The Conversation between Shahrazād and Shahriyār). Tehran: Daftar-e pazhuheshi-ye farhanghā, 1382/2003.

Sims, Eleanor, with Boris I. Marshak and Ernst J. Grube: *Peerless Images: Persian Painting and Its Sources.* New Haven, London: Yale University Press, 2002.

Sironval, Margaret: "Histoire des princes Amgiad et Assad." In: *Communications* 39 (1984) 125-140.

Vakiliyān, Aḥmad (ed.): *Farhang-e mardom.* vol. 2,2-3 (1382/2003).

Waugh, Earle H.: "Alexander in Islam: The Sacred Persona in Muslim Rulership *adab*." In: *Subject and Ruler: The Cult of the Ruling Power in Classical Antiquity.* ed. by Alastair Small. Ann Arbor: Oxbow, 1996. 237-253.

Yamanaka, Yuriko: "From Evil Destroyer to Islamic Hero: The Transformation of Alexander the Great's Image in Iran." In: *Annals of [the] Japan Association for Middle Eastern Studies* 8 (1993) 55-87.

Zokā', Yaḥyā: *Zendegi va āsār-e ostād-e Ṣani' al-molk 1229-1283 h.q.*/Life and Works of Sani'ol-Molk 1814-1866. ed. by Cyrus Parham. Tehran: Markaz-e nashr-e dāneshgāhi/Sāzmān-e Mirās-e farhangi-ye keshvar, 1382/2003.

<hr>

FURTHER READING

Criticism

Bochman, Victor. "The Jews and *The Arabian Nights*." *Ariel* 103 (1996): 39-47.

Examines Jewish origins of *The Arabian Nights* and notes the widespread presence of Arabic-speaking Jews throughout seventh- and eighth-century Europe and the Middle East.

Boone, Joseph A. "Framing the Phallus in the *Arabian Nights*: Pansexuality, Pederasty, Pasolini." In *Translations/Transformations: Gender and Culture in Film and Literature East and West,* edited by Valerie Wayne and Cornelia Moore, pp. 23-33. Honolulu: University of Hawaii Press, 1993.

Emphasizes stereotypes of homoeroticism in Eastern culture as presented by *The Arabian Nights* and Pier Paulo Pasolini's filmed version of the book.

Chraïbi, Aboubakr. "Texts of the *Arabian Nights* and Ideological Variations." *Middle Eastern Literatures* 7, no. 2 (July 2004): 149-57.

Traces ancient Indian and Near Eastern origins of tales featured in medieval texts of *The Arabian Nights*.

Marzolph, Ulrich. "Narrative Strategies in Popular Literature: Ideology and Ethics in Tales from the *Arabian Nights* and Other Collections." *Middle Eastern Literatures* 7, no. 2 (July 2004): 171-82.

Probes the Westernization and abbreviation of stories in both *The Arabian Nights* and the fourteenth-century collection known as *Hikayat al-cajiba*.

Parker, Margaret R. *The Story of a Story across Cultures: The Case of the Doncella Teodor.* London: Tamesis, 1996, 153 p.

Explains the origins of "Abu Al-Husn and His Slave-Girl Tawaddud."

Langston Hughes
1902-1967

(Full name James Mercer Langston Hughes) American short story writer, poet, novelist, playwright, autobiographer, and author of children's books.

The following entry provides an overview of Hughes's short fiction. For additional information on his short fiction career, see *SSC*, Volume 6.

INTRODUCTION

A prolific and versatile author, Hughes was a seminal figure in the Harlem Renaissance movement, a period of groundbreaking artistic achievement among African Americans in the 1920s. Although he is perhaps most famous for his poetry, Hughes wrote within a broad range of genres, underscoring the individuality, humanity, strength, and accomplishments of African Americans throughout his oeuvre. Hughes's short fiction is venerated for its incorporation of jazz and blues motifs, inventive use of African American vernacular, and colorful depictions of everyday life in the black community.

BIOGRAPHICAL INFORMATION

Hughes was born in Joplin, Missouri, to James Nathaniel and Carrie Mercer Langston Hughes. His parents separated soon after his birth, and his father moved to Mexico, where he lived the rest of his life. Consequently, Hughes was left in the care of his maternal grandmother in Lawrence, Kansas. Following his grandmother's death in 1910, Hughes lived briefly with various relatives before moving in with his mother and stepfather in Lincoln, Illinois. The family soon moved to Cleveland, Ohio, where Hughes attended Central High School. It was during this time that Hughes composed his first short story and contributed poetry to the school literary magazine. Hughes stayed with his father in Mexico during the summer of 1919 but became disheartened by his father's racially intolerant attitudes. Following his graduation from high school, Hughes returned to Mexico and taught English while composing poems and essays for the NAACP-sponsored magazine *Crisis*. In 1921, he enrolled in English literature classes at Columbia University in New York City but dropped out after his freshman year, attributing his scholastic struggles to the distractions of the burgeoning African

American artistic scene known as the Harlem Renaissance. He signed up to work on a merchant freighter bound for West Africa in 1923 and traveled the world, spending much of the following year in France and Italy. Upon returning to the United States in 1925, Hughes settled in Washington, D.C.; he received poetry prizes from the periodicals *Opportunity* and *Crisis* during the summer of that year. He soon attracted the attention of critic and art patron Carl Van Vechten, who helped Hughes with the publication of his first book, a collection of poetry entitled *The Weary Blues* (1926). The next year, along with author Zora Neale Hurston, Hughes became one of the founders of *Fire!!*, a short-lived literary journal devoted to the study of African American culture. In 1929 Hughes earned a B.A. from Lincoln University in Pennsylvania.

During the late 1920s he began publishing his first short stories and made the acquaintance of Charlotte Osgood Mason, an elderly white widow he referred to as "Godmother." Mason became Hughes's friend and patron during the composition of his first novel, *Not without Laughter* (1930), which won the Harmon gold medal for literature, but the two parted ways shortly after its publication. Hughes traveled to the Soviet Union in 1932 and began working as a journalist in Moscow. He was profoundly inspired by D. H. Lawrence's story collection *The Lovely Lady* and started developing the tales that would be published upon his return to the United States as *The Ways of White Folks* (1934). Around this time Hughes also took a strong interest in the dramatic arts, writing the play *Mulatto*, which was produced in 1935. Although his focus subsequently turned back to poetry for most of his remaining career, Hughes introduced one of his most popular characters in a 1943 piece published in the black-owned newspaper *Chicago Defender*. The character, Jesse B. Semple—nicknamed "Simple"—became a staple of Hughes's regular newspaper column. In 1951 Hughes published *Montage of a Dream Deferred*, a collection of verse that has been credited with influencing the Civil Rights Movement. The NAACP awarded Hughes the prestigious Spingarn Medal in 1960, and President Lyndon Johnson appointed Hughes the American representative to the 1966 First World Festival of Negro Arts, held in Dakar, Senegal. Hughes died of cancer in New York City at the age of sixty-five.

MAJOR WORKS OF SHORT FICTION

Hughes addressed his chief thematic concerns of race relations and cultural divisions in *The Ways of White Folks*. In the fourteen satirical tales that comprise this collection, Hughes explored the interplay of race, class, and gender in America, depicting the attitudes and actions of white society as hypocritical and insensitive. He expressed his disillusionment with white patronage in the autobiographically inspired story "The Blues I'm Playing," in which an aspiring pianist breaks away from her condescending and controlling patron. "Slave on the Block" satirizes the superiority/inferiority psychology of white society through the tale of Luther, a young, black man employed by a white, bohemian couple. Subtexts of both racial and sexual tension are present as the wife poses Luther as a slave for her painting. Though the employers believe themselves to be liberal and tolerant, their treatment of Luther reveals a denigrating, sanctimonious, and callous attitude toward race. Other stories highlight the despair of well-deserving African Americans who pass through life virtually unnoticed by white society. The unsung hero of "Cora Unashamed," for instance, is a black housekeeper who struggles against the eradication of her cultural identity. The hardships of oppressed people and the brutality of racism are highlighted in the stories "Father and Son" and "Home." "Father and Son," which is based on Hughes's play, *Mulatto*, emphasizes the dangers of societal prejudices against racially mixed children with a narrative

that culminates in murder, suicide, and madness. "Home" tells of a young musician who returns to the southern town of his youth after spending time abroad refining his talent and intellect. The locals, white and black alike, feel threatened by his education and presumed elitism; he is subsequently falsely accused of rape and is lynched.

The stories in Hughes's next collection, *Laughing to Keep from Crying* (1952), continue the author's thematic focus on racial and social injustice. Critics divide the stories of this volume into two categories: those with an overtly militant message which advocate defiance against the white establishment, and those which depict black adolescents struggling with the complexities of ethnic identity. In "On the Road," a rebellious vagrant has a visionary encounter with a "deity" who promotes radical views on race and equality. The story echoes the emergent revolutionary consciousness and burgeoning political activism of the black community in 1950s America. "African Morning" is a symbolic and visually evocative tale of a mulatto boy grappling with thoughts of suicide due to his paradoxical racial heritage. The protagonist transcends his despair through a spiritual epiphany. *Something in Common* (1963) broadens Hughes's exploration of bigotry to include homosexual intolerance, and consists of selections from the previous volumes in addition to eight new stories.

The "Simple" stories are acknowledged as the vehicle through which Hughes reached his widest and most diverse audience. These short and fast-paced sketches feature a series of dialogues between Jesse B. Semple—a hardworking laborer who has moved to Harlem from the South—and his educated acquaintance, Boyd, who presents the viewpoint of a cultured, black liberal. Originally appearing in the *Chicago Defender* newspaper, these tales were assembled in the popular collections *Simple Takes a Wife* (1953), *Simple Stakes a Claim* (1957), and *Simple's Uncle Sam* (1965). In these stories, Hughes juxtaposed Simple's crude realism and instinctive race consciousness with Boyd's broadminded sophistication and tolerance to create a humorous interplay between the characters and to illustrate two distinct approaches to establishing racial identity.

CRITICAL RECEPTION

Commentators concur that Hughes's short stories, distinguished by their enduring portraits of the triumphs and challenges of African Americans in a whitedominated society, have contributed to his reputation as one of the most influential authors of his generation. Scholars often remark on the similarities between his work and blues music, citing the dramatic irony, rhythmic structure, and elements of folk heritage inherent in both. Hughes's representation of women has been studied with more mixed commentary. While some reviewers praise Hughes's representation of strong, courageous female characters, other commentators fault Hughes for reinforcing a negative image of black women as helpless pawns forever trapped in the psychology of the old South. Conversely, some scholars commend Hughes for his significant insights into culturally established notions of masculinity, emphasizing the influence of W. E. B. Du Bois and D. H. Lawrence on his depiction of African American men. Hughes's unflinching commentary on racism and his cynical and embittered tone in the favorably received collection *The Ways of White Folks* is also a point of discussion for critics. Susan Neal Mayberry's analysis, for instance, focuses on Hughes's creative experiments with narrative voice, specifically that of a child, to demonstrate the "ignorance, intolerance, pietism, condescension, blindness, and racism" of white society. Other critics have assessed Hughes's exploration of the conflicts within parent/child relationships from a Freudian perspective, emphasizing the author's portrayal of miscegenation and its complicated impact on the oedipal triangle.

PRINCIPAL WORKS

Short Fiction

The Ways of White Folks 1934
Simple Speaks His Mind 1950
Laughing to Keep from Crying 1952
Simple Takes a Wife 1953
Simple Stakes a Claim 1957
The Best of Simple 1961
Something in Common, and Other Stories 1963
Simple's Uncle Sam 1965
*The Collected Works of Langston Hughes. 16 vols. 2001

Other Major Works

The Weary Blues (poetry) 1926
Fine Clothes to the Jew (poetry) 1927
Not without Laughter (novel) 1930
The Dream Keeper and Other Poems (poetry) 1932
Popo and Fifina: Children of Haiti [with Arna Bontemps] (juvenilia) 1932
Mulatto (play) 1935
The Big Sea: An Autobiography (autobiography) 1940
Shakespeare in Harlem (poetry) 1942
Montage of a Dream Deferred (poetry) 1951

I Wonder as I Wander: An Autobiographical Journey (autobiography) 1956
Simply Heavenly (play) 1957
Ask Your Mama: 12 Moods for Jazz (poetry) 1961

*Volumes 7, 8, and 15 contain Hughes's short stories.

CRITICISM

Heather Hathaway (essay date 1989)

SOURCE: Hathaway, Heather. "'Maybe Freedom Lies in Hating': Miscegenation and the Oedipal Conflict." In *Refiguring the Father: New Feminist Readings of Patriarchy,* edited by Patricia Yaeger and Beth Kowaleski-Wallace, pp. 153-67. Carbondale: Southern Illinois University Press, 1989.

[*In the following essay, Hathaway studies the relationship between mulatto children and their fathers in Charles Chesnutt's "The Sheriff's Children" and Hughes's "Father and Son," suggesting that both stories employ a Freudian concept of taboo.*]

"I dearly loved my master, son," she said.

"You should have hated him," I said.

"He gave me several sons," she said, "and because I loved my sons I learned to love their father though I hated him too."

"I too have become acquainted with ambivalence," I said. . . . "Maybe freedom lies in hating."

Ralph Ellison, *Invisible Man*

Plagued by a history of prejudice, interracial relations in the United States are turbulent and disturbing. Blacks have hated whites; whites have hated blacks—but this is not the "freedom to hate" of which Ellison speaks in *Invisible Man.* Ellison addresses an issue of even greater complexity: that of black/white relations within the family structure, or miscegenation. Rooted in the Latin words *miscere,* meaning "to mix," and *genus,* meaning "race," miscegenation describes the cohabitation or marriage between persons of different races. In miscegenous relationships, kinship and race rhetoric overlap and conflict. While it is important to know who *you* are when I choose you as a spouse, it is equally and sometimes more important to know who *I* am in order to be sure of our consanguineal and racial compatibility. The choice of a mate is affected by both the incest taboo and the rules governing exogamy, those customary or legal injunctions that prohibit marriage outside a specific group, clan, or race. Miscegenous parent/child relationships are equally intricate. Mixed blood provokes a simultaneous confirmation and denial of kinship bonds: the very life of a mulatto offspring confirms a blood tie, yet the exogamy taboo against acknowledging this tie prohibits that same relationship. Miscegenation creates, yet destroys, the family.

Mulatto literature, focusing on the children of miscegenous relationships, provides a channel through which to study interracial relations bound within consanguinity. The peculiar relation between race and kin that such writing addresses, particularly in its depiction of plantation societies, offers, according to Simone Vauthier, the most "suitable setting for the staging of 'realistic' incestuous dramas, since, if bastardy is a common enough phenomenon, in no modern society has the silence of the father been to the same extent a factor in the development and structuration of the social organism."[1] The role of the father in mulatto literature is particularly intriguing since it involves both the problems that accompany the coupling of incest and miscegenation, as well as the intricacies of the "traditional" oedipal triangle. The desire to kill the father for sleeping with the mother is intensified by the rejection of the "black" son by the "white" father because of racial "impurities." The violation of identity caused by miscegenation exacerbates oedipal motivations.[2]

Both Charles Chesnutt's pre-Freudian short story entitled "The Sheriff's Children" (1889) and Langston Hughes's post-Freudian tale entitled **"Father and Son"** (1934)[3] bind miscegenation and incest via the oedipal complex. A reconstructive feminist reading of these texts enables us to explore how the characters and plots designed by Chesnutt and Hughes work toward reforming the image of "the father" into a tangible and conquerable figure. It will reveal how both mulatto protagonists, in literally destroying invisible patriarchal symbols, essentially redefine their own fathers as visible, vulnerable, and undeniably carnal human beings. In both tales the white father begins as an abstraction; his detached position symbolizes the oppressive legality on which interracial kinship and social structures are based. Compelled by motives jointly rooted in the oedipal complex and a history of subjugation, both protagonists challenge the role of "the father" to the point where he can no longer function only in the abstract. Confrontation by the son insists upon recognition from and subsequent redefinition of "the father." Finally, a reexamination of these plots will lead to a deeper understanding of how, using the Freudian models on which the stories were unknowingly and knowingly constructed, interracial unions have often oppressed not just women but their children as well.

In most cases, male mulattoes are represented in literature as violent, dynamic, and vengeful, while female mulattoes "tragically" reject their ambiguous relationship to family and race through suicide. Judith Berzon, in *Neither White Nor Black: The Mulatto in American Fiction*,[4] provides numerous examples of mulatto characters in fiction and classifies them along gender lines. Her generalization that there are "almost no male suicides" is disproved, however, by the two tales discussed here. In both cases, the "militant" male mulattoes choose death over a life with no name, no lineage, no home. Charles Chesnutt's "The Sheriff's Children" tells the story of a mulatto taken prisoner for his suspected murder of a white community leader, Captain Walker. A vengeance-seeking white mob surrounds the jail in which the mulatto is being held and demands his release. The sheriff, firmly committed to his civic duty, refuses the mob entry but provokes their gunfire. During the battle the prisoner seizes the sheriff's weapon and reveals his identity as the man's son. Just as the mulatto appears willing to murder his father, the sheriff's white daughter, Polly, enters and shoots but does not kill her half brother. The sheriff then bandages the mulatto's wound, returns him to his cell, and spends a harrowing night contemplating his own conflicting obligations as father and civil servant. Resolving to assist this black child whom he unconscionably betrayed by selling into slavery, the sheriff decides to use his influence to secure the acquittal of the mulatto. But the law-enforcer is too late in acknowledging his progeny—the mulatto has committed suicide in the night.

Langston Hughes's **"Father and Son"** describes a similar confrontation. Bert, the mulatto son of a plantation owner named Colonel Norwood, returns home for the summer after having been sent away for six years because he called his father "papa" in front of guests. A rebellious twenty-year-old, Bert is determined to claim his birthright as the colonel's son. Continually violating codes required of blacks on the plantation, he moves freely through the front door of the house despite the colonel's orders that no blacks enter, exit, or even cross the front porch. Bert offers to shake hands with his father and he identifies himself as a Norwood to both tenants and townspeople. Tension between father and son mounts all summer until finally a dispute between Bert and a white postal clerk provokes hostility from the colonel's friends and results in a climactic confrontation between parent and child. Norwood threatens to kill Bert, but the son murders the father first. He attempts escape with the help of his mother, Cora, but is trapped by a lynch mob and chooses to take his own life rather than to die at their hands.

Both Chesnutt's and Hughes's tales illustrate the complexities of oedipal relationships when race intervenes. Both pose a black son against a white father, and in so doing, set the stage for a conflict not only between father and son but also between consanguinity and race.[5] Freud's *Totem and Taboo* illuminates the relationships between incest and miscegenation, progenitor and progeny, black and white, as it reveals how social taboos add to the explosiveness of the oedipal triangle. Among the primary objectives of taboo are the "guarding [of] chief acts of life—birth, initiation, marriage and sexual functions, and the like, against interference" and the "securing of unborn infants and young children"—the securing of kin—"who stand in a specially sympathetic relation with one or both parents, from the consequences of certain actions." Violation of a taboo results in the "taboo itself [taking] vengeance."[6]

The mulatto son of the sheriff, and Bert, the mulatto in **"Father and Son,"** are personifications of the taboo violation between their black mothers and white fathers, and as such "stand in a specially sympathetic relation with both parents," belonging fully to the race of neither. The sheriff's son's intended and Bert's actual murder of their fathers represent, in part, "taboos taking vengeance" for white men's "interference" in "chief acts of life." The white fathers violate rights of birth and initiation by denying their paternity; they violate Western laws of marriage and sexuality by refusing both to acknowledge and wed the mothers of their children.

Both Chesnutt's and Hughes's mulatto sons become "taboo" themselves as products of taboo liaisons; similarly, the two are "taboo*ed*" by both black and white society. This inference is difficult to document in "The Sheriff's Children" because the mulatto son is in jail and may be "taboo*ed*" for his potential criminality as well as for his mixed blood. In **"Father and Son,"** however, Bert is carefully placed in situations where he is ostracized by blacks and whites alike. Whites are afraid of his cataclysmic temper; blacks and other mulattoes, most specifically his brother Willie who has opted for a black identity, are afraid "with a fear worse than physical . . . of the things that happen around Bert" (113). In systems of taboo, the practice of "transference" results in an individual who has "transgressed one of these prohibitions" becoming in turn prohibited himself, "as though the whole of the dangerous charge had been transferred over to him. This power is attached to all 'special' individuals, such as kings, priests, or new born babies."[7] Bert, as a personification of the miscegenation taboo violated by his parents, has essentially "transgressed the prohibition" simply by being, and thus becomes comparably prohibited. As the "new born baby" of a black/white liaison, the "dangerous charge" has been "transferred over to him": the taboo and the "taboo*ed*" become one. Visibly representing an infraction of rules prohibiting miscegenation, Bert, as the taboo object, "takes vengeance" upon his father. But as "taboo*ed*" by the social transference of prohibitions, he must also die himself.

The oedipal components of incest expressed in miscegenous relationships are illustrated in "The Sheriff's Children" by the very fact that the mulatto has *not* killed

Captain Walker, the man of whose murder he is originally accused. If the mulatto's motivations for homicide were merely the destruction or avenging of white power structures, he would have murdered the captain or any other white man, for that matter. But he seeks only the life of his father. The speech delivered by the sheriff to the angry mob foreshadows the central issue of the story: "'All right, boys, talk away. You are all strangers to me, and I don't know what business you can have.' The sheriff did not think it necessary to recognize anybody in particular on such an occasion; the question of identity sometimes comes up in the investigation of these extra-judicial executions" (74). As Robert Bone argues, the mulatto son is actually the "stranger" and the one whom the sheriff has never thought it "necessary to recognize." The question of "identity" plagues the father's conscience, and his decision, though tardy, to free his son is actually an "extra-judicial" activity in that it violates his civic duty as sheriff.[8]

Prior to the patricide attempts, the mulatto is alternately referred to as "the nigger," "the negro," and "the prisoner" by the sheriff, the lynchers, and the narrator. Only once, in a nonspecific description of Captain Walker's murder related by the narrator, is the term "mulatto" applied (63). At the point of confrontation between the sheriff and his son, however, the words "mulatto" and "prisoner" are those predominantly used to describe the son. This juxtaposition semantically reflects the peculiar position of the mulatto as imprisoned by black and white society. Because of his simultaneous "sameness" and "otherness," he is neither wholly rejected nor wholly accepted by either group. Furthermore, the introduction of "mulatto" at the point of oedipal conflict emphasizes the kinship ties between father and son.

The following dialogue between the "prisoner" and the sheriff reflects the complexity of their relationship as father to son, as black to white:

> "Good God!" [the sheriff] gasped, "you would not murder your own father?"
>
> "My father?" replied the mulatto, "it were well enough for me to claim the relationship, but it comes with poor grace from you to ask anything by reason of it. What father's duty have you ever performed for me? Did you give me protection . . . freedom . . . [or] money? . . . *You* sold *me* to the rice swamps."
>
> "I at least gave you the life you cling to," murmured the sheriff.
>
> "Life?" said the prisoner, with a sarcastic laugh. "What kind of life? You gave me your own blood, your own features. . . . You gave me a white man's spirit, and you made me a slave, and crushed it out. . . . I owe you nothing . . . and it would be no more than justice if I should avenge upon you my mother's wrongs and my own. But I still hate to shoot you."
>
> (84-87 passim)

The issues involve not solely transgressions of kinship systems in the rejection of son by father and lifelong denial of paternity, and not solely offenses against race in the enslavement of blacks by whites. Rather, they involve simultaneous violations of *both* kin and race through the selling into slavery of son by father; the reckless passing on and entrapment of a "white" spirit in a "black" body in a society that "despise[s] . . . scorn[s] . . . and set[s] aside" (86) biracial individuals; and finally, the essential uxoricide of the black mother by the white father.

But the mulatto prisoner is unsuccessful in his patricide attempt; he is preempted by his half sister, Polly. Allusions to Greek myth in Chesnutt's tale expose oedipal elements intrinsic to miscegenation as the intervention of race adds a new dimension to the older, traditional equations. Polly (whose name echoes Polynices), is also involved in an oedipal relationship with the sheriff. Recalling the devotion that Antigone feels for Oedipus her father/brother, Polly displays comparable adoration for the sheriff, her father/husband. I refer to him as such because of the telling descriptions of the interaction between Polly and the sheriff throughout the story that imply a relationship reminiscent of one between husband and wife rather than between father and daughter. Significantly, there is no mother—black or white—present in the sheriff's family. In a traditional triangle the mulatto son is allied with the maternal line, and in this miscegenous trio that alliance is even stronger because of mother and son's shared and socially stigmatizing color. Thus Polly, in attempting to kill her mixed-blooded brother, symbolically seeks vengeance upon the entire maternal line with whom she is in contest for the father.

Resembling Oedipus's need for redemption, the sheriff is overcome by conscience as he tries to envision a way to "in some degree, atone for his crime against this son of his—against society—against God" (93). But Oedipus atones only for crimes against "society" and "God"—for the social crime of incest and the divine crime of murder. The sheriff, as the white miscegenator who is aware of the existence of his mulatto son, must atone for an additional crime against his child—the denial of paternity, and therefore of the son's identity. The intervention of race adds a more personal dimension to the traditional equation since the two figures in conflict, "white" father and "black" son, are both alive and both conscious of their relationship.

Finally, just as Antigone buries her brother in defiance of Creon's edict, the sheriff is tempted to value claims of kinship over the order of the polis when he considers letting "the prisoner" escape. But in the end civic duty (white law) overrules personal rectitude (paternal responsibility), and though the sheriff has developed a plan to absolve himself of some guilt, the forces of atonement are never put into action, because the mulatto son has chosen death over a life with "no name, no father, no mother" (92).

Hughes's **"Father and Son"** discloses other oedipal elements common to miscegenation. In Sophocles, the verbalization of incest increases the horror that surrounds it. Though the act itself is taboo, vengeance need not be taken until Oedipus's murder of his father, marriage to his mother, and fathering of his sisters are acknowledged through speech. Only the actual recognition and expression of these "sins" set the forces of punishment in motion. A similar pattern underscores **"Father and Son."** The white father, Norwood, continually abdicates his responsibilities as parent by referring to his children as "your" kids, as "Cora's brats," as "yellow-bastards." The "sin" for which Bert first gets subjugated by his father (at an age of great Freudian significance, not surprisingly) is that of verbally acknowledging his own ancestry. He calls his father "papa" in front of guests, and receives a slap that "made him see stars and darkness. . . . As though he were brushing a fly out of the way, the Colonel had knocked him down under the feet of the horses" (116).

Norwood's punishment of Bert conversely provokes the son to reassert his identity as the colonel's child. Early in life Bert realizes that his playmates "were named after their fathers, whereas he . . . bore the mother's name, Lewis. He was Bert Lewis—not Bert Norwood" (115). Bert strongly identifies with his mother as mutual victim as he grows to understand that his father's denial of paternity is crucial to the maintenance of the entire oppressive, Southern social structure. Vauthier explains: "if black, which is non-white, can look non-black, nay white, then the opposition white/non-white shows up as problematical. . . . The social structure insofar as it determines status according to race, i.e. color, is jeopardized. . . . The place of the white individual within the race-based social scheme and hence his very identity are threatened by the mere existence of a white Negro."[9]

Bert's recognition of this incites him to assert his heritage rebelliously, in defiance of both familial and socially imposed diminutions of his ancestry, of his very identity. He challenges Norwood's denial of paternity as well as the entire paternalistic structure every time he enters through the front door, every time he offers to shake hands with or speak to his father, every time he refers to Norwood as his "old man." Most blatantly, Bert asserts that he is a "Norwood"; he takes his father's name. As Mr. Higgins, the postal clerk, describes to Norwood: "He said last week, standin' out on my corner, he wasn't *all* nigger no how; said his name was Norwood—not Lewis, like the rest of Cora's family; said your plantation would be his when you passed out—and all that kind o' stuff, boasting to the niggers listening about you being his father" (123).

Motivated by similar rebelliousness the mulatto son in "The Sheriff's Children" is shocked when the sheriff refers to himself, at last, as the mulatto's father: "My father?" replied the mulatto. . . . "What father's duty have you ever performed for me? Did you ever *give me your name*?" (85, emphasis mine). In an inversion of Freud's discussion about certain societal practices of changing names after death to avoid vengeance,[10] never *giving* the name in the first place acknowledges neither the life nor the taboo violation.

Both fictionally and historically slaves and mulattoes have been stereotyped as having no origins, implying the denial of any birthright to blacks by the entire social system of slavery. The black "pickaninnies" in Dion Boucicault's 1861 drama, "The Octoroon," for example, are described as children who have no heritage: "dem black tings never was born at all; dey swarmed one mornin' on a sassafras tree in the swamp" (3). A similar conversation occurs between Topsy and Miss Ophelia in *Uncle Tom's Cabin or, Life Among the Lowly*. In response to Ophelia's question, "Who was your mother?," Topsy replies, "Never had none! . . . Never was born! . . . never had no mother, nor father, nor nothin" (355-56). Lines of descent are obscured in the case of blacks—and by conjecture—mulattoes especially.[11] According to Vauthier, "the planter may scatter his seed indiscriminately; as long as he refuses to acknowledge his off-spring, he can keep his blood-line pure and his dynastic order working."[12] She goes on to explain that by "refusing to acknowledge his slave son, the father fails to transmit with his surname what Lacan calls the Name-of-the-Father—[that is], the universal law that prohibits incest."[13] Failure to transmit the Name-of-the-Father not only obscures kinship lines, complicating relationships of affinity and consanguinity, but it is precisely what opens the door for a reenactment of the oedipal drama.

Both Chesnutt's and Hughes's mulattoes breach the "silence of the father," crucial to the maintenance of a paternalistic society, as they challenge denials of filiation by attempting to enact the oedipal goal. Additionally, as nameless mulatto children, Bert and the sheriff's son stand outside the law prohibiting incest. Their status as taboo objects is amplified by their existence beyond the circle of taboo liaisons; they are neither black nor white—they are both. This biracial pariah identity psychically allies these mulatto children with the mother who, as a black woman in Southern plantation society, represents a similar taboo against which white men must guard themselves under the rules governing exogamy.

Ambivalence is a crucial factor in both systems of taboo and the oedipal complex,[14] and provides another link between miscegenation and incest. At the same time that we revere, adore, or admire a leader or ruler, we are also seized by latent hostility and anger at this leader/father's superiority and power over us. We both love and hate our enemies; simultaneously we seek and fear vengeance upon them. Norwood is clearly ambivalent about Bert. Upon his son's arrival at the plantation, Norwood schemes to stay in the library for a number of minutes in an effort to avoid appearing anxious to see his child: "Colonel Norwood never would have admitted, even to himself, that he was standing in his doorway waiting for this half-Negro son to come home. But in truth that is what he was doing. . . . Not once [since being sent away to school] had [Bert] been allowed to come back to Big House Plantation. The Colonel had said then that never did he want to see the boy. But in truth, he did" (106). Norwood acknowledges the similarities in their appearance and temperament with a modicum of pride: "This boy had been . . . the most beautiful of the lot, the brightest and the baddest of the Colonel's five children . . . Handsome and mischievous, [and] favoring too much the Colonel in his ways" (106). The sheriff in "The Sheriff's Children" is equally torn between love and hatred for his offspring. "He knew whose passions coursed beneath that swarthy skin and burned in the black eyes opposite his own. He saw in this mulatto . . . he, himself" (86). The paradoxes implied in hating their sons' "otherness" and loving their "sameness" results in Norwood's inability to kill his son and in the sheriff's compulsion to "atone" for his "sin." Both are bound by a responsibility to kin.

Obviously, however, the same is not true for the mulatto progeny. As Werner Sollors has noted, the oedipal triangle requires "the unmarried son [to] confront the father who possesses the mother [in order] to approach the riddle of his own existence."[15] This tension is expressed in the dialogues between the fathers and the sons that directly precede the shots of death in both stories. The sheriff's son screams in rage: "you gave me a black mother. Poor wretch! She died under the lash, because she had enough womanhood to call her soul her own. . . . I should avenge upon you my mother's wrongs and my own" (86, 87).

Bert expresses similar sentiments in the dynamic scene preceding his murder of Norwood. The colonel demands from Bert an explanation for his behavior in town, warning him to "talk right." When Bert asks what he means by "talk[ing] right," the Colonel snaps:

> "I mean talk like a nigger should to a white man."
>
> "Oh, but I'm not a nigger, Colonel Norwood," Bert said, "I'm your son."
>
> The old man frowned at the boy in front of him. "Cora's son," he said.
>
> "Fatherless?" Bert asked.
>
> "Bastard," the old man said. . . . "You black bastard."

"I've heard that before." Bert just stood there. "You're talking about my mother."

(pp. 126-27)

In the 1928 dramatic version of the tale entitled *Mulatto* the oedipal tension over the mother is even more apparent:

ROBERT:

. . . I'm your son.

NORWOOD:

(Testily) You're Cora's boy.

ROBERT:

Women don't have children by themselves.

NORWOOD:

Nigger women don't know the fathers. You're a bastard. . . .

ROBERT:

. . . (Slowly) You're talking about my mother.

NORWOOD:

I'm talking about Cora, yes. Her children are bastards.

ROBERT:

(Quickly) And you're their father. (Angrily) How come I look like you if you're not my father? . . . You had no right to raise that cane today when I was standing at the door of this house where *you* live, while *I* have to sleep in a shack down the road with the field hands. (Slowly) But my mother sleeps with you.

NORWOOD:

You don't like it?

ROBERT:

No, I don't like it.

NORWOOD:

What can you do about it?

ROBERT:

(After a pause) I'd like to kill all the white men in the world.[16]

Both Bert and the sheriff's son hate their fathers *because* they sleep with (or "kill") their mothers. But this is not merely oedipally motivated. In the traditional oedipal triangle the son hates the father who possesses the mother in marriage; when miscegenation becomes a factor under the economy of slavery, the desire for retaliation magnifies: the son must avenge both figurative and literal possession of mother by father. In miscegenous oedipal plots the son is allied with his mother because both are defined as "black" while the father is

placed in a different social category. Lines of filiation are affected insofar as oedipal ambitions are fulfilled through the son's greater social similarity to the maternal line. Thus in both tales the mothers, viewed as mutually tabooed and victimized figures by their mulatto sons, are absolved of blame. For the mulattoes, interracial sex is not the ultimate evil; rather, the rejection of parental and spousal responsibility by the socially dominant, white, male miscegenator is the crime that cannot be excused. As Bert cries in Hughes's 1949 operatic rendition of the same story, *The Barrier,* "not in Georgia nor anywhere else / Should a man deny his son," for such a denial is an offense against both son and mother.

By murdering his father, Bert transfers his hatred to "all the white men in Georgia" on whom he wants to wreak similar vengeance, fusing what Vauthier describes in a different context as "the Oedipal fantasies of [patricide] and the dream of social redress."[17] The mulatto son's desire "to kill all the white men in the world" expresses his attempt to prohibit not only miscegenation and incest, but also to destroy the entire social system of slavery based on the literal possession of one human being by another. The death of both the sheriff and Norwood—indeed, the imagined death of all white men—would mean the death of unrecognized consanguinity through miscegenation and the complications that result from it. More significantly, it would mean the death both of the white, male, rule—of law—as well as of the racist patriarchal order that denies its own paternity. Most interestingly, the murder of white father by black son dismantles the alliance between "the father" as lawmaker, as governor, as ruler, by transforming *him* into the vulnerable, victimized role that the mother and son once occupied. The obfuscation of kinship lines through incest and miscegenation is transformed into a symbolic destruction of an entire social system through the fulfillment of oedipal ambitions.

On one level, Charles Chesnutt's "The Sheriff's Children" and Langston Hughes's **"Father and Son"** help to reveal the complexities that result from a superimposition of race on an already elaborate oedipal triangle by disclosing the additional tensions that exist when black and white, son and lover, leader and enemy are all embodied within the same consanguineal bond. Racial differences between father and son, given the history of tension between black and white in America, create both an additional barrier between parent and child as well as an additional motivation for oedipal desires to kill the father. Justifying the violation of race by creating an artificial familial construct through a paternalistic interpretation of slavery, Southern society simultaneously built into its culture the opportunity for systematic denial of those consanguine bonds that actually did exist. Desiring straightforward acts of racial segregation and white paternalism, the South was paradoxically a land of amalgamation, fundamentally rooted in the denial of paternity.

On another level, the characters created by Chesnutt and Hughes foreshadow the goals of many contemporary feminist writers. By confronting and killing the literal and figurative fathers of a patriarchal familial and social structure, these mulatto men essentially attack the image of "the father" as one who is detached and intangible—as one who is the abstraction of law and power. In this sense at least, these two black male writers can be considered allies of all women who strive to attain the social ideal of equality.

Notes

This paper grew out of a seminar entitled "Kinship and Literature" led by Werner Sollors in the fall of 1986 at Harvard University. I am greatly indebted to Professor Sollors for his inspiration, encouragement, and wisdom, as well as for generously providing me with a copy of his article, "'Never Was Born': The Mulatto, An American Tragedy?," which has since been published in the *Massachusetts Review*, 27:293-316.

1. Simone Vauthier, "*Textualité et Stereotypes*: Of African Queens and Afro-American Princes and Princesses: Miscegenation in *Old Hepsy*," *Publications du Conseil Scientifique de la Sorbonne Nouvelle*, Paris, 3 (1980): 91.

2. It is interesting to note that few if any narratives address this issue from the opposite perspective: a "black" father and a "white" son. The absence of such reversed tales indicates the degree and direction of racism in this country.

3. Unless otherwise stated, excerpts by Charles W. Chesnutt are quoted from "The Sheriff's Children," contained in *The Wife of His Youth and Other Stories of the Color Line* (Boston: 1899; repr. Ann Arbor: University of Michigan Press, 1968). Excerpts by Langston Hughes are quoted from *Something in Common and Other Stories* (New York: Hill and Wang, First American Century Series edition, 1963). Subsequent references will be cited in the text.

4. Judith Berzon, *Neither White Nor Black: The Mulatto in American Fiction* (New York: New York University Press, 1978) 74.

5. Werner Sollors, "'Never Was Born': The Mulatto, An American Tragedy?," *Massachusetts Review* 27:306. The presence of the father in the story itself, which thereby allows him an active role in the drama, is in contrast to Dion Boucicault's 1861 play entitled "The Octoroon" (Miami: Mnemosyne Publishing, first Mnemosyne reprinting from a copy in the Fisk University Library Negro Collection, 1969) and another of Chesnutt's stories concerning mulattoes entitled "Her Virginia Mammy" (also contained in *The Wife of His Youth and Other Stories of the Color Line*). Here, the "sinning" white fathers, Mr. Peyton and Mr. Stafford, are conveniently freed from taking responsibility for their paternity through death. Again, the gender difference between the "tragic" and "militant" mulatto is suggested, since both these tales involve a mulatto heroine. The absence of the father precludes interaction, which in some ways forces "tragic" responses on the part of the mulatto because there is no white paternal figure to confront directly with the issue of patrimony.

6. Sigmund Freud, *Totem and Taboo: Some Points of Agreement between the Mental Lives of Savages and Neurotics* (1913; transl. James Strachey, New York: Norton, 1950), 19, 20.

7. Freud, *Totem and Taboo*, 22.

8. Robert Bone, *Down Home: A History of Afro-American Short Fiction from Its Beginnings to the End of the Harlem Renaissance* (New York: Putnam's, 1975), 96-97.

9. Vauthier, "Textualité," 88-89 passim.

10. Freud, *Totem and Taboo*, 54-57.

11. For a more detailed discussion of mulatto genealogies in literature, see Werner Sollors's article cited in note 5 of this chapter. For a large-scale attempt to show the status of slaves in general as "never [having been] born," see Orlando Patterson, *Slavery and Social Death: A Comparative Study* (Cambridge: Harvard University Press, 1982).

12. Vauthier, "Textualité," 84.

13. Vauthier, "Textualité," 90.

14. Freud, *Totem and Taboo*, 29-30, 157.

15. Sollors, *Massachusetts Review* 27:308.

16. Arthur P. Davis explains in his classic essay, "The Tragic Mulatto Theme in Six Works of Langston Hughes" (*Phylon* 16 [1955], 195-204, reprinted in *Five Black Writers*, ed. Donald B. Gibson [New York: New York University Press, 1970]), that Hughes developed the mulatto theme in a variety of genres including poetry, drama, and opera. The play entitled *Mulatto* is contained in *Five Plays by Langston Hughes*, ed. Webster Smalley (Bloomington: Indiana University Press, First Midland Book edition, 1968), 1-37. This excerpt is found on pages 23-24.

17. Vauthier, "Textualité," 90.

Steven C. Tracy (essay date spring 1993)

SOURCE: Tracy, Steven C. "Blues to Live By: Langston Hughes's 'The Blues I'm Playing.'" *The Langston Hughes Review* 12, no. 1 (spring 1993): 12-18.

[*In the following essay, Tracy examines the interplay between morality, aesthetics, and identity in "The Blues I'm Playing."*]

In his short story **"The Blues I'm Playing,"** from *The Ways of White Folks* (1934), Langston Hughes presents us with a compelling portrait of two women whose approaches to life and art cause them to sever a relationship that could have continued to be advantageous to each of them. In elderly white patron Mrs. Dora Ellsworth, who was based partially on Hughes's ex-patron Charlotte Mason, Hughes portrays a widow whose lack of fecundity, both physiologically and creatively, abetted by beliefs in Platonic and Manichaean dualism, leads her to exercise a Nietzschean "master morality" and to adopt an artistic aesthetic, art for art's sake, that divorces art from the living of life. In Oceola Jones, Hughes shows a quietly rebellious woman who subverts a number of sexual and racial stereotypes and in the process succeeds in defining herself and challenging Mrs. Ellsworth's aesthetic. Through Oceola, Hughes demonstrates how a positive self- and racial image brings about self-confidence, success, and a unified vision of life. Oceola declares her independence from the strictures of Mrs. Ellsworth, but just as surely declares her dependence on Pete and her community for the support she needs to help make her what she can be; and the community recognizes the need it has for Oceola—a need she sets about fulfilling. She has, then, not only the freedom but the courage to choose her direction. And it is in the blues that Oceola finds the artistic freedom, range of emotion, and intellectual and spiritual energy equal to expressing her feelings about the nature of existence.

Hughes makes it clear that Mrs. Ellsworth is, in a sense, trying to be a mother to her young charges, Oceola and Antonio Bas, because of her own emotional aridity and loneliness. Because her wealthy husband is dead and she has no children of her own, Mrs. Ellsworth, feeling deserted, unfulfilled, and bitter, allows her own personal barrenness to direct her young charges away from personal relationships and life-directed thoughts that would interfere with her domination and away from their movement *toward* their own art, so that they can give birth to things out of their minds and not their bodies. She has adopted, clearly, the Platonic mind/body dualism and, perhaps, a Manichaean dualism as well, given the regular contrast and opposition between black and white in the story.

In Ellsworth's view, the mind is associated with right, whiteness, and goodness, the body with wrong, blackness, and evil. Ellsworth views the "intrusion" of Pete,

Oceola's African American boyfriend, as the intrusion equivalent to that of a psychic and economic vampire whom she hopes to drive away by exposure to the "sunlight" of her ideas. James Emanuel speculates that "unappreciated sensitivity" (142) has led Mrs. Ellsworth to her mindset, and indeed she does seem to fear male domination in a way that suggests that she had been in some way limited personally, perhaps artistically, by her relationship with her husband. However, Mrs. Ellsworth seems to have absorbed the power relationships established by society enough to be unaware of the fact that her attitudes and actions do the same thing to her charges that (we assume) her husband did to her. She assumes, in other words, that her money, her power, gives her the right to place limits on "her" artists, as her husband's maleness, and thus dominance, had given him the right to do to her. Her "unappreciated sensitivity," if indeed she had it, did not teach her to appreciate sensitivity that she did not understand, or care to understand, in others.

Ellsworth obviously feels it is her right and duty—indeed her place—to exercise control over artistic concerns and endeavors, not only because she has the money to do so, but because the money offers her the status of authority and intellectual superior as well. Mrs. Ellsworth is someone whose knowledge of the inherited values of Western culture in the world of art is sufficiently developed to value the accomplishments of the past masters recognized by the guardians of *her* culture, but insufficiently sympathetic to "foreign" developments that would represent real advances in art. She guards the Western past and tradition because *that* is where she is master, where she is in control. Actually, the control she has is economic, bequeathed to her by a male, her late husband; and it is this economic independence granted to her that she wishes to pass on to Oceola—but with artistic and aesthetic strings attached, a strong sexual attraction, and a desire to run Oceola's life that indicates that Mrs. Ellsworth has learned from her husband, and male authority, well. Plato asserts in *The Republic* that because art is an imitation of an imitation and thus removed from reality and eternal beauty, the person most capable of appreciating true beauty is the intellectual, not the artist. Therefore art should be subject to the control of the intellectual. And this is, in fact, what Mrs. Ellsworth wants for herself—in direct contrast to Oceola's desire to please herself, her audience, and her "people" with the variety of music they all want. To one who doesn't worry about paying the rent, playing for rent parties is uncommonly vulgar; but to one who has those worries, it is commonly voluntary.

Friedrich Nietzsche describes, in *Beyond Good and Evil,* what he believed to be the root of the problem that Hughes has torture Mrs. Ellsworth (or does she use it to torture Oceola?) and makes her what she is. She possesses what Nietzsche terms a perverted "master morality." Because she is unable to actuate her own will creatively—perhaps as a result of her husband's inability or lack of desire to understand her own forays into singing—, she seeks to substitute power over others, in Oceola's case someone she views as both an exotic and a child, for her own inability to create. This is her "sublimation" (Nietzsche's term), and it explains her "master morality," her desire to direct or control the lives of others, in terms of her own weaknesses. When she encourages Oceola to sublimate her soul, Mrs. Ellsworth does so with the weight of Plato and Nietzsche behind her, and with the desire to control Oceola's life, to have her own "period," the period of Oceola, as she calls it. Ironically, her ability to control Oceola represents for her a fecundity she lacks, and it is not difficult to see her controlling of Oceola's life as being analogous to Mrs. Ellsworth's getting her menstrual period, proving herself still capable of giving birth and thus creating something of her own. The joke here, of course, is that if she has her period she is most likely not with child, so her imagined state is an illusory one at best. When Mrs. Ellsworth first meets Oceola, she is intrigued at the thought of having a Black among *her* artists. She is an owner, or at least deludes herself that she can own people like Oceola. However, at the very point at which she deludes herself into believing that she is freeing Oceola, she is making a subtle and insidious attempt to enslave her.

Part of that attempt at enslavement draws philosophically on the ideas of Walter Pater and the Aesthetic Movement in championing the phrase and concept of art for art's sake. Separating art from some kind of useful purpose places art in a realm where the wealthy Mrs. Ellsworth, retreating from the mundane reality of life with the help of her money, can deal with it as the exclusive property of someone of her class and background who has the time to cloister herself in delicate parlors and lose herself in some imaginary artistic realm. "But you must have time," Mrs. Ellsworth tells Oceola when Oceola says that she is too busy with work to study formally (346). Later, when Hughes introduces the carpe diem theme as Mrs. Ellsworth cautions Oceola that "Art is long . . . and time is fleeting . . ." (348), Oceola replies, "Yes, ma'am . . . but I get nervous if I start worrying about time" (348). Whereas Mrs. Ellsworth worries about time—in this case Oceola's—as if it were her own, Oceola prefers not to do so, electing to concentrate on doing things as they can be done, on living more immediately, and on flowing with her life rather than flooding it nervously or frantically toward some destination that would be destroyed by the deluge. Art, then, takes its place in a continuum rather than existing outside of or over it, and takes its character from a continuum as well. The concept of pure art is totally alien to Oceola's aesthetic system. Like the idea of a "pure" race, which is very likely at least partially behind Mrs. Ellsworth's retreat from contemporary life,

pure art in Mrs. Ellsworth's case is the creation of a master mentality that is in many ways afraid of both Oceola's reality and itself.

And pure art has nothing to do, Mrs. Ellsworth believes, with syncopation, blues, jazz, or spirituals. She is decidedly not a modernist where music is concerned. For her, art must have a certain dignity and propriety of her own definition, and clearly African-American music didn't have them. The selections that Oceola played for Mrs. Ellsworth at their first audience reflected Oceola's interests: the Rakhmaninov *Prelude in C Sharp Minor,* with its melancholy and nostalgia, possesses at times a blues-like sadness; the Liszt *Etudes,* from the pen of the greatest piano virtuoso of his time, reflect his imaginative and technical advances; Ravel's *Pavanne Pour Une Enfante Defunte* demonstrates one of Ravel's lifelong sympathies with the ancient, exotic worlds and experiences of children and animals; and Handy's "St. Louis Blues," which Ellsworth would have grudgingly granted as a concession to Oceola's background and inexperience, demonstrates the popular possibilities for folk material of African-Americans. Oceola demonstrates through her selections not only her virtuosity but also her respect for imagination and innovation. Ravel himself, in fact, produced a jazz-like syncopation in *Concerto for the Left Hand,* and a G-Major piano concerto that was touched by jazz as well. It is certainly ironic that Mrs. Ellsworth is impressed by the works of classical composers like Ravel, who flirted with jazz, and with their innovations and independence, but is herself unable to break through and accept the achievements and possibilities of jazz the way Milhaud, Gershwin, Ives, and Stravinsky could. But then, she needs the cloak of respectability wrapped around what she likes, and that cloak is for her necessarily made of a heavy European fiber.

Of course, it is significant that Oceola is a pianist, since the piano is one of the few instruments that women were encouraged or allowed to play at the time. Linda Dahl discussed its importance as an artistic, but not an economic, outlet for women:

> The piano is one of the few instruments that seem more or less free of sex stereotypes to the extent that it does carry unconscious gender associations. Those associations deliver an ambiguous message. On the one hand, for example, Jelly Roll Morton recalled hesitating to take up piano for fear of being thought a "sissy;" on the other hand, though playing the piano has been approved as a desirable feminine refinement, making a professional career of it was considered decidedly unladylike and was an option reserved largely for men (59).

Rosetta Reitz points out that women "profoundly influenced many of our most distinguished male jazz pianists," citing the influence of Mamie Desdoumes on Jelly Roll Morton, the mothers of James P. Johnson and

Willie "the Lion" Smith on their sons, Mazie Mullins on Fats Waller, a grade school teacher on Fletcher Henderson, and two Washington, D.C., pianists on Duke Ellington (*Piano Singer's Blues*). Indeed, during the pre-World War II period, such outstanding women pianists as Berniece Edwards, Victoria Spivey, Myrtle Jenkins, Louise Johnson, Georgia White, Gladys Bentley, and Hociel Thomas recorded as featured artists or accompanists, demonstrating that there were women who plied their talents as pianists either as a career or an avocation; and a pianist in the sacred field, the great Arizona Dranes of the Church of God in Christ, was just one of many women whose pianistic skill graced the church services and recordings of multitudes of African-American churches. Hughes's choice, then, of the piano as an instrument for Oceola is entirely within the reality of the acceptability of the piano as an option available to women in both nonprofessional and sometimes professional areas. Playing the piano allowed Oceola to express a part of her personality that might otherwise have been repressed or gone unexplored.

From the very first words of the story, Hughes emphasizes the importance of possessing an identity, opening with the name of the woman who is the primary force of the story. Her name is important in that through it Hughes is able to provide some subtle characterization. Linda Dahl reports in *Stormy Weather* that Mary Lou Williams remembered a pianist named Oceola playing in Kansas City, and Hughes may have been familiar with that performer, though he mentions her nowhere else in his autobiographical writings. It is likely that the use of that name stems from Hughes's familiarity with the historical figure for whom nineteen towns, plus various counties, streets, a Navy destroyer, and a mountain have been named (Pratt vi): Osceola, the famous chief of the Seminole tribe in the Second Seminole War. The Seminoles counted among their tribe, friends, and allies a rather large element of African American ex-slaves who had fled largely from the abuses of the South Carolinians and felt a kinship with the Seminoles, who also not only had suffered similar abuses, but also possessed "religious, ceremonial, governmental, and mythical similarities" that had parallels to the African heritage of the slaves (Mahon 663). Those African Americans who were slaves to the Native Americans were in fact more like feudal vassals than chattel slaves, and the combination of the runaway slave problem and the relatively better treatment at the hands of the Native American masters was enough to provoke the U.S. government into declaring war on the Seminoles twice, once in 1817-18 and again in 1835-42. It was during the second war that Osceola rose to prominence because of his success in battle.

Osceola's name lends a number of associations to Hughes's character in the story. It strengthens, on one hand, the autobiographical elements of the story, given that in real life the first love of Hughes's patron Charlotte Mason was Indians, suggesting that in her interest in Oceola Mrs. Ellsworth has a parallel to the lover of primitives in Hughes's life. More important are a number of pertinent facts related to the historical figure. Although most sources report that the name "Asi-Yahola" means "black drink singer," referring to a ceremonial drink, Charles B. Cory reported in 1896 that the name signified "rising sun," and Oceola is certainly that. Not only is she, for Mrs. Ellsworth, at the beginning of a great career, ready to be polished and finished, as Ormond Hunter notes (45), like new furniture; she is also a youthful choir director and rent party pianist who loves her neighbors and neighborhood and seeks to warm her community with the heart of its own technique and passion. The Seminole chief, though, was noted for his fighting, his bravery in battle, and his war whoop—especially remarked by several commentators—, which is in stark contrast to the much more subtle, calm rebellion of the female Oceola Jones.

Oceola Jones *wonders* at Mrs. Ellsworth's generosity; merely sidesteps Ellsworth's question about the location of her biological father (on the heels of a discussion of how big Billy Kersands's mouth was, it is hard not to think about how big Ellsworth's mouth is here); politely refuses Ellsworth's first attempt to extricate her from Harlem, though she ultimately does move; puzzles over the arguments that fellow students have at the Left Bank concerning art; and patiently resists Mrs. Ellsworth's attempts to separate her and Pete. Oceola is, indeed, constantly under siege, captured for a time under the white flag of truce, like the chief was, but ultimately escaping by simply walking away—unlike the chief, who died in captivity. What is admirable about Oceola in this story is that she has the strength *not* to whoop, not to insult, not to say "none of your nasty business, white woman," not to strike out; but to state calmly her objectives and desires, to try various opportunities, to resist gently those directives with which she disagrees, and to walk away richer and with dignity without having compromised her integrity. She is self-assured, comfortable and happy with her culture and her abilities, and is thus not defensive about Ellsworth's intrusions into her private life or attitudes about her people. Her war, then, has been won in her own mind, and her confrontation with the enemy, Ellsworth (who had been informed of Oceola's presence by the great white hunter, Ormond), is a victory without bloodshed, but a victory nonetheless. The Seminole chief's victory was only a partial and posthumous one; later much romanticized and mythologized, buried with military honors, the subject of poems, plays and novels, he took on an heroic stature in American popular culture that living Native Americans might not enjoy. Most of Oceola's people were removed from their land, and Osceola died in captivity, though not without taking 1500 of the enemy and twenty million dollars in U.S. war expenses with him. Oceola Jones winds up on the verge of being married, and to return to live among "her people," with two years of professional training to her credit, and a feeling of calm with herself.

Oceola Jones's victory comes about because she refuses to let Mrs. Ellsworth define her. The opening lines of the story, with their clipped cadence and bloodless tones, reflect Ellsworth's aesthetic:

> Oceola Jones, pianist, studied under Philippe in Paris. Mrs. Dora Ellsworth paid her bills. The bills included a little apartment on the Left Bank and a grand piano.
>
> (345)

The sentences are very neat, economical, and passionless. Oceola is a pianist, nothing more—that is enough. She studies in the "correct" location with the "correct" person, and is significantly described as being "under" him, subjugated to his aesthetic values; she has an economic arrangement that removes her from the mundane worries of daily life; and she is allowed for that life only a "little" apartment, while for her art she is supplied with something "grand." At this time Oceola is not the sole beneficiary of Mrs. Ellsworth's attention. Mrs. Ellsworth is also seeking to be the patron of the significantly-named Antonio Bas, whose surname evokes associations with bas-relief, sculpture carved in a flat surface so that the figures are only slightly three dimensional. As in Shaw's *Pygmalion,* Ellsworth seeks to take the rough base and mold it in her image of what it could or ought to be; and Ellsworth wants the figure to be only slightly three dimensional, always compliant with her wishes. Bas, in fact, ends up with Mrs. Ellsworth at the conclusion of the story when the Oceola-Ellsworth relationship deteriorates, most likely because of his acquiescence rather than any special genius he might have. Mrs. Ellsworth had, after all, once dismissed a soprano because she smelled like garlic, living "to regret bitterly her lack of musical acumen in the face of garlic" (346) when the soprano later became a great success.

But Oceola avoids the Ellsworth ambush and maintains her own identity independent of Ellsworth's vision of what Oceola is or ought to be. Oceola tells Mrs. Ellsworth what she needs to know about her past and family—no more—, calmly reports her devotion and aid to Pete, sacrifices at one point her technical progress for Pete's benefit, and laments at one point "I've been away from my people so long . . . I want to live right in the middle of them again" (350). She prefers, we might say, being in bed with Pete to being in bed with Mrs. Ellsworth. Mrs. Ellsworth would characterize the preference as being for the pleasures of the body over the pleasures of the mind, an avoidance, perhaps, of her own sublimated sexual attraction to "the electric strength of that brown-black body beside her" (348).

Oceola would not employ that characterization. At their parting audience, just as Mrs. Ellsworth begins to express her fears about men, Oceola plays the blues, described by Hughes in blatantly sexual terms. It starts as a sensuous slow blues of seductively wandering fingers and "soft and lazy syncopation" (351), building to a more rollicking and driving passion, climaxing with an "earth-throbbing rhythm that shook the lilies in the Persian vases of Mrs. Ellsworth's music room" (351), returning to the slow and sensuous denouement of the blues with which she began. In Oceola's microcosmic and artistic drama, which drowns out the voice, the imperatives, of Mrs. Ellsworth and her aesthetic, we see the playing out of Oceola's own aesthetic. While Mrs. Ellsworth continues to try to define Oceola's artistry in economic terms—"Is this what I spent thousands of dollars to teach you?" (351)—Oceola emphasizes the blues as a marriage of intellectual, technical, and personal emotional impulses, a unified approach that does not compartmentalize or deny anything about her life, but builds from it, moves to its feel, swells to its height, and always returns to what is most elemental and honest about it. It is a protean force, not fixed or static in Persian vases removed from Nature to adorn in an artificial environment, but emotionally complex and broad-ranging. "These are the blues . . . I'm playing," Oceola announces, and she means that statement two ways: she is playing the blues, and now *she* is playing, from herself.

Interestingly, Hughes makes it clear that the music has a voice of its own, a message it delivers. After the first and before the last line of the message, Hughes includes the words "sang the blues" to indicate that indeed it communicates by virtue of what it is, from what tradition it comes. Rather than letting the blues act as a means of separation and unproductivity, as Mrs. Ellsworth does, Oceola fuses her sadness and hope into a work of art that affirms humanity and self pride. After all, the bass notes are said to throb like "tom-toms" (351), suggesting that the blues recall what Hughes saw as the ancient and earthy power of her African ancestors. Thus, historically, geographically, intellectually, emotionally, sexually, and artistically, the blues is represented as being both unifying and useful. Mrs. Ellsworth's response to the song doesn't make much sense practically. "If I could holler," the song begins; Mrs. Ellsworth responds that she would stand looking. In her hands (or rather mouth), the lyric's emotional construction is undercut by an unfulfilling delivery: if one can holler, why does one merely *look*? Why mention the ability to holler if in fact one has no intention of doing so? It is because she is an observer, not a creator, and someone unused to being enough in touch with herself and the meaning of her life to consider it worthy of individual, personal artistic expression. Quite appropriately, the line she supplies, "And I . . . would stand looking at the stars" (351), violates the true words lyric not only in spirit, but in form. Ellsworth's line doesn't rhyme, as do the lines of the song, probably taken from Leroy Carr's version of "How Long How Long Blues" as performed by Carr or someone like Jimmy Rushing. Ellsworth's line is clearly de-contextualized, underscoring how foreign the tradition and the spirit are to Ellsworth.

Mrs. Ellsworth has the last word in Hughes's story, but one has to wonder, as the song asks: how long she'll have it, or how long Blacks will have to suffer it.

Her speech seems little more than broken wind as she delivers her final words. The "stars in her eyes" prevent her from realizing that she is doomed to remoteness from the object of her admiration: her sense of what she and others ought to be. "How long has that evening train been gone?" the song asks. Mrs. Ellsworth didn't even know that darkness had fallen long before Oceola, having bought a railroad of her own, rode off on her own track.

Works Cited

Cory, Charles B. "The Seminole Indians." *A Seminole Sourcebook.* Ed. William C. Sturtevant. New York: Garland, 1987: 7-40.

Dahl, Linda. *Stormy Weather: The Music and Lives of a Century of Jazz Women.* New York: Pantheon Books, 1984.

Emanuel, James. *Langston Hughes.* New York: Twayne, 1967.

Hughes, Langston. "The Blues I'm Playing." *Scribner's Magazine* 95.5 (May 1934): 345-51.

Mahon, John K. "Seminole Wars." *Dictionary of Afro-American Slavery.* Eds. Randall M. Miller and John David Smith. New York: Greenwood, 1988.

Pratt, Theodore. *Seminole.* Gainesville: U of Florida P, 1953.

Reitz, Rosetta. Jacket Notes. *Piano Singer's Blues: Women Accompany Themselves.* Rosetta, RR 1303, 1982.

Hans Ostrom (essay date 1993)

SOURCE: Ostrom, Hans. *"Laughing to Keep from Crying."* In *Langston Hughes: A Study of the Short Fiction,* pp. 19-30. New York: Twayne Publishers, 1993.

[*In the following essay, Ostrom discusses the plots and themes of* Laughing to Keep from Crying *and under-scores the author's use of irony and humor.*]

OVERVIEW: MINING A COMIC VEIN

Laughing To Keep From Crying (Henry Holt, 1952) contains 24 stories, most of which had appeared earlier in such magazines as *The African, American Spectator, Crisis, Esquire, The New Yorker,* and *Story.*

A collection of Jesse B. Simple stories had appeared in 1950 from Simon and Schuster: *Simple Speaks His Mind.* Since the Simple stories represent a separate, distinct development in Hughes's short fiction, how-ever, this chapter refers to *Laughing To Keep From Crying* as the "second" collection, meaning the second gathering of stories not featuring Simple. Further, since Hughes did not fully develop Simple until later in the 1950s, there is a sense in which the collection repre-sents the middle portion of Hughes's progress as a writer of stories.

As the title of the collection suggests, Hughes seems to have decided to let his short fiction mine a vein of com-edy. One indelible impression created by *The Ways of White Folks* is of black and white Americans on un-avoidable collision courses, in every region and social class of the land. In contrast, most of the stories in *Laughing To Keep From Crying* leave the impression that black Americans will survive the collisions, and that the nature and consequences of the collisions are sometimes unpredictable. In his second collection, Hughes is by no means less unflinching in his docu-mentation of the African-American predicament, but he generally shifts the focus from destructive consequences to embodiments of resiliency.

As in the first collection, irony, often of the situational kind, plays a key role in *Laughing To Keep From Cry-ing.* The irony, however, often gravitates toward com-edy rather than satire or tragedy. To some extent, this shift in purpose or temperament reveals a desire to ac-cept and to heal. It would be overgeneralizing to say that Hughes's short fiction journeys from outrage to ac-ceptance in the years between his first and second col-lections; the transformation was not that simple, com-plete, or one-dimensional. Nonetheless, a comic spirit makes *Laughing To Keep From Crying* a much differ-ent collection of stories.

The greatest similarity between the two collections is narrative technique. As this chapter will reveal, a broader range of form exists in the second book, but overall Hughes is still writing with great directness and simplicity; he is embracing a variety of characters and settings; he is letting social criticism infiltrate and shape his fiction.

The story **"Who's Passing For Who?"** offers specific clues to the general differences and similarities between the two collections of stories. Suggesting changes in

Hughes's outlook on racial conflict, it seems a universe apart from the last story of *The Ways of White Folks,* the mythic, tragic **"Father and Son."**

In this first story of the collection, three apparently white middle-class tourists visit Harlem to "sample" black culture—a situation that is not so different from those presented in *The Ways of White Folks,* where the idea of sampling or experiencing culture was exposed as another symptom of racism. In **"Who's Passing For Who?"** one of the characters says, without irony or self-consciousness, "We've never met a Negro writer before."[1]

In the course of the story, the three tourists (Iowans, we learn) and several black artists sit down for drinks in a club. A black patron at another table strikes his female companion during an argument. One of the men defends the woman, whom he thinks is white. During the ensuing verbal argument, he finds out the woman is actually black, and he apologizes for butting in. One of the black artists then asks him why defending the woman became less important when the man found out she was black. The man storms off, leaving his friends from Iowa—a "white" couple—behind. At the end of the story, this couple reveals they are black and have been merely passing as white.

As in the stories of *The Ways of White Folks,* the ironies of the situation are obvious, the plot streamlined, the style direct, colloquial, unadorned. One chief difference, however, is that Hughes allows the essential situational irony to multiply into further ironies until the situation becomes ridiculous. Consequently, the story moves beyond the theme of whites "sampling" black Harlem culture and teases the whole question of skin color until the question unravels comically. At the end of the story, the first-person plural narrator remarks, "Whatever race they [the 'white' couple] were, they had had too much fun at our expense—even if they did pay for the drinks" (*Laughing* [*Laughing to Keep from Crying*], 7).

Does the story imply that questions of skin color are moot, promoting the stale platitude "we're all the same underneath"? No. Despite the shift toward comedy, Hughes still shows an awareness of the deep ethnic differences history, law, and economics have created. He also shows how attitudes toward women are affected by attitudes toward color.

The shift toward comedy, then, is clear, but measured. Hughes is exploring the complications, many of them potentially comic, of "race relations," but he is not playing down the existence of deep social inequities.

The use of "we" as narrator of **"Who's Passing For Who?"** to some extent contributes to the comic ethos of the story because it admits multiple perspectives on the action of the story. In a sense, this first-person plurality represents the ambivalence with which the story approaches the topic of "passing"—an ambivalence greater than in the story **"Passing"** [**"Who's Passing for Who?"**] from *The Ways of White Folks,* where the first-person epistolary form reinforces a single, isolated perspective.

"Something In Common" may be the most predictable and least satisfying story of the collection. In it, an elderly black man and an elderly white man meet in a Hong Kong bar, spar verbally, nearly come to blows, get kicked out by the British bartender, and then decide to join forces against the bartender. For the moment, nationalism is more powerful than race. The situation seems far more contrived and less believable than that in **"Who's Passing For Who?,"** and the texture of irony far less complicated. Nonetheless, the story reinforces the sense that Hughes is using irony for comic, rather than satiric, purposes.

In part because it follows the thin, predictable story, **"Something In Common," "African Morning"** is a delightful surprise and one of Hughes's most memorable stories. **"African Morning"** works with a version of "the tragic mulatto," a recurring character type in Hughes's stories and in much African-American and southern literature symbolizing the consequences and dilemmas of racism.

A young mulatto African boy is sent by his father, a white banker, on an errand to the waterfront of a city. The boy is mistaken for a prostitute's son, teased, beaten, and chased. At the end of the story, the boy confronts the tragedy of being "the color of gold" (*Laughing,* 19). He realizes that, because his mother is dead, his father will find it easy to abandon him. He then dives into a pool, wishes to drown, but bobs up like a cork; bright birds land on a branch overhead, then fly away.

"African Morning" is more visually rich and evocative than many of Hughes's stories; in it a Joycean sense of epiphany provides a strategy for closure not often seen in Hughes's short fiction. This story also depends less on situational ironies for its effect, and more on the pathos of the main character.

The symbolism of "the color of gold" is also striking because at some level both the boy and reader come to realize that in Africa, at that particular historical moment, to be a "gold" mulatto is to be, in some sense, a form of currency. That is, the boy represents literal and figurative commerce between Europe and Africa; he understands his status as mulatto has reduced him to an object in most people's eyes, a kind of human coin.

To a degree, **"African Morning"** differs from the stories that precede and follow it in the collection because it is more dramatic, even tragic, than comic. The ending of the story, however, suggests the boy's resilience, and the bright birds—which can in one sense be taken as a symbol for an unconcerned, morally neutral universe— also add an image of spontaneous beauty that relieves the dominant, somber tone. Even while working with the figure of the tragic mulatto, Hughes does not close himself off to a certain inspiriting element.

"Saratoga Rain," a highly lyrical, compressed, one- page story, offers surprises not unlike those in **"African Morning."** Evocative and imagistic, it is almost a prose- poem description of two lovers, both gamblers, who achieve a temporary peace one rainy morning in Sa- ratoga. We find out that although their relationship has been plagued by adultery and other dishonesties, they have entered a redemptive moment. **"Saratoga Rain"** will remind many readers of several Ernest Hemingway stories—"Hills Like White Elephants" or "Cat In The Rain"—which deal with troubled "modern" couples. The tone and method of closure are more generous, more positive, perhaps more earthy in Hughes's story than in these Hemingway pieces, but both writers pro- vide a highly polished, intense glimpse of a moment in conjoined lives.

"Spanish Blood" is perhaps most notable as a slice-of- Harlem-nightclub-life, and **"Heaven To Hell"** is a very light, comic monologue spoken by a woman who has been in an automobile accident with her husband. When a woman the narrator supposes to be her husband's mistress visits her, the narrator is consumed with jeal- ousy and narrow-minded piety.

"Sailor Ashore" is a more ambitious story than these other two. Set in Los Angeles, it adds another point to Hughes's immense fictional map, draws successfully on his knowledge of waterfronts and the seagoing life, and uses dialogue and colloquial language adeptly. A sailor and a prostitute—both black—meet and seek temporary solace with one another, but end up only reinforcing their sense of despair and hopelessness. In its own way, **"Sailor Ashore,"** is as poignant in its depiction of two disenfranchised characters, as **"African Morning"** is in its depiction of a tragic mulatto.

Linked with **"Sailor Ashore"** (set in Los Angeles), **"Slice Him Down"** and **"Tain't So,"** set, respectively, in Reno and Hollywood, begin to suggest what the American West meant to Hughes—less a frontier or otherwise physical landscape, more an unpredictable, embryonic social province of America. Hughes does not, to be sure, idealize the West, but he does suggest how it is a unique North American region.

"Slice Him Down" takes place in a Reno bar and fea- tures two older African-American drinking buddies whose bragging escalates into a knife fight in which layers of clothing insure no one gets seriously injured.

"Tain't So" details the visit of a "proper" Southern white woman to a black faith healer and fortune-teller in Hollywood. The essential situations keep the stories well within the comic boundaries of the collection.

Beyond North and South, however, the stories also hint at a third regional dimension to the predicament of race in America. *The Ways of White Folks* often presented racial conflict as it emerged in brutal dichotomies: master/servant; patron/artist; rich/poor; and most espe- cially, North/South.

In these stories set in the American West, racial strife and its consequences haven't disappeared: Reno has its "black" or "Negro" side of town; Los Angeles is not more economically hopeful for blacks than Chicago or New York. Nonetheless, the unrelenting nature of rac- ism is somewhat relieved, and the relief seems to spring from the relatively unhardened youth of the West. The "black" side of Reno isn't as oppressed or victimized as Harlem; the scuffle depicted in **"Slice Him Down,"** be- tween two black men, ends comically, very much a family affair. The African-American faith healer is com- fortably ensconced in flaky Hollywood, making her way.

Perhaps more importantly, a sense of blurred—if not erased—racial lines, and a region in flux emerges in these stories. Each story refers in its own way to rac- ism, but the racism has often been defanged, most obvi- ously in **"Tain't So."** And in all three stories, the social boundaries are less fixed. For instance, when Miss Lucy, the "proper" white Southern woman in **"Tain't So,"** re- marks, "I'll never in the world get used to the North. Now here's a great—my friend says great faith-healer, treating darkies!" (*Laughing,* 80), we know she is re- ally put off by a particularly western variety of north- ernness. She realizes as much herself when she discov- ers the faith healer is black, and the faith healer heals her psyche simply by disagreeing with her. Certainly, Miss Lucy's racism isn't "harmless"; no racism is, as Hughes shows repeatedly in his fiction. But Miss Lucy is harmless.

Few readers would likely call **"One Friday Morning"** or **"Professor"** the most compelling or most comic sto- ries of *Laughing To Keep From Crying*; in fact, both seem plodding and uninspired in contrast to **"African Morning," "Saratoga Rain,"** and **"On The Road."** Taken together, however, the two stories are of particu- lar note because they concern two African Americans who choose to beat the racist system by changing it from within. **"One Friday Morning"** presents a young African-American woman who wins an art award, only to have it taken away when the judging committee dis- covers her skin color. Her response? At the high school awards ceremony, she stands up, recites the Pledge of Allegiance with everyone else, and says to herself: "That is the land we must make" (*Laughing,* 95).

The story is surprisingly unironic, unembittered, even sentimental for Hughes, but it serves to prepare the way for **"Professor."** It also suggests Hughes was considering—not endorsing, but considering—methods, which did not come naturally to him, of coping with racism.

In the second of these "paired" stories, a professor from a black college visits a philanthropic white family, the Chandlers, at none other than the Booker T. Washington Hotel, in itself a symbol for working within the system.

The professor, Dr. Brown, tells the Chandlers what they want to hear and allows them to condescend to him because he knows he can get money for the impoverished college: "And the things Dr. Brown's little college needed were small enough in the eyes of the Chandlers. The sane and conservative way in which Dr. Brown presented his case delighted the philanthropic heart of the Chandlers. And Mr. Chandler and Dr. Bulwick both felt that instead of building a junior college for Negroes in their own town they could rightfully advise local colored students to go down South to that fine little campus where they had a professor of their own race like Dr. Brown" (*Laughing,* 105). The ironic tone here lets us know Hughes certainly has not lost his skepticism, even cynicism, about "the ways of white (philanthropic) folks." But as in **"One Friday Morning,"** an ambivalence toward working within the system emerges.

Hughes clearly is not enthusiastically endorsing the responses of the girl cheated out of her prize nor those of the professor who "grins and bears" condescension. But neither is he indicting or heaping scorn on them.

Instead, the stories to some extent document a social or economic form of passing that involves a figurative blending in: a willingness to take the Pledge of Allegiance at face value and push the society toward an ideal it has never tried to achieve, and to use philanthropy motivated by racism for a greater good, a willingness to "go along to get along."

Although Hughes himself briefly had a white patron, and although he worked with all manner of mainstream editors and publishers, his style was not to conform as completely or with as much docility as these two characters. Nonetheless, by admitting such conformist characters into his fictional world without satirizing them, Hughes showed a measure of disinterestedness, at least, and perhaps even generosity toward African Americans who chose to cope in ways that did not personally suit him.

In the four stories, **"Pushcart Man," "Why, You Reckon?" "Name in the Papers,"** and **"Rouge High,"** the plots are minimal, and the inclination is to fashion sketches of street life in New York City, or at least of street characters that embodied such life as Hughes viewed it.

"Pushcart Man," for instance, is a kind of prose-poem filled with street speech; it creates a miniature folk opera of numerous arguments, conversations, sales pitches, and monologues on a Harlem street. While the pushcart man constitutes a kind of unifying musical theme, there is no main character, action, or pointed message to the story. Sound, its exuberant flow, is the sense of the piece.

In **"Why, You Reckon?"** a young upper-middle-class white man is mugged and responds enthusiastically; to the befuddlement of his muggers, he thinks of the event as a way to experience black culture. Here the familiar notion of "sampling culture" returns at its most absurd, perhaps, and mugging is presented in its most pleasant light—pleasant enough to appear in *The New Yorker.*

"Name In The Papers" is a monologue spoken by a hospitalized man who has just been shot several times by a husband who discovered his wife and the speaker in compromising circumstances. The speaker is much less concerned with his ventilated body than with the possibility of having his name appear in the newspaper.

"Rouge High" depicts two prostitutes in a bar; a pimp walks in, strikes one of the women, takes money from her, and leaves. For both the women and the bartender the incident seems de rigueur. The woman then produces a money-choked wallet lifted from a customer, making it clear the pimp only thought he was getting his due. The other woman tells her that her eye is swelling from the beating and suggests she "rouge high"—move the rouge up from cheekbone to eye.

The theme of undaunted resilience, the mixture of naive and worldly-wise humor, the attention to dialect and speech patterns, and the minimalist "sketch" form in these four stories all bear strong resemblance to the Jesse B. Simple stories Hughes had begun to write for *The Chicago Defender* and which he had already collected in one book.[2]

As we have seen, one obvious difference between Hughes's first and second collections is that *Laughing To Keep From Crying* shows a shift in purpose, tone, and narrative mode, toward the comic. This shift did not mean that Hughes turned away completely from depicting the devastating consequences of racism; the stories **"African Morning"** and **"Sailor Ashore,"** already discussed, demonstrate as much. The stories **"Powder-White Faces"** and **"On The Way Home"** also go against the dominant comic grain of the collection. In fact, of all the stories in *Laughing To Keep From Crying,* these two concern themselves most deeply with the desperation racism creates.

In **"Powder-White Faces,"** Hughes creates a more deadly version of the illicit romantic situation that underlies comic stories such as **"A Good Job Gone"** or

"Name in the Papers." A Chinese-American youth who has changed his name and jumped aboard a tramp steamer relates in flashback how he murdered a white woman with whom he was involved. The motive, purely and simple, is rage at being belittled, at being called "China boy."

The story is remarkable, in part, for the way in which it addresses racist-inspired rage so directly and places racism in a context that isn't African-American. Further, it deals with a kind of ferocity that is out of key with the dominant tone of the collection.

"On The Way Home" is in no sense as violent as **"Powder-White Faces,"** but it locates itself in a similar desperation. It depicts an alcoholic African-American man whose mother is dying. Unable to bring himself to visit her, he sinks further into alcohol as the story proceeds. Like **"Powder-White Faces,"** the story makes the desperate person's point of view sympathetic, even though it may not be completely acceptable or exemplary; like most of the stories in *Laughing To Keep From Crying,* it describes the cost of a difficult life made even more difficult by a racist society.

The stories **"Mysterious Madame Shanghai," "Little Old Spy,"** and **"Baths"** do not share common themes, settings, or narrative techniques, but in one sense they belong together because they seem to spring from Hughes's restless, itinerant life. All three are reportorial in nature, though the narrative structures and points of view differ; of all the stories in the collection, these seem to be the ones least transformed by fictional reshaping.

Hughes sets **"Mysterious Madame Shanghai"** in a New York boarding house, a locale frequently used in Hughes's fiction, second only to bars. The story details the lengthy, strange, exotic relationship between a former circus performer, Madam Shanghai, and her husband. Racial or ethnic conflict has little bearing on the story; Hughes seems chiefly to be retrieving from his travels an offbeat tale of cruel love.

Much the same can be said for **"Baths,"** a story of ill-fated love set in Mexico and of **"Little Old Spy,"** which is about the menacing but, in this story at least, ultimately harmless machinations of the reactionary government in Cuba.

All three tales seem deliberately underdramatized: all three blend in with the epistemological sense of ironic acceptance that surrounds the collection; all three bear the mark of Hughes-the-reporter, Hughes-the-documenter; all three link Hughes's fiction stylistically with his two autobiographies, *I Wonder As I Wander* and *The Big Sea.*[3]

In **"The Trouble With Angels," "On the Road,"** and **"Big Meeting,"** Hughes casts a comic, almost satiric, eye toward matters of religion. Certainly, these stories

do not approach the broad, lacerating satire of **"Rejuvenation Through Joy"** (*The Ways of White Folks*), but they nonetheless collectively demonstrate Hughes's cynicism on the subject.

"The Trouble With Angels" takes us behind the scenes of a touring gospel musical drama with an African-American cast. The popular production gets booked in Washington, D.C.—where "legitimate playhouses have no accom[m]odations for 'colored people.' Incredible as it may seem, until Ingrid Bergman made her stand, Washington was worse than the Deep South in that respect" (*Laughing,* 174).

Hughes gets a lot of funny, biting mileage out of the hypocritical contrast between the spiritual piety of white audiences and the racism of unwritten public entertainment laws. He also reserves a good deal of cynical wit for the actor playing God—"this colored God who had been such a hit on Broadway" (*Laughing,* 175)—who refuses to join the cast in a strike. This God, Hughes lets us know, is quite human and does not endorse the idea of solidarity as a method of combating racism.

"Big Meeting," by comparison, is relatively free of such implied social criticism. The chief impetus of this story seems to be Hughes's wish to document, even celebrate, that genre of religious convocation known as "the tent meeting" or "camp meeting." At one point, the black narrator remarks on white people who sit in their cars at the periphery of the gathering: "The white people were silent again in their car, listening to the singing. In the dark I couldn't see their faces to tell if they were still amused or not. But that was mostly what they wanted out of Negroes—work and fun—without paying for it, I thought, work and fun" (*Laughing,* 198). This critical assessment of whites—a throwback to *The Ways of White Folks*—is the exception to the predominant tone of **"Big Meeting,"** which is celebratory. Just as **"Pushcart Man"** captures the "music" of the streets, **"Big Meeting"** captures the literal and figurative music of a tent meeting.

Despite his cynicism toward spirituality, particularly of the pious kind, and despite his Marxist leanings and his social-critic's perspective, Hughes clearly saw the healing, unifying force the tent meetings provided to working-poor African Americans in the South. **"Big Meeting"** is at once the most meticulous and generous depiction of such a meeting one is likely to find in American short fiction. It by no means represents an abrupt turn toward religion as a solution to social, economic, or racial ills, but does represent Hughes's acknowledgment of religious ritual as a legitimate source of support for the beleaguered. Whereas the comedy of **"Trouble With Angels"** edges toward satire, the comedy of **"Big Meeting"** is full of acceptance, gravitating toward encomium.

It is no wonder that **"On The Road"** is the most anthologized story from the collection, and—outside of the Jesse B. Simple stories taken as a whole—the best-known Hughes story. A superb short narrative, it shows just how successful Hughes could be in a short-story form which is in sharp contrast to the dominant modernist mode emphasizing image, style, and lyricism over plot.

"On The Road" is a parable that makes almost perfect use of techniques and tendencies found in Hughes's first two collections: the simple, direct style, the thirst for social criticism, the balance between satire and comedy, the basic, easily recognizable plot line, and the ability to create "everyman" characters.

The story depicts Sargeant, a down-and-out African-American drifter who finds himself nearly freezing to death in a snowy northern city. Sargeant tries to hammer his way into a white church to find a warm place to sleep. He sees—and talks with—Christ, in what turns out to be an hallucination.

Sargeant believes he has knocked on the church door so hard that the church has fallen down. Christ thanks him for the liberation: "You had to pull the church down to get me off the cross" (*Laughing*, 187).

Christ turns out to be as bluesy, forlorn, and folksy as Sargeant. He (Christ) is as disappointed in the climatological, social, and spiritual failings of the northern city as Sargeant is, wants to go to Kansas City. After the vision, Sargeant is rudely awakened—in jail.

"On the Road" is a nearly perfectly-wrought, understated modern parable, satisfying on several levels,—at once simple, rich, pointed, and funny. One of its "morals," of course, is a kind of implied question: When will "Christ" (Christian values) come down off the cross and out of the church to do some good in society?

Summary

Laughing To Keep From Crying represents a shift—in tone, outlook, and choice of subject—from the harshly ironic social criticism of **The Ways of White Folks** to a comic but weary, blues-influenced outlook of acceptance.

In matters of narrative technique, however, the differences between the two books are far less extreme. In his second collection, Hughes still relies on simple narrative forms—the tale, the sketch, the parable, and deliberately undramatic reportage. He also remains interested in allowing colloquial language, the blues, gospel music, and the sound and sense of "street speech" to inform the language of his short fiction.

Moreover the "cosmopolitan Hughes" remains constant in both volumes. Behind his preference for simplicity and directness in narrative form, open-minded, well-traveled geographic, political, and cultural visions re-

main constant. Indeed, one of the most profound curiosities of Hughes's short fiction is that while his narrative choices are often similar to those of self-proclaimed regionalists and local colorists, his concept of society and culture is multinational and eclectic.

Working with a variety of seemingly naive but actually very knowing characters, Hughes shows in his second collection the degree to which the "consciousness" of Jesse B. Simple—which had been taking shape since 1942 in *The Chicago Defender* columns—haunted him and shaped his writing.

Many critics have noted the irony of **Laughing To Keep From Crying** appearing in the same year as Ralph Ellison's *Invisible Man* (1952). Within the tradition of African-American writing, it was as if a torch of literary mastery were being passed from the older writer to the younger, and from simpler narrative forms to more complex, even mythic ones. While Hughes's collection was overshadowed by Ellison's monumental book, however, it is worth noting that the two writers shared an acute interest in issues of class and economics and that both relied heavily on irony as a method of rendering their fiction. Such commonalities make the books seem more like complementary expressions of a similar vision than competing works from writers of different generations. In any case, the older writer Hughes was yet to realize fully his most enduring short fiction character, one of the most indelible characters in American literature: Jesse B. Simple.

Notes

1. *Laughing To Keep From Crying* (New York: Henry Holt, 1952), 2; hereafter cited in the text as *Laughing*.

2. Arnold Rampersad, *The Life of Langston Hughes, Vol. 2: 1941-1967* (New York: Oxford University Press, 1988), 61-67; this volume hereafter cited in the text as Rampersad, 2.

3. *The Big Sea* (New York: Knopf, 1940) and *I Wonder As I Wander: An Autobiographical Journey* (New York: Hill and Wang, 1956).

Susan Neal Mayberry (essay date fall 1995)

SOURCE: Mayberry, Susan Neal. "Out of the Mouths of Babes: Children and Narrative Voice in Hughes' *The Ways of White Folks*." *The Griot* 14, no. 2 (fall 1995): 48-58.

[*In the following essay, Mayberry claims that Hughes experiments with narrative perspective in* The Ways of White Folks *to voice his anger toward American society.*]

While scholarly estimates of Langston Hughes' fiction, both during his career and subsequently, have been scarce, those who have commented recently are unanimous in their view that it has been consistently underrated.[1] During Hughes' lifetime he suffered not so much from a lack of success as from casual critical neglect, with mainstream scholars relegating him to the realm of popular writer and thus by-passing any serious consideration of his art.[2] Not only has his short fiction, as well as his poems, been excluded from college anthologies, evaluation of his writing continues to be hampered by lack of critical commentary in standard sources on recent American literature.[3] In the words of poet Onwuchekwa Jemie, the American literary establishment has dismissed Hughes as "too simple, too quaintly humorous, unserious, unreflective, parochial, limited in scope, without a metaphysic, and without profundity" (187).

Ironically, some of Hughes' least supportive critics have been of African descent. Ralph Ellison believed that Hughes had "used his emotions and sensibility more than his intellect" and actually accused him of having "stopped thinking." James Baldwin objected to his "fake simplicity," and declared himself "depressed" that Hughes had done so little with his genuine gifts (Lee 204). From his position of black ultra-nationalism, LeRoi Jones/Amiri Baraka pronounced, as Richard Wright had done about Zora Neale Hurston years before, that Hughes possessed an inadequate racial sense (Rampersad 2: 376). Even Nathan Huggins in his important work on the Harlem Renaissance recalls the debate among Harlem Renaissance intelligentsia over the use of the black vernacular when he charges that Hughes backed out of the Negro-artist dilemma by taking an anti-intellectual approach to art; opting for a freedom of subject and a personal honesty, Hughes avoided "the Scylla of formalism only to flounder in the Charybdis of folk art" (226-27). Huggins goes so far as to assert that nothing produced during the New Negro Renaissance can compare with the fruits of recent years when black writers have become "less provincial, more masterful of craft" (307).[4] What almost all critics, black and white alike, have failed to recognize is that Hughes set out to record and interpret black folk traditions, that his great achievement was to build popular literature into a significant art form. They also mistake the eiron for the fool; underneath Hughes' mask of geniality is a voice tight with rage.

The secrets of Hughes' short fiction have been more misunderstood, if not overlooked, by critics than have his poems. In the 1930s Hughes virtually abandoned poetry to concentrate on fiction and drama. Taken as a whole, his sixty-six published short stories constitute a social document "reflecting the various nuances of race relationships since 1920" (Dickinson 4). While the variety, restraint, humor, naturalness, and power of the stories have been commonly perceived, their pathos, real-

ism, and characteristic irony have not been adequately recognized in the published commentary and their stylistic traits virtually ignored (Emanuel, "Short Fiction" 148). Most of these characteristics are apparent in the earliest of Hughes' short story collections, *The Ways of White Folks* (1934). However, the technique that is and would continue to be most successful for Hughes in portraying black people colliding—sometimes humorously, more often tragically—with whites is his experimentation with narrative perspective and his eiron's voice.

David Michael Nifong points out that *The Ways of White Folks* contains seven different points of view: three first-person narrators, one omniscient narrator, various third-person narratives including an example of "selective omniscience," and a dramatic dialogue with an effaced narrator. However, the significance of Hughes' experiments with narrative voice is limited, for Nifong, to the observation that a reader would usually be able to observe point of view only by comparing "the different narrative postures in several works of art" and that it is "exciting" to discover a collection of short stories "which makes the study of point of view relatively simple" (94).

It is not just the variety in points of view, however, that makes Hughes' narrative voice so compelling in *The Ways of White Folks.* He also connects voice with theme in various of the stories and with the very structure of the collection itself. R. Baxter Miller notes that Hughes intuitively "recognizes the force in the ironic pretense to stupidity," drawing upon classical conventions such as the eiron to "deepen the political and social awareness in his fictional world" (101). Maurice Charney outlines the function and behavior of the eiron in his introduction to the experience of comedy, referring to Socrates as "the great eiron of antiquity." Socrates "plays the fool, feigns ignorance, asks seemingly innocent and childlike questions that are meant to trap you. Socratic irony is still usually defined as a pretended stupidity, a disingenuousness and false naivete [my emphasis], intended to mislead its hearers to produce a result strikingly different from what they counted on . . ." (11).[5] By assuming this posture of childlike innocence, the eiron is able, as an adult, to elicit from other adults the shock of recognized truth that typically only the child can evoke as when we say, "out of the mouths of babes." Sometimes it takes the ingenuousness of a child to startle grownups out of their blindness and complacency. Hughes is able to make shrewd use of this persona in *The Ways of White Folks* to startle white America into an awareness of the black culture struggling in its midst.[6]

Hughes' use of the child is not limited, however, merely to voice. Eight of the fourteen stories contained in the collection focus specifically on children in some fashion while the remaining six depict black adults treated by whites as children. Moreover, taken as a whole the stories shift from the submissiveness of black characters caught in a vise of white control that virtually renders them children to the sometimes violent rebellion necessary for them to become independent human beings. Hughes uses their attitudes towards children to reveal the ways of white folks: their ignorance, intolerance, pietism, condescension, blindness, and racism. He also creates from the order of the stories in the collection a social document which argues in a double-voiced discourse that black culture must acknowledge its child-like dependence on whites and reject it for independence.[7]

The Ways of White Folks begins in **"Cora Unashamed"** by focusing on the natural rightness of a mother's love for her child. In this story the black woman, Cora, is associated with the instinctual while the white townsfolk, particularly the women, sublimate the natural in favor of the social. Though single-handedly supporting her drunken father and her quarrelsome, chronically pregnant mother not to mention her seven "bratty" brothers and sisters, made mean from hunger, Cora is herself treated as a child by her white employers, the Studevants. As Hughes puts it, "there was something about the teeth in the trap of economic circumstances that kept her in their power practically all her life . . ." (4). To insure that readers not stereotype the situation, attributing Cora's economic quagmire to Southern racism, Hughes sets the story in a small, rural Iowa town in America's heartland. He also isolates Cora from other black people; the Jenkins family are, in the words of the townspeople, the "only Negroes in Melton, thank God!" (4). Described repeatedly as "humble," "gentle," and "inoffensive," Cora is submissive under white domination in all instances but one. Instinctively valuing life, she cries out or, rather, "cusses" against its violation.

Throughout the story, Cora is associated with images of nature. She "was like a tree—once rooted, she stood, in spite of storms and strife, wind, and rocks, in the earth" (4). She refers to the single event giving meaning to a life of plodding self-denial as her "Spring," a time when she took a lover, her first and the only man she "ever remembered wanting" (6). Her memories of that season are associated with meadows, orchards, sweet fields, velvet skies, katydids, crickets, and lightening bugs, and with the earthy scent of her yellow-haired, grey-eyed Joe, smelling like the horses he takes care of. Cora pays little attention to white folks' rules about miscegenation or about illegitimate, biracial children. She never expects to marry or even keep Joe upon the birth of her grey-eyed daughter, yet she does not attempt to hide her pregnancy, viewing it as no disgrace even when public reaction, both white and black, is one of outrage. Cora embraces the naturalness of the act, naming the child Josephine after the father who is driven from town and cherishing the child as "hers—a living bridge between two worlds" (7).

Hughes emphasizes the rightness of Cora's response to children as opposed to the unnatural attitude of the white folks by creating a number of parallels in the story, presenting Cora's situation in the context of seasonal cycles. Mrs. Art Studevant gives birth to a baby the same age as Josephine but, though turning her over to Cora to wet-nurse, does not allow Cora to bring her own little girl to play with Jessie, ostensibly because Cora "could get her work done better if she left her child at home" (8). When Josephine dies of whooping cough, Cora takes little Jessie as her own, "burying her dark face in the milky smell of the white child's hair" (9). Though venting her rage at God for the death of her child in a stream of curses so violent that the gravetenders at Josephine's funeral react in "startled horror," Cora is "gentle and humble in the face of life—she loved [the Studevants'] baby" (8-9). Having adopted "in her heart" the child that the Studevants reject as plump, dull, and strange, Cora stands as a "calm and sheltering tree" for Jessie who "blooms" only in the kitchen where she laughs, learns to cook wonderfully, and is sometimes even witty.

The final repetition in the story is seen in Cora's response to Jessie's own "Spring" when the girl, afraid to tell her mother she is pregnant, turns to the woman with whom everything "seemed so simple" (10). Here the technique Hughes employs to contrast the black woman's naturalness with the unnatural behavior of the Studevant females is their mode of expression. Hughes uses a third person narrator in the story to offer us insight into the various characters; Cora herself says very little. Her answer to the Studevants' incessant talking, mostly in the form of demands, is "Yes, ma'am." Her answer to the public outcry when she was pregnant with Josephine was "Let people talk" (7). Most of Cora's communication is indirect and is done to find ways to break the news of Jessie's various academic and social failures to her parents. The only direct statements made by Cora occur when she is moved by great feeling to announce life or protest death. Thus, although she is skilled at subtly communicating failures to the Studevants, she "marched into Mrs. Art's sun-porch and announced quite simply, 'Jessie's going to have a baby'" (11). Cora does not view the birth of a child as a failure.

While Cora speaks only when she is expressing natural feeling, the Studevants are restricted by social convention from voicing real emotion. They talk but reveal nothing. When the situation involves anything natural such as sex, birth, or death, they are incapable of speaking. The shock which follows Cora's announcement of Jessie's pregnancy can only be expressed non-verbally; Mrs. Art falls into "uncontrollable hysterics" while Old Lady Studevant's reaction can be perceived through her wheel-chair, which "roll[s] up, doddering and shaking with excitement" (12). Cora is immediately silenced to prevent her from speaking that which the Studevant feel is unspeakable:

"No trouble having a baby you want. I had one."

"Shut up, Cora!"

"Yes, ma'am. . . . But I had one."

"Hush, I tell you."

"Yes, ma'am."

(12)

Clearly at least the female Studevants view Jessie's unborn child, not to mention its Greek immigrant father, as unsuitable beyond expression to their status as civic leaders and church pillars. They cannot conceive of what they will not name.

Left to their devices, the woman arrange for Jessie to have an abortion under cover of a shopping trip to Kansas City. Forced to "talk a lot" to explain Jessie's thinness and pallor upon their return, Mrs. Art Studevant also starts a campaign to rid the town of unsavory tradespeople such as Greek ice-cream makers. In the midst of this "clean-up," refusing to eat and grieving for her aborted baby, Jessie dies. Biting her lips to keep from cursing while Jessie pines, Cora will not be silenced at the girl's funeral. While "Mrs. Art fell back in her chair, stiff as a board," "Cousin Nora and sister Mary sat like stones," and the menfolk scrambled to shut her up, Cora screams: "They preaches you a pretty sermon and they don't say nothin'. They sings you a song, and they don't say nothin'. But Cora's here honey, and she's gone tell 'em what they done to you. . . . They killed you and your child. I told 'em you loved it, but they didn't care" (16-17).

Hughes' eiron's mask is apparent throughout the piece, mildly, even humorously, recording white voices that treat Cora "like a dog" or describing in wide-eyed fashion Mrs. Art, prostrate with grief at Jessie's death, reviving briefly just before the services to request that Cora fix her an omelette with "a little piece of ham" to get her through the afternoon. However, the suppressed anger, barely concealed by the childlike quality of the narrator's voice, is reinforced by the ways that white folks treat children in the opening story. Not only do they elevate Latin grammar, civic problems, and church sermons above the welfare of their daughter, they are oblivious to the economic constraints they foster to ensure the dependency upon them of the woman acting as surrogate mother to their child. **"Cora Unashamed"** introduces ideas that will be repeated throughout the collection as Hughes presents various black characters caught in an unnatural dependency on whites. While Cora's declaration of independence is individual and ultimately contained, as she rejects "ha[ving] to stand" the Studevants for a "little garden" and "somehow manag[ing] to get along," the black revolution Hughes embraces by the final story is collective and contagious (3, 18).

"Cora Unashamed" is followed by six stories that continue Hughes' exploration of the various ways in which white folks dehumanize blacks, rendering them in some fashion childlike. While none of these narratives focuses on attitudes towards children as a central theme, each offers a situation in which black people are reduced by a white social or economic system to the status of children. Three of the stories, **"Slave On The Block," "Rejuvenation Through Joy,"** and **"The Blues I'm Playing,"** depict humorously or satirically the cult of the Negro, revealing the condescension of spiritually impoverished whites who marvel at the so-called "primitivism" of black people or attempt to control them through patronage. The other three, **"Home," "Passing,"** and **"A Good Job Gone,"** present young black men who must cope with the white world's relegation of them to the role of "boy." A physically and emotionally ailing musician is lynched when he forgets his place at home after spending years in Europe; a son elects to pass his own mother on the street in order to continue passing as white, sacrificing his manhood to avoid being called "boy"; a student with middle-class aspirations plays "boy" to a rich white man in exchange for his dental school tuition. Ranging from the tragicomic to the tragic, each story emphasizes the hopelessness and humiliation of grown people forced into childlike roles because of their race, indirectly extending Hughes' interest in children.

All of the stories in the remaining half of the collection rely directly on children to illustrate the ways of white folks. In two of his most experimental stories, **"Red-Headed Baby"** and **"Little Dog,"** Hughes uses children to reveal the repression of whites attracted to sexually forbidden relationships with black people. Because the central characters in both stories are blocked by prejudice or convention from acknowledging their real emotions, Hughes creates both a narrative perspective and a "child" character that will allow voice to carefully suppressed feelings. **"Red-Headed Baby"** combines first person point-of-view with a poetic internal monologue, successfully fusing, like Jean Toomer's *Cane,* fiction and poetry. Clarence's claustrophobic, futile life is suggested by the choppiness of the narrative style; his perception of his physical world reflects his own stagnation:

> Dead, dead as hell, these little burgs on the Florida coast. Lot of half-built skeleton houses left over from the boom. Never finished. Never will be finished. Mosquitoes, sand, niggers. Christ, I ought to break away from it.

(125)

Images of "hairy freckled hands" and a "dead hot breeze" depict Clarence as a poor white sailor drifting aimlessly on a tramp steamer up and down the Florida coast (125). Desperately in need of an anchor and a calm harbor but allowing himself no articulation of his needs, Clarence seeks out his former lover, a young black woman who "played like a kid" three years earlier. Prevented by his coarse existence from recognizing any softer emotions, Clarence also possesses the poor white's disdain of black people. He reassures himself that Betsy "wasn't nothin' to get excited over—last time [he] saw her" and refers to her as "this damn yellow gal," one of many "yellow wenches [he's] had" (125-26). Nonetheless, he is impatient to find her door and fearful that she will have forgotten his voice.

His self-destructive inclinations dominate as he masks his need for Betsy beneath an almost puritanical obsession with the possibility of her corruption, refusing to acknowledge that he initiated the circumstances of that corruption. Having "christened" a seventeen-year-old virgin and her mother, turning poor blacks scared of a white man in the house into hardened flesh traders, Clarence is disturbed that Betsy now flirts and drinks, that there have been other "mule[s] in [his] stall" (127). He denies both his need to reestablish a relationship with something innocent and any responsibility for having coarsened that innocence.

While Clarence's cryptic first-person sentences suggest denial, restlessness, and repression, passages of lush poetic monologue reveal his yearning for beauty. He contemplates

> Soft heavy hips. Hot and browner than the moon—good licker. Drinking it down in little nigger house Florida coast palm fronds scratching roof hum mosquitoes night bugs flies ain't loud enough to keep a man named Clarence girl named Betsy old woman named Auntie from talking and drinking in a little nigger house on Florida coast dead warm night with the licker browner and more fiery than the moon.
>
> (129)

Hughes marks Clarence's tentative impulses toward self-awareness not only with poetic passages; he introduces a character to complete the process. Although there is no way to miss that Betsy's "damn runt of a . . . red-headed blue-eyed yellow-skinned baby" is the red-haired sailor's child, Clarence cannot accept that he has fathered a son by a black woman (130). His mental turmoil is revealed in another poetic monologue as he confronts "A red-headed baby. Moonlight-gone baby. No kind of yellow-white bow-legged goggled-eyed County Fair baseball baby" (131). Unable to acknowledge his son's humanity, he reduces the child to a "stupid-faced," "bow-legged" doll created to be knocked down at a county fair and continues the violence of the image in a threat to "knock the [little bastard's] block off" when baby Clarence crawls towards him (131). If Clarence were to recognize the child as his own, he would also be forced to recognize Betsy as human, not just another "yellow jane" to be used for his pleasure and then tossed aside.

Hughes creates the child as the mirror image of the father in ways other than physical. Deaf, probably from syphilis passed from Clarence to the mother, little Clar-

ence will inherit sterility from his father in more ways than one. Although the child "can't say Da," he "ain't blind," and his unrelenting stare forces his father to re-evaluate the meaning of his life. Offered the opportunity to exchange sterility for creation, futility for purpose, Clarence cannot give up his old system of beliefs. Confronted with himself, he responds, "Get him the hell out of here pulling at my legs looking like me at me like me at myself like me red-headed as me. 'Christ!'" (131). He runs, knocking over glasses in his hurry. The story ends with Clarence's complete rejection of his son and his other self, symbolized by his need to prostitute the experience by paying for his drinks.

In **"Little Dog,"** Hughes again experiments with point of view and a child character to reveal suppressed emotion. Here the repressed white is a middle-aged spinster instead of a white-trash sailor and the "child," her fuzzy white dog. Developing his third-person narrator into a central intelligence, Hughes adopts the Jamesean technique of selective omniscience. The reader is limited to the thoughts and actions of Miss Clara Briggs, an introverted bookkeeper who fantasizes about the black janitor supplying meat for her little dog.

Hiding her fears of intimacy and involvement behind a mask of efficiency, Miss Briggs creates a regimented, self-contained world composed of an invalid mother, a job as head bookkeeper, and the occasional Women's Civics Club meeting or lecture on Theosophy. Her only experience with men being the "flat-footed old Negro gentlemen" who fuss over her nightly dinners at the Rose Bud Tea Shoppe, she is left without even female contact when her mother dies. Miss Briggs prides herself on "keeping her distance" from the movement and color that surround her park-front apartment on proving right her mother's comment that "Men'll have a hard time getting Clara" (165). Denying that she ever felt lonely, at least "not very lonely," Miss Briggs nonetheless spends more money than she intends to buy a little dog she spots in a pet shop window.

The impulse to share her life, albeit with something small and safe, leads Miss Briggs into a relationship with the big and, for her, not-so-safe black janitor whom she contracts to bring meat for her dog. As with her Negro waiters, she initially responds to the kindness of the man with the house full of children. However, Miss Briggs soon finds herself listening for his "rich voice" and the appearance of his "beautifully heavy body" upon her back porch steps (168, 172). While she is overwhelmed by the black man's sexuality, none too subtly couched in the image of the meat delivery, Miss Briggs makes every possible attempt to conceal the truth from herself. Her resistance to feelings she cannot control is so great that she literally closes the door in Joe's face when he brings the meat, refusing to allow him to see her blushing face. However, she keeps "looking at the big kind face of the janitor in her mind, perturbed that it was a Negro face, and that it stayed with her so" (171).

As with **"Red-Headed Baby,"** Hughes introduces in **"Little Dog"** a minor character who provides the reader with insight into the epiphany of the main character. In this case it is not the accusing stare of Clarence's son that leads to recognition but the anthropomorphic barks of Clara's dog. In both cases the feelings of repressed characters are articulated by their dumb "children." Prior to Miss Briggs' introduction to Joe, her dog Flips is not particularly expressive. By the time the two exchange their first few sentences, however, "Flips had already begun to jump upon [Joe] with friendly mien" (168). In addition, the occasional pitch-hitting of Joe's wife during the nightly meat deliveries causes Flips to "bark . . . rudely at her," something that Miss Briggs would obviously like the freedom to do (170). Miss Briggs' projection of emotion onto Flips becomes undeniably clear on the night of Joe's last delivery. Trembling so that she cannot come to the door to take the meat when he knocks, she manages to call to him to leave it by the sink. When Flips jumps up on her for his food, she says, "'Oh, Flips . . . I'm so hungry.' She meant to say 'You're so hungry.' So she repeated it. 'You're so hungry! Heh, Flipsy, dog?'" (172). Though hungry for the companionship and love she associates with the dog's eagerness for his dinner, Miss Briggs, like Clarence, ultimately denies any possibility for change. She will limit the hunger to where she thinks it belongs, to an animal, and begins immediately to make plans to move to a different apartment, uprooting her entire life to avoid confronting her sexual attraction to a black man.

Hughes focuses on children and narrative perspective again in **"Poor Little Black Fellow"** and **"Mother and Child"** to examine the hypocrisy beneath the pious masks of good "Christians" called upon to tolerate the ultimate signifier of another race—its children. The first paragraph of **"Poor Little Black Fellow"** defines the attitude and tone of voice that six-year-old Arnold Lee will experience throughout his childhood. When their "perfect" Negro servants, Arnold and Amanda Lee, inconveniently die, the wealthy, childless, white Pembertons, one of New England's oldest and finest families, would never dream of shirking their responsibility to rear little Arnie as their own. Reassuring themselves that the Lord is just, they accept Arnie as their Christian duty. Having gone to white servants because the "Negroes were getting so unsteady," the Pembertons are particularly responsive to Arnie because they thought they had seen in his parents "the real qualities of an humble and gentle race" (134). Although we glimpse their condescension to black people when they describe the death of Arnold, Sr. as "almost like a personal loss"; refer initially to Arnold, Jr. as "it"; and contribute to a

Negro school in honor of its simple, hard-working people, the Pembertons have not a clue. For them the perfect black person is a submissive child.

Their dehumanization of the only black child in Mapleton continues as they find ways to carry out their responsibilities as Christians while monitoring Arnie's status as a Negro. Birthday parties are held on the lawn because there is more room there. The two rooms over the stable-turned-garage make a "fine apartment for a growing boy" (140). But most pernicious is the Pembertons' concerted and collective effort to kill Arnie with kindness, an attitude that spreads throughout the town even to the children. When being "nice" to the poor little black fellow comes to symbolize for the town of Mapleton Christian charity itself, the narrator notes, "One would think that nobody in the town need ever again do a good deed: that his acceptance of a black boy was quite enough" (137).

What Arnie really symbolizes in **"Poor Little Black Fellow"** is the fallacy that black America's enforced dependency upon white America will keep black citizens subordinate, safe, childlike. As a child, Arnie senses the Pembertons' ambivalence but can do nothing about it. He is "very grateful, and very lonely," and everything "might have been all right forever had not Arnie begun to grow up" (137). With Arnie a child no longer, Mapleton is faced with a "Negro problem." There are not only taboos at home to contend with involving girls and dances and dating, but the outside world has rules about sixteen-year-old black boys. Even the Boy Scout summer camp cannot "admit Negroes" because "too many parents would object" (138). However, Arnie has lived too long in the white world to be able to cope at sixteen with the Negro charity camp apologetically substituted by the Pembertons, who rationalize the situation as "nice for [Arnie] to come to know some of his own people" (138). Filled with Boston slum kids "who cussed and fought and made fun of [Arnie] because he didn't know how to play the dozens," the camp is a harsh reminder that the Pembertons' niceness has as effectively distanced Arnie from the black world as from the white.

"Poor Little Black Fellow" is, on one level, Hughes' allegory of certain white American pseudoliberal attitudes towards black America. Offered passage on the pleasure boat, albeit second class accommodations, black Americans are considered ungrateful by their white benefactors when they refuse pity and demand selfhood. The Pembertons' real face appears in all its ugliness when Arnie pursues a reciprocal relationship with a young Romanian woman whom he meets in Paris; provoked by fury at Arnie's declaration of independence, Mr. Pemberton refers to his ward as "this nigger." Rejecting both his white "parents" and America itself at the end of his story, Arnie elects to remain in

Europe where the color line is blurred and it is "only hard to be poor" (153). A stranger in the country for which his father died, Arnie willingly forfeits the Pembertons' Christian patronage for a situation in which "Somebody had offered him something without charity, without condescension, without prayer, without distance, and without being nice" (146).

"Mother and Child" provides an ironic reversal of Arnie's situation when the "Christians" become the colored ladies of the Salvation Rock Missionary Society for the Rescue o' the African Heathen and the child is the offspring of a young black man and a married white woman. In most of his stories Hughes is careful to present at least one sympathetic white character. In **"Mother and Child"** he goes a step further to create a group of black women who are every bit as narrow and self-righteous as their white, middle-class counterparts in **"Poor Little Black Fellow."**[8] Though they profess a concern for African "heathens," their interest is more in gossip than grace. The title of the story reflects the centrality of children to the Christian myth, but the tenderness and compassion evoked by the figure of the mother and child are reduced by voices speaking in their own dialect to a "Mighty funny kind o' love" (194). Because it is biracial, a child is rejected by both black and white worlds. Effacing any narrator, Hughes responds to the gossips' assumption that "Everybody knows can't no good come out o' white and colored love" through one of the ladies at the very end of the piece (194). Drowned out by the other voices raised simultaneously in a hymn of praise for Jesus' benevolence and in a lament for the "mess" caused by the birth of a child, a single voice asks "Why don't you all say poor Douglass? Poor white woman? Poor child?" (196).

In despair of persuading adults, black or white, to acknowledge the beauty of black folk culture much less the ugliness inherent in contemporary race relations, Hughes turned away from adult fiction in the 1930s and began writing books for children who, he felt, had not yet absorbed the prejudice of their parents. He composed *Popo and Fifina* in 1932, two years before the publication of *The Ways of White Folks,* after which he wrote or coauthored five children's books. His increasing realization that children possess an unconscious racial tolerance not found among adults is apparent in two selections from *The Ways of White Folks*—**"Berry"** and **"One Christmas Eve."**

Making skillful use of the eiron in the mild voice of Milberry ("Berry") Jones, Hughes describes the "gyp game" perpetuated by white adults at the expense of white children attending Dr. Renfield's Summer Home for Crippled Children. Hired for less pay to replace the Scandinavian kitchen boy, Berry immediately becomes a "problem" for Mrs. Osborn, the camp's supervisor, who is concerned about whether a colored boy will fit

in at the Home and about where he will sleep. Although he is treated as "a work horse, a fool—and a nigger," quickly overburdened with other people's chores and assigned the more unpleasant tasks, Berry accepts his lot with uncomplaining good nature (181). However, he instinctively perceives the hypocrisy and greed of these adults posing as caretakers of broken children. He wonders about the doctor with the "movie beard," Mrs. Osborn's "grand manner" with everybody but the doctor for whom she has "eyes," and the cranky nurses complaining about the "bratty" kids and the food, admittedly inferior unless some parent or visitor is about. Oblivious to any barriers of color, young Berry attempts to counter their neglect of the children with affection and play. Though jobs are scarce and hunger abundant, he worries about the phoniness of the place, thinking he "wouldn't even stay there and work if it wasn't for the kids" (183). The children respond instinctively in kind, completely unconcerned about the color of Berry's skin.

Despite his industry and the children's love for him, the youngster loses his job, a ready scapegoat when a child falls from his wheelchair through little or no fault on Berry's part. With a white world that cripples children and a black savior sacrificed because of his Christian love, the story becomes, as Miller contends, an example of "Judeo-Christian tragedy rooted in the sociohistory of Black America during the mid-1930s" (103). Its conclusion is neither truly tragic nor resolved comically. Never seen by the white adults for his humanity, Berry illustrates the possibility of transforming potential tragedy into comedy with the restorative power of storytelling. Associated with sunshine as opposed to the bleak rain of the corrupted white adults, Berry extends messianic overtones to a story which illustrates the incompatibility of the love by and of children with racial intolerance.

"One Christmas Eve" poignantly contrasts the meaning of the holiday typifying Christian love and hope as the birth of a child for black as opposed to white children. Opening with the laughter and excitement of a white woman and her children returning home late to dinner after last-minute Christmas shopping, the story focuses on their maid, Arcie, whose limited plans for her own son's Christmas are jeopardized by the inconsiderate tardiness of her employer as well as her promised payment. Rushing out into the snow after washing the supper dishes, Arcie collects little Joe at their roominghouse to take him downtown to see the Christmas decorations and purchase a few small gifts. Though he asks, as children will, for everything he sees, Joe wants most to experience Christmas by seeing Santa Claus.

Left outside the store while his mother shops, Joe wanders back to a movie theater for whites only. At this point in the story, the voice shifts to that of the child struck with wonder at the presence of Santa Claus giving away gifts to the white children in the lobby of the theater. So overcome that he rushes right up to the man, Joe is frightened when Santa, amused by the pickaninny, shakes a rattle fiercely in his face and laughs with the rest of the crowd at his startled reaction.

Slamming white hypocrisy through the behavior of its secular symbol of Christmas, Hughes also defines Santa Claus as the figure of the northern philanthropist. Several poems in *Ask Your Mama* depict Santa Claus as a liberal benefactor to blacks as well as whites, a nice fellow—except that he has no gifts for the children of the welfare poor. Welcoming only a token participation which allows blacks no real share of the power, Santa offers no protection at all from the harshness of ghetto life.⁹ Hughes is not only able to suggest in his vignette the isolation of the poor black child from the privileges associated with Christmas, presenting Joe as surrounded, like Bigger Thomas, with "too many people, all white people, moving like white shadows in the snow, a world of white people" (206). He also reinforces the innocence of children to the ways of prejudice. Little Joe is not to be in the white folks' movie, and he receives his first instruction in such racial discrimination from Santa Claus.

"Father and Son," the last and longest selection from *The Ways of White Folks,* serves a dual purpose in the collection. Containing all of Hughes' ideas about American race relations as typified in attitudes towards children, it incorporates the naturalness of a mother's love for her child, the problems of white patronage and the status of "boy" for young black men, white sexual repression and miscegenation, the hypocrisy of middle-class Christians, and the unconscious racial tolerance of illustrations of white control over blacks in the form of a call for revolution.

Echoing **"Cora Unashamed," "Father and Son"** reintroduces a strong, nurturing woman named Cora, whose child will be sacrificed to the social constraints of the white world. However, the focus shifts in this story from the nobility of the black mother who values the lives of her daughters, regardless of their color, to the ignominy of the white father who brings death to his biracial sons. Abandoning the eiron's childlike voice for a forceful, omniscient narrator, Hughes becomes a more directive commentator of a thinly veiled political allegory. His presentation of the generically-named "Big House Plantation" and its inhabitants allows them to function as historical archetypes, models of America's racial past and present.

The text of **"Father and Son"** revolves around the homecoming of Bert, the twenty-year-old son of Colonel Tom Norwood, a white plantation owner, and Cora-lee Lewis, his black housekeeper. The conflict arises when Bert expects to be treated like the well-educated

man he is and refuses to be a "white folks' nigger" (221). Bert's pride and his father's obstinacy lead to patricide, Cora's mental breakdown, Bert's suicide, and the lynching of both Bert's dead body and the live body of his brother Willie—the perfect "white folks' nigger."

Hughes uses plantation mythology in the story to construct an allegorical subtext as valid in 1930 as 1830, suggesting that the position of black Americans did not change significantly with Emancipation. This subtext allies the white world with the patriarch whose control is reflected in the hierarchy of Big House Plantation. Colonel Tom is the type of the white slaveowner, oppressor, and defender of the status quo. The black world is associated with the plantation concubine, mother to generations of African-Americans, whose strength is derived from her abilities to nurture, sustain, and endure but is ultimately contained by the white male. Although Cora is technically not a slave, she has been Colonel Tom's mistress for thirty years, and her economic dependence upon him makes him her master. Caught between the two worlds, the black male is rendered impotent, without the nurturing power of the black female nor the political and economic authority of the white male. Hughes offers us the two options open to such men. Willie chooses to remain a "white folks' nigger," and Bert speaks for revolution.

As offspring of the white Everyman and the black Everywoman, Willie and Bert are products of American history. Like his parents, Willie succumbs to the plantation structure; relegated by his white father to the life of a "black boy" outside the Big House, he appears stupid, obedient, and fearful of Colonel Tom. Bert, on the other hand, is "the most beautiful of the lot, the brightest and the badest of the Colonel's five children, lording it over the other children, and sassing not only his colored mother, but his white father, as well" (208). Described as "ivory" or "yellow" with a temperament like his father's, Bert is undeniably drawn to and in conflict with both white and black worlds. While the other characters remain almost suspended in plantation time, Bert exists very much in the twentieth century. Happier away at school, he is associated with travel, motion, and change. He arrives at the plantation on a train and frequently drives the "new Ford" Colonel Tom himself almost never uses. In historical terms, Bert represents the "Negro problem" of Hughes' generation. Created by the white father, patronized but denied patrimony, the son grows up to demand his birthright. In the larger context, Bert is the modern African-American demanding his rights from a society that claims to be democratic but functions on established racist values.

Hughes presents Bert as an agent of revolutionary change, a topic that colleagues like Ellison and Baraka accused him of avoiding and one that has been neglected in his scholarship. Editing his "Uncollected Social Protest Writings," many of which were published in left-wing journals and never anthologized, Faith Berry comments that Hughes was responding not only to the disillusionment with capitalism common among artists of the 1930s but also to his travels to Russia, China, and Spain (xxii). Consistent with his outspoken work of this period, Hughes' narrator directly addresses the reader in section V of **"Father and Son"** to create a powerful metaphor of social upheaval. Bert becomes the "certain liquid" or "certain powder" that causes the community to explode (227). Hughes' image of the community as a "test tube" reinforces the pervasiveness of Bert's ideas; like a solution in a crucible, the community is converted into something completely different when Bert is added to it: "Oh, test tube of life! Crucible of the South, find the right powder and you'll never be the same again . . ." (228).

The ending of the story illustrates Hughes' vision of the dynamics of social revolution. The right catalyst forces black people to confront the injustice and indignity of their situation and facilitates the bewildering possibility of not being a "white folks' nigger." Challenged, those in power move to reassert it. White people resort to their old control tactics of fear and religious revivals only to find them insufficient. Despite or perhaps because of their relationship, even their attraction, to each other, white father and black son will finally shake hands like "steel meeting steel" when the son refuses to be a child any longer (229). Briefly removing his eiron's mask in **"Father and Son,"** Hughes reveals his fury at American whites' treatment of blacks as children, the blatant or subtle ways that white folks have maintained power. Unlike Alexander or Christ or Lenin, Bert dies anonymously in the cause of change, one more black boy shown his place in the social order. However, Hughes' tone is ominous at the conclusion of ***The Ways of White Folks.*** Black mothers will desert the white father to support their sons' fight for independence, even if it means they must make a place for them to die. And when the white father refuses to acknowledge his black sons, he, too, will die and will leave no legacy.

Notes

1. In his pioneering study, James Emanuel compares Hughes' unanalyzed powers as a short story writer with his known competence as a poet and assesses the published observations of the stories as "generally mediocre, sometimes observant, and here and there briefly penetrating" (Hughes 55, 172). Donald Dickinson notes in his 1972 bio-bibliography that, aside from Emanuel's unpublished dissertation on the short stories and several brief articles in *Phylon,* no scholarly studies are available in English (4-5). R. Baxter Miller's 1989 book confesses that "even the ablest scholars have ignored the secrets of [Hughes' practice and theory" (6).

2. While Hughes is mentioned in several commentaries on black achievement written by black authors during the height of his career, no discussion of his work can be found in such basic sources of the same period as Alfred Kazin, *On Native Grounds* (1942); Robert Spiller, et al., *The Literary History of the United States* (1948); Arthur Quinn, *The Literature of the American People* (1951).

3. I have located only two articles on *The Ways of White Folks* in the PMLA since 1963.

4. While more recent scholars such as David Levering Lewis and Houston A. Baker, Jr. disagree with Huggins when he cites provinciality and narrowness as causes for a failed Harlem Renaissance, neither focuses on a serious reassessment of Hughes' work.

5. Reviewer Babette Deutsche failed to see the eiron in the fool's mask when she suggested that Hughes' writing suffered too much from "a kind of cultivated naivete" (Lee 204). Recordings of Hughes' voice reading poetry and in commentary effectively illustrate that his eiron's mask fits so well as to be mistaken for his face.

6. Charney's theories of the eiron and comedy might well be applied to African-American socio-literary traditions of narrative and comedy as they are manipulated to create personae and to subvert. Hughes' eiron's voice finds close relatives in Charles Chesnutt's old storyteller (*The Conjure Woman*), Paul Laurence Dunbar's "mask," Zora Neale Hurston's folk voices, and Toni Morrison's revisionary myths.

7. Nathaniel Hawthorne describes a similar rejection of innocence for experience in "My Kinsman, Major Molineux" when the childlike Robin must participate in violence against the father figure to declare himself a man. This story can also be read on a symbolic level as an allegory of revolution, in this case of pre-revolutionary America declaring its independence from England.

8. Hughes' explicit depictions of both narrow-minded blacks and the gross hypocrisy of white patronage place him ahead of his time, prefiguring works such as Toni Morrison's *Tar Baby.* His prescience might further explain the general critical devaluing of his short fictions.

9. See "Ode to Dinah" (28) and "Ride, Red, Ride" (14-15).

Works Cited

Baker, Jr., Houston A. *Modernism and the Harlem Renaissance.* Chicago: U of Chicago P, 1987.

Charney, Maurice. *Comedy High and Low: An Introduction to the Experience of Comedy.* New York: Oxford UP, 1978.

Dickinson, Donald C. *A Bio-bibliography of Langston Hughes.* Rev. 2nd ed. Hamden, Ct.: Archon, 1972.

Emanuel, James. *Langston Hughes.* New York: Twayne, 1967.

Emanuel, James. "The Short Fiction of Langston Hughes." *Langston Hughes: Black Genius.* Ed. Therman B. O'Daniel.

Huggins, Nathan Irvin. *Harlem Renaissance.* New York: Oxford UP, 1971.

Hughes, Langston. *Ask Your Mama.* New York: Knopf, 1969.

Hughes, Langston. *Good Morning Revolution.* Ed. Faith Berry. New York: Lawrence Hill, 1973.

Hughes, Langston. *The Ways of White Folks.* New York: Knopf, 1933. New York: Vintage, 1990.

Jemie, Onwuchekwa. *Langston Hughes: An Introduction to the Poetry.* New York: Columbia UP, 1973.

Lee, A. Robert. "'Ask Your Mama': Langston Hughes, the Blues and Recent Afro-American Literary Studies." *Journal of American Studies* 24 (1990): 199-209.

Lewis, David Levering. *When Harlem Was In Vogue.* New York: Oxford UP, 1979.

Miller, R. Baxter. *The Art and Imagination of Langston Hughes.* Lexington: UP of Kentucky, 1989.

Nifong, David Michael. "Narrative Technique and Theory in *The Ways of White Folks.*" *Black American Literature Forum* 15.2 (1981): 93-96.

Rampersad, Arnold. *The Life of Langston Hughes.* 2 vols. New York: Oxford UP, 1986-88.

Joyce Ann Joyce (essay date 1995)

SOURCE: Joyce, Joyce Ann. "Race, Culture, and Gender in Langston Hughes's *The Ways of White Folks.*" In *Langston Hughes: The Man, His Art, and His Continuing Influence,* edited by C. James Trotman, pp. 99-107. New York: Garland Publishing, Inc., 1995.

[*In the following essay, Joyce analyzes the black female characters in "Cora Unashamed," "The Blues I'm Playing," and "Father and Son" in terms of Hughes's commentary on racial and gender relations.*]

Set in Iowa, New York, New Jersey, the Florida coast, New England, Ohio, Chicago, and Georgia, Langston Hughes's *The Ways of White Folks* emerges as a collection of satirical short stories that gives a comprehensive glimpse of the various manifestations of race relations throughout the United States and within all the different class strata of white society. Cited in Volume I of Arnold Rampersad's *The Life of Langston Hughes,* some of the reviews of the collection demonstrate the highly mixed reactions of white readers to any black literature that acutely depicts white hypocrisy, corruption, or insensitivity. While Herschel Brickell in the *North American Review* commented that the collection represented "some of the best stories that have appeared in this country in years" (290), and Horace Gregory asserted that the stories revealed a "spiritual prose style and an accurate understanding of human character" (290), Sherwood Anderson, on the other hand, wrote, in the *Nation,* "My hat is off to you in relation to your own race" (290). Anderson, according to Rampersad, thought that the whites in Hughes's collection were caricatures. "And Martha Gruening, a prominent white liberal, deplored the fact that [Hughes] saw whites as either sordid and cruel, or silly and sentimental" (290).

Both the negative and highly positive reviews testify to the breadth and depth of Hughes's collection. The fourteen stories that make up *The Ways of White Folks* explore the psychological depth of the multileveled behavioral codes that govern the interaction between blacks and whites and that describe the inferiority/superiority paradigm that makes up white consciousness. The reaction of white readers and critics attests to the degree to which the title of the collection draws attention away from Hughes's black characters, whose purpose is to illuminate "the ways of white folk." Because the artistry of Hughes's stories differs greatly from Richard Wright's—particularly in tone and mood—we do not quickly see the similarity between Hughes's and Wright's depiction of racism. Although *The Ways of White Folks* is satirically humorous and progresses through the beautiful merger of prose and poetry, it, too, like much of Wright's naturalistic fiction, reveals a world in which whites do not understand their behavior, in which they are not in touch with themselves, and, thus, in which they are both physically dangerous to blacks and psychologically dangerous to themselves and to blacks.

While Wright's *Uncle Tom's Children,* published five years after Hughes's collection, features two black women protagonists only (Sarah in "Long Black Song" and Aunt Sue in "Bright and Morning Star"), Hughes's *The Ways of White Folks* presents numerous black and white women characters, demonstrating the integral role white women play in propagating social and moral racial codes that affect the lives of both black women and men. In fact, a black or a white woman is either the protagonist or a pivotal character in every story in *The Ways of White Folks.*

In describing the multifaceted manifestations of racism found among all classes of whites across the United States, *The Ways of White Folks* emerges as an ingenious analysis of the interrelationship between race, class, and gender. *Racism*, interestingly enough, is a cultural and political phenomenon rooted in the merger of the concepts of race and culture. Whereas *race* denotes a "local geographic or global human population distinguished as a more or less distinct group by genetically transmitted physical characteristics" or a "group of people united or classified together on the basis of common history, nationality, or geographical distribution" (*American Heritage Dictionary*, 1020), *culture* refers to "the totality of socially transmitted behavior patterns, arts, beliefs, institutions, and all other products of human work and thought characteristic of a community or population" (*American Heritage Dictionary*, 348). *Racism*, then, signifies the merger of race and culture. In *The Ways of White Folks*, Langston Hughes adroitly demonstrates how white people with a common history and shared physical characteristics stifle their own lives and those of the blacks around them by continuing the legacy of behavioral patterns and beliefs that propagate their self-hatred, their hypocrisy, and their insensitivity and the paradox of inferiority/superiority that describes their interaction with blacks.

What is perhaps most striking about *The Ways of White Folks* is both the amount of space Hughes gives to women characters and his depiction of how racism and class have affected their lives. Despite Hughes's lack of any mention of his sexual life in *The Big Sea* and in *I Wonder as I Wander*, despite the confusing critical discussions about his alleged homosexuality, and despite his condescending, perhaps even sexist comment "Girls are funny creatures" in reference to Zora Neale Hurston in *The Big Sea*, his characterizations of both black and white women in *The Ways of White Folks* reveal a profound mind artistically capable of identifying with the intricacies of female consciousness and of censuring female participation in the cultural behavioral patterns that stifle their humanity. Even though all of the fourteen stories in the collection contain female characters, both black and white, and though eleven of the stories feature black women characters, it is interesting that three of the most powerful and moving stories in the collection have black women as major characters. It is through the experiences of these black women that we can clearly view "the ways of white folk."

Of the fourteen stories, **"Father and Son," "Cora Unashamed,"** and **"The Blues I'm Playing"** emerge as those with the most sustained treatment of black female characters. **"Cora Unashamed"** and **"Father and Son,"** appropriately begin and end the collection. Despite the fact that Hughes titles the collection *The Ways of White Folks*, he begins and ends the book with black women characters who are strikingly different from each other and who serve as points of reference for the female characters in the other stories. Except for Oceola in **"The Blues I'm Playing,"** all the other black women characters lack the dignity and wisdom of Cora in **"Cora**

Unashamed" and struggle to overcome Cora's poverty as well as Coralee Lewis's entrapment in **"Father and Son."**

While Cora of **"Cora Unashamed,"** the protagonist of the first story, is self-assured, courageous, loving, and wise, Coralee Lewis, the mother figure in **"Father and Son,"** is disappointingly weak, and her failure to censure her white lover/master before his death results in his death as well as the death of her two sons. Though Cora represents a traditional depiction of the black woman, Coralee emerges as a rather strikingly nontraditional, equally as convincing portrait of the black woman before and after slavery. During slavery, Coralee is just a young girl on the then young Colonel Norwood's plantation. He marries a young woman from whom he becomes isolated, and the slaves begin to gossip because Norwood and his young wife fail to have children. Norwood, like John Dutton in Margaret Walker's *Jubilee*, goes to the slave quarters to have his sexual desires fulfilled by Livonia, who also has four black lovers because she loves to love. Coralee's reaction to talk of Livonia's affair with Norwood clearly suggests that some black women during slavery welcomed a sexual union with their masters: "Cora heard all this and in her mind a certain envy sprang up. Livonia! Huh! Cora began to look more carefully into the cracked mirror in her mother's cabin. She combed her hair and oiled it better than before. She was seventeen then" (208). When Cora took milk to the Big House after this, "she tried to look her best" (208). Later during a party at the Big House, Coralee takes a walk out in the woods near the house. Young Norwood, who is restless, takes a walk and ends up near Coralee, sitting under a huge oak tree. Norwood approaches her, asks who she is, takes her face in his hands, and has sex with her.

It is not appropriate to say that he seduces her. For Coralee clearly desired Norwood long before he knew of her existence. When Coralee is pregnant with her first child, she tells her mother of her situation. Her mother's response suggests the black woman's dilemma before and after slavery. Coralee's mother says, "It's better'n slavin' in the cotton fields. . . . I's known colored women what's wore silk dresses and lived like queens on plantations right here in Georgy . . ." (210). Although Coralee's actions and her mother's attitude are not characteristic of all African American women during and after slavery, they do suggest the attitude and behavior of some black women, those women who fell prey to the conditions of their environment.

Hughes, however, goes further than to demonstrate that all slave women were not repulsed by the sexual advances of their masters. He also shows the price they and their offspring paid for this sexual union. After Bert, one of Coralee and the Colonel's four children, shoots the Colonel, he then shoots himself in order not to be lynched by the mob that pursues him. As a result of all the trauma, Coralee retreats inside herself and goes mad. The lynch mob not only lynches Bert, but his brother Willie, too. Willie had always acted humbly in order not to antagonize whites. Set during early Reconstruction, **"Father and Son"** dramatizes the complexity of the black woman's history. For as a young slave woman, Coralee has no dreams of a life outside the plantation. A sexual liaison with the slave master opens up opportunities that allow for a specious level of comfort. Thus, after slavery Coralee is able to convince Norwood to send her four children away to school, yet she and those of her children who returned to the plantation never moved beyond the status of slaves in Colonel Norwood's perception and treatment of them. Coralee completely acquiesces to his racism and attempts to instill her fears and cowardice into her offspring.

Even though Colonel Norwood and his son Bert are the two main characters as suggested by the title of the short story, Coralee's situation helps us appreciate the depth of the Colonel's racism and the inexorable cultural taboos that prevent him from marrying her and accepting her offspring as his own.

Quite unlike Coralee, Cora, the central character of **"Cora Unashamed,"** challenges white society in very different ways. Despite the fact that Cora's financial situation and her home environment are as wretched as Coralee's, on some level Cora realizes that she can make choices about how she lives her life. Cora's brothers have deserted the family leaving Cora to take care of an ailing mother and an alcoholic father.

Hughes dramatizes Cora's self-assurance and her courage by contrasting her with the wealthy Studevant women for whom she works as a domestic in a small, rural town in Iowa, 150 miles from Sioux City. While the Studevant women are hypocritical, elitist, and insensitive, Cora is humble, strong, and generous, particularly with her sincere love for people. Cora and Mrs. Studevant give birth, around the same time, to daughters, both of whom Cora nurses. After Cora's baby dies, she devotes all of her attention and love to Jessie, the Studevant child, who is seriously neglected by her mother and the rest of her family. When Jessie becomes pregnant, she seeks comfort in Cora, who tells Mrs. Studevant of her daughter's pregnancy. Mrs. Studevant first faints and later collects herself enough to tell the town that she and Jessie are going on a shopping trip to Kansas City, where they actually go for an abortion.

Jessie returns from the trip a different person. And her death is due more to a broken heart over the loss of her child than from any surgical complications. Hughes uses natural imagery to suggest Jessie's and Cora's wholesomeness as opposed to the narrow-mindedness

and unnaturalness of Mrs. Studevant, her mother, and her older daughter. When we first meet Cora, the narrator explains that she was "like a tree—once rooted, she stood, in spite of storms and strife, wind, and rocks in the earth" (3-4). And when there is a discussion about Jessie's going away to normal school after high school, the tree again represents Cora's stability, strength, and her natural ability to love: "Cora hated to think about her going away. In her heart she had adopted Jessie. In that big and careless household it was always Cora who stood like a calm and sheltering tree for Jessie to run to in her troubles" (9). Natural imagery also suggests the difference between Jessie's and Cora's wholesome attitude toward love-making and pregnancy and the Studevants' attitude. The narrator describes Cora's thoughts as she thinks of Jessie: "Then Spring came in full bloom, and the fields and orchards at the edge of Melton stretched green and beautiful to the far horizon. Cora remembered her own Spring, twenty years ago, and a great sympathy and pain welled up in her heart for Jessie, who was the same age that Josephine would have been, had she lived" (13).

A moving portrayal of the interrelationship between race, culture, and gender, **"Cora Unashamed"** dramatizes how the Studevant women's elitism and insensitivity cause them to ignore Jessie's needs and motivate their attempt to instill their cultural values in Jessie. And just as it is forbidden for a young, unmarried woman of their class and race to become pregnant outside of wedlock, it is equally forbidden for the Studevants, like Colonel Norwood, to consider Cora, a black woman, a human being even though she nurses their child and is responsible for the full care of their home.

The Studevants are not as wealthy as the Mrs. Dora Ellsworth of **"The Blues I'm Playing."** When Mrs. Ellsworth discovers Oceola Jones, a young black woman violinist, she is enthralled with Oceola's blackness as much as she is with Oceola's musical skill. Mrs. Ellsworth appoints herself as Oceola's patron and attempts to control Oceola's life. When she learns that Oceola does not charge rent to her lover/boarder, Mrs. Ellsworth assumes that Pete Williams, a Pullman porter, saving money for medical school, is exploiting Oceola. Having always had the many comforts that money can buy, Mrs. Ellsworth denies herself an emotional life and is thus incapable of understanding or appreciating Oceola's relationship with Pete. Mrs. Ellsworth is a voyeur who lives vicariously through the lives of those she patronizes, though she needs to control them in order to do so. Because she is racist and elitist, she attempts to lure Oceola away from Pete by taking her to Paris and convincing her to move away from Harlem, where she frequently plays for churches and at parties.

Mrs. Ellsworth, however, is unsuccessful in destroying or even penetrating the core of Oceola's love for herself, for Pete, for black people, and for black culture.

Oceola informs Mrs. Ellsworth that she and Pete are going to get married and invites Mrs. Ellsworth to the wedding. But Mrs. Ellsworth informs them that, although she will be unable to attend, she will send a nice gift. It seems that she must go to Florence to meet her new young protégé, "a charming white-haired boy from Omaha whose soul has been crushed in the West" (117). But Mrs. Ellsworth believes herself to be superior to Oceola and the latest protégé. Rather than seeing them as human beings, she unknowingly treats them as objects to comfort her in her loneliness. Yet, Oceola, like Cora in **"Cora Unashamed,"** is not ashamed of her emotional life or her culture. She uses her music to celebrate life rather than to avoid it.

In **"The Blues I'm Playing,"** Langston Hughes displays his deep knowledge of music and the arts in both the African American and Euro-American traditions. But his love of black music, well illustrated at the end of **"The Blues I'm Playing,"** suggests that Hughes is not just writing short stories so that white people can read about themselves; he also writes to pay tribute to the lives of the many "ladies' maids and truck drivers, laundry workers and shoe shine boys, seamstresses and porters" (*Big Sea*, 233) that he met at rent parties in Harlem and on Seventh Street in Washington, D.C. Oceola's playing a blues song at the end of the novel and Mrs. Ellsworth's preference to stand and look at the stars rather than sing of love nicely contrasts Hughes's idea of art with the Euro-centric notion of "art for art's sake." His portraits of black women like Cora, Coralee, and Oceola underscore the reason why Hughes is one of the few black writers read continuously by a large number of blacks in the underclass. They recognize that he is writing to them as much as about them. And the attention he gives to black women in *The Ways of White Folks* reveals Hughes's understanding that the African American woman is the chord that unites the historical triad of race, culture, and gender.

Works Cited

"Culture." *The American Heritage Dictionary of the English Language.* Boston: Houghton Mifflin, 1971.

Hughes, Langston. *The Big Sea.* 1940. Rpt. New York: Hill & Wang, 1963.

———. *The Ways of White Folks.* 1934. Rpt. New York: Vintage Books, 1971.

"Race." *The American Heritage Dictionary of the English Language.* Boston: Houghton Mifflin, 1971.

Rampersad, Arnold. *The Life of Langston Hughes: Volume I: 1902-1941: I, Too, Sing America.* New York: Oxford University Press, 1986.

R. Baxter Miller (essay date 1995)

SOURCE: Miller, R. Baxter. "The Physics of Change in 'Father and Son.'" In *Langston Hughes: The Man, His Art, and His Continuing Influence,* edited by C. James Trotman, pp. 131-40. New York: Garland Publishing, Inc., 1995.

[In the following essay, Miller explores subtexts of physics and illuminates references to historical personages in "Father and Son."]

> What happens to a dream deferred?
> Does it dry up
> like a raisin in the sun?
> Or fester like a sore—
> And then run?
> Does it stink like rotten meat?
>   . . . . .
> Maybe it just sags
> like a heavy load.
> *Or does it explode?*[2]

Langston Hughes, probably the most brilliant poet of African American dreams, voices curiosity about the physical world. Riddled with decay and stench, the world contains an almost magical mystique of purpose. At times the qualities seem to defy even the certain principles of gravity. For physics has seemed to be the science of energy and of the relation of it to matter, though the definition is imperfect. To understand energy would mean to have a command of all physics as well. The science of energy, in the most complete sense, includes all science. Natural philosophy, the earlier name for physics, once included a greater range of other sciences. But eventually they became specialized as chemistry, metallurgy, astronomy, meteorology, and geology. Since about 1870 physics has become narrowed to the current scope, though the process of disciplinary separation continues. Certain areas of physics, for example, developed during the construction of the nuclear bomb during World War II. Soon afterward they began to divide off into an independent branch of nuclear engineering designed to produce nuclear power. Nevertheless, the interconnections between physics and other sciences are so intimate that it is impossible ever to separate them completely. And, in tracing the denotation of the word *physic* through Middle English back to Latin, we discover that *physic* signifies not only natural science but the healing art of medicine as well. I propose that **"Father and Son,"** the concluding story of *Ways of White Folks* (1934), enacts a physics of genius. The quality is the creative principle that enters human history in order to transform it. While this genius is indeed a form of energy, it is energy *willed*. Sometimes its form is liquid, like the blood of violent history and murder that flows. But more important, genius has the characteristic of an artistic self-consciousness that determines its flow. Genius, in this instance, is a biological and creative compulsion to speak across empty spaces and provoke our forebears to answer inquiries about our belonging and our destiny. **"Father and Son"** is really about the nice complements of figurative and literal change in the world. The fiction depicts the way that the debate over the change by father and son explores which one of the two will indeed control the physical properties of language and, hence, the definitions of humanity.

At the risk of an overly biographical reading, Hughes's life provides a few clues to the persistent recurrence of physics in his subtexts. First of all, his father had insisted during the early twenties that the younger Hughes, then a carefree student at Columbia University, become an engineer.[3] Indeed, the poet would eventually write out vicariously the father's demand for him to be a kind of scientist. Perhaps Langston Hughes, the son, was always answering James Hughes, the father. The poet was proposing that he was, as his kind, the unacknowledged legislator of the world.

Second, the graduation by Langston Hughes from Lincoln University in 1929 had so brilliantly lyricized the distinction between the physical and spiritual realms. For a senior survey Hughes had researched the way that most black students at Lincoln had preferred to be taught by white professors. A famous old graduate of the institution, while objecting to the nakedness of the factual presentation, had cautioned: "You don't get things out of white folks that way" (310). When the poet had dissented, the elder had asserted that the writer would eventually understand once he was "out of college awhile." The predecessor "crosses" the landscape, the mirror image of the poet's own torment, just as the dreamer faces the physical world. Having never contemplated the demands for compromise, the writer wonders: "For bread how much of the spirit must one give away?" (310). The autobiographer searches for answers through the signs of nineteenth-century abolitionism: "I began to think back to Nat Turner, Harriet Tubman, Sojourner Truth, John Brown, Fred Douglass—*folks* [my italics] who left no *buildings* behind them—only a *wind of words* fanning *the bright flame of the spirit* down the *dark lanes of time*" (310).

Bert Lewis, the mulatto son of Colonel Thomas Norwood and Cora Lewis, a black sharecropper, returns home in **"Father and Son"** for the summer from the Institute, a run-down boarding school for blacks during the early thirties.[4] When the protagonist was a young boy, the Colonel had made a habit of physically abusing him, often knocking the son beneath the feet of horses on the grounds. The son grows up to violate the manners and customs prescribed for blacks, hence disrupting the established place for them within the hierarchy of power. His father forbids him to go back to school in Atlanta after the summer recess. During a brief encounter in the local post office, a clerk gives Bert twelve cents of change, too little for the purchase of eight three-cent stamps. Bert objects to the mistake on her part, prompting a hostile reaction by whites in the town. Mr. Higgins, a friend of the Colonel, phones the plantation to report the presumably disgusting expression of self-determination by Bert. In the following confrontation at home, Bert strangles his white father and shoots himself at night before a mob can lynch him. But the vigilantes, deprived of their pleasure, string up Willie Lewis, Bert's older brother by eight years.[5] Ironically, the Colonel leaves "no heirs" because all of his illegitimate offspring are black.

To read more deeply, "Bert arrives, at once the most beautiful . . . brightest . . . and badest son." The Colonel retreats to the library (knowledge, writing) to consult with books of both a "literary" and "business" nature. Through three different viewpoints of consciousness (by Colonel, Bert, and Cora) we hear the echoed child abuse of the father who knocked the son beneath the feet of the horses, emblems of id and masculine power. We see the greeting of the father by the son at evening, the time of the setting sun, in a diurnal foreshadowing of death. Hence, the fiction presents specifically the end for Bert, the son of Norwood, and universally the Son of Man. What makes for the skillful structure is first the prophesy of change by the lyrical narrator and then the coming of change in the form of the disowned son. One subplot takes up the process of explosive change—exciting leaps forward in the experimentation of the imagination—and a complementary subplot confines itself to a rather furious debate about money. The hidden evil in the story is capitalistic greed.

The physics of change voices itself against the silent enemy. The moment of prophecy achieves the majestic grandeur of great elegy while the storyteller celebrates those geniuses who energize the world. When they have passed from history, "You feel sick and lonesome and meaningless." Though the teller prepares his reader for the subsequent narrative about a sharecropper's son, the type implies the tragic poet. The rhetorical question, punctuated by parallelism, slows the directness:

> In the chemistry lab at school, did you ever hold a test tube, pouring in liquids and powders and seeing nothing happen until a *certain* powder is poured in and then everything begins to smoke and fume, bubble and boil, hiss to foam, and sometimes even explode? The tube is suddenly full of action and movement and life. Well, there are people like those certain liquids or powders; at a given moment they come into a room, into a town, even a country—and the place is never the same again. Things bubble, boil, change. Sometimes the whole world is changed. Alexander came. Christ. Marconi. A Russian, named Lenin.
>
> (220)

Experimentation, in other words, must derive imaginatively from a flowing concept of life. The revolutionary or artist of bold innovation, like Bert Lewis, instigates change in the social world, just as a true catalyst sparks transformation in a scientific experiment.

In a way, indeed, each of Hughes's four references was a physicist. Alexander the Great (356 B.C.), king of Macedon (now northeast Greece, southeast Yugoslavia, and southwest Bulgaria), was probably the greatest general of ancient times. By the time he was thirty-two, he had founded an empire ranging from India to the Adriatic Sea. Born the son of King Philip II and Olympia, an Epirote princess, he had a magnetic personality. He was intensely willful and mystical in thought as well as in practical action. A student of Aristotle, he pursued scientific investigations, and he doctored the sick. He looked forward to Jesus Christ, the second figure of the Christian Trinity of God the Father, God the Son, and God the Holy Spirit. Marchese Guglielmo Marconi (b. Bologna, Italy, April 25, 1874; d. Rome, July 20, 1937) refers to the specialization of physics more directly. As the son of Giuseppe Marconi, a successful businessman (as was James Hughes, Langston's father), and Annie Jameson, the youngest daughter of Andrew Jameson of Ireland, Marchese studied at home during his early years. Later at Leghorn, Italy, he deliberated about physics under the direction of Professor Vencenzo Rosa. Marconi also met with Professor Augusto Righi who was, at the University of Bologna, a pioneer in the research of electromagnetic waves.

Though Marconi was never officially a student at any university, in 1894 he browsed a journal containing an article about experiments by Heinrich Hertz on electronic waves. Inspired to try Hertzian concepts for the purposes of communication, Marconi returned home to Pontecchio to test his theory. During several months in 1895 (the year of Booker T. Washington's speech of racial accommodation in Atlanta, Georgia), Marconi completed his apparatus, transmitting signals through the air from one end of his house to the other. Then he did the same again from the house to the garden. Marconi, who in 1909 would share the Nobel Prize for Physics with Ferdinand Braun of Germany, helped usher in the age of wireless telegraphy. He was, in other words, the founder of radio, and he prophesied the emergence of television.

Whatever the differences, each of the four men had a quality of genius. Vladimir Ilich Lenin (b. Simrisk [now Ulyanovsk] Russia, April 22, 1870; d. Gorki, near Moscow, January 21, 1924), for example, had been the Russian thinker whose activities had proved instrumental in the revolution of 1917. While Lenin was a less talented writer and speaker than was his colleague, Leon Trotsky (1870-1940), Lenin had a genius that enabled him to withstand temporary setbacks. Indeed, Lenin held to the ideals and goals that once laid the foundations of Soviet totalitarianism. While Lenin had intended to liberate humanity from various forms of oppression, he had assisted really in shaping these very limitations in other ways.

Taken together the references are sometimes ironic and even contradictory. Alexander, the doctor and charismatic leader, was a conquering soldier; Christ proposed that the meek were blessed, so they would inherit the earth; Marconi abused the genius of his talent by helping his native homeland, guided by the fascist Benito Mussolini, during World War II; Lenin was certainly a fashionable name to the proletarian Left in the America of the thirties, though his dream brought about the murder of thousands. Even Bert makes the mistake of thinking that he deserves his rights because he is Norwood's bastard son, but the real reason is that he is a human being. So it is that Bert's presence disrupts the revival that Norwood arranges in order to restore the status quo on the plantation. Hence, blacks are "not *quite* the same as they had been in the morning. And never to be the same again."

To return to the inciting moment at the post office, the sales clerk does not expect to argue with African Americans. Bert keeps to his principles, "holding out the incorrect change." She becomes quite irritated while "counting the change." Now seeing the "change," she recognizes the error. But, observing the bluish grey eyes on a black man, she screams. She resents the signs of his educated privilege. As her head falls forward in the manner of the violated Southern belle, two or three white men attempt to remove Bert from line. While striking out at the whites to give one of them a bloody mouth, rather awkwardly, Bert "remembers" once he had been a football *player*. Then the female clerk screams again. The melodrama, in other words, waxes too high, the hysteria suggesting a stigma of gender. Finally, she "recovers" to narrate the tale: "Oh, my God! it was terrible." Why the delay? For a fleeting moment, I believe, she thinks about changing her Southern world. She faces, in other words, the same dilemma as Bert, though her psychic energy releases itself negatively (228).

While Norwood calls for the continued *narrative* of the status quo, Bert and Cora respond with the *narrating* of change. Even as the story proceeds, the tale prepares to finish, "The day that ends our story." So for now the notepad is cleared for a new story of American race relations to be written. Near the end, Thomas Norwood must exit his library—the emblem of learning, arts, and business—to yell his disgust at Sam, the house black. Almost hopelessly, the father brandishes a stick at Bert, who lunges in the family Ford down the road. By now the burning, blazing summer has supplanted the cool water in which Cora has washed plums. The earth, so "flooded" with the early heat of autumn, "shimmers" to prepare for the eventual flow of Norwood's blood. The Colonel, with a pistol from his open drawer, faces the waning of his own sexual power "strengthless and limp."

After Bert shoots himself, thereby depriving the mob of the presumed delight of lynching him, Cora addresses the dead Colonel, whose body lies prostrate on the floor before her. As she pulls the body feverishly, Talbot bursts in upon the scene. When he has Jim, a friend, call in to town in order to arrange for a posse, Cora realizes that "night had come." In a soliloquy with the dead Colonel, she bids him to rise, reminding him of all the occasions for which she served him well in bed, and demanding recompense now in the form of her son's life. From far off in the distance, she hears the hounds pursuing Bert while the body at her feet remains now unmoving. Finally, she goes upstairs in the mansion and leaves the Colonel's corpse lying on the floor for a long time. While she continues to hear the barking of the hounds, she prepares a hiding place in the attic for Bert, who she knows will come home to die. When Cora says "night had come," the statement extends to the metaphysical universe.

Cora speaks of "my boy" or "our boy" fleeing the lyncher's rope. But the Colonel talks about Cora's children, Cora's child, and the boy. She asks Bert to enact a law of physics—to run—as an expression of genetic bonding as true as running water. By the time of his flight back from the outside world, once the mob has cut him off from the swamp, he finishes orgasmically—"coming back" to his "father's house." Hence, he has completed the brilliant word acrostic[6] that the omniscient narrator began:

> "Lawd, chile, Bert's come home . . ."

> "Lawd, chile, and he said . . ."

> "Lawd, chile, he said . . ."

> "Lawd, chile . . ."

> "Lawd . . ."

An acrostic, literally a stairway, makes sense when read vertically from any angle. The 119th Psalm, the stanzas of which are arranged according to the Hebrew alphabet, is the earliest known illustration of the kind. Historically, the acrostic means a written composition, typically a poem, in which the various letters of lines can be read to spell out different words from those of the literal denotation. Verses of religion and love poems appeared in Europe for many years until the last century, during which time the form became unfashionable. Indeed, perhaps much of the boring literalness of twentieth-century discourse can be explained by the death of the acrostic, resisting stubbornly the idea that we can ever reduce human existence to scientific writing, to the narrow confines of linear space. Today the design of the acrostic appears most often in word puzzles. Perhaps one of the best-known is the *Double-Crostic*, by Elizabeth S. Kingsley, published in the *Saturday Review* for 1934.

Once read from the left corner at the top, then to the right at the bottom, the verbal graphic of Hughes's narrator in **"Father and Son"** ends in despair, "Lawd . . ." the expression, in the descent from the left corner at the bottom, then straight on up to the top, reveals an equal despair for the acknowledged God from whom no explanation will come: "Lawd . . . Lawd." When the descent leads downward, from the top of the second column to the bottom, an equally tragic wail sounds through human generations, "chile . . . / chile . . ." As with the fall implied in the second column, the folk regression in the third one ends in tragic nothingness, "Bert's / and / he said. . . ." Only the pattern from the far right corner to the far left one, then from the bottom left corner to the top right, promises Judaeo-Christian redemption: "Come home . . . / he said / he said / he said / Lawd, chile / Lawd, chile . . . / Lawd" "Lawd . . . / chile . . . he said . . . / and he said . . . / come home. . . ." From the hum in the quarters, the voices have expanded to the totality of God with the wave effects of radio and the telegraphy of change. Already the narrator has told us that Jesus hadn't borne the cross so well since World War I. What he means was that so many African Americans had died to make the world safe for democracy they wanted the elusive freedom that had seemed to go up in smoke. Was it the red summer of 1919 that the Colonel had remembered one day when seeing his son "coming back from the river"?

At once Langston Hughes achieves in **"Father and Son"** the grandeur of lyric and the subtle understatement of great fiction. The rare fusion signifies genius shaping itself through words. No doubt Bert exudes in more violent fashion the same quiet energy that the character Berry, the signature[7] of Langston Hughes, exemplifies in a tale about crippled children. Elsewhere, Roy Williams, a gifted violinist, comes "home" to die in a story by that title.[8] In "Ask Your Mama" (1961), the poetic cantor asserts, "Come what may Langston Hughes" (41-42). By 1965, only two years before the writer's death, the storyteller brings genius down to earth once more. Lynn Clarisse, a fiction in a Semple tale, abandons gaiety in a New York cafe—a clean, well-lighted place—to return to the sit-ins of the South. Indeed, even Semple himself, a medium of laughter for over twenty years, has fallen silent, scarred by the urgency of the times.[9] Almost always the poetic gift of Langston Hughes has remarkable resilience in the face of change. In time, Hughes believed, the human spirit would prevail. Once more it would take shape as the physics of his Dream.

Notes

1. Other variants of the same theme include *Mulatto*, the play that was completed in draft by 1930, though it was only produced on Broadway in 1935, and "The Barrier," an unpublished libretto.

See Sybil Ray Ricks, "A Textual Comparison of Langston Hughes' *Mulatto,* 'Father and Son,' and 'The Barrier,'" *Black American Literature Forum* 15 (Fall 1981): 101-103; David Michael Nifong, "Narrative Technique and Theory in *The Ways of White Folks,*" *Black American Literature Forum* 15 (Fall 1981): 93-96; R. Baxter Miller, *The Art and Imagination of Langston Hughes* (Lexington: University Press of Kentucky, 1989), 104-109; Richard K. Barksdale, *Praisesong of Survival* (Urbana: University of Illinois Press, 1992). The standard biographies are Faith Berry, *Langston Hughes: Before and Beyond Harlem* (Westport, CT: Lawrence Hill, 1993); Arnold Rampersad, *The Life of Langston Hughes,* 2 vols. (New York: Oxford University Press, 1986, 1988).

2. Langston Hughes, "Harlem," *Selected Poems* (New York: Vintage Books, 1959, 1974), 268.

3. Langston Hughes, *The Big Sea* (New York: Knopf, 1940; Hill & Wang, 1986).

4. Actually, the feel of the story seems to be much more that of the period of Reconstruction following the Civil War that had taken place between April 12, 1861, through April 9, 1865.

5. The eldest, Bertha, had traveled north with the Jubilee Singers, suggesting Fisk University though she supposedly went to school in Atlanta as well, and remained in Chicago; Sailie, the youngest and Bert's junior by three years, returned to college in Atlanta.

6. *See also* James Emanuel, "The Literary Experiments of Langston Hughes," *CLA Journal* 11 (June 1967): 335-344.

7. Hughes dedicates the volume to his California Patron, Noel Sullivan: "The ways of white folks, / I mean some white folks . . ." [signed] BERRY.

8. *Ways of White Folks,* respectively, 32-48, 171-812.

9. Richard K. Barksdale, "Comic Relief in Langston Hughes' Poetry," *Black American Literature Forum* 15 (Fall 1981): 108-111.

Donna Akiba Sullivan Harper (essay date 1995)

SOURCE: Harper, Donna Akiba Sullivan. "Introduction: 'Day-after-Day Heroism.'" In *Not So Simple: The "Simple" Stories by Langston Hughes,* pp. 1-19. Columbia: University of Missouri Press, 1995.

[*In the following essay, Harper outlines the origins, development, and critical evaluation of Hughes's recurring character Jesse B. Semple.*]

The words *simple* and *simplicity* recur in analyses of Langston Hughes's works. A disturbing consequence of this trend has been an exclusion of Hughes's works as texts for modern criticism, a dismissal of Hughes as being too simple to merit literary analysis.[1] While several critics have focused on Hughes, only Ron Baxter Miller has devoted an entire book to a complex analysis of Hughes's poetry in terms of the most recent critical strategies. What Miller and other devoted Hughes scholars know is that Hughes's works possess the illusion of simplicity—a sleight that hides a depth of complex uses of language, psychology, sociology, and history. With his literary illusion, Hughes demonstrates what Richard Wright considered to be a desirable "complex simplicity."[2]

A primary example of Hughes's deceptive simplicity is the character whose name and history represent the illusion of being simple. Thoughtful reflection upon the stage of Hughes's career during which he launched the character, upon the historical period that shaped the character, and upon the stages of the character's development will begin an appropriate consideration of why Jesse B. Semple, "Simple," was really *not* so simple.

During the 1940s, the decade of the second world war, Langston Hughes was in his forties and had achieved a significant measure of success. He was well educated, honored, active in many areas of writing, and had published thirteen books in different genres. A biobibliographical note in *What the Negro Wants,* published in 1944, included the following details about him:

> He studied one year at Columbia and was graduated from Lincoln University [Pennsylvania] in 1929. His alma mater conferred upon him the degree of Litt. D. in 1943. He is a member of The Authors' Guild, the Dramatists' Guild, ASCAP, the Advisory Council of the Writers' War Board, the Music War Committee, and the board of the magazine *Common Ground.* Mr. Hughes has contributed to the *Saturday Evening Post, Survey Graphic, Esquire, New Yorker, Nation, New Republic, Crisis, Opportunity, Theatre Arts, Poetry,* and *Common Ground.* He wrote in collaboration with Clarence Muse the scenario for *Way Down South.* His play, *Mulatto,* ran for a year at the Vanderbilt Theatre, New York. *Don't You Want to be Free?* gave 135 performances at the Harlem Suitcase Theatre. His historical pageant, *For This We Fight,* was presented at Madison Square Garden, June 7, 1943. His works, all published by Knopf, are *The Weary Blues, The Dream Keeper, Shakespeare in Harlem,* **The Ways of White Folks,** *Not Without Laughter* and his autobiography, *The Big Sea.*[3]

This list omits *Fine Clothes to the Jew,* his second volume of poetry, which was out of print at that time and which had drawn nasty criticism and even condemnation. In addition, the list omits six slim and mostly topical volumes of poems published with several small firms before 1944. Even with its gaps, however, this biographical statement indicates those achievements of which Hughes felt proudest at the beginning of the 1940s and reveals the variety of genres in which he had already been published—poetry, short stories, novels, song lyrics, and drama. Despite his versatility, he was best known then and remains best known now as a poet. However, his poetry in the 1940s received little praise and was found to be cynical, sad, and—at best—a subtle blending of tragedy and comedy.[4]

The 1940s, however, gave Hughes a new area of fame and achievement. Viewing the decade retrospectively in the headnote about Hughes in their anthology, James A. Emanuel and Theodore L. Gross praise the creation of Jesse B. Semple as a major accomplishment in Hughes's career:

> None of these books of the 1940's, and none of the awards or positions that came to Hughes then—the thousand-dollar grant from the American Academy of Arts and Letters in 1946, the posts as poet-in-residence at Atlanta University in 1947 and as "resource teacher" at the Laboratory School of the University of Chicago in 1949—distinguish the decade so much as the one night that the author spent at a Harlem bar near his St. Nicholas Avenue address. That night in 1942, the one great fictional character that Hughes was to conceive, Harlemite Jesse B. Semple, was born when the poet heard "Simple's" prototype tell a girlfriend about his job making cranks in a New Jersey war plant.[5]

Without question, Simple was "the one great fictional character" Hughes offered to the literary world. The note goes on to compare Simple to other notable creations: "Soon his vividness on paper had a wholeness and a reality that would rank him with Huck Finn, Mr. Dooley, and Uncle Remus." This praise reflects the critical consensus about the Simple stories, which feature humorous dialogues between Jesse B. Semple (pronounced Jessie B. Sample) and a usually unnamed straight man, or foil.

Literary critics, scholars, and Hughes's fellow artists have praised Jesse B. Semple as "the most famous character in black fiction" and the Simple stories as "Langston Hughes's greatest contribution to American culture." For example, Arthur P. Davis, the pioneer in criticism of Simple, summarizes in his 1974 book, "Most critics feel that the Simple series is Hughes's best work in fiction and that Simple is his greatest single creation."[6]

What makes Simple such a notable creation? The dozens of critical assessments echo the opinion that Jesse B. Semple represents the Negro[7] everyman—the average Harlem citizen—and most of them elaborate upon the value of such a characterization. Simple is an ordinary working black man representative of the masses of black folks in the 1940s. Like many other blacks, he

has migrated to Harlem from the South. He therefore vividly remembers the racism he experienced in Dixie and celebrates the opportunities for African Americans in the North.

In the same way that racism shadows even the new economic and political freedom Simple finds in the North, his troublesome romantic past inhibits his new love life. He has left but not divorced an exploitative and unloving wife, and therefore he cannot satisfy the requests of his highly respectable lady-friend, Joyce, to marry her. Joyce aspires toward culture and home-ownership, and she eschews the nightly beer outings Simple enjoys. The corner bar offers Simple more than beer, however. The relaxation there compensates for his daily routine of hard work for minimal pay, and he is also able to exchange ideas in the bar, where he discourses at length in his own straightforward way about the world, the nation, and his own life. Through his narrations Simple introduces a large (and heavily female) supporting cast: guardian Aunt Lucy, estranged wife Isabel, best girl Joyce, good-time girl Zarita, landlady Madam Butler, society lady Mrs. Sadie Maxwell-Reeves, early love interests Mabel and Cherie, and cousins F. D., Minnie, and Lynn Clarisse. Simple also finds a way to include a reference to race in almost every conversation, much to the dismay of the foil.

Ananias Boyd, as the foil eventually came to be known, is a college-educated man who remains in the neighborhood bar late into the night "observing life for literary purposes" (*Best* [*The Best of Simple*], 12). He is articulate, moderate, and generally in better financial shape than Simple. He has never lived in the South, and he does not speak often about his job or his love life. He usually just listens to Simple and questions him, but on some topics he argues with him in an effort to help his outspoken friend appreciate the broader view of whatever topic he is addressing. Every so often, however, Simple's point of view is inarguable, so the foil ends up agreeing with him, thereby emphasizing the wisdom of Simple's point.

Hughes began the Simple columns having conversations himself with his fictional Simple Minded Friend. Gradually his own college-educated, widely traveled persona was transferred to Simple's bar buddy/foil, and as Hughes became more careful in crafting his Simple stories, he more and more consistently created for the bar buddy a distinct personality and distinct language marked by a refined, occasionally stuffy diction. Confusion sometimes arises over whether the bar buddy should be called "Boyd," since Hughes did not call him that in most of the Simple columns but eventually gave him that name for dramatic purposes when he produced his Simple play, *Simply Heavenly,* in 1957. The confusion is intensified by the fact that Simple mentions in some of the early stories a fellow roomer named Ezra

Boyd; the Boyd in the play is Ananias Boyd. In his last collection of Simple stories, *Simple's Uncle Sam,* Hughes ended up calling the foil by the name Boyd.

An important note about Boyd is that his college education does not alienate him from the masses. Whereas Sterling Brown notes that Hughes sharply satirizes Aunt Tempy in *Not without Laughter* as a high-tone striver and does not treat her with sympathy,[8] Boyd, who because of his college education and elevated language could be suspected of being a striver, is likeable, although he remains far less rounded than Simple. The characterization of alienated, high-and-mighty strivers in the Simple saga is restricted to a minor figure in the play *Simply Heavenly,* a character known only as "Character." Even the society-minded Joyce and the ultimate society lady, Mrs. Sadie Maxwell-Reeves, gain some sympathy in their portrayal as strivers in the stories, but Character, described as "a snob," or "that character trying to make people think he's educated," elicits ridicule and scorn from the other people in the bar Simple frequents in the play. Speaking with an affected dialect, he asks for "a thimble of Scawtch," as Bodiddly mocks, which is a drink order "like the English," the bartender announces. Miss Mamie proudly contrasts Character with Boyd: "One thing I like about Boyd here, even if he is a writer, he ain't always trying to impress folks. Also he speaks when he comes in a public place."[9] Simple not only tolerates the foil's education, he draws upon it. On the other hand, he feels comfortable reprimanding his bar buddy when he perceives an exaggerated erudition or any other offensive air surfacing. The foil, then, emerges as a sympathetically presented upwardly mobile, college-educated persona.

Simple's intimate interaction with the foil—a very different sort of person from himself—becomes an important factor in Simple's genuine humanity and in the reader's ability to appreciate it. When Boyd and Simple converse in "that poor man's club that is a bar," the beer equalizes them. Thus, we have an environment that creates a "suspension of hierarchal precedence" in some ways similar to the "Carnival" period M. M. Bakhtin discusses. In the local bar, Simple and Boyd experience what Bakhtin finds in the carnival atmosphere: "a special form of free and familiar contact . . . among people who were usually divided by the barriers of caste, property, profession, and age." With these and the barriers of education and geographic origins broken down, the corner bar creates an atmosphere "for new, purely human relations. These truly human relations were not only a fruit of imagination or abstract thought; they were experienced." With the foil and Simple in the bar, equality was not merely imagined, it was truly experienced. The intrusion of "Character" talking about "stereotypes" in the bar in *Simply Heavenly* illustrates that Boyd was an equal, a peer, in the bar.[10]

This formula of "free and familiar" dialogue and interchange between these significantly different men began on February 13, 1943, when the *Chicago Defender* published Hughes's first dialogue with his "Simple Minded Friend." This "very happy creation" was an experiment in Hughes's weekly editorial column, "Here to Yonder."[11] Favorable response from readers and encouragement from John Sengstacke, publisher and editor of the *Defender* [*Chicago Defender*], led Hughes to continue to develop this Simple character. Within three years, he sought to publish his first book-length collection of the Simple episodes, which proved to be anything but simple. Nevertheless, Hughes persevered.

He revised and condensed the columns. He improved characterization and enhanced the distinctions between the vernacular language of Simple and the measured and educated diction of the Hughes persona/foil/Boyd. The result of his years of improvement and design was *Simple Speaks His Mind,* published in 1950, the first of six books and one play to collect as literature the ideas originating in the popular columns recording the conversations of Simple and the foil. The success of that first book led to the publication of others: *Simple Takes a Wife,* in 1953; *Simple Stakes a Claim,* in 1957; the play *Simply Heavenly,* in 1957; *The Best of Simple,* featuring selections from the three earlier volumes, in 1961; and *Simple's Uncle Sam,* in 1965. These works have been anthologized and performed extensively in the United States and have enjoyed numerous translations.

The premise of the Simple stories appeals as the primary step in the human quest for peace, understanding, and common ground: two men from different educational and cultural backgrounds meet on an equal plane, exchange ideas, develop a friendship, and bridge the gap between them. Each society has its own barriers, whether they be barriers of education, gender, class, sexual preference, or physical ability. By observing Simple and Boyd, readers vicariously experience themselves overcoming the barriers in their own world, reaching out to someone different, and finding in that person a friend.

Significantly, though, Hughes broke through these barriers while remaining within the Afrocentric sphere he had claimed as his preferred medium. Despite their differences, the foil and Simple are both black in a racially unbalanced society. Thus, one barrier is broken, but the larger one remains. In a way, the Simple premise renders permanent the chasm between the races. The two main characters seldom encounter whites. They exist in a world within a world: Harlem, the separate black community in New York City. Perhaps a celebration of the longevity of the Simple stories sadly witnesses the continuity of American race prejudice. Contemporary readers of the Simple tales repeatedly affirm that they know someone like Simple. How can a Simple still exist in the 1990s—so many years after all the laws were passed to permit the vote, to end the poll tax, to end the restrictive covenant in housing, to end discrimination in military service, education, and employment? Why do so many readers in the 1990s still recognize in Simple someone they know? Could the racial oppression against which Simple railed continue to exist? Yes, racism remains in full force, proclaims the public outcry about the 1992 acquittal of four white Los Angeles policemen who had been videotaped beating Rodney King, a black man they pulled over on the highway.

On the other hand, recognizing someone "exactly like Simple" may not necessarily mean recognizing a working-class African American suffering from racial oppression. Fans of Simple range far beyond the African American residents of Harlem. They span the globe. Therefore, Simple's appeal can be termed universal. Readers can see in Simple's racial oppression the same kinds of forces that oppress people sexually, economically, ethnically, or because of physical limitations. Perhaps the humor in Simple's tales allows us to laugh at the continuing hypocrisy of American proclamations of "liberty and justice for all," even in the face of vehement objections to President Bill Clinton's earliest efforts to allow openly gay people to serve in the U.S. armed forces. Perhaps we hope for common ground with Simple, projecting from his desire to see a black general pinning medals on a white soldier (**"Simple on Military Integration,"** *Best,* 81) a gay American's dream to see an openly gay general pinning medals on a straight soldier. Whether fifty years have left new black faces in the same old racially oppressed places or whether the name of the oppression has changed for some readers, the publication history of Simple tells us that Langston Hughes succeeded with his creation. Whether readers focus on the sameness of the race of Simple and Boyd or not, somehow, because these two different men become allies, their side of the racial barrier becomes a more humane and more appealing place to be. This study will examine Hughes's success from both a race-centered and a universal vantage point.

The extensive success in translation and the endurance in publication of the Simples stories become all the more astonishing when we take into account Simple's origins: the Negro press. Unlike any other significant fictional creation, Jesse B. Semple originated as an occasional feature in a weekly column that Hughes wrote for the *Chicago Defender,* a medium that served average African Americans. New York City publishers became involved later in the process, but Simple's origins rested with average African American readers in cities and in rural areas throughout the country, and even serving in the nation's armed forces abroad. One might assume that a character crafted to suit such a narrow audience would be too provincial, too ethnic, or other-

wise too limited to appeal to a broader audience. However, the opposite has proven true. As Hughes himself commented, "A fictional character can be ever so ethnic, ever so local and regional, and still be universal in terms of humanity." As early as 1949, G. Lewis Chandler called Hughes a synecdochist because he could use the racial as a means to achieve the universal.[12]

A major part of Simple's "humanity" stems from his ordinariness. He was then and remains the kind of person many of us recognize. Hughes not only captured Simple's ordinary qualities, but he also imbued them with dignity, humor, and goodness. He was able to bring these qualities to the creation of Simple because he maintained his own racial pride and his sense of humor. Moreover, he enjoyed the ordinary black folks he met on his many lecture tours, as well as those among whom he made his home in Harlem. As Arna Bontemps wrote in 1952, "Few people have enjoyed being Negro as much as Langston Hughes." In his more politically charged analysis, Richard Wright links Hughes's upbringing and job history to his appreciation for ordinary African Americans: "Unlike the sons and daughters of Negro 'society,' Hughes was not ashamed of those of his race who had to scuffle for their bread. The jerky transitions of his own life did not admit of his remaining in one place long enough to become a slave of prevailing Negro middle-class prejudices." Because he loved, respected, and identified with ordinary African Americans, Hughes was able to represent faithfully the attitudes and the speech patterns of the Negro everyman, an ordinary Harlem resident. Blyden Jackson thoroughly praises Simple's ordinariness, claiming, "Whether or not [Simple] is truly like most ordinary Negroes, he is certainly, in both form and substance, what many ordinary Negroes were at least once prepared to concede without rancor that they thought they were. At least, to that extent, Simple must be accounted a folk Negro's concept of the folk Negro."[13]

Jackson finds Simple's ordinariness praiseworthy because "at the very heart of American racism there seems to be an assumption of the most dangerous import: to wit, that there are no Negroes who are average people." In Jackson's analysis, this dangerous racist view assumes that blacks are either *exceptional* (e.g., Ralph Bunche or Marian Anderson) or—especially in fiction—*grotesque*:

> people whose distinctive stigma is failure, so that the prevailing conclusion to a Negro's tale of Negro life is catastrophe—Bigger Thomas awaiting execution; Lutie Johnson, Ann Petry's heroine in *The Street,* fleeing the corpse of the would-be seducer she has just murdered; Bob Jones, in *If He Hollers Let Him Go,* on his way to enforced military service; the Invisible Man submerged, and lost, in his hole in the ground.

In contrast to those exceptionally good and talented Negroes and those plagued with failure, Jackson finds Simple to be "an ordinary person who is a Negro."[14]

In the final volume of Simple stories, Simple himself elucidates the distinctions between such people as Ralph Bunche, Thurgood Marshall, Martin Luther King Jr., and himself:

> I am proud to be represented by such men, if you say they represent me. But all them men you name are *way* up there, and they do not drink beer in my bar. I have never seen a single one of them men on Lenox Avenue in my natural life. So far as I know, they do not even live in Harlem. I cannot find them in the telephone book. They all got private numbers. . . . And I bet they have not been to the Apollo since Jackie Mabley cracked the first joke.

("Coffee Break," *Return*
[*The Return of Simple*], 102-3)

Simple, of course, enjoys "Moms" Mabley and Lenox Avenue. By all accounts, he is an ordinary Harlem resident. The especially fascinating thing about Simple, however, is that he always masters his circumstances. He may not be able to change his racist countrymen or create better employment opportunities for himself, but he refuses to be defeated by oppression. The victorious attitude of this ordinary man clearly exceeds any racial or national boundaries, thereby proving useful as inspirational literature in many cultures. As Hans Ostrom points out, when Hughes created Simple he was "deconstructing other typical images of the African-American male, as [Blyden] Jackson suggests. So if Hughes was holding up a mirror to urban, working-class African-American men, he was also smashing the false images of 'the Negro' which white society had created."[15] Hughes wanted to show heroism and greatness, and he saw such greatness among the common people. More significantly, he saw such heroism as a tool for survival rather than as some final blaze of bravado before ultimate death and destruction. Instead of a Claude McKay "If We Must Die" heroism, his Simple demonstrates a Langston Hughes "Still Here" heroic achievement.

> I've been scarred and battered.
> My hopes the wind done scattered.
> Snow has friz me, sun has baked me.
>   Looks like between 'em
>   They done tried to make me
> Stop laughin', stop lovin', stop livin'—
>   But I don't care!
>   *I'm still here*![16]

Hard work and exposure to the elements could scar or batter or freeze a person, but when that person could envision a better future for his or her offspring, somehow the hardships had to be endured. In Hughes's opinion, such endurance constituted a kind of "day-after-day

heroism of work and struggle and the facing of drudgery and insult that some son or daughter might get through school and acquire the knowledge that leads to a better life where opportunities are brighter and work is less drab, less humiliating, and less hard." George E. Kent considers these survivors of daily drudgery to be typical of Hughes's vision, which emphasizes "a lifesmanship that preserves and celebrates humanity in the face of impossible odds."[17]

Besides capturing daily living, such portrayals could also inspire daily living. In his 1937 "Blueprint for Negro Writing," Richard Wright lambasted educated Negroes who had never considered that the creative works of their writers should have been guides for their daily living. Because black readers failed to expect inspiration from literature, African American writers produced works that became either "hallmark[s] of 'achievement'" or pleas to "white America for justice." Wright found that "rarely was the best of this writing addressed to the Negro himself." Instead, African American instruction emerged from the black church or black folklore, either of which produced "racial wisdom" that was transmitted orally from one person to the next. Consequently, "two separate cultures sprang up: one for the Negro masses, unwritten and unrecognized; and the other for the sons and daughters of a rising Negro bourgeoisie, parasitic and mannered." With his genuine and ordinary hero, Simple, and with his oral or folk structure embedded within the "self-conscious" literary structure, Hughes ended that split and combined the two traditions. Oluropo Sekoni, a specialist in African and African American literary and cultural semiotics, finds that Hughes employed a "post-representational imagination" with which he was able to reconcile the contradictions between two aesthetic traditions—the folk tradition, represented by Simple, and the middle-class tradition, voiced by the foil. As Susan L. Blake points out, the Simple stories allowed Hughes to enhance the folk tradition, converting the telling of the tale into a written document that becomes a unifying tool for social change. The literature, universal and critically acclaimed, represented the voices and values of the Negro masses and channeled them into a victorious, self-controlled instrument.[18]

Langston Hughes deliberately created in Simple an African American who was victorious over the major oppression of racism and the many indignities of his life because he had become self-conscious about his role as a writer and about the historical impact of his characters. Hughes had articulated what he championed as "The Need for Heroes" in the *Crisis* a little over a year before he began writing his weekly column for the *Chicago Defender*. In the article, he declared:

> The written word is the only record we will have of this our present, or our past, to leave behind for future generations. It would be a shame if that written word

in its creative form were to consist largely of defeat and death. Suppose *Native Son*'s Bigger Thomas (excellently drawn as he is) was the sole survivor on the bookshelves of tomorrow? Or my own play, *Mulatto,* whose end consists of murder, madness, and suicide? If the best of our writers continue to pour their talent into the tragedies of frustration and weakness, tomorrow will probably say, on the basis of available literary evidence, "No wonder the Negroes never amounted to anything. There were no heroes among them."[19]

Blyden Jackson's praise of Simple certainly complements Hughes's own assessment that literary heroes were needed. Jackson found that, in *Not without Laughter,* in the Simple stories, and in most of his other writing, "Hughes never succumbed to the monstrous error of arguing that, because race prejudice is itself monstrous, it has made Negroes monsters."[20] To the contrary, Simple remained quite attractively human. He merely complained about his troubles—personal, national, and racial. As Simple describes himself, "I am no dangerous man. I am what folks calls an ordinary citizen. Me, I work, pay my rent, and taxes, and try to get along" (**"American Dilemma," *Return,*** 75).

It is worth noting that Simple—like many other ordinary African Americans—did not limit his negative evaluations to white people or to white racism. As one critic points out, "When Simple is not exposing the folly and injustice of the white world, he is unveiling the foolish social climbing, moral hypocrisy, and spiritual emptiness . . . of . . . blacks."[21] Thus, Simple remains victorious without becoming blind to the problems surrounding him.

How could such a problem-conscious character have such universal appeal over the years? Richard K. Barksdale credits Hughes's perception of humor as the attribute that permitted the author to present such a well-balanced character:

> Hughes was more than a poetic dramatist; he had a comic vision that enabled him to cover the pain and suffering of black urban existence with protective layers of wit, humor, and sympathetic understanding. The characters he presented . . . are error-ridden, often fearful, and yet filled with a good-humored acceptance of their own frailties. So in their small, unheroic ways they negotiate the complicated systems and bureaucracies burdening the black citizen in the biggest ghetto in America's largest city. This they do with a certain amount of bravado, a certain amount of humility, and a certain amount of good humor.[22]

The points being made in these various critical assessments are that Simple is both ordinary and black, and that he survives with his racial integrity despite racism. He is "a MAN, strong and unafraid, who did not die a suicide, or a mob-victim, or a subject for execution, or a defeated humble beaten-down human being."[23] Hugh-

es's literary achievement is the creation of a character—very much a composite of real ordinary black men—who displays a well-rounded personality despite the negative impact of prejudice. Critical acclaim for this achievement persists fifty years after Simple's creation. This study should amplify the reasons for appreciating Hughes's accomplishment with Simple.

One aspect of that accomplishment has been virtually absent from public scrutiny, however. That hidden achievement is the actual translation of the character from one who sparkled in the *Chicago Defender* to one who retains his effervescence in book form. First finding a publisher willing to bring out the tales and then polishing Simple's character to satisfy editors for that publisher proved to be lengthy and arduous tasks for Hughes.

By learning about the original columns as they appeared in the newspaper, readers can correct the false impression so easily gained from scholarly references that indicate that readers followed Simple "week after week in the columns of the *Defender.*"[24] Simple did not appear every week in the column, much to the dismay of his most ardent fans. Hughes wrote mostly nonfiction editorials, only adding Simple as a feature to help him reach readers who might hold views strongly opposed to his own. By examining the early versions of Simple, along with the different types of columns Hughes wrote at the same time, we can better evaluate how Simple fit into Hughes's plan for communicating with the readers of the *Defender.* The initial impetus for publication of the stories in book form was enthusiastic fans and an interested publisher. Based on their enthusiasm, Hughes began in 1945 to envision his dialogues as material for a book. This vision led him to increase Simple's appearances in the *Chicago Defender* from eleven in 1943 to twenty-three in 1949—one nearly every other week.

When we recognize in the newspaper those episodes that have been collected into one of the five volumes of Simple stories, we can also correct another false impression. Some writers, in explaining briefly that the Simple columns were later collected into books, may give the false impression that all the columns were merely copied from the newspaper and then lumped together for the Simple books. Hughes certainly attempted that easy method. With dozens of writing projects occurring simultaneously, he wanted nothing more than to staple and mail his existing columns and call that sheaf of paper a new book. Indeed, when he began to envision the Simple stories as a book in 1945, he advised his literary agent to distribute the manuscript, which was merely a collection of unrevised columns. However, publishers wisely refused to grant him the luxury of presenting those journalistic gems as book-length literature.

Instead, Hughes was compelled to select carefully the episodes he would include. A comparison of the original columns and the episodes preserved in books shows that many of the columns were omitted from the collected editions. Moreover, the collected versions reflect substantial editing and revising. In addition, to enhance story line and character development, Hughes wrote some entirely new episodes specifically for his first collection of Simple stories. When we fail to appreciate the effort and attention required to produce the enduring collections of Simple stories, we diminish our understanding of the craft that resulted in the creation of the Simple books. Hughes did not churn out Simple columns week after week, nor did his columns transfer directly from newspaper to book. Failure to examine the columns accurately and thoroughly has resulted in decreased appreciation for Hughes's political commentary and for his artistic abilities.

Another consequence of the critical focus upon the book-length collections of Simple stories is that scholars have neglected to analyze the pragmatic and artistic concerns that led Hughes to transform topical columns into enduring fiction. While he dealt with actual events of the 1940s and addressed the racially homogeneous audience of the black press when he created Simple, Hughes later revised his creation so that Simple could communicate effectively outside of that context of time and audience. These revisions offer literary scholars a significant means for evaluating the craft of Langston Hughes, and the history of the revision process soundly refutes any mistaken impressions that the Simple stories were hastily or carelessly assembled. In some instances, particular stories deserve a reexamination in light of the original dialogues published in the *Defender*. Additionally, each published volume ultimately represents a stage in a process, not just a fixed piece of literature.

To evaluate the revision process, this study takes advantage of the *Chicago Defender* and *New York Post* versions of Simple—which have always been available to critics—and it provides information from manuscripts, drafts, and editorial suggestions housed in the extensive James Weldon Johnson Collection at Yale University and unavailable to most scholars until the 1980s. The identity of the foil, the distinctive speech patterns of Simple and the foil, Simple's name, and the specific details of Simple's background and day-to-day life were not evident in the earliest days of the column, but they later crystallized in the books. Comparisons of the same episodes taken from column to book will reveal many of the creative innovations Hughes employed to insure that Simple could break away from the weekly newspaper setting. The lengthy processes of negotiating for the initial book contract and the arduous work of revising the manuscript for publication reveal the extent to which

Hughes blended his artistic integrity with the suggestions of his agent and his editors to craft a work of fiction richly deserving of the critical acclaim it has received.

The Simple stories have not been unanimously celebrated, however. From the earliest days of his appearance in the *Chicago Defender* to the present, Hughes's Simple has gained both detractors and fans. Hughes remains best known as a poet, and many who love his poetry find the Simple tales excessively earthy, obvious, or prone to perpetuate stereotypes with demeaning dialect and unattractive behavior. Such readers wonder why Hughes ever put the character into print, and wonder even more why publishers have continued to reproduce the error Hughes made. Other fans of Hughes may not dislike the character, but they remain oblivious to Simple. For example, actor Danny Glover in 1992 read from Hughes's poetry for a one-hour program. When asked by an audience member whether he ever included the Simple stories in his readings, he replied that he was not familiar with Simple.[25] How has a creation so highly acclaimed failed to gain greater significance in the common public perception of Hughes's reputation?

Among readers acquainted with Simple, not all relish his perpetual focus on race or his use of black vernacular. For example, some readers enjoy or identify with the style of the dialogues or even the focus upon a humble common man, comparing the Simple episodes with other stories they know and have enjoyed, such as Sholem Aleichem's *Tevye the Dairyman and The Railroad Stories*, Garrison Keillor's stories, or Leo Rosten's *The Education of Hyman Kaplan*. Such readers appreciate the craft and the universality of the creation, although they may not always enjoy the subject matter or the dialect.

However, as long ago as the 1940s, Simple has attracted ardent fans and promoters who promised that he would become a classic, an immortal fixture in literature. Langston Hughes may have begun to believe these zealous prophesies by the time he died in 1967, since by then his Simple Minded Friend had grown to fill five published books, a musical play, and a comedy play without music, and had been translated and performed in dozens of languages throughout the world. The even more remarkable achievement is the continued vitality of this character. ***The Best of Simple*** remains in print, ***The Return of Simple*** has recently been published, and *Simply Heavenly* continues to be performed. These accomplishments confirm the universality of the Harlem everyman as Hughes carefully portrayed him. Moreover, these accomplishments testify to the perseverance and resilience of the author, who contended with several publishers, waged numerous battles over "rights," and weathered countless theatrical obstacles to achieve this list of publication and literary endurance for Simple.

While the germ that sprouted into the first Simple column may have appeared to Hughes rather easily when he conversed with a fellow in the neighborhood bar, the actual saga of Simple shows that the translation of folk characters and vernacular narration into universally celebrated fiction required both talent and tenacity on the part of the author.

Besides unraveling the process through which Simple evolved, this study will show readers that they may love only the tip of the Hughesian literary iceberg. The shelf life of books being what it is, the general public in the 1990s tends to know Jesse B. Semple as he is preserved in *The Best of Simple* or as he is presented on stage in *Simply Heavenly*. These vehicles offer likeable presentations of both Simple and the lively supporting cast; however, episodes from *Simple Takes a Wife* and *Simple's Uncle Sam* that were not included in *The Best of Simple* provide several powerful and unmatched presentations of female characters. Other episodes from the newspaper columns never reached permanence in any book form; these columns, too, offer other important dimensions of Simple and his supporting cast.[26]

The Best of Simple, which is still in print, continues to reach generations of readers further and further removed from the climate of racial segregation from which Simple sprang. How then do current generations of readers view Simple? Does this character continue to teach, to amuse, and to entertain readers? Do the Simple episodes capture African American culture and American life in ways that will lead future generations of readers to enjoy them, making Simple immortal like Shakespeare's Romeo or Dickens's Scrooge? What qualities have already sustained readership for decades after the author's death?

This examination of Jesse B. Semple traces the initial appearance of the character within the weekly column Hughes wrote for the *Chicago Defender.* We follow the character to a manuscript form that is rejected by several publishers until it gains a warm and benevolent reception from the editors at Simon and Schuster. This publisher gives the world the first two book-length collections of Simple stories. We then follow Simple to Rinehart for a third volume and to Hill and Wang for the final two volumes Hughes compiled. We see Simple expand from his birthplace in the *Chicago Defender* to publication in a "white" paper, the *New York Post,* and into syndication in a variety of newspapers. We also note Simple's appearance on stage—even on Broadway—and on television. The summary comes easily, but the actual publication and production history was anything but "simple."

Beyond the historical tracking, this examination also delves into the characterization of Jesse B. Semple and the foil, as well as the women in Simple's life and his cousins. By exposing the less common episodes, we will uncover a complexity and a depth that belie the surface appearance of simplicity.

The exploration of characterization will inevitably lead to an evaluation of Hughes's use of language, humor, and social history in these tales. To demonstrate the amount of time and talent Hughes invested, a few scenes will be followed through several drafts to their published form.

Finally, critical reception of the Simple episodes will be interspersed throughout this discussion. Both the formal criticism from scholars such as Arthur Paul Davis and the informal criticism from hundreds of fan letters preserved in Yale University's James Weldon Johnson Collection and the New York Public Library's Schomburg Center for Research in Black Culture will highlight the popular and the insulting messages that the Simple tales communicated.

Readers already familiar with Simple should return to him filled with a new appreciation for his history and his depth. Readers not yet acquainted with him should find him required reading after learning how carefully he has been drawn and how attractive he has been since 1943 to readers all over the world.

Notes

1. For example, many recent critical works by Henry Louis Gates Jr. barely mention Hughes, if they mention him at all.

2. Wright, "Blueprint for Negro Writing," 60.

3. Rayford Logan, ed., *What the Negro Wants,* 348.

4. Edward J. Mullen, ed., *Critical Essays on Langston Hughes,* 12-13.

5. Emanuel and Gross, eds., *Dark Symphony: Negro Literature in America,* 195-96.

6. Roger Rosenblatt, *Black Fiction,* 103; Eugenia Collier, "A Pain in His Soul: Simple as Epic Hero," in Therman B. O'Daniel, ed., *Langston Hughes: Black Genius,* 131; Davis, *From the Dark Tower: Afro-American Writers, 1900 to 1960,* 69.

7. Throughout this book, the terms *Negro, black,* and *African American* will be used interchangeably. While political implications would place different connotations on those racial designations, in this text, the reader should regard them as synonyms for Americans of African heritage.

8. Brown, *The Negro in American Fiction* (Washington: The Associates in Negro Folk Education, 1937).

9. LH [Langston Hughes], *Five Plays by Langston Hughes,* 123-24.

10. "Simple's Long Trek to Broadway," in *Simply Heavenly* MSS [Manuscripts], JWJ [The Langston Hughes Papers, James Weldon Johnson Collection, Beinecke Rare Book and Manuscript Library, Yale University]; Bakhtin, *Rabelais and His World,* trans. Helene Iswolsky (Bloomington: Indiana University Press, 1984), 10.

11. Arna Bontemps praised the Simple Minded Friend as a "very happy creation" in a letter to LH, February 22, 1943, in Charles H. Nichols, ed., *Arna Bontemps-Langston Hughes Letters, 1925-1967,* 121.

12. LH, "Simple Again"; Chandler, "Selfsameness and a Promise."

13. Bontemps, "Black and Bubbling," in Mullen, ed., *Critical Essays,* 80; Wright, "Forerunner and Ambassador," review of *The Big Sea,* in Michel Fabre, *Richard Wright Books and Writers* (Jackson, Miss.: University Press of Mississippi, 1990), 214; Jackson, "A Word about Simple," 111.

14. Jackson, "A Word," 115-17.

15. Ostrom, *Langston Hughes: A Study of the Short Fiction,* 44.

16. "Still Here," *Selected Poems of Langston Hughes,* 123.

17. LH, "The Need for Heroes," 206; Kent, *Blackness and the Adventure of Western Culture,* 56-57.

18. Wright, "Blueprint," 53-56; Sekoni, "Africanisms and the Post-Modernist Dimension of the Harlem Renaissance"; Blake, "Old John in Harlem: The Urban Folktales of Langston Hughes," in Mullen, ed., *Critical Essays,* 168, 175.

19. "Need for Heroes," 184.

20. Jackson, "A Word," 118.

21. Charles A. Watkins, "Simple: The Alter Ego of Langston Hughes," 21.

22. Barksdale, *Langston Hughes: The Poet and His Critics,* 86.

23. LH, "Need for Heroes," 184.

24. Jackson, "A Word," 111.

25. Questions and response from Glover's reading at Georgia State University, Wednesday, May 27, 1992. Since February 1994, Glover has included Simple in his Hughes readings.

26. Hill and Wang published *The Return of Simple,* a new collection of sixty-two Simple episodes, in July 1994. In this new book, episodes include some from previously published books, but none that were published in *Best.* Twenty-five of the stories have never before been included within a book-length collection. This new collection should ameliorate readers' lack of acquaintance with those episodes.

Abbreviations

Because *The Best of Simple* and the recently published *The Return of Simple* offer the most convenient means by which the general reader may access the Simple stories, whenever possible all page references will be to these volumes rather than to the earlier volume under discussion. When the Simple stories under discussion do not appear in either of these two collections, they will be cited as they appear in other published volumes, and any episodes not collected in any book will be cited according to their newspaper publication.

The following editions and abbreviations were used in citations throughout the book:

Collections of Simple stories by Langston Hughes:

Mind: *Simple Speaks His Mind.* New York: Simon and Schuster, 1950

Wife: *Simple Takes a Wife.* New York: Simon and Schuster, 1953

Claim: *Simple Stakes a Claim.* New York: Rinehart, 1957

Best: *The Best of Simple.* New York: Hill and Wang, 1961

Sam: *Simple's Uncle Sam.* New York: Hill and Wang, 1965

Return: *The Return of Simple,* ed. Akiba Sullivan Harper. New York: Hill and Wang, 1994

Frequently named publications:

CD: *Chicago Defender*

Post: *New York Post*

Repository for papers, manuscripts, and correspondence of Hughes and other terms used in association:

JWJ: The Langston Hughes Papers, James Weldon Johnson Collection, Beinecke Rare Book and Manuscript Library, Yale University

MS: Manuscript

MSS: Manuscripts

LH: Langston Hughes

Arnold Rampersad (essay date 1996)

SOURCE: Rampersad, Arnold. Introduction to *Short Stories of Langston Hughes,* by Langston Hughes, edited by Akiba Sullivan Harper, pp. xiii-xix. New York: Hill and Wang, 1996.

[In the following essay, Rampersad traces Hughes's early attempts at short story writing and documents themes of bigotry and intolerance in The Ways of White Folks.*]*

Langston Hughes undoubtedly saw himself first and foremost as a poet, and consistently devoted himself to the art of poetry for virtually all of his adult life. At the same time, in his evident desire for literary virtuosity he also clearly regarded few areas of literature as being utterly outside his province as a writer. Accordingly, he was a prolific essayist, dramatist, librettist and lyricist, and writer of fiction.

Indeed, Hughes possessed such a profound interest in and commitment to the art of fiction that even if he had never published a single poem, he would probably still have a place of relative prominence in African-American literary history as the author of not only two novels, *Not Without Laughter* (1930) and *Tambourines to Glory* (1958), but also more than fifty short stories. In his lifetime, these stories formed the basis of his three published collections: *The Ways of White Folks* (1934), *Laughing to Keep from Crying* (1952), and *Something in Common and Other Stories* (1963).

In addition, Hughes's devotion to the art of fiction is sharply illustrated by his development over twenty years, mainly in his weekly newspaper columns in the *Chicago Defender* and other newspapers, of the fictional character Jesse B. Semple, or Simple. In these sketches Hughes created an unforgettable world revolving about Simple, with distinctive characters, situations, and plots that rival in vividness many similar worlds created by other talented writers of fiction. These newspaper sketches, deftly edited, became the raw material for five collections of sketches in Hughes's lifetime, starting with *Simple Speaks His Mind* in 1950. One should also remember Hughes's fiction for children, notably his *Popo and Fifina,* a story about Haiti written with his friend Arna Bontemps and published in 1932.

Hughes's interest in fiction surfaced early in his writing career—almost as early as his poetry. Writing in his first volume of autobiography, *The Big Sea* (1940), Hughes credited his reading of fiction (specifically the thrill of reading and understanding, after some effort, a story in French by Guy de Maupassant) with awakening him in his high-school years to the possibilities of a career for himself as a writer. "I think it was de Maupassant," he declared, "who made me really want to be a writer and write stories about Negroes, so true that people in far-away lands would read them—even after I was dead."

Nevertheless, his first short stories had nothing to do with race. Although Hughes later apparently forgot about them, he published at least two short stories in high school, in the Central High School *Monthly* magazine, when he lived in Cleveland, Ohio, between 1916 and 1920. One extant story, perhaps vicariously autobiographical, is **"Seventy-five Dollars,"** about a lonely boy who pines for a happier, higher life, which his family, mired in poverty, would deny him. Another extant story is **"Mary Winosky,"** which was ostensibly based on a newspaper report about a humble scrubwoman who left at her death the sum of eight thousand dollars, at that time a remarkable amount for a person in her position. Mary Winosky is a lonely, pathetic European immigrant who, after being deserted by her husband, dies heartbroken when the news comes that he has been killed in the Great War. In both stories, Hughes exhibits a keen sense of the tragedy of life, and of the toll that poverty can take on the human spirit. Both stories are sentimental and idealistic narratives, the work of a tender sensibility seeking expression in fiction.

In the next few years, or during the first half of the decade of the 1920s, Hughes seemed to ignore the writing of fiction as he tirelessly laid the foundation of his career and identity as a poet. That foundation became solid with the publication of his first collection of verse, *The Weary Blues,* in 1926 and of his second, *Fine Clothes to the Jew,* a year later. In the summer and fall of 1926, with his first book behind him, and the next virtually finished, Hughes applied himself to fiction. One likely reason for this turn was his presence then as a student at Lincoln University, Pennsylvania (from which he would graduate in 1929), and his enrollment there in a course called "The Short Story," which included the writing of original narratives. However, Hughes was also following a trend which saw the younger writers of the Harlem Renaissance move increasingly toward fiction, after the earlier successes of Hughes, Countee Cullen, and Claude McKay, in particular, as poets.

In this venture into fiction in 1926, Hughes planned to write a series of six stories which would draw on his own experience in 1923 as a young seaman serving on a freighter sailing up and down the coast of West Africa. Of the six stories planned, Hughes finished only four, but these four were striking. Including **"The Young Glory of Him"** and **"Luani of the Jungles,"** the stories reflect not only the exoticism of Hughes's African adventure but also the spirit of independence that dominates his landmark essay "The Negro Artist and the Racial Mountain," which was published in *The Nation* in June of 1926. That essay trumpeted the call for younger black writers to remember both their racial background and their need for a bold independence as artists. Certainly these stories seek to be daring. In contrast to the lachrymose subject matter of his high-school fiction, their typical themes, ironically expressed, include miscegenation, sexual promiscuity, adultery, and the turmoil of sexual repression, all set against a steamy backdrop of tropical warmth and fecundity.

These short stories done, Hughes seemed to set aside the form once again, and to set aside the writing of fiction itself. Then, about two years later, in 1928, he turned to an even more ambitious project in narration. With the fierce encouragement of his domineering white patron Mrs. Charlotte Mason, or Godmother, as she liked to be called, who had taken Hughes up the year before, he went to work on what would be his first novel, *Not Without Laughter.* This story of a young African-American boy, Sandy, growing up in the Midwest with his grandmother and her daughters—with not infrequent visits from his fun-loving, guitar-strumming father—is one of the most affecting and skillfully drawn novels of the Harlem Renaissance. However, Hughes would later characterize it as personally perhaps the least favorite of his books. Two possible reasons come to mind here, although Hughes himself did little to explain his remark. One reason was the unfortunate association of *Not Without Laughter* with his patron, with whom he broke disastrously just about the time the novel appeared. The other was that Hughes never relished the special challenge intrinsic in composing long narratives. Finding the demands of the novel oppressive, he was much more at home with the comparatively lesser demands of the typical short story.

If he disliked writing his novel, he took more pleasure in his task a year or so later when he wrote *Popo and Fifina* with Arna Bontemps. And yet pleasure was probably not his principal motive. Both men appear to have approached the writing of this children's book mainly as a job, during a time of financial need that would grow only more serious during the Depression. Increasingly, in fact, Hughes would see himself as a professional writer, and the short story as one of the more reliable sources of immediate income. If he eventually joked about himself as a "literary sharecropper," then short stories became an important cash crop. This is not to negate the force of inspiration in Hughes's art, including his fiction. After all, the 1930s were the decade of Hughes's most devoted political radicalism, and his sensitivity to racial wrong and to the beauty of black culture was a constant in his life. *Popo and Fifina,* as well as most of his other stories of the era, shows not only Hughes's ideological commitment but also his classic ability to subsume with grace even the most vexing questions of politics and social action within an art rooted in his love of, and commitment to, people of African descent.

Hughes's finest short-story collection, *The Ways of White Folks,* sprang from a mixture of the accidental and the peculiarly personal. In the winter of 1933, living in Moscow, he was reading *The Lovely Lady,* a collection of short stories by the English writer D. H. Lawrence, when both the title story and the story "The Rocking Horse Winner" (as he later wrote in his second volume of autobiography, *I Wonder as I Wander*) "made my hair stand on end." The uncanny resemblance between the grasping old Pauline Attenborough in "The Lovely Lady" and Hughes's own patron Godmother

was so compelling to him that "I could not put the book down, although it brought cold sweat and goose-pimples to my body." Immediately he started writing a story based loosely on his bittersweet experiences with Mrs. Mason in the tormented world of white patronage and black American personality and art.

The first story Hughes wrote was **"Slave on the Block,"** about a silly white Greenwich Village couple whose fantasies of black life and their own existence collide with reality in the persons of their resentful black cook and an insolent young black man who has been made to serve as a model for a sculpture of a slave on an auction block undertaken by the white woman, a dilettante. **"Cora Unashamed"** tells of the searing isolation and sexual deprivation of a forty-year-old black woman living among whites in the Midwest.

The element of cynicism and bitterness in these stories (unprecedented in degree among Hughes's works) and in other stories written in Moscow marks the entire collection *The Ways of White Folks,* which Hughes completed during a year (1933-34) passed in Carmel, California, as the guest of Noel Sullivan, a wealthy but sympathetic white patron of the arts who became one of his closest friends. Hughes's relationship with Mrs. Mason is probably most vividly represented among these stories in **"The Blues I'm Playing,"** in which a musically gifted young black woman finally defies her rich, elderly white patron to marry the man she loves. Perhaps inspired by this investigation of patronage to push even more deeply into the issue of race, Hughes also composed and included in the volume the lengthy story **"Father and Son,"** about a white man in the South and his black "wife" and their children, including the tormented, rebellious son who eventually slays his father.

The Ways of White Folks (a title that surely winks at that of W. E. B. Du Bois's epochal volume of 1903, *The Souls of Black Folk*) was well received by critics. In the *North American Review,* Herschel Brickell hailed it as including "some of the best stories that have appeared in this country in years." In the *Saturday Review,* Vernon Loggins, the author of the recent scholarly study *The Negro Author* (1931), declared the book to be Hughes's strongest work to date. Horace Gregory saluted Hughes for a "spiritual prose style" and for showing such an "accurate understanding of human character" that the book suggested genius. However, the evident anger against racism and racist whites in *The Ways of White Folks* did not please everyone, including some blacks. The prominent African-American scholar Alain Locke, while also praising the book, ventured the opinion that "greater artistry, deeper sympathy and less resentment, would have made it a book for all times." In *The Nation,* the novelist Sherwood Anderson applauded Hughes's depiction of blacks ("My hat is off to you in relation to your own race") but not his depiction of whites, which was mainly caricature, according to Anderson. And even the liberal social activist Martha Gruening deplored the fact, as she saw it, that Hughes showed whites as "either sordid and cruel, or silly and sentimental."

Not long after the appearance of *The Ways of White Folks* in 1934, and following the death of his father in Mexico, Hughes spent several months there. In this time, he devoted himself to translating short stories by various young Mexican writers. However, his attempts to place these stories in North American journals came to nothing; to his dismay, he discovered that a market for Latin American fiction did not yet exist in the United States. Back home, he continued to write stories from time to time, but during the rest of the 1930s clearly emphasized drama rather than fiction or even poetry. The emphasis on drama followed the appearance on Broadway in 1935 of his sensational play about miscegenation in the South, *Mulatto* (the lengthy story **"Father and Son,"** in *The Ways of White Folks,* is a fictional treatment of the dramatic text, which Hughes had written around 1930-31).

Thereafter, Hughes would not publish stories with any marked regularity, nor would he write them in any single, concentrated effort as was the case with *The Ways of White Folks.* Both *Laughing to Keep from Crying* in 1952 and *Something in Common* in 1963 would comprise old and new stories. Without diminishing his literary reputation in any way, neither volume attracted much more than passing attention from literary critics.

If Hughes did not rush to repeat the experience of writing *The Ways of White Folks,* the sardonic and satirical tone of most of the stories in that volume became firmly established in his subsequent body of short stories. Occasionally, as in **"Thank You, M'am,"** about a black boy on the verge of a life of delinquency who is rehabilitated by an upstanding, kindly black woman, Hughes struck a sentimental note as he sought to contribute to the literature of black social uplift rather than reflect his anger against racism. The biting satire of a story such as **"Rejuvenation thru Joy,"** in *The Ways of White Folks* (about gullible whites with money and a con-man trading on their fantasies), is also abundantly present in Hughes's later work. Sometimes satire is inspired by Hughes's rage against racism, but in **"Blessed Assurance,"** for example, it springs from his mordant desire to lampoon both homosexual desire as outlandishly expressed in some instances within the black church and the homophobic intolerance and ignorance of many middle-class blacks. In the story, a father lashes out in bewilderment and rage against the evident gayness of his son, a sweet-voiced singer in a church choir.

Looking back on the body of Hughes's short fiction, it is noticeable that, on the whole, the short story served both as a professional outlet and as a way for him to express some of his more complex moods as he faced the world. While the themes of his poetry range from radical political anger to an almost ethereal lyricism, the range of his fiction is in some respects narrower. On the one hand, none of the stories, for example, preaches radical socialism, as in the manner of Richard Wright in his *Uncle Tom's Children*; on the other, very few of the stories "rise" entirely above race, or seek to do so.

This relative narrowness gives much of his short fiction a peculiar force in penetrating the world described in it. In his short stories, Hughes was generally far less didactic than in much of his poetry. He is typically the cool, sometimes cold, and occasionally even cruel observer of the human scene. Ever mindful of the distorting effects of racism and social injustice on people, he was often more concerned in his fiction with depicting, from a distance, the follies and foibles of human beings trapped by their prejudices and their inability or unwillingness to imagine and live by a vivid sense of the ideal.

Tayari A. Jones (essay date fall/spring 1999-2001)

SOURCE: Jones, Tayari A. "Beyond the Privilege of the Vernacular: A Textual Comparison of the Characterization of Bondswomen in *Their Eyes Were Watching God* and 'Father and Son.'" *The Langston Hughes Review* 16, nos. 1 & 2 (fall/spring 1999-2001): 71-80.

[*In the following essay, Jones contends that the relationship between Cora and Colonel Norwood in "Father and Son" reveals Hughes's misconception of black women as voiceless victims of a "plantation" mindset.*]

One point to begin examining the place, tradition, and significance of the vernacular in African American critical and fictive discourses is to recall the Harlem Renaissance debates on the problem of racial representation in African American expressive culture. In Alain Locke's epochal anthology, *The New Negro,* Du Bois's "Criteria of Negro Art," James Weldon Johnson's preface to his *Book of American Negro Poetry,* Langston Hughes's "The Negro Artist and the Racial Mountain," and Zora Neale Hurston's "Characteristics of Negro Expression," the problem of image and language in African American art forms a generational, ideological, and gendered divide in the era of the New Negro.

The older generation of Black artists and critics such as W. E. B. Du Bois declared that all art is propaganda and that African American artists should create works that represent the race with its "best foot forward" by using forms and symbols that emanate from within the culture. The writers of this period sought to define themselves and their race with their creative offerings. *The New Negro* by Alain Locke was to be the manifesto of the period. In his introduction to this important volume, Locke asserts that *The New Negro* "aims to document the New Negro culturally and socially." He suggests that this documentation will cause the white population to reevaluate their perception of African Americans:

> Liberal minds today cannot be asked to peer sympathetically into the darkened cave of a segregated race life. That was yesterday. Nor must they expect to find a mind and soul so bizarre and alien as the mind of a savage or even as refreshing and pleasant as the mind of a child or a peasant. That too was yesterday and the day before.
>
> (xxvi)

Du Bois believes that bringing about this change of opinion is the sole purpose of art:

> All art is propaganda and ever must be, despite the wailing of the purists. I do not care a damn for any art that is not used for propaganda. But I do care when propaganda is confined to one side and the other is stripped and silent.
>
> (66)

Needless to say, this was an aesthetic that sought to subvert representations of African Americans and their culture from scientific, philosophic, and minstrel discourses as well as their mainstream literary propaganda vehicles.

In "The Negro Artist and the Racial Mountain," Langston Hughes spoke for many of "the younger Negro Artists" when he proclaimed his own and their emancipation from the propagandistic, thus restrictive, use of Black sounds and images in art. If there is a modernist birth of Black vernacular art and criticism, then this Hughes essay is a signal moment in making African American expressive culture new. Of course, newness in artistic production means revising significant models of exemplary figures.

One of these models would be position and significance of dialect in African American art. For the prior limits of Black vernacular expressions, one might look to the turn of the turn-of-the-century dialect poetry of Paul Laurence Dunbar, an African American poet. Dunbar received national recognition with a collection of poems called *Lyrics of Lowly Life,* which was published with an introduction by William Dean Howells, the "Dean of American Letters." Dunbar, according to Howells, was "the first man of pure African blood to experience Negro life aesthetically, and express it lyrically" (xvii). Howell's praise of Dunbar is bittersweet, however. Howells writes:

> It appears to me that there is a precious difference in temperament between the races which it would be a great pity to ever lose, and that this is best preserved and most charmingly suggested by Mr. Dunbar in those pieces of his where he studies the moods and traits of his race in its own accent of our English. We call such pieces dialect pieces . . . but they are . . . delightful attempts and failures for the written and spoken language.

In short, Howells praised Dunbar for documenting his own race's inferiority so charmingly. This distressed Dunbar greatly. His previous book of poems was called *Oak and Ivy*; the standard English poems were to be the oak and the dialect pieces the ivy. But Howells had insisted that in the dialect poems, Dunbar was "most himself," and the standard English poems were not "a significant contribution to American Literature" (xviii). Only dialect was considered to be authentically African American.

James Weldon Johnson was aware of the position occupied by dialect in the mainstream imagination. Unlike his contemporaries, Locke and Du Bois, he proposed a revision of the use of dialect rather than a wholesale condemnation and abandonment of the form:

> They [African American authors] are trying to break away from not Negro dialect itself but the limitation of Negro dialect imposed by the fixing effects of long convention. . . . What the colored poet in the United States needs to do is something like what Synge did for the Irish: he needs to find a form that will express the racial spirit by symbols from within rather than by symbols from without such as the mere mutilation of English spelling and pronunciation.
>
> (41)

Amidst the American Civil Rights and Black Power Movements, critics and artists began to recover and reassess the works of many African American writers. However, Dunbar's poetic reputation was not enhanced by the new Black Aesthetic critics who sought to create a politically progressive African American literary and cultural tradition. Viewed as a poetic relic, Dunbar's work was shunned by Black Aesthetic critics for the same reasons that Johnson foresaw more than a generation earlier. However, many critics of the sixties and seventies embraced the use of dialect in the works of both Hurston and Hughes. The difference, I think, is that Dunbar's writing was clearly written to entertain a white audience, and thus appears historically and culturally inauthentic. (Notice that Howells refers to "our" English in contrast to Dunbar's.) Hurston and Hughes were celebrated by the next wave of black writers and critics because they seemed to be writing truthfully about black life and history for the benefit of black readers, and were not concerned with the reception of their work by white readers.

However, a close reading of texts written by Hurston and Hughes suggests that these two icons of vernacular literature produced work that addressed white supremacist ideas about race and racism in radically different ways. The works of Hurston and Hughes are often coupled because of their opposition to the *New Negro* "best foot forward" position. However, they differ greatly in their representations of the crucial figure in any significant attempt to creatively characterize African American culture in a historically meaningful way: the portrayal of black women. More specifically, they differ in dramatizing the meaning of freedom in the lives of black women. Of course the most profitable site to examine this difference occurs in depictions of woman who have experienced life as bondswomen and freedwomen. Nanny, in Hurston's *Their Eyes Were Watching God,* and Cora, in Hughes's short story **"Father and Son,"** are mothers whose children are the products of relations with their masters: Nanny's is forced, and Cora's an act of her seductive intent. Hurston's portrait of Nanny is strikingly similar to Harriet Jacobs's self-portrait in *Incidents in the Life of a Slave Girl.* I will argue that Hughes's dramatization of Cora tends to reinforce white supremacist stereotypes of black women and their sexuality.

Hughes's **"Father and Son"** turns on the tensions that develop between the plantation owner, Colonel Norwood, and his and Cora's mulatto son, Bert. Norwood refuses to acknowledge Bert, or any of the other four children that he has had by Cora, as his own. A sense of *noblesse oblige* and shared bloodlines compels Norwood to send Bert away to school. When Bert returns to the plantation during a summer break, he seeks to claim publicly and privately his humanity and his father's acknowledgment of his paternity. After demanding service normally reserved for white men in town, he walks through the front door of his home like a white man instead of through the back door like a servant. The results are predictable.

Yet, the relationship of Colonel Norwood and Bert's mother, Cora, is "not a story to be passed on." Hughes presents a spousal relationship between the African American woman who lives on a plantation and the man who has complete control of every aspect of her life. The implication of this seemingly consensual relation suggests that such women could refuse such liaisons.[1]

Cora's initial attraction to the Colonel is as mundane as a teenager's infatuation. Hughes writes:

> Gossip has begun to say that the young Colonel had taken up with the cook's daughter . . . Livonia. Cora heard all of this and a certain envy sprang up. Livonia! Huh! Cora began to look more carefully into the cracked mirror in her mother's cabin. She combed her hair and oiled it better than before. . . . When she took milk to the Big House now, she tried to look her best.

That Cora's response to the gossip surrounding the Colonel's relationship with Livonia arouses merely envy is significant. Obviously, she had never had any experience to suggest to her that the young Colonel was any different from any other young man she may have been interested in. No one warned her about the possible consequences of such a liaison. Had they, she certainly would not have labored so assiduously to make herself more conspicuous and seductive. Compare Hughes's narrative of attraction with that of Harriet Jacobs in her autobiography:

> [My master] announced his intention to take his youngest daughter to sleep in his apartment. It was necessary that a servant sleep in the same room. I was selected for that office. . . . I had hitherto succeeded in eluding my master though a razor was often held to my throat to force me to change this policy. At night, I slept beside my great Aunt, where I felt safe. . . . He was well aware how I prized my refuge by the side of my great Aunt and was determined to dispossess me of it.
>
> (110)

This passage, a recollection of the real-life experiences of a female slave, describes a terrified teenager. As well, the young girl could find protection in the other women in bondage. Obviously, young women were not left to find out the realities of plantation life on their own. This tradition of older women guiding and protecting younger women is further illustrated in *Their Eyes Were Watching God.* Nanny, an emancipated slave woman who no longer lives on the plantation but lives in a Jim Crow world, pledges herself to shelter Janie, who is not old enough to "know where harm is at" (13). Harm, in this case, is sexual exploitation. Janie, like Cora, is an innocent adolescent who understands sexuality merely as a blossoming of life: "Oh to be a pear tree—any tree—in bloom! With kissing bees and the singing of the beginning of the world! She was sixteen. She had glossy leaves and bursting buds" (11). Nanny, whose glossy leaves have been reduced to "the standing roots of some old tree ravished by storm" by her own sexual abuse during slavery, and later, the sexual abuse of her daughter, reprimands Janie in such a way as to make an innocent "kiss across the gatepost seem like a manure pile after the rain" (12).

Cora, on the other hand, is encouraged by her mother to become sexually involved with the Colonel. When she tells her mother that she is pregnant, the woman reacts as if her daughter has received some great honor:

> The old woman was glad. "It's better'n slaving in the cotton fields," she said. "I's known colored women what's worn silk dresses right here in Georgy."

This scene hardly serves as a generalizable gloss on upward mobility as expressed in Nanny's desire that Janie "pick from a higher bush and a sweeter berry" (13). Moreover, in slave narratives concubinage is not a coveted state. Silk dresses are hardly ample reward for the harsh repercussions that accompany being the mother of an obviously mulatto child.

Both Jacobs and Hurston concur that sexually exploited slave women are in a position of double jeopardy. Jacobs passionately declares that she

> would rather drudge out her life on a cotton plantation, til the grave opened to give [her] rest than to live with an unprincipled master and a jealous mistress.
>
> (49)

Hurston captures this sentiment through Nanny's punishment at the hand of the wife of her children's father when she sees that the child is a mulatto. Nanny recounts her mistress's reaction. "First thing in d mornin' de overseer will take you to the whipping post and cut the hide offa yo' yaller back."[2]

The wrath of the plantation mistress is not the only possible reprisal a black woman faced. Although it is not apparent in **"Father and Son,"** there was a strict African American moral code on the plantation that served to restrict such expressions of female sexuality. In Hughes's story, the servants all laugh upon learning that "The cook's daughter, . . . Livonia, had taken up with the Colonel. . . . Livonia had four or five Negro lovers, too. And she wasn't faithful to anybody—just liked to love" (215). This scenario repeats and reinforces the stereotype of Africans having no respect for monogamy and marriage. Historian Paula Giddings observes:

> Black women were seen as having all of the inferior qualities of white women with none of the virtue. One writer (in *The Independent*) wrote "Black women have the brains of children and the passions of women. . . . They are steeped in ignorance and savagery and wrapped about with moral vices." Another in 1902 writes, "I sometimes hear of a virtuous Negro woman but the idea is absolutely inconceivable to me."
>
> (Giddings 82)

In Jacobs's and Hurston's texts Linda (Harriet Jacobs) and Janie are both severely reprimanded for what is interpreted as licentious behavior. Nanny slaps Janie's face "violently" while accusing her of wanting "to kiss and hug and feel around with first one man and then another" (13). When her grandmother discovers Linda's premarital affair she exclaims, "I had rather see you dead than to see you as you are now. You are a disgrace to your dead mother" (57). With this she tears the mother's wedding ring from Linda's hand. Linda is later reunited with her grandmother but she notes that her grandmother "did not say 'I forgive you'"; instead, "she looked at [Linda] with her eyes full of tears and murmured (sic), 'Poor child!'" (58).

Punishment for private acts were not only administered by the immediate family. Licentious behavior could result in the offender being thrown out of the church congregation. On some plantations, the slaves would punish a woman that was "loose" by making her the subject of a song warning her to amend her behavior (Giddings 84).

The practice of putting the woman "in song" and the ethical code supporting it, though based on African culture, was largely influenced by the Victorian notion of ladyhood. Purity was one of the primary tenets of what would later be dubbed "The Cult of True Womanhood." Black women were determined to resist the stereotyped image of themselves as immoral and lascivious by striving to be as loyal to the cult as the most pious big house mistress (Giddings 87). When Janie becomes embarrassed after Nanny asks if she is pregnant, Nanny tells her, "You ain't got nothing to be ashamed of, honey, youse uh married 'oman. You got your lawful husband *same as Mis' Washburn*[3] or anybody else" (21). The fact that Janie's marriage is legal like a white woman's legitimizes it and gives Janie permission to be sexual.

Like Nanny, Jacobs's women are able to resist racism through individual coercive effort. Since they are without material advantages, they use their voices to assert power. Cora, however, lacks what Joanne M. Braxton calls "sass" (386). Jacobs demonstrates how a person who has no tangible weapons uses words as self-defense. In one instance, Linda's master demands, "Do you know that I have the right to do as I like with you—that I can kill you if I please?" Negotiating for respect, Linda replies: "You have tried to kill me, and I wish you had; but you have no right to do as you like with me" (62). Sass is an effective tool that allows Linda to preserve her self-esteem and to increase the psychological distance between herself and the master. She uses sass the way Frederick Douglass uses his hands and feet, as a means of expressing her resistance (Braxton 386).

Since *Their Eyes* [*Their Eyes Were Watching God*] is not set on the plantation, we do not know if Nanny uses her voice to resist the advances of the master. But we do know that she is aware of her voice as a tool of exerting power. She tells Janie, "Ah wanted to preach a sermon about colored women sittin' high, but there wasn't no pulpit" (15). Nanny does get to preach her sermon to a congregation of one: Janie. She is able to convince Janie to marry so that Janie would not be "used for a work-ox or a brood sow."

Cora does not use her voice to liberate herself like Jacobs or to liberate her children like Nanny. Indeed, she speaks very little in the tale. When she does speak, it is to protect her son from his father or to express her submission to the master. Not only do her words reflect her cowardice and complacency but they indicate a sense of complicity in her oppression. At one point, she urges the headstrong Bert to "be like Willie" who is—in Bert's words—"A White folks' nigger" (237). Throughout the text, Cora's silence and speech are indistinguishable from representations of black women in any white racist text. She is a breeder for the southern white aristocracy.

Even as the story ends and Cora does find her voice, it lacks sass; Cora has gone insane. Her soliloquy is proof of her insanity. She rails against the then-dead Colonel. The madness relieves her of her inhibitions. But in this candid state, she does not speak of her own condition. Instead, she expresses her anger at the Colonel's treatment of Bert. Cora, in her dementia, admonishes the Colonel's "purple-white" body (244):

> You's cruel, Tom. . . . I might a-knowed it—you'd be like that sending ma boy out to die. . . . Well, you won't mistreat him no more. . . . I'm gonna make a place for him. . . . Don't you come to ma bed either no more a-tall. I calls for you to help me now, Tom, and you just lays there. . . . Whenever you called *me* in the night, I came to you. Goddam you, Tom Norwood.
>
> (247)

Cora's hysteria has relieved her of her inhibitions, and she fears no punishment. Yet, she still fails to acknowledge the wrongs against her.

Why, then, does Hughes imagine so different a scenario for Cora than Hurston and Jacobs imagine for their heroines? The difference between resistance and acquiescence to sexual commodification is of no small creative consequence. Instead, it suggests Hughes's devaluation of black women's sexuality. While he recognizes that women's sexuality is frequently commodified, he does not characterize the injustice. The entire narrative rests upon the assumption that women gladly barter their bodies in exchange for material rewards and that this exchange is possibly just. No irony is intended here as Cora loses her only means of support and two of her sons to the lynch mob; moreover, the resolution of the story finds that Cora is not an heir to the Colonel's estate.

Hughes's characterization of female commodification of their sexuality is not restricted to **"Father and Son."** The image of the woman as prostitute is prevalent in Hughes's poetry. "Sister" contains the lines, "Did it ever occur to you, son / the reason Marie runs around with trash / is that she wants some cash?" Another poem, "Dancer," reads "When you are no good for dough, they [the women] go." These poems suggest that women are aware of their bodies as commodities even if the naive men are not. Finally, "Ultimatum" shows the empowerment of a man once he understands this:

> Baby, how come you can't see me
> when I am paying your bills
> each and every week
> If you got somebody else
> tell me—
> Else I'll cut you off
> without your rent
> I mean without a cent

I have argued that the relationship between Cora and the Colonel is more coercive than the one described in "Ultimatum." In the case of the slave woman-master relationships, Hughes seem oblivious to the power dynamics in that sustain the system. Interestingly enough, many critics—male and female—have shared the author's perspective. One critic remarks that the Colonel and Cora have a "thirty year affair" (James 66). Another borrows Hughes's definition of Cora as the Colonel's "mistress" (Nifong 94). A third even writes that Cora's "mind refers to the first night that he *made love*[4] to her" (Ricks 103). The expressions *mistress, affair,* and *made love* imply mutuality and romance, and fail to suggest that the relationship between Bert's biological parents is an atypical relationship.

Hughes and the critics have failed to closely examine the reality of the slave woman or those in coercive situations. The subject of miscegenation is often written about but much of the literature on the subject concerns the fate of the offspring or even the fate of the woman after the children are born. Very little examines the *relationship* between the women and the men. Recent studies of interviewing techniques of ex-slaves have indicated that researchers shied away from discussions of this subject (Morton).

Without a close examination of the reality of legally or de facto "enslaved" woman, critics and artists like Hughes tend to frame the relationship in a context with which they are already familiar. The result is a cartoonish picture that is antithetical to the testimony of women's slave narratives and separates Hughes's vision from that of Hurston and Jacobs. The women writers see the slave woman as an oppressed but subtly powerful person. Though racism and sexism—in the words of Hurston—keeps her from "fulfillin [her] dreams of whut a woman oughta be and oughta do . . . Nothing can stop her from wishin" (15). The female writers document the slave woman's vulnerability at the hands of men who control her without stripping her of her strength and personal worth. Nanny and Linda's predicaments do not stop them from "wishin" and fighting. This "wishin" motivates them to use whatever weapons they have to enforce their version of justice. Though neither woman is able to triumph completely, each is able to improve her life significantly so that she and the succeeding generation would not have to suffer so again.

A more charitable reading of Hughes's characterization of Cora situates it in the African American male tradition of black woman portraiture between that of slave narratives such as Frederick Douglass's 1845 *Narrative* and Richard Wright's *Black Boy* (1945). In Douglass's text it can be argued that the representations of slave women function primarily as objects of white male desire and brutality. The presence of black women alert both Douglass and his readers to the inhumanity of slavery without allowing the women to express anything more than their basic desires. In *Black Boy* the central function of Wright's mother and grandmother is to teach and physically reinforce "the ways of white folks," so that the young man will survive to be a man. As with Douglass, miscegenation figures in the Hughes genealogy as well as this story of a white father and his black son. In this sense, Bert, the male tragic mulatto, can be read as a fictional refiguration of Hughes's sense of liminality in early twentieth century America. As a tragic mulatto tale, **"Father and Son"** is also about the relationships of Cora and her sons and daughter. With the notable exception of the unusual and long-standing romantic yearnings Cora has for Colonel Norwood, one looks in vain for any expression of her desires beyond satisfying those of the Colonel, and protecting the lives of their children. While Hurston's Nanny cautiously arranges Janie's initial marriage to insure her granddaughter's financial security, she is also concerned with having her granddaughter achieve the legal and cultural status that was denied black women during slavery and its aftermath in both fictive discourse and the real world.

Contemporary creative writers and critics of African American literature have followed the lead of Hurston and Hughes in choosing to privilege the vernacular as the site for the production and analysis of black sounds, images, and performances. However, locating a convivial and productive site for African American literary activities only begins the obligations of writers and critics to attend to the gendered politics of form and the form of politics produced if we are to avoid the bones of contention that may inhibit the production of a useful and beautiful literature.

Notes

1. Some readers may object that Cora is not "owned" by the Colonel since the story is set after emancipation. I would agree that she is not *legally* chattel. However, her situation is sufficiently similar to the inhuman condition of human bondage to be described as such. Cora and her family live on a "plantation" under the authority of a man sometimes referred to as "Massa" who is aided by an "overseer" (207, 238, 222). Further, her family has been in his servitude for at least three generations. The Colonel declares that "if [the servants] turn in crops they get a living."

2. Here, Nanny is quoting her mistress. The speech pattern here is Nanny's but the words are her mistress's.

3. Italics mine.

4. Italics mine.

Works Cited

Braxton, Joanne M. "Harriet Jacobs's *Incidents in the Life of a Slave Girl Written by Herself*: The Re-

Definition of the Slave Narrative Genre." *Massachusetts Review: A Quarterly of Literature, the Arts, and Public Affairs.* Summer 1986.

Du Bois, W. E. B. "The Criteria of Negro Art." *Within the Circle* (60-68). First published in *Crisis.* 32 (October 1926).

Foster, Francis. "'In Respect to Families': Differences in the Portrayals of Women by Male and Female Narrators." *Black American Literature Forum.* Summer 1981. 66-70.

Howells, William Dean. Introduction. *Lyrics of Lowly Life.* By Paul Lawrence Dunbar. New York: Citadel Press, 1993.

Hughes, Langston. "Father and Son." *The Ways of White Folks.* New York: Vintage Books, 1990. 207-55.

———. "The Negro Artist and the Racial Mountain." *Within the Circle.* (55-59). First published in *The Nation* 122 (1926).

Hurston, Zora Neale. *Their Eyes Were Watching God.* New York: Harper and Row, 1990.

———. "Characteristics of Negro Expression." *Within the Circle.* (79-94). First published in Nancy Cunard, ed. *The Negro: An Anthology.* London, 1934.

Jacobs, Harriet. *Incidents in the Life of a Slave Girl Written by Herself.* Miami, FL: Mnemosyne Publishing Company, 1969.

Johnson, James Weldon. Preface. *The Book of American Negro Poetry.* New York: Harcourt Brace, 1969.

Locke, Alaine, ed. *The New Negro.* New York: Simon and Schuster, 1992.

Mitchell, Angelyn, ed. *Within the Circle: An Anthology of African-American Literary Criticism from the Harlem Renaissance to the Present.* Durham, NC: Duke University Press, 1994.

Morton, Patricia, ed. *Discovering the Women in Slavery: Emancipating Perspectives on the American Past.* Athens: University of Georgia Press, 1996.

Nifong, David M. "Narrative Technique and Theory in *The Ways of White Folks.*" *Black American Literature Forum.* Fall 1981. 93-96.

Ricks, Sybil Ray. "A Textual Comparison of Langston Hughes's *Mulatto,* 'Father and Son,' and 'The Barrier.'" *Black American Literature Forum.* Fall 1981. 101-3.

Jane Olmsted (essay date 2000)

SOURCE: Olmsted, Jane. "Black Moves, White Ways, Every Body's Blues: Orphic Power in Langston Hughes's *The Ways of White Folks.*" In *Black Orpheus:*

Music in African American Fiction from the Harlem Renaissance to Toni Morrison, edited by Saadi A. Simawe, pp. 65-89. New York: Garland Publishing, Inc., 2000.

[*In the following essay, Olmsted considers the transformational power of music in* The Ways of White Folks.]

> The written word is a power, and to use that
> power for false purposes would seem to me to
> be morally wrong.
>
> —Langston Hughes, *The Dream Keeper*

Much of what has been written about Langston Hughes and the blues focuses on his poetry. Few extended analyses address his fiction, and only one critic that I have found mentions orphic power in relation to Hughes's fiction. Referring to the musician Roy's mother in the short story **"Home,"** R. Baxter Miller (1976) says that her perspective is one of "three variations of the theme on music and art in Hughes' short fiction: contemplation, orphic power, and anticipation of Messianic Presence." Because Roy's mother is religious, "she is well-suited for making an observation concerning myth. In Roy's music, she perceives an orphic power" (33). This "orphic" power is present in Hughes's use of the blues as ethos and aesthetic in several, if not all, of the stories in *The Ways of White Folks* (1933).

This collection is, according to some, Hughes's "harshest" critique of White people. But this is a limited observation at best. Hughes is not interested solely in pointing out the flaws of White folks in relation to Black folks (a rather simple task), but rather in examining their relation to the blues, if a relationship not rooted in acquisitiveness and appropriation is possible at all. Sterling Brown makes clear, "You can't play the blues until you have paid your dues," and LeRoi Jones (Amiri Baraka) (1963) writes that "[b]lues means a Negro experience" (both quoted in Alan Dundes, 470). In citing these two spokespersons, Alan Dundes (1990) suggests that "[i]f being a Negro is a prerequisite to playing the blues, it may also be one for understanding all the nuances of the blues." Despite any universal truths that the blues can offer listeners/participants who are not Black, the heart of the blues is the lived experience of Black people—not necessarily all Black people; as such, it is rooted in, derived from, and lived through Black consciousness. In fact, LeRoi Jones marks the "beginning of blues as one beginning of American Negroes . . . the Negro's experience in this country in his English is one beginning of the Negro's conscious appearance on the American scene" (xii). Still, the blues is a widely popular, broadly reflective aesthetic that is likely, as Jones argues, to reveal "something about the essential nature of the Negro's existence in this country . . . as well as something about the essential nature of this

country, i.e., society as a whole" (x).[1] The extent to which an "essential nature" can avoid turning into a totalizing narrative is as relevant to the blues as anything else.

These observations seem fruitful as a way of setting the stage for my own discussion of Hughes's first collection of stories, *The Ways of White Folks.* First, to what extent is a "blues ideology" important to the stories, and how might one characterize it? For instance, does it, as Miller suggests, partake of orphic power? What is the relation between the Black middle class, the "common" folk, and Hughes's blues aesthetics? What is the dynamic between the White bourgeoisie and Black folk and the blues? Finally, how does the notion of mobility—migration, touring, uprootedness, searching, or domesticity—help us to understand this collection of stories as one "grounded" in or, perhaps, "processed" as the blues?

Some consider the "Simple" stories of the 1940s (first published in the *Chicago Defender* under a column Hughes titled "Here to Yonder" and later published separately) to reflect a blues perspective about life, particularly in the overlay of humor and sadness. Hughes himself said: "For sad as Blues may be, there's almost always something humorous about them—even if it's the kind of humor that laughs to keep from crying" (quoted in Klotman 1975, 76). Jess B. Simple explains the blues and his own connection to the blues tradition this way:

> The blues can be real sad, else real mad, else real glad, and funny, too, all at the same time. I ought to know. Me, I growed up with the blues. Facts is, I heard so many blues when I were a child until my shadow was blue. And when I were a young man, and left Virginia and runned away to Baltimore, behind me came the shadow of the blues.
>
> (from **"Simple's Uncle Sam,"** quoted in Klotman 1975, 76)

Even Simple's name, Jess Be Simple, reflects Hughes's philosophy about his art, particularly his use of the blues: "[W]here life is simple, truth and reality are one" (Hughes 1940, 311). In fact, Simple's simplicity, his everyday-folks intelligence, was the most significant source of his appeal, in part because he countered the prevailing racist stereotypes that Black people were either exceptional or grotesque (Blyden Jackson, cited in Harper 1995, 9). Richard Wright emphasizes Hughes's affinity to the common folk—not only to explain his appeal, but to indicate the link between his life and his art:

> Unlike the sons and daughters of Negro "society," Hughes was not ashamed of those of his race who had to scuffle for their bread. The jerky transitions of his own life did not admit of his remaining in one place long enough to become a slave of prevailing Negro middle-class prejudices.
>
> (quoted in Harper 1995, 9)

Two strands of experience and perspective provide the underlying power of *The Ways of White Folks.* First, the stories were written during a period of intense social awareness and sensitivity. *Ways* [*The Ways of White Folks*] was published in 1933—eight years after Langston Hughes's first book and three years after the extended and painful termination of his relationship with his White patron, Mrs. Osgood Mason. Most of the stories had appeared in a variety of periodicals between 1931 and 1934; three stories were written in a creative burst in 1931, when Langston Hughes was living in Moscow; still others were written immediately after his return from the Soviet Union. Arnold Rampersad (1986) notes the influence of D. H. Lawrence's collection of stories, *The Lovely Lady* (1927), which Hughes read while he was in Moscow:

> In Lawrence's stories Hughes saw not only something of the face of his tormentor, Charlotte Mason, but also glimpses of his own neuroses. . . . Now he stressed the volatile mixture of race, class, and sexuality behind not only his troubles with Mrs. Mason, but also the rituals of liberal race relations in the United States.
>
> (269)[2]

Coming on the heels of one of the most significant disappointments of his life and awakened, perhaps, by Lawrence's direct criticisms in fiction of bourgeois privilege, Hughes in this collection of short stories seems to have pulled into sharp focus a significant perspective about modern Black-White relations. Rampersad's chronology of Hughes's life in *The Collected Poems of Langston Hughes* (1994) notes that 1931 marked "a major ideological turn to the left," a change of consciousness that surely found its way into his stories (10).

Second, Hughes's passion for the blues as a necessary expression of Black consciousness, and music in general as an orphic metaphor for human capacity—to free our spirits from conformity and worse oppressions—seems to have acted as a catalyst for the creative, "chemical reaction"[3] that makes the collection so powerful. He had already demonstrated his intention to integrate the blues into his poetry, not only in *The Weary Blues* (1926) (which received good reviews) but in *Fine Clothes to the Jew* (1927) as well, which was criticized in the African American press "because of its emphasis on allegedly unsavory aspects of the blues culture" (Hughes 1994, 9). Such criticism undoubtedly reflects the tensions about representation that simmered throughout the period. Hughes contended in "The Negro Artist and the Racial Mountain" (1926/1972):

> These common people are not afraid of spirituals, as for a long time their more intellectual brethren were, and jazz is their child. They furnish a wealth of colorful, distinctive material for any artists because they still hold their individuality in the face of American standardizations. . . . And perhaps these common people will give to the world its truly great Negro artist, the one who is not afraid to be himself. Whereas the better-class Negro would tell the artist what to do, the people at least let him alone when he does appear.
>
> (168-69)

The "low-down folks" were the first blues people, and they continue to be the subjects of its lyrics—in fact, part of the appeal even for the "better-class" listeners may be an identification with the vulnerable singer/persona who survives (and thrives). Furthermore, "the beauty, unpretentiousness, and vivacity of the folk could be infused [Hughes hoped] into the all-too-reserved middle-class African-American; but the complex social interaction between environment and ethos made a complete sympathy and understanding nearly impossible" (Tracy 1988, 47-48). Thus, the orphic power of the blues has its limitations: mere listening, no matter how polite, won't take one anyplace.

Class tensions are strongly woven into the race themes promised in "the ways of white folks," which echoes Du Bois' "souls of black folks" and suggests a focus on the interrelations between the two races. To address these issues, I would like to focus on four stories, which meet at least one of the following criteria: the blues is either explicitly mentioned or evoked; some facet of Black-White attitudes about art is explored; mobility is associated with a particular aesthetic, whether it be Black, White, or some syncretic blend. Since I will not be considering the stories one at a time, but rather together as they help to answer the specific questions, a brief orientation of each story now may prove useful later.

"Home" is about Roy Williams, a brilliant violinist, who returns home after a stint performing in Europe. He becomes increasingly ill as he witnesses the contrast between the starving poor in Vienna, Berlin, and Prague, and the music-consuming, wealthy audiences. Longing to see his mother again, he arrives home to be confronted with the local version of racism, which leads ultimately to his murder when he is seen shaking hands with the one person who truly understands his music, a White woman. Collapsing social and racial barriers, the orphic power of Roy's music (which is classical rather than the blues) allows the two to share an understanding that even his mother cannot grasp. Before the mob attacks, however, he offers two feverish performances, a concert at a local church and a duet with the music teacher at the White high school—clearly an outrage to certain townspeople. **"Rejuvenation through Joy"** tells the story of a scam by two con artists, Sol and Eugene Lesche, who establish a colony for wealthy White patrons who are eager to get their "souls fixed up." What's missing in people's lives is joy (they've been "ennui'ed" to death), and the secret to joy is the primitive, located in the Negro's "amusing and delightful rhythms," which can unharden the most hardened arteries, just as Orpheus was able to soften the most resistant gods in the underworld.

The third story, **"The Blues I'm Playing,"** is the first story most critics refer to when they consider Hughes's use of the blues in his fiction. Oceola Jones is such a talented pianist that she is taken under the wing of a wealthy White patron, a Mrs. Dora Ellsworth, an obvious allusion to Mrs. Mason, Hughes's "godmother" (a term she insisted on being called). Oceola, although successfully groomed for classical performance, has an annoying tendency to enjoy the blues, and her sweetheart (even though Mrs. Ellsworth is convinced he is draining her musical talent), and to embrace a simpler and less pretentious art aesthetic than the one in vogue among expatriates in Europe. The two perspectives are beautifully juxtaposed in the closing pages of the story, when Oceola performs for the last time in Mrs. Ellsworth's home. As Beethoven and Chopin give way to the "soft and lazy syncopation of the blues," Mrs. Ellsworth's rising voice and claims about how much Oceola is giving up are insufficient to counter Oceola's own convictions that the blues are right for her.

Finally, in **"Red-Headed Baby,"** the White sailor Clarence returns after three years to the rundown home of the Black woman he had "christened," hoping for some sexual entertainment—despite his strongly ambivalent feelings about the "skeleton houses . . . in the nigger section . . . at the edge of town" (Hughes 1933/1990, 132). The very short story is characterized by Clarence's stream-of-consciousness ramblings juxtaposed with compressed dialogue. His visit is cut short when a red-headed, deaf baby with yellow skin appears at the door. Horrified at seeing himself in the tiny child, Clarence stumbles away, throwing down enough money to pay for the drink he'd already consumed, suggesting that he is attempting to pay off the family for the new addition as well as his own conscience.

My first set of questions, then, is, to what extent is a "blues ideology" important to the stories, and how might one characterize it? What is the relation between the Black middle-class, the "common" folk, and Hughes's blues aesthetics? Tracy (1988) offers the following summary of the conflicting definitions and analyses of the blues:

> Many people have attempted to define and analyze the blues, and their interpretations of what the blues are and do sometimes clash with each other. There is some truth in what the writers say, but their attempts to make their pronouncements absolute can be their downfall. Some say all blues are sad. Others claim that they are happy. This one says they are political; that one, apolitical. The blues, it is said, are a personal expression. No, comes the reply, they express the values of the

> group. Dramatic dialogues. Self-catharsis. Audience catharsis. Dance music. Devil music. Truth. The truth is, the blues can be all of these things. . . . [The blues] have a depth and breadth that reflect a range of emotion, experience, and imagination, so all blues should not be treated as if they are the same.

(75)

For Hughes, the blues seems generally to have been a "resource, as part of a folk past, or as part of a common past being lost to upwardly mobile blacks who were being trained away from their roots" (Tracy, 113). In his first autobiography, *The Big Sea* (1940), Hughes describes the music and the milieu of Seventh Street as a sharp contrast with the "conventional-mindedness" and "pretentiousness" of the upper-class Blacks of Washington, DC: on this "long, old, dirty street, where the ordinary Negroes hang out," the songs are "gay songs, because you had to be gay or die; sad songs, because you couldn't help being sad sometimes. . . . Their songs . . . had the pulse beat of the people who keep on going." The kind of music that Hughes cared about has a power and momentum that sustains:

> Like the waves of the sea coming one after another, always one after another, like the earth moving around the sun, night, day-night, day-night, day-forever, so is the undertow of black music with its rhythm that never betrays you, its strength like the beat of the human heart, its humor and its rooted power.

(208-209)

Thus, two points emerge here: the blues are the folk roots from which African Americans can take pride, identity, sustenance, memories; and the blues are a modality, a rhythm that "never betrays" (even when it surprises), a power that is as basic, or essential, as a life force. Such a mystical quality is both difficult to quantify and susceptible to misuse.[4] However, it is a characteristic of the orphic, for just as Orpheus was protected as long as he trusted his music (his ear) and was betrayed by his eye when he turned to look back at his wife, the blues' fidelity to the ear suggests that limiting it to race, to what we see as difference, the color of our skin, betrays its "essential life force."

In **"The Blues I'm Playing,"** the point about folk roots as a source of strength and pride is most strongly demonstrated. The story examines the construction of Oceola's identity as a musician. The dramatic question is whether Oceola can hold out against Mrs. Ellsworth's demands that she conform to her ideas about music—this conformity, of course, will be paid for handsomely. Mrs. Ellsworth's desires are fairly easily dissembled and include a strong wish to exhibit her wealth as a collector of *artists* (rather than *art* objects); moreover, her keen interest in the Black Oceola is laden with sexual overtones. At no point in the story is Oceola a willing object: she is suspicious every step of the way—of being the recipient of White patronage, of the concept of art for art's sake (as well as contemporary Black artists' notions that art would "break down color lines [or] . . . save the race and prevent lynchings"), and of Mrs. Ellsworth's attempts to get her to give up her home and relations with her people (Hughes 1933/1990, 113). Unlike Mrs. Ellsworth's conception of art (and beauty), where "[a]rt is bigger than love," "[m]usic, to Oceola, demanded movement and expression, dancing and living to go with it" (121, 114). Music is not about contemplation of distant, abstract concepts, as Mrs. Ellsworth conceives it, where one stands "looking at the stars," but rather a directly accessible expression of humanity: "'No,' said Oceola *simply*. . . . 'This is mine. . . . How sad and gay it is. Blue and happy. . . . How white like you and black like me. . . . How much like a man. . . . And how like a woman. . . . Warm as Pete's mouth'" (emphasis added 122-23). It's difficult to imagine a more beautifully expressed appreciation for music, especially in the context of the story. My closing with "warm as Pete's mouth" (though Oceola goes on to say, "These are the blues . . . I'm playing") is intentional, for it hearkens back to an earlier reference in the story, when the narrator offers a snippet from Oceola's past, a memory, presumably, of a member of her stepfather's minstrel band—his mouth, in fact, which was "the biggest mouth in the world . . . and [he] used to let Oceola put both her hands in it at the same time and stretch it" (104). A gesture that is at once humorous and richly symbolic, it assures us that one must enter the body of music—its rhythm, its warm, wet, sexual reality—in order for the music to enter, sustain, and nourish the spirit. For Mrs. Ellsworth, controlling Oceola's music is a way of controlling her sexuality (a point I will return to later); because she is unable to and since Oceola's music is both sensual and sexual, Mrs. Ellsworth's bourgeois sensibilities are deeply unsettled—one of the aspects of orphic power.

Approaching the perspective of the blues as an embodied aesthetic expression from quite the opposite direction, Hughes, in **"Rejuvenation through Joy,"** satirizes a whole range of trendy, appropriative practices of the White (and Black) bourgeoisie. Portrayed as clever tricksters capitalizing on the "vogue of Harlem," Lesche and Sol contrive to rip off—in effect to patronize—the White patrons not only of the Black "primitivism" but also of any sort of promising intellectual titillation that any new sort of cult might offer. For clients "who had known nothing more joyous than Gurdijieff (*sic*),"[5] for those who had sought the answer in "self-denial cults," psychoanalysis, or "under Yogi," the Colony of Joy would provide what all the other methods were lacking: lectures about joy, private consultations, "authentic" performances by "real" blues artists; but most important, perhaps, actual rhythm exercises where audience members could look up at Lesche, the "New Leader," and find themselves "a-tremble" from

doing "those slow, slightly grotesque, center-swaying exercises" that would give them (despite some awkwardness and feeling of silliness that they would eventually get over) that "Negro joy."

Despite the humor in this story (partly provided by the audacity of the two trickster figures), it is against this kind of appropriation that Hughes's anger in *The Ways of White Folks* is most brutal—and effective—though it is expressed indirectly, through irony. The bitterness named in a poem like "Militant"—published at about the same time (1930) as the stories in this collection were either being written or were germinating—is apparent in *Ways.* The poem reads in part as follows: "Let all who will / Eat quietly the bread of shame. / I cannot, / Without complaining loud and long, / . . . And so my fist is clenched / Today— / To strike your face" (Hughes 1994, 131). Such direct attack is less characteristic of the blues than an ironic stance that cuts as deep but with greater control, finesse, and humor. Ostrum (1993) notes that in addition to seeing "Hughes's use of irony in a modernist context . . . one may also see it . . . as part of a long-standing African tradition of ironic discourse" (7). Citing Henry Louis Gates, Jr.'s well-known analysis of Hughes's poem "Ask Your Mama," Ostrum concludes that Hughes had an "affinity for an ironic, deceptively sophisticated 'blues' worldview," which he claims (though he doesn't elaborate) is apparent in his short fiction as well as in his poetry (7).

I will be dealing with what I see as the best example of dramatic irony in the next section, but would like to mention a few other instances here. Verbal irony—a basic ingredient of the blues, expressing the singer's relation to life and hardship—appears in the references to Mrs. Ellsworth as a "[p]oor dear lady" (she's hardly either). One can imagine Hughes chuckling (in film clips he's often smiling, and that smile often plays across his face) when he first conceived of her requesting a copy of the White-authored *Nigger Heaven* so she could learn something about what it is to be "Negro" (106). The characterization of the White people in **"Slave on the Block"** practically drips with irony—despite the brutal accuracy of the depiction of their racist attitudes: "So they went in for the Art of Negroes—the dancing that had such jungle life about it, the songs that were so simple and fervent, the poetry that was so direct, so real" (19). Despite White couples' "affection" for them, the "Negroes didn't seem to love" them (20). A final example of ironic wordplay occurs in **"Red-Headed Baby"** in the use of *mule*: Clarence wonders *to himself* "if she [Betsy] had another mule in my stall," and the mother, as though she had access to his thoughts, tells him that the liquor is "strong enough to knock a mule down" (127, 128). Since the root word of *mulatto* is *mule,* and the story is about the making of mulattos (Betsy's story would seem to be a rewriting of her own mother's story), an additional ironic layer is that Clarence himself, with his freckles and red hair, is a bit of a mulatto as well.

In both **"The Blues I'm Playing"** and **"Slave on the Block,"** the White "patrons" show no compunction for violating the most basic and decent notions about privacy. The painter and her husband, without a moment's hesitation, can, because they want him to sing for their guests, barge into the basement bedroom of their maid, where she and the "boy on the block" are making love; furthermore, they have the presumption to "condone" their behavior because "[i]t's so simple and natural for Negroes to make love" (27). Mrs. Ellsworth asks Oceola every sort of personal question on their first visit because from the very outset she has every intention of possessing her—and because privacy is a privilege of race and class. Even the music reviewer who finds Oceola for her, and who snoops around for Mrs. Ellsworth in order to see who Oceola's roomer is, is named Ormond Hunter. Prowling, preying, aiming, shooting, killing, capturing, displaying, these characters are vicious and the consequences of their actions extremely hazardous. As James Baldwin (1988) said, "You have to be very, very, very, very careful about people bearing gifts." Langston Hughes had learned this the hard way, and I see it as a tribute to other Black artists—and perhaps a bit of revisionist personal history—that he would, in Oceola, create a character who held her own against a wealthy White woman with an appetite for Black artists.

Thus far I have focused on three elements of the blues—folk roots, rhythm, and irony—that have the potential of working against an arrogant Euro-American ideology, of subverting the status quo and liberating blues people from its constraints. Before I turn to the second framing question, I would like to consider a story in which music, let alone the blues, does not appear explicitly at all. Yet **"Red-Headed Baby"** is subtly informed by the kind of blues sensibility described above, in both its location in the broken-down, Black side of town and its narrative style, which is distinctive from all the styles in *The Ways of White Folks.*[6] Faith Berry, one of Hughes's biographers, commented that "two of Hughes's constant companions were talent and love" (Baldwin 1988). It is love and talent that keep this story from either spinning out of control or spiraling into deep depression.

Although it is told from the perspective of a White sailor, the story makes no apology for the living conditions or actions of the woman, Betsy, to whom he has returned after three years for a night of sexual entertainment—and, considering the depth of his loneliness, perhaps for companionship as well. From the conclusions that Clarence is able to draw about the changes that have occurred over the three years, it's clear that the woman has become a prostitute, has taken up drinking

and providing alcohol for her male guests, has begun wearing makeup, and has learned how to flirt. There's nothing glamorous about her life, nor is there an attempt to make her pathetic; one might point to a downward spiral, but one might as well recognize the tough survival of those for whom sex and race privileges are not conferred. Her surroundings are exotic—there are "flowers and vines all over," suggesting fertility and vitality, the surf sounds in the background, and the moon shines—yet these potentially romantic symbols are undermined by the mosquitoes, sand, and the suggestion of a community "left over from the boom" (125). Certainly James A. Emanuel (1971) identified accurately Hughes's "faithful and artistic presentation of both racial and national [and, I would argue, gender] truth—[as the] successful mediation, that is, between the beauties and the terrors of life around him" (153).

In that overlay of beauty and degradation, as well as the nonapologetic depiction of these poor folks, is the love that Hughes felt for his people, indeed all people. As one of the most vivid depictions of loneliness in *Ways,* **"Red-Headed Baby"** exemplifies the way in which "the blues expressed his [Hughes's] loneliness, his desire to get in touch with his people and himself again, his hope, determination, and pride in people who accomplish what they can as well as they can despite limitations, even if it is *crying*" (Tracy 1988, 111-12). Clarence is deeply lonely, and despite the crassness of his internal characterization of Betsy—"It don't take them yellow janes long to get old and ugly" (126); "Be funny if she had another mule in my stall" (127)—he is just about as brutal about himself: "Only a white man with red hair—third mate on a lousy tramp" (129). When he recognizes the child as his own, his mounting panic culminates in his characterization of his offspring as one of those "dolls you wham at three shots for a quarter in the County Fair half full of licker and can't hit nothing" (132). In fact, Hughes stated in a letter to James A. Emanuel that

> I feel as sorry for them [Whites] as I do for the Negroes usually involved in hurtful . . . situations. Through at least one (maybe only one) white character in each story, I try to indicate that "they are human, too." . . . the sailor all shook up about his **"Red-Headed Baby."** . . . What I try to indicate is that circumstances and conditioning make it very hard for whites, in interracial relationships, each to his "own self to be true."
>
> (150)

In "The White Ones," a poem written in 1924, Hughes affirms that "I do not hate you, / For your faces are beautiful, too. / I do not hate you, / Your faces are whirling lights of loveliness and splendor, too" (Hughes 1994, 37). And, one might add, for Clarence: your face, too, has seen the pain. An ineffectual, lonely, alcoholic wanderer, Clarence, too, has some blues to sing—unfortunately it seems unlikely that he is able to *hear* them, so caught up is he in what the eye beholds.

The method that Hughes employs to let us hear Clarence's blues is to juxtapose an internal stream of consciousness with the minimalist, compressed dialogue between himself, Betsy, and the old woman, "Auntie." The story opens with paragraphs that alternate between Clarence's complaints and memories of Betsy and his surrealistic impressions of his surroundings, for instance:

> Feet in the sand. Head under palms, magnolias, stars. Lights and the kid-cries of a sleepy town. Mosquitoes to slap at with hairy freckled hands and a dead hot breeze, when there is any breeze.
>
> "What the hell am I walkin' way out here for? She wasn't nothing to get excited over. . . ."
>
> Crossing the railroad track at the edge of town. Green lights. Sand in the road, seeping into oxfords and the cuffs of dungarees.

(Hughes 1933/1990, 125-26)

More reminiscent of some of the passages in Toomer's *Cane*, the story also sounds a bit like Joyce's *Ulysses*, as Nifong (1981) notes (94). What makes this a reflection of a blues style as opposed to a literary device being practiced by such modernists as James Joyce and John Dos Passos?[7] I'm not so concerned with separating the two, and I suspect doing so would require an elaborate explication and comparison that would not be useful here. Instead, I would like simply to reflect on two parallels that seem to me to make the blues connection valid. First, one of the characteristics of blues singers is "to have thrown together verses in a haphazard manner, to have sung the verses in a stream-of-consciousness style, and to have followed a loose, associative, nonlogical progression" (Tracy 1988, 90). Second, the juxtaposition of internal thought (which, as I demonstrated above, includes both Clarence's memories and his awareness of his external surroundings) with sparsely presented dialogue suggests that, for Hughes, "black music put people in touch with themselves and the universe, that it united the internal and external" (116). Such a call and response, in this case between the state of mind, expressed as an internal monologue, and external events, expressed as dialogue, makes **"Red-Headed Baby"** a powerful example of blues playing out in fiction.

The second question—What is the relation between White bourgeoisie and Black folk, the blues, the "Black experience"?—first takes us back to the stories in which White art patrons/consumers of Black art figure most strongly.

It is one thing for Hughes to refer to the rhythm of Black music, "its strength like the beat of the human heart, its humor and its rooted power," and quite an-

other for it to be appropriated by White people who would use "the primitive" as a means of narrowing Black people's humanity to a misunderstood fragment—moreover, doing so for the precise reason that they can then project what they are most uncomfortable about themselves onto African Americans. Marianna Torgovnick, in *Gone Primitive: Savage Intellects, Modern Lives* (1990), posits that "Western thinking frequently substitutes versions of the primitive for some of its deepest obsessions—and this becomes a major way in which the West constructs and uses the primitive for its own ends" (18). She is particularly interested in African "primitivism" in relation to "Western" (read: White) constructions of power, and this is precisely what Lesche and Sol identify as the most salable commodity to which they have access: treatments that include "music, the best music, jazz, real primitive jazz out of Africa (you know, Harlem)," and which will heal through a mystical "aliveness, the beat of Africa as expressed through the body" (84, 85). In a story like **"Rejuvenation through Joy"** it is easy to see why Ralph Ellison (1940) would have characterized the "Harlem Renaissance" not as a Black thing at all, but as a faddish White construction.[8]

Hughes's frustration at the commodification of the blues is also expressed in "Note on Commercial Theatre," written some six years after *Ways,* but nonetheless in keeping with themes therein. The poem begins, "You've taken my blues and gone— / And you fixed 'em / So they don't sound like me. / Yep, you done taken my blues and gone." The "you" seems clearly to be the White middle class, though it is possible that certain Black artists might also co-opt an "authentic" blues style for more mainstream tastes. The "me" does not, however, seem to be Hughes, but rather the common Black folk, whom Hughes is urging to find and claim their own voice: "But someday somebody'll / Stand up and talk about me, / And write about me— / . . . I reckon it'll be / Me myself! / Yes, it'll be me" (Hughes 1994, 215-16). As late as 1960, Hughes would write, "I do not understand the tendency today that some Negro artists have of seeking to run away from themselves, of running away from us, of being afraid to sing our songs, paint our own pictures, write about ourselves" (quoted in Tracy 1988, 46). Hughes's belief in Black artists' power not only to articulate their own aesthetic but to make themselves the subjects of their own art is implicit in his critique in *Ways* of false or inappropriate spokespersons and disingenuous collectors or consumers. Distinguishing between a genuine blues aesthetic and a false claim to it can lead one to chase the truth in ever more tightly binding circles: are the blues, rooted in African American history and culture, only for those with black skin or "black experience"? Can a person with white skin transcend the arrogance of White supremacy? Can one, for that matter, be both Black and White at once? Stories like **"Home," "Red-Headed**

Baby," and **"Rejuvenation through Joy"** show that Hughes understood the complexity of these questions and refused to answer in finite, and therefore reductive, terms.

In both **"The Blues I'm Playing"** and **"Slave on the Block,"** the dominant method of revealing White commodification of Black sexuality is through dramatic irony. For both Mrs. Ellsworth and the painter, their consumption of Black sexuality is invisible to them because they are unable to recognize (as the readers are) that their own "deepest obsessions"—and longings—have been projected onto the Black subjects (or objects, depending on how one is using the terms). Mrs. Ellsworth, sleeping next to Oceola one night when circumstances put them together, is aroused by the "electric strength of that brown-black body beside her," though she confounds her desire with motherly feelings (Hughes 1933/1990, 111). Longing for her difference—"she looked like nothing Mrs. Ellsworth had ever been near before. Such a rich velvet black, and such a hard young body!" (112)—Mrs. Ellsworth can only compensate by controlling her utterly, in fact, by taking away the source of her strength, her commitment to and love for her "common roots." The painter in **"Slave on the Block"** is similarly obsessed with the body of the Black man who is fatuously hired as a gardener; his body seems to her to express the "soul and sorrow of his people," his "childlike," "natural" earthiness, something to be "captured" in her ridiculous, stereotypical paintings (24). Toward the end of the story, the painter, confronted by the Black man's naked torso, is humorously reduced to a series of muted, only remotely orgasmic "Ohs!"

Hughes's treatment of the confrontation between Black and White sexuality takes a more sinister turn in **"Home,"** a story that not only reveals the deadly element in White attitudes about Black sexuality, but also deals with the blues and music from the perspective of a Black man who has left his "folk roots" for the greater success and acceptance available in Europe. Turning now to **"Home"** will therefore set the stage for the final section, on blues and mobility.

In spite of Hughes's professed and easily discernible ambivalence about the Black middle class, particularly those who would leave their folk roots behind in search of White acceptance and social conformity, there is no blanket disavowal or blame, and this is most evident in **"Home."** Roy Williams is probably the most victimized, and one of the loneliest, of Hughes's characters—Ostrum (1993) calls him the "purest victim" and identifies the purpose of the story as a political one: "[B]lack men get lynched in America . . . because of the psychosexual dimensions of racism in America, dimensions 'white America' refuses to confront" (52). What seems particularly ironic is that Roy, more than any of the

other Black characters in the book, seems to have embraced White values and lifestyle: he comes home with white gloves on; bright stickers and tags in languages the folks back home can't read are stuck to his bags and violin case. He even carries a cane (perhaps another ironic gesture at Jean Toomer). He plays classical music that no one but the White music teacher can understand. Perhaps there's less irony here than predictable reaction of a racist gang of "rednecks" facing their own worst nightmare: a Black man more successful than they—"an uppity nigger" (36).

Like Roy, Hughes himself went to Europe, and though he barely scraped by while Roy seems to have achieved success (poor people beg him for money, women offer themselves to him for money), both suffered debilitating illnesses (or nervous breakdowns) in the face of supreme disappointment. For Hughes—three years before the publication of **Ways**—his six-month attempt to mend his relationship with Mrs. Mason resulted in his second almost complete collapse (the first had occurred in the context of his painful and intensely conflicted relation with his father some ten years earlier). Rampersad (1986) writes that "[t]ouching bottom in his despair, Hughes felt his body wracked by the emotional strain; nausea haunted his stomach" (188); and later, "A new wave of illness overtook Hughes—a chronic toothache, tonsillitis, an upset stomach" (192). Hughes's account of the break-up with Mrs. Osgood in *The Big Sea* (1940) suggests a fairly clean break, but in truth "the length of time he suffered had much to do with the lasting impact of this crisis on him" (193). Without jumping to inappropriate conclusions about the autobiographical aspects of **"Home,"** it does seem to me likely that Hughes is particularly sympathetic to Roy's predicament.

Roy may have arrived home well dressed, but physically he is in ruin. Emanuel (1971) describes him as "the sensitive, gifted little Negro violinist who finds the world too 'rotten' for his survival, . . . a doomed purveyor of beauty into the midst of European decay and hometown American racism" (154). Roy may demonstrate an impulse to "adopt white values to achieve social and economic stability in the white world" (47).[9] When Roy sits down to play his "first concert in America," a stream of consciousness similar to what occurs in **"Red-Headed Baby,"** reflects not only his fevered state but his deeper despair at having failed to achieve "the broken heart of a dream come true not true" or the blessing of his mother, who had cried when he joined the minstrel show, cried when got a job in a nightclub jazz band, and prayed when he told her of his trip to Berlin. For her, music should serve God: "Honey, when you plays that violin o' your'n it makes me right weak, it's so purty. . . . Play yo' violin, boy! God's done give you a gift!" (37). For Roy, however, music is a tough mistress: "a street-walker named Music. . . . Listen, you bitch, I want you to be beautiful as the moon in the night on the edge of the Missouri hills. I'll make you beautiful . . ." (41). Ironically, both Roy and his mother believe in the orphic power of music—in her case, to unify humans with God, and in his, to merge with nature, both of which transcend culturally defined barriers.

In articulating Roy's struggle to express what is within, to communicate beauty that others may not recognize, Hughes may have been echoing his own challenge as an artist. Emanuel (1971) writes that "what he wanted to accomplish in his art [was] to interpret 'the beauty of his own people,' a beauty . . . that they were taught either not to see or not to take pride in" (152). The desire and deep commitment to achieve that goal made Mrs. Mason's rejection all the more painful, particularly because Hughes (1940) had counted her as a true friend and was now discovering that she had the *potential* power to turn him into someone he wasn't: "She wanted me to be primitive and know and feel the intuitions of the primitive. . . . I was only an American Negro—who had loved the surface of Africa and the rhythms of Africa—but I was not Africa" (325). Unable to sustain anger—"Violent anger makes me physically ill"—he nonetheless became ill. The betrayal he felt is evident in his poignant and simple declaration, "I thought she'd liked me, my patron. But I guess she only liked my writing, and not even that any more" (327-28).

One of the historically definitive moments in Black-White relations in the United States is represented at the end of **"Home,"** when Roy is punished for responding to the White music teacher's greeting. The "white young ruffians with red-necks" attack him and murder him, and in their duplicity the community defends them, immediately constructing one of the narratives on which White supremacy depends: White women need White male protection from Black men. Roy was "talking . . . insulting . . . attacking . . . RAPING A WHITE WOMAN" (48). Emanuel (1971) describes the ending of **"Home"** as "a savagery that tends to obscure the profound interplay between life and art which thematically deepens the action" (154). Here, the most threatening Black man is the one (the artist) who interprets not only his own immediate culture but the universals—beauty or truth or love—that link us all, if and when the established barriers between us are undermined. Such is the role of the musician. In Plato's *Republic,* the artist, especially the musician (let alone the Black musician), is the most subversive. As interpreters, Roy and Hughes require support, in order to survive and thrive; mobility, in order to achieve perspective and to meet a wider audience; and, for lack of a better word, freedom to create (interpret) in whatever form and using whatever subject seems right, according to their own developing aesthetic. Needless to say, each of these is fraught with a range of conflicts and uncertainties that arise from the era's particular constructions of race,

class, and gender. Hughes writes: "Freedom / Is a strong seed / Planted / In a great need" ("Freedom 1," in Hughes 1994, 289). As I understand *freedom* here, it has to do with absence: absence of strings such as a wealthy Mrs. Mason controlled; absence of barriers such as racism creates. The presence created by such absence is the place where artists and musicians move.

Finally, I would like to consider how the notion of mobility—migration, touring, uprootedness, searching, or domesticity—might help us to understand *The Ways of White Folks* as one "grounded" in—or, better, "processed" as the blues. All of the four stories that I am focusing on depend on mobility, but the specific flavor is very much dependent on the characters as they *move* within and between the various settings of the stories. These "flavors" are all central to the blues as well, "leaving/travel/journey" being one of five pervasive themes, according to Stanley Hyman (cited in Tracy 1988, 86). Naming even a few examples reveals how thoroughly the theme of mobility permeates a blues ideology: wanderlust; upward mobility; moving from South to North, from North to South, from rural to urban; being forced from Africa, returning to Africa; spiraling downward into alcoholism, despair, suicide; reaching upward for the stars; feeling trapped, busting loose; riding the rails, Jim Crow, porters; hitchhiking; homesickness; gypsies, bums, globe trotters; running from the law, from the landlord, from lovers. When Hughes writes, "Road, road, road, O! / On the No-thern road. / These Mississippi towns ain't / Fit fer a hoppin' toad," the repetition becomes a lover's croon (or a madman's cries), and the closing humorous rhyme of *toad* with *road* suggests the singer is low-down, close to the road himself, and maybe just as ugly ("Bound No'th Blues," in Hughes 1994, 76).

In **"Home"** and **"The Blues I'm Playing,"** both musicians travel to Europe to be trained by the best, to be cultivated. There, Oceola and Roy meet two lessons of the international scene that Hughes himself confronted. In Paris, Oceola wonders why the intellectuals argue so much about life and art. "Oceola merely lived—and loved it. Only Marxian students seemed sound to her for they, at least, wanted people to have enough to eat." This relates to Oceola's folk belief that art and life are not separate; "the rest of the controversies, as far as she could fathom, were based on air" (112). Roy's sharp lesson occurs when he returns home, emphasizing the point I made above about freedom as absence: "He heard some one mutter, 'Nigger.' His skin burned. For the first time in half a dozen years he felt his color. He was home" (37). Hughes writes about a similar experience upon moving to Washington after having lived in Europe and Mexico, where none of the White people he lived and slept with "seemed any the worse for it." Back in the United States, he couldn't even get a cup of coffee, let alone be served in a White restaurant. Not only did the segregation practices of White society thrust barriers in every direction, but the upper-class Blacks "were on the whole as unbearable and snobbish a group of people" as he had ever met—a circumstance that he suspected was "so precarious . . . that . . . it had to be doubly reinforced" (206-07). His own ambiguous location as both of the folk and hobnobbing with the intellectual leaders[10] is suggested in the lines "Success is a great big beefsteak / With onions on it, / And I eat" ("Success," in Hughes 1994, 108).

In **"Rejuvenation through Joy"** mobility is the ticket for Lesche and Sol, who are introduced to the idea of the Colony of Joy in their travels in Europe. Lesche's resume is itself a remarkable study in mobility. Contrary to the publicity stories, Lesche has not been to Africa; instead, he worked first in a circus, driving a Roman chariot in performance and crossing the United States twice daily, from Indianapolis to Los Angeles. There he got a "softer" job posing for artists in an art colony and swimming with the rich, which provides the inspiration for his next job, giving swimming lessons to the wealthy at Sol's gym. From there the two go to Paris ("a long way from California" 78) and finally back to New York, where the primitive spirit of Africa will transport, under their care, White patrons to joy.

Clarence, the sailor in **"Red-Headed Baby,"** is only temporarily holed up in a life of travels, providing the occasion for the story. For both him and Roy, one of the costs of mobility is lonesomeness; another is isolation, the sense that they have no home. Even though Roy longs for home, home is more than he bargained for and less than he needed. Clarence has no home except the "damned coast-wise tramp . . . the lousy tramp" from which he has fled for a bit of love (and perhaps some domesticity). Fleeing house and child as he does at the end, domesticity seems hardly what he longs for, yet there is a subtle tone of longing throughout. As he makes his way through the Black community in the beginning of the story, he notices the "kid-cries of a sleepy town" and later the "nigger-cries in the night" (125, 126). Even when he has Betsy in his lap, his thoughts wander inside, outside, inside again to the moon, the house, the bugs, the women, the house, the coast, the moon—"A blanket of stars in the Florida sky—outside. In oil-lamp house you don't see no stars" (129). Since the blues element in the inside/outside motif has already been discussed, I will simply add that the sounds and images reflect Clarence's melancholy and deep feelings of loss because he is "outside" belonging. Domesticity also figures in Oceola's blues aesthetic, since she is unable to see marriage and family as incompatible with artistic success. Far from being drained by love, her blues are fed by it. For Roy, his despair at Europe's disparity between the haves and the have nots manifests itself as homesickness, a longing for his mother. As Hughes describes it in "Homesick

Blues," "Homesick blues is / A terrible thing to have. / To keep from cryin' / I opens ma mouth an' laughs" (Hughes 1994, 72).

Mobility, then, is a multifaceted element of the blues and of **Ways**. I hope to show that this element is also central to a Black, and particularly a blues, aesthetic—in contrast to a White or Eurocentric sensibility. In "Introduction to Black Aesthetics in Music," Jimmy Stewart (1972) characterizes the art of White culture as a stance "against life and art. That is why none of the world's non-white peoples have ever evolved museums" (80). Whether or not this is entirely accurate, the whole idea of collecting and display, as James Clifford (1988) has demonstrated, reveals "crucial processes of Western identity formation" (220). In other words, "collecting has long been a strategy for the deployment of a possessive self, culture, and authenticity" (218). Along this vein, Janheinz Jahn (1961) writes:

> Now in Europe in the last few centuries art has come to a large extent under the dictatorship of the spectator, of the collector. . . . For [the artist] the completed work, that of his [or her] predecessors also, is always only a stage, a transition; in retrospect it becomes a preparatory exercise. For the connoisseur, on the other hand, the work of art is a work in itself, by reference to which he [or she] compares, measures, and develops aesthetic laws.
>
> (172)

Such a distinction is apparent in the sensibilities of Oceola and Mrs. Ellsworth, who is every bit the collector—not of objects of art, but of humans as objects of art. Her thoughts are filled with Oceola, but they are the thoughts of the connoisseur: she finds Oceola fascinating because she has never helped an artist like her. Oceola is her most recent acquisition, and as such Mrs. Ellsworth must not only have her but display her, too. Thus, she orders dresses for Oceola in colors that look good with black skin. Here again is the erotic imagination at work, for in "dressing" Oceola, she is also undressing her. Oceola is a product; if she weren't, Mrs. Ellsworth would be concerned with such "incidentals" as her feelings and desires; she would want to *listen* to her, her stories, her reactions—and her music rather than the degree to which she has "mastered" the classics.

Hughes's aesthetics itself changed over time. Early on he settled on his basic criterion, which Rampersad (1986) describes: "At the center was a vigilance about the need to find new ways, based on a steadfast loyalty to the forms of black culture, to express black consciousness—and, in so doing, to assist at its passage into the hostile modern world" (102). Rampersad's language—"center," "steadfast" contrasting with "forms" and "passage"—suggests a tension between certainty and doubt, between an art that has a folk center and one that moves into the modern world. Miller (1976) notes the inconsistency of Hughes's essays: "first, that the absence of art is a revolutionary warning; second, that art can be a means for changing reality; third, and paradoxically, that art is powerless to change reality; and fourth, that an art of aesthetic beauty cannot also be an art of social change" (35). Later, Miller notes, Hughes would reject the last premise. This emphasizes the important point that despite any "center" or "steadfastness," any discussion of aesthetics needs to consider its evolution or process.

Stewart (1972) approaches this particular dynamic this way:

> Art, in our sense, must be understood as the accomplishment of creating, the operation of creating. What results therefrom is merely the momentary residue of that operation—a perishable object and nothing more, and anything else you might imbue it with (which the white aesthetic purports to do) is nothing else but mummification. The point is—and this is the crux of our two opposing conceptions of being—that the imperishability of creation is not in what is created, is not in the art product, is not in the *thing* as it exists as an object, but in the procedure of its becoming what it is.
>
> (84)

It's easy to point to a person's evolving consciousness—I doubt any artist, let alone thinking person, can stand in one place for long and still remain an effective artist or thinker—but quite a bit trickier to quantify a modality like movement or an aesthetic of motion in an artist's work, particularly when that artist is a writer, whose very words are fixed on the paged, printed in a book, published and the shelved—unlike music, which "has no property as physical matter . . . [F]orms that utilize words . . . lack the simultaneity one encounters in the musical experience." Although an art form like painting (or poetry or fiction) can go through the motions of denying its fixity, Stewart suggests that attempts by artists like Jackson Pollock and Pablo Picasso to emphasize the "'action' aspect in its production" are rather desperate means to resurrect an "exhausted tradition" (85).

I think it's more than that, at least in the case of the written word. Reading is not done in isolation from other activities that allow us to participate in art, not from painting and certainly not from music. In this sense, through their audiences as well as their artists, art forms talk to each other. Performance art, as a case in point, often integrates many forms, bringing them to life in a dynamic exchange. A 1996 performance at the University of Minnesota Weisman Art Museum of Langston Hughes's *Ask Your Mama* (1961) demonstrated this point beautifully. Taking the words and notes on the literary and musical page and the images of paintings and sculptures from slides, the performers conjured

meaning out of fixity and made it dance . . . and sing . . . and although we in the audience were "fixed" in our chairs, our eyes and ears were drinking it up.

Even words on the page are not so fixed as all that. Read a story at two different points in your life, and see if they're the same. Read between the lines, and see if they're empty. I suggest that these stories are both located in and move through a blues aesthetic, that Oceola and Roy and Clarence and Lesche are blues performers of their lives: "I feels de blues a comin', / Wonder what de blues'll bring" ("Hey!" in Hughes 1994, 112).

Despite James Baldwin's memorable comment about the blues—"If it becomes a quotation it becomes irrelevant"—it's "becoming" that we're talking about here.

Notes

1. For a discussion about the controversy that arose in the August 1990 issue of *Guitar Player,* in which a guest editorial piece argued that anyone who isn't Black can only be a "convincing, expressive copyist" of the blues tradition, see Garon (1996). He affirms this position, saying, "[T]he very specific forms of torture, beating, lynching, slavery, mistreatment, and general discrimination that white Americans had visited upon the blacks had . . . produced the blues. Indeed, it was the very resistance to this genocidal tendency of white culture that had brought the blues into existence. Only the very specific sociological, cultural, economic, psychological, and political forces faced by working-class black Americans—forces permeated with racism at their every turning—produced the blues. *Nothing else did!*" (170).

2. Hans Ostrom (1993) links this "midcareer" collection to modernists T. S. Eliot and Ezra Pound, particularly in its "unyielding use of irony," though the causes of Hughes's "dissociation from the mainstream" was different from theirs. Ostrom goes on to note "the book's edge of social criticism [which] associates Hughes with . . . Sinclair Lewis and John Dos Passos, whose work also revealed acute social conscience" (5). Lawrence, however, is the "most specific link between Hughes's writing and modernism" (5-6).

3. This is Ostrom's term to describe the fusion of Hughes's growing political awareness and the encounter with Lawrence's fiction.

4. For more explication, see Janheinz Jahn's *Muntu* (1961), particularly his explanation of rhythm as a modality (164-169) and his discussion of Hughes's use of the blues (200-204). Jahn sees Hughes's poetry as an artistic balancing of an African "spiritual style" and a Western "agitation style" (204). See also Tracy's (1988) interpreta-

tion and employment of Jahn as part of his analysis (62-64). Despite Jahn's oft-cited overgeneralizing of African religious systems, Tracy finds useful his interpretation of the blues as "an assertion of autonomy and the desire to consolidate one's power in a world where one's power is in danger of being lost" (63).

5. This not very oblique reference to Jean Toomer underscores the fact that Hughes's anger in this story is merely masked by the many, and, in some cases, dripping, instances of irony. In his biography of Hughes, Rampersad (1986) notes that "[t]he Gurdjieff movement had already begun to bleach a talent that would never again approach the achievement of *Cane*; in addition, the light-skinned Toomer had started to deny his race. After Horace Liveright called him a promising Negro writer, Toomer was furious: 'I insist that you never use such a word, such a thought again.' Perhaps Langston heard of Toomer's attitude; certainly he eventually would write of him only with amused contempt" (120).

6. See Nifong for a brief and very positive analysis of the range of narrative styles in *Ways*. He notes the "incredible variety of perspectives," which I would argue further demonstrates the collection's overall blues sensibility.

7. The degree to which "modernist" is associated with a White avant-garde is suggested by any brief survey of tables of contents in White-authored books on modernism. But Ishmael Reed (1972) makes it clear that "[a] slave told a whopper about a hurricane that 'went on about its nevermind' long before James Joyce thought of punning Homer" (381).

8. In his review of *The Big Sea*, Ellison (1940) described the "Negro Renaissance" as a "'discovery' of the Negro by wealthy whites, who in attempting to fill the vacuum of their lives made the 1920's an era of fads. Negro music, Negro dancing, primitive Negro sculpture, and Negro writing became the vogue" (20).

9. I pull this from Tracy's (1988) analysis of the competing impulses that in the Simple stories are demonstrated by the three main characters. A fuller quotation follows:

> Hughes seems to be using the three to represent alternate impulses within his own mind: he is the artist-creator using his rational observer-commentator (Boyd) to describe the alternate impulses to retain ethnic identity (Jess) and adopt white values to achieve social and economic stability in the white world (Joyce).
>
> Hughes's problem, then, was to try to reconcile the three in his art. In his blues poems, he attempted to speak like one audience (the folk) and

interpret to another (the black middle class), but this technique created a problem. . . . [H]e was not actually referring his audience back to the folk totally. Rather, he was creating a middle ground that presented his audience with an enlightened professional poet's version of the unpretentious folk. (47)

10. Tracy (1988) notes that "[i]t was Hughes's wish that the beauty, unpretentiousness, and vivacity of the folk could be infused into the all-too-reserved middle-class African-American; but the complex social interaction between environment and ethos made a complete sympathy and understanding nearly impossible."

"Therefore, Hughes's intention to unite the intellectuals and near-intellectuals with the folk, to create the unity he felt necessary to the identity and progress of his people, was a difficult prospect. . . ." (47-48)

Works Cited

Baldwin, James. *Langston Hughes: The Dream Keeper.* Video. Voices & Visions series of The Annenberg/CPB Collection, 1988.

Clifford, James. "On Collecting Art and Culture." In *The Predicament of Culture: Twentieth-Century Ethnography, Literature, and Art,* by James Clifford, 215-52. Cambridge: Harvard University Press, 1988.

Dundes, Alan, ed. *Mother Wit from the Laughing Barrel: Readings in the Interpretation of Afro-American Folklore.* Jackson: University Press of Mississippi, 1990.

Ellison, Ralph. "Stormy Weather." Review of *The Big Sea,* by Langston Hughes. *New Masses,* 24 September 1940, 20-21.

Emanuel, James A. "The Short Fiction of Langston Hughes." In *Langston Hughes, Black Genius: A Critical Evaluation,* edited by Therman B. O'Daniel, 145-56. New York: William Morrow, 1971.

Garon, Paul. "White Blues." In *Race Traitor,* edited by Noel Ignatiev and John Garvey, 163-175. New York: Routledge, 1996.

Harper, Donna Akiba Sullivan. *Not So Simple: The "Simple" Stories by Langston Hughes.* Columbia: University of Missouri Press, 1995.

Hughes, Langston. *The Big Sea.* New York: Hill and Wang, 1940.

———. "The Negro Artist and the Racial Mountain." *Nation* 122 (1926): 692-94. Reprinted in *The Black Aesthetic,* edited by Addison Gayle, 167-72. New York: Doubleday, 1972.

———. *The Ways of White Folks* (1933). New York: Vintage, 1990.

———. *The Collected Poems of Langston Hughes.* Edited by Arnold Rampersad and David Roessel. New York: Vintage Books, 1994.

Jahn, Janheinz. *Muntu: African Culture and the Western World.* New York: Grove Weidenfeld, 1961.

Jones, Leroi. *Blues People: Negro Music in White America.* New York: William Morrow, 1963.

Klotman, Phillis R. "Langston Hughes's Jess B. Semple and the Blues." *Phylon* (March 1975): 68-77.

Miller, R. Baxter. "'A Mere Poem': 'Daybreak in Alabama,' A Resolution to Langston Hughes's Theme of Music and Art." *Obsidian: Black Literature in Review* 2, no. 2 (1976): 30-37.

Nifong, David Michael. "Narrative Technique and Theory in *The Ways of White Folks.*" *Black American Literature Forum* 15, no. 3 (Fall 1981): 93-96.

Ostrum, Hans. *Langston Hughes: A Study of the Short Fiction.* New York: Twayne, 1993.

Rampersad, Arnold. *The Life of Langston Hughes: I, Too, Sing America.* Vol. 1, 1902-1941. New York: Oxford University Press, 1986.

Reed, Ishmael. "Can a Metronome Know the Thunder or Summon a God?" In *The Black Aesthetic,* edited by Addison Gayle, 381-382. New York: Doubleday, 1972.

Stewart, Jimmy. "Introduction to Black Aesthetics in Music." In *The Black Aesthetic,* edited by Addison Gayle, 77-91. New York: Doubleday, 1972.

Torgovnick, Marianna. *Gone Primitive: Savage Intellects, Modern Lives.* Chicago: University of Chicago Press, 1990.

Tracy, Steven C. *Langston Hughes and the Blues.* Urbana: University of Illinois Press, 1988.

Kate A. Baldwin (essay date winter 2002)

SOURCE: Baldwin, Kate A. "The Russian Connection: Interracialism as Queer Alliance in Langston Hughes's *The Ways of White Folks.*" *Modern Fiction Studies* 48, no. 4 (winter 2002): 795-824.

[*In the following essay, Baldwin investigates the influence of D. H. Lawrence's "The Lovely Lady," communist notions of self-identity, and culturally determined concepts of sexual transgression on Hughes's portrayal of intimacy and masculinity in* The Ways of White Folks.]

The blood of Pushkin
Unites
The Russian and the Negro
In art.
Tomorrow
We will be united anew
In the Internationale.

                    —Julian Anissimov, "Kinship"

The gentlemen who wrote lovely books about
the defeat of the flesh and the triumph of the spirit
    [. . .]
will kindly come forward and
Speak about the Revolution—where flesh triumphs
    [. . .]
And the young by the hundreds of thousands are free
from hunger to grow and study and love and propa-
    gate, bodies
and souls unchained without My Lord saying a com-
    moner shall never
marry my daughter or the Rabbi crying cursed be the
    mating of
Jews and
Gentiles or Kipling writing never the twain shall
    meet—
For the twain have met.

                    —Langston Hughes, "Letter to the Academy"

In June of 1932 Langston Hughes posted a telegram to his friend Louise Thomspon that read, "hold that boat 'cause to me it's an Ark" (qtd. in Rampersad 241). The boat in question was the *Europa,* bound for Berlin, and beyond that for Leningrad and Moscow. Scheduled on board were Thompson and the group of would-be actors she had organized to participate in a proposed, Soviet-funded film project titled *Black and White.* The image of an "ark" that Hughes proposes in his description of the steamship illustrates the fact that Hughes was eager to depart from US shores, excited about the artistic and social potential a Soviet adventure might bring him.

Hughes's sojourn to the Soviet Union, a trip that ended up covering a year, from June 1932 to June 1933, has been acknowledged in biographical accounts. Indicating the significance of this experience to Hughes's development as a writer, Faith Berry has described the Soviet period as "among the most productive of his literary career" (189).[1] While in the Soviet Union, Hughes produced poetry, essays, and fiction, including the poem "Letter to the Academy," the Soviet-published "A Negro Looks at Soviet Central Asia," and several of the short stories later published in the collection **The Ways of White Folks,** including **"Cora Unashamed," "Slave on the Block,"** and **"Poor Little Black Fellow."** Despite Hughes's prolific output during his Soviet experience, however, the specific ramifications of this journey on his writing from the early thirties, particularly the stories that were written in Moscow and immediately following Hughes's return to the US in 1933, have remained virtually unexplored.[2]

While in the Soviet Union, Hughes was exposed to the exhilarations of a society in progress, the reconstruction of the Soviet citizen, and the Leninist conception of internationalism. Combined, these interventions into the Russian social status quo created a heady atmosphere of possibility, of subjectivity under formation. The *novyi Sovetskii chelovek* (new Soviet person) augured a reconfiguration of the family, and Lenin's internationalism promised interracial alliances in the name of global solidarity. As the poem "Kinship," written by Julian Anissimov and translated by Hughes, suggests, partnerships between "the Russian" and "the Negro" promised a shift from biologically determined links (that is, those fabricated through blood) to politically determined ones.[3] The idea of reconstructed kinships emerges with equal force in Hughes's Moscow-composed "Letter to the Academy" in which cross-racial unions beget a heretofore taboo meeting of the "twain." The influence of these interventions into conventional mappings of the familial and the racial can be traced throughout the prose pieces that Hughes produced during this period. The Soviet project provided an impetus for rethinking the intimacies associated with family and race as given demarcators of an inherent connection between group members and for skewing these naturalized categories. In their place, Hughes's stories offer the interracial and reconfigured kinship structures as alliances and formations through which to suggest a differently affiliated black masculine subjecthood. In these stories, many of which were collected into **The Ways of White Folks,** interracial coalitions between "black" and "white" promoted by the Internationale are reformed to explore and trouble sexually proscriptive boundaries between blacks and whites in the defiantly anti-Internationale zone, the United States.[4] As Siobhan Somerville has elaborated in her work on the complicities between racial and sexual-oriented ascriptions of identity, "the often unstable division between homosexuality and heterosexuality circulates as part of [the] exploration of the barriers to desire imposed by the color line" (11). Drawing on Somerville's pioneering work, my interests are in the ways, in Hughes's work from this period, an unstable division between black and white, exemplified in the rhetoric of Soviet internationalism, circulates as part of Hughes's writerly exploration of the barriers to desire and identification imposed by sexual ascription. In this essay reclaiming a slighted portion of the historical background of Hughes's oeuvre is key to resituating his work from the 1930s and to thinking through the way this work articulates alternative modalities of desire. Rather than approaching this project with a retrospective eye toward pinning down Hughes's sexuality through empirical evidence or ascribing to his texts a correlated identity, my methodology follows the advisory articulated by Kaja Silverman, who asks us "to approach history always through the refractions of desire and identification, and to read race and class insistently in relation to

sexuality" (300). Hughes's experiences in the Soviet Union—his encounters with new modes of subjectivity and, with the impetus of authors such as Anissimov and D. H. Lawrence, explorations of the familial—promoted a rethinking of interracial alliances, kinship structures, and black American masculinity: these formative restructurings emerge in his work as the Russian connection.

THE SOULS OF BLACK MEN

Upon Hughes's arrival in Moscow in 1932 the preeminent paradigm for understanding black American consciousness was that of "double consciousness," a concept articulated powerfully by W. E. B. Du Bois in his 1903 *The Souls of Black Folk.* Double consciousness in Du Bois arises out of an awareness of an irresolvable twoness, a sense of being both American and black, two categories that remained both institutionally and ideologically mutually exclusive. As I have discussed elsewhere, in *Souls* [*The Souls of Black Folk*], Du Bois's revelation of a veil that signifies double consciousness establishes straightaway a representative means of thematizing not only African-American consciousness— but more precisely black male consciousness.[5] Although this is one of the most-often cited passages from Du Bois, what Henry Louis Gates, Jr. has termed the "urtext of the African American experience" (xvii), the fact that this revelation comes about through a specific configuration of aborted interracial desire is often overlooked. A young girl's refusal to exchange visiting cards with Du Bois provokes the narrator's sense of difference "from the others, or like, mayhap, in heart and life and longing, but shut out from their world by a vast veil" (*Souls* 2). In this seminal scene, desire operates in at least a two-fold manner: it is depicted as both cross-racial and heterosexual. Both of these desires are simultaneously proffered and denied; both are structurally mandated and disavowed ("I had thereafter no desire to tear down that veil, to creep through" [2]). They seem to accord to one another a reciprocal degree of necessity, of compulsion, so that both are mutually constituting. Black masculine desires for sameness, recognition by, and equality to the privileged space implied by the absent but constitutive presence of white male heterosexuality, by which citizenship and national belonging are defined, are meted out across the figure of white femininity.[6] In affixing black masculinity to the body of white femininity, Du Bois reiterates a social logic wherein the coupling of black man/white woman is inherently and always about a specific kind of desire—for a black man to have commerce with a white woman who denies him recognition and likewise access through a sense of social propriety or taboo. The normativization of this illicit desire is related to its larger social proscription in that prohibition creates the ground for its instantiation as a regulatory force. In the 1896 ruling of *Plessy v. Ferguson*, the majority opinion found that the object of the Fourteenth Amendment "could not have been intended to abolish distinctions based upon color, or to enforce social, as distinguished from political equality, or a commingling of the two races" (Brown 50). In barring social from political equality in terms of a fear of racial "commingling," this ruling revealed the extent to which white anxiety about black male desire was inherently couched in a heteronormative paradigm. Du Bois's pattern echoes the larger cultural taboo of racial commingling, using proscription as the generative source for its normativizing compulsion and likewise taking up not only its interdiction but also its terms of heteronormativity. In Du Bois's configuration, heterosexuality is the tacit binding agent, an organizing structure of social membership, albeit in this case a denied membership, based in mutual recognition.[7]

In repeatedly querying and rewriting this primal scene of identification in *The Ways of White Folks,* Hughes taps into the ways in which, within the very structure of representative black masculine desire, slippage offers a possibility for difference.[8] By constantly replaying and reshuffling the Du Boisian frames of black masculinity Hughes's work in *The Ways of White Folks* detects in Du Bois's enumeration of the barriers to intimacy a foregrounding of desire as an expression not of a private selfhood, but of a publicly ordained one. Hughes's work reveals the constitutive scene of double consciousness as a mediation between private and public displays of the heteronormative impulses behind the Du Boisian formation of a black masculine consciousness. In this light, the black male/white female coupling is always about the public nature of this dyad—how the private voicings in Du Bois (such as "heart and life and longing" (*Souls* 2) are the expression of social mandates. Varied formations of cross-racial desire emerge in several of Hughes's short stories to summon a possibility of rearticulating the heteronormative impulse of the Du Boisian interracial dyad. Drawing on the energizing reformulations of the Internationale, interracial alliances structurally haunt Hughes's stories as a kind of queer presence.[9]

GETTING BETWEEN

In order to more fully explain the ways in which Hughes's work performs this rearticulation of Du Bois, it is necessary to reiterate the importance of the Russian connection. Upon his return to Moscow after several months' travel in Soviet Central Asia, Langston Hughes received a copy of Lawrence's collection of stories, *The Lovely Lady,* from his friend Marie Seton. In his autobiographical *I Wonder as I Wander,* Hughes recalls that the Lawrence stories affected him deeply:

> I had never read anything of Lawrence's before, and was particularly taken with the title story. [. . .] The possessive terrifying elderly woman in 'The Lovely

Lady' seemed in some ways to be so much like my former Park Avenue patron that I could hardly bear to read the story, yet I could not put the book down, although it brought cold sweat and goose-pimples to my body. [. . .] "If D. H. Lawrence can write such psychologically powerful accounts of folks in England, that send shivers up and down my spine, maybe I could write stories like his about folks in America."

> (*Wonder* [*I Wonder as I Wander*] 213)

Before exploring in detail the specificities of Hughes's enthrallment with Lawrence's stories, however, I want to pause and draw attention to the ways in which from their very inception the Moscow-influenced stories collected in *The Ways of White Folks* can be read as reconfiguring the bonds between the interracial and the heterosexual in the Du Boisian dyad.

I Wonder as I Wander introduces Lawrence with a section titled "D. H. Lawrence Between Us." This positioning of Lawrence underscores the way in which Hughes's "us"—a liaison with a woman he calls Natasha—is altered by the incursion of Lawrence's stories into their affair. *The Lovely Lady* effectively triangulates the circuit of desire between Natasha and Hughes, interrupting their programmatic interracial, male/female affair as Hughes's words (deceptively?) describe it. Emphatically unlike the fantasy of white femininity fulfilled that might be suggested superficially by Hughes's relationship with Natasha, however, his experiences with cross-racial alliances in the Soviet Union did not serve as a means to simply refute the socially constrictive boundaries and laws against miscegenation that provided the building blocks for black male exclusion from the entitlements of citizenship in the United States. His memoir does not decorously celebrate unmediated access to white women as the driving credential of internationalism's potentialities (although certainly for some this was a hallmark of Soviet difference).[10] Rather, what the setting provides is a repositioning of this very circuit of desire as mandatory, an opportunity to rub against and articulate a space between the routes of desire paradigmatic of the black male/white female coupling.

Natasha, a woman whom Hughes describes in *I Wonder as I Wander* in clearly ambivalent terms as "buxom," "Slavic—not beautiful, not ugly" (201) and "fun and wholesome in body as an apple" (212), appears briefly as the subject of Hughes's "Moscow Romance." Defying the Du Boisian convention of the desirous yet spurned male suitor, Hughes clearly delineates her as the aggressor with "a one track mind. Without advance warning, Natasha simply came to my room in the New Moscow Hotel one night when I was out—and was in bed when I got back" (*Wonder* 201). What is more interesting than seeking out the empirical details or authenticity of this intimacy between Hughes and Natasha is the way this relationship and its foreclosure provide a frame for reading the work undertaken in Hughes's stories. As Hughes recollects, he was so caught up in the reading of Lawrence and the composition of his own stories that he "really did not want to be bothered with an almost nightly female visitor" (*Wonder* 214). The plenitude implied here (and denied Hughes in the United States)[11] is cut short, its potential pleasures disavowed by more pressing investments: Hughes continues, "Another and more possessive 'Lovely Lady' from D. H. Lawrence's stories had come between us" (*Wonder* 214). Hughes illustrates how a willful femininity provides the impetus and charge to disrupt a cross-racial, heterosexual bond, and Hughes's authorial fascination with such displays of feminine willfulness as elaborated in Lawrence's "The Lovely Lady" becomes a stepping stone to his rearticulation of this lure in *The Ways of White Folks*. Irreverent and uncouth exhibitions of femininity create a magnetic force that enables a commingling of cross-gender identification and desire that proves more compelling than the cross-racial, heterosexual configuration proffered by Natasha.

THE LADY'S POSSESSIONS

What was it about Lawrence's stories that Hughes found so compelling? Let us first consider the "possessive" femininity outlined in the character of Mrs. Pauline Attenbourough, the character from whom the story, as well as the collection, takes its title. Part of the reason Hughes may have identified so strongly with this story may be due to the ambiguously charged relationship Lawrence depicts, in "The Lovely Lady," between an elderly dowager and her younger, impressionable protégé. Although the relationship detailed in "The Lovely Lady" is between a mother and son, as Hughes himself notes, the resonances with Hughes's own relationship to Charlotte Osgood Mason, his benefactress with whom he had severed ties shortly before leaving for Moscow, ring clearly. Commenting on a power structure in which monied age beguiles and renders hapless dependent youth, and the ways such structural inequities co-mingle desire and its disavowal, Lawrence zeros in on what he portrays as the terrifying, seductive powers of a financially empowered matriarchal femininity.

In fact the maternal possessiveness outlined in "The Lovely Lady" veers into the destructive. Pauline Attenborough is described as "a mother murdering her sensitive sons, who were fascinated by her: the Circe!" (Lawrence 23). Robert, the younger of these two sons, sums up Pauline in the following manner: "She fed on life. She has fed on me as she fed on [my brother] Henry. She put a sucker into one's soul, and it sucked up one's essential life" (40). Awestruck by such all-encompassing matriarchal power, to which men are mere casualties, Robert is "sucked" dry of his vitality. In inverse relation to Robert's increasing vapidity,

Pauline seems to grow more and more enlivened. Mrs. Attenborough is so thorough in her possessiveness that she inhabits not only her own identity, but also that of those around her. In this sense, Pauline's feeding on her children is cannibalistic, an act of consumption that repeatedly seeks to satisfy the demands of an ego for more. But, unlike the popular 1930s Freudian interpretation of strong mothers who dominate their sons into weak-willed automatons (an account which clearly drew upon Freud's theorizations of connections between orality and cannibalism), Pauline's appetite lacks the requisite desire to become the other through its incorporation. Instead, we can think of Pauline as more akin to the vampiristic, a structure of desire and identification outlined by Diana Fuss. Fuss describes the vampiristic as a cultural figure for identification that differs from cannibalism in that rather than simply incorporating the other, the vampire transforms her victims into fellow vampires. Fuss writes,

> Vampirism works like an inverted form of identification—identification pulled inside out—where the subject, in the act of interiorizing the other simultaneously reproduces itself in that other. Vampirism is both other-incorporating and self-reproducing; it delimits a more ambiguous space where desire and identification appear less opposed than coterminous, where the desire to be the other (identification) draws its very sustenance from the desire to have the other.
>
> (730)

The characterization of Mrs. Attenborough both enables us to draw connections between Fuss's elaboration of vampirism and to designate differently configured modalities of desire. To be sure, Mrs. Attenborough thrives on the life-blood of those around her, incorporating their vitality into her own and fortifying the illusion of agelessness through her acts of ingestion: "at seventy-two Pauline Attenbourough could still sometimes be mistaken, in the half light, for thirty" (Lawrence 11). Yet her identification with (desire to be) these others is more ambiguous. The reproduction of self that her fits of appetite enact are less imperfect replications of herself—the reflection of the vampiristic within Robert—than partial failures to create the dialectical processes that would ensure Robert's own vampirism. Robert seems poised to rebel against his mother, an indication that he might, indeed, be like her, but throughout the story he is constrained to tired and effete ineffectuality. Rather than an invigorating bite, his mother's mouth-work has produced stasis, paralysis "in a lifelong confusion" (18). Mrs. Attenborough's suggestive affiliation to but divergence from Fuss's powerful model of vampirism is the result of her excessive acquisitiveness, her incorporation of the other as self-fulfilling, and an inability to allow for any trace of the otherness of the other.

Mrs. Attenborough's preying powers are depicted as sufficient to unhinge the conventional heterosexual plot, to come between characters seemingly destined to be partnered. Her position between Hughes and Natasha structurally parallels her abutting between Robert and his female suitor, Cecilia. Rather than an altruistic intervention, this interruption hinges on a possessive relationship to identity: a desire to have in order to assert transcendent being. According to Robert's description of her, for Pauline there is no difference between being and having. Partial fulfillments of one another, they run in seamless continuity. Her sense of self extends beyond the body and merges with the accumulation of rich appointments by which she has surrounded herself. As Lawrence writes, Pauline was "a devoted collector of beautiful and exotic things," who "really had a passion and a genius for loveliness, whether in texture or form or colour, [and] had laid the basis of her future on her father's collection. She had gone on collecting, buying where she could, and selling to collectors and to museums. She was one of the first to sell old, weird African wooden figures to the museums" (25). These descriptions elaborate on Pauline's predilection for possessing objects so that her possessive relationship to identity is also implicitly one of (imperialist) plunder: "all collectors pieces—Mrs. Attenborough had made her own money, dealing privately in pictures and furniture and rare things from barbaric countries" (16). She has cultivated a self in which "being" equals "having," and the violence of this possessiveness leaves others behind as furniture, décor, or accoutrements arranged to set off her supreme subjecthood. A fantasy of the other as aestheticized, pliable object enables the superiority of the mother as peerless subject. In fact, by having so much, Pauline is constantly in excess of being: this is a point reiterated at the story's end when Pauline leaves her fortune not to her son but to the endowment of the Pauline Attenborough Museum, a denouement that befits her identificatory apparatus.

On the other hand, Robert's lack—of resources, of resourcefulness, and, significantly, of heterosexual desire—appears to be experienced as a complete deficit of identity, of selfhood: he is thoroughly dependent and libidinally effaced in contrast to Pauline's voracious displays of self-ownership. For example, when Robert is confronted by Cecilia, who desires to marry him, Robert admits, "I know that I am no lover of women." He makes the comment "with sarcastic stoicism [. . .] but even she did not know the shame it was to him. 'You never try to be!' she said. Again his eyes changed uncannily. 'Does one have to try?' he said" (29). Although the story may suggest that Pauline Attenborough's tenacious grasp has left Robert tellingly bereft of agency, it also gives us reason to believe otherwise. Robert's subjectivity is not a replication of his mother's willful performance of self, the transformation wrought by "the mysterious little wire that worked between Pauline's will and her face" (12). As the object of his mother's drive to become "lovely," he is neither possessive nor

object-oriented. For this reason his mother remains peripheral to the locus of his identity. Juxtaposed to Mrs. Attenborough's sense of fulfillment through objects is Robert's fascination with *process*. Robert, a barrister, delights in the "weird old processes" of litigation and legal intricacies. This interest seems to offer some kind of orientation for his "habitual feeling that he was in the wrong place: almost like a soul that has got into the wrong body" (14).[12] Robert finds solace in the law, not the easily defined options between right and wrong, but rather the nuances, awkwardnesses, and slippages, the processes akin to those at work in the flux of desire, of identity in formation, of a self dispossessed. In spite of Robert's protestations, the story between himself and his mother is not simply about Mrs. Attenborough usurping his desire, but about Robert's fascination with his mother to the point of abandon, that is, the conflict between her "having" way and his penchant for foregoing identity as an achieved object (14).

The idea of Robert as a character who defies Mrs. Attenborough's imperatives for subjecthood is substantiated towards the end of the tale when we learn that Robert is the illegitimate son of Pauline and an Italian priest. In fact, this strand of illegitimacy seems to course throughout the "The Lovely Lady." It is the specter that subtends Robert's "shame" over not being a "man:" "He was ashamed that he was not a man. And he did not love his mother" (18). Robert's refusal of familial intimacy between mother and son and his refusal to reiterate her model of self-possession figures him multiply as the "miscegenated" or "queer" offspring of a socially forbidden coupling. This layered contravening of social sanctions resonates with the implicit taboo of the Du Boisian dyad, while suggestively insinuating a means of rewriting that configuration. The idea of powerful femininity that so captivated Hughes in the title story runs throughout the *Lovely Lady* collection in which women are depicted as possessing "a strange muscular energy" that annihilates men (97). Bringing together the shame associated with a lack of normative heterosexual desire and the driving force of a "strange female power that had nothing to do with parental authority" (92), "The Lovely Lady" provides an impetus for rethinking the routings of desire and identification within the family: for defamiliarization, as it were, for making strange the familial.

Recoding the Familial

Questions of literal defamiliarization were at the heart of the unprecedented social transformation and artistic experimentation that characterized the Soviet Union in the 1920s. Much of this activity was connected to the New Economic Policy, or NEP (1921-28), which came to distinguish an era in which bold challenges were made to strict Bolshevik doctrine, and a modified capitalism was reintroduced to jump-start the nation's economy. Caught up in this flurry of reconstruction was the idealized citizen—*the novyi Sovetskii chelovek*—the Soviet worker cum proletariat, and a utopian aspiration for the abolishment of petty bourgeois individualism. Even beyond the era of NEP, Stalin recognized that a reconstituted nation required a reconstituted citizen, and his hope was that by emphasizing a new iconography of the depersonalized subject, a new Soviet citizen that supported and represented the collective interests of the people would emerge. One of the ways that individualist bourgeois tendencies were purportedly subverted was through the reconstruction not only of bodies, but also of urban topography—the creation of new parks, public thoroughfares, and high-rises.[13] The latter were to be dwelling spaces that undermined "the structure of the bourgeois family," in its place "instituting the relationships of proletarian comradeship" (Boym 127). In fact, much emphasis was placed on the family as the locus of the reproduction of individualism, and thus as the necessary site of intervention.[14] In 1926 a new Family Code was introduced, a document that espoused radically reformulated conceptions of the family and its social counterpart, marriage. Although not all bureaucrats or intelligentsia agreed on the proper place of family in the emergent society, most rejected what they termed "bourgeois piety." As Richard Stites has commented, "In comparison with both Roman and Anglo-Saxon legal traditions, the code was truly radical. Western family law was generally designed to penalize extra-marital unions by means of property, inheritance, legitimacy, and even fornication laws. The Soviets, on the contrary, recognized them as an established and by no means repugnant fact" (370). By subtending the existence of extra-marital liaisons, the Soviet Union implicitly challenged compulsory advocation of monogamy, and left open the possibility for intimacies outside the proper bounds of the conjugal bedroom. Similarly, in granting full freedom of divorce to either partner, the Soviets abolished "the concept of guilt, the humiliating delays, and the publicity," elsewhere associated with the procedure (Stites 369). In a characteristically ambiguous summation of the era, one critic describes the reformulation of family in the 1920s as an experiment "which sought to socialize family functions and explore new modes of personal relationships" (Attwood 71). Although neither of these scholars make this connection, these interventions into the structures subtending marriage produced a correlative intervention into the affective emotions conventionally associated with matrimony; and by releasing the "guilt" and "shame" commonly paired with its dissolution they also provided a release for those similarly inflected emotions associated with "unconventional" erotic drives and impulses. As Stites notes, "The measure won the general approval of the Russian urban intelligentsia, Bolshevik and otherwise, who despised the hypocrisy of tsarist and western bourgeois marriage laws" (369). While So-

viet Russia was not a promised land for libidinal drives that did not conform to a norm, it is possible that within the language of societal reconstruction spaces for non-normative identities were articulated alongside their prescripted others.

As families were confined to *kommunalkas,* the communal apartments for which the Soviet era is renowned, the reworking of familial intimacy became standard issue: the very idea of privacy was undermined through the assertion of its public display. Forced into "unnatural" alliances with one another, previous strangers became aunts, uncles, cousins. The paradigm of family was extended and distended to move beyond its rote association with genealogy and blood heritage. Similarly, a reconstruction of the national family was underway. The grouping of unindustrialized, economically dispersed republics into a multifederated union of Soviet "peoples" produced an "integration of nations and nationalities into a single community and thus, for the first time in history, creat[ed] a truly multinational culture" (Kelly et al. 10). Theoreticians gauged that the success of multinationalism within the socialist Union was possible, as traits and cultural norms formerly seen as innately divisive were reconfigured into potentialities for future federation. In his work on materialist theory and heredity, for example, N. P. Posnanski claimed that "even naturally caused differences of birth, e.g. racial, can and must be abolished by a new historical development" (qtd. in Attwood 59). While we must remain skeptical of the presuppositions and logic of the "natural" herein, we can at the same time register in Posnanski's terms a desire to unseat tired theories of the natural, and of race, as strictly biological: an attempt to reconfigure alliances through material processes as agent of and product of the Internationale. Though far from an explicit endorsement of alternative sexualities, the Internationale provided a space for queer identifications coded through interracial, differently familial, heretofore unimagined and unimaginable, alliances across previously proscriptive boundaries.

The Lawrence Connection

Bringing together Lawrence's exploration of possessiveness and a Soviet reordination of selfhood, Hughes's stories, within their exploration of the interracial, offer a theory of self-dispossession as a response to the stultifying constraints of white supremacy outlined in *The Ways of White Folks* and as a means of refiguring the bonds of Du Boisian black masculinity. If we see in Lawrence's story a preoccupation with strong femininities, it is to be sure equally a preoccupation with feminine possessiveness, that is, with the concept of self-possession as a condition of subjecthood. And as discussed above, Hughes pinpoints his fascination with "The Lovely Lady" as located in the vicinity of such "possessive" femininity. That this feature of Lawrence's story should stand out for Hughes in Moscow in 1933 makes sense: self-possession, or more precisely, self-ownership, as a means of articulating autonomy was precisely at issue in Bolshevik theorization of subjectivity in which the collective was prized over the individual. Such theorization offered a critique of liberal notions of the self in which self-ownership is the goal. A disbanding of personal property and its ideologies was especially salient to a critic, like Hughes, of the residual slave-owning structures underlying US attitudes toward property and likewise citizenship. Given the historical property status of blacks in the US, a goal of self-ownership would seem the obvious and necessary counter to the delimitations of property laws subtending the national ideology of citizenship. Thus to explore a theory of self-dispossession as counter to the goal of self-ownership challenges expected avenues of retribution.[15] Hughes explores this dilemma throughout, refusing to supply a definitive answer, but gesturing toward a rebuttal of liberal notions of selfhood that subtend whiteness as the standard bearer of subjecthood and belonging. Thus what emerges in Lawrence as a preoccupation with strong femininities reappears in a highly altered form in *The Ways of White Folks*.[16]

Although the Russian connection has been largely occluded from Hughes scholarship, two critics have commented upon Hughes's Russia-originated relationship to Lawrence. Both, however, have summarily dismissed the dynamics of influence at work in Hughes's stories that emerged in response to his reading of Lawrence. Faith Berry concedes that Hughes was "overwhelmingly influenced by D. H. Lawrence" (18), but later qualifies this influence when she writes that this was "more emotionally than stylistically" (188). In the end for Berry, Hughes's work "bears little resemblance" to that of Lawrence (188). Similarly, Leo Hamalian, who is more extensive in his exploration of the authorial relationship, reduces the significance of Lawrence's work to a concern with "domineering, hateful parents" and the ways that "our revered authority figures, representing a society run on a money ethic, can best educate the younger generation in violation and murder" (587-88). While acknowledging a terrain of contiguity, Berry and Hamalian overlook the subtle dynamics of desire and identification within the familial, the exploration of non-normative female/male relationships, the specters of illegitimate offspring, and the ways Hughes implicitly connected these narrative circuits to the querying of relationships between black and white underway in the Internationale.

In his stories Hughes was self-admittedly aspiring to the "same hair raising manner" of character and situation as Lawrence's stories (*Wonder* 213). To accomplish this effect while focusing not on Britain but on the United States, Hughes's work strays from the standard shorthand used to describe black American masculine

consciousness. Two of the most pointed cases of reconfigured interracial alliances that bear on a rearticulated black masculinity emerge in **"Slave on the Block"** and **"Home."** **"Slave on the Block"** was written in Moscow in 1933, and **"Home"** was written shortly after Hughes's return to the United States. Recollecting the constraints of Du Bois's interracial dyad, and the reconfigured "queer" contours of feminine identified masculinity insinuated by Lawrence, these stories establish their Russian connection through explorations of the interracial. Each story offers a differently eroticized bond between the interracial couple, suggesting emotional alliances through aberrant sexual behavior, and toys with this filiation as an expression of reconfigured black male subjectivity.

In **"Slave on the Block,"** Anne is an artist who "thought in terms of pictures," an indication that she cannot get outside visual representation as a means of mapping identity; and indeed when she first meets Luther, she "could hardly see the boy, it being dark in the hall, and he being dark, too" (21). Luther's presence establishes a critique of modernity's insistence on the immediate readability of the racialized body, but it also enables this episteme's (unjust) elaboration through Anne's persistent inability to "see" Luther. "Come in and let us see you" (22), Anne pleads, an indication that she will remain affixed to a modern means of extrapolating and producing meaning through surface, visible signs (22). What Anne and her husband do see is that Luther is "the essence in the flesh" of Negro-ness (21), and in their excitement to bring this essence into proximity to them, they make "a place for him to sleep in the basement by the furnace" (23). This mingling of the desire for proximity and the barriers to it erected by the mediation of racial stereotypes in Anne's fascination with Luther produce the story's key tension: the dialectic between her mounting erotic attachment to Luther and her attempt to produce his image as a warding off of this illicit desire. We see these proclivities at work when Anne summons the courage to ask Luther to undress:

> Anne could stare at him at leisure when he was asleep. One day she decided to paint him nude, or at least half nude. A slave picture, that's what she would do. The market at New Orleans for a background. And call it 'The Boy on the Block'. [. . .] She wanted to paint him now representing to the full the soul and sorrow of his people. She wanted to paint him as a slave about to be sold. And since slaves in warm climates had no clothes, would he please take off his shirt.
>
> (24)

Anne uses artistic license to access an idealized image as an excuse to disrobe her subject. At the same time this very image of Luther—the slave on the block—provides both a partial barrier to Anne's increasing desire and a means of further incitement. "It's too marvelous!" (25) Anne delights when she sees Luther's naked torso, and thereafter Luther is allowed to neglect his house-boy duties and simply pose for Anne's delectation.

Anne's fantasy of Luther as her self-fulfilling spectacle of desire comes crashing down when Luther explicitly directs his own erotic arrows. When Anne learns that Luther is sleeping with their maid, Mattie, her jealousy is tempered by rationalization. She "condones them" because "it's so simple and natural for Negroes to make love" (27), and the Carraways "prided themselves on being different, artists, you know, and liberal-minded people" (28). Anne decides to "keep" Luther in spite of his libidinal truancy (27). However, when Luther's erotic attachments bar her completion of "The Boy on the Block," she grows frustrated. She notes that Luther "had grown a bit familiar lately" (27), an indication that Luther has become too proximate within this "different"-oriented household. It is clear that Luther not only has transgressed limits of Anne's fantasized image of blackness, but that this image relies on a possessive relationship between the artist and her object. Mattie is a source of comeuppance for Anne, who must temper her desire for Luther through the knowledge that he desires not her but the black maid. In order to stave off this threat to white femininity, Anne indulges in a fantasy of blackness as proximate, as "familiar," by welcoming Luther into her home. But she simultaneously asserts the superiority of her whiteness, her model of self-ownership, through the act of aestheticization.

Unlike the "ur"-bond between black male/white female as contingent on denied male access, Luther's interest in Anne can be interpreted as disinterest. He is unmoved by her advances, disengaged from her model of desire as acquisitiveness. Indeed, Luther construes Anne's desire—which can only be expressed as possessiveness—as "too strange:" "They is mighty funny," he comments (25). The modality of Anne's fascination with, indeed fetishization of, Luther's body, is odd to Luther, who refuses and remains impermeable to her (socially mandated) structures of representation and desire. Hughes notes that, "They didn't like the Carraways. [. . .] They didn't understand the vagaries of white folks, neither Luther nor Mattie, and they didn't want to be bothered trying" (25). As this passage exemplifies, throughout the story Luther is accorded a kind of false simplicity, a seeming unawareness of and apathy toward the "vagaries of white folks." However, Luther's lackadaisical attitude toward Anne can be read at the same time as a reflection of a subjecthood that knows these "vagaries" all too well. In other words, Luther's indifference reads as at once a refusal to cohere to a pattern that turns on the vagaries of desire and identification implicit in a verb such as "like"—"They didn't like the Carraways"—and structurally reiterates the prohibition against interracial desire and its sanctioned reinforcement through law and violence. While

Luther's disinterest demonstrates his ex-centric position vis-à-vis a Du Boisian pattern of black male subjectivity, it also places him precariously within the larger cultural proscription endorsed through lynching and anti-miscegenation laws. But, at the crossroads of these related but far from isomorphic forces, Luther presents the possibility of aberration, of sexual transgression from the bond of interracial heternormative desire that reads, only superficially, as complicit with the strictures of white supremacy. His disinterest is a calculated strategy to deflect the tune of social taboos, and reflects the structural inequalities that confer between white women and black men.

Luther's interventions into the familial reveal further aberration from white imperatives. As if sensing Luther's refusal to conform to a presupposed model of filiation, the Carraways' liberal attitudes toward a reworked familial unit establish limits. This is made starkly clear through the imposition of Michael's mother into their household. Mrs. Carraway Sr. accuses Luther of overstepping implied boundaries: "I never liked familiar Negroes," she declares (29). Her objection to Luther as too familiar summons Luther's eviction from the family. The story depicts the limits of familiarity accorded objects of desire, thereby remarking upon the contiguous yet asymmetrical relations between subject positions accorded "black men" and "white women" in the spectrum of a model in which subjectivity is based on self-possession. At the same time the story reads against these constraints, not only by portraying Luther's disinterest in such models, but also through Anne's response to Luther's exit, which can only be read as melancholic: her plea to have Luther stay reveals itself as the fear of losing an object of desire through which she orients her own subjectivity. Anne is tongue-tied:

> She looked at Luther. His black arms were full of roses he had brought to put in the vases. He had on no shirt. "Oh!" His body was ebony [. . .]. "Oh", Anne moaned distressfully, "my 'Boy on the Block.'"
>
> (31)

Anne's lost object of fantasy (based as it is on demoralizing representations of the black other) threatens to unseat a racial superiority inextricably bound to her sense of self; its loss, the lost Luther, is experienced as a potential loss of self, of a self-dispossessed.

In the fall of 1933 Hughes had returned to the United States and taken up residence in Carmel, California, where he worked assiduously to complete the stories triggered by his Soviet journey. Arnold Rampersad comments that "the whirlwind of fiction that started in Moscow with his reading of D. H. Lawrence carried Hughes through long sessions at his typewriter during the fall in Carmel" (282). By December Hughes had completed a manuscript draft of what would become *The Ways of*

White Folks, a collection that included the Moscow stories in addition to several that up to that time he had been unable to publish stateside.[17] Among these stories, **"Home"** signals Hughes's interest in thinking through the complexities of returning to the States after his encounters abroad, and in so doing takes up the idea of self-dispossession to forward it as an alternative model of subjectivity altogether. This story summons the Du Boisian black male/white female dyad as a site of intimate negotiation between self and other to elucidate a disavowal of possessive subjecthood. In so doing the story rewrites this coupling, refusing its recognition-based model as linked to heteronormative bonds articulated as the improperly interracial. **"Home"** is the story of young violinist, Roy, who, stricken with a mortal illness returns home from Europe. Upon his arrival he is immediately marked as different, foreign, unreadable: "When the boy came back there were bright stickers and tags in strange languages the home folks couldn't read all over his bags" (33). This unreadability becomes the mirror of Roy's articulation of selfhood in which recognition is always under erasure. The story is filled with abstract hallucinatory moments that break from the third person narrative to introduce a first person stream-of-consciousness in which people and objects mingle and merge and cross-gender identifications circulate with racial taboos. Commissioned to play a concert for his hometown, Roy fantasizes deliriously while on-stage:

> This is the *Meditation from Thaïs* by Massenet. . . . This is the broken heart of a dream come true not true. This is music, and me, sitting on the door-step of the world needing you. . . . O, body of life and love with black hands and brown limbs and white breasts and a golden face with lips like a violin bowed for singing. Steady, Roy! It's hot in this crowded church and you're sick as hell. . . . This, the dream and the dreamer, wandering in the desert from Hopkinsville to Vienna in love with a streetwalker named Music. . . . Listen, you bitch, I want you to be as beautiful as the moon in the night on the edge of the Missouri hills. [. . .] You don't look like Thaïs, you scrawny woman in a cheap coat and red hat staring up at me from the first row. [. . .] What is it you want the music to give you? What do you want from me? . . . This is Hopkinsville, Missouri. . . . Look at all those brown girls back there in the crowd of Negroes, leaning toward me and the music. First time most of them ever saw a man in evening clothes, black or white. First time most of them ever heard the *Meditation from Thaïs*. First time they ever had one of their own race come home from abroad playing a violin. See them looking proud at me and Music over the heads of the white folks in the first rows, over the head of the white woman in the cheap coat and red hat who knows what Music's all about. . . . Who are you, lady?
>
> (40-42)

Roy's first-person hallucination distinguishes itself from the narrative that has preceded it, creating a private space by calling attention to itself as such. This formal abruption of the third person narrative reveals the extent to which Roy's private musings are simultaneously a public iteration. The provenance of Roy's thoughts as public is reinforced not only by the location of them as part of his performance in the music hall (where the hallucination could itself be seen as constitutive of the self-constituting performative), but also through the larger structural plot of the story. Closing with the violent realization of white presuppositions about a black male/white female dyad—that such a couple can only and always be interpreted as about masculine voraciousness and feminine fear—reconfirms the inseparability between private and public enactments of black masculine selfhood. In spite of his desires to created a space unimpeded by public mandate, voiced powerfully in his delirium, Roy is all too aware of this interpretive model: it has come to structure what he calls "home" and thus structures Hughes's story of the same name. Roy's mortal illness, the fact that we are told that he is doomed to die from the outset of the story, becomes an expression not so much of mysterious ill-health but of the inescapability of public intervention into, regulation of, his "private" life. Roy's glance into the mirror before he leaves for his ill-fated evening stroll becomes an expression of his accepting the destiny of his racial bearing, even as the face staring back at him poses a strong counter-model to this interpretation: "Roy lighted the light, the better to see himself in the warped mirror of the dresser. Ashy pale his face was that had once been brown. His cheeks were sunken" (45). The image looking back at Roy from the "warped mirror" has been distended, retaining only a faint resemblance to the white fantasy of its racialized counterpart. His hallucinations offer an alternative narrative, but one that Roy, set on a course to encounter a violent death, seems resigned to renounce.

In the delirious musings cited above, Roy's thoughts offer glimpses of an alternative model of black masculine selfhood. In the first part of the hallucination, the word "this" works as a transitional term to indicate the contiguities between music, Roy, and the "scrawny woman in a cheap coat and red hat." The bond created between them suggests the enticement and risk imbedded within the interracial coupling, but these inducements are charged with a flux of identity and desire, creating a scene in which the dream becomes the dreamer, the music the prostitute, the music the dream, Roy the streetwalker, and so on. In order for these crossings to proceed, Roy's axis of vision summons another visual point of contact: "all those brown girls back there in the crowd of Negroes [. . .] looking proud at me." The collective gaze of brown girls marveling at Roy who hails "from abroad" recalls the recognition under erasure poised by the story's opening scene in which white people "wonder about the brown-skinned young man" with the "stickers and tags in strange languages the home folks couldn't read" (33). Whereas within white disdain there lurks a specter of violence against black males who present differently, who are not immediately or transparently readable, within the gaze of the brown girls (who are, as Roy admits, equally unable to "read" him) there remains a sense, however superfluous, of racial connectedness that soars "over the heads of the white folks" (42).

In this vein Hughes introduces into the Du Boisian dyad of black male/white female the interloping gaze and presence of black femininity, a presence remarkably absent from the scene of Du Bois's production of black masculinity. Rather than posing the insinuating look of violence proffered by the implied white masculine overseer in Du Bois's configuration, these girls offer mute pride. It is as if the girls are necessary collective witnesses to the transformation underway here: witnesses whose "look" is full of pride, albeit based in partial misrecognition.[18] For Roy's hallucinatory meanderings cut short any material connection between himself and the brown girls by focusing his identificatory gaze on the white woman in the front row. The girls may swell with possessive pride at the thought of one of "their own" dressed in a tuxedo and playing classical music, but this sense of affiliation is unmoored by their inability to comprehend anything other about Roy than the fact that his skin looks, like their own, brown. This filiation, based as it is on "looking," turns out to be an insufficient basis for identification. The inadequacy of visual mechanisms to determine connections in **"Home"** recalls Hughes's critique of Anne's dependency on this episteme in **"Slave on The Block."** When Roy figuratively addresses Mrs. Reese to say, "You don't look like Thaïs," he underscores the unreliability of visual sources of association. Thaïs, the heroine of Massenet's opera of the same name, was an Egyptian dancer of questionable reputation, and Roy's depiction of Mrs. Reese as both proximate to but different from Thaïs insinuates the instability of the category of looking. She may not look like Thaïs, if Roy imagines as he might that Thaïs has brown skin, but she is associatively linked through music to the prostitute, who links back to Roy, the music's source. This association proves more powerful than that between Roy's brown skin and that of the girls. The addressee, "you," here remains the white woman, who together with Roy is constitutive of an "us," whereas the brown girls become the "them": "See them looking proud at me" (42).

Thus the negotiation of intimacy finally at play comes to be about the decidedly non-possessive relationship between Roy and the woman who stands out, who seems, unlike the others, to know what it's "all about" (42). Elizabeth Povinelli's work on intimacy is helpful here. In her work that traces the links between personal and social filiations, between intimacy as a form of recognition that validates the self and as a form of recognition that validates one's relationship to others within a given community (a "We-The-People"), Povinelli explains how intimate love came to be based on intimate recognition. She writes,

> to assert the bond of love was to assert simultaneously a rejection of social utility. [. . .] Along with being a form of orientation and attachment, intimacy is the dialectic of this self-elaboration. Who am I in relation to you? This question and its cognates lift up a reflexive ego in the act of asking and stitch it to a world of others. The question is performative in the strict sense. In the act of asking Who Am I, the I is constituted.

(230-31)

The kind of co-dependency between "private" longings and social recognition that Povinelli describes is, again, reinforced in Du Bois's model. In the scene of Roy's performance of Thaïs, however, Roy turns the tables on Du Bois's recognition-based model of subjectivity. Rather than asking "who Am I?" Roy asks, "who are you, lady?" This question is to be sure self-constituting, but in backwards fashion: the who am I is constituted in the moment of asking not simply who are you, but who is *she*? There is a merging, enfolding of subjectivities here, a flux of identificatory objects and desires; punctuated only intermittently by Roy's attempt to remain "steady" (40). She, it turns out, is the one who knows Music, and correlatively, a differently identified sense of subjectivity suggested by the "bitch" and her "tawdry" red hat. This lyrical, delirium-based selfhood recalls Robert's object-less identity in emergence. It is identified as Roy's difference, his "red" internationalism, his unreadableness, and his refusal of recognition through prescripted models of gender, racial, and sexual ascription. The intimate space carved out here between Roy and Mrs. Reese defies Du Bois's ideal of intimate, heteronormative recognition as key to black masculine selfhood. In the same way that he refuses self-possession as key to subjecthood, Hughes bars intimacy as recognition.[19] Hughes disentwines the subjective I based on intimacy (Du Bois's model) from the I of a self dispossessed. The latter, in the character of Roy, navigates differently this relationship between self and other, allowing for their commingling and cross-identification, a "knowing" without mutual recognition or a desire to possess. This formulation offers a powerful critique of the model of white citizenship as based in a relationship to selfhood in which self-possession and recognition by the other create mutual consensus of the "we" in "We the People." Hughes disbands this idea/model by challenging it through differently configured intimacies, problematizing this formative Du Boisian moment in which the narration of black masculinity organizes a structure of social membership based in heteronormative impulses voiced as a desire for recognition. Hughes's intervention into the familial arrives here in the middle of Roy's delirium. The introduction of Ma into the flux of hallucinatory language promises a place, a location for the maternal bond: "You remember, Ma

[. . .] you remember that Kreisler record we had on the phonograph with the big horn when I was a kid? Nobody liked it but me, but you didn't care how many times I played it, over and over. . . . Why did you pray all night when I told you we had a contract to go to Berlin and work in a cabaret there? [. . .] And didn't I send you money home?" (41). In the process of defamiliarizing her, Ma's space is usurped or overwhelmed by a more enticing association, that between Roy and Mrs. Reese, one that suggests an emotional alliance created through aberrant sexual behavior, a refusal to conform to "white" ways of recognizing interracial desire.[20]

As I mention above, a kinship between Roy and Mrs. Reese becomes cruelly, violently reinforced at the story's end when Roy and Mrs. Reese exchange partial greetings on the street and Roy is subsequently lynched for a purportedly errant display of black male desire. In depicting this denouement, the story offers a key rereading of the Du Boisian dyad of black man/white woman as based, in **"Home,"** on a misrecognition of desire. What the white folks see when they observe Roy and Mrs. Reese takes on a life of its own. Consider how Hughes's language here escalates to make this point through the use of voice, point of view, and speculation. A seemingly unmediated flow of opinion gathers momentum transforming the benign act of talk in the following spectrum: talking/insulting/attacking/RAPING. In operation there is a need to turn the unreadable Roy into a codifiable (and forbidden) display of black masculinity as sexual aggressor, to fulfill the larger cultural mandate that promises violence as retribution for fantasized desire.[21] Likewise his punishment is the evisceration of his corporeality, the "feminization" of his body, so that it "hung like a violin for the wind to play" (49). Rescue from the purported danger posed to Mrs. Reese by Roy signals a mode by which white concerns about preserving white femininity summon a familiar Lacanian paradigm: As Slavoj Žižek rephrases it, "Lacan's thesis that 'there is no sexual relationship' means precisely that the structure of the 'real' sexual act (of the act with a flesh-and-blood partner) is already inherently phantasmatic—the 'real' body of the other serves only as a support for a phantasmatic projection" (21). In replaying this compulsory projection of white male fantasy, and its counterprojection articulated by Du Bois, Hughes offers a renarration of African-American masculinity, a disarticulation of the bonds of phantasmatic projection, and a rewriting of interracial, cross-gender desire as a site for alliances through aberration from the norm. These stories offer a "bond" of sexual transgression, a means of articulating queer emotional alliances through the identifications that emerge therein. Drawing on the utopian impulses of Soviet society in the 1930s, Hughes's stories unite the urges behind reconfigured subjectivity announced by the *novyi Sovetskii chelovek* with the queer contours of a feminine-identified masculinity suggested by

Lawrence to offer a differently affiliated black American masculine subjecthood. Political coalitions between blacks and whites proposed by the Internationale are adjusted to explore the interdictions of sexual boundaries between black and white in the United States. As readers of these stories we are invited to explore the different modalities of desire and identification that Hughes's characters bring to life, to investigate the ways in which Hughes's depictions of interracial alliances, infused with the possibilities of the Internationale, enable a vocabulary for meditating upon queer desire and its social disavowal.

Notes

1. Attesting to the validation of his writing career he found in the USSR, and significantly contrasting this validation with his struggles as a writer in the United States, Hughes recalls, "I made more from writing in Moscow in terms of buying power than I have ever earned within the same period anywhere else" (*Wonder* 196).

2. See Baldwin. In my book I focus specifically on Hughes's negotiation of interstices between Du Bois's black masculine veil and the feminine, Orientalist veil of Central Asia in Hughes's writings about Soviet Central Asia, and the way the latter enabled Hughes to theorize an alternative black masculine subjectivity through feminine identification and the Soviet project of unveiling.

3. Hughes partnered himself with other Russian authors, most notably in his translations of Vladimir Mayakovsky and Boris Pasternak. See, for example, his translation of Pasternak's "Beloved" in *I Wonder as I Wander* (197), and (with the assistance of Lydia Filatova) Mayakovsky's "Black and White," "Syphilis," and "Hygiene" (the latter in *Wonder* 198). The originals are in the Special Collections at Fisk University Library.

4. As Michael Uebel notes, "crossing racial, class, and national boundaries, and most significantly, the lines imposed by normative sexuality and erotic practice, is a vital, empowering act of social critique," but little scholarly attention has been focused on linking identificatory boundary crossing to the specific national borders crossed in work such as Hughes's (8).

5. The argument elaborated here is a reformulation of the one I make in *Beyond the Color Line and the Iron Curtain*.

6. On the privileges of white masculinity as a disembodied entitlement of citizenship and the correlative ways in which black masculinity is forced to embody otherness, see Wiegman.

7. As others have noted, Du Bois's example is based on a Hegelian model of dialectical recognition. See, for example, Gilroy 50-58.

8. Judith Butler argues that heterosexuality secures its success by eliciting and simultaneously disavowing its abject, interiorized, and ghostly other, homosexuality. In a similar fashion, Hughes's stories reread the compulsorily heterosexual in the Du Boisian dyad to summon key links between the aberrance of interraciality and the aberrance of non-hetero desire that remain otherwise under erasure. See Butler 106.

9. My use of "heteronormative" here and elsewhere is informed by the work of Lauren Berlant and Michael Warner who underscore the elasticity and divergence within the category of heterosexuality even as the category works as a unifying and privileged location for a national idiom of "rightness." They write, "by heteronormativity we mean the institutions, structures of understanding, and practical orientations that make heterosexuality seem not only coherent—that is, organized as a sexuality—but also privileged. [. . .] It consists less of norms that could be summarized as a body of doctrine than of a sense of rightness produced in contradictory manifestations—often unconscious, immanent to practice or to institutions" (548). The term "queer" here suggests ruptures of "normalcy" often associated with heteronormativity, spaces in which interventions into the heteronormative provide the possibility for inhabiting a differently configured black masculine subjectivity.

10. In his unpublished manuscript "Russia and America: An Interpretation," one of the first things W. E. B. Du Bois notes about Russia is that "women sit beside me quite confidently and unconsciously" (27). Many African-American men (including several from the *Black and White* troupe) who ventured to the Soviet Union in the 1930s because of the job opportunities there had affairs with and/or married Soviet women.

11. In his essay "Moscow and Me," Hughes makes the comparison explicit. He writes that "to dance with a white woman in the dining room of a fine restaurant and not be dragged out by the neck—is to wonder if you're really living in a city full of white folks" (64). Noting the difference between white attitudes toward blacks in the US and the USSR, Hughes then queries the adequateness of a term like "white" to describe Moscow's residents, "But then the papers of the other lands are always calling the Muscovites red" (64).

12. A parallel between Robert's self-description and that of the "invert" further underscores the queer contours of Robert's subjecthood. Robert's words echo the model of the invert that emerged in the late nineteenth century and reduced complex gender identifications to binary structures so that an "invert" identified a person as a woman's soul

trapped in a man's body or vice versa. See Duggan. And in the 1920s and 30s Freudian theory popularized the idea of homosexuality as inversion. See Freud, especially 2-14.

13. See Attwood and Kelly.

14. Examples of artistic renditions of the new family include Evgeni Zamiatin's *We* (1920), Yuri Olesha's *Envy* (1927), and Abram Romm's *Bed and Sofa* (1927). See also Matich.

15. In *The Possessive Investment in Whiteness*, George Lipsitz uses the phrase "possessive investment" to demarcate both literal and figural advantages afforded whites by the social fact of whiteness as profit-bearing. He writes, "whiteness has a cash value: it accounts for advantages that come to individuals through profits made from housing secured in discriminatory markets, through the unequal educations allocated to children of different races, through insider networks that channel employment opportunities to the relatives and friends of those who have profited most from present and past racial discrimination, and especially through *intergenerational transfers of inherited wealth* that pass on the spoils of discrimination to succeeding generations" (vii; emphasis added).

16. Throughout the collection, women's voices, points of view, and agencies are ceded central roles. Cora in "Cora Unashamed," Cora in "Father and Son," and Vivi in "Poor Little Black Fellow" are all examples of revivified feminine presences who bear with them transformative and transforming powers in relationship to the people around them.

17. "Home" was rejected by *Harper's, American Mercury, Atlantic Monthly, Scribner's,* and *Forum.* When it finally was accepted for publication by *Esquire* in 1934, one reviewer commented, "Why is it that authors think it is their function to lay the flesh bare and rub salt in the wound? [. . .] Most people read for pleasure, and certainly there is no pleasure here" (qtd. in Rampersad 282).

18. In *Beyond the Color Line and the Iron Curtain* I explore the importance to Hughes's work in *The Ways of White Folks* of asserting black female agency as key to the reconstruction of black masculinity. In "Home" and "Slave on the Block" this can be seen in the presence of Mattie and the "brown girls" in Roy's audience, all of who structurally intervene in the absenting of black femininity from Du Bois's representative paradigm of black masculinity.

19. Perhaps this is one of the reasons that Hughes's stories are generally read (and critically dismissed) as overly simple—a means of signifying impersonal and likewise expendable.

20. In the story "Cora Unashamed," Hughes pursues the idea of interracial bonds created through sexual transgression. Between the protagonist Cora (who is black) and the daughter of the family Cora works for (who is white) he creates structurally parallel tales to forge an "interracial" alliance based on their aberrant sexual behavior (both have interracial affairs) that challenges the conventional basis of the familial bond.

21. In some ways Roy's story offers a parable for what Judith Butler has described as the mechanism of heterosexuality's "success." Seen in this way, heterosexuality (or, in the case of "Home," white consensus) secures this success by summoning and simultaneously erasing its abject other, homosexuality (in this case Roy). See Butler 106.

Works Cited

Anissimov, Julian. "Kinship." Trans. Langston Hughes. *International Literature* 4 (1933): 61.

Attwood, Lynne. "The New Soviet Man and Woman." *Soviet Sisterhood.* Ed. Barbara Holland. Bloomington: Indiana UP, 1985: 54-77.

Attwood, Lynne, and Catriona Kelly. "Programmes for Identity: The 'New Man' and 'New Woman.'" *Constructing Russian Culture in the Age of Revolution: 1881-1940.* Ed. Catriona Kelly and David Shepherd. Oxford: Oxford UP, 1998. 256-90.

Baldwin, Kate. *Beyond the Color Line and the Iron Curtain: Reading Encounters between Black and Red, 1922-1963.* Durham: Duke UP, 2002.

Berlant, Lauren, and Michael Warner. "Sex in Public." *Critical Inquiry* 24 (1998): 547-66.

Berry, Faith. *Langston Hughes: Before and Beyond Harlem.* New York: Random, 1995.

Boym, Svetlana. *Common Places: Mythologies of Everyday Life in Russia.* Cambridge: Harvard UP, 1994.

Brown, Henry Billings. "Majority Opinion in Plessy v. Ferguson." *Desegregation and the Supreme Court.* Ed. Benjamin Munn Ziegler. Boston: Heath, 1958. 50-51.

Butler, Judith. *Gender Trouble: Feminism and the Subversion of Identity.* New York: Routledge, 1990.

Du Bois, W. E. B. *The Souls of Black Folk.* 1903. New York: Bantam, 1989.

———. "Russia and America: An Interpretation." *The W. E. B. Du Bois Papers.* Amherst: U of Massachusetts. 1-318. Microfilm 85, frames 395-527.

Duggan, Lisa. "Theory in Practice: The Theory Wars, or Who's Afraid of Judith Butler?" *Journal of Women's History* 10.1 (1998): 9-19.

Freud, Sigmund. *Three Essays on the Theory of Sexuality.* Trans. James Strachey. New York: Basic, 1962.

Fuss, Diana. "Fashion and the Homospectatorial Look." *Critical Inquiry* 18 (1992): 713-37.

Gates, Henry Louis, Jr. "Introduction: Darkly as through a Veil." Du Bois, *The Souls of Black Folk* vii-xxix.

Gilroy, Paul. *The Black Atlantic: Modernity and Double Consciousness.* Cambridge: Harvard UP, 1993.

Hamalian, Leo. "D. H. Lawrence and Black Writers." *Journal of Modern Literature* 16 (1990): 579-96.

Hughes, Langston. *I Wonder as I Wander.* New York: Thunder Mouth, 1956.

———. *The Ways of White Folks.* 1933. New York: Vintage, 1962.

———. "Moscow and Me." *International Literature* 4 (1933): 61-66.

———. "Letter to the Academy." *International Literature* 5 (1933): 112.

Kelly, Catriona, Hilary Pilkington, David Shepherd, and Vadim Volkvo. "Why Cultural Studies?" *Russian Cultural Studies.* Ed. Catriona Kelly and David Shepherd. Oxford: Oxford UP, 1998. 1-17.

Lawrence, D. H. *The Lovely Lady.* 1930. London: Secker, 1932.

Lipsitz, George. *The Possessive Investment in Whiteness: How White People Profit From Identity Politics.* Philadelphia: Temple UP, 1998.

Matich, Olga. "Remaking the Bed: Utopia in Daily Life." *Laboratory of Dreams: The Russian Avant-Garde and Cultural Experimentation.* Ed. John E. Bowlt and Olga Matich. Stanford: Stanford UP, 1996. 59-80.

Povinelli, Elizabeth. "Notes on Gridlock: Genealogy, Intimacy, Sexuality." *Public Culture* 14 (2002): 215-38.

Rampersad, Arnold. *The Life of Langston Hughes, Vol. 1, 1902-1941.* Oxford: Oxford UP, 1986.

Silverman, Kaja. *Male Subjectivity at the Margins.* New York: Routledge, 1992.

Somerville, Siobhan. *Queering the Color Line: Race and the Invention of Homosexuality in American Culture.* Durham: Duke UP, 2000.

Stites, Richard. *The Women's Liberation Movement in Russia: Feminism, Nihilism, and Bolshevism, 1860-1930.* Princeton: Princeton UP, 1978.

Uebel, Michael. "Men In Color: Introducing Race and the Subject of Masculinities." Ed. Harry Stecopoulos and Micahel Uebel. *Race and the Subject of Masculinities.* Durham: Duke UP, 1997. 1-16.

Wiegman, Robyn. *American Anatomies: Theorizing Race and Gender.* Durham: Duke UP, 1995.

Žižek, Slavoj. "Introduction: The Spectre of Ideology." *Mapping Ideology.* Ed. Slavoj Žižek. London: Verso, 1994. 1-33.

S. D. Blackford (review date winter 2003)

SOURCE: Blackford, S. D. Review of *The Collected Works of Langston Hughes, Vol. 15: The Short Stories,* by Langston Hughes, edited by R. Baxter Miller. *The Virginia Quarterly Review* 79, no. 1 (winter 2003): 23.

[*In the following review, Blackford praises Hughes's writing as "fresh, provocative, and enjoyable," but deems the collection poorly edited.*]

All but eight of Hughes' 58 short stories originally appeared in the three collections the celebrated African American writer published before his death in 1967: *The Ways of White Folks* (1934); *Laughing to Keep from Crying* (1952); and *Something in Common and Other Stories* (1963). The limited editorial apparatus of this volume [*The Collected Works of Langston Hughes, Vol. 15: The Short Stories*] consists of sparse annotation, a chronology of Hughes' life, an index of titles, a brief introduction by Arnold Rampersad, and a one-page "Note on the Text," in which Miller notes that "All spellings, capitalization, punctuation, and word compounding have been retained as they originally appeared, although obvious typographical errors have been corrected." But, skepticism is warranted by the editor's own typo of "stores" for "stories" on the previous line. The volume's structure is also problematic. Miller retains the original order of the stories as they appeared in the three volumes mentioned above, but the uncollected ones—Hughes' earliest works—appear at the end of the book, hindering a systematic analysis of stylistic development, and their texts derive from Akiba Sullivan Harper's *Langston Hughes: Short Stories* (1996). Happily, the quality of Hughes' writing shines through, and the short stories remain fresh, provocative, and enjoyable. Simple narratives in form, they capture the complexity of race relations in America, as well as the joys and sorrows of life, by championing the culture of working-class blacks and celebrating its life-affirming values.

Kimberly Banks (essay date fall 2004)

SOURCE: Banks, Kimberly. "'Like a violin for the wind to play': Lyrical Approaches to Lynching by Hughes, Du Bois, and Toomer." *African American Review* 38, no. 3 (fall 2004): 451-65.

[*In the following essay, Banks compares the stylized depictions of lynching in stories by Hughes, Jean Toomer, and W. E. B. Du Bois, emphasizing the lynching victims' shared aspirations for upward mobility and their interactions with an intolerant community.*]

Langston Hughes, W. E. B. Du Bois, and Jean Toomer experiment stylistically in their representations of lynching. The event of lynching can be understood both as an act existing within a symbolic system created by white people and as a moment within a trajectory of advancement pursued by black people. Within a system where black people attempt to make sense of the meaning of lynching, their symbolic understanding of the event is very different from that of its white participants. Schematizing lynching into black and white symbolic values highlights lynching as an act that polarizes groups and establishes rigid boundaries. Such schematization enables me to discuss literary repetition among black male writers and elucidate differences among these writers.

Critics have tended to focus on representations of lynching in the late-nineteenth and mid-to-late twentieth centuries. In *Exorcising Blackness,* Trudier Harris discusses efforts by Richard Wright, John Widemann, Toni Morrison, and David Bradley to rewrite the lynching ritual. More recently critics such as Sandra Gunning and Erika M. Miller have concentrated on the importance of women writing about lynching in the post-Reconstruction period, and in their collection *Strange Fruit: Plays on Lynching by American Women,* Judith L. Stephens and Kathy A. Perkins also focus on women's representations of lynching. But despite the increasing interest in representations of lynching in literature, very few scholars have focused on the early twentieth century. Stephens asserts that "lynchings reached their peak in 1892 when 255 individuals (155 black victims, 100 white) were killed by lynch mobs" (8). Harris makes the point that "as lynchings decreased—in a general way, though there were periodic rises—in the twenties, thirties, and forties, and as black writers searched for a distinct tradition and symbolism of their own, lynching and burning scenes reflect stylistic experimentation, symbolic language, and multiple levels of interpretation" (71). Barbara Foley complicates Harris's explanation of experimentation in the early twentieth century by highlighting the fact that "the early 1920s signaled if anything an increase in economic exploitation and racial violence: Throughout the South there were in 1921 more lynchings than there had been in any year since 1909" (190). Thus, writers like Hughes, Du Bois, and Toomer did not experiment because the threat of lynching was no longer tangible. Rather, their efforts are consistent with the increasing interest in literary style in the early twentieth century, and these experiments with lyricism enabled them to affirm the humanity of the lynching victim while also illustrating the brutality of the lynch mob. Lyricism shifts the symbolic importance of lynching from the perpetrators to the victim and restores his/her humanity.

Hughes, Du Bois, and Toomer explore conflicts that precipitate lynching. In doing so, they de-emphasize their male characters' sexual desire for white women and focus instead on their desire for social and economic advancement. Barbara Foley has challenged the long-standing impression of lynching by asserting that, "contrary to popular belief, the great majority of lynchings (more than seventy-five percent) were committed not in response to allegations of the rape of white women by black men, but in reaction to black acts of defiance against white abuse, both physical and economic" (187). In **"Home,"** Langston Hughes focuses on the musical attainment of Roy Williams as a classical violinist. In "The Coming of John," W. E. B. Du Bois emphasizes John Jones's attainment of a liberal education. Finally, in "Blood-Burning Moon," Jean Toomer highlights Tom Burwell's desire for land and a family. The protagonists of **"Home,"** "Of the Coming of John," and "Blood-Burning Moon," respectively, struggle against economic and educational constraints. The act of lynching highlights the inconsistency of punishing a man because he strives for improvement. All three protagonists meet the same end because they struggle instead of being satisfied with their proscribed social place.

I have organized this article into three sections: the dream, the return, and the denial of community. The dream section explores the desires and aspirations of each protagonist in terms of his aspirations for economic and educational advancement. Hughes, Du Bois, and Toomer refute the assertion that black men are driven by animal instincts and individualize their motivations. In doing so, they represent a spectrum of black masculinity. This spectrum de-sexualizes black masculinity. Racial obstacles forestall the realization of the protagonists' dreams. Each protagonist seeks to surmount obstacles to advancement by returning to a community or to origins, whether that community is literally one of a geographical home or figuratively one of a familial home. The return is complicated by the fact that each protagonist hopes to accomplish something new through the return. Each brings his dream of economic and/or educational advancement back to the community in hopes of transforming it. The return is not so much a return to place as a replacement and repositioning that would allow each protagonist to realize his dream. The return belies the promise of a change in geography. Acquiring an education, working the entertainment circuit, or working a brutalizing job demands that each protagonist leave a geographical safety zone. However, when they return home, what was once a geographical safety zone is no longer safe. The return is meant to fulfill a promise rather than recreate the past.

Each protagonist is unable to fulfill his dream through the return, which produces a denial of community. The denial is not an absolute denial, which would mean isolation. Rather, the local black community is unable to assimilate the protagonist's ideas about change, whereas the local white community refuses to accept the protagonist's change in social status. And because of the local white community's refusal, each protagonist is lynched.

Presumably the lynching eliminates the protagonist's different social status and affirms the distance between the protagonist and the local black community. However each protagonist's attempt to fulfill his dreams through a return underscores a continual process of social negotiation. Although each local black community does not accept the protagonist's ideas about social change, they are willing to argue and struggle about those ideas. Therefore, in the representations of lynching by Hughes, Du Bois, and Toomer, the social act of lynching, as an act of terror directed toward a local black community, fails to forestall the social change, the danger each protagonist represents. The act of lynching does not eradicate the debates about social change that the protagonist instigates. In other words, the social act of lynching does not rob the protagonist of his humanity; indeed, by making the lynching a lyrical moment, Hughes, Du Bois, and Toomer contrast the protagonist's humanity against the inhumanity of the mob.

THE DREAM

Each protagonist from the short stories by Hughes, Du Bois, and Toomer articulates his dreams in terms that retain his humanity. In Hughes's short story, Roy sees his ability to play classical music as a contribution to a global cultural exchange in which black men are equal and valued participants. Du Bois's John also sees himself participating in a global cultural exchange. He envisions such participation in terms of audience. He can be transported and whole listening to Wagner's music. While Tom in Toomer's short story does not participate in a global cultural exchange, he envisions a geographical, social, and familial space off limits to the economic and social inequalities and injustices he must face on a daily basis. Hughes, Du Bois, and Toomer draw the reader into each protagonist's dream because each one is fairly rational and reasonably sought.

Roy's choice of the violin and classical music is significant as a source of inspiration and hope to bridge racial exclusiveness. Not long after his return to Hopkinsville, Missouri, from Europe, Roy gives a classical concert at his mother's home church, Shiloh Church, which offers segregated seating: "Poor white folks" pay fifty cents and sit in front, and "even poorer Negroes" pay twenty-five cents and sit behind them. Such an environment is the antithesis of Roy's dream. Section five of the short story, which reveals his tumbling into despair, is a mixed reflection on how he got away from Hopkinsville and the situation he finds himself in now. His dream of Carnegie Hall and Salle Gaveau is contrasted with the present reality of Shiloh Church. Roy hears a performing voice in his head as he plays his concert. This internal voice allows Hughes to register Roy's split in consciousness as it occurs. Roy still attaches the same energy and hope to his music although it has changed locations. The opening line of the section, "Hello, Mr. Brahms on a violin from Vienna at a colored church in Hopkinsville, Missouri" (39), suggests an announcer's voice rather than a personal reflection. It also reinforces Roy's distance from his own performance at the moment. Roy plays the meditation from "Thaïs" by Massenet to reflect "the broken heart of a dream come true not true" (40). Through his selection, he expresses the distorted way a dream can come true and nevertheless be false. Roy plays out his despair to an audience insensitive to the significance of his music. The only connection that his music makes with the audience comes through the music teacher, Miss Reese. Roy sees her as "the white woman in the cheap coat and red hat who knows what music's all about." At the end of the concert, instead of exultation, Roy feels acute sickness. He "was shaking a little and his eyes burned and he wanted terribly to cough. Pain shot across his shoulders. But he smiled his concert-jazz-band smile. . . . And he held out a feverish hand" (42). Roy finds refuge in the role of performer and at least feels some satisfaction in Miss Reese's understanding. He vaguely hopes that his performance in Hopkinsville will bridge a social gap it was unable to bridge in Europe.

There is a gap between his dream of his success and his present reality back in Missouri, which creates nightmarish effects, culminating in his lynching. Considering that the short story is an elaboration of Hughes's dream poetry, it is surprising that **"Home"** has not been discussed more carefully in the criticism. Roy addresses his performance to "Mr. Brahms," who is able to reach a wide variety of people through his composition "Thaïs." However Roy feels limited in his ability to reach people through his interpretation of that composition. Mr. Brahms can realize his dream through virtual travel to Hopkinsville, Missouri, but Roy's dream dies in his interpretation of the music to the audience there. The realization of Roy's dream would have occurred through his presentation of the music to a sophisticated European or American audience. Such an audience would have appreciated not only Roy's technical skill, but also his transgression of social boundaries by being a black musician playing classical music very well. In particular, Roy plays Thaïs's meditation and addresses it as "body of life and love with black hands and brown limbs and white breasts and a golden face with lips like a violin bowed for singing" (40). Roy would like to be able to travel across cultures and racial boundaries in

the same way Brahms' music reaches across the Atlantic Ocean. The movement across racial boundaries is particularly important in the figuration of the music as black, brown, white, and golden. The image of white breasts replaces the use of the white female in classic lynch narratives with the image of a cultural artifact. German music is designated European, and when it travels to the United States it becomes white. This particular negative, racial translation puts Roy in danger. His desire to play the violin originates in another kind of cultural translation that occurs through the records of Fritz Kreisler. Kreisler's record spurs Roy to want to learn the violin in Berlin.

When Roy notices the music teacher in the audience, he asks, "'What is it you want the music to give you? What do you want from me?'" (42). Roy does not become as powerful as the music in his interpretation of the music. He cannot extend its reach to remedy the segregated seating at Shiloh Church. Even as Miss Reese understands the power of Brahms, she has trouble accepting Roy as a vessel. She shakes Roy's hand, but her compliment is limited: ". . . she spoke of symphony concerts in St. Louis, of the fact that she was a teacher of music, of piano and violin, but that she had no pupils like Roy, that never in the town of Hopkinsville had anyone else played so beautifully" (43). Her frame of reference is limited compared to Roy's. Miss Reese can only speak of one of Missouri's big cities. Rather than complimenting Roy in terms of the performers in St. Louis, she compliments him in terms of Hopkinsville, where there is no question of rivalry since Roy is unique in his interests and attainments. Even with the guarded nature of her compliment, Roy appreciates her understanding of music, which is also unique and unparalleled in Hopkinsville.

Where Hughes reveals Roy's dream through its displacement in Hopkinsville, Du Bois emphasizes John's dream in "In the Coming of John" through its development away from his hometown. John comes to realize his potential, only to have that realization undercut by a subsequent realization that few opportunities exist for black men to excel. When John leaves for school, "full half the black folk followed him proudly to the station, and carried his queer little trunk and many bundles. And there they shook and shook hands, and the girls kissed him shyly and the boys clapped him on the back . . . he pinched his little sister lovingly, and put his great arms about his mother's neck" (246-47). There is a clear affection and affinity between John and those he leaves, but this affinity is worn away over the years of John's absence. While he is unsuccessful in school, he remains unchanged from when he first left his hometown. Once he is suspended for a semester and works in the city, he attacks his studies with more determination and earnestness and becomes successful. With this success his hometown comes to represent "the choked and narrow life" (250-51). Such a major transformation in John's perspective leads him away from the jovial and good-natured boy he was to the serious and contemplative man. To the same degree that Hughes defines manhood through compassion, Du Bois defines manhood through intellectual curiosity. With the attainment of manhood, John is no longer fit for life in his hometown.

One of the central questions of the short story is how the intellect confronts the irrationality of racial violence. Gavin Jones suggests that articulation of racial violence is the answer because it is only through articulation that self-consciousness can occur. At the same time, he argues that articulation must be ambiguous if it is to address the paradoxes of the color line. Language does not provide the range of ambiguity provided by music, which offers a different grammar of articulation. Language can illuminate the inconsistencies that accompany racial violence without providing a method for eradicating the violence. If racial violence is illogical, then its challenge and refutation must also be illogical, which paves the way for the importance of music and lyricism as representations of lynching. Although John begins to satisfy his intellectual curiosity at the Wells Institute, it is only in New York at the performance of Wagner's music that he realizes the potential within the world: "The infinite beauty of the wail lingered and swept through every muscle of his frame, and put it all a-tune. . . . A deep longing swelled in all his heart to rise with that clear music out of the dirt and dust of that low life that held him prisoned and befouled. If he could only live up in the free air where birds sang and setting suns had no touch of blood!" (252). Music provides the momentary imaginative realization of an ideal that is thwarted from social realization. Music transports John away from illogical racial boundaries, supposedly boundaries of blood, to an equalizing spiritual plane.

In Toomer's "Blood-Burning Moon," Tom Burwell does not try to transcend social restrictions. He believes that the separate social arenas for black and white people can be equal. Unlike Roy, who finds his dream displaced in Hopkinsville, or John, who finds no room for the realization of his dream, Tom attempts to make the social fiction of "separate but equal" apply to his employer Bob Stone. Tom would like to build a life with Louisa as his wife. Louisa is ambivalent about Tom because she puts that relationship on a par with her relationship with Bob Stone. Since Bob Stone is white and has inherited the legacy of being plantation master, his relationship to Tom is structured by his control over Tom's desire for a plot of land to sharecrop. Tom seeks to divorce his economic relationship to Bob from his position of romantic rival for Louisa's affections. Tom tells Louisa that a day will come when "'my bales will buy yo what y gets from white folks now'" (30). He

believes that he will have a level economic playing field once he can farm a plot of land.

One of Tom's co-workers explains that "'Tom Burwell's been on the gang three times fo cuttin men'" (32), and Tom's connection to his knife emerges as an obvious synecdoche. When his friends tease him about Louisa and Bob Stone, he "whip[s] out a long knife and would have cut them to shreds if they hadnt ducked into the woods" (29). Tom's ultimate self-expression occurs through his knife, which reflects his limited options. Tom forms community with the men around the stove, but that community is fragile, as represented by his willingness to start a knife-fight. Because Tom is both working-class and inarticulate in "Blood-Burning Moon," Peckham sees his character as stereotypical. What marks Tom as in danger of being stereotypical is his Bad Man status in the community, someone who fights and totes a knife, willing to cut anyone who crosses him. This mythological image is called into question through Tom's relationship to Louisa. The Bad Man provides occasions for eruptions of racial conflict. However Tom's relationship with Louisa provides an occasion for racial conflict that lacks provocation. Tom's desire for Louisa also contributes to his conflict with Bob because it puts him on equal status with Bob. Ironically, it is Bob who is the first to pull a knife during their fight, which reinforces the similarity between the two characters rather than their difference. For a black man to be a "Bad Man," he seeks equality with powerful white men.

The individual struggles of Roy Williams, John Jones, and Tom Burwell are representative of various ways black men seek social equality. Roy Williams believes that by learning the violin and becoming a concert violinist interpreting Brahms that he will be able to bridge both socio-economic and racial divides. His inability to serve as an absolute and complete bridge weakens him physically. He would like his music to build a common community as an antidote to the community of the lynch mob. John Jones hopes to bridge the racial divide through his status as a teacher. John sees becoming a teacher in his hometown as a consolation for being unable to participate in the wider world, represented by Wagner's *Lohengrin*. John hopes to serve as a bridge between that wider world and his students. Tom Burwell is in a position of public prominence because he carries a knife and has been on the chain gang. Black men in "Blood-Burning Moon" watch him with anticipation because they know his girlfriend Louisa is also seeing the white Bob Stone. Despite Tom's experience of Georgia justice, he needs to believe in the possibility of farming his own land and raising his family without interference from white people. Tom identifies a private sphere that is off-limits to white people. This private sphere includes not only Louisa, but also his livelihood, farming. Tom challenges the racist logic that makes every aspect of black people's lives open to the master's scrutiny. These protagonists challenge fundamental relationships between black and white people.

RETURNING HOME

For each protagonist, the return home highlights how his dream clashes with social reality. The premise of human equality on which each protagonist's dream is based is a premise denied in social reality. Roy might play Bach and Mozart beautifully, but his performance is reduced to the performance of a "nigger," code for non-human, and his music interpreted as "funny pieces." John might present an eloquent statement of the commonalities among humankind, but in doing so he relativizes the importance of Christianity and religion, thereby alienating his audience, who subsequently holds him up to scorn. Tom might represent the proverbial white knight in shining armor in his defense of Louisa against Bob, but his courage to confront Bob comes to be interpreted as insolence, punishable by death. Instead of the ugly evil monster, Bob is the (despicable?) king. The terms in which each protagonist articulates his dream are perverted for competing political aims, and these subversive dreams are demonized through such reinterpretation.

In **"Home,"** Roy Williams is a prodigal son who comes home to die. Instead of the jubilant return garnered to the son in Jesus' parable, Roy faces a familial and racial legacy of enslavement and segregation. Roy has held a higher social status than that held by all other Hopkinsville residents, but his greeting in Hopkinsville is from white loafers surrounding the train platform who make it clear that he is not wanted. They ask a series of questions, such as, "'Where you been, boy?,'" "'What'd yuh come back for?,'" and "'I hope [your mother's] gladder to see yuh than we are'" (36). Roy says nothing in response, but "he fe[els] dizzy and weak" and attributes the increasing vehemence of his cough to "the smoke and dust of travel" (37). The inability to respond to these latent threats makes Roy internalize them and grow weaker.

Hughes, Du Bois, and Toomer explain the phenomenon of lynching within the racial legacy of enslavement and segregation. What should have been Roy's triumphant return from Europe becomes like John's homecoming in W. E. B. Du Bois's "Of the Coming of John"—an occasion for increasing tension and hostility. In Du Bois's story Judge Henderson tells John Jones that "'by God! We'll hold them under if we have to lynch every Nigger in the land'" (258). The ideas of home and home-coming that are so crucial to each short story ironically reinforce the displacement of the black male characters. They are returning home, but it is a home to which they will never belong because they have lost their places by leaving. Like John, Roy can neither be-

come reincorporated into the local black community, nor can he assume a higher position in a hierarchy that always restricted black people to the lowest rungs of the social ladder. John returns home, but he compares his position to that of Esther before the king begging for the salvation of the Jews. Like in Esther 4:16, John thinks, "I will go in to the King, which is not according to the law; and if I perish, I perish" (254). Embedded in this passage is the sentiment that both the law and those who make and/or enforce it can be unjust. Such injustice must be challenged at any cost.

Such a sense of injustice can be applied to the process of interpretation. The turning point in **"Home"** is Roy's performance for Miss Reese's students at the local white high school. Miss Reese has been instructing them on classical music, and Roy is invited to the white high school to make that music come alive. The narrator explains that "Roy played. But it was one of those days when his throat was hot and dry, and his eyes burned. He had been coughing all morning and, as he played, his breath left him and he stood covered with a damp sweat. He played badly" (44). At the white high school, Roy is no longer able to play the music he loves with gusto, considering the context in which he plays. His music loses its ability to salve the gap in understanding between black and white in the town of Hopkinsville. While Miss Reese bravely cheers his work, he no longer feels as though he is communicating through his art. The narrator reflects on the children's responses, thereby confirming the alienation and even hostility of his audience:

> The students went home that afternoon and told their parents that a dressed-up nigger had come to school with a violin and played a lot of funny pieces nobody but Miss Reese liked. They went on to say that Miss Reese had grinned all over herself and cried, "Wonderful!" And had even bowed to the nigger when he went out!
>
> (44)

Instead of an artist, Roy is simply a "nigger" who incongruously for them was dressed up. His music is no longer music and only "funny pieces" that none of them understands or wants to. Yet the woman who Roy's mother identifies as "an old maid musicianer" (43) not only liked these pieces but lost control of herself by smiling indiscriminately and bowing to Roy as another human being. Whereas during Roy's concert at Shiloh Church, his survey and reaction to the audience are given through the detail of prose poetry, his performance at the school is not given an interior perspective and does not register his consciousness of student activity. Failure to register both Roy's and the audience's consciousness at the moment of performance reinforces the lack of communication between them.

Both John and Roy are expected to assume minstrel masks, one function of which is the assurance of predictability. Yet upon their returns, neither John nor Roy acts in a predictable fashion. When John arrives in Altamaha, Georgia, the town is perplexed by his preoccupation. He does not take the time to gossip and chat with everyone who meets him at the station. The white townspeople are suspicious of John from the beginning, shaking their heads each time someone refers to his education. When he arrives at Wells Institute, he is described as "loud and boisterous, always laughing and singing, and never able to work consecutively at anything" (248). Du Bois equates John's good-spirited nature with a lack of consciousness, and, for both Du Bois and Toomer, lynching is part of a process of what Toomer labels "southern awakening" (33). Rather than lynching's signifying the end of consciousness, it marks a new awakening that others attempt to defer and subvert. In **"Home,"** when Roy arrives in Hopkinsville in his own private Pullman car, the local white men are sorry to see him come. Hughes makes a clear distinction between the first paragraph, in which he refers to the main character as "the boy," and the second paragraph, which specifies the name Roy Williams. In his performance at the black church, Roy plays a selection from Massenet, and at his performance at the white high school, he plays selections from Bach and Mozart. His selections of music, combined with his habit of wearing a formal tuxedo on the street, signal that he is out of his place as a black man because he is more educated and cultured than Hopkinsville's other residents. His assumption of a concert performance identity, learned and developed in Europe, has permanently replaced the minstrel performance that at one time he knew by heart, but discarded. In contrast to the minstrel performance, Roy's social performance upon his return to Hopkinsville is in many ways a kind of grand finale performance to his life.

For Du Bois to define manhood intellectually, John must dissociate himself from his schoolmates to the same extent that he sought their company before the change, for manhood requires solitary reflection and contemplation. The transformation in intellect brings a transformation in how John sees the world around him, and particularly the color line. A number of changes occur in John's outward perception: "He first noticed now the oppression that had not seemed oppression before, differences that erstwhile seemed natural, restraints and slights that in his boyhood days had gone unnoticed or been greeted with a laugh" (250). In addition to gaining seriousness, the genial, good-natured boy becomes a sarcastic and bitter man. John grimly sets his teeth to accept the work of transforming the black children of Altamaha into responsible citizens. His dream is the attainment of the sort of citizenship embodied in the equality, fraternity, and liberty of the French Revolution.

Du Bois shows John's solitary struggle for self-development, a struggle against restrictions that transforms him into a man, as a prelude to his lynching. Upon John's return to Altamaha, local white men want to remind John of his boyhood status. The estrangement accompanying John's return is similar to the estrangement that accompanies Roy's return to Hopkinsville, but John is also estranged from the black community. When John arrives at the station, he is preoccupied with the Jim Crow accommodations. Immediately the "sordidness and narrowness of it all seized him." As a result, "he looked in vain for his mother, kissed coldly the tall, strange girl who called him brother, spoke a short, dry word here and there; then, lingering neither for hand-shaking nor gossip, started silently up the street, raising his hat merely to the last eager old aunty, to her open-mouthed astonishment" (255). The disaster of his arrival is compounded by his speech at the Baptist Church. He wants the audience to move beyond religious differences and even the importance of religion itself. As a result, an old religious gentleman from the community holds John up to scorn "for trampling on the true Religion, and he realized with amazement that all unknowingly he had put rough, rude hands on something this little world held sacred" (257). Because Du Bois isolates John from the black community, lynching becomes an anomaly not only because very few black people could gain an education, but also because only someone educated would dare confront the system and be conscious of its injustice. However there is hope that John has influenced his sister Jennie and the students of his school.

Articulation, in the form of intellectual and cultural attainment, does not doom John, but it is a problem in "Of the Coming of John" insofar as it fails to solve the race problem. Racial violence, since it is not logical, will not yield to the logic of articulation. Arnold Rampersad has argued that "the finest achievement of the story is its rendition of the emotional and spiritual paralysis that overtakes John from the beginning of his education" (76). But John very admirably negotiates the expectations of his teachers at the Wells Institute, as his emotional and spiritual center shifts to classical literature and classical music. Ronald Radano argues that, "while holding the secrets to power and knowledge, culture can also—as the reason behind a history of enslavement—turn against its possessor" (78). John comes to recognize the power of the irrational while attempting to teach in the South. Indeed, it is the force of the irrational that makes him realize that he should leave for the North. And his intellectual training serves him well as he negotiates the Southern racial system, pushing against its vulnerable points. Thus, rather than representing a "deathly trance" (Posnock 339), John's return to Wagner at the end of the short story ironically expresses hope and faith in the American ideal of equality. Rather than representing paralysis or death, John's turn to classical music is a turn to a spiritual reserve of strength.

Toomer's representation of lynching challenges Du Bois's strong class-based notion of understanding injustice. Tom Burwell is a member of the working class, and he believes he has the right to have a relationship with a black woman without anyone, white or black, interfering in that relationship. Tom is just as much an outsider as John, not because of his education but because of his propensity to fight. Just as members of the Altamaha community cannot relate to John's intellectual achievement, members of Toomer's rural Georgia community cannot relate to Tom's aggression and sense of outrage. The sense of justice that seizes Tom is not rooted in Louisa's desires. Kathie Birat compares Tom's and Bob's fantasies of Louisa and concludes that Tom's words "prove his superiority" (127). However, his desire, expressed with "'Ise carried y with me into th fields, day after day, an after that, an I sho can plow when yo is there, an I can pick cotton'" (30), only heightens the difference between forms of violence committed toward women and men. Tom is forced to labor in the fields without adequate recompense or a way to seek such recompense, whereas by working as a domestic in the Stone household, Louisa is subject to both economic and sexual exploitation. Yet another kind of violence is committed when Louisa cannot discuss her sexual exploitation as such and seek protection from such violation. Readers who want to make Tom into "a true black man" (Solard 556), a harmless peasant, blunt the danger that he represents. Tom is not able to articulate his desire for Louisa or his sense of outrage when he thinks of Bob Stone. When Tom asks Louisa if the rumors about her and Bob are true, he does not challenge her expression of naïveté; he simply affirms that the rumors are a lie. He explains that "'white folks aint up t them tricks so much nowadays. Godam better not be. Leastawise not with you. Cause I wouldn't stand f it. Nassur'" (30). The inevitable is constantly deferred until the moment of confrontation is determined to lead to death. Tom cannot let awareness of his economic exploitation blur into an understanding of Louisa's sexual exploitation. And when he does understand the connection between the two, he attempts to function as Louisa's protector.

Although Louisa, Tom, and Bob are supposed to represent a love triangle, the triangle is complicated by Louisa's lack of attachment to either suitor. In his discussion of identity in *Cane*, Jeff Webb explains that there is "a division that argues for a basic equivalence between the social forces that would transform him into ashes and linguistic or literary forces that transform her into metaphors. The social and the linguistic, in other words, are twin emblems of the destruction of identity

in 'Portrait in Georgia'" (211). Webb's observations about this poem extend into the story that follows it, "Blood-Burning Moon." Louisa, like so many of Toomer's black women characters, is constructed as a blank slate that men project their desires onto. Rather than being separate from the parts of *Cane* that focus on portraits of women, Toomer's exploration of lynching is a way of exploring equally violent forms of desire. Linda Wagner-Martin makes the point that "Toomer uses the erotic to approach the political" (26). The first section of the story, Louisa's, explains that, "by measure of that warm glow which came into her mind at the thought of [Bob Stone], he had won her . . . [yet] the fact was that [Tom Burwell] held her to factory town more firmly than he thought. His black balanced, and pulled against, the white of Stone, when she thought of them" (28). Ironically, Toomer is able to represent Louisa as both demur and hyper-sexual within the same passage. And she is able to be both because she is indifferent to which one she is.

The idea of familial return that Toomer uses in "Blood-Burning Moon" complicates ideas around geographical return. If the geographical return is an attempt to fulfill a new dream in an old place, then the familial return is an attempt to produce new familial relationships by discarding the distanced intimacy fostered during slavery. The danger is that the new family form will reproduce the dynamics of the master-mistress relationship. Unlike Carma in Toomer's story of the same name, Louisa does not negotiate with men for freedom and security. Louisa naïvely enjoys the fact that Bob's whiteness pulls against Tom's blackness. After Tom's death, Louisa loses her naïveté and seeks to build community around a conscious understanding of racial violence. Louisa's transformation over the course of the short story throws Tom's relationship ideal into question. Each of them seeks a relationship that has no models. Tom only knows that Bob's presence mires their relationship in patterns of slavery, whereas Louisa is initially unaware of such a pattern. Tom seeks to alter the terms by which black men and women relate to one another, and his efforts eventually transform Louisa's understanding. In contrast to the myth of black men raping white women, Tom dies in order to foster new, mutual, long-term relationships between black men and women.

Both Toomer and Du Bois emphasize the importance of white men losing the power associated with being the master of a plantation to explain the occurrence of lynching. Toomer is more explicit about this transition as he describes Bob's shift in consciousness as becoming "consciously a white man's" (31). Through this consciousness, Bob envisions his power to rape Louisa during the days of slavery, thereby establishing his current relationship to Louisa as parallel to the one before Emancipation. Bob conceptualizes his relationship to

Louisa in terms of violence, specifically rape. He understands her as a "nigger gal" (32) in order to heighten his sense of power over her and her exoticism. He thinks that "no nigger had ever been with his girl. He'd like to see one try. Some position for him to be in. Him, Bob Stone, of the old Stone family, in a scrap with a nigger over a nigger girl" (32). Bob recognizes that he is entering uncharted territory by articulating his relationship to Louisa as one of both violence and mutuality. Louisa is both his victim and his girlfriend. While asserting the power to claim a black man's girlfriend, he also claims an exclusive relationship with Louisa. John Henderson's attempt to rape Jennie in "Of the Coming of John" is not so fully articulated as Bob Stone's relationship with Louisa. John Henderson has a similar family background to Bob Stone, and this unspoken background enables Du Bois to take the racial history in the South for granted. The attempt to assert an exclusive relationship betrays a change in power dynamics. Stone's exercise of power is excessive as a response to his loss of power over black people's everyday movements.

Denial of Community

Lynching serves as the climax to each of these short stories, and the stories themselves try to establish a context for understanding lynching, how and why it happens. None of the protagonists in these stories lets the threat of lynching outweigh his sense of moral responsibility. Once Tom cuts Bob across the throat and he staggers away in search of help, Tom waits by the factory door for the mob. When the black John Jones kills the white John Henderson in Du Bois's short story, Jones waits on the tree stump for the mob. There is a grand sense of responsibility with both characters in that they will not sacrifice their sense of moral responsibility to save their lives. Once they protect themselves or their female lover or sister, they await the immoral consequences. Such a sense of unjustly dying for the sake of justice is highlighted in Toomer's title *Cane*. Wagner-Martin calls attention to the fact that "the noun *cane* also is a homonym for the Biblical *Cain,* whose character suggests the bloody destruction of brotherhood and introduces the concept of immoral violence" (19). The title's echo also suggests that retribution will come in future generations. Thus, lynching is an unjust punishment that the protagonists of these short stories nonetheless accept. Toomer expresses Tom's immortalization by describing "only his head, erect, lean, like a blackened stone" (34) over the flames consuming his body. Tom is just as implacable in his resistance as is Bob in his assertion of domination. Ultimately it is the lynch mob that must face retribution.

The importance of white young men asserting domination is also important in Hughes's story **"Home."** Roy's final encounter with Miss Reese is late at night on the main street of the town. Since Roy is accustomed to

staying up late and going to bed at dawn, he has trouble sleeping at night, so he develops the habit of dressing up for a performance and walking the streets of Hopkinsville alone. On the night of his lynching, he runs into Miss Reese as she emerges from a drug store. The narrator explains that "forgetting he wasn't in Europe, he took off his hat and his gloves, and held out his hand to this lady who understood music. They smiled at each other, the sick young colored man and the aging music teacher in the light of the main street" (47). The term *forgetting* is ingenuous in its use, for it echoes the accusation that someone is "forgetting his/her place." In fact, Roy extends his hand because he remembers his place as a human being, but the town's residents are unable to see either Roy or Miss Reese as people—one is a "nigger" and the other an "old maid"—and this makes it inevitable that they would want to destroy their relationship. Since Roy and Miss Reese recognize one another as equals, the town must reconfigure Roy's status so that he understands his inferiority. Young men emerging from the local theater spot Roy Williams and Miss Reese talking across the street and immediately assault Roy. The crowd "objected to a Negro talking to a white woman—insulting a White Woman—attacking a WHITE woman—RAPING A WHITE WOMAN" (47-48). Not only does the crowd project its violence into the interaction between the black man and the white woman, Miss Reese becomes white in the passage. In other contexts, she is only an old maid and subjected to derision, but because she and Roy have developed a relationship of mutual respect, she becomes white and someone to be revered if only to more securely identify Roy as a symbol, the source of a warning to other black people in town. As the "white young ruffians with rednecks, open sweaters, and fists doubled" (47) continually knock Roy down, "his mouth was full of blood and his eyes burned" (48). This description is not very different from the image of him "shaking a little and his eyes burn[ing] and he want[ing] terribly to cough" (42) or the image of him with "throat . . . hot and dry" and "eyes burn[ing]" (44). The constant cough suggests not only the hot dry throat but also the phlegm and other bodily fluids that are purged through the mouth in sickness. The mouth full of blood is a release for the dry cough. The similarity between the physical violence of the mob and the economic violence toward the poor in Europe is highlighted through the similarity in Roy's response.

The white mob hangs Roy from a tree, but the final paragraph of the short story suggests he died otherwise. The narrator explains that he "began to choke on the blood in his mouth" (49). The importance of the choking is larger than the lynching. Roy had been dying slowly in various ways since Vienna. When compared to the passive violence of watching people starve, the final physical violence of the lynching is a relief. In coming home maybe Roy sought the violence of the

South rather than the impersonal violence of major cities. Given the insulting reactions of white men on his arrival in town, Roy knows wearing evening wear every night on his walks about town will prompt violence. Roy hears the mob as "the roar of their voices and the scuff of their feet were split by the moonlight into a thousand notes like a Beethoven sonata" (49). In other words, Roy hears the music that he loves in the very sounds of the people who are going to kill him. The final image of Roy's body is the image of his instrument, the violin: "His brown body, stark naked, strung from a tree at the edge of town" is intended to serve as a warning to other black people in Hopkinsville as well as white single women, especially educated women like Miss Reese. But the second half of the sentence claims something else. Roy's body "hung there all night, like a violin for the wind to play" (49). His body becomes the vessel for his song. Critic Susan Koprince describes how "the final image of the story . . . combines both violence and beauty, both horror and mystic calm. Similarly, the moon serves to create an ironic background of beauty against which the violence of the white mob stands in relief" (17). Yet this moon imagery works in conjunction with images of Roy's physical illness and his relationship to his music. These various images reinforce one another and affirm the release of death and beauty of life for Roy, compared to the brutal hatred that compels the mob to take his life.

The final image in Du Bois's "Of the Coming of John" is equally majestic. Judge Henderson decides to close John's school after hearing about his teaching the French Revolution. His son then relates the story of John sitting in the orchestra at a show in New York City. After his school is abruptly closed in the middle of a lesson, John walks the town. Du Bois then establishes the calm of the environment: "The great brown sea lay silent. The air scarce breathed. The dying day bathed the twisted oaks and mighty pines in black and gold. There came from the wind no warning, not a whisper from the cloudless sky" (262). John hears cries from his sister Jennie and sees her struggling in John Henderson's grasp. He stills the grasp with the blow of a tree limb. He walks his sister home and tells his mother that he is going north. Once John returns to the sight of killing John Henderson, north becomes symbolic of freedom after death. Similar to the music of the mob in **"Home,"** John hears the music of Lohengrin's swan in the mob's approach. The swan echoes Toomer's invocation of a swan's song in the South and Hughes's use of violins to express the paradoxical way a dream can come true and remain unrealized. For John in the concert hall, "when at last a soft sorrow crept across the violins, there came to him the vision of a far-off home, the great eyes of his sister, and the dark drawn face of his mother. And his heart sank below the waters, even as the sea-sand sinks by the shores of Altamaha, only to be lifted aloft again with that last ethereal wail of the

swan that quivered and faded away into the sky" (253). John harks back to this moment as he waits for the mob.

As John waits and "as the sheen of the starlight stole over him, he thought of the gilded ceiling of that vast concert hall, heard stealing toward him the faint sweet music of the swan. Hark! Was it music, or the hurry and shouting of men? Yes, surely! Clear and high the faint sweet melody rose and fluttered like a living thing, so that the very earth trembled as with the tramp of horses and murmur of angry men." John hears the music in his head as counterpoint to the galloping horses. When the judge leads the pack with the rope, John only pities him. John closes his eyes, turns toward the sea and "the world whistle[s] in his ears" (263). It is the world of the opera and the music and New York City, a world which represents possibilities to John and contrasts with the racism and hatred of the judge. John positions himself as superior at the moment of his death if only because he is willing and working to achieve justice and equality.

Unlike in **"Home"** and "Of the Coming of John," where the protagonist experiences both the pain of lynching and the victory of artistic sublimation, those two ideas are separately characterized in "Blood-Burning Moon." Although Tom waits at the well, with the approach of the mob, he understands that he is prey to be captured, bound, and roasted. Both the stench of burning flesh and the roar of the crowd waft over to Louisa as she reaches the steps of her home. Based on the way the other two stories resolve the relationship between lynching and art, Louisa is confirmed as Tom's counterpart at the end of the story. Both his burning and the crowd's yells call to her, and she awakens to the consequences of her relationship with Bob Stone in a way that was not possible in the first section of the short story. That her awakening is in response to Tom rather than the crowd is made clear with the information that Louisa "did not hear [the ghost of a yell], but her eyes opened slowly" (35). This awakening is not the romantic awakening to the scent of cane. Barbara Foley explains that "the scent of cane suffuses the landscape and sweetens its inhabitants, transmuting their suffering into beauty and signaling their fusion with nature" (185). Such an understanding of the power of the cane is undermined and mocked in "Blood-Burning Moon," where the scent of cane is substituted with the scent of burning flesh. The substitution belies the calmness and innocence of existence in the South.

At the story's beginning, Louisa sings to ward off an omen, like other black women. Louisa is mentioned by name but she holds no separate identity. At the end of the story, the full moon is still an omen, but unlike the "Negro women [who] improvised songs against its spell" (28), Louisa asks "where were they, these people?" (35). These people disappeared after they witnessed Tom cutting Bob's throat. This sense of witness and complicity disappears in **"Home"** and "Of the Coming of John." Both Miss Reese and Jennie are not mentioned once the crowd attacks Roy and John kills John Henderson. In "Blood-Burning Moon," the witness is uncomfortable: "Negroes who had seen the fight slunk into their homes and blew the lamps out" (33). Louisa actually waits at the well with Tom. When the mob comes, "Louisa [i]s driven back" (34). Why Louisa is driven back is enigmatic and is meant to be enigmatic because she could have been lynched with Tom since it was common knowledge that Tom, Louisa, and Bob formed a triangle. Once Louisa reaches home, "she'd sing, and perhaps they'd come out and join her" (35). She sings to her black neighbors who hide in fear. She sings with the courage of Tom Burwell, although he is dead. Her singing reflects the dual message of his death, which is to be afraid of inequality and to be emboldened and fight for equality. Louisa is still singing at the end of the short story and that she sings alone highlights the problem of the omen. The omen has not been fulfilled through Tom's death. Rather, the omen will be fulfilled through the black people hiding in their houses with the lights turned out. The refrain

> Red nigger moon. Sinner!
> Blood-burning moon. Sinner!
> Come out that fact'ry door.

ends each of the three sections of the story. Its presence at the very end of the tale still calls out for someone to "come out that fact'ry door." Louisa thinks that "perhaps Tom Burwell would come" (35). Such a hope points to the importance of his legacy. His coming is not literal, only figurative. The literal coming is embodied in the members of the mob which lynches Tom. Of course, it is only within an imaginative space that a vision can exist of mob and witnesses coming together. Unfortunately, they come together through their representatives Tom Burwell and Bob Stone, whose antagonism remains unresolved at the end of the story even as Louisa's ambivalence has shifted. No longer does she simply confuse Tom and Bob in her mind, but she calls out to the communities they laid claim to. She remains the center of a communal circle fraught with tension and friction.

Interpretation is clearly a politically motivated act in each short story. Each protagonist's dream is spelled out in explicit detail. Upon each protagonist's return to his hometown, local men reinterpret their dreams in such a way that the local white and black communities feel threatened. Such reinterpretation denies the protagonists' attempts to achieve justice and equality. However the ending of each short story is unsettling, not only in its representation of lynching, but also in its charge to interpret lynching. The decision to represent

lynching in lyrical terms prompts readers to see lynching as a loss of social power. Lynching is a desperate social act, instigated through fear of social equality.

Works Cited

Birat, Kathie. "'Giving the Negro to Himself': Medium and 'Immediacy' in Jean Toomer's *Cane*." *Q/W/E/R/T/Y* 7 (1997): 121-28.

Du Bois, W. E. B. *The Souls of Black Folk.* 1903. New York: Penguin, 1969.

Foley, Barbara. "'In the Land of Cotton': Economics and Violence in Jean Toomer's *Cane*." *African American Review* 32 (1998): 181-98.

Gunning, Sandra. *Race, Rape, and Lynching: The Red Record of American Literature, 1890-1912.* New York: Oxford UP, 1996.

Harris, Trudier. *Exorcising Blackness: Historical and Literary Lynching and Burning Rituals.* Bloomington: Indiana UP, 1984.

Hughes, Langston. *The Ways of White Folks.* 1933. New York: Vintage, 1990.

Jones, Gavin. "'Whose Line Is It Anyway?': W. E. B. Du Bois and the Language of the Color Line." *Race Consciousness: African American Studies for the New Century.* Ed. Judith Jackson Fossett and Jeffrey A. Tucker. New York: New York UP, 1997. 19-34.

Koprince, Susan. "Moon Imagery in *The Ways of White Folks*." *Langston Hughes Review* 1.1 (1982): 14 17.

Miller, Erika M. *The Other Reconstruction: Where Violence and Womanhood Meet in the Writings of Wells-Barnett, Grimké, and Larsen.* New York: Garland, 2000.

Peckham, Joel B. "Jean Toomer's *Cane*: Self as Montage and the Drive toward Integration." *American Literature* 72 (2000): 275-90.

Perkins, Kathy A., and Judith L. Stephens, eds. *Strange Fruit: Plays on Lynching by American Women.* Bloomington: Indiana UP, 1998.

Posnock, Ross. "How It Feels to Be a Problem: Du Bois, Fanon, and the 'Impossible Life' of the Black Intellectual." *Critical Inquiry* 23 (1997): 323-49.

Radano, Ronald. "Soul Texts and the Blackness of Folk." *Modernism/Modernity* 2.1 (1995): 71-95.

Rampersad, Arnold. *The Art and Imagination of W. E. B. Du Bois.* Cambridge: Harvard UP, 1976.

Toomer, Jean. *Cane.* 1923. New York: Liveright, 1975.

Wagner-Martin, Linda. "Toomer's *Cane* as Narrative Sequence." *Modern American Short Story Sequences: Composite Fictions and Fictive Communities.* Ed. J. Gerald Kennedy. Cambridge: Cambridge UP, 1995. 35-51.

Webb, Jeff. "Literature and Lynching: Identity in Jean Toomer's *Cane*." *ELH* 67 (2000): 205-28.

FURTHER READING

Criticism

Franke, Thomas L. "The Art of Verbal Performance: A Stylistic Analysis of Langston Hughes's 'Feet Live Their Own Life.'" *Language and Style* 19, no. 4 (fall 1986): 377-87.

Explores thematic implications of Hughes's short story "Feet Live Their Own Life."

Malcolm, Cheryl Alexander. "The Politics of Passing in the Short Fiction of Langston Hughes and Bernard Malamud." In *Cultural Policy, or the Politics of Culture?*, edited by Agata Preis-Smith and Piotr Skurowski, pp. 321-26. Warsaw: University of Warsaw, Institute of English Studies, 1999.

Compares Hughes's short story "Passing" to Bernard Malamud's "The Lady of the Lake," focusing on themes of ethnic identity.

Miyakawa, Felicia M. "'Jazz at Night and the Classics in the Morning': Musical Double-Consciousness in Short Fiction by Langston Hughes." *Popular Music* 24, no. 2 (May 2005): 273-78.

Discusses the incorporation of musical elements in Hughes's short stories.

Ramsey, Priscilla. Review of *The Collected Works of Langston Hughes, Vol. 15: The Short Stories,* by Langston Hughes, edited by R. Baxter Miller. *The Journal of African American History* 88, no. 1 (winter 2003): 82-4.

Extols the social relevance of Hughes's short fiction and recounts the initial critical response to *The Ways of White Folks*.

Walker, Carolyn P. "Liberating Christ: Sargeant's Metamorphosis in Langston Hughes's 'On the Road.'" *Black American Literature Forum* 25, no. 4 (winter 1991): 745-52.

Analyzes Hughes's symbolic use of snow and references to Christ in "On the Road," highlighting poetic details in the story.

Alistair MacLeod
1936-

Canadian short story writer and novelist.

The following entry provides an overview of Mac-Leod's short fiction.

INTRODUCTION

Although he has published relatively little over a career spanning nearly thirty years, MacLeod is viewed as one of the most accomplished writers in Canada. His fiction centers on the lives and struggles of the mining and fishing communities of Nova Scotia, reflecting the Gaelic heritage and rural values cultivated by the descendants of Highland Scots who settled the area more than two centuries ago. MacLeod's stories typically relate the physical and psychological alienation experienced by the inhabitants as they cope with harsh natural environments and foreboding occupational hazards. His narratives often emphasize the power of the past upon the present and give voice to the displaced communities of society's outermost regions.

BIOGRAPHICAL INFORMATION

MacLeod was born in North Battleford, Saskatchewan, Canada. His parents were natives of Cape Breton Island, Nova Scotia, and they returned there while MacLeod was still a boy. As he grew up, MacLeod experienced first-hand the hardships of the mining and logging communities, which he has drawn upon in his writing. After graduating from high school, he entered Nova Scotia Teachers' College and taught on Port Hood Island, near Cape Breton. Between 1957 and 1960, he attended St. Francis-Xavier University in Antigonish, where he earned two bachelor's degrees. In 1961, MacLeod received a master's degree from the University of New Brunswick and accepted a position at Nova Scotia Teachers' College, where he taught English until 1963. In 1966, MacLeod moved to the United States, teaching English at the University of Indiana while studying at the University of Notre Dame for a doctorate degree, which he received in 1968. The following year, MacLeod accepted a faculty position in the English department at the University of Windsor, Ontario, and began to publish short stories and poems in literary periodicals. In 1976, he completed his first collection of short stories, *The Lost Salt Gift of Blood*. His next vol-

ume, *As Birds Bring Forth the Sun,* was published ten years later in 1986. In 2000, MacLeod gathered his previously published stories in a comprehensive anthology, *Island.* Since then, he has served on the English faculty at the University of Windsor and has edited fiction for the *University of Windsor Review.*

MAJOR WORKS OF SHORT FICTION

Each of the seven stories in *The Lost Salt Gift of Blood* are narrated by a young man who must decide whether to stay within the traditional confines of his community or to strike out on a new path. For example, MacLeod's most popular and anthologized story, "The Boat," details a young man's decision either to continue the family profession as a fisherman or to leave home for a job at a large university. While his father, a singer of traditional Gaelic songs, encourages him to leave, his mother coerces him to stay home. Just as he is about to commit to the old social structure of his hometown, his father's drowned body washes ashore. Although this event prompts the protagonist to accept the university job, he remains haunted by a sense of guilt as he recounts the tale. Narrated in the present tense, "The Vastness of the Dark" concerns a young man who resigns himself to working in the mining community in which he was raised. In "The Return," a boy travels with his parents to the mining region of his father's youth. Juxtaposed with the clean and proper environment of their Montreal household, the rugged life of the miners on Cape Breton Island opens the boy's eyes to a strange world of which he is distantly a part. "In the Fall" involves one of MacLeod's typically sympathetic father figures whose beloved family horse must be sacrificed to the slaughterhouse for a meager economic gain.

Similar themes of ancestry, hardship, and pivotal life choices are evident in *As Birds Bring Forth the Sun*. For instance, "The Closing Down of Summer" features a miner's contemplations about going abroad for a potentially lethal job in the South African diamond mines. In "The Tuning of Perfection," a 78-year-old folklorist named Archibald is offered an opportunity to sing traditional Gaelic songs on a television program. When he discovers that he must shorten and rearrange the songs to suit the preferences of the show's producers, Archibald declines to participate and keeps his ancestral integrity intact. "As Birds Bring Forth the Sun" is narrated by a more self-consciously stylized voice and features elements of maritime folklore. Opening during the nineteenth century, the story recounts the history of a family consumed by a sense of ancient, mystical doom. This ominous tone is more strongly pronounced in the collection's final story, "Vision," which uses an intricate, postmodern narrative structure to record five generations of a family consistently plagued by disfigurement and blindness. The introduction of a betrayed ancestor's spirit as both the origin of the curse and the protector of the family represents a departure from the realism employed in MacLeod's other stories.

First published in *The Lost Salt Gift of Blood: New & Selected Stories* (1988), the title story of *Island* features a female protagonist, MacLeod's first, who recounts the story of her unusual life. After falling in love and bearing a child with a red-haired fisherman, she is left spiritually distraught upon learning of his death. Emotionally destitute, she gives away her child, and leads a lonely and eccentric life tending a lighthouse. Eventually, another red-haired man comes to her, identifies himself as her grandson, and helps her to escape her solitude. The story contains elements of mysticism and naturalism, both of which are representative of MacLeod's body of work. In addition to collecting MacLeod's previously published stories, *Island* also contains a new tale, "Clearances," which centers on an elderly widower as he reminisces about his life, marriage, and experiences in World War II.

CRITICAL RECEPTION

Critics have acknowledged MacLeod as among the finest contemporary Canadian writers of short fiction. In particular, reviewers have praised MacLeod's ability to conjure a sense of physical isolation and displacement, admiring—as commentator Jim Hannan has—his depiction of "the often hauntingly lonesome lives people lead even amid tight-knit families and small communities." They have also commended MacLeod's portrayal of loss and its attendant grief, observing his deeply traditional perspective on family heritage and the art of storytelling. Other reviewers have applauded MacLeod's description of past historical events in the present tense, a narrative technique that conveys the relevance of cultural and personal memories. Critic David Stevens has detected a melancholy sense of the past, especially in MacLeod's characterization of male protagonists, noting that his fiction focuses "so often and intently on the dilemma of male characters coming of age within the regional community, characters who must make the impossible decision to stay or leave." A few critics have found MacLeod's prose style too sentimental, and his tendency to leave his stories open-ended has been deemed overly cryptic. However, many scholars have praised MacLeod's authentic portrayal of the cultural decline in Nova Scotia specifically, and the loss of traditional Canadian values in general.

PRINCIPAL WORKS

Short Fiction

The Lost Salt Gift of Blood 1976
As Birds Bring Forth the Sun and Other Stories 1986
The Lost Salt Gift of Blood: New & Selected Stories 1988
Island: The Collected Short Stories of Alistair MacLeod 2000
Island: The Complete Stories 2001

Other Major Works

No Great Mischief (novel) 1999

CRITICISM

David Stevens (essay date spring 1996)

SOURCE: Stevens, David. "Writing Region Across the Border: Two Stories of Breece Pancake and Alistair

MacLeod." *Studies in Short Fiction* 33, no. 2 (spring 1996): 263-71.

[*In the following essay, Stevens compares the protagonists, settings, and themes of Breece Pancake's "Trilobites" and MacLeod's "The Boat," underscoring the influence of regional community on identity.*]

In a Tennessee folk tale from the early twentieth century, a Yankee traveling salesman receives a dose of regional wisdom when his car breaks down in the southern backwoods.

> Judging from the last hour of his trip, the salesman decided his best chance of reaching civilization lay in abandoning the road and cutting through the surrounding forest, which he did, only to find himself hopelessly lost minutes later. Luckily a young farm-boy was hunting nearby and offered to guide the salesman to the nearest service station. Grateful for this rescue, the salesman tried to strike up a conversation with the boy along the way. "That's a mighty fine rifle you have," he told the boy, who shrugged and responded, "It's the same rifle my granddad carried in the Civil War."
>
> Duly impressed, the salesman asked if he could take a look at it, so the boy stopped and handed him the gun. The salesman turned it over in his hands. "That's a good-looking barrel to have gone through the Civil War," he said.
>
> "Oh, it's not the same barrel," the boy rejoined. "Granddad put on a new one not too far back."
>
> The salesman fingered the gun respectfully. "Well, it's still a fine wood stock to have lasted all these years," he offered.
>
> "I s'pose," the boy responded, "but my daddy put that stock on not five years before giving it to me."
>
> The salesman scratched his head. "I see. Well, it's still a mighty nice trigger to have stayed easy all this time."
>
> The boy shook his head. "I put that on just last month."
>
> At this final admission, the salesman returned the firearm, practically beside himself with amusement. "Son, I hate to say this, but that rifle's practically new."
>
> The boy took it solemnly. "Nosir, it's the same gun my granddad carried in the Civil War."[1]

The story of the gun has always struck me as profound, in particular for the way it seems to inform the process of identity-construction in the regional community. The salesman, the outsider who has no sense of the community or its spirit, reduces his understanding of the rifle to an assessment of its use-value after he has determined that it was not, in fact, carried through the Civil War. For the boy, however, the rifle remains both a figurative and literal intersection of past and present, not so important because it dates his ancestry as far back as the War Between the States, but because it provides him with a tangible link to that ancestry, a link that justifies his present occupation of the land and con-

tinually articulates his relationship to it. The gun is not, as the salesman would contend, mere memorabilia, but a symbol of the hunting and fighting, with their implicit emphasis on reading the landscape, in which the boy's ancestors participated and in which the boy now participates in order to survive. History for the boy, then, becomes not only dates and facts, but a genetic tie to the land itself, his inheritance of the gun representing an external affirmation of his passage into manhood and his ascent into this physical, almost life-and-death, relationship.

This kind of understanding, of course, allows the boy to navigate the woods where the salesman cannot, and his clear vision of the forest implies a clarity and rationality about his correspondent sense of history, symbolized by the gun. Nonetheless, there remains a side of me that sympathizes with the salesman; in his world of contracts and premiums, the gun can only be a gun, and its worth is dictated almost solely by the changes that have been made to it, changes which in this case serve only to decrease its value. Moreover, if the gun is symbolic of the land and the people who occupy it, then the salesman's comment strikes even more sinisterly at the changing value of the regional community itself. The various alterations to the rifle correspond to the succession of generations within the community, a succession in which sons and daughters are born and raised only to remain the same as their parents. Given the salesman's reading, we have to wonder if this hereditary transference is representative of the strong sense of historical identity and affection that the boy espouses or a kind of cultural and emotional stasis, the regional character's inability to become other than what he or she is inexorably programmed to be. Obviously the salesman is a perfect contrast to the boy—the representative of progress, the man with an eye to the future—and though we may at first balk at his rejection of the spiritual for a more economically efficient analysis of the community's worth, we cannot refute the validity of this practical side, born out demographically these last 50 or 60 years by the expansion of cities and suburbs and the literal eclipse of many rural cultures.[2]

In this way, the story of the gun clearly illustrates the kind of terrain, both physical and psychic, which the regional character must comprehend and navigate. Finally, there are two people lost in that Tennessee forest: the salesman trapped by his ignorance of the geography and refusal to recognize in his surroundings the energy and passions of an entire people, and the boy in his inability to look beyond *that same* sense of history or to prevent the devaluation of the landscape and its residents that the salesman represents. Given the disparate, almost diametric, nature of these two readings, it is not surprising that the fiction of Breece Pancake and Alistair MacLeod—the former from West Virginia, the latter from Nova Scotia—should focus so often and intently on the dilemma of male characters coming of age within the regional community, characters who must make the impossible decision to stay or leave. Admittedly repulsed by their parents' harsh lifestyles as well as the decline of the surrounding landscape, such young men cannot escape their devotion to family and community either, recognizing as they do the components of their own identities that only the region can supply.

This sense of futility is captured succinctly by Colly, the narrator of Pancake's story, "Trilobites," when he says of farming: "It just don't do to work your ass off at something you're no good at" (Pancake 25). In the story, Colly is left to run the family farm after his father's death, but, unable to produce the same amount of crops as his father did and confronted by increasingly desperate finances, he is ultimately forced to acquiesce to the wishes of his mother who wants to sell the farm and move to Akron. Nevertheless, despite his failure, Colly acknowledges intuitive ties to the region and to history. As he begins his tale, he looks out across the Teays River valley and focuses on the foothills in the distance, saying of one particularly:

> It took over a million years to make that smooth little hill, and I've looked all over it for trilobites. I think how it has always been there and always will be, at least for as long as it matters. The air is smoky with summertime. A bunch of starlings swim over me. I was born in this country and I have never much wanted to leave.
>
> (21)

The rest of the story finds him wavering in self-doubt, because, though he wants profoundly to remain, he can neither articulate the reason behind his desire nor substantiate—to his mother or to himself—his hereditary claim upon the land. His search for a trilobite, which frames the entire narrative, points to his need for a specific piece of the past that will inform his present, somehow justifying his sense of historical determinism, but his failure to find even one causes him to perceive history as a kind of generality to which, finally, he can articulate no rational connection. The trilobites—fossilized insects, displaced, absent—stand in for the dead father, whose place Colly can assume no more effectively than he can retrieve the past. Slowly the lines between prehistory and history dim as both seem equally distant and powerless to inform his quest for identity.

Nonetheless, Colly can never fully disconnect his belief in the importance of the past and continues to seek within history a kind of redemption to his life. He agrees, for instance, to go out with Ginny, his high school sweetheart who now lives in Florida, in the hope of rekindling their former passion, a passion that moved him long ago to inscribe her yearbook with the message, "We will live on mangoes and love." But Ginny offers him no more satisfaction than his search for the trilobites, and his inability either to re-establish a relationship with her or to let her go completely only reiterates his relationship to the region and to history, his desire for escape combated by his intense determination to locate some promise of renewal within the land itself. When he asks her if she ever looks in her yearbook, she responds with a laugh that she does not remember where she put it. The yearbook is Colly's link to his own history and to his once satisfying relationship with Ginny; in asking her if she ever looks at it, he again seeks a validation of that past, a reciprocation of the simultaneous agony and love that would justify his staying in the region.

But Ginny does not recognize his request or, if she does, refuses to offer him this connection. For her, to recognize her former feelings would be to question her own rejection of the land and to undermine the newfound freedom that she associates with her life in Florida. And though Colly finds this response cowardly, in confronting Ginny he is finally forced to acknowledge that aspect of himself that is also frightened, that desperately requires escape. Thus he responds to Ginny and to his own feelings with an inarticulate yet meaningful act of violence,[3] an act that represents his will both to resist and to submit: "I slide her to the floor," he says. "Her scent rises to me, and I shove crates aside to make room. I don't wait. She isn't making love, she's getting laid. All right, I think, all right. Get laid" (35). With his internal struggle offered external expression, Colly can at last admit that he was wrong, as his father was wrong, to return to the land, and his story ends with an assertion of identity finally independent from the history that has constrained him all along: "I'll spend tonight at home. I've got eyes to shut in Michigan—maybe even Germany or China, I don't know yet. I walk, but I'm not scared. I feel my fear moving away in rings of time for a million years" (37).

Like Colly, the narrator of Alistair MacLeod's **"The Boat"** finds himself caught between his wish to heed his ancestral calling—in this case to become a fisherman—and his fear of the physical dangers and emotional desolation that would result from the fulfillment of this wish. His tale is constructed mostly from boyhood memories as, early on, he reveals that he "teaches at a great Midwestern university" (MacLeod [*The Lost Salt Gift of Blood*] 105). Unlike "Trilobites," then, **"The Boat"** does not require us to wait until the end for his declaration of escape; nor must we hypothesize about his eventual fate, which appears, if not satisfying, at least successful. Nonetheless, his insistence on reinvoking the past and its implicit sense of guilt suggests that he has left behind only the physical aspects of the regional community, not the psychological ones. In the opening lines of the story, he claims,

There are times even now, when I awake at four o'clock in the morning with the terrible fear that I have over-slept; when I imagine that my father is waiting for me in the room below the darkened stairs or that the shore-bound men are tossing pebbles against my window while blowing their hands and stomping their feet against the frozen steadfast earth.

(105)

He is not, in other words, just recounting history but confessing the way his past is continually revisited upon his present, a past that is constructed wholly through his relationships to his family and to the landscape on which it depends for survival, a past in which the earth remains "steadfast" though frozen while he appears uncertain and unreliable.

From the beginning of the tale, history is figured in terms of the landscape, particularly the sea, through which both sides of the narrator's family gauge their lives. His mother, he says, "was of the sea as were all of her people, and her horizons were the very literal ones she scanned with her dark and fearless eyes" (108-09), while his father had always been a fisherman, "just like [his] uncles and all of the men that formed [his] past" (124). In effect, the sea becomes a blood relation as well as the vehicle that transcends the family's temporal moment and links its members to past and future. The boat of the story's title, then, is important both in the physical bond it offers the family to the sea and in its larger role as signifier of historical identity.[4] Its name, for instance, is the same as the mother's maiden name, and the narrator notes that it was "called after her as another link in the chain of tradition" (107). By extension, this close association of boat and mother makes the fisherman's daily chore of entering and handling the boat a very sexual one and suggests that the passage of the boat and an understanding of the sea from father to son is as important to the survival of the family, at least relative to their historic notions of identity, as the act of procreation itself.[5] As a result, the narrator's rejection of the sea becomes not merely a break with tradition but a rupture in the generational infrastructure; by disowning the sea, he disowns his family as well.

Such a disjunction, of course, is not wholly his fault, but reciprocated by the community he leaves behind. Within the story, the narrator's mother in particular will not accept her son's desire for escape and continues even after he is gone to anticipate his return, holding fast to her faith that the sea will ultimately provide. As the narrator explains, "it is not an easy thing to know that your mother looks on the sea with love and on you with bitterness because the one has been so constant and the other so untrue" (124). The mother's feelings stem from her larger desire to maintain order as her world, in many ways, deteriorates about her. She "runs her house as her brothers ran their boats, everything

. . . clean and spotless," and her compulsive neatness suggests her general belief that everything has its place, that her place and the place of her family are, and will always remain, the region of her birth. For her, the sea becomes the consummate gauge of safety and stability, preventing her from seeing, as do both her husband and son, its highly treacherous and physically chaotic nature. Though we sympathize with her desperate attempts to hold onto the Gaelic culture of her past, we realize these attempts to be no more successful than if she would order the sea itself. We realize finally that her horizons—"those very literal ones" that physically seem quite broad—are really somewhat narrow and, as reflected by the dying landscape, emotionally stifling.

Juxtaposed against the mother's insistence on order is the father's embrace of chaos, symbolized by his bedroom, a room of "disorder and disarray" that seems in contrast to the rest of the house "like a rock of opposition in the sparkling waters of a clear deep harbour" (111). Naturally, the mother despises this room, yet she does so mostly because the room is also the home's library and because the books threaten the simplistic world vision that unites her idea of family indelibly with a maritime existence. Indeed, all of her children discover the room, and all later go on to discover a world outside the confines of her limited imagination, their small movements in and out of the library punctuated finally by a larger movement from the region. Unlike the children, however, the father cannot make this last movement, even though his philosophical horizons are much broader than his wife's. In his room there is only one small window, which looks out over the sea, suggesting that somehow his literal horizons—his job, his boat, his family—have been forced over his figurative ones.

The Gaelic culture that to this point has seemed exclusively endangered suddenly becomes sinister and constrictive, as does the sea itself, framing the second half of the narrator's dilemma to stay or go. While looking at a photograph of his father taken on a beach, for instance, the narrator says of the sea that "it seemed very far away from him or else he was so much in the foreground that he seemed too big for it" (117), and only then does he realize that his father had possessed greater aspirations than he had ever guessed, that his father's covertly expressed desire to attend university had not been an idle one, that part of his father's life had been irrevocably stolen by the sea. This cycle is made complete by the story's end, when the father drowns, finally giving to the water in body what has been required all along in spirit. Yet this final demand is also the one that the narrator cannot tolerate, which he refuses to let the sea make of him. Of this moment he concludes, "it is not easy to know that your father was found on November twenty-eighth, ten miles to the north and wedged between two boulders at the base of the rock-strewn cliffs where he had been hurled and slammed so many many times" (125). With this vision, he offers his final rejection, despite his mother's pleas, of the regional community.

To me, however, such an ending seems a bit too tidy. Ultimately we understand the narrator to reject tradition for greater self-direction and volition—that is, to give up his old identity in order to form a new and independent one. But how free is this decision in reality? Throughout the story, the father has encouraged his son to give up the sea life for an education, and, at one moment when the narrator promises to return to school only when his father no longer needs help on the boat, the old man replies, "I hope you will remember what you've said" (122). As MacLeod himself has noted, this brief but resonant admonition suggests the possibility of the father's suicide, in which case the son's final decision would not be self-directed at all but forged again by the will of his ancestors.[6] And even if the father's death is accidental, the narrator's continual meditation upon his past within the present and his reluctance to give history shape except when contextualized by the familiar confines of the sea suggest that he has never truly left the regional community, that he yet stands motionless in his Cape Breton house perched in the doorway of his father's bedroom, unable to accept the notions of either chaos or order and the articulations of his own identity, which that place represents.

The same thing, to go back for a moment, might be said of Colly's decision as well. Though he ends his story with a decision to discover the external world, we know from what we have seen in Ginny or his mother's vision of Akron that the external world is hardly the promised land for which he searches. Moreover, the places Colly vows to go—Michigan, Germany, China—are the same places to which his father had gone in World War II, places where his father experienced a violence at least comparable to that of West Virginia, places that he swore he'd never leave but did, places that ultimately caused his death (in the form of an undetected shell fragment that later passed to his brain). In this light, Colly's comprehensive rejection of the landscape remains somewhat dubious because, like his father, it seems he will return to it continuously, if only in his mind.

Finally, the process of navigating physical space, like the process of history, becomes a circular one, and both Colly and the narrator of **"The Boat"** seem to be drawn unavoidably back to that point from which their quest for identity began. Their emphasis is placed on the external landscape because it mirrors so closely the internal one, giving—in its landmarks, its rivers, plowed fields, machines, and even graves—physical definition to the deep sense of time and heritage, self and permanence, felt by its residents. The land ultimately is the common denominator of the community, to which all can relate, into which many identities are invested and circulated and made one. It exacts the blood and sweat of those who work it and gives back a kind of yield, thus simulating the process of human life itself as well as the passage of historical identity from generation to generation. In short, it is a point of common reference, a place to come to, an acknowledgment of a kinship and friendship made possible by the earth itself. But when that landscape deteriorates, when it is dying, when it becomes overwhelmingly capricious and savage, or even when it is changed by the waves of progress, the correspondent landscape of the mind is left suspended and isolated. Ultimately, and put simply again, the problem of the displaced regional character is not so much building a new life as building a new home, a much more soulful project that takes considerably longer and that can never fully escape the intense sense of loss and destruction from which it proceeds.

Notes

1. The tale of the "same old gun" pervades Southern folk history, having first been told in its present form at the beginning of the nineteenth century and handed down to the present (like the gun itself) with only minor variations. The story as I have recorded it is a variant of the probable original in which the gun dates back to the Revolutionary—not the Civil—War and the salesman is more a generic traveler (Botkin 6). Other versions of the tale change its subject slightly, as in "my grandfather's axe" or "the cane-bottomed chair," which Wright Morris employs in *The Home Place*. Whatever the version, though, I would argue that both the endurance of the story and its widespread usage suggest its fundamental importance (at least metaphorically) in the way that regional characters define themselves and the world around them. In this sense, the boy's connection to his grandfather through the gun is not only a matter of personal history but a signifier of communal, national/political, and mythic identity as well.

2. For a clear introduction to the tradition of rural-urban tension in literature in English, see Raymond Williams's *The Country and the City*.

3. Ellesa Clay High, in particular, addresses the method by which male characters in Pancake's fiction almost always resort to symbolic violence against other people or animals in order to express their rage both at the literal decline of the regional community and at their own impotence to prevent such a decline.

4. The close connection of "family" and "land" in regional writing cannot be overstated. MacLeod, in several interviews, has pointed to the importance of heredity in the regional community, but

the heredity of which he speaks is not merely the passing of family name and rite from father to son. Heredity means a kind of genetic transference of historical identity beyond the confines of family relations, through the landscape itself. As one of the characters in MacLeod's "The Vastness of the Dark" tells his son during the boy's first trip to a coal mine: "Once you start it takes a hold of you, once you drink underground water, you will always come back to drink some more. The water gets in your blood. It is in all our blood. We have been working in the mines here since 1873."

5. Interestingly, in both writers, the figure of landscape as mother—in its guise as provider and its relationship to the father—is reinforced by an actual mother in the text, dissatisfied with her son's uncertainties and continually mindful of his responsibility to assume his father's role, if only to satisfy her. Naturally, the son desperately wishes to fulfill her desire but recognizes this fulfillment to be, at least for him, largely taboo.

6. For a more detailed analysis, see Colin Nicholson, "Alistair MacLeod" or "Signatures of Time: Alistair MacLeod and his Short Stories."

Works Cited

Botkin, B. A. *A Treasury of Southern Folklore.* New York: American Legacy, 1949.

High, Ellesa Clay. "A Lost Generation: The Appalachia of Breece D'J Pancake." *Appalachian Journal: A Regional Studies Review* 13 (1985): 34-40.

MacLeod, Alistair. *The Lost Salt Gift of Blood.* Toronto: McClelland, 1989.

Nicholson, Colin. "Signatures of Time: Alistair MacLeod and his Short Stories." *Canadian Literature* 107 (1985): 90-101.

———. "Alistair MacLeod." *Journal of Commonwealth Studies* 21 (1986): 188-200.

Pancake, Breece. *The Stories of Breece D'J Pancake.* New York: Holt, 1977.

Williams, Raymond. *The Country and the City.* New York: Oxford UP, 1973.

Christian Riegel (essay date summer 1998)

SOURCE: Riegel, Christian. "Elegy and Mourning in Alistair MacLeod's 'The Boat.'" *Studies in Short Fiction* 35, no. 3 (summer 1998): 233-40.

[*In the following essay, Riegel studies the elegiac elements of "The Boat," delineating its narrative structure in terms of the narrator's engagement with the processes of mourning.*]

Readers of Alistair MacLeod have identified "an abiding sense of loss and regret. . . . [and] a pervasive sense of sadness" (Nicholson 98) in the writing, as well as the "proximity of most characters to . . . the final elemental darkness threatening to reduce all hopes to one uniform and meaningless conclusion" (Berces 116). MacLeod's short stories are pervasively somber in that they depict a culture that is in a gradual loss or erosion of value. Colin Nicholson considers MacLeod to be "involved in a kind of historical elegizing, playing a pibroch in his own behalf" (99). The "Scottish-Canadian genealogical explorations" (Gittings 93) that largely comprise MacLeod's short stories, as both laments of a lost past and as fictional chronicles of that past, have the function of memorializing the personal—and familial—as well as social history of the narrators and their ancestors. Many of MacLeod's narrators can be considered to be mourning, and the stories that they tell are an activity of that process; that is, telling stories has the function of helping a narrator memorialize the dead and thus partially work through feelings of grief. MacLeod's stories, however, have not received sustained analysis in terms of mourning, or in terms of their elegiac elements, beyond initial thematic identification. In this paper I will explore the narrator's engagement in **"The Boat"** from the collection ***The Lost Salt Gift of Blood*** with this memorializing by delineating the structural elements that allow this story to be identified as a work of mourning, and by exploring the narrator's engagement with processes of mourning—processes that force him to examine his fundamental sense of self.

In a useful conception, Freud defines mourning as work—both in the sense of an action and as an object—a dual connotation that the German word for mourning, *Trauerarbeit*, supports even more forcefully than the English term does. Thus, mourning is considered as work that needs completing and, in some cases, mourning work can be the result of the action, such as, for example, a literary representation. The textual form that is most readily identified as a "work" of mourning is the elegy. The notion that mourning itself is work implies active involvement by the individual in the processes of grief. While elegy is most commonly associated with poetic forms, it is, as one theorist points out, "a literary genre that has become increasingly marked by blurred boundaries" (Smythe 4); and fiction that incorporates elements of elegy is termed fiction-elegy. Formally, fiction-elegy is "fundamentally trans-generic in that it brackets other genres in their modal form while retaining elegy as the generic 'dominant'" (6). The dominant genre, then, elegy "is a verbal presentation or staging of emotion wherein the detached speaker engages the audience with the intent of achieving some form of cathartic consolation." In tragedy, for example, where mourning is central, "it is the structure of the text that makes catharsis possible" (3). As a "staged performance of grief-work structure is [also] partially functional" (3) in forms that incorporate elegy. Peter Sacks points out that "the objective of an elegy is . . . to displace the urgent psychological currents of its work of mourning into the apparently more placid, authentically organized currents of language" (14). Forms that incorporate elements of elegy channel the emotional responses to death into a structure (the creative work) that can more effectively deal with the loss, and that offers a means for working through the loss. Thus, the work of mourning involves the active ordering and structuring of information into a narrative construction that will enable—or, at least attempt—consolation.

As a work of mourning, **"The Boat"** is structured around the narrator's grief for the loss of his father. The narrator's means of coping with his emotional state is by telling a story that explores his relationship with his father, mother and ancestral tradition; these relationships are fraught with conflict and ambivalence, for the narrator documents a period in his life where he must choose between upholding old beliefs and forging his own path in life. In this sense, the story he tells is effectively a coming of age tale—stories that document a period frequently associated with troubled identity and competing life choices. His story, however, is additionally complicated by grief, as the narrator's coming of age experience is fundamentally altered by the death of the father. In the present of the text the narrator has made clear career and lifestyle choices (far away from the traditional world of his youth), but he has not come to terms with the significance of his father's passing, and he still feels a fundamental unease with his life.

The narrator's situation parallels definitions of mourning where mourning is described as an action where the individual, in response to a death or serious loss, "calls into question the meaningfulness and reality of the social frameworks in which they participate" (Mellor 13). The result of the serious loss is "the shattering of a sense of ontological security." Ontological security, according to Anthony Giddens, refers to an individual's "sense of order and continuity in relation to events in which they participate in their day-to-day lives" (cited by Mellor 12). The opening of the story chronicles the contemporary life of the narrator, establishes the fundamental unease that he feels in his daily life, and comments on his continual questioning of his chosen career and lifestyle. **"The Boat"** begins with the moment of "terrible fear" (105) that awakens the narrator, and the confusion he feels as he comes to an awareness of his surroundings. The link between the narrator's feelings of being "foolishly alone" and the absence of his father is underscored here. The narrator describes his frequent early morning awakenings where he faces "the terrible fear that I have overslept . . . [and] that my father is waiting for me" (105) in a manner that suggests an action that has become reflexive after years and years of constant early mornings to go fishing with his father

and the other men: "There are times when I am half out of bed and fumbling for socks and mumbling for words before I realize that I am foolishly alone, that no one waits at the base of the stairs and no boat rides restlessly in the waters of the pier" (105).

In the second paragraph of the story the narrator comments on the preoccupation with death that accompanies these moments, further keying the importance of his father's death to the storytelling. As he states, "I am afraid to be alone with death" which necessitates his rising from bed and departure for an all-night restaurant in search of company. The narrator uses images that are laden with connotations of death to depict his predicament, mirroring his emotional state: "At such times only the gray corpses on the overflowing ashtray beside my bed bear witness to the extinction of the latest spark and silently await the crushing out of the most recent of their fellows" (105). As the narrator moves into the story of his past, he juxtaposes his current unease with the elements of his past that trouble him. As the day dawns, he focuses on "the countless things one must worry about when he teaches at a great Midwestern university" (106), contextualizing his occupation and geographical location—both far removed from the world of his childhood and adolescence. With daylight comes the certainty that the past is far removed from the present, that it is "only shadows and echoes . . . the cuttings from an old movie made in the black and white of long ago," and with daylight comes "all kinds of comforting reality to prove" that the past is long gone. Despite being figments of his imagination, however, the "call and the voices and the shapes and the boat" had the semblance of reality for the narrator during those early morning hours. Thus, the narrator's assertion that the "day will go by as have all the days of the past ten years" (106) is in part an empty conclusion, offering no resolution to his malaise, for the narrator implies that there have been many similar days, and no consolation or resolution has been attained—therefore, more days like this one can be expected. The role of the storytelling is to fill in the "shadows and echoes" that haunt him, to revisit the old movie in an attempt to come to grips with it.

The opening and closing paragraphs of **"The Boat"** frame the narrator's story. While the narrator's story literally takes up the most space in the text, the frame emphasizes the thematic ordering of the story and provides context. The beginning of **"The Boat"** emphasizes the continuing presence of the father's influence on the narrator, while he is forever physically absent, and the ending of the story contextualizes the absence by figuring the father's corpse. The figuration of the corpse—by being written—is an attempt at bringing presence to the father; although in the attempt the paradoxical nature of the signifying process is highlighted, for the body can never literally be recovered. It can, however, be figured textually which results in narrative signification. The feelings of emotional instability caused by grief at the beginning of the story, and the figuration of the corpse at the end serve as focalizers for the storytelling. The images of the discovery of his father's corpse are harrowing in their graphic description:

> [It is not] easy to know that your father was found on November twenty-eighth, ten miles to the north and wedged between two boulders at the base of the rock-strewn cliffs where he had been hurled and slammed so many times. His hands were shredded as were his feet which had lost their boots to the suction of the sea, like the grass on graves, upon the purple, bloated mass that was his face. There was not much left of my father, physically, as he lay there with the brass chains on his wrists and the seaweed on his hair.
>
> (125)

The images of the father provide insight into the significance of the narrator's fear and emotion in the opening lines, for the story ends with the graphic description of the discovery of the father's corpse. And it is this image that informs and frames the emotional unease that the narrator is feeling at the opening, for the description of the corpse points to several key thematics of the story, and of the narrator's life: the father's feelings of otherness with the sea, and the narrator's conflicted feelings about tradition. The images reflect the ravages of the sea on bodies, what here literally is a body mutilated by sea, but also function metaphorically to describe the effects that sea, boat, and father, have had on the narrator's conflicted identity—what could be termed a mutilated identity.

Read retrospectively, the images from the closing of the story combine with the opening unease to focalize the narrative and provide context for the narrator's storytelling. The father's mutilated body signifies the narrator's own sense of mutilation in respect to his past and his sense of self.

His father, in death, represents the narrator's epiphanic realization earlier in the summer that his father's occupation was foreign to him, and that he would have chosen otherwise if possible. The father's alienation from his livelihood is complete—both physical and emotional:

> My father did not tan—he never tanned—because of his reddish complexion, and the salt water irritated his skin as it had for sixty years. He burned and reburned over and over again and his lips cracked so that they bled when he smiled, and his arms, especially the left, still broke out into oozing salt-water boils. . . . The chafe-preventing bracelets of brass linked chain that all men wore about their wrists in early spring were his the full season and he shaved but painfully once a week.
>
> (121)

The bodily rejection of the occupation is manifested as fear in the son for he realizes that this may be his fate as well.

In the present the narrator is feeling conflicted about his dereliction of the family tradition, on his mother's side, of fishing and working on the ocean. This has led to his estrangement from his mother. The exploration of his father's death, and the son's involvement in that summer's activities, becomes an exploration of the narrator's conflicted identity in relation to the roles that he performs in life. As David Stevens notes, "his insistence on reinvoking the past and its implicit sense of guilt suggests that he has left behind only the physical aspects . . . not the psychological ones" (267). He "teaches at a great Midwestern university"—as far away from the ocean as one can get on this continent, and figuratively, in a profession that prioritizes mental activity over physical work. He in effect rejects all that his mother understands and respects in life: a sense of nicely ordered history and tradition embodied in honest hard work on the sea. The mother is comfortable in the "immaculate order" of the house, but does not understand "the disruptive chaos of the single room that was my father's" (108), for the father's room represents a link to the world outside the traditional life that gives meaning to the mother: "My mother despised the room and all it stood for and she had stopped sleeping in it after I was born. She despised disorder in rooms and in houses and in hours and in lives, and she had not read a book since high school" (111). She loses each of her daughters to this link with the outside world, and, eventually, her son: "One by one they went. My mother had each of her daughters for fifteen years, then lost them for two and finally forever. None married a fisherman" (117). And so, the narrator's exploration of his father's death necessarily involves an examination of his mother's feelings of rejection towards him, and of all that she stands for. It is an explicit rejection of tradition and the limiting force that tradition can have on a society and culture, but it is also a lament for the (inevitable) loss of tradition in the face of modernization and change.

While the mother holds out hope that her son may yet return to fish on "the grounds to which the *Jenny Lynn* once went" (124); and the community, still strong in its conservative belief in tradition, upholds that sense of hope, for the grounds "remain untouched and unfished as they have for the last ten years" (124). For indeed, the grounds represent a long line of family tradition: "For if there are no signposts on the sea in storm there are certain ones in calm and the lobster bottoms were distributed in calm before any of us can remember and the grounds my father fished were those his father fished before him and there were others before and before and before" (124). These grounds, by the mother and community, "are held to be sacred," further underscoring the sense that the narrator is rejecting not only tradition, but the notion of a natural symbiotic relationship between sea and humans.

The opening of the story focuses on the reflexive awakening of the narrator and his temporal confusion. Near the end of the story, however, this scene is deconstructed by the narrator and the effect of that awakening is shifted. The scene is narrated as one of a number of fleeting moments in the son's short fishing career—a point that is clearly elided early in the story. The narrator, in this section of the story, "joined my father then for the trawling season" (120) part of the way through the summer, as he had to finish school first. The description of the early mornings in the narrator's story itself belies the scene as he describes it in the opening paragraph, for in the opening he thinks of his father waiting for him while the narrator oversleeps. But in the description in the textual past, his father does not wait for him; rather, it is the fishermen from the community who provide the impetus for the narrator's work:

> The men would come tramping by our house at 4:00 a.m. and we would join them and walk with them to the wharf and be on our way before the sun rose out of the ocean where it seemed to spend the night. If I was not up they would toss pebbles to my window and I would be embarrassed and tumble downstairs to where my father lay fully clothed atop his bed. . . . He would make no attempt to wake me himself.
>
> (120)

The narrator remembers that his father had little interest or passion for the work he performed. One of the key memories he has of his father is of his epiphanic awareness that his father is not doing what he would like in life: "And I saw then, that summer, many things that I had seen all my life as if for the first time and I thought that perhaps my father had never been intended for a fisherman either physically or mentally" (121). Caught between this realization, and his mother's approbation of his choice to quit school to fish, the narrator romanticizes the father's life—projecting his own sentiments onto his father's situation: "I thought it was very much braver to spend a life doing what you really do not want rather than selfishly following forever your own dreams and inclinations" (122). With this realization he decides to give up his "silly shallow selfish dream" of completing high school to enter into tradition and fish. With the death of his father, however, he abandons fishing for a life of education and books. As the narrator's story attests, the conflict between his mother's desires, and his father's wishes, as well as his own uncertainty, has remained for many years after this period of his life. The continuing grief that the narrator feels in relation to the loss of his father is in large part due to these unresolved conflicts.

The early morning awakening of the narrator is paralleled a second time in the story by the description of the mother, who also awakens when the fishing day begins—but for other reasons: "She lies awake in the early morning's darkness when the rubber boots of the men scrunch upon the gravel as they pass beside her house on their way down to the wharf" (19). The narrator's story, ostensibly, came out of the mourning for his father, but the description of his mother lying awake in the mornings underscores the importance of the sense of loss that the narrator feels at having given up his traditional role. For indeed, it is the mother—even in the present—who lies awake at the bottom of the stairs waiting for the son to get up to fish. And part of the narrator's sense of loss comes from his mother's rejection of him: "it is not an easy thing to know that your mother looks upon the sea with love and on you with bitterness because the one has been so constant and the other so untrue" (19).

The narrator of **"The Boat"** engages in memorializing his personal and familial ancestry out of a need to work through deep feelings of loss that haunt his emotions years after their occurrence. The processes of memorializing, however, are fraught with complexity, for the narrator shows ambivalence in his relation to the cultural and social traditions that he is attempting to memorialize; in effect, the narrator is involved in an elemental crisis of his ontological status—a crisis that he realizes is not necessarily consolable for he finds no resolution to his conflicted identity. John J. Clayton argues that "all expressive art is an attempt to end discords in its creator, to feed some hunger or cope with an experience that feels overwhelming, feels intensely dissonant—to express that experience and so gain control. . . . [Art] is the act of coping" (3). MacLeod's narrator, however, seems more concomitant in his uneasy relationship with his past to what George Steiner has called the "failure of consolation" (Schleifer 2), what he terms the "crises of word and meaning" (cited by Schleifer 1) that "have disrupted traditional Western apprehensions of the possibilities of transcendental significance in experience" (Schleifer 2). The narrator, responding to feelings of grief, attempts to articulate loss through narrative with the hope that the process will prove fruitful. At the heart of this story lies the narrator's attempts at ordering his past into a text that will provide needed consolation; but his failure to do so comments on his unease at marking a past that will unalterably signify his present and future. In effect, he presents a fear of closure—the final word on his ontological status—but he still is compelled to, in fact must, respond to the emotions that overcome him. The elusiveness of consolation in recent narratives of mourning is expressed by Smythe: for these writers "'consolation,' if it can be called that, is acquired in the reader's recognition of form, and in the apprehension of the meaning of loss in its relationship to presence" (10). And thus, the narrator's mourning is enacted not as a process requiring, or even offering the possibility of, closure or resolution, but as a process that enables the exploration of loss, the past, and identity.

Works Cited

Berces, Francis. "Existential Maritimer: Alistair Mac-Leod's *The Lost Salt Gift of Blood.*" *Studies in Canadian Literature* 16.1 (1991): 114-28.

Clayton, John J. *Gestures of Healing: Anxiety and the Modern Novel.* Amherst: U of Massachusetts P, 1991.

Freud, Sigmund. "Mourning and Melancholia." *The Freud Reader.* Ed., Peter Gay. New York: Norton, 1989. 584-89.

Gittings, Christopher. "Sounds in the Empty Spaces of History: The Highland Clearances in Neil Gunn's 'Highland River' and Alistair MacLeod's 'The Road to Rankin's Point.'" *Studies in Canadian Literature* 17.1 (1992): 93-105.

MacLeod, Alistair. "The Boat." *The Lost Salt Gift of Blood.* New Canadian Library. Toronto: McClelland and Stewart, 1976. Rpt. 1992. 105-25.

Mellor, Philip. "Death in High Modernity: The Contemporary Presence and Absence of Death." *The Sociology of Death.* Ed., David Clark. Oxford and Cambridge: Blackwell, 1993. 11-30.

Nicholson, Colin. "Signatures of Time: Alistair MacLeod and His Short Stories." *Canadian Literature* 107 (1985): 90-101.

Sacks, Peter. *The English Elegy.* Baltimore: Johns Hopkins UP, 1985.

Schleifer, Ronald. *Rhetoric and Death: The Language of Modernism and Postmodern Discourse Theory.* Urbana: U of Illinois P, 1990.

Smythe, Karen E. *Figuring Grief: Gallant, Munro, and the Poetics of Elegy.* Montreal and Kingston: McGill-Queen's UP, 1992.

Stevens, David. "Writing Region Across the Border: The Two Stories of Breece Pancake and Alistair MacLeod." *Studies in Short Fiction* 33 (1996): 263-71.

Laurie Kruk (essay date 1999)

SOURCE: Kruk, Laurie. "Hands and Mirrors: Gender Reflections in the Short Stories of Alistair MacLeod and Timothy Findley." In *Dominant Impressions: Essays on the Canadian Short Story,* edited by Gerald Lynch and Angela Arnold Robbeson, pp. 137-50. Ottawa: University of Ottawa Press, 1999.

[*In the following essay, Kruk analyzes the representation of masculine identity in Timothy Findley's "Stones" and MacLeod's "The Boat."*]

What do the short stories of Alistair MacLeod and Timothy Findley have in common, and how do they "reflect" and "reflect on" gender? Seemingly old-fashioned MacLeod, his roots in the oral tradition and Cape Breton's Celtic culture, described by Michael Ondaatje as "one of the best short story writers in Canada"[1] . . . and Findley, a publicly gay or homosexual writer,[2] whose critically popular work has been described as both "postmodernist" in form and "feminist" in outlook? While Findley has been noted for creating "remarkable women" possessing "hyper-realistic sight," as one critic puts it (Murray 217), the heterosexual MacLeod's work is presented from a distinctively masculine (though not masculin*ist*) perspective. Aside from the excellence of the stories in question, initially, their differences are more apparent than any similarities. Yet I propose to argue that the visually-oriented Findley and the verbally-oriented MacLeod travel over some of the same territory. Both writers, for instance—whether comfortable or not with the increasingly fuzzy term "realist writer"—believe strongly in getting at the "real." In interview, MacLeod described realist writing simply as "telling the truth as I happen to see it" ("Exiles" 159); Findley redefined "realism" as placing "the anchor in the *real* heart, the *real* spirit and the *real* turmoil of *real* life" ("Edge" 18).[3] At the same time, Findley added—not surprisingly, given his earlier acting career—that "theatricality" is a "very positive thing" and "writing is a performance art" ("Edge" 19, 3). Consequently, Findley appears to approach the issue of gender identity from the view endorsed by Judith Butler in *Gender Trouble,* one described as "performative—that is, constituting the identity it is purported to be. In this sense, gender is always a doing, though not a doing by a subject who might be said to preexist the deed" (24-25). Obviously, neither writer presents the rigorously deconstructive philosophy Butler advocates; both men, it must be acknowledged, may be characterized as adhering to "a metaphysics of substance that confirms the normative model of humanism as the framework for feminism" (20). Indeed, that is the framework within which I am operating. I take a largely social psychology approach to the discussion of gender and treat these male authors' "gender reflections" as aspects of this (largely) realist fiction's ability—for this (female) reader, at least—to be a compelling "representation" of certain aspects of our lives as men and women, lives which are both emphatically embodied and culturally constructed.[4]

Yet Findley's emphasis on the *performative* aspects of writing does point to a significant divergence in outlook from MacLeod. And this divergence will be revealed through my focus on their "reflection" of gender relations and identities in their short stories. That is to say, while MacLeod's treatment of men and women returns us, powerfully, to our physical and sensual existence, Findley probes the performative aspects of our social and sexual roles as gendered beings. In her review of *Dinner Along the Amazon,* Barbara Gabriel writes, "Findley's most radical politics are the politics of gender" (89). He utilizes his admittedly "other" perspective, as a gay man, to reflect on the ways that gender roles entrap both sexes. In *Headhunter,* his heroine Fabiana declares, "It's a drag act—men pretending to be men—women pretending to be women" (341). Alternatively, MacLeod's short stories frequently draw our attention to his characters' work-marked *hands.* This repeated detail creates a synecdochic effect that reinforces the presentation of his very physical characters as not only shapers of, but also shaped by, the surrounding natural world. Meanwhile, one of Findley's guiding metaphors appears to be the *mirror,* linked in turn to his recurring theatrical motif of masks in particular and performance in general. Having established their difference in approach to gender identities and relations, by means of an overview of this contrasting imagery, I will analyze a story by each author that addresses similar concerns about masculine identity. The stories to be discussed offer moving variations on the shared theme of the lost, sacrificed father: MacLeod's acclaimed **"The Boat"** (*Gift* [*The Lost Salt Gift of Blood*]) and Findley's "Stones" (*Stones*).[5]

Short stories are often neglected by literary critics, viewed as drafts for novels, or as supplements to that legitimate project. Certainly MacLeod, who has built his career writing only short stories, thus far,[6] disproves this view. His stories owe much to the oral tradition, and as Janice Kulyk Keefer notes, "Often he seems to sing rather than tell his stories" (182). By incorporating into his prose sonorous Gaelic rhythms and folkloric repetition, MacLeod enters the company of bards and storytellers. Except for two (**"The Tuning of Perfection"** [**Birds** (**As Birds Bring Forth the Sun**)] **"The Golden Gift of Grey"** [**Gift**]), all of MacLeod's stories take advantage of the intensity of a first-person narrator. More importantly, all of them focus on a male protagonist, heightening their "autobiographical," and masculine, quality.[7] By contrast, Findley's short stories are more varied in form and style, and may be described as exploring the "experimental" aspect of the modern short story in its more self-consciously literary development. The first things Findley wrote were short stories, just as his earliest reading experiences involved "the self-contained entity, [the story] that is taken at one dose" ("Edge" 1). The fact that several of his stories were related to plays he wanted to write ("Daybreak at Pisa," "Out of the Silence" [*Dinner*]; see also "Edge" 116), or novels such as *The Last of the Crazy People* (1967) ("Lemonade" [*Dinner*]) and *Headhunter* (1993) ("Dinner Along the Amazon" [*Dinner*]) does not diminish them as separate entries in this genre. But it does suggest that his stories may be more justly seen as experiments in narrative and subject matter. Mary Louise Pratt has suggested that the short story is the place "to

introduce new (and possibly stigmatized) subject matters into the literary arena" (187). If that is true, then the exploration of such matters would appear here first. For instance, in Findley's "Minna and Bragg" and "A Gift of Mercy" (*Stones*), he introduces, for the first time, an explicitly homosexual protagonist; two later Minna and Bragg stories tackle issues of gay identity and its contradictions ("A Bag of Bones," "Come as You Are" [*Dust to Dust*]; see also the collection's "Dust"). While homosexuality was either hinted at (or the heterosexuality of his characters subtly questioned) in other places within the Findley canon, Bragg is the first male protagonist whose homosexuality is not only evident but also central to the story. At the same time, while increasingly open about his own homosexuality, Findley defies narrow categorization. He notes that "I'm not turning my back on [homosexuality], and I'm perfectly happy to have it said, 'He is a homosexual' in any biographical material. But I just don't think I want to be collected exclusively in gay anthologies. . . . I want my world to be wider than my sexuality" ("Edge" 9-10).

In making "The Case for Men's Studies," Harry Brod has said, "While women have been obscured from our vision by being too much in the background, men have been obscured from our vision by being too much in the foreground" (41). This intriguing insight has motivated my exploration of the two authors' portrayal of men. If MacLeod's tendency is to focus on the totality of the individual's freedoms and limitations, Findley's stories highlight the contradictions and burdens of what social psychologists call the "sex or gender role" (Pleck). There is ample evidence within his fiction that Findley's distinctive perspective as a gay man leads him to treat sympathetically women trapped or exploited by sexual stereotyping, as well as to probe deeply into traditional social or cultural expectations of men. Don Murray has delineated Findley's "optical imagery," and its relationship to themes of physical and psychic survival. He includes among it the use of sight "to locate oneself, especially in stories where mirrors are prominent, in order to confirm one's existence" (201). Thus, Findley's use of the mirror in his stories aptly "reflects" his special consciousness not simply of problems of psychological identity, but of the constructedness of gender identity.[8] For instance, in "Lemonade" (*Dinner*), Renalda Dewey's descent into alcoholism and rejection of her son appears to be facilitated by her own entrapment by a gender role that has outlived its usefulness. The woman described as formerly "one of the most beautiful . . . you could see anywhere in the world," loses her main audience after her husband is killed in the Second World War. Her main activity within the home consists of her morning "performance" as wealthy lady and adored mother. She must reconstruct her feminine identity, with the aid of cosmetics, before her lonely son can enter the sanctuary of her bedroom.

Looking in the mirror, for her, becomes a confirmation of the success of her role-playing, yet, increasingly, this image is no longer sufficient: "She looked into the mirror. It was as though she couldn't find herself there. She had to go very close to it and lean one hand against the table to steady herself and she had to almost close her eyes before she found what she was looking for" (15). Her eventual suicide is foreshadowed by her stagnation in a kind of role-playing that lacks the appropriate audience, trapping her in a static, silent image like the "floating figure in a Japanese print . . . the mime" she resembles as she prepares her toilette.

Similarly, the poet Annie Bogan, in "The Book of Pins" (*Dinner*), neurotically obsessed with controlling or "pinning" her environment, focusses on her image in a mirror across the room, which is once again described as "Japanese" (237).[9] She seeks the mirror's confirmation that she is not only "dressed" and "erect" but "immensely real" (248). The story draws attention to her obsession with mirrors by starting and finishing, in a kind of chiasmus, with the same description of the same old women reflected in the mirrors in the hotel lobby. Her fascination with "fixing" or "pinning" the world around her into artistic figures gives Annie a kind of sterile self-absorption that would be dangerous to others if it were not ample evidence of the (suicidal) fragility of her own psyche.

Vivien Eliot, in "Out of the Silence" (*Dinner*) also stares into her mirror for long periods of time, as if questioning not only her sanity, but the contribution of male-dominated society (represented by both husband and doctor), to the undermining of that sanity. This use of the mirror reflection to offer reassurance regarding the achievement of a proper social or sexual image reappears in several places in Findley's short stories. "Dinner Along the Amazon" 's Fabiana summarizes her acceptance of a passive role as the woman "chosen" by the desiring suitor with her reference to her younger self as always "sitting in the front seat, watching in the mirror" (290). "Almeyer's Mother" (*Stones*) finds comfort in watching herself—in the mirror—lunching with her son and daughter-in-law in the stately Royal Ontario Museum cafeteria. The image freezes them in their appropriate social and gender roles as a family. "*This is us*, the picture informed her, *sitting where we belong*" (177). In "Losers, Finders, Strangers at the Door" (*Dinner*), Daisy McCabe, struggling to maintain her ladylike role as "Mrs. Arnold McCabe" against her despairing rage at the situation her husband's unusual sexual desires have placed her in, refers bitterly to the confirmation of her mirror that "the loveliness—the innocence" is gone. In her case, the innocence may really be the ignorance of people's true complexity: a knowledge that is stifled by rigid gender identities, Findley suggests.

Men, too, are presented gazing into mirrors in Findley's stories, but often in a dramatization of a questioning, rather than a confirmation, of their various roles or personae, including gender roles. Bragg, in "A Gift of Mercy" (*Stones*), glances in the mirror "the way most people do who don't want to see themselves" (36); Ishmael, in "Hello Cheeverland, Goodbye" (*Dinner*) briefly regards "his whole self" with horror in the bathroom mirror before turning away (185). And in "Masks" (*Stones*), the reclusive Professor Glendenning catches a glimpse in the mirror of the "unmasked" self that he discovers later when trying on the Japanese fox masks at the Royal Ontario Museum (66). In a more explicit example of the imprisoning potential of gender roles, Bud, in "Real Life Writes Real Bad" (*Stones*), is obsessed with the monstrous form his male body appears to present: "Every time he looked [in a mirror], you might have thought he'd never seen himself in mirrors or photographs before. . . . He always cringed while peering at himself through narrowed eyes—a voyeur watching through a window. 'Look at his hands!' he would say, *as if the person in the mirror wasn't him*, 'Look at the size of his bloody hands, Neil!'" (156, emphasis added). Bud's alienation from his (reflected) body underscores his own emotional imbalance, while symbolizing men's equal entrapment in gender roles or identities that may not fit their needs or personalities.

Alistair MacLeod, on the other hand, draws our attention precisely to *that* other: the life of the body, male or female, within the larger, natural environment. This dynamic is frequently figured by the *hand*. Gender roles in his fictional world appear to follow the age-old prescription of men's and women's separate spheres: the woman ruling the household and the man providing for his family by means of physically demanding, dangerous work. However, in the harsh, maritime environment of the stories, these roles are equally important. So while this segregation of the sexes into traditional roles clearly has a restrictive aspect—often forcing the next generation away from the community, to escape rigid gender roles through formal education and greater opportunities—it also strengthens, grounds and ennobles those who stay. While Findley directs our attention to seeing, and, more politically, to *being* seen, MacLeod reminds us, with his focus on the hand, of *doing*: shaping, but also being shaped by, one's environment. MacLeod's stories evoke a time and place where people do not pay, as many urban professionals now do, for "the pleasures of perspiration" ("**The Closing Down of Summer**," *Birds* 23) and one's physical nature is an integral factor in determining success, or even survival. The body in MacLeod's world serves an important purpose, in its capability and endurance, and is not simply a token in the social games that Findley's more privileged, urbanized people have leisure to play. Indeed, in the same way that memories are often experienced as being carried by the physical body, these stories might be described as "embodied" narratives. For at the beginning of **"Vision"** (*Birds*), MacLeod describes not "the time around scars," as Michael Ondaatje did in the poem of that name, but the psychic scar, "medallion of . . . emotion," that forms around a powerfully told story. The scarring wound that MacLeod introduces to make his storytelling analogy is, not surprisingly, inflicted on the hand (**"Vision,"** *Birds* 128).

Just as the hands are scarred, but also strengthened, by their labour, so MacLeod's people are moulded into roles that, if narrow, still carry deep satisfactions for some. MacLeod's stories are deemed by Colin Nicholson "elemental fictions" (90) and Janice Kulyk Keefer also uses the word "elemental" to describe the embrace between husband and wife that occurs at the end of **"In the Fall"** (*Gift*). There, the wife's long hair is associated with "the wind and snow whirling round them," as well as the mane of the loyal horse the husband agrees to sell for slaughter. It at first appears that MacLeod is propagating the familiar (and in much feminist analysis) patriarchal linking of women with nature. Yet his descriptive focus on the detail of the hand, and the animal and natural world surrounding his characters, is applied to both men and women. It reinforces MacLeod's vision of humanity as inevitable participants within the cycle of nature, however foolishly we ignore and defy or disrupt it.

Nicholson observes that in MacLeod's stories "identity and relationships are very much prefigured in imagery associated with the human hand" (93). But hands themselves feature as key indices in MacLeod's stories, not just of choice of work but of character, and of gender role, with its mixture of limitations and opportunities. Returning to **"In the Fall,"** Janice Kulyk Keefer remarks on the correlation of gender role with hand description: "The narrator tells us how, whenever his mother does speak, 'She does something with her hands. It is as if the private voice in her can only be liberated by some kind of physical action'" (184). Although this detail does suggest an entrapment in the daily domestic work of the traditional, rural woman's role, elsewhere MacLeod's heroines are described, along with their hands, as strong and independent and decidedly practical, in the face of their men's tendency toward impetuous schemes and sentimental loyalties. Hands, those most subtle and supple of tools, are more often described as defined by their labour in these stories. The father's left hand and arm are enlarged by his work as a stevedore in **"In the Fall"** (*Gift*), while the miner father of **"The Vastness of the Dark"** (*Gift*) has lost "the first two fingers from his right hand" (25) in an accident with dynamite. Violence flows from the paternal hand in this story as well, as the narrator describes his father inadvertently injuring him by flailing out in his sleep and once, in a drunken rage, putting his hand through a window. This defiantly self-destructive act

suggests the father's wordless protest at his entrapment by both economic circumstances and gender role. The damage done to the father's hand is more than symbolic of latent frustration, however, as mother and son together pray "that no tendons were damaged and that no infection would set in because it was the only good hand that he had and all of us rode upon it as perilous passengers on an unpredictably violent sea" (33). As if emphasizing all that rides on the work of the hand, the hands of MacLeod's people are almost always large, even "gigantic" (**"The Vastness of the Dark,"** *Gift* 28) or "massive" (**"The Golden Gift of Grey,"** *Gift* 101), as are the people. Even the women share in this characteristic, having "powerful, almost masculine hands" (**"Vastness,"** [**"The Vastness of the Dark"**] *Gift* 37) or "strong brown hands" (**"Vision,"** *Birds* 142).

As well, the divided state within a family is represented, in **"The Return"** (*Gift*), by means of a division of hands: Alex's right hand is squeezed almost painfully by his nostalgic father as they arrive by train in his home village. All the while, he is aware of his left hand lying peacefully, painlessly, beside his urban, unimpressed mother's right, "on the green upholstered cushion" (72). Alex's grandmother has "powerful hands," while his grandfather's are described as "very big" (76); the strength with which they each swing Alex up into the air when they greet him reveals a life of—and their pride in—hard physical work. The grandfather's grimy hugging of Alex after his shift at the mine, a hug which tests the boy's endurance and covers him in coal dust— marking him with the traces of a masculine gendered economy—expresses the ambivalence many of MacLeod's protagonists feel toward their birthplaces, and the traditional gender roles associated with them. Like the hug, these places comfort but also constrict. It is no accident that the callous and vulgar salesman, heading back to Toronto, who offers the hero a ride in **"The Vastness of the Dark"** (*Gift*) is described as having "very white and disproportionately small" hands (42). If hands in MacLeod are an index of character as well as lifestyle, then his "very white" hands reflect not simply his class, but also his personal inferiority to the local people he so easily dismisses, including the widowed women whose loneliness he exploits. MacLeod's stories present an elegiac treatment of a passing way of life, not simply an economic one, but also a philosophical or spiritual one. If his characters share certain traits, as suggested by the detail of the hand, this is in the interest of impressing on the reader, by the folk-tale technique of repetition, the image of a community of men and women who were not simply strong, but big—a bigness which clearly has a spiritual or emotional quality. As he says of the doomed animal breeder in **"As Birds Bring Forth the Sun"** (*Birds*), "He was a man used to working with the breeding of animals, with the guiding of rams and bulls and stallions and often with the funky smell of animal semen heavy on his *large* *and gentle hands*" (120, emphasis added). The conjunction of largeness and gentleness is significant, as it suggests not the stereotypical male role of aggressor, but a controlled, channelled strength. And the detail of the smell of animal semen reinforces the stories' presentation of human and animal world not as separate spheres, but linked and interacting. MacLeod's love for his people brings into being stories that, in their solemn beauty and widespread appeal (translated into languages as diverse as Russian and Urdu [Pakistani]: "Exiles" 3), testify to the life-giving power of fiction.

Despite their different interests, Findley and MacLeod have each written a story that presents, from a first-person perspective, the son's relationship with a father whose end defines a conflict between the individual man and his society's vision of "Manhood." But here, Findley puts aside the image of the mirror to address the male gender role, and how it is "reflected" from father to son, through a pattern of natural imagery—flowers, stones, hands, the sea—more common in MacLeod's work. David Max, father of Ben Max, the narrator of "Stones," contentedly runs a flower shop along with his wife and three children on the outskirts of Rosedale until the Second World War comes along. When it does, he is among the first to sign up. His theatrical announcement, "Children . . . I am going to be a soldier" (200), suggests a certain pride in putting on a role that is still rewarded in the theatre of our society. Ben is frightened, but his older brother, Cy, "crowed with delight and yelled with excitement. He wanted to know if the war would last until *he was a man* and could join his father at the front" (200, emphasis added).

This contrast between the two brothers is exploited by the father when he returns, four years later, discharged from duty for deserting his men at the disastrous battle of Dieppe. In a grim ceremony that seems to parody the theatrical moment in which David Max announced his decision to join in the war, he is paraded in the Exhibition grounds before his family with other discharged, wounded men. Already seen as a "failure" as a male, Ben now bears the brunt of his disturbed father's wrath. For as if recognizing in his younger son his own weakness, the alcoholic father, stigmatized by his "dishonourable discharge," turns on Ben. When Ben obeys his terse orders unquestioningly, the father taunts him with the notion of rebellion, which would threaten the filial bond but strengthen Ben's presumed masculinity through a display of defiance. The crisis occurs when David Max drunkenly assaults his younger son: "One night, he came into the bedroom where I slept in the bunk-bed over Cy and he shouted at me *why don't you fight back?* Then he dragged my covers off and threw me onto the floor against the bureau" (212). This attack reveals the savagery released in a shame-filled man who failed to "do his duty" and die with his men. Before the battle of Dieppe, Ben learns, his father, a Cap-

tain, was considered a "natural leader" and it was asserted that his men "would have followed him anywhere" (215).[10] Once David's dream of upholding the law of honour, based upon the stoical aspect of the male gender role,[11] is shattered, all he can do is take out his frustrations on his too-obedient son, in the guise of instilling in him the more useful, as it now appears, law of the jungle.

David Max's self-hatred next leads him to assault his wife viciously. This attack is precipitated by a humiliating confrontation with a survivor of Dieppe determined to pronounce publicly Max's cowardice. That evening, the children find their mother "lying on the sofa . . . *her hands* broken because she had used them trying to fend off the blows" of the hammer he attacked her with (214, emphasis added). David is then institutionalized in the Asylum for the Insane on Queen Street. Turning away from his family, he joins other outcasts of society—gender rebels: "whores and derelicts"—and dies unmourned by his children. Only Ben, the "failure" at masculinity, cares enough to carry out his father's last request. David Max asked if his ashes might be put with the blood of the men who died at Dieppe: among the stones.

The stones of the title first suggest coldness or hardheartedness, as in Ben's lament that, despite his father's behaviour, "I would have loved a stone" (218). This makes the placement of his ashes among the "treacherous" stones ironically apt to his son: "*Why not,* I thought. *A stone among stones.*" A stone can also be a weapon; in the story "War" (*Dinner*) which Lorraine York has linked to this one, the young boy Neil throws stones at his father in anger at his imminent desertion of the family for service in the war. As a fact of the landscape, the stones of the beach also played a role in thwarting the attack, since they "jammed the tank tracks" (216). And of course, as a title, "Stones" recalls the biblical proverb which Findley brings to mind here, generally paraphrased as "Let he who is without sin, cast the first stone" (John 8:7).[12]

"Fathers cannot be cowards," Ben insists (217). Which term excludes the other? If Max remains accepted and loved as Ben's father, despite everything, then what meaning does "coward" hold for him? Surely, Findley implies, fathers endure, despite the labels society may apply to their actions. In mingling his father's ashes with those of his obedient men, the "heroes" at Dieppe, Ben finally challenges the distinction between "heroes" and "cowards" that so burdened his father.

If David Max's dilemma is that he fails to live up to an ideal of masculinity that his son comes to question, the unnamed father in **"The Boat"** lives up to his gender role all too well.[13] With the help of "the boat," the father supports his large family of six daughters and one son—the narrator, now looking back as an adult—through the summer season of lobster and trawl fishing.

The father, forty when he married, is described by his son as an old man when he is born, lending mystery to their relationship. Within the son's memory-map of the family home, the father's bedroom represents his silent protest against the harsh outdoor labour of his life. Radio and reading lamp always on, it also appears as a masculine refuge from the feminine order of the household. The unmade bed he lies on top of, the fact that "he never seemed to sleep, only to doze" implies an intellectual restlessness which his simple, seasonal life will not satisfy. The mythically described "daughters of the house," after a brief apprenticeship at home, are led by reading their father's books into a similar restlessness. Tempted by the money and excitement offered by working in the American-owned Sea Food Restaurant, they allow themselves to be wooed, won and taken away by visiting American men. And the father, MacLeod implies, appears to sympathize with his daughters, for he himself is wooed by the outside world. After he takes a group of tourists out for a ride in the *Jenny Lynn,* he succumbs to their flattery and alcohol, and entertains them with Gaelic songs dating back three hundred years. The father who has moved uncomplainingly between his life in the boat, and the life of his books, acts also as a guileless prophet of the past, amazing and shaming his listening son.

Consequently, it is with a sense of guilty duty that the son, when he turns fifteen, steps into the role that his mother's family had envisioned for him. His father wants him to continue with his studies. But the mother here reinforces "manly behaviour" to the extent that she remains loyal to the traditional ways and gender roles of the village, including an obligation that is also the son's birthright.

MacLeod has stressed the importance form plays in shaping his fiction, saying "[v]ery often, when I write stories, I write the concluding paragraph about half-way through. And I find that this more or less helps me because I think of it as, 'This is the last thing I'm going to say to the reader, this will be the last statement that I'll make—the last paragraph or the last sentence'" ("Exiles" 151). Whether or not this was the case with **"The Boat,"** its final paragraph is almost a story—or a poem—in itself. The son has promised to "remain with [his father] as long as he lived and . . . [to] fish the sea together" (122). Yet this promise perhaps serves to shorten the father's life, as his disappearance from the boat in a November squall releases the son from his noble vow. Whether by active suicide or passive exhaustion, the father appears to have sacrificed himself. The story concludes with the son's terrifying encounter with the body of the father, consumed by the sea the mother still loves:

His hands were shredded ribbons as were his feet which had lost their boots to the suction of the sea, and his shoulders came apart in our hands when we tried to move him from the rocks. And the fish had eaten his testicles and the gulls had pecked out his eyes and the white-green stubble of his whiskers had continued to grow in death, like the grass on graves, upon the purple bloated mass that was his face. There was not much left of my father, physically, as he lay there with the brass chains on his wrists and the seaweed in his hair.

(125)

The father's body has been both transformed and absorbed, the consumption of eyes and testicles recalling the ways in which his life was consumed by others. The lyrical paralleling of "brass chains on his wrists" and "seaweed in his hair" suggests an unconscious garlanding. Numerous figures of paradoxical, inverted paternal authority are here suggested, such as Lear, garlanded with weeds and wild flowers on the heath, or the royal father in Ariel's song in *The Tempest* (I.ii. 398-406). But perhaps the most important word in the description is the adverb "physically," qualifying the father's disintegration. Unlike the pronouncement by Ben Max upon *his* father's absorption by the sea, that "He is dead and he is gone" (220), the narrator's statement here implies that his father remains more alive in death. Both fathers are imaged as absorbed by the sea; both may also be described as enacting a sacrifice. In **"The Boat,"** the sacrifice is made to free the son from an unwanted social, as well as gender, role; in "Stones," "sacrifice" may be exactly what David Max failed to achieve. However, by mentally walking with his lost men, "all through hell . . . to do them honour" (218), during the bitter remainder of his life, he has absolved his son of the necessity of enacting a rigid gender role that, tightened by the demands of war, left his father "pummelled and broken" (219).

As I have shown, Timothy Findley and Alistair MacLeod are in many ways very different writers. Frequently utilizing the image of the mirror, which reinforces the overarching theme of social life as theatre, Findley emphasizes the "performative" quality of gender relations. Yet his sensitivity to our ongoing social "theatre" is based upon an underlying awareness of our original, if estranged, participation in an elemental, sacred order, seen in the natural imagery deployed in "Stones." MacLeod, drawing his artistic authority from the timeless act of storytelling, reminds us of our human rootedness . . . in a landscape, a community, a body. MacLeod's recurring focus on hands—a focus which links the two stories—connects his men and women to the natural order. By doing so, he reclaims an ancient relationship that today is urged by many, from feminists, to native healers, to environmentalists. Each male author reflects gender from an angle unique to his interests and experiences, yet the men and women their equally moving, magical stories offer us are well worth reflecting on.[14]

Notes

1. Personal communication made to me by Prof. Stan Dragland of the University of Western Ontario. Ondaatje's selection of *two* MacLeod stories, "As Birds Bring Forth the Sun" and "The Closing Down of Summer" for his anthology of Canadian stories *From Ink Lake*—they hold the significant position, respectively, of "opening" and "closing" story—clearly demonstrates his admiration.

2. On this vexed question of "identity politics," Carol Roberts notes: "Findley refuses to be called a homosexual writer and opposes the labelling of any group in society, whether based on gender, colour, nationality, or sexual orientation. He told Peter Buitenhuis in 1988, 'I'm opposed to the ghettoization of homosexuals. "Gay" is a word I loathe and detest. As a homosexual, it offends me deeply and it offends me twice deeply when other homosexuals choose that as an appellation—as an "us against them" word. It's so confining. The point is to join the human race, as my mother would say'" (Roberts 105-106). However, in our 1993 interview, Findley used *both* terms freely. I will follow his more recent practice in this essay.

3. In this paper, I will be drawing on my published interviews with both writers: "'I Want Edge': An Interview with Timothy Findley" (abbreviated to "Edge," *Canadian Literature* 148 [Spring 1996] 115-129) and "Alistair MacLeod: 'The World is Full of Exiles'" (abbreviated to "Exiles," *Studies in Canadian Literature* 20:1 [1995]: 150-159).

4. I am using representation in the sense of being "an image brought clearly to mind," although it may also include "a dramatic production or performance" (*Collins English Dictionary* 1979).

5. The following abbreviations are being used to represent the two authors' story collection titles: *Birds* for *As Birds Bring Forth the Sun and Other Stories, Gift* for *The Lost Salt Gift of Blood* and *Dinner* for *Dinner Along the Amazon.*

6. As he told me in our interview, he is presently working on a novel about Highland soldiers at the siege of Quebec, entitled *No Great Mischief If They Fall* ("Exiles" 150).

7. This bias in favour of masculine speakers or protagonists has finally been challenged in the long short story/novella (a vexed distinction) "Island," which has recently been published, by Thistledown Press (Saskatoon, 1989), in a specialty edition. Written in the third person, the story narrates the life of the last of a line of lighthouse keepers, Agnes MacPhedran.

8. The use of a mirror as a trope for identity or self-knowledge, and the quest for that identity, is a familiar one; see M. H. Abrams's *The Mirror and the Lamp.* In Findley's case, however, the questioning is frequently specifically related to *gender* roles and identities; a questioning that is perhaps more commonly seen in the writing of women.

9. Cf. her discussion of *The Butterfly Plague,* where Barbara Gabriel makes the following observation about the "Orientalist" description of the sexually ambiguous Octavius: "Associated throughout the novel with the aesthetics of the Japanese, Octavius's coding as oriental ephebe is made clearer in the first version of the novel, where he suggests these 'small, delicate Japanese faces carved in ivory and teakwood—dark Buddhas and russet warriors—golden daughters of the Mikado' (Findley 1969, 33). Yet his framing also anticipates the Lucy figure of Findley's *Not Wanted on the Voyage,* who is even more explicitly drawn as the *Onna gata* of the Japanese Kabuki theatre, that ideal stylization of the feminine, which is always performed by a man" (233).

10. "Manliness during the [Second World] War encompassed the traditional attributes of courage, endurance, toughness and a lack of squeamishness when confronted by the dangers of a raging battle. . . . An additional fear was that a soldier might be thought of as less than a man and unsuitable for soldiering if he did not perform well" (Dubbert 231).

11. In *The Forty-Nine Percent Majority,* four stereotypical attitudes associated with masculinity are said to define "the male sex role": 1. No Sissy Stuff. 2. The Big Wheel. 3. The Sturdy Oak. 4. Give 'Em Hell! The attitude David Max has *most* failed to express, out of the four, is that of being "The Sturdy Oak" in a situation in which no amount of violence or aggression could have protected him.

12. Prof. Louis MacKendrick of University of Windsor has pointed out that "stones" is also male slang for the testicles, and associated traits like bravery or daring. Gender *does* affect reading, it seems.

13. Significantly, none of the characters is given a name in "The Boat." By deliberately omitting names, MacLeod underscores the universal quality of the story's conflicts.

14. I gratefully acknowledge the assistance of the Social Sciences and Humanities Research Council of Canada, who provided funding for this research in the form of a Post-Doctoral Fellowship.

Works Cited

Abrams, M. H. *The Mirror and the Lamp: Romantic Theory and the Critical Tradition.* London: Oxford UP, 1953.

Brod, Harry. "The Case for Men's Studies." *The Making of Masculinities: The New Men's Studies.* Ed. Harry Brod. Boston: Allen and Unwin, 1987. 39-62.

Butler, Judith. *Gender Trouble: Feminism and the Subversion of Identity.* New York; London: Routledge, 1990.

David, Deborah S., and Robert Brannon, eds. *The Forty-Nine Percent Majority: The Male Sex Role.* Reading, Mass.: Addison-Wesley, 1976.

Dubbert, Joe L. *A Man's Place: Masculinity in Transition.* Englewood Cliffs, N. J.: Prentice-Hall, 1979.

Findley, Timothy. *Dinner Along the Amazon.* Markham, Ont.: Penguin, 1984.

————. *Dust to Dust: Stories.* Toronto: HarperCollins, 1997.

————. *Headhunter.* Toronto: HarperCollins, 1993.

————. *Stones.* Markham, Ont.: Penguin, 1988.

————. *The Last of the Crazy People.* Markham, Ont.: Penguin, 1967.

Gabriel, Barbara. Rev. of *Dinner Along the Amazon,* by Timothy Findley. *Canadian Fiction Magazine* (1985): 87-89.

————. "Performing the Bent Text: Fascism and the Regulation of Sexualities in Timothy Findley's *The Butterfly Plague.*" *English Studies in Canada* 20:2 (June 1995): 227-250.

Kruk, Laurie. "Alistair MacLeod: 'The World Is Full of Exiles.'" *Studies in Canadian Literature* 20:1 (1995): 150-159.

————. "'I Want Edge': An Interview with Timothy Findley." *Canadian Literature* 148 (Spring 1996): 115-129.

Kulyk Keefer, Janice. *Under Eastern Eyes: A Critical Reading of Maritime Fiction.* Toronto: U of Toronto P, 1987.

MacLeod, Alistair. *As Birds Bring Forth the Sun and Other Stories.* Toronto: McClelland and Stewart, 1976.

————. *Island.* Saskatoon, Sask.: Thistledown, 1989.

————. *The Lost Salt Gift of Blood.* Toronto: McClelland and Stewart, 1976.

Murray, Don. "Seeing and Surviving in Timothy Findley's Short Stories." *Studies in Canadian Literature* 13:2 (1988): 200-222.

Nicholson, Colin. "Signatures of Time: Alistair MacLeod and His Short Stories." *Canadian Literature* 107 (Winter 1985): 90-101.

Ondaatje, Michael, ed. *From Ink Lake: Canadian Stories Selected by Michael Ondaatje.* Toronto: Lester and Orpen Dennys, 1990.

————. "The Time Around Scars." *There's a Trick with a Knife I'm Learning to Do: Poems 1963-78.* New York: Norton, 1979. 19.

Pleck, Joseph. *The Myth of Masculinity.* Cambridge, Mass.; London: MIT Press, 1981.

Pratt, Mary Louise. "The Short Story: The Long and the Short of It." *The New Short Story Theories.* Ed. Charles E. May. Athens, Ohio: Ohio UP, 1994. 91-113.

Roberts, Carol. *Timothy Findley: Stories from a Life.* Toronto: ECW Press, 1994.

York, Lorraine M. *Front Lines: The Fiction of Timothy Findley.* Toronto: ECW, 1991.

Jane Urquhart (essay date 2001)

SOURCE: Urquhart, Jane. "The Vision of Alistair MacLeod." In *Alistair MacLeod: Essays on His Works,* edited by Irene Guilford, pp. 36-42. Toronto: Guernica Editions Inc., 2001.

[*In the following essay, Urquhart discusses the themes and prose style of the collection* As Birds Bring Forth the Sun.]

Each time I read the stories in **As Birds Bring Forth the Sun and Other Stories,** I am struck by the largeness of Alistair MacLeod's main characters. This is not only a largeness of physical stature but also, and more important, a largeness of soul, a generosity of spirit. Reflective and emotional without being self-conscious, his men are intimate, not just with women and children, but with the rough beauty of their geography, the old sorrows of their family legends, the sanctity of work, the mating cycles and slaughter of their animals: in short, with life itself. Although the presence of the "anima" in general is strong and benign in these stories, they are really about the masculine spirit, its strengths and its vulnerabilities. Time and again we are put in mind of the old Celtic heroes, of Oisin arguing ethics with Saint Patrick or of Finn McCool mourning the loss of his beloved dog Bran. And yes, at the same time, we are brought into closer contact with the men who are part of our own world and who are our friends and our family.

Like many other Canadians of Irish or Scottish background, MacLeod himself was brought up in the midst of a tribal, Celtic family much given to remembering the past and measuring the present in terms of it. In such families the tales of previous generations are told spontaneously and repetitively as a means of establishing both geographically and emotionally where the family has been, where it is now, and where it is going. In MacLeod's fiction the "voice" of the oral tradition is never far away and in some cases is as close as the opening sentences of a story. "Once there was a family with a Highland name who lived beside the sea," we are told in **"As Birds Bring Forth the Sun."** "And the man had a dog of which he was very fond." In the space of a few short sentences we, the readers, have joined the family, have entered the rooms of their houses, and have gathered together to hear the remainder of the tale. By the time the story is finished, the identification is so complete that we feel the hair rising on the backs of our own necks and hear the claws of the *cù mòr glas,* the big grey dog, scratching at our own doors. Moreover, a brilliant transformation has taken place. By skillfully interweaving past and present, recurring images and sensual detail, MacLeod creates a complex tapestry out of a seemingly simple and much-told family tale.

MacLeod's stories have been called—albeit with great admiration—traditional, even conservative, by a literary world cluttered with theories and "isms." They are, however, in their portrayal of an ancestral past that continually affects the present and in their sense of deep yearning for forsaken landscapes, as fresh and complex as the present moment. We Canadians are, after all, a nation composed of people longing for a variety of abandoned homelands and the tribes that inhabited them, whether these be the distant homelands of our recent immigrants, the abducted homelands of our natives peoples, the rural homelands vacated by the post-war migrations to the cities, or the various European or Asian homelands left behind by our earliest settlers. All of us have been touched in some way or another by this loss of landscape and of kin, and all of us are moved by the sometimes unidentifiable sorrow that accompanies such a loss. We are also moved, however, by the comfort we are afforded when an artist of the calibre of Alistair MacLeod carries such sorrowful and penetrating themes towards us in his gentle and capable hands.

These themes are not only Canadian ones, of course, they are universal—migration having always been a part of the human experience—and in MacLeod's stories, as in all great art, the universal becomes clearer and sharper when we are brought into intimate contact with the particular. I am always impressed, for instance, by the tension MacLeod creates in this country of vast distances and brutal weather by the anticipated journey home. A young man wishing to return to Cape Breton for Christmas from a job on Ontario lake freighters is dependent on the Great Lakes freezing, on the one hand, and on the highways being free of crippling blizzards on the other. A boy relies on a golden dog to guide him towards his warm kitchen and away from his death on a partly frozen sea. A crew of shaft and development miners knows that if one of them dies underground, as is so often the case, his comrades will make the dangerous winter journey to ferry the broken body back to the

ancestral graveyard. A group of scattered relatives is aware that they will attempt to drive the long highways home to attend the funeral of a loved one despite the fear that the journey will be rendered impossible by winter, circumstance, change, or the fact that the return itself may be almost too painful to be borne. As the exiled narrator in **"Winter Dog"** laments:

> Should we be forced to drive tonight, it will be a long, tough journey into the wind and the driving snow which is pounding across Ontario and Quebec and New Brunswick and against the granite coast of Nova Scotia. Should we be drawn by death, we might well meet our own.

And in the middle of the long, multi-layered, and disturbing story entitled **"Vision,"** the grandfather quotes the poem reputed to have been uttered thirteen hundred years ago by Saint Colum Cille upon his exile from Ireland:

> There is a grey eye
> Looking back on Ireland,
> That will never see again
> Her men or her women.
>
> Early and late my lamentation,
> Alas, the journey I am making;
> This will be my secret bye-name
> "Back turned on Ireland."

MacLeod's stories are resonant with the lamentations of exiles, and strong within these lamentations is the desire to preserve that which was, and even that which is, against the heartbreaking ravages of time; to preserve, not necessarily with factual accuracy, but rather with something that one can only call, trite though it sounds, emotional truth. Like the fishermen in **"Vision"** and in the interests of this goal, MacLeod defines his boundaries by making use of "the actual river" when it suits his purposes or, when it does not, "an earlier imaginary river which [he] can no longer see." Hence a tale from the past sheds as much clear light on a character or a situation as a contemporary word or deed and, in the end, preservation is accomplished by establishing the timelessness of legend.

To explore timelessness, preservation and emotional truth is among the purest of literary intentions and, because of this, the seven stories in *As Birds Bring Forth the Sun and Other Stories* seem to move effortlessly from the author's heart to the page and then to leap back from the page into the heart of the reader. This is not to suggest that there is anything resembling a "stream-of-consciousness" approach in the writing. In fact, MacLeod is so "care-full," in the true sense of the word, that quite the opposite is true. All of the stories have been "tuned to perfection" both technically and emotionally and with such care that they burst into sensual life as we read. We see and feel the cold, wet nose of the beloved dog, the delicate form of an embryo calf exposed within the slaughtered body of its mother, captured lobsters moving awkwardly on the floor of a fishing boat. But, most important, we are witness to a deepness of caring that binds man to woman, father to son, man to animal, and humanity to kin and landscape.

The depth of caring that is examined in *As Birds Bring Forth the Sun and Other Stories* is as much active as it is reflective in its expression. All the protagonists are men whose lives are inexorably bound to the physical: the netting of fish, the husbandry of animals, the carving of rock from the bowels of the earth. Almost immediately the reader comes to trust the heavy, muscular presence of such men who in many cases carry the history of their physicality around with them in the form of wounds or scars. Even the entry of a family story concerning old sorrows into the mind and memory of a young man is described actively, physically, and compared to wounds and scars. "You know," says the narrator in **"Vision,"** "the future scar will be forever on the outside while the memory will remain, forever, deep within." By associating memory with blood and body, MacLeod suggests that emotion is biological and genetic and can never, therefore, be connected to that which is ephemeral or casual.

In the end it is this utter absence of the casual that gives MacLeod's stories their enormous power and raises them to the level of myth. **"Second Spring"** is much more than the tale of a Maritime boy "smitten with the calf club wish." It reaches back through time to all the sacred bulls and cows that have existed in Celtic, Greek, and Eastern myth. The *cù mòr glas,* which in the title story operates, for one family, as a sort of canine banshee, is equally Finn McCool's great dog Bran loping across the Giant's Causeway from Ireland to Scotland and Charon's dog Cerebus guarding the gates to the underworld and keeping watch over the River Styx. In **"Vision"** references to second sight, blindness, memory and a constant shifting of understanding call to mind the blindfolded figure of justice and cause us to examine the nature of perception itself.

One winter night I was fortunate enough to hear Alistair MacLeod read from new fiction. I took home that evening images of knives and forks being placed on a kitchen floor by children playing store, a nocturnal winter landscape viewed through glass, and, in the distance, one lantern going dark and another coming to rest far out on the ice. Like the old masters in W. H. Auden's "Musée des Beaux Arts," MacLeod is never wrong about suffering and understands "how it takes place / While someone else is eating or opening a window or just walking dully along;" or "how everything turns away / Quite leisurely from the disaster." But it is not the leisurely turning away that commands the focus of MacLeod's attention. Somewhere around the middle

of the piece he read that night, he described a dog whose passion leads him to a tragedy as final as the one that visited his lantern-carrying owners. Someone, a grandfather I believe, says, "It was in those dogs to care too much, to try too hard," meaning that this exaggerated trying and caring was bred into such dogs in Scotland over 150 years ago. Sitting in the audience, I was suddenly convinced that MacLeod was describing not only a certain breed of dog but all his characters, animal and human, and the writer himself, engaged in his craft.

That is what we want from our best authors: not merely that they care and try but that they care *too* much and try *too* hard, that the intensification of feeling and of meaning manifest itself in their hearts and in their work. We come away from the stories in *As Birds Bring Forth the Sun and Other Stories* with that desire completely satisfied, our own world view intensified, enlarged, and enriched. And we come away understanding more clearly "the twisted strands within the rope," the difficult, "tangled twisted strands of love."

Colin Nicholson (essay date 2001)

SOURCE: Nicholson, Colin. "Re-Sourcing the Historical Present: A Postmodern Turn in Alistair MacLeod's Short Fiction." In *Alistair MacLeod: Essays on His Works,* edited by Irene Guilford, pp. 95-111. Toronto: Guernica Editions Inc., 2001.

[*In the following essay, Nicholson describes the interplay between the mythic past and the historical present in MacLeod's stories.*]

As Clearance-driven emigration from historic Scotland's Highlands and Islands into Canada transmutes into economically pressurised out-migration from contemporary Nova Scotia, transitions from Gaelic to English regularly marked by the need to gloss surviving Celtic phrase and saying constitute textual equivalences for an ethnic displacement out of which Alistair MacLeod forges his fictions (Davidson 41). Imagined voices alert to the linguistic, cultural and ontological networks that construct their interactive environments also disclose, in the example of the university teacher who narrates **"The Boat,"** inescapable contexts for scripted speech-acts: "I say this now with a sense of wonder at my own stupidity in thinking I was somehow free" (MacLeod [*The Lost Salt Gift of Blood*] 12). In the same story, a father already fifty-six years old at the time of the narrator's conception, thematises genealogy as a compressed and formative temporality where the surviving son's autonomy is problematised as a permanent mediation through prior representation. For Cape Breton communities produced by "Ireland's discontent and Scotland's Highland Clearances and America's War of Independence" (3-4), writing in which the personal is always already historical articulates identity, conflict and relationship. Because MacLeod's narrators tell tales that unfold myths of origin connecting them with a Highland past, the collective unconscious of an imagined historical community significantly constructs present selfhood and landscape out of remembered event.

When the miner MacKinnon who narrates **"The Closing Down of Summer"** thinks of his mining gang as "Greek actors or mastodons of an earlier time. Soon to be replaced or else perhaps to be extinct" (225), he describes by implication Archibald, seventy-eight-year-old descendant of an immigrant who, in **"The Tuning of Perfection,"** has "come to be regarded as 'the last of the authentic old-time Gaelic singers' and is still remembered as 'the man from Skye'" (229). Since his discovery by folklorists twenty years before the opening of the story Archibald has been repeatedly interviewed and written about in articles typically entitled "Cape Breton Singer: The Last of His Kind" (234-5). The Scottish folklorist Calum MacLean, brother of the Gaelic poet Sorley MacLean, spent a lifetime gathering and recording the songs and stories of domestic Gaeldom and produced in 1958 a Highland memoir that has a bearing on Archibald's place in MacLeod's Nova Scotian fiction:

> A new culture had penetrated the Rough Bounds (*Garbhchriochan*) of the Gael, and was sweeping before it all traces, all memories of the past. Before it became too late, I had to recover something that would give our contemporaries and the generations of the future some picture of that past. My sources of information were not to be guide-books, travellers' accounts or the prejudiced writings of formal historians. They had to be living sources breathing the air and treading the soil of [the Highlands] . . . In the past, generation after generation of them returned slowly to the dust and left not one single record of what they ever knew or learned about their *patria*. Without doubt the transmission of knowledge had proceeded orally for centuries . . . The process was about to cease because the younger generation was no longer interested in its continuance. The culture of Hollywood has certainly influenced youth in [the Highlands] today.
>
> (99)

Archibald has already passed into print: his appearance on television would produce a further integration into North American contemporaneity but entail a loss of cultural and personal definition. The terms and tactics by which MacLeod's self-identifying subjects relate their constructed identities to imagined communities becomes a significant part of what these stories are about, including Archibald's unwillingness or inability to change his singing for performance in a medium organised by people who know little and care less about how Gaelic actually signifies.

So it seems fitting that **"As Birds Bring Forth the Sun"** should explore in more detail the continuance of Gaelic myth and legend into modern, metropolitan Canada. On his travels around Scotland, Calum MacLean talked to a shepherd in the mainland district of Morar, south of the Isle of Skye, who laughed on being asked if he were afraid of meeting the legendary Grey Dog of Meoble:

> The Grey Dog of Meoble makes its appearance when any one of the MacDonalds of Morar, the seed of Dugald, is about to die. There are several people still living who maintain that they have really seen the mysterious dog . . . Over two hundred years ago a MacDonald of Meoble had a grey hound. He had to leave to take part in some campaign and at the time of his leaving, the hound was in pup. When he left, the bitch swam out to an island on Loch Morar and there gave birth to a litter. Months went by and MacDonald returned home again, but his greyhound was missing. He happened to go to the very island where the bitch had her litter. The pups had now grown up into huge dogs, and not recognising their master, attacked and killed him before the mother appeared on the scene. Ever since that time the Grey Dog has appeared as an omen of death.
>
> (138)

Off the western coast of South Morar stands the Island of Eigg which Alistair MacLeod's ancestors left for Cape Breton in the 1790s, and by beginning the title story of his second volume with the simplicity of "Once there was a family with a Highland name who lived beside the sea," MacLeod makes regional identifications at once territorially specific and mythically resonant. "And the man had a dog of which he was very fond. She was large and grey, a sort of staghound from another time" (134). Scottish story surfaces in Canadian retelling which preserves original narrative circumstance as well as the Gaelic *cù mòr glas*—the big grey dog—and thereby harks back to ancestral orality as it becomes the "big grey dog of death" in metropolitan North American text. Each time a violent death occurs in the family, the *cù mòr glas a' bhàis* is ritually invoked. Since the first owner is our narrator's great-great-great-grandfather, the legend is experienced as a family affair. A genealogical fiction produces a fiction of genealogy that has been internalised as self-definition: "With succeeding generations it seemed the spectre had somehow come to stay and that it had become *ours*—not in the manner of an unwanted skeleton in the closet from a family's ancient past but more in the manner of something close to a genetic possibility" (144).

The story called **"Island"** concentrates themes of personal and linguistic survival and of cultural marginalisation in a study of isolation that also involves the origins and impulse of myth. Using patterns of repetition and return that characterise oral narratives, the writing rigorously presents experiential, climatic and environmental actuality, but filters them through the uncertain perception of a focalising protagonist. When Agnes first sees her lover from a kitchen window, "she wrapped the damp dish towel around her hand as if it were a bandage and then she as quickly unwrapped it again" (85), a gesture re-enacted in the different circumstances of the story's end. Repetition prevaricates temporality, interrogating sameness and difference across the passage of time. When altered circumstance challenges surviving modes of self-apprehension, **"Island"** blurs generic boundaries between realist study in the psychology of loneliness and ghost-story, exploring the effects of changed conditions on unchanging structures of belief and assumption. Desire and frustrated motherhood combine to shift realism towards fantasy; and imaginary relationships to determining conditions come to seem as fully determining as the material circumstances which stimulated the imaginings. When Agnes looks towards the mainland:

> Because of her failing sight and the nature of the weather she was not sure if she could really see it. But she had seen it in all weathers and over so many decades that the image of it was clearly in her mind, and whether she actually saw it or remembered it, now, seemed to make no difference.

(79)

As discriminations between what is imagined and what is perceived dissolve, specific threshold modifies into uncertain hinterland while ontology becomes identified through topography. "Gradually, with the passage of the years, the family's name as well as their identity became entwined with that of the island . . . As if in giving their name to the island they had received its own lonely designation in return" (83-4).

If writing has been considered from Plato onwards as constituting a threat to the living presences of authentic—spoken—language, in these Nova Scotian versions it structures the necessary here and now for marginalised subjectivities recording their own vanishing trace. MacLeod's speaking subjects are written as they insist that they are saying, so that writing in this usage does not "displace the *proper place* of the sentence, the unique time of the sentence pronounced *hic et nunc* by an irreplaceable subject," but becomes instead the only possible medium of that irreplaceable subject's utterance (Derrida 281). The return of the repressed is repeatedly figured as Gaelic phrase and cadence in acts of narration paradoxically concerned to preserve Celtic memory by transposing its signifying systems into English. What then happens is that the lucid constructions of single speaking subjects cannot be reduced to an order of univocal (single-voiced) truth. MacLeod's speakers make their language; but they do not make it in contexts of their own choosing: precursor forms constantly ghost concretely rendered self-presences whose evanescence is thereby indelibly inscribed. Reconstructing a Christmas memory for his eleven-year-old self on a small farm on the west coast of Cape Breton is not easy for the adult, self-aware narrator of **"To Everything There Is a Season"**:

> My family had been there for a long, long time and so it seemed had I. And much of that time seems like the proverbial yesterday. Yet when I speak on this Christmas 1977, I am not sure how much I speak with the voice of that time or how much in the voice of what I have since become. And I am not sure how many liberties I may be taking with the boy I think I was. For Christmas is a time of both past and present and often the two are imperfectly blended. As we step into its nowness we often look behind.

(111)

Where it is impossible to remember the consciousness of childhood, it will be correspondingly inconceivable that cultural ancestry can be present in easily recoverable forms. MacLeod himself is living on the edges in this writing, probing a margin of thought and being where past and present blend a seeming contrast between myths of origin and the rigours of continuity. "How many thousands of days," asks Benedict Anderson, "passed between infancy and early adulthood vanish beyond direct recall! . . . Out of this estrangement comes a conception of personhood, *identity* . . . which, because it cannot be 'remembered,' must be narrated." Awareness of being embedded in secular, serial time: "with all its implications of continuity, yet of 'forgetting' the experience of this continuity . . . engenders the need for a narrative of 'identity'" (204-205). Embedding in serial time involves writing and that in turn leads vocal spontaneity into scripted record. The miner MacKinnon, while repeatedly emphasising speech and its difficulties—"It is difficult to explain . . ." (215); "We will not have much to say . . ." (219); "I would like to tell . . ." (219)—is unable to enter "deeply enough" into the significations of the Zulu dancing he witnessed in Africa. This narrator feels trapped in the prison-house of a language he deploys expertly to communicate his feelings. His vivid self-representation in English comes to haunt a narrative that is itself entombed: the reader is participating—as recurrently in these tales—in the singing silence of a generally suppressed confessional. MacKinnon's interior monologue is a mark both of isolation from his family and of his stoical attitude and stance towards a Gaeldom felt to be terminal in his immediate group. Underground, Gaelic is the preferred sound-world, but in this narration the submerged breaks surface to speak English with compelling fluency.

The different stories related in **"Vision"** endorse Walter Ong's suggestion that "in all the wonderful worlds that writing opens, the spoken word still resides and lives. Written texts all have to be related somehow, directly or indirectly, to the world of sound, the natural habitat of language, to yield their meanings . . . Writing can never dispense with orality." *Rhetorike,* "speech-art," originally referred to oral tactics and strategies, but became a product of writing when schematised in, for example, Aristotle's *Art of Rhetoric,* as an organised "art" or science. So from the beginning, it can be argued, writing did not reduce orality but enhanced it (Ong 8). But, typically, as MacLeod brings into focus the mode of production of story, the effect of story upon self, and the making of self through the making of story expose narrative identity as deferral. In these interactions ongoing self-construction competes with already constructed versions of self. As ways of seeing and saying shape ways of being, blindness and insight come into contention: memory, self-definition and cultural derivation constitute subjectivity as process, in which origin is always duplicitous. **"Vision"** blends memory into continuity, speech into writing and story into creed, where our narrator's hold on the remembered story and on the circumstances of that remembering is as powerful as but no more powerful than the story's hold upon him. It is, moreover, not one story but several, so that univocality generates the plurality which makes single voices possible. This speaker is as much produced by other narratives as he is a producer of his own and these tensions are represented as physical pain in a collision between memory, cognition and imagined story. MacLeod's text weaves its patterns of repetition in ways that both sustain and entrap, and Walter Benjamin's reminder to us that *textum* originally signified web is relevant: "For an experienced event is finite—at any rate, confined to one area of experience; a remembered event is infinite, because it is only a key to everything that happened before it and after it" (202). Shifting configurations of space, time and selfhood involve the reader in unfixed boundaries between storied memory and myth, and between legend, history and genealogy, so that what we think we know at any given moment is subject to slippage. Reference is made to "a quoted story from the time" being recalled (145), and we are regaled by a story of uncertain provenance and insecure definition told by our narrator's friend Kenneth Mac-Allester when they were schoolboys, about his grandmother's distant ancestor from Scotland, a man with second sight (in the Gaelic given here *Da Shealladh*); a telling that combines narrative indeterminacy with compelling detail of recall. Existing in more than one version, the legendary protagonist in this embedded tale is himself uncertainly identified, being called either MacKenzie or Munro (though "his first name was Kenneth"), who could see spatially distant synchronic events as well as those of the future by looking through a hole in a magical white stone. Prophetic in the particular sense that it prescribes something that will subsequently happen to the teller of this tale, the eye that this legendary prophet placed to the stone for his visions "was *cam* or blind in the sense of ordinary sight." In the story as told between the two boys walking home from school, murderous violence also produces a prophecy concerning the end of a family-line that would come about "when there was a deaf-and-dumb father who would outlive his four sons" (148). The two boys arrive

home from school still talking about this story and Kenneth's mother then produces Walter Scott's version of the tale, to which our remembering narrator "did not pay much attention" although he can remember and quote lines which refer to the father and his four doomed sons:

> Thy sons rose around thee in light and in love
> All a father could hope, all a friend could approve;
> What 'vails it the tale of thy sorrows to tell?
> In the springtime of youth and of promise they fell!
>
> (Scott 647-8)

Attention to the source of these lines helps to focus some of the ways in which **"Vision"** prevaricates self-definition with myths of derivation.

Walter Scott's poem, "Farewell to Mackenzie, High Chief of Kintail" begins: "Farewell to Mackenneth, great Earl of the North," suggesting a link with the name of our remembering narrator's story-telling friend. Already written in 1810, the poem is dated 1815 and is described as being "From the Gaelic" and composed, as a prefatory note explains: "by the Family Bard upon the departure of the Earl of Seaforth, who was obliged to take refuge in Spain, after an unsuccessful effort at insurrection in favour of the Stuart family, in the year 1718." Scott's knowledge of Gaelic was tenuous at best, so the status of his translations—which he described as "Saxonising"—is not easily determinable (Grierson 398-9). But when the historical Francis Humberston Mackenzie died in 1815, having outlived four sons of high promise, his title died with him and Scott was prompted to write an additional six stanzas called an "Imitation of the Preceding Song" and publish the ten stanzas together. It is from these added lines that the MacLeod story-within-a-story quotes. The evidence suggests that Mackenzie lost his hearing at the age of twelve and he died, Scott records in a letter, with "all his fine faculties lost in paralytic imbecility" (Lockhart 18-19). Scott alludes to a prophecy dating from the time of Charles II according to which in the days of a deaf and dumb Caberfae (Gaelic name for the chief of the Mackenzie clan) the male line would come to an end. Whatever intertextual relationships we think we detect, we see through a glass darkly: Gaelic inscription commemorating failed political insurrection and consequent exile shifts almost one hundred years later into Scott's verses elegising the demise of a family's claim to clan leadership. As quoted in MacLeod's text, the tale is embellished with suspicions of sexual intrigue, second-sight prophecies and catastrophic revenge, which do not figure in earlier versions. Fact transmutes to fantasy in transitions from song to script, and fictions from time past and another country shape fictions closer to the present of this Nova Scotian immigrant community. We are returned to the now of the telling of the first remembered story by our narrator's father as he waits with his remembering son to unload their lobster catch at the end of the fishing season.

The remembered story begins with repeated concern about whether Canna Point can actually be seen at the moment of telling. In one of the tale's most persistent gestures, visibility and perception are at a premium. Named after the Hebridean island of Canna, "the green island" where most of its original settlers were born (149), it is also the birthplace of our narrator's grandmother. So memory, genealogy and story combine to produce contending senses of blindness and insight, of different locales, of continuity and discontinuity, of belonging and separation, of rootedness and exile over time and in specified space. But any grounding sense of place is destabilised in other ways: whereas an island called Canna is situated off the western coast of Scotland, there is no corresponding Canna Point in Nova Scotia—it is a fictional *topos* contributing to the blurring of boundaries between actually existing topography and the realia of fiction. Time also seems repeatedly to be dissolving in this text, from "that long-ago time" at the end of one paragraph to "about this time of year" at beginning of the next and then to the present registration of "by that time" and the discovery of letters "from another distant time" followed by the past of "at that time" in the paragraph which follows (149-50). The remembered story then fissures—or seems to fissure—to allow space for a digression about Syrian and Lebanese peddlers "in the early years of the century" who would act as message carriers between isolated communities, prefiguring just such an act of communication later in the remembered story. When story prefigures story, both time and space become fluid and metaleptically transferable. Introducing legend and superstition about the Irish figure Columba cross-fertilises myth with a supposed initiating encounter between Celtic Christianity and Gaeldom in the Scottish Highlands; and in **"Vision"** belief departs from evidence, and faith joins hands with fantasy to produce again a process of fleeting metalepsis, at once serial, circular and overlapping. Legend encrusting around Columba offers a bewildering variety of possibilities from which **"Vision"** selects and constructs its particular preferences; thereby bringing into question the status of event of record in relation to the inventive power of recording narrative. The grandfather's story to two children on the fictional locale of Canna Point includes English language translations of verses from an anonymous twelfth-century Irish poem whose words are put into the mouth of a Columba reflecting upon his banishment:

> There is a grey eye
> Looking back on Ireland,
> That will never see again
> Her men or her women.
>
> Early and late my lamentation,
> Alas, the journey I am making;
> This will be my secret bye-name
> "Back turned on Ireland."

(162)

Again exile's desiring gaze and again the impossibility of actual return. We are in realms where Celtic twilight stretches back to thickest fog and where a maze of more or less improbable legends composes a scripted territory where fairy-tale and faith intersect. The possible battle in which Columba may have fought and to which the grandfather in **"Vision"** refers, has been read as representing strife between Christian and Druid and, deriving as they do from an era when anything was conceivable if it came dressed in the language of the miraculous, the interpretative possibilities of these remembered episodes and events begin to appear limitless. But in the tissue of visions, prophecies and predictions encountered in the early stages of developing Celtic belief-systems relating to Columba and a Christianising drift from Ireland to Scotland, the attribution to him of *Da Shealladh,* the second sight, and the claim that he, too, "used a stone to 'see' his visions" (161), is seemingly the invention of the story-telling grandfather in MacLeod's tale: an encryption of myth as accretions of memory and circlings of narrative that interpellates the reader as participant observer in processes of fictionalisation where language enshrines event in preferred forms, writing embalms memory and the text traces myth in the making. The survival of myth as potent repository for individual and ethnic identity and continuity is rehearsed when the listening children ask their story-telling grandfather whether he knew Columba: "sometimes I feel I know him and I think I see him as well" (162). We begin to understand Michel Foucault's impatience with the construing faith of those who wish for a secret origin beyond any apparent beginning: "so secret and fundamental that it can never be quite grasped in itself. Thus one is led inevitably, through the naiveté of chronologies, towards an ever-receding point that is never itself present in any history; this point is merely is its own void" (25). If the coming of Columba to what is now known as Scotland signifies an extended historical moment of the grafting of Christian sign and ritual onto pagan precedent, in the grandfather's reference to the Scottish diaspora when inhabitants of "the green isle" were scattered "all over the world," we read subsequent survivals of related structures of self-perception: "But some of us are here. That is why this place is called Canna and we carry certain things within us" (163). "Here" is a fictional inscription and no equivalencies are easy in this writing.

"Vision" allegorises cultural derivation. As time passes and memory is activated for the two boys now returned to their home in Kintail (also a real Scottish place fictively transposed to Cape Breton): "the details blended in with their own experience . . . they could see the fire . . . sometimes they imagined her . . . they heard her call in their imagination and in their dreams." These dreams then become a shared experience in which they hear the blind woman calling "*Co a Th'ann? . . . Who's there?*" And one night they dreamed they heard themselves answer. "*Se mi-fhin*" they heard themselves say with one voice. "It is myself" (167): dream-state self-identifications constitute self-definition. **"Vision"** is similarly produced on the page as a text our remembering narrator half creates and half receives: "This, I guess, is my retelling of the story told by the young man of Canna to my father and his brother at a time when they were young and on the verge of war . . . The story was told in Gaelic, and as the people say, 'It is not the same in English,' although the images are true" (172). And when we are subsequently told that the grandfather from Canna, *Mac an Amharuis,* the son of uncertainty, died aged more than one hundred, unable to recognise, either by sight or sound, any of the people around him, we glide back intertextually to Walter Scott's Chief of Kintail dying in not dissimilar circumstances, though **"Vision"** does not disclose this information on its own narrative surfaces. Fiction articulates with fiction, narrative copulates with memory, legend coalesces with genealogy:

> When I began this story I was recounting the story which my father told to me as he faced the green hills of Canna on the last day of the lobster season a long time ago. But when I look on it now I realise that all of it did not come from him, exactly as I have told it, on that day.
>
> (173)

"Vision" is a supple enactment in fiction of the overlapping and ultimately inseparable procedures of recall by which history encrusts into legend, legend shades into myth and remembered story imbricates speaking selves; origins retreat into different tellings, and subjectivity derives from hybridising intertexts: "This has been the telling of a story about a story but like most stories it has spun off into others and relied on others and perhaps no story ever really stands alone" (177). "To tell a story," Alessandro Portelli points out, "is to take arms against the threat of time . . . the telling of a story preserves the teller from oblivion . . . Time is one of the essential things stories are about" (Tonkin 3). As MacLeod's narrators talk of a past, they reveal a shaped and shaping continuity that figures ontological entrapment for speakers who are as much shaped as shaping because the first-person narratives they utter are intertextual derivations from prior story.

Works Cited

Anderson, Benedict. *Imagined Communities: Reflections on the Origin and Spread of Nationalism.* London: Verso, rev. ed., 1991.

Benjamin, Walter. "The Image of Proust." *Illuminations: Essays and Reflections.* Trans. Harry Zohn. New York: 1968.

Davidson, Arnold. "As Birds Bring Forth the Story: The Elusive Art of Alistair MacLeod." *Canadian Literature* 119 (Winter, 1988).

Derrida, Jacques. *Of Grammatology* (1967). Trans. Gayatri Chakravorty Spivak. Baltimore: Johns Hopkins University Press, 1976.

Grierson, H. J. C., ed. *Letters of Sir Walter Scott.* Vol. 2: 1808-11. London: 1932.

Foucault, Michel. *The Archaeology of Knowledge.* London: 1972.

Lockhart, J. G. *Life of Sir Walter Scott.* Vol v. Edinburgh: 1839.

MacLean, Calum I. *The Highlands.* Edinburgh: 1990.

MacLeod, Alistair. *The Lost Salt Gift of Blood: Collected Stories.* London: 1991.

Ong, Walter J. *Orality and Literacy: The Technologizing of the Word.* London: 1982.

Scott, Sir Walter. *Poetical Works.* Edinburgh: 1849.

Tonkin, Elizabeth. *Narrating Our Pasts: The Social Construction of Oral History.* Cambridge: 1992.

Jim Hannan (review date winter 2002)

SOURCE: Hannan, Jim. Review of *Island: The Complete Stories,* by Alistair MacLeod. *World Literature Today* 76, no. 1 (winter 2002): 147-48.

[*In the following review, Hannan praises the subtle prose of* Island, *emphasizing MacLeod's compassionate rendering of his characters.*]

Some sense of the precise restraint Alistair MacLeod practices in his fiction can be gleaned from the title of this splendid collection [*Island*] and from the fact that the sixteen stories comprising his complete short fiction have been published over the course of thirty years. Set primarily in Cape Breton, Nova Scotia, these stories address the islands people inhabit as well as the often hauntingly lonesome lives people lead even amid tight-knit families and small communities. The stories draw continuously upon oral history and exhibit an unostentatious gift of storytelling, but they also dwell frequently upon isolation, independence, and eloquent silences that testify to the difficulty of telling: "I have said farewells to our children . . . and wept outwardly and inwardly for all I have not said or done and for my own clumsy failure at communication." MacLeod consistently finds the delicate but powerful balance between the volubility of the storyteller and the silences of the reticent. In a quiet, unassuming way, these stories leave the reader feeling like the narrator who remembers when he first really hears a story, when it "more or less became *mine* . . . went into me in such a way that I knew it would not leave again."

MacLeod peoples his stories with miners, farmers, fishermen, with people who labor in what he elsewhere calls the "killing professions," where bodies are injured and lives lost in sudden yet expected accidents. Many of the stories recall childhood experiences or family tales, but MacLeod minimizes nostalgia and idealization with his clear-sighted, pragmatic sensibility and a prose style simultaneously steady, earthy, and poetic. In this collection there are stories about a boy whose dog saves him in a fierce storm; about a young man whose imminent death hastens his grandmother's demise; about a man's refusal to sing the old Gaelic songs in an inauthentic, commercial form. MacLeod's genius transcends the immediate subject matter of his stories to ruminate upon love, desire, despair, doubt, solitude, grief. He evinces throughout an overriding compassion for his characters, for their way of life, for the animals with which they live and die, and for—I can't help but think—his readers, who profit from his steadiness, his eye for the compelling amid the ordinary, his capacious understanding and acceptance of the multitude of human emotions, motives, failures, and achievements.

MacLeod's quiet, careful prose, his ethical sensibility, and his generous compassion account for only part of the effect of his stories, because they are also marked by a constant violence, a violence of passion, of dangerous occupations, of the brute desire of animals to mate, of the elements, and of history. Taken in its multiplicity and repetition, this becomes an almost quotidian violence, resolutely not sensational or exploitative, but rather a constant in lives that seldom submit to the control of individuals. A miner describes his work as "the beauty of motion of the edge of violence, which by its very nature can never long endure" but which constantly recurs. Death is a regular occurrence in these stories, as children, parents, and lovers succumb to a life tempered by harsh weather, arduous and dangerous labor, remoteness, and drunkenness. Neither sentimental nor ideological, MacLeod pays homage to the laboring body, damaged, sometimes badly mutilated, but resolute in its capacities and accomplishments.

"What is the significance of ancestral islands, long left and never seen?" one of MacLeod's narrators wonders. This question lies behind these stories, behind these characters who live in a new world haunted by the family names, accents, place names, songs, anecdotes, and lingering Gaelic that evoke their ancestral Scotland. While MacLeod narrates a world strongly demarcated by these inherited characteristics, he wisely and compellingly speaks to readers far removed from Cape Breton with his memorable and strikingly humane stories.

Laurent Lepaludier (essay date spring 2002)

SOURCE: Lepaludier, Laurent. "The Everyday in 'The Closing Down of Summer' by Alistair MacLeod." *Journal of the Short Story in English*, no. 38 (spring 2002): 39-55.

[*In the following essay, Lepaludier examines the philosophical, literary, and aesthetic implications of the quotidian in "The Closing Down of Summer."*]

"To every thing there is a season, and a time to every purpose under heaven"

(Ecclesiastes, III, 1)

Studying the theme and poetics of the everyday in Alistair MacLeod's stories is particularly appropriate because they are often set in the Cape Breton area in Nova Scotia and describe the life of its inhabitants. As Elizabeth Lowry points out, Alistair MacLeod is "an astute observer of a very specific local setting (. . .); of its landscape and industry, its closed communities, quotidian tragedies and domestic disappointments."[1] The everyday is usually connected with the idea of stability in terms of setting—the home, the workplace or the usual haunts. A familiar setting may find a corresponding structure in time—the repetitive and iterative modes expressed in semantic, verbal, adverbial or adjectival ways. In drawing a picture of how a group of Canadian miners spend their holidays in their native place on the west coast of Cape Breton, **"The Closing Down of Summer"** highlights unchanging traditions and portrays social habits. Yet this short story conveys a sense of change, notably through its title which suggests a passage to another season. A study of the poetics of the quotidian and of its significance is bound to tackle the question of the representation of time but also the theme of the changeable and the unchangeable, the particular and the universal, to try and interpret the philosophical, symbolic or aesthetic implications of the story. The narrative constructs the everyday of a community as dual, as this essay will first show. If duality suggests potential changes, it is confirmed by a paradoxical impression that the quotidian works as a form of transience rather than one of stability. Whether the everyday can be transcended is the last question addressed in this study.

Constructing the Everyday

The quotidian is obviously a matter of time. In this story, what occurs every day or just about every day is not mainly expressed in the preterite—only a section is—but in the present tense. The use of the present strikes the reader because it is unusual in narratives and because it is regularly used throughout the story: "Here on this beach, on Cape Breton's west coast, there are no tourists." (7)[2] This statement presenting a fact—the specific assertive value of the present tense—also suggests in the context an unchanging characteristic of the place which seems to be taken from a documentary—the generic value of the present tense establishing a characteristic or a usual fact[3]. Other statements describe the scenery and the miners' attitude in the present tense too, bringing together an unchangeable setting and an attitude shown as a regular and unchanging habit: "The golden little beach upon which we lie curves in a crescent for approximately three-quarters of a mile and then terminates at either end in looming cliffs." (8) Also close to a present of description in the following instance, the telling of habits is expressed through iterative forms enhancing the recurrence of events:

At the south cliff a little brook ends its journey and plummets almost vertically some fifty feet into the sea. Sometimes after our swims or after lying too long in the sand we stand underneath its fall as we would a shower, feeling the fresh water fall upon our heads and necks and shoulders and running down our bodies' lengths to our feet which stand within the sea.

(9)

Different aspects of the present tense can also be found in consecutive sentences with the same blurring effect: indeed one is tempted not to make a difference between the descriptive assertion, the general characteristic and the daily routine of holidays:

Beside us on the beach lie [descriptive] the white Javex containers filled with alcohol. It is the purest of moonshine made by our relatives back in the hills and is impossible to buy [general]. It comes to us [habit] only as a gift or in exchange for long past favours (. . .) It is as clear as water [descriptive], and a teaspoonful of it when touched by a match will burn with the low blue flame of a votive candle until it is completely consumed, leaving the teaspoon hot and totally dry.

(10)

It is noteworthy as well that the modal "will" is here used to depict a present habit and not the future.

The use of the present tense does not correspond to the creation of a background to a singular event. In fact, it is sustained—apart from the section in the preterite—and together with the present perfect, shapes the structure of the story. Indeed, one can find it on page 12 ("Out on the flatness of the sea we can see the fishermen going about their work"), 17 ("In my own white house my wife does her declining wash among an increasingly bewildering battery of appliances."), 27 ("I must not think too much of death and loss, I tell myself repeatedly."), and in the very last pages. The iterative meaning of the present tense is often highlighted by adverbs of frequency or phrases such as "unaccountable times" (9). The story does not have a singulative value: it is meant to convey a sense of the usual, to depict the daily life of these miners on holiday. No singular event occurs to disturb the regular order of things.

The description of the setting also shapes the everyday, creating familiar landscapes or seascapes. Actually the quotidian is not that of the home with its domestic activities—the women's everyday in the story. It is that of the men's haunts outside. The beach, the brooks with their trout, the gardens, what they hear about tourists, highways, cars, motels and lobster traps are part of the men's daily life. The plural, often used, also contributes to the evocation of recurrent activities seen in their multiple and iterative aspects. Besides, taking showers under a fall displaces the domestic into outside natural surroundings. The "quiet graveyards that lie inland" are also their concern because the miners are the ones who take the dead back home.

The narrative voice which constructs familiar time and setting is first identified as collective. Six pages have to be read before finding the first person of the singular "I." The first person of the plural controls the narration almost from the very beginning: "We have been here for most of the summer." (7-8) Its use continues consistently over the next pages, alternating with the singular in most personal episodes until the very end. Even though the singular has an importance, it essentially illustrates the plural: what concerns the narrator—the loss of his brother, memories about his father, remarks about his wife—is typical, usual. It also appears that the narrator is the miners' authority, not an authoritarian leader at all, but someone who discreetly signals what the collective spirit has already decided, as the conditions of their departure show at the end of the short story. Obviously his function is essentially collective. His words "strike the note for (. . .) the translation of personal experience into motifs which have a collective significance."[4] His voice is thus much more the voice of a community of men than that of an individual, which contributes very much to the originality of the narrative, particularly in an enunciation that sounds both immediate and timeless because of its general value[5].

The collective self present in the narration reflects upon itself and the everyday of a community treated as a whole. If individual bodies are a matter of concern, it is because of their collective value, for they are "our bodies" (9). The narrative depicts them as though they were not separate: "We have arms that cannot raise above our heads" (9). Numbers matter more than individuals ("many of us", "few of us"). Singularity has been lost to the collective being of the community, which further enhances the importance of routines. The everyday defines the community.

The everyday in Cape Breton functions as a point of reference for another sort of daily life, away from home, the daily round of mining work. General remarks such as "we are perhaps the best crew of shaft and development miners in the world" (8) or "our crew is known as McKinnon" (26) evoke the mining trade. Occasionally—but seldom—is mining an object of iterative description in the present ("when we work we are often twelve hours in the shaft's bottom or in the development drifts and we do not often feel the sun." (9). It is the mining work that holds the community of men together in its daily round. The presence of everyday work also transpires in the sentence "we are all still in good shape after a summer of idleness" (8) The miners' bodies bear the marks of the other—and more lasting—quotidian: the skin, the hair, the scars, the limbs testify to this other daily activity:

Bodies that when free of mud and grime and the singed-hair smell of blasting powder are white almost to the colour of milk or ivory. Perhaps of leprosy. (. . .) Only the scars that all of us bear fail to respond to the healing power of the sun's heat. (. . .) Many of us carry one shoulder permanently lower than the other where we have been hit by rockfalls or the lop of the giant clam that swings down upon us in the narrow closeness of the shaft's bottom. And we have arms that we cannot raise above our heads and touches of arthritis in our backs and in our shoulders, magnified by the water that chills and falls upon us in our work. Few of us have all our fingers and some have lost either eyes or ears from falling tools or discharged blasting caps or flying stone or splintering timbers.

(9)

Bodies bridge the gap between the miners' two lives: "We are always intensely aware of our bodies" (10). The other link is memory, which functions in connection with bodies: "Lying now upon the beach we see the external scars on ourselves and on each other and are stirred to the memories of how they occurred." (10) The permanence of the marks of the daily routine of work impinges upon that of the summer holidays.

The miners' life at work surges when brought into contrast with the domestic routine of the narrator's wife:

> Her kitchen and her laundry room and her entire house gleam with porcelain and enamel and an ordered cleanliness that I can no longer comprehend. Little about me or about my work is clean or orderly and I am always mildly amazed to find the earnings of the violence and dirt in which I make my living converted into such meticulous brightness (. . .) For us most of our working lives are spent in rough, crude bunk-houses thrown up at the shaft-head's site. Our bunks are made of two-by-fours (. . .) Such rooms are like hospital wards (. . .).
>
> (17)

His working life is also contrasted with that of his children and comes in the form of a wish:

> I have always wished that my children could see me at work. That they might journey down with me in the dripping cage to the shaft's bottom or walk the eerie tunnels of the drifts that end in walls of staring stone. And that they might see how articulate we are in the accomplishment of what we do.
>
> (23)

Everyday work also permeates life at home, as the episode of the narrator's father's coffin falling down upon the bearers recalls the dangers of mining. The irony of the choice of such a trade does not escape the narrator's notice: "I was aware even then of the ultimate irony of my choice." He dropped out of the university because he wanted to "burst out", "to feel that I was breaking free" and chose precisely to "spend his working days in the most confined of places" (25).

If the miners' everyday life is dual, that of their families bears the mark of permanence. The adverb "permanently" typifies the life of the narrator's wife: "Now my wife seems to have gone permanently into a world of avocado appliances and household cleanliness and vi-

carious experiences provided by the interminable soap operas that fill her television afternoons." (18) The miners are estranged from the daily round of their families' activities. Their sons will live completely differently from them. The wives' and the sons' everyday, characterised by permanence and security, function as foils to the miners' dual and seasonal quotidian with its risky aspect. Indeed, in constructing the miners' everyday, the narrative conveys the transience of the quotidian.

THE TRANSIENCE OF THE EVERYDAY

Time seems to be hinging on the present moment. The title of the short story evokes an end suggesting the closing down of a shop, a factory, a club or the termination of an activity. A sense of impermanence is conveyed by the use of the progressive form as in "We are lying now in the ember of summer's heat and in the stillness of its time." (12) The instantaneous and temporary value[6] is reinforced by the temporal deictic "now" and the image of the ember expressing the end of summer. The present moment is felt as protracted and precarious. The present tense can also intimate the provisional character of the everyday:

> The sun no longer shines with the fierceness of the earlier day (. . .) Evening is approaching. The sand is whipped by the wind (. . .) We flinch and shake ourselves and reach for our protective shirts (. . .) In the sand we trace erratic designs and patterns with impatient toes.
>
> (27)

Transience also connotes the perspective on the quotidian implied in the use of the present perfect. If it brings together past and present[7] it also defines a time-bound and short-lived period: "All summer it has been very hot. So hot that the gardens have died and the hay has not grown and the surface wells have dried to dampened mud. The brooks that flow to the sea have dried to trickles." (7) This feeling of the passing of time, on being on the edge is sustained throughout the story with a very consistent use of the present perfect together with the present. This is reinforced by adverbs denoting mutability such as "still", "not yet", "as yet", etc.

The ephemeral nature of the everyday is thematically illustrated by the seasonal quality of the period described. The characteristics of the end of summer suggest the round of the seasons, creating a sense of expectancy even at the very beginning of the story: "We have been here for most of the summer. Surprised at the endurance and consistency of the heat. Waiting for it to break and perhaps to change the spell." (7-8). The slight changes in the weather signal the end of the holidays. The narration underlines the transitory character of the period: "Still we know that the weather cannot last much longer and in another week the tourists will be gone and the school will reopen and the pace of life will change." (8) Implied in the seasonal inscription of time is the cyclical nature of the everyday. There is indeed a time for everything, a time for work and a time for idleness—which is coming to an end. The miners' bodies themselves bear the mark of a long summer approaching its end as recalled by the permanence of the scars:

> All summer we have watched our bodies change their colour and seen our hair grow bleached and ever lighter. Only the scars that all of us bear fail to respond to the healing power of the sun's heat. They seem to stand out even more vividly now, long running pink welts that course down our inner forearms or jagged sawtooth ridges on the taut calves of our legs.
>
> (9)

The theme of transience seeps into the very description of the landscape with verbs suspiciously redolent of the end as in "The golden little beach (. . .) terminates at either end in looming cliffs." (8) Or again in "At the south cliff a little brook ends its journey" (9).

The quotidian holiday routine is beset by foreshadowing and memories of the other everyday, that of mining. The scars on the miners' bodies remind them of accidents: "memories of how they occurred" (10). Remembrances are conjured up in the form of analepses, either singulative—i.e. referring to one event—or iterative—i.e. referring to an habitual one (with the use of "would" and adverbs of frequency as in page 13). They bring the quotidian past of work into the present. But what awaits them in the near future is anticipated. It is sometimes implied in the use of the present tense characterising the miners' life, sometimes announced by the modal "will" as is their future employment in Africa: "In Africa it will be hot too, in spite of the coming rainy season, and on the veldt the heat will shimmer and the strange, fine-limbed animals will move across it in patterns older than memory." (16) The determinant "the" implies knowledge of a place familiar to the narrator. Because "will" sometimes announces the future and sometimes characterises the miners' activities, the gap between present and future tends to be reduced, suggesting the invasion of daily work into an idle everyday.

The everyday is fraught with intimations of death, past and future. Memories of death, the ultimate passage, surge from the familiar setting itself: "In the quiet graveyards that lie inland the dead are buried. Behind the small white wooden churches and beneath the monuments of polished black granite they take their silent rest." (12) The lexical field of death conjures up immediately the death of fellow miners: "Death in the shafts and in the drifts is always violent and very often the body is crushed or so blown apart that it cannot be reassembled properly for exposure in the coffin." (13)

Then through analepses, the narrator recalls the deaths of miners in Ontario's Elliot Lake and Bancroft uranium shafts "some twenty years ago." (13) There follows another flashback to the time when the narrator's younger brother died in Newfoundland "fifteen years ago." (14) The memory expands over two pages.

Such memories together with the unchanging everyday life of his wife remind the narrator of the fleeting nature of time: "It is difficult to explain to my wife such things and we have grown more and more apart with the passage of years." (17) The estrangement from his children encourages the same feeling:

> (. . .) And of how I lie awake at night aware of my own decline and of the diminishing of the men around me. For all of us know we will not last much longer and that it is unlikely that we will be replaced in the shaft's bottom by members of our own flesh and bone.
>
> (22)

The discrepancy between the songs his family sing and those he knows inevitably evokes death:

> There was always a feeling of mild panic on hearing whole dance floors of people singing aloud songs that had come and flourished since my departure and which I had never heard. As if I had been on a journey to the land of the dead.
>
> (19)

Even the Celtic revival, which should have brought together the older and the younger generation, is "a revival that is very different from our own" (20) and the narrator feels closer to the Zulus than to his own sons. A sense of an oncoming death permeates the narrator's comments: "I would like to tell my wife and children something of the way my years pass by on the route to my inevitable death." (22) In a comparison, he pictures himself as "a gladiator who fights away the impassiveness of water as it drips on darkened stone." (22) So it is not simply the idle quotidian of holidays that is at stake but his life. The narrator cannot help facing death in his risky work—and in the narrative itself:

> I must not think too much of death and loss, I tell myself repeatedly. For if I am to survive I must be as careful and calculating with my thoughts as I am with my tools when working so far beneath the earth's surface. I must always be careful of sloppiness and self-indulgence lest they cost me dearly in the end.
>
> (27)

In that context, the change in the weather takes on a symbolic dimension. The waves breaking upon the beach, the wind in their faces and the approaching evening lead to questions expressed as direct thought ambiguously evoking change and death: "Perhaps this is what we have been waiting for? Perhaps this is the end and the beginning?" (27) The wind and the men's

sigh are actually compared further on: "There is a collective sigh that is more sensed than really heard. Almost like distant wind in far-off trees." (28). The waves
stand as a symbol of death in the miners' eyes as they
destroy the shapes of their bodies in the sand:

> The waves are higher now and are breaking and crest-
> ing and rolling farther in. They have obliterated the
> outlines of our bodies in the sand and our footprints of
> brief moments before already have been washed away.
> There remains no evidence of what we have ever been.
> It is as if we have never lain, nor ever walked nor ever
> thought what thoughts we had. We leave no art or mark
> behind. The sea has washed its sand slate clean.
>
> (28)

If the signs of death are sometimes implicit in the oblit-
eration of the outlines of the bodies and of the foot-
prints, they are explicitly commented upon.

The visit to the churchyards, the farewells and the journey to Toronto in the cars take on a symbolic dimension. The miners, numbed with moonshine, undertake a
night journey to the land of the dead, ready to face their
doom and the narrator feels "like a figure in some me-
diaeval ballad who has completed his formal farewells
and goes now to meet his fatalistic future." (30) The
fifteenth century Gaelic song which surges like a "towering, breaking wave" (31) illustrates the theme of the
journey towards death:

> I wend to death, knight stith in stour;
> Through fight in field I won the flower;
> No fights me taught the death to quell-
> I wend to death, sooth I you tell.
>
> I wend to death, a king iwis;
> What helpes honour or worlde's bliss?
> Death is to man the final way-
> I wende to be clad in clay.
>
> (31)

The dirge which concludes the short story echoes in the
reader's ears and comments upon the symbolic value of
the title: the closing down of summer might be permanent and not just seasonal. The miners' everyday is
never seen as trivial for it is endowed with a transcendent dimension.

TRANSCENDING THE EVERYDAY

A miner's life is not devoid of a confrontation with the
customary. It might be a harsh life with its "twelve-
hour stand-up shifts" (10) or the rudimentary housing
conditions—the "rough bunkhouses" (17)—or the trite-
ness of community living with its "snoring and coughing or spitting into cans" (17). The narrator even confesses it might lack originality: "Perhaps we are
becoming our previous generation?" (18) Yet the everyday is transcended by work. Expressing his wish that

his children could see him at work, the narrator celebrates the miners' achievements as with a litany, repeating the same structural pattern at the beginning of
each sentence:

> That they might journey down with me in the dripping
> cage to the shaft's bottom or walk the eerie tunnels of
> the drifts that end in walls of staring stone. And that
> they might see how articulate we are in the accom-
> plishment of what we do. That they might appreciate
> the perfection of our drilling and the calculations of
> our angles and the measuring of our powder, and that
> they might understand that what we know through eye
> and ear and touch is of a finer quality than any infor-
> mation garnered by the most sophisticated of mining
> engineers with all their elaborate equipment.
>
> (23-4)

The isotopy of scientific precision illustrates and cor-
roborates that of perfection. Work is indeed magnified.
The "joy of breaking through" and the pride of "liberating resources" enhance the "glamour" of professionals
living a nomadic life that "sedentary" people cannot understand. The miners' work attains an aesthetic perfection that transcends the quotidian. The isotopy of perfection is here connected with that of beauty:

> (. . .) there is perhaps a certain eloquent beauty to be
> found in what we do. (. . .) It is perhaps akin to the
> violent motion of the huge professional athletes on the
> given days or nights of their many games. Men as huge
> and physical as we are; polished and eloquent in the
> propelling of their bodies towards their desired goals
> and in their relationships and dependencies on one an-
> other but often numb and silent before the microphone
> of their sedentary interviewers.
>
> (24)

The movements of the bodies transcend the utilitarian
to reach an elaborate rhetoric needing sophisticated interpreters. Ironically, only the miners themselves seem
to be in a capacity to appreciate their own performance
in dark and enclosed tunnels. The modalising adverb
"perhaps"—used twice—barely contains the temptation
of grandiloquence. For work magnifies the MacKinnons
and endows them with the qualities of mythic heroes.

The narration verges on myth-making, defamiliarising
the MacKinnons' quotidian working life and giving it a
magnified status. They form a sort of tribe of nomads,
only comparable perhaps to this other tribe of fishermen
with whom they exchange favours. In the tribe each individual finds his purpose in the collective being. The
personal pronoun "we" gathers and defines the community of miners. The narrator certainly feels closer to the
Zulus than to his own family. He takes interest in the
nomads of Africa. He is attentive to their bodies, their
shouts and their eyes and reads their feelings in their
dance. The bond between tribal men is implied in the
sentence: "Hoping to find there a message that is recog-

nisable only to primitive men." (20) Their bodies "magnified" (9) by the work and full of scars resemble the bodies of warriors. Their status is given epic proportions. Their working clothes make them "loom even larger than we are in actual life" (29). As primitive men, the MacKinnons form a tribe of warriors like their Scottish ancestors on the "battlefield of the world" (11), fighting "adversary" walls (25). They have their own rules and seem to be above the laws applying to ordinary citizens, speeding and drinking moonshine, "seldom fined or in odd instances allowed to pay our speeding fines upon the spot." (11) Adventurers and treasure-hunters, they can be found in Haiti, in Chile, in the Congo, in Bolivia, in Guatemala, in Mexico, in Jamaica or in South-Africa—the enumeration magnifies their importance. The narrator compares himself to "a gladiator who fights always the impassiveness of water" (22). He also feels like a figure in a medieval ballad "who goes to meet his fatalistic future" (30). In fact, the miners belong to a timeless, hence mythical world for they also feel "As if we are Greek actors or mastodons of an earlier time. Soon to be replaced or else perhaps extinct." (29). The significance of their lives must be appreciated in relation with the Ancient times, the Middle Ages or the timelessness of tribal consciousness. The phone calls announcing the deaths of miners lose their specificity in time. The comparison with the ballads and folktales underlines their unchanging truth and testifies to their timelessness:

> The darkness of the midnight phone call seems somehow to fade with the passing of time, or to change and be recreated like the ballads and folktales of the distant lonely past. Changing with each new telling as the tellers of the tales change, as they become different, older, more bitter or more serene. It is possible to hear descriptions of phone calls that you yourself have made some ten or fifteen years ago and to recognize very little about them except the undeniable kernel of truth that was at the centre of the messages they contained.
>
> (14-5)

The notion of telling as recreation participates in the mythical conception of time and rituals. The miners' working life seems to unroll in archaic time, free from the bonds of change or progress, or from the tyranny of the fleeting moment. Yet **"The Closing Down of Summer"** conveys the sense of a coming end. To exorcise the fleeting of time and share in the world of myth, the miners perform rituals of many kinds.

Drinking is treated as a community ritual, a sort of bond connecting the miners with their families back in the hills or with the fishermen who act out "their ancient rituals" (12) and with whom they trade alcohol for fish. Moonshine cannot be bought and, because of its symbolic value in the eyes of the community, it is essentially a sign of social belonging, part and parcel of the rituals of barter and mourning: "It comes to us as a

gift or in exchange for long-past favours: bringing home of bodies, small loans of forgotten dollars, kindnesses to now-dead grandmothers." (10) It burns with the purity and religious significance of "a votive candle" (10). The miners also carry it along with them in their cars on their way to Toronto as they leave, as a sort of viaticum or part of a rite of passage since the departure takes on a dimension of death. The postcards sent home, although they only "talk about the weather continents and oceans away" (21-2) participate in the ritual of exchange with the younger children: "postcards that have as their most exciting feature the exotic postage stamps sought after by the younger children for games of show and tell." (22).

The MacKinnons perform their "rituals of farewell" (29) at the end of their holidays. These rituals have the power to transform everyday life, to give it a holy dimension because they imply a belief in the invisible. Visiting the banks, checking out the dates on the insurance policies, gathering the working clothes, but also visiting the churches or standing by the graves constitute the different steps of a rite of passage which reveals the spiritual nature of the everyday. Indeed the narrator realises that "we have become strangely religious in ways that border close on superstition." (29) The various objects—Christian or pagan symbols—taken along keep the miners close to their ancestors and their past in a timeless and archaic dimension:

> We will take with us worn family rosaries and faded charms and loop ancestral medals and crosses of delicate worn fragility around our scar-lashed necks and about the thickness of our wrists, seemingly unaware of whatever irony they might project. This too seems but a further longing for the past, far removed from the "rational" approaches to religion that we sometimes encounter in our children.
>
> (29)

These sacred objects keep the miners in touch with their homeland and families in spite of the distances and differences. This is also true of the sprigs of spruce trees "wedged within the grillework of our cars or stuck beneath the headlight bulbs". (11) The sprigs bring together the everyday of summertime and the ordinary working days. What is collected by chance is deliberately given significance, made sacred and ritualised: "We will remove them and take them with us to Africa as mementoes or talismans or symbols of identity." (11) The rather unspecified value attached to the sprigs brings together the roots, the sacred, the homeland and the identity of the community. The significance of the quotidian must be found in this connection. This is expanded in a comparison with their ancestors:

> Much as our Highland ancestors, for centuries, fashioned crude badges of heather or of whortleberries to accompany them on the battlefields of the world. Per-

haps so that in the closeness of their work with death they might find nearness to their homes and an intensified realization of themselves.

(11)

The meaning of life is inseparable from death, expressed in the many rituals of death evoked or remembered in this short story.

Visits to churchyards, wakes, "youthful photographs" (13) or the yellow telegram "kept in vases and in Bibles and in dresser-drawers beneath white shirts", "[A] simple obituary of a formal kind" (15) both recall and exorcise death. Mourning joins in with a cult of the dead and of the ancestors. Memories of burials, such as that of the narrator's younger brother, link up with the conditions and dangers of mining in a compelling manner. The collapse of the grave, with the sliding earth and cracking wood, evokes the brother's death and a miner's typical professional risks:

> The next day at his funeral the rain continued to fall and in the grave that received him the unsteady timbers and the ground they held so temporarily back seemed but an extension of those that had caused his life to cease.
>
> (16)

It is in those rites of death that the everyday routine finds its profound significance as a struggle against death and the proud continuation of community traditions.

Daily life is also transcended through Gaelic music and folktales. Gaelic songs constitute a link with the past. The miners remember them from their early youth; they sing them on the beach, on their journey and at work. They differ from the songs of the modern hit-parades in that they are "so constant and unchanging and speak to us as the privately familiar." (19) Their presence in their childhood and youth and their continuity in mature age certainly accounts for their familiarity. The Gaelic language of their Scottish forebears had been instilled into them but came up in the isolation of the shafts:

> As if it had sunk in unconsciously through some osmotic process while I had been unwittingly growing up. Growing up without fully realizing the language of the conversations that swirled around me. Now in the shafts and on the beach we speak it almost constantly though it is no longer spoken in our homes.
>
> (19)

The "ballads and folktales of the distant lonely past" (14) come up as a point of comparison to account for the meaning of phone calls. Traditional music, when the bagpipe-player plays "Flowers of the Forest" causes "the hair to bristle on the backs of our necks" (14) awakening a sense of social identity and prompting

people to speak the Gaelic language in outbursts of mourning farewells. Contrary to an artificial summer-culture "Celtic Revival", the MacKinnons experience a descent into their remote past, the depths of their archaic nature and community spirit: "Singing songs in an archaic language as we too became more archaic and recognising the nods of acknowledgement and shouted responses as coming only from our friends and relatives." Although the songs are "for the most part local and private" and would lose "almost all of substance in translation", they reach for the universal as the narrator hopes, referring to a quotation from his daughter's university textbook. It is because the archaic or mythical constitutes the universal foundation of the particular, the local or the private. The Gaelic songs and folktales revive the past and the present in a timeless mythic transformation. In singing in Gaelic, the men's quasi-unconscious incantation reaches the depths of the collective unconscious in which they experience a sense of the familiar: "After a while they begin to sing in Gaelic, singing almost unconsciously the old words that are so worn and so familiar." (30) Time is thus ritually abolished and the everyday acquires another dimension since it shares in the traditional expression of a community. The quotidian mining work and the singing in Gaelic are but two ways of using traditional tools: "They seem to handle them [the old words] almost as they would familiar tools." (30)

In the fifteenth-century Gaelic song which concludes the short story, life—and the everyday—is seen as a journey towards death: "I wend to death". In the perspective of the short story, it is the miners' everyday which is endowed with epic overtones: *knight stith in stour / Through fight in field I won the flower / No fights me taught the death to quell*". The alliteration in [kl] in "*clad in clay*" draws attention on the final word "*clay*" as both the symbol of death and the familiar element of mining work, the word combining the metaphysical and the everyday.

It is the Cape Breton miners' quotidian life of labour, which haunts the whole story. The miners' summertime everyday only finds significance in relation to it. It shows the transience of life which can be transcended by everyday work itself, by myth-making and rituals. The purpose of the narrative is not simply to construct the everyday. It aims at giving a voice to often felt but unexpressed feelings of identity. Miners do not speak directly in this short story. Yet through an essentially collective voice ("we") mixed with a discreet personal one, with recourse to the experience of a community, their rituals, gestures, traditions, myths, songs or language, the narrative recreates folk culture—as "the ballads and the folktales of the lonely distant past" (14) would, not reproducing bygone legends but seeing the archaic in the contemporary. Thus Alistair MacLeod participates in what John Barth called "the literature of replenishment".

Notes

1. Elizabeth Lowry, "Little Red Boy", a review of MacLeod's *Island: Collected Stories* and *No Great Mischief, The London Review of Books,* 20 September 2001, 21.

2. All references to "The Closing Down of Summer" are taken from *As Birds Bring Forth the Sun & Other Stories,* Toronto: McClelland & Stewart, (1986), 1992, 7-31 and are given parenthetically in the text.

3. These notions are taken from Jean-Rémi Lapaire & Wilfrid Rotgé, *Linguistique et grammaire de l'anglais,* Toulouse: Presses Universitaires du Mirail, 1991, 393-404.

4. Elizabeth Lowry, *ibid.*

5. See Randolph Quirk & Sidney Greenbaum, *A University Grammar of English,* Harlow: Longman, 1973, 41.

6. Randolph Quirk & Sidney Greenbaum, *op. cit.,* 41.

7. See Jean-Rémi Lapaire & Wilfrid Rotgé, *op. cit.,* 457.

Works Cited

Lapaire, Jean-Rémi & Wilfrid Rotgé. *Linguistique et grammaire de l'anglais.* Toulouse: Presses Universitaires du Mirail, 1991, 393-404.

Lowry, Elizabeth. "Little Red Boy", a review of MacLeod's *Island: Collected Stories* and *No Great Mischief, The London Review of Books,* 20 September 2001, 21-2.

MacLeod, Alistair. "The Closing Down of Summer". *As Birds Bring Forth the Sun & Other Stories.* Toronto: McClelland & Stewart, (1986), 1992, 7-31.

Quirk, Randolph & Sidney Greenbaum. *A University Grammar of English.* Harlow: Longman, 1973.

Karl Miller (essay date spring 2002)

SOURCE: Miller, Karl. "From the Lone Shieling: Alistair MacLeod." *Raritan* 21, no. 4 (spring 2002): 149-61.

[In the following essay, Miller surveys the themes, characters, and historical background of MacLeod's works.]

"The Canadian Boat Song" was not written by a Canadian. It is a poem of exile, which expresses the sorrow of those who suffered as a result of the Clearances, of the expulsion of crofters from the Highlands and Islands of Scotland which began in the later eighteenth century and went on for a hundred years. But it is the work neither of a Canadian nor of a Scottish Highlander. It has been attributed to city-dwelling D. M. Moir, who was a contributor to *Blackwood's Magazine,* where the poem appeared in their serial symposium, the "Noctes Ambrosianae," in September 1829. It has also been attributed to John Gibson Lockhart, Walter Scott's biographer and a condemner of the Clearances.

The poem was introduced by the pseudonymous "Christopher North" (John Wilson) with the explanation that it had come to them together with a letter "from a friend of mine now in Upper Canada. He was rowed down the St. Lawrence lately, for several days on end, by a set of strapping fellows, all born in that country, and yet hardly one of whom could speak a word of any tongue but the Gaelic." The poem was described as a translation of one of their songs. As for the friend, he seems to have been the novelist John Galt, at that time a colonial ruler of Upper Canada, who was a friend of Moir's.

Some of the poem is beautiful, and has remained memorable:

> From the lone shieling of the misty island
> Mountains divide us, and the waste of seas—
> Yet still the blood is strong, the heart is Highland,
> And we in dreams behold the Hebrides.

A letter of Lockhart's, from Inverness, indicates that these lines may have been known to him in 1821: "The room is cold, my hand shakes, the pen is Highland."

Children had been banished, the poem says, "that a degenerate Lord might boast his sheep." In came these lucrative sheep. Out went his smallholders, his crofters. A Hebridean schoolteacher of mine in Edinburgh, Hector MacIver, a gifted and sophisticated man, was, I felt, so moved by the poem that he had to convey that he couldn't abide its outsider's romantic sentimentality, though he *could* abide, and would recite, Wordsworth's poem about the solitary Highland girl, singing and reaping in the harvest field. His ancestors had been ousted from Uig in the Hebrides, in the 1850s, by "one of the most humane of Highland landlords," he'd been told, who was just following the fashion for eviction. It seems that they took away with them in their boat the rafters of their house.

I am going on about the "plaintive numbers" of "The Canadian Boat Song" because the "old, unhappy, far-off things" which it commemorates have continued to matter very much, and because its history suggests that nationality is the mother of complication. As in my own case, that of someone who is Scottish and Irish and British. The Scots have recently devolved themselves, though they have yet to desist from electing people to the Westminster Parliament; and there are Scots who wish to separate from England and be their own nation—themselves alone. That would, in my view, be a wrong move rooted in a phobic tribalism, an atavistic and ahistorical tribalism, moreover. The Scots have never been one nation, but always at least two. Scotland, Wales, and England share an island, and have run as a not intractable union, *e pluribus,* for three hundred years. Ireland is another story.

The Highland North-West of Scotland, still residually Gaelic-speaking, has been culturally very different from the Lowlands, whether urban or rural. Hector had as much trouble speaking the Scots of Robert Burns as Noel Coward would have had. Highlanders were strange when I was young in Edinburgh, their Gaelic speech far stranger than French or German. They were "clannish." My family used to refer to my sophisticated teacher as "the cheuchter," an ugly word of Gaelic origin which meant a rustic or a hick. Since they were half-Irish, they might have seen themselves as not wholly alien to the Hebridean sector of the Gaeltacht—the Celtic common culture which had once spanned the Irish Sea. But they didn't. As I grew up, I grew to be interested in the Irish writers of the modern world, while repelled by the style or movement known as the Celtic Twilight.

This account is not offered as a way of staking a claim to write about the fiction of Alistair MacLeod, which I intensely admire, and in which "The Canadian Boat Song" has a place. Since I started to read him, his fiction has been widely welcomed in Canada and in America, and he is read in Britain too; and most of his readers in all three countries must feel no less implicated than I am in the tribal or national significance of what he does. He is a Canadian of Scottish-Gaelic-speaking stock whose forefathers settled with compatriots on Cape Breton Island, a northern region of Nova Scotia, early in the nineteenth century. His fiction tells how these compatriots have since sent sons and daughters down the Atlantic sea coast to the south, throughout the North American hinterlands, and as far afield as mines blasted from the bowels of South Africa.

His first story, **"The Boat,"** was published in 1968 in the *Massachusetts Review.* Having worked as a teacher, logger and miner, he took to teaching literature and creative writing at the University of Windsor, Ontario. He is the author of sixteen stories—which appeared in two collections later amalgamated and chronologically arranged in a third, *Island*—and of a novel, *No Great Mischief,* which appeared in 2000. His writings are concerned with the clannishness of the old country and of the new country to which it has been transferred, with a hostility toward city life, with the activities of boys, parents, the old, with the sexual lives of strapping fellows and old fellows, and of animals, with the ice that

surrounds his island and some small island offshore. The ice grips and relaxes. It joins and it sunders the two islands. It can be walked over, sleighed over. It is good at drowning you. A moving episode in the novel has parents and their boy crossing the ice at night, with lights. One single, stationary light is suddenly seen from the opposite shore.

The deaths described in this heart-shaking passage represent a pivotal point in the dynastic history evident in his fiction. The passage captures MacLeod's sense of a way of life wrung from hardship, expedient, danger, and disaster. His books are elemental and ancient. They go back to the world of Odysseus, to Homer's Ithaca. They tell you what his people have to do in order to survive and to bear with what they've got, how they catch fish, fight or sit drinking. And these people do all this without being made to seem simple or naive, or like specialists in survival.

The clan in the novel is a sept of the MacDonalds—as who should say, the MacLeods. I said to him, when I met him once, that I'd been reading an intriguing account of a nineteenth-century MacLeod, only to be told by him that there were lots of different MacLeods in the world; he may have thought I was some more than usually flitter-mouse publicist come to ingratiate myself, who needed to be made aware that a clan was a serious business. But then I knew that already from his books.

The narrator of the novel—the *ille bhig ruaidh,* or little red boy—is a survivor from the disaster of the drowning, together with his brother Calum, a key dynast and a drinker. In the course of a call home from a uranium mine on the Canadian Shield, the narrator talks to his Grandpa, a man of the senses, a comic foil to the other grandparent, known to the book in his austerity as Grandfather. Grandpa gives the narrator the customary admonitions on the subject of clan solidarity, fortified with a quotation from the "Boat Song," from "that poem your grandfather is always quoting: 'Yet still the blood is strong, the heart is Highland.' I hope you remember that." "Yes," replies the narrator, a man of few conversational words. "I remember that." Grandpa says what Robert the Bruce, the hammer of the English, said at the battle of Bannockburn in 1314, Scotland's most familiar date: "My hope is constant in thee, Clan Donald." Grandma comes on the line to teach some more lessons: "Blood is thicker than water, as you've heard us say." Yes, he has.

Kinship comes first. Duty is important, and is bound up with kinship. It is important to be stoical. The narrator of **"The Boat"** provides a portrait of his father, a fisherman opposed and disapproved of by his bitter wife. Eventually there's this: "And then there came into my heart a very great love for my father and I thought it was very much braver to spend a life doing what you really do not want rather than selfishly following forever your own dreams and inclinations." To drink is to care, runs a further suggestion—to care about family, and because of it.

That poem is mentioned again in another story, which speaks of the "stretches of mountain and water" that may lie between relatives and "those they love" ("loved ones" is a term that, formerly suspect, has gained a new currency in the era of terrorist attack). They lie between these Nova Scotian families and the shielings of their ancestors. Gaels love those they love, it can seem here, and the bardic poetry of the Celtic past is full of how much they hate their enemies. They are not ecumenical. They are not multicultural.

A sharp sense of this is felt in **"The Return,"** which recounts a family visit to a mining town on Cape Breton by an exogamous lawyer from Montreal, his rich wife, and his young son, who tells the story. As they change trains on the island, a blond youth is noticed singing-drunk, and is hurried past by the wife. They are then brought before the tribunal of their not very forbearing ancestors. The son's tall, white-haired granny, smelling of soap and water and hot rolls, casts up her own son's turning out of his alcoholic brother from his Montreal mansion. Her son defends himself: "If I were by myself he could have stayed forever." This is a forever comparatively free from dreams and inclinations; and there's a hint that he might prefer it to what he has—that he might prefer to care for his alcoholic brother. (Care for such a brother, for Calum, is the situation from which *No Great Mischief* unfolds.) Very softly, his mother rejoins:

> But it seems that we can only stay forever if we stay right here. As we have stayed to the seventh generation. Because in the end that is all there is—just staying. I have lost three children at birth but I've raised eight sons. I have one a lawyer and one a doctor who committed suicide, one who died in coal beneath the sea and one who is a drunkard and four who still work the coal like their father and those four are all that I have that stand by me. It is these four that carry their father now that he needs it, and it is these that carry the drunkard, that dug two days for Andrew's body and that have given me thirty grandchildren in my old age.

There's a "just staying forever" in this comma-less endlessness of "and"s. MacLeod can seem shy of commas.

Such is the granny's stand against the axiomatically bad outside world, against the daughter-in-law of the corporate lifestyle, to which her lost son the lawyer is literally wedded. MacLeod gives her very good tunes—very good, if at moments magniloquently biblical, condemnations and dirges. But it would be wrong to decide that the story lacks a sense of what is quenching and constraining in the grandmother's fanatical insistence.

In **"The Tuning of Perfection"** is a righteous old man, Archibald, a widower whose early loss bereaves him for life, whose house sits on a high hill overlooking the sea, on the site of his family's original settlement, and who is a singer of the old Gaelic songs as he believes they have always been sung. He and a coil of relations are invited to take part in a televised folk festival, whose earringed producer, one of the new men, wants their songs cut, in order to stave off boredom. Archibald removes the group from the festival. "He thought of the impossibility of trimming the songs and of changing them and he wondered why he seemed the only one in his group who harbored such concerns." The spot goes to a rival group led by the scarred and wily Carver.

The old man is now alone on his high place, sequestered in a fashion reminiscent of the no-surrender family of anti-statists, holed up in the American West, who lost a son to their besiegers not long ago. He hears a car and prepares to defend himself, measuring his distance in the kitchen from a poker, which he hefts as if it were an "ancient sword." His visitors are Carver and his mates, fresh from a car-park scrap, who want to make peace with the old man. Archibald is not mocked in the story, while seeming a little far-out. Hanging on to the old songs is seen as understandable, and more.

Where there's a clan, there's an enemy, and the enemy, in MacLeod's fiction, is the city, with its affluence, its television producers, its publicists, its no time for long songs, its intolerance of drunken relatives. The narrator of *No Great Mischief* (MacLeod's genius does not extend to his titles) embraces the guilty role of a society dentist who had once been down the mines and on Cape Breton's braes. The risk MacLeod has run, as a writer, is that of yielding to the paranoia of the tribe and the special pleading of the tribe, of the small tribe of kin and clan and the larger one of expatriate Gaeldom. It's a risk against which he guards himself.

His pictures of a collective and individual humanity are among the finest literary achievements of their time, a finer achievement than many currently famous, a relief from the novel of soliloquy which has been in favor, with its reluctance to dramatize and to get out of the author into other people. The lives he describes are more patient, but no narrower, than other lives. He is on their side, but doesn't portray a chosen people, or point to a political program. He knows that the days of a spoken Gaelic may be numbered, but his books bear witness to the survival of the Gaelic tradition: there are as many Gaelic writers as there were fifty years ago, and there are colleges devoted to Celtic studies—on the island of Skye, for instance—after the long years of proscription.

The patience of Highlanders, fierce fighters as they have been, has exposed them to exploitation, from the second Jacobite rebellion to the First World War. They fought for their enemies, for their Hanoverian victors, their exploiting chiefs, in regiments raised by local gentries. Few of them had much at stake in the Great War of 1914 (1314 may have been different), where once again it was no great mischief if they fell—which, as the novel explains, is what General Wolfe said of the Highlanders who stormed the Heights of Abraham for him against the French.

On both sides of the Atlantic, MacLeod's fiction might possibly be used to make the separatist or devolutionary case from which his fiction refrains. Perhaps there's a risk here too. Last summer, in Edinburgh, Gore Vidal was heard singing the praises of small nations, having shortly before been singing those of the Oklahoma bomber Timothy McVeigh—of the Clan or Klan McVeigh, one might add, with an eye on Walter Scott's gift of fiery crosses and other feudal customs to the American South. McVeigh's action was in some degree tribal, in some degree a secession, a declaration of independence. And it was a reminder that small nations have their tribal antecedents and characteristics, and that they have their faults. Guess what would have happened to its black population if the American South had managed to secede; guess what must be happening now in Belarus. There seems no likelihood of a Nova Scotia *libre,* of a tribal state there of the kind that continues to come about. Strikingly, there's not a word in these books about the politics of Canada: it's as if MacLeod's Highlanders have lived separate lives in that respect, for all their exposure to urban and foreign environments. Tribe, though, is mostly family in his fictions, and the conception of family to be found in them is some distance from the tribalism encountered among modern political parties, as the remains of an old story.

The enemy in MacLeod's fiction has a complex history, which begins with Bonny Prince Charlie and the Forty-Five rebellion, when some of the clans rose in support of a Stuart invasion of Hanoverian Britain, charged and looted their way down into England, turned back toward their glens, and suffered under "Butcher" Cumberland at the battle of Culloden, and under the persecution that ensued. The attempt to impose a divine-right-of-kings, foreign-faith despotism on a country largely averse to it had failed. MacLeod is not a Jacobite. His Charlie is not the "unfortunate Prince" of literature and legend. He is under no illusions about the leaders whom his Highlanders served in 1745, or thirteen years later, when they fought bravely for King George, under their old enemy, Wolfe.

The Clearances started to spread with the pacification of the Highlands after Culloden—a battle long ago, if you like, but the horror of this dispossession is at the present day an unexpired sentiment, if not a visceral emotion. The dispossession is everywhere in MacLeod's writings. His novel describes the arrival on Cape Breton of the forced-out founder of its expatriate dynasty.

A guide to this Fall from Eden was supplied in 1990 by David Craig with his excellent book, *On the Crofters' Trail,* where he plays the part of an Old Mortality, in search of the Clearance Highlanders and of their descendants in Scotland and in Canada. Alistair MacLeod is shown summering in Inverness County, Cape Breton, among family and friends, and off with the writer to the "demonic" Hiberno-Scottish fiddle music of a country dance. Craig spells out a memorial on a pile of shingle stones.

> PIONEER
> DONALD MACLEOD
> HIS WIFE
> JANET MACPHERSON
> APPLIED FOR
> AND GRANTED 1808-11
> A SECTION OF
> THIS THE GOOD EARTH
> TRADITION AND
> CULTURE ENRICHED
> THE LAND OF
> THEIR ADOPTION

Craig has a rare eye for northern landscape, for the wild place and the cultivated place, for every last sweet spot left behind by the cleared Highlanders. This is an essential skill, given his subject. "Stags were roaring from the slopes of Beinn Dubhain in the damson-dark October gloaming": the prose is richer than MacLeod's, and there may be those for whom the note of threnody and outrage recurs too often. But it's a book that embarrasses such objections.

Poor agricultural land, a rising population—economic historians have argued that the traditional Highland economy was doomed, and that innovation, "improvement," and dispersal had to happen. But there did not have to be the dispersal that took place. Chiefs became landlords and investors, and legally unprotected tenants were treated with widespread and prolonged brutality, which has been seen by many Scots as Holocaust-like. Clan values never recovered in Scotland. "The real chieftains were no more," wrote one observer in the last year of the nineteenth century; and clansmen had refused to join in the game of imitation chieftainship. The clans regrouped, and made a life in various new worlds, where the heart was Highland, where there was hardship, but where there was no lordship. Among the destinations for the country's unwanted at that time was Australia, whose government recently turned away a boatload of refugees from terror.

The story **"Vision"** (1986) gathers up MacLeod's main concerns. He is attached to an aesthetic in which one story gives rise to another; this is what stories are like, he believes. So **"Vision"** is three stories or more. And it has two Cannas: one a Scottish Western Isle, and one in Nova Scotia. At the start of the story a father points out the second of these places, with its green hills. "Yes," says his son. "I see it. There it is." At an earlier point two boys, brothers, one of them this father, have gone to their Canna to visit grandparents, who are hard to find. They are diverted to a certain bleak house:

> Framed in the doorway was a tall old woman clad in layers of clothing, even though it was summer, and wearing wire-framed glasses. On either side of her were two black dogs. They were like collies, though they had no white markings. . . . The boys would have run away but they were afraid that if they moved, the dogs would be upon them, so they stayed where they were as still as could be. The only sound was the tense growling of the dogs. "*Co a th'ann?*" she said in Gaelic. "Who's there?"

The boys leave this tall old woman, who is blind, and the next thing they experience is the sight of their grandfather masturbating in his barn. His wife is kind to the boys, frosty to the onanist. Gradually the lives of the three old people are unforgettably laid bare.

Their grandfather tells the boys about the original Canna, and about second-sighted Saint Columba, whose chapel was on the island, and who grieved for a departure from Ireland:

> Early and late my lamentation,
> Alas, the journey I am making;
> This will be my secret bye-name
> "Back turned on Ireland."

The old man proves to have been an illegitimate child who grew up to become a rider of stallions, and a stallion himself, the lover of the blind woman and of other women. He had been known as Mac an Amharuis, Son of Uncertainty. The boys learn this at a tribunal where they are seeking to enlist in the Great War. They enlist. One loses a leg. The other—the man on the boat who was later to point out the green hills of Canna—is blinded in the Second World War. The story ends with one of MacLeod's knockdown interclan fights in the Legion Hall frequented by veterans.

This is a story about sight and the loss of sight, a theme which seems related to a preoccupation with the power of sexual passion and with its dark outcomes. These include, in this case, the uncertainties of a dynastic succession. There may be an air of contrivance to the way in which the observant fisherman of the opening pages is only later discovered to be blind. A small difficulty, this—comparable, perhaps, as one of MacLeod's few possible aberrations, to the discovery by the family in the novel that their house has been set on fire. By one of the French Canadians with whom the MacDonalds are at feud? The arsonists are never identified, and the subject is dropped.

MacLeod likes to write about sexual activity. Even his old men are sexually unspent—a state, I notice, for which writers seldom have much time. Husbands and wives do it, and other people too. Animals do it. A cow moans and bawls her passion from the barn, till the day arrives when the farmer helps a bull's penis into her with his own large hand. Bulls advance snorting and drooling with lust. Eagle mates are tender and companionate. When the comic grandfather returned to Cape Breton in his youth, he used to get an erection at the very sight of the island. In these fictions is an *Amor vincit omnia* which is neither fanciful nor exhibitionist. It is all true. Passion is duly awarded its exhaustions and its dark and cursing outcomes.

The animals in the books are as clannish as the dynasties are, as loyal to their human beings as the human beings are to their kinsfolk, and, without being in the least anthropomorphized, as much of a living presence, almost every one of them an individual. The story of the mother dog who leaps on her old master to lick his face, and thereby excites her sons to tear his throat out, has great resonance. When, elsewhere, a lighthouse-keeper's daughter rises in the night to go to the neighboring shanties to make love for the one and only time with a distant relative, soon to die in a logging accident in Maine, we are told more about the body of the dog by her bed than we are about the man's. "The eyes of the dog seemed to glow in the dark and she felt the cold wetness of its nose when she extended her hand beyond the boundary of the bed. She could smell the wetness of its coat, and when she moved her hand across its head and down its neck the water filmed upon her palm." What goes on in the shanty is nevertheless perfectly in focus. She spends the rest of her life as a keeper of the light until the Government automates it. On one occasion she is taken sexually by some fisherman; no word of blame or indeed comment is expressed. Then she disappears from the world of her relatives.

Alistair MacLeod must be doing all right: slurs have started to appear. I have seen a letter in a newspaper reproaching him for a geographical error in the return visit to Scotland that occurs in his novel. He has also been complained of for producing an ambience of males: it seems clear to me that his tall old women are even more important to his fiction than his old men. One important woman, a widow of long standing, is dying on her farm at Rankin's Point, and is visited by a grandson, Calum, also dying, his blood "diseased." Her husband's blood is still remembered, as it stained the road to the farm, many years before. Her blood relations press her to enter a nursing home, but she wants to tough it out at Rankin's Point, until she is found dead on the same road by Calum, after a family reunion with jigs and reels, where the fiddle is played in the old way, but where the young ones have brought guitars. Here is a tribal intransigence, tracked by death, and encircled by later generations who haven't deserted her but in whom the Highland blood may no longer be as strong as it was once. The scene reminds me of a possibly Celtic dream I have had, in which an aunt of mine dies on her own in an ancient shieling, on a hill.

I am writing this in Brittany, where there's a place named Gael and an Inter-Celtic festival is advertised with a harp-hefting poster (I used to hate harps when I was a boy, not so much now). The Breton language is a form of Gaelic, and a million Bretons are said to speak it. In a nearby village, ten families each lost three or more sons in the war of 1914—another case of "no great mischief." Then, in the castled town of Josselin, I came across a pair of young women playing the flute and the accordion beside the church door, with a casket at their feet for francs. I was overcome with joy. Very good musicians they were, and they were very good musicians for hours on end, with no song heard more than once. Sarah and Rachel, Jewish perhaps, have the memories of Early Modern Scottish ballad reciters. The group is called by a Breton name, Kan Ha Distroy, and their songs are presented as Breton and as *tradition-elles*. They are, in fact, from all over the complicated Celtic diaspora: there were Scottish, Irish, and French Canadian songs that day, as well as French.

MacLeod's singers are not remote from these memorious young women. These women don't sound nostalgic. They sell tapes of their music, and may perhaps trim some of their songs. It may be that, unlike Archibald, they belong to the media. At the same time, they are enabling a civilization to survive, even if its old language is to cease to be a vernacular. Alistair MacLeod is doing this too. I hope he would see them as sisters.

FURTHER READING

Criticism

MacLeod, Alistair, and John DeMont. "'It's Like Being in Love': One of the World's Great Writers Reflects on His Art—and His Life." *Maclean's* 116, no. 12 (24 March 2003): 40.

> MacLeod discusses *No Great Mischief,* his work habits, and his teaching career.

Steinberg, Sybil S. Review of *Island: The Complete Stories,* by Alistair MacLeod. *Publishers Weekly* 247, no. 51 (18 December 2000): 54.

> Assesses the strengths of the setting, characters, and themes of *Island.*

Sutherland, Fraser. Review of *As Birds Bring Forth the Sun,* by Alistair MacLeod. *The Canadian Forum* 66, no. 761 (August/September 1986): 35-6.

> Discusses the mythical, rather than naturalistic, quality of *As Birds Bring Forth the Sun* with respect to the collection's style and themes.

Sutherland, John. "Out with the Tide." *New York Times Book Review* (18 February 2001): section 7, p. 6.

> Evaluates the strengths of *Island.*

Towey, Cathleen A. Review of *Island: The Complete Stories,* by Alistair MacLeod. *Library Journal* 126, no. 1 (January 2001): 159-60.

> Commends the characters and language of *Island.*

Young, Alan R. "Varieties of Nova Scotian Experience: Thomas Raddall and Alistair MacLeod." *Dalhousie Review* 67, nos. 2/3 (summer/fall 1987): 340-44.

> Provides an overview of *As Birds Bring Forth the Sun,* demonstrating the significance of the collection's setting and exile theme.

Additional coverage of MacLeod's life and career is contained in the following sources published by Thomson Gale: *Contemporary Authors,* **Vol. 123;** *Contemporary Canadian Authors,* **Vol. 1;** *Contemporary Literary Criticism,* **Vols. 56, 165;** *Dictionary of Literary Biography,* **Vol. 60;** *DISCovering Authors: Canadian Edition; DISCovering Authors Modules: Most-studied Authors; Literature Resource Center; Major 20th-Century Writers,* **Ed. 2;** *Major 21st-Century Writers,* **(eBook) 2005;** *Reference Guide to Short Fiction,* **Ed. 2; and** *Twayne Companion to Contemporary Literature in English,* **Ed. 1:2.**

Constance Fenimore Woolson
1840-1894

(Also wrote under the pseudonym Anne March) American short story writer, novelist, travel writer, and author of children's books.

The following entry provides an overview of Woolson's short fiction.

INTRODUCTION

A grandniece of the first major American novelist, James Fenimore Cooper, Woolson was among the most respected women writers in the United States during the last quarter of the nineteenth century. Her stories and novels depart from the sentimental romanticism of her contemporaries, and concern such topical, often controversial issues as race relations, industrialization, women's status in society, and American imperialism. Pioneering a type of realism known as "local color," Woolson evoked the distinctive sights and sounds of specific locales in the Great Lakes region, the American Southeast, and northern Italy as an integral means of developing her characters' motivations and personalities. Woolson's popularity and critical reputation has diminished since her death, but contemporary feminist scholarship has renewed interest in Woolson's fiction, particularly her struggle to reconcile female authorship with nineteenth-century gender roles.

BIOGRAPHICAL INFORMATION

The youngest of six daughters born in Claremont, New Hampshire, to Charles Jarvis Woolson and Hannah Cooper Pomeroy, Woolson lost three sisters to scarlet fever within a month after her birth in 1840. Like other pioneers during the nineteenth century, the family moved to the western frontier to start over and settled in Cleveland, Ohio, where Woolson attended Miss Hayden's School. During the 1850s, she completed her formal education at the Cleveland Female Seminary. Woolson then entered Madame Chegary's School in New York City and graduated with honors in 1858. When the Civil War erupted in 1861, she worked for the Union cause, constantly moving between Cleveland and New York City until 1865. After her father's death in 1869, Woolson published travel sketches in the *Daily Cleveland Herald* and contributed short stories to such journals as *Harper's* and the *Atlantic Monthly*. In 1871 she began a

two-year respite with her maternal relatives in Cooperstown, New York. Two years later, she traveled with her invalid mother throughout the southeastern United States before they settled in St. Augustine, Florida. She then began collecting short stories for publication in her first book, *Castle Nowhere* (1875). After her mother died in 1879, Woolson left America for Europe where she spent the rest of her life, alternating between Italy and England while frequenting tourist destinations and circulating among American expatriate communities in Switzerland, Austria, France, and Greece. In 1880, she published her second volume of short fiction, *Rodman the Keeper*. That year, Woolson also met the English author Henry James, whom she befriended professionally, and perhaps romantically, regularly corresponding with him and periodically visiting him until her death. With his guidance, Woolson wrote longer works during the 1880s, publishing the novels *Anne* (1882), *East Angels* (1886), and *Jupiter Lights* (1889). Meanwhile, she crisscrossed Europe and continued to write short stories, which were posthumously published in the collections *The Front Yard* (1895) and *Dorothy, and Other Italian Stories* (1896). In January 1894, Woolson either fell or leapt to her death from a second floor window at her residence in Venice, Italy, while suffering from influenza and depression.

MAJOR WORKS OF SHORT FICTION

Woolson's short stories correspond with her own experiences in the Old Northwest Territories (the Great Lakes region), the Reconstruction South, and the newly wealthy American expatriate communities of Europe. Despite the different settings, a number of themes inform her short fiction, including a keen awareness of landscapes and environmental issues, sensitivity toward the complexities of race in American culture, suspicion of social pretensions afforded by wealth or heredity, and concern for the status of women, particularly as professional writers. The stories comprising *Castle Nowhere* are among the earliest American literary representations of the nineteenth-century Great Lakes frontier. Observing the region's transition from the forested wilderness of fur traders and French missionaries to the cleared settlements of farmers first and industrialists later, some stories deal with the inevitable cultural conflicts between European Americans and the indigenous peoples living there. Many stories also broach the subject of women's roles in frontier society. In "The Lady of Little

Fishing," Woolson's revision of Bret Harte's "The Luck of Roaring Camp," character development is closely tied to the description of the primeval wilderness. After a mysterious woman suddenly arrives at a men's primitive outpost and introduces culture and civilized manners into the otherwise brutish surroundings, she falls in love with one of the men, which shatters the other men's illusions about womanhood. The camp soon reverts to its old ways, and the woman dies brokenhearted—a fate common for many of Woolson's strong, female characters.

Generally recognized as the first fiction written by a Northerner about the South after the Civil War, the stories collected in *Rodman the Keeper* articulate the cultural tensions confronting Americans during the Reconstruction era. Although many stories try to accommodate the various realities of the post-Civil War South for a mainly Northern audience, some do not. For instance, the title story fairly spreads blame among Yankees, Rebels, and freed slaves alike; "King David" follows the futile attempts of a Northern schoolteacher to educate freed slaves in a formerly Confederate town as a fellow Yankee opens a liquor store. Many stories trace the hazards of clinging to worn-out illusions. Set at a crumbling plantation, "In the Cotton Country" recounts a conversation between a Northern woman and a Southern widow who relates the destruction of her family's livelihood and the shattered illusions of neighbors assisting her. In "Up in the Blue Ridge," a Northern woman rescues her morally reprehensible Southern cousin from certain death because she refuses to let go of outdated notions about devotion to family. Other stories in *Rodman the Keeper* reflect Woolson's innovations with controversial subjects, including "Felipa," which feminist critics have read as an early example of nineteenth-century lesbian fiction, and "The South Devil," which superficially concerns the superstitions surrounding a fabled Florida swamp but actually represents Woolson's experiments with the concept of authorship, the limits of art, and the temptations of literary fame.

Originally published in *Lippincott's Magazine* in 1880, Woolson's uncollected story "Miss Grief" is perhaps her most famous work and a perennial favorite among readers. In it, a pompous male author, whom many critics have mistakenly identified as Henry James, receives a manuscript from an unknown, dying female writer. Astounded by the woman's talents, he begins to edit the work in order to market it to a wider audience when he suddenly abandons the project because he feels his skills are no match for hers. After the woman dies, he honors her request to seal her manuscripts in her grave. Set among various cosmopolitan communities of expatriate Americans in Italy, the stories of the posthumous collections *The Front Yard* and *Dorothy* expose American ignorance of the international world. Many of these sto-

ries also continue to explore the status of female genius in a culture that refused to recognize it. In both "The Street of the Hyacinth" and "At the Château of Corinne," the female protagonists sacrifice their professional and personal ambitions when they marry aloof, dismissive men.

CRITICAL RECEPTION

Woolson's works have received diminishing attention since her death, with more recent scholarship focusing on feminist studies. However, some critics acknowledge Woolson's use of local color as an important precursor of Regional American Literature. Testifying to Woolson's talent for description, Evelyn Thomas Helmick has argued that "her real accomplishment is in her evocation of that sense of place that is an accomplishment confined to a few." Detractors have complained that Woolson's Southern stories perpetuate stereotypes about the region despite the well-documented prevalence of early-Reconstruction-era prejudice against the South. Feminist critics have applauded Woolson's innovative examinations of gender roles, especially in relation to the constraints on female authorship during the nineteenth century. Additional scholarship has centered on Woolson's friendship with Henry James and the question of literary influence.

PRINCIPAL WORKS

Short Fiction

Castle Nowhere: Lake-Country Sketches 1875
Rodman the Keeper: Southern Sketches 1880
For the Major: A Novelette 1883
The Front Yard, and Other Italian Stories 1895
Dorothy, and Other Italian Stories 1896
For the Major, and Selected Short Stories 1967
Women Artists, Women Exiles: "Miss Grief" and Other Stories 1988
Constance Fenimore Woolson: Selected Stories and Travel Narratives 2004

Other Major Works

The Old Stone House [as Anne March] (juvenilia) 1873
Anne: A Novel (novel) 1882
East Angels: A Novel (novel) 1886
Jupiter Lights: A Novel (novel) 1889
Horace Chase: A Novel (novel) 1894
Mentone, Cairo and Corfu (travel essays) 1896

CRITICISM

Evelyn Thomas Helmick (essay date 1969)

SOURCE: Helmick, Evelyn Thomas. "Constance Fenimore Woolson: First Novelist of Florida." In *Feminist Criticism: Essays on Theory, Poetry and Prose,* edited by Cheryl L. Brown and Karen Olson, pp. 233-43. Metuchen, N.J.: The Scarecrow Press, Inc., 1978.

[*In the following essay, originally published in* The Carrell *in 1969, Helmick traces the influence of northern Florida pervading Woolson's literary aesthetics.*]

In the *Atlantic Monthly* of 1875 appeared a series of papers called "An English Sportsman in Florida," describing this exotic peninsula in precise detail. Such description was not a novelty, for men had written accounts of their journeys into Florida from the beginning of its exploration: the list includes Sidney Lanier, John James Audubon, John Bartram, Jonathan Dickinson; it reaches back to Cabeza de Vaca's *Adventures in the Unknown Interior of America* published in 1555. But immediately preceding the English sportsman's article in that March 13 issue of the *Atlantic* was something truly new in literature—a short story with a Florida setting. The significant fiction of the state, in fact, begins with the author of that story, Constance Fenimore Woolson, who captured in novels, short stories, and poems the *genius loci* of northern Florida.[1] The Florida fiction is the best work of a writer highly praised in her day by such critics as Henry James and William Dean Howells and judged as late as 1929 "one of the finest novelists that America thus far has produced."[2]

Miss Woolson—or Fenimore, as her friend Henry James called her and as her great-uncle, James Fenimore Cooper had been called—began to publish in national periodicals in 1870 with stories of the Lake Country near Cleveland, where her family had moved a few months after her birth in New Hampshire in 1840. Her first collection of stories (after the prize-winning *Old Stone House* for children) was *Castle Nowhere: Lake Country Sketches* in 1875. Before that time, however, she and her mother and sister had begun to spend much of each year in St. Augustine, with frequent visits to the Carolinas, Tennessee, and Georgia. From this experience came her second collection, *Rodman the Keeper: Southern Sketches,* in 1880. After her mother's death she sailed for Europe, where she lived in Italy and England, producing an astonishing number of books before she died in 1896. These works include the novels *Anne, East Angels, Jupiter Lights,* and *Horace Chase*; a novelette, *For the Major*; two story collections, *The Front Yard and Other Italian Stories* and *Dorothy and Other Italian Stories*; and a book of travel sketches, *Mentone, Cairo, and Corfu.*

As the titles of the story collections indicate and even a cursory examination of the novels reveals, Miss Woolson was fascinated with places. And through the whole of her life, the place that seemed to mean most to her was Florida. Soon after she arrived in St. Augustine in 1873, she wrote to a friend:

> The life here is so fresh, so new, so full of certain wild freedom. I walk miles through the hummocks, where it looks as though no one had ever walked before, gathering wild flowers everywhere, or sitting down under the pine trees to rest in the shade. . . . You know the ocean is new to me and I am so fond of it already that I feel as if I never cared to go inland any more.[3]

Her admiration for the area continued undiminished during her residence there, so that she could write to her literary mentor, Edmund Clarence Stedman, just a month after her arrival in Europe that she wanted to return to Florida to live as soon as possible:

> I am only waiting to store up a little more money; then I shall return; buy a wee cottage down there; set up a crane and three orange-trees; & never stir again.[4]

No wonder, then, that some of her most vital work sprang from a Florida background.

Her earliest writing about the state appeared in verse form in *Harper's Magazine, Galaxy,* and *Appleton's Journal* soon after she settled in St. Augustine. The poems, written in careful rhythm and rhyme and full of inversion and nineteenth-century poetic diction, nevertheless evoke some remarkable pictures. The fourth stanza of "Pine Barrens," is one example:

> Abroad upon the Barrens the saw-palmetto reddens
> The ground with arméd ranks that firm for centuries
>   have stood;
> They kneel and pray to Heaven that their sins may be
>   forgiven,
> Their long green knives in readiness, bold outlaws of
>   the wood!

That the pine barrens were more than mere landscape to her is apparent in the last stanza of "The Florida Beach":

> Alone, alone, we wander through
>   The southern winter day.
> The ocean spreads his mighty blue,
>   The world is far away:
> The tide comes in,—the birds fly low,
>   As if to catch our speech—
> Ah Fate! why must we ever go
> From the beautiful Florida Beach?

Other descriptive poems about the Florida landscape, all published between 1874 and 1876, are "Yellow Jessamine," "The Ancient City," and "The Ocklawaha." "Dolores" is a narrative poem about a Minorcan woman and a surgeon in the Union Army who saves her child.[5]

Miss Woolson soon turned to short stories as the way to relate her Florida experience, a fortunate change because of her greater skill and originality in prose than in poetry. There are four stories with north Florida settings,[6] and they grow progressively more permeated with a sense of the mystery of the natural surroundings and of the role of environment in men's lives. **"Miss Elisabetha"** is the story of a proud northern spinster who rears her lover's son to be a gentleman in the town of Beata along the Warra River. Two other women challenge her for control of Theodore; Miss Elisabetha is victorious over the prima donna who wants to teach him opera in Europe but is defeated by the beautiful, uneducated Minorcan girl who marries him, provides him with a large brood of lazy, ignorant, happy children, and sends him to an early death. They tolerantly regard Miss Elisabetha, who tirelessly works in the household, as a "species differing from theirs, but good in its way, especially for work." Here is Miss Woolson's constantly recurring theme of the way in which men's origins confer certain lifelong character traits. The Minorcan character is treated again in **"Felipa,"** a story of a wild southern child who falls in love with a northerner and tries to kill both herself and him when she learns of his impending marriage to a northern woman. Contrast between the northern and southern temperaments is important in the next Florida story Miss Woolson wrote, **"Sister St. Luke."** Pedro, a lighthouse keeper, is married to Malvyna, a New England woman, whom his Minorcan friends and relatives regard as a "woman of wonder—of an energy unfathomable." Even her seven-year-old New England bonnet is trimmed with a "durable" green ribbon and a "vigorous" wreath of artificial flowers. The characterization of Pedro and Malvyna provides most of the interest in the story, whose plot focuses on the heroism during a storm of Sister Luke, a timid nun from a nearby convent who is nursed by Malvyna during an illness.

The most powerful of the Florida short stories without doubt is **"The South Devil,"** which moves quickly toward the skillfulness of the novels, and which contains the germs of the themes developed more fully in them. Contrast between the northern and southern character is central to the plot. Mark Deal, a northerner, works from daylight until dusk ("and was probably the only white man in the State who did") to create order and beauty in his plaza and to care for his southern step-brother Carl, whom he has only recently met. Carl sleeps most of the day, works not at all, and gambles away Mark's savings in one card game. But his strongest and strangest vice is an attraction to the evils of the South Devil, the poisonous cypress swamp nearby. Mark's two excursions into the swamp to rescue Carl give Miss Woolson an opportunity to display her powers of description:

> They passed under the gray and solemn cypresses, rising without branches to an enormous height, their far foliage hidden by the moss, which hung down thickly in long flakes, diffusing the sunshine and making it silvery like mist; in the silver swung the air-plants, great cream-colored disks, and wands of scarlet, crowded with little buds, blossoms that looked like butterflies, and blossoms that looked like humming-birds, and little dragonheads with grinning faces. Then they came to the region of the palms; these shot up, slender and graceful, and leaned over the stream the great aureum ferns growing on their trunks high in the air. Beneath was a firmer soil than in the domain of the cypresses, and here grew a mat of little flowers, each less than a quarter of an inch wide, close together, pink, blue, scarlet, yellow, purple, but never white, producing a hue singularly rich, owing to the absence of that colorless color which man ever mingles with his floral combinations, and strangely makes sacred alike to the bridal and to death. . . . The air was absolutely still; no breeze reached these blossoming aisles; each leaf hung motionless. The atmosphere was hot, and heavy with perfumes. It was the heart of the swamp, a riot of intoxicating, steaming, swarming, fragrant, beautiful, tropical life, without man to make or mar it. All the world was once so, before man was made.

> [pp. 191-192]

Her ambivalent feelings toward the tropical land, so prominent in the novels, begin to become apparent in this tale, even slightly in the description of the swamp. The end of the passage quoted reveals another of Miss Woolson's themes: the awareness of the long history of the Florida peninsula. One paragraph of **"The South Devil"** prods the reader into an immediate awareness of that history; as Mark notices fifty-year-old furrows in his field, the author comments:

> There are many such traces of former cultivation in Florida; we come suddenly upon old tracks, furrows, and drains in what we thought primeval forest; rosebushes run wild and distorted old fig-trees meet us in a jungle where we supposed no white man's foot had ever before penetrated; the ruins of a chimney gleam whitely through a waste of thorny chaparral. It is all natural enough, if one stops to remember that fifty years before the first settlement was made in Virginia, and sixty-three before the Mayflower touched the shores of the New World, there were flourishing Spanish plantations on this Southern coast,—more flourishing apparently, than any the indolent peninsula has since known. But one does not stop to remember it; the belief is imbedded in all our Northern hearts that because the narrow, sun-bathed State is far away and wild and empty, it is also new and virgin, like the lands of the West; whereas it is old,—the only gray-haired corner our country holds.

> [p. 175]

The consciousness of the past and of the beauties of the unspoiled land are two ever-relevant themes for readers of Miss Woolson's fiction. A final theme of **"The South Devil,"** one recurring frequently in her stories, is consummately Victorian and dates her work for the contemporary reader. The idea of sacrifice, often to no purpose, appears again and again. In this last Florida short story, Carl takes a fatal walk through the swamp to post a letter, thinking perhaps he can redeem his worthless life by informing his cousin that Mark loves her. Often such sacrifices seem to be made only to prove strength of character.

Such unattractive, if not improbable, martyrs are perhaps part of the reason Miss Woolson's work is seldom read today. The problems with her books are undoubtedly those characteristics which made them popular in her own day. Her characters, in exercising a restraint admirable to the Victorian mind, seem wooden and unreal; the endless feminine analysis of emotions and motivations becomes comic after a while; the plots become too circumstantial to bear. If, however, the reader is able to recognize and isolate the Victorian elements, as, for example, a playgoer might recognize the conventions of British comedy, he or she can still find much to enjoy and appreciate in a Woolson novel. The humor alone often makes her stories worth the reading. Much of her humor is very subtle, and mildly malicious, as in her description of Felicité, the French woman, who looked as though she would like to be wicked: "In reality, however, she was harmless, for one insatiable ambition within her swallowed up all else, namely, the ambition not to be middle-aged. As she was forty-eight, the struggle took all her time" (p. 228). Another example in the same novel, *Horace Chase,* is the party given by a local St. Augustine do-gooder for the Indians held prisoner at Fort St. Marco. The company commander has wisely chosen only six of the Indians for the party, and the hostess tries to convert them:

> 'If I could only speak to them in their own tongue!' she said, yearningly. And the long sentences, expressive of friendship, which she begged the interpreter to translate to them, would have filled a volume. The interpreter, a very intelligent young man, obeyed all her requests with much politeness. 'Tell them then we *love* them,' said Mrs. Kip. 'Tell them that we think of their *souls.*'
>
> The interpreter bowed; then he translated as follows: 'The white squaw says that you have had enough to eat, and more than enough; and she hopes that you won't make pigs of yourselves if anything else is offered—especially Drowning Raven!'

[pp. 183-184]

The reader who values a subtle wit, or one frequently not so subtle, will find much in Woolson.

But her real accomplishment is in her evocation of that sense of place that is an accomplishment confined to a few: Thomas Hardy with the heaths of England, Sarah Orne Jewett with Vermont, Willa Cather with Nebraska, and Marjorie Kinnan Rawlings with rural Florida. Miss Woolson's ability to see and to describe brings early Florida to life. Such scenes as the annual search for the first jessamine in early St. Augustine not only add flavor to her novels, but serve to reinforce both character

and structure, as Hardy's Egdon Heath so often does. The Florida settings in two novels—*East Angels* entirely and *Horace Chase* in part—control the characters, the action, the morality, the tone of the stories. Miss Woolson, so often labeled a local colorist, does much more than skilfully describe an unknown region. For her, a sense of place pervades every area of life.

True, by the time of *East Angels* of 1886 and *Horace Chase* of 1894, her powers of descriptive writing are developed fully enough to be pleasurable in themselves. She can describe the movements of a character in *East Angels*:

> He went to look at some camellias, whose glossy leaves formed a thicket at a little distance; on the other side of this thicket he discovered a crape-myrtle avenue, the delicate trees so choked and hustled by the ruder foliage which had grown up about them that they stood like captives in the midst of a rabble, broken-hearted and dumb.

[pp. 48-49]

She is able to weave her descriptions into the very fabric of her story without intrusion upon the action or change in pace. A trip in a canoe from *East Angels,* for example, shows her skill:

> Lightly it sped out towards deep water, the slightest motion sent it forward; its sides were of such slender thickness that the two men could feel the breathing of the great soft stream, which had here a breadth of three miles, though in sight, both above and below, it widened into six. These broad water stretches were tranquil; from shore to shore the slow, full current swept majestically on; and even to look across the wide, still reaches, with the tropical forests standing thickly on their low strands, was a vision of peace for the most troubled human soul.
>
> Kildee plover flew chattering before the canoe while they were still near land. Far above in the blue a bald-headed eagle sailed along. Lanse chose to go out to the centre of the stream—Lanse never skirted the edge of anything; reaching it, he turned southward, and they voyaged onward for nearly an hour.

[p. 410]

Such scenes interested northern readers of 1886, many of whom, like one of the characters in *East Angels,* must have supposed there was nothing worth their personal consideration south of Philadelphia.

With her two Florida novels, both popularly and critically acclaimed, Miss Woolson was able to capture the interest of northerners in the state. The novels, like the stories, are conventional and somewhat sentimental in characterization and plot. *East Angels* tells of the romances and marriages of two women: the shallow southerner Garda Thorne who marries unthinkingly twice, the second time to a Spaniard whom she respects little, and the patient, noble northerner Margaret Harold who stands by a husband even after he has deserted her twice, although she loves another man. *Horace Chase,* only partly set in Florida, is the story of a young woman married to an older successful man. When a younger colleague encourages her infatuation, it is the husband who sacrifices his pride after a near-indiscretion confessed by his wife. It would seem nearly impossible to make such slim plots interest a reader in 1970; yet they do, chiefly because Miss Woolson's appreciation of surroundings and her insight into the relationship between place and character make fascinating study.

Beyond her ability to describe clearly those exotic sights and smells which intrigued her in Florida, she brings to the novels careful observation of the groups of people she found there. The Minorcans appear as colorful embodiments of an indolent, sunny landscape. The southern Negroes, particularly in *East Angels,* are carefully and attractively drawn. Their speech, at times as incomprehensible in Miss Woolson's printed version as it is aurally, has been called a "careful philological study." She observed with care the new immigrants to Florida, sometimes with admiration, sometimes with disdain, as in *East Angels:*

> This new class counted within its ranks at present the captains and crews of the northern schooners that were beginning to come into that port for lumber; the agents of land-companies looking after titles and the old Spanish grants; speculators with plans in their pockets for railways, with plans in their pockets for canals, with plans in their pockets (and sometimes very little else) for draining the swamps and dredging the Everglades, many of the schemes dependent upon aid from Congress, and mysteriously connected with the new negro vote. In addition there were the first projectors of health resorts, the first northern buyers of orange groves: in short, the pioneers of that busy, practical American majority. . . .
>
> [p. 54]

Of special interest to the modern reader is Miss Woolson's wide knowledge of Florida history. Her awareness of the region's past expressed in **"The South Devil"** pervades most of her southern stories. In **"Sister St. Luke"** the structure of a lighthouse affords the opportunity to tell the history of Pelican Island as each alteration and addition to the lighthouse is analyzed. In *East Angels* the tracing of a deed back to the original Spanish settlers becomes an informative lesson. Miss Woolson tries to make the reader as conscious of Florida's history as is Evert Winthrop in that novel:

> There was—he could not deny it—a certain comparative antiquity about this southern peninsula which had in it more richness of color and a deeper perspective than that possessed by any of the rather blank, near, little backgrounds of American history farther north. This was a surprise to him. Like most New Englanders,

he had unconsciously cherished the belief that all there was of historical importance, of historical picturesqueness even, in the beginnings of the republic, was associated with the Puritans from whom he was on his father's side descended, was appended to their stately hats and ruffs, their wonderful perseverance, their dignified orthography, the solemnities of their speech and demeanor.

> [p. 15]

In *Horace Chase,* the "ancient city," as Miss Woolson calls St. Augustine, provides historical comment, with much focus on Fort San Marco and the Indian past.

The Florida environment exerts its influence on the present just as much in these novels. Miss Woolson's major theme in all her southern work is the contrast between the northern and southern temperaments. *East Angels* opens with a contrast between the regions and soon adapts the doctor's point of view: "to him the difference between New England and the South was as wide, whether considered geographically, psychologically, or historically, as that between the South and Japan." The indolent, sweet-natured Garda Thorne of that novel is a natural product of the pine-barrens who lacks the fortitude to cope with adversity. Her mother, described by Henry James, as "the little starved yet ardent daughter of the Puritans, who has been condemned to spend her life in the land of the relaxed," expends her dying breath in an attack on the region:

> Oh! I so hate and loathe it all—the idle, unrealizing, contented life of this tiresome, idle coast. They amounted to something once, perhaps; but their day is over, and will never come back. They don't know it; you couldn't make them believe it even if you should try. That is what makes you rage—they're so completely mistaken and so completely satisfied!
>
> [p. 219]

Florida is variously referred to in these stories as the land of the lotus eaters, the land of the alligators, and "this miserable little half-afloat land." And its shortcomings affect its inhabitants. In *Horace Chase,* the infatuation of the young wife Ruth occurs in St. Augustine "by fatality." Her comment that the winter in that town was the happiest of her life is ironic, since her infatuation destroys both her health and her happiness. In *East Angels,* Evert Winthrop behaves impulsively during a ride through the Monnlungs swamp and declares that a man is not responsible for his actions in such a place.

Miss Woolson's ambivalence makes her observations of Florida more interesting than unmitigated praise might. Perhaps she was trying for the balance of a Thomas Hardy, whom she admired as a writer and of whom she wrote, "his landscapes have no moral meanings." Her final personal judgment appears in a letter to Stedman from Europe in 1877:

I hardly appreciated myself, until I was separated from it, how much I loved that warm hazy peninsula where I spent five long happy winters. . . .

Her admiration was combined with her skill to capture a spirit of early Florida which we might otherwise never know.

Notes

Reprinted by permission of the author and publisher from *The Carrell* 10 (1969), 8-18.

1. Two Florida novels by William Gilmore Sims (*The Lily and the Totem* and *Vasconselos*) and one by James Fenimore Cooper (*Jack Tier: or the Florida Reef*) preceded Miss Woolson's work, but Sims' books were historical romances and Cooper's was a sea story with little description of the state.

2. John Hervey, *Saturday Review of Literature* (October 12, 1929).

3. Clare Benedict, *Voices out of the Past,* vol. 1 of *Five Generations* (London, 1930), pp. 230-231.

4. This letter is reprinted in Rayburn S. Moore, *Constance F. Woolson* (New York, 1963), p. 27.

5. The Florida poems and the periodicals in which they originally appeared are: "Yellow Jessamine," *Appleton's Journal,* March 1874; "Dolores," *Appleton's Journal,* July 1874; "The Florida Beach," *The Galaxy,* October 1874; "Pine Barrens," *Harper's Magazine,* December 1874; "The Ancient City," *Harper's Magazine,* December 1874 and January 1875; "The Ocklawaha," *Harper's Magazine,* January 1876.

6. The Florida stories and the periodicals in which they originally appeared are: "Miss Elisabetha," *Appleton's Journal,* September 1875; "Felipa," *Lippincott's Magazine,* June 1876; "Sister St. Luke," *The Galaxy,* April 1877; "The South Devil," *The Atlantic Monthly,* February 1880.

Cheryl B. Torsney (essay date spring 1987)

SOURCE: Torsney, Cheryl B. Introduction to "'Miss Grief,'" by Constance Fenimore Woolson. *Legacy* 4, no. 1 (spring 1987): 11-13.

[*In the following essay, Torsney discusses the literary precedents and cultural contexts of "Miss Grief," highlighting its subversion of patriarchal literary conventions.*]

In the late nineteenth-century Constance Fenimore Woolson was famous. Her friend Henry James wrote that Woolson was the only novelist writing in English

whom he read besides William Dean Howells (3:29), and he published an essay on her alongside sketches of such luminaries as Turgenev, Daudet, and George Eliot in *Partial Portraits* (1888). Until recently, however, few modern readers have considered Woolson's writing on its own merits, in part because the biography of her constructed by Leon Edel has discouraged a serious reading of her work. In his award-winning life of James, Edel caricatures Woolson; he portrays her as an old, pitiable spinster who chased the literary lion James across the Continent from their first meeting in the spring of 1880 to her death in January 1894, as the result of a fall from the second-story window of her Venetian residence. Edel implies that the fall was the consequence of Woolson's unrequited love for James (3:363). The real story is quite different: Woolson was suffering from influenza, hereditary depression, and financial woes, and if, in fact, she committed suicide, Henry James had little to do with it.[1] The myth of the lion and the spinster, however, resulted in Woolson's writing being largely ignored until recently.

Renewed interest in nineteenth-century women's writing is gaining recognition for Woolson's work, beginning with her 50-some short stories, most of which were published in four nineteenth-century collections.[2] One of the best of these is the uncollected "'Miss Grief,'" first published in *Lippincott's Magazine* (May 1880) and reprinted in *Stories by American Authors* (1884), ***For the Major and Selected Short Stories,*** edited by Rayburn S. Moore (1967), and here.

Set in Rome, the story is narrated by a smug, expatriated American writer, who is confounded by the visits of a strange woman whose name he understands as "Miss Grief." When finally admitted to his home, Miss Grief importunes the narrator to act as her literary agent for a drama entitled "Armor." He reads it to discover in the work of his bedraggled countrywoman "the divine spark of genius," which he himself lacks. His belief in her talent is further substantiated when he reads her other work. In all of her writings, however, he detects some "fault or lack," which forms the basis for rejections from prospective publishers of Miss Grief's work. When the narrator attempts to rewrite her work himself, he discovers that his "own powers were not equal to the task, or else that her perversities were as essential a part of her work as her inspirations, and not to be separated from it." In the meantime, Miss Grief, whose real name is Aaronna Moncrief, is dying. The writer goes to her hovel, lies to her about the acceptance of the drama for publication, and promises to bury the rest of her work with her. He does, in fact, bury her manuscripts, save "Armor," which he locks up in a case.

Of the few critics who have taken up this story, most use a biographical approach, frequently discussing the question of influence.[3] Although "'Miss Grief'" was actually written before Constance Fenimore Woolson met Henry James, Rayburn S. Moore insists on a resemblance between the narrator and the Master: both men have inherited wealth, understand social convention, imitate Balzac in their own work, consider psychological motivation paramount, use Woolson's metaphor "the figure in the carpet" (156, n. 27). Moreover, as John Dwight Kern has noted, Woolson's work in "'Miss Grief'" demonstrates that she is "one of the few writers of the time who practised what he [James] preached" (178). Predictably, Leon Edel ignores the method of "'Miss Grief,'" arguing instead that Woolson had, like the title character, an "exalted notion of her own literary powers" (2:417).

Although Kern (117) credits the master-disciple theme of "'Miss Grief'" with predating by eight years James's "The Lesson of the Master," neither he, Moore, nor Edel really argues for Woolson's literary influence on James, as does Sharon Dean. She asserts that James had both Woolson and her fiction, particularly "'Miss Grief,'" in mind when he wrote not only "The Aspern Papers" and "The Lesson of the Master," two artist tales, but also "The Beast in the Jungle" and "The Jolly Corner," two tales of missed opportunities for salvation (7-8). According to Dean, Miss Grief is the narrator's alter-ego: "When he denies grief, he also denies suffering genius and accepts instead the shallow emptiness represented by Isabel," the narrator's fiancée (8).[4] Dean believes that James learned the concept of the alter-ego, which he later used to develop his ghost stories, from Woolson's "'Miss Grief.'"

But the story does more than simply illustrate influence or, as Kern writes, exemplify "the martyrdom of an artist who refuses to compromise her principles for the sake of popular success" (117). "'Miss Grief'" attempts to subvert male literary mythology. Both the goal of subversion and its implications for political and social institutions are lost on the self-centered, love-struck narrator. He, who declares himself "good tempered, well-dressed, sufficiently provided with money and amiably obedient to all the rules and requirements of 'society,'" is incapable of dealing with an uneventempered, poorly dressed, insufficiently provided for woman, who flouts the rules and requirements of society. Though more successful than she, he is forced to admit that the "authoress" has more power. An obvious representative of the ruling class, he strives to maintain his hegemony by possessing and locking up Miss Grief's text of selfhood.

Throughout the story the narrator attempts to exercise his power over Miss Grief: by refusing to grant her access to him; by renaming her; by acting as her intermediary in such a way as to pretend to champion her efforts while actually undermining them; by forcing her to rely on him for sustenance; by taking control of her

production. The pattern is reminiscent of the politico-economic design of a slave state. (At one point, in fact, the narrator decides to call the downtrodden writer "Aunt," a title frequently given to slave retainers in the pre-Civil War and later South.) Thus, we can read "'Miss Grief'" as a script of classic class conflict. The lower classes have the potential for power but the upper class robs them of it because political convention is on its side. Since in this story the upper class is male and the underclass female, the dimension of gender becomes primary.

Because she is a writer, Miss Grief tries to assert her power in the literary sphere, the publishing world serving as a metaphor for other patriarchal institutions, such as class. Aaronna Moncrief and her writing attempt to overturn male literary mythology, beginning with the religious traditions of the Old and New Testaments, and moving on to the secular traditions of the courtly and domestic romances. For example, Aaronna Moncrief, a woman, is cast as the Creator, full of original power and possessing "the divine spark." In a play on a New Testament story, the narrator, a this-worldly literary god, cannot resurrect his countrywoman as Jesus will do for Lazarus after a visit to the home of his sisters, one of whom is named Martha, like Miss Grief's companion. Moreover, the narrator casts his and Miss Grief's relationship in the tradition of courtly literature, using its conventions and inserting his actions in place of the heroic variable, in order to maintain control; however, *she* courts the narrator, not vice versa, and *she,* not he, is the soldier for art, the armored knight. Furthermore, Miss Grief violates all of the narrator's expectations about women and women writers by subverting social convention and by being, herself, unpretty and noncompliant. By undermining these various mythologies in numerous ways, Miss Grief insists upon her own power.

"'Miss Grief'" is the first story Constance Fenimore Woolson wrote after moving abroad. More stories, novels, poems, and travel sketches followed. Indeed, she was so well-known when she died that *Harper's Bazaar* ran a full-page portrait in her memory. Today's readers will celebrate that, unlike the unread Miss Grief, Constance Fenimore Woolson is once more available.

Notes

1. See my essay "Henry James and Constance Fenimore Woolson: The Traditions of Gender" in *Patrons and Protégées,* edited by Shirley Marchalonis forthcoming from Rutgers University Press, January 1988.

2. Joan Weimer is editing a collection of Woolson's short fiction to be published by Rutgers University Press.

3. Joan Myers Weimer, "Women Artists as Exiles in the Fiction of Constance Fenimore Woolson,"

Legacy 3.2 (Fall 1986), appeared too late for me to consider it in this discussion.

4. The narrator's fiancée is named Ethelind in the original. Her name may have been changed to Isabel in the later versions because Ethelinda is the name of the artist-heroine of Woolson's "The Street of the Hyacinth" (1882).

Works Cited

Dean, Sharon. "Constance Fenimore Woolson and Henry James: The Literary Relationship." *Massachusetts Studies in English* 7 (1980).

Edel, Leon. *Henry James: The Conquest of London: 1870-1881.* Vol. 2. 1962; rpt. New York: Avon, 1978.

———. *Henry James: The Middle Years, 1882-1895.* Vol. 3. 1962; rpt. New York: Avon Books, 1978.

James, Henry. *Henry James Letters (1883-1895).* Ed. Leon Edel. Vol. 3. Cambridge: Belknap, 1980.

Kern, John Dwight. *Constance Fenimore Woolson: Literary Pioneer.* Philadelphia: U of Pennsylvania P, 1934.

Moore, Rayburn S. *Constance Fenimore Woolson.* New York: Twayne, 1963.

Joan Myers Weimer (essay date 1988)

SOURCE: Weimer, Joan Myers. Introduction to *Women Artists, Women Exiles: "Miss Grief" and Other Stories,* by Constance Fenimore Woolson, edited by Joan Myers Weimer, pp. ix-xlvii. New Brunswick, N.J.: Rutgers University Press, 1988.

[*In the following essay, Weimer provides an overview of Woolson's life and career, assessing her achievements within the context of her lifelong struggles against depression and the patriarchal literary tradition.*]

In January of 1894, ill with typhoid fever, possibly delirious, Constance Fenimore Woolson leapt or fell from her balcony in Venice and died without regaining consciousness. She was fifty-three years old. The violence of her death horrified her intimate friend Henry James, who believed that she had committed suicide. Thirteen years later, he was still making pilgrimages to her grave in the Protestant Cemetery in Rome, which he found "the most beautiful thing in Italy . . . that very particular spot below the great grey wall, the cypresses and time-silvered pyramid. It is tremendously, inexhaustibly touching—its effect never fails to overwhelm" (Edel 3: 377).

Woolson was, however, a number of contradictory women besides the one whose life had so touched and whose death had so overwhelmed Henry James. One

was a novelist so successful in her day that *Harper's* gave her a thousand-dollar bonus on her first novel and begged her for more fiction than she could produce,[1] yet so obscure today that even feminist scholars ignore her. Another was a major innovator in American literary realism, yet singled out for her essential conservatism (James 178). She was adventurous and independent, spending the last fourteen years of her life in Florence and Venice, Oxford and London, Switzerland and Egypt; but she also longed for a little cottage in Florida with all her own things about her. Most paradoxically, Woolson was a highly articulate spokeswoman for the first generation of American women writers who saw themselves as artists, even while she remained strongly male-identified, leaning on her connection with her famous great-uncle James Fenimore Cooper[2] and attaching herself to the most important male writers of her own time.

Trying to understand Woolson through her male connections, however, is to see her through a distorting androcentric lens. Her response to Cooper, James, and other male literary giants was as critical and analytical as it was admiring; by appropriating and transforming some of their key images and themes, she critiqued and revised their work. Furthermore, she was at least as much affected by her personal and literary relations with women as she was by her links with men—so much so that her life and work comprise a complex response to the male and female cultures and literary traditions available to a woman writer after the Civil War.[3]

Woolson saw clearly that all these contexts were charged with conflict for women writers. Her fiction and letters show such women caught between their desire to compete with male artists and their ingrained sense of their own inadequacy; between their vision of a society that suppressed and silenced women and their need to write what male editors would publish and pay for; between their sense of the isolation and alienation of "woman's sphere" and their desire for homes and children. She saw too that women writers were torn between their admiration for male writers and texts and their need to reject or revise them in order to clear a space for their own art. Her life and work answer her own question: "Why do literary women break down so?" (letter to Stedman, 23 July 1876).

* * *

Woolson's own struggle to prevent physical and emotional breakdown can be traced to the beginning of her life. Within three weeks of her birth in Claremont, New Hampshire, in 1840, scarlet fever killed three of her five older sisters. Her mother could never talk about the tragedy, and her father told the children that "a 'something' went out of her that week that was lost forever" (Benedict 3: 42). Woolson's birthdays must always have been celebrated in the shadow of her sisters' deaths and her mother's sad alteration. By the time she reached puberty, sixth-born Constance had become the eldest. She had watched three other sisters die, one in infancy, one after three months of marriage, one after giving birth to her second child. As she approached womanhood, she came to associate marriage and child-bearing with death. These experiences may help explain why she later avoided intimacy with men, whose love seemed to kill, or with women, who died and left her.

Woolson's solitary habits also have roots in her intense relations with her parents. She adored her handsome, dashing father. Shortly after his death when she was twenty-nine, she prepared "A Brief Sketch of the Life of Charles Jarvis Woolson. Written by his daughter" (Benedict 3: 94-101). In the "Brief Sketch," Woolson emphasized traits of his that the two of them shared: a talent for "close observation of nature," a love of adventurous travel, a "ready wit, and keen sense of humour," and "the fortitude with which he bore the trials of life," trials she also shared (loss of loved ones, deafness, depression, financial insecurity). She describes her father as a paragon of physical and intellectual superiority; it seems she could never find a man who was his equal. She wrote to her friend Edmund Clarence Stedman, "My idea of love is, unfortunately, so high, that, like my idea of the office of minister, nothing or nobody ever comes up to it" (23 July 1876).

Much of Woolson's early fiction features father-daughter relations. While the bonds between fathers and daughters are very strong, almost incestuous, the fathers themselves are remarkably weak, as in *Anne* (1880) and *For the Major* (1882). Their deficiencies leave a vacuum in which their daughters must exercise power, just as Jarvis Woolson's death enabled his daughter to discover that she could earn her living by her pen. The incompetence of these adored fictive fathers may also come from Woolson's sense of her father's inability to protect his children from early deaths, while the criminality of the father in **"Castle Nowhere"** (1875) suggests that she saw her father's love as an attempt to expiate this weakness.

Mothers are much less prominent in Woolson's fiction, although their surrogates are everywhere: guardians, aunts both benevolent and vicious, and independent spinsters who nurture young women. This displacement may reflect Woolson's strong ambivalence toward her own mother. On the positive side was Hannah's role as a literary precursor, both as a niece of Fenimore Cooper and in her own right. Hannah's talent for close observation, her good memory, lively imagination, and deft turn of phrase appear in a large manuscript volume of "Recollections" of her childhood and early years of marriage, writings which Constance greatly admired. At the height of her own career, she wrote her niece about "the desire I have to arrange and publish—probably

added to one of my own books—a few of the pages included in the MS volume of her 'recollections' that Mother bequeathed to you. . . . They have a simplicity and reality of style that is very remarkable, and that my best efforts cannot approach" (Benedict 3: 120). Woolson appears to have seen herself as fulfilling her mother's literary ambitions.

The negative side of Hannah's legacy lay in her conspicuous preference for her one son over her many but short-lived daughters. Hannah's longing for a son probably determined the unusually large size of her family; she recalled that she "could not persuade Mr. Woolson to feel as disappointed" as she about the sex of their first eight children (Benedict 3: 161). When she finally produced a male heir, Hannah wrote, "Congratulations poured in—after eight little girls comes the one boy: predictions of wonderful things by him to be accomplished, verses written upon his birth, etc." (Benedict 3: 166). Named for his father, Charly was always the center of his mother's life. In her late thirties, after nearly a decade of devoting herself to her mother's care, Constance wrote bitterly that her mother's "whole happiness, even her life I might almost say, depends, and always has depended upon how Charly is and how he feels" (letter to Samuel Mather, 24 Feb. 1877). Woolson appears to have driven herself all her life to outstrip her living sister and brother while trying to fulfill the promise of her six dead sisters.

However, her childhood was far from grim. The happier side of it can be glimpsed in her mother's account of a home where the family gathers "after tea with games and stories for the little ones until their bedtime, then music or reading or conversation with pleasant 'callers' for the older ones" (Benedict 3: 149). As a schoolgirl at the Cleveland Seminary, Woolson was "the center of a select admiring group, a girl at once fun-loving and dignified . . . whose school essays read in her low, cultivated voice held [her schoolmates] in rapt attention" (Guilford, "Notes" ["Notes in Memory of Miss Woolson"]).

Woolson took these early writings very seriously. A classmate remembered "the flush of pleasure on Connie's face as her audience breaks into open applause after one of her characteristic essays" was read aloud (Guilford, *Story of a Cleveland School* 76-77). Many years later, she thanked her remarkable teacher Linda Guilford for "the pains you took with my crude compositions; the clearness with which you made my careless eyes notice the essential differences between a good style and a bad one" (Benedict 3: 42). When she graduated at the head of her class at Madame Chegaray's fashionable New York school, and her father took the family on a long celebratory trip to "the fashionable resorts around Boston," she seemed to care more about writing when and where she pleased than about her success as "great belle."

Woolson was twenty-one when the Civil War broke out. She wrote that "the war was the heart and spirit of my life, and everything has seemed tame to me since" (letter to Stedman, 1 Oct. 1876). That excitement extended to a young soldier who had been a childhood friend, but it was only the "glamor that the war threw over the young officers who left their homes to fight" that "made me fancy I cared for him" (letter to Samuel Mather, Jan. 1891). She never again admitted to a romantic attachment to any man.

Very little is known about Woolson in her twenties. She lived with her family in Cleveland, helped run a fair to raise money for medical supplies for Union troops, visited New York, went driving with her father and walking and rowing by herself, and described herself half-ironically to a girlhood friend as a "desolate spinster" (Benedict 2: 19). Certainly she continued her avid reading; probably she began to experiment with writing in different literary genres. But like many other women of her time, only when her father's death left her and her mother with "precarious means" (Benedict 3: 19) did she find the occasion and opportunity, and perhaps the excuse, to publish essays and stories. Their quality suggests she had been working on them for some time.

Within a year of her father's death, when she was thirty, she broke into *Harper's New Monthly Magazine* with **"The Happy Valley,"** a sketch of the Zoarites in Ohio, whom she had visited with her father, and into *Putnam's Magazine* with a sketch of Mackinac Island, where the family had vacationed. She also wrote lively accounts, "From Our Special Woman Correspondent," for the *Daily Cleveland Herald,* based on impressions gathered while she and her mother lived in New York after the family home in Cleveland was broken up.

Within five years, she could write of the "success that has come to me, limited of course, but very great when you think that it lifts all pecuniary cares off my mind. With the money I earn by my pen, Mother and I are entirely comfortable in our quiet way; without it, we should be very much cramped, and every day an anxiety" (Benedict 3: 119). She is obviously proud of her ability to take over her father's role as provider for her mother and herself.

Uncertain where her talents lay, she experimented for a long time with the available literary genres. A successful early venture was in children's literature; her first book, *The Old Stone House* (1873), won a prize of $1000. This genre was very congenial to her: "All of my life . . . I have been a teller of stories to children. Endless stories; stories that went on for months and years,—oral serials" (letter to Mary Mapes Dodge). But she had greater ambitions. In the same year, she published her first two stories for adults. Both **"Solomon"** and **"St. Clair Flats"** feature women stranded in the

wilderness with visionary husbands. By 1877 Woolson was also publishing anonymous reviews and criticism in the "Contributor's Club" of the *Atlantic Monthly.* She was deeply interested in the theater, and in the 1880s considered collaborating on a play with Henry James. She published a great deal of poetry, mostly undistinguished except in its effort to present American locales, legends, and dialects in elaborate meters like Poe's.[4]

The best of Woolson's work grows out of her interest in a distinctly female genre: the regional sketch, which aimed to describe as faithfully as possible a narrow piece of life.[5] Because she led a nomadic life in the South and in Europe from the time she began to write for a living, she never focused, as most of the women regionalists did, on a single geographic area. But she entered deeply and seriously into every place she lived or visited. She set most of her early stories in the American equivalents of desert islands: Mackinac Island in Lake Michigan, a mining camp on an island in Lake Superior, a solitary house in a salt marsh on Lake Huron, a cotton plantation abandoned after Sherman's march, a Southern cemetery for Union soldiers. Many of these stories focus on the relations of people who are geographically, socially, and emotionally stranded with visitors from less isolated situations, dramatizing the effect that dominant and muted cultures have on each other.[6] The isolated settings also function as metaphors for women's various forms of exile—from themselves, from their society, from their art—and for Woolson's sense of herself as a homeless outcast.

That feeling seemed to take root during the decade she spent wandering with her mother in the South after her father died. New York had proved too cold for Hannah's health, and too expensive, so they visited Virginia, the Carolinas, Tennessee, and Georgia, eventually settling in St. Augustine, Florida. Living in boarding houses, they met interesting literary figures such as Edmund Clarence Stedman and Elizabeth Stuart Phelps, and fabulously wealthy visitors who interested Woolson only as objects of satire.[7] To a friend's hint that she might be engaged, she replied, "Nobody is at my feet at all, do'nt be satirical. . . . I am as truly out of that kind of talk as a nun. I go about a great deal, but always as an 'observer,' 'a very superior person,' and that sort of thing" (Benedict 2: 242).

Increasingly, she disliked going into society. By age thirty-six she had decided that "To enjoy society a woman must be either personally attractive, gifted with conversational powers, or else must *think* herself one or both, whether she is in reality or not. I do not come under any of those heads. Result: do'nt care for society at all. . . . I keep away from all chance callers and flee all invitations. . . . I am very strongly 'New Hampshire' in all my ways. I have a row of tall solemn

Aunts up there, silent, reserved, solitary, thin, and a little grim; I am as much like them as the kind of life I lead will allow" (Hubbell 732).

Her niece Clare Benedict, however, who lived with Woolson for months at a time and was an intimate friend, describes her in totally different terms: "Holding a curiously low opinion of her own personal appearance, she was nevertheless considered by others to be unusually attractive, physically . . . her charm was potent and well-nigh irresistible. . . . [She was] endowed by nature with a passionate, even stormy temperament, together with a keenly analytical mind. . . . Like all creative artists, she suffered from periodical fits of acute depression, but her powers of enjoyment were correspondingly high, and her interests were many and catholic" (Benedict 2: xiii-xv). Even allowing for the niece's inclination to canonize her aunt, Benedict's description of Woolson's personal attractiveness, complex temperament, and capacity for charm matches the woman who emerges from Woolson's letters and photographs much better than the satiric self-portraits. Woolson's self-rejection may have grown in part from the guilty survivor's sense of worthlessness, while her solitary inclinations were reinforced by her decade of displacement in the South.

An important aspect of that displacement was cultural. She found Southern literary taste impossibly provincial, and Southern politics painful, writing to her friend, the Southern poet Paul Hamilton Hayne, "Don't you think that for a red hot abolitionist, republican and hard-money advocate, I have behaved well down here in Dixie during these last three long years?" (Easter 1876). She behaved well too in accommodating to the dull routines of her mother's life, but repeatedly described herself as "starving" for culture (letter to Hayne, 14 May 1876). She also found a rich source of untouched material for fiction in the South's struggles to recover from the Civil War five years after the surrender at Appomattox. Although one of the Harper brothers warned her "'of all things' to avoid the subject of the war in connection with the South" (letter to Stedman, 23 July 1876), she ignored his advice and found material there for some of her strongest fiction, such as **"Rodman the Keeper"** (1877) and **"In the Cotton Country"** (1876).[8]

Her ability to treat both Northerners and Southerners with balanced sympathy and irony probably grew from her feeling that they were linked by the emotional intensity of the Civil War years. She wrote Hayne, "What days they were. After all, we *lived* then. It is in vain for our generation to hope to be any other than 'people who remember'" (23 July 1875).

Still, she longed to break away from the South and to travel abroad. Resigned and somewhat resentful, she was stuck with her mother in the South while her brother Charly was making trips to Europe and to California, writing to ask her for money, and destroying his health—with morphine, Woolson believed. His letters so "appalled" and "terrified" his sister that she lived "in a state of constant trouble and dread" (letter to Samuel Mather, 30 Jan. 1877).

Such sibling and oedipal tensions animate much of Woolson's fiction. In **"The South Devil"** (1880, *Rodman the Keeper*), for instance, a hard-working man sacrifices himself for his thoroughly selfish and immature younger brother because the lad reminds him of his own lost beloved—as Charly reminded Constance of her father. Woolson identifies with both brothers, giving the younger her own artistic temperament and her longings for flight and irresponsibility. While such feelings—stunningly transformed into images of a deadly but beautiful swamp—give this story its force, they pushed all her novels but one into melodrama.[9]

Woolson's compulsive focus on the interrelated themes of irrational guilt, self-sacrifice, and the refusal of love can be traced to her clearly understood but unresolved family drama: passion for her father ambivalently transferred to her brother, guilt and inordinate expectations of herself growing out of her sisters' deaths, longing for her mother's love mixed with resentment of her mother's preference for the men of the family. At the same time, she knew that these themes could empower literature, and she used them deliberately: "The most dramatic effects are those that indicate suppressed passion—hounds are ready to slip the leash. They are utilized by Browning; they channelize the Puritan repression in Hawthorne" (Benedict 2: 108).

She also understood and shared Hawthorne's guilt over using as material for art the experience of other human beings who could not be intimately observed without damaging their lives and the observer's own integrity. In her own fiction Woolson revises Hawthorne's major tales about this "unpardonable sin"—*The Scarlet Letter* in **"Peter the Parson"** (1874) and "Rappaccini's Daughter" in **"Castle Nowhere"** (1875). She also creates women narrators who prey on their subject matter like vampires in such stories as **"Jeannette"** (1874), **"Wilhelmena"** (1874), and **"In the Cotton Country."**[10]

In her guilt as an artist, as well as her guilt as a daughter and sister, can be found the roots of Woolson's self-rejection and reclusiveness. It would certainly have been hard for a woman so entangled in these conflicts to accept herself or to form adult attachments. Here too are sources, along with her biological inheritance from her father and grandfather, of the devastating depressions that darkened her life for months at a time and that contributed to her early death, probably by suicide.

* * *

The depressions began during her thirties. She "lost a whole year and more, owing to the depressed state of my mind" after finishing her first novel *Anne* (letter to Stedman, 16 Sept. 1877). She wrote to her girlhood friend Arabella Washburn, "Don't fancy I am sad all the time. Oh no. I am much too busy and too full of plans of all kinds. But at times, in spite of all I can do, this deadly enemy of mine creeps in, and once in, he is master. I think it is constitutional, and I know it is inherited" (Benedict 3: 244). She also inherited another cause of depression from her father—deafness, which came to her in her forties. It added to her isolation—"It is only old friends who will take the trouble to speak in a trumpet"—and soon she was not well enough to see anyone because of prolonged infections brought on by attempts to use artificial eardrums whose pain made her think she "should be mad, or dead, before morning" (letter to Baldwin, 5 Feb. 1892).

She struggled fiercely against depression, and developed three remedies for it. The first was simply to hang on and outlive despair with "simple courage. . . . (I am determined never to outlive my own)" (letter to Baldwin, 15 June 1892). The second was travel, which she used extensively, and successfully, most of her life. After the death of her mother, when she was forty, she left for Europe and never returned to America. Until her own death in 1894, she spent cool months in Italy, warm months in England and Switzerland, and traveled to other exotic locales. She sometimes disliked this rootless life—"it is a curious fate that has made the most domestic woman in the world . . . a wanderer for nearly twenty years" (letter to Katherine Mather, 2 July 1893)—and was often tempted to return to America. But she also loved "the romance & color" of Europe: "What do you say to my trying Algiers next winter? Would'nt that be a bold move!" (Petry 47).

Her third remedy for depression, the "evil spirit that haunts all creative minds," was to pump up one's self-esteem. She advised the poet Paul Hamilton Hayne, ill, impoverished, and despairing, to "Think of yourself highly. . . . The greatest artists are nerved to their greatest works by a sublime consciousness of a belief in their own powers" (10 Jan. 1876).

Unsurprisingly, she saw depression as an occupational hazard for women writers, for whom such self-esteem was all but impossible. Although she must have known that male writers broke down too, she thought women who wrote were predisposed to depression. When she heard that the writer Elizabeth Stoddard was ill, she asked Edmund Stedman, "Why do literary women break down so? . . . It almost seems as though only the unhappy women took to writing" (23 July 1876). Some illnesses came from the physical work of writing long manuscripts by hand. "Too constant pen-work" (letter to Stedman, 24 Feb. 1887) brought considerable pain and a right arm whose muscles "tangle themselves with the nerves of the same locality and the two hold a witches' dance together that sends me to bed and keeps me there" (Benedict 2: 41). Some women even lost the ability to use words. Woolson notes that her "(comparatively) small trouble of lameness sinks into nothingness beside the terrible nervous prostration" her friend Frances Hodgson Burnett suffered every time she finished writing a book; bedridden for six months, she could not produce the right names for things (letter to Samuel Mather, n.d.). Such a loss of control over language, or over one's writing arm, vividly expresses the "anxiety of authorship" that Gilbert and Gubar (49) believe afflicted nineteenth-century women writers.[11]

Women writers also suffered, Woolson thought, from losing their femininity. After spending an evening with Elizabeth Stoddard and Mary Mapes Dodge at the home of Edmund Stedman, she wrote to him:

> How much prettier and lovelier a thousand times over was Mrs. Stedman in every motion, look and tone than the best we other three could do! What *is* the reason that if we take up a pen we seem to lose so much in other ways? . . . But perhaps it is 'compensation'; as we gain money, or fame, just so surely must we lose that which in our hearts we prize a great deal more.
>
> (28 Sept. 1874)

One might dismiss this uncharacteristically formulaic language as a mixture of flattery and fishing if Woolson hadn't also presented herself to another spinster as an old maid whose necessary literary labors unfitted her to attract a man and reap the usual womanly rewards. She wrote Guilford from Oxford on the birth of a niece, "Oxford and rooms and writing a novel are poor things compared to a baby" (Guilford, "Notes").

While she regretted not having children and a home, she showed no signs of willingness to exchange her independent, adventurous life for them. Although often lonely, she never formed a "Boston marriage" as so many of her contemporaries did, finding the love and support indispensable to the artist in a long-term relationship with another woman. She saw such a partnership close up in the relationship of Alice James and Katherine Loring, and must have known of many others, but she never lived for extended periods with any woman but her mother, nor is there much correspondence to be found with women other than her relatives, although there may well be letters that have been lost. She seems to have rejected the domestic world of womanly bonds which had sustained her mother out of a complex mixture of feelings: resentment at the ways that world had disappointed her as daughter and sister and as artist; longing for a wider, more adventurous life of independence and travel; and fear from childhood of losing women she loved.

She never participated directly in the women's movement, but she showed a cautious sympathy with it. She satirized herself, in a very funny letter, for giving in to her sister and spending a lot of money on a silk suit, which failed to conceal her identity as a literary (and therefore dowdy) woman; but she also laughed at Elizabeth Stuart Phelps for adopting dress reform.[12] She sent her sonnet "To George Eliot" to the *New Century for Women,* a journal supporting woman suffrage. And while she let Henry James think she "would never lend her voice to the plea . . . for a revolution which should place her sex in the thick of the struggle for power" ("Miss Woolson"), she wrote his sister Alice that she was in favor of medical education for women but that men and women should receive such education together. "It is the only way, in my opinion, to widen the feminine mind. . . . Do not suppose from that that I think the feminine mind inferior to the masculine. For I do not. But it has been kept back, & enfeebled, & limited, by ages of ignorance, & almost servitude" (Strouse 260).

Most of Woolson's deep attachments were to men, mostly distinguished in or connected with the arts, all safely married except for the entrenched bachelor, Henry James. Correspondence attests to the complex relations she had with Dr. William Wilberforce Baldwin, an American physician living in Florence who treated such noted Americans as Henry James, Samuel Clemens, Edith Wharton, and William Dean Howells (Petry 57n3); with Edmund Clarence Stedman, the eminent critic and poet; with John Hay, who held high posts in the Lincoln, McKinley, and Roosevelt administrations, and who wrote sketches, fiction, and verse as well as a ten-volume study of Lincoln; and with Paul Hamilton Hayne. Her sustained friendships with these remarkable men indicate how readily she was accepted as writer, thinker, and woman, as well as her ambition to achieve eminence like theirs, possibly with their help.[13]

Her hope of meeting Henry James was one factor that impelled her to travel to Europe in 1879. Despite her devastation from her mother's recent death and despite her habitual aversion to society, she managed before leaving America to obtain a letter of introduction to James from his cousin, Henrietta Pell-Clark. James was then the distinguished author of stories, articles, reviews, and several novels, though he had not yet written his major work. Woolson was then the established author of two volumes of short stories and a novel appearing serially in *Harper's.* They met in Florence in the spring of 1880, where despite James's numerous social and professional obligations, "he found time to come in the mornings and take me out; sometimes to the galleries or churches, and sometimes just for a walk in the beautiful green Cascine. . . . He has been perfectly charming to me" (Benedict 2: 184-185).

Woolson had long been fascinated by James's work. Only a few months before they met, she had written a perceptive and appreciative review of his novel *The Europeans* for the *Atlantic.* Three years later she could tell him that "The deepest charm of your writings to me" is that "they voice for me—as nothing else ever has—my own feelings. . . . Your writings . . . are my true country, my real home. And nothing else ever fully is—try as I may to think so" (7 May 1883). For four months in 1886 and 1887 she and James actually shared a home, a villa she was renting outside Florence. Although James told Woolson's sister that these had been "the most charmed and appeased, the most gratified and rewarded and beguiled days that [Woolson] . . . ever passed" (Benedict 3: 338n), they must also have been replete with powerful and mixed feelings on both sides.

For Woolson saw James's personal limitations with her usual clarity, and let him know about them. She told him gently in letters, indirectly in a group of stories about women artists, and with devastating accuracy in journals that James read after her death:

> Imagine a man endowed with an absolutely unswerving will; extremely intelligent, he *comprehends* passion, affection, unselfishness and self-sacrifice, etc., perfectly, though he is himself cold and a pure egoist. He has a charming face, a charming voice, and he can, when he pleases, counterfeit all these feelings so exactly that he gets all the benefits that are to be obtained by them.
>
> (Benedict 2: 135)

She was as openly ambivalent toward the writer as she was toward the man. In the four letters she wrote him that James failed to destroy, she grovels before his genius, and then tells him how she hates him for it. She insists that "the utmost best of my work cannot touch the hem of your first or poorest" (30 Aug. 1882). But she also writes with astounding frankness,

> I do'nt think you appreciated . . . the laudation your books received in America, as they came out one by one. We little fish did! We little fish became worn to skeletons owing to the constant admonitions we received to regard the beauty, the grace, the incomparable perfections of all sorts and kinds of the proud salmon of the pond; we ended by hating that salmon.
>
> (12 Feb. 1882)

In many ways, Woolson's relationship with James exemplifies tensions between male and female writers of their time. For example, James expresses his own mixed feelings about Woolson as woman and as writer, and about successful women writers generally, in his revealing essay "Miss Woolson" (1888). He contrasts women's struggle for admission to "various offices, colleges, functions, and privileges" with their success in gaining "admission into the world of literature: they are there in force; they have been admitted, with all the honours, on a perfectly equal footing. In America, at least, one feels tempted to exclaim that they are in themselves the world of literature." He is sure that Woolson shares his opinion, that except for the "strength of the current which today carries both sexes" to write books, she would not be "competing for the literary laurel" because she believes that women are "by their very nature only too much exposed"—he doesn't say to what—even in their confinement in the home. James claims that she would not "lend her voice to the plea for further exposure—for a revolution which should place her sex in the thick of the struggle for power."

James's essay warns Woolson against struggling for power, against competing with him, against exposing her feelings, while praising her female characters who "try and provide for the happiness of others (when they adore them) even to their own injury." After Woolson's death, James came to believe that she had made such sacrifices for him and that in his egotism he had refused to see her love or seize the salvation it offered him. He dramatized this very situation in "The Beast in the Jungle," whose central theme he took from an entry he found in Woolson's journal—"To imagine a man spending his life looking for and waiting for his 'splendid moment.' . . . But the moment never comes" (Benedict 2: 144-45)—and whose climactic scene of revelation he set at Woolson's grave.

James seemed to think that Woolson had sacrificed opportunities to meet and marry other men because of her absorption in him, but it is doubtful that she could ever have married anyone. Still, she did compromise herself in a way for James. She told him, "I do not come in as a literary woman at all, but as a sort of—admiring aunt. I think that expresses it" (letter to James, 12 Feb. 1882). What this comment expressed was her need to avoid rejection as both a literary competitor and a demanding woman, a need so great that she was willing to sacrifice her literary and sexual identities to it. This denial injured her personally and professionally and surely contributed—along with her ill health, financial worry, history of depression, and philosophical approval of suicide as "the open door"[14]—to her violent death at age fifty-three.

Just after her death, her stricken and guilty friends described her life as wretched. John Hay saw her as a "thoroughly good, and most unhappy woman, with a great talent, bedeviled by disordered nerves. She . . . had not as much happiness as a convict" (Petry 17). And James saw her as never perfectly sane, always so depressed that his feeling for her was largely concern and anxiety (Edel 3: 361). Her own accounts confirm that she was often desperately unhappy.[15] But she was also a witty, irreverent, impertinent woman who enjoyed life passionately. Her psychological doubleness—anguished and amused, home-rooted and restless—was

underlined by her complicated dual national identities—a Northerner in the South, an American in Europe. She transforms these facts of her life into the insights of her fiction.

* * *

From the 1870s to the early 1890s, a wide and varied readership eagerly awaited stories and novels by Constance Fenimore Woolson as they appeared in the leading American literary magazines. Her contemporaries placed her among the best writers of their time. Alice James asked to have Woolson's story **"Dorothy"** read to her in the last days of her life, and Henry James wrote to William Dean Howells that the only English language writers he read were Howells himself and Woolson. By putting his essay on her with studies of George Eliot, Turgenev, Emerson, Stevenson, and Maupassant in his *Partial Portraits,* James indicated that he thought her equally worthy of consideration. By today's standards, she deserves to be ranked with such contemporaries as Sarah Orne Jewett, Mary E. Wilkins Freeman, Rebecca Harding Davis, Elizabeth Stuart Phelps, and Kate Chopin. The five novels, four volumes of short stories, and numerous sketches, poems, and reviews she published in her lifetime show her to be an extraordinary observer, a superb stylist, and a shrewd and witty critic of prevailing mores and ideologies.

Why was Woolson so prominent in her own time and so invisible in ours? Possibly she has been misread, in both periods, as a conservative advocate of womanly repression in the name of self-control, and of masochistic self-sacrifice in the name of goodness. Woolson's contemporaries had been taught to admire women like her "heroic" characters who endured "great sacrifice" and "intense suffering with so much fortitude" (Benedict, *Appreciations* 87). Although some women writers saw that such sacrifices were "actually demoralizing and debilitating" (Kelley 251), such widely read novelists as Augusta Evans Wilson and Caroline Lee Hentz glorified such self-abnegating women. By adding their voices to the chorus of approval for selfless women, they helped to console women for their loss of a wider world than the home, while discouraging them from forsaking their assigned domestic sphere.

Modern readers have failed to perceive that Woolson's fiction is not an endorsement but a radical critique of this ideology, and a brilliant analysis of the dynamics of self-sacrifice in women's lives. Her most complex analysis of female selflessness is in her best novel, *East Angels* (1886), whose heroine conceals her struggle for freedom and her rebellion against male authority behind the unassailable veneer of self-sacrifice. Woolson's pervasive irony is subtle enough in this novel that so astute a critic as James could choose to overlook it and praise the book for making "real and natural a transcendent, exceptional act . . . in which the sense of duty is raised to exaltation" ("Miss Woolson"). Woolson's journals, however, make explicit what James missed: "Self-denial is giving up what one really likes. Search for the secret taste of each person, and see if *that* is indulged! If it is, there is no self-denial, no matter how ascetic the man (or woman) may appear to be" (Benedict 2: 110).[16]

Woolson scrutinizes not only the main pillar of domestic ideology, self-sacrifice, but also its base: love. In her fiction, heterosexual love infantilizes women, although the love of daughters and sisters for their fathers and siblings empowers them. In *Jupiter Lights* (1889), for example, a woman capable of shooting a crazed alcoholic and rescuing a baby from a drifting boat in a tempest is reduced, when she falls in love, to the helpless child her lover wants her to be. But in *Horace Chase* (1893), a crippled woman finds the strength to haul her sister off a mountain ledge. In her fiction love sometimes excuses women for venturing beyond prescribed roles, as in *Anne,* where the heroine has to become a detective to clear her lover's name. Or it requires a woman to exaggerate prescribed roles, as when Madame Carroll imitates the ideal of the child-woman to preserve her husband's vital illusions in *For the Major.* But in no case does Woolson accept the patriarchal love plot in which the heroine finds earthly salvation through the love of a good man.

* * *

The stories reprinted here represent the range of Woolson's best work, and feature her most characteristic theme: women's struggles against the isolation and alienation that she saw as inevitable consequences of confinement to the places and ideas of "woman's sphere." Her expanding vision of this struggle unites the three regions she made her own—the Great Lakes, the South, and Europe. The first three stories, from her first volume of collected fiction, *Castle Nowhere: Lake-Country Sketches* (1875), center on isolated women living on tiny islands in the Great Lakes. While the later stories feature women artists who struggle with the patriarchal norms that silence women's voices, these early stories examine the male literary texts that encode women's marginality. By alluding to the work of Francis Bacon, Hawthorne, Bret Harte, and the literary domestics,[17] she makes them her own, revises their assumptions about women, and creates her own art in the space she has cleared. Of all her precursors, her great-uncle Cooper pressed hardest on her imagination.

Annette Kolodny points out that before women writers could construct their own fantasies of the meaning of the wilderness, they had to deal with the mythic figure who already dominated that terrain: the solitary hunter based on Daniel Boone and given imaginative form by Cooper (224). Literary domestics writing frontier fic-

tion, such as E. D. E. N. Southworth and Maria Cummins, tamed and refined the mighty hunter by bringing him "out of the woods and into town" and by redefining the meaning of the hunt (Kolodny 224).

Woolson, however, went much further; she undermined the hero's claim to heroism. She turns Cooper's solitary woodsman into a recreational hunter and parodies as Romantic affectation his desire to live "close to the great heart of nature." She turns Leatherstocking's sententious morality into the religious fanaticism of Waiting Samuel in **"St. Clair Flats"** or the tortured theology of Old Fog in **"Castle Nowhere."** She transforms his obtusely clear conscience into the haunted consciousness of Reuben Mitchell in **"The Lady of Little Fishing."** Most important, she brings Cooper's marginalized, silenced women to the center of her narratives, sometimes as realistic characters who tell their own stories of loss and endurance, sometimes as mythic figures enacting symbolic dramas. As she creates new tales out of old texts, she reveals the effects on a woman writer of the literary traditions available to her.

"The Lady of Little Fishing" (1874) contains a brilliant image of a writer simultaneously demolishing the work of her predecessors and nourishing herself on it. Woolson's narrator uses buildings of an abandoned town on an island in Lake Superior as fuel to cook his meals while shaping a story from the events that took place there. By giving this action to a man, Woolson evades its aggressiveness, but at the same time she confronts directly the most indigestible part of Cooper's legacy: his portrait of the ideal female as a pious half-wit. Woolson transforms his Hetty Hunter, who thinks she can persuade the Indians to stop taking scalps by reading the Bible to them, into an eloquent woman missionary who imposes civilized behavior on Indians as well as on hunters and trappers, and who, like Hetty, is not harmed by them.

Woolson rewrites *The Deerslayer* to explore the possibility that men might listen to a full-witted woman—say, to a writer like herself. She concludes that even lawless, depraved men will hang on a woman's words just as long as they see the woman as an angel, a sexless, wholly spiritual being. Then they will even cook for this madonna, nurse her when she's ill, build a meetinghouse for her to conduct services, and become docile, sexless children for her. But once she falls in love with one of them, she loses her power over both the man and herself. When she throws herself at the feet of a man who does not love her, her rhetorical degradation is as great as her personal fall: "Oh, take me with you! Let me be your servant—your slave—anything—anything, so that I am not parted from you, my lord and master, my only, only love!" Although love is shown to be a terrible affliction, the Lady dies not of love but of shame.

Love leads the Lady not only to the loss of her dignity and verbal power but also to the devastating revelation that she was not God's instrument in the wildernesses of America and of men's hearts. The story thus comments not only on Cooper but on the strategy of some of Woolson's female precursors, the so-called literary domestics, who excused their unladylike entry into man's public sphere by claiming that they wrote because God had called on them to save souls (Kelley 295). Woolson suggests not only that God's instruments may be deluded, but that they can retain their power only by sacrificing their capacity for love. The story also undercuts the ideology of the woman as "the angel of the house." Woolson's angelic Lady is not confined to any home but takes the whole wilderness for her sphere. Her role is not to sacrifice herself for men but to save them by her preaching. And the story subverts the stand of the literary domestics that a woman's selfless love of one man gives her power over him, and through him, in the world. In Woolson's tale, neither love nor moral influence gives a woman power or security. The Lady fades into a troubling memory about whom men construct stories of their own.[18]

The second of the *Lake-Country Sketches* [*Castle Nowhere: Lake-Country Sketches*] reprinted here, **"Castle Nowhere"** (1875), also focuses on love and religion, but in this story the woman knows nothing of good and evil. The theologian, called Old Fog, is a murderer who thinks he expiates his crime by tenderly raising an abandoned child, although he commits further murders because the girl's "delicate life must be delicately nurtured." In a review in the *Atlantic,* William Dean Howells objected to the "subtle confusion of all the conceptions of right and wrong" created by Old Fog's morality (737), and the character's disbelief in eternal punishment brought Woolson "at least twenty awful letters. . . . Is it possible that I am to be held personally responsible for the theology and morality of all my characters?" (Benedict 2: 20).

She was herself ambivalent about **"Castle Nowhere,"** writing to Stedman that trying "to make the new story more 'ideal' . . . makes me feel as though I was telling a thousand lies" (20 Jan. 1875), while telling Hayne that she thought "it is my best" (letter of May 1875). The story—a novella, in fact—is a remarkable record of Woolson's confrontation as a committed realist with the possibilities of the mythic and romantic. She here rejects the romantic idea that one can escape a historical identity as "somebody" and become "nobody" or "anybody." She tests the assertion of her young hunter Jarvis Waring, that "we can be anybody we please," by confronting him with the ultimate "nobody"—Old Fog, who has deliberately destroyed his civilized identity—and the ultimate "anybody"—Fog's daughter Silver,

whose identity is only potential because she has grown up on a floating castle surrounded by deep water, knowing only four people and five books.

Woolson also entertained and rejected the possibility of being "nowhere" rather than one particular "somewhere"—a possibility that challenges the basis of regionalist writing. "Nowhere" is outside geography, history, religion, society, and culture. There, sinful father and innocent daughter can live happily together until "somebody"—a potential suitor for the daughter—invades, bringing with him a variety of cultural "somewheres" that eventually destroy "nowhere." Jarvis brings the world of Scripture to the wilderness when he identifies Silver as Rachel and himself as Esau, and explains to Silver the meaning of death and resurrection. The world of mythology enters through allusions to Sisyphus, Psyche, and Sleeping Beauty. The world of patriarchy is exemplified by the polygamous Mormons on nearby Beaver Island, while Silver's name indicates that she, like Mormon women, is merely a medium of exchange between men. The world of art is only another form of struggle between men and of male dominance over women: Fog steals Jarvis's copy of Shakespeare's sonnets and a Titian miniature for Silver, who learns "womanly feelings" from the way male art structures love and loss. The sole female influence to balance this male perspective is a doubly disqualified woman—a mute ex-slave.

Whether she is "nowhere" or "somewhere," then, a woman's effort to become "somebody" is severely constrained. But in this novella Woolson does clear a space where women's identities can develop by revising two prominent male fictions in which women are severely repressed: Hawthorne's "Rappaccini's Daughter" and, once more, Cooper's *Deerslayer.* Her critique of Cooper here goes beyond changing a female born with weak brains into a normal woman kept ignorant by a man. While featuring in her title the floating castle prominent in *The Deerslayer,* Woolson centers her tale on what is peripheral in Cooper: the relations of a criminal father and the daughter he raises in the wilderness. She turns the antagonism Cooper imagined between the Hutter girls and Tom into a possessive love between father and daughter whose incestuous tendencies must be halted by a young suitor. And unlike Tom Hutter's horrible slow death from scalping—exactly what he deserves for scalping Indian women and children for bounties—Old Fog dies peacefully in Silver's loving arms. The suggestion is that Woolson, and possibly God, can forgive crimes committed in the name of devotion.

Her use of Hawthorne is more searching. As in "Rappaccini's Daughter," the heroine of **"Castle Nowhere"** lives in a bower of flowering plants which she kisses and talks to because her father's crimes have deprived her of all human companionship. Like Dr. Rappaccini,

Fog is a father willing to sacrifice other men as he has sacrificed his daughter to his own objectives. But unlike the poisonous Beatrice, whose soul may or may not be pure, Silver is utterly innocent. And unlike Hawthorne, Woolson questions whether men of the world could really be satisfied with the pure, cloistered women who were their ideal.

To this end, she loads Silver with archetypes of female innocence until the girl staggers under the weight. Silver is even more innocent than the unfallen Eve, because her father has withheld from her all knowledge of death and of God's word. She is like Sleeping Beauty, with her purity guarded by a hedge of water instead of thorns, like Psyche kept in solitude for the delight of one man and mysteriously provided with delicate food and gorgeous gowns. Woolson's tale makes it clear that the cultural ideal of female innocence limits both male and female development by preventing women's self-realization and by mating men with grown-up children. Silver may have no more opportunity to develop or express herself than Rappaccini's daughter or the Hutter girls, but Woolson, in her strenuous revision of patriarchal texts, has prepared a space where women's identities may develop, where their voices may eventually be heard.

A woman tells her own experience of the wilderness in the last of the *Lake-Country Sketches* reprinted here. The heroine of **"St. Clair Flats"** (1873) has given up her parents, her baby's grave, and even mementoes of life in civilization because her husband considers them "vanity." He has changed her first as well as last name, and even taken away her title of "Mrs." presumably because the spirits that led him into the wilderness tell him that marital relations are also "vanity." Although Samuel belittles Roxana's domain—he tells visiting hunters that the "woman will attend to your earthly concerns"—Roxana has come to like the spirits who tell Samuel of a thousand years of joy about to begin in America, when it becomes a new Eden. But she also does her best to realize Eden in the present, miraculously providing fresh butter and down pillows on a tiny island at the center of a labyrinth of marshy channels.

Woolson makes this remote spot speak not only of the conflict between flesh and spirit, but also of the related struggles between female and male, the practical and the visionary, the comic and the romantic, the mobile and the stationary, the historic and the mythic. These concerns are superbly illustrated by the imagery of the St. Clair Flats, and by an astonishing range of allusion to myth and legend, Old and New Testament, history and literature. Like the effect of these male texts on a woman writer, the Flats are beautiful but bewildering, fascinating but disorienting: "It is an ocean full of land,—a prairie full of water,—a desert full of verdure."

The story is an elegy for two American myths, one essentially male, the other female. When Woolson's hunter returns to the Flats several years later, he finds no sign of the new American Eden Samuel had waited for, but rather a victory of commerce over the spirit. An ugly and efficient canal cuts through the beautiful channels of the marsh; a lighthouse of "ncw and prosaic brick" replaces the picturesque fortress on stilts. Nor has Roxana's fantasy of making the wilderness into a domestic garden prevailed; she and Samuel have vanished, and her cheerful home is a ruin. Woolson's lyrical prose is her tribute to the beauty and futility of these dreams.

* * *

The next three stories reprinted here, collected in 1880 in *Rodman the Keeper: Southern Sketches,* are set in the post-Civil War South. They all feature women artists who are exiles not only from their homes but from themselves, cut off from self-knowledge and relationships so devastating that solitude is preferable. Ultimately, these repressions exile them from their own art. But while the plots depict female failure, the style and point of view assert Woolson's growing self-consciousness and self-confidence. She replaces the male narrators of the *Lake-Country Sketches* with female narrators or with a female character's point of view. And she analyzes the debilitation of her women artists in an authorial voice that is assured, ironic, and in control. This striking discrepancy between form and content raises questions about the degree to which Woolson identified herself with these failed women artists.

The comedy that dances around **"Miss Elisabetha"** (1875) indicates Woolson's distance from a woman who exercises her art exclusively in the domestic sphere. In her characteristic comic style, prominent in all her novels but rare in her short stories, Woolson reveals the absurdities of the elderly spinster while simultaneously evoking sympathy for her. Perfectly confident in her superiority as a descendant of an old New York Dutch family, Miss Elisabetha marches along dusty Florida roads in her ancient brocade dress, accompanied by a bodyguard of black children, prepared to "grind to powder" the opera singer who threatens to take away the spinster's talented ward, Doro. But this beautiful prima donna also gets comic treatment. A parody of male fantasies of female perfection, she materializes on a beach sitting on a tiger skin, dressed in purple velvet, singing like an angel. In reality she is very much like Miss Elisabetha in her self-importance.

Woolson's technique is to point out such similarities in apparently opposite characters. These women confront each other as representatives of two different social orders, one based on old family distinction, the other on new individual accomplishment. They also represent the differing worlds of high art and domestic art. But in fact their common ground as women is more important than the difference in the music they admire and perform; both women are brilliant performers of roles invented by others, and both obey the rules of male art. Miss Elisabetha is merely out-of-date. She reproduces the stylized trills and quavers her music master taught her forty years before, because she has lived in a cultural vacuum and has not heard newer music. In the same way, she practices female domestic arts, along with their supporting values of self-sacrifice and self-satisfaction, because she does not know that the young man for whom she labors will find other women's arts more appealing than hers.

While Woolson respects the domestic art that enables Miss Elisabetha to offer a comfortable life and a wider future to Doro, she sees that it is doomed to fail along with the rigid system of values it expresses because they make no allowance for nature or spontaneity. When Doro chooses marriage to a Minorcan girl over a life as an opera singer or as a cultivated gentleman, high art, bourgeois art, and domestic art all fall before the simple melody she sings in a voice "as full of rich tones as a peach is full of lusciousness." But his choice of luscious nature is no more fulfilling than Elisabetha's choice of puritanical discipline. If Doro is caged by the limits of the sensuous life he chooses, his guardian is enslaved by her rigid habits that keep her laboring even after Doro's death, and in silence—a sure sign that her arts, and the domestic and familial values that supported them, have failed in a world that doesn't value them.

* * *

Woolson stands in no such distant relationship to the would-be woman artist who narrates **"In the Cotton Country"** (1876). This narrator is a slightly fictionalized version of Woolson herself at that time: a displaced Northerner in the post-Civil War South, a "solitary pedestrian" whose own sense of homelessness is so great that she follows a flock of crows, thinking, "The crows at home—that would be something worth seeing." They lead her not to their home but to a house whose wretched situation "all alone on a desolate waste . . . inspired me with—let us call it interest and I went forward." One might also call it a fascination with solitude even greater than her own, and a need to discover if such deprivation could be endured. The narrator seems to be looking for an image of what she herself would become if she succumbed to her own inclinations toward solitude.

What she finds is a terrifying image of immobilized despair. A once-wealthy Southern woman is living in the dilapidated cabin of her former overseer, unable even to find relief in work like Miss Elisabetha because of her

training in pride and indolence on a prosperous plantation. Two-thirds of the story is the bitter monologue forced from her by the narrator. The other third deals with the narrator's compulsive need to hear the other woman's story, and to find a way out of her own isolation by retelling it to an audience she urgently invokes. "I have written stories of imagination, but this is a story of fact, and I want you to believe it. It is true, every word of it, save the names given, and, when you read it, you whose eyes are now upon these lines, stop and reflect that it is only one of many life-stories like unto it." Abandoning her fictional frame, asserting the truth of her narrative, seizing the reader by the shoulders, Woolson indicates that she is seeking a way out of her own isolation by reaching an audience through the pain of a woman even more exiled than herself.

The situation vividly recalls Hawthorne's admission that he hoped through his writing to "open an intercourse with the world" (preface to *Twice Told Tales*, 587), and his conviction that "somewhere among your fellow creatures, there is a heart that will receive yours into itself" (Blodgett 182). Woolson's story also documents the guilt that accompanies this strategy. To conceal from herself the fact that she is actually exploiting the Southern woman's loneliness and despair, the narrator tells herself that she is a "Sister of Charity . . . bearing balm and wine and oil for those who suffer."[19]

The third Southern story reprinted here is one of Woolson's finest, and her most courageous confrontation of the connection between art and sexuality. In **"The Lady of Little Fishing,"** Woolson had suggested that a woman who allows herself to love a man becomes an ordinary woman whose words have no weight with men. In **"Felipa"** (1876), she indicates that lovelessness limits a woman artist as much as love, and that love for other women is likely to be as disabling as love for men. What appears to us as lesbian or bisexual feeling in **"Felipa"** would not have startled Woolson's contemporaries, since women's romantic friendships were not regarded with suspicion until a later era. Two years after writing **"Felipa,"** Woolson drew attention to the power of the love women can feel for each other in a review she wrote for the *Atlantic* of Alice Perry's novel *Esther Pennefather* (1878). She called the novel a ridiculous book with an original subject: "the singular power one woman sometimes has over another" until they marry and look back at "that old adoration which was so intense and so pure, so self-sacrificing and so far away" (503). **"Felipa"** dramatizes what the review suggests: women who love women lose them to men. This story, like **"In the Cotton Country,"** confirms Woolson's conviction that intimacy with either men or women cannot last but can only betray. It also reveals her conviction that the best protection against such loss is accepting homelessness and habitual solitude, while trying to forge an art that links the writer with the human community.

Catherine, the heroine of **"Felipa,"** describes herself as an "artist, poor and painstaking," living a "poor gray life" in the shadow of her friend Christine, who uses her to show off her own beauty and power over others. If Christine is Catherine's foil, her alter ego is Felipa, the Minorcan child they meet in Florida, who rejects patriarchal forms of religion and art by making a goddess out of palmetto leaves and worshipping her. In her passionate attachment to both Christine and her suitor Edward, Felipa also rejects approved heterosexual behavior. Felipa's sexual ambiguity, implied by her name and made explicit by her equal passion for the man and the woman, is secretly shared by Catherine, but the woman artist is properly socialized to repress such desires, to be "gentle," "quiet and good," to accept a "respectable, orderly doll" as an adequate representation of female possibilities, and to do her modest sketching at the seashore, where women who are no man's mate can occupy a sliver of no-man's-land.

Catherine thinks she can escape her smoldering sexual longings by turning to art, which she uses to evade her feelings rather than to understand or transform them. But Felipa understands that art can poison when it is used to repress rather than to express feeling. When Christine finally accepts Edward's marriage proposal, Catherine pretends to be glad, but Felipa eats the "poison things" in Catherine's paint box, and then stabs Edward's arm with Catherine's little dagger. Catherine insists that since Felipa loved the man and the woman "both alike," her love "is nothing; she does not know." But the child's grandfather realizes that "it was two loves, and the stronger thrust the knife." Catherine also has "two loves," and "does not know" what she feels because she cannot admit to any of her feelings. A failed woman and a failed artist, her attempts to capture on canvas the subtleties of the salt-marsh or Felipa's complex character can only be "hopeless efforts."

Woolson's identification with her women artist characters is more complex in this story than in either **"Miss Elisabetha"** or **"In the Cotton Country"** because here both the repressed woman painter and her wild alter ego Felipa represent parts of Woolson herself. The story is their joint production, with its energy and passion coming from the child, and its form from the woman. Transforming these Dionysian and Apollonian tendencies into female terms, Woolson decides that neither one by itself can produce art. For the rest of her career, she would continue to search for ways in which they could collaborate.

* * *

The last three stories come from Woolson's years abroad, when her own personal and artistic horizons were expanding. As she continued to explore ways

women might wield power through words, she kept raising chilling questions about women and art. If a woman wants passionately to be an artist, but is told she lacks talent, what kind of life can she make for herself in the shadow of great art and criticism by men? The heroine of **"The Street of the Hyacinth"** (1882) is an independent New Woman with the courage to confront male-sanctified artistic taste from the time of the Romans to her own, but when men convince her that her work is hopelessly mediocre, she abandons it. What use can a woman artist make of the genius of women of another age? **"At the Château of Corinne"** (1886) invokes the most influential female texts affirming women's art—Elizabeth Barrett Browning's *Aurora Leigh* and Madame de Staël's *Corinne*—but neither their words nor their examples can save the woman artist of the story from having to marry and give up her writing. If a woman writer has enormous power, would her work be perceived as being so flawed by the anomaly of genius in woman that it would fail to find an audience? In **"Miss Grief'"** (1880) the only satisfaction possible for a woman genius is to die happily deceived that her work has at last found a publisher.

These stories were written in the early years of Woolson's difficult relationship with Henry James and feature successful male writers and critics who resemble James. Their complex realism shows James's positive effect on Woolson's technique, while their plots insist on the negative effect of his arrogance and the patriarchy that sustained it. In two of the stories, the heroine marries the James-like character, but it is clear in both cases that this solution is a "downfall."

Ettie Macks comes from her tiny Western town to live in **"The Street of the Hyacinth"** in Rome to study masterpieces by men as part of her education as a painter. A series of male mentors persuade her that she has not a shred of talent, and at the end she succumbs to marriage to an art critic she loves but cannot respect. The imagery of hyacinths throughout suggests that rather than finding fulfillment, she has suffered "a great downfall" from her "superhuman" heights of integrity. She is like the street of the Hyacinth, pulled down so it would no longer "disfigure" the Pantheon ("the magnificent old Pagan temple" it adjoined). In "Pagan" mythology, Hyacinthus suffered a downfall worse than Ettie's at the hands of his loving mentor, Apollo, who accidentally killed him while teaching him to throw the discus. In this story, the Apollonian principle is purely destructive. On the street of the Hyacinth, Ettie's mentor has slain his beloved's faith in herself as artist and woman. Her female self-assertion would evidently "disfigure" the monumental principles of male culture which her mentor upholds as both art critic and suitor. Nor is the Dionysian principle more enabling, since Ettie's passion for her destructive mentor contributes to her "downfall."

Ettie's independence and seriousness of purpose are like Woolson's own, while her ambivalent relationship with her mentor reflects Woolson's experience with Henry James. But in Ettie's social and intellectual naïveté, her inability to find an audience that can appreciate her art, or her eventual belief in its hopeless mediocrity, there is no resemblance to Woolson. Woolson may here be speculating about what might happen if she married James, and concluding that marriage would end her career without satisfying her desire to love a man she could also respect, a "downfall" on both counts.

* * *

Woolson created another male mentor who persuades a woman to give up her artistic ambitions, not because her writing is judged to be bad—Woolson never reveals its quality—but because he believes that genius in women is a disfigurement or a delusion. In the character of John Ford in **"At the Château of Corinne,"** Woolson combines Henry James's arrogant charm and dislike of women writers with Edmund Stedman's "entire disbelief in the possibility of true fiery genius in women" (letter to Stedman, 23 July 1876). The story's heroine, Katharine Winthrop, is less like Woolson than any of her other artist heroines, in her artistic dilettantism, leisured life, and abundant suitors.

The plot centers on Katharine's need to choose between independence and literary ambition on the one hand, and marriage to John Ford on the other—a man who detests the idea of female genius and dislikes female independence. Both these attributes are symbolized by Madame de Staël and her heroine Corinne. They were admired by women as different as Elizabeth Cady Stanton and Harriet Beecher Stowe, and also attacked in a popular magazine of the time which warned that while women with minds "equal to any human undertaking" exist, "happily these giants of their kind are rare" (*Young Lady's Companion,* Welter 76). The magazine reflected the popular wisdom that women who go beyond male-defined limitations become monsters. Ford expresses this view in a torrent of misogyny which recalls a similar speech, with a similar ironic function, in Elizabeth Barrett Browning's immensely influential verse novel, *Aurora Leigh.*[20] The overblown rhetoric Woolson assigns Ford is a clear sign of her disapproval of his stereotypical masculinity, while the space she gives his violent opinions indicates her belief that such opinions were a very serious obstacle to women writers.

The structure of the story indicates Woolson's regret that modern women lack the means of a Madame de Staël to develop their genius. The story is built on four visits to Staël's place of exile at Coppet, each marking a decline in Staël's influence and Katharine's independence. Her story, worked out in Staël's shadow, has the same outcome as Ettie's, in the shadow of the Pantheon

and the galleries of great male painters. Neither male nor female models of greatness seem of much help to women who would be artists but are persuaded that they have no talent and that their only recourse is marriage to men unable to accept independence or talent in women.

Woolson wrote one tale about a woman writer of undisputed genius. **"'Miss Grief'"** (1880) is narrated by a self-satisfied male author who models himself on Balzac but writes only "delightful little studies of society." He misreads the name of the woman seeking his help in getting her play published, turning Miss Crief into Miss Grief. And she does bring grief to him. Although he tells himself that he is fortunate because "she, with the greater power, failed—I with the less, succeeded," he knows, like the corrupted artist in Henry James's "The Lesson of the Master" (1888), what it means to have everything but "the great thing . . . the sense of having done the best" (135).

Miss Crief's first name, Aaronna, is also significant: "My father was much disappointed that I was not a boy, and gave me as nearly as possible the name he had prepared—Aaron." That name would have linked the child with the authority of the first high priest of Israel. Because Aaron had the verbal powers Moses lacked, God empowered him to lead and judge his people along with Moses. Woolson implicitly compares Aaronna's works to Aaron's elaborate priestly garb when her narrator likens the woman's writings to "a case of jeweller's wares set before you, with each ring unfinished, each bracelet too large or too small for its purpose, each breastpin without its fastening, each necklace purposely broken." When assumed by a woman, the ornaments which symbolized priestly power appear to male eyes only as ruined treasures. Woolson's simile also recalls the "rings of gold" Aaron collected from the Israelites and "fashioned . . . with a graving tool" into a golden calf. Aaron, however, evades responsibility for this act of artistry, telling Moses that he "threw the gold into the fire and there came out this calf" (Exodus 32:24). But Aaronna cannot escape the consequences of her conscious and deliberate artistry. For the discrepancy between her vision and male-defined norms, she is punished with obscurity and poverty.

This story recasts the relation between the Dionysian and the Apollonian artist which Woolson first considered in **"Felipa."** This time the wild genius belongs to a mature woman, but it succeeds no more than when it belonged to a wild child. In **"'Miss Grief,'"** however, the socially conforming male artist wins a measure of love and success, both of which were denied to Catherine, his female equivalent in **"Felipa."** Mediocre men fare much better in Woolson's fiction than either mediocre or brilliant women.

Woolson here imagines a more direct collaboration between the genius and the conformist than in **"Felipa."** The male narrator of **"'Miss Grief'"** tries to correct what he sees as disfiguring faults in the woman's brilliant play, to make it acceptable to a publisher. He finds, however, that at least for a man of his limited talents, the flaws are inseparable from the genius. It is like "taking out one especial figure in a carpet: that is impossible, unless you unravel the whole." As Leon Edel has observed, James took Woolson's metaphor of the "figure in a carpet" for the title of his own tale about the elusive nature of genius. But James gave his male genius, Hugh Vereker, fame and disciples. Miss Crief has neither, because in a woman, genius is perceived as deforming. Her Dionysian imagination, which is "unrestrained, large, vast, like the skies or the wind," cannot be tamed enough to communicate with the public she needs, and brings her only grief.

Characteristically, given her paradoxical and divided nature, Woolson identified with both these characters, and separated herself from both of them. She shared Miss Crief's grief but neither her genius nor her failure. She shared the narrator's success but not his complacent obtuseness. She may have identified with his failure to do the best work of which he was capable, not from lack of dedication but from a fear that her own wildness, like Miss Crief's genius, would have alienated the audience she so urgently needed. Unlike her male mentors, Woolson believed in women's genius, but saw it as so compromised by the patriarchy of her time that it could appear only in distorted forms, and could bring only grief to its possessors.

She believed that women in the past had produced art of distinctive greatness, which could inspire women's genius in the future. Early in her career, she wrote a sonnet, "To George Eliot" (1876), which describes a woman's genius as a combination of the "colossal" power of a Michelangelo with the "finely traced" beauty created by "woman-hands," and concludes, "A myriad women light have seen, / And courage taken, because *thou* has been!" This mixture of power and tenderness is what Woolson hoped her own legacy would be. A month before her death, she thought again of the "giant's work" that a woman could do, and wrote, "I should like to turn into a peak when I die, to be a beautiful purple mountain, which would please the tired, sad eyes of thousands of human beings for ages" (Benedict 2: xvi). Woolson's mountain is not like Shelley's Mont Blanc, embodying the male poet's verbal and sexual power, but like her conception of George Eliot's genius, both maternal and masculine. It suggests that she saw the struggles between gender and genre as not only damaging but also as fruitful.

Notes

1. Biographical material on Woolson is very limited. Unless otherwise indicated, my discussion is based on the following sources: *Five Generations (1785-*

1923), the three-volume collection of Woolson family documents edited by Woolson's niece Clare Benedict, and indicated henceforth as Benedict; *Appreciations,* Benedict's collection of readers' responses to those volumes; *The Life of Henry James* by Leon Edel and his edition of James's letters; John D. Kern, *Constance Fenimore Woolson: Literary Pioneer*; Rayburn S. Moore, *Constance Fenimore Woolson*; and Doris Faber's unpublished biography of Woolson. Unpublished letters are designated in the bibliography by the collections in which they appear.

2. Woolson's uncertainty about her ability to equal Cooper as well as her desire to hitch a ride on his fame appear in an early letter to a publisher: "I would rather not have my name appear with the article, but if it is necessary, please give only 'Constance Fenimore' as I have taken that for a nom de plume" (letter to Mary L. Booth, 2 Feb. 1871).

3. Woolson discussed in her reviews and letters and debated in her fiction the work of her immediate male and female predecessors. Her "gods" are Dickens, Cooper, Emerson, Hawthorne, and Turgenev; Madame de Staël, Charlotte Brontë, George Eliot, George Sand, and Elizabeth Barrett Browning. Of her contemporaries, she finds more to admire in the work of men than of women. She praises Bret Harte's Western tales but insists she is not imitating him; reads and reprints as epigraphs to her stories poems by young Southern men; admires the criticism, fiction, and biography written by her eminent friends Edmund Clarence Stedman and John Hay; reviews the writings of Henry James and tells him they form "my true country, my real home" (Edel 3: 93). She is neutral about or critical of many of her women contemporaries. In her journal, she told herself, "Have all the scenes as distinctly American as S. Jewett, and Miss Wilkins . . . but more realistic," and faulted Rebecca Harding Davis for creating unbelievable characters ("Mottoes"). In letters, she mentions Elizabeth Stuart Phelps, Louisa May Alcott, Mary Mapes Dodge, Frances Hodgson Burnett, Violet Paget ("Vernon Lee"), Elizabeth Stoddard, and Mrs. Oliphant, without giving any opinion of their work. She marvels however that anyone can read the mass of "words, words, words" Augusta Evans Wilson inflicted on her readers, and wonders how readers who liked such writing could ever like her own (letter to Hayne, 10 Jan. 1876).

4. An ambitious book-length poem, *Two Women* (1872), interesting for its reversal of stereotypes, contrasts an experienced woman's generosity with an innocent woman's narcissism. Even more inter-

esting is "The Florida Beach" (1874, Benedict 3: 458), which identifies the woman writer with a lighthouse keeper, suggesting that she is visible, even essential, to an audience she cannot see from her position where land meets sea at the margins of culture.

5. For a suggestive account of regionalism as a women's art form, see Ammons xx-xxii.

6. The distinction between "muted" and "dominant" cultures is made by Shirley and Edwin Ardener, and used by Elaine Showalter to describe the relationship between male and female cultures (261).

7. "Aspinwalls, Stewarts, Rhinelanders, Astors . . . are arriving and we are beginning to breathe that tiresome atmosphere of gold dust and ancestors which has oppressed us for two long winters. I always feel like a fraud when I go sailing with, say, six or eight incomes of six figures and the like" (Benedict 3: 235, 247).

8. Woolson set all her novels in different parts of the South, and prided herself on letters she received from Southerners "about the truthfulness of the 'Southern' part" of *East Angels.* "It is indeed exactly accurate; I have described nothing that is not a literal transcript from life" (letter to Samuel Mather, 18 Mar. 1886).

9. The heroine of her first novel, *Anne,* also written during the years when Charly was writing "appalling" letters, chooses as her lover a man as indolent, careless, irresponsible, and immature as Charly, a character who seems to exist only to give Anne opportunities to show her superior strength and character. An adored scapegrace son provides the complications of the plot of Woolson's second novel, *For the Major* (1883); the heroine of Woolson's fourth novel, *Jupiter Lights* (1889), is tormented by her incestuous passion for her father, her brother, and her brother's son; and her last novel, *Horace Chase* (1893), features the death of a brother from brain fever. Only *East Angels* (1886) is free of these concerns.

10. I discuss these stories and themes in my "Women Artists as Exiles" 6.

11. In *The Madwoman in the Attic,* Gilbert and Gubar argue that women writers had to develop strategies to evade their own anxiety about their right to write at all, in the face of patriarchal assumptions that only men had the necessary authority to be authors.

12. "I did not want the thing at all, but there are so many grand people here, and Clara does not like it unless I am respectable. I could ill afford the gown, and hated paying for it dreadfully. . . .

What remark do you suppose was made about that time by two ladies staying in the same house who did not know me at all? 'Is not that lady opposite us at table a literary person? We have felt sure she was an authoress, and not only that, but there is something about her which makes us think that she was the daughter of a clergyman!' Now then, *they* had on short black alpaca gowns, their noses were sharp and red at the tips, and they wore glasses and had gristly hands. Ages 40 and 50 perhaps. Wasn't it disgusting? After all my trouble and spent money! Elizabeth Stuart Phelps is here again this winter and she is 'Dress Reform.' I am going to be 'Dress Reform' hereafter, in spite of Clara. Dress Reform means two dresses, *et praeterea nihil*" (Benedict 3: 242).

13. More letters have survived to these four men than to Woolson's closest male friend, Henry James, because he destroyed all but four of her letters as well as his letters to her which were in her possession when she died. Despite the paucity of extant correspondence, this relationship has received extensive treatment in Leon Edel's biography of James. But Edel distorts the relationship nearly as much as he misrepresents Woolson's writing, which he describes as "prosy and banal . . . without style, and with an extreme literalness," lacking "ease and the richer verbal imagination . . . minute and cluttered" (2: 203). He presents Woolson as desperately "reaching out to a man younger than herself" (2: 87) who was grateful for her devotion but evasive of the demands of a woman Edel calls an "elderly spinster" though she was only three years older than James. The reality is less stereotypical and more complex.

14. Woolson heavily marked a passage in her copy of *The Teaching of Epictetus* (135) which justifies suicide:

> "when, it may be, that the necessary things are no longer supplied, that is the signal for retreat: the door is opened, and God saith to thee, *Depart.*"
>
> "'Whither?'"
>
> "To nothing dreadful, but to the place from whence thou camest—to things friendly and akin to thee, to the elements of Being."

Someone—probably Clare Benedict—cut out the pages on death and suicide before donating the volume to the Woolson Collection at Rollins College.

15. When Charly died in his thirties in 1883, for example, the news of the death of this brother whom she had hardly seen as an adult "made me suffer more than I have ever suffered in my life. . . . For a time, it seemed to me that I could not rally from the depression it caused; and that it was

hardly worth while to try" (letter to Samuel Mather, 16 Jan. 1884).

16. The wretched ascetic minister in "Peter the Parson" (1874, *Castle Nowhere*), for example, seems to sacrifice physical comforts and love for his religion. But when he dies trying to save a thief who had crippled him from a lynch mob, Woolson shows that he is not a martyr but a suicide. He hates his life because he has failed to conquer either the miners' disbelief or his own "proud, evil body." Woolson's readers thought he deserved better, but she stuck to her guns: "under the abuse which has been showered upon me for my 'brutal' killing of 'Peter the Parson,' I have steadily maintained to myself that both in an artistic and truthful-to-life point of view my ending of the story was better than the conversion of the miners, the plenty to eat, and the happy marriage proposed by my critics" (Benedict 2: 23).

17. Mary Kelley gives this name to the best-selling women writers of the 1850s, 1860s, and 1870s, who published fiction that affirmed the values of women's domestic sphere.

18. "The Lady of Little Fishing" has long been admired, but for the wrong reasons. Fred L. Pattee thinks that Woolson improved on Bret Harte's story, "The Luck of Roaring Camp"—which tells of a group of rough miners reformed by their responsibility for a baby—because of the superiority of the "real motif of [her] story": that women perversely care only for the men who care nothing for them (*Short Story* 255). The story's "real motif" is not that, and Woolson directly criticized Harte's sentimental Victorian idea that a miner could be brought to salvation by an innocent baby—or a pure woman. More radically, Woolson corrected Harte's depiction of the baby's unwed mother as "a very sinful woman" whose death in childbirth was a divine punishment for her sins (69); the chasteness of Woolson's Lady implies that her own death is a punishment for her sin of thinking herself above such human necessities as love and sex.

19. Woolson's longing to interact with the women whose misery she studies in this and other stories such as "Jeannette" and "Wilhelmena" (*Castle Nowhere*) contrasts with Hawthorne's inclination to be an invisible observer. In an early sketch, "Sights from a Steeple," his narrator thinks that "the most desirable mode of existence might be that of a spiritualized Paul Pry, hovering invisible round men and women, witnessing their deeds, searching into their hearts, borrowing brightness from their felicity and shade from their sorrow, and retaining no emotion peculiar to himself" (404). Hawthorne later resisted this tendency in

himself, and in later works he showed such isolated observers as Ethan Brand, Roger Chillingworth, Rappaccini, and Young Goodman Brown as damned souls.

20. This story is a tribute to Elizabeth Barrett Browning as well as to Madame de Staël. Woolson was annoyed by Stedman's condescension to Elizabeth Barrett Browning: "Mr. Stedman does not really believe in woman's genius. His disbelief peeps through every line of the criticism below, whose essence is—'She did wonderfully well for a woman'" (Benedict 2: 93).

Selected Bibliography

MAJOR WORKS BY CONSTANCE FENIMORE WOOLSON

Anne. 1880. New York: Harper, 1882.

Castle Nowhere: Lake-Country Sketches. Boston: Osgood, 1875.

Dorothy and Other Italian Stories. New York: Harper, 1896.

East Angels. New York: Harper, 1886.

For the Major. New York: Harper, 1883.

The Front Yard and Other Italian Stories. New York: Harper, 1895.

Horace Chase. New York: Harper, 1894.

Jupiter Lights. New York: Harper, 1889.

Letters to Dr. William Wilberforce Baldwin. MA 3564. The Pierpont Morgan Library, New York.

Letter to Mary L. Booth. 2 Feb. 1871. General MSS Misc., Princeton University Library.

Letter to Mary Mapes Dodge. n.d. Donald and Robert M. Dodge Collection of Mary Mapes Dodge. Princeton University Library.

Letters to John Hay in Alice Hall Petry, "'Always, Your Attached Friend': The Unpublished Letters of Constance Fenimore Woolson to John and Clara Hay." *Books at Brown* 29-30 (1982-83): 11-108.

Letters to Paul Hamilton Hayne. Duke University Library.

Letters to Henry James. William James Papers. Houghton Library, Harvard University.

Letters to Katherine and Samuel Mather. Mather Family Papers. Western Reserve Historical Society, Cleveland.

Letters to Edmund Clarence Stedman. Edmund Clarence Stedman Papers, Rare Book and Manuscript Library, Butler Library, Columbia University.

"'Miss Grief.'" *Lippincott's Magazine* 25 (May 1880): 574-85.

"Mottoes. Maxims. Reflections." Woolson Papers. Rollins College.

Review of *Esther Pennefather.* Contributors' Club, *Atlantic* 42 (Oct. 1878): 502-03. Benedict 2: 65-67.

Review of Henry James's *The Europeans.* Contributors' Club, *Atlantic* 43 (Feb. 1879): 259. Benedict 2: 55-56.

Rodman the Keeper: Southern Sketches. 1880. Harper, 1886.

"To George Eliot." *The New Century for Women* 2 (20 May 1876): 1.

Two Women. 1862. New York: Appleton, 1877, 1890.

Note: A complete bibliography of Woolson's works is in Kern 180-94.

SOURCES AND FURTHER READINGS

Ammons, Elizabeth, ed. *How Celia Changed Her Mind and Selected Stories.* By Rose Terry Cook. New Brunswick: Rutgers UP, 1986.

Auerbach, Nina. Rev. of *Rediscovered Fiction by American Women: A Personal Selection.* Ed. Elizabeth Hardwick. *Nineteenth Century Fiction* 33 (Mar. 1979): 475-83.

Benedict, Clare, ed. *Appreciations.* London: privately printed, 1941.

———, ed. *Five Generations (1785-1923).* 3 vols. London: privately printed, 1930, 1932.

Blodgett, Harold. "Hawthorne as Poetry Critic: Six Unpublished Letters to Lewis Mansfield." *American Literature* 30 (Mar. 1958): 37-59.

Browning, Elizabeth Barrett. *Aurora Leigh.* Ed. Cora Kaplan. London: Women's Press, 1982.

Dean, Sharon. "Constance Fenimore Woolson and Henry James: The Literary Relationship." *Massachusetts Studies in English* 7.3 (1980): 1-9.

Edel, Leon. *The Life of Henry James.* 5 vols. Philadelphia: Lippincott, 1953-72.

Epictetus. *The Teaching of Epictetus: Being the "Encheiridion" of Epictetus, with Selections from the "Dissertations" and "Fragments."* Trans. and ed. T. W. Rolleston. London: Walter Scott, 1888.

Gilbert, Sandra, and Susan Gubar. *The Madwoman in the Attic.* New Haven: Yale UP, 1979.

Guilford, Linda T. "Notes in Memory of Miss Woolson." TS. Western Reserve Historical Society, Cleveland.

———. *The Story of a Cleveland School from 1848 to 1881.* Cambridge: John Wilson, 1890.

Harte, Bret. "The Luck of Roaring Camp." *Poems and Prose of Bret Harte.* London: War, Lock and Tyler, 1872.

Hawthorne, Nathaniel. *Selected Tales and Sketches.* Ed. Hyatt Waggoner. New York: Holt, 1970.

Howells, William Dean. Review of "Castle Nowhere." *Atlantic* 35 (June 1875): 736-37.

Hubbell, Jay B. "Some New Letters of Constance Fenimore Woolson." *New England Quarterly* 14 (Dec. 1941): 715-35.

James, Henry. "The Lesson of the Master" (1888) in *Henry James: Stories of Writers and Artists,* ed. F. O. Matthiessen. New York: New Directions, n.d.

———. *Henry James: Letters.* Ed. Leon Edel. 3 vols. Cambridge: Harvard UP, 1974, 1975, 1980.

———. "Miss Woolson." First published as "Miss Constance Fenimore Woolson" in *Harper's Weekly* 31 (12 Feb. 1887): 114-15. Rpt. in *Partial Portraits.* London: Macmillan, 1888.

Kelley, Mary. *Private Woman, Public Stage: Literary Domesticity in Nineteenth-Century America.* New York: Oxford UP, 1984.

Kennedy, Elizabeth Marie. *Constance Fenimore Woolson and Henry James: Friendship and Reflections.* Diss. Yale U, 1983.

Kern, John D. *Constance Fenimore Woolson: Literary Pioneer.* Philadelphia, U of Pennsylvania P, 1934.

Kolodny, Annette. *The Land before Her: Fantasy and Experience of the American Frontier 1630-1860.* Chapel Hill: U of North Carolina P, 1984.

Moore, Rayburn S. *Constance Fenimore Woolson.* New York: Twayne, 1963.

Pattee, Fred Lewis. "Constance Fenimore Woolson and the South." *South Atlantic Quarterly* 38 (1939): 131-41.

———. *The Development of the American Short Story: An Historical Survey.* New York: Harper, 1923.

Petry, Alice Hall. "'Always, Your Attached Friend': The Unpublished Letters of Constance Fenimore Woolson to John Hay." *Books at Brown* 29-30 (1982-83): 11-108.

Showalter, Elaine. "Feminist Criticism in the Wilderness." *Feminist Criticism: Essays on Women, Literature and Theory.* Ed. Elaine Showalter. New York: Pantheon, 1985.

Strouse, Jean. *Alice James: A Biography.* Boston: Houghton, 1980.

Weimer, Joan Myers. "Women Artists as Exiles in the Fiction of Constance Fenimore Woolson." *Legacy* 3.1 (Fall 1986): 3-15.

Weir, Sybil B. "Southern Womanhood in the Novels of Constance Fenimore Woolson." *Mississippi Quarterly* (1976): 559-68.

Welter, Barbara. "Anti-Intellectualism and the American Woman 1800-1860." In *Dimity Convictions: The American Woman in the Nineteenth Century.* Athens: Ohio UP, 1976.

Wood, Ann Douglas. "The Literature of Impoverishment: The Women Local Colorists in America 1865-1914." *Women's Studies* 1 (1972): 3-45.

Caroline Gebhard (essay date 1992)

SOURCE: Gebhard, Caroline. "Constance Fenimore Woolson Rewrites Bret Harte: The Sexual Politics of Intertextuality." In *Critical Essays on Constance Fenimore Woolson,* edited by Cheryl B. Torsney, pp. 217-33. New York: G. K. Hall & Co., 1992.

[*In the following essay, Gebhard examines the intertextual relationship between Woolson's "The Lady of Little Fishing" and Bret Harte's "The Luck of Roaring Camp," demonstrating how the former appropriates the literary style and sexual politics of the latter for its own purposes.*]

> I have such a horror of "pretty," "sweet" writing that I should almost prefer a style that was ugly and bitter, provided that it was also *strong.*
>
> —Constance Fenimore Woolson[2]

> The mechanics of amorous vassalage require a fathomless futility. . . . (If I acknowledge my dependency, I do so because for me it is a means of *signifying* my demand: in the realm of love, futility is not a "weakness" or an "absurdity": it is a strong sign: the more futile, the more it signifies and the more it asserts itself as strength.)
>
> —Roland Barthes, *A Lover's Discourse*[3]

[1]Four years after *The Luck of Roaring Camp and Other Stories* (1870) appeared, a young woman published a story in the *Atlantic Monthly* about an all-male camp deep in the woods that undergoes a miraculous transformation. In **"The Lady of Little Fishing,"** Constance Fenimore Woolson rewrote Bret Harte's story of Roaring Camp.[4] This was not just any story she chose to rewrite. "The Luck of Roaring Camp" established the style that was Harte's trademark. And it was also the story that one may say without too much exaggeration started the literary equivalent of the California Gold Rush. Harte's enormously popular fiction helped initiate the production of a fabulous Wild West that still continues today.[5] Harte's Roaring Camp is, of course, no place for a lady. Indeed, the reaction of the young woman who first proofread the story nearly persuaded the pub-

lisher not to print it.[6] On his side, Harte of the *Overland Monthly* had little use for ladies meddling in fiction; Patrick D. Morrow notes, "Hardly a single female-authored book failed to elicit some snide comment."[7]

Yet the first to study his effects most closely and the first to seize upon the possibilities for reworking "The Luck of Roaring Camp" itself was nevertheless a well-bred young woman with literary ambitions. Descended from a distinguished Eastern family, which included one of America's best-known novelists, James Fenimore Cooper, Constance Fenimore Woolson was a woman who impressed the men in her literary circle (which included the critic E. C. Stedman and later Henry James) as being a woman of taste and refinement. Yet she chose as one of her first literary models a writer who seems in every way the opposite of what one would expect to appeal to such a woman. Critics have generally interpreted Woolson's obvious borrowing from Harte's fiction as yet another case of a master-disciple relationship, reminding us of how often women are cast in the role of disciple to a male "master."[8] Close attention to the nineteenth-century literary context for Woolson's bold maneuver, as well as an examination of her revision of the male fantasy that Harte mines in "The Luck of Roaring Camp," however, suggests that the relationship between these two writers cannot be understood as a case of literary discipleship; rather Woolson's conscious intertextual play with Harte's text is better read as a woman writer's bid for both literary popularity and mastery.

Woolson's rewriting of the story that made Harte famous represents an American woman writer's attempt at the outset of her career to appropriate the style and success of a popular male writer for her own, quite different literary purposes. How different they were may be gauged by the tale Woolson made from her source, but before we can consider how **"The Lady of Little Fishing"** revises the male fantasy elaborated in "The Luck of Roaring Camp," we must first situate the moment of her response to Harte, in the context of late nineteenth-century literary culture and of her own struggle to succeed as a professional writer after the Civil War.

I

In 1870 on the strength of the sensation caused by "The Luck of Roaring Camp" and a few other pieces published in the *Overland Monthly,* William Dean Howells offered the brash Western writer an unheard-of $10,000 for the *Atlantic Monthly*'s exclusive rights to his fiction for one year. The celebrated contract confirmed that he had scored not only a phenomenal popular success but also a critical one. To see why contemporaries were so taken by Bret Harte, it is only necessary to quote Howells: "Readers who were amazed by the excellent quality of the whole magazine were tempted to cry out most of all over 'The Luck of Roaring Camp,' and the subsequent papers by the same hand, and to triumph in a man who gave them something new in fiction."[9] The "something new" was not only Harte's locales—"the revolver-echoing cañon, the embattled diggings, the lawless flat, and the immoral bar"—but also his ability to render these places and the people in them who were formerly beneath literary notice not only inoffensive, but positively charming to middle-class tastes, especially to masculine tastes. Howells interprets Harte's literary coup as primarily a triumph of those masculine tastes, supposing that women generally would not "find his stories amusing or touching" because of the "entirely masculine temper" of Harte's sensibility. He imagines that "perhaps some woman with an unusual sense of humor would feel the tenderness, the delicacy, and the wit that so win the hearts of his own sex," but he assumes that Harte's brand of humor and "the robust vigor and racy savor of the miner's vernacular" must "chiefly commend itself" to a masculine mind.

There is no doubt, however, that Woolson not only admired Harte's work, she made use of it. In **"Misery Landing,"** her hero takes to the woods, armed with Thomas à Kempis, French and German philosophy, and last, but not least, a volume of Bret Harte. In *Castle Nowhere* (1875), her first volume of short fiction, she chose to reprint this story and four others that deliberately echo Harte. **"Castle Nowhere"** and **"St. Clair Flats"** employ male narrators who adopt a narrative stance similar to Harte's to relate their encounters with society's outcasts in fantastic, remote settings. The fourth tale, **"Peter the Parson,"** though much bleaker than anything Harte ever wrote, recounts an instance of frontier justice in a mining camp, a subject Harte had treated earlier.[10] The last, and often praised, story in the volume, **"The Lady of Little Fishing,"** is, as I have noted, a recognizable revision of Harte's most famous tale. But it was not, I think, his "ferocious drollery" that interested Woolson, for unlike Harte's stories, Woolson's tales of encampments on the outskirts of civilization have a somber feel. Whether or not Howells was right in surmising that Harte primarily appealed to male readers, it is clear that he appealed to Woolson, but most likely not for the reasons that Howells imagines.

Woolson's self-conscious adoption of a popular male writer rather than a popular female one as a literary role model is significant in view of the literary marketplace in post-Civil War America. The generation of women writers who had succeeded in dominating the marketplace in the 1850s through their immense popularity still enjoyed a large following in the 1870s. If Bret Harte and other Westerners were making inroads into the nation's magazines of high culture, E. D. E. N. Southworth and other popular women writers still held their own.[11] Woolson did not lack female literary mod-

els, and we must therefore read her readiness to admire Harte in conjunction with her desire to reject her countrywomen as literary precursors. In the early stages of her career as a writer, Woolson was anxious to dissociate herself from the sentimental subjects and style of expression associated with women.

How Woolson felt about the prospect of being relegated to a female literary sphere is clear from her anger as a young woman; she later remembered "how sore" she felt when her "demi-god"—one of her male professors at school—delivered "an hour's eulogy of Miss Alcott's 'Little Women.'" She added that she thought such works "had their own sphere, and that it was a very high one," but it was not that of Shakespeare or Milton or of the great writers of fiction.[12] Her painful sensitivity about the commendation of particular types of women's writing suggests that she interpreted such extravagant praise as false, masking a fundamental disbelief in the power of women to write works of genius outside their "own" sphere.[13] Although her first book was a prize-winning children's book, Woolson had no intention of becoming trapped within this traditionally female literary sphere.[14] "I have the idea that women run too much into mere beauty at the expense of power," she confided to a male poet and friend, admitting, "the result is, I fear, that I have gone too far the other way; too rude; too abrupt."[15]

When she began to publish, Woolson also worried that she would be rejected by the majority of readers because she refused to write as a woman was expected to write. Significantly, she imagined this rejecting reader as female. She once confessed that "a dear good aunt" of hers "unconsciously to herself" always represented to Woolson "the immense general class of readers." She was afraid that female readers like her aunt who confounded "'Christian Reid' with the great Charles of the same name," who were "devoted to Mrs. Southworth," and who thought the books Woolson admired "queer" and "stupid" ("stupid," Woolson explains, was her aunt's verdict on *Middlemarch*) would have little patience with anything she cared to write.[16] For a woman who aimed at making a living as a professional writer, these were not idle fears. In the 1870s, her father recently dead, Woolson was beginning to depend on income from her writing; without it, she recognized that she and her mother "should be very much cramped . . . every day an anxiety."[17] She was never financially secure despite her critical success as a writer, yet she always saw her writing as something she did not primarily do for money. Her personal correspondence makes plain Woolson's dedication to her art. She once wrote her niece, "I don't suppose any of you realize the amount of time and thought I give to each page of my novels; every character, every word of speech and of description is thought of, literally for years."[18] Woolson at times bows to the old view that writing makes a woman unfeminine: "What *is* the reason that if we take up a pen we seem to lose so much in other ways?" Woolson once wondered, certain that her friend, Stedman, must be glad *his* wife was not a writer.[19] But she is not afraid to see herself as an artist in pursuit of greatness, an ambition that very few women in America would have owned a generation earlier.

It must be said, however, that Woolson is not fair to her female predecessors; as Nina Baym and others have suggested, the women of Woolson's generation owed a great deal to the example of women like Southworth whose successful careers as professional writers created the conditions for the literary ambitions of the women of the next generation. Nor is it fair to characterize the "women's fiction" these writers produced as nothing but "'pretty,' 'sweet' writing."[20] Yet the very success of "women's fiction" threatened Woolson. To make a place for herself as a woman with high artistic ambitions, she felt compelled to reject the previous generation of American women's writing. Male writers, such as her contemporary Henry James, engaged in similar revaluations and rejections, as is evident in James's commentary on Nathaniel Hawthorne. But for a woman, the rejection of a popular feminine literary mode meant risking disapproval and even courting literary oblivion. Readers brought up on the happy endings of women's fiction, she feared, would find her fiction "queer" or "stupid," and indeed, for one early story, she reports that readers and critics alike "showered" abuse upon her for her "'brutal killing of Peter the Parson.'" Yet even such an overwhelmingly negative response as this, she asserted, could not make her abandon "an artistic and truthful-to-life point of view," though it violated "'the plenty to eat and the happy marriage'" popular with the public.[21]

Woolson was willing to risk her readers' disapproval; her self-conscious adoption of the ultramasculine style of Bret Harte is part of her declaration of literary independence from the "feminine sphere" of literature. Harte struck her—and many of her contemporaries as well—as "new and unconventional."[22] To Woolson, Harte's writing seemed as far as it was possible to be from the "pretty and sweet" stories supposed the natural province of women. To a modern eye, Harte's tales easily reveal a strain of sentimentality not so different from that usually ascribed to nineteenth-century women's writing, but Harte's genius was to discover that the sentimental could be given new life if the heart of gold were put into unexpected places—the rough miner or the unreclaimed prostitute. But to Woolson who had grown up spending the summer along the Great Lakes, where the wild life of the fur trade had not yet been forgotten, the uncouth characters and rugged scenes of Harte's fiction represented freedom to a woman writer.

Woolson used Harte as a point of departure for her early work. But she adamantly rejected the idea that she was Harte's disciple. "In spite of all I said to you," she once explained to Stedman, "I do *not* plead guilty to imitating Harte." She added that Harte "was the sensation of the hour, that was all."[23] Woolson was also well aware that Harte did not fulfill his early promise as a writer; in a later letter to Stedman, she writes that she "felt she could not desert her old favorite," but she admits, "I am afraid to read 'Gabriel Conroy'; I skimmed a little of it, and it seemed so disappointing."[24] Yet critics have usually been content to read Woolson as Harte's disciple; very few have seen any complexity in her conscious use of Harte's work. This judgment is all the more ironic, in the light of these same critics' willingness to admit that in rewriting Harte's popular story, she "bettered" the work of her "master."[25] Joan Myers Weimer is the notable exception, arguing that Woolson in revising Harte's popular tale performs a radical critique of the assumptions that lie behind his fiction.[26] But Weimer does not acknowledge that in Harte's writing, Woolson found much to admire and much that she could use. Her transformation of "The Luck of Roaring Camp" into **"The Lady of Little Fishing"** offers a glimpse into the sexual politics of literary intertextuality, both as practiced in nineteenth-century America and as carried on in contemporary criticism.

It is telling that the relation of these two American writers, one a man at the height of his popularity, the other a woman in the process of defining herself as a writer, was never realized as a literary friendship and that the relationship, such as it was, remained one-sided, in the mind of the woman writer alone. According to her biographer Rayburn S. Moore, Harte's name "occurs frequently" in Woolson's correspondence, but she did not occupy anything like this place in Harte's life; indeed, he seems never to have taken notice of her existence.[27] The two apparently never met, despite their sharing a good friend in John Hay.[28] It is even more telling that twentieth-century critics, despite their often judging Woolson as the better writer, have persisted in seeing theirs as a relationship in which intertextuality works only in one way, from "master" Harte to "disciple" Woolson (later in her career, according to some critics, she graduates from being Harte's disciple to being Henry James's[29]). Woolson's rewriting of "The Luck of Roaring Camp," however, deserves to be read as a woman writer's daring gambit. She was not only interested in capturing for herself Harte's readership and his critical success; she rewrites his story to make it serve her needs as a woman and as a writer in late nineteenth-century America. Her pointed reiteration of Harte's narrative situation in **"The Lady of Little Fishing"** invites a comparative reading, but the crucial and all-important difference in Woolson's text—the insertion of "the Lady's" voice and with it female desire into Harte's male text—testifies to the ambition of her project: to rewrite nineteenth-century American culture from a woman's point of view.

II

"The Luck of Roaring Camp" has a long critical history. Nineteenth-century critics tended to see it as a story of "noble" pathos, praising its evocation of "the spirit of early California life." Twentieth-century critics have been less unanimous in their praise. Although Fred Lewis Pattee reads the story as an important contribution to the American short story, other critics, such as Cleanth Brooks and Robert Penn Warren, have discussed it as an example of the failure of sentimental writing. In the late sixties and seventies, critics seeking to rehabilitate Bret Harte defended the story as a well-constructed "parable," although whether the story is to be read as a parable of Christian values, Manifest Destiny, or Victorian progress, or even as a parody of these pieties, is contested.[30] But Woolson's revision of this story suggests that she interprets "The Luck of Roaring Camp" in terms of nineteenth-century sexual politics,[31] an interpretation moreover fully in line with many modern interpretations of "classic" American fiction. For example, both Leslie Fiedler and Judith Fetterley, though from opposite points of view, see canonical American literature as retelling a central male fantasy, the escape to a paradise without women.[32]

In Harte's story the fantasy takes the form of a regression to a golden summer of childhood, where there is no separation from the mother: men and baby live happily together, in a womblike valley high in the Sierras.[33] The instrument of the camp's transformation is the baby, and the deepest instinct, the means by which paradise is recaptured, the desire to merge with the mother. Harte's narrative is staged as a gentleman's monologue, with the reader imagined as a mirror of the narrator, a gentleman at his elbow, who can be trusted to see the story as he sees it, despite certain aspects in questionable taste (the introduction of the camp prostitute and her illegitimate baby). The humor of this story depends upon the gentleman's holding himself—and the reader—at a safe distance from "them." The high literary tone of the gentleman-narrator—"deaths were by no means uncommon in Roaring Camp, but . . . this was the first time that anybody had been introduced into the camp *ab initio*" (2)—assures us that we ought not to take the likes of French Pete, Stumpy, and Kentuck seriously, but rather we should enjoy the ludicrous spectacle of a bunch of rough men reduced to cooing over a baby.

Woolson instead sets up the tale as a dialogue between two male narrators, one, a young man in his twenties, and the other, a man in his fifties. In her tale, the instrument of change is not a baby, but a beautiful woman. Harte's story proffers the fantasy that the forbidden wish to return to the womb can—if only briefly—be satisfied. Woolson's tale, however, dramatizes that such wishes cannot really be satisfied, for they are always already subject to a reality principle. The very harshness

of her setting, deep winter on an island in Lake Superior, contrasts with Harte's. Although Woolson's camp represents an imaginary space of freedom, where male and female might meet and love as equals, finally, however, Woolson's story does not offer us a wish fulfillment at all. Hers is a cautionary tale about the damage that erotic fantasies sanctioned by the dominant culture can do, especially when they are substituted for social relations between men and women that are always more complex than ideology admits or fantasy allows.

The dialogic frame of her story allows Woolson to explore the dominant configurations of male and female fantasies in nineteenth-century American culture from multiple points of view. The frame narrator, the young man who hears the tale, is a figure of the narcissism of the male. He is under the delusion that everything is there for his amusement. Choosing this voice to frame the tale is a brilliant stroke, for it both provides the reader a measure of the egocentric behavior of the young man in the narrated story as well as invites the reader to side with the fantastic tale over his callow certainty. Struck by the "stupendous" fact that he had not even been born when the story the older man tells took place, he is clearly too immature to grasp fully what he is about to hear. Yet Woolson also suggests that the other male narrator is limited as well. Like some American incarnation of the Ancient Mariner, he is strangely obsessed by the story he is telling; at the end, it seems clear that he returns to tell the tale because he has only now begun to understand what happened there. But he also represents the dominance of masculine desire in American culture as he lives to tell the story, and it is his version of the events that survives.

Male desire, however, makes up only half the story. Through the filter of a dialogue between these two men, Woolson gives speech and desire to a woman. Only the remembered words of "our Lady" enable the reader to make sense of the events: In this curiously mediated way, her female creator represents female desire. By making the woman's voice central to the story, however, Woolson breaks Harte's illusion of a self-sufficient all-male world and so provides an alternative vision to the meaning of the West in America. The space beyond the borders of civilization represented by the freedom of the all-male camp, as Woolson's tale attests, becomes all too easily the place where dominant, middle-class culture once more plays out its enslaving fantasies.

In her revision, Woolson subtly undermines Harte's version of the American fantasy of a happy, all-male existence uncomplicated by women by exposing that this fantasy depends upon women—upon women being silenced and excluded. Not only can there not be a story without a woman in it—even Harte's story, after all, needs a woman to produce the wonderful baby—but also Woolson insists, the woman *is* the story. When the frame narrator discovers that his companion was actually one of the builders of the ghost town, he is astounded:

"Was n't a meeting-house an unusual accompaniment?"

"Most unusual."

"Accounted for in this case by—"

"A woman."

"Ah!" I said in a tone of relish; "then of course there is a story?"[34]

It might be argued that Woolson once more reinscribes the woman as object, as the body of the fiction, upon whom men write their desires, but Woolson deliberately complicates the dominance of what Laura Mulvey has called the male gaze.[35] The privileged position of the male gaze is undercut by being split between two male narrators, neither of whom moreover seems entirely worthy of the reader's trust. Unlike Harte, who gives his narrator literary airs that suggest he is superior to the story he tells, Woolson repeatedly shows up the pretensions of the frame narrator. "Ruins are rare in the New World; I took off my hat. 'Hail, homes of the past!'" the young man declares, when he comes across these unlikely remains of a town in the wilderness (3). His jejune posturing throughout forces the reader to realize how limited his perspective is. The second male narrator, who materializes out of nowhere, also invites the reader's doubts. His obsession with the story he tells suggests a rigidity that is as suspect as the young man's jocular familiarity.

In "The Luck of Roaring Camp," Harte excises the woman early in the story. "The less said of her the better," Harte's narrator comments, adding, "She was a coarse, and it is to be feared, a very sinful woman" (1). In his tale, the woman never says a single word; there is no place for a woman to speak or to signify what, if any, desires she might have. Harte portrays the men as "boys" who happily return to the innocent companionship of their own sex once the camp prostitute dies in childbirth. The feminine, displaced onto nature and removed from the realm of complex adult relationships, remains at a safe distance. But Woolson sees male-female relationships as the main drama, imagining no escape from eros, even in the most remote wilderness. True, the men on their island in Lake Superior do manage for a time to live a relatively simple life without women: "there was n't any nonsense at Little Fishing— until *she* came," as the old man puts it (6). But this is only illusory, for Woolson's narrative reveals that such "nonsense"—that is desire, that which is not entirely subject to reason—is what lies at the great heart of nature, and indeed the heart of all stories.

"The Lady" miraculously appears in the camp one night, heeding the call that she must preach the gospel in every camp on Lake Superior. The men enshrine her as a saint, giving her the best wigwam and surrounding it with pine saplings, as if she were a medieval virgin to be protected by walls and moats. Almost overnight, civilization flowers, with log houses and a church springing up where there had only been shanties. The old man recalls, "It seemed as though she was not of this earth, so utterly impersonal was her interest in us, so heavenly her pity" (8). But Woolson's story exposes male worship of a pure and pious womanhood as a fatal illusion. When their "Lady" falls in love with one of the trappers, she awakens to her own erotic desire. For her, it is a slow, tortuous process, like spring coming to the Great Lakes, and she does not fully comprehend what is happening to her. It becomes clear to the camp, although it is not yet clear to her, that their Lady is in love, and with the one young man who is oblivious to her. The men feel bitterly betrayed. She has shown herself to be "nothing but a woman." In a dramatic scene in the church, the men confront her with the truth. When the angry men have the man brought to her, the impetuous object of her desire rejects her: "'What is she to me? Nothing. A very good missionary, no doubt; but *I* don't fancy women preachers. You may remember that *I* never gave in to her influence; *I* was never under her thumb. *I* was the only man in Little Fishing who cared nothing for her!'" (22). As he tries to leave, she prostrates herself at his feet, begging him to take her with him. He rejects her, leaving her to pine away and die. At the end of this story, the reader is not surprised to learn—although his listener is very surprised—that the man who has narrated these events of thirty years ago, the only man who has come back after all these years to find their Lady's grave, is the young man who once so absolutely refused her. What are we to make of this story of the Lady's humiliation?

Even though the men are made furious by the discovery that their Lady, too, is driven by carnal desire, this is not because the men have succeeded, as Harte's miners do, in actually banishing eros. The transformation of a camp of hardened men into the pure joys of collective boyhood that in Harte's story is dramatized as a real possibility is shown up in Woolson's story as a sham. Her tale shows us that desire has only gone underground; the men's fury is unleashed not because they have been truly reformed and are therefore hurt by her "betrayal," but because the exposure of her erotic need forces into the open what the men would prefer to hide from themselves: the true source of her power all along has been sexual, not spiritual. On both sides, erotic desire has been sublimated in a dangerous and idolatrous game: the Lady believes she is holy and above desire, and the men, who would have her so, worship her as a god.

On one level, then, the story unveils an allegory of how the Cult of True Womanhood operated in nineteenth-century American culture.[36] Absorbed in the business of making an aggressively capitalist enterprise pay off (as hunters and trappers, they participate in a not-so-symbolic rape of the wilderness), the men seize upon her as an ideal of womanhood to bless their godless activities. Safely shut up within her home/church, the Lady is allowed to wield her "influence," but only over domestic and spiritual matters, which the story suggests is a narrow realm indeed. The men attend church on Sunday and adopt more gentlemanly manners, but the business of killing and trapping goes on exactly as before. In making her into the icon of "Our Lady," the men mystify her actual position in relation to themselves, which is in reality analogous to the animals they trap and profit from, for she, too, has been converted into an object of symbolic value. She is not a human being to whom they must respond, or with whom they must play any of the difficult roles of brother, husband, or friend, but a conveniently distant object of desire. At one point, the Frenchman in the camp disabuses another trapper, who imagines that what he feels for their Lady is similar to what he would feel for a sister; relations with one's actual sister, the trapper makes clear, are never so simple. The Frenchman says of his own sister: "We fight like four cats and one dog; *she is the cats*" (37). As long as their Lady is content to remain an idol and the men are willing to sublimate their desire, civilization of a sort can prosper. But the cost of such a civilization erected upon women denying their bodies may be read in the tortured relations between the sexes that the story portrays as the norm.

Yet men are not wholly to blame for this arrangement, for women—especially "ladies," that is, middle class women—Woolson suggests, are themselves complicit in a social order that chiefly values them as objects to display and desire. Under the delusion that her influence over the men is "heavenly," the Lady wills her isolation and seeks out her martyrdom as a saint. But she is the one, the story shows, who in the end pays the most dearly for her own participation in the process that turns her into an object and denies her an autonomous subjectivity. The cost of True Womanhood is the loss of physical and sexual vitality. In the beginning, the Lady is pale, bloodless, almost a ghost. The only sign of life—as with Hawthorne's Hester—is her hair, but only a little of it is allowed to glimmer through her white cap. But when she falls in love, her female sexuality emerges as she stands before them "crowned only by her golden hair" (16), more like Lady Godiva than the Virgin Mary. Woolson manages the climax with great power, as hatred, rape, and violence seem about to erupt as the Lady falls from grace and admits to desire.

But something else happens. The woman speaks and strikes the men "dumb," disrupting this male text of possession and desire. The Lady's discourse is that of the traditional masculine "amorous vassalage" that Roland Barthes analyzes so well in *A Lover's Discourse*,

which in fact *requires* "a fathomless futility." Barthes reminds us that the lover's acknowledgment of dependency becomes "a means of *signifying* demand" for "in the realm of love, futility is not a 'weakness' or an 'absurdity': it is a strong sign: the more futile, the more it signifies and the more it asserts itself as strength."[37] Yet it is shocking that a woman, a "lady," would appropriate this discourse, and all the more shocking because her gesture of submission is nevertheless a claim to power.[38] Clasping her beloved's ankles, she lays her face on his shoes and begs him to "let me be your servant—your slave—anything—anything, so that I am not parted from you, my Lord and master, my only, only love" (22); paradoxically, however, she signifies her strength in this gesture of total erotic self-abasement, which, in its extremity and futility, not only bespeaks an enormous demand, but also testifies that she is the men's equal in desire.

The female author enables the woman to speak, but the radical import of her words is that in speaking her desire, she does not reveal herself as Woman, as Other; rather she reveals that men and women are the same. When the Lady positions herself in the male role of humble suitor at the beloved's feet, she inverts the hierarchy of social meaning based on a belief in the "natural" difference between the sexes: predatory, amorous males in pursuit of passionless female prey. By suing for her lover's favor, she shatters the image of woman as a cold and distant mistress, unwittingly laying bare the power relations implicated in the culture's discourse of romantic desire. This role reversal betrays that this discourse is grounded in male power over women, in which "true" women, like slaves, are presumed to have no autonomous desires that might give rise to desires at variance with the dominant order. This is why Woolson represents the Lady's erotic speech act as so potentially disruptive; the spectacle of women desiring as men desire threatens to overturn a hierarchy based on female subordination and thus to remake the dominant social order. The potency of this threat explains the extraordinary measures the men take to erase all traces of what happened: "They tore down her empty lodge and destroyed its every fragment; in their grim determination they even smoothed over the ground and planted shrubs and bushes, so that the very location might be lost" (23). But Woolson proposes, contrary to Harte, that women can never be wholly silenced, entirely erased.

Nevertheless, no good comes of the Lady's attempt to express herself as a desiring subject. She suffers the same fate as the silent prostitute in Harte's story: abandonment and death. **"The Lady of Little Fishing"** comes uncomfortably close to supporting the ideology of True Womanhood: for women who fall through sexual desire, the consequences are betrayal and death. And yet Woolson's story resists any simple reading, for both desire and danger are confirmed. The very structure of the story commemorates a woman speaking: what is left after everything else has been destroyed is a voice that tells of woman's desire. The Lady remains, however, an enigmatic sign of contradiction: at once chaste and betrayed, dying and asking forgiveness from the men, but never renouncing desire, she hovers at the boundaries of True Womanhood, both fallen and unfallen, desiring and pure, false missionary and true woman.

III

Despite Woolson's radical rewriting of Bret Harte's "The Luck of Roaring Camp," however, she draws back from the most radical possibilities. Although she has inserted a woman's voice into Harte's text, she has also changed Harte's prostitute, "Cherokee Sal," a lower-class woman of a different race, into a middle-class, white woman missionary. And though she mostly avoids Harte's tendency to render the lower class as humorous grotesques, she, like Harte, has made the lower-class woman invisible; the prostitute, mute in Harte's tale, has been dropped out of her story entirely. Yet her intertextual play with Harte's structure and style in **"The Lady of Little Fishing"** represents Woolson's effort to fashion a bold, new literary language for herself. Her apprentice tale is stunning in the sheer array of speech that she tries out, although it must be admitted that the attempt to reflect the Euro-American conquest of the West is sometimes strained. The Frenchman talks like a bad cartoon; the Dutchman is hardly more successful. Woolson is at her best when she breathes into her characters the sound of colloquial American English: "Say, Frenchy, have you got a sister," one man says to another, and a little later, someone tells him, "Shut up your howling, Jack" (13). By turning the structure and the assumptions of Harte's famous story inside out, Woolson accomplishes in this best of her early tales what will become a characteristic double maneuver in her fiction: the deconstruction of the male gaze as blind and limited, and the oblique representation of women's suffering.

Woolson would soon drop Harte as a literary model, but she did not abandon her interest in representing sexual politics. In her later work, she dramatizes the toll on women in conventional relations between the sexes, exploring the woman who plays the part of the girl-wife in *For the Major* (1883), the woman who feels she must remain a true wife to the man who has deserted her years earlier in *East Angels* (1886), the woman who loves her batterer in *Jupiter Lights* (1889), and the woman undone by a romantic obsession in *Horace Chase* (1894).

Constance Fenimore Woolson's work richly deserves a new reading. Although she sometimes universalizes female experience in troubling ways, making middle-

class, white women speak for all women, a feminist reappraisal must not underestimate the daring and subtlety of her fiction in post-Civil War America. In identifying with a male writer and setting herself apart from other writers of her sex, Woolson saw herself as choosing art over popularity and power over beauty. It was a deliberate and risky choice to make early in her career. Defending herself to her closest female friend for a supposed "want of morality" in a story she had published, she explained, "I want you to think of me not as your old friend, when you read my writings, but as a 'writer,' like anyone else. For instance, take 'Adam Bede' . . . Would you like to have a friend of yours the author of such a story? Dealing with such subjects? And yet it was a great book."[39] Later in her career, Woolson's fictions about women artists suggest that she had begun to confront the sexual politics not just of being a woman in the nineteenth century but also of being a woman writer; stories such as **"Miss Grief"** (1880) and **"At the Château of Corinne"** (1887) reveal how impossible it is for a woman to be read as a "writer like anyone else." Fifteen years after she championed Harte's fiction, her comment on Louisa May Alcott from the vantage of her own long struggle to succeed as an artist indicates that she had at last begun to read her female compatriots in a different light. Greatly impressed by Alcott's *Life and Letters,* she wrote, "What heroic, brave struggles. And what a splendid success."[40] One might with justice say the same of Woolson.

Notes

1. I wish to thank Julie Bates Dock, R. James Goldstein, and Paula V. Smith for their suggestions.

2. Constance Fenimore Woolson's letter to Mrs. [Arabella Carter] Washburn is quoted in *Five Generations (1785-1923),* ed. Clare Benedict, vol. 2 (London: Ellis, 1930), 21. Hereafter cited as *Five Generations.*

3. Roland Barthes, *A Lover's Discourse: Fragments,* trans. Richard Howard (New York: Hill and Wang, 1978), 82.

4. Constance Fenimore Woolson, "The Lady of Little Fishing," *Atlantic Monthly* 34 (September 1874):293-305. "The Luck of Roaring Camp" first appeared in the San Francisco journal Harte edited, *Overland Monthly,* 1st series, 1, no. 2 (August 1868):183-89. Fields and Osgood made it the title story of the first volume of Francis Bret Harte's collected tales, *The Luck of Roaring Camp, and Other Sketches* (Boston: Fields, Osgood, 1870).

5. Patrick D. Morrow has noted Harte's great influence upon popular film and television, in *Bret Harte,* Boise State College Writers Series 5 (Boise, Idaho: Boise State College, 1972), 7. For his most recent assessment of Harte's place in American

literature, see "Bret Harte, Mark Twain, and the San Francisco Circle," *A Literary History of the American West* (Fort Worth: Texas Christian University Press, 1987), 339-58.

Other important appraisals include Margaret Duckett, *Mark Twain and Bret Harte* (Norman: University of Oklahoma Press, 1964); James K. Folsom, *The American Western Novel* (New Haven: College and University Press, 1966); Fred Lewis Pattee, *The Development of the American Short Story* (New York: Harper, 1923); George R. Stewart, Jr., *Bret Harte: Argonaut and Exile* (Boston: Houghton Mifflin, 1931), and Franklin Walker, *San Francisco's Literary Frontier* (New York: Knopf, 1939).

6. Harte tells how the printer did not return the proofs to him, but instead tried to convince the publisher of the *Overland Monthly* not to print a story "so indecent, irreligious, and improper that his proof-reader—a young lady—had with difficulty been induced to continue its perusal." See "General Introduction," *The Writings of Bret Harte,* vol. 1 (Boston and New York: Houghton Mifflin, 1896), xiii. Harte's youthful indignation at such female-inspired interference had softened over the years, and in this introduction, he stretched forth "the hand of sympathy and forgiveness" even to "the gentle proof-reader, that chaste and unknown nymph" (xv).

7. Patrick D. Morrow, *Bret Harte: Literary Critic* (Bowling Green, Ohio: Bowling Green State University Popular Press, 1979), 68.

8. See *Patrons and Protégées: Gender, Friendship, and Writing in Nineteenth-Century America,* ed. Shirley Marchalonis (New Brunswick and London: Rutgers University Press, 1988); for a feminist rethinking of Woolson's relationship with Henry James, see especially in this collection, Cheryl B. Torsney, "The Traditions of Gender: Constance Fenimore Woolson and Henry James,"

9. William Dean Howells, "Reviews and Literary Notices" (review of *The Luck of Roaring Camp, and Other Sketches*), *Atlantic Monthly* 25 (May 1870):633-35.

10. In Harte's "Tennessee's Partner," first published in the *Overland Monthly* and collected in *The Luck of Roaring Camp, and Other Sketches,* the hanging of Tennessee by the enraged citizens of Sandy Bar is softened by the sentimental ending, his partner's hope of meeting him in heaven. "Peter the Parson," Woolson's story of frontier justice, by contrast, emphasizes mob cruelty as the miners stone to death a frail and unpopular Episcopal priest.

11. "The most widely read writers of the post-Civil War decades, we should remember, were not Howells or James but domestic writers like Mrs. Southworth, Caroline Lee Hentz, and Mary Jane Holmes," writes Richard H. Brodhead, "Literature and Culture," *Columbia Literary History of the United States,* ed. Emory Elliott et al. (New York: Columbia University Press, 1988), 469.

12. Woolson's letter to Miss [Linda T.] Guilford is quoted in *Five Generations,* vol. 2, 42-43.

13. Woolson commented acidly that her friend E. C. Stedman had revealed that he did "not really believe in woman's genius," for the essence of his criticism of Elizabeth Barrett Browning is "'She did wonderfully well for a woman'"; from Woolson's marginalia quoted in *Five Generations,* vol. 2, 93.

14. *The Old Stone House* (Boston: D. Lothrop, 1873); Woolson did not publish the book under her own name, but under the pseudonym "Anne March," perhaps an indirect tribute to Louisa May Alcott and her novel of the March girls, but also a means of distancing herself from a genre perceived as female.

15. Woolson's letter to South Carolina poet Paul Hamilton Hayne is dated May Day, 1875, and is quoted in Jay B. Hubbell, "Some New Letters of Constance Fenimore Woolson," *New England Quarterly* 14 (December 1941):718. Hereafter cited as "Some New Letters."

16. Woolson's letter to Hayne is dated 16 January 1876, and is quoted in "Some New Letters," 728.

17. Woolson's letter to [Mrs. Samuel Livingston (Elizabeth Gwinn)] Mather is quoted in *Five Generations,* vol. 1, 229.

18. Woolson's letter to Katharine Livingston Mather is quoted in *Five Generations,* vol. 2, 52. Mary P. Edwards Kitterman, quoting Woolson's teacher, Linda Guilford, argues that Woolson felt that the "'only way in which she could fulfill her soul destiny' was as a literary artist." See "Henry James and the Artist Heroine in the Tales of Constance Fenimore Woolson," *Nineteenth-Century Women Writers of the English-Speaking World* (Westport, Conn.: Greenwood, 1986), 54.

19. Woolson's letter to E. C. Stedman is dated 28 September 1874, and is quoted in Laura Stedman and George M. Gould, *Life and Letters of Edmund Clarence Stedman,* vol. 1 (New York: Moffat, Yard, 1910), 521-22.

20. Helen Waite Papashvily, *All the Happy Endings* (New York: Harpers, 1956) was the first to see discontent beneath the surface of nineteenth-

century women's fiction, but Nina Baym must be credited with the first major reinterpretation of the tradition, *Woman's Fiction: A Guide to Novels by and about Women in America, 1820-1870* (Ithaca: Cornell University Press, 1978). "The flowering of this fiction," Baym writes, "created the ground from which, after the Civil War, a group of women who were literary artists developed" (298). Baym also argues that this women's fiction is not about romance and courtship, but about women learning to survive on their own. See also Mary Kelley, *Private Woman, Public Stage: Literary Domesticity in Nineteenth-Century America* (New York: Oxford University Press, 1984).

21. Woolson's letter to Samuel Mather is quoted in *Five Generations*, vol. 2, 23.

22. Woolson puts this praise of Bret Harte's fiction into the mouth of her male protagonist in "Misery Landing," *Harper's New Monthly Magazine* 48 (May 1874):866: "Strange that it should be so, but everywhere it is the cultivated people only who are taken with Bret. But they must be imaginative as well as cultivated; routine people, whether in life or in literature, dislike anything unconventional or new."

23. Woolson's letter to E. C. Stedman is dated 28 September 1874, and is quoted in Rayburn S. Moore, *Constance Fenimore Woolson* (New York: Twayne, 1963), 120-21. Hereafter cited as *Constance Fenimore Woolson.*

24. Woolson's letter is quoted in *Constance Fenimore Woolson,* 121.

25. Woolson is represented by Carlos Baker in *A Literary History of the United States,* ed. Robert Spiller et al., 4th rev. ed. (New York: Macmillan, 1974), as a lesser "imitator" of Bret Harte (868). Even her biographer Rayburn S. Moore views her as Harte's disciple, although he credits her in "The Lady of Little Fishing" with bettering "the work of one of her masters" (*Constance Fenimore Woolson,* 50). Although some critics have seen Woolson as improving upon Harte's story, very few have seen that she does more than make the characters or the ending more plausible. Fred Lewis Pattee, in *The Development of the American Short Story,* judges "The Lady of Little Fishing" as a "model short story" because it makes Harte's "grotesque situation" more "of a peep into the heart of life" when it reveals that "woman" is "'the same the world over!'" (255). Claude M. Simpson also sees Woolson's story as more realistic than its predecessor because she resolves the story "by the strictly human device of disenchantment, where Harte resorted to chance calamity" (*The Local Colorists: American Short Stories 1857-1900* [New York: Harper, 1960], 130).

26. "Woolson directly criticized Harte's sentimental Victorian idea that a miner could be brought to salvation by an innocent baby—or a pure woman," Weimer argues; however, she sees Woolson's famous uncle as her major male precursor, reading "The Lady of Little Fishing" as a rewriting of Cooper. See Joan Myers Weimer, "Introduction," *Women Artists, Women Exiles: "Miss Grief" and Other Stories,* by Constance Fenimore Woolson (New Brunswick and London: Rutgers University Press, 1988), 18 n., xxvi. Although I agree with Weimer that Cooper was an important precursor for his grandniece, I argue here that Harte's fiction, not Cooper's, is the primary source for "The Lady of Little Fishing."

27. *Constance Fenimore Woolson,* 120. Harte later gave credit to Joel Chandler Harris, George Washington Cable, Thomas Nelson Page, Mark Twain, Mary Noailles Murfree, and Mary E. Wilkins Freeman for following his lead in cutting "loose from conventional methods" in order "to honestly describe the life around them"; he neglects, however, to mention Woolson. "The Rise of the 'Short Story,'" *Cornhill Magazine* 7 (July 1899):102-110. That Harte omits her name here is significant; he may be indirectly accusing Woolson of earning the label "Imitator," a term he says "could not fairly apply" to the others mentioned.

28. See Alice Hall Petry, "'Always, Your Attached Friend': The Unpublished Letters of Constance Fenimore Woolson to John and Clara Hay," *Books at Brown* 29-30 (1982-1983):11-108. John Hay was responsible for Bret Harte's being promoted to the post of United States consul in Glasgow, Scotland, according to his biographer George R. Stewart, Jr. (*Bret Harte: Argonaut and Exile,* 269-70). Harte was a notoriously absentee consul. Woolson once commented in a letter to Hayne that Bret Harte "is *not* a nice person, I am told" (quoted in *Constance Fenimore Woolson,* 121).

29. For a feminist critique of this traditional reading of the Woolson-James relationship, in addition to Torsney and Kitterman cited above, see Sharon Dean, "Constance Fenimore Woolson and Henry James: The Literary Relationship," *Massachusetts Studies in English* 7 (1980):1-9. Dean was the first to note that James borrowed from Woolson's notebooks and fiction.

30. For early reviews of "The Luck of Roaring Camp," see Anon., "Notes," *Nation* 8 (13 May 1869):376; Anon., "New Publications," *New York Times,* (30 April 1870), 11; and Anon., "American Books," *Blackwoods Edinburgh Magazine* 110 (October 1871):422-30. Twentieth-century appraisals of the story include: Pattee, *The Development of the American Short Story,* 220-44; Cleanth

Brooks, John Thibaut Purser, and Robert Penn Warren, *An Approach to Literature,* 3rd. ed. (New York: Appleton-Century-Crofts, 1952), 86-87; Allen B. Brown, "The Christ Motif in 'The Luck of Roaring Camp,'" *Papers of the Michigan Academy of Science, Arts, and Letters* 46 (1961):629-33; J. R. Boggan, "The Regeneration of 'Roaring Camp,'" *Nineteenth-Century Fiction* 22 (December 1967):271-80; and Morrow, "The Predicament of Bret Harte," *American Literary Realism, 1870-1910* 5 (1972):181-88, and "Bret Harte, Popular Fiction, and the Local Color Movement," *American Literary Realism* 8 (1973):123-31. In the last decade new readings of Harte's fiction have mostly been offered by German critics; see, for example, Klaus P. Hansen, "Francis Bret Harte: Ironie und Konvention," *Arbeiten aus Anglistik und Amerikanistik* 9, no. 1 (1984):23-37.

31. Jeffrey F. Thomas has noted that Henry Adams was the first to see Harte's fiction as an exploration of sexuality; Adams singled out Harte and Whitman as the only American writers who dared to treat sex as a force. "Bret Harte and the Power of Sex," *Western American Literature* 8 (1973):91-109. See also *The Education of Henry Adams,* ed. Ernest Samuels (Boston: Houghton Mifflin, 1973), 385. Like Adams, Thomas locates the "power of sex" mainly in women; unlike Adams, however, and unlike Woolson in her fiction, Thomas does not explore what it means for the woman herself to serve as the site of sexuality in American culture.

32. See Leslie Fiedler, *Love and Death in the American Novel,* 3rd. rev. ed. (New York: Stein and Day, 1982), and Judith Fetterley, *The Resisting Reader: A Feminist Approach to American Fiction* (Bloomington: Indiana University Press, 1978). Fetterley's more recent book, *Provisions: A Reader from 19th-Century American Women* (Bloomington: Indiana University Press, 1985), attempts to redefine the field of American literature by offering new critical introductions to and selections from the work of nineteenth-century women.

33. Harte's description of the geography not only recalls the womb but is also linked with "the suffering woman" in labor: "The camp lay in a triangular valley between two hills and a river. The only outlet was a steep trail over the summit of a hill." "The Luck of Roaring Camp," *The Writings of Bret Harte,* vol. 1, 3. All quotations are from this edition and hereafter will be cited by page number in the text.

34. "The Lady of Little Fishing," *Women Artists, Women Exiles,* 5; all quotations are from this edition and will be cited hereafter by page number in the text. Weimer follows the text of the story as Woolson revised it for publication in *Castle Nowhere: Lake Country Sketches* (Boston: Osgood, 1875); I cite Weimer's volume because this is the first time in more than twenty years that a new and authoritative edition of Woolson's work is available to the general reader.

35. Laura Mulvey has analyzed how "the male gaze" controls the narrative perspective in film: "In a world ordered by sexual imbalance, pleasure in looking has been split between active/male and passive/female. The determining male gaze projects its fantasy onto the female figure." "Visual Pleasure and Narrative Cinema," *Narrative, Apparatus, Ideology: A Film Theory Reader,* ed. Philip Rosen (Columbia University Press, 1986), 203. The essay was first published in *Screen* 16, no. 3 (Autumn 1975):6-18.

36. See Barbara Welter, "The Cult of True Womanhood: 1820-1860," *American Quarterly* 18 (1966):151-74.

37. Barthes, *A Lover's Discourse: Fragments,* trans. Richard Howard, p. 82.

38. Weimer interprets the Lady's speech differently, as representing "the loss of dignity and verbal power," "Introduction," *Women Artists, Women Exiles,* p. xxvii. She elaborates this view in "Women Artists as Exiles in the Fiction of Constance Fenimore Woolson," *Legacy: A Journal of Nineteenth-Century Women Writers,* 3, No. 2 (Fall 1986), 3-15.

39. Woolson to Mrs. [Arabella Carter] Washburn, quoted in *Five Generations,* vol. II, p. 20. Woolson is defending "Castle Nowhere," the title story she wrote for the first volume of her collected fiction.

40. Woolson's letter to [Miss Linda T. Guilford] is quoted in *Five Generations,* vol. II, p. 43.

Linda Grasso (essay date June 1994)

SOURCE: Grasso, Linda. "'Thwarted Life, Mighty Hunger, Unfinished Work': The Legacy of Nineteenth-Century Women Writing in America." *ATQ* n.s. 8, no. 2 (June 1994): 97-118.

[*In the following essay, Grasso compares the frustrated literary ambitions of the female protagonists in "Miss Grief" and Mary Wilkins Freeman's "The Poetess" with the plight of nineteenth-century American women writers.*]

Nothing remains to tell that the poor Welsh puddler once lived, but this figure of the mill-woman cut in korl. I have it here in a corner of my library. I keep it hid behind a curtain,—it is such a rough, ungainly thing. Yet there are about it touches, grand sweeps of outline, that show a master's hand. Sometimes,—to-night, for instance,—the curtain is accidentally drawn back, and I see a bare arm stretched out imploringly in the darkness, and an eager, wolfish face watching mine: a wan, woful face, through which the spirit of the dead korl-cutter looks out, with its thwarted life, its mighty hunger, its unfinished work.

(64)—Rebecca Harding Davis,
Life in the Iron Mills, 1861

In the last twenty years of the nineteenth century, two white women writers published stories that feature writing women who were destroyed, both in body and in spirit, by intrusive, publicly sanctioned male authority figures. In Mary Wilkins Freeman's "The Poetess" (1880), it is a young minister who propels the protagonist, Betsey Dole, to burn all her poetry; in Constance Fenimore Woolson's **"Miss Grief"** (1891), it is a smug, self-satisfied writer and critic, suggestively styled on the career of Henry James, who ruins Miss Crief's chance of public recognition and literary success. Not only does the writers' choice of the male authority figures as minister and critic suggest the ways in which cultural authority was institutionalized and then shifted in the course of the nineteenth century from the religious to the secular realm, the power struggle between the well-fed men and the "starving" women poignantly expresses the angered anxiety that a number of late nineteenth-century women writers were feeling when they began to assert their right to become "artists" in male defined terms. Although many "new women" writers were determined to move beyond the limited literary world of their forebears, they found that their newly-defined artistic endeavors were thwarted by two related sources: male colleagues who resented the threat of encroachment on their exclusive preserve, and a male-dominated publishing industry that continued to assess their work based on rigidly defined gendered categories.[1]

The Freeman and Woolson stories metaphorically encapsulate how "new women" writers responded to the "mighty hungers" of such frustrated artistry. Poised on the brink of modernity, Freeman and Woolson bequeath a legacy of the nineteenth-century writing woman's defiance, struggle, and cultural contribution that is both tortured and compromised. Although they create protagonists who write very different texts for very different reasons, both writers conclude that it doesn't matter whether a woman stays within acceptably "feminine" imaginative genres, or crosses the boundary into male-defined artistic territory. Regardless of how and what the writing woman writes, she—as well as her stories—are condemned to death in the annals of a literary history that only men record.

Yet both writers portray their protagonists' death and literary defeat ambiguously. For even though Betsy

Dole and Miss Crief die with their work burnt and buried, their stories of wasted possibility live in much the same way Rebecca Harding Davis' "rough, ungainly" figure of the mill-woman "lives": each bears witness to thwarted achievement. When the concealing curtain "is accidentally drawn back" in these two stories, then, a similar grief-stricken indignation is revealed, but it is an indignation that is much more explicit. Paradoxically, while Davis' moral outrage is poignantly conveyed through one symbolic structure—the sculpture of the mill-woman created from the refuse of an inhumane and corrupt industrial system—Woolson's and Freeman's is diffused through imagery and effect. Nevertheless, because Davis can not confront her own anger as a "thwarted" female artist directly, she uses the tragic story of a working-class male artist as a way of distancing and containing her own frustration and rage.

Such displacement does not exist in the Freeman and Woolson stories; on the contrary, the woman writer's frustrated artistry is depicted with controlled yet seething rage. The change is significant, for the more overt expression of anger about the writing woman's status signals a paradigmatic shift in women's imaginative visions. Beginning in the post-bellum period, power struggles between men and women are no longer ameliorated by forgiveness or the belief in the innate goodness of the human heart; arrogant, sadistic, atheistic men are no longer converted through the goodness, patience, and humility of charitable women; there is no longer sustaining hope in a female community organized around an ethos of nurture and care; and there is no longer redemptive power in women's suffering and sacrificing of self. Instead, Freeman and Woolson decry the waste of the sacrificed female self; they underscore the deadly effects man-made institutions and aesthetic standards have had on the writing woman's sense of self and literary productivity. And they obviously want revenge—the very act of telling the woman's story guarantees that retribution will be done. The culprits are identified; blame is apportioned; and in the end, even though the writing woman's life and work are lost, her dignity remains intact. In this way Freeman and Woolson ennoble their own position as women writers, for their failures and achievements become part of a much larger legacy of thwarted lives, mighty hungers, and unfinished works.

The protagonists in "A Poetess" and **"Miss Grief"** remind us that there are two opposing realms of possibility for women writers in the nineteenth century. Like the enormously popular sentimental poet, Lydia Sigourney, Freeman's "poetess" writes well within the bounds of female discourse; thus she occupies the socially acceptable end of the spectrum. Woolson's "writer," on the other hand, is more like the anomalous, iconoclastic polemicist Margaret Fuller. Because her attitudes and practices conflict with gendered ideals of domesticity and selflessness, she occupies the transgressive "other" end of the spectrum.

Betsey Dole's and Miss Crief's opposing positions are most apparent in the different ways each perceives "success," the writing process, and the relationship to her readers. Unlike Miss Crief who believes in her own talent so much that she seeks out a well-known author and critic as a mentor, "the poetess" Betsey Dole does not want fame. Even though she was "born with the wantin' to write poetry" (384), she is not ambitious in the same way Miss Crief is. To her, seeing one of her poems printed and framed is equivalent to being published "in one of the great magazines" (381). Approval from the people in her immediate community—not the editors and critics of the established literary world that Miss Crief wants validation from—matters most to Betsey. Writing poems that are "the very genius of gentle, old-fashioned, sentimental poetry" (378), her pleasure is derived from responding to the needs and requests of others. It is they, in fact, who literally determine the subject and content of what she writes. For example, when the grieving mother, Mrs. Caxton, comes and asks Betsey to "write a few lines" as a memorial to her dead son, she is very specific about what she wants the poem to say.

> You could mention how—handsome he was, and good, and I never had to punish him but once in his life, and how pleased he was with his little new suit, and what a sufferer he was, and—how we hope he is at rest—in a better land.
>
> (376)

By underscoring this relationship between reader and writer, Freeman depicts "sentimental" writing as a highly social, interactive endeavor, very different from the kind of inspired, individualistic, "artistic" writing Woolson envisions Miss Crief creating.

Such an integral relationship between writer and reader has immediate rewards. When Betsey fulfills Mrs. Caxton's wishes, especially by "work[ing] that in about his new suit so nice" (381), Mrs. Caxton is so appreciative, she is moved to tears. "It's beautiful, beautiful," she says as she cries, "It's jest as comfortin' as it can be" (381). Hearing Mrs. Caxton's praise, Betsey feels "as if her poem had been approved and accepted by one of the great magazines. She had the pride and self-wonderment of recognized genius" (381). What is clear is that even though Betsey does not harbor dreams of literary posterity in the same way Miss Crief does, writing is vital to her sense of self as well as her self-esteem. Living a pinched, meager, solitary life, writing sentimental poetry is Betsey Dole's life-line. It gives her a way to deflect concentrating on life's inadequacies—how little food she has to eat, or how she can't afford to buy paper or clothes—by providing the kind of structure, purpose, and intellectual engagement that would otherwise not exist.

Freeman is explicit about the life-sustaining role writing plays in Betsey Dole's life. Shortly after Mrs. Caxton leaves, Betsey eagerly begins to work:

> [She] got an old black portfolio and pen and ink out of the chimney cupboard, and seated herself to work. She meditated, and wrote one line, then another. Now and then she read aloud what she had written with a solemn intonation. She sat there thinking and writing, and the time went on. The twelve-o'clock bell rang, but she never noticed it; she had quite forgotten the bread and jelly.
>
> (378)

After a sleepless night "altering several lines in her mind," the next day she spends hours meticulously copying the poem "on both sides of note-paper, in a neat, cramped hand," and then delivers it to Mrs. Caxton, all neatly rolled and "tied . . . with a bit of black ribbon" (380). In this lovingly rendered evocation of each detail of the writing process—from inception to execution to delivery—Freeman shows that writing sentimental poetry not only gives Betsey a way to make her life meaningful, it also gives her a way to interact, to connect—*to be of value, and to feel herself valued*—to her immediate community.

By sympathetically portraying the writing of sentimental poetry as a highly social act that serves important social functions for both the writing woman and her community, Freeman provides an interpretation of the sentimental literary legacy radically different from the pejorative one that many twentieth-century scholars have formulated. There is no better summary of how sentimental literature has been maligned "by the male-dominated scholarly tradition" than Jane Tompkins' pithy analysis in *Sensational Designs: The Cultural Work of American Fiction, 1790-1860*. According to Tompkins:

> In reaction against [the female sentimentalists'] world view, and perhaps even more against their success, twentieth-century critics have taught generations of students to equate popularity with debasement, emotionality with ineffectiveness, religiosity with fakery, domesticity with triviality, and all of these, implicitly, with womanly inferiority.
>
> (123)

Freeman's depiction of sentimental writing in "A Poetess" provides even more evidence for Tompkins' main contention—that when considered within the parameters of its cultural context, sentimental literature performed important "cultural work" for both its creators and their audiences. For in Freeman's vision, the ability to connect with other human beings by ministering comfort—to "enter into [another's] feelin's considerable" (379) by validating their every-day experiences through the written-word—plays a crucial function in a society that does not provide emotional and economic support for all its members. It is not incidental that Betsey Dole is an aged, poverty-stricken spinster, eating "scarcely more than her canary-bird," living on an "income [which] was almost infinitesimal" (382). Nor is it incidental that most antebellum, white women writers wrote in a "sentimental" style in order to make a living. Even though Betsey Dole "had never received a cent for her poems" because "she had not thought such a thing possible" (382), many of her living counterparts in antebellum America did not share this experience. On the contrary, they benefited from the financial as well as the emotional rewards that writing sentimental literature made possible. Nevertheless, by making a link between the economic and social status of the writing woman and a sentimental ethos, Freeman compels a reexamination of a sentimental legacy that brings the function of sentimentality in America—including the question of aesthetics—into full view.

Given that Freeman is considered part of the first generation of women writers who self-consciously begins to perceive themselves as "artists," it is noteworthy that she takes up the issue of sentimentality. To begin with, the rendering of a "sentimental poetess" as "old fashioned" and "obsolete" suggests Freeman's sense of a profoundly changed American literary landscape. Secondly, that she chose to embody the past literally in an aged and feeble woman suggests her acute awareness of literary sentimentality as a highly gendered, specifically female tradition that she, as a woman writing in its wake, has to come to terms with. That late nineteenth-century women writers such as Freeman and Woolson had to reckon with a "feminine" literary legacy is a crucial point that Ann Douglas Wood makes in an influential early study of "sentimental" and "local color" women writers. In her interpretation, the local colorists saw themselves in hostile opposition to the sentimentalists who came before them. She quotes Woolson complaining that previous women writers had "favored the beautiful at the expense of strength," and that, in her view, their literature obscured "the ugly," "the commonplace," and "the shockingly unpleasant" realities of life (4). She reads Mary Wilkins Freeman's "starved New England women" "using the sickly sweet trash" of sentimental poetry "as a form of opiate" (5). In essence, Douglas Wood argues that because the first generation of "serious" women writers reject a "sentimental" tradition with nothing to replace it with, their imaginative visions are barren, sterile, and pathetic. Without the kind of ideological imperative that motivated their predecessors, she argues, the "local color" women writers become "corpse watchers," their writing an indulgence in nostalgia, a way to unburden despair (32).

A decade later, Josephine Donovan countered Douglas Woods' unrelentingly bleak interpretation by publishing *New England Local Color Literature: A Woman's Tra-*

dition. Where Douglas Wood sees impoverishment and self-destruction, Donovan sees ingenuity and willfulness. To her, "local color" women writers "create a counter world . . . that nourished strong, free women"; when considered a cohesive "school," their literature can be read as a complex response to a male-centered industrial and technological society that was threatening to obliterate their world view and value systems (3). Not withstanding their differences, however, Donovan, like Douglas Wood, sees the "local color" writers as creating a "counter-tradition" to "sentimentality"—that "other" tradition characterized by such "weakening indulgence[s]" as "melodramatic emotionalism" and "romantic hyperbole" (33).

While both studies remain significant contributions to the scholarship on nineteenth-century American women's literature, the problem with Douglas Woods' and Donovan's analyses is that their focus is on the cleavages, breakages, and discontinuities that sever generations, rather than on the linkages, affiliations, and sympathies that bind them. Their interest is in delineating the dividing lines that separate one generation of writers from the other; they concentrate on the development of "schools," the theoretical approaches to craft, the changing ideologies that undergird each generation's visions. By doing so, what they miss are the muted boundaries, the overlaps, the ambiguities. The "local color" women writers may well have been writing against the "sentimentalists"—vehemently rejecting their values and visions of what literature should do and be—but as "A Poetess" poignantly demonstrates, this rejection was not as clear-cut nor as unsympathetically accomplished as Douglas Wood and Donovan would have us believe. Indeed, one of the best illustrations of this complicated response is the way Freeman foregrounds the question of aesthetics in "A Poetess."

Unlike the standard caricature of the weeping black-bonneted sermonizer, Freeman's "sentimental poetess" is far from a stock figure. Betsey Dole is a willful and determined character who is given subjectivity through dialogue and behavior. There are reasons why she behaves as she does. Thoughtful and resourceful, her choices are made based on what she needs to survive from day to day. Yet Freeman makes it clear that these needs are more than just physical: Betsey Dole's attempt to cultivate a self-contained world of beauty is a repeated motif throughout the story. Freeman illustrates this point by underscoring Betsey's valiant efforts to maintain dignity and control over her appearance and environment. The minutely detailed description of Betsey's visiting attire is a good example. Although on the one hand the narrator tells us that Betsey does not mind wearing the same costume, unaltered, for the past twenty years because "the old satisfied her" (380), on the other, each color-coordinated accessory is notably rendered. Betsey's dress pattern consists of "delicate bunches of faded flowers on a faded green ground"; she wore "a narrow green felt ribbon around her long waist" and "a green barege bonnet"; and "she carried a small green parasol with a jointed handle" (380). Thus, on the surface the costume is "obsolete, even in the little country village where she lived," yet underneath there is the implication that Betsey once cared, and still cares, about her public appearance.

That the matching color is green and that Betsey wears the costume to deliver her finished poem are both highly significant because throughout the story green symbolizes beauty, a love of growing things, and a peaceful and productive environment within which to work. In this way Freeman uses the color green to signify the creation of a life that is not only meaningful, but also aesthetically pleasing. The evocative descriptions of Betsey's garden, her love of flowers, and her appreciation of sunlight all suggest how important beautiful, living things are to her and her ability to be productive. For example, at one point, Betsey becomes so absorbed in her work that she forgets to eat:

> The light in the room was din and green . . . Great plumy bunches of asparagus waved over the tops of the looking-glass; a framed sampler, a steel engraving of a female head taken from some old magazine, and sheaves of dried grasses hung on or were fastened to the walls; vases and tumblers of flowers stood on the shelf and table. The air was heavy and sweet.
>
> (378)

The light in the room is alive with presence; the "plumy bunches of asparagus" suggest the freedom of flight; and the richly perfumed air provides the kind of nourishment her meager food supply can't come close to equaling. Here Freeman shows how Betsey Dole creates a world of beauty for herself by ennobling a bleak and dreary life with flowers, sweet smells, and useful work.

But descriptions of the beautiful that sustain life are always in tension with the deprivation and poverty that "cut if off." Images of a life circumscribed, bordered, and caged pervade the story. Mrs. Caxton is unable to see Betsey because "the view to the side [of the house] was in a measure cut off" (374). Betsey's canary trills and chirps from within his cage, and she "buries" the ashes of her poems in the urn-like, covered, sugar bowl. By juxtaposing images of enclosure and openness within the same scenes, Freeman highlights the tug-of-war between poverty and beauty that characterizes Betsey's life. For example, Betsey's garden-patch "was a gay spangle with sweet-peas and red-flowering beans, and flanked with feathery asparagus," and the entry to her house "was full of green light . . . and bristling with grasses and flowers and asparagus stalks" (374). Yet, because she has "more flowerin' beans than eatin

ones'" (375), she doesn't have enough to eat; and the entry that is flooded with light is "small and square and unfurnished, except for a well-rubbed old card-table against the back wall" (374). It is Freeman's portrayal of Betsey Dole's struggle to maintain the beautiful in spite of the ugly—in essence, the will to create her own aesthetic—that invests her "sentimental poetess" with dignity and integrity.

It is only when Betsey Dole can no longer define her own standards of beauty that the ugly wins out. Images of murder and cold convey Betsey's defeat. As soon as Mrs. Caxton reports that "Sarah Rogers says that the minister told her Ida that that poetry you wrote was jest as poor as it could be," Betsey "sat looking at Mrs. Caxton as a victim whom the first blow had not killed might look at her executioner. Her face was like a pale wedge of ice between her curls" (383). The ultimate tragedy of the story, then, is when Betsey takes "to heart" the minister's judgment that her literary activity "wa'n't worth nothing" (386), and she loses the will to create her own warmth—a potent symbol of the death of self-sufficiency. After destroying everything she had ever written—"all the love-letters that had passed between her and life" (385),—she becomes permanently ill and cold, with nothing left to live for. Even the change of seasons signals Betsey's demise: "It was now late August. Before October it was quite generally recognized that Betsey Dole's life was nearly over" (385). As summer turns into fall, she lies shivering, coughing, and silent, awaiting death with only one request: "she kept asking if the minister got home" (385). What happens between Betsey and the minister when the two finally meet provides the key to Freeman's vision of how American culture had changed over the course of the nineteenth century.

The pernicious effects of the abuse of privilege—no matter how unintentional—between those in power and those without, is what the story's denouement is all about. It is highly ironic that Freeman uses the "meeting" between Betsey and the minister to underscore what divides them—a total lack of communication. They meet for very different purposes and with very different intentions. For Betsey, it is a way to get revenge; for the minister, it is a professional obligation. That he clearly doesn't understand why she calls him, nor how his authority has impacted on her life, underscores how oblivious this young male authority figure is of his own power, as well as the needs of his elderly, female constituency. When Betsey asks him if he will "tend to" having the sugar bowl that contains the ashes of her poetry "buried with [her]," not only does he "not once suspect his own connection with the matter," he assumes Betsey is "out of [her] head" (386). While she is forcing a confrontation by literally leaving the "ashes" of her life "in his hands," he remains "bewildered," "confused," and "embarrassed."

Freeman makes it clear that the minister is part of a new generation that does not understand Betsey Dole's values and experiences. "[S]peak[ing] in the stilted fashion, yet with a certain force by reason of his unpolished honesty" (386), the "awkward" young minister communicates in a different language and performs a different function from that of the sentimental poetess. It is here that Freeman's critique becomes most explicit, for the contrast between Betsey Dole's ability to minister comfort in comparison to the minister's is striking indeed. Whereas Betsey is able to plumb the depths of empathy to such an extent that she can imagine herself in the sufferer's place, the minister makes no such attempt. He dutifully does what he is asked to do; he responds sympathetically to what he doesn't understand; but not once does he try to "enter into [Betsey's] feelin's considerable" (379). Unlike the community's female "minister" of comfort, the institutionally trained male minister is not empathetic. Yet, it is he—the young man who speaks "in the stilted fashion"—who is published in a magazine. And it is he who is in the position to make the kind of judgments that facilitate new cultural tastes. By casting the representative of the "new" as a murderer oblivious of his crime, Freeman suggests that an aesthetic based on blinded individualism and "unfeeling standards" has literally obliterated the more socially empathetic, culturally useful aesthetic of sentimentality.

Freeman chooses to dramatize the ultimate conflict between Betsey and the minister as a power struggle that makes issues of subjectivity, agency, victimization, and oppression primary. This struggle in itself provides an important clue to Freeman's perception of how embattled gender relations were at the turn of the century. Even more telling though is that she sees an integral relationship between self-sufficiency and the ability and desire to write. It is highly significant that in addition to asking the minister to make sure the ashes of her poems are buried along with her body, Betsey Dole also asks that he write a poem about her after she's dead. No longer able to envision herself as productive, active, alive, and in control, she had "been thinkin' that mebbe [her]—dying was goin' to make [her]—a good subject for—poetry" (387). In this request, Freeman shows Betsey Dole's transformation from the writer to the written about, from the subject of her own life to the object in another's rendering. The only way Betsey can continue to exist is by becoming the subject-matter of a male-authored text; the only way she can express anger is through self-destructive revenge. By connecting the demise of a "sentimental aesthetic" with the "death" of the writing woman's subjectivity and freedom of expression, Freeman implies that her literary predecessors may have had more autonomy than she and her contemporaries—the "realistic" writers who are meeting new male-defined standards of literary excellence. Dramatizing Betsey Dole's fight for honor, revenge, and literary integrity may well have been Freeman's way of paying tribute to a female legacy that was becoming more and more devalued and obsolete as the culture's needs changed.

On the other end of the literary spectrum is the brilliant, eccentric, incorrigible Miss Crief who is so ambitious she seeks out a successful male writer and critic in the hope that he will help her enter professional publishing. Unlike Betsey Dole who "had not enough imagination" (378) to experiment with imagery, content, and form, Miss Crief is intuitive, insightful, and extraordinarily original. According to the critic who narrates the story, her dramas, stories, and poetry are the result of an "inspired mind" (256). Reading them for the first time, he feels "thrilled" by their "earnestness, passion, and power" (256). Gifted with the "divine spark of genius" (257), her writing contains "originality and force" (259). Unrestricted in subject matter, her poems are "unrestrained, large, vast, like the skies or the wind" (265). In Woolson's deftly ironic hands, Miss Crief becomes the archetype of the unrecognized, uniquely original, literary genius who is more concerned with translating her own vision into "art" than attending to her readers' wishes and expectations. To her, gaining access to an audience means validation and appreciation of her talent, nothing more. As an artist with a unique vision, the writing process is a solitary and individualistic endeavor; it happens in isolation; the inspiration is from within. Her relationship with her readers is one-sided— she offers them profound insight and wisdom. In essence, Woolson's description of Miss Crief's literary powers is the epitome of what is now known as the "modernist" aesthetic.

Yet, even though Miss Crief creates literature that meets all the standards of a male-defined aesthetic that values wide-ranging, transcendent "universal" themes, ambiguity, complexity, and originality, her plight is remarkably similar to that of Betsey Dole's. Like Betsey, Miss Crief is a feeble, poverty-stricken, writing woman who lives in a constant state of physical and spiritual hunger. She and her aunt, whom the narrator assumes is her "maid," rent a room in "one of the most wretched quarters of the city, the abode of poverty, crowded and unclean" (266). Also like Betsey, Miss Crief does not dress in current fashion; she has very few clothes, and not enough food to eat. As the narrator constantly reminds us, in her rain-drenched, shabby old clothes and emaciated state, Miss Crief is "a very depressing object" (253) to a literary man who is good tempered, well dressed, sufficiently provided with money, and amiably obedient to all the rules and requirements of "society" (248). Miss Crief, like Betsey Dole, values the opinion of a powerful, male authority figure. Although Miss Crief self-consciously seeks out the male narrator as a mentor, whereas Betsey receives the minister's judgment indirectly, both women are profoundly affected by what these men think of their work. Indeed, after hearing the narrator praise her drama, Miss Crief confesses that "if your sentence had been against me, it would have been my end" (258). And both Betsey Dole and Miss Crief live isolated, economically precarious existences on the margins of society, with writing as their only source of sustenance.

Woolson underscores the life-sustaining role that writing plays in Miss Crief's life by using descriptions of hunger and satiation in the same way Freeman uses descriptions of Betsey's writing process and environment. While in both stories the physical hunger of the writing woman signifies social and economic deprivation, in **"Miss Grief"** it is also a metaphor for artistic starvation. Over and over again throughout the story, Woolson shows that Miss Crief is starved not only by the lack of basic necessities such as food, clothing, and housing, she is also starved by the lack of opportunity, recognition, and influence denied to the writing woman. Woolson achieves this effect by dramatically juxtaposing the male narrator's privileged access to food in contrast to Miss Crief's pitiful need of it. In a scene that suggests transubstantiation, the Christian conversion of bread and wine into the body and blood of Christ, when Miss Crief drinks wine and eats "a bit of bread" in the cozy warmth of the narrator's study, she is literally transformed into a vital being. As the narrator comments, once she has eaten "she began to show new life" (257). What he fails to see, however, is that Miss Crief's "new life" has more to do with the artistic nourishment he provides than with the physical. For according to his own account, only after he has pronounced Miss Crief's drama "full of original power," and told her how he "sat up half the night reading it," does she begin to "look warm" (257). Only then does Miss Crief experience triumph and exude confidence. "As she spoke the word 'drama,' a triumphant brightness came into her eyes" (258); standing "in the center of the room" she insists on reciting her drama, ending with "a triumphant smile" (259). Unbeknownst to the myopic narrator, Miss Crief is being "fed" in two ways simultaneously: she is physically invigorated by having enough food to eat, and she is emotionally revived after ingesting his sought-after praise.

Woolson connects physical and emotional satiation through the metaphor of hunger in other ways as well. At the end of the story, it is highly significant that when the narrator lies to Miss Crief by telling her that her drama has been accepted for publication, she asks for food. "It's the first time she's asked for food in weeks," Aunt Martha tells the narrator, but she cannot provide it because there is literally nothing in the apartment to eat. According to the narrator:

> [Aunt Martha] opened a cupboard door vaguely, but I could see nothing within. "What have you for her?" I asked with some impatience, though in a low voice.

> "Please God, nothing!" answered the poor old woman, hiding her reply and her tears behind the broad cupboard door. "I was going out to get a little something when I met you."

> "Good Heavens! is it money you need? here, take this and send; or go yourself in the carriage waiting below."
>
> (267)

Once again, Woolson not only draws a relationship between physical and spiritual deprivation, she does so by mocking the narrator's ability to resuscitate Miss Crief. The implication is that because he has not bothered to get back to Miss Crief concerning her work, she has been slowly dying of starvation. But once he is made aware of her condition, he does not hesitate to offer all his resources. In a scene that satirizes the traditional "rescue" of the penniless, besieged maiden by the rich and powerful "prince," he orders fruit, flowers, wine, and candles to assuage his guilty conscience and make her suffering more bearable. The ultimate irony, however, is that the narrator continues to "starve" Miss Crief by providing "food" that is poisonous with lies.

By suggesting such an integral connection between the physical and the spiritual, Woolson uses Christian imagery to convey Miss Crief's relationship to the narrator. Just as bread and wine miraculously made into the body and blood of Christ feeds both the body and the soul, so, too, does the narrator's food and praise miraculously "feed" both the body and soul of Miss Crief. In this sense, Miss Crief is the faithful female disciple to the narrator's all-giving, all-powerful masculine Christ. For once she imbibes his physical and spiritual nourishment, she is transformed from impoverished beggar to well-fed innovator. In another sense, however, Miss Crief, and not the narrator, is the Christ-like figure. For as soon as the narrator has faith in her talent, she is resurrected and glories in triumph. In the same way that Jesus Christ, the sacrificed son, trusts God the father, the narrator's "belief in her genius" (258) is all Miss Crief needs to roll away the stone from her tomb-like existence and rise to new heights of confidence. The essential problem, however, is that the narrator, unlike the truly faithful, is too malicious to be worthy of such trust.

Exposing the fallacy of Miss Crief's "faith" in the male critic as mentor is one of Woolson's most important political messages. Using the audacious narrative device of having the male narrator tell the writing woman's story, along with the devastating irony of Christian symbolism, Woolson makes it clear that when women desire to compete with men in the male world, they participate in their own sacrifice. As Christ is tempted by the devil, Miss Crief is lured by the narrator's position in relation to her own. Indeed, as she confesses on her deathbed, it was because of "the contrast" between their two positions that she became obsessed with meeting him in the first place:

You were young—strong—rich—praised—loved—successful: all that I was not. I wanted to look at you—and imagine how it would feel. You had success—but I had the greater power. Tell me, did I not have it?

(268)

Miss Crief hungers for power, recognition, and prestige, but when she attempts to become the agent of her own desires, she is duped and destroyed by a man who is not even her equal. The implication is that the desire to "feel" male power and privilege leads to self-destruction, and in Woolson's late nineteenth-century vision, there is nothing socially redemptive about such an act.

The specifically gendered nature of Miss Crief's deprivation and waste of talent repeatedly suggests the ritual of Christian sacrifice in which Christ suffers and dies for sins he does not commit. Several times throughout the story, the narrator smugly admits that although he has achieved visibility and success as a writer and critic, it is Miss Crief who "possessed the divine spark of genius" (257), and "the greater power" (268). Yet, in the end, her identity, history, and literary achievements are distorted, buried and destroyed *by him*. It is he, after all, who not only gets her name wrong from their first meeting to their last—referring to her as **"Miss Grief"** all along—it is also he who literally tells her story. In this context, Miss Crief becomes a female Christ-figure who is sacrificed so that less talented men like the narrator can succeed. Without subjectivity and point of view, it's as if she lives out Betsey Dole's fate: in the same way that Betsey may become the object of the minister's poetic renderings, Miss Crief becomes the object of the narrator's imagination.

That the story-teller's angle of vision is highly subjective is a point Woolson makes continually through the device of the male narrator. She demonstrates why control of narrative point-of-view is so powerful by showing how the narrator sees selectively, picking and choosing what *he* deems is important to know, see, and tell. In one of the most poignantly ironic statements in the story, after Miss Crief's death, the narrator claims: "I never knew more of her history than is written here. If there was more that I might have learned, it remained unlearned, for I did not ask" (268-269). Pompous, self-centered, and totally self-serving, the narrator constructs Miss Crief according to his own notions of what a writing woman is supposed to be. Woolson repeatedly exposes his patronizing ideas about women by showing how he constructs theories which are based on nothing more than his own biased assumptions. When he learns, for example, that Miss Crief has persisted in trying to meet him day after day, he assumes that she is peddling carvings or lace; when she shames him into reading her manuscript, he responds in the same way the minister does to Betsey Dole: he thinks she's mad; and when the

traditionally conventional "young lady" he is courting does not behave as he expects, he becomes "exasperated," "standing, as it were, on a desolate shore, with nothing but a handful of mistaken inductions wherewith to console myself" (250).

Accordingly, the male narrator as expert, official interpreter is relentlessly undermined. Even though it is his voice that dominates the narrative—shaping and controlling Miss Crief's story—Woolson makes it clear that his perceptions and point of view must always be questioned. By depicting him as myopic, egocentric, and undeserving, she mocks the sanctified, authoritarian, male voice, suggesting that if Miss Crief's story had been narrated from a different angle of vision, it would have been told differently indeed. Equally significant, the use of the male narrator repeatedly calls attention to the erasure of the writing woman's voice. Like Freeman, Woolson dramatizes the writing woman's loss of power by foregrounding issues of voice and subjectivity. But, unlike Freeman, she does so by invoking Biblical themes and stories.

Sacrificed and betrayed, the Christ-like Miss Crief is deceived by the thieving Judas-like male narrator. In one of the most brilliant twists of the story, Woolson has Miss Crief appoint the narrator her literary executor as she lies dying. Believing that her drama has been accepted for publication, she had "never known what it was . . . to be fully happy until now" (267). But she feels this way only because she believes in the narrator's fictions, the most pernicious of which is that he has her interests at heart. When confronted with the dying woman's questions about the fate of her work, the narrator is unable to tell her the truth. Instead, he fabricates "a romance invented for the occasion"—one that "none of [his] published sketches could compare with . . ." (267). After her death, he keeps the entrusted drama in a "locked case" with instructions that it should be "destroyed unread" upon his death, for he "could not bear that . . . anyone should cast so much of a thought of scorn upon the memory of the writer, . . . [his] poor dead, 'unavailable' unaccepted 'Miss Grief'" (269). The ultimate act of betrayal is the appropriation of Miss Crief in every way possible: the narrator destroys her work to protect his own privileged position; he robs her of subjectivity so that he can valorize his own authority; and, most significantly, he replaces her voice with his own. In Woolson's vision, the inspired female genius has as much hope as the unimaginative sentimental poetess when it comes to "battling" men in the literary marketplace.

And a battle it is. Not only does Woolson deftly portray the relationship between the narrator and Miss Crief as a deathly contest of wills, to make the point even more obvious, military references and war imagery abound. There is no doubt indeed that Woolson uses such suggestive and powerful devices to convey an important message about gendered literary politics at the turn of the century in which men and women were literally "battling" over literary turf and aesthetic terrain.[2] The weapons and strategies of the "battle" are delineated chiefly through the exchanges between the two characters. From their very first encounter, Miss Crief and the narrator engage in a tenacious power struggle in which each tests the other's position and endurance. Unlike the seemingly benign minister in "A Poetess," who is oblivious of his own power and privilege, Woolson's male narrator is fiercely protective of his acquired domain. The persistent effort Miss Crief must make to capture his initial intention underscores this point. In the beginning, when the narrator first learns of her visits, he imagines her as nothing more than an eccentric and bothersome intruder; it takes eight tries before she wins entry into his parlor. And the only reason he finally consents to see her is because he's curious about this visitor who "had sacrificed her womanly claims by her persistent attacks upon my door" (250). Even before they had any physical contact, the narrator perceives Miss Crief's desire to meet him as an "attack."

The contract between the man in his cozy, protected parlor and the woman outside in the rain, clamoring to get in, depicts brilliantly an inversion of the ideology of "separate spheres," in which women supposedly inhabit—happily—the home and men, the world. Similarly, the title of Miss Crief's drama repudiates the notion of gender-prescribed imaginative boundaries: "[The manuscript was] in the form of a little volume, and clearly written; on the cover was the word 'Armour' in German text, and underneath, a pen-and-ink sketch of a helmet, breast-plate, and shield" (255). Miss Crief steps into the realm of masculine metaphor, using images more appropriate to the "male sphere" of epic, war, and conquest than to the "female sphere" of domesticity, moral compliance, and self-abnegation. In Woolson's vision, the ante-bellum ideal of men and women peacefully coexisting from within their "separate spheres" is transformed into the image of men and women angrily hurling separate spears.

There is no question that both Miss Crief and the narrator are aiming at each other. In yet another powerfully charged battle, the two spar over the question of whether or not Miss Crief's dramas, stories, and poems should be edited and reconceptualized. To the narrator's discerning eye, the drama contained "faults" that were "many and prominent" (256); the poems were "marred by some fault or lack which seemed wilful perversity, like the work of an evil sprite. . . . [Each was like a] ring unfinished, [a] bracelet too large or too small for its purpose, [a] breastpin without its fastening, [a] necklace purposely broken" (262); and the prose story had an implausible plot and characters. To Miss Crief, however, her imaginative renderings perfectly express her

vision; uninterested in correcting the "bad points" and improbabilities to suit readers' expectations, she wants the work published as is. She responds to the author's pronouncement that the drama has "faults," by quietly stating, "I was not aware there were any" (258); and when he insists she "cut out" a character from one of the stories, she refuses because the character "belongs to the story so closely that he cannot be separated from it" (263). In the end, Miss Crief's tenacity wears out the narrator; after repeating his critique a second time and still not getting any results, he concludes that "she simply could not see the faults of her own work, any more than a blind man can see the smoke that dims a patch of blue sky" (259). But Woolson makes it clear that it is the narrator and not Miss Crief whose aesthetic sights are impaired. For when the narrator takes up upon himself to "alter and improve" Miss Crief's texts without her knowledge and permission, he finds that no amount of "amend[ing], alter[ing], [leaving] out, put[ing]in, piec[ing], condensc[ing] [or] lengthen[ing]" does any good. After all his effort, he is forced to conclude that his edits and revisions could never "approach . . . Miss Grief's own work just as it stood" (264).

In addition to exposing the narrator's arrogant assumptions about his own superior capabilities and judgments, Woolson also makes it clear that the disagreement that takes place in the narrator's parlor is a depiction in miniature of the larger culture's unequal gender relations in the literary marketplace. In other words, what could seemingly be a conflict of visions between two individuals is really something much larger; the power struggle between Miss Crief and the narrator symbolizes a power struggle between those who have the power to disseminate values and administer institutions and those who don't. For example, before the narrator attempts to "improve" Miss Crief's work, he sends the drama and story to a friend who edits a monthly magazine. The editor has the same reaction as the narrator: he rejects the texts for publication because they have too many faults to please "a public 'lamentably' fond of amusement" (264). Here we see Woolson suggesting not only that market demands of a commercial culture affect the creation of literary standards but also how influential "literary men" are in creating and perpetuating those standards. To implicate the male publishing industry in the devaluation of standards even further, Woolson quotes the pompous double-talk in the rejection and has the narrator comment that even he "doubt[ed] if [the editor] knew himself what he meant" (264).

Woolson's scathing critique of late nineteenth-century literary politics is not achieved solely through cleverly suggestive ironic devices, however. It is articulated directly by Miss Crief's companion, Aunt Martha. It is she who boldly confronts the narrator when they meet by chance, on the street, after many months of no contact. Although he had promised Miss Crief he would try to find her a publisher, when he wasn't successful, he lost interest. Now, after much time has passed, he encounters Miss Crief's aunt and inquiries about her. In a tirade remarkable for its explicit expression of rage, Aunt Martha responds by accusing him of stealing her niece's ideas:

> "And as to who has racked and stabbed her, I say you, you-you literary men!" She had put her old head inside my carriage, and flung out these words at me in a shrill, menacing tone. "But she die in peace in spite of you." she continued. "Vampires! you take her ideas and fatten on them, and leave her to starve. You know you do—you who have had her poor manuscripts these months and months!"
>
> (266)

Woolson's choice of images is not subtle; each evokes some form of violent intrusion to both the body and the soul. Racking and stabbing, the "literary men" torture and murder their female victims. They are Anti-Christs—the "vampires" who diabolically steal the vital life-blood of other human beings. Robbed of her genius, the writing woman is left "to starve," nailed to her own cross. But, like Christ, she does not die in vain, for her "sacrifice" will not be for naught. Although she can not tell her own story in her own voice, there is hope that future generations of writing women may be spared a similar sacrifice if they are attentive to Aunt Martha's outburst. In this respect, both the direct and indirect expression of anger in this story is key to social change.

It is significant that it is Miss Crief's female relative whom Woolson chooses as spokesperson of the writing woman's "grief" and rage. In the same way women have historically tended to the dead, cleansing and preserving the body for burial, Aunt Martha "tends to" the writing woman's rage by providing a conduit for its expression. In yet another ironic twist, the narrator's assumption that Aunt Martha is Miss Crief's "maid" has a dual meaning: while she is not a subservient caretaker in the traditional sense, she performs an essential "care-taking" function none the less. By naming the enemy and the consequences of the deathly battle, she preserves a story of agency and victimization that succeeding generations of writing women need to know. It is she, then, who ultimately effects Miss Crief's "resurrection" because it is she who suggests that the writing woman's story can not be suppressed, buried, or destroyed.

Miss Crief's and Betsey Dole's plight as writing women battling a male-controlled literary market-place, whose values, standards, and practices make women's lives and visions negligible, helps us locate a critical turning-point in the history of American women's literature. In these two stories, the major "crisis of being" is not internalized solely within the female protagonist or her

woman-centered world.[3] Instead, what I would like to call a "crisis of confrontation" is projected outward, into an imaginative universe that includes female protagonists in undisguised competition with male opponents. Such a shift in vision signals the ending of an ante-bellum female literary culture rooted in an ideology based on separatism and difference from men and heralds the beginning of a "modernist" female literary culture that aspires to join men as equals and peers on common ground. Ironically, however, what these two stories ultimately suggest is that at the same time "new women" writers begin to claim the emotional and artistic freedom to feel and express anger without a protective "mask," they also begin to create female protagonists who are paralyzed by defeat and despair. For in the ante-bellum tradition, women's "masked" anger inspired public-spirited representations of triumphant protagonists and a transformed America; but in the post-bellum tradition, women's "unmasked" anger about the individual sacrificed self results in visions of death and isolated inarticulation.

The above Freeman and Woolson stories provide an intimate, telescopic view of the conclusions that historians and literary scholars have drawn about the social, cultural, and political changes that begin to occur in the post-civil war period but that are not fully manifested until the 1920s. There is a general consensus that these years mark a new era in women's history and literature. The creation of mass culture leisure activities provides public spaces where rigid boundaries between races, sexes, and classes begin to break down; more and more white, middle-class women gain access to the workplace and educational institutions; the ideology of "separate spheres" begins to collapse as a younger generation of "new" women claim they are more like, rather than unlike, men. In essence, this shift from a homosocial to a heterosocial world of work, leisure, and gender relations has a profound impact on how women perceive themselves and their worlds, which in turn greatly affects their literary productions. By the 1920s, for example, the ante-bellum belief that human nature could be perfected through the exercise of "good, moral feeling"—an ideology rooted in evangelical moral reform fervor and transcendentalist notions of the sanctity of the individual—was considered at best quaint, at worst, culpable for modern society's ills. Replacing this idealistic, visionary notion of human capability was a rationalistic, evolutionary, bureaucratic sense of human agency that no longer gave credence to the idea that women could exercise power through uniquely female moral virtues. When an ideology that claimed its basis of power in an ethos of feeling was rejected and replaced by both men and women—albeit for different reasons—so too was a tradition of ante-bellum women's activism, culture, and ways of thinking.

The profoundly different meaning of Christian sacrifice that the Freeman and Woolson stories encode provides the most telling evidence of how these changes affected the imaginings of late nineteenth-century women writers. To the previous generation, ideas about self-sacrifice were based on both a secular and religious rhetoric that deemed public interests more important than private desires. Using the paradigm of the martyred Christ as a prototype, this previous generation believed that when a woman sacrificed her own needs for the sake of her family's, she was assuring the success of American democracy. By instilling the most important tenants of Republican virtue in her family members, the self-sacrificing wife and mother could perform the most sacred form of public honor and responsibility. Such an ideology assumes different inflections in different imaginative visions, but most writers share a common assumption that self-sacrifice is a praiseworthy virtue. Catharine Maria Sedgwick, in her novel *Hope Leslie,* for example, equates self-sacrifice with the noblest form of heroism; in *Uncle Tom's Cabin,* Harriet Beecher Stowe envisions the sacrifice of self as the ultimate form of salvation from the sins of slavery; even such authors of slave narratives, as Mattie J. Jackson, Harriet Jacobs, and Lucy Delaney, valorize mothers for sacrificing their own freedom to insure that of their children's.

But for Freeman and Woolson, the notion of self-sacrifice has a radically different meaning. Instead of signifying accomplishment, in their vision, self-sacrifice results in a sacrificed self. Instead of a visionary ideal that has the potential to mold human thought and behavior, self-sacrifice becomes a literary device used to express anger at insensitive and conniving male competitors. In Freeman and Woolson's stories, the writing woman's sacrifice by no means leads to some higher moral good; rather, it provokes a reassessment of literary history from a wronged woman's point of view. Written at precisely the time that aesthetic standards were becoming institutionalized and professionalized, the implication in the Woolson story that a male-narrated version of the writing woman's story may well be a fiction is potent indeed.

By imaging Christian sacrifice as a symbol of waste, deprivation, and erasure of subjectivity, Freeman and Woolson anticipate a profound shift in ideologies of womanhood that occurred between the ante-bellum and modern eras. Their notion that a sacrificed female self is something to mourn and protest is completely at odds with an ante-bellum ideology of sacrifice as selfless heroism. Beginning in the post-bellum period, but not coming into full expression until the 1920s, a "modern" woman demanded the right to claim and fashion an independent self who could also express anger at men. The Freeman and Woolson stories provide unique insight into how difficult it was for many women to relinquish traditional notions of inferiority while at the same time embracing new ideas of equality. Both portray protagonists who unwittingly participate in their own sacrifice—Betsey by asking to become the subject of the minister's poem, and Miss Crief by appointing the male narrator as her literary executor. Thus, both are examples of a conflict between self-actualization and self-denial, between agency and victimization, a conflict which is literally physicalized in the depiction of their wasted, hungry bodies.

Yet, in the end, the stories bequeath a legacy of hope, not despair. Because there is no idealized conclusion, the conflict, tension, and anger are projected outward onto the reader, and it is he or she who must ultimately make sense of the writing woman's sacrificed self. In this process, the reader experiences the anger the sacrificed woman is denied, and her story "lives" to prevent further acts of female sacrifice. In essence then, whereas in the ante-bellum period women shaped and designed the notion of sacrifice to mask anger, by the last quarter of the nineteenth century, a new generation of writers begins to use it for the opposite purpose. Once a way to cope with powerlessness, by the post-bellum period sacrifice becomes a way to expose it. Nonetheless, sacrifice is still not depicted without ambivalence.

The closing image of "A Poetess" is of Betsey Dole's canary "chirping faster and faster until he trilled into a triumphant song" (387).[4] This image seems enigmatic at first, but it doesn't take long to realize that it encapsulates one of the story's most important messages: that from the "cage" of her poverty and powerlessness, in the end, Betsey Dole triumphs. Similar to the use of caged birds in so many other poems and stories written by women, here the canary is an emblem of contradictory meanings: imprisonment and despair, hope and freedom. But the canary in this story means something more: it is a symbol of Betsey Dole's "caged" anger. With so little to sustain her, once her tenuous link to life is broken, Betsey's anger turns inward, and she decides to destroy that which is most precious to her, her writing. Yet, because her anger works on two different levels, Betsey's act of suicide is also an act of survival: her personal, internalized anger becomes the vehicle through which the public reader can recognize and express her own. Thus, while on the one hand the writing woman's anger is "caged," on the other, the reason why the bird "trills triumphantly in song" is because the anger is communicated to the reader and released from within the story itself. In this way it enters the culture and motivates social change. A similar process is at work in the Woolson story through the device of the male narrator. Here, too, the expression of anger works on two levels. As in "A Poetess," the writing woman herself does not voice her own rage, but the overall effect is that the reader is stunned into awareness through the circuitous route led by the unreliable narrator.

Thus the most important legacy that the Freeman and Woolson stories bequeath is that the writing woman will always be imperiled unless her voice, vision, and anger are incorporated into public history. Rebecca Harding Davis intuitively understood this when she wrote *Life in the Iron Mills* in 1861. In that text, she haltingly exposes the writing woman's thwarted, mighty, and unfinished anger when she imagines the statue of the naked, ungainly female mill-worker hidden behind a curtain that was only "sometimes" "accidentally drawn back." Thirty years later, Freeman and Woolson continue the unmasking process that Rebecca Harding Davis began. What makes their late nineteenth-century rendering different, however, is that the writing woman's anger is no longer "hidden," and its exposure is far from "accidental."

Notes

I wish to thank Mari Jo Buhle, Thadious Davis, Ruth Feldstein, David Hirsch, Louise Newman, and Lyde Cullen Sizer for their generous and insightful comments on different versions of this article.

1. Elizabeth Ammons provides an excellent overview of the period in the introduction to *Conflicting Stories: American Women Writers at the Turn into the Twentieth Century.*

2. Gilbert and Bugar see this gendered battle as paradigmatic of the modern sexual literary relationship. In their words, "both male and female writers increasingly represented women's unprecedented invasion of the public sphere as a battle of the sexes, a battle over a zone that could be defined as a no man's land" (4).

3. "Crisis of being" is Mary Kelley's phrase. In her analysis, the "crisis" occurs because nineteenth-century "literary domestics" are unable to reconcile a sense of self as both a public "creator of culture" and a private "domestic" woman. The ultimate dilemma is that they are private, domestic, familial women writing about private, domestic, familial lives for public consumption. Even though they create a new public role for themselves and the pressing issues of their lives, they are unable to conceive of themselves as doing so. Thus, they resort to denial, subterfuge, and secrecy in both their private and public writings.

4. Although the New American Library reprint edition of "A Poetess" reads that the canary *"thrilled* into a triumphant song," I have used "trilled" here because that is what is used in an 1897 edition of Wilkins' *A New England Nun and Other Stories* (159). I am indebted to David Hirsch for pointing out this discrepancy.

Works Cited

Ammons, Elizabeth. *Conflicting Stories: American Women Writers at the Turn into the Twentieth Century.* New York: Oxford University Press, 1991.

Davis, Rebecca Harding. *Life in the Iron Mills,* ed. with a biographical interpretation by Tillie Olsen. New York: The Feminist Press, 1985.

Donovan, Josephine. *New England Local Color Literature: A Woman's Tradition.* New York: Frederick Ungar, 1983.

Freeman, Mary Wilkins. "The Poetess," reprinted in *Short Fiction of Sara Orne Jewett and Mary Wilkins Freeman,* ed. and introduced by Barbara H. Solomon. New York: New American Library, 1979.

————. *A New England Nun and Other Stories.* New York: Harper & Brothers, 1897.

Gilbert, Sandra M., and Susan Gubar. *No Man's Land: The Place of the Woman Writer in the Twentieth Century, Volume 1: The War of the Worlds.* New Haven: Yale University Press, 1988.

Kelley, Mary. *Private Woman, Public Stage: Literary Domesticity in Nineteenth-Century America.* New York: Oxford University Press, 1984.

Tompkins, Jane. *The Cultural Work of American Fiction: 1790-1860.* New York: Oxford University Press, 1985.

Wood, Ann Douglas. "The Literature of Impoverishment: The Women Local Colorists in America 1865-1914." *Women's Studies* 1 (1972): 3-45.

Woolson, Constance Fenimore. "Miss Grief," reprinted in *Women Artists, Women Exiles: Miss Grief and Other Stories,* ed. and introduced by Joan Myers Weimer. New Brunswick: Rutgers University Press, 1988.

Sharon L. Dean (essay date 1995)

SOURCE: Dean, Sharon L. "The Marriage Question." In *Constance Fenimore Woolson: Homeward Bound,* pp. 99-136. Knoxville: The University of Tennessee Press, 1995.

[*In the following essay, Dean focuses on Woolson's attitudes toward marriage, divorce, and free love as they relate to the author's representations of family home life.*]

Using the different locations of her fiction, Woolson asks questions about the impact of region and ethnicity on the search for a home. Even more, she embeds all her work with questions about the impact of gender on this search. Woolson knew that to be born female in the nineteenth century meant that the boundaries of one's home would be limited—by access to property and education, by expectations within the family and the community, by socially defined cultural and artistic norms. Because her artistic temperament found its strongest voice in observation of the present rather than in an imagined past and because that present included both the boundaries placed on women and an increasingly vocal objection to those boundaries, Woolson could use her position as observer to its greatest advantage. When she wrote about isolated western communities, about the South, or about Europe, when she wrote about African Americans or American Indians or Spanish Americans, she wrote primarily from external observation. Even her emphasis on the geographical features of the landscape were, by definition, external observations. But when she wrote about women's issues, she could combine the external with the private struggles of one who knew what it felt like to be born female and to encounter the boundaries that limited the female's search for home.

Of all the gender questions Woolson raises, the one that most closely connects her to her sociocultural milieu is the marriage question. Woolson knew that most of her female contemporaries looked for the physical sanctuary of home in marriage. But when she turned her powers of observation onto the forces that pressured women to marry, she had to endure the criticism of the male literary establishment that defined these forces as a less than profound subject for fiction. When, for example, Henry James wrote his generally favorable review of Woolson in the February 12, 1887, edition of *Harper's Weekly,* he criticized her for limiting women's choices by too often having them choose marriage: Miss Woolson, he says, "likes the unmarried . . . but she likes marriages even better." For him, Woolson was not revolutionary in her portraits of women: rather than adding further complications to women's lives, she was content to explore the complications that already existed for women "fenced in by the old disabilities and prejudices."[1]

James's criticism represents the dilemma of the female novelist. For a woman, to center on the marriage question is to write in ways that are not revolutionary; for a male, to center on the marriage question is to explore how society constructs the social and psychological reality of women's lives. What James defines as Woolson's weakness, others define as James's strength, for he, too, centered most of his novels about women around issues of marriage. In *Henry James and the "Woman Business,"* Alfred Habegger has ably demonstrated that many of James's plots were appropriated from nineteenth-century women's fiction and that these enabled him to develop his fantasy of orphaned girl and father-lover. Like James, whose father was deeply involved in the mid-nineteenth-century debate about the

nature of marriage, Woolson came of age in an era that asked questions about what constituted the family home by examining the roles of husband and wife in marriage, by arguing about the legitimacy of divorce, and by experimenting with free-love communities. And like James, Woolson found her literary home by exploring the context of these debates.

Habegger's study of James provides ample historical background about the nineteenth-century debates on marriage that Henry James Sr. was so involved with and that serve as backdrop to the social realism of Henry Jr. and of Woolson. This was an age that drew on the doctrines of Charles Fourier, a figure lurking behind Hawthorne's Blithedale community. Fourier, a French socialist, believed that a variety of models were needed for sexual relationships among men and women, including models that allowed free love. Drawing on Fourier-like doctrines, a Vermonter named John Noyes founded, in 1848, the Oneida Community in New York. Noyes preached that monogamy was selfish and that men and women should be able to share sexual partners. The Oneida Community practiced free love until the confusion about children's paternity became too uncomfortable. Although the general public accommodated male infidelities, it feared sexual freedom within communal experiments like Oneida because these threatened to undermine established definitions of home and family by offering sexual freedom to both men and women. So, too, did the practice of birth control. Despite the support of birth control in infamous journals like *Woodhull and Claflin's Weekly,* in the larger society, authorities were prosecuting physicians and midwives not just for performing abortions but also for dispensing information about birth control—their fear being that immigrant populations were changing the ethnic profile of the family by outproducing white Anglo-Saxon Protestants.[2] At the same time that free-love experiments were flourishing and birth control was being used, Mormon communities with their advocacy of male polygamy were being established as another kind of threat to the traditional-marriage home. Woolson never portrayed free-love communities, but she did look at the way the Mormon and Zoarite communities impacted on women's lives and at the implications of a double-standard of sexual behavior. And although she never directly addressed the issue of birth control, she did often comment on attitudes that scorned large broods of immigrant or French or Hispanic children.

When Woolson began writing, she had decided that she would never marry and that she would not, therefore, have to make decisions about divorce should her husband prove unfaithful or her marriage unsatisfactory. Nor would she be pressured to increase the Anglo-American population. When she made her decision to pursue her home through writing rather than through marriage, Woolson freed herself to write about how marriage decisions impact on women's ways of finding home. She saw how in the West, the culture encouraged that people should be happy, free, able to pursue a new life, thus able freely to seek divorce.[3] Yet the more the West became socialized, the more it adopted eastern standards of marriage. Woolson depicts this most explicitly in a story titled **"Lily and Diamond,"** which sounds as if it will be a Wild West adventure, but which instead shows the tension between those who want freedom in the West, saying that "[s]urely in a country-town . . . , we can do as we please," and those who want fashionable society, saying about the same resort, "[s]urely in a city of one hundred thousand inhabitants, or in a summer hotel containing more than a hundred people, we owe it to ourselves to preserve all social requirements intact" (477). Society wins the day in the story as its female protagonists engage in rivalry for a man. The diamond figure, an older woman who has been widowed, loses the man and marries as society believes she wants while the young lily figure wins him. He minimalizes her act of bravery in following him in a storm when he says, "And so she came out alone in her cockleshell skiff, with those soft little fists, to rescue a great, strong man like me, in a steady old sail-boat like the scud, did she?" (482). The West may offer the dream of freedom for women, but Woolson knew that its marriage norms too often imitated the East and imposed similar kinds of strictures on women that made the married home the expected one.

Just which pieces about marriage, divorce, and sexuality Woolson read is unknown, but given the currency of these debates in the context of debates about women's suffrage, including those conducted at women's conventions in Cleveland while Woolson was still living there, she would have been well-aware of the issues. It is likely that she also learned that Henry James Sr. had joined the debate about divorce. James argued that monogamy was really promiscuous when, as so often was the case, it forced sex with no love; sexuality without marriage, on the other hand, could be endorsed when love was involved. James, according to Habegger, came under public scrutiny when he was referenced in an 1852 book by Marx Edgeworth Lazarus called *Love vs. Marriage,* which argued for variety in sexual partners. James, who had had Lazarus to dinner, did not, in fact, endorse such practices, advocating instead a spiritualized sexuality. He countered Lazarus publicly in a *New York Tribune* article called "The Marriage Question," in which he defended monogamy. Men, he said, will always be disappointed in marriage because women cannot fulfill the idealized promise they held before marriage. Marriage binds men to less than what they dreamed of; at the same time, however, it is a disciplining institution through which men can ultimately transcend physical and selfish desire.[4]

When discussing Woolson's attitude toward marriage and divorce, it is important to note that even though figures say that nine of ten women in the nineteenth century married, both the westward movement and the Civil War made it more difficult in eastern and southern sections of the United States for them to do so: in 1850, for example, there were twenty thousand more women than men in the United States, by 1870 that number had risen to fifty thousand, and by 1880 to sixty-six thousand (Chambers-Schiller 334). When James criticized Woolson's attention to issues of marriage, he missed the crucial fact that much of Woolson's fiction involves an explanation of the expectations that women marry and the conscious decisions of women who subvert these expectations by choosing what Joan Weimer calls "homelessness and habitual solitude" over human relationships, particularly those involving marriage.[5] One of Woolson's first stories, **"Cicely's Christmas,"** is almost allegorical in its recognition of the pressures on women to marry, presenting the plight of a single woman in the city who resists a suitor who prefers his inventions to her, only to find herself face to face on Christmas with the lot of an unmarried woman: she finds that women's restaurants are closed on Christmas Day and is forced to lunch in an overpriced restaurant, where she is stared at for being alone; she leaves the theater because the men on either side of her accost her; she has her purse stolen; she has supper alone in her room; and, as a final insult, she discovers a man who has been flirting with her flirting with someone else. When the inventor returns, it is no wonder that she accepts an unsuitable marriage over an equally unsuitable spinsterhood.

Woolson knew that it was difficult for women to find a home outside of marriage, and she often couches her anger at the expectation for marriage in satire. In one of her most satirical pieces, **"Matches Morganatic,"** a suitor declares his love in overblown lines like "Idol of my life, give me a smile—no, not a smile, for I could not see it in the darkness [the man is so nearsighted he would not be able to see it in the light]; but give me your hand, your lily hand, that I may know I am not despised" (524). Another couple banter about a woman's obedience in marriage only to have the woman accept marriage when a Confederate commander kidnaps her and her suitor and forces them to marry as a condition for their release. Woolson uses this as a way to force marriage onto a couple who love each other and to satisfy audiences who love the marriage plot. But the satirical level is so high that she subverts that plot by having marriage becomes a metaphor for battle, surrender, and optionlessness. Given society's expectations, it is no wonder that so many of Woolson's characters fail to live up to their pledge that they "will never marry for a home" (9).

Woolson's treatment of marriage centers less on demographics than on how the search for marital relationships often results in betrayal, not only of men toward women, but also of women toward each other in the competition for suitable partners. Still, this does not imply that Woolson disliked marriage. In a letter to her nephew Sam Mather near the end of her life, she called it "the best thing in life; it's the only thing worth living for; this is the sincere belief—& the result of observations of one who has never had it."[6] One could easily read this as evidence that Woolson yearned for marriage, perhaps to Henry James; however, the attention she paid to observing society's attitudes about marriage and to observing individual marriages in order to write about women's decisions to marry more likely point simply to an increased awareness about the difficulties women who do not marry face. John Kern wonders if the sense of loss Woolson reveals in so many of her stories indicates a shattered love affair, but there is no evidence for this (34). Woolson made a conscious decision early in her life not to marry. She never expressed regret over her broken relationship with Col. Zeph Spaulding when she was in her early twenties and, later in her life, referenced him as a childhood friend, saying that the "glamor that the war threw over the young officers who left their homes to fight . . . made me fancy that I cared for him."[7] A letter to her friend Arabella Carter Washburn seems to be quashing a rumor about suitors, though it is unclear if they are suitors to herself or to her sister Clara, who, Woolson tells Washburn, she believes will never remarry, being contented with her life as it is (Kern 51).

Joan Weimer thinks that Woolson associated marriage and childbirth with death because of her family tragedies, but given the fact that she was nearly thirty before her father died and that her mother lived another ten years, this may be overstated. (*MG* [*Women Artists, Women Exiles:* "*Miss Grief*" *and Other Stories*] x). Two stories can serve as better explanations on Woolson's decision not to marry. One, "**Hepzibah's Story**,"[8] probably written between 1871 and 1873 but never published, portrays a woman who nursed her family, especially her father, during the Civil War even though her caretaking duties prevented her from following Theodore, the man she loves, west. Finally released by the deaths of her father and mother, she joins Theodore, only to discover that he loves someone else when she overhears a conversation between the two lovers. Theodore is willing to fulfill his promise and marry Hepzibah, but Woolson avoids this through the device of a fire that causes a denouement that prevents the marriage. The other story, "**Ballast Island**,"[9] published in 1873 when Woolson was still tied to the caretaking of her mother, portrays two lovers who discover a solitary woman, Miss Jonah, on Ballast Island. Like Hepzibah, Miss Jonah had overheard her fiancé making love to another woman, in this case her sister. Miss Jonah re-

leases her fiancé by feigning her drowning and then retreating to the island. Where Hepzibah's act is tied to self-sacrifice, Miss Jonah's is tied to independence, and the message it gives to the lovers is that they should seek in their marriage the kind of freedom she has found in solitude. Where Hepzibah is like Hawthorne's spinster who nurses Clifford and loses herself in the process, Miss Jonah, like her biblical namesake, defies authority and, in a subversion of the story, thrives.

Reading "**Hepzibah's Story**" psycho-biographically, we can argue that Woolson's ties to her own mother and father, her sense of obligation to care for them, plus her own tendencies toward melancholy and solitude made her decide not just to refuse marriage to her soldier friend (or readily accept his rejection of her), but also to build a wall around herself that would discourage other marriage proposals, and, after the death of both parents, allow her to build an independent life. If we knew Woolson's emotional attitudes toward potential marriage partners, we would know more about a particular woman in the nineteenth century. What we have, instead, is the evidence of her fiction that generalizes about the impact of marriage on women's lives in the nineteenth century. Three more of her short stories are of particular interest here, one for its exposure of sentimental views of marriage, one for its exploration of marriage in an experimental community, and one for its exploration of how marriage is often the result of sexual blackmail. Each helps us to understand Woolson's response to the tremendous pressures on women to find marital homes, whether or not these homes are likely to provide happiness.

In "**Up in the Blue Ridge**," collected in *Rodman the Keeper*, Woolson manipulates the melodramatic form so that this story of a glamorous lover saving a damsel in distress is filled with humor and irony that subverts the sentimental marriage plot. The damsel in question is Honor Dooris, a woman who has found her potential marriage partner in the hills where she used to vacation before the Civil War. The melodrama involves her protecting the man she loves from her bootlegging cousin, who is about to murder him. Honor ends up marrying this man, preferring him to the northerner Stephen Wainwright, who also is beginning to love her. Despite the intrigue, Woolson undercuts any notion of a great passionate love both in Honor's relationship and in Stephen's relationship to the widow Adelaide Kellinger, who has caused the melodrama in order to prevent Stephen from declaring his love for Honor. Honor's choice of husband

> ended well; that is, he married her after a while, took her away to the North, and was, on the whole, a good husband. But from first to last, he ruled her, and she never became quite the beauty that Mrs. Kellinger intended her to be, because she was too devoted to him, too absorbed in him, too dependent upon his fancies, to

collect that repose and security of heart which are necessary to complete the beauty of even the most beautiful women.

(Rodman [Rodman the Keeper] 338)

With Honor married to her southern lover, Woolson implies that Stephen Wainwright will eventually, with no fanfare, marry Adelaide Kellinger. "This woman loved him," says the narrator; "the other [Honor] would never have given him more than gratitude" for saving her cousin from being murdered. "What would you have?" (**Rodman** 339). Neither, one would like to say, for although the settled, unpassionate premarital relationship between Stephen and Mrs. Kellinger seems natural, Woolson undercuts it, suggesting that social expectations hinder a natural relationship between an eligible woman and an eligible man. The omniscient narrator describes the "natural" relationship between Stephen and Mrs. Kellinger:

> If he asked a question, she answered with the plainest truth she could imagine; if he asked an opinion, she gave the one she would have given to her most intimate woman-friend (if she had had one); if she was tired, she did not conceal it; if she was out of temper, she said disagreeable, sharp-edged things. She was, therefore, perfectly natural? On the contrary, she was extremely unnatural. A charming woman does not go around at the present day in a state of nature mentally any more than physically; politeness has become a necessary clothing to her. Adelaide Kellinger never spoke to her cousin [Wainwright] without a little preceding pause, during which she thought over what she was going to say; and, as Stephen was slow to speak also, their conversations were ineffective, judged from a dramatic point of view.

(Rodman 279)

From a dramatic point of view, Woolson finally says in **"Up in the Blue Ridge,"** sentiment and melodrama are fine; in real life, steady, mature, rather dull marital relationships are the norm—perhaps to be preferred, but only as long as society expects men and women to marry.

Woolson was never so liberal a thinker—or so sure of her status with her publishers—that she examined open marriage systems or free love in her fiction, though there are undertones in many of her novels about the impulse toward sexual freedom. She did, however, look rather closely at the Zoarite system that disconnected marriage and human relations in general from sexuality. The German Zoarites settled in Ohio around 1819 and, soon realizing that it was not practical to ban sexual intercourse entirely, advocated it only for purposes of procreation. Woolson often visited this community with her father and, though she admired its peaceful ways, she realized, especially after the Civil War, that the community's young people would become restless under its austerity. In a letter to Arabella Washburn, she is saddened that the Zoarites objected to what she thought a respectful sketch of them called **"The Happy Valley"** (Benedict 2:273).

The Zoarites would have found Woolson's story **"Wilhelmina,"** in the *Castle Nowhere* collection, even more disturbing because of its exposure of the Zoarite's privacy and its focus on the restlessness of their youth under a rigid marriage system. The story has Wilhelmina, who has grown up in the community but is not German, wait for her lover Gustav to return from the Civil War, where he has gone because the Zoarites, though pacifist, were pressured into sending men. Gustav gladly fought, but he returns now unwilling to accept Zoarite ways. He rejects Wilhelmina and the community for a more worldly woman, and Wilhelmina is bullied into marrying a widower with five children, shortly after which she dies. The narrator has misread Wilhelmina by believing her when she says she is "contented" in this charming but dull life, for there is no evidence that she stops loving Gustav. The narrator believes, "So were they taught from childhood, and I was about to say—they knew no better; but, after all, is there anything better to know?" (*CN* [*Castle Nowhere*] 277). This is the sentimental view, and if the narrator thinks it so charming, we must ask why she wants to take Gustav and Wilhelmina out of the community and educate them. She faults Gustav for his attraction to a woman whose photograph she sees as frivolous. But the photograph also forces her to recognize that women do foolish things for love and that she herself has done so: "If it had not been for this red-cheeked Miss Martin in her gilt beads! 'Why is it that men will be such fools?' I thought. Up sprung a memory of the curls and ponderous jet necklace I sported at a certain period of my existence, when John—I was silenced . . ." (*CN* 298). There is no evidence that the narrator has made an ideal match herself, traveling without her husband as she does when she visits the Zoarite community for its charm. What Woolson yearns for is for Wilhelmina to be content within the Zoarite community, for her to be able to be who she is and still to marry for love, and not to be scorned for being uncultivated, as she is by both the narrator and Gustav. At the same time, she sees how impossible this is. As Carolyn VanBergen has demonstrated in an essay on **"Wilhelmina"** and **"Solomon,"** another Zoarite story, Woolson undercuts the nostalgia for the unity of the Zoarite community by showing how it suffocates diversity and creates disharmony rather than love.[10] These tightly controlled communal homes—like Catholic nunneries—attracted Woolson, but she knew that, with or without marriage, such a home would become her prison.

Even Woolson's early short fiction frequently portrays marriages that are unfulfilling whether because, like Honor's in **"Up in the Blue Ridge,"** they do not reach their early promise or because, like Wilhelmina's, they are forced by social expectations that endorse marriages of convenience. Woolson reveals another very troubling aspect of marriage when she recognizes that it often occurs under circumstances of sexual or emotional blackmail. The pattern occurs in much of her fiction—for example, in **"Jeannette"** and **"Peter the Parson"** in *Castle Nowhere* and in the novels *Anne, East Angels,* and *Horace Chase.* The story **"Misery Landing"** from *Castle Nowhere* best illustrates the issue. It involves a narrator who finds letters of John Jay, an aristocrat, who escapes his unrequited love for a society woman by building an isolated hut on an island cliff in Lake Superior. A young man, George Bram, saves himself from a storm by climbing a ladder to John's house. Subsequently, John tries to educate him for a role in the larger world, but George has fallen in love with a local girl, Martha, and does not want to leave Misery Landing. Martha does not love George, however, but both John and George practice emotional blackmail so that she accepts George anyway. George's blackmail is perhaps subconscious, occurring when he is about to die because Martha has not accepted him. Woolson recognized that the loss of a loved one could hasten one's death—her sister Emma, who married someone her parents at first objected to because he was ill, died soon after her husband.[11] But there is no evidence that Emma married, like Martha, to save her husband from death because of unrequited love, and such a motive is one that Woolson would have disapproved of.

Woolson's life and fiction reflect a belief that one could and should face up to disappointment and live. Thus she makes John's sexual blackmail blatant and uses it to represent the worst aspects of male-female relationships. John takes it upon himself to find Martha and bring her back to George so that George will live. Then he leaves the two of them at Misery Landing and ends up himself marrying the woman who had refused him, the implication being that she accepts him for his money even though he originally wanted her love as well. Of course, this does not represent a triumph for him, but he has gotten vicarious revenge by forcing marriage onto Martha. John's view of women is decidedly sexist. They are frivolous and false, "an inferior race" (*CN* 223) who are "all alike" (*CN* 228) and who "cannot learn, or rather unlearn" (*CN* 223). Men have two choices: they can be tyrannized by women as George is because of his love, or they can enslave them, as John finally decides on doing. That John is an artist furthers the barb, for he has chosen to shape the lives of two people he does not respect. He is no Thoreauvian nature lover who prefers commoners to aristocrats. He loves Bret Harte but marvels that only "cultivated people . . . are taken with Bret" (*CN* 219), suggesting that Harte's readers condescend to these primitive character types. George is John's bit of local color, worthy to be shaped while Martha, without beauty, is not. John is one of Woolson's earliest versions of male attitudes

toward unattractive women: "A homely woman is a complete mistake, always: a woman should always be beautiful, as a man should always be strong" (*CN* 215). Martha, with little choice, becomes Martha of the Bible, serving rather than loving.

Because Woolson saw so clearly and so satirically how real-life and fictional marriage plots manipulated women into false homes, her short fiction presents a decidedly bleak view of marriage. It is not, however, marriage that Woolson opposes, but only the pressure to marry. In some of her short fiction, there are glimmers of success in marriage. The settled marriage of Stephen Wainwright and the widow Mrs. Kellinger is dull, but stable, and there is hope within limited lifestyles for the unions in stories like **"Castle Nowhere," "Jeannette," "Old Gardiston,"** and **"Miss Elisabetha,"** to name just a few. Much of Woolson's uncollected short fiction ends in marriages that promise to be successful, but this fiction, written early in her career, tends to be formulaic and the marriages either unimpassioned (**"Black Point"**) or between childlike women and older men (**"Miss Vedder"**). It is interesting, as well, that childlike women, whether they marry or not, are often less naïve about sexuality than their deeper counterparts, having, as the omniscient narrator says of a flirtatious girl in **"A Flower of the Snow,"** "[t]en times more knowledge of the world, twenty times more coquetry . . . than . . . the educated woman of twenty-six," who eventually marries the story's hero (79).

Woolson's European short fiction continues to explore the marriage-plot in ways that show resistance to the idea of a happy ending, but in the novels written during the same period, the view of marriage is more complex and more positive. In them, Woolson, like most of her contemporary women writers, endorses women's role of holding together homes, particularly marital homes.[12] While in the short fiction, as Joan Weimer has shown,[13] Woolson's most interesting women, all artists, choose not to marry, in the novels, they almost always choose a home equated with marriage. Woolson is not abandoning the broader sphere of the female that Weimer sees her developing in her short fiction; rather, she is using the longer novel form to reconcile independence with the idea of a marital home.

Because she was also quite aware that "nine-tenths of the great mass of readers care *only* for the love story" (Benedict 2:103) and because she had to please these readers to maintain her financial independence, Woolson needed to reconcile her sense of the rewards of independence despite loneliness with the tastes of the audience of her day. As she wrestled in each of her novels with the expectations of her audience and her own conflicting needs for home and independence, Woolson broke out of what James called the "old disabilities and prejudices" by stepping back to observe the implications of the choice for a home that is equated with marriage. Because she continued to long for a home outside of marriage, she also asked, particularly in her last novel, how a woman can possess a home that is not equated with marriage.

Like so much of the fiction written by males canonized in American literature, each of Woolson's longer pieces of fiction juxtaposes naïve or shallow girl-women with women more aware of the ambiguities of life. The girl figures always choose marriage, and through them, Woolson reveals her ability to understand why women did not often exercise other kinds of choices. Woolson's niece Clare Benedict describes her aunt's capacity for understanding all types of women as an "intense sympathy with and understanding of all . . . moral and intellectual aspirations, that [enabled her] to draw out of people the best that was in them, while giving them in return the most inspiring and comforting comprehension" (Benedict 2:xiv). Such a capacity for comprehension is even more apparent in Woolson's portraits of complex women. While the girl-women in the novels are interesting but similar, each of the complex heroines provides a different focus on the issues involved when a woman desires or is expected by her society to desire a marital home. Woolson's character pairings show her observing closely how women compromise as they seek homes and show her struggling with issues involving kinship, sexuality, violence, and loneliness.

Woolson's novel *Anne* develops the marriage plot around intricate twists and turns that would keep its momentum in serialization. The title character is engaged to a childhood friend, Rast Pronando, on Mackinac Island and is relieved when he elopes with her sister, Tita. In New York, where she lives with an aunt and attends school, she rejects the proposal of another suitor, Gregory Dexter, and falls in love with Ward Heathcote, who marries her best friend, Helen Lorrington, but is reunited with Anne when his wife is murdered. Rather than being purely melodramatic, the plot allows Woolson to explore a society in which women exist for marriage or can find financial security only within marriage. Anne's long interlude at a private, but fashionable watering hole in New York gives Woolson ample opportunity to reveal the kinds of things that attract men to women: beauty, coyness, discreet rather than ostentatious fashion. Because the possibility of home is equated with marriage, Woolson reveals not only how women use these devices in their pursuit of a husband, but also how ruthless they can be in their pursuits. The novel's shallow, though hardly naïve, girl figure, Helen Lorrington, articulates the feelings that plague all of women's relationships: Helen befriends the title character Anne because "Anne admired her, and was at the same time neither envious nor jealous, and from her youth

she [Helen] had been troubled by the sure development of these two feelings, sooner or later, in all her girl companions" (161).

Several plot complications suggest how often women's jealousy or fear leads them to betray one another if they equate home with marriage. Anne's aunt subverts Anne's engagement because her fiancé is the son of the man her aunt once loved and had hoped to make a home with, and Anne's half-sister, Tita [Angelique], is another shallow girl who like the island girl in **"A Flower of the Snow"** has "twenty times more coquetry" than Anne, so much so that she elopes with Anne's fiancé. An even worse betrayal comes from Helen, who tells Heathcote, the man both she and Anne have fallen in love with, that the Angelique whose marriage notice has appeared in the newspaper is really Anne and thereby wins Heathcote for her own husband. At the same time, however, Woolson seems loath to condemn any woman who manipulates for love, understanding as she does how much women's lives depend on marriage and how much better marriages are likely to be if they are based on love. She does, though, readily expose falseness, and it is interesting to note that all the admirable men in this novel prefer Anne's honesty and independence to the coquetry of the fashionable young women frequenting the New York resort. Woolson might have ended *Anne* with Helen Lorrington's marriage to the man Anne loves, thus being consistent with her versions of exiles from home in the short fiction. Instead, she reunites Anne and Helen. Believing Heathcote dead, they become honest with each other and share the bond of suffering. Through their bond, Woolson suggests that although women often betray each other in their search for the security of home, they also can be honest with each other. Although betrayal severs friendship, honesty redeems it and draws them into a closer relationship than they might otherwise have had.

Through more plot twists, including Helen's murder and Heathcote's arrest and acquittal for this, Woolson eventually manages to unite Anne and Heathcote in marriage. Joan Weimer objects to this union, finding Heathcote "a character who seems to exist only to give Anne opportunities to show her superior strength and character" (*MG* xli). But Gregory Dexter is no more appropriate a match for Anne. He is too much a father figure and represents Woolson's rejection of the older-man/younger-woman motif that was so current in the fiction of the day. In fact, one of the striking things about Woolson's fiction is how often she develops the opposite motif, that of the older woman/younger man, the best example being the marriage of Prudence Wilkins in her story **"The Front Yard"** to a man eighteen years her junior. Woolson was quite aware that older women could be attracted to younger men. Earlier in the century, there had been Margaret Fuller and the Marquis Angelo Ossoli, who was ten years younger than she. Woolson had arrived in Europe at the time that George Eliot was being much talked about for marrying John Cross, a man twenty-one years her junior. In Florence, she watched the novelist Ouida making a "goose of herself . . . by falling in love with a young Italian 20 years younger than herself."[14] Likewise, for Prudence, love for a younger man is disastrous but explicable by "her having already become the captive of this handsome, this irresistible, this wholly unexpected Tonio, who was serving as a waiter in the Perugian inn" (*FY* [*The Front Yard*] 5).[15]

Although Ward Heathcote is also older than Anne, in his early thirties compared to Dexter's late thirties and Anne's eighteen, Woolson chose his character type carefully. He is, as Weimer has noted, like Woolson's prodigal brother Charlie (*MG* xli) and, therefore, seems younger and in need himself of growing up before he can enter into an adult marriage. His marriage to Helen, a childhood friend, is much what Anne's marriage to Rast, her childhood friend, might have become, an exercise in duty rather than love. It is the kind of marriage that Woolson may have imagined for herself had she married Zeph Spaulding. Despite Heathcote's love for Anne, the novel presents him as faithful to Helen. At the same time, however, it suggests an undercurrent of a double standard. When people observe Anne at Heathcote's trial, they see her as evidence of Helen's obligation to endure her husband's infidelity: Anne represents "one of those concealed trials which wives of 'men of the world' were obliged to endure"; that is, the man's affair with "a girl of the lower class, beautiful, and perhaps in her way even respectable" (478). To underscore the inappropriateness of such a double standard, Woolson gives as the reason for Anne's aunt's refusal to marry Rast's father the fact that during their short engagement he ran around with a "common girl—a market gardener's daughter" (182).[16] Woolson is documenting not just the double standard here, but also how much the ideal of the true and virtuous woman was a social construct of the middle and upper classes. Elsewhere in her fiction, however, she does suggest that sexuality outside of wedlock is not confined to the exploitation of poor women, and even Anne is nearly seduced by Heathcote until his honor forces him to tell her that he has married Helen.

Woolson wants to provide Anne a relationship based on openness, freedom, sexuality, and maturity, thus in choosing Heathcote's name, she echoes Emily Brontë's name Heathcliff. She would also have known that Cooper had given the name Heathcote to the Puritan family in *The Wept of Wish-ton-Wish*. She echoes Cooper's background of Indian warfare in the background of the Civil War, and Mark Heathcote Jr., who falls in love with a woman who was saved from Indian capture instead of his sister, prefigures Ward Heathcote. But Cooper's Heathcote is a minor character only, and Woolson's Heathcote, though not as sinister as Heathcliff, is blasphemous rather than pious, a religious doubter, a man locked into an inappropriate marriage and haunted by a love associated with the natural—though not the supernatural—environment. Anne is attracted to Heathcote in the first place because with her he can discuss his deepest and most unorthodox feelings, represented in a discussion they have in which they question the nature of God. Like Brontë's Catherine Earnshaw to Heathcliff, she is also attracted to him because he has no family whose expectations he must fulfill. Heathcote and Anne, however, both must mature before they marry. Helen serves as the disciplining force for Heathcote, and their marriage represents what Henry James Sr. saw as the nature of marriage, a state in which a man's instincts are spiritualized by the care of a loving wife. Besides becoming freed from his marriage to Helen, Heathcote must learn to treat Anne as a woman, not a child, a word he often uses when wooing her and, indeed, Anne must become more than a child. The two encounter each other several times on a train and each encounter brings them a step further into maturity and equality until Heathcote, unlike Dexter, drops the word *child* in reference to her. An early scene in the novel has Anne in a tableaux vivant dressed as the Goddess of Liberty and Heathcote holding her up, when the ladder she is on nearly falls. What Woolson implies by the end of the novel is that Anne must find liberty before she finds connection, something she and Heathcote both finally do. Imprisoned at first by her engagement, Anne gains the freedom of temporary spinsterhood and is able to free Heathcote from the prison of his marriage that has been represented metaphorically in his literal imprisonment for a crime he did not commit.

Once Anne proves Heathcote's innocence, they join together in a marriage that is liberating rather than imprisoning. Anne's choice of Heathcote is similar to her half-sister Tita's elopement, a choice made despite what society defines as sensible. A significant difference in the choice, however, is that society would define Anne's choice as morally acceptable. It is important that the marriage takes place on Mackinac Island, Anne's girlhood home, one which would have been a limiting home had she married her girlhood fiancé. Because Anne has been independent and intelligent, hers is not the limiting fate that fulfills women like Helen and Tita; rather, it is one that combines freedom and responsibility at the same time that it satisfies a reader's desire for romantic adventure within or outside of marriage. As Cheryl Torsney has so ably pointed out in a discussion of *Anne* and Henry James's *The Portrait of a Lady*—novels the two were composing at the start of their friendship—Anne, unlike Isabel Archer, "assert[s] her identity in the real world": she names herself and uses the active voice to say, "I, Anne, take thee, Ward, to my wedded husband, to have and to hold, from this day forward" (539).[17]

Woolson presents a radical vision in *Anne* because she refuses to criticize Helen for betraying friendship and Tita for betraying kinship. However, she endorses Anne as the heroine who follows the conventionally moral path no matter the cost to herself, and she rewards her by providing her what we judge will become a mature, satisfactory, even romantic home within marriage. In *For the Major,* she continues to explore the kinds of choices women make to establish marital homes, but now with a heroine whose behavior might be considered less socially acceptable. Again, she juxtaposes the girl figure with a woman whose life circumstances are more complex. Sara Carroll is one of Woolson's least complex girl figures and her virtue is rewarded by marriage to the man she loves. Sara is of minor interest in the novella, far more conventional than Tita or Helen, but providing her with a home via marriage enables Woolson to validate her simplicity because it is accompanied by honesty. In her conventional morality, Sara is more like Anne than Helen or Tita, but this morality is never really tempted. Sara's stepmother, Madame Carroll, might be compared to Helen and Tita in the sense that she must compromise standards of behavior in order to gain a husband. However, because Woolson has focused on Madame Carroll, we see her not just following self-gratification but also weighing the consequences of her actions within both a social and familial context. Unlike Helen and Tita, Madame Carroll is honest with herself even though she is not truthful with those around her.

For the Major explores an interesting angle toward marriage and home because Madame Carroll articulates so explicitly the reasons why many women act the way they do. Through her, Woolson finds a voice that helps us to understand her own unwillingness to belittle any of the decisions her female characters make regarding marriage. Left with a sickly daughter to support, Madame Carroll teaches, working as hard as she can, but finding that she can do no more than feed her child. As she says to her stepdaughter Sara, "I had strained every nerve, made use of all my poor little knowledge and my trifling accomplishments; I had worked as hard as I possibly could; and the result of all my efforts was that I had barely succeeded in getting our bread from day to day, with nothing laid up for the future, and the end of my small strength near at hand" (*Major* [*For the Major*] 342). At this point in her life, she meets, through a friend, Major Carroll, in front of whom she pretends to be younger than she is. She also leads Major Carroll to believe she has had only one child, the daughter who dies shortly after her marriage to the major. In reality, she also has a son who finds her at Major Carroll's home in Far Edgerley. When the son dies and the major's ill-health deteriorates into senility, Madame Carroll reveals the truth to Sara. In a final plot twist, we learn that Madame Carroll has either never married the major or, more likely, married him not knowing her

first husband was still alive. Woolson downplays the bigamy and the illegitimacy of her child by the major, reminding us of these only when Madame Carroll (re)marries the senile Major at a bedside ceremony.

Madame Carroll's actions have hardly been what we want to admire: living a lie based on feminine appearance to satisfy a man. Yet the portrait is sympathetic because Woolson has shown us that although loving has required Madame Carroll to be false, it has not required hypocrisy. Explaining her position to Sara, Madame Carroll displays the kind of integrity Woolson wanted us to see in her:

> [The major] saw in me a little blue-eyed, golden-haired girl-mother, unacquainted with the dark side of life, trusting, sweet. It was this very youth and child-like look which had attracted him, man of the world as he was himself, and no longer young. I feared to shatter his dream. In addition, that part did not seem to me of any especial consequence; I knew that I should be able to live up to his ideal, to maintain it not only fully, but longer, probably, than as though I had been in reality the person he supposed me to be.
>
> (*Major* 341)

By having Madame Carroll become only superficially a child-wife, permanently youthful and beautiful but also fully aware of the implications of her pretense, Woolson has focused on her observations about the things that matter to the major's kind of world. It is the men in that world who, as Sybil Weir has noted, end up being the most deeply scarred, for where "the woman is aware that the sentimental disguise masks her actual self, the man is robbed of self-knowledge." For Weir, the major's son Scar, a shortening of Scarborough, "a sickly and effeminate child," serves as a metaphor for the perversity of relationships where men treat women as children (141). Given this demeaning social expectation, is it really so awful, Woolson suggests, to choose honest pretense and service as a more viable way of living than self-delusion or loneliness and poverty? Madame Carroll is not, at the core, false or childlike, for she knows that she is not a person who possesses a "lofty kind of vision which sees only the one path, and that the highest." Instead, she sees "all the shorter paths, lower down, that lead to the same place—the cross-cuts." "[T]he great things, the wide view," says Madame Carroll, "are beyond me." She is not fitted for "struggle" but can "work and plan and accomplish . . . only when sheltered—sheltered in a home, no matter how plain, protected from actual contact with the crowd," where there is always "brutality" (*Major* 342-43). Some of Woolson's more limited characters may take a superficial kind of high road; Madame Carroll outdistances them because she understands how much societal expectations have shaped her own decisions in securing a home.

By the time she wrote her third novel, *East Angels,* Woolson had been in Europe long enough to observe the differences in American and European marriages, one of which was the extent to which European marriages served as avenues through which women could lead more open and freer lives. One of the great themes of the nineteenth century, worked out most fully by Henry James, was what happened to innocent Americans faced with the darker experience of Europe. In a remarkably clear and candid letter to Mrs. Samuel Livingston Mather, her brother-in-law's second wife, Woolson suggests how this applies to females by talking about the differences between American and European attitudes toward marriage. Florence, she writes, "is no place for *young* young ladies; they have no liberty, and can hardly speak unless spoken to, can go nowhere alone, and flirtation is—for them—unknown; if they indulge in it, they lose their reputation; the only thing they can do is to marry and they generally do that at least once," provided, of course, that they have dowries. In Florence, Woolson continues, "the married women, and in fact all older women, whether married or not have a much better time" than those in America. The problem, however, is that no matter how old they are, if

> they have a little money, especially, they are never secure, but are considered proper subjects of discussion [for marriage] as long as they live! These, of course, are the widows and old maids; as to the married ladies, there is a great deal of flirtation going on. What our young ladies amuse themselves with at home, the married ladies amuse themselves with here. It is all very curious and, to a looker-on like me, amusing.
>
> (Benedict 2:26-27)

Embedded within Woolson's comments is her awareness that European marriages give women a license for sexuality, protection from unwanted advances, and freedom of choice and movement. One thinks especially of the European-style marriage of the Touchetts in James's *The Portrait of a Lady,* where Mrs. Touchett feels free to travel as she chooses, merely dropping in now and again to visit her husband.

For nineteenth-century American women, marriage carried expectations of women's fidelity and decorum even if husbands were unfaithful. Married women could not pursue freer life-styles than unmarried ones, nor could they resort to divorce if marriages were unsuccessful, unless they wanted to flout the prevailing social attitudes that condemned divorce. Henry James's Aunt Kate (Catherine Walsh), for example, had married at age forty but quickly separated from her husband, Capt. Charles Marshall, to rejoin the James family as a valued companion-nurse. The grounds for the separation are unknown, but one wonders if Marshall may have been abusive and if Woolson used this as background to *Jupiter Lights.* Whatever the grounds for separation, it was unusual for Walsh to leave her husband even though she never pursued a formal divorce.

The alternative to the quiet separation of Catherine Walsh and Charles Marshall is represented in the example of Harriet Beecher Stowe's brother Henry Ward Beecher, whose affair midcentury with his parishioner Libby Tilton triggered a highly publicized and scandalous trial, the kind of scandal a decorous family would want to avoid.[18] Even though society in the nineteenth century was debating the divorce question and Henry James Sr. for a time advocated divorce, the majority of society vehemently opposed it and avoided scandal. Nina Baym has noted the tendency of reviewers in the nineteenth century to respond negatively to books about divorce,[19] and Woolson herself documented in her notebook an idea for a story about society rejecting a divorced woman (Benedict 2:134). After the Civil War, Howells dared to treat divorce in *A Modern Instance* (1882), but even Kate Chopin's *The Awakening* (1899), which caused a furor among her contemporaries for its refusal to condemn a woman's adultery, avoids treating divorce. It was not until the turn of the century that divorce became a more open topic in fiction, with Edith Wharton, herself divorced in 1913, using it in such works as "The Other Two" (1904), *The Custom of the Country* (1913), and *The Age of Innocence* (1920).

Woolson knew that many marriages, whether European or American, were imperfect. Given this fact and the prohibitions against divorce, her fiction considers the compensations a marriage of convenience, like that of the Touchetts, can give a woman. Her story **"A Florentine Experiment"** illustrates some of the issues such marriages raise, issues she explores more fully later in her novel *East Angels.* Both works center on characters named Margaret, as if Woolson is consciously showing two avenues of responding to the notion of a marriage of convenience. The choice of name makes it tempting to speculate that Woolson was paying homage to Margaret Fuller, a woman whose life was similar to her own and whose life-style reflected many of her fictional concerns. Even more than Woolson, Fuller had been educated and shaped by a father. She was never interested in fiction and had more of a reputation as a conversationalist than a writer, but, like Woolson, she had been a journalist, had traveled to and written about the Great Lakes in *Summer on the Lakes* (1844), and had settled in Italy. Unlike Woolson, Fuller married, but only after she had borne her husband's child out of wedlock. Earlier in her life, she also had a strong attachment to Emerson, and her relationship to him, like Woolson's to James has been misinterpreted as one of unrequited love. Recent reassessments of that relationship see Emerson as Fuller's distant but intellectually compatible friend in much the same way that James was Woolson's. Fuller's sense of herself as homeless in a society that expected women to be what she could not be would have attracted Woolson. She may have discussed Fuller and her death by drowning in 1850 with James, who thought Fuller a disturbing force working on his psyche.[20]

"A Florentine Experiment" is one of Woolson's most Jamesian stories, heavily ironic with multiple levels of interpretive possibilities, as it leads its Margaret to home and a happy ending Woolson knew her audiences wanted. But, as is so often the case in Woolson's fiction, there is a distinct qualification to this happy ending. The story opens with Margaret Stowe talking to her friend Beatrice Lovell, a woman with money. Beatrice is quick to let Margaret know how much higher her status is as a widow rather than, like Margaret, as a spinster: "'You have beautiful theories, I know; but in my *experience*' (Mrs. Lovell slightly underlined this word as if in opposition to the 'theories' of her friend) 'the people who have those deeper sort of feelings you describe are almost always unhappy'" (502). Margaret's theory involves loving someone "deeply and jealously, and to the exclusion of all the rest" (502). Beatrice, with the status of a widow and the freedom and money to travel, is uninterested in love, so much so that she gives Margaret a letter from a suitor, Trafford Morgan. Later, Margaret meets Morgan and, we surmise, falls in love with him. He assumes she loves him and tells her that he, however, loves someone else. Margaret recoils at Morgan's arrogance and denies her love, claiming that she was cultivating an interest in him in order to forget someone else she loved. They part and in the interim before they meet again Beatrice marries. When Margaret and Morgan do meet again, he asks her to be the subject of his Florentine Experiment and allow him to forget another woman by trying to fall in love with her. Eventually, he proposes to her, saying he hasn't exactly fallen in love with her but that he does care for her and, once again showing his arrogance, saying he wants to marry her because she loves him. Again they part, and when they meet for the third time Margaret's aunt tries her own experiment, telling Morgan that Margaret is engaged. This time when Morgan proposes, he admits that he has finally figured out that he loved Margaret all along.

"A Florentine Experiment" is so heavily ironic that it is difficult to know if and when either of these characters loves the other, though Woolson does seem, finally, to agree with Morgan who comes to realize that to "marry without love" is a "wretched thing" (529) and to suggest that Margaret will simply hold out against Morgan until she is sure he really loves her. What is interesting, though, is that Woolson is also aware that marriage protects women from unwanted advances and, at least in Europe, that marriages of convenience allow women greater avenues toward freedom. We have no evidence that she ever seriously considered marriage while in Europe, though we do know that John Hay tried to arrange a marriage with Clarence King, and we

surmise that there must have been speculation about her and James. Although he thought Woolson in love with King, Hay also calls her a "very clever person, to whom men are a vain show."[21] King had the reputation of a libertine and, had a marriage been arranged, Woolson might have found in him a husband willing to give her her liberty. But King was secretly married and Woolson probably had not met him when she wrote **"A Florentine Experiment."** Nor did she need King as a model, for almost immediately upon her arrival in Europe, she recognized the easy attitude toward marriages of convenience. As Morgan says in his first marriage proposal: "If [marriage] fails—if you are not happy—I promise not to hold you in the slightest degree. You shall have your liberty untrammeled, and, at the same time, all shall be arranged so as to escape comment. I will be with you enough to save appearances; that is all. In reality you shall be entirely free" (524).

One of the tensions in **"A Florentine Experiment"** involves the issue of sexual freedom. Although Woolson addressed the issue of marriage and sexuality only obliquely in her fiction, she does not ignore sexuality. Morgan's willingness to allow Margaret freedom if the marriage fails implies that, at least initially, the marriage will be sexual. John Kern believed that the "lovers in Miss Woolson's stories are so completely untroubled by amorous desires that the reader may be forgiven for suspecting their virility" (129), but Carolyn VanBergen has recently shown that this is not the case. In her discussion of the sexual and economic metaphors in *Horace Chase,* VanBergen finds ample metaphors through which Woolson could locate her characters' sexuality.[22] Early in her career, Woolson had written a provocative story, **"On the Iron Mountain,"** that examines the role of sexuality within marriage. The protagonist, Helen Fay, is magnetic, restless, metaphorically sexual. At one point, she "seemed to be all pulse; pulses throbbed in her throat and the blood leaped through her veins" (228). In the story, Woolson develops the character of a mesmerist, who quiets Helen's sexuality and brings her so much under his control that she is willing to run away with him. His motive, however, is to force her other lover to acknowledge sexuality. The problem, though, is that for a woman sexuality becomes a loss of control over the self; it puts Helen first into the power of the mesmerist, then into the protection of a husband with whom she will be able to express sexuality only because he has been coerced by the mesmerist into giving his wife permission for sexuality. Throughout the story, Woolson associates Helen, the namesake of the woman whose beauty wields power over men, with the goddess Diana, who exacts revenge upon Actaeon when he sees her naked. The associations are ironic, for Helen gains autonomy neither through passion nor through chastity. Only if women can control their own sexuality can they find their own power.

Woolson's fullest and most sophisticated working out of the relationship of home to issues of sexuality, marriages of convenience, and the problem of divorce occurs in *East Angels,* not just through her treatment of that novel's heroine, Margaret Harold, but also through another examination of the girl-woman. Here, Woolson's girl-woman, Garda Thorne, defies society's mores to pursue the man she loves. Garda's defiance makes her, like Tita and Helen in *Anne,* more interesting than the simply virtuous Sara Carroll. Through both Garda and Margaret, Woolson hints at the sexual dimension implied in a marital home and at how that home may fulfill or stifle a woman's sexuality. One of the reasons Garda pursues marriage is that she is pursuing her sexuality, a trait most of Woolson's predecessors denied their fictional girl figures. In fact, Nina Baym's research on reviewers of pre-Civil War novels finds hostility among reviews to any treatment of sexuality.[23] Woolson subverts nineteenth-century literary models and expectations by suggesting that sexuality fulfills these limited women precisely because they do not need wider avenues for fulfillment. Furthermore, Woolson suggests that beautiful women have greater choices in finding their ideal marriage/sex partners. The beginning of *East Angels* contains a passage that articulates this view, one Woolson was especially sensitive to because, portrait evidence to the contrary, she thought herself lacking in beauty:[24] "For in their hearts women always know that of all the gifts bestowed upon their sex that of beauty has so immeasurably the greatest power that nothing else can for one moment be compared with it, that all other gifts of whatsoever nature and extent, sink into insignificance and powerlessness beside it" (19).

The question *East Angels* poses at first is what will become of the beautiful, sheltered, natural, restless Garda Thorne. Encouraged by her mother to become interested in a rich northerner, thirty-five-year-old Evert Winthrop, Garda complies. But enter Lucian Spenser, who engages in a brief flirtation with Garda. Spenser soon leaves Florida, the setting for the novel, and is enticed into marriage by a woman who has told him she is dying, but gets well after their marriage. This relationship is not central to the novel; however, it again reflects Woolson's sense of the sexual or emotional blackmail used to achieve marriage as well as her insight into how dull a life a woman can lead if she allows her family to dictate that she be reserved and wait for a suitably rich mate. When Garda can no longer pretend to love Winthrop, she breaks her engagement, taking what would seem a noble stance: "Everybody in the world seems to tell lies but me. . . . And everybody else seems to prefer it" (392). But nobility requires deeper feelings than Woolson develops in Garda. Because she does not have these deeper feelings, Woolson can reward her truthfulness simply by having Spenser's wife die and Garda marry him. In an unexpected plot twist, Spenser himself dies, but Garda finds a suit-

able second marriage to a handsome former admirer. By highlighting the dashing manners and physical handsomeness of both Garda's husbands, Woolson implies that being an honest and virtuous girl-wife is compatible with sexuality. In fact, sexuality becomes all the more crucial for wives whose intellectual dimension remains undeveloped. If one must marry to find a home, the sexual dimension to marriage should be fulfilling rather than endured for the sake of that home.

Unlike Garda, Margaret Harold does not find a fulfilling sexuality within her marital home but, instead, discovers how sexuality threatens to destroy a home. Margaret's husband, Lanse,[25] has had a long-standing affair in Europe, one she is expected to allow him, striving only to keep it secret so that his good name—and their facade of a good marriage—will be protected. But Margaret, who discovers soon after marriage that she does not love her husband, will have none of this double standard. Lanse leaves her for Europe and forbids her to follow him. When he eventually returns to America and Margaret, he remains oblivious to Margaret's growth and her needs. He cannot understand that his presence is painful to her, for he is willing to allow her to lead the life she is used to while he leads the life he wants. Thus, he believes, they can have a model marriage. Yet Lanse immediately contradicts this notion by insisting that Margaret conform to his notions of how she should dress, turning her into an ornament much as Henry James's Gilbert Osmond tried to turn Isabel Archer into an object for his collection. After all, Lanse has married Margaret for "her profile" (438) rather than for love. He dresses her according to his wishes and is pleased that she is such a "beautiful object" (440). Unlike Madame Carroll in **For the Major,** who finds this kind of role a satisfying one, Margaret finds it stifling, especially because she has fallen in love with Evert Winthrop during Lanse's absence. A scene between Margaret and Winthrop exudes the kind of passion Margaret is capable of feeling and that Garda's more fulfilling marriages contain. Lost in the sexually charged atmosphere of a swamp, Margaret and Winthrop acknowledge their mutual passion, but this is never consummated because Margaret chooses to remain faithful to Lanse. The scene in the swamp clarifies how much this loyalty betrays Margaret's natural instincts, but because she has refused to acknowledge Lanse's instincts to love another woman, she cannot act on similar feelings in herself. Lanse's parallel devotion to this other woman is long-standing, thus he leaves Margaret a second time. When he returns as an invalid, his illness suggests that the marriage will remain nonsexual.

Woolson uses Margaret's decision not to divorce Lanse, despite her unhappiness within the marriage, to illustrate how complex women's tendency to self-sacrifice can be. In an otherwise favorable review of *East Angels,* William Dean Howells criticizes Woolson's portrayal of Margaret as a sacrificial woman: "Neither Margaret nor Winthrop her lover appeals to our sympathy, perhaps because we cannot believe in them; they form for us the one false note of the book."[26] Woolson objects in a letter to John Hay that she "could not expect Mr. Howells to like 'Margaret,' for he does not believe in 'Margarets,'—he has never perceived they exist" (Petry 87, 30 July 1886). Nor, it seems, does Rayburn Moore believe they exist. He admits his own impatience with Margaret even as he recognizes the problem of dismissing her and thus denying the "generous impulses of feminine nature."[27] To accept Howells's or Moore's view is to dismiss Woolson's subtle portrayal of self-sacrifice, especially when the stakes of finding a satisfactory home are so high for women. Henry James serves as a better guide for understanding Woolson's position. He believes that she spends too much time in *East Angels* on feminine matters of love, but he also sees that if we "repudiate" Margaret, we deny "that a woman *may* look at life from a high point of view," deny "that there *are* distinguished natures."[28] Sybil Weir explains the matter from a more contemporary perspective, saying that we have lost the "religious referent available to Woolson" and that Woolson "saw clearly that it was almost always the woman, either motivated by a principle higher than self-love or forced by necessity, who was called upon to make the sacrifice" (565).

Unlike most interpreters of Margaret's refusal to divorce and remarry, Joan Weimer argues that Margaret is attempting to choose autonomy within her bleak marriage over enslavement in a loving marriage to Winthrop.[29] This is a welcome interpretation because, typical of Woolson's fiction, the issue of self-sacrifice in *East Angels* is never clear-cut, and when James recognizes that there is a temptation to repudiate Margaret's choice to remain in her marital home, he realizes that Woolson is ambivalent about the value of women's sacrificial nature. A narrative passage from *East Angels* about Margaret's sacrifice and her friend Dr. Kirby's response to it illustrates one side of the issue:

> There are women who are capable of sacrificing themselves, with the noblest unselfishness in great causes, who yet, as regards the small matters of every-day life, are rather uncomfortable to live with; so much so, indeed, that those who are under the same roof with them are driven to reflect now and then upon the merits of the ancient hermitages and caves to which in former ages such characters were accustomed to retire. . . .

> The Doctor had had these saints as his patients more than once, he knew them perfectly. But here was a woman who had sacrificed her whole life to duty, who felt constantly the dreary ache of deprivation; but who yet did not think in the least, apparently, that these things freed her from the kindly efforts, the patience, the small sweet friendly attempts which made home comfortable.

(565-66)

As admiring as Dr. Kirby's view is, Woolson knew that it is only one part of the issue. Garda takes an opposite view, believing that sacrifice is silly, that "two whole lives [have been] wasted—and all for the sake of an idea" (579). Winthrop takes yet another angle: "Women are better than men; in some things they are stronger. But that's because they are sustained . . . by their terrible love of self-sacrifice; I absolutely believe there are women who *like* to be tortured" (588).

Had Woolson simply admired sacrifice and seen it played out in martyrdom, she might have chosen to end her novel with either reward or doom. Instead, the ambiguous last line of *East Angels* shows Margaret still married to Lanse, never again meeting Winthrop, engaged in this cutting dialogue:

> "Do you know that you've grown old, Madge, before your time?"

> "Yes, I know it."

> "Well—you're a good woman," said Lanse.

(591)

Margaret has sacrificed and lost love, has been tempted into the "terrible love of self-sacrifice" that is the mark of the "good" martyr. But something stronger than martyrdom also works in Margaret, much as it works in James's Isabel Archer, whose apparent choice to return to her marriage Woolson echoes. Like Isabel, Margaret had married naïvely, believing in fidelity only to discover opposing values in her husband and, again like Isabel, when she chooses with full knowledge to remain married, she upholds the value she believes reflected in the marriage vow, no matter her husband's cynicism about such vows. She wishes she could be like Garda, who "puts the rest of us (women, I mean) to shame—the rest of us with our complicated motives, and involved consciences" (244). But Margaret knows society too well to be like Garda and can analyze what lies beneath society's codes. She understands that part of the necessity to remain married comes from the stigma that would have been attached to her divorcing a man who, in her words, has not been physically abusive, who has not been an alcoholic, and who has not exerted a negative influence on any children (531).

An interesting commentary on society's attitudes occurs in *East Angels* when Winthrop overhears an older woman speaking to a younger one on a train: "*We* [women] do not exhibit our charms—which should be sacred to the privacy of the boudoir [i.e., the home]—in the glare of lecture-rooms; *we* prefer to be, and to *remain,* the low-voiced retiring mothers of a race of giant sons whom the Muse of History will immortalize in the character of soldier, statesman, and divine" (536). Aware of the frequency of this attitude, Margaret must struggle to find a place for herself in a society that allows her

neither independence through divorce nor the fulfillment she might find in a public sphere "in the glow of
lecture-rooms" or in a career analogous to the male occupations of "soldier, statesman, and divine." Woolson
clearly does not endorse the attitude of the women on
the train, and she may be suggesting that change can
come only from a younger generation of women.
Through Margaret's "complicated motives, and involved
conscience" and Garda's naïveté, she may also be suggesting that as the younger generation carves a public
sphere for women it consider the implications of this on
the private sphere of the home. To widen society's acceptance of divorce for reasons of incompatibility would
be to undermine the value of marriage in maintaining
the private sphere. As a more public sphere has opened
for women in the twentieth century, Woolson might
well have predicted the difficulties women would face
when they have to balance home and work, particularly
if they have to do so as single mothers.

In *East Angels,* Woolson shows the price Margaret pays
for upholding the sanctity of marriage her readers expected her to uphold. One of these readers wrote Woolson that she wanted the author to allow Lanse to be
"taken" in order to provide a happy ending and still endorse the sanctity of marriage. Woolson answered this
reader, saying that it is more realistic not to have Lanse
die (Kern 88). She does not uphold the sanctity of marriage herself as much as she shows the degree to which
women like Margaret have internalized society's norms.
She does not make Margaret a "good" woman who finds
sacrifice easy because she did not value easy sacrifice,
believing, instead, that people are not especially good if
what they do comes easily. Margaret is the genuine article—a person whose impulse to goodness involves
great pain. Her marriage of convenience brings her no
happiness, but it does bring some reward. Although the
marriage and, along with it, her relationship to Lanse's
hostile aunt are painful, Margaret also has gained something for herself. Three months before Lanse's return to
the marriage, Margaret decides not to return to the isolated New England home of the deceased grandmother
who raised her and has instead purchased East Angels
in her own name. Knowing that a sense of place may
help her replace her lack of a satisfying marital home,
she tells Winthrop, "I shall do very well here if I have
the place to think about . . . I shall have the land cultivated; perhaps I shall start a new orange grove" (524).
At the same time, she also accuses Winthrop of wanting
"no woman to lead a really independent life" (524).

Lanse's return undercuts Margaret's independence, but
because he is now an invalid, she can still maintain
control over her property. In fact, the narrative mentions a new orange grove just before Margaret tells
Winthrop that she will remain married to Lanse (538).
As much as Margaret sacrifices, her choice has had its
compensations. We know that she has learned to live

with the pain of Winthrop's loss because she counsels
Garda that she, too, will learn to live with the loss of
her first husband. She is even willing to have Winthrop
marry Garda, and Winthrop reads this as a reflection of
how much "you women think . . . of a home" (587).
By the end of *East Angels,* Margaret has gained a richer
home than she had in the past because both Lanse and
his aunt have learned to treat her more kindly and because Garda, whom she cares about, is also likely to return to Florida and add the rootedness of place to the
home she has in her new marriage. More important,
Margaret has gained the integrity of the self-knowledge
that, eight years after her refusal of Winthrop, though
she is old before her time, she has become so for reasons that go beyond her personal happiness.

Early nineteenth-century novels, if they treated wom-
en's sexuality at all, tended to ghettoize it into nonmari-
tal relationships that necessitated retribution. Woolson's
subtle, but still clear, acknowledgement of a legitimate
sexual dimension in a character like Garda Thorne
moves toward the openness at the end of the century of
novelists such as Edith Wharton and Kate Chopin. Like
her depiction of sexuality, her depiction of marital abuse
moves beyond the polemics of early novels that suggest
that wives must somehow endure abuse or work toward
the reformation of alcoholic husbands. Issues of alcohol
abuse and its impact on domestic violence were widely
discussed throughout the nineteenth century. Early in
the century, crusades against alcohol often sensationalized the problem in ways that titillated rather than reformed. David Reynolds has called this tendency to
sensationalize under the guise of reform "immoral didacticism" aimed at a "public accustomed to having its
reform well spiced with violence and sex." Temperance
works in this genre include "Horrid Case of Intemper-
ance," published in the *Salem Gazette,* showing a
"drunkard burned to a crisp by a blacksmith's fire";
Mary L. Fox's *Ruined Deacon* (1834), showing the
downfall of an alcoholic deacon, and novels with titles
like *Letters from the Alms House* (1841), *Confessions of
a Reformed Inebriate* (1844), *Confessions of a Rum-
Seller* (1845), and *The Glass* (1849) that include wife
beating and murder, psychopathological visions and insanity, child murder, and a case of self-cannibalism
brought about by an abuse victim's being locked in a
closet. Even Walt Whitman wrote a temperance novel
called *Franklin Evans,* and Poe's "The Cask of Amon-
tillado" and "The Black Cat" are derivative of the genre
(Reynolds 65-73). Cathy Davidson has studied less-
sensationalized novels and found that wives were expected to endure abuse rather than seek divorce.[30]

E. D. E. N. Southworth provides a living example of a
woman who gained independence as a writer but chose
not to seek divorce from a husband who had abandoned
her and her small children.[31] So, too, does the notorious
case involving Mansfield and Ellen Walworth, an elite

couple from Saratoga Springs, New York. Mansfield's father, Reuban Hyde Walworth, had been Chancellor of New York State and a friend of Cooper, Emerson, and Lincoln. When Reuban remarried, the young Mansfield met and soon married the daughter of his new stepmother. A novelist whose book *Mission of Death* (1853) went through twelve editions, Mansfield became an alcoholic and an abuser. The situation not only prompted Ellen to leave the marriage and open a school to support herself, in 1873 it also prompted the couple's nineteen-year-old son Frank to shoot his father. The case was highly publicized, including a lengthy piece in *Frank Leslie's Illustrated Newspaper* (June 21, 1873). Given the Walworth family's connection to Cooper and Mansfield's position as a novelist, Woolson would surely have been familiar with this situation. Cases like this triggered crusades against alcohol, which gained huge support among women, especially in the 1870s, when Ohio became one of the centers of activism and the birthplace of the WCTU. Women were tending to become politically involved and, by law, could ask that an alcoholic husband not be served at local saloons.[32]

Woolson first addressed the idea of wife abuse obliquely in a story called **"King Log."** She does not name the source of the abuse, but her readers would have inferred alcoholism. The story deals with the reaction of a man whose sister has been trapped in an abusive marriage and who hears that the woman who broke her engagement to him has nearly succumbed to the same kind of marriage. More interesting is Woolson's portrayal of wife and child abuse in *Jupiter Lights,* in which the source of the abuse is alcohol. The novel is Woolson's most problematic, for it seems to endorse stereotypical attitudes about women as martyrs even if martyrdom requires enduring abuse. Yet beneath the surface of *Jupiter Lights,* we see Woolson struggling to come to grips with the issues of how women damage themselves when they remain in abusive relationships. Although the plot is melodramatic, *Jupiter Lights* neither titillates nor advocates wifely endurance. The novel examines how its girl-figure, Cicely Bruce Morrison, chooses not between sexuality and home or sexuality or home, but between sexuality/violence/home and loneliness.

Throughout *Jupiter Lights,* Woolson questions the conventional attitudes her characters too often display. In the novel, the widowed Cicely has broken protocol by marrying Ferdinand Morrison before she has gone through the appropriate mourning period for her first husband, Eve's brother. She lives for only a few months with Ferdie before returning to her home at Jupiter Lights, Georgia. Eventually, she tells Eve that Ferdie, when drunk, has abused both herself and her son by Bruce, Jack. That Woolson was concerned about how marriage could be a physical threat as well as a refuge for women is evidenced in *East Angels* when she has Margaret declare that she has no grounds such as abu-

siveness or alcoholism for divorce. Woolson voices her dissent from this attitude when she has Eve indicate her disgust in a sarcastic comment: "And marriage makes everything perfectly safe . . . ?" (73). Just how abusive husbands and fathers can be is evidenced in the extent of Cicely's and Jack's injuries. Woolson does not sensationalize them but makes them realistic and serious: scars on Cicely's breast and shoulder and a broken arm for Jack that Cicely says "was easily set. Nobody ever knew about it, I never told" (79). And here, of course, is the problem. Although everyone who knows him loves and defends Ferdie, he misuses other people's money, misuses alcohol, misuses women, misuses children, misuses himself. The qualities Cicely and others love in Ferdie—his vitality, his handsome devil-may-care passion—are the very qualities that lead him to violence.

Although Woolson does not endorse Cicely's loyalty to Ferdie, she does accept the misconception that to break the violence may well be to break the man. Ferdie's half-brother, for example, says that "[d]runkards are death to the women—to the wives and mothers and sisters; but some of 'em are more lovable than lots of the moral skin-flints that go nagging about, saving a penny, and grinding everybody but themselves. The trouble with Ferdie was that he was born without any conscience, just as some people have no ear for music; it was a case of heredity . . ." (339).[33] But Woolson's novel is not just another addition to temperance arguments that expect women to shoulder the burden of keeping men away from alcohol. It portrays alcoholism as hereditary and debilitating at the same time that it sees the danger of understanding the alcoholic, loveable or not. Thus Cicely's attitude of pretending that violence within the home does not exist by never speaking of the violence results only in a perpetuation of the cycle of violence.

Centering on the issues of home as kindred and home as violence, Woolson deepens her insights into how women pursue homes in her portrait of Cicely's more complex counterpart, Eve Bruce, her sister-in-law by her first marriage. Eve comes to meet Cicely for the first time after her brother's death, already disliking her for having married her brother and causing her, she believes, to lose the only family and connection to the feeling of home she has had. In fact, Eve's motive is to take her nephew Jack from his mother and build a home for herself with the child. Joan Weimer reads this as the result of Eve's incestuous fixation on her father, her brother, and her brother's child (*MG* xli). Though I do not like the term incestuous—Jack after all is only a toddler—Eve does seem to me a victim of social attitudes that expect female children to reify male family members and to appoint themselves as family caretakers. In that role, Eve breaks all taboos against violence when she discovers Ferdie chasing Cicely and Jack with a knife during one of his drunken rampages and shoots him. That Woolson has Eve rather than Cicely attack Ferdie enables her to focus on issues of passion and violence. Violence begets violence so that Eve finds she can shoot Ferdie, and Cicely, believing Eve wants Ferdie dead, strikes Eve. Cicely's passion is itself destructive and irrational. Not only does she excuse Ferdie on the basis that his violence "seldom happens" (80), she also believes herself "free; no one has any authority over me except Ferdie" (130). What she does not see is the extent to which this authority makes her not free.

Woolson uses Eve's gradual awakening to a passionate love for Ferdie's brother Paul Tennant to counterpoint Cicely's love for Ferdie. John Kern sees this working out of the plot as melodramatic, but it is so only if one fails to connect it to the issue of violence toward women, a subject he does not even identify as part of the plot of *Jupiter Lights* (90-92). Early on, Eve thinks of Cicely's wish that she drop her cold demeanor and learn the power of love: "To wish her [Eve] a love like her [Cicely's] own, this seemed almost a curse, a malediction . . . ; to love any man so submissively was weakness, but to love as Cicely loved, that was degradation" (90). Eve's anger here at Cicely is a revolt "against the injustice of all the ages, past, present, and to come, towards women" (90). But Eve's love for Paul is just as powerful as Cicely's for Ferdie. Like Cicely's, Eve's love tempts her to ignore social controls—at one point she meets Paul in the woods, the implication being that she is ready to have a sexual affair, and for a time she is willing to lie to him to ensure her happiness. Eve likes Paul's despotism, but only to a point. She claims that she wants someone stronger than herself, a protector. But if one has a despotic protector and no power, then the protector becomes the destroyer. What Woolson uses Eve to achieve is a relationship that will bring support at the same time that it brings independence and personal power.

Paul does not have Ferdie's outward abusiveness, but he has similar faults that Eve knows about, condemns, and loves him in spite of. He trifles with other women, assuming that a sexual double standard is okay if the other woman is a peasant girl. The double-standard theme is strong enough that Woolson has Ferdie involved in a liaison; Paul's friend Hollis Clay, who also loves Eve, nearly seduces a barmaid; and Cicely's friend Judge Abercrombie condemns Ferdie's infidelity only because it, unlike his own, has touched a wife. Paul also trifles with Eve, treating her "like a child" he "long[s] to take care of" (325) and like a person who will, of course, bend to his will.

Only by having Eve love Paul can Woolson provide a way for her to understand how Cicely can continue to desire a home with Ferdie. But because she possesses a deeper nature than Cicely, Eve refuses to be bound to Paul in contrast to Cicely's bondage in love. She fears she will become a woman whose love will destroy her integrity and make her yet another victim of love, another woman who will accept a marital home, whatever the cost to her personal safety and integrity. "Once your wife," she says to Paul, "I know that I should stay on, even if it were only to fold your clothes,—to touch them; to pick up the burnt match-ends you had dropped, and your newspapers; to arrange the chairs as you like to have them. I should be weak, weak—I should follow you about" (324).

Woolson makes Eve's decision to leave Paul, because she believes she has killed his half-brother, strong enough that we have no question about its seriousness. Eve cannot marry Paul until Woolson provides a deus ex machina revealing that Eve did not murder Ferdie. The question we must ask is why provide this and save her from becoming, like Margaret Harold, a genuine martyr, one whose sacrifice is not easy, but hard, causing a great deal of personal pain. On a simple level, the answer may be that Woolson knew her readers would expect it. But as concerned as she was with the question of home, it is consistent that Woolson find a way to provide Eve a home that will not be one of bondage. She cannot give her Jack, for she needs Jack to provide Cicely with a home and for Eve to make her own home with them would be to enter into a different kind of bondage with a woman who hates her. Nor does Woolson want Eve to marry Paul's friend Hollis, a man who loves her but who is too much an older father figure and whom she does not love. The only home Even can have consistent with her character is with Paul, but on her terms, not his. These terms include economic independence—Eve has an inheritance; social independence—she has broken society's code by shooting Ferdie; and physical power—she has rescued Jack from a near drowning without the help of a man.

Woolson reunites Paul and Eve at the end of *Jupiter Lights* in a scene that allows her to speak out against violence, suggesting that women like Cicely who have been tempted to tolerate violence for the sake of love and home have traded too much. Paul knocks down a priest at a charitable institution to get to Eve to tell her the truth about the real cause of Ferdie's death. This institution is an inappropriate refuge for someone of Eve's passionate nature and is, in fact, itself exploitative, largely, Woolson hints, interested in Eve's money. The woman in charge of the institution stops Paul just as he is about to force open the door that is blocking him from Eve: "Your violence has been unnecessary—the violence of a boor!" (347). Paul "laugh[s] in her face," opens the door, and takes "Eve in his arms" (347). Like the woman who blocks the door, we want to say, yes, his violence is, like Ferdie's, "the violence of a boor." But we also must surmise that despite, or maybe even because of, this display of violence, Paul wins Eve in a way that Woolson's readers might find satisfyingly dramatic. Woolson does not naïvely dismiss Paul's violence but, instead, shows the extent to which women commit themselves to relationships and the extent to which readers romanticize this kind of violence as evidence of love. But because Woolson has linked violence to Ferdie in a more instructive way, she forces us to remember that to be bound to home can constitute the kind of bondage that love has been for Cicely. Because she has earlier made Eve strong enough to resist the bondage of love, we hope that she will marry Paul, and escape the bondage of an institution that is also not a viable home for her, in a union that will allow him to see that violence should not be equated with loving passion.

In her portrait of the girl-woman in *Horace Chase,* Woolson does not expand beyond issues she has previously addressed, and though the novel reads well—it is her funniest, filled with the sarcastic and cynical wit that marks the majority of her fiction—it is also her least textured, as if she has reconciled herself to the inevitability of social codes that deny women autonomy and dignity. In this novel, Woolson explicitly links sexuality with shallowness. Ruth Franklin is spoiled, indulged, entirely natural; she is unconcerned about the implications of sexuality and acts however she wants without thinking about social forms. Like an indulged child, she has her way in marrying Horace Chase, who is much her senior, not in any search for home, but because she finds him fun to be with. Woolson exposes the attitude that it is appropriate for older men to marry younger women by having a minor character constantly remark on how women age in ways that men do not. This is similar to the comment that Lanse Harold makes in *East Angels* about marrying a girl fourteen years his junior because he "always had a fancy for young girls" though he despairs because they all seem to grow up (413). The irony, of course, is that, contrary to the male viewpoint, Woolson shows that women are far better off when they do grow up, whether this means losing their beauty or not.

In *Horace Chase,* Ruth can easily accept the older Horace because he has money and can indulge her frivolous nature. Predictably, Ruth discovers that she has a sexual nature that Horace is not fulfilling and falls in love with his partner, the younger Walter Willoughby, a man who flirts with her but ultimately marries the woman he really loves. Ruth's awakening to her sexuality, late and outside her "happy" marriage, anticipates by five years Kate Chopin's theme in *The Awakening.* But, because she remains a childlike character, Ruth never gains Edna Pontellier's awareness of the implications of sexuality outside of marriage. Horace, the father figure, is really the right man for this nonspeculative woman whose limited view of happiness is so

different from Chopin's and from Woolson's own. Still, Woolson refuses to condescend: given her upbringing and personality, Ruth is suited only for play love. If Ruth is not cut out for a higher view of life or for enduring and growing through suffering, she at least has the integrity of her feelings and whims. She suffers and nearly dies because of her love for Walter, but because Horace proves to be such a tolerant husband, she is protected from exposure to society and whisked off to Europe, where we assume she begins to rebuild herself. Importantly, she tells Horace that she cannot promise she will not do something similar again and, given her character, we expect that she would follow her sexual instinct. Still, she is honest and fresh, and she may attain the kind of happiness denied the person who possesses the deeper intelligence Woolson was cursed by herself.

The marriage of Ruth's brother Jared to Genevieve Franklin represents an inversion of the marriage between Horace and Ruth, one in which the male feels that the freedom he has longed for as a sailor has been curbed by a serious-minded wife who pursues her passion not for business but for philanthropy. In the process of gaining the kind of home she wants in marriage, she forces her husband, Jared Franklin, into a life-style he is unsuited for and thinks so little of his well-being that she is indirectly responsible for his death. Genevieve is the kind of wife Henry James Sr. seemed to extol, someone who has "her principles and plans . . . and her rules" (121), a dull do-gooder who would like to stay put and run charitable institutions, solicit donations for worthy causes, and keep an eye on the clergy, all kinds of reform she can pursue from within the socially accepted realm of the home. And yet, in her limited way, Genevieve loves Jared, and even as Woolson blames her, she does show that Genevieve has used her power to find freedom within her marriage to pursue an independent life. Still, Woolson is not so sympathetic to this philanthropist type as Henry James Sr. In fact, she suspected philanthropy as just another form of self-indulgence, writing in her notebook that people are philanthropic because this is what they enjoy being and that they are, therefore, not less self-indulgent than anyone who pursues a personal interest (Benedict 2:112). Woolson sees both Genevieve and Jared as victims of society's expectations. Society has taught them to value men according to how successfully they support a family, whether or not this material dimension provides a satisfying marital relationship, a sense of kinship, or even a permanent place to live. Jared's mother has valued the male within the home so much that she dotes on her son as the only male left in the family and even dies when he dies, as if to say that without a male there can be no home. Significantly the name of her home is *L'Hommedieu,* for home equates with the men she thinks necessary to support it.

Woolson's own character is apparent in all her complex heroines, but the personal connection is the strongest in her portrait of Ruth's sister, Dolly Franklin. She is the only major character in the novels who remains unmarried, and through her Woolson looks again at how the idea of home includes the importance of kindred and the importance of place. She had touched on both these issues before—in *Jupiter Lights,* for example, through Eve's longing for her dead brother in the guise of his child and in *East Angels* in Margaret's purchase of a house—but never without involving as well the idea of a marital home.

As the only unmarried woman in the novel not treated comically, Dolly Franklin represents Woolson's answer for how to reconcile home and independence, a reconciliation closest to the one Woolson sought for herself. She represents the same kind of strong woman that Woolson provides in her other novels in the portraits of Anne, Madame Carroll, Margaret Harold, and Eve Bruce. However, Dolly hasn't the sexual passion of any of these women. Speculation about Henry James to the contrary, at this point in her life Woolson seems less interested in seeing what passion calls forth in a woman than in what steadfast intelligence calls forth. Dolly's intelligence is especially nurtured because her arthritis-like condition, perhaps a metaphor for Woolson's tendency to depression and her habit of loneliness, has limited her options even more than society has limited them. Woolson surely intended Dolly's name to be ironic, for she is no pale, doll-like invalid, but with her acute and lively observations sounds much like Alice James. Even though Horace Chase dismisses her as a meddling spinster, she has superior insight about others and sees why Ruth and many like her need to marry men who will indulge them. At the end of the novel, Dolly reveals not just intelligence but also physical and moral strength when during a storm she saves Ruth, who has tried to run to Walter Willoughby. Dolly returns her to Horace, cautioning her not to tell him the truth because she underestimates his integrity and believes he, like most of society, will reject Ruth. Instead, Horace forgives Ruth and continues to love and value her as his wife. Because Ruth and Horace will now leave *L'Hommedieu* for Europe, Dolly has saved Ruth's marital home at the price of her own last ties to kindred.

Early in *Horace Chase,* Dolly articulates her understanding of how women tend to find homes and, therefore, of why Ruth's marital home is so important. In her comments, she locates the theme that permeates all of Woolson's novels: "Have you ever noticed . . . that the women who sacrifice their lives so nobly to help humanity seldom sacrifice one small thing, and that is a happy home? Either they do not possess such an article, or else they have spoiled it by quarrelling with every individual member of their families" (19). Through all

her novels, Woolson presents a consistent vision of women who are homeward bound in the sense that they fight to find or to keep a home. When they sacrifice at all, as in the cases of Anne for Helen's marriage and Eve Bruce for her own integrity, they do so before they have found a home or, as with Madame Carroll's sacrifice of conventional honesty and Margaret Harold's sacrifice of love, they do so for a home.

Read in the light of Dolly's need to reconcile home and independence, the last paragraph of *Horace Chase* becomes more than just melodrama: "Horace Chase put Dolly aside—put her aside forever. He lifted his wife in his arms, and silently bent his head over hers as it lay on his breast" (419). The image of the wife, protected in the arms of her husband, represents the standard role for women in the nineteenth century, the one Woolson's readers would most value. But the image of a cast-aside woman is a fitting one in a society in which women have been so bound to the need for home that many feared that to remain unmarried was to bind them to homelessness and loneliness. Marriage represented to most of Woolson's contemporaries less the danger of limitedness and compromise than the promise of legitimized sexuality, social status, or security. But Woolson's portrait of Dolly Franklin, the woman who by the death of her parents and her brother and the marriage of her younger sister becomes the owner of *L'Hommedieu,* represents a different way to find a home, one that Woolson had touched on most explicitly in *East Angels.* In that novel, not only does Margaret Harold become rooted to East Angels, but Garda Thorne returns to it, and, before her death, Garda's widowed mother found satisfaction in performing household maintenance normally associated with men. That Dolly is cast aside by Horace, that she has no husband and now will lose her tie to kindred, just as Woolson had lost so many of her own ties to kindred, does not mean that she must be homeless. Woolson did not live to write a novel in which she examined closely the struggles a woman like Dolly Franklin might confront as she becomes bound to a home defined as the rootedness of place. But she clearly looked forward to this kind of home for herself, hoping to buy her own little cottage in Florida or to rent a permanent villa in Venice. Had illness, and possibly suicide brought on by her sense of homelessness, not cut short her life, she may have found herself bound to a home that did not limit her as it did so many of her characters.

Notes

1. James, *Partial Portraits,* 179, 182.

2. Victoria Woodhull, an Ohioan who had been involved with her mother in mesmeric exhibitions, was so outrageous by nineteenth-century standards that she ran for the presidency. She and her sister, Tennessee Claflin, published *Woodhull and Claf-*

lin's Weekly between 1870 and 1876, a magazine that advocated suffrage, birth control, and free love.

3. For a discussion of divorce patterns, see Glenda Riley, *Divorce: An American Tradition* (New York: Oxford Univ. Press, 1991).

4. Alfred Habegger, *Henry James and the "Woman Business"* (New York: Cambridge Univ. Press, 1989), 27-62.

5. Joan Myers Weimer, "Women Artists as Exiles in the Fiction of Constance Fenimore Woolson," *Legacy* 3, no. 2 (Fall 1986): 3-15, quoted 6.

6. Cited in Moore, *Constance F. Woolson,* 153-54. Letter dated 21 Jan. 1891.

7. Cited in *MG* [Weimer, Joan Myers, ed. *Women Artists, Women Exiles: "Miss Grief" and Other Stories,* by Constance Fenimore Woolson. New Brunswick, N.J.: Rutgers Univ. Press, 1988.] xiii. Letter to Sam Mather dated 21 Jan. 1891.

8. Robert Gingras, "'Hepzibah's Story': An Unpublished Work by Constance Fenimore Woolson," *Resources for American Literary Study* 10 (1980): 33-46. Two other uncollected stories—"A Flower of the Snow" and "Black Point"—involve an incident in which a woman overhears the man she loves in a liaison with another woman, but in both stories, these are minor flirtations and the marriages take place. The pattern is frequent enough to invite speculation that Woolson overheard Zeph Spaulding in a liaison with another woman.

9. See Victoria Brehm, "Island Fortress: The Landscape of the Imagination," in *Critical Essays,* ed. Torsney, 172-86 for a discussion of western freedom represented in the female lighthouse keeper of Ballast Island.

10. Carolyn VanBergen, "Constance Fenimore Woolson and the Next Country," *Western Reserve Studies* 3 (1988): 86-92.

11. See Benedict 1:67 for a discussion of Emma's marriage.

12. For discussions of fictional presentations of women's domestic roles, see especially Nina Baym, *Novels, Readers, and Reviewers: Responses to Fiction in Antebellum America* (Ithaca, N.Y.: Cornell Univ. Press, 1984); *Woman's Fiction: A Guide to Novels by and about Women in America, 1820-1870* (Ithaca, N.Y.: Cornell Univ. Press, 1978); and Mary Kelley, *Private Woman, Public Stage: Literary Domesticity in Nineteenth-Century America* (New York: Oxford Univ. Press, 1984).

13. *MG.*

14. WRHS [Mather Family Papers, 1834-1967, Western Reserve Historical Society, Cleveland, OH]. Letter to Sam Mather dated 24 Mar. 1887.

15. Leon Edel makes it seem as if Woolson is significantly older than James, but she is just three years older, hardly enough to be considered an older woman chasing a younger man. Edel, *Life of Henry James* 3:87.

16. John Dwight Kern, *Constance Fenimore Woolson: Literary Pioneer* (Philadelphia: Univ. of Pennsylvania Press, 1934), 42, identifies the model for Rast as John Biddle (1883-86), the son of Edward Biddle, who in 1819 married the stepdaughter of the French Joseph Bailey. Bailey's wife—the girl's mother—was an American Indian.

17. Torsney, *Constance Fenimore Woolson,* 44.

18. For a discussion of Catherine Walsh's marriage, see Strouse, *Alice James,* 33-35. For a discussion of the Beecher-Tilton scandal, which was exposed by Victoria Woodhull, see Douglas, *Feminization of American Culture,* 241-43.

19. Baym, *Novels, Readers, and Reviewers,* 184.

20. Margaret Fuller's sense of herself as a misfit led to enough unhappiness that her death on a burning ship may have been a choice to die rather than to be rescued and returned to the United States where she was so out of place. Her personality prompted her friend Rebecca Spring to continue to dream of her fifty years after her death. I have found no reference to Woolson meeting Rebecca Spring, but her choice of the name Roberta Spring for a woman who is a misfit in "A Transplanted Boy" is provocative. A letter from Woolson to Henry James dated 12 Feb. 1882 indicates that she had spoken to Richard Henry Dana about Fuller and Emerson (Edel, ed., *Letters of Henry James* 3:528). For a discussion of how much Margaret Fuller's life-style was at odds with the nineteenth century, see Douglas, *Feminization of American Culture,* 259-88. For a discussion of the Fuller-Emerson relationship, see Dorothy Berkson, "'Born and Bred in Different Nations': Margaret Fuller and Ralph Waldo Emerson," in *Patrons and Protégées,* ed. Marchalonis, 3-30.

21. Letter from John Hay to Henry Adams dated 22 Nov. 1882. Quoted in Fred Kaplan, *Henry James: The Imagination of Genius* (New York: William Morrow, 1992), 254.

22. Carolyn VanBergen, "Getting Your Money's Worth: The Social Marketplace in *Horace Chase,*" in *Critical Essays,* ed. Torsney, 234-44.

23. Baym, *Novels, Readers, and Reviewers,* 181-90. Alfred Habegger (*Gender, Fantasy and Realism in American Literature* [New York: Columbia Univ.

Press, 1982], 15-20) thinks Baym overstates this prohibition against sexuality and reads the marriage proposal itself as a symbol of sexuality. Although his interpretation seems accurate, it does not negate the fact that any overt innuendo about sexuality remained taboo.

24. Woolson often spoke of herself as unattractive. Photographs of famous writers circulated widely in the nineteenth century, and those of Woolson indicate otherwise. The Granger Collection (381 Park Avenue South, New York, N.Y. 10016) possesses copies of some, including the ones reproduced in this text. All are in profile, apparently Woolson's way of responding to what Clare Benedict called her "curiously low opinion of her own personal appearance" (Benedict 2:xv).

25. The early model for Lanse (Lawrence) may be Lawrence Vickery in "Bro" (Rodman), a man who has European entanglements.

26. Petry, "'Always, Your Attached Friend,'" 88. The Howells' review appears in *Harper's,* Aug. 1886.

27. Moore, *Constance F. Woolson,* 97.

28. James, *Partial Portraits,* 190.

29. Weimer, "The 'Admiring Aunt,'" in *Critical Essays,* ed. Torsney, 203-16. Weimer reads *East Angels* in conjunction with James's *The Europeans.*

30. See Cathy N. Davidson, *Revolution and the Word: The Rise of the Novel in America* (New York: Oxford Univ. Press, 1986) for a discussion of wifely endurance of alcoholic husbands in Helena Well's *Constantia Neville; or the West Indian* (1800) and S. S. B. K. Wood's *Amelia; or the Influence of Virtue* (1802).

31. See Joanne Dobson, ed., *The Hidden Hand or, Capitola the Madcap,* by E. D. E. N. Southworth (New Brunswick, N.J.: Rutgers Univ. Press, 1988).

32. Information on the Walworth case is on exhibit at the Walworth Memorial Museum at Congress Park, Saratoga Springs, New York. See also Ruth Bordin, "'A Baptism of Power and Liberty': The Women's Crusade of 1873-1874," in *Woman's Being,* ed. Kelley, 283-95 for a discussion of Ohio's role in the temperance crusade of 1873-74.

33. Woolson believed in the hereditary nature of certain psychological traits and thought her own bouts of depression to be hereditary (Moore, *Constance F. Woolson,* 36). In a 16 Jan. 1876 letter to Paul Hamilton Hayne, she links "'Depression,' that evil spirit that haunts all creative minds" with the need for "the close appreciative warm belief & praise of . . . family" (Hubbell 728-29).

Bibliography

Baym, Nina. *Novels, Readers, and Reviews: Responses to Fiction in Antebellum America.* Ithaca, N.Y.: Cornell Univ. Press, 1984.

———. *Woman's Fiction: A Guide to Novels by and about Women in America,* 1820-1870. Ithaca, N.Y.: Cornell Univ. Press, 1978.

Benedict, Clare. *Appreciations.* Leatherhead, Surrey: F. B. Benger, 1941.

———. *Five Generations (1785-1923).* 3 vols. London Ellis, 1929-30, 1932. Vol. 1, *Voices Out of the Past.* Vol. 2, *Constance Fenimore Woolson.* Vol. 3, *The Benedicts Abroad.*

Berkson, Dorothy. "'Born and Bred in Different Nations': Margaret Fuller and Ralph Waldo Emerson." *Patrons and Protégées: Gender, Friendship, and Writing in Nineteenth-Century America,* edited by Shirley Marchalonis, 3-30. New Brunswick, N.J.: Rutgers Univ. Press, 1988.

Bordin, Ruth. "'A Baptism of Power and Liberty': The Women's Crusade of 1873-1874." In *Woman's Being, Woman's Place,* ed. Kelley, 283-95.

Brehm, Victoria. "Island Fortress: The Landscape of the Imagination." In *Critical Essays,* ed. Torsney, 172-86. First published in *American Literary Realism* 22 (1990): 51-66.

Davidson, Cathy N. *Revolution and the Word: The Rise of the Novel in America.* New York: Oxford Univ. Press, 1986.

Dobson, Joanne. Introduction to *The Hidden Hand or, Capitola the Madcap,* by E. D. E. N. Southworth. New Brunswick, N.J.: Rutgers Univ. Press, 1988.

Douglas, Ann. *The Feminization of American Culture.* New York: Knopf, 1977.

Edel, Leon. *The Life of Henry James.* 5 vols. Philadelphia: Lippincott, 1953-72.

Habegger, Alfred. *Gender, Fantasy and Realism in American Literature.* New York: Columbia Univ. Press, 1982.

———. *Henry James and the "Woman Business."* New York: Cambridge Univ. Press, 1989.

Hubbell, Jay B., ed. "Some New Letters of Constance Fenimore Woolson." *New England Quarterly* 14 (Dec. 1941): 715-35.

James, Henry. *The Letters of Henry James.* Edited by Leon Edel. 3 vols. Cambridge: Harvard Univ. Press, 1974-1980.

———. *Partial Portraits.* 1887. Reprint, Ann Arbor: Univ. of Michigan Press, 1970.

Kaplan, Fred. *Henry James: The Imagination of Genius.* New York: William Morrow, 1992.

Kelley, Mary, ed. *Private Woman, Public Stage: Literary Domesticity in Nineteenth-Century America.* New York: Oxford Univ. Press, 1984.

———. *Woman's Being, Woman's Place: Female Identity and Vocation in American History.* Boston: G. K. Hall, 1979.

Kern, John Dwight. *Constance Fenimore Woolson: Literary Pioneer.* Philadelphia: Univ. of Pennsylvania Press, 1934.

Marchalonis, Shirley, ed. *Patrons and Protégées: Gender, Friendship, and Writing in Nineteenth-Century America.* New Brunswick, N.J.: Rutgers Univ. Press, 1988.

Moore, Rayburn S. *Constance F. Woolson.* New Haven, Conn.: Twayne, 1963.

Petry, Alice Hall. "'Always, Your Attached Friend': The Unpublished Letters of Constance Fenimore Woolson to John and Clara Hay." *Books at Brown* 29-30 (1982-83): 11-107.

Riley, Glenda. *Divorce: An American Tradition.* New York: Oxford Univ. Press, 1991.

Strouse, Jean. *Alice James: A Biography.* Boston: Houghton Mifflin, 1980.

Torsney, Cheryl B. *Constance Fenimore Woolson: The Grief of Artistry.* Athens: Univ. of Georgia Press, 1989.

———, ed. *Critical Essays on Constance Fenimore Woolson.* New York: G. K. Hall, Macmillan, 1992.

VanBergen, Carolyn. "Constance Fenimore Woolson and the Next Country." *Western Reserve Studies* 3 (1988): 86-92.

———. "Getting Your Money's Worth: The Social Marketplace in *Horace Chase.*" In *Critical Essays,* ed. Torsney, 234-44.

Weimer, Joan Myers. "Women Artists as Exiles in the Fiction of Constance Fenimore Woolson." *Legacy* 3, no. 2 (Fall 1986): 3-15.

———, ed. *Women Artists, Women Exiles: "Miss Grief" and Other Stories,* by Constance Fenimore Woolson. New Brunswick, N.J.: Rutgers University Press, 1988.

Woolson, Constance Fenimore. *Anne.* New York: Harper and Brothers, 1882; New York: Arno, 1977. First published in *Harper's New Monthly Magazine* 62-64 (Dec. 1880-May 1882).

———. "Ballast Island." *Appletons' Journal* 9 (28 June 1873): 833-39.

———. "Black Point." *Harper's New Monthly Magazine* 59 (June 1879): 84-97.

———. *Castle Nowhere: Lake Country Sketches.* Boston: J. R. Osgood, 1875. (Published as *Solomon, and Other "Lake Country" Sketches* [Odessa, Ontario: J. Reish & Sons, 1897]). New York: Harper & Bros., 1899. New York: Garrett Press, 1969.

———. "Cicely's Christmas." *Appletons' Journal* 6 (30 Dec. 1871): 753-58.

———. *East Angels.* New York: Harper and Brothers, 1886. First published in *Harper's New Monthly Magazine* 70-77 (Jan. 1885-May 1886).

———. "A Florentine Experiment." *Atlantic Monthly* 46 (Oct. 1880). Also in *Dorothy and Other Italian Stories,* by Woolson; and *Five Generations,* by Benedict, vol. 2: 192-99.

———. "A Flower of the Snow." *Galaxy* 17 (Jan. 1874): 76-85.

———. *For the Major.* In *For the Major and Selected Short Stories,* ed. Moore, 259-367. First published in *Harper's New Monthly Magazine* 65-66 (Nov. 1882-Apr. 1883).

———. *The Front Yard and Other Italian Stories.* New York: Harper and Brothers, 1895; New York: Books for Libraries Press, 1969.

———. "The Happy Valley." *Harper's New Monthly Magazine* 41 (July 1870): 282-85. Also in *Five Generations,* by Benedict, vol. 1: 268-76.

———. "'Hepzibah's Story': An Unpublished Work by Constance Fenimore Woolson." Edited by Robert Gingras. *Resources for American Literary Study* 10 (1980): 33-45.

———. *Horace Chase.* New York: Harper and Brothers, 1894; Upper Saddle River, N.J.: Literature House, 1970. First published in *Harper's New Monthly Magazine* 86-87 (Jan. 1893-Aug. 1893).

———. *Jupiter Lights.* New York: Harper and Brothers, 1889; New York: AMS Press, 1971. First published in *Harper's New Monthly Magazine* 78-79 (Jan. 1889-Sept. 1889).

———. "King Log." *Appletons' Journal* 9 (18 Jan. 1873): 97-101.

———. "Lily and Diamond." *Appletons' Journal* 8 (2 Nov. 1872): 477-83.

———. "Matches Morganatic." *Harper's New Monthly Magazine* 61 (Mar. 1878): 517-31.

———. "Miss Grief." In *Women Artists, Women Exiles,* ed. Weimer, 248-69. First published in *Lippincott's Magazine* 25 (May 1880): 574-85. Also in *For the Major,* ed. Moore, 123-43; and Cheryl B. Torsney, *Legacy* 4, no. 1 (Spring 1987): 11-25.

———. "Miss Vedder." *Harper's New Monthly Magazine* 58 (Mar. 1879): 590-601.

————. "On the Iron Mountain." *Appletons' Journal* 9 (15 Feb. 1873): 225-30.

————. *Rodman the Keeper: Southern Sketches.* New York: D. Appleton, 1880; New York: Harper & Bros. 1886; New York: Garrett Press, 1969.

Karen Weekes (essay date spring 2000)

SOURCE: Weekes, Karen. "Northern Bias in Constance Fenimore Woolson's *Rodman the Keeper: Southern Sketches*." *Southern Literary Journal* 32, no. 2 (spring 2000): 102-15.

[*In the following essay, Weekes discusses the influence of prevalent Reconstruction-era prejudice against the South on the characters and plots of* Rodman the Keeper.]

Constance Fenimore Woolson is praised for her accuracy in depicting a variety of locales, including the northern "lake country," Italy, and the South, but her tales of the South are especially remarked upon for their realistic portrayals. Her collection of short stories *Rodman the Keeper: Southern Sketches* (1880) was hailed as "the first adequate presentation to the North without sentimentality or local prejudice of southern conditions during the decade after 1865" (Pattee 134). A northern sojourner in this region, Woolson spent the years 1873-1879 in the deep South, caring for her invalid mother. As the two women traveled throughout Georgia, the Carolinas, and Florida, Woolson gathered material for her southern writings, eventually producing travel sketches, three novels, a novelette, and fifteen short stories all based on aspects of this area (Rowe 58). Northern interest in things southern had been spurred by Union soldiers' travels into the region as well as an awareness that the destructiveness of the war and subsequent impoverishment had doomed this entire culture, with its "pathos and grandeur of a lost civilization" (Rowe xix). Northern periodicals including *Scribner's*, *Harper's*, and *Atlantic Monthly* sent writers and illustrators into the South to report on its conditions.[1] Accounts rendered immediately after the Civil War tended to be critical of the South:

> In the prewar period tensions among various sections of the country precluded the acceptance by a northern audience of any sympathetic depiction of the South in fiction. This was also true immediately after the war, when many nonsoutherners still thought of southerners as heathens who must be 'democratized' or further punished for their transgressions. In fact, southerners' continued resistance to northern influence only intensified the predominant opinion that the South must be rescued and the way cleared for the implementation of Reconstruction governments.
>
> (Rowe xvii)

In the latter part of the 1860s, southerners were perceived as ready to revolt anew, and northern readers and publishers were hostile to conciliatory representations of the region (Silber 40, 41; Buck 208). However, as the legislation of Reconstruction stumbled and progressed, more and more northerners began to evince sympathy for the dispossessed southerners.[2] Once the South was no longer a political threat, it could be romanticized and idealized: "A culture which in its life was anathema to the North, could in its death be honored" (Buck 208). Essays and fiction in the 1870s began to be less politically critical and more interested in preserving a record of the quickly-fading southern values, society, and way of life.

Woolson wrote her stories in this latter period, and reviews both at the time of and since the publication of *Rodman* [*Rodman the Keeper*] have repeatedly described her work as epitomizing this sympathy and sensitivity for the South. But the collection belies this assessment; it manifests the harsher, earlier attitude much more strongly than the sympathetic, later one. In almost all of these stories, a northern "caretaker" intervenes to provide physical, emotional, or financial salvation to needy, denigrated southern figures. More often than not, a heroic male is entangled romantically with a recalcitrant belle, enacting a patriarchal metaphor that dominates much of the writing of this period. "This image of marriage between northern men and southern women stood at the foundation of the late-nineteenth-century culture of conciliation and became a symbol which defined and justified the northern view of the power relations in the reunified nation," since the South was perennially cast in the role of the female, or submissive, partner (Silber 6-7). Nina Silber points out that this familiar metaphor emphasized "traditional notions of domestic harmony" while enabling the North to enshrine "the image of their victory in this metaphor, using it to reflect the political and economic leverage they hoped to exercise over Dixie" (10). She argues that this marital focus expressed the hopes of the North that an emotional "reunion" would take place, thus allowing Yankees to "submerg[e] . . . politics beneath images and metaphors that wallowed in compassion and claimed to take the high ground of emotion as opposed to the low ground of party positioning" (55). Casting the South as a damsel in distress who is in desperate need of rescue by a northern soldier or businessman reifies and naturalizes the power imbalance extant in the conquered states.

Even without consideration of gender dynamics, the repetition of a central conflict between a southern indigent and a northern redeemer is hardly sympathetic to the South; indeed, most of these stories portray southerners as victims of their own weakness, indolence, and pride. Either they are ultimately convinced of the respectability and desirability of northern values such as thrift, industry, and pragmatism, or they die. Both conclusions signify the death of an Old South that somehow deserves to perish: not simply for its participation in slavery, but for its peculiar, proud resistance to its fate.

None of the nineteenth-century northern criticism notes this thematic aspect, which is not surprising given the pervasive fictional metaphor of the time and the encouraging response to sympathetic treatments of the South. Reviews instead burgeon with praise for the "truthfulness" (rev. of *Rodman, Dial* 13) of the accounts. The stories "are all of the South, and though the writer is a Northern woman they more thoroughly represent the South as it is than anything of the kind that has been written since the war" ("Southern Sketches" 28). Her long-time friend Henry James credits Woolson for speaking out "in the light of the *voicelessness* of the conquered and reconstructed South. Miss Woolson strikes the reader as having a compassionate sense of this pathetic dumbness" (182). However, even in the twentieth century, critics have persisted in reading this collection as an original and strikingly sympathetic rendering of southern characters and situations. Rayburn Moore asserts that "few of those who shared Miss Woolson's Republican principles in the 1870's were able to be so fair to the fallen enemy" (55). Anne Rowe includes Woolson in a list of authors who "reflect the second-stage treatment of the South—that of rapt praise and overt idealization of the escapist, faraway country" (xx-xxi). Woolson is praised repeatedly for her "sympathy and knowledge" of the South (Hubbell 735),[3] yet her southern characters lack the diversity and inherent virtue of those of Mary Noailles Murfree, Kate Chopin, or Grace Elizabeth King. Her black characters conform to a "childlike lackey stereotype," while poor white characters are almost completely omitted (they are, however, described in one story as having "long, clay-colored faces, lank yellow hair, and half-open mouths" as well as "ignorance and dense self-conceit" [261]) (Rowe 59, 61).

There are several possible explanations for the contemporaneous assessments stating that Woolson had accurately depicted the South of the 1870s. These reviews were largely the products of magazine writers who, along with their readers, were unfamiliar with the South and were part of a culture that strongly desired to idealize this region. This area was a new source for local color writing, a type of realism that depended heavily upon carefully chosen detail: Paul Buck recounts that "new writers seemed intent upon doing little more than describe in simple language the many local diversities of the national scene" (196). The depiction of environment is one of Woolson's strongest talents, and another possibility is thus that these reviews are products of

writers who were enchanted into disregard of Woolson's hyperbolic characters and plots by her fine descriptions. Rowe argues that:

> The realism in her stories . . . derives largely from her careful descriptions of place which create the impression that the author has superimposed the tale upon a very realistic setting. . . . In contrast to her treatment of setting, the development of characterization in Woolson's stories and novels is often superficial and stereotyped.
>
> (58-59)

The majority of Woolson's critics do not draw this distinction between her strengths and weaknesses, instead limiting their focus to her striking depictions of place. James notes that Woolson's accurate descriptions are the result of "a remarkable minuteness of observation and tenderness of feeling on the part of one who evidently did not glance and pass, but lingered and analysed" (179). Woolson does have a gift for evoking the sensory offerings of the South. Anyone who has ever experienced Georgia humidity, for example, will recognize the veracity of this passage: "One April day the heat was almost insupportable; but the sun's rays were not those brazen beams that sometimes in Northern cities burn the air and scorch the pavements to a white heat; rather were they soft and still; the moist earth exhaled her richness, not a leaf stirred, and the whole level country seemed sitting in a hot vapor-bath" (15). And northerners who imagined the vanished possibilities of the southern way of life were indulged with Romantic visions: "Overlooking the tide-water river stands an old house, gleaming white in the soft moonlight; the fragrance of tropic flowers floats out to sea on the land-breeze, coming at sunset over the pine-barrens to take the place of the ocean winds that have blown all day long, bringing in the salt freshness to do battle with the hot shafts of the sun and conquer them" (75).

Unfortunately, Woolson rarely treats the South's citizens with the same appreciation and generosity that she shows its climate and gothic houses. Although various critics argue that Woolson censures northerners and southerners equally (Richardson 26, Stephan 3, Rowe 67) and that she is more even-handed in her criticism of northern traits in her longer works, in *Rodman the Keeper* proud southerners, and especially southern women, are forced to an emotional capitulation that few northerners have to endure. In an 1880 review, B. Phillips compliments Woolson on her familiarity with southern life and scenery, then examines her characters with this surprising result: "Where the author shows real genius is in that finer appreciation of Southern women. Miss Woolson evinces a very touching sympathy for her Southern sisters" (25). This sympathy may be evoked by her presentation of their hardships and endurance, but is more than negated by their stereotypical stubbornness, willfulness, hatred, and laziness. Joan Meyers Weimer recognizes that the plots of these stories "depict female failure" (xxxi). Woolson here participates in another of the fictional formulae of early Reconstruction: northerners often attributed southern women with having "weak moral fiber and poor work habits" (Silber 9) and a spiteful character (Silber 6). Speaking of Woolson's novels, Sybil Weir notes that "the strong, mature women are all Northern; the self-indulgent, irresponsible women . . . are all Southern" (141). This inconsistency in characterization actually applies to many of Woolson's short stories, and to her male characters as well as females.

Of the ten stories in the collection, the first four and the last one show the most obvious early-Reconstruction bias. All of these stories have a northerner who provides physical and financial salvation to a needy southerner. **"Rodman the Keeper"** is the story of a Federal soldier who cares for a national cemetery and for a wounded, dying Confederate soldier, Ward DeRosset. The dichotomy between the northern and southern cultures is made clear at the beginning of the story, when Rodman remembers commenting on the "shiftless ways" of the South:

> He had seen with his New England eyes the magnificence and carelessness of the South, her splendor and negligence, her wealth and thriftlessness. . . . Everywhere magnificence went hand in hand with neglect.
>
> "We have no such shiftless ways," he would remark, after he had furtively supplied a prisoner with hardtack and coffee.
>
> "And no such grand ones, either," Johnny Reb would reply.
>
> (11)

As Peter Morris Stephan explains the regional pride evidenced in this exchange, "Southerners identify with their locale, either the region or the state. The Northerners identify with the nation as a whole. . . . For the Southerners, pride is a prime mover; it leads to their thinking their way of life is not only good, but the best, if not the best ever. Miss Woolson's Northerners, rather than believing they have arrived at perfection, keep working at bettering their conditions" (73-74). The conflict between the organized, methodical North, embodying a relentless, puritan work ethic, and the indolent, bitter South is especially clear in these first stories.

Rodman is the keeper of a national cemetery in the South, which no white southerner ever visits (freed slaves honor the graves on Memorial Day). Ironically, this story is apparently based on the national cemetery in Andersonville, Georgia which was often visited by Confederates who decorated the graves not only of the southern dead but the northern as well.[4] Woolson herself wrote that "I go often to the soldier's graves. I can-

not bear to think that they are so soon forgotten; as they are, at the North . . ." (Moore 152). Woolson has transformed the northerners' neglect of the dead into a negative trait of southerners.

Rodman's antagonist in the story is Bettina, the ridiculously proud niece of Ward. Rodman blames her for Ward's own self-defeating pride, accusing him of being influenced by "the small venom of a woman, that here, as everywhere through the South, is playing its rancorous part" (27). Although critics have noted the melodrama in Bettina's rhetoric and actions (Perry 26), some see her extreme character as evidence of Woolson's view of the southern woman as trapped by her preference for living in a lost past (Dean, "Southern Sketches" 281); her bitterness at her lost lifestyle is the "venom" that is poisoning the northerner's attempts to rehabilitate the South and the southern man's attempt to accept the new order. None of Woolson's males are cursed with the stubbornness and smallness of heart that her southern belles display.

Another example of rancorous southern woman clinging to the past is Gardis Duke, the "guardian" of southern tradition in **"Old Gardiston."** She is consumed with "foolish pride" (136) in her pathetic attempts to exemplify a lifestyle that is beyond her means. But Gardis has a fierceness in her obsession with the past that her male cousin lacks; after Yankee soldiers have dined at her table, she burns the clothes she wore as hostess, exclaiming to herself, "So perish also the enemies of my country!" (123). Melodramatic episodes such as this make Bettina and Gardis both appear "like [what] one finds oftener in poor novels than in real life" (Perry 26). Southern women are portrayed as romantic and proud, hoping for princes and knights (131) to rescue them from their idle, melancholy pasts. Gardis *is* rescued: the Federal Captain Newell saves her small household from starving through his thrifty management of the family's business affairs, and then he marries the desolate and humbled Gardis. This conclusion is termed by Sharon Dean one of Woolson's "rare happy endings" because of Gardis's final refusal to continue to be victimized as "guardian of the noble southern past" (*Homeward Bound* 40). And Rowe argues:

> Coming as [Woolson] did to describe and praise, not to convert, there was no need for Woolson's southerners to capitulate to northern lovers. A romantic theme typical of her short stories and novels shows the southerner as a beautiful young girl, very similar to De Forest's Lillie Ravenel, although perhaps more indolent. The northerner is usually a wealthy man, always older, often self-made, who is fascinated by the girl's charm and languor.
>
> (68-69)

Gardis, however, does clearly "capitulate" to her northern suitor, and only when she is a victim *in extremis*: her house has been burned, her beloved cousin is dead, and she has nowhere else to turn. The "noble southern past" she has so fiercely and proudly guarded has been obliterated entirely, so she submits at last to the sensitive, wise, strong North, embodied in the Union soldier whose very name, Newell, marks him as the personification of a "new" order replacing tradition and signals his ability to heal the ills of Gardis and her region.

"Sister St. Luke" features a female northern savior who is assisted by two other northerners in the care of a meek southern nun. Sister St. Luke is an incredibly timid woman steeped in Catholic rather than social tradition. The northerner Melvyna, a former nurse, brings the sick nun back to health, but it is Melvyna's energy and drive, not her nursing ability, that gain her the respect of the community. The Minorcans, natives to the north Florida coast, are "too indolent to do anything more than smoke, lie in the sun, and eat salads heavily dressed with oil" (45). The amiable Pedro is overshadowed by his "quick, enterprising" northern wife (43). The natives are awed: "Had he not married a woman of wonder—of an energy unfathomable?" (46). Melvyna is assisted in her energetic attempts to wean Sister St. Luke from the pagan Catholic church by two northern men. Yet they fail in their efforts to break her bonds with tradition. Even after she heroically saves the men's lives in a storm, it is they who physically and emotionally "save" her, by enabling her to return to the convent through a generous financial contribution. Her character shows a streak of courage buried under fear and reticence and an unshakable tenacity in her beliefs. She believes in the traditions of the church and in her imagined bond with the other nuns; this stubborn clinging to ideas both true and false, particularly when they relate to the past, is a trait of many of Woolson's southerners.

The last story in the collection, **"Up in the Blue Ridge,"** shows southerners obsessed with this loyalty to false ideas of the past. The main southern character, Honor Dooris, saves the life of her cousin, a member of an esteemed family. The act is seen in a clearer light when one remembers that this "distinguished" man is a moonshiner and a murderer, yet he is still assisted by Honor and by the minister of the community. Blind family loyalty and tarnished honor are negative aspects of southern character in this story. A northerner, Stephen Wainwright, intervenes as the financial protector of Honor and her entire town, and once again a male financial savior becomes emotionally involved with a stubborn, tradition-bound southerner. Eventually Honor unknowingly rejects Stephen, but through her marriage to the northerner Royce she exchanges one northern protector for another.

Another northerner who tries to direct the life of a southerner is Miss Elisabetha, in the story by the same name. Elisabetha, the legal guardian of Doro (Theodore), a southerner, rules their household with the characteristic thrift and industry that Woolson portrays in Rodman, Melvyna, and other northerners. Elisabetha tends to her orange groves in person, and as a result "not one orange was lost," as opposed to "the annual waste of the other proprietors, an ancient and matter-of-course waste, handed down from father to son" (80). She sends her servant, Pedro, to sell oranges to "the lazy housewives" who, along with their husbands, waste the mornings in idle talk. She also braids palmetto to supplement her income, showing her unusual industry: "her long fingers, once accustomed to the work, accomplished as much in a week as Zanita Perez and both her apprentices accomplished in two" (81). Elisabetha is compared to the Minorcans of the South rather than plantation-bred southerners, but the idleness and shiftlessness on the part of non-northerners is still clear.

Another typical trait of Woolson's northerners is that of exemplary organization, which Elisabetha epitomizes. Elisabetha's rigidity and formality make her somewhat ridiculous: "Woolson reveals the absurdities of the elderly spinster while simultaneously evoking sympathy for her" (Weimer xxxi). However, Woolson gives the unhappy Elisabetha a much more sympathetic treatment than she does the Minorcan whom Doro eventually marries. Doro's love for his bride, Catalina, part of a thriftless, lazy family, drags Doro to his ruin in a haze of ease and shiftlessness. His new family is "careless, idle, ignorant . . . asking for nothing, planning not at all, working not at all, but loving each other in their own way, contented to sit in the sunshine, and laugh, and eat, and sing, all the day long" (104). Revealing a bias himself, Lyon Richardson explains that "the young husband settles down to *the regional* slothfulness and indolence, and soon children grow wild on the estate" (28, emphasis added). Elisabetha gives them her savings and works to support them. She is rewarded, in a sense, by Doro's last words: "I have had nothing to wish for" (104). Her goal of caring for him and gratifying his wishes has been met. Elisabetha's hopeless grief at the tragedy of the loss of Doro's ambition encourages sympathy with the pathetic, industrious figure of Elisabetha, the northerner who fails in her larger caretaking mission of helping Doro to realize a cultural purpose.

Another northern caretaker whose quest is futile is David King in the story **"King David."** David has come from the North to educate and provide medicine for the freedmen (another case of physical healing by a northerner). Unfortunately, he ultimately fails and, humiliated, returns to the North.[5] David, like Elisabetha, is a pathetic character, and prejudiced in his own way. However, Elisabetha and he in all their weaknesses still exhibit traits superior to those of the southerners in their stories. David's own prejudice is a source of shame rather than the source of violence and pride as evoked in his foil, the planter Harnett Ammerton. According to Robert Gingras, Woolson implies, through her characterization of Ammerton, that he "was entitled to his role as master because of his higher intelligence and cultivation" and that he "represents the last element of refinement in the area, surrounded as he is by poor whites, carpetbaggers, naive Northern missionaries like King, and surly freedmen—blacks who are consistently compared to animals in their behavior" (136). But this ignores the fact that Woolson's depiction of blacks and poor whites is consistently stereotypical, as well as the response that Ammerton's statements would evoke in Woolson's northern readers of 1880. He says that the freedmen "must be taken care of, worked, and fed, as we work and feed our horses—precisely in the same way" that they "have not capacity for anything save ignorance"; and that "they are an inferior race by nature; God made them so" (262-263). This characterization hardly shows Woolson's "sympathy for the old order of the South," and when Ammerton joins with other planters to form an association for the protection of the whites, it is difficult to believe that northern readers aware of the fear-driven lynchings of Reconstruction would find this move "entirely justified" as Gingras asserts (136; see also Rowe 67).

Proud and violent passions erupt in **"Felipa"** in a quite different way. Aside from the healing of a physical wound, northerners in this tale are not true caretakers of Felipa, who "betrays that impetuosity of temperament which is natural to one of her [Minorcan] race" (Kern 61). Instead, by introducing their culture without giving Felipa any hope of achieving her new desire to be a continuing part of their lives, without being willing to "save" her, they devastate her simple world. The North's supplanting of the southern way of life is clear in **"Old Gardiston"** as well, but at least in that story the southerner is given love to replace the loss of family and past; Felipa is abandoned between two cultures. Her rejection by the beautiful, sophisticated northerners is too much for her to bear, and she kills herself.

Two more stories in the collection, **"Bro"** and **"The South Devil,"** also include negative representations of the South. **"Bro"** lacks a northern caretaker, but one of the main characters in the story is said to be like her northern father: organized, habitual, and persevering. She is academically bright and perceptive about others, whereas the southerners around her "were either too indolent or too good-natured to make those conscientious studies of their neighbors which are demanded by the code of morals prevailing on the coast farther north" (222). **"The South Devil"** features a northern caretaker, Mark Deal, but no southerner for whom he cares. Still Mark enacts the industrious northern role in contrast to the lazy southern one: "[Mark] worked . . . every day from daylight until dusk, and was probably the only white man in the State who did" (143). His German half-brother's refusal to become energetic or materially ambitious is partly due to his obsession with the south-

ern swamp; his artistic, passive nature is shaped by the narcotic influence of this sensual but dangerous area. Dean comments:

> Woolson uses Mark and Carl [the half-brother] to locate contrasting responses to the South. Carl can respond to the artistic mystery of the swamp because he can accept the South as it is. However, Woolson recognizes that Carl's response is not necessarily "better" than Mark's. . . . Woolson is also clear that the southern swamp represents something stifling and sinister, a spur to the exploitative, nonproductive side of Carl's character. This danger, Woolson implies, must be courted. The artist must be open to beauty and seduction and terror . . . open to a South that Woolson knows can touch the soul.
>
> (*Homeward Bound* 43-44)

Significantly, the character who is able to appreciate and immerse himself in this element of the South dies as a result of this very immersion.

Woolson repeatedly maintained the accuracy of these southern stories, beginning with the preface to the volume in which she states that "as far as they go they record real impressions" ([5]). If she actually perceived southerners being sometimes gracious, courageous, or talented, but more often lazy, incompetent, bitter, or stubborn, and always in desperate need of northern assistance, then it is hard to reconcile that view of the South with the one presented in **"In the Cotton Country."** Woolson strongly asserts the truth of this particular tale: "I have written stories of imagination, but this is a story of fact, and I want you to believe it. It is true, every word of it . . . and when you read it . . . stop and reflect that it is only one of many life-stories like unto it" (184). This story is an anomaly in the collection, featuring a southern heroine who survives through energy and determination. Her only acceptance of northern help is when she asks the narrator to take her child and raise him "in your rich, prosperous North" (196). She chooses to remain a part of her broken past, which is typical for a Woolson southerner, but she herself is never broken. She never surrenders to indolence, bitterness, or passivity; this resistance is certainly atypical for Woolson's southerners.

Woolson has rightfully been praised for the realism of many of her recorded impressions of the South; her descriptions of decaying houses and lush landscapes are detailed and credible. Her southern characters may even be accurately drawn as individuals, but collectively the stories show the inherent northern bias of the early Reconstruction era against southerners. **"In the Cotton Country"** presents an alternative for southern characters; despite this, Woolson focuses almost exclusively on the weak, the slothful, or the obsessed. According to Buck, the literary 1880s signify "a transition from a critical attitude to a complete espousal of the tradition of a South of heroism and beauty" (229). Woolson's tales depict the faded beauty of the southern land, but rarely find heroes native to this region.

Northern characters in her stories are often stereotypical, but their traits are generally positive ones that evoke a puritan work ethic.[6] As Dean points out, "whether male or female, both northerners and southerners may represent extreme forms of behavior" (*Homeward Bound* 36). She continues:

> Aware of her position as an outsider, a single woman who has lost her home, [Woolson] was sensitive to southern loss; aware of the newness of western communities, she quickly perceived the age and tradition of southern ones. . . . This, of course, does not mean that she was free from bias. She implies that the south will never adopt the democratic openness she located as part of the hope for western settlement. . . . She imaged a South far more likely to be immersed in social stratification or locked in the enmity that is the legacy of the Civil War.[7]
>
> (*Homeward Bound* 34)

Woolson's sketches show a South incapable of helping itself; story after story portrays needy, proud, or lazy southerners relying on the strength of the North to save them. Woolson's sympathy might lie with the South, but in ***Rodman the Keeper,*** her sensitivity to variations in character and theme surely lie elsewhere.

Notes

1. For a fuller discussion of northern writing about the Reconstruction-era South, see Anne Rowe's excellent introduction to her book *The Enchanted Country: Northern Writers in the South, 1865-1910.* Paul Buck's seminal *The Road to Reunion: 1865-1900* (222-226) also offers a comprehensive treatment of this topic.

2. Nina Silber points out the classism implicit in many of these attitudinal shifts toward the South: "When northerners looked at the South in the postwar years, they cultivated specific types of images and promoted a specific version of reunion that was best suited to Yankee needs. They transformed their anger against the southern aristocracy into feelings of pity and respect, ultimately sentimentalizing the unhurried and leisurely lifestyles of the planter class. Moreover, in light of the social turbulence of the Gilded Age, northerners were not unmindful of the type of class and racial authority which southern planters had apparently exercised over their subordinates; they learned to respect the southern elite for what they saw as an authoritative yet harmonious relationship with their slaves. . . . To some extent, sentimental suffering merely masked a deeply rooted sense of class snobbery. Many middle- and upper-class

northerners claimed to be captivated by the idea of southern suffering, but most were fascinated by the image of wealthy southerners who had experienced such great losses. Southern planters aroused northern pity because of their drastically altered circumstances and because it seemed so unfortunate for such a well-mannered and highly bred people to have suffered so much" (6, 52).

3. See also Simms 362, Richardson 25-26, Dean, *Homeward Bound* 35, Rowe 67, and Kern 71.

4. Andersonville is clearly the setting of the story. There are only three national cemeteries located by Confederate prison sites: Andersonville, GA; Salisbury, NC; and Florence, SC. Woolson gives a figure of 14,321 interred, a figure exceeding that of any of the national cemeteries, but which is quite close to the total at Andersonville. Geographical indications in the story also point to Andersonville as the only possible basis in fact for this prison. However, Woolson could not give the actual name of the cemetery for thematic reasons. Andersonville was visited by both northerners and southerners, as a reporter remarked in the *Sumter Republican* on 4 July 1879. It was not visited in numbers as vast as those of Florence or Salisbury, but neither was it ignored or forgotten by Yankees or Confederates. If Woolson had represented the cemetery as visited by both sides, though, she would have removed some of Rodman's isolation and diminished the theme of dichotomy and resentment between the North and South.

5. As John Dwight Kern explains: "Miss Woolson knew the South quite well enough to realize that the good intentions and idealism of men like David King were misdirected, and that the negroes, freed suddenly after generations of slavery, were the easy prey of demagogues. . . . Very few northerners of the time, except Miss Woolson, were in a position to recognize the fact that misguided and untimely idealism was as harmful to the emancipated [sic] slaves as the machinations of the unprincipled carpet-baggers" (75). Sharon Dean adds that Woolson "knew that she was an outsider and that she could read dangers inherent in people like David King, who, for all their idealism, displayed the same kind of missionary zeal that had sought to destroy Indian cultures in the name of education" (*Homeward Bound* 64).

6. Two remarkably different readings of Woolson's southern works are found in the criticism of Anne Rowe and Peter Morris Stephen. Rowe, in an evaluation of Woolson's entire southern canon, contends that Woolson's South is "the land of milk and honey, the unspoiled Eden of a preindustrial world, a place that northerners cursed with the

work ethic and the puritan scruple might dream about and view from afar, but never enter. . . . The indolence, the sensuousness of a more relaxed life, the very unprogressiveness, become for the industrializing, materialistic Yankee a veritable rebuke" (73). Stephen, on the other hand, argues that Woolson "shows a North that is apparently the superior region, by virtue of its winning of the War and its spreading of its wealth and ideology throughout the defeated region. That the passing of the old is sad, she does not deny. But that the inevitable coming of the new is not so sad, she also tries to make clear" (176-177).

7. Dean adds that Woolson goes on to "expose the biases of more colonial-minded northerners," citing Harold Chase as an example (34). This point seems more evident in the southern novels of Woolson than in her short stories in this collection.

Works Cited

Buck, Paul H. *The Road to Reunion: 1865-1900.* Boston: Little, Brown, 1937.

Dean, Sharon L. "Constance Woolson's Southern Sketches." *Southern Studies* 25 (1986): 274-283.

————. *Constance Fenimore Woolson: Homeward Bound.* Knoxville: U of Tennessee P, 1995.

Gingras, Robert. "Constance Fenimore Woolson's Literary Achievement as a Short Story Writer." Diss. Florida State U, 1980.

Hubbell, Jay B. *The South in American Literature, 1607-1900.* Durham: Duke UP, 1954.

James, Henry. *Partial Portraits.* 1888. Westport, CT: Greenwood, 1970.

Kern, John Dwight. *Constance Fenimore Woolson: Literary Pioneer.* Philadelphia: U of Pennsylvania P, 1934.

Moore, Rayburn S. *Constance Fenimore Woolson.* New York: Twayne, 1963.

Pattee, Fred Lewis. "Constance Fenimore Woolson and the South." *South Atlantic Quarterly* 38 (Apr. 39): 130-141.

Perry, Thomas Sergeant. "Some Recent Novels." *Atlantic Monthly* 46 (July 1880): 124-125. Reprinted in Torsney 26-27.

Phillips, B. "[Review of *Rodman the Keeper: Southern Sketches*]." *New York Times* 11 June 1880: 3. Reprinted in Torsney 25.

Review of *Rodman the Keeper: Southern Sketches,* by Constance Fenimore Woolson. *The Dial* May 1880: 13-14.

Richardson, Lyon N. "Constance Fenimore Woolson: 'Novelist Laureate' of America." *South Atlantic Quarterly* 39 (1940): 18-36.

Rowe, Anne E. *The Enchanted Country: Northern Writers in the South, 1865-1910.* Baton Rouge: Louisiana State UP, 1978.

Silber, Nina. *The Romance of Reunion: Northerners and the South, 1965-1900.* Chapel Hill: U of North Carolina P, 1993.

Simms, L. Moody, Jr. "Constance Fenimore Woolson on Southern Literary Taste." *Mississippi Quarterly* 22 (1969): 362-366.

Stephan, Peter Morris. "Comparative Value Systems in the Fiction of Constance Fenimore Woolson." Diss. U of New Mexico, 1976.

Torsney, Cheryl, ed. *Critical Essays on Constance Fenimore Woolson.* New York: G. K. Hall, 1992.

"Southern Sketches." *Literary World* (Boston) 3 July 1880: 223. Reprinted in Torsney 28.

Weir, Sybil. "Southern Womanhood in the Novels of Constance Fenimore Woolson." *Mississippi Quarterly* 19 (1976): 559-568. Reprinted in Torsney 140-147.

Weimer, Joan Myers. "Introduction." *Women Artists, Women Exiles: "Miss Grief" and Other Stories.* New Brunswick: Rutgers UP, 1988.

Woolson, Constance Fenimore. *Rodman the Keeper: Southern Sketches.* New York, 1880.

Paul Crumbley (essay date 2003)

SOURCE: Crumbley, Paul. "Haunting the House of Print: The Circulation of Disembodied Texts in 'Collected by a Valetudinarian' and 'Miss Grief.'" In *American Culture, Canons, and the Case of Elizabeth Stoddard,* edited by Robert McClure Smith and Ellen Weinauer, pp. 83-104. Tuscaloosa: The University of Alabama Press, 2003.

[In the following essay, Crumbley studies the connection between the failed health of the female protagonists in "Miss Grief" and Elizabeth Stoddard's "Collected by a Valetudinarian."]

In "Collected by a Valetudinarian" and **"Miss Grief,"** Elizabeth Stoddard and Constance Fenimore Woolson build short stories around texts that never appear.[1] The female narrator of Stoddard's 1870 "Collected" ["Collected by a Valetudinarian"] reads a dead woman's diary chronicling the deceased author's creation of a novel that the narrator deems unpublishable but that nonetheless powerfully relates "the truth about us women"

(306). Similarly, the male narrator of Woolson's 1880 **"Miss Grief"** is deeply moved by a female writer's unruly manuscripts that he nevertheless ultimately rejects because "her perversities were as essential a part of her work as her inspirations" (265). These disembodied texts haunt the stories in which they figure primarily through the effect they have on those who read, write, and hear them. By pointing to manuscript compositions that have great power but are incapable of print publication, these stories achieve two objectives of particular importance to nineteenth-century American women writers: they illuminate the extent to which print conventions constrain literary representation, and they draw attention to human experience—in these instances, female—that lies outside the protocols of print culture. By presenting female authors who are from the beginning sickly and who eventually die unpublished, Stoddard and Woolson connect failed female health to the inadequate circulation of a print record that embodies the experiences of real women.

For both writers, then, literary circulation emerges as a central underlying trope in which the health of the nonconforming female writer is linked to the reading public she relies on for the absorption and dissemination of her work. Simply stated, the healthy circulation of literature requires that all persons who acknowledge its value act as transmitters within a circuit connecting private creation to public benefit. Cast in this light, one of the most intriguing dimensions of both stories is their investigation of gift-based distribution as an alternative to consumer-based print publication. In *The World of the Gift,* Jacques T. Godbout explains that gift networks can indeed "transform the producer-user relationship" from a "binary utilitarian" system to one that operates "according to rules that are not those of the public institution and differ from it essentially in not making a distinction between . . . producer and consumer" (166). Such an alternative system offers writers a means to distribute uncensored writing through readers who actively collaborate in the circulation of texts. Consequently, gift distribution provides a means of assessing the practical viability of even the most severely limited circulation as a means of preserving unruly female texts. What these stories show, however, is that the ultimate benefit to the individual writer and the culture she inhabits must be assessed according to the potential collaborator's effectiveness in expanding circulation.

Stoddard and Woolson stress the importance of audience by presenting female writers who conduct their artistic lives outside conventional print culture, a position which means that neither writer enjoys the luxury of public support nor the pain of public rejection; instead, they fear not the loss of a public readership but, rather, the possibility of no readership whatsoever. While male authors like Herman Melville and Nathaniel Hawthorne also struggled with questions of artistic integrity—in

their personal lives as well as in their fiction—their positions differed significantly since they both achieved public recognition by successfully utilizing existing systems for print circulation. This meant that for them, the problem lay in making those systems responsive to artistic innovation, not in gaining access in the first place.[2] In her discussion of Stoddard's public and critical reception, Lisa Radinovsky points out that Stoddard herself knew only too well how difficult it was for a nonconforming female writer to win a public readership. While critics received her novels positively, Stoddard's bold rejection of "the pious, pure, submissive and domestic" ideal conveyed by the Cult of True Womanhood cost her dearly in terms of public support: "eccentric women like Stoddard were often stigmatized as unnatural, unwomanly threats to middle-class ideals . . . especially when their unorthodox views entered the public sphere" (Radinovsky, "Against All Odds" 266). When Stoddard's narrator learns that the female artist, Alicia Raymond, is "a woman of genius" (289) and Woolson's narrator identifies the protagonist in that story as a woman who "possessed the divine spark of genius" (257), both characters are immediately set apart as eccentrics and, therefore, suspect. As Radinovsky notes in her discussion of Stoddard, "The very few women who were described as geniuses were apt to be called diseased, vulgar, coarse, and unwomanly, as if they could not be both geniuses and real women" ("Against All Odds" 267). Radinovsky demonstrates the currency of this view by citing the following statement from Cesare Lombroso's 1863 book *The Man of Genius*: "there are no women of genius; the women of genius are men."

In keeping with this theory, the female narrator in "Collected" describes the setting where the deceased writer composed her novel as an isolated haven where "neither laws nor men could trouble a solitary stranger," at the same time concluding that the author could never "have been induced to publish anything" even though "we should have a better literature" if she did (307). Likewise, in **"Miss Grief,"** the male author who narrates the story acknowledges that the dying Miss Moncrief "had the greater power" (268)—despite her rejection of all his editorial advice—but nonetheless arranges to have her unpublished drama "destroyed unread" upon his death (269). Sharon L. Dean illustrates Woolson's sensitivity to the inhibiting presence of editorial demands by referring to a letter Woolson wrote to Henry James in which she objects that even at the turn of the century it was impossible for a woman to be "a complete artist" (186). In a manner entirely consistent with this statement, "Collected" and **"Miss Grief"** show that print culture in nineteenth-century America was so resistant to the original contributions of female writers that even the most talented among them could be deprived of cultural support.[3]

Lawrence Buell and Sandra Zagarell have observed the strong parallels "in attitude, upbringing and milieu" that link Stoddard's life to that of Emily Dickinson, who is arguably the best-known nineteenth-century writer to have declined print publication (Buell and Zagarell xii).[4] Striking as the biographical similarities are, the links uniting Dickinson to the fictional authors of Stoddard's and Woolson's stories may be even more impressive. Through her correspondence, for instance, Dickinson clearly engaged in the sort of gift-based circulation that Alicia Raymond and Aarona Moncrief attempted. Especially in her letters to Helen Hunt Jackson and Thomas Wentworth Higginson, the differences between gift and commercial economies emerge with stunning clarity. The Jackson correspondence shows the successfully published Jackson attempting to secure print publication for a clearly resistant Dickinson. Having explained to Jackson that she is "unwilling" and "incapable" (*The Letters of Emily Dickinson* 563), Dickinson repeatedly asks Higginson's assistance in eluding Jackson's efforts (562-63, 566). Similarly, in her earlier letters to Higginson, Dickinson famously declared that "to publish" was "foreign to my thought, as Firmament to Fin" (408). Though she clearly desired communication with both Jackson and Higginson, Dickinson appears to have been much more interested in gift circulation than print publication.[5] Ironically, Dickinson's sustained correspondence with Higginson—who consistently doubted her readiness to enter print—was a primary reason her work has endured, as his editorial collaboration with Mabel Loomis Todd ultimately secured a broad public readership. In this sense, then, Dickinson exemplifies the circulation potential that remains unrealized in "Collected" and **"Miss Grief."**

The degree to which Stoddard and Woolson are concerned with the exclusion of female authors from positions of cultural authority may be seen through the way both stories present vague and disturbingly disembodied roles for central female characters. This approach draws attention to the near invisibility of women not fully engaged in authorized forms of female conduct, while also magnifying the double bind whereby women writers who seek print visibility must conform to the social expectations that prevent female originality from becoming part of the official literary record. In Stoddard's case, the "valetudinarian" protagonist is an ailing widow who discovers comfort in the presence of another widow, both of whom appear to confirm one well-known female stereotype, that of the helpless widow. Miss Grief, Woolson's semi-eponymous woman writer (whose real name is Moncrief), is an aging spinster whose actual life is so clouded by culturally imposed stereotypes about spinster authors that the conventional male narrator appears incapable of viewing her as a distinct individual. These framing procedures establish a pervasive cultural inclination to erase the presence of nonconforming women, an inclination that women writ-

ers must overcome if their writing is to succeed in conveying a more accurate picture of the lives American women actually lived. This is precisely the point Helen Hunt Jackson makes in her poem "Found Frozen," in which her speaker describes the way "they who loved her with all the love / Their wintry natures had to give" erase the suffering of a deceased woman's actual life by writing "across her grave / Some common record which they thought was true" (20). Perhaps it was her desire to displace the false but all too common public record of women's lives that prompted Jackson to seek publication for Dickinson.

From the opening pages of "Collected," Stoddard draws attention to the way conventions that inform the "common record" collectively obscure female identity. After not having revealed the narrator's name for the first fifth of the story, Stoddard finally does so after giving her married name first, revealing her first name in the following paragraph. And in the paragraph after that we learn that Alicia Raymond, the female writer of genius, has lost what limited fame had been hers when her father died and all efforts to promote her work ceased (288-89). To show that the concealment of a distinctive female identity revealed in these instances is a pervasive feature of society, Stoddard includes within her narrator's gaze both the "occasional" village woman who "now and then appeared" wrapped in shawls (285) and her future friend, Helen Hobson, whom the narrator describes as bearing "a shadowy resemblance to myself, in as much as she was dressed in mourning and looked delicate and feeble" (288). By linking the anonymous village woman to the narrator and her friend, who are also village women—at least temporarily—Stoddard's opening pages convey the general impression of a society in which women fail to achieve full embodiment.

This impression of cultural disembodiment is further reinforced when the ever-present hotel manager, Mr. Binks, introduces the narrator and Mrs. Hobson with the twin observations "Birds of a feather flock together" and "By your looks I conclude you have them 'ere mysterious complaints which make women so unaccountable. My wife was the same; first and last, she cost me a couple of hundred in patent medicines" (288). Not only does Binks automatically categorize all ill women as of a single type, but he appears to have no clear recollection of distinguishing personal features that would set his own wife apart from other similarly constituted women. Instead, he points to the inconvenient expense of patent medicines that he clearly views as the natural resort of all similarly indisposed women. Throughout his conversation he conveys a good-natured patronage of female quirkiness even as his words inadvertently reveal how commercial enterprise accommodates precisely the eccentricities he so derisively dismisses. Apparently without conscious forethought, his words show that these very eccentricities of the female constitution define the type of woman who purchases patent medicines and frequents the establishment upon which his livelihood depends, thus providing an economic foundation for the perpetuation of female enfeeblement.

Despite the humorous presence of Mr. Binks (he provokes Helen and Eliza's first laughter [288]), his comic relief underscores the easy dismissal of fictional females that all too clearly illustrates a widespread social denial of female seriousness, a denial often debilitating for female authors in the real world. Woolson provocatively identified Stoddard as an example of the negative effect writing can have on female health when, upon hearing that Stoddard was ill in 1876, she asked Edmund Clarence Stedman, "Why do literary women break down so?" (qtd. in Weimer xviii). Joan Myers Weimer further demonstrates Woolson's awareness that she formed one of a community of women writers who suffered debilitating somatic responses to writing by quoting a letter Woolson wrote to Samuel Mather. In that letter, Woolson states that while she suffered the "(comparatively) small trouble of lameness," her suffering "sinks to nothingness beside the terrible nervous prostration her friend Frances Hodgson Burnett suffered every time she finished writing a book" (xix). Cheryl B. Torsney gives special emphasis to the extent that Woolson saw discomfort as an accompaniment of writing: "The happiest women I have known belonged to two classes; the devoted wives and mothers, and the successful flirts, whether married or single; such women never write" (19).

The awareness registered in these passages informs the approach Stoddard and Woolson develop in "Collected" and **"Miss Grief,"** showing that for each woman the relation of writing to health raised important questions; but as we shall see, the stories' explorations of health and writing tend to view the questions themselves as more productive than attempts to resolve them. Lying as they do behind the events of each story, these questions enable both writers to oppose mind-body and text-body binaries as a way of evoking heteroglossia unique to the female writer's contemplation of public utterance. Mikhail M. Bakhtin's definition of "heteroglossia" as the closest "conceptualization as is possible of that locus where centripetal and centrifugal forces collide" (428) here applies to the multiple conflicting discourses that Stoddard and Woolson use to frame the experience of dissenting woman writers. Among these, the pressure to present a fictional self consistent with society's expectation of a privatized domestic woman runs up against the woman writer's desire to reach an audience responsive to writing that seriously challenges conventional knowledge through innovations in style and content. Most pointedly, both stories also show that, far from promoting female health, privatization

can, in fact, have a negative effect by foreclosing communication and thus thwarting expressive impulses the exercise of which is essential to overall health.

As Cynthia Davis has advised in her analysis of medical science and literary form, the serious effort to "examine bodily and narrative forms as analogous entities" (3) must proceed with the understanding "that medical definitions of embodied identity were—contrary to received knowledge—both complicated and unstable" (2). Nowhere is the instability of medical definitions more evident than in Edward H. Dixon's popular medical advice book, *Woman and Her Diseases.* "From her position in the social scale," he writes in his introduction, "she is subjected to so many causes of physical degeneration from the evident design of nature . . . that it seems but an act of humanity to make an effort for her instruction in some of the evils that so constantly beset her" (5). In her assessment of Dixon, Diane Price Herndl states, "Like other books in the genre, Dixon's reveals the conflicting messages of medical thought" whereby "woman is both innately sick and responsible for her poor health" (35).[6] Pronouncements like Dixon's, which Herndl sees as typifying nineteenth-century medical science, have led her to agree with numerous other critics who also view "patriarchal culture as potentially sickening for women and as defining women as inherently sick, especially when they resist its norms" (7).[7] Notable contemporaries of Stoddard and Woolson, who also understood writing as linked to the debilitating influence of patriarchal culture, include Charlotte Perkins Gilman and Edith Wharton, both of whom Herndl describes as having written "illness into their texts, leaving themselves apart from it, not invalid women" (128). The most famous and perhaps the most public declaration of a woman writer's rejection of the patriarchal medical establishment is Gilman's explanation in "Why I Wrote the Yellow Wallpaper?" that she wrote that work with the express purpose of rejecting S. Weir Mitchell's rest cure, founded "on the solemn advice to 'live as domestic a life as far as possible,' to 'have but two hours' intellectual life a day,' and 'never to touch pen, brush or pencil again as long as I lived'" (348). Davis presents Louisa May Alcott, Dr. Harriot K. Hunt, and Margaret Fuller as similarly taking up the pen "in hopes of not simply minimizing or escaping suffering but alleviating it" (55). As these observations suggest, Stoddard and Woolson reflect a sensitivity to the connection of writing with health that found broad support in advice literature, as well as in the work of other women writers.

Stoddard gives special attention to the internal psychological and emotional forces that further complicate the management of female bodies by not limiting her analysis to external social and cultural forces that seek to dictate women's behavior. More disturbing even than the near invisibility of women is the experience of interior turmoil that Stoddard urges her readers to associate with a disruption of mental faculties. The first sentence of "Collected" quickly injects evidence of the narrator's troubled search for a vanished self that directly links health to emotional state and sets up the narrator's contradictory thought process. She describes herself as revisiting "an old village on our sea-board" where she actively seeks "something lost, *i.e.,* health and to appease a heart disquieted by grief," in pursuit of which she will "remain as long as the perturbed ghosts, my present rulers, [will] permit" (285). Here we see that the narrator, Eliza Sinclair, perceives herself as simultaneously having "lost" health while also passively submitting to "ghosts" that dictate her actions. We soon learn that though Eliza ostensibly wishes to recover the health and equanimity of her past, she is guided by the words of "the medieval Balzac" whose advice to "*Hide your life*" she takes to heart, stating her intent to "lose myself" in the woods and sand barrens where she knows she will find "arrow-heads, and the Indian skulls" of a once-flourishing culture (286). Stoddard's determination to establish a parallel between the artifacts of Native American culture and the fate that Eliza faces compels consideration of the crucial role self-awareness plays in making possible the circulation of texts that then become critical to the historical survival of cultures. The near erasure of Native American culture from the cultural landscape of the United States portends a similar future for women's culture if steps are not taken to secure the stories capable of perpetuating an accurate account of life within that culture.

Throughout "Collected," Stoddard interweaves passages establishing the pernicious influence of widely held beliefs about the sanctity of women's private lives that are not only incommensurate with female experience but that can have the effect of preventing women from acknowledging the authority of their own histories. The first of these takes the form of an exchange between Eliza Sinclair and Helen Hobson in which both appear to understand that female history is a private matter: "Mrs. Hobson never told me her history; I never asked it. Having no wish to reveal mine, why should I demand hers?" (288). Mr. Binks's words succeed this exchange with a disclosure that once again associates female sickness with monetary value while effectively defining the cultural vacuum that surrounds the experiences of women who deviate from the mainstream. "I am an inquisitive man," he avers, "but I never asked Mrs. Hobson a question, and I am never going to. She is as good as gold, and as sick as Lazarus" (289). Mrs. Hobson herself then observes the cultural outcome of such punctilious determination not to violate female privacy when she reports Binks's often-repeated pronouncement that "one half of the world does not know how the other half lives" (289). Once again, the story asks readers to think about the internal contradictions that prevent a woman like Helen Hobson from realizing

that her own refusal to communicate details of her personal history makes her complicit in the social denial of female embodiment that she so deplores.

Like "Collected," **"Miss Grief"** quickly conveys the impression that culturally based assumptions that bear directly on female embodiment and literary circulation obscure the actual composition of women's lives, only Woolson makes an even more pronounced effort to show that male assumptions about women diminish the visibility of all women, not merely the "eccentric" or the marginal. To achieve this end, Woolson sets her work in cosmopolitan Rome, uniting two divergent poles of the female social spectrum by introducing the drab Miss Moncrief and the sparkling Isabel Abercrombie in the same paragraph. Doing so juxtaposes the "eccentric and unconventional," "shabby, unattractive, and more than middle-aged" Moncrief with the socially brilliant, youthful, and much-sought-after future wife of the narrator (249, 251). Upon first mention, Miss Moncrief is identified not by the visiting card conventionally left by members of polite society but by an orally transmitted name that is garbled as it circulates from the manservant to the narrator. That the female writer's name is altered from Moncrief to "Grief" conveys the grief encountered by female writers who seek a clear viewing of their work. However, the narrator applies the mispronounced name to himself only, waggishly punning that he shall continue to "not be at home" to grief "if she continues to call" (249). Such quick translation into the interior domain of male thought is consistent with the story's opening line, in which the narrator readily admits "that I am conceited" and shortly thereafter acknowledges that he is "amiably obedient to all the rules and requirements of 'society'" (248).

Woolson makes her point that male authors like her narrator introduce into their writing false assumptions about female behavior by showing that this particular author is unable to continue composing once he actually encounters a woman whose behavior is inconsistent with the pattern that guides his thoughts. This violation of supposed norms takes place when Isabel Abercrombie, the woman he is courting, does not act as he thinks she should. "I had constructed a careful theory of the young woman's characteristics in my own mind, and she had lived up to it delightfully until the previous evening, when with one word she had blown it to atoms and taken flight, leaving me standing, as it were, on a desolate shore, with nothing but a handful of mistaken inductions wherewith to console myself. I could not write, and so I took up a French novel (I modeled myself a little after Balzac)" (250).

In a manner consistent with both the Stoddard and the Woolson stories, the offending conduct is not described. Similarly, the ultimate concealment of Miss Moncrief's writing and Alicia Raymond's novel will further demonstrate that only socially acceptable forms of female embodiment make their way onto the printed page. In this context, the narrator's recourse to Balzac functions to expose both the narrowness of his own conception of female behavior and the precarious foundations of any exclusively male effort to depict female experience realistically. Given the narrator's deliberate modeling of himself on Balzac, we can also see embedded in this passage Woolson's implied assertion that the circulation of male-authored texts reinforces notions of female embodiment badly in need of the corrective balance offered by a female point of view. We may also detect here a parallel with Stoddard's allusion to Balzac, wherein she also uses the influential male writer to illuminate the way literary representation can negatively inform social expectation.

What is required to balance the influence of Balzac, however, is not merely the presence of female writers; rather, Woolson and Stoddard appear to share a desire for women writers who enjoy the consultative power of a Balzac. For this reason, the problem at the heart of both stories turns on the ability of a female writer who possesses original literary power to achieve the circulation essential to becoming as influential as a major male writer. For Miss Moncrief, the path to circulation begins with an established male writer whose work she respects. "I have read every word you have written," she eventually declares to the narrator upon meeting him after seven failed attempts (252). She then describes a particular passage within the narrator's work that "was secretly [his] favorite," despite the fact that an otherwise adoring public "had never noticed the higher purpose of this little shaft, aimed not at the balconies and lighted windows of society, but straight up toward the distant stars." In response, the narrator admits that "she had understood me—understood me almost better than I had understood myself." Following this exchange, the narrator grudgingly acknowledges, "You have bestowed so much of your kind attention upon me that I feel your debtor" (253). He then acts to remove the debt by offering his services, indicating an effort at reciprocity through his willingness to assist with the contents of a box he knows contains a manuscript: "It may be there is something I can do for you—connected possibly with that little box." At this point, Miss Moncrief responds with words that undermine the narrator's proposal of a materially based reciprocal exchange by introducing the possibility of an alternative, non-material economy. Instead of graciously accepting whatever limited assistance he can provide, she acknowledges that while his opinion may be of little value "in a business way," it might nonetheless "be—an assistance personally."[8] These words bring into Woolson's text a set of values that oppose the leveling force of marketplace reciprocity with the singularity of a personal gesture.

By posing the possibility that personal response may provide a preferred alternative to commercial publication, Woolson introduces the discourse of gift exchange that brings with it an alternative form of circulation. According to the definition of gift Lewis Hyde has provided in *The Gift,* an essential feature of gift exchange is the opening of a special relation with the world and others achieved fully through circulation, so that the gift is "consumed" through an exchange process not dependent on abstract value (9).[9] To track this kind of circulation, it is important to shift attention from publication and print distribution to affective response and the establishment of community identity. Godbout's definition of the gift as "any circulation of goods or services with no guarantee of recompense in order to create, nourish, recreate social bonds between people" (20) might usefully be applied to the above circumstance involving Miss Moncrief and the narrator. Woolson's displacement of the impersonal "business" dimension of commercial exchange with Miss Moncrief's desire for something more like understanding, sympathy, or even friendship reflects the extent that the story deliberately examines the power gifts have to create significant social bonds.

However, as Stoddard's and Woolson's stories have raised the issue of authorial influence, we ought to examine the ways in which the circulation of gifts contributes to the establishment of hierarchical relationships. Annette B. Weiner provides just such an analysis by distinguishing between "alienable properties" that may be "exchanged against each other" and "inalienable possessions" that function as "repositories of genealogies and historical events, their unique, subjective identity [giving] them absolute value placing them above the exchangeability of one thing for another" (33). As Weiner makes clear, the category of inalienable possessions is broad, containing language in the form of "myths . . . songs, and the knowledge of dances," as well as material objects like "human bones, sacred stones" and "woven fabrics" (37). Ownership of these inalienable possessions introduces difference into the otherwise reciprocal exchange of gifts by investing certain gifts with a power that radiates from the inalienable possession. In Weiner's words, "the motivation for reciprocity is centered not in the gift per se, but in the authority invested in keeping inalienable possessions" (40). The outcome is a social system within which the ownership of inalienable possessions "makes the authentication of difference rather than the balance of equivalence the fundamental feature of exchange." Within such a system, the distribution of gifts may serve to affirm the superior authority of one giver despite the superficial appearance of equivalence. If, as Hyde has argued, talent and inspiration are gifts just as the ability fully to appreciate a work of art is (xi-xii), then Miss Moncrief's perception of the narrator's instance of isolated brilliance initiates an exchange of gifts that may coincidentally reveal a fundamental difference based on authorial power that here acts as an inalienable possession. As Mary Louise Kete has argued in *Sentimental Collaborations,* for nineteenth-century Americans "the inalienable possession of a self fundamental to liberalism is produced through a free circulation of gifts of the self" (53). In the case of Stoddard and Woolson, the inalienable possession is the self's power to produce literature that sets the gifts of certain writers apart from the products of lesser talents.

To assess fully the presence or absence of such a distinction and its bearing on Miss Moncrief's status as a writer capable of literary influence, we need to examine the narrator's response to the manuscripts she gives him. Much to his surprise, the narrator finds that he is unable to put down the drama Miss Moncrief hands him at the conclusion of their first meeting. He stays up half the night reading it, and Woolson's words clearly convey his astonishment: "No one could have been more surprised than I was to find myself thus enthusiastic" (256). When Miss Moncrief returns to his rooms to hear his judgment, he provides additional language that not only expresses his appreciation for her gift but also acknowledges that she possesses ability beyond his own. "It seemed so pitiful that she should be trembling there before me—a woman who possessed the divine spark of genius, which I was by no means sure (in spite of my success) had been granted to me—that I felt as if I ought to go down on my knees before her, and entreat her to take her proper place of supremacy at once" (257).

Up to this point, the narrator has merely reciprocated by reading her work after having learned that she has read his. The unexpected discovery that hers is the greater talent, however, upsets the system of reciprocity, creating a dilemma for the narrator, who now sees both that Miss Moncrief has the inalienable possession of literary power and that commercial success has not proven his ownership of a similar ability. Despite this discovery, he resists the impulse to acknowledge her superiority openly and, instead, denies the difference by attempting the impossible task of employing his inferior talent to make her work commercially palatable. This effort is, of course, doomed from the beginning, leaving the frustrated narrator to admit, "I began; and utterly failed" (264).

Woolson's decision to focus on the narrator's recognition of Miss Moncrief's talent, in combination with his inability to give the work a form suitable for publication, establishes one of the central economic conflicts that ultimately impede the public circulation of works by nonconforming women. To understand this conflict, it is important to look at the way Miss Moncrief ceases to have an interest in the publication of her work and seems content to die happy in the knowledge that her

gift has been received by at least one writer whose ability she respects. This difference in point of view becomes evident after the narrator falsely informs the dying Miss Moncrief that he has found a publisher for her drama (266). He assumes that lying to her about publication will make her happy, but the text does not support such a conclusion. Miss Moncrief does admit that she had "never known what it was . . . to be fully happy until now," but she makes this admission *after* the narrator has told her a story (267). At the moment she first hears his lie that her drama has been accepted, her response to the narrator is, "Tell me." He then fulfills her wish with "a romance invented for the occasion," one with which he readily admits "none of [his] published sketches could compare." In his own mind, he acknowledges that the telling of this lie "will stand among my few good deeds . . . at the judgment seat." What Woolson seems to be showing here is that Miss Moncrief is grateful for the story the narrator has spun, for the return of the gift of story, rather than for the news of publication. Had publication been her aim, she would surely have urged the publication of her other manuscripts, but this she does not do. Instead, she designates the narrator as executor for one work only, her drama; her other manuscripts, which she describes as her "poor dead children," are, in her words, to be buried with her, "unread, as I have been" (268). This final statement conveys Miss Moncrief's understanding that the real story of her life has never been read and that the revisions she knows to have been undertaken by the narrator have at least partially erased the distinctive features of her life. She knows, in other words, that beyond helping the narrator tell a better story than anything he has previously published, her life has failed to enter circulation and become part of the official record of her culture. Equally important, her description of her manuscripts as "dead children" indicates her awareness that her flesh-and-blood existence is intimately linked to the successful circulation of her art.

In "Collected," the positive health benefits that potentially follow from circulation do not register in the author, Alicia Raymond, who has died before the story begins, but rather in Eliza, the person who receives from Helen the gift of Alicia's diary. Following her initial reading of Alicia's diary, Eliza ponders the possibility that reading the work has placed her in contact with forces capable of improving her health: "Maybe I am sent here to be aided by her," she wonders out loud to Helen (296). Helen's response seems to confirm the power Eliza has detected: "'Be then,' she exclaimed, 'my atonement,'" as if Eliza's reception of the gift has provided the proper channel for a force that Helen has been unable to accommodate. If this is the case, both women are shown to benefit either physically or spiritually from the continued circulation of the diary. One question, then, that the Stoddard and Woolson texts both pose is whether the immediate gratification experienced by the writer, or the long-term benefits to readers that come through circulation within a restricted community of able readers, actually provides an affirmation of authorial power sufficient to justify a lifetime of public obscurity. The physical and emotional suffering so apparent in the female authors at the centers of these stories necessarily vexes any answering of this question.

Stoddard's presentation of a gift-based distribution system does, however, provide evidence of some immediate benefit to readers, though any ultimate assessment of the system must be based on the degree to which the distinctive force of the author begins to influence public culture. As Ellen Weinauer astutely observes in her analysis of "Collected by a Valetudinarian," Stoddard situates literary circulation within a gift economy constituted by "an extended, affectively-connected, mixed gender family" made up of Helen, Eliza, Alicia's brother, and his bride-to-be, Julia (168). What is more, Stoddard appears interested in providing a set of gifts uniquely suited to cultural circulation. The first and most prominent gift is the house where Alicia Raymond and her brother lived for six years. Significantly, the house is located on "Bront's Point" (293), suggesting a link to the Brontë family. When we learn that the house was given to Helen (290), that it is the house where Alicia's mother was born (292, 293), and that Helen would like Eliza to assess the value of the manuscripts the house contains (295), we recognize the basic features of a gift economy with potential public appeal. We also see that the house metonymically and materially links Alicia's manuscripts at the same time that it provides a matrilineal line of descent that might prove valuable in defining a literary history patterned on the Brontë family. Accordingly, the house acquires significance as the locus within which Alicia's talent serves as the inalienable possession that infuses her multiple manuscripts with a potency like that which Helen has earlier attached to "a scrap of [Charlotte Brontë's] handwriting" (290).

The significance of Charlotte Brontë, both as a female writer and as the emblem of female literary history, has already been established by the time the circuit of gift exchange that involves the house and manuscripts enters the story. At the time Alicia Raymond is first mentioned, Helen immediately compares her artistic struggle with that of Charlotte Brontë, giving special emphasis to the way the entire family, including both parents, shared hardships prior to any public recognition of literary greatness (289-90). In making these associations, Helen appears to be reflecting on her own blood relation to Alicia, who was her cousin. It is also at this moment in the text that Helen announces her possession of "a scrap of [Charlotte Brontë's] handwriting," thereby introducing into the text the circulation of gifts within an economy founded on the inalienable possession of

literary ability. Helen's observation that "Alicia discerned a world of beauty and truth that made an everlasting happiness for her great soul, as did Charlotte Brontë" (290) shows that in her mind the two families possess a common history and that perhaps her own life might be touched by a like greatness. With clear signs of eagerness, then, both Helen and Eliza seek to emulate this sterling example of female artistic achievement. "'Dear Helen,' Eliza queries, 'how shall we idlers be taught this ideal happiness?'" (290). This is the question that immediately precedes the introduction of the primary gifts in Stoddard's story, both of which acquire meaning as part of Helen and Eliza's efforts to embody the truth that guided Alicia Raymond, thus bringing into the story an authoritative precedent for literary embodiment descending not from Balzac but from Brontë.

The movement of the house and the manuscripts from Alicia to Helen to Eliza potentially affirms each woman's inclusion within an expanding female group whose identity springs from recognition of the power dispensed by the house and the gifted writer. In this way, material and non-material, house and inspired art, body and mind are fused, the value of the one entering into and informing the other. Such a pairing of binaries indicates the way group identity and the proper management of the gift economy can transform discarded manuscripts into a potent literary corpus capable of bringing hope and health to Eliza and Helen, thus unifying producer and consumer in the manner pointed to by Godbout. Viewed from this perspective, Stoddard's story demonstrates that the proper circulation of texts within a gift economy corresponds significantly with the health of those whose role it is to oversee expanded distribution. In this particular case, the management of Alicia's house—descending at it does from mother to daughter and located on Bront's Point—and the treatment given the manuscripts become important symbolic indexes that register the reverence or lack thereof shown for the female body.

Stoddard presents the challenge circulation poses to Eliza and Helen through the answers Helen provides to Eliza's questions about how the two of them might acquire the "ideal happiness" Alicia discovered (290). Helen's response is both direct and revealing: "As soon as we can be made to believe that what is called material or positive happiness is no more truthful or exact than that named visionary or romantic happiness." Through these words, Helen admits that "we" have more confidence in the happiness rooted in materiality than in that arising from the spirit. This crucial and potentially destructive self-awareness reveals a fundamental dualism at odds with the collapse of binaries so essential to embodiment within a gift economy. It comes as no surprise, then, that immediately following Helen's observation, Eliza steps out of the female circle of perception and describes the picture she imagines the two women present within the gaze of Mr. Binks. "We were a couple of faded, middle-aged women, clad in black garments," she resignedly acknowledges. "Why should such indulge in aspirations for happiness, or the expectation of doing any farther [*sic*] work in this gay world?" In like fashion, Helen describes the house and its surroundings as void of spiritual promise: "[Alicia] gave it to me; the spot, worthless as it is, has chained me; the ground about it is barren; nobody would think of bringing it under cultivation." In what appears to be a last fleeting effort to locate spiritual potential within the house and dispel an entrenched mind-body dualism, Helen proposes that she and Eliza inhabit the home together: "'Suppose, Eliza,'—and Helen brightened at the thought—'that you and I should occupy the house?'" Eliza dismisses this proposal in language that effectively communicates her view that the house has become an empty shell: "But we should have to leave out the genius which has made such an impression upon you, and, I confess, upon me also." These quick exchanges illustrate the extent to which Eliza and Helen—despite their hopes—see the house as utterly vacated by the vitality that once dwelt within. This failure to perceive within the structure any seeds for future growth reflects the extent to which each woman has lost confidence in the generative power of Alicia's art and of her own body, adopting, instead, the male construction that casts them as "faded, middle-aged women" who entertain no "aspirations for happiness." Finally, Eliza's rejection of Helen's offer of joint habitation suggests that for her the weight of individual resignation exceeds her ability to imagine the generative power of collective effort. In this way, the two women fail to meet Helen's challenge to accept the reality of visionary truth that they must embody if they are to promote the further circulation of Alicia's manuscripts.

In the light of this shared resignation, Helen's decision to sell the house comes as no surprise. As she explains to Eliza, "Since you came I have decided to settle my affairs so far as that old place is concerned. When Alicia's papers are looked over and every thing removed I will sell the house. When you leave the town I will go also, for I can no longer endure it" (295). The logic behind Helen's actions suggests that for her, a future in the old house may have been possible if someone capable of comprehending Alicia's writing had been willing to take up residence with her; she needs to know that the house is the locus for significant artistic accomplishment that she has sensed but cannot fully confirm. Following Eliza's refusal, Helen is left with the haunting sense of having had a passing acquaintance with greatness, a sense that she is incapable of translating into the basis for meaningful future action. In terms of the circulation of gifts, the sale of the house in combination with the imperfect union of the two women suggests a failure to discover the potential for cultural reproduction so central to the circulation of gifts. As Weiner has succinctly stated, "The processes of cultural

reproduction involve the heroic ability to reproduce more of one's self or one's group through time by asserting difference while defining an historical past that looks unchanging" (48). By selling the house and failing to embody visionary truth, Eliza and Helen relinquish the difference offered by Alicia's talent and accept, rather, the sameness society imposes on "faded, middle-aged women, clad in black garments" (290). They also fail in their effort to follow the path that Alicia took, the path that Stoddard presents as descending from Brontë rather than Balzac.

In the closing pages, the story provides what might be the purest example of a gift exchange directly affecting Alicia Raymond. Significantly, the event takes place in the pages of Alicia's diary, a work that Buell and Zagarell have described as growing out of Stoddard's own "manuscript journal" (Stoddard, *The Morgesons and Other Writings* 308 n. 8), thus positioning this particular gift exchange in that portion of the story that most nearly approximates the actual author's own life. For this reason, the details of the scene bear close scrutiny as a source of information about Stoddard's personal understanding of the circulation potential inherent in gift exchange. On the second-to-last page of the story, Alicia reads to Julia, her brother Alton's fiancée: "[Julia] clapped her hands at first, then grew silent; as I read on her delicate cheek crimsoned, her eyes blazed, she moved near me, took my hand, and kissed it" (306). After the reading, Julia expresses her astonishment at Alicia's courage in daring to "tell the truth about us women." Along with her surprise at Alicia's courage, however, Julia also expresses her amazement that a woman as reclusive as Alicia could write with such discernment about shared female experience. "I did not know that one could create without experience," she remarks. To which Alicia enigmatically replies, "Nor can one; like Ulysses, I am part of all that I have seen; and much good it has done me, hasn't it?" This reference to Tennyson's Ulysses is followed shortly, in the last diary entry, with words that allude to yet another literary traveler, this time Melville's Queequeg,[10] after whom she patterns her own signature: "Alicia Raymond—her mark."[11] Through this gesture, Stoddard would appear to be conflating the fame of the classic hero with the obscurity of Ishmael's native companion whose language escapes the interpretive powers of the Americans who surround him. Alicia herself appears entirely aware of the fact that while her work possesses power comparable to that of classic literature, it may ultimately fail to enter circulation and to contribute to the life of the culture embodied in its pages. Nevertheless, she does remark in her diary that she is "glad" that Julia now "knows a thought of mine," expressing in these words the momentary happiness that the imparting of her gift has afforded her. In consideration of the fact that Alicia's words take the form of diary entries that expand on Stoddard's own journal, we may conclude that Stoddard has not only established a personal link with Alicia Raymond but also presented through Alicia the difficult authorial challenge of weighing the immediate gratification of limited circulation against the delayed gratification of extended circulation that might follow publication. Helen may well sum up the high stakes at play in such a quandary when she comments on the sort of fame Alicia had so far been denied: "Talk about Chatterton and Keats—if they did not live in their lifetime, they do now, while Alicia's memory only exists in mine and that of her brother" (289).

For both Stoddard and Woolson, the central struggle of the nonconforming female artist lies in balancing contrary requirements: that writing take place outside the demands of social convention while retaining contact with a public readership sufficient to ensure cultural consumption. Weinauer effectively poses Stoddard's authorial predicament, writing that "it is, finally, as much the lack of consumption as consumption itself that threatens the author" (174). However, Weinauer's conclusion that through "Collected" Stoddard's "reworking her own journal and representing it as Alicia's" enables her to circulate "a most 'private' text in a most public forum: *Harper's New Monthly Magazine*" (176), overlooks not only the fate of Alicia's novel but her health as well. Even so, Weinauer's analysis does usefully flesh out authorial alternatives that appear in Stoddard as well as in Woolson. According to Weinauer, "Eliza does not merely 'collect' and preserve the diary: she publishes it, including it in her story" (176). Weinauer further argues that Stoddard's inclusion of her own journal in Alicia's diary blurs "the lines between private and public property" so that when "Alica Raymond makes a gift of her [diary] . . . so too does Stoddard make a gift of herself" (177). What is, perhaps, most interesting is that Weinauer's logic might also be applied to Woolson's story, yielding the conclusion that her narrator acts as Eliza does by incorporating the private writing of Miss Moncrief in his public story. The implication, then, is that like Stoddard, Woolson, too, discovers the means to circulate a private truth within a public medium. Due, however, to the fact that both stories contain literary works that never appear, the circulation Weinauer outlines is incomplete: that is, it fails to embody the female work Stoddard and Woolson describe in their stories.

Trapped by the desire to produce honest accounts of female experience in an era that demanded standardized narratives of women's lives, writers like Stoddard and Woolson chose to write about the inability to embody texts that delivered more of the truth about nonconforming women than print culture would allow. In this regard, "Collected by a Valetudinarian" and **"Miss Grief"** emerge as narratives that not only detail the multiple vexations faced by female writers but also provide accounts of a cultural illness that affected many women. As illness narratives, the texts proceed as if their authors were patients describing the conditions of their enfeeblement, hoping that among their readers will be doctors capable of diagnosing and correcting the problem. Gay Wilentz has written in *Healing Narratives* that through such narratives "it is hoped that something lost, in this case one's health, can be regained through the doctor's interpretation" (16). Indeed, Stoddard's opening lines in "Collected" so closely resemble Wilentz's contemporary phrasing that it is difficult not to read them as an appeal for diagnostic assistance: "Traveling this year in search of something lost, *i.e.,* health . . . I revisited an old village on our sea-board for the first time in many years" (285). Perhaps the primary achievement of these short stories is that through them Stoddard and Woolson provide modern readers with the description of an ailment for which nineteenth-century culture could offer no effectual cure.

Notes

1. "Collected by a Valetudinarian" first appeared in *Harper's New Monthly Magazine* in 1870. All quotations are from Stoddard, "Collected by a Valetudinarian," in *The Morgesons and Other Writings.* "Miss Grief" appeared in 1880 in the short-story collection titled *Rodman the Keeper* (Torsney 70-72). All quotations are from Woolson, *Women Artists, Women Exiles: "Miss Grief" and Other Stories.*

2. Much has been written about Melville's and Hawthorne's struggles to sustain the popular and critical acclaim they received for their early publications. For more on Melville's struggle, see especially "Melville's Misanthropy" in Brown, *Domestic Individualism.* For more on Hawthorne, see Brodhead, *The School of Hawthorne,* particularly "Late Hawthorne, or the Woes of the Immortals."

3. In an 1876 letter to Elizabeth Allen, Stoddard describes the devastating effect poor sales had on her confidence: "No one knows what a literary ambition I had, nor how my failure has broken me" (*The Morgesons and Other Writings* 344). This sentiment is echoed in an 1891 letter to Stedman in which she makes it clear that critical praise is no substitute for the failure to achieve broad public circulation: "The failure of my novels is the 'black drop,' when they are praised, and it chokes me into silence" (*The Morgesons and Other Writings* 337).

4. See also Weinauer 172.

5. For a more detailed discussion of the gift economy and the Dickinson-Jackson correspondence, see my essay "'As if for you to choose—': Conflicting Textual Economies in Dickinson's Correspon-

dence with Helen Hunt Jackson." For a more in-depth discussion of parallels linking Dickinson's correspondence with Higginson to Woolson's "Miss Grief," see the conclusion to my book *Inflections of the Pen: Dash and Voice in Emily Dickinson*.

6. Of the numerous examples from advice literature that blame women for their physical enfeeblement, I will cite two here: William A. Alcott's 1838 book *The Young Wife, or Duties of Woman in the Marriage Relation,* especially his chapter "Domestic Economy" (152-77); Reverend Daniel Wise's 1869 *The Young Lady's Counsellor: Or, Outlines and Illustrations of the Sphere, the Duties, and the Dangers of Young Women,* especially 152-99.

7. Other critics who have pointed out the debilitating influence patriarchal culture has had on female health include Gilbert and Gubar in *Madwoman in the Attic,* Smith-Rosenberg in *Disorderly Conduct,* Ehrenreich and English in *Complaints and Disorders,* and Showalter in *The Female Malady.*

8. Other instances of Miss Moncrief's ambivalent relationship to publication appear on 254, 259, and 263. In each of these passages, an argument can be made that Moncrief actually seeks the publication of her work. My position is that the logic of gift exchange in combination with the undeniable ambiguity of these passages supports the conclusion that she only appears to desire publication in an effort to pacify the narrator.

9. What Hyde means by "consumed" is that the gift "moves from one hand to another with no assurance of anything in return" (9); in this way, the relationship between giver and receiver differs from that of the marketplace, where the giver expects an equivalent return. In the gift economy, the giver surrenders all expectations of a specific return; the transmission of the gift is the consummation beyond which the giver expects nothing. However, as Marcel Mauss has pointed out in his study of the gift, the circulation of gifts within a social system proceeds according to general principles: "In the distinctive sphere of our social life we can never remain at rest. We must always return more than we receive; the return is always bigger and more costly" (63). Given this dynamic of gift exchange, we can observe the movement of the gift that Miss Moncrief has bestowed on the narrator to see if he, indeed, meets and, thus, confirms the demands of the gift-based economy.

10. There is ample evidence to support the likelihood that Stoddard read *Moby-Dick.* As Zagarell points out, Stoddard published "a brief sketch in the Duyckinck brothers' *Literary World* in 1852" ("Profile" 42) within months of the *Literary World*'s "two-part review" of *Moby-Dick,* written by Evert Duyckinck, that caused Melville such distress (Robertson-Lorant 290). That Stoddard was a "distant cousin" of Nathaniel Hawthorne, to whom she sent a complimentary copy of *The Morgesons* ten years later (Zagarell, "Profile" 43), suggests that she was aware of his literary tastes and knew of his friendship with Melville, as well as his support for *Moby-Dick* during the period she wrote for *Literary World.* As an experimenter in stylistics and form herself, Stoddard would almost certainly have read the work that attracted so much attention. The fact that Stoddard's husband, Richard Stoddard, worked for the New York Custom House at the same time Melville did and that he wrote a review of *John Marr and Other Sailors* in 1888 lends further support to the idea that Elizabeth Stoddard was familiar with Melville's published work (Robertson-Lorant 501, 587).

11. The obvious allusion is to the chapter in *Moby-Dick* titled "His Mark." In this chapter, Queequeg signs the ship's articles by making a mark that duplicates a tattoo on his arm. To show Queequeg's mark, Melville included a hand-drawn representation of the tattoo surrounded by Captain Peleg's words, also written by hand: "His Quohog mark" (85). Melville's surrounding of the exotic Queequeg's mark by the hand of an enterprising capitalistic male may have had special resonance for Stoddard's Alicia, who was about to release her manuscripts on a journey of unknown destination while she herself, like Queequeg, was about to set sail on a journey from which she would never return (Stoddard, *The Morgesons and Other Writings* 307). Equally intriguing is the fact that the tattoo forms part of a language imprinted on Queequeg's body which Melville later describes as "a complete theory of the heavens and the earth, and a mystical treatise on the art of attaining truth" (366). This, in combination with the fact that Queequeg remains "a riddle . . . unsolved to the last" (366-67), may have recommended to Stoddard that she use Melville to show that like Queequeg's "treatise on the art of attaining truth," Alicia's "world of beauty and truth" (Stoddard, *The Morgesons and Other Writings* 290) would also fade from the world unread by her contemporaries.

Works Cited

Alcott, William A. *The Young Wife, or Duties of a Woman in the Marriage Relation.* Boston: George W. Light, 1838.

Bakhtin, Mikhail M. *The Dialogic Imagination: Four Essays by M. M. Bakhtin.* Trans. Caryl Emerson and Michael Holquist. Austin: U of Texas P, 1981.

Brodhead, Richard H. *The School of Hawthorne.* New York: Oxford UP, 1986.

Brown, Gillian. *Domestic Individualism: Imagining Self in Nineteenth-Century America.* Berkeley: U of California P, 1990.

Crumbley, Paul. "'As if for you to choose—': Conflicting Textual Economies in Dickinson's Correspondence with Helen Hunt Jackson." *Women's Studies: An Interdisciplinary Journal* 31 (2002): 743-57.

———. *Inflections of the Pen: Dash and Voice in Emily Dickinson.* Lexington: UP of Kentucky, 1997.

Davis, Cynthia J. *Bodily and Narrative Forms: The Influence of Medicine on American Literature, 1845-1915.* Stanford: Stanford UP, 2000.

Dean, Sharon L. *Constance Fenimore Woolson.* Knoxville: U of Tennessee P, 1995.

Dickinson, Emily. *The Letters of Emily Dickinson.* 3 vols. Ed. Thomas H. Johnson and Theodora Ward. Cambridge: Belknap P of Harvard UP, 1958.

———. *The Poems of Emily Dickinson.* 3 vols. Ed. Thomas H. Johnson. Cambridge: Harvard UP, 1951, 1955.

Dixon. Edward H. *Woman and Her Diseases, from the Cradle to the Grave: Adapted Exclusively to Her Instruction in the Physiology of Her System, and All Diseases of Her Critical Periods.* 10th ed. Philadelphia: John E. Potter, 1866.

Ehrenreich, Barbara, and Deirdre English. *Complaints and Disorders: The Sexual Politics of Sickness.* Old Westbury, NY: Feminist P, 1973.

Gilbert, Sandra, and Susan Gubar. *Madwoman in the Attic: The Woman Writer and the Nineteenth-Century Literary Imagination.* New Haven: Yale UP, 1979.

Gilman, Charlotte Perkins. "Why I Wrote the Yellow Wallpaper?" *The Yellow Wallpaper.* Ed. Dale M. Bauer. New York: Bedford, 1988. 348-49.

Godbout, Jacques T. *The World of the Gift.* Trans. Donald Winkler. Montreal: McGill-Queen's UP, 1998.

Herndl, Diane Price. *Invalid Women: Figuring Feminine Illness in American Fiction and Culture, 1840-1940.* Chapel Hill: U of North Carolina P, 1993.

Hyde, Lewis. *The Gift: Imagination and the Erotic Life of Property.* New York: Vintage, 1983.

Jackson, Helen Hunt. *Verses.* Boston: Roberts Brothers, 1875.

Kete, Mary Louise. *Sentimental Collaborations: Mourning and Middle-Class Identity in Nineteenth-Century America.* Durham: Duke UP, 2000.

Mauss, Marcel. *The Gift: Forms and Function of Exchange in Archaic Societies.* Trans. Ian Cunnison. Glencoe: Free P, 1954.

Radinovsky, Lisa. "Against All Odds: Elizabeth Stoddard as Obstructed Creator." *Women, Creators of Culture.* Ed. Ekaterini Georgoudaki and Domna Pastourmatzi. Thessalonika: Hellenic Association of American Studies, 1997.

Robertson-Lorant, Laurie. *Melville: A Biography.* New York: Clarkson Potter, 1996.

Showalter, Elaine. *The Female Malady: Women, Madness, and English Culture, 1830-1980.* New York: Pantheon, 1985.

Smith-Rosenberg, Carroll. "The Female World of Love and Ritual: Relations between Women in Nineteenth-Century America." *Disorderly Conduct: Visions of Gender in Victorian America.* New York: Oxford UP, 1985. 53-76.

Stoddard, Elizabeth. "Collected by a Valetudinarian." *Harper's New Monthly Magazine* Dec. 1870: 96-105.

———. "Collected by a Valetudinarian." *The Morgesons and Other Writings, Published and Unpublished.* Ed. Lawrence Buell and Sandra A. Zagarell. Philadelphia: U of Pennsylvania P, 1984. 285-308.

———. "Journal, 1866." *The Morgesons and Other Writings, Published and Unpublished.* Ed. Lawrence Buell and Sandra A. Zagarell. Philadelphia: U of Pennsylvania P, 1984. 347-58.

Torsney, Cheryl B. *Constance Fenimore Woolson: The Artistry of Grief.* Athens: U of Georgia P, 1989.

Weimer, Joan Myers. Introduction. *Women Artists, Women Exiles: "Miss Grief" and Other Stories.* By Constance Fenimore Woolson. New Brunswick: Rutgers UP, 1988. xi-xlviii.

Weinauer, Ellen. "Alternative Economies: Authorship and Ownership in Elizabeth Stoddard's 'Collected by a Valetudinarian.'" *Studies in American Fiction* 25 (1997): 167-82.

Weiner, Annette B. *Inalienable Possessions: The Paradox of Keeping-While-Giving.* Berkeley: U of California P, 1992.

Wilentz, Gay. *Healing Narratives: Women Writers Curing Cultural Dis-ease.* New Brunswick: Rutgers UP, 2000.

Wise, Daniel. *The Young Lady's Counsellor: Or, Outlines and Illustrations of the Sphere, the Duties, and the Dangers of Young Women.* Cincinnati: Hitchcock and Walden, 1869.

Woolson, Constance Fenimore. *Women Artists, Women Exiles: "Miss Grief" and Other Stories.* Ed. Joan Meyers Weimer. New Brunswick: Rutgers UP, 1988.

Zagarell, Sandra A. "Profile: Elizabeth Drew Barstow Stoddard (1823-1902)." *Legacy* 8.1 (1991): 39-49.

Bertram Wyatt-Brown (essay date 2003)

SOURCE: Wyatt-Brown, Bertram. "Lowering Birds at the Dawn of Modernism: Constance Fenimore Woolson and Kate Chopin." In *Hearts of Darkness: Wellsprings of a Southern Literary Tradition*, pp. 181-208. Baton Rouge: Louisiana State University Press, 2003.

[*In the following essay, Wyatt-Brown discusses the significance of Woolson's and Kate Chopin's writings in the development of Southern literature.*]

> The voice of the sea is seductive, never ceasing, whispering, clamoring, murmuring, inviting the soul to wander in abysses of solitude. . . . A bird with a broken wing was beating the air above, reeling, fluttering, circling disabled down, down to the water.
>
> —Kate Chopin

> Some people think that women are the cause of modernism, whatever that is.
>
> —*New York Evening Sun,* 13 February 1917

In the late-nineteenth-century American South, women writers—not their male colleagues—were the first "moderns" of southern literature.[1] More accurately we might label them transitional romanticists or transitional modernists, for they stood halfway between the old literary ways and the new. At the start, though, a word should be said about the use of "modernism" in this text, as well as the preceding era of a sentimental character. Modernism is a slippery term, as the *New York Evening Sun* journalist suggested in 1917. The same could be said of sentimentalism. Some critics have discovered that the latter, even with its vaunted tone and soft-core sense of reality, has more merit than previously thought—as in Harriet Beecher Stowe's *Uncle Tom's Cabin,* which is seen by some as not mere gush but the powerful controlling mechanism that gives great moral thrust to the anti-slavery message.[2] At the other pole, modernist fiction, fully expressed, would leave no emotion, no sexual desire, no perverse thought, no act of violence, corruption, or betrayal unwritten and unexamined. In the chaos of a war-torn, disillusioned era, modernist writers found themselves clinging to art, not for its own sake but as the sole bearable reality.[3] Even if William Faulkner, of the succeeding generation, did not push these concerns as far as my remarks might suggest, he and the other southern male writers of the 1920s and 1930s did probe deeply into the meaningless, surreal horrors of which human beings are capable. That was a mode not available to writers like Twain, Harris, and Porter.

Those to be explored in this chapter and the next—chiefly Constance Woolson, Kate Chopin, Willa Cather, and Ellen Glasgow—could not completely repudiate the

Victorian culture into which they were born. Grace King of New Orleans, another forerunner of modernism, once had a novel on the Reconstruction era rejected in the 1880s. She had omitted the obligatory sweetheart theme. William Dean Howells, dean of literary conventionality, counseled the inquiring, frustrated Grace King, "Just rip the story open and insert a love story. It is the easiest thing to do in the world. Get a pretty girl and name her Jeanne, that name always takes! Make her fall in love with a Federal officer and your story will be printed at once!" Likewise, the novelist Sarah Dorsey, who belonged to the literary clan of Percys and Ellises of Louisiana and Mississippi, faced the admonitions of her publishers. Upon threat of rejection, she dutifully altered a novel's closure. Perhaps because of the change, *Athalie* (1872) was a financial success. From her plantation, Elkridge, at Lake St. Joseph, Louisiana, she wrote a friend, "The ending was made to please the Publishers who said that there was complaint made against my *endings* as being always too *sad.*" Even E. D. N. Southworth of Virginia, the most popular romantic female novelist of the era, had run into similar problems. She sometimes created flagrantly dissolute female characters who set no moral example for virginal readers.[4]

Valiantly the women writers with whom we are concerned here struggled, with mixed success, to break the mold. To be sure, Freud and Marx had no place in their scheme of things. Kraft-Ebbing and Havelock Ellis did not inhabit their library shelves. Indeed, sex belonged in the domain of the unspoken. That degree of restraint could be interpreted as delicacy, not timidity. Seldom did these writers reveal their inner lives even as they explored in fiction the dark places of the mind. In this authorial troupe reticence reflected their honor-conscious sense of privacy inherited from parents and forbears. It was a most treasured aspect of genteel observance. Nonetheless, these four writers represented a significant advance toward a modernist sensibility. In creating plots, the new breed would not seek to convert the ungodly, conveniently kill off characters with otherwise unacceptable fates, punish adulteresses, and reward saintly heroines with appropriately stalwart life-partners in the manner of Sarah Dorsey or Augusta Evans. In fact, the fin-de-siècle writers in these two chapters ordinarily put aside customary male-female connections. Nor did they consider that the transcendent goal of art was morally to uplift society. Nearly all their work exhibited an almost fatalistic pessimism. Even though they retained more than a touch of romanticism in their work, their questioning of the verities far outdistanced that of their much more sentimental female predecessors.[5] The latter portrayed the downside of feelings as a temporary setback. The mood would eventually pass, or at least the story would end in some sort of unambiguous closure, even if that were death, the final inevitability. The late-nineteenth-century southern women writers mentioned already, and others too numerous to treat here, explored emotional circumstances in many shapes and varying degrees of tenure with subtlety, irony, grace, and originality.[6]

In any event, the inauguration of this literary insurgency preceded the Faulknerian flowering by a generation. The literary historian Carol Manning contends that to use the two world wars as benchmarks for the Southern Renaissance, the long-accepted paradigm, is to distort reality. Also the customary privileging of male over female writers has unjustly bounded the chronology of the southern efflorescence. Yet somehow the notion that the turn-of-the-century women novelists—as a coterie of like-minded intellectuals—were the first to adopt an almost modern sensibility still awaits full recognition in the textbooks and in the general discussion of southern literature.[7]

* * *

With regard to the formation of a large female intellectual community, what united these significant women authors? By no means are we dealing here with a select Concord-like circle of high-minded friends. Carol Manning points out that few if any meeting places existed in the South for women intellectuals. Actually, there were some gatherings of female writers in Virginia, but none achieved the eminence of the salons that Charlotte Lynch Botta and Caroline Sturgis and Maria Weston Chapman organized in ante-bellum New York and Boston. As early as the 1840s, however, in the slave South, Elizabeth DuPuy, later one of the first professional, highly prolific female authors, organized a work-exchanging group of plantation women in Natchez, Mississippi.[8] Southern women relied on the usefulness of relationships, carefully nurtured. They held a deep respect for family and treasured the passing down of wisdom from mother to daughter. The southern daughter, sister, and mother were taught to enjoy experiencing many aspects of life vicariously through the dreams and actions of their fathers, brothers, and sons. Even the most venturesome were not as individualistic as perhaps these southern women writers liked to imagine themselves to be. Northern Civil War families followed a similar pattern. The historian Anne C. Rose observes of Yankee society, "The Civil War inspired a generation caught between sagging faith" and opportunities for "heroic adventure," although "reliance on family" remained vibrant in northern breasts, too. Yet with a strong civil society of associations, clubs, fraternities, and church agencies promoting one noble cause or another, life in the North differed from that in the South in a lesser dependency on kinfolk loyalties.[9]

To make up for the lack of a literary community or a sympathetic social and familial environment, these post-Civil War southern female artists turned their eyes northward and even to foreign parts for inspiration. One reason for this look elsewhere was a dissatisfaction with the politically driven ideologies that the great conflict had aroused and that continued to dominate popular fiction. On the northern side were the romances of Albion Tourgée and John William De Forest. They presented the moral imperatives of abolitionist sentiment, which had little attraction for the southern group. However worthy that cause might have been, the fiction of its adherents seemed polemically designed and artistically deficient, particularly to Constance Woolson, a northern woman writing about the South. Though scarcely a veteran himself, Henry James thought that in the North, at least, grand causes, holy zealotry, and glorious statesmanship held no one in awe or reverence anymore. He expected that the American would become "a more critical person than his complacent and confident grandfather."[10] In any case, these different perspectives fashioned a kind of hybridity, a blurring of the boundary between northern and southern writing. Michael Kreyling points out that in this period Henry Adams, Henry James, and John W. De Forest among other authors composed "significant works in Southern fiction"—James's *The Bostonians,* for instance. Kreyling argues that this time of transition and sectional reconciliation, however costly it was for African American advance, prepared the way for a less parochial national literature.[11] That transformation from old ways of thinking and writing could benefit the southern writers most particularly. It drew them away from the Anglo-provincialism of the Walter Scott and Bulwer-Lytton mode.

Of course, the proponents of the ruling southern paradigm of the Lost Cause had little use for northern abolitionist fiction writers' celebration of racial uplift and emancipation by warfare. Yet they would have agreed with the lament of Reconstruction novelist Albion Tourgée, champion of the freedmen's cause, in 1888: "The man who fights and wins is only common in human esteem. The downfall of empire is always the epoch of romance." As if to prove his point, Alabama romancer Augusta Evans replied to a Confederate widow's complaint about the tragic effect of the war on her life, asking did she really want her dead husband to return to her if it meant depriving him of the "cradling arms of glory" in the battle for "our precious cause?"[12]

Constance Woolson complained to Paul Hamilton Hayne, dean of southern letters, about the sentimental women writers, North or South: "I generally throw half across the room all the new novels of the day." The undiscriminating reader—including her own kinfolk—Woolson grumbled, preferred Evans's *Infelice* to George Eliot's masterpiece, *Middlemarch.* Her New England aunt dismissed Eliot's work as "stupid!" Woolson exploded, "What in the world *can* any cultivated reader see in that mass of words, words, words" that constitutes Evans's *Infelice*?[13] Southern women writers, she thought, "seemed to me exaggerated in style, and too full of a certain spirit, which I can best describe perhaps by saying that their heroes are always [overly] knightly—for the real life of to-day." She might have appreciated Porter's satirical portrait of Major Pendleton Talbot. Before the war, Woolson had conversed endlessly with young southern maidens at a New York City boarding school, and they spoke with simplicity, vivaciousness, and charm. But their gossip did not at all match the starchy and inauthentic dialogue found in Augusta Evans's pious *St. Elmo* (1866) or the 783-page southern gothic *The Household of Bouverie; or, The Elixir of Gold* (1860) by Catherine Ann Warfield of Kentucky.[14]

Instead of using literature as a platform for pushing political and moral ideals, the turn-of-the-century women writers sought to professionalize their craft. As a result, they found an affinity between the ideas and destinies of the South and New England. That discovery helped to bridge the time-honored fault-lines of slavery and secession. The distinctions between the literary North and South were beginning to erode. In fact, all four of the novelists with whom we are concerned in this chapter and the next—Woolson, Chopin, Cather, and Glasgow—felt themselves to be exiles from their place of birth and were therefore disinclined to march under some sectionally-inspired ideological banner. For most of her adult career, Woolson, a New Englander, sojourned in the South and Europe, calling no place home. Chopin had left a border state to spend her life in Louisiana. Cather's family moved from Virginia to the distant Great Plains. Although Glasgow lived for a time in New York, she returned to Richmond but always felt herself an alien in her homeland.

The common situation of exile or dislocation helps to explain the freeing up of these women's minds, the breaking of a stultifying provincialism and local conformity. Yet it also meant alienation from the new environment—a repulsion that sometimes brought on more than tolerable distress. Despite the pain, such a reaction assisted creativity. It offered an agreeable sense of apartness, a satisfaction with the independence of mind and heart that solitude provided instead of servile dependence on the company of others. Emily Toth, Kate Chopin's biographer, for instance, perceptively observes that her novelist's heroines seem most self-possessed when by themselves. In Chopin's story "The Maid of Saint Phillippe," a motherless young woman refuses to accept a most eligible mate because "she has breathed free air and 'was not born to be the mother of slaves.' . . . In the end, she strides toward the rising sun, alone."[15]

Among the women writers, the old communal style of kinship bonding had been severed. Instead they discovered independence of spirit, and they forged new ties,

largely based on gender. That process helped to draw the foursome into a kind of common and disciplined artistic detachment, and in learning self-reliance, they developed a receptivity to an unsentimental, realistic mode. Speaking of Constance Woolson, critic Fred Lewis Pattee argues, "'Realism' had come to her as it had come to Flaubert and the French pioneers, as a personal experience, not as a manner learned from imitation."[16] In the latter part of the nineteenth century, the aspiring writer found realism an almost essential outlook. With regard to sexual and maternal feelings, it should be fair to say that three of these four women yearned little for married life and child-rearing. Instead they preferred that composition should dominate their working lives. Glasgow remarked that "the maternal instinct, sacred or profane, was left out of me by nature when I was designed." Cather pointed out to a reporter, "A writer has to hide and lie and almost steal in order to get time to work in—and peace of mind to work with." At as early as twenty-two, Cather had felt herself "utterly alone upon the icy heights where other beings cannot live." Reclusive, especially at the close of her life, she customarily refused to be interviewed.[17] Only Kate Chopin married and bore children. Yet, as if domesticity interfered too often in her professional pursuit, she achieved her major work after the sudden death of her husband. Like her mother, as Toth observes, Chopin did not remarry but relished the uninterrupted life of the mind that an empty household afforded—with offspring grown and gone.[18]

These women were all outsiders looking in as through a glass barrier at their family heritage, their earlier social surroundings, and their former selves as well as at the world around them. That sort of imaginative exercise, which required a skeptical, questioning persistence, would never have occurred to their romantic female predecessors. Yet that sense of distance and isolation stimulated a search outside familiar boundaries. With a freedom that the antebellum writers, riven by sectional tensions, never enjoyed, post-Civil War northern and southern women writers began to create a new literary community. Most notably, Sarah Orne Jewett, Mary Wilkins Freeman, and Constance Fenimore Woolson, the latter of which is the only writer discussed here to venture South from the North, became personal friends with various southern sisters in the literary profession. Kate Chopin was a particular champion of "Miss Wilkins." Laughingly, she tried to forgive her friend for inspiring mediocre imitators "*ad nauseam.*" Being at least in their day more prominent than the aspiring southern writers, women like Jewett and Freeman exercised considerable influence on their protégées.

Absorbing novels and short stories of northern women authors was a means to stretch a hand of friendship across the postwar sectional divide. The southerners earnestly sought to discover grounds for reconciliation. They did so in a personal way and not by fictionally pairing off hero and heroine of the former warring sections in happy wedlock as Howells had recommended. In addition, these women writers wished to gain national, not just regional, audiences. They, of course, had little choice. The main publishing houses for fiction, female and otherwise, were located in New York, Philadelphia, and Boston, not New Orleans, Charleston, or Richmond. Nonetheless, the more contacts they had outside their region, the more realistic was their goal.

As a partial result of these associations and readings, sensitive southern artists discerned that the real drama did not lie in uncritical restoration of the antebellum ideals nor in the actualities of Yankee industrialization and New South wealth. Rather, through fictional representation, they began to dramatize the lives of those left behind or otherwise severed from the center of things and thought they ought to be explored, celebrated, or rendered tragic. Representations of older people—some sliding toward death—appear more often in their fiction than vigorous youthful folks seeking love and recognition.[19] Such choices had only momentary vogue, however, as male authors gravitated toward themes that involved more passion than reflection, more action in war, politics, and business than contemplation of the plight of a woman ensnared in monotonous domesticity.

Just as late-nineteenth-century southerners were losing their grip on the old values of chivalric honor, highmindedness, kinship loyalties, and Stoic resolve, so too were New Englanders abandoning a heritage of Puritan sanctity and communitarianism. In *Mind and the American Civil War: A Meditation on Lost Causes,* Lewis Simpson observes that southern loss of power as a result of the great contest spelled doom even for some of the victors. A serious erosion of status had been already underway in antebellum New England. Economic and political power was draining out of Boston and Concord and toward New York and the spacious hinterlands beyond. In a sense both sections—at least their rural backlands—shared the common fate of peripheral terrain. In her short fiction Jewett showed how New Englanders were becoming strangers to each other as a once tightly bound social and familial order unraveled. The literary historian John Seelye explains that, for Jewett and later for Edith Wharton, the northeastern section had become "a region of cellar holes and second-growth forests where farms had once stood, its former inhabitants long gone away toward the West, leaving behind elderly people only, waiting to occupy a hard-earned place in the graveyard."[20]

The subjects of northern fin-de-siècle women's fiction may have exercised an influence on similar work in the South. Take, for instance, Mary Wilkins Freeman's classic story "The Village Singer." The tale relates the dis-

placement of the aged but vital Candace Whitcomb in a New England town. She has been the church soloist for forty years but has recently lost her post. That ostensibly trifling mark of local prestige, Freeman narrates, had "been as much to her as Italy was to Napoleon." Yet, "on her island of exile," that is, her house next to the church, "she was still showing fight." With a voice that almost drowns out the meek soloist next door during the congregational hymn-singing, Candace accompanies herself on her own organ. To the distress of the churchgoers, they cannot help but hear Candace at full volume. Though strong-willed to the end, she repents on her deathbed her conduct on Sunday morning a week before. Candace exults, however, that her replacement, the mousey, piping Alma, had "flatted a little" on the last hymn.[21] The old spirit is still aflame, but Freeman sought a larger meaning. New England life outside the urban centers, she implied, no longer had its ancient integrity. In particular, the old—largely poor and uncelebrated—were the losers. Something almost claustrophobic invades Freeman's depictions of crabbed, aging, failed lives. We find similar stories in the southern library of the same period. The novels and stories of Kate Chopin and Ellen Glasgow would deal—famously, in fact—with brave people with still greater problems: lost hopes, broken lives, and a deteriorating social order, only these tales were set in the South.

* * *

Constance Fenimore Woolson (1840-1890), James Fenimore Cooper's great-niece, has been designated by Fred Pattee as "the first Southern writer of the new period."[22] Following that classification, I treat her in greater depth than Chopin, the more familiar author. As a Yankee and only temporary resident in the South, she might be said to represent the crossing-over or merging aspect of the post-Civil War literary landscape. This was an era when southern writers traveled or at least looked hopefully northward for professional inspiration. Sometimes northern women writers discovered like-minded artists in the southern backlands. It is no exaggeration to say that, with her reclusive but highly observant nature, Woolson understood the southern white mentality better than the more sentimental southern women romancers of her time. Personal experience and a great degree of self-knowledge played a part in that understanding. Woolson was herself subject to the same inner doubts, sense of loss, and dislocation that she found in the inhabitants of the Reconstruction South.

Although quite popular in the late 1870s to the 1890s, Woolson has had only a minor revival in recent years. Her reputation benefits from the rediscovery of nineteenth-century women writers in general. In her own day, she became almost an adopted southerner. Woolson published fifteen short stories set in the region and utilized that locale for scenes and references in several of her novels. For instance, her most fully realized book-length fiction, *East Angels,* published to a wide readership in 1886, was set in "Gracias-a-Dios" or St. Augustine, Florida, her favorite spot in America. Margaret Harold, the protagonist, is by no means the self-renouncing heroine that southern writer Augusta Evans so often portrayed. She exclaims, "When have *I* been permitted myself to be disagreeable? When have I ever failed to be kind? I have always repressed myself." At another point she likens herself to a slave: "Oh, to be somewhere . . . anywhere where I can breathe and think as I please—as I really am! Do you want me to die without ever having been myself—my real self—even for one day!"[23]

Nor did Woolson portray the South as a prewar paradise or a romantically decaying country. She recognized the problems of postwar mourning and the former Rebels' sense of meaningless defeat. Sometimes she was overly sympathetic. Her poem "At the Smithy" gives a dramatic but sentimental account of a blacksmith who has lost his sons in the conflict. Hayne spoke of it as unusually "full of '*grit,*' vigor, and almost *manly verve.*"[24] Set in heroic couplets, the poem does not actually deserve such enthusiasm.[25]

While her early stories, like the blacksmith poem, were overburdened with conventional formulas, Woolson moved swiftly away from clichés to take more a cold-eyed inspection of post-Civil War southern society. "Literature," she wrote, "must not refuse to deal with the ugly and the commonplace and even the shockingly unpleasant. It is all in life and therefore not to be avoided."[26] In *East Angels,* Mrs. Thorne, a penurious northern woman stranded in Florida, for instance, has to hide her disgust with southern mean-spiritedness and suspicion in order to support herself and daughter: "I swallowed everything. I even swallowed slavery—I, a New England girl, abolitionist to the core! It was the most heroic thing I ever did in my life." With a remarkable intensity, Mrs. Thorne curses "the idle, unrealizing, contented life of this tiresome, idle coast!"[27] This was not the picture of the sunny South that Henry Flagler would have wanted advertised as he built his luxury hotels at St. Augustine.

As far as Woolson was concerned, both sections, but especially the South, grossly underrated females' capabilities. She wrote her friend Alice, Henry James's neurasthenic sister, that education should be taught equally to both sexes in the same space. It was the only way "to widen the feminine mind. Do not suppose that I think the feminine mind inferior to the masculine. For I do not. But it has been kept back, & enfeebled, & limited, by ages of ignorance & almost servitude."[28]

Such an attitude and clarity of focus enabled Woolson to develop a greater interest in the southern mentalité than any of the other female northern writers. Anne

Rowe, an otherwise discerning critic, however, finds her characters stereotypical. She calls Woolson's approach to southern life sentimental and even mythical about the splendor of antebellum planter culture. Rowe laments the artist's withdrawal from the antislavery spirit of Tourgée's and De Forest's Reconstruction novels.[29] But as an artist, not ideologue, Woolson had reason to flesh out the ambiguities and reject the good-versus-evil representations of the morally inspired writer. A different perspective led her to write of what she saw but did not necessarily admire in her renderings of southern white defeat, descent into poverty, and nostalgia for a past that could never be restored.

Woolson formed her perceptions of this tragic state of southern affairs through her conversations with members of the southern planter class, once proud and wealthy, now bitter and poor. To be sure, she was conservative in opinions about race and other matters. Born in 1840, she was little different from the other women writers mentioned here in failing to meet twenty-first-century standards of equity in relation to African Americans and perhaps other minorities. Nevertheless, out of necessity she had become quite adventurous in the management of her single life. Taking care of an invalid and gloom-tormented mother, she dwelt briefly in various parts of this country and abroad. Like her mother, she had a highly pronounced tendency toward depression.

No less serious a problem was the series of family losses that deeply wounded so sensitive and intellectual a soul. In Woolson's first month of life, three of her sisters died of scarlet fever, plunging the family into extended grief. When Woolson was twelve, an older sister died of tuberculosis, a disease contracted from her husband. Another sister lost her life in childbirth the next year. In 1869, when Woolson was twenty-nine, her father expired. When Alice James lost her father, Woolson commiserated, "A daughter feels [such a loss] . . . more than a son of course, because her life is so limited, so bounded by home life."[30]

Extraordinarily reserved and prudent to a fault, Woolson never married, and her relations with such men as southern writer Paul Hamilton Hayne were confined to mutual intellectual and professional interests.[31] She looked upon matrimony as a form of boredom and torturing dependence, not of mutual love. "If there is anything I dread," she once confessed, "it is a new acquaintance. I evade, and avoid, and back away from everybody." Feeling too inadequate to play the sexual game, she wrote Paul Hayne, "To enjoy society a woman must be either personally attractive, gifted with conversational powers, or else must *think* of herself as one or both, whether she is in reality or not. I do not come under any of those heads. Result, don't care for society at all." When she thought of how much southerners loved to talk and visit, she was reminded of the contrasting nature of her New Hampshire aunts: "silent, reserved, solitary, thin, and a little grim; I am as much like them as the kind of life I lead will allow."[32]

No doubt Woolson's lack of frivolity was in part owing to her chronic melancholy, a malady that affected others in the Woolson line besides her often baleful mother. She once cursed "this deadly enemy of mine [which] creeps in, and once in, he is master." These periods of deep sadness left her "overweighted with a sort of depression that comes unexpectedly, and makes everything black." She had grown up in a household where laughter seldom echoed and smiles were rare. Referring to the gloom that pervaded her family, she wrote, "My grandfather gave up to it and was a dreary useless man; my father battled it all his life."[33] Adding to her wretchedness was an increasing deafness that shut out the sometimes comforting noises of the world, leaving her in empty silence.

From 1873 to 1879, to overcome the succession of ordeals, Constance and her suffering mother, who died in the latter year, moved like nomads through the southern states, living out of trunks and portmanteaux. The pair also traveled throughout Europe, England, and North Africa. Yet all her life Woolson longed to settle in a cottage in Florida. For a time, she made her experiences in the South a prime source of her fiction. Reflecting her own feelings as a struggling female artist in a male world, she fashioned some of her complex female characters as chiefly solitary and romantic—but soon bitterly disillusioned—figures. Often their self-sacrifices, necessitated by social convention and male demand, did not end in typical Victorian uplift. Her many women readers found that twist against fashion dramatic and appealing. To be sure, not all her stories express ambiguity, indeterminacy. Some followed the usual happy post-Civil War formula of the southern belle who proudly rejects, then succumbs to the charms of, a handsome Union officer.[34]

"In the Cotton Country" (1876), however, represents a more serious aesthetic turn. In it we find a narrator who, as the intellectual historian Ann Douglas observes, has "almost an uncontrollable need to . . . get at some stifled part of herself, mysteriously locked in" another woman's travails. This troubled quest makes her "capable not only of pain but of creativity." The epigraphs opening **"In the Cotton Country"** consist of verses by Paul Hamilton Hayne and Henry Timrod. They quote hymns of exaltation for the Carolina landscape. Woolson's intention was to contrast the subsequent story of death and wretchedness with the smiling poems. It would seem that William Faulkner was not the first to use the decaying southern plantation manor to symbolize the South's postwar downslide into moral decay and impoverishment. Poe, of course, had used the image for

different purposes—to symbolize the dissolution of an anguished mind, for instance, in "The Fall of the House of Usher." Others, like John Pendleton Kennedy and William Gilmore Simms, exploited the decrepit mansion to underline the passing of an old aristocracy.[35] Woolson, however, depicted a very real situation—the downfall of once prominent families in the vortex of war and violence—almost modernistic in its detail and existential depth. In the story, the South Carolina residence—a "very plain abode" rather than the grand mansion that occupies most romances—"seemed to have fallen to the hands of Giant Despair. 'Forlorn' was written over its lintels, and 'without hope' along its low roof-edge."[36] The family house had been razed by Yankee troops. The former residents were reduced to living in the overseer's lodging, a not uncommon situation in actual fact.

The story creates a desolate but not a gothic atmosphere. The mood is heightened by the unreliability of the narrator, a northern woman whose depressive nature is severe enough to seem a snake-pit of the soul. Like Woolson herself, the protagonist has been wandering through the defeated South as a "solitary pedestrian." Lacking a home of her own, the lonely narrator pursues a flock of crows, an image often adopted to symbolize the depressive condition. "The crows at home," Woolson has the speaker sigh nostalgically, "—that would be something worth seeing."[37] The southern creatures magically lead the northern visitor, a fruitless seeker of contentment in her own life, toward the ravaged house and its grieving, embittered occupant.

The use of this powerful imagery to signify the desperation of a tortured soul might be said to link the past romanticisms of Poe's "Raven" and Chapman's "War Eagle" to similar and equally compelling winged representations in the literature of Woolson's time and beyond it into modern letters. Two quick examples may serve to reveal the connection. In the closing lines of *The Awakening* (1899), Kate Chopin invokes a similar metaphor, as quoted in the epigraph opening this chapter. A bird with a broken wing falls into the sea as Edna Pontellier prepares to drown herself. In the mid-twentieth century the Virginian William Styron also made use of the feathered harbinger. Confined to walking the earth, clucking, flightless birds appear to Peyton Loftis in her last psychotic fantasy in *Lie Down in Darkness* as she moves toward the open window of a deserted warehouse in Harlem: "I turn in the room and see them come across the tiles, dimly prancing, fluffing up their wings, I think: my poor flightless birds, have you suffered without soaring on this earth? Come then and fly." The distracted Peyton imagines the creatures miraculously taking wing as she leaps in her own doomed flight.[38]

To return to the Woolson story, the unforgiving widow, the head of her household, has good reason for anger and grief. Despite an initial reluctance, she tells her intrusive guest a tale of heartache and death. The Clayton Cotesworths, her once proud and wealthy family, lost all their men in distant battle and local skirmish. The survivors had been nearly overrun by a slave uprising late in the war. These are not presented as heroic moments. Rather, they are treated as events that might occur in any war. Gray-haired and gaunt, the widow is described as looking twice her youthful age. The foolish rush of the widow's half-mad father had earlier prompted approaching Union troops to cut him down in a fusillade. A lonely survivor with a quiet, solitary boy—her orphaned nephew—to raise, the widow mourns her fate. In the closing lines of the story, she warns the narrator, "Let us alone; we will watch the old life out with her [the South], and when her new dawning comes, we shall have joined our dead, and all of us, our errors, our sins, and our sufferings will be forgotten."[39]

In Woolson's narrative, dreams of a New South do not arise. Referring to **"In the Cotton Country,"** she reported, "I have written stories of imagination, but this is a story of fact. It is true, every word of it, save the names given." The dull grayness of a decaying house and an unmarked grave symbolize Confederate defeat. But the narrator, who represents the triumphant North, offers no contrasting signal of happiness. She may think of herself as a "Sister of Charity" laden with "balm and wine and oil for those who suffer," but actually she has extracted from the old woman her tragic story because she compulsively seeks out others even more miserable and solitary than she is herself.[40] The literary critic Joan Weimer, who is most perceptive about **"In the Cotton Country,"** proposes that Woolson's "narrator finds only confirmation of her unstated beliefs that human connection cannot last but can only betray, and that the best protection against such loss is accepting homelessness and habitual solitude."[41] The Edwardian novelist E. M. Forster would make primary in his fiction a sense of the need for human connection. Woolson, though, saw little possibility for fulfillment of that ideal. She was always an exile, an isolate.

One reason that she found the Florida landscape so compelling a subject to write about was her recognition of its compatibility with her own solitary spirit. The swamps that she describes in *East Angels* and in the torturous story **"The South Devil"** are not so much gothic exaggerations as genuine descriptions of the fetid mass of tropical terrors that her characters pass through. She was gifted in natural descriptions; she wrote what she saw. William Dean Howells publicly thought otherwise, but Woolson rejoined, "Mr Howells is mistaken in thinking the situation fantastic [in *Castle Nowhere*]; the islands, the fogs, the false lights, the wreckers, the Mormons are all exactly from *real life,* true descriptions."[42] Even her positive word-paintings capture the spirit of

the sight, such as her passage about the St. Johns river in Florida, "where palms stand along the shores in groups, outlined against the sky, which has a softness unknown in the North." The Florida pine barrens were not for her: "dull, desolate expanses, without beauty or use."[43]

Woolson was equally at home with the political conflicts of the day. She did not translate them into moral lessons in the manner of Tourgée but explored them with almost a scientific detachment. In **"King David,"** another piece of short fiction about the South, she grasps the tragic degeneration in the late Reconstruction years of carpetbaggers' dreams of racial peace and African American uplift. The story involves the moral collapse of an abolitionist's grammar school for the freed people at a hamlet ironically renamed by the former slaves as Jubilee. The community moves from idealistic promise to disillusionment on all sides. The deterioration has been engineered by planter hostility to black independence. Yet more than so easy an explanation of failure is involved. **"King David"** is basically an allegory of the death of New England ideals. It also offers an implied criticism of the new era in which a cynically Yankee-like "New South" materialism is beginning to flourish. The narrator explains that in their naïveté most of the field-hands are easily fooled in that remote backwater. Yet under the guidance of the New England teacher, they for a time have been successfully striving to create a better life.

The white abolitionist teacher at Jubilee is David King. The name underscores the story's allegorical character. By setting a stern but saintly example, the missionary has guarded his pupils and parents from the postwar chaos of hard drinking and random violence. A rascally northerner, though, brings to the sleepy community new temptations that will crush all advances for the simple freed people. He opens a store to sell liquor to the men and "trashy finery" to the gullible young girls. "The women of Jubilee," Woolson writes, "more faithful than the men, still sent their children to [David King's] school; but they did it with discouraged hearts, poor things! Often now they were seen with bandaged heads and bruised bodies, the result of drunken blows from husband or brother."[44]

The local whites blame the freed people's dissolute behavior on the dedicated abolitionist schoolmaster, not the storekeeper and his array of consumer goods. In a confrontation between the two northern whites, the freed people side with the owner of the store. Sadly David King realizes that "they had taught him a great lesson, the lesson of a failure." Only one black woman stands in the road at his departure. She hands him some flowers. Momentarily he is touched but quickly sees that she is "unmoved" and motivated simply by curiosity at his leaving. When he returns to his Yankee home, the villagers gossip about how he had abruptly returned and taken up the duties of running the district school. "'Has he now?' they say. 'Didn't find the blacks what he expected, I guess.'" They are no more sympathetic than the southerners, black and white, whom he had left in Jubilee.[45]

While Woolson's sympathies lay with the white missionary teacher, she recognized that instruction of a people beset by poverty, narrow agrarian horizons, recent bondage, and unremitting white vigilance and terrorizing was a daunting venture. Moreover, as the narrator makes clear, the laborers prefer a teacher of their own race. That fact David King finally has to admit to himself. The story remains a telling commentary on the clash between some age-old sectional ideals—a rigid code of chivalry and race subordination on the one hand, and a well-meaning but uncomprehending Yankee utopian principle on the other. Union victory, Woolson implied, could not overcome the tragic weight of racial traditions of inequity and oppression. The victors, she avers, brought to the South not only a reforming spirit but also a sinister consumer mentality. The tale further illustrates her capacity to render irony. Woolson recognized that "the mind dreams; life mocks the dream," in the words of an observant critic.[46] Certainly that was David King's fate.

Although Woolson admired some aspects of southern custom and life—even at times its wildness—she found the people provincial, indolent, and meanspirited.[47] Like the Cotesworth widow, too many of them were immersed in the past and unable to deal successfully with the present. Woolson compared her own New England heritage very critically to the white southerners' insistence on form and appearance over substance and reality. Perhaps she was expressing something of Yankee self-righteousness, but not without seeing through its own demise in a New England whose rural young people were heading west or to urban centers. In her novel *For the Major,* for instance, she deals effectively with the immaturity and empty-headedness of southern women, whose men like them that way. But she creates a situation more complex than that. Woolson indicates that the men are bereft, too. They are unable to revitalize their war-ravaged community and live too much on memories of happy times long vanished. An old carriage symbolizes the deterioration of Far Edgerley, the low-country settlement. The Carroll family, whose members own the broken-down vehicle, do not even have mules, much less horses, to pull it. Since the Carrolls "lived all the year round now upon one of their sea islands, whose only road through the waste of old cotton fields was most of the time overflowed, they had nothing to draw it upon."[48]

Woolson captures in this and other works a mood that was very prevalent in the defeated South—despite the almost frenzied weaving of Lost Cause tapestries.[49] With subtlety and keen precision, the short-fiction writer undermined the sentimental forms and showed how inauthentic the stereotypes were. In her stories, the southern gentleman can accept only a woman who matches the youthful innocence and purity of the stylized belle. A full-fledged woman with intellect and opinions would be too much for him to handle. Yet ultimately Woolson's women submit to the demands that the world imposes on their sex—but not without recognizing and inwardly lamenting the high price paid for being unfree, never true to themselves.[50] Her own sense of displacement and loss was acute. As the critic Joan Weimer puts it, like many of her female characters, Woolson remained throughout her life a perpetual exile.[51]

Unfortunately, the native New Englander's self-esteem was insufficient to sustain her. In 1894, ill from both typhoid and influenza, she suffered from a particularly severe attack of dejection. Cold weather and lack of sun had a severe effect on her—a problem associated with chronic depression. She once wrote Samuel Mather, a Cleveland, Ohio, relation, "Let the air grow really cold," as it was in the fall, 1894, "and down I go towards the gates of death."[52] She killed herself by leaping from the balcony of her Venetian villa.[53] Shrinking from the stigma attached to suicide, Woolson's relations insisted that delirium from disease provoked her to swoon and fall. She had not merely dropped, however, but had jumped from the height. Upon hearing the news, Henry James, with whom Woolson had possibly fallen vainly in love, was horrified, mystified, and guilt-ridden. At once he wrote his friend Francis Boott, "Pitiful victim of chronic melancholy as she was (so that half one's friendship for her was always anxiety), nothing is more possible than that, in illness, this obsession should abruptly have deepened into suicidal mania."[54] Later, he wrote his brother William, "My own belief is that she had been on the very verge of suicide years ago." Had it not been for a few important friendships, he guessed, she would not have lived as long as she did. But for all his speculations, he knew that his rejection of her love for him played a part.[55] Every year, Henry James visited her grave and, as an epitaph perhaps, wrote the mordant short story "The Beast in the Jungle," with its melancholy, sexless, semi-autobiographical hero John Marcher.[56]

For good reason, then, Woolson, single and unfulfilled in her own sexual longings, chose for a time the defeated South for her settings—a preference over her prospering northern homeland. Southern destiny matched her own foreboding feelings of alienation and isolation. She did not end her own life out of a loss of creative energy or worries about her place in the profession of writing. Rather she fell victim to a neurological and an emotional disease that, when under control, had stimulated her extraordinary imaginative gifts.[57]

* * *

Unlike Woolson, Kate Chopin (1850-1904) moved into the lower South not from New England but from Missouri, where North and South had fiercely clashed for dominance in the great civil conflict of her young life. That migration, as we shall also see in the case of Willa Cather, deeply affected Chopin's art even more than Woolson's sojourn in the Southeast. Yet both shared the fate of many artists—melancholia and a close acquaintance with death. Chopin's father, Thomas O'Flaherty, a prominent St. Louis, Missouri, commission merchant, died in a train accident on All Saints' Day, 1855. His daughter was only five at the time she went with the family to the Catholic cathedral for his funeral. The event drew her aristocratic and devout mother closer to the daughter who had so admired and loved her father. A Chopin biographer comments, "In the silence of deep distress in the mother's heart and strange wonder in the child's, a sympathy awoke that never ceased and never grew less while the mother lived."[58]

The understanding of others' pain is a noteworthy and poignant characteristic of Chopin's fiction. That gift for empathy may well have grown from her childhood wrestling with loss and sorrow and their reconciliation through the means of love. Further deepening the grief of the household was the death of Kate's younger sister when Kate was only five or six. The loss was bound to have a serious emotional impact (though her biographers make little of it). In addition, Kate was only twelve when her Rebel brother died of typhoid in a Yankee prison camp, a third loss that she found "crushing." For several years she refused to leave home, did not attend school, read romances voraciously in the attic, and composed poems and essays on the theme of sudden and early mortality. After Thomas O'Flaherty's death, the house was always a place of "subdued sadness."[59]

After her emergence from that period of intense grief, Chopin fell into episodes of despair only occasionally. The incidents did not seem to interrupt her work or even last very long. It seems significant, however, that her most famous work, *The Awakening,* was written after the loss of her husband. Given her artistic resilience after this blow, one might speculate that her disciplined effort of creation acted in some way as a restorative. We cannot know for certain. Professional writer as she was—but also southern in her self-restraint—she was extremely taciturn about her innermost feelings. Chopin admitted that she "would never be confidential except for the purpose of misleading."[60]

To a remarkable degree, the record of Kate Chopin's losses and sufferings had a compensatory effect. The Louisiana writer developed a sympathy for the displaced in that society—working-class Creoles and African American women. In her short stories, she treats them without sentimentality. The male characters are often handsome but also violent and abusive. Armand Aubigny, Désirée's plantation-owner husband in the grim, interracial tale "Désirée's Baby," presents a salient example. The story concerns something seldom talked about in the nineteenth century—the verbal and emotional abuse toward women of which domineering and unloving men are capable. It also treats in fresh manner the inhumanity of racial prejudice. The brief, understated story tells of how Désirée, a beautiful child-bride of unknown parentage, gives birth to a baby—a firstborn male—to the vast pleasure, initially, of Armand. By the time the infant reaches three months, however, the child shows distinctly Negroid features. Armand, whom Désirée worships, turns viciously against mother and son. Others in the household and neighborhood follow his venomous example. Shorn of all support and distraught over Armand's smoldering hatred, Désirée walks fatally into the waters of the bayou, holding her infant in her arms.

To destroy all memory associated with the disgraced wife, the proud plantation owner has a bonfire made of the things she has loved. Then, as the flames burn fiercely, Armand discovers a hidden note, not from Désirée, but an old letter from his mother to her husband. The last lines read, "I thank the good God for having so arranged our lives that our dear Armand will never know that his mother, who adores him, belongs to the race that is cursed with the brand of slavery."[61] Fashioned in the style of Guy de Maupassant, the few pages of text became a professional success. The story opened the author to the magazines and publishing houses of the North.[62] Yet like other unconventional southern women writers of her time, Kate Chopin had to defy such editorial guardians of the genteel tradition as Richard Watson Gilder in New York. Seeking acceptance in the greater publishing world meant compromises with her own art. Intimidated, she destroyed one novel and several short stories. The texts presumably violated the code of feminine delicacy.[63]

Nevertheless, Chopin stayed the course reasonably well. While Woolson's male figures seemed at times to border on stock characters, the same could by no means be said of Chopin's. The Creoles with whom she populated her tales are on the whole a little slow in the head. Yet they may be kind—for instance, the nineteen-year-old Gilma Germain in "Dead Man's Shoes." By and large the black women in her stories are powerful Dilsey-like figures, deftly rendered. Perhaps influenced by Mary Freeman's work, she also wrote movingly about lone women. One such story, "The White Eagle," was written after she had suffered several deaths of those close to her and following the controversial reception of *The Awakening.* It is about a young girl whose only companion is a cast-iron bird with a knowing, almost human expression. Even after the protagonist has lost all her property, her youth, and her wealthy friends, the eagle inhabits a corner of her decrepit single room. After her death, the bird presides over her grave, still gazing "with an expression which in a human being would pass for wisdom."[64] This bird is not the frightening apparition of Poe's Raven or Woolson's crows but a protective companion. Yet it, too, personifies death and sadness all the same.[65]

Regarding her most famous work, *The Awakening,* Chopin should be remembered for what Cynthia Wolff calls her "ruthless fidelity" in portraying "the disintegration" of the heroine Edna Pontellier's "character."[66] The author helped to change fictional heroines dramatically from the earlier mode of modesty and self-sacrifice for their men. Gustave Flaubert's Emma Bovary had likewise striven in vain rebellion by engaging in adulterous passion. Flaubert's masterpiece closes with the agonized deaths of the lovers, who never achieve the romantic passion they anticipated. Such figures, male and female, demonstrated the "dissociation of the artist's imagination from the world about, a disengagement that originated in the fiction-writer's own psychological essence," as Michael Ignatieff observes.[67]

Despite Edna's infidelity, some critics see her as an ennobled figure, made majestic by her death as a form of spiritual liberation. That is a misreading. Nor is Edna, as some claim, a victim of schizophrenia. Her feelings of an inner emptiness spring from a depressive nature, a state of mind that leaves her no peace, no outlet. To be sure, she is more than a bundle of neurotic symptoms. Edna Pontellier is certainly no Madame Bovary except in the most superficial respects—both being unhappy women, resentful of the obtuseness of their husbands. Unlike Emma Bovary, however, Edna Pontellier is not engaged in self-indulgent boredom, shallow-mindedness, or simple lust. Chopin's authorial sentiments about Edna are both positive and negative. Like William Styron was later to be, particularly in *Lie Down in Darkness* and *Sophie's Choice,* Chopin was intrigued and repelled by her main character's condition of melancholia and suicidal inclination.[68] Flaubert was much more outspoken than Chopin in linking his writing to his own depressive tendency. The melancholy bachelor, for instance, explained that he found in the practice of art a kind of agonized compulsion: "As to my mania for work, I'll compare it to a rash. I keep scratching myself and yelling as I scratch. It's pleasure and torture combined."[69] Chopin may have felt that way but, ladylike, kept her own counsel.

There was an elusiveness in Chopin's fiction. She left it to the reader to divine a character's inner life. The Louisiana writer offered no conveniently unambiguous account, no indisputable portrait of the heroine in *The Awakening.* We do know, however, that Edna Pontellier

has been motherless from an early age, and that her sense of aloneness has not been assuaged by her rather tyrannical and distant father. Like Chopin, who came from Missouri, a state neither quite northern nor fully southern, her heroine Edna is a relative newcomer to the lower South—from Kentucky, far from the Creole society that she finds so estranging. Her Presbyterian upbringing contrasts with the Catholicism surrounding her. Moreover, her husband, Léonce, has no deep feeling for her or perhaps for anyone. We are given these clues about her troubled life, and yet somehow Chopin has Edna remain mysterious. The reader has to witness Edna's seemingly triumphant wading into the enveloping bosom of the sea, not altogether certain that the ending is justified in the narrative itself. That horrifying decision to end life makes clear that this young wife of a prosperous, if diffident and self-absorbed, gentleman sees herself as a meaningless failure. But why? As is the case of other transitional women writers of her generation and very much like Willa Cather in the next, Chopin wants us to supply the meaning ourselves.

In her poignant and doomed flight out of her marital cage, Edna becomes what we might now call a nearly modern woman. She tries an affair with the ambivalent Robert LeBrun that inevitably fades away. Meanwhile, she attempts an independent, artistic life under the tutelage of Mademoiselle Reisz, the imperious and dedicated professional. She finds a motherly figure in Adèle Ratignolle. Edna discovers, however, that their friendship does not fill the emptiness within.[70] Like her infatuation with Robert, all these endeavors to overcome the inner dread come to nothing.

Without career, without roots in the society into which her marriage took her, without an education that might provide a sense of intellectual discipline, and without a circle of like-minded women to give her strength, she cannot master or understand her own feelings. Emancipating death beckons instead. As Kate Chopin divined, perhaps out of her own suffering, suicides like Edna Pontellier, in making the decision to depart life, feel their irresolution, anxiety, and panic disappear. They march out of this world, not exactly with a song in their hearts, but at least with a sense that the excruciating pain of living, which girdles them, will vanish like clouds shrinking in a radiant sun. For too many would-be or actual suicides, including creative writers, death offers a remedy. As the analyst Kay Redfield Jamison reports, self-dissolution seems the "best and final response to bale and weariness."[71]

Regrettably, the ambiguity, irony, and psychological realism in *The Awakening* that we now admire made it very difficult for the Victorian reader to understand. The public was unprepared to approve wholeheartedly so radical an experiment in fiction. Although there were exceptions elsewhere, *The Awakening* was greeted in southern reviewing venues with unanimous scorn and horror. Even the perceptive Willa Cather, a fellow southern novelist, savagely denounced Chopin's greatest work. Perhaps for Cather, herself a woman beset by times of profound depression, the moods and plight of Edna Pontellier were all too familiar—dangerously so. In truculent terms, she condemned the fictional work as a sorry imitation of *Madame Bovary* with a theme both "trite and sordid." Cather interpreted the main character as a self-indulgent, spoiled young matron. Edna, she asserted, was suffocating under the weight of her own dependence on romance. Cather missed entirely Chopin's theme of how a woman, unloved, displaced, and forlorn in an indifferent world, could become a stranger to herself, alien to her own feelings.[72]

The suicidal closure of *The Awakening* utterly baffled and even infuriated its nineteenth-century pre-Freudian readers.[73] Members of the St. Louis Fine Arts Club went so far as to blackball its author. Outwardly Chopin took the rejection she received from every side with a degree of "ironic insouciance," as Edmund Wilson phrased it. "I never dreamed," she later wrote half-facetiously, "of Mrs. Pontellier making such a mess of things and working out her own damnation as she did. If I had had the slightest intimation of such a thing I would have excluded her from the company."[74] It was typical of Chopin's repressiveness to detach herself from her characters, as if someone might suspect that she was represented in her own fiction. After the barrage of criticism, however, she never attempted another major work. She wrote a friend, "I have had a severe spell of illness and am only now looking about and gathering up the scattered threads of a rather monotonous existence."[75] Chopin's masterpiece surely entitles her to be considered more than just a slight forerunner of modernism. She was a major contributor to a necessary transitional movement with its own integrity, one that Ellen Glasgow and Willa Cather carried forward to eminent effect.

Notes

1. Such fin-de-siècle American authors as Theodore Dreiser, Jack London, and Stephen Crane also belonged to this innovative coterie, but they seem to have had little influence on the southern literary scene. I owe this point to Charles Joyner.

2. See Jane Tompkins, *Sensational Designs: The Cultural Work of American Fiction, 1790-1860* (New York: Oxford University Press, 1985), 122-46; David Leverenz, *Manhood and the American Renaissance* (Ithaca, N.Y.: Cornell University Press, 1989), 19-20; Suzanne Clark, *Sentimental Modernism: Women Writers and the Revolution of the Word* (Bloomington: Indiana University Press, 1991), 1-4.

3. See Astradur Eysteinsson, *The Concept of Modernism* (Ithaca, N.Y.: Cornell University Press, 1990), 9.

4. See Susan Coultrap-McQuin, *Doing Literary Business: American Women Writers in the Nineteenth Century* (Chapel Hill: University of North Carolina Press, 1990), 50-78; Sarah A. Dorsey to Edward Lyulph Stanley of Alderley Hall, 8 April 1872, Stanley Family Collection, Ryl. Eng. MS 1094, R 84307, John Rylands University Library of Manchester. See also Bertram Wyatt-Brown, *The House of Percy: Honor, Melancholy, and Imagination in a Southern Family* (New York: Oxford University Press, 1994), 130-2. Howells quoted in Michael Kreyling, *Figures of the Hero in Southern Narrative* (Baton Rouge: Louisiana State University Press, 1987), 78.

5. See, for instance, James Woodress, who considers Willa Cather's later fiction as less affirmatively "Romantic," as he puts it, than her earlier novels. James Woodress, *Willa Cather: A Literary Life* (Lincoln: University of Nebraska Press, 1987), 483.

6. Given more space, I could have chosen a much larger group that would have included Grace King, Ruth McEnery Stuart, Amélie Rives, the poet Charlotte Eliot (T. S. Eliot's mother), Frances Newman, and Mary Johnston. Moreover, there was a whole set of politically minded female writers too. Sarah Barnwell Elliott (1848-1928) was an exceptionally gifted novelist. Her first and bestselling work, *The Felmeres* (1879), dealt realistically with the fall of the Confederacy and its aftermath. Influenced by Constance Woolson, Elliott's fiction treated the state of the post-Civil War South with close attention to unique detail, authentic local dialects, few resorts to sentimental stereotypes, and a muting of moral uplift. See Clara Childs MacKenzie, *Sarah Barnwell Elliott* (Boston: Twayne, 1980), 31-49.

7. Carol S. Manning, "The Real Beginning of the Southern Renaissance," in *The Female Tradition in Southern Literature,* ed. Carol S. Manning (Urbana: University of Illinois Press, 1993), 37-56. As early as 1979 Michael O'Brien had noted the achievements of the fin-de-siècle southern writers, both male and female—Chopin and Joel Chandler Harris, for instance—naming them the true founders of a regional literary efflorescence. See Michael O'Brien, *The Idea of the American South, 1920-1941* (Baltimore: Johns Hopkins University Press, 1979), 11.

8. The Virginia salons were pointed out to me by Susan Donaldson, 4 July 2001. See also Susan Emiston and Linda D. Cirino, *Literary New York: A History and Guide* (Boston: Houghton Mifflin, 1976), 39, and Wyatt-Brown, *The House of Percy,*

109-10, 123-4, 155-8; Manning, "Real Beginning of the Southern Renaissance," in *The Female Tradition,* ed. Manning, 49.

9. Anne C. Rose, *Victorian America and the Civil War* (New York: Cambridge University Press, 1992), 184.

10. Henry James, *Hawthorne* (New York: Scribners, 1880), 139-40.

11. Michael Kreyling, "Southern Literature: Consensus and Dissensus," *American Literature* 60 (March 1988): 88.

12. Tourgée quoted by David Blight, *Race and Reunion: The Civil War in American Memory* (Cambridge, Mass.: Harvard University Press, 2001), 220. Evans quoted in Elizabeth Moss, *Domestic Novelists in the Old South: Defenders of Southern Culture* (Baton Rouge: Louisiana State University Press, 1992), 193.

13. Mary R. Reichart, *A Web of Relationship: Women in the Short Fiction of Mary Wilkins Freeman* (Jackson: University Press of Mississippi, 1992), 21; Woolson quoted in Anne Goodwyn Jones, *Tomorrow Is Another Day: The Woman Writer in the South, 1859-1936* (Baton Rouge: Louisiana State University Press, 1981), 52. Admittedly, these aspiring women professionals like Woolson were neglecting the quality and subtleties in the sentimentalists' works that only lately have been appreciated. See, for further enlightenment, Susan Donaldson, *Competing Voices: The American Novel, 1865-1914* (New York: Twayne, 1998); David Shi, *Facing Facts: Realism in American Thought and Culture, 1850-1920* (New York: Oxford University Press, 1995); and Alfred Habegger, *Gender, Fantasy, and Realism in American Literature* (New York: Columbia University Press, 1982).

14. Constance Fenimore Woolson to Paul Hamilton Hayne, "All Saints Day" 1875[?], in "Some New Letters of Constance Fenimore Woolson," ed. Jay Hubbell, *New England Quarterly* 14 (December 1941): 725, 726, and 728. Woolson elaborated on the character of the antebellum southern belles she knew at school, noting how a Charlestonian belle, in bed reading, called a maid downstairs to shut a bedroom door that she could easily have shut herself. Slavery induced that sort of thoughtlessness, Woolson concluded in her letter to Hayne (p. 726). See also Wyatt-Brown, *The Literary Percys: Family History, Gender, and the Southern Imagination* (Athens: University of Georgia Press, 1994), 83-6.

15. Emily Toth, "Kate Chopin Thinks Back Through Her Mothers: Three Stories by Kate Chopin," in *Kate Chopin Reconsidered: Beyond the Bayou,* ed.

Lynda S. Boren and Sara de-Saussure Davis (Baton Rouge: Louisiana State University Press, 1992), 17.

16. Fred Lewis Pattee, "Constance Fenimore Woolson and the South," *South Atlantic Quarterly* 38 (April 1939):132.

17. Quoted in L. Brent Bohlke, "Introduction," in *Willa Cather in Person: Interviews, Speeches, and Letters,* ed. Bohlke (Lincoln: University of Nebraska Press, 1986), xxvi, and also in Terry Castle, "Pipe Down Back There!" *London Review of Books,* 14 December 2000, p. 15. See the interesting interpretation of Sharon O'Brien, *Willa Cather: The Emerging Voice* (New York: Oxford University Press, 1987), who claims that the novelist was an active lesbian. See also Katrina Irving, "Displacing Homosexuality: The Use of Ethnicity in Willa Cather's *My Ántonia,*" *Modern Fiction Studies* 36 (Spring 1990), 91-102. Cf. Ellen Glasgow, *The Woman Within: An Autobiography,* ed. Pamela R. Matthews (1954; Charlottesville: University Press of Virginia, 1994), 108. Glasgow attributed her unwillingness to bear children to her growing deafness, an inheritable condition in her view.

18. Toth, "Kate Chopin Thinks Back," 15-25.

19. See Joyce Jensen, "Economics in Literature," *New York Times,* 4 December 2000, A2.

20. Lewis F. Simpson, *Mind and the American Civil War: A Meditation on Lost Causes* (Baton Rouge: Louisiana State University Press, 1989); Helen Fiddyment Levy, *Fiction of the Home Place: Jewett, Cather, Glasgow, Porter, Welty, and Naylor* (Jackson: University Press of Mississippi, 1992), 31-63; John Seelye, *Memory's Nation: The Place of Plymouth Rock* (Chapel Hill: University of North Carolina Press, 1998), 566.

21. Mary E. Wilkins Freeman, "The Village Singer," in *Selected Stories,* ed. Marjorie Pryse (New York: Norton, 1983), 138.

22. Pattee, "Woolson and the South," 135.

23. Sybil B. Weir, "Southern Womanhood in the Novels of Constance Fenimore Woolson," *Mississippi Quarterly* 30 (Fall 1976): 566. I am much indebted to the author of this fine article for her useful insights. Quotations are from Constance Fenimore Woolson, *East Angels* (New York: Harper Bros., 1886), 497, 591.

24. Paul Hamilton Hayne to Margaret J. Preston, 25 October 1875, in *A Man of Letters in the Nineteenth-Century South: Selected Letters of Paul Hamilton Hayne,* ed. Rayburn S. Moore (Baton Rouge: Louisiana State University Press, 1982), 130.

25. Constance Fenimore Woolson, "At the Smithy. (Pickens County, South Carolina, 1874)," *Appleton's Journal* 12 (5 September 1874), 289-90.

26. Quoted in Ann Douglas Wood, "The Literature of Impoverishment: The Women Local Colorists in America, 1865-1914," *Women's Studies* 1 (1972): 4.

27. Woolson, *East Angels,* 219, 223.

28. Quoted in Jean Strouse, *Alice James: A Biography* (Boston: Houghton Mifflin, 1980), 260.

29. Anne Rowe, *The Enchanted Country: Northern Writers in the South, 1865-1910* (Baton Rouge: Louisiana State University Press, 1978), 54-73.

30. Quoted in Strouse, *Alice James,* 202n.

31. Cheryl B. Torsney, *Constance Fenimore Woolson: The Grief of Artistry* (Athens: University of Georgia Press, 1989), 15-6; John Dwight Kern, *Constance Fenimore Woolson: Literary Pioneer* (Philadelphia: University of Pennsylvania Press, 1975), 161; Rayburn S. Moore, *Constance Fenimore Woolson* (New York: Twayne, 1963), 23-4.

32. Woolson to Hayne, 10 September 1876, in "Some New Letters of Constance Fenimore Woolson," ed. Hubbell, 732; see also Kern, *Woolson,* 51.

33. Constance Fenimore Woolson, quoted in *Women Artists, Women Exiles: "Miss Grief" and Other Stories by Constance Fenimore Woolson,* ed. Joan Myers Weimer (New Brunswick, N.J.: Rutgers University Press, 1988), xviii, xxiii. See Helen Taylor, *Gender, Race, and Region in the Writings of Grace King, Ruth McEnery Stuart, and Kate Chopin* (Baton Rouge: Louisiana State University Press, 1989), 21, 39-40, 103, 105, 122-6, 163; Jones, *Tomorrow Is Another Day,* 146-7; see also Woolson to Hayne, "All Saints' Day," 1875[?], in "Some New Letters of Constance Fenimore Woolson," ed. Hubbell, 727.

34. Torsney, *Woolson,* 20.

35. I thank Susan Donaldson for pointing out the different uses to which the mansion in decline was put in southern literature.

36. Constance Fenimore Woolson, "In the Cotton Country," in her *Rodman the Keeper: Southern Sketches* (1880; New York: AMS Press, 1971), 181.

37. Woolson, "In the Cotton Country," in *Women Artists, Women Exiles,* ed. Weimer, 134.

38. Kate Chopin, *The Awakening: An Authoritative Text, Contexts, Criticism,* ed. Margaret Culley (1899; New York: W. W. Norton, 1976), 113; William Styron, *Lie Down in Darkness* (1951; New York: Viking, 1968), 386.

39. Woolson, "In the Cotton Country," in *Rodman the Keeper,* 196.

40. Ibid., 184; Kern, *Woolson,* 73. Kern points out that in the title story, "Rodman the Keeper," Woolson creates a female character whose bitterness and seething resentment against the victors were not at all untypical of white southerners during the post-Civil War years. At a national cemetery in the South where lay the remains of fourteen thousand Union troops, the figure signs a guest book with a fiery accusation against the soldiers who "killed my father, my three brothers, my cousins." They had sown ruin and desolation "upon our neighborhood, all our State, and all our country," which would never submit its irreconcilable spirit to the blue-coated enemy. Quoted in Kern, *Woolson,* 74.

41. John Myers Weimer, "Women Artists as Exiles in the Fiction of Constance Fenimore Woolson," *Legacy* 3 (Fall 1986): 6.

42. Woolson to Hayne, 15 June 1875, in "Some New Letters of Constance Fenimore Woolson," ed. Hubbell, 720.

43. Quoted in Pattee, "Woolson and the South," 137-8.

44. Woolson, "King David," in *Rodman the Keeper,* 267.

45. Ibid., 274-5.

46. Joan Acocella, *Willa Cather and the Politics of Criticism* (Lincoln: University of Nebraska Press, 2000), 21.

47. Weir, "Southern Womanhood in the Novels of Constance Fenimore Woolson," 559.

48. Constance Fenimore Woolson, *For the Major and Selected Short Stories,* ed. Rayburn S. Moore (1883; New Haven: Yale University Press, 1967), 260. Anne Rowe offers an entirely different interpretation of this work. She claims that Woolson sustained from beginning to end the illusion of an "idealized presentation of a finer life" to be located in the Old South. See Anne E. Rowe, *The Enchanted Country,* 66.

49. See Bertram Wyatt-Brown, *The Shaping of Southern Culture: Honor, Grace, and War, 1760s to 1890s* (Chapel Hill: University of North Carolina Press, 2001), chapters 11 and 12.

50. Torsney, *Woolson,* 14-21, 23.

51. See Weimer, ed., *Women Artists, Women Exiles,* 3-16.

52. Woolson to Samuel Mather, n.d., in *Constance Fenimore Woolson: Five Generations (1785-1923),* ed. Clare Benedict, 3 vols. (London: G. White, 1923), 2:48.

53. Weimer, "Women Artists as Exiles," 3-16; Weir, "Southern Womanhood in the Novels of Constance Fenimore Woolson," 559-68.

54. Leon Edel, *Henry James: A Life* (New York: Harper, 1977), 391-2.

55. Ibid., 392.

56. Torsney, *Woolson,* 1, 11, 20, 14-7; Edel, *Henry James,* 603-11, 793; idem, *Henry James: The Master, 1901-1916* (New York, Avon, 1972), 135; Henry James, "The Beast in the Jungle (1903)," in Henry James, *Collected Stories,* 2 vols. (New York: Knopf, 1999) 2:737-84.

57. The potential suicide cannot produce clear thought or reason toward hope: "Neuropsychologists and clinicians have found that people when depressed think more slowly, are more easily distracted, tire more quickly in cognitive tasks, and find their memory wanting." Kay Redfield Jamison, *Night Falls Fast: Understanding Suicide* (New York: Knopf, 1999), 92. See also Edwin S. Shneidman, ed., *Essays in Self-Destruction* (New York: Science House, 1967).

58. Per Seyersted, *Kate Chopin: A Critical Biography* (Baton Rouge: Louisiana State University Press, 1969), 17.

59. Emily Toth, *Kate Chopin* (1990; Austin: University of Texas Press, 1993), 34; Seyersted, *Kate Chopin,* 16-30.

60. Quoted in Seyersted, *Kate Chopin,* 61.

61. Kate Chopin, "Désirée's Baby," in *Complete Works,* ed. Per Seyersted (Baton Rouge: Louisiana State University Press, 1969), 245.

62. Seyersted, *Kate Chopin,* 54.

63. See Taylor, *Gender, Race, and Region,* 148-9.

64. Chopin, "The White Eagle," in *Complete Works,* ed. Seyersted, 673.

65. See Heather Kirk Thomas, "'What Are the Prospects for the Book?': Rewriting a Woman's Life," in *Kate Chopin Reconsidered,* ed. Boren and Davis, 51-2. Thomas thinks the view that Chopin suffered a depression after the publication of *The Awakening* is much overblown. She cites as evidence to the contrary Chopin's shrewd and meticulous real-estate deals, declining physical as opposed to emotional health, and the production of further short stories. These factors, Thomas says, should dispel the notion of a Chopin under special mental stress. Indeed, that might be so, and her essay is worth serious attention. Yet the poems and stories like "The White Eagle" (all impressive artistically), written after *The Awakening,* suggest

otherwise. They concern issues of death and sadness, but why should they not? After all, she had ample reason to feel unappreciated, and her physical declension might well have made her less resilient emotionally.

66. Cynthia Griffin Wolff, "Thanatos and Eros: Kate Chopin's *The Awakening,*" *American Quarterly* 25 (October 1973): 450.

67. B. F. Bart, ed., *Madame Bovary and the Critics: A Collection of Essays* (New York: New York University Press, 1966); Michael Ignatieff, "Paradigm Lost," *Times Literary Supplement,* 4 September 1987, p. 939.

68. See Bertram Wyatt-Brown, "William Styron's *Sophie's Choice,* Poland, and Depression," Fourteenth Annual International Conference on Literature and Psychoanalysis, Bialystok, Poland, 10 July 2000, published in *Southern Literary Journal* 34 (Fall 2001):56-67; idem, "The Desperate Imagination: Writers and Melancholy in the Modern American South," in *Southern Writers and their Worlds,* ed. Christopher Morris and Steven G. Reinhardt (University Station: Texas A & M Press, 1996), 57-77 (also reprinted in paperback by Louisiana State University Press, 1998).

69. Ignatieff, "Paradigm Lost," 939; Stanley W. Jackson, *Melancholia and Depression: From Hippocratic Times to Modern Times* (New Haven: Yale University Press, 1986); Julia Kristeva, *Black Sun: Depression and Melancholia* (New York: Columbia University Press, 1989).

70. See Virginia Ross, "Kate Chopin's Motherless Heroine," in *Southern Mothers: Fact and Fiction in Southern Women's Writing,* ed. Nagueyalti Warren and Sally Wolff (Baton Rouge: Louisiana State University Press, 1999), 51-63; Elaine Showalter, "*The Awakening*: Tradition and the Female Talent," in *Sister's Choice: Tradition and Change in American Women's Writing* (New York: Oxford University Press, 1991), 73.

71. Jamison, *Night Falls Fast,* 100.

72. "Kate Chopin," in Willa Cather, *Stories, Poems, and Other Writings* (New York: Library of America, 1992), 910-2. Cather's fury blinded her from recognizing that Chopin was not playing a variation on the theme of adultery in the old-fashioned style of the "scribbling" sorority. In all fairness, though, it should be pointed out that Chopin was not above similarly hostile reactions to contemporary writers. She roundly denounced Thomas Hardy's *Jude the Obscure* (1897). It was, she claimed, "immoral" and dangerous for children to read. See Taylor, *Gender, Race, and Region,* 150-1.

73. Toth, *Kate Chopin*, 336-52; Otis B. Wheeler, "The Five Awakenings of Edna Pontellier," *Southern Review* 11 (January 1975): 118-28; Kate Chopin, *The Awakening* (1899; New York: Avon, 1972), 189.

74. *Kate Chopin's Private Papers,* ed. Emily Toth and Per Seyersted (Bloomington: Indiana University Press, 1998), 296.

75. Toth, *Kate Chopin*, 87, 126, 239, 361 (quotation), 377-8.

Anne E. Boyd (essay date 2004)

SOURCE: Boyd, Anne E. "'*Recognition* is the thing': Seeking the Status of Artist; Making Friends with the Male Literary Elite." In *Writing for Immortality: Women and the Emergence of High Literary Culture in America*, pp. 186-202. Baltimore: The Johns Hopkins University Press, 2004.

[*In the following essay, Boyd explores the motives for and consequences of several nineteenth-century women writers' professional relationships with literary men, detailing the competition and anxiety that characterized Woolson's friendship with Henry James.*]

Alcott, Phelps, Stoddard, and Woolson each hoped to gain from their friendships with literary men varying degrees of advice, encouragement, help in getting published, favorable reviews, assistance with payments from publishers, camaraderie, and a less tangible quality—a sense of belonging to "the literary race." They wanted above all to be taken seriously. One way to achieve this was to befriend some of the nation's foremost male literary figures, as many women writers of their generation did. The most famous example, of course, is Emily Dickinson's relationship with Thomas Wentworth Higginson, whose *Atlantic* essay "Letters to a Young Contributor" conveyed his willingness to help unknown women writers. His generous encouragement in his position as an editorial assistant at the magazine and as a key figure in the emerging high literary culture was extended to Alcott, Phelps, Harriet Prescott Spofford, Helen Hunt Jackson, and many others. Jackson called him "my mentor—my teacher—the one man to whom & to whose style, I chiefly owe what little I have done in literature." It was also not uncommon for women writers to view their male mentors as father figures. John Greenleaf Whittier, who also used his ties to the *Atlantic* hierarchy to help young women writers get published and to give them the confidence they needed to pursue serious literary careers, was a fatherly mentor to Phelps, Sarah Orne Jewett, Lucy Larcom, and Celia Thaxter. Jewett, for instance, thought of herself as Whittier's "honorary daughter,"[1] just as Emma Lazarus and

Alcott thought of themselves as Emerson's. Likewise, Henry Wadsworth Longfellow was an advocate of many talented women writers, including Phelps and Sherwood Bonner, and Stedman proved to be one of the literary men most generous in lending his aid to struggling women writers, providing inestimable encouragement and aid to Stoddard and Woolson, as well as Lazarus. Most often, these literary friendships originated in the men's overtures, but on occasion they were initiated by the women themselves, who approached their idols in the hopes of finding a literary mentor or companion. Such was the case not only between Dickinson and Higginson but also between Bonner and Longfellow, Woolson and Henry James, and Lazarus and Emerson. It also was not unheard of for women writers to send their publications to the most esteemed male writers, just as Walt Whitman famously had done when he sent his *Leaves of Grass* to Emerson. Lazarus sent her first book of poems to Emerson, Stoddard sent *The Morgesons* to Nathaniel Hawthorne, and Rebecca Harding Davis sent her first story, "Life in the Iron Mills," to Hawthorne as well.

Despite the tremendous encouragement that many struggling women writers received from established literary men, their relationships reveal that they were always on unequal footing. Many women writers stood in awe of the more experienced and more successful male authors and editors whose attention they courted. They often approached such men with servile gratitude for any notice they received and with self-deprecating comments about their own meager abilities. An example of this attitude of inferiority is visible in a letter that Alcott wrote to Higginson's wife: "Please give him my hearty thanks for the compliment; also for the many helpful & encouraging words which his busy & gifted pen finds time to write so kindly to the young beginners who sit on the lowest seats in the great school where he is one of the best & friendliest teachers." As Alcott's words indicate, the relationships between male and female writers were likely to be that of teacher and pupil. Dickinson, who frequently sought out male "Masters," "preceptors," and "tutors," wrote letters to Higginson, which also convey the self-abasement of the student:

> Would you have the time to be the "friend" you should think I need? I have a little shape—it would not crowd your desk—nor make much racket as the Mouse, that dents your Galleries—
>
> If I might bring you what I do—not so frequent to trouble you—and ask you if I told it clear—'twould be control, to me—. . .
>
> But, will you be my Preceptor, Mr. Higginson?[2]

Phelps's many relationships with powerful literary men particularly illuminate the support based on the implicit barriers to equality that marked most of these friendships. Early in her career, Phelps received letters of congratulations from Higginson and Whittier for her first story in the *Atlantic Monthly,* signaling a new beginning for her as a serious author. She went on to become a member of the circle of *Atlantic* authors who congregated at James and Annie Fields's house on Charles Street in Boston, where she cultivated friendships with many of the preeminent writers she admired. Chief among them were Whittier, Longfellow, and Oliver Wendell Holmes, all older men who essentially served as paternal substitutes. She carried on a long-term correspondence with each of these men that reveals her great admiration for them. Because they were older and already recognized as foremost among America's poets, it was inevitable that her relationships with them would be unequal. She often sent her work to them and solicited their advice, many times receiving well-meaning but nonetheless condescending responses. Longfellow, for example, told her that a poem she sent him was "simple and sweet," and Holmes wrote to her that her collection of stories (probably *Men, Women, and Ghosts*) was written from "your true woman's heart," describing "emotional complications" that only women could understand, suggesting his inability to appreciate her stories. Often he and Longfellow drew attention to her sex when addressing her or responding to her work, offering comments that pointed out the barrier between them. In her letters to them, as well, the inequality was palpable, as her following comment to Longfellow reveals: "It was more than kind in you [to write]—with your lame arm; which is almost as antagonistic to letter-writing as my lame brain."[3]

Phelps's relationship with Whittier, however, was more equitable. "Dr. Holmes and Mr. Longfellow have been very kind to me," she once wrote to him. "But no one is just like you." His appreciation of her work meant more to her than anyone else's, "except my father." His praise for one of her books "made me feel as if I hadn't lived or worked in vain." But Phelps at times also wrote to him in tones suggesting that he could never be a comrade or peer. When she asked him for his picture and sent hers to him, she wrote, "My picture will be of small interest to you, but yours will be an inspiration to me, like the measure of a Hebrew prophet . . . that especial picture of you that I [request] looks as if 'you could not sin'—'because you were born of God.' Forgive me for saying so much about it."[4]

Despite her humility and deference to Holmes, Longfellow, and Whittier, Phelps was not shy about telling the world she was friends with these luminaries. Chapter 8 of her autobiography focuses on her reminiscences about them. "Of our great pentarchy of poets, one—Lowell—I never met; and of another—Emerson—my personal knowledge, as I have said, was but of the slightest." But, she exulted in writing, "With the remaining three I had differing degrees of friendship; and to speak of them is still a privilege full of affectionate

sadness." She recalled a luncheon with Holmes and Whittier at which she was so awed she was unable to open her mouth. "[M]y speech seemed a piece of intrusion on the society of larger planets, or a higher race than ours," she claimed, indicating the extent of the disparity she felt between their world and hers. Phelps also publicized her relationships with these men in magazine articles, perhaps at least partially out of a desire to gain recognition by connecting herself in the public's mind with some of America's leading authors, as Susan Coultrap-McQuin has argued.[5]

Interestingly, Phelps had no such reverence for her male contemporaries, as is evidenced by the critique of William Dean Howells's theories of literature in her autobiography and the scathing attack on Henry James's biography of Hawthorne that she wrote for the *Independent.* In this latter piece, she charged that "[t]o defend our great novelist against our little teller of tales were a Quixotic waste of knight-errantry. The critic's imperfect appreciation of a nature and a work so foreign in h[e]ight, breadth, and depth to his own, is a small matter."[6] It is rare, indeed, to see a woman writer of this period venting such vituperation on a male writer. In her relationships with three of America's already canonized poets and in her defense of Hawthorne, we can see Phelps's reverence for the "select few" who had established America's high literature. But as her generation came of age as authors, Phelps was ready to compete in the marketplace and in the critical realm with younger male writers. Howells and James were not established masters but peers with whom she felt emboldened to do battle.

In stark contrast to Phelps's distinction between towering older masters and younger rivals, Woolson sought out and nourished relationships with the up-and-coming male writers of her day, particularly Stedman, Howells, and James. Her highest esteem was reserved for James, with whom she had a notoriously complicated relationship. While Woolson admired James as ardently as Phelps did Whittier, she also, at least initially, hoped for a literary friendship based on mutual respect and equality. Her deep reverence for him, however, did not preclude feelings of competitiveness. Her three stories that grew out of her relationship with James—**"Street of the Hyacinth," "At the Château of Corinne,"** and **"'Miss Grief'"**—offer the most striking literary exploration by any woman writer of this period of the obstacles women faced as they sought men's acceptance as peers in the literary world.

Woolson and James met in late April 1880 and remained friends until her death in 1894. Unfortunately, from what may have been a voluminous correspondence, only four letters have survived, all written by Woolson. As a result, efforts to understand the nature of their friendship have been largely speculative. For decades, the most popular depiction of the James-Woolson relationship came from James's foremost biographer, Leon Edel, who argued that Woolson harbored a deep desire for intimacy with James that was not reciprocated. Edel portrays Woolson as a "flirt" who "clung to [James] in a kind of pathetic dependency" and as someone who competed with him, possessing "a certain exalted notion of her own literary powers."[7] Recent feminist scholars have objected to Edel's portrayal of Woolson as a love-starved spinster pursuing the reluctant James all over Europe, insisting instead that she possessed a strong sense of herself as an author and sought out James for literary companionship and support, not love. "'Miss Grief'" (1880) offers a particularly rich fund of evidence to support the latter view. And if read in light of the time in which it was written, the story strongly suggests that Woolson had serious doubts about the ability of James, a writer whom she admired above all others, to provide the literary and personal support she craved at a pivotal point in her life as she moved to Europe, alone after her mother's death. In addition, the story reveals that even before they became friends she felt compelled to challenge his critically acclaimed constructions of women.

Having spent a decade perfecting the regional sketch and writing her first novel, in 1879 Woolson was ready to take on an international project, perhaps inspired by the European writing of Henry James. She had written two anonymous reviews of James's *Europeans* for the *Atlantic* in 1879, one of which declared: "There is a great satisfaction in seeing a thing well done, and both in the substance and in the style of his books, Mr. James always offers an intellectual treat to appreciative readers; of course it is obvious that he writes only for the cultivated minority." In her review, Woolson claims membership in this minority, granting herself the status of an authoritative reader of James.[8] Their subsequent personal relationship, mirroring those between many other male and female writers, was marked by her attempts to prove herself one of the "cultivated minority" for whom James was writing.

Less than a week after she arrived (with her sister and niece) in London, this relatively reclusive woman went to Henry James's door with a letter of introduction from his cousin. But James was in Paris, and he returned just as Woolson left for the Riviera in search of a warmer climate. They would not meet until five months later (late April 1880), in Florence. It is very possible that Woolson wrote "'Miss Grief'" during this interval between her first attempt to introduce herself to James and their eventual meeting, but she may have written it even before she left for Europe. In either case, the characters and subject matter make clear that the story was written in anticipation of meeting the great writer.

Although the story must have been written before Woolson met James (it appeared in the May 1880 issue of *Lippincott's,* two or three weeks after they first met), there are unmistakable similarities between James and the male writer who is the narrator of the story. The unnamed male author has inherited money as James had and does not need to depend solely on income from his writings; he writes "delightful little studies of society," as James did; and he claims, "I model myself a little on Balzac," as James's 1875 essay "Honoré de Balzac" indicated James did. Moreover, the male writer mentions two of his stories, "Old Gold" and "The Buried God," which featured antiquities and artifacts, as did James's "Last of the Valerii" (1874). And in the opening sentences of "'Miss Grief'" the male narrator describes himself as a "literary success," which James had recently become with the sensational publication of *Daisy Miller.* But these are all qualities that Woolson could have known from James's works and reputation as well as from their mutual friends Howells and John Hay.[9]

The fact that the narrator is not based on the actual James she personally came to know becomes even clearer when this earlier Jamesian character is contrasted with those versions Woolson created afterward in **"Street"** [**"Street of the Hyacinth"**] and **"Château"** [**"At the Château of Corinne"**]. In these later stories we are introduced to male figures who more closely resemble the kind of cool, detached, even arrogant personality James appears to have possessed. Raymond Noel and John Ford, who convince Ettie and Katherine that they have neither talent nor the right to pursue careers as artists, were modeled on the man with whom she had developed an intense relationship and who, she learned, had a more inflexible position on women writers than she had imagined. In contrast, the male writer featured in "'Miss Grief,'" while reluctant to admit an "authoress" into his home, nonetheless admires her genius; he may be wary, but he never denies her talent or insists on the incompatibility of womanhood and art.

Although there are also similarities between the woman writer in the story and Woolson, there are also important differences. Chief among them is that Aaronna Moncrief, who goes by Miss Crief, is impoverished and unpublished and needs the narrator's assistance in launching her career, whereas Woolson had become well known in America as a writer of short stories and poetry and had just finished writing her first novel, slated for publication by Harper and Brothers. Therefore, rather than being simply an autobiographical projection, this story allowed Woolson to experiment with themes that reflect her anxiety about meeting James. More than anything else, Miss Crief represents Woolson's ideas about James's biases toward "authoresses."

In **"Miss Grief,"** Woolson depicts the efforts of a forlorn female author to gain the help of a successful male writer in publishing her work. As in **"Street"** and **"Châ-**

teau," his perspective is privileged, but here it dominates to an even greater extent, for he is the narrator, speaking directly to the reader without the intervention of a limited omniscient narrator as in the other two stories. However, Woolson still finds ways to undercut his authority. The title itself, **"Miss Grief,"** is the name the male writer chooses for her. But the quotation marks Woolson places around the name call his perspective into question. This story is clearly his version of events, which may be distorted. The fact that the story is told through his eyes again distances the reader from the woman's experience and neutralizes her anger. As many critics have noted, this story in particular points a damning finger at the male literary world for its neglect of women writers. For Woolson to raise her voice and point that finger directly would have been too provocative, especially as she prepared to meet James, the current darling of the literary world. So, instead of directly telling her story of betrayal and exclusion, Miss Crief remains relatively silent. We experience her grief primarily through the male narrator, who at virtually every turn belittles and ridicules her in his own mind.

Initially, the male writer is put off by Miss Crief's tenacity in seeking an interview. But her ragged, impoverished appearance gains his pity. From the beginning, he believes she is "mad" (254) and insists on calling her "Miss Grief," using the name to suggest the grief she seems to cause him; however, the name most potently conveys the grief that she herself is experiencing, for her suffering pales in comparison to his. Contributing to her grief is his inability to recognize her as a peer. Instead of accepting her as a fellow writer, he constantly contrasts her with Isabel Abercrombie, the highly desirable, conventional woman he is courting. Whereas Isabel is young and attractive, Miss Crief is her exact opposite: "shabby, unattractive, and more than middle-aged" (251). When Miss Crief seeks entrance to the house, the narrator suspects she is some sort of saleswoman who wants to sell him antiques. But she slowly reveals that she has come for another purpose. "I am your friend," she insists. "I have read every word you have written." And she begins to demonstrate her admiration for him by reciting a passage from his work that happens to be the narrator's favorite. Here, like Woolson herself, she displays a deeper understanding and appreciation for his work than did the general public, who "had never noticed the higher purpose of this little shaft, aimed not at the balconies and lighted windows of society, but straight up toward the distant stars." Indeed, he admits that she "understood me almost better than I had understood myself" (252). By showing a genuine appreciation for his work, she gains his attention, and he agrees to read some of her work, including a drama, "Armor," the title of which signifies her need to protect herself from the blows of the male-dominated

literary world and, by extension, perhaps even his own response to her work. Fortunately, he admires the drama and agrees to help her.

When he delivers his judgment of her work as "full of original power," Miss Crief begins to cry, "her whole frame shaken by the strength of her emotion" (257). Hanging over the side of the chair, she seems to have nearly lost consciousness, and the narrator fortifies her with wine and biscuit. What truly revives her, however, is his continued praise. Like Mary Hathorne in Phelps's "Rejected Manuscript," Miss Crief has been, essentially, dying of critical neglect. With no one to appreciate her work, she has lost the will and the means to live. As she tells the narrator, "My life was at a low ebb: if your sentence had been against me, it would have been my end. . . . I should have destroyed myself" (258). His praise alone, however, proves to be insufficient to sustain her. She will receive no thousand-dollar check, as Mary does, another key to the woman writer's survival. For her works prove to be unpublishable. Despite "the divine spark of genius" that he believes her works possess (257), he sees "faults" that must be corrected to gain the acceptance of an editor or publisher (258). "To me originality and force are everything," he tells her, echoing Ettie Macks in **"Street,"** "but the world at large will not overlook as I do your absolutely barbarous shortcomings on account of them" (259). The "world at large," namely the male literary elite, demands the kind of training and adherence to forms and rules that also prohibit Ettie from entering the art world.

However, Miss Crief refuses to acknowledge any faults in her work or allow the narrator to make any changes. Exasperated by her "obstinacy," he gives up and decides to pass her works on to some of his friends in publishing, convinced that, flaws notwithstanding, they possess "originality and force" (259). But the pieces are rejected. The writer, therefore, decides on his own to revise them, but he soon discovers he cannot "'improve' Miss Grief" (265). Shortly thereafter, he learns that she is dying of poverty and starvation. Her aunt, a powerless protector, expresses the anger that Miss Crief is herself incapable of voicing: "Your patronizing face shows that you have no good news," the aunt tells him, "and you shall not rack and stab her any more on *this* earth." He is confused and wonders of whom she is speaking. "I say you, *you*,—You literary men!" she replies. "Vampires! you take her ideas and fatten on them, and leave her to starve" (265-266). After this speech, the male writer's guilt compels him to tell Miss Crief that some of her work has been accepted for publication. Thus deluded, she makes the writer her literary executor and asks him to bury the rest of her unpublished work with her, which he does. Before she dies, she tells him, "Did you wonder why I came to you? It was the contrast. You were young—strong—rich—praised—

loved—successful: all that I was not. I wanted to look at you—and imagine how it would feel. You had success—but I had the greater power" (268). As the story closes, he reflects on his own "good fortune," for he has succeeded not only in his career but in his personal life by winning Isabel as his wife.

Why was the injustice done to women writers at the hands of the male literary world on Woolson's mind as she anticipated meeting James for the first time? For one, she knew that James received favors and recognition that women writers rarely did. As she wrote to Paul Hamilton Hayne, "Mr Hurd, of Hurd & Houghton [the publishers of the *Atlantic*] . . . has let out that Howells [editor of the *Atlantic*] has 'favorites.' Chief among them at present, Henry James, Jr. I suspect there is a strong current of favoritism up there." More telling is what she wrote many years later to James himself: "I don't think you appreciated, over there, among the chimney pots, the laudation your books received in America as they came out one by one. (We little fish did! We little fish became worn to skeletons owing to the constant admonitions we received to regard the beauty, the grace, the incomparable perfection of all sorts and kinds of the proud salmon of the pond; we ended by hating that salmon.)"[10] There is an unmistakable strain of envy in this passage, as there is in "**Miss Grief.**" These comments and Miss Crief's insistence that she possessed "the greater power" also suggest that the envy arose from the feeling that she was eclipsed by more established but not necessarily more talented male writers.

Edel's argument that as Woolson began her friendship with James she "felt herself, on some strange deep level, to be competing" with him is on the mark, although Edel fails to understand the context for this competition. It is likely that Woolson detected the rivalry in James's own writings before she ever met him. As Alfred Habegger points out in *Henry James and the "Woman Business,"* James was himself competing with women writers in general by adopting the themes of women's fiction and in a sense "correct[ing]" and "answer[ing]" them. As Habegger puts it, "James's own narratives have all along professed great authority on the subject of women." In a letter to James in 1882, Woolson accused him of treading on her literary territory. "How did you ever dare write a portrait of a lady," she remonstrated. "Fancy any woman's attempting a portrait of a gentleman! Wouldn't there be a storm of ridicule!"[11] At this time her first novel, *Anne,* and James's novel, *The Portrait of a Lady,* were being issued as books, both having been published serially in periodicals almost simultaneously from the late 1880 through 1881, and both dealing with the attempts of young women to find their place in the world.

But even when she wrote "**Miss Grief,**" Woolson seems to have felt that James's work was competing

with, perhaps even exploiting, women's fiction, including her own, and achieving recognition at the expense of women authors. To her, the failure of women writers like herself to achieve James's stature was primarily due to the contemporary conventional attitudes toward women writers and not the quality or subjects of their work. For example, James had recently become wildly popular in both Britain and the United States as the author of *Daisy Miller.* Edel reflects the prevailing nineteenth-century response to the story when he writes, "James had discovered nothing less than 'the American girl'—as a social phenomenon, a fact, a type."[12] No doubt Woolson was aware that a generation of women writers before James, legitimate claimants to this achievement, never received the recognition that he now did. The aunt's accusation to the male narrator that he, as a male writer, is part of a class of "vampires" that "take her [Miss Crief's] ideas and fatten on them, and leave her to starve" (266) makes more sense when read in this context.

On the other hand, Woolson also indicated her deep appreciation for James's writings: "they voice for me—as nothing else ever has—my own feelings; those that are so deep—so a part of me, that I cannot express them, and do not try to . . . they are my true country, my real home," she wrote to him in 1883.[13] Her sentiment that James possessed a greater power than herself to voice her own emotions is reminiscent of the male narrator's view in "**Miss Grief**" that Miss Crief understood his work better than he himself did. Woolson felt such a deep affinity for James's writing that she seemed to have hoped for some reciprocity of understanding, a sort of meeting of the minds hinted at, indeed longed for, by Miss Crief. But Woolson's male narrator, while recognizing Miss Crief's "greater power," fails to comprehend the nature of her achievement, hoping instead to fix her work. The male writer's desire to "improve" Miss Crief indicates the real doubts Woolson had about James's ability to view her as an intellectual equal deserving of respect and admiration rather than paternalistic correction.

This lack of appreciation is revealed in the narrator's prejudices against women writers and his constant comparison of Miss Crief to Isabel Abercrombie. From the beginning of the story, he tries to make Miss Crief conform to his preconceptions of her, fearing that she may possess a supernatural power to control him. But this irrational fear is undercut by his own observations of her. Shortly after she reveals that she is an author looking for his assistance, he begins to perceive her as a threat: "'She is mad,' I thought. *But she did not look so, and she had spoken quietly, even gently.* 'Sit down,' I said, moving away from her. I felt as if I had been magnetized; *but it was only the nearness of her eyes to mine, and their intensity*" (254; italics added). Just as he forms an opinion of her, he contradicts himself, suggesting that his impressions are based on prejudice rather than on facts. This passage reveals not only the narrator's unwarranted fear of the power the mysterious woman might have over him but also his inability to overcome his preconceived notions of women. Shortly thereafter, when confronted by Isabel's unpredictability, he is incapable of comprehending her as well, and he comes home confused about himself and her: "it was foggy without, and very foggy within. What Isabel really was, now that she had broken through my elaborately built theories, I was not able to decide" (255). Furthermore, he has already found a scapegoat as his excuse: when he sees Miss Crief's name on her manuscript, "A. Crief," he thinks, "A Grief . . . and so she is. I positively believe she has brought all this trouble upon me: she has the evil eye" (253). She too is part of his "elaborately built theories." To his relief, though, his temporary uncertainty about Isabel's true nature wanes, and he sees her again as the "sweet" (269), simple woman who knows her place.

The narrator of "'**Miss Grief**'" here strongly resembles some of James's early male characters, most notably Winterbourne in *Daisy Miller* and Rowland Mallet in *Roderick Hudson.* For these men, as Priscilla L. Walton says about *Roderick Hudson,* "women function as the Other, the 'unknowable.'" All try, without much success, to understand enigmatic young American women. Just as Winterbourne in *Daisy Miller* is irritated when he learns that Daisy is spending much time with an Italian would-be suitor, so the male writer in "'**Miss Grief**'" is upset when Isabel presumably flirts with "a certain young Englishman" (255). At issue are the "true" feelings of these women. The same is the case in *Roderick Hudson,* as Rowland attempts to deduce Christina's intentions with respect to his friend Roderick. Are these women displaying their "real" selves, or are they, as Christina is accused of being, merely superb actresses? Are they displaying, as Rowland muses about Christina, "touching sincerity or unfathomable coquetry?" The answer to this question was of the utmost importance because it indicated on which side of the fault line between angel and prostitute—between "safe and unsafe," as Rowland says—these women would come down.[14] Understanding these mysterious women, therefore, was a way of classifying and containing them. Once they were understood, they could be controlled.

Drawing on Victorian conventions, James often had his heroes classify light and dark women: the former asexual and a potential wife, the latter sexual and not marriageable. The female sex, therefore, is divided into those who can be married and those who must be shunned.[15] The narrator of "'**Miss Grief**'" clearly evaluates Aaronna in these terms and is confused by her: "A woman—yes, a lady—but shabby, unattractive, and more than middle-aged" (251). In other words, she is not marriageable, but she is respectable. The problem

the narrator faces is how to understand this woman who nonetheless has "sacrificed her womanly claims" by persistently coming to see him (250). He confronts the same kind of problem that Noel will in the later "**Street**" in trying to understand the motives of the forward Ettie. As in that work, Woolson was aware that forward women forfeited men's esteem. The task for the woman writer was to stake out a new territory, to be taken for neither prospective wife nor sexually free woman, rather as fellow author. Woolson critiques the angel/whore dichotomy by creating a heroine who fits in neither category despite the narrator's attempts to classify her as a dangerous, "evil" woman. By portraying Aaronna with nothing to offer the man who is drawn to women for their ornamental function, Woolson declares that the woman writer does not desire the kind of attention beautiful young women receive. She tries to get the male writer to accept her as a *writer,* not as a *woman.* For if he views her as a woman, then any understanding between the two as writers is forever lost, as Noel's insistence on viewing Ettie as a woman precludes any relationship between them as artists.

Even more indicative of the narrator's unwillingness to accept women as writers is his clear preference for Isabel Abercrombie and the type of womanhood she assumes in his imagination. For instance, he is "glad" that Isabel neither likes nor understands Miss Crief's poetry, because it points to the contrast between the two women. Miss Crief's poetry is "unrestrained, large, vast, like the skies or the wind. Isabel was bounded on all sides, like a violet in a garden bed. And I liked her so" (265). Interestingly, his description of Miss Crief's poems resembles the ambition he had harbored for his own sketch that Miss Crief admiringly recited to him on her first visit. Like the narrator, Miss Crief's writing indicates that she too is reaching for "the distant stars" rather than the general public (252), a sign of their competition with each other. Such an ambition, he assumes, is not desirable in a woman. Instead, he prefers the woman happy in the "bounded" world Isabel inhabits, the woman who neither competes with him nor challenges his perception of her, just as Oswald preferred Lucille to Corinne and John Ford preferred Sylvia to Katherine.

Most male authors, Woolson perceived, were probably not ready to accept someone like her as an equal, in terms of ambition and serious devotion to literature. She would have to tread carefully, then, as she approached James. Indeed, she did not, as she later wrote to him, "come in as a literary woman at all, but as a sort of—of admiring aunt," despite being only three years older than he.[16] Having by then apparently given up on the possibility of a mutually supportive literary friendship with him, she limited herself to trying to be his ideal reader. But Woolson allowed Miss Crief to be what she did not dare herself: Miss Crief did not humble herself before the master, and she refused to let him correct or appropriate her art. In this way, then, she resembles Dickinson, who would not let Higginson alter her verse, no matter how much she admired his expertise. Ultimately, though, Miss Crief fails to interest the narrator in herself as a writer, displaying the deep ambivalence Woolson harbored about James's ability to look past her gender and receive her as a literary companion and equal. For while the male writer senses Miss Crief's "greater power," he also perceives her presence in his life as a "grief," and he is more than happy to bury her work with her when she dies, indicating how dangerous he thinks her writings are. Isabel's inability to understand Miss Crief's poetry is a great relief, and he hides the rest of her works from view, eager to extinguish the latent power that lurks within them.

In contrast to Edel's depictions of Woolson's amorous motives for seeking out a friendship with James, "**Miss Grief**" suggests that Woolson hoped for (although she did not expect) his understanding of and respect for her literary work and perhaps even some recognition of her genius. In 1884, Woolson wrote to the writer John Hay of her eagerness to find a kindred literary spirit and how rare such an occurrence had been in her life: "I shd. be so glad to have some talks with you . . . I am terribly alone in my literary work. There seems to be no one for me to turn to. It is true that there are only two or three to whom I wd. turn!" That Henry James was by that time one of the few with whom she would have liked to form a literary friendship is certain, but the meaning of the sentence is clear: he was not what she had hoped he would be; there is "no one" with whom to share her literary life. Even more telling are her 1883 letters to James in which she admonishes him for his inability to respond directly to her questions and carry on a real conversation, even about his work. She does not bother to ask him to respond to her work. Her August 30, 1882, letter to him remarks that in his brief replies to her very long letters there is "no allusion to anything I have said," indicating that her involved, carefully crafted responses to *The Portrait of a Lady* in her previous letter have gone unnoticed by him and, therefore, that James refused to reply to her as an appreciate and discerning reader. He would not allow theirs to be a writers' friendship based on the free exchange of opinions concerning their art, despite her clear desire to establish such a relationship.[17]

Woolson's predictions in "**Miss Grief**" of how James would view her as a woman writer were correct. His destruction of many of her personal effects and letters after her death is eerily anticipated by the male narrator's burial of Miss Crief's writings, indicating that Woolson was aware of how dangerous men perceived the woman writer's words to be. Her extant letters to him and his essay "Miss Woolson," in which he assesses her work as "essentially conservative," indicate

that she was correct in doubting his ability to accept her as a writer and a woman.[18] In her depictions of Jamesian men in "**Street**" and "**Château**," she wrestled with the problem of his potential power to extinguish her creative life. That she was able to overcome his judgment of women authors is a testament to her strong identity as a writer. Nevertheless, it is fair to say that the lack of appreciation and understanding she received from him contributed not only to her own personal and vocational grief but also to her marginalization at a time when the canon of American literature was taking shape. In "**Miss Grief**" she uncannily forecast her fate and those of her female contemporaries: misunderstanding by male writers and rejection by the cultural forces of posterity. In addition, "**Miss Grief**" expresses the anxiety that many women writers of her generation felt about approaching and befriending their male cohorts as well as their disbelief in men's ability to consider them equals in the literary world.

While Woolson seems largely to have accepted the terms James offered her in order to remain his friend, Stoddard was much more demanding of her male author friends; she was not afraid even to break off relationships with them when they refused to acknowledge her worth as a peer. It was primarily from the circle of her husband's friends that she sought appreciation and help, believing that these men would be her passport to a significant literary reputation. As she later wrote, "*I have been made the little that I am, by my association with literary men.*" These associations introduced her to the ideal of the sanctity of the author's profession, and she was inspired by their seriousness. This is probably why she dedicated her first novel to "My Three Friends, the three poets, Richard, Bayard, George" (her husband, Bayard Taylor, and George Boker). Her desire to "prove to you males that I [am] your comrade" drove much of her early ambition.[19] She yearned for the fellowship of an experienced and successful author whom she could admire and from whom she could learn. But most of the male authors she met did not live up to her expectations.

At the beginning of Stoddard's writing career, two of the chief obstacles to her success, she felt, were "the contemptuous silence of [my] husband [and] the incredulity of all [my] male acquaintances." She had particularly rocky relationships with Boker and Taylor. She wanted their help in building up her reputation, and she asked them to write reviews for her, but she was not always happy with the results. And while they initially tried to support her budding "genius," her lack of respect for them and their condescending criticisms of her work led to great conflicts. When Taylor criticized *The Morgesons* (in a private letter to her), and she wrote to him scathingly in return, he protested that he was "a friend who loves you, who appreciates your genius." Nonetheless, he and Taylor resented her strong-willed, outspoken nature, and they made her gender an integral part of their attacks on her, calling her behind her back "the Pythoness" and "the Sybil," and in one dispute with her and Richard assuming that "E. D. B. S. is at the bottom of this witches [*sic*] cauldron, stirring up her old hell-broth."[20]

Taylor, especially, tried to put Stoddard in her place: "[I now see] the intensely *feminine* character of your mind," he wrote her. "With all your power and daring—with an intimate knowledge of the nature of men which few women attain—you are *woman* to the smallest fibre of your brain." In this attack, Taylor gave her the greatest insult he could muster. Knowing that she was desperately trying to distinguish herself as an exceptional woman writer, he told her that she would always be beneath him and all other men, that she could never escape her sex and hence her inferiority. By doing so, he denied her any individuality and any distinction as an author. As she later wrote to Stedman, "He said what Caliban might have said, had he been an American author, to Miranda, when he got mad with her, and had the male vanity of wishing to crush her. . . . All I ever did against him—was to decry his immense vanity—to say that he was not a great writer." Years later she would confide to a friend that "[n]o person in this world has ever hurt and wounded us [her and her husband] individually as BT."[21]

The writer she most admired, Nathaniel Hawthorne, died shortly after the publication of her first novel. She had dared to send him a copy of *The Morgesons* and was delighted to receive an approving letter in return. He told her that he was "very glad to hear that you are writing another novel, and [I] do not doubt that something good and true will come of it." This letter was the "one immortal feather in my cap," she later wrote, the one sign of recognition that she had received from the powers on high. To prove her worth to her fellows who so neglected her, she included portions of the letter in her preface to *The Morgesons* when it was republished in 1901. However, Hawthorne had not lived long enough to be a sustaining influence on her career.[22]

In the 1870s and after it was Stedman who proved to be Stoddard's greatest supporter. He was a poet, critic, and editor who was coming into his own during this decade. He went on to become a very influential force in the New York literary world. It was to him that Stoddard owed "it all," she believed, when her reputation was recuperated in the 1890s. Although Stedman participated in some of the sniping about Elizabeth behind her back, and although she was unhappy with an early review he wrote of *The Morgesons,* she grew to feel that he believed in her more than any of her other peers. She also respected him as an author more than the other men she met and had a strong "ambition to please" him in verse, which she did. He wrote in his diary, "Read Mrs. Stod-

dard's poems. Have seen nothing so good from an American woman." He also felt strongly about her novels, writing to James Russell Lowell that he thought *Two Men* "artistic and powerful" and full of "genius." Most importantly, though, he did not belittle her or condescend to her. He respected her ambition, and she informed him, "it is a true comfort to have you understand and appreciate me as *no other has.*" While Richard had given "up hope," Stedman's faith in her never waned, she believed.[23] In the late 1880s and the 1890s, when Stedman helped her to republish her novels, he proved to be the kind of friend and mentor Miss Crief had looked for. He wrote a laudatory introduction to the republication of *Two Men* in 1888, which helped bring it to the attention of reviewers. And when he published *An American Anthology, 1787-1900* (1900), he included eight of Stoddard's poems, representing her prominently among the important American poets.[24]

Alcott, Phelps, Stoddard, and Woolson all felt that they needed the help of powerful men to advance their careers and reputations. But just as Alcott's *Diana and Persis* leaves the question open of whether Diana and her new supporter, Stafford, develop a romantic relationship, the issue of romance was always the subtext in friendships between single male and female writers. Woolson knew this in her relationship with James, and she tried to defuse the issue by assuring him that she felt herself to be a "sort of . . . admiring aunt" to him, and nothing more. This may also be why Phelps felt most comfortable approaching older men who would be surrogate fathers rather than potential husbands. As the only married woman, Stoddard probably was more successful at gaining the support of one of her male peers because personal intimacy was less of an issue. Because he was a friend of her husband as well, Stedman could give her advice, praise her writing, and work on her behalf without the appearance of impropriety.

Notes

1. Jackson quoted in Alfred Habegger, *My Wars Are Laid Away in Books: The Life of Emily Dickinson* (New York: Random House, 2001), 555-556. Jewett quoted in Paula Blanchard, *Sarah Orne Jewett: Her World and Her Work* (Reading, MA: Addison-Wesley, 1994), 112.

2. LMA [Louisa May Alcott] to Mary E. Channing Higginson, Oct. 18, [1868], in *The Selected Letters of Louisa May Alcott,* ed. Joel Myerson, Daniel Shealy, and associate ed. Madeleine B. Stern (Athens: University of Georgia Press, 1995), 118. Dickinson to T. W. Higginson, June 7, 1862, in Emily Dickinson, *The Letters of Emily Dickinson,* ed. Thomas H. Johnson (Cambridge: Harvard University Press, 1965), 409.

3. Henry Wadsworth Longfellow to ESP [Elizabeth Stuart Phelps], Apr. 6, 1876, BPL [Boston Public Library, Department of Rare Books and Manu-

scripts, Boston, MA]. Oliver Wendell Holmes to ESP, Oct. 29, 1879, in John T. Morse, *Life and Letters of Oliver Wendell Holmes* (Boston: Houghton, Mifflin, 1896), 260-261. ESP to Longfellow, May 17, n.y., bMS Am 1340.2 (5815), MH [Houghton Library, Harvard University, Cambridge, MA].

4. ESP to John Greenleaf Whittier, Dec. 7, 1879, UVA [Clifton Waller Barrett Library, Albert and Shirley Small Special Collections Library, University of Virginia, Charlottesville, VA]. ESP to Whittier, Dec. 22, 1879, Mar. 13, 1868, Apr. 5, 1878, bMS Am 1844 (325), MH.

5. ESP, *Chapters from a Life* (Boston: Houghton, Mifflin, 1895), 153, 166. Susan Coultrap-McQuin, "Elizabeth Stuart Phelps" (Ph.D. diss., University of Iowa, 1979), 136.

6. For her critique of Howells, see ESP, *Chapters*, 260-264. ESP, "The Man without a Country," *Independent* 32 (May 6, 1880): 1-2.

7. Leon Edel, *The Life of Henry James*, 5 vols. (Philadelphia: Lippincott, 1953-72), 2:411-412, 417.

8. In 1875 Woolson remarked to her friend Paul Hamilton Hayne that James was among her favorite authors; quoted in Jay B. Hubbell, ed., "Some New Letters of Constance Fenimore Woolson," *New England Quarterly* 14 (Dec. 1941): 724. CFW [Constance Fenimore Woolson], "The Contributors' Club," *Atlantic Monthly* 43 (Jan. 1879): 106-108; (Feb. 1879): 259.

9. CFW, "'Miss Grief'" (1880), in *Women Artists, Women Exiles: "Miss Grief" and Other Stories by Constance Fenimore Woolson*, ed. Joan Myers Weimer (New Brunswick, NJ: Rutgers University Press, 1988), 248, 250. Subsequent references will be made in the text. In *The Life of Henry James*, Edel points out two of the similarities noted here, and he argues that the story "reflects a close reading of Henry's work" (2:416).

10. CFW to Paul Hamilton Hayne, Feb. 13, [1876], in Hubbell, "Some New Letters," 730. CFW to Henry James, Feb. 12, 1882, in *The Letters of Henry James*, ed. Leon Edel (Cambridge: Harvard University Press, 1974-80), 3:529.

11. Edel, *Life of Henry James*, 2:417. Alfred Habegger, *Henry James and the "Woman Business"* (Cambridge: Cambridge University Press, 1989), 25, 4. CFW to Henry James, Feb. 12, 1882, in Edel, *Letters of Henry James*, 3:535.

12. Edel, *Life of Henry James*, 2:309.

13. CFW to Henry James, May 7, 1883, in Edel, *The Letters of Henry James*, 3:550-551.

14. Priscilla L. Walton, *Disruption of the Feminine in Henry James* (Toronto: University of Toronto Press, 1992), 38. Henry James, *Roderick Hudson*, in *Henry James, Novels 1871-1880*, ed. William T. Stafford (New York: Library of America, 1983), 293, 301-302, 270. (This edition reproduces the original American publication in 1875.)

15. See Walton, *Disruption*, 41.

16. Woolson to James, Feb. 12, [1882], in Edel, *Letters of Henry James*, 3:528.

17. CFW to John Hay, January 27, 1884, in Alice Hall Petry, "'Always Your Attached Friend': The Unpublished Letters of Constance Fenimore Woolson to John and Clara Hay," *Books at Brown* 29-30 (1982-1983): 65. CFW to Henry James, August 30, 1882, in Edel, *Letters of Henry James*, 3:542.

18. Henry James, "Miss Woolson," in *Women Artists, Women Exiles*, 271, first published as "Miss Constance Fenimore Woolson," in *Harper's Weekly* (Feb. 12, 1887): 114-115.

19. EBS [Elizabeth Barstow Stoddard] to Elizabeth Akers Allen, [1873-74], in *The Morgesons and Other Writings, Published and Unpublished*, ed. Lawrence Buell and Sandra Zagarell (Philadelphia: University of Pennsylvania Press, 1984), 341. Dedication to *The Morgesons* quoted in Matlack, "Literary Career," 223. EBS to ECS [Edmund Clarence Stedman], Nov. 3, n.y., NYCol-SC [Stedman Collection, Columbia University, Rare Book and Manuscript Library, Butler Library, New York, NY].

20. EBS, *Daily Alta California*, Nov. 18, 1855; quoted in Matlack, "Literary Career," 156. (While she spoke here to the "courageous woman" author, she clearly did so from personal experience.) Bayard Taylor to EBS, Nov. 21, 1862, Rare and Manuscript Collections, Carl A. Kroch Library, Cornell University Library, Ithaca, NY. For the names they called her, see Matlack, 448, 466.

21. Bayard Taylor to EBS, Feb. 27, 1863, Rare and Manuscript Collections, Carl A. Kroch Library, Cornell University Library, Ithaca, NY. EBS to ECS, May 1, 1865, NYCol-SC. EBS to Julia Dorr, July 31, 1881, VTMC [Albernethy Library, Special Collections, Middlebury College, Middlebury, VT].

22. Nathaniel Hawthorne to EBS, Jan. 26, 1863, Berg Collection of English and American Literature, New York Public Library, New York, NY, Astor, Lenox, and Tilden Foundations. See 1901 preface in *The Morgesons*, 262. EBS to Lillian Whiting, June 20, n.y., BPL.

23. EBS to Julia Dorr, Oct. 5, [1888], VTMC. ECS believed that EBS was dissatisfied with his review of *The Morgesons*, according to a letter to Thomas

Bailey Aldrich, quoted in Matlack, "Literary Career," 221. EBS to ECS, Nov. 25, n.y., NYCol-SC. ECS's diary quoted in Matlack, 192. ECS to James Russell Lowell, quoted in Matlack, 440. EBS to ECS, [Oct. or Nov. 1887], NYCol-SC. EBS to Julia Dorr, Oct. 5, [1888], VTMC.

24. Stedman's 1901 introduction to Stoddard's novels is included in his *Genius and Other Essays* (New York: Moffat, Yard, 1911). ECS, ed., *An American Anthology, 1787-1900* (Boston: Houghton, Mifflin, 1900).

FURTHER READING

Criticism

Boren, Lynda S. "'Dear Constance,' 'Dear Henry': The Woolson/James Affair—Fact, Fiction, or Fine Art?" *Amerikastudien* 27, no. 4 (1982): 457-66.

Reconstructs the "virtuous attachment" between Woolson and Henry James deduced from the fictional treatment of their relationship in her "A Florentine Experiment" and his "The Beast in the Jungle" as well as from four surviving letters written by Woolson to James.

Buonomo, Leonardo. "The Other Face of History in Constance Fenimore Woolson's Southern Stories." *Canadian Review of American Studies* 28, no. 3 (1998): 15-29.

Treats historical implications of Woolson's portrayal of the American South in her short fiction.

Dean, Sharon L. *Constance Fenimore Woolson and Edith Wharton: Perspectives on Landscape and Art.* Knoxville: University of Tennessee Press, 2002, 268 p.

Compares the treatment of aesthetics and landscape architecture in works by Woolson and Edith Wharton.

Gingras, Robert. "'Hepzibah's Story': An Unpublished Work by Constance Fenimore Woolson." *Resources for American Literary Study* 10, no. 1 (spring 1980): 33-46.

Speculates about the date and the circumstances surrounding the composition of "Hepzibah's Story."

Kitterman, Mary P. Edwards. "Henry James and the Artist-Heroine in the Tales of Constance Fenimore Woolson." In *Nineteenth-Century Women Writers of the English-Speaking World,* edited by Rhoda B. Nathan, pp. 45-59. Westport, Conn.: Greenwood Press, 1986.

Discusses the representation of female artistry in Woolson's stories in light of her relationship with James.

Torsney, Cheryl B. "'Whenever I Open a Book and See "Hoot, Mon," I Always Close It Immediately': Constance Fenimore Woolson's Humor." *Studies in American Humor* 3, no. 9 (2002): 69-81.

Examines local color and comedic characters in Woolson's fiction.

Additional coverage of Woolson's life and career is contained in the following sources published by Thomson Gale: *Dictionary of Literary Biography,* **Vols. 12, 74, 189, 221;** *Literature Resource Center; Nineteenth-Century Literature Criticism,* **Vol. 82; and** *Reference Guide to American Literature,* **Ed. 4.**

How to Use This Index

The main references

> **Calvino, Italo**
> 1923-1985 .... CLC **5, 8, 11, 22, 33, 39,**
> **73; SSC 3, 48**

list all author entries in the following Thomson Gale Literary Criticism series:

AAL = *Asian American Literature*
BG = *The Beat Generation: A Gale Critical Companion*
BLC = *Black Literature Criticism*
BLCS = *Black Literature Criticism Supplement*
CLC = *Contemporary Literary Criticism*
CLR = *Children's Literature Review*
CMLC = *Classical and Medieval Literature Criticism*
DC = *Drama Criticism*
FL = *Feminism in Literature: A Gale Critical Companion*
GL = *Gothic Literature: A Gale Critical Companion*
HLC = *Hispanic Literature Criticism*
HLCS = *Hispanic Literature Criticism Supplement*
HR = *Harlem Renaissance: A Gale Critical Companion*
LC = *Literature Criticism from 1400 to 1800*
NCLC = *Nineteenth-Century Literature Criticism*
NNAL = *Native North American Literature*
PC = *Poetry Criticism*
SSC = *Short Story Criticism*
TCLC = *Twentieth-Century Literary Criticism*
WLC = *World Literature Criticism, 1500 to the Present*
WLCS = *World Literature Criticism Supplement*

The cross-references

> See also CA 85-88, 116; CANR 23, 61;
> DAM NOV; DLB 196; EW 13; MTCW 1, 2;
> RGSF 2; RGWL 2; SFW 4; SSFS 12

list all author entries in the following Thomson Gale biographical and literary sources:

AAYA = *Authors & Artists for Young Adults*
AFAW = *African American Writers*
AFW = *African Writers*
AITN = *Authors in the News*
AMW = *American Writers*
AMWR = *American Writers Retrospective Supplement*
AMWS = *American Writers Supplement*
ANW = *American Nature Writers*
AW = *Ancient Writers*
BEST = *Bestsellers*
BPFB = *Beacham's Encyclopedia of Popular Fiction: Biography and Resources*
BRW = *British Writers*
BRWS = *British Writers Supplement*
BW = *Black Writers*
BYA = *Beacham's Guide to Literature for Young Adults*
CA = *Contemporary Authors*
CAAS = *Contemporary Authors Autobiography Series*
CABS = *Contemporary Authors Bibliographical Series*
CAD = *Contemporary American Dramatists*
CANR = *Contemporary Authors New Revision Series*
CAP = *Contemporary Authors Permanent Series*
CBD = *Contemporary British Dramatists*
CCA = *Contemporary Canadian Authors*
CD = *Contemporary Dramatists*
CDALB = *Concise Dictionary of American Literary Biography*

CDALBS = Concise Dictionary of American Literary Biography Supplement
CDBLB = Concise Dictionary of British Literary Biography
CMW = St. James Guide to Crime & Mystery Writers
CN = Contemporary Novelists
CP = Contemporary Poets
CPW = Contemporary Popular Writers
CSW = Contemporary Southern Writers
CWD = Contemporary Women Dramatists
CWP = Contemporary Women Poets
CWRI = St. James Guide to Children's Writers
CWW = Contemporary World Writers
DA = DISCovering Authors
DA3 = DISCovering Authors 3.0
DAB = DISCovering Authors: British Edition
DAC = DISCovering Authors: Canadian Edition
DAM = DISCovering Authors: Modules
   DRAM: Dramatists Module; **MST:** Most-studied Authors Module;
   MULT: Multicultural Authors Module; **NOV:** Novelists Module;
   POET: Poets Module; **POP:** Popular Fiction and Genre Authors Module
DFS = Drama for Students
DLB = Dictionary of Literary Biography
DLBD = Dictionary of Literary Biography Documentary Series
DLBY = Dictionary of Literary Biography Yearbook
DNFS = Literature of Developing Nations for Students
EFS = Epics for Students
EXPN = Exploring Novels
EXPP = Exploring Poetry
EXPS = Exploring Short Stories
EW = European Writers
FANT = St. James Guide to Fantasy Writers
FW = Feminist Writers
GFL = Guide to French Literature, Beginnings to 1789, 1798 to the Present
GLL = Gay and Lesbian Literature
HGG = St. James Guide to Horror, Ghost & Gothic Writers
HW = Hispanic Writers
IDFW = International Dictionary of Films and Filmmakers: Writers and Production Artists
IDTP = International Dictionary of Theatre: Playwrights
LAIT = Literature and Its Times
LAW = Latin American Writers
JRDA = Junior DISCovering Authors
MAICYA = Major Authors and Illustrators for Children and Young Adults
MAICYAS = Major Authors and Illustrators for Children and Young Adults Supplement
MAWW = Modern American Women Writers
MJW = Modern Japanese Writers
MTCW = Major 20th-Century Writers
NCFS = Nonfiction Classics for Students
NFS = Novels for Students
PAB = Poets: American and British
PFS = Poetry for Students
RGAL = Reference Guide to American Literature
RGEL = Reference Guide to English Literature
RGSF = Reference Guide to Short Fiction
RGWL = Reference Guide to World Literature
RHW = Twentieth-Century Romance and Historical Writers
SAAS = Something about the Author Autobiography Series
SATA = Something about the Author
SFW = St. James Guide to Science Fiction Writers
SSFS = Short Stories for Students
TCWW = Twentieth-Century Western Writers
WLIT = World Literature and Its Times
WP = World Poets
YABC = Yesterday's Authors of Books for Children
YAW = St. James Guide to Young Adult Writers

Literary Criticism Series
Cumulative Author Index

Anderson, C. Farley
See Mencken, H(enry) L(ouis); Nathan, George Jean

Anderson, Jessica (Margaret) Queale
1916- .... **CLC 37**
See also CA 9-12R; CANR 4, 62; CN 4, 5, 6, 7

Anderson, Jon (Victor) 1940- .... CLC 9
See also CA 25-28R; CANR 20; CP 1, 3, 4; DAM POET

Anderson, Lindsay (Gordon)
1923-1994 .... **CLC 20**
See also CA 125; 128; 146; CANR 77

Anderson, Maxwell 1888-1959 .... TCLC 2, 144
See also CA 105; 152; DAM DRAM; DFS 16, 20; DLB 7, 228; MAL 5; MTCW 2; MTFW 2005; RGAL 4

Anderson, Poul (William)
1926-2001 .... **CLC 15**
See also AAYA 5, 34; BPFB 1; BYA 6, 8, 9; CA 1-4R, 181; 199; CAAE 181; CAAS 2; CANR 2, 15, 34, 64, 110; CLR 58; DLB 8; FANT; INT CANR-15; MTCW 1, 2; MTFW 2005; SATA 90; SATA-Brief 39; SATA-Essay 106; SCFW 1, 2; SFW 4; SUFW 1, 2

Anderson, Robert (Woodruff)
1917- .... **CLC 23**
See also AITN 1; CA 21-24R; CANR 32; CD 6; DAM DRAM; DLB 7; LAIT 5

Anderson, Roberta Joan
See Mitchell, Joni

Anderson, Sherwood 1876-1941 .. SSC 1, 46; TCLC 1, 10, 24, 123; WLC
See also AAYA 30; AMW; AMWC 2; BPFB 1; CA 104; 121; CANR 61; CDALB 1917-1929; DA; DA3; DAB; DAC; DAM MST, NOV; DLB 4, 9, 86; DLBD 1; EWL 3; EXPS; GLL 2; MAL 5; MTCW 1, 2; MTFW 2005; NFS 4; RGAL 4; RGSF 2; SSFS 4, 10, 11; TUS

Andier, Pierre
See Desnos, Robert

Andouard
See Giraudoux, Jean(-Hippolyte)

Andrade, Carlos Drummond de ..... CLC 18
See Drummond de Andrade, Carlos
See also EWL 3; RGWL 2, 3

Andrade, Mario de .... TCLC 43
See de Andrade, Mario
See also DLB 307; EWL 3; LAW; RGWL 2, 3; WLIT 1

Andreae, Johann V(alentin)
1586-1654 .... **LC 32**
See also DLB 164

Andreas Capellanus fl. c. 1185- .... CMLC 45
See also DLB 208

Andreas-Salome, Lou 1861-1937 ... TCLC 56
See also CA 178; DLB 66

Andreev, Leonid
See Andreyev, Leonid (Nikolaevich)
See also DLB 295; EWL 3

Andress, Lesley
See Sanders, Lawrence

Andrewes, Lancelot 1555-1626 .... LC 5
See also DLB 151, 172

Andrews, Cicily Fairfield
See West, Rebecca

Andrews, Elton V.
See Pohl, Frederik

Andreyev, Leonid (Nikolaevich)
1871-1919 .... **TCLC 3**
See Andreev, Leonid
See also CA 104; 185

Andric, Ivo 1892-1975 .... CLC 8; SSC 36; TCLC 135
See also CA 81-84; 57-60; CANR 43, 60; CDWLB 4; DLB 147; EW 11; EWL 3; MTCW 1; RGSF 2; RGWL 2, 3

Androvar
See Prado (Calvo), Pedro

Angela of Foligno 1248(?)-1309 .... CMLC 76

Angelique, Pierre
See Bataille, Georges

Angell, Roger 1920- .... CLC 26
See also CA 57-60; CANR 13, 44, 70, 144; DLB 171, 185

Angelou, Maya 1928- ... BLC 1; CLC 12, 35, 64, 77, 155; PC 32; WLCS
See also AAYA 7, 20; AMWS 4; BPFB 1; BW 2, 3; BYA 2; CA 65-68; CANR 19, 42, 65, 111, 133; CDALBS; CLR 53; CP 4, 5, 6, 7; CPW; CSW; CWP; DA; DA3; DAB; DAC; DAM MST, MULT, POET, POP; DLB 38; EWL 3; EXPN; EXPP; FL 1:5; LAIT 4; MAICYA 2; MAICYAS 1; MAL 5; MAWW; MTCW 1, 2; MTFW 2005; NCFS 2; NFS 2; PFS 2, 3; RGAL 4; SATA 49, 136; TCLE 1:1; WYA; YAW

Angouleme, Marguerite d'
See de Navarre, Marguerite

Anna Comnena 1083-1153 .... CMLC 25

Annensky, Innokentii Fedorovich
See Annensky, Innokenty (Fyodorovich)
See also DLB 295

Annensky, Innokenty (Fyodorovich)
1856-1909 .... **TCLC 14**
See also CA 110; 155; EWL 3

Annunzio, Gabriele d'
See D'Annunzio, Gabriele

Anodos
See Coleridge, Mary E(lizabeth)

Anon, Charles Robert
See Pessoa, Fernando (Antonio Nogueira)

Anouilh, Jean (Marie Lucien Pierre)
1910-1987 . **CLC 1, 3, 8, 13, 40, 50; DC 8, 21**
See also AAYA 67; CA 17-20R; 123; CANR 32; DAM DRAM; DFS 9, 10, 19; DLB 321; EW 13; EWL 3; GFL 1789 to the Present; MTCW 1, 2; MTFW 2005; RGWL 2, 3; TWA

Anselm of Canterbury
1033(?)-1109 .... **CMLC 67**
See also DLB 115

Anthony, Florence
See Ai

Anthony, John
See Ciardi, John (Anthony)

Anthony, Peter
See Shaffer, Anthony (Joshua); Shaffer, Peter (Levin)

Anthony, Piers 1934- .... CLC 35
See also AAYA 11, 48; BYA 7; CA 200; CAAE 200; CANR 28, 56, 73, 102, 133; CPW; DAM POP; DLB 8; FANT; MAICYA 2; MAICYAS 1; MTCW 1, 2; MTFW 2005; SAAS 22; SATA 84, 129; SATA-Essay 129; SFW 4; SUFW 1, 2; YAW

Anthony, Susan B(rownell)
1820-1906 .... **TCLC 84**
See also CA 211; FW

Antiphon c. 480B.C.-c. 411B.C. .... CMLC 55

Antoine, Marc
See Proust, (Valentin-Louis-George-Eugene) Marcel

Antoninus, Brother
See Everson, William (Oliver)
See also CP 1

Antonioni, Michelangelo 1912- .... CLC 20, 144
See also CA 73-76; CANR 45, 77

Antschel, Paul 1920-1970
See Celan, Paul
See also CA 85-88; CANR 33, 61; MTCW 1; PFS 21

Anwar, Chairil 1922-1949 .... TCLC 22
See Chairil Anwar
See also CA 121; 219; RGWL 3

Anzaldua, Gloria (Evanjelina)
1942-2004 .... **CLC 200; HLCS 1**
See also CA 175, 227; CSW; CWP; DLB 122; FW; LLW; RGAL 4; SATA-Obit 154

Apess, William 1798-1839(?) .... NCLC 73; NNAL
See also DAM MULT; DLB 175, 243

Apollinaire, Guillaume 1880-1918 .... PC 7; TCLC 3, 8, 51
See Kostrowitzki, Wilhelm Apollinaris de
See also CA 152; DAM POET; DLB 258, 321; EW 9; EWL 3; GFL 1789 to the Present; MTCW 2; RGWL 2, 3; TWA; WP

Apollonius of Rhodes
See Apollonius Rhodius
See also AW 1; RGWL 2, 3

Apollonius Rhodius c. 300B.C.-c. 220B.C. .... CMLC 28
See Apollonius of Rhodes
See also DLB 176

Appelfeld, Aharon 1932- ... CLC 23, 47; SSC 42
See also CA 112; 133; CANR 86; CWW 2; DLB 299; EWL 3; RGSF 2; WLIT 6

Apple, Max (Isaac) 1941- .... CLC 9, 33; SSC 50
See also CA 81-84; CANR 19, 54; DLB 130

Appleman, Philip (Dean) 1926- .... CLC 51
See also CA 13-16R; CAAS 18; CANR 6, 29, 56

Appleton, Lawrence
See Lovecraft, H(oward) P(hillips)

Apteryx
See Eliot, T(homas) S(tearns)

Apuleius, (Lucius Madaurensis)
125(?)-175(?) .... **CMLC 1**
See also AW 2; CDWLB 1; DLB 211; RGWL 2, 3; SUFW

Aquin, Hubert 1929-1977 .... CLC 15
See also CA 105; DLB 53; EWL 3

Aquinas, Thomas 1224(?)-1274 ..... CMLC 33
See also DLB 115; EW 1; TWA

Aragon, Louis 1897-1982 .... CLC 3, 22; TCLC 123
See also CA 69-72; 108; CANR 28, 71; DAM NOV, POET; DLB 72, 258; EW 11; EWL 3; GFL 1789 to the Present; GLL 2; LMFS 2; MTCW 1, 2; RGWL 2, 3

Arany, Janos 1817-1882 .... NCLC 34

Aranyos, Kakay 1847-1910
See Mikszath, Kalman

Aratus of Soli c. 315B.C.-c. 240B.C. .... CMLC 64
See also DLB 176

Arbuthnot, John 1667-1735 .... LC 1
See also DLB 101

Archer, Herbert Winslow
See Mencken, H(enry) L(ouis)

Archer, Jeffrey (Howard) 1940- .... CLC 28
See also AAYA 16; BEST 89:3; BPFB 1; CA 77-80; CANR 22, 52, 95, 136; CPW; DA3; DAM POP; INT CANR-22; MTFW 2005

Archer, Jules 1915- .... CLC 12
See also CA 9-12R; CANR 6, 69; SAAS 5; SATA 4, 85

Archer, Lee
See Ellison, Harlan (Jay)

Archilochus c. 7th cent. B.C.- .... CMLC 44
See also DLB 176

Auchincloss, Louis (Stanton) 1917- .. **CLC 4, 6, 9, 18, 45; SSC 22**
See also AMWS 4; CA 1-4R; CANR 6, 29, 55, 87, 130; CN 1, 2, 3, 4, 5, 6, 7; DAM NOV; DLB 2, 244; DLBY 1980; EWL 3; INT CANR-29; MAL 5; MTCW 1; RGAL 4

Auden, W(ystan) H(ugh) 1907-1973 . **CLC 1, 2, 3, 4, 6, 9, 11, 14, 43, 123; PC 1; WLC**
See also AAYA 18; AMWS 2; BRW 7; BRWR 1; CA 9-12R; 45-48; CANR 5, 61, 105; CDBLB 1914-1945; CP 1, 2; DA; DA3; DAB; DAC; DAM DRAM, MST, POET; DLB 10, 20; EWL 3; EXPP; MAL 5; MTCW 1, 2; MTFW 2005; PAB; PFS 1, 3, 4, 10; TUS; WP

Audiberti, Jacques 1899-1965 .... **CLC 38**
See also CA 25-28R; DAM DRAM; DLB 321; EWL 3

Audubon, John James 1785-1851 . **NCLC 47**
See also ANW; DLB 248

Auel, Jean M(arie) 1936- .... **CLC 31, 107**
See also AAYA 7, 51; BEST 90:4; BPFB 1; CA 103; CANR 21, 64, 115; CPW; DA3; DAM POP; INT CANR-21; NFS 11; RHW; SATA 91

Auerbach, Erich 1892-1957 .... **TCLC 43**
See also CA 118; 155; EWL 3

Augier, Emile 1820-1889 .... **NCLC 31**
See also DLB 192; GFL 1789 to the Present

August, John
See De Voto, Bernard (Augustine)

Augustine, St. 354-430 .... **CMLC 6; WLCS**
See also DA; DA3; DAB; DAC; DAM MST; DLB 115; EW 1; RGWL 2, 3

Aunt Belinda
See Braddon, Mary Elizabeth

Aunt Weedy
See Alcott, Louisa May

Aurelius
See Bourne, Randolph S(illiman)

Aurelius, Marcus 121-180 .... **CMLC 45**
See Marcus Aurelius
See also RGWL 2, 3

Aurobindo, Sri
See Ghose, Aurabinda

Aurobindo Ghose
See Ghose, Aurabinda

Austen, Jane 1775-1817 ...... **NCLC 1, 13, 19, 33, 51, 81, 95, 119, 150; WLC**
See also AAYA 19; BRW 4; BRWC 1; BRWR 2; BYA 3; CDBLB 1789-1832; DA; DA3; DAB; DAC; DAM MST, NOV; DLB 116; EXPN; FL 1:2; GL 2; LAIT 2; LATS 1:1; LMFS 1; NFS 1, 14, 18, 20, 21; TEA; WLIT 3; WYAS 1

Auster, Paul 1947- .... **CLC 47, 131**
See also AMWS 12; CA 69-72; CANR 23, 52, 75, 129; CMW 4; CN 5, 6, 7; DA3; DLB 227; MAL 5; MTCW 2; MTFW 2005; SUFW 2; TCLE 1:1

Austin, Frank
See Faust, Frederick (Schiller)

Austin, Mary (Hunter) 1868-1934 . **TCLC 25**
See also ANW; CA 109; 178; DLB 9, 78, 206, 221, 275; FW; TCWW 1, 2

Averroes 1126-1198 .... **CMLC 7**
See also DLB 115

Avicenna 980-1037 .... **CMLC 16**
See also DLB 115

Avison, Margaret (Kirkland) 1918- .. **CLC 2, 4, 97**
See also CA 17-20R; CANR 134; CP 1, 2, 3, 4, 5, 6, 7; DAC; DAM POET; DLB 53; MTCW 1

Axton, David
See Koontz, Dean R.

Ayckbourn, Alan 1939- ...... **CLC 5, 8, 18, 33, 74; DC 13**
See also BRWS 5; CA 21-24R; CANR 31, 59, 118; CBD; CD 5, 6; DAB; DAM DRAM; DFS 7; DLB 13, 245; EWL 3; MTCW 1, 2; MTFW 2005

Aydy, Catherine
See Tennant, Emma (Christina)

Ayme, Marcel (Andre) 1902-1967 ... **CLC 11; SSC 41**
See also CA 89-92; CANR 67, 137; CLR 25; DLB 72; EW 12; EWL 3; GFL 1789 to the Present; RGSF 2; RGWL 2, 3; SATA 91

Ayrton, Michael 1921-1975 .... **CLC 7**
See also CA 5-8R; 61-64; CANR 9, 21

Aytmatov, Chingiz
See Aitmatov, Chingiz (Torekulovich)
See also EWL 3

Azorin .... **CLC 11**
See Martinez Ruiz, Jose
See also DLB 322; EW 9; EWL 3

Azuela, Mariano 1873-1952 .. **HLC 1; TCLC 3, 145**
See also CA 104; 131; CANR 81; DAM MULT; EWL 3; HW 1, 2; LAW; MTCW 1, 2; MTFW 2005

Ba, Mariama 1929-1981 .... **BLCS**
See also AFW; BW 2; CA 141; CANR 87; DNFS 2; WLIT 2

Baastad, Babbis Friis
See Friis-Baastad, Babbis Ellinor

Bab
See Gilbert, W(illiam) S(chwenck)

Babbis, Eleanor
See Friis-Baastad, Babbis Ellinor

Babel, Isaac
See Babel, Isaak (Emmanuilovich)
See also EW 11; SSFS 10

Babel, Isaak (Emmanuilovich) 1894-1941(?) . **SSC 16, 78; TCLC 2, 13, 171**
See Babel, Isaac
See also CA 104; 155; CANR 113; DLB 272; EWL 3; MTCW 2; MTFW 2005; RGSF 2; RGWL 2, 3; TWA

Babits, Mihaly 1883-1941 .... **TCLC 14**
See also CA 114; CDWLB 4; DLB 215; EWL 3

Babur 1483-1530 .... **LC 18**

Babylas 1898-1962
See Ghelderode, Michel de

Baca, Jimmy Santiago 1952- . **HLC 1; PC 41**
See also CA 131; CANR 81, 90, 146; CP 7; DAM MULT; DLB 122; HW 1, 2; LLW; MAL 5

Baca, Jose Santiago
See Baca, Jimmy Santiago

Bacchelli, Riccardo 1891-1985 .... **CLC 19**
See also CA 29-32R; 117; DLB 264; EWL 3

Bach, Richard (David) 1936- .... **CLC 14**
See also AITN 1; BEST 89:2; BPFB 1; BYA 5; CA 9-12R; CANR 18, 93; CPW; DAM NOV, POP; FANT; MTCW 1; SATA 13

Bache, Benjamin Franklin 1769-1798 .... **LC 74**
See also DLB 43

Bachelard, Gaston 1884-1962 ...... **TCLC 128**
See also CA 97-100; 89-92; DLB 296; GFL 1789 to the Present

Bachman, Richard
See King, Stephen

Bachmann, Ingeborg 1926-1973 .... **CLC 69**
See also CA 93-96; 45-48; CANR 69; DLB 85; EWL 3; RGWL 2, 3

Bacon, Francis 1561-1626 .... **LC 18, 32**
See also BRW 1; CDBLB Before 1660; DLB 151, 236, 252; RGEL 2; TEA

Bacon, Roger 1214(?)-1294 .... **CMLC 14**
See also DLB 115

Bacovia, George 1881-1957 .... **TCLC 24**
See Vasiliu, Gheorghe
See also CDWLB 4; DLB 220; EWL 3

Badanes, Jerome 1937-1995 .... **CLC 59**
See also CA 234

Bagehot, Walter 1826-1877 .... **NCLC 10**
See also DLB 55

Bagnold, Enid 1889-1981 .... **CLC 25**
See also BYA 2; CA 5-8R; 103; CANR 5, 40; CBD; CN 2; CWD; CWRI 5; DAM DRAM; DLB 13, 160, 191, 245; FW; MAICYA 1, 2; RGEL 2; SATA 1, 25

Bagritsky, Eduard .... **TCLC 60**
See Dzyubin, Eduard Georgievich

Bagrjana, Elisaveta
See Belcheva, Elisaveta Lyubomirova

Bagryana, Elisaveta .... **CLC 10**
See Belcheva, Elisaveta Lyubomirova
See also CA 178; CDWLB 4; DLB 147; EWL 3

Bailey, Paul 1937- .... **CLC 45**
See also CA 21-24R; CANR 16, 62, 124; CN 1, 2, 3, 4, 5, 6, 7; DLB 14, 271; GLL 2

Baillie, Joanna 1762-1851 ...... **NCLC 71, 151**
See also DLB 93; GL 2; RGEL 2

Bainbridge, Beryl (Margaret) 1934- . **CLC 4, 5, 8, 10, 14, 18, 22, 62, 130**
See also BRWS 6; CA 21-24R; CANR 24, 55, 75, 88, 128; CN 2, 3, 4, 5, 6, 7; DAM NOV; DLB 14, 231; EWL 3; MTCW 1, 2; MTFW 2005

Baker, Carlos (Heard) 1909-1987 .... **TCLC 119**
See also CA 5-8R; 122; CANR 3, 63; DLB 103

Baker, Elliott 1922- .... **CLC 8**
See also CA 45-48; CANR 2, 63; CN 1, 2, 3, 4, 5, 6, 7

Baker, Jean H. .... **TCLC 3, 10**
See Russell, George William

Baker, Nicholson 1957- .... **CLC 61, 165**
See also AMWS 13; CA 135; CANR 63, 120, 138; CN 6; CPW; DA3; DAM POP; DLB 227; MTFW 2005

Baker, Ray Stannard 1870-1946 .... **TCLC 47**
See also CA 118

Baker, Russell (Wayne) 1925- .... **CLC 31**
See also BEST 89:4; CA 57-60; CANR 11, 41, 59, 137; MTCW 1, 2; MTFW 2005

Bakhtin, M.
See Bakhtin, Mikhail Mikhailovich

Bakhtin, M. M.
See Bakhtin, Mikhail Mikhailovich

Bakhtin, Mikhail
See Bakhtin, Mikhail Mikhailovich

Bakhtin, Mikhail Mikhailovich 1895-1975 .... **CLC 83; TCLC 160**
See also CA 128; 113; DLB 242; EWL 3

Bakshi, Ralph 1938(?)- .... **CLC 26**
See also CA 112; 138; IDFW 3

Bakunin, Mikhail (Alexandrovich) 1814-1876 .... **NCLC 25, 58**
See also DLB 277

Baldwin, James (Arthur) 1924-1987 . **BLC 1; CLC 1, 2, 3, 4, 5, 8, 13, 15, 17, 42, 50, 67, 90, 127; DC 1; SSC 10, 33; WLC**
See also AAYA 4, 34; AFAW 1, 2; AMWR 2; AMWS 1; BPFB 1; BW 1; CA 1-4R; 124; CABS 1; CAD; CANR 3, 24; CDALB 1941-1968; CN 1, 2, 3, 4; CPW; DA; DA3; DAB; DAC; DAM MST, MULT, NOV, POP; DFS 11, 15; DLB 2, 7, 33, 249, 278; DLBY 1987; EWL 3;

EXPS; LAIT 5; MAL 5; MTCW 1, 2; MTFW 2005; NCFS 4; NFS 4; RGAL 4; RGSF 2; SATA 9; SATA-Obit 54; SSFS 2, 18; TUS

Baldwin, William c. 1515-1563 .... **LC 113**
See also DLB 132

Bale, John 1495-1563 .... **LC 62**
See also DLB 132; RGEL 2; TEA

Ball, Hugo 1886-1927 .... **TCLC 104**

Ballard, J(ames) G(raham) 1930- . **CLC 3, 6, 14, 36, 137; SSC 1, 53**
See also AAYA 3, 52; BRWS 5; CA 5-8R; CANR 15, 39, 65, 107, 133; CN 1, 2, 3, 4, 5, 6, 7; DA3; DAM NOV, POP; DLB 14, 207, 261, 319; EWL 3; HGG; MTCW 1, 2; MTFW 2005; NFS 8; RGEL 2; RGSF 2; SATA 93; SCFW 1, 2; SFW 4

Balmont, Konstantin (Dmitriyevich)
1867-1943 .... **TCLC 11**
See also CA 109; 155; DLB 295; EWL 3

Baltausis, Vincas 1847-1910
See Mikszath, Kalman

Balzac, Honore de 1799-1850 ... **NCLC 5, 35, 53, 153; SSC 5, 59; WLC**
See also DA; DA3; DAB; DAC; DAM MST, NOV; DLB 119; EW 5; GFL 1789 to the Present; LMFS 1; RGSF 2; RGWL 2, 3; SSFS 10; SUFW; TWA

Bambara, Toni Cade 1939-1995 .... **BLC 1; CLC 19, 88; SSC 35; TCLC 116; WLCS**
See also AAYA 5, 49; AFAW 2; AMWS 11; BW 2, 3; BYA 12, 14; CA 29-32R; 150; CANR 24, 49, 81; CDALBS; DA; DA3; DAC; DAM MST, MULT; DLB 38, 218; EXPS; MAL 5; MTCW 1, 2; MTFW 2005; RGAL 4; RGSF 2; SATA 112; SSFS 4, 7, 12, 21

Bamdad, A.
See Shamlu, Ahmad

Bamdad, Alef
See Shamlu, Ahmad

Banat, D. R.
See Bradbury, Ray (Douglas)

Bancroft, Laura
See Baum, L(yman) Frank

Banim, John 1798-1842 .... **NCLC 13**
See also DLB 116, 158, 159; RGEL 2

Banim, Michael 1796-1874 .... **NCLC 13**
See also DLB 158, 159

Banjo, The
See Paterson, A(ndrew) B(arton)

Banks, Iain
See Banks, Iain M(enzies)
See also BRWS 11

Banks, Iain M(enzies) 1954- .... **CLC 34**
See Banks, Iain
See also CA 123; 128; CANR 61, 106; DLB 194, 261; EWL 3; HGG; INT CA-128; MTFW 2005; SFW 4

Banks, Lynne Reid .... **CLC 23**
See Reid Banks, Lynne
See also AAYA 6; BYA 7; CLR 86; CN 4, 5, 6

Banks, Russell (Earl) 1940- .... **CLC 37, 72, 187; SSC 42**
See also AAYA 45; AMWS 5; CA 65-68; CAAS 15; CANR 19, 52, 73, 118; CN 4, 5, 6, 7; DLB 130, 278; EWL 3; MAL 5; MTCW 2; MTFW 2005; NFS 13

Banville, John 1945- .... **CLC 46, 118**
See also CA 117; 128; CANR 104; CN 4, 5, 6, 7; DLB 14, 271; INT CA-128

Banville, Theodore (Faullain) de
1832-1891 .... **NCLC 9**
See also DLB 217; GFL 1789 to the Present

Baraka, Amiri 1934- .... **BLC 1; CLC 1, 2, 3, 5, 10, 14, 33, 115, 213; DC 6; PC 4; WLCS**
See Jones, LeRoi
See also AAYA 63; AFAW 1, 2; AMWS 2; BW 2, 3; CA 21-24R; CABS 3; CAD; CANR 27, 38, 61, 133; CD 3, 5, 6; CDALB 1941-1968; CP 4, 5, 6, 7; CPW; DA; DA3; DAC; DAM MST, MULT, POET, POP; DFS 3, 11, 16; DLB 5, 7, 16, 38; DLBD 8; EWL 3; MAL 5; MTCW 1, 2; MTFW 2005; PFS 9; RGAL 4; TCLE 1:1; TUS; WP

Baratynsky, Evgenii Abramovich
1800-1844 .... **NCLC 103**
See also DLB 205

Barbauld, Anna Laetitia
1743-1825 .... **NCLC 50**
See also DLB 107, 109, 142, 158; RGEL 2

Barbellion, W. N. P. .... **TCLC 24**
See Cummings, Bruce F(rederick)

Barber, Benjamin R. 1939- .... **CLC 141**
See also CA 29-32R; CANR 12, 32, 64, 119

Barbera, Jack (Vincent) 1945- .... **CLC 44**
See also CA 110; CANR 45

Barbey d'Aurevilly, Jules-Amedee
1808-1889 .... **NCLC 1; SSC 17**
See also DLB 119; GFL 1789 to the Present

Barbour, John c. 1316-1395 .... **CMLC 33**
See also DLB 146

Barbusse, Henri 1873-1935 .... **TCLC 5**
See also CA 105; 154; DLB 65; EWL 3; RGWL 2, 3

Barclay, Alexander c. 1475-1552 .... **LC 109**
See also DLB 132

Barclay, Bill
See Moorcock, Michael (John)

Barclay, William Ewert
See Moorcock, Michael (John)

Barea, Arturo 1897-1957 .... **TCLC 14**
See also CA 111; 201

Barfoot, Joan 1946- .... **CLC 18**
See also CA 105; CANR 141

Barham, Richard Harris
1788-1845 .... **NCLC 77**
See also DLB 159

Baring, Maurice 1874-1945 .... **TCLC 8**
See also CA 105; 168; DLB 34; HGG

Baring-Gould, Sabine 1834-1924 ... **TCLC 88**
See also DLB 156, 190

Barker, Clive 1952- .... **CLC 52, 205; SSC 53**
See also AAYA 10, 54; BEST 90:3; BPFB 1; CA 121; 129; CANR 71, 111, 133; CPW; DA3; DAM POP; DLB 261; HGG; INT CA-129; MTCW 1, 2; MTFW 2005; SUFW 2

Barker, George Granville
1913-1991 .... **CLC 8, 48**
See also CA 9-12R; 135; CANR 7, 38; CP 1, 2, 3, 4; DAM POET; DLB 20; EWL 3; MTCW 1

Barker, Harley Granville
See Granville-Barker, Harley
See also DLB 10

Barker, Howard 1946- .... **CLC 37**
See also CA 102; CBD; CD 5, 6; DLB 13, 233

Barker, Jane 1652-1732 .... **LC 42, 82**
See also DLB 39, 131

Barker, Pat(ricia) 1943- ...... **CLC 32, 94, 146**
See also BRWS 4; CA 117; 122; CANR 50, 101; CN 6, 7; DLB 271; INT CA-122

Barlach, Ernst (Heinrich)
1870-1938 .... **TCLC 84**
See also CA 178; DLB 56, 118; EWL 3

Barlow, Joel 1754-1812 .... **NCLC 23**
See also AMWS 2; DLB 37; RGAL 4

Barnard, Mary (Ethel) 1909- .... **CLC 48**
See also CA 21-22; CAP 2; CP 1

Barnes, Djuna 1892-1982 .... **CLC 3, 4, 8, 11, 29, 127; SSC 3**
See Steptoe, Lydia
See also AMWS 3; CA 9-12R; 107; CAD; CANR 16, 55; CN 1, 2, 3; CWD; DLB 4, 9, 45; EWL 3; GLL 1; MAL 5; MTCW 1, 2; MTFW 2005; RGAL 4; TCLE 1:1; TUS

Barnes, Jim 1933- .... **NNAL**
See also CA 108; 175; CAAE 175; CAAS 28; DLB 175

Barnes, Julian (Patrick) 1946- . **CLC 42, 141**
See also BRWS 4; CA 102; CANR 19, 54, 115, 137; CN 4, 5, 6, 7; DAB; DLB 194; DLBY 1993; EWL 3; MTCW 2; MTFW 2005

Barnes, Peter 1931-2004 .... **CLC 5, 56**
See also CA 65-68; 230; CAAS 12; CANR 33, 34, 64, 113; CBD; CD 5, 6; DFS 6; DLB 13, 233; MTCW 1

Barnes, William 1801-1886 .... **NCLC 75**
See also DLB 32

Baroja (y Nessi), Pio 1872-1956 .... **HLC 1; TCLC 8**
See also CA 104; EW 9

Baron, David
See Pinter, Harold

Baron Corvo
See Rolfe, Frederick (William Serafino Austin Lewis Mary)

Barondess, Sue K(aufman)
1926-1977 .... **CLC 8**
See Kaufman, Sue
See also CA 1-4R; 69-72; CANR 1

Baron de Teive
See Pessoa, Fernando (Antonio Nogueira)

Baroness Von S.
See Zangwill, Israel

Barres, (Auguste-)Maurice
1862-1923 .... **TCLC 47**
See also CA 164; DLB 123; GFL 1789 to the Present

Barreto, Afonso Henrique de Lima
See Lima Barreto, Afonso Henrique de

Barrett, Andrea 1954- .... **CLC 150**
See also CA 156; CANR 92; CN 7

Barrett, Michele .... **CLC 65**

Barrett, (Roger) Syd 1946- .... **CLC 35**

Barrett, William (Christopher)
1913-1992 .... **CLC 27**
See also CA 13-16R; 139; CANR 11, 67; INT CANR-11

Barrett Browning, Elizabeth
1806-1861 ... **NCLC 1, 16, 61, 66; PC 6, 62; WLC**
See also AAYA 63; BRW 4; CDBLB 1832-1890; DA; DA3; DAB; DAC; DAM MST, POET; DLB 32, 199; EXPP; FL 1:2; PAB; PFS 2, 16, 23; TEA; WLIT 4; WP

Barrie, J(ames) M(atthew)
1860-1937 .... **TCLC 2, 164**
See also BRWS 3; BYA 4, 5; CA 104; 136; CANR 77; CDBLB 1890-1914; CLR 16; CWRI 5; DA3; DAB; DAM DRAM; DFS 7; DLB 10, 141, 156; EWL 3; FANT; MAICYA 1, 2; MTCW 2; MTFW 2005; SATA 100; SUFW; WCH; WLIT 4; YABC 1

Barrington, Michael
See Moorcock, Michael (John)

Barrol, Grady
See Bograd, Larry

Barry, Mike
See Malzberg, Barry N(athaniel)

Barry, Philip 1896-1949 .... **TCLC 11**
See also CA 109; 199; DFS 9; DLB 7, 228; MAL 5; RGAL 4

Bart, Andre Schwarz
See Schwarz-Bart, Andre

Behrman, S(amuel) N(athaniel)
1893-1973 .... **CLC 40**
See also CA 13-16; 45-48; CAD; CAP 1;
DLB 7, 44; IDFW 3; MAL 5; RGAL 4

Bekederemo, J. P. Clark
See Clark Bekederemo, J(ohnson) P(epper)
See also CD 6

Belasco, David 1853-1931 .... **TCLC 3**
See also CA 104; 168; DLB 7; MAL 5;
RGAL 4

Belcheva, Elisaveta Lyubomirova
1893-1991 .... **CLC 10**
See Bagryana, Elisaveta

Beldone, Phil ''Cheech''
See Ellison, Harlan (Jay)

Beleno
See Azuela, Mariano

Belinski, Vissarion Grigoryevich
1811-1848 .... **NCLC 5**
See also DLB 198

Belitt, Ben 1911- .... **CLC 22**
See also CA 13-16R; CAAS 4; CANR 7,
77; CP 1, 2, 3, 4; DLB 5

Belknap, Jeremy 1744-1798 .... **LC 115**
See also DLB 30, 37

Bell, Gertrude (Margaret Lowthian)
1868-1926 .... **TCLC 67**
See also CA 167; CANR 110; DLB 174

Bell, J. Freeman
See Zangwill, Israel

Bell, James Madison 1826-1902 .... **BLC 1;
TCLC 43**
See also BW 1; CA 122; 124; DAM MULT;
DLB 50

Bell, Madison Smartt 1957- ...... **CLC 41, 102**
See also AMWS 10; BPFB 1; CA 111, 183;
CAAE 183; CANR 28, 54, 73, 134; CN
5, 6, 7; CSW; DLB 218, 278; MTCW 2;
MTFW 2005

Bell, Marvin (Hartley) 1937- .... **CLC 8, 31**
See also CA 21-24R; CAAS 14; CANR 59,
102; CP 1, 2, 3, 4, 5, 6, 7; DAM POET;
DLB 5; MAL 5; MTCW 1

Bell, W. L. D.
See Mencken, H(enry) L(ouis)

Bellamy, Atwood C.
See Mencken, H(enry) L(ouis)

Bellamy, Edward 1850-1898 ..... **NCLC 4, 86,
147**
See also DLB 12; NFS 15; RGAL 4; SFW
4

Belli, Gioconda 1948- .... **HLCS 1**
See also CA 152; CANR 143; CWW 2;
DLB 290; EWL 3; RGWL 3

Bellin, Edward J.
See Kuttner, Henry

Bello, Andres 1781-1865 .... **NCLC 131**
See also LAW

**Belloc, (Joseph) Hilaire (Pierre Sebastien
Rene Swanton)** 1870-1953 .... **PC 24;
TCLC 7, 18**
See also CA 106; 152; CLR 102; CWRI 5;
DAM POET; DLB 19, 100, 141, 174;
EWL 3; MTCW 2; MTFW 2005; SATA
112; WCH; YABC 1

Belloc, Joseph Peter Rene Hilaire
See Belloc, (Joseph) Hilaire (Pierre Sebastien Rene Swanton)

Belloc, Joseph Pierre Hilaire
See Belloc, (Joseph) Hilaire (Pierre Sebastien Rene Swanton)

Belloc, M. A.
See Lowndes, Marie Adelaide (Belloc)

Belloc-Lowndes, Mrs.
See Lowndes, Marie Adelaide (Belloc)

Bellow, Saul 1915-2005 ...... **CLC 1, 2, 3, 6, 8,
10, 13, 15, 25, 33, 34, 63, 79, 190, 200;
SSC 14; WLC**
See also AITN 2; AMW; AMWC 2; AMWR
2; BEST 89:3; BPFB 1; CA 5-8R; 238;
CABS 1; CANR 29, 53, 95, 132; CDALB
1941-1968; CN 1, 2, 3, 4, 5, 6, 7; DA;
DA3; DAB; DAC; DAM MST, NOV,
POP; DLB 2, 28, 299; DLBD 3; DLBY
1982; EWL 3; MAL 5; MTCW 1, 2;
MTFW 2005; NFS 4, 14; RGAL 4; RGSF
2; SSFS 12; TUS

Belser, Reimond Karel Maria de 1929-
See Ruyslinck, Ward
See also CA 152

Bely, Andrey .... **PC 11; TCLC 7**
See Bugayev, Boris Nikolayevich
See also DLB 295; EW 9; EWL 3

Belyi, Andrei
See Bugayev, Boris Nikolayevich
See also RGWL 2, 3

Bembo, Pietro 1470-1547 .... **LC 79**
See also RGWL 2, 3

Benary, Margot
See Benary-Isbert, Margot

Benary-Isbert, Margot 1889-1979 .... **CLC 12**
See also CA 5-8R; 89-92; CANR 4, 72;
CLR 12; MAICYA 1, 2; SATA 2; SATA-
Obit 21

Benavente (y Martinez), Jacinto
1866-1954 .... **DC 26; HLCS 1; TCLC 3**
See also CA 106; 131; CANR 81; DAM
DRAM, MULT; EWL 3; GLL 2; HW 1,
2; MTCW 1, 2

Benchley, Peter 1940- .... **CLC 4, 8**
See also AAYA 14; AITN 2; BPFB 1; CA
17-20R; CANR 12, 35, 66, 115; CPW;
DAM NOV, POP; HGG; MTCW 1, 2;
MTFW 2005; SATA 3, 89, 164

Benchley, Peter Bradford
See Benchley, Peter

Benchley, Robert (Charles)
1889-1945 .... **TCLC 1, 55**
See also CA 105; 153; DLB 11; MAL 5;
RGAL 4

Benda, Julien 1867-1956 .... **TCLC 60**
See also CA 120; 154; GFL 1789 to the
Present

Benedict, Ruth (Fulton)
1887-1948 .... **TCLC 60**
See also CA 158; DLB 246

Benedikt, Michael 1935- .... **CLC 4, 14**
See also CA 13-16R; CANR 7; CP 1, 2, 3,
4, 5, 6, 7; DLB 5

Benet, Juan 1927-1993 .... **CLC 28**
See also CA 143; EWL 3

Benet, Stephen Vincent 1898-1943 ..... **PC 64;
SSC 10, 86; TCLC 7**
See also AMWS 11; CA 104; 152; DA3;
DAM POET; DLB 4, 48, 102, 249, 284;
DLBY 1997; EWL 3; HGG; MAL 5;
MTCW 2; MTFW 2005; RGAL 4; RGSF
2; SUFW; WP; YABC 1

Benet, William Rose 1886-1950 ..... **TCLC 28**
See also CA 118; 152; DAM POET; DLB
45; RGAL 4

Benford, Gregory (Albert) 1941- ..... **CLC 52**
See also BPFB 1; CA 69-72, 175; CAAE
175; CAAS 27; CANR 12, 24, 49, 95,
134; CN 7; CSW; DLBY 1982; MTFW
2005; SCFW 2; SFW 4

Bengtsson, Frans (Gunnar)
1894-1954 .... **TCLC 48**
See also CA 170; EWL 3

Benjamin, David
See Slavitt, David R(ytman)

Benjamin, Lois
See Gould, Lois

Benjamin, Walter 1892-1940 .... **TCLC 39**
See also CA 164; DLB 242; EW 11; EWL
3

Ben Jelloun, Tahar 1944-
See Jelloun, Tahar ben
See also CA 135; CWW 2; EWL 3; RGWL
3; WLIT 2

Benn, Gottfried 1886-1956 .. **PC 35; TCLC 3**
See also CA 106; 153; DLB 56; EWL 3;
RGWL 2, 3

Bennett, Alan 1934- .... **CLC 45, 77**
See also BRWS 8; CA 103; CANR 35, 55,
106; CBD; CD 5, 6; DAB; DAM MST;
DLB 310; MTCW 1, 2; MTFW 2005

Bennett, (Enoch) Arnold
1867-1931 .... **TCLC 5, 20**
See also BRW 6; CA 106; 155; CDBLB
1890-1914; DLB 10, 34, 98, 135; EWL 3;
MTCW 2

Bennett, Elizabeth
See Mitchell, Margaret (Munnerlyn)

Bennett, George Harold 1930-
See Bennett, Hal
See also BW 1; CA 97-100; CANR 87

Bennett, Gwendolyn B. 1902-1981 .... **HR 1:2**
See also BW 1; CA 125; DLB 51; WP

Bennett, Hal .... **CLC 5**
See Bennett, George Harold
See also DLB 33

Bennett, Jay 1912- .... **CLC 35**
See also AAYA 10; CA 69-72; CANR 11,
42, 79; JRDA; SAAS 4; SATA 41, 87;
SATA-Brief 27; WYA; YAW

Bennett, Louise (Simone) 1919- .... **BLC 1;
CLC 28**
See also BW 2, 3; CA 151; CDWLB 3; CP
1, 2, 3, 4, 5, 6, 7; DAM MULT; DLB 117;
EWL 3

Benson, A. C. 1862-1925 .... **TCLC 123**
See also DLB 98

Benson, E(dward) F(rederic)
1867-1940 .... **TCLC 27**
See also CA 114; 157; DLB 135, 153;
HGG; SUFW 1

Benson, Jackson J. 1930- .... **CLC 34**
See also CA 25-28R; DLB 111

Benson, Sally 1900-1972 .... **CLC 17**
See also CA 19-20; 37-40R; CAP 1; SATA
1, 35; SATA-Obit 27

Benson, Stella 1892-1933 .... **TCLC 17**
See also CA 117; 154, 155; DLB 36, 162;
FANT; TEA

Bentham, Jeremy 1748-1832 .... **NCLC 38**
See also DLB 107, 158, 252

Bentley, E(dmund) C(lerihew)
1875-1956 .... **TCLC 12**
See also CA 108; 232; DLB 70; MSW

Bentley, Eric (Russell) 1916- .... **CLC 24**
See also CA 5-8R; CAD; CANR 6, 67;
CBD; CD 5, 6; INT CANR-6

ben Uzair, Salem
See Horne, Richard Henry Hengist

Beranger, Pierre Jean de
1780-1857 .... **NCLC 34**

Berdyaev, Nicolas
See Berdyaev, Nikolai (Aleksandrovich)

Berdyaev, Nikolai (Aleksandrovich)
1874-1948 .... **TCLC 67**
See also CA 120; 157

Berdyayev, Nikolai (Aleksandrovich)
See Berdyaev, Nikolai (Aleksandrovich)

Berendt, John (Lawrence) 1939- ...... **CLC 86**
See also CA 146; CANR 75, 93; DA3;
MTCW 2; MTFW 2005

Beresford, J(ohn) D(avys)
1873-1947 .... **TCLC 81**
See also CA 112; 155; DLB 162, 178, 197;
SFW 4; SUFW 1

Bishop, John Peale 1892-1944 ..... **TCLC 103**
See also CA 107; 155; DLB 4, 9, 45; MAL 5; RGAL 4

Bissett, Bill 1939- .... **CLC 18; PC 14**
See also CA 69-72; CAAS 19; CANR 15; CCA 1; CP 1, 2, 3, 4, 5, 6, 7; DLB 53; MTCW 1

Bissoondath, Neil (Devindra)
1955- .... **CLC 120**
See also CA 136; CANR 123; CN 6, 7; DAC

Bitov, Andrei (Georgievich) 1937- ... **CLC 57**
See also CA 142; DLB 302

Biyidi, Alexandre 1932-
See Beti, Mongo
See also BW 1, 3; CA 114; 124; CANR 81; DA3; MTCW 1, 2

Bjarme, Brynjolf
See Ibsen, Henrik (Johan)

Bjoernson, Bjoernstjerne (Martinius)
1832-1910 .... **TCLC 7, 37**
See also CA 104

Black, Robert
See Holdstock, Robert P.

Blackburn, Paul 1926-1971 .... **CLC 9, 43**
See also BG 1:2; CA 81-84; 33-36R; CANR 34; CP 1; DLB 16; DLBY 1981

Black Elk 1863-1950 .... **NNAL; TCLC 33**
See also CA 144; DAM MULT; MTCW 2; MTFW 2005; WP

Black Hawk 1767-1838 .... **NNAL**

Black Hobart
See Sanders, (James) Ed(ward)

Blacklin, Malcolm
See Chambers, Aidan

Blackmore, R(ichard) D(oddridge)
1825-1900 .... **TCLC 27**
See also CA 120; DLB 18; RGEL 2

Blackmur, R(ichard) P(almer)
1904-1965 .... **CLC 2, 24**
See also AMWS 2; CA 11-12; 25-28R; CANR 71; CAP 1; DLB 63; EWL 3; MAL 5

Black Tarantula
See Acker, Kathy

Blackwood, Algernon (Henry)
1869-1951 .... **TCLC 5**
See also CA 105; 150; DLB 153, 156, 178; HGG; SUFW 1

Blackwood, Caroline (Maureen)
1931-1996 .... **CLC 6, 9, 100**
See also BRWS 9; CA 85-88; 151; CANR 32, 61, 65; CN 3, 4, 5, 6; DLB 14, 207; HGG; MTCW 1

Blade, Alexander
See Hamilton, Edmond; Silverberg, Robert

Blaga, Lucian 1895-1961 .... **CLC 75**
See also CA 157; DLB 220; EWL 3

Blair, Eric (Arthur) 1903-1950 .... **TCLC 123**
See Orwell, George
See also CA 104; 132; DA; DA3; DAB; DAC; DAM MST, NOV; MTCW 1, 2; MTFW 2005; SATA 29

Blair, Hugh 1718-1800 .... **NCLC 75**

Blais, Marie-Claire 1939- .... **CLC 2, 4, 6, 13, 22**
See also CA 21-24R; CAAS 4; CANR 38, 75, 93; CWW 2; DAC; DAM MST; DLB 53; EWL 3; FW; MTCW 1, 2; MTFW 2005; TWA

Blaise, Clark 1940- .... **CLC 29**
See also AITN 2; CA 53-56, 231; CAAE 231; CAAS 3; CANR 5, 66, 106; CN 4, 5, 6, 7; DLB 53; RGSF 2

Blake, Fairley
See De Voto, Bernard (Augustine)

Blake, Nicholas
See Day Lewis, C(ecil)
See also DLB 77; MSW

Blake, Sterling
See Benford, Gregory (Albert)

Blake, William 1757-1827 . **NCLC 13, 37, 57, 127; PC 12, 63; WLC**
See also BRW 3; BRWR 1; CD-BLB 1789-1832; CLR 52; DA; DA3; DAB; DAC; DAM MST, POET; DLB 93, 163; EXPP; LATS 1:1; LMFS 1; MAI-CYA 1, 2; PAB; PFS 2, 12; SATA 30; TEA; WCH; WLIT 3; WP

Blanchot, Maurice 1907-2003 .... **CLC 135**
See also CA 117; 144; 213; CANR 138; DLB 72, 296; EWL 3

Blasco Ibanez, Vicente 1867-1928 . **TCLC 12**
See Ibanez, Vicente Blasco
See also BPFB 1; CA 110; 131; CANR 81; DA3; DAM NOV; EW 8; EWL 3; HW 1, 2; MTCW 1

Blatty, William Peter 1928- .... **CLC 2**
See also CA 5-8R; CANR 9, 124; DAM POP; HGG

Bleeck, Oliver
See Thomas, Ross (Elmore)

Blessing, Lee (Knowlton) 1949- .... **CLC 54**
See also CA 236; CAD; CD 5, 6

Blight, Rose
See Greer, Germaine

Blish, James (Benjamin) 1921-1975 . **CLC 14**
See also BPFB 1; CA 1-4R; 57-60; CANR 3; CN 2; DLB 8; MTCW 1; SATA 66; SCFW 1, 2; SFW 4

Bliss, Frederick
See Card, Orson Scott

Bliss, Reginald
See Wells, H(erbert) G(eorge)

Blixen, Karen (Christentze Dinesen)
1885-1962
See Dinesen, Isak
See also CA 25-28; CANR 22, 50; CAP 2; DA3; DLB 214; LMFS 1; MTCW 1, 2; SATA 44; SSFS 20

Bloch, Robert (Albert) 1917-1994 .... **CLC 33**
See also AAYA 29; CA 5-8R, 179; 146; CAAE 179; CAAS 20; CANR 5, 78; DA3; DLB 44; HGG; INT CANR-5; MTCW 2; SATA 12; SATA-Obit 82; SFW 4; SUFW 1, 2

Blok, Alexander (Alexandrovich)
1880-1921 .... **PC 21; TCLC 5**
See also CA 104; 183; DLB 295; EW 9; EWL 3; LMFS 2; RGWL 2, 3

Blom, Jan
See Breytenbach, Breyten

Bloom, Harold 1930- .... **CLC 24, 103**
See also CA 13-16R; CANR 39, 75, 92, 133; DLB 67; EWL 3; MTCW 2; MTFW 2005; RGAL 4

Bloomfield, Aurelius
See Bourne, Randolph S(illiman)

Bloomfield, Robert 1766-1823 ..... **NCLC 145**
See also DLB 93

Blount, Roy (Alton), Jr. 1941- .... **CLC 38**
See also CA 53-56; CANR 10, 28, 61, 125; CSW; INT CANR-28; MTCW 1, 2; MTFW 2005

Blowsnake, Sam 1875-(?) .... **NNAL**

Bloy, Leon 1846-1917 .... **TCLC 22**
See also CA 121; 183; DLB 123; GFL 1789 to the Present

Blue Cloud, Peter (Aroniawenrate)
1933- .... **NNAL**
See also CA 117; CANR 40; DAM MULT

Bluggage, Oranthy
See Alcott, Louisa May

Blume, Judy (Sussman) 1938- .... **CLC 12, 30**
See also AAYA 3, 26; BYA 1, 8, 12; CA 29-32R; CANR 13, 37, 66, 124; CLR 2, 15, 69; CPW; DA3; DAM NOV, POP; DLB

52; JRDA; MAICYA 1, 2; MAICYAS 1; MTCW 1, 2; MTFW 2005; SATA 2, 31, 79, 142; WYA; YAW

Blunden, Edmund (Charles)
1896-1974 .... **CLC 2, 56; PC 66**
See also BRW 6; BRWS 11; CA 17-18; 45-48; CANR 54; CAP 2; CP 1, 2; DLB 20, 100, 155; MTCW 1; PAB

Bly, Robert (Elwood) 1926- .... **CLC 1, 2, 5, 10, 15, 38, 128; PC 39**
See also AMWS 4; CA 5-8R; CANR 41, 73, 125; CP 1, 2, 3, 4, 5, 6, 7; DA3; DAM POET; DLB 5; EWL 3; MAL 5; MTCW 1, 2; MTFW 2005; PFS 6, 17; RGAL 4

Boas, Franz 1858-1942 .... **TCLC 56**
See also CA 115; 181

Bobette
See Simenon, Georges (Jacques Christian)

Boccaccio, Giovanni 1313-1375 ... **CMLC 13, 57; SSC 10, 87**
See also EW 2; RGSF 2; RGWL 2, 3; TWA; WLIT 7

Bochco, Steven 1943- .... **CLC 35**
See also AAYA 11; CA 124; 138

Bode, Sigmund
See O'Doherty, Brian

Bodel, Jean 1167(?)-1210 .... **CMLC 28**

Bodenheim, Maxwell 1892-1954 .... **TCLC 44**
See also CA 110; 187; DLB 9, 45; MAL 5; RGAL 4

Bodenheimer, Maxwell
See Bodenheim, Maxwell

Bodker, Cecil 1927-
See Bodker, Cecil

Bodker, Cecil 1927- .... **CLC 21**
See also CA 73-76; CANR 13, 44, 111; CLR 23; MAICYA 1, 2; SATA 14, 133

Boell, Heinrich (Theodor)
1917-1985 ... **CLC 2, 3, 6, 9, 11, 15, 27, 32, 72; SSC 23; WLC**
See Boll, Heinrich (Theodor)
See also CA 21-24R; 116; CANR 24; DA; DA3; DAB; DAC; DAM MST, NOV; DLB 69; DLBY 1985; MTCW 1, 2; MTFW 2005; SSFS 20; TWA

Boerne, Alfred
See Doeblin, Alfred

Boethius c. 480-c. 524 .... **CMLC 15**
See also DLB 115; RGWL 2, 3

Boff, Leonardo (Genezio Darci)
1938- .... **CLC 70; HLC 1**
See also CA 150; DAM MULT; HW 2

Bogan, Louise 1897-1970 .... **CLC 4, 39, 46, 93; PC 12**
See also AMWS 3; CA 73-76; 25-28R; CANR 33, 82; CP 1; DAM POET; DLB 45, 169; EWL 3; MAL 5; MAWW; MTCW 1, 2; PFS 21; RGAL 4

Bogarde, Dirk
See Van Den Bogarde, Derek Jules Gaspard Ulric Niven
See also DLB 14

Bogosian, Eric 1953- .... **CLC 45, 141**
See also CA 138; CAD; CANR 102; CD 5, 6

Bograd, Larry 1953- .... **CLC 35**
See also CA 93-96; CANR 57; SAAS 21; SATA 33, 89; WYA

Boiardo, Matteo Maria 1441-1494 .... **LC 6**

Boileau-Despreaux, Nicolas 1636-1711 . **LC 3**
See also DLB 268; EW 3; GFL Beginnings to 1789; RGWL 2, 3

Boissard, Maurice
See Leautaud, Paul

Bojer, Johan 1872-1959 .... **TCLC 64**
See also CA 189; EWL 3

Bok, Edward W(illiam)
1863-1930 .... **TCLC 101**
See also CA 217; DLB 91; DLBD 16

Boker, George Henry 1823-1890 . **NCLC 125**
See also RGAL 4

Boland, Eavan (Aisling) 1944- .. **CLC 40, 67, 113; PC 58**
See also BRWS 5; CA 143, 207; CAAE 207; CANR 61; CP 1, 7; CWP; DAM POET; DLB 40; FW; MTCW 2; MTFW 2005; PFS 12, 22

Boll, Heinrich (Theodor)
See Boell, Heinrich (Theodor)
See also BPFB 1; CDWLB 2; EW 13; EWL 3; RGSF 2; RGWL 2, 3

Bolt, Lee
See Faust, Frederick (Schiller)

Bolt, Robert (Oxton) 1924-1995 ...... **CLC 14; TCLC 175**
See also CA 17-20R; 147; CANR 35, 67; CBD; DAM DRAM; DFS 2; DLB 13, 233; EWL 3; LAIT 1; MTCW 1

Bombal, Maria Luisa 1910-1980 .... **HLCS 1; SSC 37**
See also CA 127; CANR 72; EWL 3; HW 1; LAW; RGSF 2

Bombet, Louis-Alexandre-Cesar
See Stendhal

Bomkauf
See Kaufman, Bob (Garnell)

Bonaventura .... **NCLC 35**
See also DLB 90

Bonaventure 1217(?)-1274 .... **CMLC 79**
See also DLB 115; LMFS 1

Bond, Edward 1934- .... **CLC 4, 6, 13, 23**
See also AAYA 50; BRWS 1; CA 25-28R; CANR 38, 67, 106; CBD; CD 5, 6; DAM DRAM; DFS 3, 8; DLB 13, 310; EWL 3; MTCW 1

Bonham, Frank 1914-1989 .... **CLC 12**
See also AAYA 1; BYA 1, 3; CA 9-12R; CANR 4, 36; JRDA; MAICYA 1, 2; SAAS 3; SATA 1, 49; SATA-Obit 62; TCWW 1, 2; YAW

Bonnefoy, Yves 1923- . **CLC 9, 15, 58; PC 58**
See also CA 85-88; CANR 33, 75, 97, 136; CWW 2; DAM MST, POET; DLB 258; EWL 3; GFL 1789 to the Present; MTCW 1, 2; MTFW 2005

Bonner, Marita .... **HR 1:2**
See Occomy, Marita (Odette) Bonner

Bonnin, Gertrude 1876-1938 .... **NNAL**
See Zitkala-Sa
See also CA 150; DAM MULT

Bontemps, Arna(ud Wendell)
1902-1973 .. **BLC 1, 18; HR 1:2**
See also BW 1; CA 1-4R; 41-44R; CANR 4, 35; CLR 6; CP 1; CWRI 5; DA3; DAM MULT, NOV, POET; DLB 48, 51; JRDA; MAICYA 1, 2; MAL 5; MTCW 1, 2; SATA 2, 44; SATA-Obit 24; WCH; WP

Boot, William
See Stoppard, Tom

Booth, Martin 1944-2004 .... **CLC 13**
See also CA 93-96, 188; 223; CAAE 188; CAAS 2; CANR 92; CP 1, 2, 3, 4

Booth, Philip 1925- .... **CLC 23**
See also CA 5-8R; CANR 5, 88; CP 1, 2, 3, 4, 5, 6, 7; DLBY 1982

Booth, Wayne C(layson) 1921-2005 . **CLC 24**
See also CA 1-4R; CAAS 5; CANR 3, 43, 117; DLB 67

Borchert, Wolfgang 1921-1947 .... **TCLC 5**
See also CA 104; 188; DLB 69, 124; EWL 3

Borel, Petrus 1809-1859 .... **NCLC 41**
See also DLB 119; GFL 1789 to the Present

Borges, Jorge Luis 1899-1986 ... **CLC 1, 2, 3, 4, 6, 8, 9, 10, 13, 19, 44, 48, 83; HLC 1; PC 22, 32; SSC 4, 41; TCLC 109; WLC**
See also AAYA 26; BPFB 1; CA 21-24R; CANR 19, 33, 75, 105, 133; CDWLB 3; DA; DA3; DAB; DAC; DAM MST,

MULT; DLB 113, 283; DLBY 1986; DNFS 1, 2; EWL 3; HW 1, 2; LAW; LMFS 2; MSW; MTCW 1, 2; MTFW 2005; RGSF 2; RGWL 2, 3; SFW 4; SSFS 17; TWA; WLIT 1

Borowski, Tadeusz 1922-1951 .... **SSC 48; TCLC 9**
See also CA 106; 154; CDWLB 4; DLB 215; EWL 3; RGSF 2; RGWL 3; SSFS 13

Borrow, George (Henry)
1803-1881 .... **NCLC 9**
See also DLB 21, 55, 166

Bosch (Gavino), Juan 1909-2001 ..... **HLCS 1**
See also CA 151; 204; DAM MST, MULT; DLB 145; HW 1, 2

Bosman, Herman Charles
1905-1951 .... **TCLC 49**
See Malan, Herman
See also CA 160; DLB 225; RGSF 2

Bosschere, Jean de 1878(?)-1953 ... **TCLC 19**
See also CA 115; 186

Boswell, James 1740-1795 ... **LC 4, 50; WLC**
See also BRW 3; CDBLB 1660-1789; DA; DAB; DAC; DAM MST; DLB 104, 142; TEA; WLIT 3

Bottomley, Gordon 1874-1948 ..... **TCLC 107**
See also CA 120; 192; DLB 10

Bottoms, David 1949- .... **CLC 53**
See also CA 105; CANR 22; CSW; DLB 120; DLBY 1983

Boucicault, Dion 1820-1890 .... **NCLC 41**

Boucolon, Maryse
See Conde, Maryse

Bourdieu, Pierre 1930-2002 .... **CLC 198**
See also CA 130; 204

Bourget, Paul (Charles Joseph)
1852-1935 .... **TCLC 12**
See also CA 107; 196; DLB 123; GFL 1789 to the Present

Bourjaily, Vance (Nye) 1922- .... **CLC 8, 62**
See also CA 1-4R; CAAS 1; CANR 2, 72; CN 1, 2, 3, 4, 5, 6, 7; DLB 2, 143; MAL 5

Bourne, Randolph S(illiman)
1886-1918 .... **TCLC 16**
See also AMW; CA 117; 155; DLB 63; MAL 5

Bova, Ben(jamin William) 1932- ...... **CLC 45**
See also AAYA 16; CA 5-8R; CAAS 18; CANR 11, 56, 94, 111; CLR 3, 96; DLBY 1981; INT CANR-11; MAICYA 1, 2; MTCW 1; SATA 6, 68, 133; SFW 4

Bowen, Elizabeth (Dorothea Cole)
1899-1973 . **CLC 1, 3, 6, 11, 15, 22, 118; SSC 3, 28, 66; TCLC 148**
See also BRWS 2; CA 17-18; 41-44R; CANR 35, 105; CAP 2; CDBLB 1945-1960; CN 1; DA3; DAM NOV; DLB 15, 162; EWL 3; EXPS; FW; HGG; MTCW 1, 2; MTFW 2005; NFS 13; RGSF 2; SSFS 5; SUFW 1; TEA; WLIT 4

Bowering, George 1935- .... **CLC 15, 47**
See also CA 21-24R; CAAS 16; CANR 10; CN 7; CP 1, 2, 3, 4, 5, 6, 7; DLB 53

Bowering, Marilyn R(uthe) 1949- .... **CLC 32**
See also CA 101; CANR 49; CP 4, 5, 6, 7; CWP

Bowers, Edgar 1924-2000 .... **CLC 9**
See also CA 5-8R; 188; CANR 24; CP 1, 2, 3, 4, 5, 6, 7; CSW; DLB 5

Bowers, Mrs. J. Milton 1842-1914
See Bierce, Ambrose (Gwinett)

Bowie, David .... **CLC 17**
See Jones, David Robert

Bowles, Jane (Sydney) 1917-1973 ..... **CLC 3, 68**
See Bowles, Jane Auer
See also CA 19-20; 41-44R; CAP 2; CN 1; MAL 5

Bowles, Jane Auer
See Bowles, Jane (Sydney)
See also EWL 3

Bowles, Paul (Frederick) 1910-1999 . **CLC 1, 2, 19, 53; SSC 3**
See also AMWS 4; CA 1-4R; 186; CAAS 1; CANR 1, 19, 50, 75; CN 1, 2, 3, 4, 5, 6; DA3; DLB 5, 6, 218; EWL 3; MAL 5; MTCW 1, 2; MTFW 2005; RGAL 4; SSFS 17

Bowles, William Lisle 1762-1850 . **NCLC 103**
See also DLB 93

Box, Edgar
See Vidal, (Eugene Luther) Gore
See also GLL 1

Boyd, James 1888-1944 .... **TCLC 115**
See also CA 186; DLB 9; DLBD 16; RGAL 4; RHW

Boyd, Nancy
See Millay, Edna St. Vincent
See also GLL 1

Boyd, Thomas (Alexander)
1898-1935 .... **TCLC 111**
See also CA 111; 183; DLB 9; DLBD 16, 316

Boyd, William (Andrew Murray)
1952- .... **CLC 28, 53, 70**
See also CA 114; 120; CANR 51, 71, 131; CN 4, 5, 6, 7; DLB 231

Boyesen, Hjalmar Hjorth
1848-1895 .... **NCLC 135**
See also DLB 12, 71; DLBD 13; RGAL 4

Boyle, Kay 1902-1992 .... **CLC 1, 5, 19, 58, 121; SSC 5**
See also CA 13-16R; 140; CAAS 1; CANR 29, 61, 110; CN 1, 2, 3, 4, 5; CP 1, 2, 3, 4; DLB 4, 9, 48, 86; DLBY 1993; EWL 3; MAL 5; MTCW 1, 2; MTFW 2005; RGAL 4; RGSF 2; SSFS 10, 13, 14

Boyle, Mark
See Kienzle, William X(avier)

Boyle, Patrick 1905-1982 .... **CLC 19**
See also CA 127

Boyle, T. C.
See Boyle, T(homas) Coraghessan
See also AMWS 8

Boyle, T(homas) Coraghessan
1948- .... **CLC 36, 55, 90; SSC 16**
See Boyle, T. C.
See also AAYA 47; BEST 90:4; BPFB 1; CA 120; CANR 44, 76, 89, 132; CN 6, 7; CPW; DA3; DAM POP; DLB 218, 278; DLBY 1986; EWL 3; MAL 5; MTCW 2; MTFW 2005; SSFS 13, 19

Boz
See Dickens, Charles (John Huffam)

Brackenridge, Hugh Henry
1748-1816 .... **NCLC 7**
See also DLB 11, 37; RGAL 4

Bradbury, Edward P.
See Moorcock, Michael (John)
See also MTCW 2

Bradbury, Malcolm (Stanley)
1932-2000 .... **CLC 32, 61**
See also CA 1-4R; CANR 1, 33, 91, 98, 137; CN 1, 2, 3, 4, 5, 6, 7; CP 1; DA3; DAM NOV; DLB 14, 207; EWL 3; MTCW 1, 2; MTFW 2005

Bradbury, Ray (Douglas) 1920- .... **CLC 1, 3, 10, 15, 42, 98; SSC 29, 53; WLC**
See also AAYA 15; AITN 1, 2; AMWS 4; BPFB 1; BYA 4, 5, 11; CA 1-4R; CANR 2, 30, 75, 125; CDALB 1968-1988; CN 1, 2, 3, 4, 5, 6, 7; CPW; DA; DA3; DAB; DAC; DAM MST, NOV, POP; DLB 2, 8;

EXPN; EXPS; HGG; LAIT 3, 5; LATS
1:2; LMFS 2; MAL 5; MTCW 1, 2;
MTFW 2005; NFS 1, 22; RGAL 4; RGSF
2; SATA 11, 64, 123; SCFW 1, 2; SFW 4;
SSFS 1, 20; SUFW 1, 2; TUS; YAW

Braddon, Mary Elizabeth
1837-1915 .... **TCLC 111**
See also BRWS 8; CA 108; 179; CMW 4;
DLB 18, 70, 156; HGG

Bradfield, Scott (Michael) 1955- .... **SSC 65**
See also CA 147; CANR 90; HGG; SUFW
2

Bradford, Gamaliel 1863-1932 .... **TCLC 36**
See also CA 160; DLB 17

Bradford, William 1590-1657 .... **LC 64**
See also DLB 24, 30; RGAL 4

Bradley, David (Henry), Jr. 1950- .... **BLC 1;
CLC 23, 118**
See also BW 1, 3; CA 104; CANR 26, 81;
CN 4, 5, 6, 7; DAM MULT; DLB 33

Bradley, John Ed(mund, Jr.) 1958- . **CLC 55**
See also CA 139; CANR 99; CN 6, 7; CSW

Bradley, Marion Zimmer
1930-1999 .... **CLC 30**
See Chapman, Lee; Dexter, John; Gardner,
Miriam; Ives, Morgan; Rivers, Elfrida
See also AAYA 40; BPFB 1; CA 57-60; 185;
CAAS 10; CANR 7, 31, 51, 75, 107;
CPW; DA3; DAM POP; DLB 8; FANT;
FW; MTCW 1, 2; MTFW 2005; SATA 90,
139; SATA-Obit 116; SFW 4; SUFW 2;
YAW

Bradshaw, John 1933- .... **CLC 70**
See also CA 138; CANR 61

Bradstreet, Anne 1612(?)-1672 ...... **LC 4, 30;
PC 10**
See also AMWS 1; CDALB 1640-1865;
DA; DA3; DAC; DAM MST, POET; DLB
24; EXPP; FW; PFS 6; RGAL 4; TUS;
WP

Brady, Joan 1939- .... **CLC 86**
See also CA 141

Bragg, Melvyn 1939- .... **CLC 10**
See also BEST 89:3; CA 57-60; CANR 10,
48, 89; CN 1, 2, 3, 4, 5, 6, 7; DLB 14,
271; RHW

Brahe, Tycho 1546-1601 .... **LC 45**
See also DLB 300

Braine, John (Gerard) 1922-1986 . **CLC 1, 3,
41**
See also CA 1-4R; 120; CANR 1, 33; CD-
BLB 1945-1960; CN 1, 2, 3, 4; DLB 15;
DLBY 1986; EWL 3; MTCW 1

Braithwaite, William Stanley (Beaumont)
1878-1962 .... **BLC 1; HR 1:2; PC 52**
See also BW 1; CA 125; DAM MULT; DLB
50, 54; MAL 5

Bramah, Ernest 1868-1942 .... **TCLC 72**
See also CA 156; CMW 4; DLB 70; FANT

Brammer, Billy Lee
See Brammer, William

Brammer, William 1929-1978 .... **CLC 31**
See also CA 235; 77-80

Brancati, Vitaliano 1907-1954 .... **TCLC 12**
See also CA 109; DLB 264; EWL 3

Brancato, Robin F(idler) 1936- .... **CLC 35**
See also AAYA 9, 68; BYA 6; CA 69-72;
CANR 11, 45; CLR 32; JRDA; MAICYA
2; MAICYAS 1; SAAS 9; SATA 97;
WYA; YAW

Brand, Dionne 1953- .... **CLC 192**
See also BW 2; CA 143; CANR 143; CWP

Brand, Max
See Faust, Frederick (Schiller)
See also BPFB 1; TCWW 1, 2

Brand, Millen 1906-1980 .... **CLC 7**
See also CA 21-24R; 97-100; CANR 72

Branden, Barbara .... **CLC 44**
See also CA 148

Brandes, Georg (Morris Cohen)
1842-1927 .... **TCLC 10**
See also CA 105; 189; DLB 300

Brandys, Kazimierz 1916-2000 .... **CLC 62**
See also CA 239; EWL 3

Branley, Franklyn M(ansfield)
1915-2002 .... **CLC 21**
See also CA 33-36R; 207; CANR 14, 39;
CLR 13; MAICYA 1, 2; SAAS 16; SATA
4, 68, 136

Brant, Beth (E.) 1941- .... **NNAL**
See also CA 144; FW

Brant, Sebastian 1457-1521 .... **LC 112**
See also DLB 179; RGWL 2, 3

Brathwaite, Edward Kamau
1930- .... **BLCS; CLC 11; PC 56**
See also BW 2, 3; CA 25-28R; CANR 11,
26, 47, 107; CDWLB 3; CP 1, 2, 3, 4, 5,
6, 7; DAM POET; DLB 125; EWL 3

Brathwaite, Kamau
See Brathwaite, Edward Kamau

Brautigan, Richard (Gary)
1935-1984 .... **CLC 1, 3, 5, 9, 12, 34, 42;
TCLC 133**
See also BPFB 1; CA 53-56; 113; CANR
34; CN 1, 2, 3; CP 1, 2, 3, 4; DA3; DAM
NOV; DLB 2, 5, 206; DLBY 1980, 1984;
FANT; MAL 5; MTCW 1; RGAL 4;
SATA 56

Brave Bird, Mary .... **NNAL**
See Crow Dog, Mary (Ellen)

Braverman, Kate 1950- .... **CLC 67**
See also CA 89-92; CANR 141

Brecht, (Eugen) Bertolt (Friedrich)
1898-1956 ..... **DC 3; TCLC 1, 6, 13, 35,
169; WLC**
See also CA 104; 133; CANR 62; CDWLB
2; DA; DA3; DAB; DAC; DAM DRAM,
MST; DFS 4, 5, 9; DLB 56, 124; EW 11;
EWL 3; IDTP; MTCW 1, 2; MTFW 2005;
RGWL 2, 3; TWA

Brecht, Eugen Berthold Friedrich
See Brecht, (Eugen) Bertolt (Friedrich)

Bremer, Fredrika 1801-1865 .... **NCLC 11**
See also DLB 254

Brennan, Christopher John
1870-1932 .... **TCLC 17**
See also CA 117; 188; DLB 230; EWL 3

Brennan, Maeve 1917-1993 ... **CLC 5; TCLC
124**
See also CA 81-84; CANR 72, 100

Brenner, Jozef 1887-1919
See Csath, Geza
See also CA 240

Brent, Linda
See Jacobs, Harriet A(nn)

Brentano, Clemens (Maria)
1778-1842 .... **NCLC 1**
See also DLB 90; RGWL 2, 3

Brent of Bin Bin
See Franklin, (Stella Maria Sarah) Miles
(Lampe)

Brenton, Howard 1942- .... **CLC 31**
See also CA 69-72; CANR 33, 67; CBD;
CD 5, 6; DLB 13; MTCW 1

Breslin, James 1930-
See Breslin, Jimmy
See also CA 73-76; CANR 31, 75, 139;
DAM NOV; MTCW 1, 2; MTFW 2005

Breslin, Jimmy .... **CLC 4, 43**
See Breslin, James
See also AITN 1; DLB 185; MTCW 2

Bresson, Robert 1901(?)-1999 .... **CLC 16**
See also CA 110; 187; CANR 49

Breton, Andre 1896-1966 .. **CLC 2, 9, 15, 54;
PC 15**
See also CA 19-20; 25-28R; CANR 40, 60;
CAP 2; DLB 65, 258; EW 11; EWL 3;
GFL 1789 to the Present; LMFS 2;
MTCW 1, 2; MTFW 2005; RGWL 2, 3;
TWA; WP

Breytenbach, Breyten 1939(?)- .. **CLC 23, 37,
126**
See also CA 113; 129; CANR 61, 122;
CWW 2; DAM POET; DLB 225; EWL 3

Bridgers, Sue Ellen 1942- .... **CLC 26**
See also AAYA 8, 49; BYA 7, 8; CA 65-68;
CANR 11, 36; CLR 18; DLB 52; JRDA;
MAICYA 1, 2; SAAS 1; SATA 22, 90;
SATA-Essay 109; WYA; YAW

Bridges, Robert (Seymour)
1844-1930 .... **PC 28; TCLC 1**
See also BRW 6; CA 104; 152; CDBLB
1890-1914; DAM POET; DLB 19, 98

Bridie, James .... **TCLC 3**
See Mavor, Osborne Henry
See also DLB 10; EWL 3

Brin, David 1950- .... **CLC 34**
See also AAYA 21; CA 102; CANR 24, 70,
125, 127; INT CANR-24; SATA 65;
SCFW 2; SFW 4

Brink, Andre (Philippus) 1935- . **CLC 18, 36,
106**
See also AFW; BRWS 6; CA 104; CANR
39, 62, 109, 133; CN 4, 5, 6, 7; DLB 225;
EWL 3; INT CA-103; LATS 1:2; MTCW
1, 2; MTFW 2005; WLIT 2

Brinsmead, H. F(ay)
See Brinsmead, H(esba) F(ay)

Brinsmead, H. F.
See Brinsmead, H(esba) F(ay)

Brinsmead, H(esba) F(ay) 1922- ...... **CLC 21**
See also CA 21-24R; CANR 10; CLR 47;
CWRI 5; MAICYA 1, 2; SAAS 5; SATA
18, 78

Brittain, Vera (Mary) 1893(?)-1970 . **CLC 23**
See also BRWS 10; CA 13-16; 25-28R;
CANR 58; CAP 1; DLB 191; FW; MTCW
1, 2

Broch, Hermann 1886-1951 .... **TCLC 20**
See also CA 117; 211; CDWLB 2; DLB 85,
124; EW 10; EWL 3; RGWL 2, 3

Brock, Rose
See Hansen, Joseph
See also GLL 1

Brod, Max 1884-1968 .... **TCLC 115**
See also CA 5-8R; 25-28R; CANR 7; DLB
81; EWL 3

Brodkey, Harold (Roy) 1930-1996 .. **CLC 56;
TCLC 123**
See also CA 111; 151; CANR 71; CN 4, 5,
6; DLB 130

Brodsky, Iosif Alexandrovich 1940-1996
See Brodsky, Joseph
See also AITN 1; CA 41-44R; 151; CANR
37, 106; DA3; DAM POET; MTCW 1, 2;
MTFW 2005; RGWL 2, 3

Brodsky, Joseph . **CLC 4, 6, 13, 36, 100; PC
9**
See Brodsky, Iosif Alexandrovich
See also AMWS 8; CWW 2; DLB 285;
EWL 3; MTCW 1

Brodsky, Michael (Mark) 1948- .... **CLC 19**
See also CA 102; CANR 18, 41, 58; DLB
244

Brodzki, Bella ed. .... **CLC 65**

Brome, Richard 1590(?)-1652 .... **LC 61**
See also BRWS 10; DLB 58

Bromell, Henry 1947- .... **CLC 5**
See also CA 53-56; CANR 9, 115, 116

Bryant, William Cullen 1794-1878 . **NCLC 6, 46; PC 20**
See also AMWS 1; CDALB 1640-1865; DA; DAB; DAC; DAM MST, POET; DLB 3, 43, 59, 189, 250; EXPP; PAB; RGAL 4; TUS

Bryusov, Valery Yakovlevich 1873-1924 .... **TCLC 10**
See also CA 107; 155; EWL 3; SFW 4

Buchan, John 1875-1940 .... **TCLC 41**
See also CA 108; 145; CMW 4; DAB; DAM POP; DLB 34, 70, 156; HGG; MSW; MTCW 2; RGEL 2; RHW; YABC 2

Buchanan, George 1506-1582 .... **LC 4**
See also DLB 132

Buchanan, Robert 1841-1901 .... **TCLC 107**
See also CA 179; DLB 18, 35

Buchheim, Lothar-Guenther 1918- .... **CLC 6**
See also CA 85-88

Buchner, (Karl) Georg 1813-1837 .... **NCLC 26, 146**
See also CDWLB 2; DLB 133; EW 6; RGSF 2; RGWL 2, 3; TWA

Buchwald, Art(hur) 1925- .... **CLC 33**
See also AITN 1; CA 5-8R; CANR 21, 67, 107; MTCW 1, 2; SATA 10

Buck, Pearl S(ydenstricker) 1892-1973 ...... **CLC 7, 11, 18, 127**
See also AAYA 42; AITN 1; AMWS 2; BPFB 1; CA 1-4R; 41-44R; CANR 1, 34; CDALBS; CN 1; DA; DA3; DAB; DAC; DAM MST, NOV; DLB 9, 102; EWL 3; LAIT 3; MAL 5; MTCW 1, 2; MTFW 2005; RGAL 4; RHW; SATA 1, 25; TUS

Buckler, Ernest 1908-1984 .... **CLC 13**
See also CA 11-12; 114; CAP 1; CCA 1; CN 1, 2, 3; DAC; DAM MST; DLB 68; SATA 47

Buckley, Christopher (Taylor) 1952- .... **CLC 165**
See also CA 139; CANR 119

Buckley, Vincent (Thomas) 1925-1988 .... **CLC 57**
See also CA 101; CP 1, 2, 3, 4; DLB 289

Buckley, William F(rank), Jr. 1925- . **CLC 7, 18, 37**
See also AITN 1; BPFB 1; CA 1-4R; CANR 1, 24, 53, 93, 133; CMW 4; CPW; DA3; DAM POP; DLB 137; DLBY 1980; INT CANR-24; MTCW 1, 2; MTFW 2005; TUS

Buechner, (Carl) Frederick 1926- . **CLC 2, 4, 6, 9**
See also AMWS 12; BPFB 1; CA 13-16R; CANR 11, 39, 64, 114, 138; CN 1, 2, 3, 4, 5, 6, 7; DAM NOV; DLBY 1980; INT CANR-11; MAL 5; MTCW 1, 2; MTFW 2005; TCLE 1:1

Buell, John (Edward) 1927- .... **CLC 10**
See also CA 1-4R; CANR 71; DLB 53

Buero Vallejo, Antonio 1916-2000 ... **CLC 15, 46, 139; DC 18**
See also CA 106; 189; CANR 24, 49, 75; CWW 2; DFS 11; EWL 3; HW 1; MTCW 1, 2

Bufalino, Gesualdo 1920-1996 .... **CLC 74**
See also CA 209; CWW 2; DLB 196

Bugayev, Boris Nikolayevich 1880-1934 .... **PC 11; TCLC 7**
See Bely, Andrey; Belyi, Andrei
See also CA 104; 165; MTCW 2; MTFW 2005

Bukowski, Charles 1920-1994 ... **CLC 2, 5, 9, 41, 82, 108; PC 18; SSC 45**
See also CA 17-20R; 144; CANR 40, 62, 105; CN 4, 5; CP 1, 2, 3, 4; CPW; DA3; DAM NOV, POET; DLB 5, 130, 169; EWL 3; MAL 5; MTCW 1, 2; MTFW 2005

Bulgakov, Mikhail (Afanas'evich) 1891-1940 ..... **SSC 18; TCLC 2, 16, 159**
See also BPFB 1; CA 105; 152; DAM DRAM, NOV; DLB 272; EWL 3; MTCW 2; MTFW 2005; NFS 8; RGSF 2; RGWL 2, 3; SFW 4; TWA

Bulgya, Alexander Alexandrovich 1901-1956 .... **TCLC 53**
See Fadeev, Aleksandr Aleksandrovich; Fadeev, Alexandr Alexandrovich; Fadeyev, Alexander
See also CA 117; 181

Bullins, Ed 1935- .... **BLC 1; CLC 1, 5, 7; DC 6**
See also BW 2, 3; CA 49-52; CAAS 16; CAD; CANR 24, 46, 73, 134; CD 5, 6; DAM DRAM, MULT; DLB 7, 38, 249; EWL 3; MAL 5; MTCW 1, 2; MTFW 2005; RGAL 4

Bulosan, Carlos 1911-1956 .... **AAL**
See also CA 216; DLB 312; RGAL 4

Bulwer-Lytton, Edward (George Earle Lytton) 1803-1873 .... **NCLC 1, 45**
See also DLB 21; RGEL 2; SFW 4; SUFW 1; TEA

Bunin, Ivan Alexeyevich 1870-1953 ... **SSC 5; TCLC 6**
See also CA 104; DLB 317; EWL 3; RGSF 2; RGWL 2, 3; TWA

Bunting, Basil 1900-1985 ...... **CLC 10, 39, 47**
See also BRWS 7; CA 53-56; 115; CANR 7; CP 1, 2, 3, 4; DAM POET; DLB 20; EWL 3; RGEL 2

Bunuel, Luis 1900-1983 ... **CLC 16, 80; HLC 1**
See also CA 101; 110; CANR 32, 77; DAM MULT; HW 1

Bunyan, John 1628-1688 ..... **LC 4, 69; WLC**
See also BRW 2; BYA 5; CDBLB 1660-1789; DA; DAB; DAC; DAM MST; DLB 39; RGEL 2; TEA; WCH; WLIT 3

Buravsky, Alexandr .... **CLC 59**

Burckhardt, Jacob (Christoph) 1818-1897 .... **NCLC 49**
See also EW 6

Burford, Eleanor
See Hibbert, Eleanor Alice Burford

Burgess, Anthony . **CLC 1, 2, 4, 5, 8, 10, 13, 15, 22, 40, 62, 81, 94**
See Wilson, John (Anthony) Burgess
See also AAYA 25; AITN 1; BRWS 1; CD-BLB 1960 to Present; CN 1, 2, 3, 4, 5; DAB; DLB 14, 194, 261; DLBY 1998; EWL 3; RGEL 2; RHW; SFW 4; YAW

Burke, Edmund 1729(?)-1797 .... **LC 7, 36; WLC**
See also BRW 3; DA; DA3; DAB; DAC; DAM MST; DLB 104, 252; RGEL 2; TEA

Burke, Kenneth (Duva) 1897-1993 ... **CLC 2, 24**
See also AMW; CA 5-8R; 143; CANR 39, 74, 136; CN 1, 2; CP 1, 2, 3, 4; DLB 45, 63; EWL 3; MAL 5; MTCW 1, 2; RGAL 4

Burke, Leda
See Garnett, David

Burke, Ralph
See Silverberg, Robert

Burke, Thomas 1886-1945 .... **TCLC 63**
See also CA 113; 155; CMW 4; DLB 197

Burney, Fanny 1752-1840 .... **NCLC 12, 54, 107**
See also BRWS 3; DLB 39; FL 1:2; NFS 16; RGEL 2; TEA

Burney, Frances
See Burney, Fanny

Burns, Robert 1759-1796 ... **LC 3, 29, 40; PC 6; WLC**
See also AAYA 51; BRW 3; CDBLB 1789-1832; DA; DA3; DAB; DAC; DAM MST, POET; DLB 109; EXPP; PAB; RGEL 2; TEA; WP

Burns, Tex
See L'Amour, Louis (Dearborn)

Burnshaw, Stanley 1906- .... **CLC 3, 13, 44**
See also CA 9-12R; CP 1, 2, 3, 4, 5, 6, 7; DLB 48; DLBY 1997

Burr, Anne 1937- .... **CLC 6**
See also CA 25-28R

Burroughs, Edgar Rice 1875-1950 . **TCLC 2, 32**
See also AAYA 11; BPFB 1; BYA 4, 9; CA 104; 132; CANR 131; DA3; DAM NOV; DLB 8; FANT; MTCW 1, 2; MTFW 2005; RGAL 4; SATA 41; SCFW 1, 2; SFW 4; TCWW 1, 2; TUS; YAW

Burroughs, William S(eward) 1914-1997 .. **CLC 1, 2, 5, 15, 22, 42, 75, 109; TCLC 121; WLC**
See Lee, William; Lee, Willy
See also AAYA 60; AITN 2; AMWS 3; BG 1:2; BPFB 1; CA 9-12R; 160; CANR 20, 52, 104; CN 1, 2, 3, 4, 5, 6; CPW; DA; DA3; DAB; DAC; DAM MST, NOV, POP; DLB 2, 8, 16, 152, 237; DLBY 1981, 1997; EWL 3; HGG; LMFS 2; MAL 5; MTCW 1, 2; MTFW 2005; RGAL 4; SFW 4

Burton, Sir Richard F(rancis) 1821-1890 .... **NCLC 42**
See also DLB 55, 166, 184; SSFS 21

Burton, Robert 1577-1640 .... **LC 74**
See also DLB 151; RGEL 2

Buruma, Ian 1951- .... **CLC 163**
See also CA 128; CANR 65, 141

Busch, Frederick 1941- ... **CLC 7, 10, 18, 47, 166**
See also CA 33-36R; CAAS 1; CANR 45, 73, 92; CN 1, 2, 3, 4, 5, 6, 7; DLB 6, 218

Bush, Barney (Furman) 1946- .... **NNAL**
See also CA 145

Bush, Ronald 1946- .... **CLC 34**
See also CA 136

Bustos, F(rancisco)
See Borges, Jorge Luis

Bustos Domecq, H(onorio)
See Bioy Casares, Adolfo; Borges, Jorge Luis

Butler, Octavia E(stelle) 1947- .. **BLCS; CLC 38, 121**
See also AAYA 18, 48; AFAW 2; AMWS 13; BPFB 1; BW 2, 3; CA 73-76; CANR 12, 24, 38, 73, 145; CLR 65; CN 7; CPW; DA3; DAM MULT, POP; DLB 33; LATS 1:2; MTCW 1, 2; MTFW 2005; NFS 8, 21; SATA 84; SCFW 2; SFW 4; SSFS 6; TCLE 1:1; YAW

Butler, Robert Olen, (Jr.) 1945- ...... **CLC 81, 162**
See also AMWS 12; BPFB 1; CA 112; CANR 66, 138; CN 7; CSW; DAM POP; DLB 173; INT CA-112; MAL 5; MTCW 2; MTFW 2005; SSFS 11

Butler, Samuel 1612-1680 .... **LC 16, 43**
See also DLB 101, 126; RGEL 2

Butler, Samuel 1835-1902 .... **TCLC 1, 33; WLC**
See also BRWS 2; CA 143; CDBLB 1890-1914; DA; DA3; DAB; DAC; DAM MST, NOV; DLB 18, 57, 174; RGEL 2; SFW 4; TEA

Butler, Walter C.
See Faust, Frederick (Schiller)

Canfield, Dorothea F.
    See Fisher, Dorothy (Frances) Canfield
Canfield, Dorothea Frances
    See Fisher, Dorothy (Frances) Canfield
Canfield, Dorothy
    See Fisher, Dorothy (Frances) Canfield
Canin, Ethan 1960- .... **CLC 55; SSC 70**
    See also CA 131; 135; MAL 5
Cankar, Ivan 1876-1918 .... **TCLC 105**
    See also CDWLB 4; DLB 147; EWL 3
Cannon, Curt
    See Hunter, Evan
Cao, Lan 1961- .... **CLC 109**
    See also CA 165
Cape, Judith
    See Page, P(atricia) K(athleen)
    See also CCA 1
Capek, Karel 1890-1938 .... **DC 1; SSC 36;
    TCLC 6, 37; WLC**
    See also CA 104; 140; CDWLB 4; DA;
    DA3; DAB; DAC; DAM DRAM, MST,
    NOV; DFS 7, 11; DLB 215; EW 10; EWL
    3; MTCW 2; MTFW 2005; RGSF 2;
    RGWL 2, 3; SCFW 1, 2; SFW 4
Capote, Truman 1924-1984 . **CLC 1, 3, 8, 13,
    19, 34, 38, 58; SSC 2, 47; TCLC 164;
    WLC**
    See also AAYA 61; AMWS 3; BPFB 1; CA
    5-8R; 113; CANR 18, 62; CDALB 1941-
    1968; CN 1, 2; CPW; DA; DA3; DAB;
    DAC; DAM MST, NOV, POP; DLB 2,
    185, 227; DLBY 1980, 1984; EWL 3;
    EXPS; GLL 1; LAIT 3; MAL 5; MTCW
    1, 2; MTFW 2005; NCFS 2; RGAL 4;
    RGSF 2; SATA 91; SSFS 2; TUS
Capra, Frank 1897-1991 .... **CLC 16**
    See also AAYA 52; CA 61-64; 135
Caputo, Philip 1941- .... **CLC 32**
    See also AAYA 60; CA 73-76; CANR 40,
    135; YAW
Caragiale, Ion Luca 1852-1912 ...... **TCLC 76**
    See also CA 157
Card, Orson Scott 1951- .... **CLC 44, 47, 50**
    See also AAYA 11, 42; BPFB 1; BYA 5, 8;
    CA 102; CANR 27, 47, 73, 102, 106, 133;
    CPW; DA3; DAM POP; FANT; INT
    CANR-27; MTCW 1, 2; MTFW 2005;
    NFS 5; SATA 83, 127; SCFW 2; SFW 4;
    SUFW 2; YAW
Cardenal, Ernesto 1925- .... **CLC 31, 161;
    HLC 1; PC 22**
    See also CA 49-52; CANR 2, 32, 66, 138;
    CWW 2; DAM MULT, POET; DLB 290;
    EWL 3; HW 1, 2; LAWS 1; MTCW 1, 2;
    MTFW 2005; RGWL 2, 3
Cardinal, Marie 1929-2001 .... **CLC 189**
    See also CA 177; CWW 2; DLB 83; FW
Cardozo, Benjamin N(athan)
    1870-1938 .... **TCLC 65**
    See also CA 117; 164
Carducci, Giosue (Alessandro Giuseppe)
    1835-1907 .... **PC 46; TCLC 32**
    See also CA 163; EW 7; RGWL 2, 3
Carew, Thomas 1595(?)-1640 . **LC 13; PC 29**
    See also BRW 2; DLB 126; PAB; RGEL 2
Carey, Ernestine Gilbreth 1908- ...... **CLC 17**
    See also CA 5-8R; CANR 71; SATA 2
Carey, Peter 1943- .... **CLC 40, 55, 96, 183**
    See also CA 123; 127; CANR 53, 76, 117;
    CN 4, 5, 6, 7; DLB 289; EWL 3; INT CA-
    127; MTCW 1, 2; MTFW 2005; RGSF 2;
    SATA 94
Carleton, William 1794-1869 .... **NCLC 3**
    See also DLB 159; RGEL 2; RGSF 2
Carlisle, Henry (Coffin) 1926- .... **CLC 33**
    See also CA 13-16R; CANR 15, 85
Carlsen, Chris
    See Holdstock, Robert P.

Carlson, Ron(ald F.) 1947- .... **CLC 54**
    See also CA 105, 189; CAAE 189; CANR
    27; DLB 244
Carlyle, Thomas 1795-1881 ..... **NCLC 22, 70**
    See also BRW 4; CDBLB 1789-1832; DA;
    DAB; DAC; DAM MST; DLB 55, 144,
    254; RGEL 2; TEA
Carman, (William) Bliss 1861-1929 ... **PC 34;
    TCLC 7**
    See also CA 104; 152; DAC; DLB 92;
    RGEL 2
Carnegie, Dale 1888-1955 .... **TCLC 53**
    See also CA 218
Carossa, Hans 1878-1956 .... **TCLC 48**
    See also CA 170; DLB 66; EWL 3
Carpenter, Don(ald Richard)
    1931-1995 .... **CLC 41**
    See also CA 45-48; 149; CANR 1, 71
Carpenter, Edward 1844-1929 .... **TCLC 88**
    See also CA 163; GLL 1
Carpenter, John (Howard) 1948- ... **CLC 161**
    See also AAYA 2; CA 134; SATA 58
Carpenter, Johnny
    See Carpenter, John (Howard)
Carpentier (y Valmont), Alejo
    1904-1980 . **CLC 8, 11, 38, 110; HLC 1;
    SSC 35**
    See also CA 65-68; 97-100; CANR 11, 70;
    CDWLB 3; DAM MULT; DLB 113; EWL
    3; HW 1, 2; LAW; LMFS 2; RGSF 2;
    RGWL 2, 3; WLIT 1
Carr, Caleb 1955- .... **CLC 86**
    See also CA 147; CANR 73, 134; DA3
Carr, Emily 1871-1945 .... **TCLC 32**
    See also CA 159; DLB 68; FW; GLL 2
Carr, John Dickson 1906-1977 .... **CLC 3**
    See Fairbairn, Roger
    See also CA 49-52; 69-72; CANR 3, 33,
    60; CMW 4; DLB 306; MSW; MTCW 1,
    2
Carr, Philippa
    See Hibbert, Eleanor Alice Burford
Carr, Virginia Spencer 1929- .... **CLC 34**
    See also CA 61-64; DLB 111
Carrere, Emmanuel 1957- .... **CLC 89**
    See also CA 200
Carrier, Roch 1937- .... **CLC 13, 78**
    See also CA 130; CANR 61; CCA 1; DAC;
    DAM MST; DLB 53; SATA 105
Carroll, James Dennis
    See Carroll, Jim
Carroll, James P. 1943(?)- .... **CLC 38**
    See also CA 81-84; CANR 73, 139; MTCW
    2; MTFW 2005
Carroll, Jim 1951- .... **CLC 35, 143**
    See also AAYA 17; CA 45-48; CANR 42,
    115; NCFS 5
Carroll, Lewis ..... **NCLC 2, 53, 139; PC 18;
    WLC**
    See Dodgson, Charles L(utwidge)
    See also AAYA 39; BRW 5; BYA 5, 13; CD-
    BLB 1832-1890; CLR 2, 18; DLB 18,
    163, 178; DLBY 1998; EXPN; EXPP;
    FANT; JRDA; LAIT 1; NFS 7; PFS 11;
    RGEL 2; SUFW 1; TEA; WCH
Carroll, Paul Vincent 1900-1968 ...... **CLC 10**
    See also CA 9-12R; 25-28R; DLB 10; EWL
    3; RGEL 2
Carruth, Hayden 1921- ..... **CLC 4, 7, 10, 18,
    84; PC 10**
    See also CA 9-12R; CANR 4, 38, 59, 110;
    CP 1, 2, 3, 4, 5, 6, 7; DLB 5, 165; INT
    CANR-4; MTCW 1, 2; MTFW 2005;
    SATA 47
Carson, Anne 1950- .... **CLC 185; PC 64**
    See also AMWS 12; CA 203; DLB 193;
    PFS 18; TCLE 1:1
Carson, Ciaran 1948- .... **CLC 201**
    See also CA 112; 153; CANR 113; CP 7

Carson, Rachel
    See Carson, Rachel Louise
    See also AAYA 49; DLB 275
Carson, Rachel Louise 1907-1964 .... **CLC 71**
    See Carson, Rachel
    See also AMWS 9; ANW; CA 77-80; CANR
    35; DA3; DAM POP; FW; LAIT 4; MAL
    5; MTCW 1, 2; MTFW 2005; NCFS 1;
    SATA 23
Carter, Angela (Olive) 1940-1992 ...... **CLC 5,
    41, 76; SSC 13, 85; TCLC 139**
    See also BRWS 3; CA 53-56; 136; CANR
    12, 36, 61, 106; CN 3, 4, 5; DA3; DLB
    14, 207, 261, 319; EXPS; FANT; FW; GL
    2; MTCW 1, 2; MTFW 2005; RGSF 2;
    SATA 66; SATA-Obit 70; SFW 4; SSFS
    4, 12; SUFW 2; WLIT 4
Carter, Nick
    See Smith, Martin Cruz
Carver, Raymond 1938-1988 ..... **CLC 22, 36,
    53, 55, 126; PC 54; SSC 8, 51**
    See also AAYA 44; AMWS 3; BPFB 1; CA
    33-36R; 126; CANR 17, 34, 61, 103; CN
    4; CPW; DA3; DAM NOV; DLB 130;
    DLBY 1984, 1988; EWL 3; MAL 5;
    MTCW 1, 2; MTFW 2005; PFS 17;
    RGAL 4; RGSF 2; SSFS 3, 6, 12, 13;
    TCLE 1:1; TCWW 2; TUS
Cary, Elizabeth, Lady Falkland
    1585-1639 .... **LC 30**
Cary, (Arthur) Joyce (Lunel)
    1888-1957 .... **TCLC 1, 29**
    See also BRW 7; CA 104; 164; CDBLB
    1914-1945; DLB 15, 100; EWL 3; MTCW
    2; RGEL 2; TEA
Casal, Julian del 1863-1893 .... **NCLC 131**
    See also DLB 283; LAW
Casanova, Giacomo
    See Casanova de Seingalt, Giovanni Jacopo
    See also WLIT 7
Casanova de Seingalt, Giovanni Jacopo
    1725-1798 .... **LC 13**
    See Casanova, Giacomo
Casares, Adolfo Bioy
    See Bioy Casares, Adolfo
    See also RGSF 2
Casas, Bartolome de las 1474-1566
    See Las Casas, Bartolome de
    See also WLIT 1
Casely-Hayford, J(oseph) E(phraim)
    1866-1903 .... **BLC 1; TCLC 24**
    See also BW 2; CA 123; 152; DAM MULT
Casey, John (Dudley) 1939- .... **CLC 59**
    See also BEST 90:2; CA 69-72; CANR 23,
    100
Casey, Michael 1947- .... **CLC 2**
    See also CA 65-68; CANR 109; CP 2, 3;
    DLB 5
Casey, Patrick
    See Thurman, Wallace (Henry)
Casey, Warren (Peter) 1935-1988 .... **CLC 12**
    See also CA 101; 127; INT CA-101
Casona, Alejandro .... **CLC 49**
    See Alvarez, Alejandro Rodriguez
    See also EWL 3
Cassavetes, John 1929-1989 .... **CLC 20**
    See also CA 85-88; 127; CANR 82
Cassian, Nina 1924- .... **PC 17**
    See also CWP; CWW 2
Cassill, R(onald) V(erlin)
    1919-2002 .... **CLC 4, 23**
    See also CA 9-12R; 208; CAAS 1; CANR
    7, 45; CN 1, 2, 3, 4, 5, 6, 7; DLB 6, 218;
    DLBY 2002
Cassiodorus, Flavius Magnus c. 490(?)-c.
    583(?) .... **CMLC 43**
Cassirer, Ernst 1874-1945 .... **TCLC 61**
    See also CA 157

Chapman, John Jay 1862-1933 .... TCLC 7
See also AMWS 14; CA 104; 191
Chapman, Lee
See Bradley, Marion Zimmer
See also GLL 1
Chapman, Walker
See Silverberg, Robert
Chappell, Fred (Davis) 1936- .... CLC 40, 78,
162
See also CA 5-8R, 198; CAAE 198; CAAS
4; CANR 8, 33, 67, 110; CN 6; CP 7;
CSW; DLB 6, 105; HGG
Char, Rene(-Emile) 1907-1988 .... CLC 9, 11,
14, 55; PC 56
See also CA 13-16R; 124; CANR 32; DAM
POET; DLB 258; EWL 3; GFL 1789 to
the Present; MTCW 1, 2; RGWL 2, 3
Charby, Jay
See Ellison, Harlan (Jay)
Chardin, Pierre Teilhard de
See Teilhard de Chardin, (Marie Joseph)
Pierre
Chariton fl. 1st cent. (?)- .... CMLC 49
Charlemagne 742-814 .... CMLC 37
Charles I 1600-1649 .... LC 13
Charriere, Isabelle de 1740-1805 .. NCLC 66
See also DLB 313
Chartier, Alain c. 1392-1430 .... LC 94
See also DLB 208
Chartier, Emile-Auguste
See Alain
Charyn, Jerome 1937- .... CLC 5, 8, 18
See also CA 5-8R; CAAS 1; CANR 7, 61,
101; CMW 4; CN 1, 2, 3, 4, 5, 6, 7;
DLBY 1983; MTCW 1
Chase, Adam
See Marlowe, Stephen
Chase, Mary (Coyle) 1907-1981 .... DC 1
See also CA 77-80; 105; CAD; CWD; DFS
11; DLB 228; SATA 17; SATA-Obit 29
Chase, Mary Ellen 1887-1973 .... CLC 2;
TCLC 124
See also CA 13-16; 41-44R; CAP 1; SATA
10
Chase, Nicholas
See Hyde, Anthony
See also CCA 1
Chateaubriand, Francois Rene de
1768-1848 .... NCLC 3, 134
See also DLB 119; EW 5; GFL 1789 to the
Present; RGWL 2, 3; TWA
Chatelet, Gabrielle-Emilie Du
See du Chatelet, Emilie
See also DLB 313
Chatterje, Sarat Chandra 1876-1936(?)
See Chatterji, Saratchandra
See also CA 109
Chatterji, Bankim Chandra
1838-1894 .... NCLC 19
Chatterji, Saratchandra .... TCLC 13
See Chatterje, Sarat Chandra
See also CA 186; EWL 3
Chatterton, Thomas 1752-1770 .... LC 3, 54
See also DAM POET; DLB 109; RGEL 2
Chatwin, (Charles) Bruce
1940-1989 .... CLC 28, 57, 59
See also AAYA 4; BEST 90:1; BRWS 4;
CA 85-88; 127; CPW; DAM POP; DLB
194, 204; EWL 3; MTFW 2005
Chaucer, Daniel
See Ford, Ford Madox
See also RHW
Chaucer, Geoffrey 1340(?)-1400 .. LC 17, 56;
PC 19, 58; WLCS
See also BRW 1; BRWC 1; BRWR 2; CD-
BLB Before 1660; DA; DA3; DAB;
DAC; DAM MST, POET; DLB 146;
LAIT 1; PAB; PFS 14; RGEL 2; TEA;
WLIT 3; WP

Chavez, Denise (Elia) 1948- .... HLC 1
See also CA 131; CANR 56, 81, 137; DAM
MULT; DLB 122; FW; HW 1, 2; LLW;
MAL 5; MTCW 2; MTFW 2005
Chaviaras, Strates 1935-
See Haviaras, Stratis
See also CA 105
Chayefsky, Paddy .... CLC 23
See Chayefsky, Sidney
See also CAD; DLB 7, 44; DLBY 1981;
RGAL 4
Chayefsky, Sidney 1923-1981
See Chayefsky, Paddy
See also CA 9-12R; 104; CANR 18; DAM
DRAM
Chedid, Andree 1920- .... CLC 47
See also CA 145; CANR 95; EWL 3
Cheever, John 1912-1982 ..... CLC 3, 7, 8, 11,
15, 25, 64; SSC 1, 38, 57; WLC
See also AAYA 65; AMWS 1; BPFB 1; CA
5-8R; 106; CABS 1; CANR 5, 27, 76;
CDALB 1941-1968; CN 1, 2, 3; CPW;
DA; DA3; DAB; DAC; DAM MST, NOV,
POP; DLB 2, 102, 227; DLBY 1980,
1982; EWL 3; EXPS; INT CANR-5;
MAL 5; MTCW 1, 2; MTFW 2005;
RGAL 4; RGSF 2; SSFS 2, 14; TUS
Cheever, Susan 1943- .... CLC 18, 48
See also CA 103; CANR 27, 51, 92; DLBY
1982; INT CANR-27
Chekhonte, Antosha
See Chekhov, Anton (Pavlovich)
Chekhov, Anton (Pavlovich)
1860-1904 .... DC 9; SSC 2, 28, 41, 51,
85; TCLC 3, 10, 31, 55, 96, 163; WLC
See also AAYA 68; BYA 14; CA 104; 124;
DA; DA3; DAB; DAC; DAM DRAM,
MST; DFS 1, 5, 10, 12; DLB 277; EW 7;
EWL 3; EXPS; LAIT 3; LATS 1:1; RGSF
2; RGWL 2, 3; SATA 90; SSFS 5, 13, 14;
TWA
Cheney, Lynne V. 1941- .... CLC 70
See also CA 89-92; CANR 58, 117; SATA
152
Chernyshevsky, Nikolai Gavrilovich
See Chernyshevsky, Nikolay Gavrilovich
See also DLB 238
Chernyshevsky, Nikolay Gavrilovich
1828-1889 .... NCLC 1
See Chernyshevsky, Nikolai Gavrilovich
Cherry, Carolyn Janice 1942-
See Cherryh, C. J.
See also CA 65-68; CANR 10
Cherryh, C. J. .... CLC 35
See Cherry, Carolyn Janice
See also AAYA 24; BPFB 1; DLBY 1980;
FANT; SATA 93; SCFW 2; SFW 4; YAW
Chesnutt, Charles W(addell)
1858-1932 .... BLC 1; SSC 7, 54; TCLC
5, 39
See also AFAW 1, 2; AMWS 14; BW 1, 3;
CA 106; 125; CANR 76; DAM MULT;
DLB 12, 50, 78; EWL 3; MAL 5; MTCW
1, 2; MTFW 2005; RGAL 4; RGSF 2;
SSFS 11
Chester, Alfred 1929(?)-1971 .... CLC 49
See also CA 196; 33-36R; DLB 130; MAL
5
Chesterton, G(ilbert) K(eith)
1874-1936 . PC 28; SSC 1, 46; TCLC 1,
6, 64
See also AAYA 57; BRW 6; CA 104; 132;
CANR 73, 131; CDBLB 1914-1945;
CMW 4; DAM NOV, POET; DLB 10, 19,
34, 70, 98, 149, 178; EWL 3; FANT;
MSW; MTCW 1, 2; MTFW 2005; RGEL
2; RGSF 2; SATA 27; SUFW 1
Chettle, Henry 1560-1607(?) .... LC 112
See also DLB 136; RGEL 2

Chiang, Pin-chin 1904-1986
See Ding Ling
See also CA 118
Chief Joseph 1840-1904 .... NNAL
See also CA 152; DA3; DAM MULT
Chief Seattle 1786(?)-1866 .... NNAL
See also DA3; DAM MULT
Ch'ien, Chung-shu 1910-1998 .... CLC 22
See Qian Zhongshu
See also CA 130; CANR 73; MTCW 1, 2
Chikamatsu Monzaemon 1653-1724 ... LC 66
See also RGWL 2, 3
Child, L. Maria
See Child, Lydia Maria
Child, Lydia Maria 1802-1880 .. NCLC 6, 73
See also DLB 1, 74, 243; RGAL 4; SATA
67
Child, Mrs.
See Child, Lydia Maria
Child, Philip 1898-1978 .... CLC 19, 68
See also CA 13-14; CAP 1; CP 1; DLB 68;
RHW; SATA 47
Childers, (Robert) Erskine
1870-1922 .... TCLC 65
See also CA 113; 153; DLB 70
Childress, Alice 1920-1994 . BLC 1; CLC 12,
15, 86, 96; DC 4; TCLC 116
See also AAYA 8; BW 2, 3; BYA 2; CA 45-
48; 146; CAD; CANR 3, 27, 50, 74; CLR
14; CWD; DA3; DAM DRAM, MULT,
NOV; DFS 2, 8, 14; DLB 7, 38, 249;
JRDA; LAIT 5; MAICYA 1, 2; MAIC-
YAS 1; MAL 5; MTCW 1, 2; MTFW
2005; RGAL 4; SATA 7, 48, 81; TUS;
WYA; YAW
Chin, Frank (Chew, Jr.) 1940- .... AAL; CLC
135; DC 7
See also CA 33-36R; CAD; CANR 71; CD
5, 6; DAM MULT; DLB 206, 312; LAIT
5; RGAL 4
Chin, Marilyn (Mei Ling) 1955- .... PC 40
See also CA 129; CANR 70, 113; CWP;
DLB 312
Chislett, (Margaret) Anne 1943- ...... CLC 34
See also CA 151
Chitty, Thomas Willes 1926- .... CLC 11
See Hinde, Thomas
See also CA 5-8R; CN 7
Chivers, Thomas Holley
1809-1858 .... NCLC 49
See also DLB 3, 248; RGAL 4
Choi, Susan 1969- .... CLC 119
See also CA 223
Chomette, Rene Lucien 1898-1981
See Clair, Rene
See also CA 103
Chomsky, (Avram) Noam 1928- ..... CLC 132
See also CA 17-20R; CANR 28, 62, 110,
132; DA3; DLB 246; MTCW 1, 2; MTFW
2005
Chona, Maria 1845(?)-1936 .... NNAL
See also CA 144
Chopin, Kate .... SSC 8, 68; TCLC 127;
WLCS
See Chopin, Katherine
See also AAYA 33; AMWR 2; AMWS 1;
BYA 11, 15; CDALB 1865-1917; DA;
DAB; DLB 12, 78; EXPN; EXPS; FL 1:3;
FW; LAIT 3; MAL 5; MAWW; NFS 3;
RGAL 4; RGSF 2; SSFS 2, 13, 17; TUS
Chopin, Katherine 1851-1904
See Chopin, Kate
See also CA 104; 122; DA3; DAC; DAM
MST, NOV
Chretien de Troyes c. 12th cent. - . CMLC 10
See also DLB 208; EW 1; RGWL 2, 3;
TWA
Christie
See Ichikawa, Kon

Connelly, Marc(us Cook) 1890-1980 . **CLC 7**
See also CA 85-88; 102; CAD; CANR 30; DFS 12; DLB 7; DLBY 1980; MAL 5; RGAL 4; SATA-Obit 25

Connor, Ralph .... **TCLC 31**
See Gordon, Charles William
See also DLB 92; TCWW 1, 2

Conrad, Joseph 1857-1924 ..... **SSC 9, 67, 69, 71; TCLC 1, 6, 13, 25, 43, 57; WLC**
See also AAYA 26; BPFB 1; BRW 6; BRWC 1; BRWR 2; BYA 2; CA 104; 131; CANR 60; CDBLB 1890-1914; DA; DA3; DAB; DAC; DAM MST, NOV; DLB 10, 34, 98, 156; EWL 3; EXPN; EXPS; LAIT 2; LATS 1:1; LMFS 1; MTCW 1, 2; MTFW 2005; NFS 2, 16; RGEL 2; RGSF 2; SATA 27; SSFS 1, 12; TEA; WLIT 4

Conrad, Robert Arnold
See Hart, Moss

Conroy, (Donald) Pat(rick) 1945- ... **CLC 30, 74**
See also AAYA 8, 52; AITN 1; BPFB 1; CA 85-88; CANR 24, 53, 129; CN 7; CPW; CSW; DA3; DAM NOV, POP; DLB 6; LAIT 5; MAL 5; MTCW 1, 2; MTFW 2005

Constant (de Rebecque), (Henri) Benjamin 1767-1830 .... **NCLC 6**
See also DLB 119; EW 4; GFL 1789 to the Present

Conway, Jill K(er) 1934- .... **CLC 152**
See also CA 130; CANR 94

Conybeare, Charles Augustus
See Eliot, T(homas) S(tearns)

Cook, Michael 1933-1994 .... **CLC 58**
See also CA 93-96; CANR 68; DLB 53

Cook, Robin 1940- .... **CLC 14**
See also AAYA 32; BEST 90:2; BPFB 1; CA 108; 111; CANR 41, 90, 109; CPW; DA3; DAM POP; HGG; INT CA-111

Cook, Roy
See Silverberg, Robert

Cooke, Elizabeth 1948- .... **CLC 55**
See also CA 129

Cooke, John Esten 1830-1886 .... **NCLC 5**
See also DLB 3, 248; RGAL 4

Cooke, John Estes
See Baum, L(yman) Frank

Cooke, M. E.
See Creasey, John

Cooke, Margaret
See Creasey, John

Cooke, Rose Terry 1827-1892 ...... **NCLC 110**
See also DLB 12, 74

Cook-Lynn, Elizabeth 1930- .... **CLC 93; NNAL**
See also CA 133; DAM MULT; DLB 175

Cooney, Ray .... **CLC 62**
See also CBD

Cooper, Anthony Ashley 1671-1713 .. **LC 107**
See also DLB 101

Cooper, Dennis 1953- .... **CLC 203**
See also CA 133; CANR 72, 86; GLL 1; HGG

Cooper, Douglas 1960- .... **CLC 86**

Cooper, Henry St. John
See Creasey, John

Cooper, J(oan) California (?)- .... **CLC 56**
See also AAYA 12; BW 1; CA 125; CANR 55; DAM MULT; DLB 212

Cooper, James Fenimore 1789-1851 .... **NCLC 1, 27, 54**
See also AAYA 22; AMW; BPFB 1; CDALB 1640-1865; DA3; DLB 3, 183, 250, 254; LAIT 1; NFS 9; RGAL 4; SATA 19; TUS; WCH

Cooper, Susan Fenimore 1813-1894 .... **NCLC 129**
See also ANW; DLB 239, 254

Coover, Robert (Lowell) 1932- ...... **CLC 3, 7, 15, 32, 46, 87, 161; SSC 15**
See also AMWS 5; BPFB 1; CA 45-48; CANR 3, 37, 58, 115; CN 1, 2, 3, 4, 5, 6, 7; DAM NOV; DLB 2, 227; DLBY 1981; EWL 3; MAL 5; MTCW 1, 2; MTFW 2005; RGAL 4; RGSF 2

Copeland, Stewart (Armstrong) 1952- .... **CLC 26**

Copernicus, Nicolaus 1473-1543 .... **LC 45**

Coppard, A(lfred) E(dgar) 1878-1957 .... **SSC 21; TCLC 5**
See also BRWS 8; CA 114; 167; DLB 162; EWL 3; HGG; RGEL 2; RGSF 2; SUFW 1; YABC 1

Coppee, Francois 1842-1908 .... **TCLC 25**
See also CA 170; DLB 217

Coppola, Francis Ford 1939- ... **CLC 16, 126**
See also AAYA 39; CA 77-80; CANR 40, 78; DLB 44

Copway, George 1818-1869 .... **NNAL**
See also DAM MULT; DLB 175, 183

Corbiere, Tristan 1845-1875 .... **NCLC 43**
See also DLB 217; GFL 1789 to the Present

Corcoran, Barbara (Asenath) 1911- .... **CLC 17**
See also AAYA 14; CA 21-24R, 191; CAAE 191; CAAS 2; CANR 11, 28, 48; CLR 50; DLB 52; JRDA; MAICYA 2; MAIC-YAS 1; RHW; SAAS 20; SATA 3, 77; SATA-Essay 125

Cordelier, Maurice
See Giraudoux, Jean(-Hippolyte)

Corelli, Marie .... **TCLC 51**
See Mackay, Mary
See also DLB 34, 156; RGEL 2; SUFW 1

Corinna c. 225B.C.-c. 305B.C. ...... **CMLC 72**

Corman, Cid .... **CLC 9**
See Corman, Sidney
See also CAAS 2; CP 1, 2, 3, 4, 5, 6, 7; DLB 5, 193

Corman, Sidney 1924-2004
See Corman, Cid
See also CA 85-88; 225; CANR 44; DAM POET

Cormier, Robert (Edmund) 1925-2000 .... **CLC 12, 30**
See also AAYA 3, 19; BYA 1, 2, 6, 8, 9; CA 1-4R; CANR 5, 23, 76, 93; CDALB 1968-1988; CLR 12, 55; DA; DAB; DAC; DAM MST, NOV; DLB 52; EXPN; INT CANR-23; JRDA; LAIT 5; MAICYA 1, 2; MTCW 1, 2; MTFW 2005; NFS 2, 18; SATA 10, 45, 83; SATA-Obit 122; WYA; YAW

Corn, Alfred (DeWitt III) 1943- .... **CLC 33**
See also CA 179; CAAE 179; CAAS 25; CANR 44; CP 3, 4, 5, 6, 7; CSW; DLB 120, 282; DLBY 1980

Corneille, Pierre 1606-1684 ... **DC 21; LC 28**
See also DAB; DAM MST; DFS 21; DLB 268; EW 3; GFL Beginnings to 1789; RGWL 2, 3; TWA

Cornwell, David (John Moore) 1931- .... **CLC 9, 15**
See le Carre, John
See also CA 5-8R; CANR 13, 33, 59, 107, 132; DA3; DAM POP; MTCW 1, 2; MTFW 2005

Cornwell, Patricia (Daniels) 1956- . **CLC 155**
See also AAYA 16, 56; BPFB 1; CA 134; CANR 53, 131; CMW 4; CPW; CSW; DAM POP; DLB 306; MSW; MTCW 2; MTFW 2005

Corso, (Nunzio) Gregory 1930-2001 . **CLC 1, 11; PC 33**
See also AMWS 12; BG 1:2; CA 5-8R; 193; CANR 41, 76, 132; CP 1, 2, 3, 4, 5, 6, 7; DA3; DLB 5, 16, 237; LMFS 2; MAL 5; MTCW 1, 2; MTFW 2005; WP

Cortazar, Julio 1914-1984 ... **CLC 2, 3, 5, 10, 13, 15, 33, 34, 92; HLC 1; SSC 7, 76**
See also BPFB 1; CA 21-24R; CANR 12, 32, 81; CDWLB 3; DA3; DAM MULT, NOV; DLB 113; EWL 3; EXPS; HW 1, 2; LAW; MTCW 1, 2; MTFW 2005; RGSF 2; RGWL 2, 3; SSFS 3, 20; TWA; WLIT 1

Cortes, Hernan 1485-1547 .... **LC 31**

Corvinus, Jakob
See Raabe, Wilhelm (Karl)

Corwin, Cecil
See Kornbluth, C(yril) M.

Cosic, Dobrica 1921- .... **CLC 14**
See also CA 122; 138; CDWLB 4; CWW 2; DLB 181; EWL 3

Costain, Thomas B(ertram) 1885-1965 .... **CLC 30**
See also BYA 3; CA 5-8R; 25-28R; DLB 9; RHW

Costantini, Humberto 1924(?)-1987 . **CLC 49**
See also CA 131; 122; EWL 3; HW 1

Costello, Elvis 1954- .... **CLC 21**
See also CA 204

Costenoble, Philostene
See Ghelderode, Michel de

Cotes, Cecil V.
See Duncan, Sara Jeannette

Cotter, Joseph Seamon Sr. 1861-1949 .... **BLC 1; TCLC 28**
See also BW 1; CA 124; DAM MULT; DLB 50

Couch, Arthur Thomas Quiller
See Quiller-Couch, Sir Arthur (Thomas)

Coulton, James
See Hansen, Joseph

Couperus, Louis (Marie Anne) 1863-1923 .... **TCLC 15**
See also CA 115; EWL 3; RGWL 2, 3

Coupland, Douglas 1961- .... **CLC 85, 133**
See also AAYA 34; CA 142; CANR 57, 90, 130; CCA 1; CN 7; CPW; DAC; DAM POP

Court, Wesli
See Turco, Lewis (Putnam)

Courtenay, Bryce 1933- .... **CLC 59**
See also CA 138; CPW

Courtney, Robert
See Ellison, Harlan (Jay)

Cousteau, Jacques-Yves 1910-1997 .. **CLC 30**
See also CA 65-68; 159; CANR 15, 67; MTCW 1; SATA 38, 98

Coventry, Francis 1725-1754 .... **LC 46**

Coverdale, Miles c. 1487-1569 .... **LC 77**
See also DLB 167

Cowan, Peter (Walkinshaw) 1914-2002 .... **SSC 28**
See also CA 21-24R; CANR 9, 25, 50, 83; CN 1, 2, 3, 4, 5, 6, 7; DLB 260; RGSF 2

Coward, Noel (Peirce) 1899-1973 . **CLC 1, 9, 29, 51**
See also AITN 1; BRWS 2; CA 17-18; 41-44R; CANR 35, 132; CAP 2; CBD; CD-BLB 1914-1945; DA3; DAM DRAM; DFS 3, 6; DLB 10, 245; EWL 3; IDFW 3, 4; MTCW 1, 2; MTFW 2005; RGEL 2; TEA

Cowley, Abraham 1618-1667 .... **LC 43**
See also BRW 2; DLB 131, 151; PAB; RGEL 2

Cowley, Malcolm 1898-1989 .... **CLC 39**
See also AMWS 2; CA 5-8R; 128; CANR 3, 55; CP 1, 2, 3, 4; DLB 4, 48; DLBY 1981, 1989; EWL 3; MAL 5; MTCW 1, 2; MTFW 2005

Cowper, William 1731-1800 ..... **NCLC 8, 94; PC 40**
See also BRW 3; DA3; DAM POET; DLB 104, 109; RGEL 2

Cox, William Trevor 1928-
  See Trevor, William
    See also CA 9-12R; CANR 4, 37, 55, 76,
    102, 139; DAM NOV; INT CANR-37;
    MTCW 1, 2; MTFW 2005; TEA

Coyne, P. J.
  See Masters, Hilary

Cozzens, James Gould 1903-1978 . **CLC 1, 4,**
    11, 92
    See also AMW; BPFB 1; CA 9-12R; 81-84;
    CANR 19; CDALB 1941-1968; CN 1, 2;
    DLB 9, 294; DLBD 2; DLBY 1984, 1997;
    EWL 3; MAL 5; MTCW 1, 2; MTFW
    2005; RGAL 4

Crabbe, George 1754-1832 .... **NCLC 26, 121**
    See also BRW 3; DLB 93; RGEL 2

Crace, Jim 1946- .... **CLC 157; SSC 61**
    See also CA 128; 135; CANR 55, 70, 123;
    CN 5, 6, 7; DLB 231; INT CA-135

Craddock, Charles Egbert
  See Murfree, Mary Noailles

Craig, A. A.
  See Anderson, Poul (William)

Craik, Mrs.
  See Craik, Dinah Maria (Mulock)
  See also RGEL 2

Craik, Dinah Maria (Mulock)
    1826-1887 .... **NCLC 38**
    See Craik, Mrs.; Mulock, Dinah Maria
    See also DLB 35, 163; MAICYA 1, 2;
    SATA 34

Cram, Ralph Adams 1863-1942 ..... **TCLC 45**
    See also CA 160

Cranch, Christopher Pearse
    1813-1892 .... **NCLC 115**
    See also DLB 1, 42, 243

Crane, (Harold) Hart 1899-1932 .... **PC 3;**
    TCLC 2, 5, 80; WLC
    See also AMW; AMWR 2; CA 104; 127;
    CDALB 1917-1929; DA; DA3; DAB;
    DAC; DAM MST, POET; DLB 4, 48;
    EWL 3; MAL 5; MTCW 1, 2; MTFW
    2005; RGAL 4; TUS

Crane, R(onald) S(almon)
    1886-1967 .... **CLC 27**
    See also CA 85-88; DLB 63

Crane, Stephen (Townley)
    1871-1900 ...... **SSC 7, 56, 70; TCLC 11,**
    17, 32; WLC
    See also AAYA 21; AMW; AMWC 1; BPFB
    1; BYA 3; CA 109; 140; CANR 84;
    CDALB 1865-1917; DA; DA3; DAB;
    DAC; DAM MST, NOV, POET; DLB 12,
    54, 78; EXPN; EXPS; LAIT 2; LMFS 2;
    MAL 5; NFS 4, 20; PFS 9; RGAL 4;
    RGSF 2; SSFS 4; TUS; WYA; YABC 2

Cranmer, Thomas 1489-1556 .... **LC 95**
    See also DLB 132, 213

Cranshaw, Stanley
  See Fisher, Dorothy (Frances) Canfield

Crase, Douglas 1944- .... **CLC 58**
    See also CA 106

Crashaw, Richard 1612(?)-1649 .... **LC 24**
    See also BRW 2; DLB 126; PAB; RGEL 2

Cratinus c. 519B.C.-c. 422B.C. ..... **CMLC 54**
    See also LMFS 1

Craven, Margaret 1901-1980 .... **CLC 17**
    See also BYA 2; CA 103; CCA 1; DAC;
    LAIT 5

Crawford, F(rancis) Marion
    1854-1909 .... **TCLC 10**
    See also CA 107; 168; DLB 71; HGG;
    RGAL 4; SUFW 1

Crawford, Isabella Valancy
    1850-1887 .... **NCLC 12, 127**
    See also DLB 92; RGEL 2

Crayon, Geoffrey
  See Irving, Washington

Creasey, John 1908-1973 .... **CLC 11**
  See Marric, J. J.
    See also CA 5-8R; 41-44R; CANR 8, 59;
    CMW 4; DLB 77; MTCW 1

Crebillon, Claude Prosper Jolyot de (fils)
    1707-1777 .... **LC 1, 28**
    See also DLB 313; GFL Beginnings to 1789

Credo
  See Creasey, John

Credo, Alvaro J. de
  See Prado (Calvo), Pedro

Creeley, Robert (White) 1926-2005 .. **CLC 1,**
    2, 4, 8, 11, 15, 36, 78
    See also AMWS 4; CA 1-4R; 237; CAAS
    10; CANR 23, 43, 89, 137; CP 1, 2, 3, 4,
    5, 6, 7; DA3; DAM POET; DLB 5, 16,
    169; DLBD 17; EWL 3; MAL 5; MTCW
    1, 2; MTFW 2005; PFS 21; RGAL 4; WP

Crenne, Helisenne de 1510-1560 .... **LC 113**

Crevecoeur, Hector St. John de
  See Crevecoeur, Michel Guillaume Jean de
  See also ANW

Crevecoeur, Michel Guillaume Jean de
    1735-1813 .... **NCLC 105**
    See Crevecoeur, Hector St. John de
    See also AMWS 1; DLB 37

Crevel, Rene 1900-1935 .... **TCLC 112**
    See also GLL 2

Crews, Harry (Eugene) 1935- ..... **CLC 6, 23,**
    49
    See also AITN 1; AMWS 11; BPFB 1; CA
    25-28R; CANR 20, 57; CN 3, 4, 5, 6, 7;
    CSW; DA3; DLB 6, 143, 185; MTCW 1,
    2; MTFW 2005; RGAL 4

Crichton, (John) Michael 1942- .... **CLC 2, 6,**
    54, 90
    See also AAYA 10, 49; AITN 2; BPFB 1;
    CA 25-28R; CANR 13, 40, 54, 76, 127;
    CMW 4; CN 2, 3, 6, 7; CPW; DA3; DAM
    NOV, POP; DLB 292; DLBY 1981; INT
    CANR-13; JRDA; MTCW 1, 2; MTFW
    2005; SATA 9, 88; SFW 4; YAW

Crispin, Edmund .... **CLC 22**
  See Montgomery, (Robert) Bruce
    See also DLB 87; MSW

Cristofer, Michael 1945- .... **CLC 28**
    See also CA 110; 152; CAD; CD 5, 6; DAM
    DRAM; DFS 15; DLB 7

Criton
  See Alain

Croce, Benedetto 1866-1952 .... **TCLC 37**
    See also CA 120; 155; EW 8; EWL 3;
    WLIT 7

Crockett, David 1786-1836 .... **NCLC 8**
    See also DLB 3, 11, 183, 248

Crockett, Davy
  See Crockett, David

Crofts, Freeman Wills 1879-1957 .. **TCLC 55**
    See also CA 115; 195; CMW 4; DLB 77;
    MSW

Croker, John Wilson 1780-1857 .... **NCLC 10**
    See also DLB 110

Crommelynck, Fernand 1885-1970 .. **CLC 75**
    See also CA 189; 89-92; EWL 3

Cromwell, Oliver 1599-1658 .... **LC 43**

Cronenberg, David 1943- .... **CLC 143**
    See also CA 138; CCA 1

Cronin, A(rchibald) J(oseph)
    1896-1981 .... **CLC 32**
    See also BPFB 1; CA 1-4R; 102; CANR 5;
    CN 2; DLB 191; SATA 47; SATA-Obit 25

Cross, Amanda
  See Heilbrun, Carolyn G(old)
    See also BPFB 1; CMW; CPW; DLB 306;
    MSW

Crothers, Rachel 1878-1958 .... **TCLC 19**
    See also CA 113; 194; CAD; CWD; DLB
    7, 266; RGAL 4

Croves, Hal
  See Traven, B.

Crow Dog, Mary (Ellen) (?)- .... **CLC 93**
  See Brave Bird, Mary
    See also CA 154

Crowfield, Christopher
  See Stowe, Harriet (Elizabeth) Beecher

Crowley, Aleister .... **TCLC 7**
  See Crowley, Edward Alexander
    See also GLL 1

Crowley, Edward Alexander 1875-1947
  See Crowley, Aleister
    See also CA 104; HGG

Crowley, John 1942- .... **CLC 57**
    See also AAYA 57; BPFB 1; CA 61-64;
    CANR 43, 98, 138; DLBY 1982; FANT;
    MTFW 2005; SATA 65, 140; SFW 4;
    SUFW 2

Crowne, John 1641-1712 .... **LC 104**
    See also DLB 80; RGEL 2

Crud
  See Crumb, R(obert)

Crumarums
  See Crumb, R(obert)

Crumb, R(obert) 1943- .... **CLC 17**
    See also CA 106; CANR 107

Crumbum
  See Crumb, R(obert)

Crumski
  See Crumb, R(obert)

Crum the Bum
  See Crumb, R(obert)

Crunk
  See Crumb, R(obert)

Crustt
  See Crumb, R(obert)

Crutchfield, Les
  See Trumbo, Dalton

Cruz, Victor Hernandez 1949- ... **HLC 1; PC**
    37
    See also BW 2; CA 65-68; CAAS 17;
    CANR 14, 32, 74, 132; CP 1, 2, 3, 4, 5,
    6, 7; DAM MULT, POET; DLB 41; DNFS
    1; EXPP; HW 1, 2; LLW; MTCW 2;
    MTFW 2005; PFS 16; WP

Cryer, Gretchen (Kiger) 1935- .... **CLC 21**
    See also CA 114; 123

Csath, Geza .... **TCLC 13**
  See Brenner, Jozef
    See also CA 111

Cudlip, David R(ockwell) 1933- .... **CLC 34**
    See also CA 177

Cullen, Countee 1903-1946 . **BLC 1; HR 1:2;**
    PC 20; TCLC 4, 37; WLCS
    See also AFAW 2; AMWS 4; BW 1; CA
    108; 124; CDALB 1917-1929; DA; DA3;
    DAC; DAM MST, MULT, POET; DLB 4,
    48, 51; EWL 3; EXPP; LMFS 2; MAL 5;
    MTCW 1, 2; MTFW 2005; PFS 3; RGAL
    4; SATA 18; WP

Culleton, Beatrice 1949- .... **NNAL**
    See also CA 120; CANR 83; DAC

Cum, R.
  See Crumb, R(obert)

Cumberland, Richard
    1732-1811 .... **NCLC 167**
    See also DLB 89; RGEL 2

Cummings, Bruce F(rederick) 1889-1919
  See Barbellion, W. N. P.
    See also CA 123

Cummings, E(dward) E(stlin)
    1894-1962 .. **CLC 1, 3, 8, 12, 15, 68; PC**
    5; TCLC 137; WLC
    See also AAYA 41; AMW; CA 73-76;
    CANR 31; CDALB 1929-1941; DA;
    DA3; DAB; DAC; DAM MST, POET;
    DLB 4, 48; EWL 3; EXPP; MAL 5;
    MTCW 1, 2; MTFW 2005; PAB; PFS 1,
    3, 12, 13, 19; RGAL 4; TUS; WP

Douglas, Leonard
See Bradbury, Ray (Douglas)

Douglas, Michael
See Crichton, (John) Michael

Douglas, (George) Norman
1868-1952 .... **TCLC 68**
See also BRW 6; CA 119; 157; DLB 34, 195; RGEL 2

Douglas, William
See Brown, George Douglas

Douglass, Frederick 1817(?)-1895 ..... **BLC 1; NCLC 7, 55, 141; WLC**
See also AAYA 48; AFAW 1, 2; AMWC 1; AMWS 3; CDALB 1640-1865; DA; DA3; DAC; DAM MST, MULT; DLB 1, 43, 50, 79, 243; FW; LAIT 2; NCFS 2; RGAL 4; SATA 29

Dourado, (Waldomiro Freitas) Autran
1926- .... **CLC 23, 60**
See also CA 25-28R; 179; CANR 34, 81; DLB 145, 307; HW 2

Dourado, Waldomiro Freitas Autran
See Dourado, (Waldomiro Freitas) Autran

Dove, Rita (Frances) 1952- . **BLCS; CLC 50, 81; PC 6**
See also AAYA 46; AMWS 4; BW 2; CA 109; CAAS 19; CANR 27, 42, 68, 76, 97, 132; CDALBS; CP 7; CSW; CWP; DA3; DAM MULT, POET; DLB 120; EWL 3; EXPP; MAL 5; MTCW 2; MTFW 2005; PFS 1, 15; RGAL 4

Doveglion
See Villa, Jose Garcia

Dowell, Coleman 1925-1985 .... **CLC 60**
See also CA 25-28R; 117; CANR 10; DLB 130; GLL 2

Dowson, Ernest (Christopher)
1867-1900 .... **TCLC 4**
See also CA 105; 150; DLB 19, 135; RGEL 2

Doyle, A. Conan
See Doyle, Sir Arthur Conan

Doyle, Sir Arthur Conan
1859-1930 . **SSC 12, 83; TCLC 7; WLC**
See Conan Doyle, Arthur
See also AAYA 14; BRWS 2; CA 104; 122; CANR 131; CDBLB 1890-1914; CMW 4; DA; DA3; DAB; DAC; DAM MST, NOV; DLB 18, 70, 156, 178; EXPS; HGG; LAIT 2; MSW; MTCW 1, 2; MTFW 2005; RGEL 2; RGSF 2; RHW; SATA 24; SCFW 1, 2; SFW 4; SSFS 2; TEA; WCH; WLIT 4; WYA; YAW

Doyle, Conan
See Doyle, Sir Arthur Conan

Doyle, John
See Graves, Robert (von Ranke)

Doyle, Roddy 1958- .... **CLC 81, 178**
See also AAYA 14; BRWS 5; CA 143; CANR 73, 128; CN 6, 7; DA3; DLB 194; MTCW 2; MTFW 2005

Doyle, Sir A. Conan
See Doyle, Sir Arthur Conan

Dr. A
See Asimov, Isaac; Silverstein, Alvin; Silverstein, Virginia B(arbara Opshelor)

Drabble, Margaret 1939- ...... **CLC 2, 3, 5, 8, 10, 22, 53, 129**
See also BRWS 4; CA 13-16R; CANR 18, 35, 63, 112, 131; CDBLB 1960 to Present; CN 1, 2, 3, 4, 5, 6, 7; CPW; DA3; DAB; DAC; DAM MST, NOV, POP; DLB 14, 155, 231; EWL 3; FW; MTCW 1, 2; MTFW 2005; RGEL 2; SATA 48; TEA

Drakulic, Slavenka 1949- .... **CLC 173**
See also CA 144; CANR 92

Drakulic-Ilic, Slavenka
See Drakulic, Slavenka

Drapier, M. B.
See Swift, Jonathan

Drayham, James
See Mencken, H(enry) L(ouis)

Drayton, Michael 1563-1631 .... **LC 8**
See also DAM POET; DLB 121; RGEL 2

Dreadstone, Carl
See Campbell, (John) Ramsey

Dreiser, Theodore (Herman Albert)
1871-1945 .... **SSC 30; TCLC 10, 18, 35, 83; WLC**
See also AMW; AMWC 2; AMWR 2; BYA 15, 16; CA 106; 132; CDALB 1865-1917; DA; DA3; DAC; DAM MST, NOV; DLB 9, 12, 102, 137; DLBD 1; EWL 3; LAIT 2; LMFS 2; MAL 5; MTCW 1, 2; MTFW 2005; NFS 8, 17; RGAL 4; TUS

Drexler, Rosalyn 1926- .... **CLC 2, 6**
See also CA 81-84; CAD; CANR 68, 124; CD 5, 6; CWD; MAL 5

Dreyer, Carl Theodor 1889-1968 ...... **CLC 16**
See also CA 116

Drieu la Rochelle, Pierre(-Eugene)
1893-1945 .... **TCLC 21**
See also CA 117; DLB 72; EWL 3; GFL 1789 to the Present

Drinkwater, John 1882-1937 .... **TCLC 57**
See also CA 109; 149; DLB 10, 19, 149; RGEL 2

Drop Shot
See Cable, George Washington

Droste-Hulshoff, Annette Freiin von
1797-1848 .... **NCLC 3, 133**
See also CDWLB 2; DLB 133; RGSF 2; RGWL 2, 3

Drummond, Walter
See Silverberg, Robert

Drummond, William Henry
1854-1907 .... **TCLC 25**
See also CA 160; DLB 92

Drummond de Andrade, Carlos
1902-1987 .... **CLC 18; TCLC 139**
See Andrade, Carlos Drummond de
See also CA 132; 123; DLB 307; LAW

Drummond of Hawthornden, William
1585-1649 .... **LC 83**
See also DLB 121, 213; RGEL 2

Drury, Allen (Stuart) 1918-1998 .... **CLC 37**
See also CA 57-60; 170; CANR 18, 52; CN 1, 2, 3, 4, 5, 6; INT CANR-18

Druse, Eleanor
See King, Stephen

Dryden, John 1631-1700 ..... **DC 3; LC 3, 21, 115; PC 25; WLC**
See also BRW 2; CDBLB 1660-1789; DA; DAB; DAC; DAM DRAM, MST, POET; DLB 80, 101, 131; EXPP; IDTP; LMFS 1; RGEL 2; TEA; WLIT 3

du Bellay, Joachim 1524-1560 .... **LC 92**
See also GFL Beginnings to 1789; RGWL 2, 3

Duberman, Martin (Bauml) 1930- ..... **CLC 8**
See also CA 1-4R; CAD; CANR 2, 63, 137; CD 5, 6

Dubie, Norman (Evans) 1945- .... **CLC 36**
See also CA 69-72; CANR 12, 115; CP 3, 4, 5, 6, 7; DLB 120; PFS 12

Du Bois, W(illiam) E(dward) B(urghardt)
1868-1963 ..... **BLC 1; CLC 1, 2, 13, 64, 96; HR 1:2; TCLC 169; WLC**
See also AAYA 40; AFAW 1, 2; AMWC 1; AMWS 2; BW 1, 3; CA 85-88; CANR 34, 82, 132; CDALB 1865-1917; DA; DA3; DAC; DAM MST, MULT, NOV; DLB 47, 50, 91, 246, 284; EWL 3; EXPP; LAIT 2; LMFS 2; MAL 5; MTCW 1, 2; MTFW 2005; NCFS 1; PFS 13; RGAL 4; SATA 42

Dubus, Andre 1936-1999 ..... **CLC 13, 36, 97; SSC 15**
See also AMWS 7; CA 21-24R; 177; CANR 17; CN 5, 6; CSW; DLB 130; INT CANR-17; RGAL 4; SSFS 10; TCLE 1:1

Duca Minimo
See D'Annunzio, Gabriele

Ducharme, Rejean 1941- .... **CLC 74**
See also CA 165; DLB 60

du Chatelet, Emilie 1706-1749 .... **LC 96**
See Chatelet, Gabrielle-Emilie Du

Duchen, Claire .... **CLC 65**

Duclos, Charles Pinot- 1704-1772 .... **LC 1**
See also GFL Beginnings to 1789

Dudek, Louis 1918-2001 .... **CLC 11, 19**
See also CA 45-48; 215; CAAS 14; CANR 1; CP 1, 2, 3, 4, 5, 6, 7; DLB 88

Duerrenmatt, Friedrich 1921-1990 ... **CLC 1, 4, 8, 11, 15, 43, 102**
See Durrenmatt, Friedrich
See also CA 17-20R; CANR 33; CMW 4; DAM DRAM; DLB 69, 124; MTCW 1, 2

Duffy, Bruce 1953(?)- .... **CLC 50**
See also CA 172

Duffy, Maureen (Patricia) 1933- ...... **CLC 37**
See also CA 25-28R; CANR 33, 68; CBD; CN 1, 2, 3, 4, 5, 6, 7; CP 7; CWD; CWP; DFS 15; DLB 14, 310; FW; MTCW 1

Du Fu
See Tu Fu
See also RGWL 2, 3

Dugan, Alan 1923-2003 .... **CLC 2, 6**
See also CA 81-84; 220; CANR 119; CP 1, 2, 3, 4, 5, 6, 7; DLB 5; MAL 5; PFS 10

du Gard, Roger Martin
See Martin du Gard, Roger

Duhamel, Georges 1884-1966 .... **CLC 8**
See also CA 81-84; 25-28R; CANR 35; DLB 65; EWL 3; GFL 1789 to the Present; MTCW 1

Dujardin, Edouard (Emile Louis)
1861-1949 .... **TCLC 13**
See also CA 109; DLB 123

Duke, Raoul
See Thompson, Hunter S(tockton)

Dulles, John Foster 1888-1959 .... **TCLC 72**
See also CA 115; 149

Dumas, Alexandre (pere)
1802-1870 .... **NCLC 11, 71; WLC**
See also AAYA 22; BYA 3; DA; DA3; DAB; DAC; DAM MST, NOV; DLB 119, 192; EW 6; GFL 1789 to the Present; LAIT 1, 2; NFS 14, 19; RGWL 2, 3; SATA 18; TWA; WCH

Dumas, Alexandre (fils) 1824-1895 ...... **DC 1; NCLC 9**
See also DLB 192; GFL 1789 to the Present; RGWL 2, 3

Dumas, Claudine
See Malzberg, Barry N(athaniel)

Dumas, Henry L. 1934-1968 .... **CLC 6, 62**
See also BW 1; CA 85-88; DLB 41; RGAL 4

du Maurier, Daphne 1907-1989 .. **CLC 6, 11, 59; SSC 18**
See also AAYA 37; BPFB 1; BRWS 3; CA 5-8R; 128; CANR 6, 55; CMW 4; CN 1, 2, 3, 4; CPW; DA3; DAB; DAC; DAM MST, POP; DLB 191; GL 2; HGG; LAIT 3; MSW; MTCW 1, 2; NFS 12; RGEL 2; RGSF 2; RHW; SATA 27; SATA-Obit 60; SSFS 14, 16; TEA

Du Maurier, George 1834-1896 ..... **NCLC 86**
See also DLB 153, 178; RGEL 2

Dunbar, Paul Laurence 1872-1906 ... **BLC 1; PC 5; SSC 8; TCLC 2, 12; WLC**
See also AFAW 1, 2; AMWS 2; BW 1, 3; CA 104; 124; CANR 79; CDALB 1865-1917; DA; DA3; DAC; DAM MST, MULT, POET; DLB 50, 54, 78; EXPP; MAL 5; RGAL 4; SATA 34

Dunbar, William 1460(?)-1520(?) .... **LC 20;
PC 67**
See also BRWS 8; DLB 132, 146; RGEL 2

Dunbar-Nelson, Alice .... **HR 1:2**
See Nelson, Alice Ruth Moore Dunbar

Duncan, Dora Angela
See Duncan, Isadora

Duncan, Isadora 1877(?)-1927 .... **TCLC 68**
See also CA 118; 149

Duncan, Lois 1934- .... **CLC 26**
See also AAYA 4, 34; BYA 6, 8; CA 1-4R;
CANR 2, 23, 36, 111; CLR 29; JRDA;
MAICYA 1, 2; MAICYAS 1; MTFW
2005; SAAS 2; SATA 1, 36, 75, 133, 141;
SATA-Essay 141; WYA; YAW

Duncan, Robert (Edward)
1919-1988 .... **CLC 1, 2, 4, 7, 15, 41, 55;
PC 2**
See also BG 1:2; CA 9-12R; 124; CANR
28, 62; CP 1, 2, 3, 4; DAM POET; DLB
5, 16, 193; EWL 3; MAL 5; MTCW 1, 2;
MTFW 2005; PFS 13; RGAL 4; WP

Duncan, Sara Jeannette
1861-1922 .... **TCLC 60**
See also CA 157; DLB 92

Dunlap, William 1766-1839 .... **NCLC 2**
See also DLB 30, 37, 59; RGAL 4

Dunn, Douglas (Eaglesham) 1942- .... **CLC 6,
40**
See also BRWS 10; CA 45-48; CANR 2,
33, 126; CP 1, 2, 3, 4, 5, 6, 7; DLB 40;
MTCW 1

Dunn, Katherine (Karen) 1945- .... **CLC 71**
See also CA 33-36R; CANR 72; HGG;
MTCW 2; MTFW 2005

Dunn, Stephen (Elliott) 1939- .. **CLC 36, 206**
See also AMWS 11; CA 33-36R; CANR
12, 48, 53, 105; CP 3, 4, 5, 6, 7; DLB
105; PFS 21

Dunne, Finley Peter 1867-1936 ...... **TCLC 28**
See also CA 108; 178; DLB 11, 23; RGAL
4

Dunne, John Gregory 1932-2003 ..... **CLC 28**
See also CA 25-28R; 222; CANR 14, 50;
CN 5, 6, 7; DLBY 1980

Dunsany, Lord .... **TCLC 2, 59**
See Dunsany, Edward John Moreton Drax
Plunkett
See also DLB 77, 153, 156, 255; FANT;
IDTP; RGEL 2; SFW 4; SUFW 1

**Dunsany, Edward John Moreton Drax
Plunkett** 1878-1957
See Dunsany, Lord
See also CA 104; 148; DLB 10; MTCW 2

Duns Scotus, John 1266(?)-1308 ... **CMLC 59**
See also DLB 115

du Perry, Jean
See Simenon, Georges (Jacques Christian)

Durang, Christopher (Ferdinand)
1949- .... **CLC 27, 38**
See also CA 105; CAD; CANR 50, 76, 130;
CD 5, 6; MTCW 2; MTFW 2005

Duras, Claire de 1777-1832 .... **NCLC 154**

Duras, Marguerite 1914-1996 . **CLC 3, 6, 11,
20, 34, 40, 68, 100; SSC 40**
See also BPFB 1; CA 25-28R; 151; CANR
50; CWW 2; DFS 21; DLB 83, 321; EWL
3; FL 1:5; GFL 1789 to the Present; IDFW
4; MTCW 1, 2; RGWL 2, 3; TWA

Durban, (Rosa) Pam 1947- .... **CLC 39**
See also CA 123; CANR 98; CSW

Durcan, Paul 1944- .... **CLC 43, 70**
See also CA 134; CANR 123; CP 1, 7;
DAM POET; EWL 3

Durfey, Thomas 1653-1723 .... **LC 94**
See also DLB 80; RGEL 2

Durkheim, Emile 1858-1917 .... **TCLC 55**

Durrell, Lawrence (George)
1912-1990 ..... **CLC 1, 4, 6, 8, 13, 27, 41**
See also BPFB 1; BRWS 1; CA 9-12R; 132;
CANR 40, 77; CDBLB 1945-1960; CN 1,
2, 3, 4; CP 1, 2, 3, 4; DAM NOV; DLB
15, 27, 204; DLBY 1990; EWL 3; MTCW
1, 2; RGEL 2; SFW 4; TEA

Durrenmatt, Friedrich
See Duerrenmatt, Friedrich
See also CDWLB 2; EW 13; EWL 3;
RGWL 2, 3

Dutt, Michael Madhusudan
1824-1873 .... **NCLC 118**

Dutt, Toru 1856-1877 .... **NCLC 29**
See also DLB 240

Dwight, Timothy 1752-1817 .... **NCLC 13**
See also DLB 37; RGAL 4

Dworkin, Andrea 1946-2005 ...... **CLC 43, 123**
See also CA 77-80; 238; CAAS 21; CANR
16, 39, 76, 96; FL 1:5; FW; GLL 1; INT
CANR-16; MTCW 1, 2; MTFW 2005

Dwyer, Deanna
See Koontz, Dean R.

Dwyer, K. R.
See Koontz, Dean R.

Dybek, Stuart 1942- .... **CLC 114; SSC 55**
See also CA 97-100; CANR 39; DLB 130

Dye, Richard
See De Voto, Bernard (Augustine)

Dyer, Geoff 1958- .... **CLC 149**
See also CA 125; CANR 88

Dyer, George 1755-1841 .... **NCLC 129**
See also DLB 93

Dylan, Bob 1941- .... **CLC 3, 4, 6, 12, 77; PC
37**
See also CA 41-44R; CANR 108; CP 1, 2,
3, 4, 5, 6, 7; DLB 16

Dyson, John 1943- .... **CLC 70**
See also CA 144

Dzyubin, Eduard Georgievich 1895-1934
See Bagritsky, Eduard
See also CA 170

E. V. L.
See Lucas, E(dward) V(errall)

Eagleton, Terence (Francis) 1943- .. **CLC 63,
132**
See also CA 57-60; CANR 7, 23, 68, 115;
DLB 242; LMFS 2; MTCW 1, 2; MTFW
2005

Eagleton, Terry
See Eagleton, Terence (Francis)

Early, Jack
See Scoppettone, Sandra
See also GLL 1

East, Michael
See West, Morris L(anglo)

Eastaway, Edward
See Thomas, (Philip) Edward

Eastlake, William (Derry)
1917-1997 .... **CLC 8**
See also CA 5-8R; 158; CAAS 1; CANR 5,
63; CN 1, 2, 3, 4, 5, 6; DLB 6, 206; INT
CANR-5; MAL 5; TCWW 1, 2

Eastman, Charles A(lexander)
1858-1939 .... **NNAL; TCLC 55**
See also CA 179; CANR 91; DAM MULT;
DLB 175; YABC 1

Eaton, Edith Maude 1865-1914 .... **AAL**
See Far, Sui Sin
See also CA 154; DLB 221, 312; FW

Eaton, (Lillie) Winnifred 1875-1954 .... **AAL**
See also CA 217; DLB 221, 312; RGAL 4

Eberhart, Richard 1904-2005 ...... **CLC 3, 11,
19, 56**
See also AMW; CA 1-4R; 240; CANR 2,
125; CDALB 1941-1968; CP 1, 2, 3, 4, 5,
6, 7; DAM POET; DLB 48; MAL 5;
MTCW 1; RGAL 4

Eberhart, Richard Ghormley
See Eberhart, Richard

Eberstadt, Fernanda 1960- .... **CLC 39**
See also CA 136; CANR 69, 128

**Echegaray (y Eizaguirre), Jose (Maria
Waldo)** 1832-1916 .... **HLCS 1; TCLC 4**
See also CA 104; CANR 32; EWL 3; HW
1; MTCW 1

Echeverria, (Jose) Esteban (Antonino)
1805-1851 .... **NCLC 18**
See also LAW

Echo
See Proust, (Valentin-Louis-George-Eugene)
Marcel

Eckert, Allan W. 1931- .... **CLC 17**
See also AAYA 18; BYA 2; CA 13-16R;
CANR 14, 45; INT CANR-14; MAICYA
2; MAICYAS 1; SAAS 21; SATA 29, 91;
SATA-Brief 27

Eckhart, Meister 1260(?)-1327(?) .. **CMLC 9,
80**
See also DLB 115; LMFS 1

Eckmar, F. R.
See de Hartog, Jan

Eco, Umberto 1932- .... **CLC 28, 60, 142**
See also BEST 90:1; BPFB 1; CA 77-80;
CANR 12, 33, 55, 110, 131; CPW; CWW
2; DA3; DAM NOV; DLB 196, 242;
EWL 3; MSW; MTCW 1, 2; MTFW
2005; NFS 22; RGWL 3; WLIT 7

Eddison, E(ric) R(ucker)
1882-1945 .... **TCLC 15**
See also CA 109; 156; DLB 255; FANT;
SFW 4; SUFW 1

Eddy, Mary (Ann Morse) Baker
1821-1910 .... **TCLC 71**
See also CA 113; 174

Edel, (Joseph) Leon 1907-1997 .. **CLC 29, 34**
See also CA 1-4R; 161; CANR 1, 22, 112;
DLB 103; INT CANR-22

Eden, Emily 1797-1869 .... **NCLC 10**

Edgar, David 1948- .... **CLC 42**
See also CA 57-60; CANR 12, 61, 112;
CBD; CD 5, 6; DAM DRAM; DFS 15;
DLB 13, 233; MTCW 1

Edgerton, Clyde (Carlyle) 1944- ...... **CLC 39**
See also AAYA 17; CA 118; 134; CANR
64, 125; CN 7; CSW; DLB 278; INT CA-
134; TCLE 1:1; YAW

Edgeworth, Maria 1768-1849 ... **NCLC 1, 51,
158; SSC 86**
See also BRWS 3; DLB 116, 159, 163; FL
1:3; FW; RGEL 2; SATA 21; TEA; WLIT
3

Edmonds, Paul
See Kuttner, Henry

Edmonds, Walter D(umaux)
1903-1998 .... **CLC 35**
See also BYA 2; CA 5-8R; CANR 2; CWRI
5; DLB 9; LAIT 1; MAICYA 1, 2; MAL
5; RHW; SAAS 4; SATA 1, 27; SATA-
Obit 99

Edmondson, Wallace
See Ellison, Harlan (Jay)

Edson, Margaret 1961- ...... **CLC 199; DC 24**
See also CA 190; DFS 13; DLB 266

Edson, Russell 1935- .... **CLC 13**
See also CA 33-36R; CANR 115; CP 2, 3,
4, 5, 6, 7; DLB 244; WP

Edwards, Bronwen Elizabeth
See Rose, Wendy

Edwards, G(erald) B(asil)
1899-1976 .... **CLC 25**
See also CA 201; 110

Edwards, Gus 1939- .... **CLC 43**
See also CA 108; INT CA-108

Edwards, Jonathan 1703-1758 .... **LC 7, 54**
See also AMW; DA; DAC; DAM MST;
DLB 24, 270; RGAL 4; TUS

Edwards, Sarah Pierpont 1710-1758 .. **LC 87**
See also DLB 200

Efron, Marina Ivanovna Tsvetaeva
See Tsvetaeva (Efron), Marina (Ivanovna)

Egeria fl. 4th cent. - .... **CMLC 70**

Egoyan, Atom 1960- .... **CLC 151**
See also AAYA 63; CA 157

Ehle, John (Marsden, Jr.) 1925- ...... **CLC 27**
See also CA 9-12R; CSW

Ehrenbourg, Ilya (Grigoryevich)
See Ehrenburg, Ilya (Grigoryevich)

Ehrenburg, Ilya (Grigoryevich)
1891-1967 .... **CLC 18, 34, 62**
See Erenburg, Il'ia Grigor'evich
See also CA 102; 25-28R; EWL 3

Ehrenburg, Ilyo (Grigoryevich)
See Ehrenburg, Ilya (Grigoryevich)

Ehrenreich, Barbara 1941- .... **CLC 110**
See also BEST 90:4; CA 73-76; CANR 16, 37, 62, 117; DLB 246; FW; MTCW 1, 2; MTFW 2005

Eich, Gunter
See Eich, Gunter
See also RGWL 2, 3

Eich, Gunter 1907-1972 .... **CLC 15**
See Eich, Gunter
See also CA 111; 93-96; DLB 69, 124; EWL 3

Eichendorff, Joseph 1788-1857 .... **NCLC 8**
See also DLB 90; RGWL 2, 3

Eigner, Larry .... **CLC 9**
See Eigner, Laurence (Joel)
See also CAAS 23; CP 1, 2, 3, 4; DLB 5; WP

Eigner, Laurence (Joel) 1927-1996
See Eigner, Larry
See also CA 9-12R; 151; CANR 6, 84; CP 7; DLB 193

Eilhart von Oberge c. 1140-c.
1195 .... **CMLC 67**
See also DLB 148

Einhard c. 770-840 .... **CMLC 50**
See also DLB 148

Einstein, Albert 1879-1955 .... **TCLC 65**
See also CA 121; 133; MTCW 1, 2

Eiseley, Loren
See Eiseley, Loren Corey
See also DLB 275

Eiseley, Loren Corey 1907-1977 .... **CLC 7**
See Eiseley, Loren
See also AAYA 5; ANW; CA 1-4R; 73-76; CANR 6; DLBD 17

Eisenstadt, Jill 1963- .... **CLC 50**
See also CA 140

Eisenstein, Sergei (Mikhailovich)
1898-1948 .... **TCLC 57**
See also CA 114; 149

Eisner, Simon
See Kornbluth, C(yril) M.

Ekeloef, (Bengt) Gunnar
1907-1968 .... **CLC 27; PC 23**
See Ekelof, (Bengt) Gunnar
See also CA 123; 25-28R; DAM POET

Ekelof, (Bengt) Gunnar 1907-1968
See Ekeloef, (Bengt) Gunnar
See also DLB 259; EW 12; EWL 3

Ekelund, Vilhelm 1880-1949 .... **TCLC 75**
See also CA 189; EWL 3

Ekwensi, C. O. D.
See Ekwensi, Cyprian (Odiatu Duaka)

Ekwensi, Cyprian (Odiatu Duaka)
1921- .... **BLC 1; CLC 4**
See also AFW; BW 2, 3; CA 29-32R; CANR 18, 42, 74, 125; CDWLB 3; CN 1, 2, 3, 4, 5, 6; CWRI 5; DAM MULT; DLB 117; EWL 3; MTCW 1, 2; RGEL 2; SATA 66; WLIT 2

Elaine .... **TCLC 18**
See Leverson, Ada Esther

El Crummo
See Crumb, R(obert)

Elder, Lonne III 1931-1996 ..... **BLC 1; DC 8**
See also BW 1, 3; CA 81-84; 152; CAD; CANR 25; DAM MULT; DLB 7, 38, 44; MAL 5

Eleanor of Aquitaine 1122-1204 ... **CMLC 39**

Elia
See Lamb, Charles

Eliade, Mircea 1907-1986 .... **CLC 19**
See also CA 65-68; 119; CANR 30, 62; CD-WLB 4; DLB 220; EWL 3; MTCW 1; RGWL 3; SFW 4

Eliot, A. D.
See Jewett, (Theodora) Sarah Orne

Eliot, Alice
See Jewett, (Theodora) Sarah Orne

Eliot, Dan
See Silverberg, Robert

Eliot, George 1819-1880 ...... **NCLC 4, 13, 23, 41, 49, 89, 118; PC 20; SSC 72; WLC**
See Evans, Mary Ann
See also BRW 5; BRWC 1, 2; BRWR 2; CDBLB 1832-1890; CN 7; CPW; DA; DA3; DAB; DAC; DAM MST, NOV; DLB 21, 35, 55; FL 1:3; LATS 1:1; LMFS 1; NFS 17, 20; RGEL 2; RGSF 2; SSFS 8; TEA; WLIT 3

Eliot, John 1604-1690 .... **LC 5**
See also DLB 24

Eliot, T(homas) S(tearns)
1888-1965 ...... **CLC 1, 2, 3, 6, 9, 10, 13, 15, 24, 34, 41, 55, 57, 113; PC 5, 31; WLC**
See also AAYA 28; AMW; AMWC 1; AMWR 1; BRW 7; BRWR 2; CA 5-8R; 25-28R; CANR 41; CBD; CDALB 1929-1941; DA; DA3; DAB; DAC; DAM DRAM, MST, POET; DFS 4, 13; DLB 7, 10, 45, 63, 245; DLBY 1988; EWL 3; EXPP; LAIT 3; LATS 1:1; LMFS 2; MAL 5; MTCW 1, 2; MTFW 2005; NCFS 5; PAB; PFS 1, 7, 20; RGAL 4; RGEL 2; TUS; WLIT 4; WP

Elisabeth of Schönau c.
1129-1165 .... **CMLC 82**

Elizabeth 1866-1941 .... **TCLC 41**

Elizabeth I 1533-1603 .... **LC 118**
See also DLB 136

Elkin, Stanley L(awrence)
1930-1995 .. **CLC 4, 6, 9, 14, 27, 51, 91; SSC 12**
See also AMWS 6; BPFB 1; CA 9-12R; 148; CANR 8, 46; CN 1, 2, 3, 4, 5, 6; CPW; DAM NOV, POP; DLB 2, 28, 218, 278; DLBY 1980; EWL 3; INT CANR-8; MAL 5; MTCW 1, 2; MTFW 2005; RGAL 4; TCLE 1:1

Elledge, Scott .... **CLC 34**

Eller, Scott
See Shepard, James R.

Elliott, Don
See Silverberg, Robert

Elliott, George P(aul) 1918-1980 .... **CLC 2**
See also CA 1-4R; 97-100; CANR 2; CN 1, 2; CP 3; DLB 244; MAL 5

Elliott, Janice 1931-1995 .... **CLC 47**
See also CA 13-16R; CANR 8, 29, 84; CN 5, 6, 7; DLB 14; SATA 119

Elliott, Sumner Locke 1917-1991 ..... **CLC 38**
See also CA 5-8R; 134; CANR 2, 21; DLB 289

Elliott, William
See Bradbury, Ray (Douglas)

Ellis, A. E. .... **CLC 7**

Ellis, Alice Thomas .... **CLC 40**
See Haycraft, Anna (Margaret)
See also CN 4, 5, 6; DLB 194

Ellis, Bret Easton 1964- ...... **CLC 39, 71, 117**
See also AAYA 2, 43; CA 118; 123; CANR 51, 74, 126; CN 6, 7; CPW; DA3; DAM POP; DLB 292; HGG; INT CA-123; MTCW 2; MTFW 2005; NFS 11

Ellis, (Henry) Havelock
1859-1939 .... **TCLC 14**
See also CA 109; 169; DLB 190

Ellis, Landon
See Ellison, Harlan (Jay)

Ellis, Trey 1962- .... **CLC 55**
See also CA 146; CANR 92; CN 7

Ellison, Harlan (Jay) 1934- ... **CLC 1, 13, 42, 139; SSC 14**
See also AAYA 29; BPFB 1; BYA 14; CA 5-8R; CANR 5, 46, 115; CPW; DAM POP; DLB 8; HGG; INT CANR-5; MTCW 1, 2; MTFW 2005; SCFW 2; SFW 4; SSFS 13, 14, 15, 21; SUFW 1, 2

Ellison, Ralph (Waldo) 1914-1994 ..... **BLC 1; CLC 1, 3, 11, 54, 86, 114; SSC 26, 79; WLC**
See also AAYA 19; AFAW 1, 2; AMWC 2; AMWR 2; AMWS 2; BPFB 1; BW 1, 3; BYA 2; CA 9-12R; 145; CANR 24, 53; CDALB 1941-1968; CN 1, 2, 3, 4, 5; CSW; DA; DA3; DAB; DAC; DAM MST, MULT, NOV; DLB 2, 76, 227; DLBY 1994; EWL 3; EXPN; EXPS; LAIT 4; MAL 5; MTCW 1, 2; MTFW 2005; NCFS 3; NFS 2, 21; RGAL 4; RGSF 2; SSFS 1, 11; YAW

Ellmann, Lucy (Elizabeth) 1956- ..... **CLC 61**
See also CA 128

Ellmann, Richard (David)
1918-1987 .... **CLC 50**
See also BEST 89:2; CA 1-4R; 122; CANR 2, 28, 61; DLB 103; DLBY 1987; MTCW 1, 2; MTFW 2005

Elman, Richard (Martin)
1934-1997 .... **CLC 19**
See also CA 17-20R; 163; CAAS 3; CANR 47; TCLE 1:1

Elron
See Hubbard, L(afayette) Ron(ald)

El Saadawi, Nawal 1931- .... **CLC 196**
See al'Sadaawi, Nawal; Sa'adawi, al-Nawal; Saadawi, Nawal El; Sa'dawi, Nawal al-
See also CA 118; CAAS 11; CANR 44, 92

Eluard, Paul .... **PC 38; TCLC 7, 41**
See Grindel, Eugene
See also EWL 3; GFL 1789 to the Present; RGWL 2, 3

Elyot, Thomas 1490(?)-1546 .... **LC 11**
See also DLB 136; RGEL 2

Elytis, Odysseus 1911-1996 .... **CLC 15, 49, 100; PC 21**
See Alepoudelis, Odysseus
See also CA 102; 151; CANR 94; CWW 2; DAM POET; EW 13; EWL 3; MTCW 1, 2; RGWL 2, 3

Emecheta, (Florence Onye) Buchi
1944- ...... **BLC 2; CLC 14, 48, 128, 214**
See also AAYA 67; AFW; BW 2, 3; CA 81-84; CANR 27, 81, 126; CDWLB 3; CN 4, 5, 6, 7; CWRI 5; DA3; DAM MULT; DLB 117; EWL 3; FL 1:5; FW; MTCW 1, 2; MTFW 2005; NFS 12, 14; SATA 66; WLIT 2

Emerson, Mary Moody
1774-1863 .... **NCLC 66**

Emerson, Ralph Waldo 1803-1882 . **NCLC 1, 38, 98; PC 18; WLC**
See also AAYA 60; AMW; ANW; CDALB 1640-1865; DA; DA3; DAB; DAC; DAM MST, POET; DLB 1, 59, 73, 183, 223, 270; EXPP; LAIT 2; LMFS 1; NCFS 3; PFS 4, 17; RGAL 4; TUS; WP

Eminescu, Mihail 1850-1889 .. **NCLC 33, 131**

Empedocles 5th cent. B.C.- .... **CMLC 50**
See also DLB 176

Empson, William 1906-1984 ... **CLC 3, 8, 19, 33, 34**
See also BRWS 2; CA 17-20R; 112; CANR 31, 61; CP 1, 2, 3; DLB 20; EWL 3; MTCW 1, 2; RGEL 2

Enchi, Fumiko (Ueda) 1905-1986 ..... **CLC 31**
See Enchi Fumiko
See also CA 129; 121; FW; MJW

Enchi Fumiko
See Enchi, Fumiko (Ueda)
See also DLB 182; EWL 3

Ende, Michael (Andreas Helmuth) 1929-1995 .... **CLC 31**
See also BYA 5; CA 118; 124; 149; CANR 36, 110; CLR 14; DLB 75; MAICYA 1, 2; MAICYAS 1; SATA 61, 130; SATA-Brief 42; SATA-Obit 86

Endo, Shusaku 1923-1996 ..... **CLC 7, 14, 19, 54, 99; SSC 48; TCLC 152**
See Endo Shusaku
See also CA 29-32R; 153; CANR 21, 54, 131; DA3; DAM NOV; MTCW 1, 2; MTFW 2005; RGSF 2; RGWL 2, 3

Endo Shusaku
See Endo, Shusaku
See also CWW 2; DLB 182; EWL 3

Engel, Marian 1933-1985 .... **CLC 36; TCLC 137**
See also CA 25-28R; CANR 12; CN 2, 3; DLB 53; FW; INT CANR-12

Engelhardt, Frederick
See Hubbard, L(afayette) Ron(ald)

Engels, Friedrich 1820-1895 .. **NCLC 85, 114**
See also DLB 129; LATS 1:1

Enright, D(ennis) J(oseph) 1920-2002 .... **CLC 4, 8, 31**
See also CA 1-4R; 211; CANR 1, 42, 83; CN 1, 2; CP 1, 2, 3, 4, 5, 6, 7; DLB 27; EWL 3; SATA 25; SATA-Obit 140

Ensler, Eve 1953- .... **CLC 212**
See also CA 172; CANR 126

Enzensberger, Hans Magnus 1929- .... **CLC 43; PC 28**
See also CA 116; 119; CANR 103; CWW 2; EWL 3

Ephron, Nora 1941- .... **CLC 17, 31**
See also AAYA 35; AITN 2; CA 65-68; CANR 12, 39, 83; DFS 22

Epicurus 341B.C.-270B.C. .... **CMLC 21**
See also DLB 176

Epsilon
See Betjeman, John

Epstein, Daniel Mark 1948- .... **CLC 7**
See also CA 49-52; CANR 2, 53, 90

Epstein, Jacob 1956- .... **CLC 19**
See also CA 114

Epstein, Jean 1897-1953 .... **TCLC 92**

Epstein, Joseph 1937- .... **CLC 39, 204**
See also AMWS 14; CA 112; 119; CANR 50, 65, 117

Epstein, Leslie 1938- .... **CLC 27**
See also AMWS 12; CA 73-76, 215; CAAE 215; CAAS 12; CANR 23, 69; DLB 299

Equiano, Olaudah 1745(?)-1797 . **BLC 2; LC 16**
See also AFAW 1, 2; CDWLB 3; DAM MULT; DLB 37, 50; WLIT 2

Erasmus, Desiderius 1469(?)-1536 ..... **LC 16, 93**
See also DLB 136; EW 2; LMFS 1; RGWL 2, 3; TWA

Erdman, Paul E(mil) 1932- .... **CLC 25**
See also AITN 1; CA 61-64; CANR 13, 43, 84

Erdrich, (Karen) Louise 1954- .. **CLC 39, 54, 120, 176; NNAL; PC 52**
See also AAYA 10, 47; AMWS 4; BEST 89:1; BPFB 1; CA 114; CANR 41, 62, 118, 138; CDALBS; CN 5, 6, 7; CP 7; CPW; CWP; DA3; DAM MULT, NOV, POP; DLB 152, 175, 206; EWL 3; EXPP; FL 1:5; LAIT 5; LATS 1:2; MAL 5; MTCW 1, 2; MTFW 2005; NFS 5; PFS 14; RGAL 4; SATA 94, 141; SSFS 14; TCWW 2

Erenburg, Ilya (Grigoryevich)
See Ehrenburg, Ilya (Grigoryevich)

Erickson, Stephen Michael 1950-
See Erickson, Steve
See also CA 129; SFW 4

Erickson, Steve .... **CLC 64**
See Erickson, Stephen Michael
See also CANR 60, 68, 136; MTFW 2005; SUFW 2

Erickson, Walter
See Fast, Howard (Melvin)

Ericson, Walter
See Fast, Howard (Melvin)

Eriksson, Buntel
See Bergman, (Ernst) Ingmar

Eriugena, John Scottus c. 810-877 .... **CMLC 65**
See also DLB 115

Ernaux, Annie 1940- .... **CLC 88, 184**
See also CA 147; CANR 93; MTFW 2005; NCFS 3, 5

Erskine, John 1879-1951 .... **TCLC 84**
See also CA 112; 159; DLB 9, 102; FANT

Eschenbach, Wolfram von
See Wolfram von Eschenbach
See also RGWL 3

Eseki, Bruno
See Mphahlele, Ezekiel

Esenin, Sergei (Alexandrovich) 1895-1925 .... **TCLC 4**
See Yesenin, Sergey
See also CA 104; RGWL 2, 3

Eshleman, Clayton 1935- .... **CLC 7**
See also CA 33-36R, 212; CAAE 212; CAAS 6; CANR 93; CP 1, 2, 3, 4, 5, 6, 7; DLB 5

Espriella, Don Manuel Alvarez
See Southey, Robert

Espriu, Salvador 1913-1985 .... **CLC 9**
See also CA 154; 115; DLB 134; EWL 3

Espronceda, Jose de 1808-1842 ..... **NCLC 39**

Esquivel, Laura 1951(?)- ... **CLC 141; HLCS 1**
See also AAYA 29; CA 143; CANR 68, 113; DA3; DNFS 2; LAIT 3; LMFS 2; MTCW 2; MTFW 2005; NFS 5; WLIT 1

Esse, James
See Stephens, James

Esterbrook, Tom
See Hubbard, L(afayette) Ron(ald)

Estleman, Loren D. 1952- .... **CLC 48**
See also AAYA 27; CA 85-88; CANR 27, 74, 139; CMW 4; CPW; DA3; DAM NOV, POP; DLB 226; INT CANR-27; MTCW 1, 2; MTFW 2005; TCWW 1, 2

Etherege, Sir George 1636-1692 . **DC 23; LC 78**
See also BRW 2; DAM DRAM; DLB 80; PAB; RGEL 2

Euclid 306B.C.-283B.C. .... **CMLC 25**

Eugenides, Jeffrey 1960(?)- .... **CLC 81, 212**
See also AAYA 51; CA 144; CANR 120; MTFW 2005

Euripides c. 484B.C.-406B.C. .... **CMLC 23, 51; DC 4; WLCS**
See also AW 1; CDWLB 1; DA; DA3; DAB; DAC; DAM DRAM, MST; DFS 1, 4, 6; DLB 176; LAIT 1; LMFS 1; RGWL 2, 3

Evan, Evin
See Faust, Frederick (Schiller)

Evans, Caradoc 1878-1945 ... **SSC 43; TCLC 85**
See also DLB 162

Evans, Evan
See Faust, Frederick (Schiller)

Evans, Marian
See Eliot, George

Evans, Mary Ann
See Eliot, George
See also NFS 20

Evarts, Esther
See Benson, Sally

Everett, Percival
See Everett, Percival L.
See also CSW

Everett, Percival L. 1956- .... **CLC 57**
See Everett, Percival
See also BW 2; CA 129; CANR 94, 134; CN 7; MTFW 2005

Everson, R(onald) G(ilmour) 1903-1992 .... **CLC 27**
See also CA 17-20R; CP 1, 2, 3, 4; DLB 88

Everson, William (Oliver) 1912-1994 .... **CLC 1, 5, 14**
See Antoninus, Brother
See also BG 1:2; CA 9-12R; 145; CANR 20; CP 2, 3, 4; DLB 5, 16, 212; MTCW 1

Evtushenko, Evgenii Aleksandrovich
See Yevtushenko, Yevgeny (Alexandrovich)
See also CWW 2; RGWL 2, 3

Ewart, Gavin (Buchanan) 1916-1995 .... **CLC 13, 46**
See also BRWS 7; CA 89-92; 150; CANR 17, 46; CP 1, 2, 3, 4; DLB 40; MTCW 1

Ewers, Hanns Heinz 1871-1943 ..... **TCLC 12**
See also CA 109; 149

Ewing, Frederick R.
See Sturgeon, Theodore (Hamilton)

Exley, Frederick (Earl) 1929-1992 .... **CLC 6, 11**
See also AITN 2; BPFB 1; CA 81-84; 138; CANR 117; DLB 143; DLBY 1981

Eynhardt, Guillermo
See Quiroga, Horacio (Sylvestre)

Ezekiel, Nissim (Moses) 1924-2004 .. **CLC 61**
See also CA 61-64; 223; CP 1, 2, 3, 4, 5, 6, 7; EWL 3

Ezekiel, Tish O'Dowd 1943- .... **CLC 34**
See also CA 129

Fadeev, Aleksandr Aleksandrovich
See Bulgya, Alexander Alexandrovich
See also DLB 272

Fadeev, Alexandr Alexandrovich
See Bulgya, Alexander Alexandrovich
See also EWL 3

Fadeyev, A.
See Bulgya, Alexander Alexandrovich

Fadeyev, Alexander .... **TCLC 53**
See Bulgya, Alexander Alexandrovich

Fagen, Donald 1948- .... **CLC 26**

Fainzilberg, Ilya Arnoldovich 1897-1937
See Ilf, Ilya
See also CA 120; 165

Fair, Ronald L. 1932- .... **CLC 18**
See also BW 1; CA 69-72; CANR 25; DLB 33

Fairbairn, Roger
See Carr, John Dickson

Fairbairns, Zoe (Ann) 1948- .... **CLC 32**
See also CA 103; CANR 21, 85; CN 4, 5, 6, 7

French, Albert 1943- .... **CLC 86**
See also BW 3; CA 167

French, Antonia
See Kureishi, Hanif

French, Marilyn 1929- .. **CLC 10, 18, 60, 177**
See also BPFB 1; CA 69-72; CANR 3, 31,
134; CN 5, 6, 7; CPW; DAM DRAM,
NOV, POP; FL 1:5; FW; INT CANR-31;
MTCW 1, 2; MTFW 2005

French, Paul
See Asimov, Isaac

Freneau, Philip Morin 1752-1832 .. **NCLC 1,**
111
See also AMWS 2; DLB 37, 43; RGAL 4

Freud, Sigmund 1856-1939 .... **TCLC 52**
See also CA 115; 133; CANR 69; DLB 296;
EW 8; EWL 3; LATS 1:1; MTCW 1, 2;
MTFW 2005; NCFS 3; TWA

Freytag, Gustav 1816-1895 .... **NCLC 109**
See also DLB 129

Friedan, Betty (Naomi) 1921- .... **CLC 74**
See also CA 65-68; CANR 18, 45, 74; DLB
246; FW; MTCW 1, 2; MTFW 2005;
NCFS 5

Friedlander, Saul 1932- .... **CLC 90**
See also CA 117; 130; CANR 72

Friedman, B(ernard) H(arper)
1926- .... **CLC 7**
See also CA 1-4R; CANR 3, 48

Friedman, Bruce Jay 1930- ...... **CLC 3, 5, 56**
See also CA 9-12R; CAD; CANR 25, 52,
101; CD 5, 6; CN 1, 2, 3, 4, 5, 6, 7; DLB
2, 28, 244; INT CANR-25; MAL 5; SSFS
18

Friel, Brian 1929- .... **CLC 5, 42, 59, 115; DC**
8; SSC 76
See also BRWS 5; CA 21-24R; CANR 33,
69, 131; CBD; CD 5, 6; DFS 11; DLB
13, 319; EWL 3; MTCW 1; RGEL 2; TEA

Friis-Baastad, Babbis Ellinor
1921-1970 .... **CLC 12**
See also CA 17-20R; 134; SATA 7

Frisch, Max (Rudolph) 1911-1991 ... **CLC 3, 9,**
14, 18, 32, 44; TCLC 121
See also CA 85-88; 134; CANR 32, 74; CD-
WLB 2; DAM DRAM, NOV; DLB 69,
124; EW 13; EWL 3; MTCW 1, 2; MTFW
2005; RGWL 2, 3

Fromentin, Eugene (Samuel Auguste)
1820-1876 .... **NCLC 10, 125**
See also DLB 123; GFL 1789 to the Present

Frost, Frederick
See Faust, Frederick (Schiller)

Frost, Robert (Lee) 1874-1963 .. **CLC 1, 3, 4,**
9, 10, 13, 15, 26, 34, 44; PC 1, 39;
WLC
See also AAYA 21; AMW; AMWR 1; CA
89-92; CANR 33; CDALB 1917-1929;
CLR 67; DA; DA3; DAB; DAC; DAM
MST, POET; DLB 54, 284; DLBD 7;
EWL 3; EXPP; MAL 5; MTCW 1, 2;
MTFW 2005; PAB; PFS 1, 2, 3, 4, 5, 6,
7, 10, 13; RGAL 4; SATA 14; TUS; WP;
WYA

Froude, James Anthony
1818-1894 .... **NCLC 43**
See also DLB 18, 57, 144

Froy, Herald
See Waterhouse, Keith (Spencer)

Fry, Christopher 1907-2005 ... **CLC 2, 10, 14**
See also BRWS 3; CA 17-20R; 240; CAAS
23; CANR 9, 30, 74, 132; CBD; CD 5, 6;
CP 1, 2, 3, 4, 5, 6, 7; DAM DRAM; DLB
13; EWL 3; MTCW 1, 2; MTFW 2005;
RGEL 2; SATA 66; TEA

Frye, (Herman) Northrop
1912-1991 .... **CLC 24, 70; TCLC 165**
See also CA 5-8R; 133; CANR 8, 37; DLB
67, 68, 246; EWL 3; MTCW 1, 2; MTFW
2005; RGAL 4; TWA

Fuchs, Daniel 1909-1993 .... **CLC 8, 22**
See also CA 81-84; 142; CAAS 5; CANR
40; CN 1, 2, 3, 4, 5; DLB 9, 26, 28;
DLBY 1993; MAL 5

Fuchs, Daniel 1934- .... **CLC 34**
See also CA 37-40R; CANR 14, 48

Fuentes, Carlos 1928- .. **CLC 3, 8, 10, 13, 22,**
41, 60, 113; HLC 1; SSC 24; WLC
See also AAYA 4, 45; AITN 2; BPFB 1;
CA 69-72; CANR 10, 32, 68, 104, 138;
CDWLB 3; CWW 2; DA; DA3; DAB;
DAC; DAM MST, MULT, NOV; DLB
113; DNFS 2; EWL 3; HW 1, 2; LAIT 3;
LATS 1:2; LAW; LAWS 1; LMFS 2;
MTCW 1, 2; MTFW 2005; NFS 8; RGSF
2; RGWL 2, 3; TWA; WLIT 1

Fuentes, Gregorio Lopez y
See Lopez y Fuentes, Gregorio

Fuertes, Gloria 1918-1998 .... **PC 27**
See also CA 178, 180; DLB 108; HW 2;
SATA 115

Fugard, (Harold) Athol 1932- . **CLC 5, 9, 14,**
25, 40, 80, 211; DC 3
See also AAYA 17; AFW; CA 85-88; CANR
32, 54, 118; CD 5, 6; DAM DRAM; DFS
3, 6, 10; DLB 225; DNFS 1, 2; EWL 3;
LATS 1:2; MTCW 1; MTFW 2005; RGEL
2; WLIT 2

Fugard, Sheila 1932- .... **CLC 48**
See also CA 125

Fujiwara no Teika 1162-1241 .... **CMLC 73**
See also DLB 203

Fukuyama, Francis 1952- .... **CLC 131**
See also CA 140; CANR 72, 125

Fuller, Charles (H.), (Jr.) 1939- .... **BLC 2;**
CLC 25; DC 1
See also BW 2; CA 108; 112; CAD; CANR
87; CD 5, 6; DAM DRAM, MULT; DFS
8; DLB 38, 266; EWL 3; INT CA-112;
MAL 5; MTCW 1

Fuller, Henry Blake 1857-1929 .... **TCLC 103**
See also CA 108; 177; DLB 12; RGAL 4

Fuller, John (Leopold) 1937- .... **CLC 62**
See also CA 21-24R; CANR 9, 44; CP 1, 2,
3, 4, 5, 6, 7; DLB 40

Fuller, Margaret
See Ossoli, Sarah Margaret (Fuller)
See also AMWS 2; DLB 183, 223, 239; FL
1:3

Fuller, Roy (Broadbent) 1912-1991 ... **CLC 4,**
28
See also BRWS 7; CA 5-8R; 135; CAAS
10; CANR 53, 83; CN 1, 2, 3, 4, 5; CP 1,
2, 3, 4; CWRI 5; DLB 15, 20; EWL 3;
RGEL 2; SATA 87

Fuller, Sarah Margaret
See Ossoli, Sarah Margaret (Fuller)

Fuller, Sarah Margaret
See Ossoli, Sarah Margaret (Fuller)
See also DLB 1, 59, 73

Fuller, Thomas 1608-1661 .... **LC 111**
See also DLB 151

Fulton, Alice 1952- .... **CLC 52**
See also CA 116; CANR 57, 88; CP 7;
CWP; DLB 193

Furphy, Joseph 1843-1912 .... **TCLC 25**
See Collins, Tom
See also CA 163; DLB 230; EWL 3; RGEL
2

Fuson, Robert H(enderson) 1927- .... **CLC 70**
See also CA 89-92; CANR 103

Fussell, Paul 1924- .... **CLC 74**
See also BEST 90:1; CA 17-20R; CANR 8,
21, 35, 69, 135; INT CANR-21; MTCW
1, 2; MTFW 2005

Futabatei, Shimei 1864-1909 .... **TCLC 44**
See Futabatei Shimei
See also CA 162; MJW

Futabatei Shimei
See Futabatei, Shimei
See also DLB 180; EWL 3

Futrelle, Jacques 1875-1912 .... **TCLC 19**
See also CA 113; 155; CMW 4

Gaboriau, Emile 1835-1873 .... **NCLC 14**
See also CMW 4; MSW

Gadda, Carlo Emilio 1893-1973 ...... **CLC 11;**
TCLC 144
See also CA 89-92; DLB 177; EWL 3;
WLIT 7

Gaddis, William 1922-1998 ... **CLC 1, 3, 6, 8,**
10, 19, 43, 86
See also AMWS 4; BPFB 1; CA 17-20R;
172; CANR 21, 48; CN 1, 2, 3, 4, 5, 6;
DLB 2, 278; EWL 3; MAL 5; MTCW 1,
2; MTFW 2005; RGAL 4

Gaelique, Moruen le
See Jacob, (Cyprien-)Max

Gage, Walter
See Inge, William (Motter)

Gaiman, Neil (Richard) 1960- .... **CLC 195**
See also AAYA 19, 42; CA 133; CANR 81,
129; DLB 261; HGG; MTFW 2005; SATA
85, 146; SFW 4; SUFW 2

Gaines, Ernest J(ames) 1933- .. **BLC 2; CLC**
3, 11, 18, 86, 181; SSC 68
See also AAYA 18; AFAW 1, 2; AITN 1;
BPFB 2; BW 2, 3; BYA 6; CA 9-12R;
CANR 6, 24, 42, 75, 126; CDALB 1968-
1988; CLR 62; CN 1, 2, 3, 4, 5, 6, 7;
CSW; DA3; DAM MULT; DLB 2, 33,
152; DLBY 1980; EWL 3; EXPN; LAIT
5; LATS 1:2; MAL 5; MTCW 1, 2;
MTFW 2005; NFS 5, 7, 16; RGAL 4;
RGSF 2; RHW; SATA 86; SSFS 5; YAW

Gaitskill, Mary (Lawrence) 1954- .... **CLC 69**
See also CA 128; CANR 61; DLB 244;
TCLE 1:1

Gaius Suetonius Tranquillus
See Suetonius

Galdos, Benito Perez
See Perez Galdos, Benito
See also EW 7

Gale, Zona 1874-1938 .... **TCLC 7**
See also CA 105; 153; CANR 84; DAM
DRAM; DFS 17; DLB 9, 78, 228; RGAL
4

Galeano, Eduardo (Hughes) 1940- . **CLC 72;**
HLCS 1
See also CA 29-32R; CANR 13, 32, 100;
HW 1

Galiano, Juan Valera y Alcala
See Valera y Alcala-Galiano, Juan

Galilei, Galileo 1564-1642 .... **LC 45**

Gallagher, Tess 1943- .... **CLC 18, 63; PC 9**
See also CA 106; CP 3, 4, 5, 6, 7; CWP;
DAM POET; DLB 120, 212, 244; PFS 16

Gallant, Mavis 1922- ..... **CLC 7, 18, 38, 172;**
SSC 5, 78
See also CA 69-72; CANR 29, 69, 117;
CCA 1; CN 1, 2, 3, 4, 5, 6, 7; DAC; DAM
MST; DLB 53; EWL 3; MTCW 1, 2;
MTFW 2005; RGEL 2; RGSF 2

Gallant, Roy A(rthur) 1924- .... **CLC 17**
See also CA 5-8R; CANR 4, 29, 54, 117;
CLR 30; MAICYA 1, 2; SATA 4, 68, 110

Gallico, Paul (William) 1897-1976 ..... **CLC 2**
See also AITN 1; CA 5-8R; 69-72; CANR
23; CN 1, 2; DLB 9, 171; FANT; MAI-
CYA 1, 2; SATA 13

Gallo, Max Louis 1932- .... **CLC 95**
See also CA 85-88

Gallois, Lucien
See Desnos, Robert

Gallup, Ralph
See Whitemore, Hugh (John)

Galsworthy, John 1867-1933 .... **SSC 22; TCLC 1, 45; WLC**
See also BRW 6; CA 104; 141; CANR 75; CDBLB 1890-1914; DA; DA3; DAB; DAC; DAM DRAM, MST, NOV; DLB 10, 34, 98, 162; DLBD 16; EWL 3; MTCW 2; RGEL 2; SSFS 3; TEA

Galt, John 1779-1839 .... **NCLC 1, 110**
See also DLB 99, 116, 159; RGEL 2; RGSF 2

Galvin, James 1951- .... **CLC 38**
See also CA 108; CANR 26

Gamboa, Federico 1864-1939 ...... **TCLC 36**
See also CA 167; HW 2; LAW

Gandhi, M. K.
See Gandhi, Mohandas Karamchand

Gandhi, Mahatma
See Gandhi, Mohandas Karamchand

Gandhi, Mohandas Karamchand
1869-1948 .... **TCLC 59**
See also CA 121; 132; DA3; DAM MULT; MTCW 1, 2

Gann, Ernest Kellogg 1910-1991 ..... **CLC 23**
See also AITN 1; BPFB 2; CA 1-4R; 136; CANR 1, 83; RHW

Gao Xingjian 1940- .... **CLC 167**
See Xingjian, Gao
See also MTFW 2005

Garber, Eric 1943(?)-
See Holleran, Andrew
See also CANR 89

Garcia, Cristina 1958- .... **CLC 76**
See also AMWS 11; CA 141; CANR 73, 130; CN 7; DLB 292; DNFS 1; EWL 3; HW 2; LLW; MTFW 2005

Garcia Lorca, Federico 1898-1936 ...... **DC 2; HLC 2; PC 3; TCLC 1, 7, 49; WLC**
See Lorca, Federico Garcia
See also AAYA 46; CA 104; 131; CANR 81; DA; DA3; DAB; DAC; DAM DRAM, MST, MULT, POET; DFS 4, 10; DLB 108; EWL 3; HW 1, 2; LATS 1:2; MTCW 1, 2; MTFW 2005; TWA

Garcia Marquez, Gabriel (Jose)
1928- .... **CLC 2, 3, 8, 10, 15, 27, 47, 55, 68, 170; HLC 1; SSC 8, 83; WLC**
See also AAYA 3, 33; BEST 89:1, 90:4; BPFB 2; BYA 12, 16; CA 33-36R; CANR 10, 28, 50, 75, 82, 128; CDWLB 3; CPW; CWW 2; DA; DA3; DAB; DAC; DAM MST, MULT, NOV, POP; DLB 113; DNFS 1, 2; EWL 3; EXPN; EXPS; HW 1, 2; LAIT 2; LATS 1:2; LAW; LAWS 1; LMFS 2; MTCW 1, 2; MTFW 2005; NCFS 3; NFS 1, 5, 10; RGSF 2; RGWL 2, 3; SSFS 1, 6, 16, 21; TWA; WLIT 1

Garcilaso de la Vega, El Inca
1539-1616 .... **HLCS 1**
See also DLB 318; LAW

Gard, Janice
See Latham, Jean Lee

Gard, Roger Martin du
See Martin du Gard, Roger

Gardam, Jane (Mary) 1928- .... **CLC 43**
See also CA 49-52; CANR 2, 18, 33, 54, 106; CLR 12; DLB 14, 161, 231; MAICYA 1, 2; MTCW 1; SAAS 9; SATA 39, 76, 130; SATA-Brief 28; YAW

Gardner, Herb(ert George)
1934-2003 .... **CLC 44**
See also CA 149; 220; CAD; CANR 119; CD 5, 6; DFS 18, 20

Gardner, John (Champlin), Jr.
1933-1982 .... **CLC 2, 3, 5, 7, 8, 10, 18, 28, 34; SSC 7**
See also AAYA 45; AITN 1; AMWS 6; BPFB 2; CA 65-68; 107; CANR 33, 73; CDALBS; CN 2, 3; CPW; DA3; DAM NOV, POP; DLB 2; DLBY 1982; EWL 3;

FANT; LATS 1:2; MAL 5; MTCW 1, 2; MTFW 2005; NFS 3; RGAL 4; RGSF 2; SATA 40; SATA-Obit 31; SSFS 8

Gardner, John (Edmund) 1926- .... **CLC 30**
See also CA 103; CANR 15, 69, 127; CMW 4; CPW; DAM POP; MTCW 1

Gardner, Miriam
See Bradley, Marion Zimmer
See also GLL 1

Gardner, Noel
See Kuttner, Henry

Gardons, S. S.
See Snodgrass, W(illiam) D(e Witt)

Garfield, Leon 1921-1996 .... **CLC 12**
See also AAYA 8; BYA 1, 3; CA 17-20R; 152; CANR 38, 41, 78; CLR 21; DLB 161; JRDA; MAICYA 1, 2; MAICYAS 1; SATA 1, 32, 76; SATA-Obit 90; TEA; WYA; YAW

Garland, (Hannibal) Hamlin
1860-1940 .... **SSC 18; TCLC 3**
See also CA 104; DLB 12, 71, 78, 186; MAL 5; RGAL 4; RGSF 2; TCWW 1, 2

Garneau, (Hector de) Saint-Denys
1912-1943 .... **TCLC 13**
See also CA 111; DLB 88

Garner, Alan 1934- .... **CLC 17**
See also AAYA 18; BYA 3, 5; CA 73-76, 178; CAAE 178; CANR 15, 64, 134; CLR 20; CPW; DAB; DAM POP; DLB 161, 261; FANT; MAICYA 1, 2; MTCW 1, 2; MTFW 2005; SATA 18, 69; SATA-Essay 108; SUFW 1, 2; YAW

Garner, Hugh 1913-1979 .... **CLC 13**
See Warwick, Jarvis
See also CA 69-72; CANR 31; CCA 1; CN 1, 2; DLB 68

Garnett, David 1892-1981 .... **CLC 3**
See also CA 5-8R; 103; CANR 17, 79; CN 1, 2; DLB 34; FANT; MTCW 2; RGEL 2; SFW 4; SUFW 1

Garnier, Robert c. 1545-1590 .... **LC 119**
See also GFL Beginnings to 1789

Garos, Stephanie
See Katz, Steve

Garrett, George (Palmer, Jr.) 1929- . **CLC 3, 11, 51; SSC 30**
See also AMWS 7; BPFB 2; CA 1-4R, 202; CAAE 202; CAAS 5; CANR 1, 42, 67, 109; CN 1, 2, 3, 4, 5, 6, 7; CP 1, 2, 3, 4, 5, 6, 7; CSW; DLB 2, 5, 130, 152; DLBY 1983

Garrick, David 1717-1779 .... **LC 15**
See also DAM DRAM; DLB 84, 213; RGEL 2

Garrigue, Jean 1914-1972 .... **CLC 2, 8**
See also CA 5-8R; 37-40R; CANR 20; CP 1; MAL 5

Garrison, Frederick
See Sinclair, Upton (Beall)

Garrison, William Lloyd
1805-1879 .... **NCLC 149**
See also CDALB 1640-1865; DLB 1, 43, 235

Garro, Elena 1920(?)-1998 .. **HLCS 1; TCLC 153**
See also CA 131; 169; CWW 2; DLB 145; EWL 3; HW 1; LAWS 1; WLIT 1

Garth, Will
See Hamilton, Edmond; Kuttner, Henry

Garvey, Marcus (Moziah, Jr.)
1887-1940 ... **BLC 2; HR 1:2; TCLC 41**
See also BW 1; CA 120; 124; CANR 79; DAM MULT

Gary, Romain .... **CLC 25**
See Kacew, Romain
See also DLB 83, 299

Gascar, Pierre .... **CLC 11**
See Fournier, Pierre
See also EWL 3

Gascoigne, George 1539-1577 .... **LC 108**
See also DLB 136; RGEL 2

Gascoyne, David (Emery)
1916-2001 .... **CLC 45**
See also CA 65-68; 200; CANR 10, 28, 54; CP 1, 2, 3, 4, 5, 6, 7; DLB 20; MTCW 1; RGEL 2

Gaskell, Elizabeth Cleghorn
1810-1865 .... **NCLC 5, 70, 97, 137; SSC 25**
See also BRW 5; CDBLB 1832-1890; DAB; DAM MST; DLB 21, 144, 159; RGEL 2; RGSF 2; TEA

Gass, William H(oward) 1924- . **CLC 1, 2, 8, 11, 15, 39, 132; SSC 12**
See also AMWS 6; CA 17-20R; CANR 30, 71, 100; CN 1, 2, 3, 4, 5, 6, 7; DLB 2, 227; EWL 3; MAL 5; MTCW 1, 2; MTFW 2005; RGAL 4

Gassendi, Pierre 1592-1655 .... **LC 54**
See also GFL Beginnings to 1789

Gasset, Jose Ortega y
See Ortega y Gasset, Jose

Gates, Henry Louis, Jr. 1950- ... **BLCS; CLC 65**
See also BW 2, 3; CA 109; CANR 25, 53, 75, 125; CSW; DA3; DAM MULT; DLB 67; EWL 3; MAL 5; MTCW 2; MTFW 2005; RGAL 4

Gautier, Theophile 1811-1872 .. **NCLC 1, 59; PC 18; SSC 20**
See also DAM POET; DLB 119; EW 6; GFL 1789 to the Present; RGWL 2, 3; SUFW; TWA

Gay, John 1685-1732 .... **LC 49**
See also BRW 3; DAM DRAM; DLB 84, 95; RGEL 2; WLIT 3

Gay, Oliver
See Gogarty, Oliver St. John

Gay, Peter (Jack) 1923- .... **CLC 158**
See also CA 13-16R; CANR 18, 41, 77; INT CANR-18

Gaye, Marvin (Pentz, Jr.)
1939-1984 .... **CLC 26**
See also CA 195; 112

Gebler, Carlo (Ernest) 1954- .... **CLC 39**
See also CA 119; 133; CANR 96; DLB 271

Gee, Maggie (Mary) 1948- .... **CLC 57**
See also CA 130; CANR 125; CN 4, 5, 6, 7; DLB 207; MTFW 2005

Gee, Maurice (Gough) 1931- .... **CLC 29**
See also AAYA 42; CA 97-100; CANR 67, 123; CLR 56; CN 2, 3, 4, 5, 6, 7; CWRI 5; EWL 3; MAICYA 2; RGSF 2; SATA 46, 101

Geiogamah, Hanay 1945- .... **NNAL**
See also CA 153; DAM MULT; DLB 175

Gelbart, Larry
See Gelbart, Larry (Simon)
See also CAD; CD 5, 6

Gelbart, Larry (Simon) 1928- .... **CLC 21, 61**
See Gelbart, Larry
See also CA 73-76; CANR 45, 94

Gelber, Jack 1932-2003 ...... **CLC 1, 6, 14, 79**
See also CA 1-4R; 216; CAD; CANR 2; DLB 7, 228; MAL 5

Gellhorn, Martha (Ellis)
1908-1998 .... **CLC 14, 60**
See also CA 77-80; 164; CANR 44; CN 1, 2, 3, 4, 5, 6 7; DLBY 1982, 1998

Genet, Jean 1910-1986 .. **CLC 1, 2, 5, 10, 14, 44, 46; DC 25; TCLC 128**
See also CA 13-16R; CANR 18; DA3; DAM DRAM; DFS 10; DLB 72, 321; DLBY 1986; EW 13; EWL 3; GFL 1789 to the Present; GLL 1; LMFS 2; MTCW 1, 2; MTFW 2005; RGWL 2, 3; TWA

Gent, Peter 1942- .... **CLC 29**
See also AITN 1; CA 89-92; DLBY 1982

Gentile, Giovanni 1875-1944 .... **TCLC 96**
See also CA 119

Gentlewoman in New England, A
See Bradstreet, Anne

Gentlewoman in Those Parts, A
See Bradstreet, Anne

Geoffrey of Monmouth c.
1100-1155 .... **CMLC 44**
See also DLB 146; TEA

George, Jean
See George, Jean Craighead

George, Jean Craighead 1919- .... **CLC 35**
See also AAYA 8; BYA 2, 4; CA 5-8R;
CANR 25; CLR 1; 80; DLB 52; JRDA;
MAICYA 1, 2; SATA 2, 68, 124; WYA;
YAW

George, Stefan (Anton) 1868-1933 . **TCLC 2,
14**
See also CA 104; 193; EW 8; EWL 3

Georges, Georges Martin
See Simenon, Georges (Jacques Christian)

Gerald of Wales c. 1146-c. 1223 ... **CMLC 60**

Gerhardi, William Alexander
See Gerhardie, William Alexander

Gerhardie, William Alexander
1895-1977 .... **CLC 5**
See also CA 25-28R; 73-76; CANR 18; CN
1, 2; DLB 36; RGEL 2

Gerson, Jean 1363-1429 .... **LC 77**
See also DLB 208

Gersonides 1288-1344 .... **CMLC 49**
See also DLB 115

Gerstler, Amy 1956- .... **CLC 70**
See also CA 146; CANR 99

Gertler, T. .... **CLC 34**
See also CA 116; 121

Gertsen, Aleksandr Ivanovich
See Herzen, Aleksandr Ivanovich

Ghalib .... **NCLC 39, 78**
See Ghalib, Asadullah Khan

Ghalib, Asadullah Khan 1797-1869
See Ghalib
See also DAM POET; RGWL 2, 3

Ghelderode, Michel de 1898-1962 ..... **CLC 6,
11; DC 15**
See also CA 85-88; CANR 40, 77; DAM
DRAM; DLB 321; EW 11; EWL 3; TWA

Ghiselin, Brewster 1903-2001 .... **CLC 23**
See also CA 13-16R; CAAS 10; CANR 13;
CP 1, 2, 3, 4, 5, 6, 7

Ghose, Aurabinda 1872-1950 .... **TCLC 63**
See Ghose, Aurobindo
See also CA 163

Ghose, Aurobindo
See Ghose, Aurabinda
See also EWL 3

Ghose, Zulfikar 1935- .... **CLC 42, 200**
See also CA 65-68; CANR 67; CN 1, 2, 3,
4, 5, 6, 7; CP 1, 2, 3, 4, 5, 6, 7; EWL 3

Ghosh, Amitav 1956- .... **CLC 44, 153**
See also CA 147; CANR 80; CN 6, 7;
WWE 1

Giacosa, Giuseppe 1847-1906 .... **TCLC 7**
See also CA 104

Gibb, Lee
See Waterhouse, Keith (Spencer)

Gibbon, Edward 1737-1794 .... **LC 97**
See also BRW 3; DLB 104; RGEL 2

Gibbon, Lewis Grassic .... **TCLC 4**
See Mitchell, James Leslie
See also RGEL 2

Gibbons, Kaye 1960- .... **CLC 50, 88, 145**
See also AAYA 34; AMWS 10; CA 151;
CANR 75, 127; CN 7; CSW; DA3; DAM
POP; DLB 292; MTCW 2; MTFW 2005;
NFS 3; RGAL 4; SATA 117

Gibran, Kahlil 1883-1931 . **PC 9; TCLC 1, 9**
See also CA 104; 150; DA3; DAM POET,
POP; EWL 3; MTCW 2; WLIT 6

Gibran, Khalil
See Gibran, Kahlil

Gibson, Mel 1956- .... **CLC 215**

Gibson, William 1914- .... **CLC 23**
See also CA 9-12R; CAD; CANR 9, 42, 75,
125; CD 5, 6; DA; DAB; DAC; DAM
DRAM, MST; DFS 2; DLB 7; LAIT 2;
MAL 5; MTCW 2; MTFW 2005; SATA
66; YAW

Gibson, William (Ford) 1948- ... **CLC 39, 63,
186, 192; SSC 52**
See also AAYA 12, 59; BPFB 2; CA 126;
133; CANR 52, 90, 106; CN 6, 7; CPW;
DA3; DAM POP; DLB 251; MTCW 2;
MTFW 2005; SCFW 2; SFW 4

Gide, Andre (Paul Guillaume)
1869-1951 ..... **SSC 13; TCLC 5, 12, 36;
WLC**
See also CA 104; 124; DA; DA3; DAB;
DAC; DAM MST, NOV; DLB 65, 321;
EW 8; EWL 3; GFL 1789 to the Present;
MTCW 1, 2; MTFW 2005; NFS 21;
RGSF 2; RGWL 2, 3; TWA

Gifford, Barry (Colby) 1946- .... **CLC 34**
See also CA 65-68; CANR 9, 30, 40, 90

Gilbert, Frank
See De Voto, Bernard (Augustine)

Gilbert, W(illiam) S(chwenck)
1836-1911 .... **TCLC 3**
See also CA 104; 173; DAM DRAM, POET;
RGEL 2; SATA 36

Gilbreth, Frank B(unker), Jr.
1911-2001 .... **CLC 17**
See also CA 9-12R; SATA 2

Gilchrist, Ellen (Louise) 1935- .. **CLC 34, 48,
143; SSC 14, 63**
See also BPFB 2; CA 113; 116; CANR 41,
61, 104; CN 4, 5, 6, 7; CPW; CSW; DAM
POP; DLB 130; EWL 3; EXPS; MTCW
1, 2; MTFW 2005; RGAL 4; RGSF 2;
SSFS 9

Giles, Molly 1942- .... **CLC 39**
See also CA 126; CANR 98

Gill, Eric .... **TCLC 85**
See Gill, (Arthur) Eric (Rowton Peter
Joseph)

Gill, (Arthur) Eric (Rowton Peter Joseph)
1882-1940
See Gill, Eric
See also CA 120; DLB 98

Gill, Patrick
See Creasey, John

Gillette, Douglas .... **CLC 70**

Gilliam, Terry (Vance) 1940- .... **CLC 21, 141**
See Monty Python
See also AAYA 19, 59; CA 108; 113; CANR
35; INT CA-113

Gillian, Jerry
See Gilliam, Terry (Vance)

Gilliatt, Penelope (Ann Douglass)
1932-1993 .... **CLC 2, 10, 13, 53**
See also AITN 2; CA 13-16R; 141; CANR
49; CN 1, 2, 3, 4, 5; DLB 14

Gilligan, Carol 1936- .... **CLC 208**
See also CA 142; CANR 121; FW

Gilman, Charlotte (Anna) Perkins (Stetson)
1860-1935 ...... **SSC 13, 62; TCLC 9, 37,
117**
See also AMWS 11; BYA 11; CA 106; 150;
DLB 221; EXPS; FL 1:5; FW; HGG;
LAIT 2; MAWW; MTCW 2; MTFW
2005; RGAL 4; RGSF 2; SFW 4; SSFS 1,
18

Gilmour, David 1946- .... **CLC 35**

Gilpin, William 1724-1804 .... **NCLC 30**

Gilray, J. D.
See Mencken, H(enry) L(ouis)

Gilroy, Frank D(aniel) 1925- .... **CLC 2**
See also CA 81-84; CAD; CANR 32, 64,
86; CD 5, 6; DFS 17; DLB 7

Gilstrap, John 1957(?)- .... **CLC 99**
See also AAYA 67; CA 160; CANR 101

Ginsberg, Allen 1926-1997 .... **CLC 1, 2, 3, 4,
6, 13, 36, 69, 109; PC 4, 47; TCLC
120; WLC**
See also AAYA 33; AITN 1; AMWC 1;
AMWS 2; BG 1:2; CA 1-4R; 157; CANR
2, 41, 63, 95; CDALB 1941-1968; CP 1,
2, 3, 4, 5, 6; DA; DA3; DAB; DAC; DAM
MST, POET; DLB 5, 16, 169, 237; EWL
3; GLL 1; LMFS 2; MAL 5; MTCW 1, 2;
MTFW 2005; PAB; PFS 5; RGAL 4;
TUS; WP

Ginzburg, Eugenia .... **CLC 59**
See Ginzburg, Evgeniia

Ginzburg, Evgeniia 1904-1977
See Ginzburg, Eugenia
See also DLB 302

Ginzburg, Natalia 1916-1991 .... **CLC 5, 11,
54, 70; SSC 65; TCLC 156**
See also CA 85-88; 135; CANR 33; DFS
14; DLB 177; EW 13; EWL 3; MTCW 1,
2; MTFW 2005; RGWL 2, 3

Giono, Jean 1895-1970 .... **CLC 4, 11; TCLC
124**
See also CA 45-48; 29-32R; CANR 2, 35;
DLB 72, 321; EWL 3; GFL 1789 to the
Present; MTCW 1; RGWL 2, 3

Giovanni, Nikki 1943- ...... **BLC 2; CLC 2, 4,
19, 64, 117; PC 19; WLCS**
See also AAYA 22; AITN 1; BW 2, 3; CA
29-32R; CAAS 6; CANR 18, 41, 60, 91,
130; CDALBS; CLR 6, 73; CP 2, 3, 4, 5,
6, 7; CSW; CWP; CWRI 5; DA; DA3;
DAB; DAC; DAM MST, MULT, POET;
DLB 5, 41; EWL 3; EXPP; INT CANR-
18; MAICYA 1, 2; MAL 5; MTCW 1, 2;
MTFW 2005; PFS 17; RGAL 4; SATA
24, 107; TUS; YAW

Giovene, Andrea 1904-1998 .... **CLC 7**
See also CA 85-88

Gippius, Zinaida (Nikolaevna) 1869-1945
See Hippius, Zinaida (Nikolaevna)
See also CA 106; 212

Giraudoux, Jean(-Hippolyte)
1882-1944 .... **TCLC 2, 7**
See also CA 104; 196; DAM DRAM; DLB
65, 321; EW 9; EWL 3; GFL 1789 to the
Present; RGWL 2, 3; TWA

Gironella, Jose Maria (Pous)
1917-2003 .... **CLC 11**
See also CA 101; 212; EWL 3; RGWL 2, 3

Gissing, George (Robert)
1857-1903 .... **SSC 37; TCLC 3, 24, 47**
See also BRW 5; CA 105; 167; DLB 18,
135, 184; RGEL 2; TEA

Gitlin, Todd 1943- .... **CLC 201**
See also CA 29-32R; CANR 25, 50, 88

Giurlani, Aldo
See Palazzeschi, Aldo

Gladkov, Fedor Vasil'evich
See Gladkov, Fyodor (Vasilyevich)
See also DLB 272

Gladkov, Fyodor (Vasilyevich)
1883-1958 .... **TCLC 27**
See Gladkov, Fedor Vasil'evich
See also CA 170; EWL 3

Glancy, Diane 1941- .... **CLC 210; NNAL**
See also CA 136, 225; CAAE 225; CAAS
24; CANR 87; DLB 175

Gordone, Charles 1925-1995 .. **CLC 1, 4; DC 8**
See also BW 1, 3; CA 93-96, 180; 150; CAAE 180; CAD; CANR 55; DAM DRAM; DLB 7; INT CA-93-96; MTCW 1

Gore, Catherine 1800-1861 .... **NCLC 65**
See also DLB 116; RGEL 2

Gorenko, Anna Andreevna
See Akhmatova, Anna

Gorky, Maxim .... **SSC 28; TCLC 8; WLC**
See Peshkov, Alexei Maximovich
See also DAB; DFS 9; DLB 295; EW 8; EWL 3; TWA

Goryan, Sirak
See Saroyan, William

Gosse, Edmund (William)
1849-1928 .... **TCLC 28**
See also CA 117; DLB 57, 144, 184; RGEL 2

Gotlieb, Phyllis (Fay Bloom) 1926- .. **CLC 18**
See also CA 13-16R; CANR 7, 135; CN 7; CP 1, 2, 3, 4; DLB 88, 251; SFW 4

Gottesman, S. D.
See Kornbluth, C(yril) M.; Pohl, Frederik

Gottfried von Strassburg fl. c.
1170-1215 .... **CMLC 10**
See also CDWLB 2; DLB 138; EW 1; RGWL 2, 3

Gotthelf, Jeremias 1797-1854 .... **NCLC 117**
See also DLB 133; RGWL 2, 3

Gottschalk, Laura Riding
See Jackson, Laura (Riding)

Gould, Lois 1932(?)-2002 .... **CLC 4, 10**
See also CA 77-80; 208; CANR 29; MTCW 1

Gould, Stephen Jay 1941-2002 .... **CLC 163**
See also AAYA 26; BEST 90:2; CA 77-80; 205; CANR 10, 27, 56, 75, 125; CPW; INT CANR-27; MTCW 1, 2; MTFW 2005

Gourmont, Remy(-Marie-Charles) de
1858-1915 .... **TCLC 17**
See also CA 109; 150; GFL 1789 to the Present; MTCW 2

Gournay, Marie le Jars de
See de Gournay, Marie le Jars

Govier, Katherine 1948- .... **CLC 51**
See also CA 101; CANR 18, 40, 128; CCA 1

Gower, John c. 1330-1408 .... **LC 76; PC 59**
See also BRW 1; DLB 146; RGEL 2

Goyen, (Charles) William
1915-1983 .... **CLC 5, 8, 14, 40**
See also AITN 2; CA 5-8R; 110; CANR 6, 71; CN 1, 2, 3; DLB 2, 218; DLBY 1983; EWL 3; INT CANR-6; MAL 5

Goytisolo, Juan 1931- .... **CLC 5, 10, 23, 133; HLC 1**
See also CA 85-88; CANR 32, 61, 131; CWW 2; DAM MULT; DLB 322; EWL 3; GLL 2; HW 1, 2; MTCW 1, 2; MTFW 2005

Gozzano, Guido 1883-1916 .... **PC 10**
See also CA 154; DLB 114; EWL 3

Gozzi, (Conte) Carlo 1720-1806 .... **NCLC 23**

Grabbe, Christian Dietrich
1801-1836 .... **NCLC 2**
See also DLB 133; RGWL 2, 3

Grace, Patricia Frances 1937- .... **CLC 56**
See also CA 176; CANR 118; CN 4, 5, 6, 7; EWL 3; RGSF 2

Gracian y Morales, Baltasar
1601-1658 .... **LC 15**

Gracq, Julien .... **CLC 11, 48**
See Poirier, Louis
See also CWW 2; DLB 83; GFL 1789 to the Present

Grade, Chaim 1910-1982 .... **CLC 10**
See also CA 93-96; 107; EWL 3

Graduate of Oxford, A
See Ruskin, John

Grafton, Garth
See Duncan, Sara Jeannette

Grafton, Sue 1940- .... **CLC 163**
See also AAYA 11, 49; BEST 90:3; CA 108; CANR 31, 55, 111, 134; CMW 4; CPW; CSW; DA3; DAM POP; DLB 226; FW; MSW; MTFW 2005

Graham, John
See Phillips, David Graham

Graham, Jorie 1950- .... **CLC 48, 118; PC 59**
See also AAYA 67; CA 111; CANR 63, 118; CP 4, 5, 6, 7; CWP; DLB 120; EWL 3; MTFW 2005; PFS 10, 17; TCLE 1:1

Graham, R(obert) B(ontine) Cunninghame
See Cunninghame Graham, Robert (Gallnigad) Bontine
See also DLB 98, 135, 174; RGEL 2; RGSF 2

Graham, Robert
See Haldeman, Joe (William)

Graham, Tom
See Lewis, (Harry) Sinclair

Graham, W(illiam) S(idney)
1918-1986 .... **CLC 29**
See also BRWS 7; CA 73-76; 118; CP 1, 2, 3, 4; DLB 20; RGEL 2

Graham, Winston (Mawdsley)
1910-2003 .... **CLC 23**
See also CA 49-52; 218; CANR 2, 22, 45, 66; CMW 4; CN 1, 2, 3, 4, 5, 6, 7; DLB 77; RHW

Grahame, Kenneth 1859-1932 ...... **TCLC 64, 136**
See also BYA 5; CA 108; 136; CANR 80; CLR 5; CWRI 5; DA3; DAB; DLB 34, 141, 178; FANT; MAICYA 1, 2; MTCW 2; NFS 20; RGEL 2; SATA 100; TEA; WCH; YABC 1

Granger, Darius John
See Marlowe, Stephen

Granin, Daniil 1918- .... **CLC 59**
See also DLB 302

Granovsky, Timofei Nikolaevich
1813-1855 .... **NCLC 75**
See also DLB 198

Grant, Skeeter
See Spiegelman, Art

Granville-Barker, Harley
1877-1946 .... **TCLC 2**
See Barker, Harley Granville
See also CA 104; 204; DAM DRAM; RGEL 2

Granzotto, Gianni
See Granzotto, Giovanni Battista

Granzotto, Giovanni Battista
1914-1985 .... **CLC 70**
See also CA 166

Grass, Guenter (Wilhelm) 1927- ... **CLC 1, 2, 4, 6, 11, 15, 22, 32, 49, 88, 207; WLC**
See Grass, Gunter (Wilhelm)
See also BPFB 2; CA 13-16R; CANR 20, 75, 93, 133; CDWLB 2; DA; DA3; DAB; DAC; DAM MST, NOV; DLB 75, 124; EW 13; EWL 3; MTCW 1, 2; MTFW 2005; RGWL 2, 3; TWA

Grass, Gunter (Wilhelm)
See Grass, Guenter (Wilhelm)
See also CWW 2

Gratton, Thomas
See Hulme, T(homas) E(rnest)

Grau, Shirley Ann 1929- .... **CLC 4, 9, 146; SSC 15**
See also CA 89-92; CANR 22, 69; CN 1, 2, 3, 4, 5, 6, 7; CSW; DLB 2, 218; INT CA-89-92; CANR-22; MTCW 1

Gravel, Fern
See Hall, James Norman

Graver, Elizabeth 1964- .... **CLC 70**
See also CA 135; CANR 71, 129

Graves, Richard Perceval
1895-1985 .... **CLC 44**
See also CA 65-68; CANR 9, 26, 51

Graves, Robert (von Ranke)
1895-1985 .. **CLC 1, 2, 6, 11, 39, 44, 45; PC 6**
See also BPFB 2; BRW 7; BYA 4; CA 5-8R; 117; CANR 5, 36; CDBLB 1914-1945; CN 1, 2, 3; CP 1, 2, 3, 4; DA3; DAB; DAC; DAM MST, POET; DLB 20, 100, 191; DLBD 18; DLBY 1985; EWL 3; LATS 1:1; MTCW 1, 2; MTFW 2005; NCFS 2; NFS 21; RGEL 2; RHW; SATA 45; TEA

Graves, Valerie
See Bradley, Marion Zimmer

Gray, Alasdair (James) 1934- .... **CLC 41**
See also BRWS 9; CA 126; CANR 47, 69, 106, 140; CN 4, 5, 6, 7; DLB 194, 261, 319; HGG; INT CA-126; MTCW 1, 2; MTFW 2005; RGSF 2; SUFW 2

Gray, Amlin 1946- .... **CLC 29**
See also CA 138

Gray, Francine du Plessix 1930- ..... **CLC 22, 153**
See also BEST 90:3; CA 61-64; CAAS 2; CANR 11, 33, 75, 81; DAM NOV; INT CANR-11; MTCW 1, 2; MTFW 2005

Gray, John (Henry) 1866-1934 ...... **TCLC 19**
See also CA 119; 162; RGEL 2

Gray, John Lee
See Jakes, John (William)

Gray, Simon (James Holliday)
1936- .... **CLC 9, 14, 36**
See also AITN 1; CA 21-24R; CAAS 3; CANR 32, 69; CBD; CD 5, 6; CN 1, 2, 3; DLB 13; EWL 3; MTCW 1; RGEL 2

Gray, Spalding 1941-2004 .... **CLC 49, 112; DC 7**
See also AAYA 62; CA 128; 225; CAD; CANR 74, 138; CD 5, 6; CPW; DAM POP; MTCW 2; MTFW 2005

Gray, Thomas 1716-1771 .... **LC 4, 40; PC 2; WLC**
See also BRW 3; CDBLB 1660-1789; DA; DA3; DAB; DAC; DAM MST; DLB 109; EXPP; PAB; PFS 9; RGEL 2; TEA; WP

Grayson, David
See Baker, Ray Stannard

Grayson, Richard (A.) 1951- .... **CLC 38**
See also CA 85-88; 210; CAAE 210; CANR 14, 31, 57; DLB 234

Greeley, Andrew M(oran) 1928- ...... **CLC 28**
See also BPFB 2; CA 5-8R; CAAS 7; CANR 7, 43, 69, 104, 136; CMW 4; CPW; DA3; DAM POP; MTCW 1, 2; MTFW 2005

Green, Anna Katharine
1846-1935 .... **TCLC 63**
See also CA 112; 159; CMW 4; DLB 202, 221; MSW

Green, Brian
See Card, Orson Scott

Green, Hannah
See Greenberg, Joanne (Goldenberg)

Green, Hannah 1927(?)-1996 .... **CLC 3**
See also CA 73-76; CANR 59, 93; NFS 10

Green, Henry .... **CLC 2, 13, 97**
See Yorke, Henry Vincent
See also BRWS 2; CA 175; DLB 15; EWL 3; RGEL 2

Green, Julian .... **CLC 3, 11, 77**
See Green, Julien (Hartridge)
See also EWL 3; GFL 1789 to the Present; MTCW 2

Green, Julien (Hartridge) 1900-1998
See Green, Julian
See also CA 21-24R; 169; CANR 33, 87;
CWW 2; DLB 4, 72; MTCW 1, 2; MTFW
2005
Green, Paul (Eliot) 1894-1981 .... **CLC 25**
See also AITN 1; CA 5-8R; 103; CAD;
CANR 3; DAM DRAM; DLB 7, 9, 249;
DLBY 1981; MAL 5; RGAL 4
Greenaway, Peter 1942- .... **CLC 159**
See also CA 127
Greenberg, Ivan 1908-1973
See Rahv, Philip
See also CA 85-88
Greenberg, Joanne (Goldenberg)
1932- .... **CLC 7, 30**
See also AAYA 12, 67; CA 5-8R; CANR
14, 32, 69; CN 6, 7; SATA 25; YAW
Greenberg, Richard 1959(?)- .... **CLC 57**
See also CA 138; CAD; CD 5, 6
Greenblatt, Stephen J(ay) 1943- ...... **CLC 70**
See also CA 49-52; CANR 115
Greene, Bette 1934- .... **CLC 30**
See also AAYA 7; BYA 3; CA 53-56; CANR
4, 146; CLR 2; CWRI 5; JRDA; LAIT 4;
MAICYA 1, 2; NFS 10; SAAS 16; SATA
8, 102, 161; WYA; YAW
Greene, Gael .... **CLC 8**
See also CA 13-16R; CANR 10
Greene, Graham (Henry)
1904-1991 .... **CLC 1, 3, 6, 9, 14, 18, 27,
37, 70, 72, 125; SSC 29; WLC**
See also AAYA 61; AITN 2; BPFB 2;
BRWR 2; BRWS 1; BYA 3; CA 13-16R;
133; CANR 35, 61, 131; CBD; CDBLB
1945-1960; CMW 4; CN 1, 2, 3, 4; DA;
DA3; DAB; DAC; DAM MST, NOV;
DLB 13, 15, 77, 100, 162, 201, 204;
DLBY 1991; EWL 3; MSW; MTCW 1, 2;
MTFW 2005; NFS 16; RGEL 2; SATA
20; SSFS 14; TEA; WLIT 4
Greene, Robert 1558-1592 .... **LC 41**
See also BRWS 8; DLB 62, 167; IDTP;
RGEL 2; TEA
Greer, Germaine 1939- .... **CLC 131**
See also AITN 1; CA 81-84; CANR 33, 70,
115, 133; FW; MTCW 1, 2; MTFW 2005
Greer, Richard
See Silverberg, Robert
Gregor, Arthur 1923- .... **CLC 9**
See also CA 25-28R; CAAS 10; CANR 11;
CP 1, 2, 3, 4, 5, 6, 7; SATA 36
Gregor, Lee
See Pohl, Frederik
Gregory, Lady Isabella Augusta (Persse)
1852-1932 .... **TCLC 1, 176**
See also BRW 6; CA 104; 184; DLB 10;
IDTP; RGEL 2
Gregory, J. Dennis
See Williams, John A(lfred)
Grekova, I. .... **CLC 59**
See Ventsel, Elena Sergeevna
See also CWW 2
Grendon, Stephen
See Derleth, August (William)
Grenville, Kate 1950- .... **CLC 61**
See also CA 118; CANR 53, 93; CN 7
Grenville, Pelham
See Wodehouse, P(elham) G(renville)
Greve, Felix Paul (Berthold Friedrich)
1879-1948
See Grove, Frederick Philip
See also CA 104; 141, 175; CANR 79;
DAC; DAM MST
Greville, Fulke 1554-1628 .... **LC 79**
See also BRWS 11; DLB 62, 172; RGEL 2
Grey, Lady Jane 1537-1554 .... **LC 93**
See also DLB 132

Grey, Zane 1872-1939 .... **TCLC 6**
See also BPFB 2; CA 104; 132; DA3; DAM
POP; DLB 9, 212; MTCW 1, 2; MTFW
2005; RGAL 4; TCWW 1, 2; TUS
Griboedov, Aleksandr Sergeevich
1795(?)-1829 .... **NCLC 129**
See also DLB 205; RGWL 2, 3
Grieg, (Johan) Nordahl (Brun)
1902-1943 .... **TCLC 10**
See also CA 107; 189; EWL 3
Grieve, C(hristopher) M(urray)
1892-1978 .... **CLC 11, 19**
See MacDiarmid, Hugh; Pteleon
See also CA 5-8R; 85-88; CANR 33, 107;
DAM POET; MTCW 1; RGEL 2
Griffin, Gerald 1803-1840 .... **NCLC 7**
See also DLB 159; RGEL 2
Griffin, John Howard 1920-1980 ..... **CLC 68**
See also AITN 1; CA 1-4R; 101; CANR 2
Griffin, Peter 1942- .... **CLC 39**
See also CA 136
Griffith, D(avid Lewelyn) W(ark)
1875(?)-1948 .... **TCLC 68**
See also CA 119; 150; CANR 80
Griffith, Lawrence
See Griffith, D(avid Lewelyn) W(ark)
Griffiths, Trevor 1935- .... **CLC 13, 52**
See also CA 97-100; CANR 45; CBD; CD
5, 6; DLB 13, 245
Griggs, Sutton (Elbert)
1872-1930 .... **TCLC 77**
See also CA 123; 186; DLB 50
Grigson, Geoffrey (Edward Harvey)
1905-1985 .... **CLC 7, 39**
See also CA 25-28R; 118; CANR 20, 33;
CP 1, 2, 3, 4; DLB 27; MTCW 1, 2
Grile, Dod
See Bierce, Ambrose (Gwinett)
Grillparzer, Franz 1791-1872 .... **DC 14;
NCLC 1, 102; SSC 37**
See also CDWLB 2; DLB 133; EW 5;
RGWL 2, 3; TWA
Grimble, Reverend Charles James
See Eliot, T(homas) S(tearns)
Grimke, Angelina (Emily) Weld
1880-1958 .... **HR 1:2**
See Weld, Angelina (Emily) Grimke
See also BW 1; CA 124; DAM POET; DLB
50, 54
Grimke, Charlotte L(ottie) Forten
1837(?)-1914
See Forten, Charlotte L.
See also BW 1; CA 117; 124; DAM MULT,
POET
Grimm, Jacob Ludwig Karl
1785-1863 .... **NCLC 3, 77; SSC 36, 88**
See also DLB 90; MAICYA 1, 2; RGSF 2;
RGWL 2, 3; SATA 22; WCH
Grimm, Wilhelm Karl 1786-1859 .. **NCLC 3,
77; SSC 36, 88**
See also CDWLB 2; DLB 90; MAICYA 1,
2; RGSF 2; RGWL 2, 3; SATA 22; WCH
**Grimmelshausen, Hans Jakob Christoffel
von**
See Grimmelshausen, Johann Jakob Christ-
offel von
See also RGWL 2, 3
**Grimmelshausen, Johann Jakob Christoffel
von** 1621-1676 .... **LC 6**
See Grimmelshausen, Hans Jakob Christof-
fel von
See also CDWLB 2; DLB 168
Grindel, Eugene 1895-1952
See Eluard, Paul
See also CA 104; 193; LMFS 2

Grisham, John 1955- .... **CLC 84**
See also AAYA 14, 47; BPFB 2; CA 138;
CANR 47, 69, 114, 133; CMW 4; CN 6,
7; CPW; CSW; DA3; DAM POP; MSW;
MTCW 2; MTFW 2005
Grosseteste, Robert 1175(?)-1253 . **CMLC 62**
See also DLB 115
Grossman, David 1954- .... **CLC 67**
See also CA 138; CANR 114; CWW 2;
DLB 299; EWL 3; WLIT 6
Grossman, Vasilii Semenovich
See Grossman, Vasily (Semenovich)
See also DLB 272
Grossman, Vasily (Semenovich)
1905-1964 .... **CLC 41**
See Grossman, Vasilii Semenovich
See also CA 124; 130; MTCW 1
Grove, Frederick Philip .... **TCLC 4**
See Greve, Felix Paul (Berthold Friedrich)
See also DLB 92; RGEL 2; TCWW 1, 2
Grubb
See Crumb, R(obert)
Grumbach, Doris (Isaac) 1918- . **CLC 13, 22,
64**
See also CA 5-8R; CAAS 2; CANR 9, 42,
70, 127; CN 6, 7; INT CANR-9; MTCW
2; MTFW 2005
Grundtvig, Nikolai Frederik Severin
1783-1872 .... **NCLC 1, 158**
See also DLB 300
Grunge
See Crumb, R(obert)
Grunwald, Lisa 1959- .... **CLC 44**
See also CA 120
Gryphius, Andreas 1616-1664 .... **LC 89**
See also CDWLB 2; DLB 164; RGWL 2, 3
Guare, John 1938- .... **CLC 8, 14, 29, 67; DC
20**
See also CA 73-76; CAD; CANR 21, 69,
118; CD 5, 6; DAM DRAM; DFS 8, 13;
DLB 7, 249; EWL 3; MAL 5; MTCW 1,
2; RGAL 4
Guarini, Battista 1537-1612 .... **LC 102**
Gubar, Susan (David) 1944- .... **CLC 145**
See also CA 108; CANR 45, 70, 139; FW;
MTCW 1; RGAL 4
Gudjonsson, Halldor Kiljan 1902-1998
See Halldor Laxness
See also CA 103; 164
Guenter, Erich
See Eich, Gunter
Guest, Barbara 1920- .... **CLC 34; PC 55**
See also BG 1:2; CA 25-28R; CANR 11,
44, 84; CP 1, 2, 3, 4, 5, 6, 7; CWP; DLB
5, 193
Guest, Edgar A(lbert) 1881-1959 ... **TCLC 95**
See also CA 112; 168
Guest, Judith (Ann) 1936- .... **CLC 8, 30**
See also AAYA 7, 66; CA 77-80; CANR
15, 75, 138; DA3; DAM NOV, POP;
EXPN; INT CANR-15; LAIT 5; MTCW
1, 2; MTFW 2005; NFS 1
Guevara, Che .... **CLC 87; HLC 1**
See Guevara (Serna), Ernesto
Guevara (Serna), Ernesto
1928-1967 .... **CLC 87; HLC 1**
See Guevara, Che
See also CA 127; 111; CANR 56; DAM
MULT; HW 1
Guicciardini, Francesco 1483-1540 ..... **LC 49**
Guild, Nicholas M. 1944- .... **CLC 33**
See also CA 93-96
Guillemin, Jacques
See Sartre, Jean-Paul
Guillen, Jorge 1893-1984 . **CLC 11; HLCS 1;
PC 35**
See also CA 89-92; 112; DAM MULT,
POET; DLB 108; EWL 3; HW 1; RGWL
2, 3

Guillen, Nicolas (Cristobal)
1902-1989 .... **BLC 2; CLC 48, 79; HLC 1; PC 23**
See also BW 2; CA 116; 125; 129; CANR 84; DAM MST, MULT, POET; DLB 283; EWL 3; HW 1; LAW; RGWL 2, 3; WP

Guillen y Alvarez, Jorge
See Guillen, Jorge

Guillevic, (Eugene) 1907-1997 .... **CLC 33**
See also CA 93-96; CWW 2

Guillois
See Desnos, Robert

Guillois, Valentin
See Desnos, Robert

Guimaraes Rosa, Joao 1908-1967 .... **HLCS 2**
See Rosa, Joao Guimaraes
See also CA 175; LAW; RGSF 2; RGWL 2, 3

Guiney, Louise Imogen
1861-1920 .... **TCLC 41**
See also CA 160; DLB 54; RGAL 4

Guinizelli, Guido c. 1230-1276 ...... **CMLC 49**
See Guinizzelli, Guido

Guinizzelli, Guido
See Guinizelli, Guido
See also WLIT 7

Guiraldes, Ricardo (Guillermo)
1886-1927 .... **TCLC 39**
See also CA 131; EWL 3; HW 1; LAW; MTCW 1

Gumilev, Nikolai (Stepanovich)
1886-1921 .... **TCLC 60**
See Gumilyov, Nikolay Stepanovich
See also CA 165; DLB 295

Gumilyov, Nikolay Stepanovich
See Gumilev, Nikolai (Stepanovich)
See also EWL 3

Gump, P. Q.
See Card, Orson Scott

Gunesekera, Romesh 1954- .... **CLC 91**
See also BRWS 10; CA 159; CANR 140; CN 6, 7; DLB 267

Gunn, Bill .... **CLC 5**
See Gunn, William Harrison
See also DLB 38

Gunn, Thom(son William)
1929-2004 . **CLC 3, 6, 18, 32, 81; PC 26**
See also BRWS 4; CA 17-20R; 227; CANR 9, 33, 116; CDBLB 1960 to Present; CP 1, 2, 3, 4, 5, 6, 7; DAM POET; DLB 27; INT CANR-33; MTCW 1; PFS 9; RGEL 2

Gunn, William Harrison 1934(?)-1989
See Gunn, Bill
See also AITN 1; BW 1, 3; CA 13-16R; 128; CANR 12, 25, 76

Gunn Allen, Paula
See Allen, Paula Gunn

Gunnars, Kristjana 1948- .... **CLC 69**
See also CA 113; CCA 1; CP 7; CWP; DLB 60

Gunter, Erich
See Eich, Gunter

Gurdjieff, G(eorgei) I(vanovich)
1877(?)-1949 .... **TCLC 71**
See also CA 157

Gurganus, Allan 1947- .... **CLC 70**
See also BEST 90:1; CA 135; CANR 114; CN 6, 7; CPW; CSW; DAM POP; GLL 1

Gurney, A. R.
See Gurney, A(lbert) R(amsdell), Jr.
See also DLB 266

Gurney, A(lbert) R(amsdell), Jr.
1930- .... **CLC 32, 50, 54**
See Gurney, A. R.
See also AMWS 5; CA 77-80; CAD; CANR 32, 64, 121; CD 5, 6; DAM DRAM; EWL 3

Gurney, Ivor (Bertie) 1890-1937 ... **TCLC 33**
See also BRW 6; CA 167; DLBY 2002; PAB; RGEL 2

Gurney, Peter
See Gurney, A(lbert) R(amsdell), Jr.

Guro, Elena (Genrikhovna)
1877-1913 .... **TCLC 56**
See also DLB 295

Gustafson, James M(oody) 1925- ... **CLC 100**
See also CA 25-28R; CANR 37

Gustafson, Ralph (Barker)
1909-1995 .... **CLC 36**
See also CA 21-24R; CANR 8, 45, 84; CP 1, 2, 3, 4; DLB 88; RGEL 2

Gut, Gom
See Simenon, Georges (Jacques Christian)

Guterson, David 1956- .... **CLC 91**
See also CA 132; CANR 73, 126; CN 7; DLB 292; MTCW 2; MTFW 2005; NFS 13

Guthrie, A(lfred) B(ertram), Jr.
1901-1991 .... **CLC 23**
See also CA 57-60; 134; CANR 24; CN 1, 2, 3; DLB 6, 212; MAL 5; SATA 62; SATA-Obit 67; TCWW 1, 2

Guthrie, Isobel
See Grieve, C(hristopher) M(urray)

Guthrie, Woodrow Wilson 1912-1967
See Guthrie, Woody
See also CA 113; 93-96

Guthrie, Woody .... **CLC 35**
See Guthrie, Woodrow Wilson
See also DLB 303; LAIT 3

Gutierrez Najera, Manuel
1859-1895 .... **HLCS 2; NCLC 133**
See also DLB 290; LAW

Guy, Rosa (Cuthbert) 1925- .... **CLC 26**
See also AAYA 4, 37; BW 2; CA 17-20R; CANR 14, 34, 83; CLR 13; DLB 33; DNFS 1; JRDA; MAICYA 1, 2; SATA 14, 62, 122; YAW

Gwendolyn
See Bennett, (Enoch) Arnold

H. D. .... **CLC 3, 8, 14, 31, 34, 73; PC 5**
See Doolittle, Hilda
See also FL 1:5

H. de V.
See Buchan, John

Haavikko, Paavo Juhani 1931- .. **CLC 18, 34**
See also CA 106; CWW 2; EWL 3

Habbema, Koos
See Heijermans, Herman

Habermas, Juergen 1929- .... **CLC 104**
See also CA 109; CANR 85; DLB 242

Habermas, Jurgen
See Habermas, Juergen

Hacker, Marilyn 1942- ...... **CLC 5, 9, 23, 72, 91; PC 47**
See also CA 77-80; CANR 68, 129; CP 3, 4, 5, 6, 7; CWP; DAM POET; DLB 120, 282; FW; GLL 2; MAL 5; PFS 19

Hadewijch of Antwerp fl. 1250- ... **CMLC 61**
See also RGWL 3

Hadrian 76-138 .... **CMLC 52**

Haeckel, Ernst Heinrich (Philipp August)
1834-1919 .... **TCLC 83**
See also CA 157

Hafiz c. 1326-1389(?) .... **CMLC 34**
See also RGWL 2, 3; WLIT 6

Hagedorn, Jessica T(arahata)
1949- .... **CLC 185**
See also CA 139; CANR 69; CWP; DLB 312; RGAL 4

Haggard, H(enry) Rider
1856-1925 .... **TCLC 11**
See also BRWS 3; BYA 4, 5; CA 108; 148; CANR 112; DLB 70, 156, 174, 178; FANT; LMFS 1; MTCW 2; RGEL 2; RHW; SATA 16; SCFW 1, 2; SFW 4; SUFW 1; WLIT 4

Hagiosy, L.
See Larbaud, Valery (Nicolas)

Hagiwara, Sakutaro 1886-1942 .... **PC 18; TCLC 60**
See Hagiwara Sakutaro
See also CA 154; RGWL 3

Hagiwara Sakutaro
See Hagiwara, Sakutaro
See also EWL 3

Haig, Fenil
See Ford, Ford Madox

Haig-Brown, Roderick (Langmere)
1908-1976 .... **CLC 21**
See also CA 5-8R; 69-72; CANR 4, 38, 83; CLR 31; CWRI 5; DLB 88; MAICYA 1, 2; SATA 12; TCWW 2

Haight, Rip
See Carpenter, John (Howard)

Hailey, Arthur 1920-2004 .... **CLC 5**
See also AITN 2; BEST 90:3; BPFB 2; CA 1-4R; 233; CANR 2, 36, 75; CCA 1; CN 1, 2, 3, 4, 5, 6, 7; CPW; DAM NOV, POP; DLB 88; DLBY 1982; MTCW 1, 2; MTFW 2005

Hailey, Elizabeth Forsythe 1938- ..... **CLC 40**
See also CA 93-96, 188; CAAE 188; CAAS 1; CANR 15, 48; INT CANR-15

Haines, John (Meade) 1924- .... **CLC 58**
See also AMWS 12; CA 17-20R; CANR 13, 34; CP 1, 2, 3, 4; CSW; DLB 5, 212; TCLE 1:1

Hakluyt, Richard 1552-1616 .... **LC 31**
See also DLB 136; RGEL 2

Haldeman, Joe (William) 1943- .... **CLC 61**
See Graham, Robert
See also AAYA 38; CA 53-56, 179; CAAE 179; CAAS 25; CANR 6, 70, 72, 130; DLB 8; INT CANR-6; SCFW 2; SFW 4

Hale, Janet Campbell 1947- .... **NNAL**
See also CA 49-52; CANR 45, 75; DAM MULT; DLB 175; MTCW 2; MTFW 2005

Hale, Sarah Josepha (Buell)
1788-1879 .... **NCLC 75**
See also DLB 1, 42, 73, 243

Halevy, Elie 1870-1937 .... **TCLC 104**

Haley, Alex(ander Murray Palmer)
1921-1992 .... **BLC 2; CLC 8, 12, 76; TCLC 147**
See also AAYA 26; BPFB 2; BW 2, 3; CA 77-80; 136; CANR 61; CDALBS; CPW; CSW; DA; DA3; DAB; DAC; DAM MST, MULT, POP; DLB 38; LAIT 5; MTCW 1, 2; NFS 9

Haliburton, Thomas Chandler
1796-1865 .... **NCLC 15, 149**
See also DLB 11, 99; RGEL 2; RGSF 2

Hall, Donald (Andrew, Jr.) 1928- ...... **CLC 1, 13, 37, 59, 151; PC 70**
See also AAYA 63; CA 5-8R; CAAS 7; CANR 2, 44, 64, 106, 133; CP 1, 2, 3, 4, 5, 6, 7; DAM POET; DLB 5; MAL 5; MTCW 2; MTFW 2005; RGAL 4; SATA 23, 97

Hall, Frederic Sauser
See Sauser-Hall, Frederic

Hall, James
See Kuttner, Henry

Hall, James Norman 1887-1951 ..... **TCLC 23**
See also CA 123; 173; LAIT 1; RHW 1; SATA 21

Hall, Joseph 1574-1656 .... **LC 91**
See also DLB 121, 151; RGEL 2

Hall, (Marguerite) Radclyffe
1880-1943 .... **TCLC 12**
See also BRWS 6; CA 110; 150; CANR 83;
DLB 191; MTCW 2; MTFW 2005; RGEL
2; RHW

Hall, Rodney 1935- .... **CLC 51**
See also CA 109; CANR 69; CN 6, 7; CP
1, 2, 3, 4, 5, 6, 7; DLB 289

Hallam, Arthur Henry
1811-1833 .... **NCLC 110**
See also DLB 32

Halldor Laxness .... **CLC 25**
See Gudjonsson, Halldor Kiljan
See also DLB 293; EW 12; EWL 3; RGWL
2, 3

Halleck, Fitz-Greene 1790-1867 .... **NCLC 47**
See also DLB 3, 250; RGAL 4

Halliday, Michael
See Creasey, John

Halpern, Daniel 1945- .... **CLC 14**
See also CA 33-36R; CANR 93; CP 3, 4, 5,
6, 7

Hamburger, Michael (Peter Leopold)
1924- .... **CLC 5, 14**
See also CA 5-8R, 196; CAAE 196; CAAS
4; CANR 2, 47; CP 1, 2, 3, 4, 5, 6, 7;
DLB 27

Hamill, Pete 1935- .... **CLC 10**
See also CA 25-28R; CANR 18, 71, 127

Hamilton, Alexander
1755(?)-1804 .... **NCLC 49**
See also DLB 37

Hamilton, Clive
See Lewis, C(live) S(taples)

Hamilton, Edmond 1904-1977 .... **CLC 1**
See also CA 1-4R; CANR 3, 84; DLB 8;
SATA 118; SFW 4

Hamilton, Elizabeth 1758-1816 ... **NCLC 153**
See also DLB 116, 158

Hamilton, Eugene (Jacob) Lee
See Lee-Hamilton, Eugene (Jacob)

Hamilton, Franklin
See Silverberg, Robert

Hamilton, Gail
See Corcoran, Barbara (Asenath)

Hamilton, (Robert) Ian 1938-2001 . **CLC 191**
See also CA 106; 203; CANR 41, 67; CP 1,
2, 3, 4, 5, 6, 7; DLB 40, 155

Hamilton, Jane 1957- .... **CLC 179**
See also CA 147; CANR 85, 128; CN 7;
MTFW 2005

Hamilton, Mollie
See Kaye, M(ary) M(argaret)

Hamilton, (Anthony Walter) Patrick
1904-1962 .... **CLC 51**
See also CA 176; 113; DLB 10, 191

Hamilton, Virginia (Esther)
1936-2002 .... **CLC 26**
See also AAYA 2, 21; BW 2, 3; BYA 1, 2,
8; CA 25-28R; 206; CANR 20, 37, 73,
126; CLR 1, 11, 40; DAM MULT; DLB
33, 52; DLBY 2001; INT CANR-20;
JRDA; LAIT 5; MAICYA 1, 2; MAIC-
YAS 1; MTCW 1, 2; MTFW 2005; SATA
4, 56, 79, 123; SATA-Obit 132; WYA;
YAW

Hammett, (Samuel) Dashiell
1894-1961 .... **CLC 3, 5, 10, 19, 47; SSC
17**
See also AAYA 59; AITN 1; AMWS 4;
BPFB 2; CA 81-84; 157; CDALB
1929-1941; CMW 4; DA3; DLB 226, 280;
DLBD 6; DLBY 1996; EWL 3; LAIT 3;
MAL 5; MSW; MTCW 1, 2; MTFW
2005; NFS 21; RGAL 4; RGSF 2; TUS

Hammon, Jupiter 1720(?)-1800(?) .... **BLC 2;
NCLC 5; PC 16**
See also DAM MULT, POET; DLB 31, 50

Hammond, Keith
See Kuttner, Henry

Hamner, Earl (Henry), Jr. 1923- ...... **CLC 12**
See also AITN 2; CA 73-76; DLB 6

Hampton, Christopher (James)
1946- .... **CLC 4**
See also CA 25-28R; CD 5, 6; DLB 13;
MTCW 1

Hamsun, Knut .... **TCLC 2, 14, 49, 151**
See Pedersen, Knut
See also DLB 297; EW 8; EWL 3; RGWL
2, 3

Handke, Peter 1942- .... **CLC 5, 8, 10, 15, 38,
134; DC 17**
See also CA 77-80; CANR 33, 75, 104, 133;
CWW 2; DAM DRAM, NOV; DLB 85,
124; EWL 3; MTCW 1, 2; MTFW 2005;
TWA

Handy, W(illiam) C(hristopher)
1873-1958 .... **TCLC 97**
See also BW 3; CA 121; 167

Hanley, James 1901-1985 ..... **CLC 3, 5, 8, 13**
See also CA 73-76; 117; CANR 36; CBD;
CN 1, 2, 3; DLB 191; EWL 3; MTCW 1;
RGEL 2

Hannah, Barry 1942- .... **CLC 23, 38, 90**
See also BPFB 2; CA 108; 110; CANR 43,
68, 113; CN 4, 5, 6, 7; CSW; DLB 6, 234;
INT CA-110; MTCW 1; RGSF 2

Hannon, Ezra
See Hunter, Evan

Hansberry, Lorraine (Vivian)
1930-1965 ... **BLC 2; CLC 17, 62; DC 2**
See also AAYA 25; AFAW 1, 2; AMWS 4;
BW 1, 3; CA 109; 25-28R; CABS 3;
CAD; CANR 58; CDALB 1941-1968;
CWD; DA; DA3; DAB; DAC; DAM
DRAM, MST, MULT; DFS 2; DLB 7, 38;
EWL 3; FL 1:6; FW; LAIT 4; MAL 5;
MTCW 1, 2; MTFW 2005; RGAL 4; TUS

Hansen, Joseph 1923-2004 .... **CLC 38**
See Brock, Rose; Colton, James
See also BPFB 2; CA 29-32R; 233; CAAS
17; CANR 16, 44, 66, 125; CMW 4; DLB
226; GLL 1; INT CANR-16

Hansen, Martin A(lfred)
1909-1955 .... **TCLC 32**
See also CA 167; DLB 214; EWL 3

Hansen and Philipson eds. .... **CLC 65**

Hanson, Kenneth O(stlin) 1922- .... **CLC 13**
See also CA 53-56; CANR 7; CP 1, 2, 3, 4

Hardwick, Elizabeth (Bruce) 1916- . **CLC 13**
See also AMWS 3; CA 5-8R; CANR 3, 32,
70, 100, 139; CN 4, 5, 6; CSW; DA3;
DAM NOV; DLB 6; MAWW; MTCW 1,
2; MTFW 2005; TCLE 1:1

Hardy, Thomas 1840-1928 .... **PC 8; SSC 2,
60; TCLC 4, 10, 18, 32, 48, 53, 72, 143,
153; WLC**
See also BRW 6; BRWC 1, 2; BRWR 1;
CA 104; 123; CDBLB 1890-1914; DA;
DA3; DAB; DAC; DAM MST, NOV,
POET; DLB 18, 19, 135, 284; EWL 3;
EXPN; EXPP; LAIT 2; MTCW 1, 2;
MTFW 2005; NFS 3, 11, 15, 19; PFS 3,
4, 18; RGEL 2; RGSF 2; TEA; WLIT 4

Hare, David 1947- . **CLC 29, 58, 136; DC 26**
See also BRWS 4; CA 97-100; CANR 39,
91; CBD; CD 5, 6; DFS 4, 7, 16; DLB
13, 310; MTCW 1; TEA

Harewood, John
See Van Druten, John (William)

Harford, Henry
See Hudson, W(illiam) H(enry)

Hargrave, Leonie
See Disch, Thomas M(ichael)

**Hariri, Al- al-Qasim ibn 'Ali Abu
Muhammad al-Basri**
See al-Hariri, al-Qasim ibn 'Ali Abu Mu-
hammad al-Basri

Harjo, Joy 1951- ..... **CLC 83; NNAL; PC 27**
See also AMWS 12; CA 114; CANR 35,
67, 91, 129; CP 7; CWP; DAM MULT;
DLB 120, 175; EWL 3; MTCW 2; MTFW
2005; PFS 15; RGAL 4

Harlan, Louis R(udolph) 1922- .... **CLC 34**
See also CA 21-24R; CANR 25, 55, 80

Harling, Robert 1951(?)- .... **CLC 53**
See also CA 147

Harmon, William (Ruth) 1938- .... **CLC 38**
See also CA 33-36R; CANR 14, 32, 35;
SATA 65

Harper, F. E. W.
See Harper, Frances Ellen Watkins

Harper, Frances E. W.
See Harper, Frances Ellen Watkins

Harper, Frances E. Watkins
See Harper, Frances Ellen Watkins

Harper, Frances Ellen
See Harper, Frances Ellen Watkins

Harper, Frances Ellen Watkins
1825-1911 ..... **BLC 2; PC 21; TCLC 14**
See also AFAW 1, 2; BW 1, 3; CA 111; 125;
CANR 79; DAM MULT, POET; DLB 50,
221; MAWW; RGAL 4

Harper, Michael S(teven) 1938- ... **CLC 7, 22**
See also AFAW 2; BW 1; CA 33-36R; 224;
CAAE 224; CANR 24, 108; CP 2, 3, 4, 5,
6, 7; DLB 41; RGAL 4; TCLE 1:1

Harper, Mrs. F. E. W.
See Harper, Frances Ellen Watkins

Harpur, Charles 1813-1868 .... **NCLC 114**
See also DLB 230; RGEL 2

Harris, Christie
See Harris, Christie (Lucy) Irwin

Harris, Christie (Lucy) Irwin
1907-2002 .... **CLC 12**
See also CA 5-8R; CANR 6, 83; CLR 47;
DLB 88; JRDA; MAICYA 1, 2; SAAS 10;
SATA 6, 74; SATA-Essay 116

Harris, Frank 1856-1931 .... **TCLC 24**
See also CA 109; 150; CANR 80; DLB 156,
197; RGEL 2

Harris, George Washington
1814-1869 .... **NCLC 23, 165**
See also DLB 3, 11, 248; RGAL 4

Harris, Joel Chandler 1848-1908 ..... **SSC 19;
TCLC 2**
See also CA 104; 137; CANR 80; CLR 49;
DLB 11, 23, 42, 78, 91; LAIT 2; MAI-
CYA 1, 2; RGSF 2; SATA 100; WCH;
YABC 1

**Harris, John (Wyndham Parkes Lucas)
Beynon** 1903-1969
See Wyndham, John
See also CA 102; 89-92; CANR 84; SATA
118; SFW 4

Harris, MacDonald .... **CLC 9**
See Heiney, Donald (William)

Harris, Mark 1922- .... **CLC 19**
See also CA 5-8R; CAAS 3; CANR 2, 55,
83; CN 1, 2, 3, 4, 5, 6, 7; DLB 2; DLBY
1980

Harris, Norman .... **CLC 65**

Harris, (Theodore) Wilson 1921- .... **CLC 25,
159**
See also BRWS 5; BW 2, 3; CA 65-68;
CAAS 16; CANR 11, 27, 69, 114; CD-
WLB 3; CN 1, 2, 3, 4, 5, 6, 7; CP 1, 2, 3,
4, 5, 6, 7; DLB 117; EWL 3; MTCW 1;
RGEL 2

Harrison, Barbara Grizzuti
1934-2002 .... **CLC 144**
See also CA 77-80; 205; CANR 15, 48; INT
CANR-15

Ivask, Ivar Vidrik 1927-1992 .... **CLC 14**
　　See also CA 37-40R; 139; CANR 24
Ives, Morgan
　　See Bradley, Marion Zimmer
　　See also GLL 1
Izumi Shikibu c. 973-c. 1034 .... **CMLC 33**
J. R. S.
　　See Gogarty, Oliver St. John
Jabran, Kahlil
　　See Gibran, Kahlil
Jabran, Khalil
　　See Gibran, Kahlil
Jackson, Daniel
　　See Wingrove, David (John)
Jackson, Helen Hunt 1830-1885 .... **NCLC 90**
　　See also DLB 42, 47, 186, 189; RGAL 4
Jackson, Jesse 1908-1983 .... **CLC 12**
　　See also BW 1; CA 25-28R; 109; CANR
　　27; CLR 28; CWRI 5; MAICYA 1, 2;
　　SATA 2, 29; SATA-Obit 48
Jackson, Laura (Riding) 1901-1991 .... **PC 44**
　　See Riding, Laura
　　See also CA 65-68; 135; CANR 28, 89;
　　DLB 48
Jackson, Sam
　　See Trumbo, Dalton
Jackson, Sara
　　See Wingrove, David (John)
Jackson, Shirley 1919-1965 . **CLC 11, 60, 87;**
　　　SSC 9, 39; WLC
　　See also AAYA 9; AMWS 9; BPFB 2; CA
　　1-4R; 25-28R; CANR 4, 52; CDALB
　　1941-1968; DA; DA3; DAC; DAM MST;
　　DLB 6, 234; EXPS; HGG; LAIT 4; MAL
　　5; MTFW 2005; RGAL 4; RGSF 2;
　　RGSF 2; SATA 2; SSFS 1; SUFW 1, 2
Jacob, (Cyprien-)Max 1876-1944 .... **TCLC 6**
　　See also CA 104; 193; DLB 258; EWL 3;
　　GFL 1789 to the Present; GLL 2; RGWL
　　2, 3
Jacobs, Harriet A(nn)
　　　1813(?)-1897 .... **NCLC 67, 162**
　　See also AFAW 1, 2; DLB 239; FL 1:3; FW;
　　LAIT 2; RGAL 4
Jacobs, Jim 1942- .... **CLC 12**
　　See also CA 97-100; INT CA-97-100
Jacobs, W(illiam) W(ymark)
　　　1863-1943 .... **SSC 73; TCLC 22**
　　See also CA 121; 167; DLB 135; EXPS;
　　HGG; RGEL 2; RGSF 2; SSFS 2; SUFW
　　1
Jacobsen, Jens Peter 1847-1885 .... **NCLC 34**
Jacobsen, Josephine (Winder)
　　　1908-2003 .... **CLC 48, 102; PC 62**
　　See also CA 33-36R; 218; CAAS 18; CANR
　　23, 48; CCA 1; CP 2, 3, 4, 5, 6, 7; DLB
　　244; PFS 23; TCLE 1:1
Jacobson, Dan 1929- .... **CLC 4, 14**
　　See also AFW; CA 1-4R; CANR 2, 25, 66;
　　CN 1, 2, 3, 4, 5, 6, 7; DLB 14, 207, 225,
　　319; EWL 3; MTCW 1; RGSF 2
Jacqueline
　　See Carpentier (y Valmont), Alejo
Jacques de Vitry c. 1160-1240 ...... **CMLC 63**
　　See also DLB 208
Jagger, Michael Philip
　　See Jagger, Mick
Jagger, Mick 1943- .... **CLC 17**
　　See also CA 239
Jahiz, al- c. 780-c. 869 .... **CMLC 25**
　　See also DLB 311
Jakes, John (William) 1932- .... **CLC 29**
　　See also AAYA 32; BEST 89:4; BPFB 2;
　　CA 57-60, 214; CAAE 214; CANR 10,
　　43, 66, 111, 142; CPW; CSW; DA3; DAM
　　NOV, POP; DLB 278; DLBY 1983;
　　FANT; INT CANR-10; MTCW 1, 2;
　　MTFW 2005; RHW; SATA 62; SFW 4;
　　TCWW 1, 2

James I 1394-1437 .... **LC 20**
　　See also RGEL 2
James, Andrew
　　See Kirkup, James
James, C(yril) L(ionel) R(obert)
　　　1901-1989 .... **BLCS; CLC 33**
　　See also BW 2; CA 117; 125; 128; CANR
　　62; CN 1, 2, 3, 4; DLB 125; MTCW 1
James, Daniel (Lewis) 1911-1988
　　See Santiago, Danny
　　See also CA 174; 125
James, Dynely
　　See Mayne, William (James Carter)
James, Henry Sr. 1811-1882 .... **NCLC 53**
James, Henry 1843-1916 .... **SSC 8, 32, 47;**
　　　TCLC 2, 11, 24, 40, 47, 64, 171; WLC
　　See also AMW; AMWC 1; AMWR 1; BPFB
　　2; BRW 6; CA 104; 132; CDALB 1865-
　　1917; DA; DA3; DAB; DAC; DAM MST,
　　NOV; DLB 12, 71, 74, 189; DLBD 13;
　　EWL 3; EXPS; GL 2; HGG; LAIT 2;
　　MAL 5; MTCW 1, 2; MTFW 2005; NFS
　　12, 16, 19; RGAL 4; RGEL 2; RGSF 2;
　　SSFS 9; SUFW 1; TUS
James, M. R.
　　See James, Montague (Rhodes)
　　See also DLB 156, 201
James, Montague (Rhodes)
　　　1862-1936 .... **SSC 16; TCLC 6**
　　See James, M. R.
　　See also CA 104; 203; HGG; RGEL 2;
　　RGSF 2; SUFW 1
James, P. D. .... **CLC 18, 46, 122**
　　See White, Phyllis Dorothy James
　　See also BEST 90:2; BPFB 2; BRWS 4;
　　CDBLB 1960 to Present; CN 4, 5, 6; DLB
　　87, 276; DLBD 17; MSW
James, Philip
　　See Moorcock, Michael (John)
James, Samuel
　　See Stephens, James
James, Seumas
　　See Stephens, James
James, Stephen
　　See Stephens, James
James, William 1842-1910 .... **TCLC 15, 32**
　　See also AMW; CA 109; 193; DLB 270,
　　284; MAL 5; NCFS 5; RGAL 4
Jameson, Anna 1794-1860 .... **NCLC 43**
　　See also DLB 99, 166
Jameson, Fredric (R.) 1934- .... **CLC 142**
　　See also CA 196; DLB 67; LMFS 2
James VI of Scotland 1566-1625 .... **LC 109**
　　See also DLB 151, 172
Jami, Nur al-Din 'Abd al-Rahman
　　　1414-1492 .... **LC 9**
Jammes, Francis 1868-1938 .... **TCLC 75**
　　See also CA 198; EWL 3; GFL 1789 to the
　　Present
Jandl, Ernst 1925-2000 .... **CLC 34**
　　See also CA 200; EWL 3
Janowitz, Tama 1957- .... **CLC 43, 145**
　　See also CA 106; CANR 52, 89, 129; CN
　　5, 6, 7; CPW; DAM POP; DLB 292;
　　MTFW 2005
Japrisot, Sebastien 1931- .... **CLC 90**
　　See Rossi, Jean-Baptiste
　　See also CMW 4; NFS 18
Jarrell, Randall 1914-1965 .... **CLC 1, 2, 6, 9,**
　　　13, 49; PC 41
　　See also AMW; BYA 5; CA 5-8R; 25-28R;
　　CABS 2; CANR 6, 34; CDALB 1941-
　　1968; CLR 6; CWRI 5; DAM POET;
　　DLB 48, 52; EWL 3; EXPP; MAICYA 1,
　　2; MAL 5; MTCW 1, 2; PAB; PFS 2;
　　RGAL 4; SATA 7

Jarry, Alfred 1873-1907 .... **SSC 20; TCLC 2,**
　　　14, 147
　　See also CA 104; 153; DA3; DAM DRAM;
　　DFS 8; DLB 192, 258; EW 9; EWL 3;
　　GFL 1789 to the Present; RGWL 2, 3;
　　TWA
Jarvis, E. K.
　　See Ellison, Harlan (Jay)
Jawien, Andrzej
　　See John Paul II, Pope
Jaynes, Roderick
　　See Coen, Ethan
Jeake, Samuel, Jr.
　　See Aiken, Conrad (Potter)
Jean Paul 1763-1825 .... **NCLC 7**
Jefferies, (John) Richard
　　　1848-1887 .... **NCLC 47**
　　See also DLB 98, 141; RGEL 2; SATA 16;
　　SFW 4
Jeffers, (John) Robinson 1887-1962 .. **CLC 2,**
　　　3, 11, 15, 54; PC 17; WLC
　　See also AMWS 2; CA 85-88; CANR 35;
　　CDALB 1917-1929; DA; DAC; DAM
　　MST, POET; DLB 45, 212; EWL 3; MAL
　　5; MTCW 1, 2; MTFW 2005; PAB; PFS
　　3, 4; RGAL 4
Jefferson, Janet
　　See Mencken, H(enry) L(ouis)
Jefferson, Thomas 1743-1826 . **NCLC 11, 103**
　　See also AAYA 54; ANW; CDALB 1640-
　　1865; DA3; DLB 31, 183; LAIT 1; RGAL
　　4
Jeffrey, Francis 1773-1850 .... **NCLC 33**
　　See Francis, Lord Jeffrey
Jelakowitch, Ivan
　　See Heijermans, Herman
Jelinek, Elfriede 1946- .... **CLC 169**
　　See also AAYA 68; CA 154; DLB 85; FW
Jellicoe, (Patricia) Ann 1927- .... **CLC 27**
　　See also CA 85-88; CBD; CD 5, 6; CWD;
　　CWRI 5; DLB 13, 233; FW
Jelloun, Tahar ben 1944- .... **CLC 180**
　　See Ben Jelloun, Tahar
　　See also CA 162; CANR 100
Jemyma
　　See Holley, Marietta
Jen, Gish .... **AAL; CLC 70, 198**
　　See Jen, Lillian
　　See also AMWC 2; CN 7; DLB 312
Jen, Lillian 1955-
　　See Jen, Gish
　　See also CA 135; CANR 89, 130
Jenkins, (John) Robin 1912- .... **CLC 52**
　　See also CA 1-4R; CANR 1, 135; CN 1, 2,
　　3, 4, 5, 6, 7; DLB 14, 271
Jennings, Elizabeth (Joan)
　　　1926-2001 .... **CLC 5, 14, 131**
　　See also BRWS 5; CA 61-64; 200; CAAS
　　5; CANR 8, 39, 66, 127; CP 1, 2, 3, 4, 5,
　　6, 7; CWP; DLB 27; EWL 3; MTCW 1;
　　SATA 66
Jennings, Waylon 1937-2002 .... **CLC 21**
Jensen, Johannes V(ilhelm)
　　　1873-1950 .... **TCLC 41**
　　See also CA 170; DLB 214; EWL 3; RGWL
　　3
Jensen, Laura (Linnea) 1948- .... **CLC 37**
　　See also CA 103
Jerome, Saint 345-420 .... **CMLC 30**
　　See also RGWL 3
Jerome, Jerome K(lapka)
　　　1859-1927 .... **TCLC 23**
　　See also CA 119; 177; DLB 10, 34, 135;
　　RGEL 2
Jerrold, Douglas William
　　　1803-1857 .... **NCLC 2**
　　See also DLB 158, 159; RGEL 2

Jordan, June (Meyer)
  1936-2002 .. **BLCS; CLC 5, 11, 23, 114; PC 38**
    See also AAYA 2, 66; AFAW 1, 2; BW 2, 3; CA 33-36R; 206; CANR 25, 70, 114; CLR 10; CP 3, 4, 5, 6, 7; CWP; DAM MULT, POET; DLB 38; GLL 2; LAIT 5; MAICYA 1, 2; MTCW 1; SATA 4, 136; YAW

Jordan, Neil (Patrick) 1950- .... **CLC 110**
    See also CA 124; 130; CANR 54; CN 4, 5, 6, 7; GLL 2; INT CA-130

Jordan, Pat(rick M.) 1941- .... **CLC 37**
    See also CA 33-36R; CANR 121

Jorgensen, Ivar
    See Ellison, Harlan (Jay)

Jorgenson, Ivar
    See Silverberg, Robert

Joseph, George Ghevarughese .... **CLC 70**

Josephson, Mary
    See O'Doherty, Brian

Josephus, Flavius c. 37-100 .... **CMLC 13**
    See also AW 2; DLB 176

Josiah Allen's Wife
    See Holley, Marietta

Josipovici, Gabriel (David) 1940- ...... **CLC 6, 43, 153**
    See also CA 37-40R; 224; CAAE 224; CAAS 8; CANR 47, 84; CN 3, 4, 5, 6, 7; DLB 14, 319

Joubert, Joseph 1754-1824 .... **NCLC 9**

Jouve, Pierre Jean 1887-1976 .... **CLC 47**
    See also CA 65-68; DLB 258; EWL 3

Jovine, Francesco 1902-1950 .... **TCLC 79**
    See also DLB 264; EWL 3

Joyce, James (Augustine Aloysius)
  1882-1941 .... **DC 16; PC 22; SSC 3, 26, 44, 64; TCLC 3, 8, 16, 35, 52, 159; WLC**
    See also AAYA 42; BRW 7; BRWC 1; BRWR 1; BYA 11, 13; CA 104; 126; CD-BLB 1914-1945; DA; DA3; DAB; DAC; DAM MST, NOV, POET; DLB 10, 19, 36, 162, 247; EWL 3; EXPN; EXPS; LAIT 3; LMFS 1, 2; MTCW 1, 2; MTFW 2005; NFS 7; RGSF 2; SSFS 1, 19; TEA; WLIT 4

Jozsef, Attila 1905-1937 .... **TCLC 22**
    See also CA 116; 230; CDWLB 4; DLB 215; EWL 3

Juana Ines de la Cruz, Sor
  1651(?)-1695 ...... **HLCS 1; LC 5; PC 24**
    See also DLB 305; FW; LAW; RGWL 2, 3; WLIT 1

Juana Inez de La Cruz, Sor
    See Juana Ines de la Cruz, Sor

Judd, Cyril
    See Kornbluth, C(yril) M.; Pohl, Frederik

Juenger, Ernst 1895-1998 .... **CLC 125**
    See Junger, Ernst
    See also CA 101; 167; CANR 21, 47, 106; DLB 56

Julian of Norwich 1342(?)-1416(?) . **LC 6, 52**
    See also DLB 146; LMFS 1

Julius Caesar 100B.C.-44B.C.
    See Caesar, Julius
    See also CDWLB 1; DLB 211

Junger, Ernst
    See Juenger, Ernst
    See also CDWLB 2; EWL 3; RGWL 2, 3

Junger, Sebastian 1962- .... **CLC 109**
    See also AAYA 28; CA 165; CANR 130; MTFW 2005

Juniper, Alex
    See Hospital, Janette Turner

Junius
    See Luxemburg, Rosa

Junzaburo, Nishiwaki
    See Nishiwaki, Junzaburo
    See also EWL 3

Just, Ward (Swift) 1935- .... **CLC 4, 27**
    See also CA 25-28R; CANR 32, 87; CN 6, 7; INT CANR-32

Justice, Donald (Rodney)
  1925-2004 .... **CLC 6, 19, 102; PC 64**
    See also AMWS 7; CA 5-8R; 230; CANR 26, 54, 74, 121, 122; CP 1, 2, 3, 4, 5, 6, 7; CSW; DAM POET; DLBY 1983; EWL 3; INT CANR-26; MAL 5; MTCW 2; PFS 14; TCLE 1:1

Juvenal c. 60-c. 130 .... **CMLC 8**
    See also AW 2; CDWLB 1; DLB 211; RGWL 2, 3

Juvenis
    See Bourne, Randolph S(illiman)

K., Alice
    See Knapp, Caroline

Kabakov, Sasha .... **CLC 59**

Kabir 1398(?)-1448(?) .... **LC 109; PC 56**
    See also RGWL 2, 3

Kacew, Romain 1914-1980
    See Gary, Romain
    See also CA 108; 102

Kadare, Ismail 1936- .... **CLC 52, 190**
    See also CA 161; EWL 3; RGWL 3

Kadohata, Cynthia (Lynn)
  1956(?)- .... **CLC 59, 122**
    See also CA 140; CANR 124; SATA 155

Kafka, Franz 1883-1924 ... **SSC 5, 29, 35, 60; TCLC 2, 6, 13, 29, 47, 53, 112; WLC**
    See also AAYA 31; BPFB 2; CA 105; 126; CDWLB 2; DA; DA3; DAB; DAC; DAM MST, NOV; DLB 81; EW 9; EWL 3; EXPS; LATS 1:1; LMFS 2; MTCW 1, 2; MTFW 2005; NFS 7; RGSF 2; RGWL 2, 3; SFW 4; SSFS 3, 7, 12; TWA

Kahanovitsch, Pinkhes
    See Der Nister

Kahn, Roger 1927- .... **CLC 30**
    See also CA 25-28R; CANR 44, 69; DLB 171; SATA 37

Kain, Saul
    See Sassoon, Siegfried (Lorraine)

Kaiser, Georg 1878-1945 .... **TCLC 9**
    See also CA 106; 190; CDWLB 2; DLB 124; EWL 3; LMFS 2; RGWL 2, 3

Kaledin, Sergei .... **CLC 59**

Kaletski, Alexander 1946- .... **CLC 39**
    See also CA 118; 143

Kalidasa fl. c. 400-455 .... **CMLC 9; PC 22**
    See also RGWL 2, 3

Kallman, Chester (Simon)
  1921-1975 .... **CLC 2**
    See also CA 45-48; 53-56; CANR 3; CP 1, 2

Kaminsky, Melvin 1926-
    See Brooks, Mel
    See also CA 65-68; CANR 16; DFS 21

Kaminsky, Stuart M(elvin) 1934- ..... **CLC 59**
    See also CA 73-76; CANR 29, 53, 89; CMW 4

Kamo no Chomei 1153(?)-1216 .... **CMLC 66**
    See also DLB 203

Kamo no Nagaakira
    See Kamo no Chomei

Kandinsky, Wassily 1866-1944 .... **TCLC 92**
    See also AAYA 64; CA 118; 155

Kane, Francis
    See Robbins, Harold

Kane, Henry 1918-
    See Queen, Ellery
    See also CA 156; CMW 4

Kane, Paul
    See Simon, Paul (Frederick)

Kanin, Garson 1912-1999 .... **CLC 22**
    See also AITN 1; CA 5-8R; 177; CAD; CANR 7, 78; DLB 7; IDFW 3, 4

Kaniuk, Yoram 1930- .... **CLC 19**
    See also CA 134; DLB 299

Kant, Immanuel 1724-1804 ..... **NCLC 27, 67**
    See also DLB 94

Kantor, MacKinlay 1904-1977 .... **CLC 7**
    See also CA 61-64; 73-76; CANR 60, 63; CN 1, 2; DLB 9, 102; MAL 5; MTCW 2; RHW; TCWW 1, 2

Kanze Motokiyo
    See Zeami

Kaplan, David Michael 1946- .... **CLC 50**
    See also CA 187

Kaplan, James 1951- .... **CLC 59**
    See also CA 135; CANR 121

Karadzic, Vuk Stefanovic
  1787-1864 .... **NCLC 115**
    See also CDWLB 4; DLB 147

Karageorge, Michael
    See Anderson, Poul (William)

Karamzin, Nikolai Mikhailovich
  1766-1826 .... **NCLC 3**
    See also DLB 150; RGSF 2

Karapanou, Margarita 1946- .... **CLC 13**
    See also CA 101

Karinthy, Frigyes 1887-1938 .... **TCLC 47**
    See also CA 170; DLB 215; EWL 3

Karl, Frederick R(obert)
  1927-2004 .... **CLC 34**
    See also CA 5-8R; 226; CANR 3, 44, 143

Karr, Mary 1955- .... **CLC 188**
    See also AMWS 11; CA 151; CANR 100; MTFW 2005; NCFS 5

Kastel, Warren
    See Silverberg, Robert

Kataev, Evgeny Petrovich 1903-1942
    See Petrov, Evgeny
    See also CA 120

Kataphusin
    See Ruskin, John

Katz, Steve 1935- .... **CLC 47**
    See also CA 25-28R; CAAS 14, 64; CANR 12; CN 4, 5, 6, 7; DLBY 1983

Kauffman, Janet 1945- .... **CLC 42**
    See also CA 117; CANR 43, 84; DLB 218; DLBY 1986

Kaufman, Bob (Garnell) 1925-1986 . **CLC 49**
    See also BG 1:3; BW 1; CA 41-44R; 118; CANR 22; CP 1; DLB 16, 41

Kaufman, George S. 1889-1961 ...... **CLC 38; DC 17**
    See also CA 108; 93-96; DAM DRAM; DFS 1, 10; DLB 7; INT CA-108; MTCW 2; MTFW 2005; RGAL 4; TUS

Kaufman, Moises 1964- .... **DC 26**
    See also CA 211; DFS 22; MTFW 2005

Kaufman, Sue .... **CLC 3, 8**
    See Barondess, Sue K(aufman)

Kavafis, Konstantinos Petrou 1863-1933
    See Cavafy, C(onstantine) P(eter)
    See also CA 104

Kavan, Anna 1901-1968 .... **CLC 5, 13, 82**
    See also BRWS 7; CA 5-8R; CANR 6, 57; DLB 255; MTCW 1; RGEL 2; SFW 4

Kavanagh, Dan
    See Barnes, Julian (Patrick)

Kavanagh, Julie 1952- .... **CLC 119**
    See also CA 163

Kavanagh, Patrick (Joseph)
  1904-1967 .... **CLC 22; PC 33**
    See also BRWS 7; CA 123; 25-28R; DLB 15, 20; EWL 3; MTCW 1; RGEL 2

Kawabata, Yasunari 1899-1972 ..... **CLC 2, 5, 9, 18, 107; SSC 17**
See Kawabata Yasunari
See also CA 93-96; 33-36R; CANR 88; DAM MULT; MJW; MTCW 2; MTFW 2005; RGSF 2; RGWL 2, 3

Kawabata Yasunari
See Kawabata, Yasunari
See also DLB 180; EWL 3

Kaye, M(ary) M(argaret)
1908-2004 .... **CLC 28**
See also CA 89-92; 223; CANR 24, 60, 102, 142; MTCW 1, 2; MTFW 2005; RHW; SATA 62; SATA-Obit 152

Kaye, Mollie
See Kaye, M(ary) M(argaret)

Kaye-Smith, Sheila 1887-1956 .... **TCLC 20**
See also CA 118; 203; DLB 36

Kaymor, Patrice Maguilene
See Senghor, Leopold Sedar

Kazakov, Iurii Pavlovich
See Kazakov, Yuri Pavlovich
See also DLB 302

Kazakov, Yuri Pavlovich 1927-1982 . **SSC 43**
See Kazakov, Iurii Pavlovich; Kazakov, Yury
See also CA 5-8R; CANR 36; MTCW 1; RGSF 2

Kazakov, Yury
See Kazakov, Yuri Pavlovich
See also EWL 3

Kazan, Elia 1909-2003 .... **CLC 6, 16, 63**
See also CA 21-24R; 220; CANR 32, 78

Kazantzakis, Nikos 1883(?)-1957 .... **TCLC 2, 5, 33**
See also BPFB 2; CA 105; 132; DA3; EW 9; EWL 3; MTCW 1, 2; MTFW 2005; RGWL 2, 3

Kazin, Alfred 1915-1998 ..... **CLC 34, 38, 119**
See also AMWS 8; CA 1-4R; CAAS 7; CANR 1, 45, 79; DLB 67; EWL 3

Keane, Mary Nesta (Skrine) 1904-1996
See Keane, Molly
See also CA 108; 114; 151; RHW

Keane, Molly .... **CLC 31**
See Keane, Mary Nesta (Skrine)
See also CN 5, 6; INT CA-114; TCLE 1:1

Keates, Jonathan 1946(?)- .... **CLC 34**
See also CA 163; CANR 126

Keaton, Buster 1895-1966 .... **CLC 20**
See also CA 194

Keats, John 1795-1821 ...... **NCLC 8, 73, 121; PC 1; WLC**
See also AAYA 58; BRW 4; BRWR 1; CD-BLB 1789-1832; DA; DA3; DAB; DAC; DAM MST, POET; DLB 96, 110; EXPP; LMFS 1; PAB; PFS 1, 2, 3, 9, 17; RGEL 2; TEA; WLIT 3; WP

Keble, John 1792-1866 .... **NCLC 87**
See also DLB 32, 55; RGEL 2

Keene, Donald 1922- .... **CLC 34**
See also CA 1-4R; CANR 5, 119

Keillor, Garrison .... **CLC 40, 115**
See Keillor, Gary (Edward)
See also AAYA 2, 62; BEST 89:3; BPFB 2; DLBY 1987; EWL 3; SATA 58; TUS

Keillor, Gary (Edward) 1942-
See Keillor, Garrison
See also CA 111; 117; CANR 36, 59, 124; CPW; DA3; DAM POP; MTCW 1, 2; MTFW 2005

Keith, Carlos
See Lewton, Val

Keith, Michael
See Hubbard, L(afayette) Ron(ald)

Keller, Gottfried 1819-1890 .... **NCLC 2; SSC 26**
See also CDWLB 2; DLB 129; EW; RGSF 2; RGWL 2, 3

Keller, Nora Okja 1965- .... **CLC 109**
See also CA 187

Kellerman, Jonathan 1949- .... **CLC 44**
See also AAYA 35; BEST 90:1; CA 106; CANR 29, 51; CMW 4; CPW; DA3; DAM POP; INT CANR-29

Kelley, William Melvin 1937- .... **CLC 22**
See also BW 1; CA 77-80; CANR 27, 83; CN 1, 2, 3, 4, 5, 6, 7; DLB 33; EWL 3

Kellogg, Marjorie 1922-2005 .... **CLC 2**
See also CA 81-84

Kellow, Kathleen
See Hibbert, Eleanor Alice Burford

Kelly, Lauren
See Oates, Joyce Carol

Kelly, M(ilton) T(errence) 1947- ...... **CLC 55**
See also CA 97-100; CAAS 22; CANR 19, 43, 84; CN 6

Kelly, Robert 1935- .... **SSC 50**
See also CA 17-20R; CAAS 19; CANR 47; CP 1, 2, 3, 4, 5, 6, 7; DLB 5, 130, 165

Kelman, James 1946- .... **CLC 58, 86**
See also BRWS 5; CA 148; CANR 85, 130; CN 5, 6, 7; DLB 194, 319; RGSF 2; WLIT 4

Kemal, Yasar
See Kemal, Yashar
See also CWW 2; EWL 3; WLIT 6

Kemal, Yashar 1923(?)- .... **CLC 14, 29**
See also CA 89-92; CANR 44

Kemble, Fanny 1809-1893 .... **NCLC 18**
See also DLB 32

Kemelman, Harry 1908-1996 .... **CLC 2**
See also AITN 1; BPFB 2; CA 9-12R; 155; CANR 6, 71; CMW 4; DLB 28

Kempe, Margery 1373(?)-1440(?) ... **LC 6, 56**
See also DLB 146; FL 1:1; RGEL 2

Kempis, Thomas a 1380-1471 .... **LC 11**

Kendall, Henry 1839-1882 .... **NCLC 12**
See also DLB 230

Keneally, Thomas (Michael) 1935- ... **CLC 5, 8, 10, 14, 19, 27, 43, 117**
See also BRWS 4; CA 85-88; CANR 10, 50, 74, 130; CN 1, 2, 3, 4, 5, 6, 7; CPW; DA3; DAM NOV; DLB 289, 299; EWL 3; MTCW 1, 2; MTFW 2005; NFS 17; RGEL 2; RHW

Kennedy, A(lison) L(ouise) 1965- ... **CLC 188**
See also CA 168; 213; CAAE 213; CANR 108; CD 5, 6; CN 6, 7; DLB 271; RGSF 2

Kennedy, Adrienne (Lita) 1931- .... **BLC 2; CLC 66; DC 5**
See also AFAW 2; BW 2, 3; CA 103; CAAS 20; CABS 3; CAD; CANR 26, 53, 82; CD 5, 6; DAM MULT; DFS 9; DLB 38; FW; MAL 5

Kennedy, John Pendleton
1795-1870 .... **NCLC 2**
See also DLB 3, 248, 254; RGAL 4

Kennedy, Joseph Charles 1929-
See Kennedy, X. J.
See also CA 1-4R; 201; CAAE 201; CANR 4, 30, 40; CWRI 5; MAICYA 2; MAIC-YAS 1; SATA 14, 86, 130; SATA-Essay 130

Kennedy, William (Joseph) 1928- ..... **CLC 6, 28, 34, 53**
See also AAYA 1; AMWS 7; BPFB 2; CA 85-88; CANR 14, 31, 76, 134; CN 4, 5, 6, 7; DA3; DAM NOV; DLB 143; DLBY 1985; EWL 3; INT CANR-31; MAL 5; MTCW 1, 2; MTFW 2005; SATA 57

Kennedy, X. J. .... **CLC 8, 42**
See Kennedy, Joseph Charles
See also AMWS 15; CAAS 9; CLR 27; CP 1, 2, 3, 4, 5, 6, 7; DLB 5; SAAS 22

Kenny, Maurice (Francis) 1929- ..... **CLC 87; NNAL**
See also CA 144; CAAS 22; CANR 143; DAM MULT; DLB 175

Kent, Kelvin
See Kuttner, Henry

Kenton, Maxwell
See Southern, Terry

Kenyon, Jane 1947-1995 .... **PC 57**
See also AAYA 63; AMWS 7; CA 118; 148; CANR 44, 69; CP 7; CWP; DLB 120; PFS 9, 17; RGAL 4

Kenyon, Robert O.
See Kuttner, Henry

Kepler, Johannes 1571-1630 .... **LC 45**

Ker, Jill
See Conway, Jill K(er)

Kerkow, H. C.
See Lewton, Val

Kerouac, Jack 1922-1969 ...... **CLC 1, 2, 3, 5, 14, 29, 61; TCLC 117; WLC**
See Kerouac, Jean-Louis Lebris de
See also AAYA 25; AMWC 1; AMWS 3; BG 3; BPFB 2; CDALB 1941-1968; CP 1; CPW; DLB 2, 16, 237; DLBD 3; DLBY 1995; EWL 3; GLL 1; LATS 1:2; LMFS 2; MAL 5; NFS 8; RGAL 4; TUS; WP

Kerouac, Jean-Louis Lebris de 1922-1969
See Kerouac, Jack
See also AITN 1; CA 5-8R; 25-28R; CANR 26, 54, 95; DA; DA3; DAB; DAC; DAM MST, NOV, POET, POP; MTCW 1, 2; MTFW 2005

Kerr, (Bridget) Jean (Collins)
1923(?)-2003 .... **CLC 22**
See also CA 5-8R; 212; CANR 7; INT CANR-7

Kerr, M. E. .... **CLC 12, 35**
See Meaker, Marijane (Agnes)
See also AAYA 2, 23; BYA 1, 7, 8; CLR 29; SAAS 1; WYA

Kerr, Robert .... **CLC 55**

Kerrigan, (Thomas) Anthony 1918- .. **CLC 4, 6**
See also CA 49-52; CAAS 11; CANR 4

Kerry, Lois
See Duncan, Lois

Kesey, Ken (Elton) 1935-2001 ... **CLC 1, 3, 6, 11, 46, 64, 184; WLC**
See also AAYA 25; BG 1:3; BPFB 2; CA 1-4R; 204; CANR 22, 38, 66, 124; CDALB 1968-1988; CN 1, 2, 3, 4, 5, 6, 7; CPW; DA; DA3; DAB; DAC; DAM MST, NOV, POP; DLB 2, 16, 206; EWL 3; EXPN; LAIT 4; MAL 5; MTCW 1, 2; MTFW 2005; NFS 2; RGAL 4; SATA 66; SATA-Obit 131; TUS; YAW

Kesselring, Joseph (Otto)
1902-1967 .... **CLC 45**
See also CA 150; DAM DRAM, MST; DFS 20

Kessler, Jascha (Frederick) 1929- ...... **CLC 4**
See also CA 17-20R; CANR 8, 48, 111; CP 1

Kettelkamp, Larry (Dale) 1933- .... **CLC 12**
See also CA 29-32R; CANR 16; SAAS 3; SATA 2

Key, Ellen (Karolina Sofia)
1849-1926 .... **TCLC 65**
See also DLB 259

Keyber, Conny
See Fielding, Henry

Keyes, Daniel 1927- .... **CLC 80**
See also AAYA 23; BYA 11; CA 17-20R, 181; CAAE 181; CANR 10, 26, 54, 74; DA; DA3; DAC; DAM MST, NOV; EXPN; LAIT 4; MTCW 2; MTFW 2005; NFS 2; SATA 37; SFW 4

Keynes, John Maynard
1883-1946 .... **TCLC 64**
See also CA 114; 162, 163; DLBD 10;
MTCW 2; MTFW 2005

Khanshendel, Chiron
See Rose, Wendy

Khayyam, Omar 1048-1131 ... **CMLC 11; PC 8**
See Omar Khayyam
See also DA3; DAM POET; WLIT 6

Kherdian, David 1931- .... **CLC 6, 9**
See also AAYA 42; CA 21-24R, 192; CAAE
192; CAAS 2; CANR 39, 78; CLR 24;
JRDA; LAIT 3; MAICYA 1, 2; SATA 16,
74; SATA-Essay 125

Khlebnikov, Velimir .... **TCLC 20**
See Khlebnikov, Viktor Vladimirovich
See also DLB 295; EW 10; EWL 3; RGWL
2, 3

Khlebnikov, Viktor Vladimirovich 1885-1922
See Khlebnikov, Velimir
See also CA 117; 217

Khodasevich, Vladislav (Felitsianovich)
1886-1939 .... **TCLC 15**
See also CA 115; DLB 317; EWL 3

Kielland, Alexander Lange
1849-1906 .... **TCLC 5**
See also CA 104

Kiely, Benedict 1919- ... **CLC 23, 43; SSC 58**
See also CA 1-4R; CANR 2, 84; CN 1, 2,
3, 4, 5, 6, 7; DLB 15, 319; TCLE 1:1

Kienzle, William X(avier)
1928-2001 .... **CLC 25**
See also CA 93-96; 203; CAAS 1; CANR
9, 31, 59, 111; CMW 4; DA3; DAM POP;
INT CANR-31; MSW; MTCW 1, 2;
MTFW 2005

Kierkegaard, Soren 1813-1855 ..... **NCLC 34, 78, 125**
See also DLB 300; EW 6; LMFS 2; RGWL
3; TWA

Kieslowski, Krzysztof 1941-1996 .... **CLC 120**
See also CA 147; 151

Killens, John Oliver 1916-1987 .... **CLC 10**
See also BW 2; CA 77-80; 123; CAAS 2;
CANR 26; CN 1, 2, 3, 4; DLB 33; EWL
3

Killigrew, Anne 1660-1685 .... **LC 4, 73**
See also DLB 131

Killigrew, Thomas 1612-1683 .... **LC 57**
See also DLB 58; RGEL 2

Kim
See Simenon, Georges (Jacques Christian)

Kincaid, Jamaica 1949- ...... **BLC 2; CLC 43, 68, 137; SSC 72**
See also AAYA 13, 56; AFAW 2; AMWS 7;
BRWS 7; BW 2, 3; CA 125; CANR 47,
59, 95, 133; CDALBS; CDWLB 3; CLR
63; CN 4, 5, 6, 7; DA3; DAM MULT,
NOV; DLB 157, 227; DNFS 1; EWL 3;
EXPS; FW; LATS 1:2; LMFS 2; MAL 5;
MTCW 2; MTFW 2005; NCFS 1; NFS 3;
SSFS 5, 7; TUS; WWE 1; YAW

King, Francis (Henry) 1923- .... **CLC 8, 53, 145**
See also CA 1-4R; CANR 1, 33, 86; CN 1,
2, 3, 4, 5, 6, 7; DAM NOV; DLB 15, 139;
MTCW 1

King, Kennedy
See Brown, George Douglas

King, Martin Luther, Jr. 1929-1968 . **BLC 2; CLC 83; WLCS**
See also BW 2, 3; CA 25-28; CANR 27,
44; CAP 2; DA; DA3; DAB; DAC; DAM
MST, MULT; LAIT 5; LATS 1:2; MTCW
1, 2; MTFW 2005; SATA 14

King, Stephen 1947- .... **CLC 12, 26, 37, 61, 113; SSC 17, 55**
See also AAYA 1, 17; AMWS 5; BEST
90:1; BPFB 2; CA 61-64; CANR 1, 30,
52, 76, 119, 134; CN 7; CPW; DA3; DAM
NOV, POP; DLB 143; DLBY 1980; HGG;
JRDA; LAIT 5; MTCW 1, 2; MTFW
2005; RGAL 4; SATA 9, 55, 161; SUFW
1, 2; WYAS 1; YAW

King, Stephen Edwin
See King, Stephen

King, Steve
See King, Stephen

King, Thomas 1943- .... **CLC 89, 171; NNAL**
See also CA 144; CANR 95; CCA 1; CN 6,
7; DAC; DAM MULT; DLB 175; SATA
96

Kingman, Lee .... **CLC 17**
See Natti, (Mary) Lee
See also CWRI 5; SAAS 3; SATA 1, 67

Kingsley, Charles 1819-1875 .... **NCLC 35**
See also CLR 77; DLB 21, 32, 163, 178,
190; FANT; MAICYA 2; MAICYAS 1;
RGEL 2; WCH; YABC 2

Kingsley, Henry 1830-1876 .... **NCLC 107**
See also DLB 21, 230; RGEL 2

Kingsley, Sidney 1906-1995 .... **CLC 44**
See also CA 85-88; 147; CAD; DFS 14, 19;
DLB 7; MAL 5; RGAL 4

Kingsolver, Barbara 1955- .... **CLC 55, 81, 130, 216**
See also AAYA 15; AMWS 7; CA 129; 134;
CANR 60, 96, 133; CDALBS; CN 7;
CPW; CSW; DA3; DAM POP; DLB 206;
INT CA-134; LAIT 5; MTCW 2; MTFW
2005; NFS 5, 10, 12; RGAL 4; TCLE 1:1

Kingston, Maxine (Ting Ting) Hong
1940- .... **AAL; CLC 12, 19, 58, 121; WLCS**
See also AAYA 8, 55; AMWS 5; BPFB 2;
CA 69-72; CANR 13, 38, 74, 87, 128;
CDALBS; CN 6, 7; DA3; DAM MULT,
NOV; DLB 173, 212, 312; DLBY 1980;
EWL 3; FL 1:6; FW; INT CANR-13;
LAIT 5; MAL 5; MAWW; MTCW 1, 2;
MTFW 2005; NFS 6; RGAL 4; SATA 53;
SSFS 3; TCWW 2

Kinnell, Galway 1927- ..... **CLC 1, 2, 3, 5, 13, 29, 129; PC 26**
See also AMWS 3; CA 9-12R; CANR 10,
34, 66, 116, 138; CP 1, 2, 3, 4, 5, 6, 7;
DLB 5; DLBY 1987; EWL 3; INT CANR-
34; MAL 5; MTCW 1, 2; MTFW 2005;
PAB; PFS 9; RGAL 4; TCLE 1:1; WP

Kinsella, Thomas 1928- .... **CLC 4, 19, 138; PC 69**
See also BRWS 5; CA 17-20R; CANR 15,
122; CP 1, 2, 3, 4, 5, 6, 7; DLB 27; EWL
3; MTCW 1, 2; MTFW 2005; RGEL 2;
TEA

Kinsella, W(illiam) P(atrick) 1935- . **CLC 27, 43, 166**
See also AAYA 7, 60; BPFB 2; CA 97-100;
222; CAAE 222; CAAS 7; CANR 21, 35,
66, 75, 129; CN 4, 5, 6, 7; CPW; DAC;
DAM NOV, POP; FANT; INT CANR-21;
LAIT 5; MTCW 1, 2; MTFW 2005; NFS
15; RGSF 2

Kinsey, Alfred C(harles)
1894-1956 .... **TCLC 91**
See also CA 115; 170; MTCW 2

Kipling, (Joseph) Rudyard 1865-1936 . **PC 3; SSC 5, 54; TCLC 8, 17, 167; WLC**
See also AAYA 32; BRW 6; BRWC 1, 2;
BYA 4; CA 105; 120; CANR 33; CDBLB
1890-1914; CLR 39, 65; CWRI 5; DA;
DA3; DAB; DAC; DAM MST, POET;
DLB 19, 34, 141, 156; EWL 3; EXPS;
FANT; LAIT 3; LMFS 1; MAICYA 1, 2;

MTCW 1, 2; MTFW 2005; NFS 21; PFS
22; RGEL 2; RGSF 2; SATA 100; SFW
4; SSFS 8, 21; SUFW 1; TEA; WCH;
WLIT 4; YABC 2

Kircher, Athanasius 1602-1680 .... **LC 121**
See also DLB 164

Kirk, Russell (Amos) 1918-1994 .. **TCLC 119**
See also AITN 1; CA 1-4R; 145; CAAS 9;
CANR 1, 20, 60; HGG; INT CANR-20;
MTCW 1, 2

Kirkham, Dinah
See Card, Orson Scott

Kirkland, Caroline M. 1801-1864 . **NCLC 85**
See also DLB 3, 73, 74, 250, 254; DLBD
13

Kirkup, James 1918- .... **CLC 1**
See also CA 1-4R; CAAS 4; CANR 2; CP
1, 2, 3, 4, 5, 6, 7; DLB 27; SATA 12

Kirkwood, James 1930(?)-1989 .... **CLC 9**
See also AITN 2; CA 1-4R; 128; CANR 6,
40; GLL 2

Kirsch, Sarah 1935- .... **CLC 176**
See also CA 178; CWW 2; DLB 75; EWL
3

Kirshner, Sidney
See Kingsley, Sidney

Kis, Danilo 1935-1989 .... **CLC 57**
See also CA 109; 118; 129; CANR 61; CD-
WLB 4; DLB 181; EWL 3; MTCW 1;
RGSF 2; RGWL 2, 3

Kissinger, Henry A(lfred) 1923- ..... **CLC 137**
See also CA 1-4R; CANR 2, 33, 66, 109;
MTCW 1

Kivi, Aleksis 1834-1872 .... **NCLC 30**

Kizer, Carolyn (Ashley) 1925- ... **CLC 15, 39, 80; PC 66**
See also CA 65-68; CAAS 5; CANR 24,
70, 134; CP 1, 2, 3, 4, 5, 6, 7; CWP; DAM
POET; DLB 5, 169; EWL 3; MAL 5;
MTCW 2; MTFW 2005; PFS 18; TCLE
1:1

Klabund 1890-1928 .... **TCLC 44**
See also CA 162; DLB 66

Klappert, Peter 1942- .... **CLC 57**
See also CA 33-36R; CSW; DLB 5

Klein, A(braham) M(oses)
1909-1972 .... **CLC 19**
See also CA 101; 37-40R; CP 1; DAB;
DAC; DAM MST; DLB 68; EWL 3;
RGEL 2

Klein, Joe
See Klein, Joseph

Klein, Joseph 1946- .... **CLC 154**
See also CA 85-88; CANR 55

Klein, Norma 1938-1989 .... **CLC 30**
See also AAYA 2, 35; BPFB 2; BYA 6, 7,
8; CA 41-44R; 128; CANR 15, 37; CLR
2, 19; INT CANR-15; JRDA; MAICYA
1, 2; SAAS 1; SATA 7, 57; WYA; YAW

Klein, T(heodore) E(ibon) D(onald)
1947- .... **CLC 34**
See also CA 119; CANR 44, 75; HGG

Kleist, Heinrich von 1777-1811 ...... **NCLC 2, 37; SSC 22**
See also CDWLB 2; DAM DRAM; DLB
90; EW 5; RGSF 2; RGWL 2, 3

Klima, Ivan 1931- .... **CLC 56, 172**
See also CA 25-28R; CANR 17, 50, 91;
CDWLB 4; CWW 2; DAM NOV; DLB
232; EWL 3; RGWL 3

Klimentev, Andrei Platonovich
See Klimentov, Andrei Platonovich

Klimentov, Andrei Platonovich
1899-1951 .... **SSC 42; TCLC 14**
See Platonov, Andrei Platonovich; Platonov,
Andrey Platonovich
See also CA 108; 232

Kubrick, Stanley 1928-1999 .... **CLC 16; TCLC 112**
  See also AAYA 30; CA 81-84; 177; CANR 33; DLB 26

Kumin, Maxine (Winokur) 1925- ..... **CLC 5, 13, 28, 164; PC 15**
  See also AITN 2; AMWS 4; ANW; CA 1-4R; CAAS 8; CANR 1, 21, 69, 115, 140; CP 2, 3, 4, 5, 6, 7; CWP; DA3; DAM POET; DLB 5; EWL 3; EXPP; MTCW 1, 2; MTFW 2005; PAB; PFS 18; SATA 12

Kundera, Milan 1929- . **CLC 4, 9, 19, 32, 68, 115, 135; SSC 24**
  See also AAYA 2, 62; BPFB 2; CA 85-88; CANR 19, 52, 74, 144; CDWLB 4; CWW 2; DA3; DAM NOV; DLB 232; EW 13; EWL 3; MTCW 1, 2; MTFW 2005; NFS 18; RGSF 2; RGWL 3; SSFS 10

Kunene, Mazisi (Raymond) 1930- ... **CLC 85**
  See also BW 1, 3; CA 125; CANR 81; CP 1, 7; DLB 117

Kung, Hans .... **CLC 130**
  See Kung, Hans

Kung, Hans 1928-
  See Kung, Hans
  See also CA 53-56; CANR 66, 134; MTCW 1, 2; MTFW 2005

Kunikida Doppo 1869(?)-1908
  See Doppo, Kunikida
  See also DLB 180; EWL 3

Kunitz, Stanley (Jasspon) 1905- .. **CLC 6, 11, 14, 148; PC 19**
  See also AMWS 3; CA 41-44R; CANR 26, 57, 98; CP 1, 2, 3, 4, 5, 6, 7; DA3; DLB 48; INT CANR-26; MAL 5; MTCW 1, 2; MTFW 2005; PFS 11; RGAL 4

Kunze, Reiner 1933- .... **CLC 10**
  See also CA 93-96; CWW 2; DLB 75; EWL 3

Kuprin, Aleksander Ivanovich 1870-1938 .... **TCLC 5**
  See Kuprin, Aleksander Ivanovich; Kuprin, Alexandr Ivanovich
  See also CA 104; 182

Kuprin, Aleksandr Ivanovich
  See Kuprin, Aleksander Ivanovich
  See also DLB 295

Kuprin, Alexandr Ivanovich
  See Kuprin, Aleksander Ivanovich
  See also EWL 3

Kureishi, Hanif 1954- .. **CLC 64, 135; DC 26**
  See also BRWS 11; CA 139; CANR 113; CBD; CD 5, 6; CN 6, 7; DLB 194, 245; GLL 2; IDFW 4; WLIT 4; WWE 1

Kurosawa, Akira 1910-1998 ..... **CLC 16, 119**
  See also AAYA 11, 64; CA 101; 170; CANR 46; DAM MULT

Kushner, Tony 1956- .... **CLC 81, 203; DC 10**
  See also AAYA 61; AMWS 9; CA 144; CAD; CANR 74, 130; CD 5, 6; DA3; DAM DRAM; DFS 5; DLB 228; EWL 3; GLL 1; LAIT 5; MAL 5; MTCW 2; MTFW 2005; RGAL 4; SATA 160

Kuttner, Henry 1915-1958 .... **TCLC 10**
  See also CA 107; 157; DLB 8; FANT; SCFW 1, 2; SFW 4

Kutty, Madhavi
  See Das, Kamala

Kuzma, Greg 1944- .... **CLC 7**
  See also CA 33-36R; CANR 70

Kuzmin, Mikhail (Alekseevich) 1872(?)-1936 .... **TCLC 40**
  See also CA 170; DLB 295; EWL 3

Kyd, Thomas 1558-1594 .... **DC 3; LC 22**
  See also BRW 1; DAM DRAM; DFS 21; DLB 62; IDTP; LMFS 1; RGEL 2; TEA; WLIT 3

Kyprianos, Iossif
  See Samarakis, Antonis

L. S.
  See Stephen, Sir Leslie

Laȝamon
  See Layamon
  See also DLB 146

Labe, Louise 1521-1566 .... **LC 120**

Labrunie, Gerard
  See Nerval, Gerard de

La Bruyere, Jean de 1645-1696 .... **LC 17**
  See also DLB 268; EW 3; GFL Beginnings to 1789

Lacan, Jacques (Marie Emile) 1901-1981 .... **CLC 75**
  See also CA 121; 104; DLB 296; EWL 3; TWA

Laclos, Pierre-Ambroise Francois 1741-1803 .... **NCLC 4, 87**
  See also DLB 313; EW 4; GFL Beginnings to 1789; RGWL 2, 3

Lacolere, Francois
  See Aragon, Louis

La Colere, Francois
  See Aragon, Louis

La Deshabilleuse
  See Simenon, Georges (Jacques Christian)

Lady Gregory
  See Gregory, Lady Isabella Augusta (Persse)

Lady of Quality, A
  See Bagnold, Enid

La Fayette, Marie-(Madelaine Pioche de la Vergne) 1634-1693 .... **LC 2**
  See Lafayette, Marie-Madeleine
  See also GFL Beginnings to 1789; RGWL 2, 3

Lafayette, Marie-Madeleine
  See La Fayette, Marie-(Madelaine Pioche de la Vergne)
  See also DLB 268

Lafayette, Rene
  See Hubbard, L(afayette) Ron(ald)

La Flesche, Francis 1857(?)-1932 ...... **NNAL**
  See also CA 144; CANR 83; DLB 175

La Fontaine, Jean de 1621-1695 .... **LC 50**
  See also DLB 268; EW 3; GFL Beginnings to 1789; MAICYA 1, 2; RGWL 2, 3; SATA 18

Laforet, Carmen 1921-2004 .... **CLC 219**
  See also CWW 2; DLB 322; EWL 3

Laforgue, Jules 1860-1887 . **NCLC 5, 53; PC 14; SSC 20**
  See also DLB 217; EW 7; GFL 1789 to the Present; RGWL 2, 3

Lagerkvist, Paer (Fabian) 1891-1974 ..... **CLC 7, 10, 13, 54; TCLC 144**
  See Lagerkvist, Par
  See also CA 85-88; 49-52; DA3; DAM DRAM, NOV; MTCW 1, 2; MTFW 2005; TWA

Lagerkvist, Par .... **SSC 12**
  See Lagerkvist, Paer (Fabian)
  See also DLB 259; EW 10; EWL 3; RGSF 2; RGWL 2, 3

Lagerloef, Selma (Ottiliana Lovisa) .... **TCLC 4, 36**
  See Lagerlof, Selma (Ottiliana Lovisa)
  See also CA 108; MTCW 2

Lagerlof, Selma (Ottiliana Lovisa) 1858-1940
  See Lagerloef, Selma (Ottiliana Lovisa)
  See also CA 188; CLR 7; DLB 259; RGWL 2, 3; SATA 15; SSFS 18

La Guma, (Justin) Alex(ander) 1925-1985 . **BLCS; CLC 19; TCLC 140**
  See also AFW; BW 1, 3; CA 49-52; 118; CANR 25, 81; CDWLB 3; CN 1, 2, 3; CP 1; DAM NOV; DLB 117, 225; EWL 3; MTCW 1, 2; MTFW 2005; WLIT 2; WWE 1

Laidlaw, A. K.
  See Grieve, C(hristopher) M(urray)

Lainez, Manuel Mujica
  See Mujica Lainez, Manuel
  See also HW 1

Laing, R(onald) D(avid) 1927-1989 . **CLC 95**
  See also CA 107; 129; CANR 34; MTCW 1

Laishley, Alex
  See Booth, Martin

Lamartine, Alphonse (Marie Louis Prat) de 1790-1869 .... **NCLC 11; PC 16**
  See also DAM POET; DLB 217; GFL 1789 to the Present; RGWL 2, 3

Lamb, Charles 1775-1834 ..... **NCLC 10, 113; WLC**
  See also BRW 4; CDBLB 1789-1832; DA; DAB; DAC; DAM MST; DLB 93, 107, 163; RGEL 2; SATA 17; TEA

Lamb, Lady Caroline 1785-1828 ... **NCLC 38**
  See also DLB 116

Lamb, Mary Ann 1764-1847 .... **NCLC 125**
  See also DLB 163; SATA 17

Lame Deer 1903(?)-1976 .... **NNAL**
  See also CA 69-72

Lamming, George (William) 1927- ... **BLC 2; CLC 2, 4, 66, 144**
  See also BW 2, 3; CA 85-88; CANR 26, 76; CDWLB 3; CN 1, 2, 3, 4, 5, 6, 7; CP 1; DAM MULT; DLB 125; EWL 3; MTCW 1, 2; MTFW 2005; NFS 15; RGEL 2

L'Amour, Louis (Dearborn) 1908-1988 .... **CLC 25, 55**
  See also AAYA 16; AITN 2; BEST 89:2; BPFB 2; CA 1-4R; 125; CANR 3, 25, 40; CPW; DA3; DAM NOV, POP; DLB 206; DLBY 1980; MTCW 1, 2; MTFW 2005; RGAL 4; TCWW 1, 2

Lampedusa, Giuseppe (Tomasi) di .... **TCLC 13**
  See Tomasi di Lampedusa, Giuseppe
  See also CA 164; EW 11; MTCW 2; MTFW 2005; RGWL 2, 3

Lampman, Archibald 1861-1899 ... **NCLC 25**
  See also DLB 92; RGEL 2; TWA

Lancaster, Bruce 1896-1963 .... **CLC 36**
  See also CA 9-10; CANR 70; CAP 1; SATA 9

Lanchester, John 1962- .... **CLC 99**
  See also CA 194; DLB 267

Landau, Mark Alexandrovich
  See Aldanov, Mark (Alexandrovich)

Landau-Aldanov, Mark Alexandrovich
  See Aldanov, Mark (Alexandrovich)

Landis, Jerry
  See Simon, Paul (Frederick)

Landis, John 1950- .... **CLC 26**
  See also CA 112; 122; CANR 128

Landolfi, Tommaso 1908-1979 .... **CLC 11, 49**
  See also CA 127; 117; DLB 177; EWL 3

Landon, Letitia Elizabeth 1802-1838 .... **NCLC 15**
  See also DLB 96

Landor, Walter Savage 1775-1864 .... **NCLC 14**
  See also BRW 4; DLB 93, 107; RGEL 2

Landwirth, Heinz 1927-
  See Lind, Jakov
  See also CA 9-12R; CANR 7

Lane, Patrick 1939- .... **CLC 25**
  See also CA 97-100; CANR 54; CP 3, 4, 5, 6, 7; DAM POET; DLB 53; INT CA-97-100

Lang, Andrew 1844-1912 .... **TCLC 16**
  See also CA 114; 137; CANR 85; CLR 101; DLB 98, 141, 184; FANT; MAICYA 1, 2; RGEL 2; SATA 16; WCH

Leonov, Leonid (Maximovich)
1899-1994 .... **CLC 92**
See Leonov, Leonid Maksimovich
See also CA 129; CANR 76; DAM NOV;
EWL 3; MTCW 1, 2; MTFW 2005

Leonov, Leonid Maksimovich
See Leonov, Leonid (Maximovich)
See also DLB 272

Leopardi, (Conte) Giacomo
1798-1837 .... **NCLC 22, 129; PC 37**
See also EW 5; RGWL 2, 3; WLIT 7; WP

Le Reveler
See Artaud, Antonin (Marie Joseph)

Lerman, Eleanor 1952- .... **CLC 9**
See also CA 85-88; CANR 69, 124

Lerman, Rhoda 1936- .... **CLC 56**
See also CA 49-52; CANR 70

Lermontov, Mikhail Iur'evich
See Lermontov, Mikhail Yuryevich
See also DLB 205

Lermontov, Mikhail Yuryevich
1814-1841 .... **NCLC 5, 47, 126; PC 18**
See Lermontov, Mikhail Iur'evich
See also EW 6; RGWL 2, 3; TWA

Leroux, Gaston 1868-1927 .... **TCLC 25**
See also CA 108; 136; CANR 69; CMW 4;
MTFW 2005; NFS 20; SATA 65

Lesage, Alain-Rene 1668-1747 .... **LC 2, 28**
See also DLB 313; EW 3; GFL Beginnings
to 1789; RGWL 2, 3

Leskov, N(ikolai) S(emenovich) 1831-1895
See Leskov, Nikolai (Semyonovich)

Leskov, Nikolai (Semyonovich)
1831-1895 .... **NCLC 25; SSC 34**
See Leskov, Nikolai Semenovich

Leskov, Nikolai Semenovich
See Leskov, Nikolai (Semyonovich)
See also DLB 238

Lesser, Milton
See Marlowe, Stephen

Lessing, Doris (May) 1919- ... **CLC 1, 2, 3, 6,
10, 15, 22, 40, 94, 170; SSC 6, 61;
WLCS**
See also AAYA 57; AFW; BRWS 1; CA
9-12R; CAAS 14; CANR 33, 54, 76, 122;
CBD; CD 5, 6; CDBLB 1960 to Present;
CN 1, 2, 3, 4, 5, 6, 7; CWD; DA; DA3;
DAB; DAC; DAM MST, NOV; DFS 20;
DLB 15, 139; DLBY 1985; EWL 3;
EXPS; FL 1:6; FW; LAIT 4; MTCW 1, 2;
MTFW 2005; RGEL 2; RGSF 2; SFW 4;
SSFS 1, 12, 20; TEA; WLIT 2, 4

Lessing, Gotthold Ephraim
1729-1781 .... **DC 26; LC 8, 124**
See also CDWLB 2; DLB 97; EW 4; RGWL
2, 3

Lester, Richard 1932- .... **CLC 20**

Levenson, Jay .... **CLC 70**

Lever, Charles (James)
1806-1872 .... **NCLC 23**
See also DLB 21; RGEL 2

Leverson, Ada Esther
1862(?)-1933(?) .... **TCLC 18**
See Elaine
See also CA 117; 202; DLB 153; RGEL 2

Levertov, Denise 1923-1997 .. **CLC 1, 2, 3, 5,
8, 15, 28, 66; PC 11**
See also AMWS 3; CA 1-4R, 178; 163;
CAAE 178; CAAS 19; CANR 3, 29, 50,
108; CDALBS; CP 1, 2, 3, 4, 5, 6; CWP;
DAM POET; DLB 5, 165; EWL 3; EXPP;
FW; INT CANR-29; MAL 5; MTCW 1,
2; PAB; PFS 7, 17; RGAL 4; TUS; WP

Levi, Carlo 1902-1975 .... **TCLC 125**
See also CA 65-68; 53-56; CANR 10; EWL
3; RGWL 2, 3

Levi, Jonathan .... **CLC 76**
See also CA 197

Levi, Peter (Chad Tigar)
1931-2000 .... **CLC 41**
See also CA 5-8R; 187; CANR 34, 80; CP
1, 2, 3, 4, 5, 6, 7; DLB 40

Levi, Primo 1919-1987 ...... **CLC 37, 50; SSC
12; TCLC 109**
See also CA 13-16R; 122; CANR 12, 33,
61, 70, 132; DLB 177, 299; EWL 3;
MTCW 1, 2; MTFW 2005; RGWL 2, 3;
WLIT 7

Levin, Ira 1929- .... **CLC 3, 6**
See also CA 21-24R; CANR 17, 44, 74,
139; CMW 4; CN 1, 2, 3, 4, 5, 6, 7; CPW;
DA3; DAM POP; HGG; MTCW 1, 2;
MTFW 2005; SATA 66; SFW 4

Levin, Meyer 1905-1981 .... **CLC 7**
See also AITN 1; CA 9-12R; 104; CANR
15; CN 1, 2, 3; DAM POP; DLB 9, 28;
DLBY 1981; MAL 5; SATA 21; SATA-
Obit 27

Levine, Norman 1923-2005 .... **CLC 54**
See also CA 73-76; 240; CAAS 23; CANR
14, 70; CN 1, 2, 3, 4, 5, 6; CP 1; DLB 88

Levine, Norman Albert
See Levine, Norman

Levine, Philip 1928- .. **CLC 2, 4, 5, 9, 14, 33,
118; PC 22**
See also AMWS 5; CA 9-12R; CANR 9,
37, 52, 116; CP 1, 2, 3, 4, 5, 6, 7; DAM
POET; DLB 5; EWL 3; MAL 5; PFS 8

Levinson, Deirdre 1931- .... **CLC 49**
See also CA 73-76; CANR 70

Levi-Strauss, Claude 1908- .... **CLC 38**
See also CA 1-4R; CANR 6, 32, 57; DLB
242; EWL 3; GFL 1789 to the Present;
MTCW 1, 2; TWA

Levitin, Sonia (Wolff) 1934- .... **CLC 17**
See also AAYA 13, 48; CA 29-32R; CANR
14, 32, 79; CLR 53; JRDA; MAICYA 1,
2; SAAS 2; SATA 4, 68, 119, 131; SATA-
Essay 131; YAW

Levon, O. U.
See Kesey, Ken (Elton)

Levy, Amy 1861-1889 .... **NCLC 59**
See also DLB 156, 240

Lewes, George Henry 1817-1878 ... **NCLC 25**
See also DLB 55, 144

Lewis, Alun 1915-1944 .... **SSC 40; TCLC 3**
See also BRW 7; CA 104; 188; DLB 20,
162; PAB; RGEL 2

Lewis, C. Day
See Day Lewis, C(ecil)
See also CN 1

Lewis, C(live) S(taples) 1898-1963 .... **CLC 1,
3, 6, 14, 27, 124; WLC**
See also AAYA 3, 39; BPFB 2; BRWS 3;
BYA 15, 16; CA 81-84; CANR 33, 71,
132; CDBLB 1945-1960; CLR 3, 27;
CWRI 5; DA; DA3; DAB; DAC; DAM
MST, NOV, POP; DLB 15, 100, 160, 255;
EWL 3; FANT; JRDA; LMFS 2; MAI-
CYA 1, 2; MTCW 1, 2; MTFW 2005;
RGEL 2; SATA 13, 100; SCFW 1, 2; SFW
4; SUFW 1; TEA; WCH; WYA; YAW

Lewis, Cecil Day
See Day Lewis, C(ecil)

Lewis, Janet 1899-1998 .... **CLC 41**
See Winters, Janet Lewis
See also CA 9-12R; 172; CANR 29, 63;
CAP 1; CN 1, 2, 3, 4, 5, 6; DLBY 1987;
RHW; TCWW 2

Lewis, Matthew Gregory
1775-1818 .... **NCLC 11, 62**
See also DLB 39, 158, 178; GL 3; HGG;
LMFS 1; RGEL 2; SUFW

Lewis, (Harry) Sinclair 1885-1951 . **TCLC 4,
13, 23, 39; WLC**
See also AMW; AMWC 1; BPFB 2; CA
104; 133; CANR 132; CDALB 1917-
1929; DA; DA3; DAB; DAC; DAM MST,
NOV; DLB 9, 102, 284; DLBD 1; EWL
3; LAIT 3; MTCW 1, 2; MTFW 2005;
NFS 15, 19, 22; RGAL 4; TUS

Lewis, (Percy) Wyndham
1884(?)-1957 .. **SSC 34; TCLC 2, 9, 104**
See also BRW 7; CA 104; 157; DLB 15;
EWL 3; FANT; MTCW 2; MTFW 2005;
RGEL 2

Lewisohn, Ludwig 1883-1955 .... **TCLC 19**
See also CA 107; 203; DLB 4, 9, 28, 102;
MAL 5

Lewton, Val 1904-1951 .... **TCLC 76**
See also CA 199; IDFW 3, 4

Leyner, Mark 1956- .... **CLC 92**
See also CA 110; CANR 28, 53; DA3; DLB
292; MTCW 2; MTFW 2005

Lezama Lima, Jose 1910-1976 .... **CLC 4, 10,
101; HLCS 2**
See also CA 77-80; CANR 71; DAM
MULT; DLB 113, 283; EWL 3; HW 1, 2;
LAW; RGWL 2, 3

L'Heureux, John (Clarke) 1934- ...... **CLC 52**
See also CA 13-16R; CANR 23, 45, 88; CP
1, 2, 3, 4; DLB 244

Li Ch'ing-chao 1081(?)-1141(?) .... **CMLC 71**

Liddell, C. H.
See Kuttner, Henry

Lie, Jonas (Lauritz Idemil)
1833-1908(?) .... **TCLC 5**
See also CA 115

Lieber, Joel 1937-1971 .... **CLC 6**
See also CA 73-76; 29-32R

Lieber, Stanley Martin
See Lee, Stan

Lieberman, Laurence (James)
1935- .... **CLC 4, 36**
See also CA 17-20R; CANR 8, 36, 89; CP
1, 2, 3, 4, 5, 6, 7

Lieh Tzu fl. 7th cent. B.C.-5th cent.
B.C. .... **CMLC 27**

Lieksman, Anders
See Haavikko, Paavo Juhani

Li Fei-kan 1904-
See Pa Chin
See also CA 105; TWA

Lifton, Robert Jay 1926- .... **CLC 67**
See also CA 17-20R; CANR 27, 78; INT
CANR-27; SATA 66

Lightfoot, Gordon 1938- .... **CLC 26**
See also CA 109

Lightman, Alan P(aige) 1948- .... **CLC 81**
See also CA 141; CANR 63, 105, 138;
MTFW 2005

Ligotti, Thomas (Robert) 1953- ...... **CLC 44;
SSC 16**
See also CA 123; CANR 49, 135; HGG;
SUFW 2

Li Ho 791-817 .... **PC 13**

Li Ju-chen c. 1763-c. 1830 .... **NCLC 137**

Lilar, Francoise
See Mallet-Joris, Francoise

**Liliencron, (Friedrich Adolf Axel) Detlev
von** 1844-1909 .... **TCLC 18**
See also CA 117

Lille, Alain de
See Alain de Lille

Lilly, William 1602-1681 .... **LC 27**

Lima, Jose Lezama
See Lezama Lima, Jose

Lima Barreto, Afonso Henrique de
1881-1922 .... **TCLC 23**
See Lima Barreto, Afonso Henriques de
See also CA 117; 181; LAW

Lima Barreto, Afonso Henriques de
See Lima Barreto, Afonso Henrique de
See also DLB 307

Limonov, Eduard
See Limonov, Edward
See also DLB 317

Limonov, Edward 1944- .... **CLC 67**
See Limonov, Eduard
See also CA 137

Lin, Frank
See Atherton, Gertrude (Franklin Horn)

Lin, Yutang 1895-1976 .... **TCLC 149**
See also CA 45-48; 65-68; CANR 2; RGAL 4

Lincoln, Abraham 1809-1865 .... **NCLC 18**
See also LAIT 2

Lind, Jakov .... **CLC 1, 2, 4, 27, 82**
See Landwirth, Heinz
See also CAAS 4; DLB 299; EWL 3

Lindbergh, Anne (Spencer) Morrow
1906-2001 .... **CLC 82**
See also BPFB 2; CA 17-20R; 193; CANR 16, 73; DAM NOV; MTCW 1, 2; MTFW 2005; SATA 33; SATA-Obit 125; TUS

Lindsay, David 1878(?)-1945 .... **TCLC 15**
See also CA 113; 187; DLB 255; FANT; SFW 4; SUFW 1

Lindsay, (Nicholas) Vachel
1879-1931 .... **PC 23; TCLC 17; WLC**
See also AMWS 1; CA 114; 135; CANR 79; CDALB 1865-1917; DA; DA3; DAC; DAM MST, POET; DLB 54; EWL 3; EXPP; MAL 5; RGAL 4; SATA 40; WP

Linke-Poot
See Doeblin, Alfred

Linney, Romulus 1930- .... **CLC 51**
See also CA 1-4R; CAD; CANR 40, 44, 79; CD 5, 6; CSW; RGAL 4

Linton, Eliza Lynn 1822-1898 .... **NCLC 41**
See also DLB 18

Li Po 701-763 .... **CMLC 2; PC 29**
See also PFS 20; WP

Lipsius, Justus 1547-1606 .... **LC 16**

Lipsyte, Robert (Michael) 1938- ...... **CLC 21**
See also AAYA 7, 45; CA 17-20R; CANR 8, 57; CLR 23, 76; DA; DAC; DAM MST, NOV; JRDA; LAIT 5; MAICYA 1, 2; SATA 5, 68, 113, 161; WYA; YAW

Lish, Gordon (Jay) 1934- ... **CLC 45; SSC 18**
See also CA 113; 117; CANR 79; DLB 130; INT CA-117

Lispector, Clarice 1925(?)-1977 .... **CLC 43; HLCS 2; SSC 34**
See also CA 139; 116; CANR 71; CDWLB 3; DLB 113, 307; DNFS 1; EWL 3; FW; HW 2; LAW; RGSF 2; RGWL 2, 3; WLIT 1

Littell, Robert 1935(?)- .... **CLC 42**
See also CA 109; 112; CANR 64, 115; CMW 4

Little, Malcolm 1925-1965
See Malcolm X
See also BW 1, 3; CA 125; 111; CANR 82; DA; DA3; DAB; DAC; DAM MST, MULT; MTCW 1, 2; MTFW 2005

Littlewit, Humphrey Gent.
See Lovecraft, H(oward) P(hillips)

Litwos
See Sienkiewicz, Henryk (Adam Alexander Pius)

Liu, E. 1857-1909 .... **TCLC 15**
See also CA 115; 190

Lively, Penelope 1933- .... **CLC 32, 50**
See also BPFB 2; CA 41-44R; CANR 29, 67, 79, 131; CLR 7; CN 5, 6, 7; CWRI 5; DAM NOV; DLB 14, 161, 207; FANT; JRDA; MAICYA 1, 2; MTCW 1, 2; MTFW 2005; SATA 7, 60, 101, 164; TEA

Lively, Penelope Margaret
See Lively, Penelope

Livesay, Dorothy (Kathleen)
1909-1996 .... **CLC 4, 15, 79**
See also AITN 2; CA 25-28R; CAAS 8; CANR 36, 67; CP 1, 2, 3, 4; DAC; DAM MST, POET; DLB 68; FW; MTCW 1; RGEL 2; TWA

Livy c. 59B.C.-c. 12 .... **CMLC 11**
See also AW 2; CDWLB 1; DLB 211; RGWL 2, 3

Lizardi, Jose Joaquin Fernandez de
1776-1827 .... **NCLC 30**
See also LAW

Llewellyn, Richard
See Llewellyn Lloyd, Richard Dafydd Vivian
See also DLB 15

Llewellyn Lloyd, Richard Dafydd Vivian
1906-1983 .... **CLC 7, 80**
See Llewellyn, Richard
See also CA 53-56; 111; CANR 7, 71; SATA 11; SATA-Obit 37

Llosa, (Jorge) Mario (Pedro) Vargas
See Vargas Llosa, (Jorge) Mario (Pedro)
See also RGWL 3

Llosa, Mario Vargas
See Vargas Llosa, (Jorge) Mario (Pedro)

Lloyd, Manda
See Mander, (Mary) Jane

Lloyd Webber, Andrew 1948-
See Webber, Andrew Lloyd
See also AAYA 1, 38; CA 116; 149; DAM DRAM; SATA 56

Llull, Ramon c. 1235-c. 1316 .... **CMLC 12**

Lobb, Ebenezer
See Upward, Allen

Locke, Alain (Le Roy)
1886-1954 .... **BLCS; HR 1:3; TCLC 43**
See also AMWS 14; BW 1, 3; CA 106; 124; CANR 79; DLB 51; LMFS 2; MAL 5; RGAL 4

Locke, John 1632-1704 .... **LC 7, 35**
See also DLB 31, 101, 213, 252; RGEL 2; WLIT 3

Locke-Elliott, Sumner
See Elliott, Sumner Locke

Lockhart, John Gibson 1794-1854 .. **NCLC 6**
See also DLB 110, 116, 144

Lockridge, Ross (Franklin), Jr.
1914-1948 .... **TCLC 111**
See also CA 108; 145; CANR 79; DLB 143; DLBY 1980; MAL 5; RGAL 4; RHW

Lockwood, Robert
See Johnson, Robert

Lodge, David (John) 1935- .... **CLC 36, 141**
See also BEST 90:1; BRWS 4; CA 17-20R; CANR 19, 53, 92, 139; CN 1, 2, 3, 4, 5, 6, 7; CPW; DAM POP; DLB 14, 194; EWL 3; INT CANR-19; MTCW 1, 2; MTFW 2005

Lodge, Thomas 1558-1625 .... **LC 41**
See also DLB 172; RGEL 2

Loewinsohn, Ron(ald William)
1937- .... **CLC 52**
See also CA 25-28R; CANR 71; CP 1, 2, 3, 4

Logan, Jake
See Smith, Martin Cruz

Logan, John (Burton) 1923-1987 .... **CLC 5**
See also CA 77-80; 124; CANR 45; CP 1, 2, 3, 4; DLB 5

Lo Kuan-chung 1330(?)-1400(?) .... **LC 12**

Lombard, Nap
See Johnson, Pamela Hansford

Lombard, Peter 1100(?)-1160(?) ... **CMLC 72**

London, Jack 1876-1916 .. **SSC 4, 49; TCLC 9, 15, 39; WLC**
See London, John Griffith
See also AAYA 13; AITN 2; AMW; BPFB 2; BYA 4, 13; CDALB 1865-1917; DLB 8, 12, 78, 212; EWL 3; EXPS; LAIT 3; MAL 5; NFS 8; RGAL 4; RGSF; SATA 18; SFW 4; SSFS 7; TCWW 1, 2; TUS; WYA; YAW

London, John Griffith 1876-1916
See London, Jack
See also CA 110; 119; CANR 73; DA; DA3; DAB; DAC; DAM MST, NOV; JRDA; MAICYA 1, 2; MTCW 1, 2; MTFW 2005; NFS 19

Long, Emmett
See Leonard, Elmore (John, Jr.)

Longbaugh, Harry
See Goldman, William (W.)

Longfellow, Henry Wadsworth
1807-1882 .... **NCLC 2, 45, 101, 103; PC 30; WLCS**
See also AMW; AMWR 2; CDALB 1640-1865; CLR 99; DA; DA3; DAB; DAC; DAM MST, POET; DLB 1, 59, 235; EXPP; PAB; PFS 2, 7, 17; RGAL 4; SATA 19; TUS; WP

Longinus c. 1st cent. - .... **CMLC 27**
See also AW 2; DLB 176

Longley, Michael 1939- .... **CLC 29**
See also BRWS 8; CA 102; CP 1, 2, 3, 4, 5, 6, 7; DLB 40

Longstreet, Augustus Baldwin
1790-1870 .... **NCLC 159**
See also DLB 3, 11, 74, 248; RGAL 4

Longus fl. c. 2nd cent. - .... **CMLC 7**

Longway, A. Hugh
See Lang, Andrew

Lonnbohm, Armas Eino Leopold 1878-1926
See Leino, Eino
See also CA 123

Lonnrot, Elias 1802-1884 .... **NCLC 53**
See also EFS 1

Lonsdale, Roger ed. .... **CLC 65**

Lopate, Phillip 1943- .... **CLC 29**
See also CA 97-100; CANR 88; DLBY 1980; INT CA-97-100

Lopez, Barry (Holstun) 1945- .... **CLC 70**
See also AAYA 9, 63; ANW; CA 65-68; CANR 7, 23, 47, 68, 92; DLB 256, 275; INT CANR-7, -23; MTCW 1; RGAL 4; SATA 67

Lopez de Mendoza, Inigo
See Santillana, Inigo Lopez de Mendoza, Marques de

Lopez Portillo (y Pacheco), Jose
1920-2004 .... **CLC 46**
See also CA 129; 224; HW 1

Lopez y Fuentes, Gregorio
1897(?)-1966 .... **CLC 32**
See also CA 131; EWL 3; HW 1

Lorca, Federico Garcia
See Garcia Lorca, Federico
See also DFS 4; EW 11; PFS 20; RGWL 2, 3; WP

Lord, Audre
See Lorde, Audre (Geraldine)
See also EWL 3

Lord, Bette Bao 1938- .... **AAL; CLC 23**
See also BEST 90:3; BPFB 2; CA 107; CANR 41, 79; INT CA-107; SATA 58

Lord Auch
See Bataille, Georges

Lord Brooke
See Greville, Fulke

Lord Byron
See Byron, George Gordon (Noel)

Lorde, Audre (Geraldine)
1934-1992 .... **BLC 2; CLC 18, 71; PC 12; TCLC 173**
See Domini, Rey; Lord, Audre
See also AFAW 1, 2; BW 1, 3; CA 25-28R; 142; CANR 16, 26, 46, 82; CP 2, 3, 4; DA3; DAM MULT, POET; DLB 41; FW; MAL 5; MTCW 1, 2; MTFW 2005; PFS 16; RGAL 4

Macdonald, John
See Millar, Kenneth
MacDonald, John D(ann)
1916-1986 .... CLC 3, 27, 44
See also BPFB 2; CA 1-4R; 121; CANR 1,
19, 60; CMW 4; CPW; DAM NOV, POP;
DLB 8, 306; DLBY 1986; MSW; MTCW
1, 2; MTFW 2005; SFW 4
Macdonald, John Ross
See Millar, Kenneth
Macdonald, Ross ..... CLC 1, 2, 3, 14, 34, 41
See Millar, Kenneth
See also AMWS 4; BPFB 2; CN 1, 2, 3;
DLBD 6; MSW; RGAL 4
MacDougal, John
See Blish, James (Benjamin)
MacDougal, John
See Blish, James (Benjamin)
MacDowell, John
See Parks, Tim(othy Harold)
MacEwen, Gwendolyn (Margaret)
1941-1987 .... CLC 13, 55
See also CA 9-12R; 124; CANR 7, 22; CP
1, 2, 3, 4; DLB 53, 251; SATA 50; SATA-
Obit 55
Macha, Karel Hynek 1810-1846 .... NCLC 46
Machado (y Ruiz), Antonio
1875-1939 .... TCLC 3
See also CA 104; 174; DLB 108; EW 9;
EWL 3; HW 2; PFS 23; RGWL 2, 3
Machado de Assis, Joaquim Maria
1839-1908 .... BLC 2; HLCS 2; SSC 24;
TCLC 10
See also CA 107; 153; CANR 91; DLB 307;
LAW; RGSF 2; RGWL 2, 3; TWA; WLIT
1
Machaut, Guillaume de c.
1300-1377 .... CMLC 64
See also DLB 208
Machen, Arthur .... SSC 20; TCLC 4
See Jones, Arthur Llewellyn
See also CA 179; DLB 156, 178; RGEL 2;
SUFW 1
Machiavelli, Niccolo 1469-1527 ... DC 16; LC
8, 36; WLCS
See also AAYA 58; DA; DAB; DAC; DAM
MST; EW 2; LAIT 1; LMFS 1; NFS 9;
RGWL 2, 3; TWA; WLIT 7
MacInnes, Colin 1914-1976 .... CLC 4, 23
See also CA 69-72; 65-68; CANR 21; CN
1, 2; DLB 14; MTCW 1, 2; RGEL 2;
RHW
MacInnes, Helen (Clark)
1907-1985 .... CLC 27, 39
See also BPFB 2; CA 1-4R; 117; CANR 1,
28, 58; CMW 4; CN 1, 2; CPW; DAM
POP; DLB 87; MSW; MTCW 1, 2;
MTFW 2005; SATA 22; SATA-Obit 44
Mackay, Mary 1855-1924
See Corelli, Marie
See also CA 118; 177; FANT; RHW
Mackay, Shena 1944- .... CLC 195
See also CA 104; CANR 88, 139; DLB 231,
319; MTFW 2005
Mackenzie, Compton (Edward Montague)
1883-1972 .... CLC 18; TCLC 116
See also CA 21-22; 37-40R; CAP 2; CN 1;
DLB 34, 100; RGEL 2
Mackenzie, Henry 1745-1831 .... NCLC 41
See also DLB 39; RGEL 2
Mackey, Nathaniel (Ernest) 1947- .... PC 49
See also CA 153; CANR 114; CP 7; DLB
169
MacKinnon, Catharine A. 1946- .... CLC 181
See also CA 128; 132; CANR 73, 140; FW;
MTCW 2; MTFW 2005
Mackintosh, Elizabeth 1896(?)-1952
See Tey, Josephine
See also CA 110; CMW 4

MacLaren, James
See Grieve, C(hristopher) M(urray)
MacLaverty, Bernard 1942- .... CLC 31
See also CA 116; 118; CANR 43, 88; CN
5, 6, 7; DLB 267; INT CA-118; RGSF 2
MacLean, Alistair (Stuart)
1922(?)-1987 .... CLC 3, 13, 50, 63
See also CA 57-60; 121; CANR 28, 61;
CMW 4; CP 2, 3, 4, 5, 6, 7; CPW; DAM
POP; DLB 276; MTCW 1; SATA 23;
SATA-Obit 50; TCWW 2
Maclean, Norman (Fitzroy)
1902-1990 .... CLC 78; SSC 13
See also AMWS 14; CA 102; 132; CANR
49; CPW; DAM POP; DLB 206; TCWW
2
MacLeish, Archibald 1892-1982 ... CLC 3, 8,
14, 68; PC 47
See also AMW; CA 9-12R; 106; CAD;
CANR 33, 63; CDALBS; DAM POET;
DFS 15; DLB 4, 7, 45; DLBY
1982; EWL 3; EXPP; MAL 5; MTCW 1,
2; MTFW 2005; PAB; PFS 5; RGAL 4;
TUS
MacLennan, (John) Hugh
1907-1990 .... CLC 2, 14, 92
See also CA 5-8R; 142; CANR 33; CN 1,
2, 3, 4; DAC; DAM MST; DLB 68; EWL
3; MTCW 1, 2; MTFW 2005; RGEL 2;
TWA
MacLeod, Alistair 1936- .. CLC 56, 165; SSC
90
See also CA 123; CCA 1; DAC; DAM
MST; DLB 60; MTCW 2; MTFW 2005;
RGSF 2; TCLE 1:2
Macleod, Fiona
See Sharp, William
See also RGEL 2; SUFW
MacNeice, (Frederick) Louis
1907-1963 .... CLC 1, 4, 10, 53; PC 61
See also BRW 7; CA 85-88; CANR 61;
DAB; DAM POET; DLB 10, 20; EWL 3;
MTCW 1, 2; MTFW 2005; RGEL 2
MacNeill, Dand
See Fraser, George MacDonald
Macpherson, James 1736-1796 .... LC 29
See Ossian
See also BRWS 8; DLB 109; RGEL 2
Macpherson, (Jean) Jay 1931- .... CLC 14
See also CA 5-8R; CANR 90; CP 1, 2, 3, 4,
5, 6, 7; CWP; DLB 53
Macrobius fl. 430- .... CMLC 48
MacShane, Frank 1927-1999 .... CLC 39
See also CA 9-12R; 186; CANR 3, 33; DLB
111
Macumber, Mari
See Sandoz, Mari(e Susette)
Madach, Imre 1823-1864 .... NCLC 19
Madden, (Jerry) David 1933- .... CLC 5, 15
See also CA 1-4R; CAAS 3; CANR 4, 45;
CN 3, 4, 5, 6, 7; CSW; DLB 6; MTCW 1
Maddern, Al(an)
See Ellison, Harlan (Jay)
Madhubuti, Haki R. 1942- ... BLC 2; CLC 6,
73; PC 5
See Lee, Don L.
See also BW 2, 3; CA 73-76; CANR 24,
51, 73, 139; CP 5, 6, 7; CSW; DAM
MULT, POET; DLB 5, 41; DLBD 8; EWL
3; MAL 5; MTCW 2; MTFW 2005;
RGAL 4
Madison, James 1751-1836 .... NCLC 126
See also DLB 37
Maepenn, Hugh
See Kuttner, Henry
Maepenn, K. H.
See Kuttner, Henry

Maeterlinck, Maurice 1862-1949 ..... TCLC 3
See also CA 104; 136; CANR 80; DAM
DRAM; DLB 192; EW 8; EWL 3; GFL
1789 to the Present; LMFS 2; RGWL 2,
3; SATA 66; TWA
Maginn, William 1794-1842 .... NCLC 8
See also DLB 110, 159
Mahapatra, Jayanta 1928- .... CLC 33
See also CA 73-76; CAAS 9; CANR 15,
33, 66, 87; CP 4, 5, 6, 7; DAM MULT
Mahfouz, Naguib (Abdel Aziz Al-Sabilgi)
1911(?)- .... CLC 153; SSC 66
See Mahfuz, Najib (Abdel Aziz al-Sabilgi)
See also AAYA 49; BEST 89:2; CA 128;
CANR 55, 101; DA3; DAM NOV;
MTCW 1, 2; MTFW 2005; RGWL 2, 3;
SSFS 9
Mahfuz, Najib (Abdel Aziz al-Sabilgi)
.... CLC 52, 55
See Mahfouz, Naguib (Abdel Aziz Al-
Sabilgi)
See also AFW; CWW 2; DLBY 1988; EWL
3; RGSF 2; WLIT 6
Mahon, Derek 1941- .... CLC 27; PC 60
See also BRWS 6; CA 113; 128; CANR 88;
CP 1, 2, 3, 4, 5, 6, 7; DLB 40; EWL 3
Maiakovskii, Vladimir
See Mayakovski, Vladimir (Vladimirovich)
See also IDTP; RGWL 2, 3
Mailer, Norman (Kingsley) 1923- . CLC 1, 2,
3, 4, 5, 8, 11, 14, 28, 39, 74, 111
See also AAYA 31; AITN 2; AMW; AMWC
2; AMWR 2; BPFB 2; CA 9-12R; CABS
1; CANR 28, 74, 77, 130; CDALB 1968-
1988; CN 1, 2, 3, 4, 5, 6, 7; CPW; DA;
DA3; DAB; DAC; DAM MST, NOV,
POP; DLB 2, 16, 28, 185, 278; DLBD 3;
DLBY 1980, 1983; EWL 3; MAL 5;
MTCW 1, 2; MTFW 2005; NFS 10;
RGAL 4; TUS
Maillet, Antonine 1929- .... CLC 54, 118
See also CA 115; 120; CANR 46, 74, 77,
134; CCA 1; CWW 2; DAC; DLB 60;
INT CA-120; MTCW 2; MTFW 2005
Maimonides, Moses 1135-1204 ..... CMLC 76
See also DLB 115
Mais, Roger 1905-1955 .... TCLC 8
See also BW 1, 3; CA 105; 124; CANR 82;
CDWLB 3; DLB 125; EWL 3; MTCW 1;
RGEL 2
Maistre, Joseph 1753-1821 .... NCLC 37
See also GFL 1789 to the Present
Maitland, Frederic William
1850-1906 .... TCLC 65
Maitland, Sara (Louise) 1950- .... CLC 49
See also BRWS 11; CA 69-72; CANR 13,
59; DLB 271; FW
Major, Clarence 1936- ... BLC 2; CLC 3, 19,
48
See also AFAW 2; BW 2, 3; CA 21-24R;
CAAS 6; CANR 13, 25, 53, 82; CN 3, 4,
5, 6, 7; CP 2, 3, 4, 5, 6, 7; CSW; DAM
MULT; DLB 33; EWL 3; MAL 5; MSW
Major, Kevin (Gerald) 1949- .... CLC 26
See also AAYA 16; CA 97-100; CANR 21,
38, 112; CLR 11; DAC; DLB 60; INT
CANR-21; JRDA; MAICYA 1, 2; MAIC-
YAS 1; SATA 32, 82, 134; WYA; YAW
Maki, James
See Ozu, Yasujiro
Makine, Andrei 1957- .... CLC 198
See also CA 176; CANR 103; MTFW 2005
Malabaila, Damiano
See Levi, Primo
Malamud, Bernard 1914-1986 .. CLC 1, 2, 3,
5, 8, 9, 11, 18, 27, 44, 78, 85; SSC 15;
TCLC 129; WLC
See also AAYA 16; AMWS 1; BPFB 2;
BYA 15; CA 5-8R; 118; CABS 1; CANR
28, 62, 114; CDALB 1941-1968; CN 1, 2,

Marley, Bob .... **CLC 17**
See Marley, Robert Nesta
Marley, Robert Nesta 1945-1981
See Marley, Bob
See also CA 107; 103
Marlowe, Christopher 1564-1593 . **DC 1; LC 22, 47, 117; PC 57; WLC**
See also BRW 1; BRWR 1; CDBLB Before 1660; DA; DA3; DAB; DAC; DAM DRAM, MST; DFS 1, 5, 13, 21; DLB 62; EXPP; LMFS 1; PFS 22; RGEL 2; TEA; WLIT 3
Marlowe, Stephen 1928- .... **CLC 70**
See Queen, Ellery
See also CA 13-16R; CANR 6, 55; CMW 4; SFW 4
Marmion, Shakerley 1603-1639 .... **LC 89**
See also DLB 58; RGEL 2
Marmontel, Jean-Francois 1723-1799 .. **LC 2**
See also DLB 314
Maron, Monika 1941- .... **CLC 165**
See also CA 201
Marquand, John P(hillips)
1893-1960 .... **CLC 2, 10**
See also AMW; BPFB 2; CA 85-88; CANR 73; CMW 4; DLB 9, 102; EWL 3; MAL 5; MTCW 2; RGAL 4
Marques, Rene 1919-1979 .. **CLC 96; HLC 2**
See also CA 97-100; 85-88; CANR 78; DAM MULT; DLB 305; EWL 3; HW 1, 2; LAW; RGSF 2
Marquez, Gabriel (Jose) Garcia
See Garcia Marquez, Gabriel (Jose)
Marquis, Don(ald Robert Perry)
1878-1937 .... **TCLC 7**
See also CA 104; 166; DLB 11, 25; MAL 5; RGAL 4
Marquis de Sade
See Sade, Donatien Alphonse Francois
Marric, J. J.
See Creasey, John
See also MSW
Marryat, Frederick 1792-1848 .... **NCLC 3**
See also DLB 21, 163; RGEL 2; WCH
Marsden, James
See Creasey, John
Marsh, Edward 1872-1953 .... **TCLC 99**
Marsh, (Edith) Ngaio 1895-1982 .. **CLC 7, 53**
See also CA 9-12R; CANR 6, 58; CMW 4; CN 1, 2, 3; CPW; DAM POP; DLB 77; MSW; MTCW 1, 2; RGEL 2; TEA
Marshall, Allen
See Westlake, Donald E(dwin)
Marshall, Garry 1934- .... **CLC 17**
See also AAYA 3; CA 111; SATA 60
Marshall, Paule 1929- .. **BLC 3; CLC 27, 72; SSC 3**
See also AFAW 1, 2; AMWS 11; BPFB 2; BW 2, 3; CA 77-80; CANR 25, 73, 129; CN 1, 2, 3, 4, 5, 6, 7; DA3; DAM MULT; DLB 33, 157, 227; EWL 3; LATS 1:2; MAL 5; MTCW 1, 2; MTFW 2005; RGAL 4; SSFS 15
Marshallik
See Zangwill, Israel
Marsten, Richard
See Hunter, Evan
Marston, John 1576-1634 .... **LC 33**
See also BRW 2; DAM DRAM; DLB 58, 172; RGEL 2
Martel, Yann 1963- .... **CLC 192**
See also AAYA 67; CA 146; CANR 114; MTFW 2005
Martens, Adolphe-Adhemar
See Ghelderode, Michel de
Martha, Henry
See Harris, Mark

Marti, Jose
See Marti (y Perez), Jose (Julian)
See also DLB 290
Marti (y Perez), Jose (Julian)
1853-1895 .... **HLC 2; NCLC 63**
See Marti, Jose
See also DAM MULT; HW 2; LAW; RGWL 2, 3; WLIT 1
Martial c. 40-c. 104 .... **CMLC 35; PC 10**
See also AW 2; CDWLB 1; DLB 211; RGWL 2, 3
Martin, Ken
See Hubbard, L(afayette) Ron(ald)
Martin, Richard
See Creasey, John
Martin, Steve 1945- .... **CLC 30, 217**
See also AAYA 53; CA 97-100; CANR 30, 100, 140; DFS 19; MTCW 1; MTFW 2005
Martin, Valerie 1948- .... **CLC 89**
See also BEST 90:2; CA 85-88; CANR 49, 89
Martin, Violet Florence 1862-1915 .. **SSC 56; TCLC 51**
Martin, Webber
See Silverberg, Robert
Martindale, Patrick Victor
See White, Patrick (Victor Martindale)
Martin du Gard, Roger
1881-1958 .... **TCLC 24**
See also CA 118; CANR 94; DLB 65; EWL 3; GFL 1789 to the Present; RGWL 2, 3
Martineau, Harriet 1802-1876 ...... **NCLC 26, 137**
See also DLB 21, 55, 159, 163, 166, 190; FW; RGEL 2; YABC 2
Martines, Julia
See O'Faolain, Julia
Martinez, Enrique Gonzalez
See Gonzalez Martinez, Enrique
Martinez, Jacinto Benavente y
See Benavente (y Martinez), Jacinto
Martinez de la Rosa, Francisco de Paula
1787-1862 .... **NCLC 102**
See also TWA
Martinez Ruiz, Jose 1873-1967
See Azorin; Ruiz, Jose Martinez
See also CA 93-96; HW 1
Martinez Sierra, Gregorio
1881-1947 .... **TCLC 6**
See also CA 115; EWL 3
Martinez Sierra, Maria (de la O'LeJarraga)
1874-1974 .... **TCLC 6**
See also CA 115; EWL 3
Martinsen, Martin
See Follett, Ken(neth Martin)
Martinson, Harry (Edmund)
1904-1978 .... **CLC 14**
See also CA 77-80; CANR 34, 130; DLB 259; EWL 3
Martyn, Edward 1859-1923 .... **TCLC 131**
See also CA 179; DLB 10; RGEL 2
Marut, Ret
See Traven, B.
Marut, Robert
See Traven, B.
Marvell, Andrew 1621-1678 .... **LC 4, 43; PC 10; WLC**
See also BRW 2; BRWR 2; CDBLB 1660-1789; DA; DAB; DAC; DAM MST, POET; DLB 131; EXPP; PFS 5; RGEL 2; TEA; WP
Marx, Karl (Heinrich)
1818-1883 .... **NCLC 17, 114**
See also DLB 129; LATS 1:1; TWA
Masaoka, Shiki -1902 .... **TCLC 18**
See Masaoka, Tsunenori
See also RGWL 3

Masaoka, Tsunenori 1867-1902
See Masaoka, Shiki
See also CA 117; 191; TWA
Masefield, John (Edward)
1878-1967 .... **CLC 11, 47**
See also CA 19-20; 25-28R; CANR 33; CAP 2; CDBLB 1890-1914; DAM POET; DLB 10, 19, 153, 160; EWL 3; EXPP; FANT; MTCW 1, 2; PFS 5; RGEL 2; SATA 19
Maso, Carole (?)- .... **CLC 44**
See also CA 170; CN 7; GLL 2; RGAL 4
Mason, Bobbie Ann 1940- ... **CLC 28, 43, 82, 154; SSC 4**
See also AAYA 5, 42; AMWS 8; BPFB 2; CA 53-56; CANR 11, 31, 58, 83, 125; CDALBS; CN 5, 6, 7; CSW; DA3; DLB 173; DLBY 1987; EWL 3; EXPS; INT CANR-31; MAL 5; MTCW 1, 2; MTFW 2005; NFS 4; RGAL 4; RGSF 2; SSFS 3, 8, 20; TCLE 1:2; YAW
Mason, Ernst
See Pohl, Frederik
Mason, Hunni B.
See Sternheim, (William Adolf) Carl
Mason, Lee W.
See Malzberg, Barry N(athaniel)
Mason, Nick 1945- .... **CLC 35**
Mason, Tally
See Derleth, August (William)
Mass, Anna .... **CLC 59**
Mass, William
See Gibson, William
Massinger, Philip 1583-1640 .... **LC 70**
See also BRWS 11; DLB 58; RGEL 2
Master Lao
See Lao Tzu
Masters, Edgar Lee 1868-1950 ...... **PC 1, 36; TCLC 2, 25; WLCS**
See also AMWS 1; CA 104; 133; CDALB 1865-1917; DA; DAC; DAM MST, POET; DLB 54; EWL 3; EXPP; MAL 5; MTCW 1, 2; MTFW 2005; RGAL 4; TUS; WP
Masters, Hilary 1928- .... **CLC 48**
See also CA 25-28R; 217; CAAE 217; CANR 13, 47, 97; CN 6, 7; DLB 244
Mastrosimone, William 1947- .... **CLC 36**
See also CA 186; CAD; CD 5, 6
Mathe, Albert
See Camus, Albert
Mather, Cotton 1663-1728 .... **LC 38**
See also AMWS 2; CDALB 1640-1865; DLB 24, 30, 140; RGAL 4; TUS
Mather, Increase 1639-1723 .... **LC 38**
See also DLB 24
Matheson, Richard (Burton) 1926- .. **CLC 37**
See also AAYA 31; CA 97-100; CANR 88, 99; DLB 8, 44; HGG; INT CA-97-100; SCFW 1, 2; SFW 4; SUFW 2
Mathews, Harry (Burchell) 1930- ..... **CLC 6, 52**
See also CA 21-24R; CAAS 6; CANR 18, 40, 98; CN 5, 6, 7
Mathews, John Joseph 1894-1979 .. **CLC 84; NNAL**
See also CA 19-20; 142; CANR 45; CAP 2; DAM MULT; DLB 175; TCWW 1, 2
Mathias, Roland (Glyn) 1915- .... **CLC 45**
See also CA 97-100; CANR 19, 41; CP 1, 2, 3, 4, 5, 6, 7; DLB 27
Matsuo Basho 1644(?)-1694 ...... **LC 62; PC 3**
See Basho, Matsuo
See also DAM POET; PFS 2, 7, 18
Mattheson, Rodney
See Creasey, John
Matthews, (James) Brander
1852-1929 .... **TCLC 95**
See also CA 181; DLB 71, 78; DLBD 13

McGinley, Patrick (Anthony) 1937- . **CLC 41**
See also CA 120; 127; CANR 56; INT CA-127

McGinley, Phyllis 1905-1978 .... **CLC 14**
See also CA 9-12R; 77-80; CANR 19; CP 1, 2; CWRI 5; DLB 11, 48; MAL 5; PFS 9, 13; SATA 2, 44; SATA-Obit 24

McGinniss, Joe 1942- .... **CLC 32**
See also AITN 2; BEST 89:2; CA 25-28R; CANR 26, 70; CPW; DLB 185; INT CANR-26

McGivern, Maureen Daly
See Daly, Maureen

McGrath, Patrick 1950- .... **CLC 55**
See also CA 136; CANR 65; CN 5, 6, 7; DLB 231; HGG; SUFW 2

McGrath, Thomas (Matthew)
1916-1990 .... **CLC 28, 59**
See also AMWS 10; CA 9-12R; 132; CANR 6, 33, 95; CP 1, 2, 3, 4; DAM POET; MAL 5; MTCW 1; SATA 41; SATA-Obit 66

McGuane, Thomas (Francis III)
1939- .... **CLC 3, 7, 18, 45, 127**
See also AITN 2; BPFB 2; CA 49-52; CANR 5, 24, 49, 94; CN 2, 3, 4, 5, 6, 7; DLB 2, 212; DLBY 1980; EWL 3; INT CANR-24; MAL 5; MTCW 1; MTFW 2005; TCWW 1, 2

McGuckian, Medbh 1950- .... **CLC 48, 174; PC 27**
See also BRWS 5; CA 143; CP 4, 5, 6, 7; CWP; DAM POET; DLB 40

McHale, Tom 1942(?)-1982 .... **CLC 3, 5**
See also AITN 1; CA 77-80; 106; CN 1, 2, 3

McHugh, Heather 1948- .... **PC 61**
See also CA 69-72; CANR 11, 28, 55, 92; CP 4, 5, 6, 7; CWP

McIlvanney, William 1936- .... **CLC 42**
See also CA 25-28R; CANR 61; CMW 4; DLB 14, 207

McIlwraith, Maureen Mollie Hunter
See Hunter, Mollie
See also SATA 2

McInerney, Jay 1955- .... **CLC 34, 112**
See also AAYA 18; BPFB 2; CA 116; 123; CANR 45, 68, 116; CN 5, 6, 7; CPW; DA3; DAM POP; DLB 292; INT CA-123; MAL 5; MTCW 2; MTFW 2005

McIntyre, Vonda N(eel) 1948- .... **CLC 18**
See also CA 81-84; CANR 17, 34, 69; MTCW 1; SFW 4; YAW

McKay, Claude .... **BLC 3; HR 1:3; PC 2; TCLC 7, 41; WLC**
See McKay, Festus Claudius
See also AFAW 1, 2; AMWS 10; DAB; DLB 4, 45, 51, 117; EWL 3; EXPP; GLL 2; LAIT 3; LMFS 2; MAL 5; PAB; PFS 4; RGAL 4; WP

McKay, Festus Claudius 1889-1948
See McKay, Claude
See also BW 1, 3; CA 104; 124; CANR 73; DA; DAC; DAM MST, MULT, NOV, POET; MTCW 1, 2; MTFW 2005; TUS

McKuen, Rod 1933- .... **CLC 1, 3**
See also AITN 1; CA 41-44R; CANR 40; CP 1

McLoughlin, R. B.
See Mencken, H(enry) L(ouis)

McLuhan, (Herbert) Marshall
1911-1980 .... **CLC 37, 83**
See also CA 9-12R; 102; CANR 12, 34, 61; DLB 88; INT CANR-12; MTCW 1, 2; MTFW 2005

McManus, Declan Patrick Aloysius
See Costello, Elvis

McMillan, Terry (L.) 1951- . **BLCS; CLC 50, 61, 112**
See also AAYA 21; AMWS 13; BPFB 2; BW 2, 3; CA 140; CANR 60, 104, 131; CN 7; CPW; DA3; DAM MULT, NOV, POP; MAL 5; MTCW 2005; RGAL 4; YAW

McMurtry, Larry 1936- .... **CLC 2, 3, 7, 11, 27, 44, 127**
See also AAYA 15; AITN 2; AMWS 5; BEST 89:2; BPFB 2; CA 5-8R; CANR 19, 43, 64, 103; CDALB 1968-1988; CN 2, 3, 4, 5, 6, 7; CPW; CSW; DA3; DAM NOV, POP; DLB 2, 143, 256; DLBY 1980, 1987; EWL 3; MAL 5; MTCW 1, 2; MTFW 2005; RGAL 4; TCWW 1, 2

McNally, T. M. 1961- .... **CLC 82**

McNally, Terrence 1939- ... **CLC 4, 7, 41, 91; DC 27**
See also AAYA 62; AMWS 13; CA 45-48; CAD; CANR 2, 56, 116; CD 5, 6; DA3; DAM DRAM; DFS 16, 19; DLB 7, 249; EWL 3; GLL 1; MTCW 2; MTFW 2005

McNamer, Deirdre 1950- .... **CLC 70**

McNeal, Tom .... **CLC 119**

McNeile, Herman Cyril 1888-1937
See Sapper
See also CA 184; CMW 4; DLB 77

McNickle, (William) D'Arcy
1904-1977 .... **CLC 89; NNAL**
See also CA 9-12R; 85-88; CANR 5, 45; DAM MULT; DLB 175, 212; RGAL 4; SATA-Obit 22; TCWW 1, 2

McPhee, John (Angus) 1931- .... **CLC 36**
See also AAYA 61; AMWS 3; ANW; BEST 90:1; CA 65-68; CANR 20, 46, 64, 69, 121; CPW; DLB 185, 275; MTCW 1, 2; MTFW 2005; TUS

McPherson, James Alan 1943- . **BLCS; CLC 19, 77**
See also BW 1, 3; CA 25-28R; CAAS 17; CANR 24, 74, 140; CN 3, 4, 5, 6; CSW; DLB 38, 244; EWL 3; MTCW 1, 2; MTFW 2005; RGAL 4; RGSF 2

McPherson, William (Alexander)
1933- .... **CLC 34**
See also CA 69-72; CANR 28; INT CANR-28

McTaggart, J. McT. Ellis
See McTaggart, John McTaggart Ellis

McTaggart, John McTaggart Ellis
1866-1925 .... **TCLC 105**
See also CA 120; DLB 262

Mead, George Herbert 1863-1931 . **TCLC 89**
See also CA 212; DLB 270

Mead, Margaret 1901-1978 .... **CLC 37**
See also AITN 1; CA 1-4R; 81-84; CANR 4; DA3; FW; MTCW 1, 2; SATA-Obit 20

Meaker, Marijane (Agnes) 1927-
See Kerr, M. E.
See also CA 107; CANR 37, 63, 145; INT CA-107; JRDA; MAICYA 1, 2; MAIC-YAS 1; MTCW 1; SATA 20, 61, 99, 160; SATA-Essay 111; YAW

Medoff, Mark (Howard) 1940- .... **CLC 6, 23**
See also AITN 1; CA 53-56; CAD; CANR 5; CD 5, 6; DAM DRAM; DFS 4; DLB 7; INT CANR-5

Medvedev, P. N.
See Bakhtin, Mikhail Mikhailovich

Meged, Aharon
See Megged, Aharon

Meged, Aron
See Megged, Aharon

Megged, Aharon 1920- .... **CLC 9**
See also CA 49-52; CAAS 13; CANR 1, 140; EWL 3

Mehta, Deepa 1950- .... **CLC 208**

Mehta, Gita 1943- .... **CLC 179**
See also CA 225; CN 7; DNFS 2

Mehta, Ved (Parkash) 1934- .... **CLC 37**
See also CA 1-4R; 212; CAAE 212; CANR 2, 23, 69; MTCW 1; MTFW 2005

Melanchthon, Philipp 1497-1560 .... **LC 90**
See also DLB 179

Melanter
See Blackmore, R(ichard) D(oddridge)

Meleager c. 140B.C.-c. 70B.C. ...... **CMLC 53**

Melies, Georges 1861-1938 .... **TCLC 81**

Melikow, Loris
See Hofmannsthal, Hugo von

Melmoth, Sebastian
See Wilde, Oscar (Fingal O'Flahertie Wills)

Melo Neto, Joao Cabral de
See Cabral de Melo Neto, Joao
See also CWW 2; EWL 3

Meltzer, Milton 1915- .... **CLC 26**
See also AAYA 8, 45; BYA 2, 6; CA 13-16R; CANR 38, 92, 107; CLR 13; DLB 61; JRDA; MAICYA 1, 2; SAAS 1; SATA 1, 50, 80, 128; SATA-Essay 124; WYA; YAW

Melville, Herman 1819-1891 ..... **NCLC 3, 12, 29, 45, 49, 91, 93, 123, 157; SSC 1, 17, 46; WLC**
See also AAYA 25; AMW; AMWR 1; CDALB 1640-1865; DA; DA3; DAB; DAC; DAM MST, NOV; DLB 3, 74, 250, 254; EXPN; EXPS; GL 3; LAIT 1, 2; NFS 7, 9; RGAL 4; RGSF 2; SATA 59; SSFS 3; TUS

Members, Mark
See Powell, Anthony (Dymoke)

Membreno, Alejandro .... **CLC 59**

Menand, Louis 1952- .... **CLC 208**
See also CA 200

Menander c. 342B.C.-c. 293B.C. .... **CMLC 9, 51; DC 3**
See also AW 1; CDWLB 1; DAM DRAM; DLB 176; LMFS 1; RGWL 2, 3

Menchu, Rigoberta 1959- .. **CLC 160; HLCS 2**
See also CA 175; CANR 135; DNFS 1; WLIT 1

Mencken, H(enry) L(ouis)
1880-1956 .... **TCLC 13**
See also AMW; CA 105; 125; CDALB 1917-1929; DLB 11, 29, 63, 137, 222; EWL 3; MAL 5; MTCW 1, 2; MTFW 2005; NCFS 4; RGAL 4; TUS

Mendelsohn, Jane 1965- .... **CLC 99**
See also CA 154; CANR 94

Mendoza, Inigo Lopez de
See Santillana, Inigo Lopez de Mendoza, Marques de

Menton, Francisco de
See Chin, Frank (Chew, Jr.)

Mercer, David 1928-1980 .... **CLC 5**
See also CA 9-12R; 102; CANR 23; CBD; DAM DRAM; DLB 13, 310; MTCW 1; RGEL 2

Merchant, Paul
See Ellison, Harlan (Jay)

Meredith, George 1828-1909 .. **PC 60; TCLC 17, 43**
See also CA 117; 153; CANR 80; CDBLB 1832-1890; DAM POET; DLB 18, 35, 57, 159; RGEL 2; TEA

Meredith, William (Morris) 1919- .... **CLC 4, 13, 22, 55; PC 28**
See also CA 9-12R; CAAS 14; CANR 6, 40, 129; CP 1, 2, 3, 4, 5, 6, 7; DAM POET; DLB 5; MAL 5

Merezhkovsky, Dmitrii Sergeevich
See Merezhkovsky, Dmitry Sergeyevich
See also DLB 295

Merezhkovsky, Dmitry Sergeevich
See Merezhkovsky, Dmitry Sergeyevich
See also EWL 3

Merezhkovsky, Dmitry Sergeyevich
1865-1941 .... **TCLC 29**
See Merezhkovsky, Dmitrii Sergeevich;
Merezhkovsky, Dmitry Sergeevich
See also CA 169

Merimee, Prosper 1803-1870 ... **NCLC 6, 65;
SSC 7, 77**
See also DLB 119, 192; EW 6; EXPS; GFL
1789 to the Present; RGSF 2; RGWL 2,
3; SSFS 8; SUFW

Merkin, Daphne 1954- .... **CLC 44**
See also CA 123

Merleau-Ponty, Maurice
1908-1961 .... **TCLC 156**
See also CA 114; 89-92; DLB 296; GFL
1789 to the Present

Merlin, Arthur
See Blish, James (Benjamin)

Mernissi, Fatima 1940- .... **CLC 171**
See also CA 152; FW

Merrill, James (Ingram) 1926-1995 .. **CLC 2,
3, 6, 8, 13, 18, 34, 91; PC 28; TCLC
173**
See also AMWS 3; CA 13-16R; 147; CANR
10, 49, 63, 108; CP 1, 2, 3, 4; DA3; DAM
POET; DLB 5, 165; DLBY 1985; EWL 3;
INT CANR-10; MAL 5; MTCW 1, 2;
MTFW 2005; PAB; PFS 23; RGAL 4

Merriman, Alex
See Silverberg, Robert

Merriman, Brian 1747-1805 .... **NCLC 70**

Merritt, E. B.
See Waddington, Miriam

Merton, Thomas (James)
1915-1968 . **CLC 1, 3, 11, 34, 83; PC 10**
See also AAYA 61; AMWS 8; CA 5-8R;
25-28R; CANR 22, 53, 111, 131; DA3;
DLB 48; DLBY 1981; MAL 5; MTCW 1,
2; MTFW 2005

Merwin, W(illiam) S(tanley) 1927- ... **CLC 1,
2, 3, 5, 8, 13, 18, 45, 88; PC 45**
See also AMWS 3; CA 13-16R; CANR 15,
51, 112, 140; CP 1, 2, 3, 4, 5, 6, 7; DA3;
DAM POET; DLB 5, 169; EWL 3; INT
CANR-15; MAL 5; MTCW 1, 2; MTFW
2005; PAB; PFS 5, 15; RGAL 4

Metastasio, Pietro 1698-1782 .... **LC 115**
See also RGWL 2, 3

Metcalf, John 1938- .... **CLC 37; SSC 43**
See also CA 113; CN 4, 5, 6, 7; DLB 60;
RGSF 2; TWA

Metcalf, Suzanne
See Baum, L(yman) Frank

Mew, Charlotte (Mary) 1870-1928 .. **TCLC 8**
See also CA 105; 189; DLB 19, 135; RGEL
2

Mewshaw, Michael 1943- .... **CLC 9**
See also CA 53-56; CANR 7, 47; DLBY
1980

Meyer, Conrad Ferdinand
1825-1898 .... **NCLC 81; SSC 30**
See also DLB 129; EW; RGWL 2, 3

Meyer, Gustav 1868-1932
See Meyrink, Gustav
See also CA 117; 190

Meyer, June
See Jordan, June (Meyer)

Meyer, Lynn
See Slavitt, David R(ytman)

Meyers, Jeffrey 1939- .... **CLC 39**
See also CA 73-76; 186; CAAE 186; CANR
54, 102; DLB 111

**Meynell, Alice (Christina Gertrude
Thompson)** 1847-1922 .... **TCLC 6**
See also CA 104; 177; DLB 19, 98; RGEL
2

Meyrink, Gustav .... **TCLC 21**
See Meyer, Gustav
See also DLB 81; EWL 3

Michaels, Leonard 1933-2003 ..... **CLC 6, 25;
SSC 16**
See also CA 61-64; 216; CANR 21, 62, 119;
CN 3, 45, 6, 7; DLB 130; MTCW 1;
TCLE 1:2

Michaux, Henri 1899-1984 .... **CLC 8, 19**
See also CA 85-88; 114; DLB 258; EWL 3;
GFL 1789 to the Present; RGWL 2, 3

Micheaux, Oscar (Devereaux)
1884-1951 .... **TCLC 76**
See also BW 3; CA 174; DLB 50; TCWW
2

Michelangelo 1475-1564 .... **LC 12**
See also AAYA 43

Michelet, Jules 1798-1874 .... **NCLC 31**
See also EW 5; GFL 1789 to the Present

Michels, Robert 1876-1936 .... **TCLC 88**
See also CA 212

Michener, James A(lbert)
1907(?)-1997 .. **CLC 1, 5, 11, 29, 60, 109**
See also AAYA 27; AITN 1; BEST 90:1;
BPFB 2; CA 5-8R; 161; CANR 21, 45,
68; CN 1, 2, 3, 4, 5, 6; DAM
NOV, POP; DLB 6; MAL 5; MTCW 1, 2;
MTFW 2005; RHW; TCWW 1, 2

Mickiewicz, Adam 1798-1855 . **NCLC 3, 101;
PC 38**
See also EW 5; RGWL 2, 3

Middleton, (John) Christopher
1926- .... **CLC 13**
See also CA 13-16R; CANR 29, 54, 117;
CP 1, 2, 3, 4, 5, 6, 7; DLB 40

Middleton, Richard (Barham)
1882-1911 .... **TCLC 56**
See also CA 187; DLB 156; HGG

Middleton, Stanley 1919- .... **CLC 7, 38**
See also CA 25-28R; CAAS 23; CANR 21,
46, 81; CN 1, 2, 3, 4, 5, 6, 7; DLB 14

Middleton, Thomas 1580-1627 ...... **DC 5; LC
33, 123**
See also BRW 2; DAM DRAM, MST; DFS
18, 22; DLB 58; RGEL 2

Migueis, Jose Rodrigues 1901-1980 . **CLC 10**
See also DLB 287

Mikszath, Kalman 1847-1910 .... **TCLC 31**
See also CA 170

Miles, Jack .... **CLC 100**
See also CA 200

Miles, John Russiano
See Miles, Jack

Miles, Josephine (Louise)
1911-1985 .... **CLC 1, 2, 14, 34, 39**
See also CA 1-4R; 116; CANR 2, 55; CP 1,
2, 3, 4; DAM POET; DLB 48; MAL 5;
TCLE 1:2

Militant
See Sandburg, Carl (August)

Mill, Harriet (Hardy) Taylor
1807-1858 .... **NCLC 102**
See also FW

Mill, John Stuart 1806-1873 .... **NCLC 11, 58**
See also CDBLB 1832-1890; DLB 55, 190,
262; FW 1; RGEL 2; TEA

Millar, Kenneth 1915-1983 .... **CLC 14**
See Macdonald, Ross
See also CA 9-12R; 110; CANR 16, 63,
107; CMW 4; CPW; DA3; DAM POP;
DLB 2, 226; DLBD 6; DLBY 1983;
MTCW 1, 2; MTFW 2005

Millay, E. Vincent
See Millay, Edna St. Vincent

Millay, Edna St. Vincent 1892-1950 ..... **PC 6,
61; TCLC 4, 49, 169; WLCS**
See Boyd, Nancy
See also AMW; CA 104; 130; CDALB
1917-1929; DA; DA3; DAB; DAC; DAM
MST, POET; DLB 45, 249; EWL 3;
EXPP; FL 1:6; MAL 5; MAWW; MTCW
1, 2; MTFW 2005; PAB; PFS 3, 17;
RGAL 4; TUS; WP

Miller, Arthur 1915-2005 ..... **CLC 1, 2, 6, 10,
15, 26, 47, 78, 179; DC 1; WLC**
See also AAYA 15; AITN 1; AMW; AMWC
1; CA 1-4R; 236; CABS 3; CAD; CANR
2, 30, 54, 76, 132; CD 5, 6; CDALB
1941-1968; DA; DA3; DAB; DAC; DAM
DRAM, MST; DFS 1, 3, 8; DLB 7, 266;
EWL 3; LAIT 1, 4; LATS 1:2; MAL 5;
MTCW 1, 2; MTFW 2005; RGAL 4;
TUS; WYAS 1

Miller, Henry (Valentine)
1891-1980 .... **CLC 1, 2, 4, 9, 14, 43, 84;
WLC**
See also AMW; BPFB 2; CA 9-12R; 97-
100; CANR 33, 64; CDALB 1929-1941;
CN 1, 2; DA; DA3; DAB; DAC; DAM
MST, NOV; DLB 4, 9; DLBY 1980; EWL
3; MAL 5; MTCW 1, 2; MTFW 2005;
RGAL 4; TUS

Miller, Hugh 1802-1856 .... **NCLC 143**
See also DLB 190

Miller, Jason 1939(?)-2001 .... **CLC 2**
See also AITN 1; CA 73-76; 197; CAD;
CANR 130; DFS 12; DLB 7

Miller, Sue 1943- .... **CLC 44**
See also AMWS 12; BEST 90:3; CA 139;
CANR 59, 91, 128; DA3; DAM POP;
DLB 143

Miller, Walter M(ichael, Jr.)
1923-1996 .... **CLC 4, 30**
See also BPFB 2; CA 85-88; CANR 108;
DLB 8; SCFW 1, 2; SFW 4

Millett, Kate 1934- .... **CLC 67**
See also AITN 1; CA 73-76; CANR 32, 53,
76, 110; DA3; DLB 246; FW; GLL 1;
MTCW 1, 2; MTFW 2005

Millhauser, Steven (Lewis) 1943- .... **CLC 21,
54, 109; SSC 57**
See also CA 110; 111; CANR 63, 114, 133;
CN 6, 7; DA3; DLB 2; FANT; INT CA-
111; MAL 5; MTCW 2; MTFW 2005

Millin, Sarah Gertrude 1889-1968 ... **CLC 49**
See also CA 102; 93-96; DLB 225; EWL 3

Milne, A(lan) A(lexander)
1882-1956 .... **TCLC 6, 88**
See also BRWS 5; CA 104; 133; CLR 1,
26; CMW 4; CWRI 5; DA3; DAB; DAC;
DAM MST; DLB 10, 77, 100, 160; FANT;
MAICYA 1, 2; MTCW 1, 2; MTFW 2005;
RGEL 2; SATA 100; WCH; YABC 1

Milner, Ron(ald) 1938-2004 ..... **BLC 3; CLC
56**
See also AITN 1; BW 1; CA 73-76; 230;
CAD; CANR 24, 81; CD 5, 6; DAM
MULT; DLB 38; MAL 5; MTCW 1

Milnes, Richard Monckton
1809-1885 .... **NCLC 61**
See also DLB 32, 184

Milosz, Czeslaw 1911-2004 .... **CLC 5, 11, 22,
31, 56, 82; PC 8; WLCS**
See also AAYA 62; CA 81-84; 230; CANR
23, 51, 91, 126; CDWLB 4; CWW 2;
DA3; DAM MST, POET; DLB 215; EW
13; EWL 3; MTCW 1, 2; MTFW 2005;
PFS 16; RGWL 2, 3

Milton, John 1608-1674 ..... **LC 9, 43, 92; PC
19, 29; WLC**
See also AAYA 65; BRW 2; BRWR 2; CD-
BLB 1660-1789; DA; DA3; DAB; DAC;
DAM MST, POET; DLB 131, 151, 281;
EFS 1; EXPP; LAIT 1; PAB; PFS 3, 17;
RGEL 2; TEA; WLIT 3; WP

Min, Anchee 1957- .... **CLC 86**
 See also CA 146; CANR 94, 137; MTFW
 2005
Minehaha, Cornelius
 See Wedekind, (Benjamin) Frank(lin)
Miner, Valerie 1947- .... **CLC 40**
 See also CA 97-100; CANR 59; FW; GLL
 2
Minimo, Duca
 See D'Annunzio, Gabriele
Minot, Susan (Anderson) 1956- ...... **CLC 44,**
 159
 See also AMWS 6; CA 134; CANR 118;
 CN 6, 7
Minus, Ed 1938- .... **CLC 39**
 See also CA 185
Mirabai 1498(?)-1550(?) .... **PC 48**
Miranda, Javier
 See Bioy Casares, Adolfo
 See also CWW 2
Mirbeau, Octave 1848-1917 .... **TCLC 55**
 See also CA 216; DLB 123, 192; GFL 1789
 to the Present
Mirikitani, Janice 1942- .... **AAL**
 See also CA 211; DLB 312; RGAL 4
Mirk, John (?)-c. 1414 .... **LC 105**
 See also DLB 146
Miro (Ferrer), Gabriel (Francisco Victor)
 1879-1930 .... **TCLC 5**
 See also CA 104; 185; DLB 322; EWL 3
Misharin, Alexandr .... **CLC 59**
Mishima, Yukio ... **CLC 2, 4, 6, 9, 27; DC 1;**
 SSC 4; TCLC 161
 See Hiraoka, Kimitake
 See also AAYA 50; BPFB 2; GLL 1; MJW;
 RGSF 2; RGWL 2, 3; SSFS 5, 12
Mistral, Frederic 1830-1914 .... **TCLC 51**
 See also CA 122; 213; GFL 1789 to the
 Present
Mistral, Gabriela
 See Godoy Alcayaga, Lucila
 See also DLB 283; DNFS 1; EWL 3; LAW;
 RGWL 2, 3; WP
Mistry, Rohinton 1952- ... **CLC 71, 196; SSC**
 73
 See also BRWS 10; CA 141; CANR 86,
 114; CCA 1; CN 6, 7; DAC; SSFS 6
Mitchell, Clyde
 See Ellison, Harlan (Jay)
Mitchell, Emerson Blackhorse Barney
 1945- .... **NNAL**
 See also CA 45-48
Mitchell, James Leslie 1901-1935
 See Gibbon, Lewis Grassic
 See also CA 104; 188; DLB 15
Mitchell, Joni 1943- .... **CLC 12**
 See also CA 112; CCA 1
Mitchell, Joseph (Quincy)
 1908-1996 .... **CLC 98**
 See also CA 77-80; 152; CANR 69; CN 1,
 2, 3, 4, 5, 6; CSW; DLB 185; DLBY 1996
Mitchell, Margaret (Munnerlyn)
 1900-1949 .... **TCLC 11, 170**
 See also AAYA 23; BPFB 2; BYA 1; CA
 109; 125; CANR 55, 94; CDALBS; DA3;
 DAM NOV, POP; DLB 9; LAIT 2; MAL
 5; MTCW 1, 2; MTFW 2005; NFS 9;
 RGAL 4; RHW; TUS; WYAS 1; YAW
Mitchell, Peggy
 See Mitchell, Margaret (Munnerlyn)
Mitchell, S(ilas) Weir 1829-1914 .... **TCLC 36**
 See also CA 165; DLB 202; RGAL 4
Mitchell, W(illiam) O(rmond)
 1914-1998 .... **CLC 25**
 See also CA 77-80; 165; CANR 15, 43; CN
 1, 2, 3, 4, 5, 6; DAC; DAM MST; DLB
 88; TCLE 1:2

Mitchell, William (Lendrum)
 1879-1936 .... **TCLC 81**
 See also CA 213
Mitford, Mary Russell 1787-1855 ... **NCLC 4**
 See also DLB 110, 116; RGEL 2
Mitford, Nancy 1904-1973 .... **CLC 44**
 See also BRWS 10; CA 9-12R; CN 1; DLB
 191; RGEL 2
Miyamoto, (Chujo) Yuriko
 1899-1951 .... **TCLC 37**
 See Miyamoto Yuriko
 See also CA 170, 174
Miyamoto Yuriko
 See Miyamoto, (Chujo) Yuriko
 See also DLB 180
Miyazawa, Kenji 1896-1933 .... **TCLC 76**
 See Miyazawa Kenji
 See also CA 157; RGWL 3
Miyazawa Kenji
 See Miyazawa, Kenji
 See also EWL 3
Mizoguchi, Kenji 1898-1956 .... **TCLC 72**
 See also CA 167
Mo, Timothy (Peter) 1950- .... **CLC 46, 134**
 See also CA 117; CANR 128; CN 5, 6, 7;
 DLB 194; MTCW 1; WLIT 4; WWE 1
Modarressi, Taghi (M.) 1931-1997 ... **CLC 44**
 See also CA 121; 134; INT CA-134
Modiano, Patrick (Jean) 1945- .... **CLC 18,**
 218
 See also CA 85-88; CANR 17, 40, 115;
 CWW 2; DLB 83, 299; EWL 3
Mofolo, Thomas (Mokopu)
 1875(?)-1948 .... **BLC 3; TCLC 22**
 See also AFW; CA 121; 153; CANR 83;
 DAM MULT; DLB 225; EWL 3; MTCW
 2; MTFW 2005; WLIT 2
Mohr, Nicholasa 1938- .... **CLC 12; HLC 2**
 See also AAYA 8, 46; CA 49-52; CANR 1,
 32, 64; CLR 22; DAM MULT; DLB 145;
 HW 1, 2; JRDA; LAIT 5; LLW; MAICYA
 2; MAICYAS 1; RGAL 4; SAAS 8; SATA
 8, 97; SATA-Essay 113; WYA; YAW
Moi, Toril 1953- .... **CLC 172**
 See also CA 154; CANR 102; FW
Mojtabai, A(nn) G(race) 1938- ..... **CLC 5, 9,**
 15, 29
 See also CA 85-88; CANR 88
Moliere 1622-1673 ..... **DC 13; LC 10, 28, 64;**
 WLC
 See also DA; DA3; DAB; DAC; DAM
 DRAM, MST; DFS 13, 18, 20; DLB 268;
 EW 3; GFL Beginnings to 1789; LATS
 1:1; RGWL 2, 3; TWA
Molin, Charles
 See Mayne, William (James Carter)
Molnar, Ferenc 1878-1952 .... **TCLC 20**
 See also CA 109; 153; CANR 83; CDWLB
 4; DAM DRAM; DLB 215; EWL 3;
 RGWL 2, 3
Momaday, N(avarre) Scott 1934- ...... **CLC 2,**
 19, 85, 95, 160; NNAL; PC 25; WLCS
 See also AAYA 11, 64; AMWS 4; ANW;
 BPFB 2; BYA 12; CA 25-28R; CANR 14,
 34, 68, 134; CDALBS; CN 2, 3, 4, 5, 6,
 7; CPW; DA; DA3; DAB; DAC; DAM
 MST, MULT, NOV, POP; DLB 143, 175,
 256; EWL 3; EXPP; INT CANR-14;
 LAIT 4; LATS 1:2; MAL 5; MTCW 1, 2;
 MTFW 2005; NFS 10; PFS 2, 11; RGAL
 4; SATA 48; SATA-Brief 30; TCWW 1,
 2; WP; YAW
Monette, Paul 1945-1995 .... **CLC 82**
 See also AMWS 10; CA 139; 147; CN 6;
 GLL 1
Monroe, Harriet 1860-1936 .... **TCLC 12**
 See also CA 109; 204; DLB 54, 91
Monroe, Lyle
 See Heinlein, Robert A(nson)

Montagu, Elizabeth 1720-1800 .... **NCLC 7,**
 117
 See also FW
Montagu, Mary (Pierrepont) Wortley
 1689-1762 .... **LC 9, 57; PC 16**
 See also DLB 95, 101; FL 1:1; RGEL 2
Montagu, W. H.
 See Coleridge, Samuel Taylor
Montague, John (Patrick) 1929- ..... **CLC 13,**
 46
 See also CA 9-12R; CANR 9, 69, 121; CP
 1, 2, 3, 4, 5, 6, 7; DLB 40; EWL 3;
 MTCW 1; PFS 12; RGEL 2; TCLE 1:2
Montaigne, Michel (Eyquem) de
 1533-1592 .... **LC 8, 105; WLC**
 See also DA; DAB; DAC; DAM MST; EW
 2; GFL Beginnings to 1789; LMFS 1;
 RGWL 2, 3; TWA
Montale, Eugenio 1896-1981 ... **CLC 7, 9, 18;**
 PC 13
 See also CA 17-20R; 104; CANR 30; DLB
 114; EW 11; EWL 3; MTCW 1; PFS 22;
 RGWL 2, 3; TWA; WLIT 7
Montesquieu, Charles-Louis de Secondat
 1689-1755 .... **LC 7, 69**
 See also DLB 314; EW 3; GFL Beginnings
 to 1789; TWA
Montessori, Maria 1870-1952 ...... **TCLC 103**
 See also CA 115; 147
Montgomery, (Robert) Bruce 1921(?)-1978
 See Crispin, Edmund
 See also CA 179; 104; CMW 4
Montgomery, L(ucy) M(aud)
 1874-1942 .... **TCLC 51, 140**
 See also AAYA 12; BYA 1; CA 108; 137;
 CLR 8, 91; DA3; DAC; DAM MST; DLB
 92; DLBD 14; JRDA; MAICYA 1, 2;
 MTCW 2; MTFW 2005; RGEL 2; SATA
 100; TWA; WCH; WYA; YABC 1
Montgomery, Marion H., Jr. 1925- .... **CLC 7**
 See also AITN 1; CA 1-4R; CANR 3, 48;
 CSW; DLB 6
Montgomery, Max
 See Davenport, Guy (Mattison, Jr.)
Montherlant, Henry (Milon) de
 1896-1972 .... **CLC 8, 19**
 See also CA 85-88; 37-40R; DAM DRAM;
 DLB 72, 321; EW 11; EWL 3; GFL 1789
 to the Present; MTCW 1
Monty Python
 See Chapman, Graham; Cleese, John
 (Marwood); Gilliam, Terry (Vance); Idle,
 Eric; Jones, Terence Graham Parry; Palin,
 Michael (Edward)
 See also AAYA 7
Moodie, Susanna (Strickland)
 1803-1885 .... **NCLC 14, 113**
 See also DLB 99
Moody, Hiram (F. III) 1961-
 See Moody, Rick
 See also CA 138; CANR 64, 112; MTFW
 2005
Moody, Minerva
 See Alcott, Louisa May
Moody, Rick .... **CLC 147**
 See Moody, Hiram (F. III)
Moody, William Vaughan
 1869-1910 .... **TCLC 105**
 See also CA 110; 178; DLB 7, 54; MAL 5;
 RGAL 4
Mooney, Edward 1951-
 See Mooney, Ted
 See also CA 130
Mooney, Ted .... **CLC 25**
 See Mooney, Edward

Mourning Dove 1885(?)-1936 .... **NNAL**
See also CA 144; CANR 90; DAM MULT; DLB 175, 221
Mowat, Farley (McGill) 1921- .... **CLC 26**
See also AAYA 1, 50; BYA 2; CA 1-4R; CANR 4, 24, 42, 68, 108; CLR 20; CPW; DAC; DAM MST; DLB 68; INT CANR-24; JRDA; MAICYA 1, 2; MTCW 1, 2; MTFW 2005; SATA 3, 55; YAW
Mowatt, Anna Cora 1819-1870 ..... **NCLC 74**
See also RGAL 4
Moyers, Bill 1934- .... **CLC 74**
See also AITN 2; CA 61-64; CANR 31, 52
Mphahlele, Es'kia
See Mphahlele, Ezekiel
See also AFW; CDWLB 3; CN 4, 5, 6; DLB 125, 225; RGSF 2; SSFS 11
Mphahlele, Ezekiel 1919- ... **BLC 3; CLC 25, 133**
See Mphahlele, Es'kia
See also BW 2, 3; CA 81-84; CANR 26, 76; CN 1, 2, 3; DAM MULT; EWL 3; MTCW 2; MTFW 2005; SATA 119
Mqhayi, S(amuel) E(dward) K(rune Loliwe) 1875-1945 .... **BLC 3; TCLC 25**
See also CA 153; CANR 87; DAM MULT
Mrozek, Slawomir 1930- .... **CLC 3, 13**
See also CA 13-16R; CAAS 10; CANR 29; CDWLB 4; CWW 2; DLB 232; EWL 3; MTCW 1
Mrs. Belloc-Lowndes
See Lowndes, Marie Adelaide (Belloc)
Mrs. Fairstar
See Horne, Richard Henry Hengist
M'Taggart, John M'Taggart Ellis
See McTaggart, John McTaggart Ellis
Mtwa, Percy (?)- .... **CLC 47**
See also CD 6
Mueller, Lisel 1924- .... **CLC 13, 51; PC 33**
See also CA 93-96; CP 7; DLB 105; PFS 9, 13
Muggeridge, Malcolm (Thomas) 1903-1990 .... **TCLC 120**
See also AITN 1; CA 101; CANR 33, 63; MTCW 1, 2
Muhammad 570-632 .... **WLCS**
See also DA; DAB; DAC; DAM MST; DLB 311
Muir, Edwin 1887-1959 . **PC 49; TCLC 2, 87**
See Moore, Edward
See also BRWS 6; CA 104; 193; DLB 20, 100, 191; EWL 3; RGEL 2
Muir, John 1838-1914 .... **TCLC 28**
See also AMWS 9; ANW; CA 165; DLB 186, 275
Mujica Lainez, Manuel 1910-1984 ... **CLC 31**
See Lainez, Manuel Mujica
See also CA 81-84; 112; CANR 32; EWL 3; HW 1
Mukherjee, Bharati 1940- ..... **AAL; CLC 53, 115; SSC 38**
See also AAYA 46; BEST 89:2; CA 107, 232; CAAE 232; CANR 45, 72, 128; CN 5, 6, 7; DAM NOV; DLB 60, 218; DNFS 1, 2; EWL 3; FW; MAL 5; MTCW 1, 2; MTFW 2005; RGAL 4; RGSF 2; SSFS 7; TUS; WWE 1
Muldoon, Paul 1951- .... **CLC 32, 72, 166**
See also BRWS 4; CA 113; 129; CANR 52, 91; CP 2, 3, 4, 5, 6, 7; DAM POET; DLB 40; INT CA-129; PFS 7, 22; TCLE 1:2
Mulisch, Harry (Kurt Victor) 1927- .... **CLC 42**
See also CA 9-12R; CANR 6, 26, 56, 110; CWW 2; DLB 299; EWL 3
Mull, Martin 1943- .... **CLC 17**
See also CA 105

Muller, Wilhelm .... **NCLC 73**
Mulock, Dinah Maria
See Craik, Dinah Maria (Mulock)
See also RGEL 2
Multatuli 1820-1887 .... **NCLC 165**
See also RGWL 2, 3
Munday, Anthony 1560-1633 .... **LC 87**
See also DLB 62, 172; RGEL 2
Munford, Robert 1737(?)-1783 .... **LC 5**
See also DLB 31
Mungo, Raymond 1946- .... **CLC 72**
See also CA 49-52; CANR 2
Munro, Alice (Anne) 1931- .... **CLC 6, 10, 19, 50, 95; SSC 3; WLCS**
See also AITN 2; BPFB 2; CA 33-36R; CANR 33, 53, 75, 114; CCA 1; CN 1, 2, 3, 4, 5, 6, 7; DA3; DAC; DAM MST, NOV; DLB 53; EWL 3; MTCW 1, 2; MTFW 2005; RGEL 2; RGSF 2; SATA 29; SSFS 5, 13, 19; TCLE 1:2; WWE 1
Munro, H(ector) H(ugh) 1870-1916 .... **WLC**
See Saki
See also AAYA 56; CA 104; 130; CANR 104; CDBLB 1890-1914; DA; DA3; DAB; DAC; DAM MST, NOV; DLB 34, 162; EXPS; MTCW 1, 2; MTFW 2005; RGEL 2; SSFS 15
Murakami, Haruki 1949- .... **CLC 150**
See Murakami Haruki
See also CA 165; CANR 102, 146; MJW; RGWL 3; SFW 4
Murakami Haruki
See Murakami, Haruki
See also CWW 2; DLB 182; EWL 3
Murasaki, Lady
See Murasaki Shikibu
Murasaki Shikibu 978(?)-1026(?) .. **CMLC 1, 79**
See also EFS 2; LATS 1:1; RGWL 2, 3
Murdoch, (Jean) Iris 1919-1999 ... **CLC 1, 2, 3, 4, 6, 8, 11, 15, 22, 31, 51; TCLC 171**
See also BRWS 1; CA 13-16R; 179; CANR 8, 43, 68, 103, 142; CBD; CDBLB 1960 to Present; CN 1, 2, 3, 4, 5, 6; CWD; DA3; DAB; DAC; DAM MST, NOV; DLB 14, 194, 233; EWL 3; INT CANR-8; MTCW 1, 2; MTFW 2005; NFS 18; RGEL 2; TCLE 1:2; TEA; WLIT 4
Murfree, Mary Noailles 1850-1922 .. **SSC 22; TCLC 135**
See also CA 122; 176; DLB 12, 74; RGAL 4
Murnau, Friedrich Wilhelm
See Plumpe, Friedrich Wilhelm
Murphy, Richard 1927- .... **CLC 41**
See also BRWS 5; CA 29-32R; CP 1, 2, 3, 4, 5, 6, 7; DLB 40; EWL 3
Murphy, Sylvia 1937- .... **CLC 34**
See also CA 121
Murphy, Thomas (Bernard) 1935- ... **CLC 51**
See Murphy, Tom
See also CA 101
Murphy, Tom
See Murphy, Thomas (Bernard)
See also DLB 310
Murray, Albert L. 1916- .... **CLC 73**
See also BW 2; CA 49-52; CANR 26, 52, 78; CN 7; CSW; DLB 38; MTFW 2005
Murray, James Augustus Henry 1837-1915 .... **TCLC 117**
Murray, Judith Sargent 1751-1820 .... **NCLC 63**
See also DLB 37, 200
Murray, Les(lie Allan) 1938- .... **CLC 40**
See also BRWS 7; CA 21-24R; CANR 11, 27, 56, 103; CP 1, 2, 3, 4, 5, 6, 7; DAM POET; DLB 289; DLBY 2001; EWL 3; RGEL 2

Murry, J. Middleton
See Murry, John Middleton
Murry, John Middleton 1889-1957 .... **TCLC 16**
See also CA 118; 217; DLB 149
Musgrave, Susan 1951- .... **CLC 13, 54**
See also CA 69-72; CANR 45, 84; CCA 1; CP 2, 3, 4, 5, 6, 7; CWP
Musil, Robert (Edler von) 1880-1942 .... **SSC 18; TCLC 12, 68**
See also CA 109; CANR 55, 84; CDWLB 2; DLB 81, 124; EW 9; EWL 3; MTCW 2; RGSF 2; RGWL 2, 3
Muske, Carol .... **CLC 90**
See Muske-Dukes, Carol (Anne)
Muske-Dukes, Carol (Anne) 1945-
See Muske, Carol
See also CA 65-68, 203; CAAE 203; CANR 32, 70; CWP
Musset, (Louis Charles) Alfred de 1810-1857 .... **DC 27; NCLC 7, 150**
See also DLB 192, 217; EW 6; GFL 1789 to the Present; RGWL 2, 3; TWA
Mussolini, Benito (Amilcare Andrea) 1883-1945 .... **TCLC 96**
See also CA 116
Mutanabbi, Al-
See al-Mutanabbi, Ahmad ibn al-Husayn Abu al-Tayyib al-Jufi al-Kindi
See also WLIT 6
My Brother's Brother
See Chekhov, Anton (Pavlovich)
Myers, L(eopold) H(amilton) 1881-1944 .... **TCLC 59**
See also CA 157; DLB 15; EWL 3; RGEL 2
Myers, Walter Dean 1937- .. **BLC 3; CLC 35**
See also AAYA 4, 23; BW 2; BYA 6, 8, 11; CA 33-36R; CANR 20, 42, 67, 108; CLR 4, 16, 35; DAM MULT, NOV; DLB 33; INT CANR-20; JRDA; LAIT 5; MAICYA 1, 2; MAICYAS 1; MTCW 2; MTFW 2005; SAAS 2; SATA 41, 71, 109, 157; SATA-Brief 27; WYA; YAW
Myers, Walter M.
See Myers, Walter Dean
Myles, Symon
See Follett, Ken(neth Martin)
Nabokov, Vladimir (Vladimirovich) 1899-1977 .... **CLC 1, 2, 3, 6, 8, 11, 15, 23, 44, 46, 64; SSC 11, 86; TCLC 108; WLC**
See also AAYA 45; AMW; AMWC 1; AMWR 1; BPFB 2; CA 5-8R; 69-72; CANR 20, 102; CDALB 1941-1968; CN 1, 2; CP 2; DA; DA3; DAB; DAC; DAM MST, NOV; DLB 2, 244, 278, 317; DLBD 3; DLBY 1980, 1991; EWL 3; EXPS; LATS 1:2; MAL 5; MTCW 1, 2; MTFW 2005; NCFS 4; NFS 9; RGAL 4; RGSF 2; SSFS 6, 15; TUS
Naevius c. 265B.C.-201B.C. .... **CMLC 37**
See also DLB 211
Nagai, Kafu .... **TCLC 51**
See Nagai, Sokichi
See also DLB 180
Nagai, Sokichi 1879-1959
See Nagai, Kafu
See also CA 117
Nagy, Laszlo 1925-1978 .... **CLC 7**
See also CA 129; 112
Naidu, Sarojini 1879-1949 .... **TCLC 80**
See also EWL 3; RGEL 2
Naipaul, Shiva(dhar Srinivasa) 1945-1985 .... **CLC 32, 39; TCLC 153**
See also CA 110; 112; 116; CANR 33; CN 2, 3; DA3; DAM NOV; DLB 157; DLBY 1985; EWL 3; MTCW 1, 2; MTFW 2005

Niven, Larry .... **CLC 8**
See Niven, Laurence Van Cott
See also AAYA 27; BPFB 2; BYA 10; DLB 8; SCFW 1, 2

Niven, Laurence Van Cott 1938-
See Niven, Larry
See also CA 21-24R, 207; CAAE 207; CAAS 12; CANR 14, 44, 66, 113; CPW; DAM POP; MTCW 1, 2; SATA 95; SFW 4

Nixon, Agnes Eckhardt 1927- .... **CLC 21**
See also CA 110

Nizan, Paul 1905-1940 .... **TCLC 40**
See also CA 161; DLB 72; EWL 3; GFL 1789 to the Present

Nkosi, Lewis 1936- .... **BLC 3; CLC 45**
See also BW 1, 3; CA 65-68; CANR 27, 81; CBD; CD 5, 6; DAM MULT; DLB 157, 225; WWE 1

Nodier, (Jean) Charles (Emmanuel) 1780-1844 .... **NCLC 19**
See also DLB 119; GFL 1789 to the Present

Noguchi, Yone 1875-1947 .... **TCLC 80**

Nolan, Christopher 1965- .... **CLC 58**
See also CA 111; CANR 88

Noon, Jeff 1957- .... **CLC 91**
See also CA 148; CANR 83; DLB 267; SFW 4

Norden, Charles
See Durrell, Lawrence (George)

Nordhoff, Charles Bernard 1887-1947 .... **TCLC 23**
See also CA 108; 211; DLB 9; LAIT 1; RHW 1; SATA 23

Norfolk, Lawrence 1963- .... **CLC 76**
See also CA 144; CANR 85; CN 6, 7; DLB 267

Norman, Marsha (Williams) 1947- . **CLC 28, 186; DC 8**
See also CA 105; CABS 3; CAD; CANR 41, 131; CD 5, 6; CSW; CWD; DAM DRAM; DFS 2; DLB 266; DLBY 1984; FW; MAL 5

Normyx
See Douglas, (George) Norman

Norris, (Benjamin) Frank(lin, Jr.) 1870-1902 .... **SSC 28; TCLC 24, 155**
See also AAYA 57; AMW; AMWC 2; BPFB 2; CA 110; 160; CDALB 1865-1917; DLB 12, 71, 186; LMFS 2; NFS 12; RGAL 4; TCWW 1, 2; TUS

Norris, Leslie 1921- .... **CLC 14**
See also CA 11-12; CANR 14, 117; CAP 1; CP 1, 2, 3, 4, 5, 6, 7; DLB 27, 256

North, Andrew
See Norton, Andre

North, Anthony
See Koontz, Dean R.

North, Captain George
See Stevenson, Robert Louis (Balfour)

North, Captain George
See Stevenson, Robert Louis (Balfour)

North, Milou
See Erdrich, (Karen) Louise

Northrup, B. A.
See Hubbard, L(afayette) Ron(ald)

North Staffs
See Hulme, T(homas) E(rnest)

Northup, Solomon 1808-1863 .... **NCLC 105**

Norton, Alice Mary
See Norton, Andre
See also MAICYA 1; SATA 1, 43

Norton, Andre 1912-2005 .... **CLC 12**
See Norton, Alice Mary
See also AAYA 14; BPFB 2; BYA 4, 10, 12; CA 1-4R; 237; CANR 68; CLR 50; DLB 8, 52; JRDA; MAICYA 2; MTCW 1; SATA 91; SUFW 1, 2; YAW

Norton, Caroline 1808-1877 .... **NCLC 47**
See also DLB 21, 159, 199

Norway, Nevil Shute 1899-1960
See Shute, Nevil
See also CA 102; 93-96; CANR 85; MTCW 2

Norwid, Cyprian Kamil 1821-1883 .... **NCLC 17**
See also RGWL 3

Nosille, Nabrah
See Ellison, Harlan (Jay)

Nossack, Hans Erich 1901-1978 .... **CLC 6**
See also CA 93-96; 85-88; DLB 69; EWL 3

Nostradamus 1503-1566 .... **LC 27**

Nosu, Chuji
See Ozu, Yasujiro

Notenburg, Eleanora (Genrikhovna) von
See Guro, Elena (Genrikhovna)

Nova, Craig 1945- .... **CLC 7, 31**
See also CA 45-48; CANR 2, 53, 127

Novak, Joseph
See Kosinski, Jerzy (Nikodem)

Novalis 1772-1801 .... **NCLC 13**
See also CDWLB 2; DLB 90; EW 5; RGWL 2, 3

Novick, Peter 1934- .... **CLC 164**
See also CA 188

Novis, Emile
See Weil, Simone (Adolphine)

Nowlan, Alden (Albert) 1933-1983 .... **CLC 15**
See also CA 9-12R; CANR 5; CP 1, 2, 3; DAC; DAM MST; DLB 53; PFS 12

Noyes, Alfred 1880-1958 .... **PC 27; TCLC 7**
See also CA 104; 188; DLB 20; EXPP; FANT; PFS 4; RGEL 2

Nugent, Richard Bruce 1906(?)-1987 .... **HR 1:3**
See also BW 1; CA 125; DLB 51; GLL 2

Nunn, Kem .... **CLC 34**
See also CA 159

Nussbaum, Martha Craven 1947- .. **CLC 203**
See also CA 134; CANR 102

Nwapa, Flora (Nwanzuruaha) 1931-1993 .... **BLCS; CLC 133**
See also BW 2; CA 143; CANR 83; CDWLB 3; CWRI 5; DLB 125; EWL 3; WLIT 2

Nye, Robert 1939- .... **CLC 13, 42**
See also BRWS 10; CA 33-36R; CANR 29, 67, 107; CN 1, 2, 3, 4, 5, 6, 7; CP 1, 2, 3, 4, 5, 6, 7; CWRI 5; DAM NOV; DLB 14, 271; FANT; HGG; MTCW 1; RHW; SATA 6

Nyro, Laura 1947-1997 .... **CLC 17**
See also CA 194

Oates, Joyce Carol 1938- .. **CLC 1, 2, 3, 6, 9, 11, 15, 19, 33, 52, 108, 134; SSC 6, 70; WLC**
See also AAYA 15, 52; AITN 1; AMWS 2; BEST 89:2; BPFB 2; BYA 11; CA 5-8R; CANR 25, 45, 74, 113, 129; CDALB 1968-1988; CN 1, 2, 3, 4, 5, 6, 7; CP 7; CPW; CWP; DA; DA3; DAB; DAC; DAM MST, NOV, POP; DLB 2, 5, 130; DLBY 1981; EWL 3; EXPS; FL 1:6; FW; GL 3; HGG; INT CANR-25; LAIT 4; MAL 5; MAWW; MTCW 1, 2; MTFW 2005; NFS 8; RGAL 4; RGSF 2; SATA 159; SSFS 1, 8, 17; SUFW 2; TUS

O'Brian, E. G.
See Clarke, Arthur C(harles)

O'Brian, Patrick 1914-2000 .... **CLC 152**
See also AAYA 55; CA 144; 187; CANR 74; CPW; MTCW 2; MTFW 2005; RHW

O'Brien, Darcy 1939-1998 .... **CLC 11**
See also CA 21-24R; 167; CANR 8, 59

O'Brien, Edna 1932- ..... **CLC 3, 5, 8, 13, 36, 65, 116; SSC 10, 77**
See also BRWS 5; CA 1-4R; CANR 6, 41, 65, 102; CDBLB 1960 to Present; CN 1, 2, 3, 4, 5, 6, 7; DA3; DAM NOV; DLB 14, 231, 319; EWL 3; FW; MTCW 1, 2; MTFW 2005; RGSF 2; WLIT 4

O'Brien, Fitz-James 1828-1862 ..... **NCLC 21**
See also DLB 74; RGAL 4; SUFW

O'Brien, Flann .... **CLC 1, 4, 5, 7, 10, 47**
See O Nuallain, Brian
See also BRWS 2; DLB 231; EWL 3; RGEL 2

O'Brien, Richard 1942- .... **CLC 17**
See also CA 124

O'Brien, (William) Tim(othy) 1946- . **CLC 7, 19, 40, 103, 211; SSC 74**
See also AAYA 16; AMWS 5; CA 85-88; CANR 40, 58, 133; CDALBS; CN 5, 6, 7; CPW; DA3; DAM POP; DLB 152; DLBD 9; DLBY 1980; LATS 1:2; MAL 5; MTCW 2; MTFW 2005; RGAL 4; SSFS 5, 15; TCLE 1:2

Obstfelder, Sigbjoern 1866-1900 .... **TCLC 23**
See also CA 123

O'Casey, Sean 1880-1964 .... **CLC 1, 5, 9, 11, 15, 88; DC 12; WLCS**
See also BRW 7; CA 89-92; CANR 62; CBD; CDBLB 1914-1945; DA3; DAB; DAC; DAM DRAM, MST; DFS 19; DLB 10; EWL 3; MTCW 1, 2; MTFW 2005; RGEL 2; TEA; WLIT 4

O'Cathasaigh, Sean
See O'Casey, Sean

Occom, Samson 1723-1792 .... **LC 60; NNAL**
See also DLB 175

Ochs, Phil(ip David) 1940-1976 .... **CLC 17**
See also CA 185; 65-68

O'Connor, Edwin (Greene) 1918-1968 .... **CLC 14**
See also CA 93-96; 25-28R; MAL 5

O'Connor, (Mary) Flannery 1925-1964 .... **CLC 1, 2, 3, 6, 10, 13, 15, 21, 66, 104; SSC 1, 23, 61, 82; TCLC 132; WLC**
See also AAYA 7; AMW; AMWR 2; BPFB 3; BYA 16; CA 1-4R; CANR 3, 41; CDALB 1941-1968; DA; DA3; DAB; DAC; DAM MST, NOV; DLB 2, 152; DLBD 12; DLBY 1980; EWL 3; EXPS; LAIT 5; MAL 5; MAWW; MTCW 1, 2; MTFW 2005; NFS 3, 21; RGAL 4; RGSF 2; SSFS 2, 7, 10, 19; TUS

O'Connor, Frank .... **CLC 23; SSC 5**
See O'Donovan, Michael Francis
See also DLB 162; EWL 3; RGSF 2; SSFS 5

O'Dell, Scott 1898-1989 .... **CLC 30**
See also AAYA 3, 44; BPFB 3; BYA 1, 2, 3, 5; CA 61-64; 129; CANR 12, 30, 112; CLR 1, 16; DLB 52; JRDA; MAICYA 1, 2; SATA 12, 60, 134; WYA; YAW

Odets, Clifford 1906-1963 ..... **CLC 2, 28, 98; DC 6**
See also AMWS 2; CA 85-88; CAD; CANR 62; DAM DRAM; DFS 3, 17, 20; DLB 7, 26; EWL 3; MAL 5; MTCW 1, 2; MTFW 2005; RGAL 4; TUS

O'Doherty, Brian 1928- .... **CLC 76**
See also CA 105; CANR 108

O'Donnell, K. M.
See Malzberg, Barry N(athaniel)

O'Donnell, Lawrence
See Kuttner, Henry

O'Donovan, Michael Francis 1903-1966 .... **CLC 14**
See O'Connor, Frank
See also CA 93-96; CANR 84

Oskison, John Milton
1874-1947 .... **NNAL; TCLC 35**
See also CA 144; CANR 84; DAM MULT;
DLB 175
Ossian c. 3rd cent. - .... **CMLC 28**
See Macpherson, James
Ossoli, Sarah Margaret (Fuller)
1810-1850 .... **NCLC 5, 50**
See Fuller, Margaret; Fuller, Sarah Margaret
See also CDALB 1640-1865; FW; LMFS 1;
SATA 25
Ostriker, Alicia (Suskin) 1937- .... **CLC 132**
See also CA 25-28R; CAAS 24; CANR 10,
30, 62, 99; CWP; DLB 120; EXPP; PFS
19
Ostrovsky, Aleksandr Nikolaevich
See Ostrovsky, Alexander
See also DLB 277
Ostrovsky, Alexander 1823-1886 .. **NCLC 30,
57**
See Ostrovsky, Aleksandr Nikolaevich
Otero, Blas de 1916-1979 .... **CLC 11**
See also CA 89-92; DLB 134; EWL 3
O'Trigger, Sir Lucius
See Horne, Richard Henry Hengist
Otto, Rudolf 1869-1937 .... **TCLC 85**
Otto, Whitney 1955- .... **CLC 70**
See also CA 140; CANR 120
Otway, Thomas 1652-1685 ... **DC 24; LC 106**
See also DAM DRAM; DLB 80; RGEL 2
Ouida .... **TCLC 43**
See De la Ramee, Marie Louise (Ouida)
See also DLB 18, 156; RGEL 2
Ouologuem, Yambo 1940- .... **CLC 146**
See also CA 111; 176
Ousmane, Sembene 1923- ... **BLC 3; CLC 66**
See Sembene, Ousmane
See also BW 1, 3; CA 117; 125; CANR 81;
CWW 2; MTCW 1
Ovid 43B.C.-17 .... **CMLC 7; PC 2**
See also AW 2; CDWLB 1; DA3; DAM
POET; DLB 211; PFS 22; RGWL 2, 3;
WP
Owen, Hugh
See Faust, Frederick (Schiller)
Owen, Wilfred (Edward Salter)
1893-1918 ... **PC 19; TCLC 5, 27; WLC**
See also BRW 6; CA 104; 141; CDBLB
1914-1945; DA; DAB; DAC; DAM MST,
POET; DLB 20; EWL 3; EXPP; MTCW
2; MTFW 2005; PFS 10; RGEL 2; WLIT
4
Owens, Louis (Dean) 1948-2002 .... **NNAL**
See also CA 137, 179; 207; CAAE 179;
CAAS 24; CANR 71
Owens, Rochelle 1936- .... **CLC 8**
See also CA 17-20R; CAAS 2; CAD;
CANR 39; CD 5, 6; CP 1, 2, 3, 4, 5, 6, 7;
CWD; CWP
Oz, Amos 1939- ...... **CLC 5, 8, 11, 27, 33, 54;
SSC 66**
See also CA 53-56; CANR 27, 47, 65, 113,
138; CWW 2; DAM NOV; EWL 3;
MTCW 1, 2; MTFW 2005; RGSF 2;
RGWL 3; WLIT 6
Ozick, Cynthia 1928- .... **CLC 3, 7, 28, 62,
155; SSC 15, 60**
See also AMWS 5; BEST 90:1; CA 17-20R;
CANR 23, 58, 116; CN 3, 4, 5, 6, 7;
CPW; DA3; DAM NOV, POP; DLB 28,
152, 299; DLBY 1982; EWL 3; EXPS;
INT CANR-23; MAL 5; MTCW 1, 2;
MTFW 2005; RGAL 4; RGSF 2; SSFS 3,
12
Ozu, Yasujiro 1903-1963 .... **CLC 16**
See also CA 112
Pabst, G. W. 1885-1967 .... **TCLC 127**
Pacheco, C.
See Pessoa, Fernando (Antonio Nogueira)

Pacheco, Jose Emilio 1939- .... **HLC 2**
See also CA 111; 131; CANR 65; CWW 2;
DAM MULT; DLB 290; EWL 3; HW 1,
2; RGSF 2
Pa Chin .... **CLC 18**
See Li Fei-kan
See also EWL 3
Pack, Robert 1929- .... **CLC 13**
See also CA 1-4R; CANR 3, 44, 82; CP 1,
2, 3, 4, 5, 6, 7; DLB 5; SATA 118
Padgett, Lewis
See Kuttner, Henry
Padilla (Lorenzo), Heberto
1932-2000 .... **CLC 38**
See also AITN 1; CA 123; 131; 189; CWW
2; EWL 3; HW 1
Page, James Patrick 1944-
See Page, Jimmy
See also CA 204
Page, Jimmy 1944- .... **CLC 12**
See Page, James Patrick
Page, Louise 1955- .... **CLC 40**
See also CA 140; CANR 76; CBD; CD 5,
6; CWD; DLB 233
Page, P(atricia) K(athleen) 1916- ...... **CLC 7,
18; PC 12**
See Cape, Judith
See also CA 53-56; CANR 4, 22, 65; CP 1,
2, 3, 4, 5, 6, 7; DAC; DAM MST; DLB
68; MTCW 1; RGEL 2
Page, Stanton
See Fuller, Henry Blake
Page, Stanton
See Fuller, Henry Blake
Page, Thomas Nelson 1853-1922 .... **SSC 23**
See also CA 118; 177; DLB 12, 78; DLBD
13; RGAL 4
Pagels, Elaine Hiesey 1943- .... **CLC 104**
See also CA 45-48; CANR 2, 24, 51; FW;
NCFS 4
Paget, Violet 1856-1935
See Lee, Vernon
See also CA 104; 166; GLL 1; HGG
Paget-Lowe, Henry
See Lovecraft, H(oward) P(hillips)
Paglia, Camille (Anna) 1947- .... **CLC 68**
See also CA 140; CANR 72, 139; CPW;
FW; GLL 2; MTCW 2; MTFW 2005
Paige, Richard
See Koontz, Dean R.
Paine, Thomas 1737-1809 .... **NCLC 62**
See also AMWS 1; CDALB 1640-1865;
DLB 31, 43, 73, 158; LAIT 1; RGAL 4;
RGEL 2; TUS
Pakenham, Antonia
See Fraser, Antonia (Pakenham)
Palamas, Costis
See Palamas, Kostes
Palamas, Kostes 1859-1943 .... **TCLC 5**
See Palamas, Kostis
See also CA 105; 190; RGWL 2, 3
Palamas, Kostis
See Palamas, Kostes
See also EWL 3
Palazzeschi, Aldo 1885-1974 .... **CLC 11**
See also CA 89-92; 53-56; DLB 114, 264;
EWL 3
Pales Matos, Luis 1898-1959 .... **HLCS 2**
See Pales Matos, Luis
See also DLB 290; HW 1; LAW
Paley, Grace 1922- .. **CLC 4, 6, 37, 140; SSC
8**
See also AMWS 6; CA 25-28R; CANR 13,
46, 74, 118; CN 2, 3, 4, 5, 6, 7; CPW;
DA3; DAM POP; DLB 28, 218; EWL 3;
EXPS; FW; INT CANR-13; MAL 5;
MAWW; MTCW 1, 2; MTFW 2005;
RGAL 4; RGSF 2; SSFS 3, 20

Palin, Michael (Edward) 1943- .... **CLC 21**
See Monty Python
See also CA 107; CANR 35, 109; SATA 67
Palliser, Charles 1947- .... **CLC 65**
See also CA 136; CANR 76; CN 5, 6, 7
Palma, Ricardo 1833-1919 .... **TCLC 29**
See also CA 168; LAW
Pamuk, Orhan 1952- .... **CLC 185**
See also CA 142; CANR 75, 127; CWW 2;
WLIT 6
Pancake, Breece Dexter 1952-1979
See Pancake, Breece D'J
See also CA 123; 109
Pancake, Breece D'J .... **CLC 29; SSC 61**
See Pancake, Breece Dexter
See also DLB 130
Panchenko, Nikolai .... **CLC 59**
Pankhurst, Emmeline (Goulden)
1858-1928 .... **TCLC 100**
See also CA 116; FW
Panko, Rudy
See Gogol, Nikolai (Vasilyevich)
Papadiamantis, Alexandros
1851-1911 .... **TCLC 29**
See also CA 168; EWL 3
Papadiamantopoulos, Johannes 1856-1910
See Moreas, Jean
See also CA 117
Papini, Giovanni 1881-1956 .... **TCLC 22**
See also CA 121; 180; DLB 264
Paracelsus 1493-1541 .... **LC 14**
See also DLB 179
Parasol, Peter
See Stevens, Wallace
Pardo Bazan, Emilia 1851-1921 .... **SSC 30**
See also EWL 3; FW; RGSF 2; RGWL 2, 3
Pareto, Vilfredo 1848-1923 .... **TCLC 69**
See also CA 175
Paretsky, Sara 1947- .... **CLC 135**
See also AAYA 30; BEST 90:3; CA 125;
129; CANR 59, 95; CMW 4; CPW; DA3;
DAM POP; DLB 306; INT CA-129;
MSW; RGAL 4
Parfenie, Maria
See Codrescu, Andrei
Parini, Jay (Lee) 1948- .... **CLC 54, 133**
See also CA 97-100, 229; CAAE 229;
CAAS 16; CANR 32, 87
Park, Jordan
See Kornbluth, C(yril) M.; Pohl, Frederik
Park, Robert E(zra) 1864-1944 ..... **TCLC 73**
See also CA 122; 165
Parker, Bert
See Ellison, Harlan (Jay)
Parker, Dorothy (Rothschild)
1893-1967 . **CLC 15, 68; PC 28; SSC 2;
TCLC 143**
See also AMWS 9; CA 19-20; 25-28R; CAP
2; DA3; DAM POET; DLB 11, 45, 86;
EXPP; FW; MAL 5; MAWW; MTCW 1,
2; MTFW 2005; PFS 18; RGAL 4; RGSF
2; TUS
Parker, Robert B(rown) 1932- .... **CLC 27**
See also AAYA 28; BEST 89:4; BPFB 3;
CA 49-52; CANR 1, 26, 52, 89, 128;
CMW 4; CPW; DAM NOV, POP; DLB
306; INT CANR-26; MSW; MTCW 1;
MTFW 2005
Parkin, Frank 1940- .... **CLC 43**
See also CA 147
Parkman, Francis, Jr. 1823-1893 .. **NCLC 12**
See also AMWS 2; DLB 1, 30, 183, 186,
235; RGAL 4
Parks, Gordon (Alexander Buchanan)
1912- .... **BLC 3; CLC 1, 16**
See also AAYA 36; AITN 2; BW 2, 3; CA
41-44R; CANR 26, 66, 145; DA3; DAM
MULT; DLB 33; MTCW 2; MTFW 2005;
SATA 8, 108

MAL 5; MAWW; MTCW 1, 2; MTFW 2005; NFS 14; RGAL 4; RGSF 2; SATA 39; SATA-Obit 23; SSFS 1, 8, 11, 16; TCWW 2; TUS

Porter, Peter (Neville Frederick)
1929- .... **CLC 5, 13, 33**
See also CA 85-88; CP 1, 2, 3, 4, 5, 6, 7; DLB 40, 289; WWE 1

Porter, William Sydney 1862-1910
See Henry, O.
See also CA 104; 131; CDALB 1865-1917; DA; DA3; DAB; DAC; DAM MST; DLB 12, 78, 79; MAL 5; MTCW 1, 2; MTFW 2005; TUS; YABC 2

Portillo (y Pacheco), Jose Lopez
See Lopez Portillo (y Pacheco), Jose

Portillo Trambley, Estela 1927-1998 .. **HLC 2**
See Trambley, Estela Portillo
See also CANR 32; DAM MULT; DLB 209; HW 1

Posey, Alexander (Lawrence)
1873-1908 .... **NNAL**
See also CA 144; CANR 80; DAM MULT; DLB 175

Posse, Abel .... **CLC 70**

Post, Melville Davisson
1869-1930 .... **TCLC 39**
See also CA 110; 202; CMW 4

Potok, Chaim 1929-2002 ... **CLC 2, 7, 14, 26, 112**
See also AAYA 15, 50; AITN 1, 2; BPFB 3; BYA 1; CA 17-20R; 208; CANR 19, 35, 64, 98; CLR 92; CN 4, 5, 6; DA3; DAM NOV; DLB 28, 152; EXPN; INT CANR-19; LAIT 4; MTCW 1, 2; MTFW 2005; NFS 4; SATA 33, 106; SATA-Obit 134; TUS; YAW

Potok, Herbert Harold -2002
See Potok, Chaim

Potok, Herman Harold
See Potok, Chaim

Potter, Dennis (Christopher George)
1935-1994 .... **CLC 58, 86, 123**
See also BRWS 10; CA 107; 145; CANR 33, 61; CBD; DLB 233; MTCW 1

Pound, Ezra (Weston Loomis)
1885-1972 .. **CLC 1, 2, 3, 4, 5, 7, 10, 13, 18, 34, 48, 50, 112; PC 4; WLC**
See also AAYA 47; AMW; AMWR 1; CA 5-8R; 37-40R; CANR 40; CDALB 1917-1929; CP 1; DA; DA3; DAB; DAC; DAM MST, POET; DLB 4, 45, 63; DLBD 15; EFS 2; EWL 3; EXPP; LMFS 2; MAL 5; MTCW 1, 2; MTFW 2005; PAB; PFS 2, 8, 16; RGAL 4; TUS; WP

Povod, Reinaldo 1959-1994 .... **CLC 44**
See also CA 136; 146; CANR 83

Powell, Adam Clayton, Jr.
1908-1972 .... **BLC 3; CLC 89**
See also BW 1, 3; CA 102; 33-36R; CANR 86; DAM MULT

Powell, Anthony (Dymoke)
1905-2000 .... **CLC 1, 3, 7, 9, 10, 31**
See also BRW 7; CA 1-4R; 189; CANR 1, 32, 62, 107; CDBLB 1945-1960; CN 1, 2, 3, 4, 5, 6; DLB 15; EWL 3; MTCW 1, 2; MTFW 2005; RGEL 2; TEA

Powell, Dawn 1896(?)-1965 .... **CLC 66**
See also CA 5-8R; CANR 121; DLBY 1997

Powell, Padgett 1952- .... **CLC 34**
See also CA 126; CANR 63, 101; CSW; DLB 234; DLBY 01

Powell, (Oval) Talmage 1920-2000
See Queen, Ellery
See also CA 5-8R; CANR 2, 80

Power, Susan 1961- .... **CLC 91**
See also BYA 14; CA 160; CANR 135; NFS 11

Powers, J(ames) F(arl) 1917-1999 ..... **CLC 1, 4, 8, 57; SSC 4**
See also CA 1-4R; 181; CANR 2, 61; CN 1, 2, 3, 4, 5, 6; DLB 130; MTCW 1; RGAL 4; RGSF 2

Powers, John J(ames) 1945-
See Powers, John R.
See also CA 69-72

Powers, John R. .... **CLC 66**
See Powers, John J(ames)

Powers, Richard (S.) 1957- .... **CLC 93**
See also AMWS 9; BPFB 3; CA 148; CANR 80; CN 6, 7; MTFW 2005; TCLE 1:2

Pownall, David 1938- .... **CLC 10**
See also CA 89-92, 180; CAAS 18; CANR 49, 101; CBD; CD 5, 6; CN 4, 5, 6, 7; DLB 14

Powys, John Cowper 1872-1963 ... **CLC 7, 9, 15, 46, 125**
See also CA 85-88; CANR 106; DLB 15, 255; EWL 3; FANT; MTCW 1, 2; MTFW 2005; RGEL 2; SUFW

Powys, T(heodore) F(rancis)
1875-1953 .... **TCLC 9**
See also BRWS 8; CA 106; 189; DLB 36, 162; EWL 3; FANT; RGEL 2; SUFW

Pozzo, Modesta
See Fonte, Moderata

Prado (Calvo), Pedro 1886-1952 ... **TCLC 75**
See also CA 131; DLB 283; HW 1; LAW

Prager, Emily 1952- .... **CLC 56**
See also CA 204

Pratchett, Terry 1948- .... **CLC 197**
See also AAYA 19, 54; BPFB 3; CA 143; CANR 87, 126; CLR 64; CN 6, 7; CPW; CWRI 5; FANT; MTFW 2005; SATA 82, 139; SFW 4; SUFW 2

Pratolini, Vasco 1913-1991 .... **TCLC 124**
See also CA 211; DLB 177; EWL 3; RGWL 2, 3

Pratt, E(dwin) J(ohn) 1883(?)-1964 . **CLC 19**
See also CA 141; 93-96; CANR 77; DAC; DAM POET; DLB 92; EWL 3; RGEL 2; TWA

Premchand .... **TCLC 21**
See Srivastava, Dhanpat Rai
See also EWL 3

Prescott, William Hickling
1796-1859 .... **NCLC 163**
See also DLB 1, 30, 59, 235

Preseren, France 1800-1849 .... **NCLC 127**
See also CDWLB 4; DLB 147

Preussler, Otfried 1923- .... **CLC 17**
See also CA 77-80; SATA 24

Prevert, Jacques (Henri Marie)
1900-1977 .... **CLC 15**
See also CA 77-80; 69-72; CANR 29, 61; DLB 258; EWL 3; GFL 1789 to the Present; IDFW 3, 4; MTCW 1; RGWL 2, 3; SATA-Obit 30

Prevost, (Antoine Francois)
1697-1763 .... **LC 1**
See also DLB 314; EW 4; GFL Beginnings to 1789; RGWL 2, 3

Price, (Edward) Reynolds 1933- ... **CLC 3, 6, 13, 43, 50, 63, 212; SSC 22**
See also AMWS 6; CA 1-4R; CANR 1, 37, 57, 87, 128; CN 1, 2, 3, 4, 5, 6; CSW; DAM NOV; DLB 2, 218, 278; EWL 3; INT CANR-37; MAL 5; MTFW 2005; NFS 18

Price, Richard 1949- .... **CLC 6, 12**
See also CA 49-52; CANR 3; CN 7; DLBY 1981

Prichard, Katharine Susannah
1883-1969 .... **CLC 46**
See also CA 11-12; CANR 33; CAP 1; DLB 260; MTCW 1; RGEL 2; RGSF 2; SATA 66

Priestley, J(ohn) B(oynton)
1894-1984 .... **CLC 2, 5, 9, 34**
See also BRW 7; CA 9-12R; 113; CANR 33; CDBLB 1914-1945; CN 1, 2, 3; DA3; DAM DRAM, NOV; DLB 10, 34, 77, 100, 139; DLBY 1984; EWL 3; MTCW 1, 2; MTFW 2005; RGEL 2; SFW 4

Prince 1958- .... **CLC 35**
See also CA 213

Prince, F(rank) T(empleton)
1912-2003 .... **CLC 22**
See also CA 101; 219; CANR 43, 79; CP 1, 2, 3, 4, 5, 6, 7; DLB 20

Prince Kropotkin
See Kropotkin, Peter (Aleksieevich)

Prior, Matthew 1664-1721 .... **LC 4**
See also DLB 95; RGEL 2

Prishvin, Mikhail 1873-1954 .... **TCLC 75**
See Prishvin, Mikhail Mikhailovich

Prishvin, Mikhail Mikhailovich
See Prishvin, Mikhail
See also DLB 272; EWL 3

Pritchard, William H(arrison)
1932- .... **CLC 34**
See also CA 65-68; CANR 23, 95; DLB 111

Pritchett, V(ictor) S(awdon)
1900-1997 ... **CLC 5, 13, 15, 41; SSC 14**
See also BPFB 3; BRWS 3; CA 61-64; 157; CANR 31, 63; CN 1, 2, 3, 4, 5, 6; DA3; DAM NOV; DLB 15, 139; EWL 3; MTCW 1, 2; MTFW 2005; RGEL 2; RGSF 2; TEA

Private 19022
See Manning, Frederic

Probst, Mark 1925- .... **CLC 59**
See also CA 130

Procaccino, Michael
See Cristofer, Michael

Proclus c. 412-485 .... **CMLC 81**

Prokosch, Frederic 1908-1989 ...... **CLC 4, 48**
See also CA 73-76; 128; CANR 82; CN 1, 2, 3, 4; CP 1, 2, 3, 4; DLB 48; MTCW 2

Propertius, Sextus c. 50B.C.-c. 16B.C. .... **CMLC 32**
See also AW 2; CDWLB 1; DLB 211; RGWL 2, 3

Prophet, The
See Dreiser, Theodore (Herman Albert)

Prose, Francine 1947- .... **CLC 45**
See also CA 109; 112; CANR 46, 95, 132; DLB 234; MTFW 2005; SATA 101, 149

Proudhon
See Cunha, Euclides (Rodrigues Pimenta) da

Proulx, Annie
See Proulx, E. Annie

Proulx, E. Annie 1935- .... **CLC 81, 158**
See also AMWS 7; BPFB 3; CA 145; CANR 65, 110; CN 6, 7; CPW 1; DA3; DAM POP; MAL 5; MTCW 2; MTFW 2005; SSFS 18

Proulx, Edna Annie
See Proulx, E. Annie

Proust, (Valentin-Louis-George-Eugene) Marcel 1871-1922 ..... **SSC 75; TCLC 7, 13, 33; WLC**
See also AAYA 58; BPFB 3; CA 104; 120; CANR 110; DA; DA3; DAB; DAC; DAM MST, NOV; DLB 65; EW 8; EWL 3; GFL 1789 to the Present; MTCW 1, 2; MTFW 2005; RGWL 2, 3; TWA

Prowler, Harley
See Masters, Edgar Lee

Prudentius, Aurelius Clemens 348-c. 405 .... **CMLC 78**
   See also EW 1; RGWL 2, 3
Prus, Boleslaw 1845-1912 .... **TCLC 48**
   See also RGWL 2, 3
Pryor, Richard (Franklin Lenox Thomas) 1940-2005 .... **CLC 26**
   See also CA 122; 152
Przybyszewski, Stanislaw 1868-1927 .... **TCLC 36**
   See also CA 160; DLB 66; EWL 3
Pteleon
   See Grieve, C(hristopher) M(urray)
   See also DAM POET
Puckett, Lute
   See Masters, Edgar Lee
Puig, Manuel 1932-1990 .... **CLC 3, 5, 10, 28, 65, 133; HLC 2**
   See also BPFB 3; CA 45-48; CANR 2, 32, 63; CDWLB 3; DA3; DAM MULT; DLB 113; DNFS 1; EWL 3; GLL 1; HW 1, 2; LAW; MTCW 1, 2; MTFW 2005; RGWL 2, 3; TWA; WLIT 1
Pulitzer, Joseph 1847-1911 .... **TCLC 76**
   See also CA 114; DLB 23
Purchas, Samuel 1577(?)-1626 .... **LC 70**
   See also DLB 151
Purdy, A(lfred) W(ellington) 1918-2000 .... **CLC 3, 6, 14, 50**
   See also CA 81-84; 189; CAAS 17; CANR 42, 66; CP 1, 2, 3, 4, 5, 6, 7; DAC; DAM MST, POET; DLB 88; PFS 5; RGEL 2
Purdy, James (Amos) 1923- .... **CLC 2, 4, 10, 28, 52**
   See also AMWS 7; CA 33-36R; CAAS 1; CANR 19, 51, 132; CN 1, 2, 3, 4, 5, 6, 7; DLB 2, 218; EWL 3; INT CANR-19; MAL 5; MTCW 1; RGAL 4
Pure, Simon
   See Swinnerton, Frank Arthur
Pushkin, Aleksandr Sergeevich
   See Pushkin, Alexander (Sergeyevich)
   See also DLB 205
Pushkin, Alexander (Sergeyevich) 1799-1837 .... **NCLC 3, 27, 83; PC 10; SSC 27, 55; WLC**
   See Pushkin, Aleksandr Sergeevich
   See also DA; DA3; DAB; DAC; DAM DRAM, MST, POET; EW 5; EXPS; RGSF 2; RGWL 2, 3; SATA 61; SSFS 9; TWA
P'u Sung-ling 1640-1715 .... **LC 49; SSC 31**
Putnam, Arthur Lee
   See Alger, Horatio, Jr.
Puttenham, George 1529(?)-1590 ...... **LC 116**
   See also DLB 281
Puzo, Mario 1920-1999 .... **CLC 1, 2, 6, 36, 107**
   See also BPFB 3; CA 65-68; 185; CANR 4, 42, 65, 99, 131; CN 1, 2, 3, 4, 5, 6; CPW; DA3; DAM NOV, POP; DLB 6; MTCW 1, 2; MTFW 2005; NFS 16; RGAL 4
Pygge, Edward
   See Barnes, Julian (Patrick)
Pyle, Ernest Taylor 1900-1945
   See Pyle, Ernie
   See also CA 115; 160
Pyle, Ernie .... **TCLC 75**
   See Pyle, Ernest Taylor
   See also DLB 29; MTCW 2
Pyle, Howard 1853-1911 .... **TCLC 81**
   See also AAYA 57; BYA 2, 4; CA 109; 137; CLR 22; DLB 42, 188; DLBD 13; LAIT 1; MAICYA 1, 2; SATA 16, 100; WCH; YAW
Pym, Barbara (Mary Crampton) 1913-1980 .... **CLC 13, 19, 37, 111**
   See also BPFB 3; BRWS 2; CA 13-14; 97-100; CANR 13, 34; CAP 1; DLB 14, 207; DLBY 1987; EWL 3; MTCW 1, 2; MTFW 2005; RGEL 2; TEA

Pynchon, Thomas (Ruggles, Jr.) 1937- ...... **CLC 2, 3, 6, 9, 11, 18, 33, 62, 72, 123, 192, 213; SSC 14, 84; WLC**
   See also AMWS 2; BEST 90:2; BPFB 3; CA 17-20R; CANR 22, 46, 73, 142; CN 1, 2, 3, 4, 5, 6, 7; CPW 1; DA; DA3; DAB; DAC; DAM MST, NOV, POP; DLB 2, 173; EWL 3; MAL 5; MTCW 1, 2; MTFW 2005; RGAL 4; SFW 4; TCLE 1:2; TUS
Pythagoras c. 582B.C.-c. 507B.C. . **CMLC 22**
   See also DLB 176
Q
   See Quiller-Couch, Sir Arthur (Thomas)
Qian, Chongzhu
   See Ch'ien, Chung-shu
Qian, Sima 145B.C.-c. 89B.C. .... **CMLC 72**
Qian Zhongshu
   See Ch'ien, Chung-shu
   See also CWW 2
Qroll
   See Dagerman, Stig (Halvard)
Quarles, Francis 1592-1644 .... **LC 117**
   See also DLB 126; RGEL 2
Quarrington, Paul (Lewis) 1953- ..... **CLC 65**
   See also CA 129; CANR 62, 95
Quasimodo, Salvatore 1901-1968 .... **CLC 10; PC 47**
   See also CA 13-16; 25-28R; CAP 1; DLB 114; EW 12; EWL 3; MTCW 1; RGWL 2, 3
Quatermass, Martin
   See Carpenter, John (Howard)
Quay, Stephen 1947- .... **CLC 95**
   See also CA 189
Quay, Timothy 1947- .... **CLC 95**
   See also CA 189
Queen, Ellery .... **CLC 3, 11**
   See Dannay, Frederic; Davidson, Avram (James); Deming, Richard; Fairman, Paul W.; Flora, Fletcher; Hoch, Edward D(entinger); Kane, Henry; Lee, Manfred B(ennington); Marlowe, Stephen; Powell, (Oval) Talmage; Sheldon, Walter J(ames); Sturgeon, Theodore (Hamilton); Tracy, Don(ald Fiske); Vance, John Holbrook
   See also BPFB 3; CMW 4; MSW; RGAL 4
Queen, Ellery, Jr.
   See Dannay, Frederic; Lee, Manfred B(ennington)
Queneau, Raymond 1903-1976 ..... **CLC 2, 5, 10, 42**
   See also CA 77-80; 69-72; CANR 32; DLB 72, 258; EW 12; EWL 3; GFL 1789 to the Present; MTCW 1, 2; RGWL 2, 3
Quevedo, Francisco de 1580-1645 .... **LC 23**
Quiller-Couch, Sir Arthur (Thomas) 1863-1944 .... **TCLC 53**
   See also CA 118; 166; DLB 135, 153, 190; HGG; RGEL 2; SUFW 1
Quin, Ann (Marie) 1936-1973 .... **CLC 6**
   See also CA 9-12R; 45-48; CN 1; DLB 14, 231
Quincey, Thomas de
   See De Quincey, Thomas
Quindlen, Anna 1953- .... **CLC 191**
   See also AAYA 35; CA 138; CANR 73, 126; DA3; DLB 292; MTCW 2; MTFW 2005
Quinn, Martin
   See Smith, Martin Cruz
Quinn, Peter 1947- .... **CLC 91**
   See also CA 197
Quinn, Simon
   See Smith, Martin Cruz
Quintana, Leroy V. 1944- ...... **HLC 2; PC 36**
   See also CA 131; CANR 65, 139; DAM MULT; DLB 82; HW 1, 2
Quintilian c. 40-c. 100 .... **CMLC 77**
   See also AW 2; DLB 211; RGWL 2, 3

Quintillian 0035-0100 .... **CMLC 77**
Quiroga, Horacio (Sylvestre) 1878-1937 ... **HLC 2; SSC 89; TCLC 20**
   See also CA 117; 131; DAM MULT; EWL 3; HW 1; LAW; MTCW 1; RGSF 2; WLIT 1
Quoirez, Francoise 1935-2004 .... **CLC 9**
   See Sagan, Francoise
   See also CA 49-52; 231; CANR 6, 39, 73; MTCW 1, 2; MTFW 2005; TWA
Raabe, Wilhelm (Karl) 1831-1910 . **TCLC 45**
   See also CA 167; DLB 129
Rabe, David (William) 1940- .. **CLC 4, 8, 33, 200; DC 16**
   See also CA 85-88; CABS 3; CAD; CANR 59, 129; CD 5, 6; DAM DRAM; DFS 3, 8, 13; DLB 7, 228; EWL 3; MAL 5
Rabelais, Francois 1494-1553 .... **LC 5, 60; WLC**
   See also DA; DAB; DAC; DAM MST; EW 2; GFL Beginnings to 1789; LMFS 1; RGWL 2, 3; TWA
Rabinovitch, Sholem 1859-1916
   See Aleichem, Sholom
   See also CA 104
Rabinyan, Dorit 1972- .... **CLC 119**
   See also CA 170
Rachilde
   See Vallette, Marguerite Eymery; Vallette, Marguerite Eymery
   See also EWL 3
Racine, Jean 1639-1699 .... **LC 28, 113**
   See also DA3; DAB; DAM MST; DLB 268; EW 3; GFL Beginnings to 1789; LMFS 1; RGWL 2, 3; TWA
Radcliffe, Ann (Ward) 1764-1823 ... **NCLC 6, 55, 106**
   See also DLB 39, 178; GL 3; HGG; LMFS 1; RGEL 2; SUFW; WLIT 3
Radclyffe-Hall, Marguerite
   See Hall, (Marguerite) Radclyffe
Radiguet, Raymond 1903-1923 ...... **TCLC 29**
   See also CA 162; DLB 65; EWL 3; GFL 1789 to the Present; RGWL 2, 3
Radnoti, Miklos 1909-1944 .... **TCLC 16**
   See also CA 118; 212; CDWLB 4; DLB 215; EWL 3; RGWL 2, 3
Rado, James 1939- .... **CLC 17**
   See also CA 105
Radvanyi, Netty 1900-1983
   See Seghers, Anna
   See also CA 85-88; 110; CANR 82
Rae, Ben
   See Griffiths, Trevor
Raeburn, John (Hay) 1941- .... **CLC 34**
   See also CA 57-60
Ragni, Gerome 1942-1991 .... **CLC 17**
   See also CA 105; 134
Rahv, Philip .... **CLC 24**
   See Greenberg, Ivan
   See also DLB 137; MAL 5
Raimund, Ferdinand Jakob 1790-1836 .... **NCLC 69**
   See also DLB 90
Raine, Craig (Anthony) 1944- .. **CLC 32, 103**
   See also CA 108; CANR 29, 51, 103; CP 3, 4, 5, 6, 7; DLB 40; PFS 7
Raine, Kathleen (Jessie) 1908-2003 .. **CLC 7, 45**
   See also CA 85-88; 218; CANR 46, 109; CP 1, 2, 3, 4, 5, 6, 7; DLB 20; EWL 3; MTCW 1; RGEL 2
Rainis, Janis 1865-1929 .... **TCLC 29**
   See also CA 170; CDWLB 4; DLB 220; EWL 3
Rakosi, Carl .... **CLC 47**
   See Rawley, Callman
   See also CA 228; CAAS 5; CP 1, 2, 3, 4, 5, 6, 7; DLB 193

Ralegh, Sir Walter
See Raleigh, Sir Walter
See also BRW 1; RGEL 2; WP

Raleigh, Richard
See Lovecraft, H(oward) P(hillips)

Raleigh, Sir Walter 1554(?)-1618 .... **LC 31, 39; PC 31**
See Ralegh, Sir Walter
See also CDBLB Before 1660; DLB 172; EXPP; PFS 14; TEA

Rallentando, H. P.
See Sayers, Dorothy L(eigh)

Ramal, Walter
See de la Mare, Walter (John)

Ramana Maharshi 1879-1950 .... **TCLC 84**

Ramoacn y Cajal, Santiago 1852-1934 .... **TCLC 93**

Ramon, Juan
See Jimenez (Mantecon), Juan Ramon

Ramos, Graciliano 1892-1953 .... **TCLC 32**
See also CA 167; DLB 307; EWL 3; HW 2; LAW; WLIT 1

Rampersad, Arnold 1941- .... **CLC 44**
See also BW 2, 3; CA 127; 133; CANR 81; DLB 111; INT CA-133

Rampling, Anne
See Rice, Anne
See also GLL 2

Ramsay, Allan 1686(?)-1758 .... **LC 29**
See also DLB 95; RGEL 2

Ramsay, Jay
See Campbell, (John) Ramsey

Ramuz, Charles-Ferdinand 1878-1947 .... **TCLC 33**
See also CA 165; EWL 3

Rand, Ayn 1905-1982 ...... **CLC 3, 30, 44, 79; WLC**
See also AAYA 10; AMWS 4; BPFB 3; BYA 12; CA 13-16R; 105; CANR 27, 73; CDALBS; CN 1, 2, 3; CPW; DA; DA3; DAC; DAM MST, NOV, POP; DLB 227, 279; MTCW 1, 2; MTFW 2005; NFS 10, 16; RGAL 4; SFW 4; TUS; YAW

Randall, Dudley (Felker) 1914-2000 . **BLC 3; CLC 1, 135**
See also BW 1, 3; CA 25-28R; 189; CANR 23, 82; CP 1, 2, 3, 4; DAM MULT; DLB 41; PFS 5

Randall, Robert
See Silverberg, Robert

Ranger, Ken
See Creasey, John

Rank, Otto 1884-1939 .... **TCLC 115**

Ransom, John Crowe 1888-1974 .. **CLC 2, 4, 5, 11, 24; PC 61**
See also AMW; CA 5-8R; 49-52; CANR 6, 34; CDALBS; CP 1, 2; DA3; DAM POET; DLB 45, 63; EWL 3; EXPP; MAL 5; MTCW 1, 2; MTFW 2005; RGAL 4; TUS

Rao, Raja 1909- .... **CLC 25, 56**
See also CA 73-76; CANR 51; CN 1, 2, 3, 4, 5, 6; DAM NOV; EWL 3; MTCW 1, 2; MTFW 2005; RGEL 2; RGSF 2

Raphael, Frederic (Michael) 1931- ... **CLC 2, 14**
See also CA 1-4R; CANR 1, 86; CN 1, 2, 3, 4, 5, 6, 7; DLB 14, 319; TCLE 1:2

Ratcliffe, James P.
See Mencken, H(enry) L(ouis)

Rathbone, Julian 1935- .... **CLC 41**
See also CA 101; CANR 34, 73

Rattigan, Terence (Mervyn) 1911-1977 .... **CLC 7; DC 18**
See also BRWS 7; CA 85-88; 73-76; CBD; CDBLB 1945-1960; DAM DRAM; DFS 8; DLB 13; IDFW 3, 4; MTCW 1, 2; MTFW 2005; RGEL 2

Ratushinskaya, Irina 1954- .... **CLC 54**
See also CA 129; CANR 68; CWW 2

Raven, Simon (Arthur Noel) 1927-2001 .... **CLC 14**
See also CA 81-84; 197; CANR 86; CN 1, 2, 3, 4, 5, 6; DLB 271

Ravenna, Michael
See Welty, Eudora (Alice)

Rawley, Callman 1903-2004
See Rakosi, Carl
See also CA 21-24R; 228; CANR 12, 32, 91

Rawlings, Marjorie Kinnan 1896-1953 .... **TCLC 4**
See also AAYA 20; AMWS 10; ANW; BPFB 3; BYA 3; CA 104; 137; CANR 74; CLR 63; DLB 9, 22, 102; DLBD 17; JRDA; MAICYA 1, 2; MAL 5; MTCW 2; MTFW 2005; RGAL 4; SATA 100; WCH; YABC 1; YAW

Ray, Satyajit 1921-1992 .... **CLC 16, 76**
See also CA 114; 137; DAM MULT

Read, Herbert Edward 1893-1968 ..... **CLC 4**
See also BRW 6; CA 85-88; 25-28R; DLB 20, 149; EWL 3; PAB; RGEL 2

Read, Piers Paul 1941- .... **CLC 4, 10, 25**
See also CA 21-24R; CANR 38, 86; CN 2, 3, 4, 5, 6, 7; DLB 14; SATA 21

Reade, Charles 1814-1884 .... **NCLC 2, 74**
See also DLB 21; RGEL 2

Reade, Hamish
See Gray, Simon (James Holliday)

Reading, Peter 1946- .... **CLC 47**
See also BRWS 8; CA 103; CANR 46, 96; CP 7; DLB 40

Reaney, James 1926- .... **CLC 13**
See also CA 41-44R; CAAS 15; CANR 42; CD 5, 6; CP 1, 2, 3, 4, 5, 6, 7; DAC; DAM MST; DLB 68; RGEL 2; SATA 43

Rebreanu, Liviu 1885-1944 .... **TCLC 28**
See also CA 165; DLB 220; EWL 3

Rechy, John (Francisco) 1934- ...... **CLC 1, 7, 14, 18, 107; HLC 2**
See also CA 5-8R; 195; CAAE 195; CAAS 4; CANR 6, 32, 64; CN 1, 2, 3, 4, 5, 6, 7; DAM MULT; DLB 122, 278; DLBY 1982; HW 1, 2; INT CANR-6; LLW; MAL 5; RGAL 4

Redcam, Tom 1870-1933 .... **TCLC 25**

Reddin, Keith 1956- .... **CLC 67**
See also CAD; CD 6

Redgrove, Peter (William) 1932-2003 .... **CLC 6, 41**
See also BRWS 6; CA 1-4R; 217; CANR 3, 39, 77; CP 1, 2, 3, 4, 5, 6, 7; DLB 40; TCLE 1:2

Redmon, Anne .... **CLC 22**
See Nightingale, Anne Redmon
See also DLBY 1986

Reed, Eliot
See Ambler, Eric

Reed, Ishmael (Scott) 1938- . **BLC 3; CLC 2, 3, 5, 6, 13, 32, 60, 174; PC 68**
See also AFAW 1, 2; AMWS 10; BPFB 3; BW 2, 3; CA 21-24R; CANR 25, 48, 74, 128; CN 1, 2, 3, 4, 5, 6, 7; CP 1, 2, 3, 4, 5, 6, 7; CSW; DA3; DAM MULT; DLB 2, 5, 33, 169, 227; DLBD 8; EWL 3; LMFS 2; MAL 5; MSW; MTCW 1, 2; MTFW 2005; PFS 6; RGAL 4; TCWW 2

Reed, John (Silas) 1887-1920 .... **TCLC 9**
See also CA 106; 195; MAL 5; TUS

Reed, Lou .... **CLC 21**
See Firbank, Louis

Reese, Lizette Woodworth 1856-1935 . **PC 29**
See also CA 180; DLB 54

Reeve, Clara 1729-1807 .... **NCLC 19**
See also DLB 39; RGEL 2

Reich, Wilhelm 1897-1957 .... **TCLC 57**
See also CA 199

Reid, Christopher (John) 1949- .... **CLC 33**
See also CA 140; CANR 89; CP 4, 5, 6, 7; DLB 40; EWL 3

Reid, Desmond
See Moorcock, Michael (John)

Reid Banks, Lynne 1929-
See Banks, Lynne Reid
See also AAYA 49; CA 1-4R; CANR 6, 22, 38, 87; CLR 24; CN 1, 2, 3, 7; JRDA; MAICYA 1, 2; SATA 22, 75, 111, 165; YAW

Reilly, William K.
See Creasey, John

Reiner, Max
See Caldwell, (Janet Miriam) Taylor (Holland)

Reis, Ricardo
See Pessoa, Fernando (Antonio Nogueira)

Reizenstein, Elmer Leopold
See Rice, Elmer (Leopold)
See also EWL 3

Remarque, Erich Maria 1898-1970 . **CLC 21**
See also AAYA 27; BPFB 3; CA 77-80; 29-32R; CDWLB 2; DA; DA3; DAB; DAC; DAM MST, NOV; DLB 56; EWL 3; EXPN; LAIT 3; MTCW 1, 2; MTFW 2005; NFS 4; RGWL 2, 3

Remington, Frederic S(ackrider) 1861-1909 .... **TCLC 89**
See also CA 108; 169; DLB 12, 186, 188; SATA 41; TCWW 2

Remizov, A.
See Remizov, Aleksei (Mikhailovich)

Remizov, A. M.
See Remizov, Aleksei (Mikhailovich)

Remizov, Aleksei (Mikhailovich) 1877-1957 .... **TCLC 27**
See Remizov, Alexey Mikhaylovich
See also CA 125; 133; DLB 295

Remizov, Alexey Mikhaylovich
See Remizov, Aleksei (Mikhailovich)
See also EWL 3

Renan, Joseph Ernest 1823-1892 . **NCLC 26, 145**
See also GFL 1789 to the Present

Renard, Jules(-Pierre) 1864-1910 .. **TCLC 17**
See also CA 117; 202; GFL 1789 to the Present

Renault, Mary .... **CLC 3, 11, 17**
See Challans, Mary
See also BPFB 3; BYA 2; CN 1, 2, 3; DLBY 1983; EWL 3; GLL 1; LAIT 1; RGEL 2; RHW

Rendell, Ruth (Barbara) 1930- .. **CLC 28, 48**
See Vine, Barbara
See also BPFB 3; BRWS 9; CA 109; CANR 32, 52, 74, 127; CN 5, 6, 7; CPW; DAM POP; DLB 87, 276; INT CANR-32; MSW; MTCW 1, 2; MTFW 2005

Renoir, Jean 1894-1979 .... **CLC 20**
See also CA 129; 85-88

Resnais, Alain 1922- .... **CLC 16**

Revard, Carter (Curtis) 1931- .... **NNAL**
See also CA 144; CANR 81; PFS 5

Reverdy, Pierre 1889-1960 .... **CLC 53**
See also CA 97-100; 89-92; DLB 258; EWL 3; GFL 1789 to the Present

Rexroth, Kenneth 1905-1982 .... **CLC 1, 2, 6, 11, 22, 49, 112; PC 20**
See also BG 1:3; CA 5-8R; 107; CANR 14, 34, 63; CDALB 1941-1968; CP 1, 2, 3; DAM POET; DLB 16, 48, 165, 212; DLBY 1982; EWL 3; INT CANR-14; MAL 5; MTCW 1, 2; MTFW 2005; RGAL 4

Reyes, Alfonso 1889-1959 .... **HLCS 2; TCLC 33**
See also CA 131; EWL 3; HW 1; LAW

Reyes y Basoalto, Ricardo Eliecer Neftali
See Neruda, Pablo
Reymont, Wladyslaw (Stanislaw)
1868(?)-1925 .... **TCLC 5**
See also CA 104; EWL 3
Reynolds, John Hamilton
1794-1852 .... **NCLC 146**
See also DLB 96
Reynolds, Jonathan 1942- .... **CLC 6, 38**
See also CA 65-68; CANR 28
Reynolds, Joshua 1723-1792 .... **LC 15**
See also DLB 104
Reynolds, Michael S(hane)
1937-2000 .... **CLC 44**
See also CA 65-68; 189; CANR 9, 89, 97
Reznikoff, Charles 1894-1976 .... **CLC 9**
See also AMWS 14; CA 33-36; 61-64; CAP
2; CP 1, 2; DLB 28, 45; WP
Rezzori (d'Arezzo), Gregor von
1914-1998 .... **CLC 25**
See also CA 122; 136; 167
Rhine, Richard
See Silverstein, Alvin; Silverstein, Virginia
B(arbara Opshelor)
Rhodes, Eugene Manlove
1869-1934 .... **TCLC 53**
See also CA 198; DLB 256; TCWW 1, 2
R'hoone, Lord
See Balzac, Honore de
Rhys, Jean 1890-1979 .... **CLC 2, 4, 6, 14, 19,
51, 124; SSC 21, 76**
See also BRWS 2; CA 25-28R; 85-88;
CANR 35, 62; CDBLB 1945-1960; CD-
WLB 3; CN 1, 2; DA3; DAM NOV; DLB
36, 117, 162; DNFS 2; EWL 3; LATS 1:1;
MTCW 1, 2; MTFW 2005; NFS 19;
RGEL 2; RGSF 2; RHW; TEA; WWE 1
Ribeiro, Darcy 1922-1997 .... **CLC 34**
See also CA 33-36R; 156; EWL 3
Ribeiro, Joao Ubaldo (Osorio Pimentel)
1941- .... **CLC 10, 67**
See also CA 81-84; CWW 2; EWL 3
Ribman, Ronald (Burt) 1932- .... **CLC 7**
See also CA 21-24R; CAD; CANR 46, 80;
CD 5, 6
Ricci, Nino (Pio) 1959- .... **CLC 70**
See also CA 137; CANR 130; CCA 1
Rice, Anne 1941- .... **CLC 41, 128**
See Rampling, Anne
See also AAYA 9, 53; AMWS 7; BEST
89:2; BPFB 3; CA 65-68; CANR 12, 36,
53, 74, 100, 133; CN 6, 7; CPW; CSW;
DA3; DAM POP; DLB 292; GL 3; GLL
2; HGG; MTCW 2; MTFW 2005; SUFW
2; YAW
Rice, Elmer (Leopold) 1892-1967 ...... **CLC 7,
49**
See Reizenstein, Elmer Leopold
See also CA 21-22; 25-28R; CAP 2; DAM
DRAM; DFS 12; DLB 4, 7; IDTP; MAL
5; MTCW 1, 2; RGAL 4
Rice, Tim(othy Miles Bindon)
1944- .... **CLC 21**
See also CA 103; CANR 46; DFS 7
Rich, Adrienne (Cecile) 1929- ... **CLC 3, 6, 7,
11, 18, 36, 73, 76, 125; PC 5**
See also AMWR 2; AMWS 1; CA 9-12R;
CANR 20, 53, 74, 128; CDALBS; CP 1,
2, 3, 4, 5, 6, 7; CSW; CWP; DA3; DAM
POET; DLB 5, 67; EWL 3; EXPP; FL 1:6;
FW; MAL 5; MAWW; MTCW 1, 2;
MTFW 2005; PAB; PFS 15; RGAL 4; WP
Rich, Barbara
See Graves, Robert (von Ranke)
Rich, Robert
See Trumbo, Dalton
Richard, Keith .... **CLC 17**
See Richards, Keith

Richards, David Adams 1950- .... **CLC 59**
See also CA 93-96; CANR 60, 110; CN 7;
DAC; DLB 53; TCLE 1:2
Richards, I(vor) A(rmstrong)
1893-1979 .... **CLC 14, 24**
See also BRWS 2; CA 41-44R; 89-92;
CANR 34, 74; CP 1, 2; DLB 27; EWL 3;
MTCW 2; RGEL 2
Richards, Keith 1943-
See Richard, Keith
See also CA 107; CANR 77
Richardson, Anne
See Roiphe, Anne (Richardson)
Richardson, Dorothy Miller
1873-1957 .... **TCLC 3**
See also CA 104; 192; DLB 36; EWL 3;
FW; RGEL 2
**Richardson (Robertson), Ethel Florence
Lindesay** 1870-1946
See Richardson, Henry Handel
See also CA 105; 190; DLB 230; RHW
Richardson, Henry Handel .... **TCLC 4**
See Richardson (Robertson), Ethel Florence
Lindesay
See also DLB 197; EWL 3; RGEL 2; RGSF
2
Richardson, John 1796-1852 .... **NCLC 55**
See also CCA 1; DAC; DLB 99
Richardson, Samuel 1689-1761 ...... **LC 1, 44;
WLC**
See also BRW 3; CDBLB 1660-1789; DA;
DAB; DAC; DAM MST, NOV; DLB 39;
RGEL 2; TEA; WLIT 3
Richardson, Willis 1889-1977 .... **HR 1:3**
See also BW 1; CA 124; DLB 51; SATA 60
Richler, Mordecai 1931-2001 .... **CLC 3, 5, 9,
13, 18, 46, 70, 185**
See also AITN 1; CA 65-68; 201; CANR
31, 62, 111; CCA 1; CLR 17; CN 1, 2, 3,
4, 5, 7; CWRI 5; DAC; DAM MST, NOV;
DLB 53; EWL 3; MAICYA 1, 2; MTCW
1, 2; MTFW 2005; RGEL 2; SATA 44,
98; SATA-Brief 27; TWA
Richter, Conrad (Michael)
1890-1968 .... **CLC 30**
See also AAYA 21; BYA 2; CA 5-8R; 25-
28R; CANR 23; DLB 9, 212; LAIT 1;
MAL 5; MTCW 1, 2; MTFW 2005;
RGAL 4; SATA 3; TCWW 1, 2; TUS;
YAW
Ricostranza, Tom
See Ellis, Trey
Riddell, Charlotte 1832-1906 .... **TCLC 40**
See Riddell, Mrs. J. H.
See also CA 165; DLB 156
Riddell, Mrs. J. H.
See Riddell, Charlotte
See also HGG; SUFW
Ridge, John Rollin 1827-1867 ...... **NCLC 82;
NNAL**
See also CA 144; DAM MULT; DLB 175
Ridgeway, Jason
See Marlowe, Stephen
Ridgway, Keith 1965- .... **CLC 119**
See also CA 172; CANR 144
Riding, Laura .... **CLC 3, 7**
See Jackson, Laura (Riding)
See also CP 1, 2, 3, 4; RGAL 4
Riefenstahl, Berta Helene Amalia 1902-2003
See Riefenstahl, Leni
See also CA 108; 220
Riefenstahl, Leni .... **CLC 16, 190**
See Riefenstahl, Berta Helene Amalia
Riffe, Ernest
See Bergman, (Ernst) Ingmar
Riggs, (Rolla) Lynn
1899-1954 .... **NNAL; TCLC 56**
See also CA 144; DAM MULT; DLB 175

Riis, Jacob A(ugust) 1849-1914 ..... **TCLC 80**
See also CA 113; 168; DLB 23
Riley, James Whitcomb 1849-1916 .... **PC 48;
TCLC 51**
See also CA 118; 137; DAM POET; MAI-
CYA 1, 2; RGAL 4; SATA 17
Riley, Tex
See Creasey, John
Rilke, Rainer Maria 1875-1926 .... **PC 2;
TCLC 1, 6, 19**
See also CA 104; 132; CANR 62, 99; CD-
WLB 2; DA3; DAM POET; DLB 81; EW
9; EWL 3; MTCW 1, 2; MTFW 2005;
PFS 19; RGWL 2, 3; TWA; WP
Rimbaud, (Jean Nicolas) Arthur
1854-1891 ... **NCLC 4, 35, 82; PC 3, 57;
WLC**
See also DA; DA3; DAB; DAC; DAM
MST, POET; DLB 217; EW 7; GFL 1789
to the Present; LMFS 2; RGWL 2, 3;
TWA; WP
Rinehart, Mary Roberts
1876-1958 .... **TCLC 52**
See also BPFB 3; CA 108; 166; RGAL 4;
RHW
Ringmaster, The
See Mencken, H(enry) L(ouis)
Ringwood, Gwen(dolyn Margaret) Pharis
1910-1984 .... **CLC 48**
See also CA 148; 112; DLB 88
Rio, Michel 1945(?)- .... **CLC 43**
See also CA 201
Rios, Alberto (Alvaro) 1952- .... **PC 57**
See also AAYA 66; AMWS 4; CA 113;
CANR 34, 79, 137; CP 7; DLB 122; HW
2; MTFW 2005; PFS 11
Ritsos, Giannes
See Ritsos, Yannis
Ritsos, Yannis 1909-1990 .... **CLC 6, 13, 31**
See also CA 77-80; 133; CANR 39, 61; EW
12; EWL 3; MTCW 1; RGWL 2, 3
Ritter, Erika 1948(?)- .... **CLC 52**
See also CD 5, 6; CWD
Rivera, Jose Eustasio 1889-1928 ... **TCLC 35**
See also CA 162; EWL 3; HW 1, 2; LAW
Rivera, Tomas 1935-1984 .... **HLCS 2**
See also CA 49-52; CANR 32; DLB 82;
HW 1; LLW; RGAL 4; SSFS 15; TCWW
2; WLIT 1
Rivers, Conrad Kent 1933-1968 .... **CLC 1**
See also BW 1; CA 85-88; DLB 41
Rivers, Elfrida
See Bradley, Marion Zimmer
See also GLL 1
Riverside, John
See Heinlein, Robert A(nson)
Rizal, Jose 1861-1896 .... **NCLC 27**
Roa Bastos, Augusto (Jose Antonio)
1917-2005 .... **CLC 45; HLC 2**
See also CA 131; 238; CWW 2; DAM
MULT; DLB 113; EWL 3; HW 1; LAW;
RGSF 2; WLIT 1
Robbe-Grillet, Alain 1922- .... **CLC 1, 2, 4, 6,
8, 10, 14, 43, 128**
See also BPFB 3; CA 9-12R; CANR 33,
65, 115; CWW 2; DLB 83; EW 13; EWL
3; GFL 1789 to the Present; IDFW 3, 4;
MTCW 1, 2; MTFW 2005; RGWL 2, 3;
SSFS 15
Robbins, Harold 1916-1997 .... **CLC 5**
See also BPFB 3; CA 73-76; 162; CANR
26, 54, 112; DA3; DAM NOV; MTCW 1,
2
Robbins, Thomas Eugene 1936-
See Robbins, Tom
See also CA 81-84; CANR 29, 59, 95, 139;
CN 7; CPW; CSW; DA3; DAM NOV,
POP; MTCW 1, 2; MTFW 2005

Ross, Martin 1862-1915
  See Martin, Violet Florence
  See also DLB 135; GLL 2; RGEL 2; RGSF 2

Ross, (James) Sinclair 1908-1996 ... **CLC 13; SSC 24**
  See also CA 73-76; CANR 81; CN 1, 2, 3, 4, 5, 6; DAC; DAM MST; DLB 88; RGEL 2; RGSF 2; TCWW 1, 2

Rossetti, Christina 1830-1894 ... **NCLC 2, 50, 66; PC 7; WLC**
  See also AAYA 51; BRW 5; BYA 4; DA; DA3; DAB; DAC; DAM MST, POET; DLB 35, 163, 240; EXPP; FL 1:3; LATS 1:1; MAICYA 1, 2; PFS 10, 14; RGEL 2; SATA 20; TEA; WCH

Rossetti, Christina Georgina
  See Rossetti, Christina

Rossetti, Dante Gabriel 1828-1882 . **NCLC 4, 77; PC 44; WLC**
  See also AAYA 51; BRW 5; CDBLB 1832-1890; DA; DAB; DAC; DAM MST, POET; DLB 35; EXPP; RGEL 2; TEA

Rossi, Cristina Peri
  See Peri Rossi, Cristina

Rossi, Jean-Baptiste 1931-2003
  See Japrisot, Sebastien
  See also CA 201; 215

Rossner, Judith (Perelman) 1935- . **CLC 6, 9, 29**
  See also AITN 2; BEST 90:3; BPFB 3; CA 17-20R; CANR 18, 51, 73; CN 4, 5, 6, 7; DLB 6; INT CANR-18; MAL 5; MTCW 1, 2; MTFW 2005

Rostand, Edmond (Eugene Alexis)
  1868-1918 .... **DC 10; TCLC 6, 37**
  See also CA 104; 126; DA; DA3; DAB; DAC; DAM DRAM, MST; DFS 1; DLB 192; LAIT 1; MTCW 1; RGWL 2, 3; TWA

Roth, Henry 1906-1995 ..... **CLC 2, 6, 11, 104**
  See also AMWS 9; CA 11-12; 149; CANR 38, 63; CAP 1; CN 1, 2, 3, 4, 5, 6; DA3; DLB 28; EWL 3; MAL 5; MTCW 1, 2; MTFW 2005; RGAL 4

Roth, (Moses) Joseph 1894-1939 ... **TCLC 33**
  See also CA 160; DLB 85; EWL 3; RGWL 2, 3

Roth, Philip (Milton) 1933- ... **CLC 1, 2, 3, 4, 6, 9, 15, 22, 31, 47, 66, 86, 119, 201; SSC 26; WLC**
  See also AAYA 67; AMWR 2; AMWS 3; BEST 90:3; BPFB 3; CA 1-4R; CANR 1, 22, 36, 55, 89, 132; CDALB 1968-1988; CN 3, 4, 5, 6, 7; CPW 1; DA; DA3; DAB; DAC; DAM MST, NOV, POP; DLB 2, 28, 173; DLBY 1982; EWL 3; MAL 5; MTCW 1, 2; MTFW 2005; RGAL 4; RGSF 2; SSFS 12, 18; TUS

Rothenberg, Jerome 1931- .... **CLC 6, 57**
  See also CA 45-48; CANR 1, 106; CP 1, 2, 3, 4, 5, 6, 7; DLB 5, 193

Rotter, Pat ed. .... **CLC 65**

Roumain, Jacques (Jean Baptiste)
  1907-1944 .... **BLC 3; TCLC 19**
  See also BW 1; CA 117; 125; DAM MULT; EWL 3

Rourke, Constance Mayfield
  1885-1941 .... **TCLC 12**
  See also CA 107; 200; MAL 5; YABC 1

Rousseau, Jean-Baptiste 1671-1741 ...... **LC 9**

Rousseau, Jean-Jacques 1712-1778 .... **LC 14, 36, 122; WLC**
  See also DA; DA3; DAB; DAC; DAM MST; DLB 314; EW 4; GFL Beginnings to 1789; LMFS 1; RGWL 2, 3; TWA

Roussel, Raymond 1877-1933 .... **TCLC 20**
  See also CA 117; 201; EWL 3; GFL 1789 to the Present

Rovit, Earl (Herbert) 1927- .... **CLC 7**
  See also CA 5-8R; CANR 12

Rowe, Elizabeth Singer 1674-1737 ..... **LC 44**
  See also DLB 39, 95

Rowe, Nicholas 1674-1718 .... **LC 8**
  See also DLB 84; RGEL 2

Rowlandson, Mary 1637(?)-1678 .... **LC 66**
  See also DLB 24, 200; RGAL 4

Rowley, Ames Dorrance
  See Lovecraft, H(oward) P(hillips)

Rowley, William 1585(?)-1626 ... **LC 100, 123**
  See also DFS 22; DLB 58; RGEL 2

Rowling, J. K. 1966- .... **CLC 137, 217**
  See also AAYA 34; BYA 11, 13, 14; CA 173; CANR 128; CLR 66, 80; MAICYA 2; MTFW 2005; SATA 109; SUFW 2

Rowling, Joanne Kathleen
  See Rowling, J.K.

Rowson, Susanna Haswell
  1762(?)-1824 .... **NCLC 5, 69**
  See also AMWS 15; DLB 37, 200; RGAL 4

Roy, Arundhati 1960(?)- .... **CLC 109, 210**
  See also CA 163; CANR 90, 126; CN 7; DLBY 1997; EWL 3; LATS 1:2; MTFW 2005; NFS 22; WWE 1

Roy, Gabrielle 1909-1983 .... **CLC 10, 14**
  See also CA 53-56; 110; CANR 5, 61; CCA 1; DAB; DAC; DAM MST; DLB 68; EWL 3; MTCW 1; RGWL 2, 3; SATA 104; TCLE 1:2

Royko, Mike 1932-1997 .... **CLC 109**
  See also CA 89-92; 157; CANR 26, 111; CPW

Rozanov, Vasilii Vasil'evich
  See Rozanov, Vassili
  See also DLB 295

Rozanov, Vasily Vasilyevich
  See Rozanov, Vassili
  See also EWL 3

Rozanov, Vassili 1856-1919 .... **TCLC 104**
  See also Rozanov, Vasilii Vasil'evich; Rozanov, Vasily Vasilyevich

Rozewicz, Tadeusz 1921- ...... **CLC 9, 23, 139**
  See also CA 108; CANR 36, 66; CWW 2; DA3; DAM POET; DLB 232; EWL 3; MTCW 1, 2; MTFW 2005; RGWL 3

Ruark, Gibbons 1941- .... **CLC 3**
  See also CA 33-36R; CAAS 23; CANR 14, 31, 57; DLB 120

Rubens, Bernice (Ruth) 1923-2004 . **CLC 19, 31**
  See also CA 25-28R; 232; CANR 33, 65, 128; CN 1, 2, 3, 4, 5, 6, 7; DLB 14, 207; MTCW 1

Rubin, Harold
  See Robbins, Harold

Rudkin, (James) David 1936- .... **CLC 14**
  See also CA 89-92; CBD; CD 5, 6; DLB 13

Rudnik, Raphael 1933- .... **CLC 7**
  See also CA 29-32R

Ruffian, M.
  See Hasek, Jaroslav (Matej Frantisek)

Ruiz, Jose Martinez .... **CLC 11**
  See Martinez Ruiz, Jose

Ruiz, Juan c. 1283-c. 1350 .... **CMLC 66**

Rukeyser, Muriel 1913-1980 . **CLC 6, 10, 15, 27; PC 12**
  See also AMWS 6; CA 5-8R; 93-96; CANR 26, 60; CP 1, 2, 3; DA3; DAM POET; DLB 48; EWL 3; FW; GLL 2; MAL 5; MTCW 1, 2; PFS 10; RGAL 4; SATA-Obit 22

Rule, Jane (Vance) 1931- .... **CLC 27**
  See also CA 25-28R; CAAS 18; CANR 12, 87; CN 4, 5, 6, 7; DLB 60; FW

Rulfo, Juan 1918-1986 .. **CLC 8, 80; HLC 2; SSC 25**
  See also CA 85-88; 118; CANR 26; CD-WLB 3; DAM MULT; DLB 113; EWL 3; HW 1, 2; LAW; MTCW 1, 2; RGSF 2; RGWL 2, 3; WLIT 1

Rumi, Jalal al-Din 1207-1273 ...... **CMLC 20; PC 45**
  See also AAYA 64; RGWL 2, 3; WLIT 6; WP

Runeberg, Johan 1804-1877 .... **NCLC 41**

Runyon, (Alfred) Damon
  1884(?)-1946 .... **TCLC 10**
  See also CA 107; 165; DLB 11, 86, 171; MAL 5; MTCW 2; RGAL 4

Rush, Norman 1933- .... **CLC 44**
  See also CA 121; 126; CANR 130; INT CA-126

Rushdie, (Ahmed) Salman 1947- .... **CLC 23, 31, 55, 100, 191; SSC 83; WLCS**
  See also AAYA 65; BEST 89:3; BPFB 3; BRWS 4; CA 108; 111; CANR 33, 56, 108, 133; CN 4, 5, 6, 7; CPW 1; DA3; DAB; DAC; DAM MST, NOV, POP; DLB 194; EWL 3; FANT; INT CA-111; LATS 1:2; LMFS 2; MTCW 1, 2; MTFW 2005; NFS 22; RGEL 2; RGSF 2; TEA; WLIT 4

Rushforth, Peter (Scott) 1945- .... **CLC 19**
  See also CA 101

Ruskin, John 1819-1900 .... **TCLC 63**
  See also BRW 5; BYA 5; CA 114; 129; CD-BLB 1832-1890; DLB 55, 163, 190; RGEL 2; SATA 24; TEA; WCH

Russ, Joanna 1937- .... **CLC 15**
  See also BPFB 3; CA 25-28; CANR 11, 31, 65; CN 4, 5, 6, 7; DLB 8; FW; GLL 1; MTCW 1; SCFW 1, 2; SFW 4

Russ, Richard Patrick
  See O'Brian, Patrick

Russell, George William 1867-1935
  See A.E.; Baker, Jean H.
  See also BRWS 8; CA 104; 153; CDBLB 1890-1914; DAM POET; EWL 3; RGEL 2

Russell, Jeffrey Burton 1934- .... **CLC 70**
  See also CA 25-28R; CANR 11, 28, 52

Russell, (Henry) Ken(neth Alfred)
  1927- .... **CLC 16**
  See also CA 105

Russell, William Martin 1947-
  See Russell, Willy
  See also CA 164; CANR 107

Russell, Willy .... **CLC 60**
  See Russell, William Martin
  See also CBD; CD 5, 6; DLB 233

Russo, Richard 1949- .... **CLC 181**
  See also AMWS 12; CA 127; 133; CANR 87, 114

Rutherford, Mark .... **TCLC 25**
  See White, William Hale
  See also DLB 18; RGEL 2

Ruyslinck, Ward .... **CLC 14**
  See Belser, Reimond Karel Maria de

Ryan, Cornelius (John) 1920-1974 ..... **CLC 7**
  See also CA 69-72; 53-56; CANR 38

Ryan, Michael 1946- .... **CLC 65**
  See also CA 49-52; CANR 109; DLBY 1982

Ryan, Tim
  See Dent, Lester

Rybakov, Anatoli (Naumovich)
  1911-1998 .... **CLC 23, 53**
  See Rybakov, Anatolii (Naumovich)
  See also CA 126; 135; 172; SATA 79; SATA-Obit 108

Rybakov, Anatolii (Naumovich)
  See Rybakov, Anatoli (Naumovich)
  See also DLB 302

Ryder, Jonathan
See Ludlum, Robert
Ryga, George 1932-1987 .... **CLC 14**
See also CA 101; 124; CANR 43, 90; CCA
1; DAC; DAM MST; DLB 60
S. H.
See Hartmann, Sadakichi
S. S.
See Sassoon, Siegfried (Lorraine)
Sa'adawi, al- Nawal
See El Saadawi, Nawal
See also AFW; EWL 3
Saadawi, Nawal El
See El Saadawi, Nawal
See also WLIT 2
Saba, Umberto 1883-1957 .... **TCLC 33**
See also CA 144; CANR 79; DLB 114;
EWL 3; RGWL 2, 3
Sabatini, Rafael 1875-1950 .... **TCLC 47**
See also BPFB 3; CA 162; RHW
Sabato, Ernesto (R.) 1911- .... **CLC 10, 23;
HLC 2**
See also CA 97-100; CANR 32, 65; CD-
WLB 3; CWW 2; DAM MULT; DLB 145;
EWL 3; HW 1, 2; LAW; MTCW 1, 2;
MTFW 2005
Sa-Carneiro, Mario de 1890-1916 . **TCLC 83**
See also DLB 287; EWL 3
Sacastru, Martin
See Bioy Casares, Adolfo
See also CWW 2
Sacher-Masoch, Leopold von
1836(?)-1895 .... **NCLC 31**
Sachs, Hans 1494-1576 .... **LC 95**
See also CDWLB 2; DLB 179; RGWL 2, 3
Sachs, Marilyn 1927- .... **CLC 35**
See also AAYA 2; BYA 6; CA 17-20R;
CANR 13, 47; CLR 2; JRDA; MAICYA
1, 2; SAAS 2; SATA 3, 68, 164; SATA-
Essay 110; WYA; YAW
Sachs, Marilyn Stickle
See Sachs, Marilyn
Sachs, Nelly 1891 1970 .... **CLC 14, 98**
See also CA 17-18; 25-28R; CANR 87;
CAP 2; EWL 3; MTCW 2; MTFW 2005;
PFS 20; RGWL 2, 3
Sackler, Howard (Oliver)
1929-1982 .... **CLC 14**
See also CA 61-64; 108; CAD; CANR 30;
DFS 15; DLB 7
Sacks, Oliver (Wolf) 1933- .... **CLC 67, 202**
See also CA 53-56; CANR 28, 50, 76;
CPW; DA3; INT CANR-28; MTCW 1, 2;
MTFW 2005
Sackville, Thomas 1536-1608 .... **LC 98**
See also DAM DRAM; DLB 62, 132;
RGEL 2
Sadakichi
See Hartmann, Sadakichi
Sa'dawi, Nawal al-
See El Saadawi, Nawal
See also CWW 2
Sade, Donatien Alphonse Francois
1740-1814 .... **NCLC 3, 47**
See also DLB 314; EW 4; GFL Beginnings
to 1789; RGWL 2, 3
Sade, Marquis de
See Sade, Donatien Alphonse Francois
Sadoff, Ira 1945- .... **CLC 9**
See also CA 53-56; CANR 5, 21, 109; DLB
120
Saetone
See Camus, Albert
Safire, William 1929- .... **CLC 10**
See also CA 17-20R; CANR 31, 54, 91

Sagan, Carl (Edward) 1934-1996 .... **CLC 30,
112**
See also AAYA 2, 62; CA 25-28R; 155;
CANR 11, 36, 74; CPW; DA3; MTCW 1,
2; MTFW 2005; SATA 58; SATA-Obit 94
Sagan, Francoise .... **CLC 3, 6, 9, 17, 36**
See Quoirez, Francoise
See also CWW 2; DLB 83; EWL 3; GFL
1789 to the Present; MTCW 2
Sahgal, Nayantara (Pandit) 1927- .... **CLC 41**
See also CA 9-12R; CANR 11, 88; CN 1,
2, 3, 4, 5, 6, 7
Said, Edward W. 1935-2003 .... **CLC 123**
See also CA 21-24R; 220; CANR 45, 74,
107, 131; DLB 67; MTCW 2; MTFW
2005
Saint, H(arry) F. 1941- .... **CLC 50**
See also CA 127
St. Aubin de Teran, Lisa 1953-
See Teran, Lisa St. Aubin de
See also CA 118; 126; CN 6, 7; INT CA-
126
Saint Birgitta of Sweden c.
1303-1373 .... **CMLC 24**
Saint Gregory of Nazianzus
329-389 .... **CMLC 82**
Sainte-Beuve, Charles Augustin
1804-1869 .... **NCLC 5**
See also DLB 217; EW 6; GFL 1789 to the
Present
**Saint-Exupery, Antoine (Jean Baptiste
Marie Roger) de** 1900-1944 .... **TCLC 2,
56, 169; WLC**
See also AAYA 63; BPFB 3; BYA 3; CA
108; 132; CLR 10; DA3; DAM NOV;
DLB 72; EW 12; EWL 3; GFL 1789 to
the Present; LAIT 3; MAICYA 1, 2;
MTCW 1, 2; MTFW 2005; RGWL 2, 3;
SATA 20; TWA
St. John, David
See Hunt, E(verette) Howard, (Jr.)
St. John, J. Hector
See Crevecoeur, Michel Guillaume Jean de
Saint-John Perse
See Leger, (Marie-Rene Auguste) Alexis
Saint-Leger
See also EW 10; EWL 3; GFL 1789 to the
Present; RGWL 2
Saintsbury, George (Edward Bateman)
1845-1933 .... **TCLC 31**
See also CA 160; DLB 57, 149
Sait Faik .... **TCLC 23**
See Abasiyanik, Sait Faik
Saki .... **SSC 12; TCLC 3**
See Munro, H(ector) H(ugh)
See also BRWS 6; BYA 11; LAIT 2; RGEL
2; SSFS 1; SUFW
Sala, George Augustus 1828-1895 . **NCLC 46**
Saladin 1138-1193 .... **CMLC 38**
Salama, Hannu 1936- .... **CLC 18**
See also EWL 3
Salamanca, J(ack) R(ichard) 1922- .. **CLC 4,
15**
See also CA 25-28R, 193; CAAE 193
Salas, Floyd Francis 1931- .... **HLC 2**
See also CA 119; CAAS 27; CANR 44, 75,
93; DAM MULT; DLB 82; HW 1, 2;
MTCW 2; MTFW 2005
Sale, J. Kirkpatrick
See Sale, Kirkpatrick
Sale, Kirkpatrick 1937- .... **CLC 68**
See also CA 13-16R; CANR 10
Salinas, Luis Omar 1937- ... **CLC 90; HLC 2**
See also AMWS 13; CA 131; CANR 81;
DAM MULT; DLB 82; HW 1, 2
Salinas (y Serrano), Pedro
1891(?)-1951 .... **TCLC 17**
See also CA 117; DLB 134; EWL 3

Salinger, J(erome) D(avid) 1919- .. **CLC 1, 3,
8, 12, 55, 56, 138; SSC 2, 28, 65; WLC**
See also AAYA 2, 36; AMW; AMWC 1;
BPFB 3; CA 5-8R; CANR 39, 129;
CDALB 1941-1968; CLR 18; CN 1, 2, 3,
4, 5, 6, 7; CPW 1; DA; DA3; DAB; DAC;
DAM MST, NOV, POP; DLB 2, 102, 173;
EWL 3; EXPN; LAIT 4; MAICYA 1, 2;
MAL 5; MTCW 1, 2; MTFW 2005; NFS
1; RGAL 4; RGSF 2; SATA 67; SSFS 17;
TUS; WYA; YAW
Salisbury, John
See Caute, (John) David
Sallust c. 86B.C.-35B.C. .... **CMLC 68**
See also AW 2; CDWLB 1; DLB 211;
RGWL 2, 3
Salter, James 1925- .. **CLC 7, 52, 59; SSC 58**
See also AMWS 9; CA 73-76; CANR 107;
DLB 130
Saltus, Edgar (Everton) 1855-1921 . **TCLC 8**
See also CA 105; DLB 202; RGAL 4
Saltykov, Mikhail Evgrafovich
1826-1889 .... **NCLC 16**
See also DLB 238:
Saltykov-Shchedrin, N.
See Saltykov, Mikhail Evgrafovich
Samarakis, Andonis
See Samarakis, Antonis
See also EWL 3
Samarakis, Antonis 1919-2003 .... **CLC 5**
See Samarakis, Andonis
See also CA 25-28R; 224; CAAS 16; CANR
36
Sanchez, Florencio 1875-1910 .... **TCLC 37**
See also CA 153; DLB 305; EWL 3; HW 1;
LAW
Sanchez, Luis Rafael 1936- .... **CLC 23**
See also CA 128; DLB 305; EWL 3; HW 1;
WLIT 1
Sanchez, Sonia 1934- .... **BLC 3; CLC 5, 116,
215; PC 9**
See also BW 2, 3; CA 33-36R; CANR 24,
49, 74, 115; CLR 18; CP 2, 3, 4, 5, 6, 7;
CSW; CWP; DA3; DAM MULT; DLB 41;
DLBD 8; EWL 3; MAICYA 1, 2; MAL 5;
MTCW 1, 2; MTFW 2005; SATA 22, 136;
WP
Sancho, Ignatius 1729-1780 .... **LC 84**
Sand, George 1804-1876 ..... **NCLC 2, 42, 57;
WLC**
See also DA; DA3; DAB; DAC; DAM
MST, NOV; DLB 119, 192; EW 6; FL 1:3;
FW; GFL 1789 to the Present; RGWL 2,
3; TWA
Sandburg, Carl (August) 1878-1967 . **CLC 1,
4, 10, 15, 35; PC 2, 41; WLC**
See also AAYA 24; AMW; BYA 1, 3; CA
5-8R; 25-28R; CANR 35; CDALB 1865-
1917; CLR 67; DA; DA3; DAB; DAC;
DAM MST, POET; DLB 17, 54, 284;
EWL 3; EXPP; LAIT 2; MAICYA 1, 2;
MAL 5; MTCW 1, 2; MTFW 2005; PAB;
PFS 3, 6, 12; RGAL 4; SATA 8; TUS;
WCH; WP; WYA
Sandburg, Charles
See Sandburg, Carl (August)
Sandburg, Charles A.
See Sandburg, Carl (August)
Sanders, (James) Ed(ward) 1939- .... **CLC 53**
See Sanders, Edward
See also BG 1:3; CA 13-16R; CAAS 21;
CANR 13, 44, 78; CP 1, 2, 3, 4, 5, 6, 7;
DAM POET; DLB 16, 244
Sanders, Edward
See Sanders, (James) Ed(ward)
See also DLB 244
Sanders, Lawrence 1920-1998 .... **CLC 41**
See also BEST 89:4; BPFB 3; CA 81-84;
165; CANR 33, 62; CMW 4; CPW; DA3;
DAM POP; MTCW 1

Schnitzler, Arthur 1862-1931 ..... **DC 17; SSC 15, 61; TCLC 4**
See also CA 104; CDWLB 2; DLB 81, 118; EW 8; EWL 3; RGSF 2; RGWL 2, 3
Schoenberg, Arnold Franz Walter 1874-1951 .... **TCLC 75**
See also CA 109; 188
Schonberg, Arnold
See Schoenberg, Arnold Franz Walter
Schopenhauer, Arthur 1788-1860 . **NCLC 51, 157**
See also DLB 90; EW 5
Schor, Sandra (M.) 1932(?)-1990 ..... **CLC 65**
See also CA 132
Schorer, Mark 1908-1977 .... **CLC 9**
See also CA 5-8R; 73-76; CANR 7; CN 1, 2; DLB 103
Schrader, Paul (Joseph) 1946- . **CLC 26, 212**
See also CA 37-40R; CANR 41; DLB 44
Schreber, Daniel 1842-1911 .... **TCLC 123**
Schreiner, Olive (Emilie Albertina) 1855-1920 .... **TCLC 9**
See also AFW; BRWS 2; CA 105; 154; DLB 18, 156, 190, 225; EWL 3; FW; RGEL 2; TWA; WLIT 2; WWE 1
Schulberg, Budd (Wilson) 1914- .. **CLC 7, 48**
See also BPFB 3; CA 25-28R; CANR 19, 87; CN 1, 2, 3, 4, 5, 6, 7; DLB 6, 26, 28; DLBY 1981, 2001; MAL 5
Schulman, Arnold
See Trumbo, Dalton
Schulz, Bruno 1892-1942 .. **SSC 13; TCLC 5, 51**
See also CA 115; 123; CANR 86; CDWLB 4; DLB 215; EWL 3; MTCW 2; MTFW 2005; RGSF 2; RGWL 2, 3
Schulz, Charles M. 1922-2000 .... **CLC 12**
See also AAYA 39; CA 9-12R; 187; CANR 6, 132; INT CANR-6; MTFW 2005; SATA 10; SATA-Obit 118
Schulz, Charles Monroe
See Schulz, Charles M.
Schumacher, E(rnst) F(riedrich) 1911-1977 .... **CLC 80**
See also CA 81-84; 73-76; CANR 34, 85
Schumann, Robert 1810-1856 ...... **NCLC 143**
Schuyler, George Samuel 1895-1977 . **HR 1:3**
See also BW 2; CA 81-84; 73-76; CANR 42; DLB 29, 51
Schuyler, James Marcus 1923-1991 .. **CLC 5, 23**
See also CA 101; 134; CP 1, 2, 3, 4; DAM POET; DLB 5, 169; EWL 3; INT CA-101; MAL 5; WP
Schwartz, Delmore (David) 1913-1966 ... **CLC 2, 4, 10, 45, 87; PC 8**
See also AMWS 2; CA 17-18; 25-28R; CANR 35; CAP 2; DLB 28, 48; EWL 3; MAL 5; MTCW 1, 2; MTFW 2005; PAB; RGAL 4; TUS
Schwartz, Ernst
See Ozu, Yasujiro
Schwartz, John Burnham 1965- .... **CLC 59**
See also CA 132; CANR 116
Schwartz, Lynne Sharon 1939- .... **CLC 31**
See also CA 103; CANR 44, 89; DLB 218; MTCW 2; MTFW 2005
Schwartz, Muriel A.
See Eliot, T(homas) S(tearns)
Schwarz-Bart, Andre 1928- .... **CLC 2, 4**
See also CA 89-92; CANR 109; DLB 299
Schwarz-Bart, Simone 1938- . **BLCS; CLC 7**
See also BW 2; CA 97-100; CANR 117; EWL 3
Schwerner, Armand 1927-1999 .... **PC 42**
See also CA 9-12R; 179; CANR 50, 85; CP 2, 3, 4; DLB 165

Schwitters, Kurt (Hermann Edward Karl Julius) 1887-1948 .... **TCLC 95**
See also CA 158
Schwob, Marcel (Mayer Andre) 1867-1905 .... **TCLC 20**
See also CA 117; 168; DLB 123; GFL 1789 to the Present
Sciascia, Leonardo 1921-1989 .. **CLC 8, 9, 41**
See also CA 85-88; 130; CANR 35; DLB 177; EWL 3; MTCW 1; RGWL 2, 3
Scoppettone, Sandra 1936- .... **CLC 26**
See Early, Jack
See also AAYA 11, 65; BYA 8; CA 5-8R; CANR 41, 73; GLL 1; MAICYA 2; MAICYAS 1; SATA 9, 92; WYA; YAW
Scorsese, Martin 1942- .... **CLC 20, 89, 207**
See also AAYA 38; CA 110; 114; CANR 46, 85
Scotland, Jay
See Jakes, John (William)
Scott, Duncan Campbell 1862-1947 .... **TCLC 6**
See also CA 104; 153; DAC; DLB 92; RGEL 2
Scott, Evelyn 1893-1963 .... **CLC 43**
See also CA 104; 112; CANR 64; DLB 9, 48; RHW
Scott, F(rancis) R(eginald) 1899-1985 .... **CLC 22**
See also CA 101; 114; CANR 87; CP 1, 2, 3, 4; DLB 88; INT CA-101; RGEL 2
Scott, Frank
See Scott, F(rancis) R(eginald)
Scott, Joan .... **CLC 65**
Scott, Joanna 1960- .... **CLC 50**
See also CA 126; CANR 53, 92
Scott, Paul (Mark) 1920-1978 ...... **CLC 9, 60**
See also BRWS 1; CA 81-84; 77-80; CANR 33; CN 1, 2; DLB 14, 207; EWL 3; MTCW 1; RGEL 2; RHW; WWE 1
Scott, Ridley 1937- .... **CLC 183**
See also AAYA 13, 43
Scott, Sarah 1723-1795 .... **LC 44**
See also DLB 39
Scott, Sir Walter 1771-1832 .... **NCLC 15, 69, 110; PC 13; SSC 32; WLC**
See also AAYA 22; BRW 4; BYA 2; CD-BLB 1789-1832; DA; DAB; DAC; DAM MST, NOV, POET; DLB 93, 107, 116, 144, 159; GL 3; HGG; LAIT 1; RGEL 2; RGSF 2; SSFS 10; SUFW 1; TEA; WLIT 3; YABC 2
Scribe, (Augustin) Eugene 1791-1861 . **DC 5; NCLC 16**
See also DAM DRAM; DLB 192; GFL 1789 to the Present; RGWL 2, 3
Scrum, R.
See Crumb, R(obert)
Scudery, Georges de 1601-1667 .... **LC 75**
See also GFL Beginnings to 1789
Scudery, Madeleine de 1607-1701 .. **LC 2, 58**
See also DLB 268; GFL Beginnings to 1789
Scum
See Crumb, R(obert)
Scumbag, Little Bobby
See Crumb, R(obert)
Seabrook, John
See Hubbard, L(afayette) Ron(ald)
Seacole, Mary Jane Grant 1805-1881 .... **NCLC 147**
See also DLB 166
Sealy, I(rwin) Allan 1951- .... **CLC 55**
See also CA 136; CN 6, 7
Search, Alexander
See Pessoa, Fernando (Antonio Nogueira)
Sebald, W(infried) G(eorg) 1944-2001 .... **CLC 194**
See also BRWS 8; CA 159; 202; CANR 98; MTFW 2005

Sebastian, Lee
See Silverberg, Robert
Sebastian Owl
See Thompson, Hunter S(tockton)
Sebestyen, Igen
See Sebestyen, Ouida
Sebestyen, Ouida 1924- .... **CLC 30**
See also AAYA 8; BYA 7; CA 107; CANR 40, 114; CLR 17; JRDA; MAICYA 1, 2; SAAS 10; SATA 39, 140; WYA; YAW
Sebold, Alice 1963(?)- .... **CLC 193**
See also AAYA 56; CA 203; MTFW 2005
Second Duke of Buckingham
See Villiers, George
Secundus, H. Scriblerus
See Fielding, Henry
Sedges, John
See Buck, Pearl S(ydenstricker)
Sedgwick, Catharine Maria 1789-1867 .... **NCLC 19, 98**
See also DLB 1, 74, 183, 239, 243, 254; FL 1:3; RGAL 4
Seelye, John (Douglas) 1931- .... **CLC 7**
See also CA 97-100; CANR 70; INT CA-97-100; TCWW 1, 2
Seferiades, Giorgos Stylianou 1900-1971
See Seferis, George
See also CA 5-8R; 33-36R; CANR 5, 36; MTCW 1
Seferis, George .... **CLC 5, 11; PC 66**
See Seferiades, Giorgos Stylianou
See also EW 12; EWL 3; RGWL 2, 3
Segal, Erich (Wolf) 1937- .... **CLC 3, 10**
See also BEST 89:1; BPFB 3; CA 25-28R; CANR 20, 36, 65, 113; CPW; DAM POP; DLBY 1986; INT CANR-20; MTCW 1
Seger, Bob 1945- .... **CLC 35**
Seghers, Anna .... **CLC 7**
See Radvanyi, Netty
See also CDWLB 2; DLB 69; EWL 3
Seidel, Frederick (Lewis) 1936- .... **CLC 18**
See also CA 13-16R; CANR 8, 99; CP 1, 2, 3, 4, 5, 6, 7; DLBY 1984
Seifert, Jaroslav 1901-1986 . **CLC 34, 44, 93; PC 47**
See also CA 127; CDWLB 4; DLB 215; EWL 3; MTCW 1, 2
Sei Shonagon c. 966-1017(?) .... **CMLC 6**
Sejour, Victor 1817-1874 .... **DC 10**
See also DLB 50
Sejour Marcou et Ferrand, Juan Victor
See Sejour, Victor
Selby, Hubert, Jr. 1928-2004 ..... **CLC 1, 2, 4, 8; SSC 20**
See also CA 13-16R; 226; CANR 33, 85; CN 1, 2, 3, 4, 5, 6, 7; DLB 2, 227; MAL 5
Selzer, Richard 1928- .... **CLC 74**
See also CA 65-68; CANR 14, 106
Sembene, Ousmane
See Ousmane, Sembene
See also AFW; EWL 3; WLIT 2
Senancour, Etienne Pivert de 1770-1846 .... **NCLC 16**
See also DLB 119; GFL 1789 to the Present
Sender, Ramon (Jose) 1902-1982 ...... **CLC 8; HLC 2; TCLC 136**
See also CA 5-8R; 105; CANR 8; DAM MULT; DLB 322; EWL 3; HW 1; MTCW 1; RGWL 2, 3
Seneca, Lucius Annaeus c. 4B.C.-c. 65 .... **CMLC 6; DC 5**
See also AW 2; CDWLB 1; DAM DRAM; DLB 211; RGWL 2, 3; TWA

Shepherd, Michael
See Ludlum, Robert
Sherburne, Zoa (Lillian Morin)
1912-1995 .... **CLC 30**
See also AAYA 13; CA 1-4R; 176; CANR 3, 37; MAICYA 1, 2; SAAS 18; SATA 3; YAW
Sheridan, Frances 1724-1766 .... **LC 7**
See also DLB 39, 84
Sheridan, Richard Brinsley
1751-1816 .... **DC 1; NCLC 5, 91; WLC**
See also BRW 3; CDBLB 1660-1789; DA; DAB; DAC; DAM DRAM, MST; DFS 15; DLB 89; WLIT 3
Sherman, Jonathan Marc 1968- .... **CLC 55**
See also CA 230
Sherman, Martin 1941(?)- .... **CLC 19**
See also CA 116; 123; CAD; CANR 86; CD 5, 6; DFS 20; DLB 228; GLL 1; IDTP
Sherwin, Judith Johnson
See Johnson, Judith (Emlyn)
See also CANR 85; CP 2, 3, 4; CWP
Sherwood, Frances 1940- .... **CLC 81**
See also CA 146, 220; CAAE 220
Sherwood, Robert E(mmet)
1896-1955 .... **TCLC 3**
See also CA 104; 153; CANR 86; DAM DRAM; DFS 11, 15, 17; DLB 7, 26, 249; IDFW 3, 4; MAL 5; RGAL 4
Shestov, Lev 1866-1938 .... **TCLC 56**
Shevchenko, Taras 1814-1861 .... **NCLC 54**
Shiel, M(atthew) P(hipps)
1865-1947 .... **TCLC 8**
See Holmes, Gordon
See also CA 106; 160; DLB 153; HGG; MTCW 2; MTFW 2005; SCFW 1, 2; SFW 4; SUFW
Shields, Carol (Ann) 1935-2003 ...... **CLC 91, 113, 193**
See also AMWS 7; CA 81-84; 218; CANR 51, 74, 98, 133; CCA 1; CN 6, 7; CPW; DA3; DAC; MTCW 2; MTFW 2005
Shields, David (Jonathan) 1956- ...... **CLC 97**
See also CA 124; CANR 48, 99, 112
Shiga, Naoya 1883-1971 .... **CLC 33; SSC 23; TCLC 172**
See Shiga Naoya
See also CA 101; 33-36R; MJW; RGWL 3
Shiga Naoya
See Shiga, Naoya
See also DLB 180; EWL 3; RGWL 3
Shilts, Randy 1951-1994 .... **CLC 85**
See also AAYA 19; CA 115; 127; 144; CANR 45; DA3; GLL 1; INT CA-127; MTCW 2; MTFW 2005
Shimazaki, Haruki 1872-1943
See Shimazaki Toson
See also CA 105; 134; CANR 84; RGWL 3
Shimazaki Toson .... **TCLC 5**
See Shimazaki, Haruki
See also DLB 180; EWL 3
Shirley, James 1596-1666 .... **DC 25; LC 96**
See also DLB 58; RGEL 2
Sholokhov, Mikhail (Aleksandrovich)
1905-1984 .... **CLC 7, 15**
See also CA 101; 112; DLB 272; EWL 3; MTCW 1, 2; MTFW 2005; RGWL 2, 3; SATA-Obit 36
Shone, Patric
See Hanley, James
Showalter, Elaine 1941- .... **CLC 169**
See also CA 57-60; CANR 58, 106; DLB 67; FW; GLL 2
Shreve, Susan
See Shreve, Susan Richards
Shreve, Susan Richards 1939- .... **CLC 23**
See also CA 49-52; CAAS 5; CANR 5, 38, 69, 100; MAICYA 1, 2; SATA 46, 95, 152; SATA-Brief 41

Shue, Larry 1946-1985 .... **CLC 52**
See also CA 145; 117; DAM DRAM; DFS 7
Shu-Jen, Chou 1881-1936
See Lu Hsun
See also CA 104
Shulman, Alix Kates 1932- .... **CLC 2, 10**
See also CA 29-32R; CANR 43; FW; SATA 7
Shuster, Joe 1914-1992 .... **CLC 21**
See also AAYA 50
Shute, Nevil .... **CLC 30**
See Norway, Nevil Shute
See also BPFB 3; DLB 255; NFS 9; RHW; SFW 4
Shuttle, Penelope (Diane) 1947- .... **CLC 7**
See also CA 93-96; CANR 39, 84, 92, 108; CP 3, 4, 5, 6, 7; CWP; DLB 14, 40
Shvarts, Elena 1948- .... **PC 50**
See also CA 147
Sidhwa, Bapsi
See Sidhwa, Bapsy (N.)
See also CN 6, 7
Sidhwa, Bapsy (N.) 1938- .... **CLC 168**
See Sidhwa, Bapsi
See also CA 108; CANR 25, 57; FW
Sidney, Mary 1561-1621 .... **LC 19, 39**
See Sidney Herbert, Mary
Sidney, Sir Philip 1554-1586 . **LC 19, 39; PC 32**
See also BRW 1; BRWR 2; CDBLB Before 1660; DA; DA3; DAB; DAC; DAM MST, POET; DLB 167; EXPP; PAB; RGEL 2; TEA; WP
Sidney Herbert, Mary
See Sidney, Mary
See also DLB 167
Siegel, Jerome 1914-1996 .... **CLC 21**
See Siegel, Jerry
See also CA 116; 169; 151
Siegel, Jerry
See Siegel, Jerome
See also AAYA 50
Sienkiewicz, Henryk (Adam Alexander Pius)
1846-1916 .... **TCLC 3**
See also CA 104; 134; CANR 84; EWL 3; RGSF 2; RGWL 2, 3
Sierra, Gregorio Martinez
See Martinez Sierra, Gregorio
Sierra, Maria (de la O'LeJarraga) Martinez
See Martinez Sierra, Maria (de la O'LeJarraga)
Sigal, Clancy 1926- .... **CLC 7**
See also CA 1-4R; CANR 85; CN 1, 2, 3, 4, 5, 6, 7
Siger of Brabant 1240(?)-1284(?) . **CMLC 69**
See also DLB 115
Sigourney, Lydia H.
See Sigourney, Lydia Howard (Huntley)
See also DLB 73, 183
Sigourney, Lydia Howard (Huntley)
1791-1865 .... **NCLC 21, 87**
See Sigourney, Lydia H.; Sigourney, Lydia Huntley
See also DLB 1
Sigourney, Lydia Huntley
See Sigourney, Lydia Howard (Huntley)
See also DLB 42, 239, 243
Siguenza y Gongora, Carlos de
1645-1700 .... **HLCS 2; LC 8**
See also LAW
Sigurjonsson, Johann
See Sigurjonsson, Johann
Sigurjonsson, Johann 1880-1919 ... **TCLC 27**
See also CA 170; DLB 293; EWL 3
Sikelianos, Angelos 1884-1951 .... **PC 29; TCLC 39**
See also EWL 3; RGWL 2, 3

Silkin, Jon 1930-1997 .... **CLC 2, 6, 43**
See also CA 5-8R; CAAS 5; CANR 89; CP 1, 2, 3, 4, 5, 6; DLB 27
Silko, Leslie (Marmon) 1948- .... **CLC 23, 74, 114, 211; NNAL; SSC 37, 66; WLCS**
See also AAYA 14; AMWS 4; ANW; BYA 12; CA 115; 122; CANR 45, 65, 118; CN 4, 5, 6, 7; CP 4, 5, 6, 7; CPW 1; CWP; DA; DA3; DAC; DAM MST, MULT, POP; DLB 143, 175, 256, 275; EWL 3; EXPP; EXPS; LAIT 4; MAL 5; MTCW 2; MTFW 2005; NFS 4; PFS 9, 16; RGAL 4; RGSF 2; SSFS 4, 8, 10, 11; TCWW 1, 2
Sillanpaa, Frans Eemil 1888-1964 ... **CLC 19**
See also CA 129; 93-96; EWL 3; MTCW 1
Sillitoe, Alan 1928- .. **CLC 1, 3, 6, 10, 19, 57, 148**
See also AITN 1; BRWS 5; CA 9-12R, 191; CAAE 191; CAAS 2; CANR 8, 26, 55, 139; CDBLB 1960 to Present; CN 1, 2, 3, 4, 5, 6; CP 1, 2, 3, 4; DLB 14, 139; EWL 3; MTCW 1, 2; MTFW 2005; RGEL 2; RGSF 2; SATA 61
Silone, Ignazio 1900-1978 .... **CLC 4**
See also CA 25-28; 81-84; CANR 34; CAP 2; DLB 264; EW 12; EWL 3; MTCW 1; RGSF 2; RGWL 2, 3
Silone, Ignazione
See Silone, Ignazio
Silver, Joan Micklin 1935- .... **CLC 20**
See also CA 114; 121; INT CA-121
Silver, Nicholas
See Faust, Frederick (Schiller)
Silverberg, Robert 1935- .... **CLC 7, 140**
See also AAYA 24; BPFB 3; BYA 7, 9; CA 1-4R, 186; CAAE 186; CAAS 3; CANR 1, 20, 36, 85, 140; CLR 59; CN 6, 7; CPW; DAM POP; DLB 8; INT CANR-20; MAICYA 1, 2; MTCW 1, 2; MTFW 2005; SATA 13, 91; SATA-Essay 104; SCFW 1, 2; SFW 4; SUFW 2
Silverstein, Alvin 1933- .... **CLC 17**
See also CA 49-52; CANR 2; CLR 25; JRDA; MAICYA 1, 2; SATA 8, 69, 124
Silverstein, Shel(don Allan)
1932-1999 .... **PC 49**
See also AAYA 40; BW 3; CA 107; 179; CANR 47, 74, 81; CLR 5, 96; CWRI 5; JRDA; MAICYA 1, 2; MTCW 2; MTFW 2005; SATA 33, 92; SATA-Brief 27; SATA-Obit 116
Silverstein, Virginia B(arbara Opshelor)
1937- .... **CLC 17**
See also CA 49-52; CANR 2; CLR 25; JRDA; MAICYA 1, 2; SATA 8, 69, 124
Sim, Georges
See Simenon, Georges (Jacques Christian)
Simak, Clifford D(onald) 1904-1988 . **CLC 1, 55**
See also CA 1-4R; 125; CANR 1, 35; DLB 8; MTCW 1; SATA-Obit 56; SCFW 1, 2; SFW 4
Simenon, Georges (Jacques Christian)
1903-1989 .... **CLC 1, 2, 3, 8, 18, 47**
See also BPFB 3; CA 85-88; 129; CANR 35; CMW 4; DA3; DAM POP; DLB 72; DLBY 1989; EW 12; EWL 3; GFL 1789 to the Present; MSW; MTCW 1, 2; MTFW 2005; RGWL 2, 3
Simic, Charles 1938- .... **CLC 6, 9, 22, 49, 68, 130; PC 69**
See also AMWS 8; CA 29-32R; CAAS 4; CANR 12, 33, 52, 61, 96, 140; CP 2, 3, 4, 5, 6, 7; DA3; DAM POET; DLB 105; MAL 5; MTCW 2; MTFW 2005; PFS 7; RGAL 4; WP
Simmel, Georg 1858-1918 .... **TCLC 64**
See also CA 157; DLB 296

Simmons, Charles (Paul) 1924- .... **CLC 57**
See also CA 89-92; INT CA-89-92

Simmons, Dan 1948- .... **CLC 44**
See also AAYA 16, 54; CA 138; CANR 53, 81, 126; CPW; DAM POP; HGG; SUFW 2

Simmons, James (Stewart Alexander) 1933- .... **CLC 43**
See also CA 105; CAAS 21; CP 1, 2, 3, 4, 5, 6, 7; DLB 40

Simms, William Gilmore 1806-1870 .... **NCLC 3**
See also DLB 3, 30, 59, 73, 248, 254; RGAL 4

Simon, Carly 1945- .... **CLC 26**
See also CA 105

Simon, Claude 1913-2005 ... **CLC 4, 9, 15, 39**
See also CA 89-92; 241; CANR 33, 117; CWW 2; DAM NOV; DLB 83; EW 13; EWL 3; GFL 1789 to the Present; MTCW 1

Simon, Claude Eugene Henri
See Simon, Claude

Simon, Claude Henri Eugene
See Simon, Claude

Simon, Myles
See Follett, Ken(neth Martin)

Simon, (Marvin) Neil 1927- ... **CLC 6, 11, 31, 39, 70; DC 14**
See also AAYA 32; AITN 1; AMWS 4; CA 21-24R; CAD; CANR 26, 54, 87, 126; CD 5, 6; DA3; DAM DRAM; DFS 2, 6, 12, 18; DLB 7, 266; LAIT 4; MAL 5; MTCW 1, 2; MTFW 2005; RGAL 4; TUS

Simon, Paul (Frederick) 1941(?)- ..... **CLC 17**
See also CA 116; 153

Simonon, Paul 1956(?)- .... **CLC 30**

Simonson, Rick ed. .... **CLC 70**

Simpson, Harriette
See Arnow, Harriette (Louisa) Simpson

Simpson, Louis (Aston Marantz) 1923- .... **CLC 4, 7, 9, 32, 149**
See also AMWS 9; CA 1-4R; CAAS 4; CANR 1, 61, 140; CP 1, 2, 3, 4, 5, 6, 7; DAM POET; DLB 5; MAL 5; MTCW 1, 2; MTFW 2005; PFS 7, 11, 14; RGAL 4

Simpson, Mona (Elizabeth) 1957- ... **CLC 44, 146**
See also CA 122; 135; CANR 68, 103; CN 6, 7; EWL 3

Simpson, N(orman) F(rederick) 1919- .... **CLC 29**
See also CA 13-16R; CBD; DLB 13; RGEL 2

Sinclair, Andrew (Annandale) 1935- . **CLC 2, 14**
See also CA 9-12R; CAAS 5; CANR 14, 38, 91; CN 1, 2, 3, 4, 5, 6, 7; DLB 14; FANT; MTCW 1

Sinclair, Emil
See Hesse, Hermann

Sinclair, Iain 1943- .... **CLC 76**
See also CA 132; CANR 81; CP 7; HGG

Sinclair, Iain MacGregor
See Sinclair, Iain

Sinclair, Irene
See Griffith, D(avid Lewelyn) W(ark)

Sinclair, Mary Amelia St. Clair 1865(?)-1946
See Sinclair, May
See also CA 104; HGG; RHW

Sinclair, May .... **TCLC 3, 11**
See Sinclair, Mary Amelia St. Clair
See also CA 166; DLB 36, 135; EWL 3; RGEL 2; SUFW

Sinclair, Roy
See Griffith, D(avid Lewelyn) W(ark)

Sinclair, Upton (Beall) 1878-1968 ..... **CLC 1, 11, 15, 63; TCLC 160; WLC**
See also AAYA 63; AMWS 5; BPFB 3; BYA 2; CA 5-8R; 25-28R; CANR 7; CDALB 1929-1941; DA; DA3; DAB; DAC; DAM MST, NOV; DLB 9; EWL 3; INT CANR-7; LAIT 3; MAL 5; MTCW 1, 2; MTFW 2005; NFS 6; RGAL 4; SATA 9; TUS; YAW

Singe, (Edmund) J(ohn) M(illlngton) 1871-1909 .... **WLC**

Singer, Isaac
See Singer, Isaac Bashevis

Singer, Isaac Bashevis 1904-1991 .. **CLC 1, 3, 6, 9, 11, 15, 23, 38, 69, 111; SSC 3, 53, 80; WLC**
See also AAYA 32; AITN 1, 2; AMW; AMWR 2; BPFB 3; BYA 1, 4; CA 1-4R; 134; CANR 1, 39, 106; CDALB 1941-1968; CLR 1; CN 1, 2, 3, 4; CWRI 5; DA; DA3; DAB; DAC; DAM MST, NOV; DLB 6, 28, 52, 278; DLBY 1991; EWL 3; EXPS; HGG; JRDA; LAIT 3; MAI-CYA 1, 2; MAL 5; MTCW 1, 2; MTFW 2005; RGAL 4; RGSF 2; SATA 3, 27; SATA-Obit 68; SSFS 2, 12, 16; TUS; TWA

Singer, Israel Joshua 1893-1944 .... **TCLC 33**
See also CA 169; EWL 3

Singh, Khushwant 1915- .... **CLC 11**
See also CA 9-12R; CAAS 9; CANR 6, 84; CN 1, 2, 3, 4, 5, 6, 7; EWL 3; RGEL 2

Singleton, Ann
See Benedict, Ruth (Fulton)

Singleton, John 1968(?)- .... **CLC 156**
See also AAYA 50; BW 2, 3; CA 138; CANR 67, 82; DAM MULT

Siniavskii, Andrei
See Sinyavsky, Andrei (Donatevich)
See also CWW 2

Sinjohn, John
See Galsworthy, John

Sinyavsky, Andrei (Donatevich) 1925-1997 .... **CLC 8**
See Siniavskii, Andrei; Sinyavsky, Andrey Donatovich; Tertz, Abram
See also CA 85-88; 159

Sinyavsky, Andrey Donatovich
See Sinyavsky, Andrei (Donatevich)
See also EWL 3

Sirin, V.
See Nabokov, Vladimir (Vladimirovich)

Sissman, L(ouis) E(dward) 1928-1976 .... **CLC 9, 18**
See also CA 21-24R; 65-68; CANR 13; CP 2; DLB 5

Sisson, C(harles) H(ubert) 1914-2003 .... **CLC 8**
See also BRWS 11; CA 1-4R; 220; CAAS 3; CANR 3, 48, 84; CP 1, 2, 3, 4, 5, 6, 7; DLB 27

Sitting Bull 1831(?)-1890 .... **NNAL**
See also DA3; DAM MULT

Sitwell, Dame Edith 1887-1964 ..... **CLC 2, 9, 67; PC 3**
See also BRW 7; CA 9-12R; CANR 35; CDBLB 1945-1960; DAM POET; DLB 20; EWL 3; MTCW 1, 2; MTFW 2005; RGEL 2; TEA

Siwaarmill, H. P.
See Sharp, William

Sjoewall, Maj 1935- .... **CLC 7**
See Sjowall, Maj
See also CA 65-68; CANR 73

Sjowall, Maj
See Sjoewall, Maj
See also BPFB 3; CMW 4; MSW

Skelton, John 1460(?)-1529 ..... **LC 71; PC 25**
See also BRW 1; DLB 136; RGEL 2

Skelton, Robin 1925-1997 .... **CLC 13**
See Zuk, Georges
See also AITN 2; CA 5-8R; 160; CAAS 5; CANR 28, 89; CCA 1; CP 1, 2, 3, 4; DLB 27, 53

Skolimowski, Jerzy 1938- .... **CLC 20**
See also CA 128

Skram, Amalie (Bertha) 1847-1905 .... **TCLC 25**
See also CA 165

Skvorecky, Josef (Vaclav) 1924- ...... **CLC 15, 39, 69, 152**
See also CA 61-64; CAAS 1; CANR 10, 34, 63, 108; CDWLB 4; CWW 2; DA3; DAC; DAM NOV; DLB 232; EWL 3; MTCW 1, 2; MTFW 2005

Slade, Bernard 1930- .... **CLC 11, 46**
See Newbound, Bernard Slade
See also CAAS 9; CCA 1; CD 6; DLB 53

Slaughter, Carolyn 1946- .... **CLC 56**
See also CA 85-88; CANR 85; CN 5, 6, 7

Slaughter, Frank G(ill) 1908-2001 ... **CLC 29**
See also AITN 2; CA 5-8R; 197; CANR 5, 85; INT CANR-5; RHW

Slavitt, David R(ytman) 1935- ...... **CLC 5, 14**
See also CA 21-24R; CAAS 3; CANR 41, 83; CN 1, 2; CP 1, 2, 3, 4, 5, 6, 7; DLB 5, 6

Slesinger, Tess 1905-1945 .... **TCLC 10**
See also CA 107; 199; DLB 102

Slessor, Kenneth 1901-1971 .... **CLC 14**
See also CA 102; 89-92; DLB 260; RGEL 2

Slowacki, Juliusz 1809-1849 .... **NCLC 15**
See also RGWL 3

Smart, Christopher 1722-1771 . **LC 3; PC 13**
See also DAM POET; DLB 109; RGEL 2

Smart, Elizabeth 1913-1986 .... **CLC 54**
See also CA 81-84; 118; CN 4; DLB 88

Smiley, Jane (Graves) 1949- ...... **CLC 53, 76, 144**
See also AAYA 66; AMWS 6; BPFB 3; CA 104; CANR 30, 50, 74, 96; CN 6, 7; CPW 1; DA3; DAM POP; DLB 227, 234; EWL 3; INT CANR-30; MAL 5; MTFW 2005; SSFS 19

Smith, A(rthur) J(ames) M(arshall) 1902-1980 .... **CLC 15**
See also CA 1-4R; 102; CANR 4; CP 1, 2, 3; DAC; DLB 88; RGEL 2

Smith, Adam 1723(?)-1790 .... **LC 36**
See also DLB 104, 252; RGEL 2

Smith, Alexander 1829-1867 .... **NCLC 59**
See also DLB 32, 55

Smith, Anna Deavere 1950- .... **CLC 86**
See also CA 133; CANR 103; CD 5, 6; DFS 2, 22

Smith, Betty (Wehner) 1904-1972 .... **CLC 19**
See also BPFB 3; BYA 3; CA 5-8R; 33-36R; DLBY 1982; LAIT 3; RGAL 4; SATA 6

Smith, Charlotte (Turner) 1749-1806 .... **NCLC 23, 115**
See also DLB 39, 109; RGEL 2; TEA

Smith, Clark Ashton 1893-1961 .... **CLC 43**
See also CA 143; CANR 81; FANT; HGG; MTCW 2; SCFW 1, 2; SFW 4; SUFW

Smith, Dave .... **CLC 22, 42**
See Smith, David (Jeddie)
See also CAAS 7; CP 3, 4, 5, 6, 7; DLB 5

Smith, David (Jeddie) 1942-
See Smith, Dave
See also CA 49-52; CANR 1, 59, 120; CSW; DAM POET

Smith, Florence Margaret 1902-1971
See Smith, Stevie
See also CA 17-18; 29-32R; CANR 35; CAP 2; DAM POET; MTCW 1, 2; TEA

Smith, Iain Crichton 1928-1998 .... **CLC 64**
See also BRWS 9; CA 21-24R; 171; CN 1,
2, 3, 4, 5, 6; CP 1, 2, 3, 4; DLB 40, 139,
319; RGSF 2

Smith, John 1580(?)-1631 .... **LC 9**
See also DLB 24, 30; TUS

Smith, Johnston
See Crane, Stephen (Townley)

Smith, Joseph, Jr. 1805-1844 .... **NCLC 53**

Smith, Lee 1944- .... **CLC 25, 73**
See also CA 114; 119; CANR 46, 118; CN
7; CSW; DLB 143; DLBY 1983; EWL 3;
INT CA-119; RGAL 4

Smith, Martin
See Smith, Martin Cruz

Smith, Martin Cruz 1942- .. **CLC 25; NNAL**
See also BEST 89:4; BPFB 3; CA 85-88;
CANR 6, 23, 43, 65, 119; CMW 4; CPW;
DAM MULT, POP; HGG; INT CANR-
23; MTCW 2; MTFW 2005; RGAL 4

Smith, Patti 1946- .... **CLC 12**
See also CA 93-96; CANR 63

Smith, Pauline (Urmson)
1882-1959 .... **TCLC 25**
See also DLB 225; EWL 3

Smith, Rosamond
See Oates, Joyce Carol

Smith, Sheila Kaye
See Kaye-Smith, Sheila

Smith, Stevie .... **CLC 3, 8, 25, 44; PC 12**
See Smith, Florence Margaret
See also BRWS 2; CP 1; DLB 20; EWL 3;
PAB; PFS 3; RGEL 2

Smith, Wilbur (Addison) 1933- .... **CLC 33**
See also CA 13-16R; CANR 7, 46, 66, 134;
CPW; MTCW 1, 2; MTFW 2005

Smith, William Jay 1918- .... **CLC 6**
See also AMWS 13; CA 5-8R; CANR 44,
106; CP 1, 2, 3, 4, 5, 6, 7; CSW; CWRI
5; DLB 5; MAICYA 1, 2; SAAS 22;
SATA 2, 68, 154; SATA-Essay 154; TCLE
1:2

Smith, Woodrow Wilson
See Kuttner, Henry

Smith, Zadie 1976- .... **CLC 158**
See also AAYA 50; CA 193; MTFW 2005

Smolenskin, Peretz 1842-1885 .... **NCLC 30**

Smollett, Tobias (George) 1721-1771 ... **LC 2,
46**
See also BRW 3; CDBLB 1660-1789; DLB
39, 104; RGEL 2; TEA

Snodgrass, W(illiam) D(e Witt)
1926- .... **CLC 2, 6, 10, 18, 68**
See also AMWS 6; CA 1-4R; CANR 6, 36,
65, 85; CP 1, 2, 3, 4, 5, 6, 7; DAM POET;
DLB 5; MAL 5; MTCW 1, 2; MTFW
2005; RGAL 4; TCLE 1:2

Snorri Sturluson 1179-1241 .... **CMLC 56**
See also RGWL 2, 3

Snow, C(harles) P(ercy) 1905-1980 ... **CLC 1,
4, 6, 9, 13, 19**
See also BRW 7; CA 5-8R; 101; CANR 28;
CDBLB 1945-1960; CN 1, 2; DAM NOV;
DLB 15, 77; DLBD 17; EWL 3; MTCW
1, 2; MTFW 2005; RGEL 2; TEA

Snow, Frances Compton
See Adams, Henry (Brooks)

Snyder, Gary (Sherman) 1930- . **CLC 1, 2, 5,
9, 32, 120; PC 21**
See also AMWS 8; ANW; BG 1:3; CA 17-
20R; CANR 30, 60, 125; CP 1, 2, 3, 4, 5,
6, 7; DA3; DAM POET; DLB 5, 16, 165,
212, 237, 275; EWL 3; MAL 5; MTCW
2; MTFW 2005; PFS 9, 19; RGAL 4; WP

Snyder, Zilpha Keatley 1927- .... **CLC 17**
See also AAYA 15; BYA 1; CA 9-12R;
CANR 38; CLR 31; JRDA; MAICYA 1,
2; SAAS 2; SATA 1, 28, 75, 110, 163;
SATA-Essay 112, 163; YAW

Soares, Bernardo
See Pessoa, Fernando (Antonio Nogueira)

Sobh, A.
See Shamlu, Ahmad

Sobh, Alef
See Shamlu, Ahmad

Sobol, Joshua 1939- .... **CLC 60**
See Sobol, Yehoshua
See also CA 200

Sobol, Yehoshua 1939-
See Sobol, Joshua
See also CWW 2

Socrates 470B.C.-399B.C. .... **CMLC 27**

Soderberg, Hjalmar 1869-1941 ...... **TCLC 39**
See also DLB 259; EWL 3; RGSF 2

Soderbergh, Steven 1963- .... **CLC 154**
See also AAYA 43

Sodergran, Edith (Irene) 1892-1923
See Soedergran, Edith (Irene)
See also CA 202; DLB 259; EW 11; EWL
3; RGWL 2, 3

Soedergran, Edith (Irene)
1892-1923 .... **TCLC 31**
See Sodergran, Edith (Irene)

Softly, Edgar
See Lovecraft, H(oward) P(hillips)

Softly, Edward
See Lovecraft, H(oward) P(hillips)

Sokolov, Alexander V(sevolodovich) 1943-
See Sokolov, Sasha
See also CA 73-76

Sokolov, Raymond 1941- .... **CLC 7**
See also CA 85-88

Sokolov, Sasha .... **CLC 59**
See Sokolov, Alexander V(sevolodovich)
See also CWW 2; DLB 285; EWL 3; RGWL
2, 3

Solo, Jay
See Ellison, Harlan (Jay)

Sologub, Fyodor .... **TCLC 9**
See Teternikov, Fyodor Kuzmich
See also EWL 3

Solomons, Ikey Esquir
See Thackeray, William Makepeace

Solomos, Dionysios 1798-1857 .... **NCLC 15**

Solwoska, Mara
See French, Marilyn

Solzhenitsyn, Aleksandr I(sayevich)
1918- .. **CLC 1, 2, 4, 7, 9, 10, 18, 26, 34,
78, 134; SSC 32; WLC**
See Solzhenitsyn, Aleksandr Isaevich
See also AAYA 49; AITN 1; BPFB 3; CA
69-72; CANR 40, 65, 116; DA; DA3;
DAB; DAC; DAM MST, NOV; DLB 302;
EW 13; EXPS; LAIT 4; MTCW 1, 2;
MTFW 2005; NFS 6; RGSF 2; RGWL 2,
3; SSFS 9; TWA

Solzhenitsyn, Aleksandr Isaevich
See Solzhenitsyn, Aleksandr I(sayevich)
See also CWW 2; EWL 3

Somers, Jane
See Lessing, Doris (May)

Somerville, Edith Oenone
1858-1949 .... **SSC 56; TCLC 51**
See also CA 196; DLB 135; RGEL 2; RGSF
2

Somerville & Ross
See Martin, Violet Florence; Somerville,
Edith Oenone

Sommer, Scott 1951- .... **CLC 25**
See also CA 106

Sommers, Christina Hoff 1950- ...... **CLC 197**
See also CA 153; CANR 95

Sondheim, Stephen (Joshua) 1930- . **CLC 30,
39, 147; DC 22**
See also AAYA 11, 66; CA 103; CANR 47,
67, 125; DAM DRAM; LAIT 4

Sone, Monica 1919- .... **AAL**
See also DLB 312

Song, Cathy 1955- .... **AAL; PC 21**
See also CA 154; CANR 118; CWP; DLB
169, 312; EXPP; FW; PFS 5

Sontag, Susan 1933-2004 ... **CLC 1, 2, 10, 13,
31, 105, 195**
See also AMWS 3; CA 17-20R; 234; CANR
25, 51, 74, 97; CN 1, 2, 3, 4, 5, 6, 7;
CPW; DA3; DAM POP; DLB 2, 67; EWL
3; MAL 5; MAWW; MTCW 1, 2; MTFW
2005; RGAL 4; RHW; SSFS 10

Sophocles 496(?)B.C.-406(?)B.C. .... **CMLC 2,
47, 51; DC 1; WLCS**
See also AW 1; CDWLB 1; DA; DA3;
DAB; DAC; DAM DRAM, MST; DFS 1,
4, 8; DLB 176; LAIT 1; LATS 1:1; LMFS
1; RGWL 2, 3; TWA

Sordello 1189-1269 .... **CMLC 15**

Sorel, Georges 1847-1922 .... **TCLC 91**
See also CA 118; 188

Sorel, Julia
See Drexler, Rosalyn

Sorokin, Vladimir .... **CLC 59**
See Sorokin, Vladimir Georgievich

Sorokin, Vladimir Georgievich
See Sorokin, Vladimir
See also DLB 285

Sorrentino, Gilbert 1929- .. **CLC 3, 7, 14, 22,
40**
See also CA 77-80; CANR 14, 33, 115; CN
3, 4, 5, 6, 7; CP 1, 2, 3, 4, 5, 6, 7; DLB 5,
173; DLBY 1980; INT CANR-14

Soseki
See Natsume, Soseki
See also MJW

Soto, Gary 1952- ... **CLC 32, 80; HLC 2; PC
28**
See also AAYA 10, 37; BYA 11; CA 119;
125; CANR 50, 74, 107; CLR 38; CP 4,
5, 6, 7; DAM MULT; DLB 82; EWL 3;
EXPP; HW 1, 2; INT CA-125; JRDA;
LLW; MAICYA 2; MAICYAS 1; MAL 5;
MTCW 2; MTFW 2005; PFS 7; RGAL 4;
SATA 80, 120; WYA; YAW

Soupault, Philippe 1897-1990 .... **CLC 68**
See also CA 116; 147; 131; EWL 3; GFL
1789 to the Present; LMFS 2

Souster, (Holmes) Raymond 1921- .... **CLC 5,
14**
See also CA 13-16R; CAAS 14; CANR 13,
29, 53; CP 1, 2, 3, 4, 5, 6, 7; DA3; DAC;
DAM POET; DLB 88; RGEL 2; SATA 63

Southern, Terry 1924(?)-1995 .... **CLC 7**
See also AMWS 11; BPFB 3; CA 1-4R;
150; CANR 1, 55, 107; CN 1, 2, 3, 4, 5,
6; DLB 2; IDFW 3, 4

Southerne, Thomas 1660-1746 .... **LC 99**
See also DLB 80; RGEL 2

Southey, Robert 1774-1843 .... **NCLC 8, 97**
See also BRW 4; DLB 93, 107, 142; RGEL
2; SATA 54

Southwell, Robert 1561(?)-1595 .... **LC 108**
See also DLB 167; RGEL 2; TEA

Southworth, Emma Dorothy Eliza Nevitte
1819-1899 .... **NCLC 26**
See also DLB 239

Souza, Ernest
See Scott, Evelyn

Soyinka, Wole 1934- .. **BLC 3; CLC 3, 5, 14,
36, 44, 179; DC 2; WLC**
See also AFW; BW 2, 3; CA 13-16R;
CANR 27, 39, 82, 136; CD 5, 6; CDWLB
3; CN 6, 7; CP 1, 2, 3, 4, 5, 6 ,7; DA;
DA3; DAB; DAC; DAM DRAM, MST,
MULT; DFS 10; DLB 125; EWL 3;
MTCW 1, 2; MTFW 2005; RGEL 2;
TWA; WLIT 2; WWE 1

Spackman, W(illiam) M(ode)
1905-1990 .... **CLC 46**
See also CA 81-84; 132

Stringer, David
See Roberts, Keith (John Kingston)
Stroheim, Erich von 1885-1957 ..... **TCLC 71**
Strugatskii, Arkadii (Natanovich)
1925-1991 .... **CLC 27**
See Strugatsky, Arkadii Natanovich
See also CA 106; 135; SFW 4
Strugatskii, Boris (Natanovich)
1933- .... **CLC 27**
See Strugatsky, Boris (Natanovich)
See also CA 106; SFW 4
Strugatsky, Arkadii Natanovich
See Strugatskii, Arkadii (Natanovich)
See also DLB 302
Strugatsky, Boris (Natanovich)
See Strugatskii, Boris (Natanovich)
See also DLB 302
Strummer, Joe 1952-2002 .... **CLC 30**
Strunk, William, Jr. 1869-1946 ...... **TCLC 92**
See also CA 118; 164; NCFS 5
Stryk, Lucien 1924- .... **PC 27**
See also CA 13-16R; CANR 10, 28, 55,
110; CP 1, 2, 3, 4, 5, 6, 7
Stuart, Don A.
See Campbell, John W(ood, Jr.)
Stuart, Ian
See MacLean, Alistair (Stuart)
Stuart, Jesse (Hilton) 1906-1984 ... **CLC 1, 8,
11, 14, 34; SSC 31**
See also CA 5-8R; 112; CANR 31; CN 1,
2, 3; DLB 9, 48, 102; DLBY 1984; SATA
2; SATA-Obit 36
Stubblefield, Sally
See Trumbo, Dalton
Sturgeon, Theodore (Hamilton)
1918-1985 .... **CLC 22, 39**
See Queen, Ellery
See also AAYA 51; BPFB 3; BYA 9, 10;
CA 81-84; 116; CANR 32, 103; DLB 8;
DLBY 1985; HGG; MTCW 1, 2; MTFW
2005; SCFW; SFW 4; SUFW
Sturges, Preston 1898-1959 .... **TCLC 48**
See also CA 114; 149; DLB 26
Styron, William 1925- .... **CLC 1, 3, 5, 11, 15,
60; SSC 25**
See also AMW; AMWC 2; BEST 90:4;
BPFB 3; CA 5-8R; CANR 6, 33, 74, 126;
CDALB 1968-1988; CN 1, 2, 3, 4, 5, 6,
7; CPW; CSW; DA3; DAM NOV, POP;
DLB 2, 143, 299; DLBY 1980; EWL 3;
INT CANR-6; LAIT 2; MAL 5; MTCW
1, 2; MTFW 2005; NCFS 1; NFS 22;
RGAL 4; RHW; TUS
Su, Chien 1884-1918
See Su Man-shu
See also CA 123
Suarez Lynch, B.
See Bioy Casares, Adolfo; Borges, Jorge
Luis
Suassuna, Ariano Vilar 1927- .... **HLCS 1**
See also CA 178; DLB 307; HW 2; LAW
Suckert, Kurt Erich
See Malaparte, Curzio
Suckling, Sir John 1609-1642 . **LC 75; PC 30**
See also BRW 2; DAM POET; DLB 58,
126; EXPP; PAB; RGEL 2
Suckow, Ruth 1892-1960 .... **SSC 18**
See also CA 193; 113; DLB 9, 102; RGAL
4; TCWW 2
Sudermann, Hermann 1857-1928 .. **TCLC 15**
See also CA 107; 201; DLB 118
Sue, Eugene 1804-1857 .... **NCLC 1**
See also DLB 119
Sueskind, Patrick 1949- .... **CLC 44, 182**
See Suskind, Patrick
Suetonius c. 70-c. 130 .... **CMLC 60**
See also AW 2; DLB 211; RGWL 2, 3

Sukenick, Ronald 1932-2004 ..... **CLC 3, 4, 6,
48**
See also CA 25-28R, 209; 229; CAAE 209;
CAAS 8; CANR 32, 89; CN 3, 4, 5, 6, 7;
DLB 173; DLBY 1981
Suknaski, Andrew 1942- .... **CLC 19**
See also CA 101; CP 3, 4, 5, 6, 7; DLB 53
Sullivan, Vernon
See Vian, Boris
Sully Prudhomme, Rene-Francois-Armand
1839-1907 .... **TCLC 31**
See also GFL 1789 to the Present
Su Man-shu .... **TCLC 24**
See Su, Chien
See also EWL 3
Sumarokov, Aleksandr Petrovich
1717-1777 .... **LC 104**
See also DLB 150
Summerforest, Ivy B.
See Kirkup, James
Summers, Andrew James 1942- .... **CLC 26**
Summers, Andy
See Summers, Andrew James
Summers, Hollis (Spurgeon, Jr.)
1916- .... **CLC 10**
See also CA 5-8R; CANR 3; CN 1, 2, 3;
CP 1, 2, 3, 4; DLB 6; TCLE 1:2
**Summers, (Alphonsus Joseph-Mary
Augustus) Montague**
1880-1948 .... **TCLC 16**
See also CA 118; 163
Sumner, Gordon Matthew .... **CLC 26**
See Police, The; Sting
Sun Tzu c. 400B.C.-c. 320B.C. ...... **CMLC 56**
Surrey, Henry Howard 1517-1574 ... **LC 121;
PC 59**
See also BRW 1; RGEL 2
Surtees, Robert Smith 1805-1864 .. **NCLC 14**
See also DLB 21; RGEL 2
Susann, Jacqueline 1921-1974 .... **CLC 3**
See also AITN 1; BPFB 3; CA 65-68; 53-
56; MTCW 1, 2
Su Shi
See Su Shih
See also RGWL 2, 3
Su Shih 1036-1101 .... **CMLC 15**
See Su Shi
Suskind, Patrick .... **CLC 182**
See Sueskind, Patrick
See also BPFB 3; CA 145; CWW 2
Sutcliff, Rosemary 1920-1992 .... **CLC 26**
See also AAYA 10; BYA 1, 4; CA 5-8R;
139; CANR 37; CLR 1, 37; CPW; DAB;
DAC; DAM MST, POP; JRDA; LATS
1:1; MAICYA 1, 2; MAICYAS 1; RHW;
SATA 6, 44, 78; SATA-Obit 73; WYA;
YAW
Sutro, Alfred 1863-1933 .... **TCLC 6**
See also CA 105; 185; DLB 10; RGEL 2
Sutton, Henry
See Slavitt, David R(ytman)
Suzuki, D. T.
See Suzuki, Daisetz Teitaro
Suzuki, Daisetz T.
See Suzuki, Daisetz Teitaro
Suzuki, Daisetz Teitaro
1870-1966 .... **TCLC 109**
See also CA 121; 111; MTCW 1, 2; MTFW
2005
Suzuki, Teitaro
See Suzuki, Daisetz Teitaro
Svevo, Italo .... **SSC 25; TCLC 2, 35**
See Schmitz, Aron Hector
See also DLB 264; EW 8; EWL 3; RGWL
2, 3; WLIT 7
Swados, Elizabeth (A.) 1951- .... **CLC 12**
See also CA 97-100; CANR 49; INT CA-
97-100

Swados, Harvey 1920-1972 .... **CLC 5**
See also CA 5-8R; 37-40R; CANR 6; CN
1; DLB 2; MAL 5
Swan, Gladys 1934- .... **CLC 69**
See also CA 101; CANR 17, 39; TCLE 1:2
Swanson, Logan
See Matheson, Richard (Burton)
Swarthout, Glendon (Fred)
1918 1992 .... **CLC 35**
See also AAYA 55; CA 1-4R; 139; CANR
1, 47; CN 1, 2, 3, 4, 5; LAIT 5; SATA 26;
TCWW 1, 2; YAW
Swedenborg, Emanuel 1688-1772 ..... **LC 105**
Sweet, Sarah C.
See Jewett, (Theodora) Sarah Orne
Swenson, May 1919-1989 ...... **CLC 4, 14, 61,
106; PC 14**
See also AMWS 4; CA 5-8R; 130; CANR
36, 61, 131; CP 1, 2, 3, 4; DA; DAB;
DAC; DAM MST, POET; DLB 5; EXPP;
GLL 2; MAL 5; MTCW 1, 2; MTFW
2005; PFS 16; SATA 15; WP
Swift, Augustus
See Lovecraft, H(oward) P(hillips)
Swift, Graham (Colin) 1949- ...... **CLC 41, 88**
See also BRWC 2; BRWS 5; CA 117; 122;
CANR 46, 71, 128; CN 4, 5, 6, 7; DLB
194; MTCW 2; MTFW 2005; NFS 18;
RGSF 2
Swift, Jonathan 1667-1745 ..... **LC 1, 42, 101;
PC 9; WLC**
See also AAYA 41; BRW 3; BRWC 1;
BRWR 1; BYA 5, 14; CDBLB 1660-1789;
CLR 53; DA; DA3; DAB; DAC; DAM
MST, NOV, POET; DLB 39, 95, 101;
EXPN; LAIT 1; NFS 6; RGEL 2; SATA
19; TEA; WCH; WLIT 3
Swinburne, Algernon Charles
1837-1909 ... **PC 24; TCLC 8, 36; WLC**
See also BRW 5; CA 105; 140; CDBLB
1832-1890; DA; DA3; DAB; DAC; DAM
MST, POET; DLB 35, 57; PAB; RGEL 2;
TEA
Swinfen, Ann .... **CLC 34**
See also CA 202
Swinnerton, Frank (Arthur)
1884-1982 .... **CLC 31**
See also CA 202; 108; CN 1, 2, 3; DLB 34
Swinnerton, Frank Arthur
1884-1982 .... **CLC 31**
See also CA 108; DLB 34
Swithen, John
See King, Stephen
Sylvia
See Ashton-Warner, Sylvia (Constance)
Symmes, Robert Edward
See Duncan, Robert (Edward)
Symonds, John Addington
1840-1893 .... **NCLC 34**
See also DLB 57, 144
Symons, Arthur 1865-1945 .... **TCLC 11**
See also CA 107; 189; DLB 19, 57, 149;
RGEL 2
Symons, Julian (Gustave)
1912-1994 .... **CLC 2, 14, 32**
See also CA 49-52; 147; CAAS 3; CANR
3, 33, 59; CMW 4; CN 1, 2, 3, 4, 5; CP 1,
3, 4; DLB 87, 155; DLBY 1992; MSW;
MTCW 1
Synge, (Edmund) J(ohn) M(illington)
1871-1909 .... **DC 2; TCLC 6, 37**
See also BRW 6; BRWR 1; CA 104; 141;
CDBLB 1890-1914; DAM DRAM; DFS
18; DLB 10, 19; EWL 3; RGEL 2; TEA;
WLIT 4
Syruc, J.
See Milosz, Czeslaw

Szirtes, George 1948- .... **CLC 46; PC 51**
See also CA 109; CANR 27, 61, 117; CP 4, 5, 6, 7

Szymborska, Wislawa 1923- ... **CLC 99, 190; PC 44**
See also CA 154; CANR 91, 133; CDWLB 4; CWP; CWW 2; DA3; DLB 232; DLBY 1996; EWL 3; MTCW 2; MTFW 2005; PFS 15; RGWL 3

T. O., Nik
See Annensky, Innokenty (Fyodorovich)

Tabori, George 1914- .... **CLC 19**
See also CA 49-52; CANR 4, 69; CBD; CD 5, 6; DLB 245

Tacitus c. 55-c. 117 .... **CMLC 56**
See also AW 2; CDWLB 1; DLB 211; RGWL 2, 3

Tagore, Rabindranath 1861-1941 .... **PC 8; SSC 48; TCLC 3, 53**
See also CA 104; 120; DA3; DAM DRAM, POET; EWL 3; MTCW 1, 2; MTFW 2005; PFS 18; RGEL 2; RGSF 2; RGWL 2, 3; TWA

Taine, Hippolyte Adolphe
1828-1893 .... **NCLC 15**
See also EW 7; GFL 1789 to the Present

Talayesva, Don C. 1890-(?) .... **NNAL**

Talese, Gay 1932- .... **CLC 37**
See also AITN 1; CA 1-4R; CANR 9, 58, 137; DLB 185; INT CANR-9; MTCW 1, 2; MTFW 2005

Tallent, Elizabeth (Ann) 1954- .... **CLC 45**
See also CA 117; CANR 72; DLB 130

Tallmountain, Mary 1918-1997 .... **NNAL**
See also CA 146; 161; DLB 193

Tally, Ted 1952- .... **CLC 42**
See also CA 120; 124; CAD; CANR 125; CD 5, 6; INT CA-124

Talvik, Heiti 1904-1947 .... **TCLC 87**
See also EWL 3

Tamayo y Baus, Manuel
1829-1898 .... **NCLC 1**

Tammsaare, A(nton) H(ansen)
1878-1940 .... **TCLC 27**
See also CA 164; CDWLB 4; DLB 220; EWL 3

Tam'si, Tchicaya U
See Tchicaya, Gerald Felix

Tan, Amy (Ruth) 1952- . **AAL; CLC 59, 120, 151**
See also AAYA 9, 48; AMWS 10; BEST 89:3; BPFB 3; CA 136; CANR 54, 105, 132; CDALBS; CN 6, 7; CPW 1; DA3; DAM MULT, NOV, POP; DLB 173, 312; EXPN; FL 1:6; FW; LAIT 3, 5; MAL 5; MTCW 2; MTFW 2005; NFS 1, 13, 16; RGAL 4; SATA 75; SSFS 9; YAW

Tandem, Felix
See Spitteler, Carl (Friedrich Georg)

Tanizaki, Jun'ichiro 1886-1965 ... **CLC 8, 14, 28; SSC 21**
See Tanizaki Jun'ichiro
See also CA 93-96; 25-28R; MJW; MTCW 2; MTFW 2005; RGSF 2; RGWL 2

Tanizaki Jun'ichiro
See Tanizaki, Jun'ichiro
See also DLB 180; EWL 3

Tannen, Deborah F(rances) 1945- .. **CLC 206**
See also CA 118; CANR 95

Tanner, William
See Amis, Kingsley (William)

Tao Lao
See Storni, Alfonsina

Tapahonso, Luci 1953- .... **NNAL; PC 65**
See also CA 145; CANR 72, 127; DLB 175

Tarantino, Quentin (Jerome)
1963- .... **CLC 125**
See also AAYA 58; CA 171; CANR 125

Tarassoff, Lev
See Troyat, Henri

Tarbell, Ida M(inerva) 1857-1944 . **TCLC 40**
See also CA 122; 181; DLB 47

Tarkington, (Newton) Booth
1869-1946 .... **TCLC 9**
See also BPFB 3; BYA 3; CA 110; 143; CWRI 5; DLB 9, 102; MAL 5; MTCW 2; RGAL 4; SATA 17

Tarkovskii, Andrei Arsen'evich
See Tarkovsky, Andrei (Arsenyevich)

Tarkovsky, Andrei (Arsenyevich)
1932-1986 .... **CLC 75**
See also CA 127

Tartt, Donna 1964(?)- .... **CLC 76**
See also AAYA 56; CA 142; CANR 135; MTFW 2005

Tasso, Torquato 1544-1595 .... **LC 5, 94**
See also EFS 2; EW 2; RGWL 2, 3; WLIT 7

Tate, (John Orley) Allen 1899-1979 .. **CLC 2, 4, 6, 9, 11, 14, 24; PC 50**
See also AMW; CA 5-8R; 85-88; CANR 32, 108; CN 1, 2; CP 1, 2; DLB 4, 45, 63; DLBD 17; EWL 3; MAL 5; MTCW 1, 2; MTFW 2005; RGAL 4; RHW

Tate, Ellalice
See Hibbert, Eleanor Alice Burford

Tate, James (Vincent) 1943- ..... **CLC 2, 6, 25**
See also CA 21-24R; CANR 29, 57, 114; CP 1, 2, 3, 4, 5, 6, 7; DLB 5, 169; EWL 3; PFS 10, 15; RGAL 4; WP

Tate, Nahum 1652(?)-1715 .... **LC 109**
See also DLB 80; RGEL 2

Tauler, Johannes c. 1300-1361 ...... **CMLC 37**
See also DLB 179; LMFS 1

Tavel, Ronald 1940- .... **CLC 6**
See also CA 21-24R; CAD; CANR 33; CD 5, 6

Taviani, Paolo 1931- .... **CLC 70**
See also CA 153

Taylor, Bayard 1825-1878 .... **NCLC 89**
See also DLB 3, 189, 250, 254; RGAL 4

Taylor, C(ecil) P(hilip) 1929-1981 .... **CLC 27**
See also CA 25-28R; 105; CANR 47; CBD

Taylor, Edward 1642(?)-1729 . **LC 11; PC 63**
See also AMW; DA; DAB; DAC; DAM MST, POET; DLB 24; EXPP; RGAL 4; TUS

Taylor, Eleanor Ross 1920- .... **CLC 5**
See also CA 81-84; CANR 70

Taylor, Elizabeth 1912-1975 ..... **CLC 2, 4, 29**
See also CA 13-16R; CANR 9, 70; CN 1, 2; DLB 139; MTCW 1; RGEL 2; SATA 13

Taylor, Frederick Winslow
1856-1915 .... **TCLC 76**
See also CA 188

Taylor, Henry (Splawn) 1942- .... **CLC 44**
See also CA 33-36R; CAAS 7; CANR 31; CP 7; DLB 5; PFS 10

Taylor, Kamala (Purnaiya) 1924-2004
See Markandaya, Kamala
See also CA 77-80; 227; MTFW 2005; NFS 13

Taylor, Mildred D(elois) 1943- .... **CLC 21**
See also AAYA 10, 47; BW 1; BYA 3, 8; CA 85-88; CANR 25, 115, 136; CLR 9, 59, 90; CSW; DLB 52; JRDA; LAIT 3; MAICYA 1, 2; MTFW 2005; SAAS 5; SATA 135; WYA; YAW

Taylor, Peter (Hillsman) 1917-1994 .. **CLC 1, 4, 18, 37, 44, 50, 71; SSC 10, 84**
See also AMWS 5; BPFB 3; CA 13-16R; 147; CANR 9, 50; CN 1, 2, 3, 4, 5; CSW; DLB 218, 278; DLBY 1981, 1994; EWL 3; EXPS; INT CANR-9; MAL 5; MTCW 1, 2; MTFW 2005; RGSF 2; SSFS 9; TUS

Taylor, Robert Lewis 1912-1998 .... **CLC 14**
See also CA 1-4R; 170; CANR 3, 64; CN 1, 2; SATA 10; TCWW 1, 2

Tchekhov, Anton
See Chekhov, Anton (Pavlovich)

Tchicaya, Gerald Felix 1931-1988 .. **CLC 101**
See Tchicaya U Tam'si
See also CA 129; 125; CANR 81

Tchicaya U Tam'si
See Tchicaya, Gerald Felix
See also EWL 3

Teasdale, Sara 1884-1933 .... **PC 31; TCLC 4**
See also CA 104; 163; DLB 45; GLL 1; PFS 14; RGAL 4; SATA 32; TUS

Tecumseh 1768-1813 .... **NNAL**
See also DAM MULT

Tegner, Esaias 1782-1846 .... **NCLC 2**

Teilhard de Chardin, (Marie Joseph) Pierre
1881-1955 .... **TCLC 9**
See also CA 105; 210; GFL 1789 to the Present

Temple, Ann
See Mortimer, Penelope (Ruth)

Tennant, Emma (Christina) 1937- .. **CLC 13, 52**
See also BRWS 9; CA 65-68; CAAS 9; CANR 10, 38, 59, 88; CN 3, 4, 5, 6, 7; DLB 14; EWL 3; SFW 4

Tenneshaw, S. M.
See Silverberg, Robert

Tenney, Tabitha Gilman
1762-1837 .... **NCLC 122**
See also DLB 37, 200

Tennyson, Alfred 1809-1892 ... **NCLC 30, 65, 115; PC 6; WLC**
See also AAYA 50; BRW 4; CDBLB 1832-1890; DA; DA3; DAB; DAC; DAM MST, POET; DLB 32; EXPP; PAB; PFS 1, 2, 4, 11, 15, 19; RGEL 2; TEA; WLIT 4; WP

Teran, Lisa St. Aubin de .... **CLC 36**
See St. Aubin de Teran, Lisa

Terence c. 184B.C.-c. 159B.C. ...... **CMLC 14; DC 7**
See also AW 1; CDWLB 1; DLB 211; RGWL 2, 3; TWA

Teresa de Jesus, St. 1515-1582 .... **LC 18**

Teresa of Avila, St.
See Teresa de Jesus, St.

Terkel, Louis 1912-
See Terkel, Studs
See also CA 57-60; CANR 18, 45, 67, 132; DA3; MTCW 1, 2; MTFW 2005

Terkel, Studs .... **CLC 38**
See Terkel, Louis
See also AAYA 32; AITN 1; MTCW 2; TUS

Terry, C. V.
See Slaughter, Frank G(ill)

Terry, Megan 1932- .... **CLC 19; DC 13**
See also CA 77-80; CABS 3; CAD; CANR 43; CD 5, 6; CWD; DFS 18; DLB 7, 249; GLL 2

Tertullian c. 155-c. 245 .... **CMLC 29**

Tertz, Abram
See Sinyavsky, Andrei (Donatevich)
See also RGSF 2

Tesich, Steve 1943(?)-1996 .... **CLC 40, 69**
See also CA 105; 152; CAD; DLBY 1983

Tesla, Nikola 1856-1943 .... **TCLC 88**

Teternikov, Fyodor Kuzmich 1863-1927
See Sologub, Fyodor
See also CA 104

Tevis, Walter 1928-1984 .... **CLC 42**
See also CA 113; SFW 4

Tey, Josephine .... **TCLC 14**
See Mackintosh, Elizabeth
See also DLB 77; MSW

Thackeray, William Makepeace
 1811-1863 .... **NCLC 5, 14, 22, 43; WLC**
 See also BRW 5; BRWC 2; CDBLB 1832-
 1890; DA; DA3; DAB; DAC; DAM MST,
 NOV; DLB 21, 55, 159, 163; NFS 13;
 RGEL 2; SATA 23; TEA; WLIT 3
Thakura, Ravindranatha
 See Tagore, Rabindranath
Thames, C. H.
 See Marlowe, Stephen
Tharoor, Shashi 1956- .... **CLC 70**
 See also CA 141; CANR 91; CN 6, 7
Thelwall, John 1764-1834 .... **NCLC 162**
 See also DLB 93, 158
Thelwell, Michael Miles 1939- .... **CLC 22**
 See also BW 2; CA 101
Theobald, Lewis, Jr.
 See Lovecraft, H(oward) P(hillips)
Theocritus c. 310B.C.- .... **CMLC 45**
 See also AW 1; DLB 176; RGWL 2, 3
Theodorescu, Ion N. 1880-1967
 See Arghezi, Tudor
 See also CA 116
Theriault, Yves 1915-1983 .... **CLC 79**
 See also CA 102; CCA 1; DAC; DAM
 MST; DLB 88; EWL 3
Theroux, Alexander (Louis) 1939- .... **CLC 2,
 25**
 See also CA 85-88; CANR 20, 63; CN 4, 5,
 6, 7
Theroux, Paul (Edward) 1941- ..... **CLC 5, 8,
 11, 15, 28, 46**
 See also AAYA 28; AMWS 8; BEST 89:4;
 BPFB 3; CA 33-36R; CANR 20, 45, 74,
 133; CDALBS; CN 1, 2, 3, 4, 5, 6, 7; CP
 1; CPW 1; DA3; DAM POP; DLB 2, 218;
 EWL 3; HGG; MAL 5; MTCW 1, 2;
 MTFW 2005; RGAL 4; SATA 44, 109;
 TUS
Thesen, Sharon 1946- .... **CLC 56**
 See also CA 163; CANR 125; CP 7; CWP
Thespis fl. 6th cent. B.C.- .... **CMLC 51**
 See also LMFS 1
Thevenin, Denis
 See Duhamel, Georges
Thibault, Jacques Anatole Francois
 1844-1924
 See France, Anatole
 See also CA 106; 127; DA3; DAM NOV;
 MTCW 1, 2; TWA
Thiele, Colin (Milton) 1920- .... **CLC 17**
 See also CA 29-32R; CANR 12, 28, 53,
 105; CLR 27; CP 1, 2; DLB 289; MAI-
 CYA 1, 2; SAAS 2; SATA 14, 72, 125;
 YAW
Thistlethwaite, Bel
 See Wetherald, Agnes Ethelwyn
Thomas, Audrey (Callahan) 1935- .... **CLC 7,
 13, 37, 107; SSC 20**
 See also AITN 2; CA 21-24R; 237; CAAE
 237; CAAS 19; CANR 36, 58; CN 2, 3,
 4, 5, 6, 7; DLB 60; MTCW 1; RGSF 2
Thomas, Augustus 1857-1934 .... **TCLC 97**
 See also MAL 5
Thomas, D(onald) M(ichael) 1935- . **CLC 13,
 22, 31, 132**
 See also BPFB 3; BRWS 4; CA 61-64;
 CAAS 11; CANR 17, 45, 75; CDBLB
 1960 to Present; CN 4, 5, 6, 7; CP 1, 2, 3,
 4, 5, 6, 7; DA3; DLB 40, 207, 299; HGG;
 INT CANR-17; MTCW 1, 2; MTFW
 2005; SFW 4
Thomas, Dylan (Marlais) 1914-1953 .... **PC 2,
 52; SSC 3, 44; TCLC 1, 8, 45, 105;
 WLC**
 See also AAYA 45; BRWS 1; CA 104; 120;
 CANR 65; CDBLB 1945-1960; DA; DA3;
 DAB; DAC; DAM DRAM, MST, POET;

DLB 13, 20, 139; EWL 3; EXPP; LAIT
 3; MTCW 1, 2; MTFW 2005; PAB; PFS
 1, 3, 8; RGEL 2; RGSF 2; SATA 60; TEA;
 WLIT 4; WP
Thomas, (Philip) Edward 1878-1917 . **PC 53;
 TCLC 10**
 See also BRW 6; BRWS 3; CA 106; 153;
 DAM POET; DLB 19, 98, 156, 216; EWL
 3; PAB; RGEL 2
Thomas, Joyce Carol 1938- .... **CLC 35**
 See also AAYA 12, 54; BW 2, 3; CA 113;
 116; CANR 48, 114, 135; CLR 19; DLB
 33; INT CA-116; JRDA; MAICYA 1, 2;
 MTCW 1, 2; MTFW 2005; SAAS 7;
 SATA 40, 78, 123, 137; SATA-Essay 137;
 WYA; YAW
Thomas, Lewis 1913-1993 .... **CLC 35**
 See also ANW; CA 85-88; 143; CANR 38,
 60; DLB 275; MTCW 1, 2
Thomas, M. Carey 1857-1935 .... **TCLC 89**
 See also FW
Thomas, Paul
 See Mann, (Paul) Thomas
Thomas, Piri 1928- .... **CLC 17; HLCS 2**
 See also CA 73-76; HW 1; LLW
Thomas, R(onald) S(tuart)
 1913-2000 .... **CLC 6, 13, 48**
 See also CA 89-92; 189; CAAS 4; CANR
 30; CDBLB 1960 to Present; CP 1, 2, 3,
 4, 5, 6, 7; DAB; DAM POET; DLB 27;
 EWL 3; MTCW 1; RGEL 2
Thomas, Ross (Elmore) 1926-1995 .. **CLC 39**
 See also CA 33-36R; 150; CANR 22, 63;
 CMW 4
Thompson, Francis (Joseph)
 1859-1907 .... **TCLC 4**
 See also BRW 5; CA 104; 189; CDBLB
 1890-1914; DLB 19; RGEL 2; TEA
Thompson, Francis Clegg
 See Mencken, H(enry) L(ouis)
Thompson, Hunter S(tockton)
 1937(?)-2005 .... **CLC 9, 17, 40, 104**
 See also AAYA 45; BEST 89:1; BPFB 3;
 CA 17-20R; 236; CANR 23, 46, 74, 77,
 111, 133; CPW; CSW; DA3; DAM POP;
 DLB 185; MTCW 1, 2; MTFW 2005;
 TUS
Thompson, James Myers
 See Thompson, Jim (Myers)
Thompson, Jim (Myers)
 1906-1977(?) .... **CLC 69**
 See also BPFB 3; CA 140; CMW 4; CPW;
 DLB 226; MSW
Thompson, Judith (Clare Francesca)
 1954- .... **CLC 39**
 See also CA 143; CD 5, 6; CWD; DFS 22
Thomson, James 1700-1748 .... **LC 16, 29, 40**
 See also BRWS 3; DAM POET; DLB 95;
 RGEL 2
Thomson, James 1834-1882 .... **NCLC 18**
 See also DAM POET; DLB 35; RGEL 2
Thoreau, Henry David 1817-1862 .. **NCLC 7,
 21, 61, 138; PC 30; WLC**
 See also AAYA 42; AMW; ANW; BYA 3;
 CDALB 1640-1865; DA; DA3; DAB;
 DAC; DAM MST; DLB 1, 183, 223, 270,
 298; LAIT 2; LMFS 1; NCFS 3; RGAL
 4; TUS
Thorndike, E. L.
 See Thorndike, Edward L(ee)
Thorndike, Edward L(ee)
 1874-1949 .... **TCLC 107**
 See also CA 121
Thornton, Hall
 See Silverberg, Robert
Thorpe, Adam 1956- .... **CLC 176**
 See also CA 129; CANR 92; DLB 231

Thubron, Colin (Gerald Dryden)
 1939- .... **CLC 163**
 See also CA 25-28R; CANR 12, 29, 59, 95;
 CN 5, 6, 7; DLB 204, 231
Thucydides c. 455B.C.-c. 395B.C. . **CMLC 17**
 See also AW 1; DLB 176; RGWL 2, 3
Thumboo, Edwin Nadason 1933- .... **PC 30**
 See also CA 194; CP 1
Thurber, James (Grover)
 1894-1961 .. **CLC 5, 11, 25, 125; SSC 1,
 47**
 See also AAYA 56; AMWS 1; BPFB 3;
 BYA 5; CA 73-76; CANR 17, 39; CDALB
 1929-1941; CWRI 5; DA; DA3; DAB;
 DAC; DAM DRAM, MST, NOV; DLB 4,
 11, 22, 102; EWL 3; EXPS; FANT; LAIT
 3; MAICYA 1, 2; MAL 5; MTCW 1, 2;
 MTFW 2005; RGAL 4; RGSF 2; SATA
 13; SSFS 1, 10, 19; SUFW; TUS
Thurman, Wallace (Henry)
 1902-1934 ..... **BLC 3; HR 1:3; TCLC 6**
 See also BW 1, 3; CA 104; 124; CANR 81;
 DAM MULT; DLB 51
Tibullus c. 54B.C.-c. 18B.C. .... **CMLC 36**
 See also AW 2; DLB 211; RGWL 2, 3
Ticheburn, Cheviot
 See Ainsworth, William Harrison
Tieck, (Johann) Ludwig
 1773-1853 .... **NCLC 5, 46; SSC 31**
 See also CDWLB 2; DLB 90; EW 5; IDTP;
 RGSF 2; RGWL 2, 3; SUFW
Tiger, Derry
 See Ellison, Harlan (Jay)
Tilghman, Christopher 1946- .... **CLC 65**
 See also CA 159; CANR 135; CSW; DLB
 244
Tillich, Paul (Johannes)
 1886-1965 .... **CLC 131**
 See also CA 5-8R; 25-28R; CANR 33;
 MTCW 1, 2
Tillinghast, Richard (Williford)
 1940- .... **CLC 29**
 See also CA 29-32R; CAAS 23; CANR 26,
 51, 96; CP 2, 3, 4, 5, 6, 7; CSW
Timrod, Henry 1828-1867 .... **NCLC 25**
 See also DLB 3, 248; RGAL 4
Tindall, Gillian (Elizabeth) 1938- ...... **CLC 7**
 See also CA 21-24R; CANR 11, 65, 107;
 CN 1, 2, 3, 4, 5, 6, 7
Tiptree, James, Jr. .... **CLC 48, 50**
 See Sheldon, Alice Hastings Bradley
 See also DLB 8; SCFW 1, 2; SFW 4
Tirone Smith, Mary-Ann 1944- .... **CLC 39**
 See also CA 118; 136; CANR 113; SATA
 143
Tirso de Molina 1580(?)-1648 .... **DC 13;
 HLCS 2; LC 73**
 See also RGWL 2, 3
Titmarsh, Michael Angelo
 See Thackeray, William Makepeace
**Tocqueville, Alexis (Charles Henri Maurice
 Clerel Comte) de** 1805-1859 .. **NCLC 7,
 63**
 See also EW 6; GFL 1789 to the Present;
 TWA
Toer, Pramoedya Ananta 1925- ...... **CLC 186**
 See also CA 197; RGWL 3
Toffler, Alvin 1928- .... **CLC 168**
 See also CA 13-16R; CANR 15, 46, 67;
 CPW; DAM POP; MTCW 1, 2
Toibin, Colm 1955- .... **CLC 162**
 See also CA 142; CANR 81; CN 7; DLB
 271
Tolkien, J(ohn) R(onald) R(euel)
 1892-1973 .... **CLC 1, 2, 3, 8, 12, 38;
 TCLC 137; WLC**
 See also AAYA 10; AITN 1; BPFB 3;
 BRWC 2; BRWS 2; CA 17-18; 45-48;
 CANR 36, 134; CAP 2; CDBLB 1914-

1945; CLR 56; CN 1; CPW 1; CWRI 5; DA; DA3; DAB; DAC; DAM MST, NOV, POP; DLB 15, 160, 255; EFS 2; EWL 3; FANT; JRDA; LAIT 1; LAIT 1; LMFS 2; MAICYA 1, 2; MTCW 1, 2; MTFW 2005; NFS 8; RGEL 2; SATA 2, 32, 100; SATA-Obit 24; SFW 4; SUFW; TEA; WCH; WYA; YAW

Toller, Ernst 1893-1939 .... **TCLC 10**
See also CA 107; 186; DLB 124; EWL 3; RGWL 2, 3

Tolson, M. B.
See Tolson, Melvin B(eaunorus)

Tolson, Melvin B(eaunorus)
1898(?)-1966 .... **BLC 3; CLC 36, 105**
See also AFAW 1, 2; BW 1, 3; CA 124; 89-92; CANR 80; DAM MULT, POET; DLB 48, 76; MAL 5; RGAL 4

Tolstoi, Aleksei Nikolaevich
See Tolstoy, Alexey Nikolaevich

Tolstoi, Lev
See Tolstoy, Leo (Nikolaevich)
See also RGSF 2; RGWL 2, 3

Tolstoy, Aleksei Nikolaevich
See Tolstoy, Alexey Nikolaevich
See also DLB 272

Tolstoy, Alexey Nikolaevich
1882-1945 .... **TCLC 18**
See Tolstoy, Aleksei Nikolaevich
See also CA 107; 158; EWL 3; SFW 4

Tolstoy, Leo (Nikolaevich)
1828-1910 . **SSC 9, 30, 45, 54; TCLC 4, 11, 17, 28, 44, 79, 173; WLC**
See Tolstoi, Lev
See also AAYA 56; CA 104; 123; DA; DA3; DAB; DAC; DAM MST, NOV; DLB 238; EFS 2; EW 7; EXPS; IDTP; LAIT 2; LATS 1:1; LMFS 1; NFS 10; SATA 26; SSFS 5; TWA

Tolstoy, Count Leo
See Tolstoy, Leo (Nikolaevich)

Tomalin, Claire 1933- .... **CLC 166**
See also CA 89-92; CANR 52, 88; DLB 155

Tomasi di Lampedusa, Giuseppe 1896-1957
See Lampedusa, Giuseppe (Tomasi) di
See also CA 111; DLB 177; EWL 3; WLIT 7

Tomlin, Lily .... **CLC 17**
See Tomlin, Mary Jean

Tomlin, Mary Jean 1939(?)-
See Tomlin, Lily
See also CA 117

Tomline, F. Latour
See Gilbert, W(illiam) S(chwenck)

Tomlinson, (Alfred) Charles 1927- .... **CLC 2, 4, 6, 13, 45; PC 17**
See also CA 5-8R; CANR 33; CP 1, 2, 3, 4, 5, 6, 7; DAM POET; DLB 40; TCLE 1:2

Tomlinson, H(enry) M(ajor)
1873-1958 .... **TCLC 71**
See also CA 118; 161; DLB 36, 100, 195

Tonna, Charlotte Elizabeth
1790-1846 .... **NCLC 135**
See also DLB 163

Tonson, Jacob fl. 1655(?)-1736 .... **LC 86**
See also DLB 170

Toole, John Kennedy 1937-1969 ..... **CLC 19, 64**
See also BPFB 3; CA 104; DLBY 1981; MTCW 2; MTFW 2005

Toomer, Eugene
See Toomer, Jean

Toomer, Eugene Pinchback
See Toomer, Jean

Toomer, Jean 1894-1967 .. **BLC 3; CLC 1, 4, 13, 22; HR 1:3; PC 7; SSC 1, 45; TCLC 172; WLCS**
See also AFAW 1, 2; AMWS 3, 9; BW 1; CA 85-88; CDALB 1917-1929; DA3; DAM MULT; DLB 45, 51; EWL 3; EXPP; EXPS; LMFS 2; MAL 5; MTCW 1, 2; MTFW 2005; NFS 11; RGAL 4; RGSF 2; SSFS 5

Toomer, Nathan Jean
See Toomer, Jean

Toomer, Nathan Pinchback
See Toomer, Jean

Torley, Luke
See Blish, James (Benjamin)

Tornimparte, Alessandra
See Ginzburg, Natalia

Torre, Raoul della
See Mencken, H(enry) L(ouis)

Torrence, Ridgely 1874-1950 .... **TCLC 97**
See also DLB 54, 249; MAL 5

Torrey, E(dwin) Fuller 1937- .... **CLC 34**
See also CA 119; CANR 71

Torsvan, Ben Traven
See Traven, B.

Torsvan, Benno Traven
See Traven, B.

Torsvan, Berick Traven
See Traven, B.

Torsvan, Berwick Traven
See Traven, B.

Torsvan, Bruno Traven
See Traven, B.

Torsvan, Traven
See Traven, B.

Tourneur, Cyril 1575(?)-1626 .... **LC 66**
See also BRW 2; DAM DRAM; DLB 58; RGEL 2

Tournier, Michel (Edouard) 1924- .... **CLC 6, 23, 36, 95; SSC 88**
See also CA 49-52; CANR 3, 36, 74; CWW 2; DLB 83; EWL 3; GFL 1789 to the Present; MTCW 1, 2; SATA 23

Tournimparte, Alessandra
See Ginzburg, Natalia

Towers, Ivar
See Kornbluth, C(yril) M.

Towne, Robert (Burton) 1936(?)- ..... **CLC 87**
See also CA 108; DLB 44; IDFW 3, 4

Townsend, Sue .... **CLC 61**
See Townsend, Susan Lilian
See also AAYA 28; CA 119; 127; CANR 65, 107; CBD; CD 5, 6; CPW; CWD; DAB; DAC; DAM MST; DLB 271; INT CA-127; SATA 55, 93; SATA-Brief 48; YAW

Townsend, Susan Lilian 1946-
See Townsend, Sue

Townshend, Pete
See Townshend, Peter (Dennis Blandford)

Townshend, Peter (Dennis Blandford)
1945- .... **CLC 17, 42**
See also CA 107

Tozzi, Federigo 1883-1920 .... **TCLC 31**
See also CA 160; CANR 110; DLB 264; EWL 3; WLIT 7

Tracy, Don(ald Fiske) 1905-1970(?)
See Queen, Ellery
See also CA 1-4R; 176; CANR 2

Trafford, F. G.
See Riddell, Charlotte

Traherne, Thomas 1637(?)-1674 .. **LC 99; PC 70**
See also BRW 2; BRWS 11; DLB 131; PAB; RGEL 2

Traill, Catharine Parr 1802-1899 .. **NCLC 31**
See also DLB 99

Trakl, Georg 1887-1914 .... **PC 20; TCLC 5**
See also CA 104; 165; EW 10; EWL 3; LMFS 2; MTCW 2; RGWL 2, 3

Trambley, Estela Portillo .... **TCLC 163**
See Portillo Trambley, Estela
See also CA 77-80; RGAL 4

Tranquilli, Secondino
See Silone, Ignazio

Transtroemer, Tomas Gosta
See Transtromer, Tomas (Goesta)

Transtromer, Tomas (Gosta)
See Transtromer, Tomas (Goesta)
See also CWW 2

Transtromer, Tomas (Goesta)
1931- .... **CLC 52, 65**
See Transtromer, Tomas (Gosta)
See also CA 117; 129; CAAS 17; CANR 115; DAM POET; DLB 257; EWL 3; PFS 21

Transtromer, Tomas Gosta
See Transtromer, Tomas (Goesta)

Traven, B. 1882(?)-1969 .... **CLC 8, 11**
See also CA 19-20; 25-28R; CAP 2; DLB 9, 56; EWL 3; MTCW 1; RGAL 4

Trediakovsky, Vasilii Kirillovich
1703-1769 .... **LC 68**
See also DLB 150

Treitel, Jonathan 1959- .... **CLC 70**
See also CA 210; DLB 267

Trelawny, Edward John
1792-1881 .... **NCLC 85**
See also DLB 110, 116, 144

Tremain, Rose 1943- .... **CLC 42**
See also CA 97-100; CANR 44, 95; CN 4, 5, 6, 7; DLB 14, 271; RGSF 2; RHW

Tremblay, Michel 1942- .... **CLC 29, 102**
See also CA 116; 128; CCA 1; CWW 2; DAC; DAM MST; DLB 60; EWL 3; GLL 1; MTCW 1, 2; MTFW 2005

Trevanian .... **CLC 29**
See Whitaker, Rod(ney)

Trevor, Glen
See Hilton, James

Trevor, William .. **CLC 7, 9, 14, 25, 71, 116; SSC 21, 58**
See Cox, William Trevor
See also BRWS 4; CBD; CD 5, 6; CN 1, 2, 3, 4, 5, 6, 7; DLB 14, 139; EWL 3; LATS 1:2; RGEL 2; RGSF 2; SSFS 10; TCLE 1:2

Trifonov, Iurii (Valentinovich)
See Trifonov, Yuri (Valentinovich)
See also DLB 302; RGWL 2, 3

Trifonov, Yuri (Valentinovich)
1925-1981 .... **CLC 45**
See Trifonov, Iurii (Valentinovich); Trifonov, Yury Valentinovich
See also CA 126; 103; MTCW 1

Trifonov, Yury Valentinovich
See Trifonov, Yuri (Valentinovich)
See also EWL 3

Trilling, Diana (Rubin) 1905-1996 . **CLC 129**
See also CA 5-8R; 154; CANR 10, 46; INT CANR-10; MTCW 1, 2

Trilling, Lionel 1905-1975 ..... **CLC 9, 11, 24; SSC 75**
See also AMWS 3; CA 9-12R; 61-64; CANR 10, 105; CN 1, 2; DLB 28, 63; EWL 3; INT CANR-10; MAL 5; MTCW 1, 2; RGAL 4; TUS

Trimball, W. H.
See Mencken, H(enry) L(ouis)

Tristan
See Gomez de la Serna, Ramon

Tristram
See Housman, A(lfred) E(dward)

Usk, Thomas (?)-1388 .... **CMLC 76**
See also DLB 146
Ustinov, Peter (Alexander)
1921-2004 .... **CLC 1**
See also AITN 1; CA 13-16R; 225; CANR
25, 51; CBD; CD 5, 6; DLB 13; MTCW
2
U Tam'si, Gerald Felix Tchicaya
See Tchicaya, Gerald Felix
U Tam'si, Tchicaya
See Tchicaya, Gerald Felix
Vachss, Andrew (Henry) 1942- .... **CLC 106**
See also CA 118, 214; CAAE 214; CANR
44, 95; CMW 4
Vachss, Andrew H.
See Vachss, Andrew (Henry)
Vaculik, Ludvik 1926- .... **CLC 7**
See also CA 53-56; CANR 72; CWW 2;
DLB 232; EWL 3
Vaihinger, Hans 1852-1933 .... **TCLC 71**
See also CA 116; 166
Valdez, Luis (Miguel) 1940- ..... **CLC 84; DC
10; HLC 2**
See also CA 101; CAD; CANR 32, 81; CD
5, 6; DAM MULT; DFS 5; DLB 122;
EWL 3; HW 1; LAIT 4; LLW
Valenzuela, Luisa 1938- .... **CLC 31, 104;
HLCS 2; SSC 14, 82**
See also CA 101; CANR 32, 65, 123; CD-
WLB 3; CWW 2; DAM MULT; DLB 113;
EWL 3; FW; HW 1, 2; LAW; RGSF 2;
RGWL 3
Valera y Alcala-Galiano, Juan
1824-1905 .... **TCLC 10**
See also CA 106
Valerius Maximus fl. 20- .... **CMLC 64**
See also DLB 211
Valery, (Ambroise) Paul (Toussaint Jules)
1871-1945 .... **PC 9; TCLC 4, 15**
See also CA 104; 122; DA3; DAM POET;
DLB 258; EW 8; EWL 3; GFL 1789 to
the Present; MTCW 1, 2; MTFW 2005;
RGWL 2, 3; TWA
Valle-Inclan, Ramon (Maria) del
1866-1936 .... **HLC 2; TCLC 5**
See del Valle-Inclan, Ramon (Maria)
See also CA 106; 153; CANR 80; DAM
MULT; DLB 134; EW 8; EWL 3; HW 2;
RGSF 2; RGWL 2, 3
Vallejo, Antonio Buero
See Buero Vallejo, Antonio
Vallejo, Cesar (Abraham)
1892-1938 .... **HLC 2; TCLC 3, 56**
See also CA 105; 153; DAM MULT; DLB
290; EWL 3; HW 1; LAW; RGWL 2, 3
Valles, Jules 1832-1885 .... **NCLC 71**
See also DLB 123; GFL 1789 to the Present
Vallette, Marguerite Eymery
1860-1953 .... **TCLC 67**
See Rachilde
See also CA 182; DLB 123, 192
Valle Y Pena, Ramon del
See Valle-Inclan, Ramon (Maria) del
Van Ash, Cay 1918-1994 .... **CLC 34**
See also CA 220
Vanbrugh, Sir John 1664-1726 .... **LC 21**
See also BRW 2; DAM DRAM; DLB 80;
IDTP; RGEL 2
Van Campen, Karl
See Campbell, John W(ood, Jr.)
Vance, Gerald
See Silverberg, Robert
Vance, Jack .... **CLC 35**
See Vance, John Holbrook
See also DLB 8; FANT; SCFW 1, 2; SFW
4; SUFW 1, 2

Vance, John Holbrook 1916-
See Queen, Ellery; Vance, Jack
See also CA 29-32R; CANR 17, 65; CMW
4; MTCW 1
**Van Den Bogarde, Derek Jules Gaspard
Ulric Niven** 1921-1999 .... **CLC 14**
See Bogarde, Dirk
See also CA 77-80; 179
Vandenburgh, Jane .... **CLC 59**
See also CA 168
Vanderhaeghe, Guy 1951- .... **CLC 41**
See also BPFB 3; CA 113; CANR 72, 145;
CN 7
van der Post, Laurens (Jan)
1906-1996 .... **CLC 5**
See also AFW; CA 5-8R; 155; CANR 35;
CN 1, 2, 3, 4, 5, 6; DLB 204; RGEL 2
van de Wetering, Janwillem 1931- ... **CLC 47**
See also CA 49-52; CANR 4, 62, 90; CMW
4
Van Dine, S. S. .... **TCLC 23**
See Wright, Willard Huntington
See also DLB 306; MSW
Van Doren, Carl (Clinton)
1885-1950 .... **TCLC 18**
See also CA 111; 168
Van Doren, Mark 1894-1972 .... **CLC 6, 10**
See also CA 1-4R; 37-40R; CANR 3; CN
1; CP 1; DLB 45, 284; MAL 5; MTCW
1, 2; RGAL 4
Van Druten, John (William)
1901-1957 .... **TCLC 2**
See also CA 104; 161; DLB 10; MAL 5;
RGAL 4
Van Duyn, Mona (Jane) 1921-2004 .. **CLC 3,
7, 63, 116**
See also CA 9-12R; 234; CANR 7, 38, 60,
116; CP 1, 2, 3, 4, 5, 6, 7; CWP; DAM
POET; DLB 5; MAL 5; MTFW 2005;
PFS 20
Van Dyne, Edith
See Baum, L(yman) Frank
van Itallie, Jean-Claude 1936- .... **CLC 3**
See also CA 45-48; CAAS 2; CAD; CANR
1, 48; CD 5, 6; DLB 7
Van Loot, Cornelius Obenchain
See Roberts, Kenneth (Lewis)
van Ostaijen, Paul 1896-1928 .... **TCLC 33**
See also CA 163
Van Peebles, Melvin 1932- .... **CLC 2, 20**
See also BW 2, 3; CA 85-88; CANR 27,
67, 82; DAM MULT
van Schendel, Arthur(-Francois-Emile)
1874-1946 .... **TCLC 56**
See also EWL 3
Vansittart, Peter 1920- .... **CLC 42**
See also CA 1-4R; CANR 3, 49, 90; CN 4,
5, 6, 7; RHW
Van Vechten, Carl 1880-1964 ... **CLC 33; HR
1:3**
See also AMWS 2; CA 183; 89-92; DLB 4,
9, 51; RGAL 4
van Vogt, A(lfred) E(lton) 1912-2000 . **CLC 1**
See also BPFB 3; BYA 13, 14; CA 21-24R;
190; CANR 28; DLB 8, 251; SATA 14;
SATA-Obit 124; SCFW 1, 2; SFW 4
Vara, Madeleine
See Jackson, Laura (Riding)
Varda, Agnes 1928- .... **CLC 16**
See also CA 116; 122
Vargas Llosa, (Jorge) Mario (Pedro)
1936- .... **CLC 3, 6, 9, 10, 15, 31, 42, 85,
181; HLC 2**
See Llosa, (Jorge) Mario (Pedro) Vargas
See also BPFB 3; CA 73-76; CANR 18, 32,
42, 67, 116, 140; CDWLB 3; CWW 2;
DA; DA3; DAB; DAC; DAM MST,
MULT, NOV; DLB 145; DNFS 2; EWL

3; HW 1, 2; LAIT 5; LATS 1:2; LAW;
LAWS 1; MTCW 1, 2; MTFW 2005;
RGWL 2; SSFS 14; TWA; WLIT 1
Varnhagen von Ense, Rahel
1771-1833 .... **NCLC 130**
See also DLB 90
Vasari, Giorgio 1511-1574 .... **LC 114**
Vasiliu, George
See Bacovia, George
Vasiliu, Gheorghe
See Bacovia, George
See also CA 123; 189
Vassa, Gustavus
See Equiano, Olaudah
Vassilikos, Vassilis 1933- .... **CLC 4, 8**
See also CA 81-84; CANR 75; EWL 3
Vaughan, Henry 1621-1695 .... **LC 27**
See also BRW 2; DLB 131; PAB; RGEL 2
Vaughn, Stephanie .... **CLC 62**
Vazov, Ivan (Minchov) 1850-1921 . **TCLC 25**
See also CA 121; 167; CDWLB 4; DLB
147
Veblen, Thorstein B(unde)
1857-1929 .... **TCLC 31**
See also AMWS 1; CA 115; 165; DLB 246;
MAL 5
Vega, Lope de 1562-1635 ... **HLCS 2; LC 23,
119**
See also EW 2; RGWL 2, 3
Vendler, Helen (Hennessy) 1933- ... **CLC 138**
See also CA 41-44R; CANR 25, 72, 136;
MTCW 1, 2; MTFW 2005
Venison, Alfred
See Pound, Ezra (Weston Loomis)
Ventsel, Elena Sergeevna 1907-2002
See Grekova, I.
See also CA 154
Verdi, Marie de
See Mencken, H(enry) L(ouis)
Verdu, Matilde
See Cela, Camilo Jose
Verga, Giovanni (Carmelo)
1840-1922 .... **SSC 21, 87; TCLC 3**
See also CA 104; 123; CANR 101; EW 7;
EWL 3; RGSF 2; RGWL 2, 3; WLIT 7
Vergil 70B.C.-19B.C. ... **CMLC 9, 40; PC 12;
WLCS**
See Virgil
See also AW 2; DA; DA3; DAB; DAC;
DAM MST, POET; EFS 1; LMFS 1
Vergil, Polydore c. 1470-1555 .... **LC 108**
See also DLB 132
Verhaeren, Emile (Adolphe Gustave)
1855-1916 .... **TCLC 12**
See also CA 109; EWL 3; GFL 1789 to the
Present
Verlaine, Paul (Marie) 1844-1896 .. **NCLC 2,
51; PC 2, 32**
See also DAM POET; DLB 217; EW 7;
GFL 1789 to the Present; LMFS 2; RGWL
2, 3; TWA
Verne, Jules (Gabriel) 1828-1905 ... **TCLC 6,
52**
See also AAYA 16; BYA 4; CA 110; 131;
CLR 88; DA3; DAM MULT; GFL 1789 to
the Present; JRDA; LAIT 2; LMFS 2;
MAICYA 1, 2; MTFW 2005; RGWL 2, 3;
SATA 21; SCFW 1, 2; SFW 4; TWA;
WCH
Verus, Marcus Annius
See Aurelius, Marcus
Very, Jones 1813-1880 .... **NCLC 9**
See also DLB 1, 243; RGAL 4
Vesaas, Tarjei 1897-1970 .... **CLC 48**
See also CA 190; 29-32R; DLB 297; EW
11; EWL 3; RGWL 3
Vialis, Gaston
See Simenon, Georges (Jacques Christian)

Wasserstein, Wendy 1950-2006 . **CLC 32, 59, 90, 183; DC 4**
See also AMWS 15; CA 121; 129; CABS 3; CAD; CANR 53, 75, 128; CD 5, 6; CWD; DA3; DAM DRAM; DFS 5, 17; DLB 228; EWL 3; FW; INT CA-129; MAL 5; MTCW 2; MTFW 2005; SATA 94

Waterhouse, Keith (Spencer) 1929- . **CLC 47**
See also CA 5-8R; CANR 38, 67, 109; CBD; CD 6; CN 1, 2, 3, 4, 5, 6, 7; DLB 13, 15; MTCW 1, 2; MTFW 2005

Waters, Frank (Joseph) 1902-1995 .. **CLC 88**
See also CA 5-8R; 149; CAAS 13; CANR 3, 18, 63, 121; DLB 212; DLBY 1986; RGAL 4; TCWW 1, 2

Waters, Mary C. .... **CLC 70**

Waters, Roger 1944- .... **CLC 35**

Watkins, Frances Ellen
See Harper, Frances Ellen Watkins

Watkins, Gerrold
See Malzberg, Barry N(athaniel)

Watkins, Gloria Jean 1952(?)- .... **CLC 94**
See also BW 2; CA 143; CANR 87, 126; DLB 246; MTCW 2; MTFW 2005; SATA 115

Watkins, Paul 1964- .... **CLC 55**
See also CA 132; CANR 62, 98

Watkins, Vernon Phillips 1906-1967 .... **CLC 43**
See also CA 9-10; 25-28R; CAP 1; DLB 20; EWL 3; RGEL 2

Watson, Irving S.
See Mencken, H(enry) L(ouis)

Watson, John H.
See Farmer, Philip Jose

Watson, Richard F.
See Silverberg, Robert

Watts, Ephraim
See Horne, Richard Henry Hengist

Watts, Isaac 1674-1748 .... **LC 98**
See also DLB 95; RGEL 2; SATA 52

Waugh, Auberon (Alexander) 1939-2001 .... **CLC 7**
See also CA 45-48; 192; CANR 6, 22, 92; CN 1, 2, 3; DLB 14, 194

Waugh, Evelyn (Arthur St. John) 1903-1966 .. **CLC 1, 3, 8, 13, 19, 27, 44, 107; SSC 41; WLC**
See also BPFB 3; BRW 7; CA 85-88; 25-28R; CANR 22; CDBLB 1914-1945; DA; DA3; DAB; DAC; DAM MST, NOV, POP; DLB 15, 162, 195; EWL 3; MTCW 1, 2; MTFW 2005; NFS 13, 17; RGEL 2; RGSF 2; TEA; WLIT 4

Waugh, Harriet 1944- .... **CLC 6**
See also CA 85-88; CANR 22

Ways, C. R.
See Blount, Roy (Alton), Jr.

Waystaff, Simon
See Swift, Jonathan

Webb, Beatrice (Martha Potter) 1858-1943 .... **TCLC 22**
See also CA 117; 162; DLB 190; FW

Webb, Charles (Richard) 1939- .... **CLC 7**
See also CA 25-28R; CANR 114

Webb, Frank J. .... **NCLC 143**
See also DLB 50

Webb, James H(enry), Jr. 1946- ...... **CLC 22**
See also CA 81-84

Webb, Mary Gladys (Meredith) 1881-1927 .... **TCLC 24**
See also CA 182; 123; DLB 34; FW

Webb, Mrs. Sidney
See Webb, Beatrice (Martha Potter)

Webb, Phyllis 1927- .... **CLC 18**
See also CA 104; CANR 23; CCA 1; CP 1, 2, 3, 4, 5, 6, 7; CWP; DLB 53

Webb, Sidney (James) 1859-1947 .. **TCLC 22**
See also CA 117; 163; DLB 190

Webber, Andrew Lloyd .... **CLC 21**
See Lloyd Webber, Andrew
See also DFS 7

Weber, Lenora Mattingly 1895-1971 .... **CLC 12**
See also CA 19-20; 29-32R; CAP 1; SATA 2; SATA-Obit 26

Weber, Max 1864-1920 .... **TCLC 69**
See also CA 109; 189; DLB 296

Webster, John 1580(?)-1634(?) ...... **DC 2; LC 33, 84, 124; WLC**
See also BRW 2; CDBLB Before 1660; DA; DAB; DAC; DAM DRAM, MST; DFS 17, 19; DLB 58; IDTP; RGEL 2; WLIT 3

Webster, Noah 1758-1843 .... **NCLC 30**
See also DLB 1, 37, 42, 43, 73, 243

Wedekind, (Benjamin) Frank(lin) 1864-1918 .... **TCLC 7**
See also CA 104; 153; CANR 121, 122; CDWLB 2; DAM DRAM; DLB 118; EW 8; EWL 3; LMFS 2; RGWL 2, 3

Wehr, Demaris .... **CLC 65**

Weidman, Jerome 1913-1998 .... **CLC 7**
See also AITN 2; CA 1-4R; 171; CAD; CANR 1; CD 1, 2, 3, 4, 5; DLB 28

Weil, Simone (Adolphine) 1909-1943 .... **TCLC 23**
See also CA 117; 159; EW 12; EWL 3; FW; GFL 1789 to the Present; MTCW 2

Weininger, Otto 1880-1903 .... **TCLC 84**

Weinstein, Nathan
See West, Nathanael

Weinstein, Nathan von Wallenstein
See West, Nathanael

Weir, Peter (Lindsay) 1944- .... **CLC 20**
See also CA 113; 123

Weiss, Peter (Ulrich) 1916-1982 .. **CLC 3, 15, 51; TCLC 152**
See also CA 45-48; 106; CANR 3; DAM DRAM; DFS 3; DLB 69, 124; EWL 3; RGWL 2, 3

Weiss, Theodore (Russell) 1916-2003 .... **CLC 3, 8, 14**
See also CA 9-12R; 189; 216; CAAE 189; CAAS 2; CANR 46, 94; CP 1, 2, 3, 4, 5, 6, 7; DLB 5; TCLE 1:2

Welch, (Maurice) Denton 1915-1948 .... **TCLC 22**
See also BRWS 8, 9; CA 121; 148; RGEL 2

Welch, James (Phillip) 1940-2003 ..... **CLC 6, 14, 52; NNAL; PC 62**
See also CA 85-88; 219; CANR 42, 66, 107; CN 5, 6, 7; CP 2, 3, 4, 5, 6, 7; CPW; DAM MULT, POP; DLB 175, 256; LATS 1:1; RGAL 4; TCWW 1, 2

Weldon, Fay 1931- . **CLC 6, 9, 11, 19, 36, 59, 122**
See also BRWS 4; CA 21-24R; CANR 16, 46, 63, 97, 137; CDBLB 1960 to Present; CN 3, 4, 5, 6, 7; CPW; DAM POP; DLB 14, 194, 319; EWL 3; FW; HGG; INT CANR-16; MTCW 1, 2; MTFW 2005; RGEL 2; RGSF 2

Wellek, Rene 1903-1995 .... **CLC 28**
See also CA 5-8R; 150; CAAS 7; CANR 8; DLB 63; EWL 3; INT CANR-8

Weller, Michael 1942- .... **CLC 10, 53**
See also CA 85-88; CAD; CD 5, 6

Weller, Paul 1958- .... **CLC 26**

Wellershoff, Dieter 1925- .... **CLC 46**
See also CA 89-92; CANR 16, 37

Welles, (George) Orson 1915-1985 .. **CLC 20, 80**
See also AAYA 40; CA 93-96; 117

Wellman, John McDowell 1945-
See Wellman, Mac
See also CA 166; CD 5

Wellman, Mac .... **CLC 65**
See Wellman, John McDowell; Wellman, John McDowell
See also CAD; CD 6; RGAL 4

Wellman, Manly Wade 1903-1986 ... **CLC 49**
See also CA 1-4R; 118; CANR 6, 16, 44; FANT; SATA 6; SATA-Obit 47; SFW 4; SUFW

Wells, Carolyn 1869(?)-1942 .... **TCLC 35**
See also CA 113; 185; CMW 4; DLB 11

Wells, H(erbert) G(eorge) 1866-1946 . **SSC 6, 70; TCLC 6, 12, 19, 133; WLC**
See also AAYA 18; BPFB 3; BRW 6; CA 110; 121; CDBLB 1914-1945; CLR 64; DA; DA3; DAB; DAC; DAM MST, NOV; DLB 34, 70, 156, 178; EWL 3; EXPS; HGG; LAIT 3; LMFS 2; MTCW 1, 2; MTFW 2005; NFS 17, 20; RGEL 2; RGSF 2; SATA 20; SCFW 1, 2; SFW 4; SSFS 3; SUFW; TEA; WCH; WLIT 4; YAW

Wells, Rosemary 1943- .... **CLC 12**
See also AAYA 13; BYA 7, 8; CA 85-88; CANR 48, 120; CLR 16, 69; CWRI 5; MAICYA 1, 2; SAAS 1; SATA 18, 69, 114, 156; YAW

Wells-Barnett, Ida B(ell) 1862-1931 .... **TCLC 125**
See also CA 182; DLB 23, 221

Welsh, Irvine 1958- .... **CLC 144**
See also CA 173; CANR 146; CN 7; DLB 271

Welty, Eudora (Alice) 1909-2001 .. **CLC 1, 2, 5, 14, 22, 33, 105; SSC 1, 27, 51; WLC**
See also AAYA 48; AMW; AMWR 1; BPFB 3; CA 9-12R; 199; CABS 1; CANR 32, 65, 128; CDALB 1941-1968; CN 1, 2, 3, 4, 5, 6, 7; CSW; DA; DA3; DAB; DAC; DAM MST, NOV; DLB 2, 102, 143; DLBD 12; DLBY 1987, 2001; EWL 3; EXPS; HGG; LAIT 3; MAL 5; MAWW; MTCW 1, 2; MTFW 2005; NFS 13, 15; RGAL 4; RGSF 2; RHW; SSFS 2, 10; TUS

Wen I-to 1899-1946 .... **TCLC 28**
See also EWL 3

Wentworth, Robert
See Hamilton, Edmond

Werfel, Franz (Viktor) 1890-1945 ... **TCLC 8**
See also CA 104; 161; DLB 81, 124; EWL 3; RGWL 2, 3

Wergeland, Henrik Arnold 1808-1845 .... **NCLC 5**

Wersba, Barbara 1932- .... **CLC 30**
See also AAYA 2, 30; BYA 6, 12, 13; CA 29-32R, 182; CAAE 182; CANR 16, 38; CLR 3, 78; DLB 52; JRDA; MAICYA 1, 2; SAAS 2; SATA 1, 58; SATA-Essay 103; WYA; YAW

Wertmueller, Lina 1928- .... **CLC 16**
See also CA 97-100; CANR 39, 78

Wescott, Glenway 1901-1987 .. **CLC 13; SSC 35**
See also CA 13-16R; 121; CANR 23, 70; CN 1, 2, 3, 4; DLB 4, 9, 102; MAL 5; RGAL 4

Wesker, Arnold 1932- .... **CLC 3, 5, 42**
See also CA 1-4R; CAAS 7; CANR 1, 33; CBD; CD 5, 6; CDBLB 1960 to Present; DAB; DAM DRAM; DLB 13, 310, 319; EWL 3; MTCW 1; RGEL 2; TEA

Wesley, John 1703-1791 .... **LC 88**
See also DLB 104

Wesley, Richard (Errol) 1945- .... **CLC 7**
See also BW 1; CA 57-60; CAD; CANR 27; CD 5, 6; DLB 38

Wilson, John 1785-1854 .... **NCLC 5**

Wilson, John (Anthony) Burgess 1917-1993
See Burgess, Anthony
See also CA 1-4R; 143; CANR 2, 46; DA3;
DAC; DAM NOV; MTCW 1, 2; MTFW
2005; NFS 15; TEA

Wilson, Lanford 1937- .. **CLC 7, 14, 36, 197;
DC 19**
See also CA 17-20R; CABS 3; CAD; CANR
45, 96; CD 5, 6; DAM DRAM; DFS 4, 9,
12, 16, 20; DLB 7; EWL 3; MAL 5; TUS

Wilson, Robert M. 1941- .... **CLC 7, 9**
See also CA 49-52; CAD; CANR 2, 41; CD
5, 6; MTCW 1

Wilson, Robert McLiam 1964- .... **CLC 59**
See also CA 132; DLB 267

Wilson, Sloan 1920-2003 .... **CLC 32**
See also CA 1-4R; 216; CANR 1, 44; CN
1, 2, 3, 4, 5, 6

Wilson, Snoo 1948- .... **CLC 33**
See also CA 69-72; CBD; CD 5, 6

Wilson, William S(mith) 1932- .... **CLC 49**
See also CA 81-84

Wilson, (Thomas) Woodrow
1856-1924 .... **TCLC 79**
See also CA 166; DLB 47

Wilson and Warnke eds. .... **CLC 65**

Winchilsea, Anne (Kingsmill) Finch
1661-1720
See Finch, Anne
See also RGEL 2

Windham, Basil
See Wodehouse, P(elham) G(renville)

Wingrove, David (John) 1954- .... **CLC 68**
See also CA 133; SFW 4

Winnemucca, Sarah 1844-1891 .... **NCLC 79;
NNAL**
See also DAM MULT; DLB 175; RGAL 4

Winstanley, Gerrard 1609-1676 .... **LC 52**

Wintergreen, Jane
See Duncan, Sara Jeannette

Winters, Arthur Yvor
See Winters, Yvor

Winters, Janet Lewis .... **CLC 41**
See Lewis, Janet
See also DLBY 1987

Winters, Yvor 1900-1968 .... **CLC 4, 8, 32**
See also AMWS 2; CA 11-12; 25-28R; CAP
1; DLB 48; EWL 3; MAL 5; MTCW 1;
RGAL 4

Winterson, Jeanette 1959- .... **CLC 64, 158**
See also BRWS 4; CA 136; CANR 58, 116;
CN 5, 6, 7; CPW; DA3; DAM POP; DLB
207, 261; FANT; FW; GLL 1; MTCW 2;
MTFW 2005; RHW

Winthrop, John 1588-1649 .... **LC 31, 107**
See also DLB 24, 30

Wirth, Louis 1897-1952 .... **TCLC 92**
See also CA 210

Wiseman, Frederick 1930- .... **CLC 20**
See also CA 159

Wister, Owen 1860-1938 .... **TCLC 21**
See also BPFB 3; CA 108; 162; DLB 9, 78,
186; RGAL 4; SATA 62; TCWW 1, 2

Wither, George 1588-1667 .... **LC 96**
See also DLB 121; RGEL 2

Witkacy
See Witkiewicz, Stanislaw Ignacy

Witkiewicz, Stanislaw Ignacy
1885-1939 .... **TCLC 8**
See also CA 105; 162; CDWLB 4; DLB
215; EW 10; EWL 3; RGWL 2, 3; SFW 4

Wittgenstein, Ludwig (Josef Johann)
1889-1951 .... **TCLC 59**
See also CA 113; 164; DLB 262; MTCW 2

Wittig, Monique 1935-2003 .... **CLC 22**
See also CA 116; 135; 212; CANR 143;
CWW 2; DLB 83; EWL 3; FW; GLL 1

Wittlin, Jozef 1896-1976 .... **CLC 25**
See also CA 49-52; 65-68; CANR 3; EWL
3

Wodehouse, P(elham) G(renville)
1881-1975 . **CLC 1, 2, 5, 10, 22; SSC 2;
TCLC 108**
See also AAYA 65; AITN 2; BRWS 3; CA
45-48; 57-60; CANR 3, 33; CDBLB
1914-1945; CN 1, 2; CPW 1; DA3; DAB;
DAC; DAM NOV; DLB 34, 162; EWL 3;
MTCW 1, 2; MTFW 2005; RGEL 2;
RGSF 2; SATA 22; SSFS 10

Woiwode, L.
See Woiwode, Larry (Alfred)

Woiwode, Larry (Alfred) 1941- ... **CLC 6, 10**
See also CA 73-76; CANR 16, 94; CN 3, 4,
5, 6, 7; DLB 6; INT CANR-16

Wojciechowska, Maia (Teresa)
1927-2002 .... **CLC 26**
See also AAYA 8, 46; BYA 3; CA 9-12R;
183; 209; CAAE 183; CANR 4, 41; CLR
1; JRDA; MAICYA 1, 2; SAAS 1; SATA
1, 28, 83; SATA-Essay 104; SATA-Obit
134; YAW

Wojtyla, Karol (Jozef)
See John Paul II, Pope

Wojtyla, Karol (Josef)
See John Paul II, Pope

Wolf, Christa 1929- .... **CLC 14, 29, 58, 150**
See also CA 85-88; CANR 45, 123; CD-
WLB 2; CWW 2; DLB 75; EWL 3; FW;
MTCW 1; RGWL 2, 3; SSFS 14

Wolf, Naomi 1962- .... **CLC 157**
See also CA 141; CANR 110; FW; MTFW
2005

Wolfe, Gene 1931- .... **CLC 25**
See also AAYA 35; CA 57-60; CAAS 9;
CANR 6, 32, 60; CPW; DAM POP; DLB
8; FANT; MTCW 2; MTFW 2005; SATA
118, 165; SCFW 2; SFW 4; SUFW 2

Wolfe, Gene Rodman
See Wolfe, Gene

Wolfe, George C. 1954- .... **BLCS; CLC 49**
See also CA 149; CAD; CD 5, 6

Wolfe, Thomas (Clayton)
1900-1938 ...... **SSC 33; TCLC 4, 13, 29,
61; WLC**
See also AMW; BPFB 3; CA 104; 132;
CANR 102; CDALB 1929-1941; DA;
DA3; DAB; DAC; DAM MST, NOV;
DLB 9, 102, 229; DLBD 2, 16; DLBY
1985, 1997; EWL 3; MAL 5; MTCW 1,
2; NFS 18; RGAL 4; SSFS 18; TUS

Wolfe, Thomas Kennerly, Jr.
1931- .... **CLC 147**
See Wolfe, Tom
See also CA 13-16R; CANR 9, 33, 70, 104;
DA3; DAM POP; DLB 185; EWL 3; INT
CANR-9; MTCW 1, 2; MTFW 2005; TUS

Wolfe, Tom .... **CLC 1, 2, 9, 15, 35, 51**
See Wolfe, Thomas Kennerly, Jr.
See also AAYA 8, 67; AITN 2; AMWS 3;
BEST 89:1; BPFB 3; CN 5, 6, 7; CPW;
CSW; DLB 152; LAIT 5; RGAL 4

Wolff, Geoffrey (Ansell) 1937- .... **CLC 41**
See also CA 29-32R; CANR 29, 43, 78

Wolff, Sonia
See Levitin, Sonia (Wolff)

Wolff, Tobias (Jonathan Ansell)
1945- .... **CLC 39, 64, 172; SSC 63**
See also AAYA 16; AMWS 7; BEST 90:2;
BYA 12; CA 114; 117; CAAS 22; CANR
54, 76, 96; CN 5, 6, 7; CSW; DA3; DLB
130; EWL 3; INT CA-117; MTCW 2;
MTFW 2005; RGAL 4; RGSF 2; SSFS 4,
11

Wolfram von Eschenbach c. 1170-c.
1220 .... **CMLC 5**
See Eschenbach, Wolfram von
See also CDWLB 2; DLB 138; EW 1;
RGWL 2

Wolitzer, Hilma 1930- .... **CLC 17**
See also CA 65-68; CANR 18, 40; INT
CANR-18; SATA 31; YAW

Wollstonecraft, Mary 1759-1797 .... **LC 5, 50,
90**
See also BRWS 3; CDBLB 1789-1832;
DLB 39, 104, 158, 252; FL 1:1; FW;
LAIT 1; RGEL 2; TEA; WLIT 3

Wonder, Stevie .... **CLC 12**
See Morris, Steveland Judkins

Wong, Jade Snow 1922- .... **CLC 17**
See also CA 109; CANR 91; SATA 112

Woodberry, George Edward
1855-1930 .... **TCLC 73**
See also CA 165; DLB 71, 103

Woodcott, Keith
See Brunner, John (Kilian Houston)

Woodruff, Robert W.
See Mencken, H(enry) L(ouis)

Woolf, (Adeline) Virginia 1882-1941 .. **SSC 7,
79; TCLC 1, 5, 20, 43, 56, 101, 123,
128; WLC**
See also AAYA 44; BPFB 3; BRW 7;
BRWC 2; BRWR 1; CA 104; 130; CANR
64, 132; CDBLB 1914-1945; DA; DA3;
DAB; DAC; DAM MST, NOV; DLB 36,
100, 162; DLBD 10; EWL 3; EXPS; FL
1:6; FW; LAIT 3; LATS 1:1; LMFS 2;
MTCW 1, 2; MTFW 2005; NCFS 2; NFS
8, 12; RGEL 2; RGSF 2; SSFS 4, 12;
TEA; WLIT 4

Woollcott, Alexander (Humphreys)
1887-1943 .... **TCLC 5**
See also CA 105; 161; DLB 29

Woolrich, Cornell .... **CLC 77**
See Hopley-Woolrich, Cornell George
See also MSW

Woolson, Constance Fenimore
1840-1894 .... **NCLC 82; SSC 90**
See also DLB 12, 74, 189, 221; RGAL 4

Wordsworth, Dorothy 1771-1855 . **NCLC 25,
138**
See also DLB 107

Wordsworth, William 1770-1850 .. **NCLC 12,
38, 111; PC 4, 67; WLC**
See also BRW 4; BRWC 1; CDBLB 1789-
1832; DA; DA3; DAB; DAC; DAM MST,
POET; DLB 93, 107; EXPP; LATS 1:1;
LMFS 1; PAB; PFS 2; RGEL 2; TEA;
WLIT 3; WP

Wotton, Sir Henry 1568-1639 .... **LC 68**
See also DLB 121; RGEL 2

Wouk, Herman 1915- .... **CLC 1, 9, 38**
See also BPFB 2, 3; CA 5-8R; CANR 6,
33, 67, 146; CDALBS; CN 1, 2, 3, 4, 5,
6; CPW; DA3; DAM NOV, POP; DLBY
1982; INT CANR-6; LAIT 4; MAL 5;
MTCW 1, 2; MTFW 2005; NFS 7; TUS

Wright, Charles (Penzel, Jr.) 1935- .. **CLC 6,
13, 28, 119, 146**
See also AMWS 5; CA 29-32R; CAAS 7;
CANR 23, 36, 62, 88, 135; CP 3, 4, 5, 6,
7; DLB 165; DLBY 1982; EWL 3;
MTCW 1, 2; MTFW 2005; PFS 10

Wright, Charles Stevenson 1932- ..... **BLC 3;
CLC 49**
See also BW 1; CA 9-12R; CANR 26; CN
1, 2, 3, 4, 5, 6, 7; DAM MULT, POET;
DLB 33

Wright, Frances 1795-1852 .... **NCLC 74**
See also DLB 73

Wright, Frank Lloyd 1867-1959 .... **TCLC 95**
See also AAYA 33; CA 174

Wright, Jack R.
See Harris, Mark

Zangwill, Israel 1864-1926 ... **SSC 44; TCLC 16**
See also CA 109; 167; CMW 4; DLB 10, 135, 197; RGEL 2

Zanzotto, Andrea 1921- .... **PC 65**
See also CA 208; CWW 2; DLB 128; EWL 3

Zappa, Francis Vincent, Jr. 1940-1993
See Zappa, Frank
See also CA 108; 143; CANR 57

Zappa, Frank .... **CLC 17**
See Zappa, Francis Vincent, Jr.

Zaturenska, Marya 1902-1982 ..... **CLC 6, 11**
See also CA 13-16R; 105; CANR 22; CP 1, 2, 3

Zayas y Sotomayor, Maria de 1590-c. 1661 .... **LC 102**
See also RGSF 2

Zeami 1363-1443 .... **DC 7; LC 86**
See also DLB 203; RGWL 2, 3

Zelazny, Roger (Joseph) 1937-1995 . **CLC 21**
See also AAYA 7, 68; BPFB 3; CA 21-24R; 148; CANR 26, 60; CN 6; DLB 8; FANT; MTCW 1, 2; MTFW 2005; SATA 57; SATA-Brief 39; SCFW 1, 2; SFW 4; SUFW 1, 2

Zhang Ailing
See Chang, Eileen
See also CWW 2; RGSF 2

Zhdanov, Andrei Alexandrovich 1896-1948 .... **TCLC 18**
See also CA 117; 167

Zhukovsky, Vasilii Andreevich
See Zhukovsky, Vasily (Andreevich)
See also DLB 205

Zhukovsky, Vasily (Andreevich) 1783-1852 .... **NCLC 35**
See Zhukovsky, Vasilii Andreevich

Ziegenhagen, Eric .... **CLC 55**

Zimmer, Jill Schary
See Robinson, Jill

Zimmerman, Robert
See Dylan, Bob

Zindel, Paul 1936-2003 ...... **CLC 6, 26; DC 5**
See also AAYA 2, 37; BYA 2, 3, 8, 11, 14; CA 73-76; 213; CAD; CANR 31, 65, 108; CD 5, 6; CDALBS; CLR 3, 45, 85; DA; DA3; DAB; DAC; DAM DRAM, MST, NOV; DFS 12; DLB 7, 52; JRDA; LAIT 5; MAICYA 1, 2; MTCW 1, 2; MTFW 2005; NFS 14; SATA 16, 58, 102; SATA-Obit 142; WYA; YAW

Zinn, Howard 1922- .... **CLC 199**
See also CA 1-4R; CANR 2, 33, 90

Zinov'Ev, A. A.
See Zinoviev, Alexander (Aleksandrovich)

Zinov'ev, Aleksandr (Aleksandrovich)
See Zinoviev, Alexander (Aleksandrovich)
See also DLB 302

Zinoviev, Alexander (Aleksandrovich) 1922- .... **CLC 19**
See Zinov'ev, Aleksandr (Aleksandrovich)
See also CA 116; 133; CAAS 10

Zizek, Slavoj 1949- .... **CLC 188**
See also CA 201; MTFW 2005

Zoilus
See Lovecraft, H(oward) P(hillips)

Zola, Emile (Edouard Charles Antoine) 1840-1902 ...... **TCLC 1, 6, 21, 41; WLC**
See also CA 104; 138; DA; DA3; DAB; DAC; DAM MST, NOV; DLB 123; EW 7; GFL 1789 to the Present; IDTP; LMFS 1, 2; RGWL 2; TWA

Zoline, Pamela 1941- .... **CLC 62**
See also CA 161; SFW 4

Zoroaster 628(?)B.C.-551(?)B.C. ... **CMLC 40**

Zorrilla y Moral, Jose 1817-1893 .... **NCLC 6**

Zoshchenko, Mikhail (Mikhailovich) 1895-1958 .... **SSC 15; TCLC 15**
See also CA 115; 160; EWL 3; RGSF 2; RGWL 3

Zuckmayer, Carl 1896-1977 .... **CLC 18**
See also CA 69-72; DLB 56, 124; EWL 3; RGWL 2, 3

Zuk, Georges
See Skelton, Robin
See also CCA 1

Zukofsky, Louis 1904-1978 ... **CLC 1, 2, 4, 7, 11, 18; PC 11**
See also AMWS 3; CA 9-12R; 77-80; CANR 39; CP 1, 2; DAM POET; DLB 5, 165; EWL 3; MAL 5; MTCW 1; RGAL 4

Zweig, Paul 1935-1984 .... **CLC 34, 42**
See also CA 85-88; 113

Zweig, Stefan 1881-1942 .... **TCLC 17**
See also CA 112; 170; DLB 81, 118; EWL 3

Zwingli, Huldreich 1484-1531 .... **LC 37**
See also DLB 179

Literary Criticism Series
Cumulative Topic Index

This index lists all topic entries in Thompson Gale's *Children's Literature Review* (CLR), *Classical and Medieval Literature Criticism* (CMLC), *Contemporary Literary Criticism* (CLC), *Drama Criticism* (DC), *Literature Criticism from 1400 to 1800* (LC), *Nineteenth-Century Literature Criticism* (NCLC), *Short Story Criticism* (SSC), and *Twentieth-Century Literary Criticism* (TCLC). The index also lists topic entries in the Gale Critical Companion Collection, which includes the following publications: *The Beat Generation* (BG), *Feminism in Literature* (FL), *Gothic Literature* (GL), and *Harlem Renaissance* (HR).

Topic Index

Topic Index

SSC Cumulative Nationality Index

ALGERIAN

Camus, Albert **9**

AMERICAN

Abish, Walter **44**
Adams, Alice (Boyd) **24**
Aiken, Conrad (Potter) **9**
Alcott, Louisa May **27**
Algren, Nelson **33**
Anderson, Sherwood **1, 46**
Apple, Max (Isaac) **50**
Auchincloss, Louis (Stanton) **22**
Baldwin, James (Arthur) **10, 33**
Bambara, Toni Cade **35**
Banks, Russell **42**
Barnes, Djuna **3**
Barth, John (Simmons) **10, 89**
Barthelme, Donald **2, 55**
Bass, Rick **60**
Beattie, Ann **11**
Bellow, Saul **14**
Benét, Stephen Vincent **10, 86**
Berriault, Gina **30**
Betts, Doris (Waugh) **45**
Bierce, Ambrose (Gwinett) **9, 72**
Bowles, Paul (Frederick) **3**
Boyle, Kay **5**
Boyle, T(homas) Coraghessan **16**
Bradbury, Ray (Douglas) **29, 53**
Bradfield, Scott **65**
Bukowski, Charles **45**
Cable, George Washington **4**
Caldwell, Erskine (Preston) **19**
Calisher, Hortense **15**
Canin, Ethan **70**
Capote, Truman **2, 47**
Carver, Raymond **8, 51**
Cather, Willa (Sibert) **2, 50**
Chabon, Michael **59**
Chandler, Raymond (Thornton) **23**
Cheever, John **1, 38, 57**
Chesnutt, Charles W(addell) **7, 54**
Chopin, Kate **8, 68**
Cisneros, Sandra **32, 72**
Coover, Robert (Lowell) **15**
Cowan, Peter (Walkinshaw) **28**
Crane, Stephen (Townley) **7, 56, 70**
Davenport, Guy (Mattison Jr.) **16**
Davis, Rebecca (Blaine) Harding **38**
Dick, Philip K. **57**
Dixon, Stephen **16**
Dreiser, Theodore (Herman Albert) **30**
Dubus, André **15**
Dunbar, Paul Laurence **8**
Dybek, Stuart **55**
Elkin, Stanley L(awrence) **12**
Ellison, Harlan (Jay) **14**
Ellison, Ralph (Waldo) **26, 79**
Fante, John **65**
Farrell, James T(homas) **28**
Faulkner, William (Cuthbert) **1, 35, 42**
Fisher, Rudolph **25**

Fitzgerald, F(rancis) Scott (Key) **6, 31, 75**
Ford, Richard **56**
Freeman, Mary E(leanor) Wilkins **1, 47**
Gaines, Ernest J. **68**
Gardner, John (Champlin) Jr. **7**
Garland, (Hannibal) Hamlin **18**
Garrett, George (Palmer) **30**
Gass, William H(oward) **12**
Gibson, William (Ford) **52**
Gilchrist, Ellen (Louise) **14, 63**
Gilman, Charlotte (Anna) Perkins (Stetson) **13, 62**
Glasgow, Ellen (Anderson Gholson) **34**
Glaspell, Susan **41**
Gordon, Caroline **15**
Gordon, Mary **59**
Grau, Shirley Ann **15**
Hammett, (Samuel) Dashiell **17**
Harris, Joel Chandler **19**
Harrison, James (Thomas) **19**
Harte, (Francis) Bret(t) **8, 59**
Hawthorne, Nathaniel **3, 29, 39, 89**
Heinlein, Robert A(nson) **55**
Hemingway, Ernest (Miller) **1, 25, 36, 40, 63**
Henderson, Zenna (Chlarson) **29**
Henry, O. **5, 49**
Howells, William Dean **36**
Hughes, (James) Langston **6, 90**
Hurston, Zora Neale **4, 80**
Huxley, Aldous (Leonard) **39**
Irving, Washington **2, 37**
Jackson, Shirley **9, 39**
James, Henry **8, 32, 47**
Jewett, (Theodora) Sarah Orne **6, 44**
Johnson, Denis **56**
Jones, Thom (Douglas) **56**
Kelly, Robert **50**
Kincaid, Jamaica **72**
King, Stephen (Edwin) **17, 55**
Lardner, Ring(gold) W(ilmer) **32**
Le Guin, Ursula K(roeber) **12, 69**
Ligotti, Thomas (Robert) **16**
Lish, Gordon (Jay) **18**
London, Jack **4, 49**
Lovecraft, H(oward) P(hillips) **3, 52**
Maclean, Norman (Fitzroy) **13**
Malamud, Bernard **15**
Marshall, Paule **3**
Mason, Bobbie Ann **4**
McCarthy, Mary (Therese) **24**
McCullers, (Lula) Carson (Smith) **9, 24**
Melville, Herman **1, 17, 46**
Michaels, Leonard **16**
Millhauser, Steven **57**
Mori, Toshio **83**
Murfree, Mary Noailles **22**
Nabokov, Vladimir (Vladimirovich) **11, 86**
Nin, Anaïs **10**
Norris, (Benjamin) Frank(lin Jr.) **28**
Oates, Joyce Carol **6, 70**
O'Brien, Tim **74**
O'Connor, Frank **5**
O'Connor, (Mary) Flannery **1, 23, 61, 82**

O'Hara, John (Henry) **15**
Olsen, Tillie **11**
Ozick, Cynthia **15, 60**
Page, Thomas Nelson **23**
Paley, Grace **8**
Pancake, Breece D'J **61**
Parker, Dorothy (Rothschild) **2**
Perelman, S(idney) J(oseph) **32**
Phillips, Jayne Anne **16**
Poe, Edgar Allan **1, 22, 34, 35, 54, 88**
Pohl, Frederik **25**
Porter, Katherine Anne **4, 31, 43**
Powers, J(ames) F(arl) **4**
Price, (Edward) Reynolds **22**
Pynchon, Thomas (Ruggles Jr.) **14, 84**
Roth, Philip (Milton) **26**
Salinger, J(erome) D(avid) **2, 28, 65**
Salter, James **58**
Saroyan, William **21**
Selby, Hubert Jr. **20**
Silko, Leslie (Marmon) **37, 66**
Singer, Isaac Bashevis **3, 53**
Spencer, Elizabeth **57**
Spofford, Harriet Prescott **87**
Stafford, Jean **26, 86**
Stegner, Wallace (Earle) **27**
Stein, Gertrude **42**
Steinbeck, John (Ernst) **11, 37, 77**
Stuart, Jesse (Hilton) **31**
Styron, William **25**
Suckow, Ruth **18**
Taylor, Peter (Hillsman) **10, 84**
Thomas, Audrey (Callahan) **20**
Thurber, James (Grover) **1, 47**
Toomer, Jean **1, 45**
Trilling, Lionel **75**
Twain, Mark (Clemens, Samuel) **6, 26, 34, 87**
Updike, John (Hoyer) **13, 27**
Vinge, Joan (Carol) D(ennison) **24**
Vonnegut, Kurt Jr. **8**
Walker, Alice (Malsenior) **5**
Wallace, David Foster **68**
Warren, Robert Penn **4, 58**
Welty, Eudora **1, 27, 51**
Wescott, Glenway **35**
West, Nathanael **16**
Wharton, Edith (Newbold Jones) **6, 84**
Wideman, John Edgar **62**
Williams, William Carlos **31**
Williams, Tennessee **81**
Wodehouse, P(elham) G(renville) **2**
Wolfe, Thomas (Clayton) **33**
Wolff, Tobias **63**
Woolson, Constance Fenimore **90**
Wright, Richard (Nathaniel) **2**
Yamamoto, Hisaye **34**

ARGENTINIAN

Bioy Casares, Adolfo **17**
Borges, Jorge Luis **4, 41**
Cortázar, Julio **7, 76**
Valenzuela, Luisa **14, 82**

Nationality Index

SSC-90 Title Index

ISBN 0-7876-8887-8

90000

9 780787 688875